Contents

II Travel information

II European driving: cut through the confusion
IV Driving regulations
VII Ski resorts

1 Route planning maps

1 Key map · Distance table

17 Road maps

17 Key map

121 City plans and urban area maps

121 Legends to city plans and urban area maps

Alicante C	121	Madrid U	135
Amsterdam CU	122	Madrid C	136
Antwerpen Antwerp C	121	Málaga C	136
Athina Athens U	122	Marseille Marseilles C	136
Athina Athens C	123	Milano Milan CU	137
Barcelona CU	123	Moskva Moscow CU	138
Basel C	123	München Munich CU	138
Beograd Belgrade C	125	Nápoli Naples CU	139
Berlin CU	124	Oslo U	139
Bordeaux CU	125	Oslo C	140
Bruxelles Brussels U	125	Paris C	140
Bruxelles Brussels C	126	Paris U	141
Budapest CU	126	Praha Prague CU	142
Dublin CU	127	Roma Rome CU	143
Düsseldorf C	127	Rotterdam C	142
Düsseldorf (Ruhrgebiet) U	128	Sankt Peterburg	
Edinburgh C	127	St Petersburg U	142
Firenze Florence C	129	Sevilla Seville C	144
Frankfurt C	129	Stockholm CU	145
Genève Geneva C	129	Strasbourg CU	144
Génova Genoa C	129	Stuttgart C	144
Göteborg Gothenburg C	130	Torino Turin U	146
Granada C	130	Torino Turin C	147
Hamburg CU	130	Venézia Venice C	146
Helsinki CU	131	Warszawa Warsaw CU	147
İstanbul U	131	Wien Vienna U	147
København Copenhagen CU	132	Wien Vienna C	148
Köln Cologne C	132	Zagreb C	148
Lisboa Lisbon CU	133	Zürich C	148
London C	133		
London U	134	C City street plan	
Luxembourg C	135	U Urban area map	
Lyon CU	135		

149 Index to road maps

www.philips-maps.co.uk

First published in 1998 by Philip's,
a division of Octopus Publishing Group Ltd
www.octopusbooks.co.uk
Endeavour House, 189 Shaftesbury Avenue, London WC2H 8JY
An Hachette UK Company
www.hachette.co.uk

Seventeenth edition 2014
First impression 2014

Cartography by Philip's
Copyright © Philip's 2014

Printed in China

*Independent research survey, from research carried out by Outlook Research Limited, 2005/06.

**Nielsen BookScan Travel Publishing Year Book 2013 data

Photographic acknowledgements:
Page II, top left Raimund Kutter / imageBROKER / Alamy · *centre* Lipowski Milan / Shutterstock · *bottom right* mladn61 / iStockphoto
Page III top centre Baiaz / iStockphoto · *centre* zstock / Shutterstock; *left* Lya_Cattel / iStockphoto · *bottom* Hugo Maes / iStockphoto

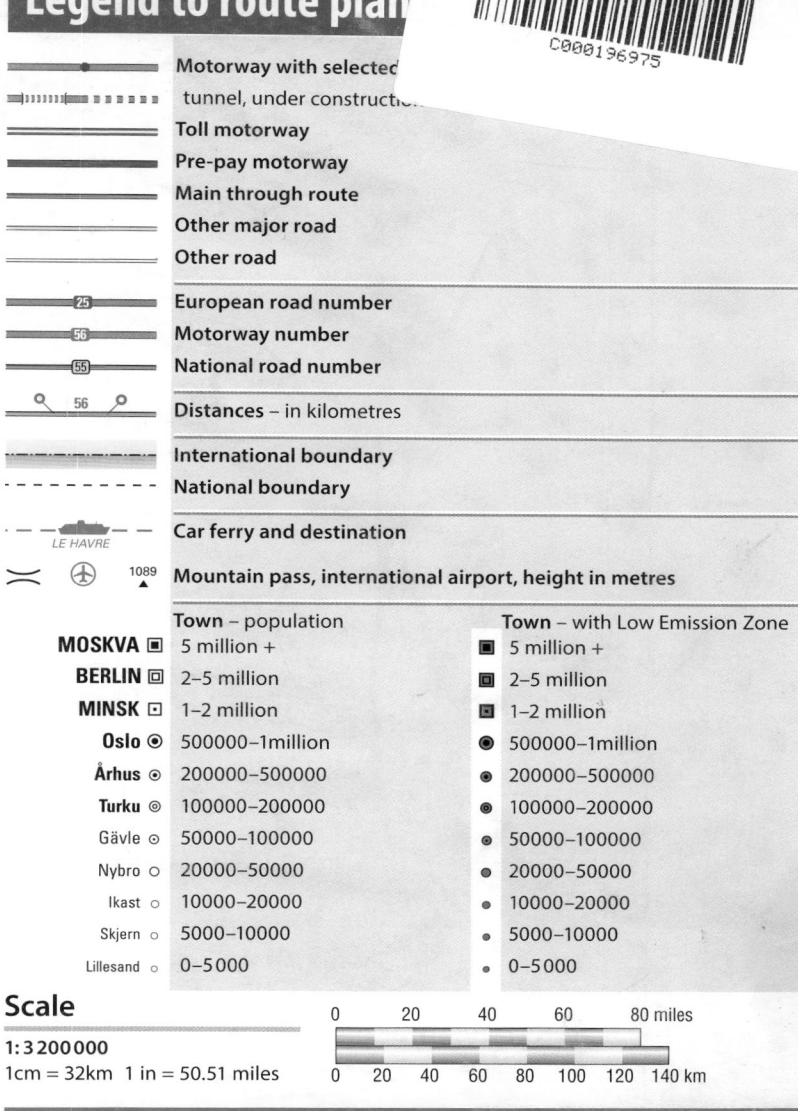

Legend to route plan[ning maps]

- Motorway with selected [junctions]
- tunnel, under construct[ion]
- Toll motorway
- Pre-pay motorway
- Main through route
- Other major road
- Other road
- 25 European road number
- 56 Motorway number
- 55 National road number
- 56 Distances – in kilometres
- International boundary
- National boundary
- LE HAVRE Car ferry and destination
- 1089 Mountain pass, international airport, height in metres

Town – population		Town – with Low Emission Zone
MOSKVA	5 million +	5 million +
BERLIN	2–5 million	2–5 million
MINSK	1–2 million	1–2 million
Oslo	500000–1million	500000–1million
Århus	200000–500000	200000–500000
Turku	100000–200000	100000–200000
Gävle	50000–100000	50000–100000
Nybro	20000–50000	20000–50000
Ikast	10000–20000	10000–20000
Skjern	5000–10000	5000–10000
Lillesand	0–5000	0–5000

Scale

1: 3 200 000
1cm = 32km 1 in = 50.51 miles

0 20 40 60 80 miles
0 20 40 60 80 100 120 140 km

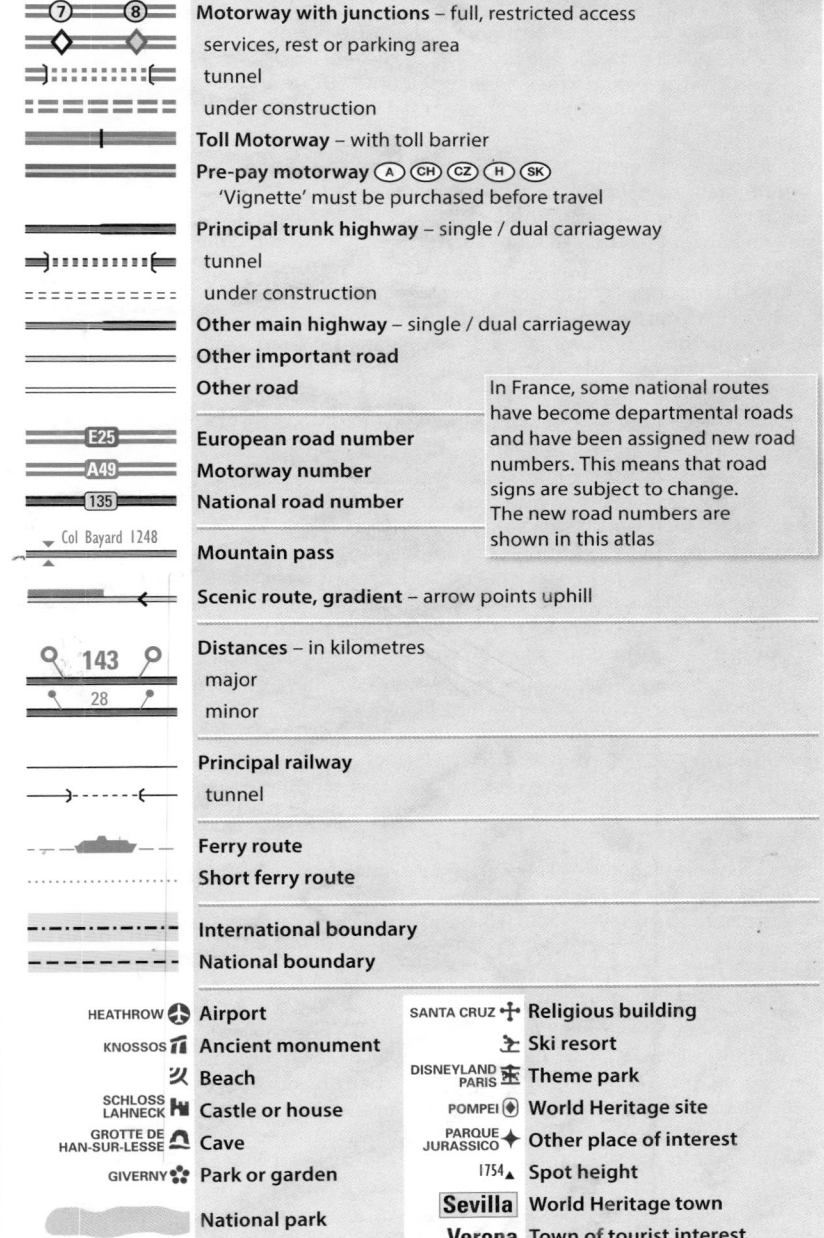

Legend to road maps pages 18–120

- 7 8 Motorway with junctions – full, restricted access
- services, rest or parking area
- tunnel
- under construction
- Toll Motorway – with toll barrier
- Pre-pay motorway A CH CZ H SK 'Vignette' must be purchased before travel
- Principal trunk highway – single / dual carriageway
- tunnel
- under construction
- Other main highway – single / dual carriageway
- Other important road
- Other road
- E25 European road number
- A49 Motorway number
- 135 National road number
- Col Bayard 1248 Mountain pass
- Scenic route, gradient – arrow points uphill
- Distances – in kilometres
  - 143 major
  - 28 minor
- Principal railway
- tunnel
- Ferry route
- Short ferry route
- International boundary
- National boundary

In France, some national routes have become departmental roads and have been assigned new road numbers. This means that road signs are subject to change. The new road numbers are shown in this atlas

HEATHROW	Airport	SANTA CRUZ	Religious building
KNOSSOS	Ancient monument		Ski resort
	Beach	DISNEYLAND PARIS	Theme park
SCHLOSS LAHNECK	Castle or house	POMPEI	World Heritage site
GROTTE DE HAN-SUR-LESSE	Cave	PARQUE JURASSICO	Other place of interest
GIVERNY	Park or garden	1754	Spot height
	National park	Sevilla	World Heritage town
	Natural park	Verona	Town of tourist interest
			Town with Low Emission Zone

Scales

1: 753 800 • Pages 18–110 and 120
1cm = 7.5km 1 inch = 12 miles

0 5 10 15 20 miles
0 5 10 15 20 25 30 35 km

1:1 507 600 • Pages 111–119
1cm = 15km, 1 inch = 24 miles

0 10 20 30 40 miles
0 10 20 30 40 50 60 70 km

European driving: cut through the confusion

Stay safe with GEM Motoring Assist

- Are you confused about European driving laws?
- How will you know what speed limits apply?
- Are you new to driving on the right hand side?
- Do you need advice about equipment requirements and which documents to take?
- Who do you call if you have an accident or break down?

Millions of us drive abroad on holiday each year. Perhaps it's a long motorway trip to the Mediterranean, a selection of historic cities and sites or a gentle tour along quiet country lanes. Whatever the purpose, it makes sense to ensure that both we and our vehicles are properly prepared for the journey.

It's not easy getting to grips with the finer points of driving in other countries, however experienced you may be as a motorist. Whether you have notched up thousands of miles of European driving or are preparing to make your first journey, the chances are you will always manage to find some road sign or legal requirement that will cause confusion.

What's more, 'driving in Europe' covers such a huge area. There are 28 countries in the European Union alone, each with its own set of road traffic laws and motoring customs. Driving in Europe can mean a spectacular and sunny coastal road that's within sight of Africa, or a snowy track amid the biting cold of the Arctic Circle, where the only others on the road are reindeer. Add to this some of the world's most congested cities, dense clusters of motorways (many with confusing numbers) and a big variation in safety standards and attitudes to risk. No wonder we often risk getting lost, taking wrong turnings or perhaps stopping where we shouldn't.

Depending on the country we're in, our errors at the wheel or our lack of familiarity with the rules of the road can sometimes bring unwelcome consequences. In any country, foreign drivers are subject to the same traffic rules as residents, enforceable in many situations by hefty on-the-spot fines and other sanctions. The situation across Europe is complex, simply because of the number of different sets of rules. For example, failure to carry a specific piece of breakdown equipment may be an offence in one country, but not in another. It's easy to see why the fun and excitement of a road trip in Europe could be spoilt by a minefield of regulations.

But we want to ensure that doesn't happen. Preparation and planning are key to a great holiday. It certainly pays to do a bit of research before you go, just to ensure you and your vehicle are up to the journey, your documents are in order and you're carrying the correct levels of equipment to keep the law enforcers happy.

Before you go

Some sensible planning will help make sure your European journey is enjoyable and – we hope – stress-free. So take some time before departure to ensure everything is in good shape: and that includes you, your travelling companions and your vehicle.

For you:

Try to become familiar with the driving laws of your holiday destination, including the local speed limits and which side of the road to drive on. You will be subject to these laws when driving abroad and if you are stopped by the police, it is not an excuse to say that you were unaware of them. Police officers in many countries have the power to impose (and collect) substantial on-the-spot fines for motoring offences, whether you are a resident or a visitor.

GEM Motoring Assist can link you direct with up-to-date information on driving in 27 different European countries (including Norway and Switzerland, who are not members of the European Union). For each country, you will find an attractive, downloadable three-page PDF document containing detailed information on driving facts, traffic laws, document and equipment requirements – and even a few simple, emergency phrases to help you if you're in difficulty. Go to **www.motoringassist.com/europe**

The Foreign and Commonwealth Office also gives country-specific travel advice (**www.gov.uk/driving-abroad**) with information on driving.

Passports

Check everyone's passport to make sure they are all valid.

Don't wait for your passport to expire. Unused time, rounded up to whole months (minimum one month, maximum nine months), will usually be added to your new passport.

New passports usually take two weeks to arrive. The Passport Office (0300 222 0000, **www.gov.uk/renew-adult-passport**) offers a faster service if you need a replacement passport urgently, but you'll have to pay a lot more.

Driving Licence

The new style photocard driving licence is valid in all European Union countries. However, you must ensure you carry both parts: the credit card-size photocard and the paper licence. The previously used pink EU format UK licence is also valid, though it may not be recognized in some areas. So if you haven't already done so, now is the time to update your old licence. For more information, contact the DVLA (0300 790 6801, **www.dft.gov.uk/dvla**)

Travel Insurance

Travel insurance is vital as it covers you against medical emergencies, accidents, thefts and cancellations, and repatriation. Ask for details before buying any travel insurance policy. Find out what it covers you for, and to what value. More important, check what's not covered. One of the key benefits of GEM membership is the excellent discount you can get on travel insurance. For more details, please visit: **www.motoringassist.com/philipsmaps**

European Breakdown Cover

Don't risk letting a breakdown ruin your European trip. Ensure you purchase a policy that will cover you for roadside assistance, emergency repair and recovery of your vehicle to the UK, wherever in Europe you may be heading. Once again, GEM members enjoy a specially discounted rate. You'll find the details at **www.motoringassist.com/philipsmaps**

EHIC

The E111 medical treatment form is no longer valid. Instead, you need an EHIC card for everyone travelling. These are free and cover you for any medical treatment you may need during a trip to another EU country or Switzerland. However, do check at the time of requiring assistance that your EHIC will be accepted. Apply online (**www.ehic.org.uk**), by telephone (0845 606 2030) or complete an application form, available from a Post office. Allow up to 14 days for the cards to arrive.

For your vehicle:

Service

It makes sense to get your car serviced before you travel. As a minimum, ensure the tyres have plenty of tread left and that water and oil levels are checked and topped up if required. Check them regularly during your time away.

Vehicle Registration Document

Police in many countries can demand that you prove you have the right to be driving your car. That means you need to show the registration document, or a suitable letter of authorization if the registration document is not in your name. Remember you should never leave the registration document in the car.

Nationality plate

Your vehicle must display a nationality plate of an approved pattern, design and size.

MOT

If your car is more than three years old, make sure you take its current MOT test certificate with you.

Insurance

If you are planning a trip to Europe, you should find that your car insurance policy provides you with the minimum amount of cover you need. But it's important to contact your insurer before you go, to confirm exactly what level of cover you have and for how many days it will be valid.

Mechanical adjustments

Check the adjustments required for your headlights before you go. Beam deflectors are a legal requirement if you drive in Europe. They are generally sold at the ports, on ferries and in the Folkestone Eurotunnel terminal, but be warned – the instructions can be a little confusing! The alternative is to ask a local garage to do the job for you before you go. If you choose this, then make sure you shop around as prices for undertaking this very simple task vary enormously.

Equipment check-list

This checklist represents GEM's suggestions for what you should take with you in the car. Different countries have different rules about what's compulsory and these rules change from time to time. So it's important to check carefully before you set out. For country-by-country guidance, visit **www.motoringassist.com/europe** or see page IV of this atlas.

- Fire extinguisher
- First aid kit
- High-visibility jacket – one for each occupant
- Two warning triangles
- Replacement bulbs and fuses
- Spare spectacles (if worn) for each driver
- Snow chains for winter journeys into the mountains
- Disposable camera and notebook. Keep in your glove compartment and record any collisions or damage for insurance purposes (if it is safe).

Contact details

Make sure you have all relevant emergency helpline numbers with you, including emergency services, breakdown assistance, the local British consulate and your insurance company. There are links to embassies and consulates around the world from the Foreign Office website. (**www.fco.gov.uk**) For information, the European emergency telephone number (our equivalent of 999) is 112.

HELP ME, PLEASE!

If you're in a difficult situation and need local help, then the following words and phrases might prove useful if language is a problem:

Do you speak English?	Parlez-vous anglais?	¿Habla usted inglés?	Parla inglese?	Sprechen Sie Englisch?
Thank you (very much)	Merci (beaucoup)	(Muchas) Gracias	Grazie (mille)	Danke (sehr)
Is there a police station near here?	Est-ce qu'il y a un commissariat de police près d'ici?	¿Hay una comisaría cerca?	C'e' un commissariato qui vicino?	Gibt es ein Polizeirevier hier in der Nähe?
I have lost my passport.	J'ai perdu mon passeport.	He perdido mi pasaporte	Ho perso il mio passaporto.	Ich have meinen Reisepass verloren.
I have broken down.	Je suis tombé en panne	Mi coche se ha averiado.	Ho un guasto.	Ich habe eine Panne.
I have run out of fuel.	Je suis tombé en panne d'essence.	Me he quedado sin gasolina.	Ho terminato la benzina.	Ich habe kein Benzin mehr.
I feel ill.	Je me sens malade.	Me siento mal.	Mi sento male.	Mir ist schlecht.

WORTH KNOWING

You will need a separate GB sticker in EU countries if your car doesn't have a registration plate containing the GB euro-symbol.

Fuel is generally most expensive at motorway service areas and cheapest at supermarkets. However, these are usually shut on Sundays and Bank Holidays. So-called '24 hour' regional fuel stations in France seldom accept payment by UK credit card, so don't rely on them if your tank is running low during a night-time journey.

If you see several fuel stations in short succession before a national border, it's likely that fuel on the other side will be more expensive, so take the opportunity to fill up.

Radar speed camera detectors are illegal in most European countries.

The insurance 'green card' is no longer required for journeys in Europe, but it is important to make sure you have contact details for your insurer in case of an accident or claim.

Speed limits in France are enforced vigorously. Radar controls are frequent, and any driver (including non-residents) detected at more than 25km/h above the speed limit can have their licence confiscated on the spot. Furthermore, if you are caught exceeding the speed limit by 50km/h, even on a first offence, you will face a term of imprisonment. • New legislation introduced in France in 2012 required every driver to carry a self-breathalyser test kit. However, the imposition of a €11 fine for failing to produce a breathalyser when required has been postponed indefinitely. So, in theory, you are required to carry a breathalyser kit, but no fine can be imposed if you don't.

In Spain you must carry two warning triangles, plus a spare pair of glasses for every driver who needs to use them.

In Luxembourg, there are specific rules relating to how you fix a satnav device to your windscreen. Get it wrong and you could be fined on the spot.

In Germany it is against the law to run out of fuel on the motorway. If you do run out, then you face an on-the-spot fine.

Norway and Sweden have particularly low limits for drink-driving: just 20mg per 100ml of blood (compared to 80 in the UK). In Slovakia, the limit is zero.

In Hungary, the limit is also zero. If you are found to be drink-driving, your driving licence will be withdrawn by police officers on the spot.

In most countries, maps and signs will have the European road number (shown in white on a green background) alongside the appropriate national road number. However, in Sweden and Belgium only the E-road number will be shown.

Denmark Cars towing caravans and trailers are prohibited from overtaking on motorways at certain times of day.

Finland Speeding fines are worked out according to your income. Access to a national database allows police at the roadside to establish a Finnish resident's income and number of dependants. Officers then impose a fine based on a specific number of days' income. • If you hit an elk or deer, you must report the collision to the police.

TOP TIPS FOR STAYING SAFE

Collisions abroad occur not just because of poor driving conditions locally, but also because we do not always take the same safety precautions as we might expect to take at home, for example by not wearing a seatbelt or by drinking and driving.

1. Plan your route before you go. That includes the journey you make to reach your destination (with sufficient breaks built in) and any excursions or local journeys you make while you're there.

2. Remember that, wherever you drive, you will be subject to the same laws as local drivers. Claiming ignorance of these laws will not be accepted as an excuse.

3. Take extra care at junctions when you re driving on the 'right side' of the road. If driving in a family group, involve every member in a quick 'junction safety check' to help reduce the risk of a collision. Having everybody in the car call out a catchphrase such as "DriLL DriLL DriLL" (Driver Look Left) on the approach to junctions and roundabouts is a small but potentially life-saving habit.

4. Take fatigue seriously. The excellent European motorway network means you can cover big distances with ease. But you must also make time for proper breaks (experts recommend a break of at least 15 minutes after every two hours of driving). If possible, share the driving and set strict daily limits to the number of driving hours. Watch a short video that explains the risks of driver fatigue: www.motoringassist.com/fatigue

5. Drink-driving limits across Europe are lower than those in the UK. The only exception is Malta, where the limit is the same (0.8mg per ml). Bear this in mind if you're flying to a holiday or business destination and plan to have a drink on the plane, as the combination of unfamiliar roads and alcohol in your bloodstream is not a safe one. It's also worth remembering that drivers who cause collisions because they were drinking are likely to find their insurance policy will not cover them.

6. Expect the unexpected. Styles of driving in your destination country are likely to be very different from those you know in the UK. Drive defensively and certainly don't get involved in any altercations on the road.

7. Don't overload your car while away, however tempting the local bargains may appear. Also, make sure you have good all-round visibility by ensuring you don't pile up items on the parcel shelf or boot, and keep your windscreen clear of dirt and dust.

8. Always wear a seatbelt and ensure everyone else on board wears one. Check specific regulations regarding the carriage of children: in some countries children under the age of 12 are not permitted to travel in the front of the car.

9. Don't use your mobile phone while driving. Even though laws on phone use while driving differ from country to country, the practice is just as dangerous wherever you are.

10. When you're exploring on foot, be wise to road safety as a pedestrian. You may get into trouble for 'jay-walking', so don't just wander across a road. Use a proper crossing, but remember that drivers may not stop for you! And don't forget that traffic closest to you approaches from the LEFT.

STOP AND GIVE WAY

Who has priority?
Make sure you keep a watchful eye on signs telling you who has priority on the road. Look for a yellow diamond sign, which tells you that traffic already on the road has priority. If you see the yellow diamond sign crossed out, then you must give way to traffic joining the road.

Priorité a droite
Despite the use of the yellow diamond signs, be aware that on some French roads (especially roundabouts in Paris), the traditional 'priorité a droite' practice is followed, even though it may no longer be legal. In theory these days, the rule no longer applies unless it is clearly signed. In practice, though, it makes sense to anticipate a driver pulling out in front of you, even though the priority may be yours.

Stop means stop!
If you come to a solid white line with an octagonal 'STOP' sign, then you must come to a complete stop. In other words your wheels must stop turning. Adherence to the 'STOP' sign is generally much more rigorously enforced in European countries than you may be used to here.

Headlight flash
Bear in mind that the practice of flashing headlights at a junction in France does not mean the same thing as it might in the UK. If another motorists flashes his headlights at you, he's telling you that he has priority and will be coming through in front of you.

Other laws and motoring advice to be aware of across Europe:

Austria Recent rules require the mandatory use of winter tyres between 1 November and 15 April.

Belgium You will have to pay to use most public toilets – including those at motorway service stations • You are not permitted to use cruise control on motorways when traffic is heavy • There are also specific penalties for close-following on motorways • Roadside drug-testing of drivers (using oral fluid testing devices) forms a regular part of any police controls.

Cyprus There have been important changes in how speeding and drink-driving are sanctioned. Cyprus now has a graduated system of speeding fines, ranging from one euro per km/h over the limit in marginal cases through to fines of up to €5,000 and a term of imprisonment for the most severe infringements. There are also graduated fines for drink-driving, ranging from fixed penalties for being slightly over the limit to terms of imprisonment and fines of up to €5,000 for the most severe.

France Any driver must be in possession of a valid breathalyser (displaying an 'BF' number), either electronic or chemical, to be shown to a police officer in case of control • All motorcycle riders and passengers must wear reflective clothing, measuring a minimum 150 square centimetres and worn on the upper part of the body. This must also be worn if they have had to stop at the side of the road • Jail terms for drivers caught at more than 50km/h above the speed limit – even first time offenders • The banning of radar detectors, with fines of €1500 for anyone using them • Increased penalties for driving while using a mobile phone.

Germany Check your fuel contents regularly as it's an offence to run out of fuel on a German motorway • It's also an offence to make rude signs to other road users.

Greece has Europe's highest accident rate in terms of the number of crashes per vehicle. Pay particular attention at traffic light junctions, as red lights are frequently ignored • All drivers detected with more than 1.10 g/l of alcohol in blood, or more than 0.60mg/l in breath will be prosecuted for the offence • Carrying a petrol can in a vehicle is forbidden.

Ireland The drink-drive limit was reduced in 2011 from 0.8 mg per ml to 0.5. • Beware of rural three-lane roads, where the middle overtaking lane is used by traffic travelling in both directions. On wider rural roads it's the accepted practice for slower vehicles to pull over to let faster traffic through.

Italy Police can impound your vehicle if you cannot present the relevant ownership documents when requested • You will need a red and white warning sign if you plan to use any rear-mounted luggage rack such as a bike rack • Zero alcohol tolerance is now applied for drivers who have held a driving licence for less than three years, as well as to drivers aged 18 to 21, professional drivers, taxi drivers and truckers.

Norway Under new legislation, police officers can perform roadside drug impairment saliva tests. There are specific limits set for the presence of 20 common non-alcohol drugs. • You'll find what amounts to a zero tolerance where drinking and driving is concerned. Only 0.1mg of alcohol per millilitre of blood is permitted (compared to 0.8 in the UK) • Speeding fines are high. For example, a driver caught at 25 km/h over the 80 km/h speed limit on a national road could expect a fine of around £600.

Portugal If you are towing a caravan, you must have a current inventory of the caravan's contents to show a police officer if requested.

Slovakia It is now mandatory to use dipped headlights on every road journey, regardless of the time of day, season or weather conditions.

Spain Motorway speed limits in Spain are 120km/h • If you need glasses for driving, then the law requires you to carry a spare pair with you in the car • It's compulsory to carry two spare warning triangles, spare bulbs for your car and reflective jackets.

Turkey Take great caution if you're driving at dusk. Many local drivers put off using their lights until it's properly dark, so you may find oncoming traffic very hard to spot • During the time of Ramadan, many people will do without food and water between the hours of sunrise and sunset. This can seriously reduce levels of alertness, especially among people driving buses, trucks and taxis.

Driving regulations

Vehicle
A national vehicle identification plate is always required when taking a vehicle abroad.

Fitting headlamp converters or beam deflectors when taking a right-hand drive car to a country where driving is on the right (every country in Europe except the UK and Ireland) is compulsory.

Within the EU, if not driving a locally hired car, it is compulsory to have either Europlates or a country of origin (e.g. GB) sticker. Outside the EU (and in Andorra) a sticker is compulsory, even with Europlates.

Documentation
All countries require that you carry a valid passport, vehicle registration document, hire certificate or letter of authority for the use of someone else's vehicle, full driving licence/International Driving Permit and insurance documentation/green card. Some non-EU countries also require a visa. Minimum driving ages are often higher for people holding foreign licences.

Licence
A photo licence (both photo and paper parts) is preferred; with an old-style paper licence, an International Driving Permit (IDP) should also be carried. In some countries, an IDP is compulsory, whatever form of licence is held. Non-EU drivers should always have both a licence and and an IDP.

Insurance
Third-party cover is compulsory across Europe. Most insurance policies give only basic cover when driving abroad, so you should check that your policy provides at least third-party cover for the countries in which you will be driving and upgrade it to the level that you require. You may be forced to take out extra cover at the frontier if you cannot produce acceptable proof that you have adequate insurance. Even in countries in which a green card is not required, carrying one is recommended for extra proof of insurance.

Motorcycles
It is compulsory for all motorcyclists and passengers to wear crash helmets. In France it may become compulsory for all motorcyclists and passengers to wear a minimum amount of reflective gear.

Other
In countries in which visibility vests are compulsory one for each person should be carried in the passenger compartment, or panniers on a motorbike, where they can be reached easily.

Warning triangles should also be carried in the passenger compartment.

The penalties for infringements of regulations vary considerably from one country to another. In many countries the police have the right to impose on-the-spot fines (ask for a receipt). Penalties can be severe for serious infringements, particularly for exceeding the blood-alcohol limit; in some countries this can result in immediate imprisonment.

In some countries, vignettes for toll roads are being replaced by electronic tags. See country details.

Please note that driving regulations often change, and that it has not been possible to cover all the information for every type of vehicle. The figures given for capitals' populations are for the whole metropolitan area.

The publishers have made every effort to ensure that the information given here was correct at the time of going to press. No responsibility can be accepted for any errors or their consequences.

The symbols used are:
- Motorway
- Dual carriageway
- Single carriageway
- Surfaced road
- Unsurfaced / gravel road
- Urban area
- Speed limit in kilometres per hour (kph). These are the maximum speeds for the types of roads listed. In some places and under certain conditions they may be considerably lower. Always obey local signs.
- Seat belts
- Children
- Blood alcohol level
- Warning triangle
- First aid kit
- Spare bulb kit
- Fire extinguisher
- Minimum driving age
- Additional documents required
- Mobile phones
- LEZ Low Emission Zone
- ★ Other information

Andorra Principat d'Andorra (AND)
Area 468 sq km (181 sq miles)
Population 85,000 **Capital** Andorra la Vella (44,000)
Languages Catalan (official), French, Castilian, Portuguese
Currency Euro = 100 cents
Website http://visitandorra.com

	Motorway	Dual carriageway	Single carriageway	Urban area
Speed limit	n/a	90	60/90	50

- Seat belts: Compulsory
- Children: Under 10 and below 150 cm must travel in an EU-approved restraint system adapted to their size in the rear
- 0.05% △ Compulsory First aid kit: Recommended
- Spare bulb kit: Compulsory Fire extinguisher: Recommended ⊖ 18
- Mobile phones: Not permitted whilst driving
- ★ Dipped headlights compulsory for motorcycles during day and for other vehicles during poor daytime visibility.
- ★ On-the-spot fines imposed
- ★ Visibility vests compulsory
- ★ Winter tyres or snow chains compulsory in poor conditions or when indicated by signs

Austria Österreich (A)
Area 83,859 sq km (32,377 sq miles)
Population 8,505,000 **Capital** Vienna / Wien (2,419,000)
Languages German (official) **Currency** Euro = 100 cents
Website www.austria.gv.at

	Motorway	Dual carriageway	Single carriageway	Urban area
Speed limit	130	100	100	50
If towing trailer under 750kg / over 750 kg				
Speed limit	100	100	100/80	50

- Seat belts: Compulsory
- Children: Under 14 and under 150cm cannot travel as a front or rear passenger unless they use a suitable child restraint; under 14 over 150cm must wear adult seat belt
- 0.049%; 0.01% if licence held less than 2 years
- △ Compulsory First aid kit: Compulsory
- Spare bulb kit: Recommended Fire extinguisher: Recommended
- ⊖ 18 (16 for mopeds)
- Mobile phones: Only allowed with hands-free kit
- LEZ On A12 motorway non-compliant vehicles banned and certain substances banned, night-time speed restrictions; Steermark province has LEZs affecting lorries
- ★ Dipped headlights must be used during the day by all road users. Headlamp converters compulsory
- ★ On-the-spot fines imposed
- ★ Radar detectors prohibited
- ★ Snow chains recommended in winter. Winter tyres compulsory 1 Nov–15 Apr in poor driving conditions
- ★ To drive on motorways or expressways, a motorway sticker must be purchased at the border or main petrol station. These are available for 10 days, 2 months or 1 year. Vehicles 3.5 tonnes or over must display an electronic tag.
- ★ Visibility vests compulsory

Belarus (BY)
Area 207,600 sq km (80,154 sq miles)
Population 9,609,000 **Capital** Minsk (2,002,000)
Languages Belarusian, Russian (both official)
Currency Belarusian ruble = 100 kopek
Website www.belarus.by/en/government

	Motorway	Dual carriageway	Single carriageway	Urban area
Speed limit	110	90	90	60*
If towing trailer under 750kg				
Speed limit	90	70	70	

*In residential areas limit is 20 km/h • Vehicle towing another vehicle 50 kph limit • If full driving licence held for less than two years, must not exceed 70 kph

- Seat belts: Compulsory in front seats, and rear seats if fitted
- Children: Under 12 not allowed in front seat and must use appropriate child restraint
- 0.00%
- △ Compulsory First aid kit: Compulsory
- Spare bulb kit: Recommended Fire extinguisher: Compulsory
- ⊖ 18
- Additional documents: Visa, vehicle technical check stamp, international driving permit, green card, health insurance. Even with a green card, local third-party insurance may be imposed at the border
- Mobile phones: Use prohibited
- ★ A temporary vehicle import certificate must be purchased on entry and driver must be registered
- ★ Dipped headlights are compulsory during the day Nov–Mar and at all other times in conditions of poor visibility or when towing or being towed.
- ★ Fees payable for driving on highways
- ★ It is illegal for vehicles to be dirty
- ★ On-the-spot fines imposed
- ★ Radar-detectors prohibited
- ★ Winter tyres compulsory; snow chains recommended

Belgium Belgique (B)
Area 30,528 sq km (11,786 sq miles)
Population 12,000,000 **Capital** Brussels/Bruxelles (1,830,000) **Languages** Dutch, French, German (all official)
Currency Euro = 100 cents **Website** www.belgium.be/en

	Motorway	Dual carriageway	Single carriageway	Urban area
Speed limit	120*	120*	90	50**
If towing trailer				
Speed limit	90	90	60	50
Over 3.5 tonnes				
Speed limit	90	90	60	50

*Minimum speed of 70kph may be applied in certain conditions on motorways and some dual carriageways
**Near schools, hospitals and churches the limit may be 30kph

- Seat belts: Compulsory
- Children: All under 19s under 135 cm must wear an appropriate child restraint. Airbags must be deactivated if a rear-facing child seat is used in the front
- 0.05%
- △ Compulsory First aid kit: Recommended
- Spare bulb kit: Recommended Fire extinguisher: Compulsory ⊖ 18
- Mobile phones: Only allowed with a hands-free kit
- ★ Cruise control is not permitted on motorways
- ★ Dipped headlights mandatory at all times for motorcycles and advised during the day in poor conditions for other vehicles
- ★ On-the-spot fines imposed
- ★ Radar detectors prohibited
- ★ Sticker indicating maximum recommended speed for winter tyres must be displayed on dashboard if using them
- ★ Visibility vest compulsory

Bosnia & Herzegovina Bosna i Hercegovina (BIH)
Area 51,197 km² (19,767 mi²) **Population** 3,872,000
Capital Sarajevo (608,000)
Languages Bosnian/Croatian/Serbian
Currency Convertible Marka = 100 convertible pfenniga
Website www.fbihvlada.gov.ba/english/index.php

	Motorway	Dual carriageway	Single carriageway	Urban area
Speed limit	120	90	90	60

- Seat belts: Compulsory if fitted
- Children: Under 12 not allowed in front seat; under 5 must use appropriate child restraint
- 0.03%
- △ Compulsory First aid kit: Compulsory
- Spare bulb kit: Compulsory ⊖ 18
- Additional documents: Visa, International Driving Permit; if driver's insurance not valid for the country, cover may be obtained at most border crossings
- Mobile phones: Prohibited
- ★ Dipped headlights compulsory for all vehicles at all times
- ★ GPS must have fixed speed camera function deactivated; radar detectors prohibited.
- ★ On-the-spot fines imposed
- ★ Visibility vest compulsory
- ★ Winter tyres compulsory 15 Nov–15 Apr; snow chains recommended

Bulgaria Bulgariya (BG)
Area 110,912 sq km (42,822 sq miles)
Population 6,925,000 **Capital** Sofia (1,454,000)
Languages Bulgarian (official), Turkish
Currency Lev = 100 stotinki
Website www.government.bg

	Motorway	Dual carriageway	Single carriageway	Urban area
Speed limit	130	90	90	50
If towing trailer				
Speed limit	100	70	70	50

- Seat belts: Compulsory in front and rear seats
- Children: Under 3s not permitted in vehicles with no child restraints; 3–10 year olds must sit in rear
- 0.05%
- △ Compulsory First aid kit: Compulsory
- Spare bulb kit: Recommended Fire extinguisher: Compulsory ⊖ 18
- Additional documents: Photo driving licence with translation and International Driving Permit; vehicle insurance specific to Bulgaria
- Mobile phones: Only allowed with a hands-free kit
- ★ Dipped headlights compulsory
- ★ Fee at border
- ★ GPS must have fixed speed camera function deactivated; radar detectors prohibited
- ★ On-the-spot fines imposed
- ★ Road tax stickers (annual, monthly or weekly) must be purchased at the border and displayed prominently with the vehicle registration number written on them.
- ★ Visibility vest compulsory

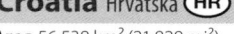

Croatia Hrvatska (HR)
Area 56,538 km² (21,829 mi²)
Population 4,471,000 **Capital** Zagreb (1,111,000)
Languages Croatian **Currency** Kuna = 100 lipa
Website croatia.hr

	Motorway	Dual carriageway	Single carriageway	Urban area
Speed limit	130	110	90	50
Under 24				
Speed limit	120	100	80	50
If towing				
Speed limit	110	80	80	50

- Seat belts: Compulsory if fitted
- Children: Children under 12 not permitted in front seat and must use appropriate child seat or restraint in rear.
- 0.00%
- △ Compulsory First aid kit: Compulsory
- Spare bulb kit: Compulsory Fire extinguisher: Recommended
- ⊖ 18
- Mobile phones: Only allowed with hands-free kit
- ★ Dipped headlights compulsory
- ★ In winter, snow chains compulsory in the mountains; snow tyres compulsory everywhere else Nov–Apr
- ★ On-the-spot fines imposed
- ★ Radar detectors prohibited
- ★ Tow bar and rope compulsory
- ★ Visibility vest compulsory

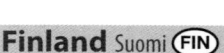

Czech Republic Česka Republica (CZ)
Area 78,864 sq km (30,449 sq miles)
Population 10,627,000 **Capital** Prague/Praha (1,211,000)
Languages Czech (official), Moravian
Currency Czech Koruna = 100 haler
Website www.vlada.cz/en/

	Motorway	Dual carriageway	Single carriageway	Urban area
Speed limit	130	130	90	50
If towing				
Speed limit	80	80	80	50

- Seat belts: Compulsory in front seats and, if fitted, in rear
- Children: Children under 36 kg and 150 cm must use appropriate child restraint. Only front-facing child retraints are permitted in the front in vehicles with airbags fitted. Airbags must be deactivated if a rear-facing child seat is used in the front.
- 0.00% △ Compulsory First aid kit: Compulsory
- Spare bulb kit: Compulsory Fire extinguisher: Compulsory
- ⊖ 18 (17 for motorcycles under 125 cc)
- Mobile phones: Only allowed with a hands-free kit
- LEZ Two-stage LEZ in Prague for vehicles over 3.5 and 6 tonnes. Permit system.
- ★ Dipped headlights compulsory at all times
- ★ GPS must have fixed speed camera function deactivated; radar detectors prohibited
- ★ On-the-spot fines imposed
- ★ Vignette needed for motorway driving, available for 1 year, 60 days, 15 days. Toll specific to lorries introduced 2006, those over 12 tonnes must buy an electronic tag
- ★ Visibility vest compulsory
- ★ Spectacles or contact lens wearers must carry a spare pair in their vehicle at all times
- ★ Winter tyres or snow chains compulsory between Nov and Apr

Denmark Danmark (DK)
Area 43,094 sq km (16,638 sq miles)
Population 5,627,000
Capital Copenhagen / København (1,997,000)
Languages Danish (official) **Currency** Krone = 100 øre
Website www.denmark.dk/en

	Motorway	Dual carriageway	Single carriageway	Urban area
Speed limit	110-130	80	80	50
If towing				
Speed limit	80	70	70	50

- Seat belts: Compulsory front and rear
- Children: Under 135cm must use appropriate child restraint; in front permitted only in an appropriate rear-facing seat with any airbags disabled.
- 0.05% △ Compulsory First aid kit: Recommended
- Spare bulb kit: Recommended Fire extinguisher: Recommended ⊖ 18
- Mobile phones: Only allowed with a hands-free kit
- LEZ Aalborg, Arhus, Copenhagen, Frederiksberg and Odense. Proofs of emissions compliance/compliant filter needed to obtain sticker. Non-compliant vehicles banned.
- ★ Dipped headlights must be used at all times
- ★ On-the-spot fines imposed
- ★ Radar detectors prohibited
- ★ Tolls apply on the Storebaeltsbroen and Oresundsbron bridges.
- ★ Visibility vest recommended

Estonia Eesti (EST)
Area 45,100 sq km (17,413 sq miles)
Population 1,314,000 **Capital** Tallinn (543,000)
Languages Estonian (official), Russian
Currency Euro = 100 cents **Website** valitsus.ee/en

	Motorway	Dual carriageway	Single carriageway	Urban area
Speed limit	n/a	90*	90	50
If full driving licence held for less than two years				
Speed limit	90	90	90	50

*In summer, the speed limit on some dual carriageways may be raised to 100/110 kph

- Seat belts: Compulsory if fitted
- Children: Children too small for adult seatbelts must wear a seat restraint appropriate to their size. Rear-facing safety seats must not be used in the front if an air bag is fitted, unless this has been deactivated.
- 0.00% △ 2 compulsory First aid kit: Compulsory
- Spare bulb kit: Recommended Fire extinguisher: Compulsory ⊖ 18
- Mobile phones: Only allowed with a hands-free kit
- ★ A toll system is in operation in Tallinn
- ★ Dipped headlights compulsory at all times
- ★ On-the-spot fines imposed
- ★ Winter tyres are compulsory from Dec–Mar. Studded winter tyres are allowed from 15 Oct–31 Mar, but this can be extended to start 1 October and/or end 30 April

Finland Suomi (FIN)
Area 338,145 sq km (130,557 sq miles)
Population 5,457,000 **Capital** Helsinki (1,403,000)
Languages Finnish, Swedish (both official)
Currency Euro = 100 cents
Website http://valtioneuvosto.fi/etusivu/en.jsp

	Motorway	Dual carriageway	Single carriageway	Urban area
Speed limit	120	100	80*	30/60
If towing				
Speed limit	80	80	80	30/60

*100 in summer • If towing a vehicle by rope, cable or rod, max speed limit 60 kph. • Maximum of 80 kph for vans and lorries • Speed limits are often lowered in winter

- Seat belts: Compulsory in front and rear
- Children: Below 135 cm must use a child restraint or seat

- 0.05%
- Compulsory
- Recommended
- Recommended
- Recommended
- 18 (motorbikes below 125cc 16)
- Only allowed with hands-free kit
- Dipped headlights must be used at all times
- On-the-spot fines imposed
- Radar-detectors are prohibited
- Visibility vest compulsory
- Winter tyres compulsory Dec–Feb

France (F)

Area 551,500 sq km (212,934 sq miles)
Population 66,616,000 **Capital** Paris (12,162,000)
Languages French (official), Breton, Occitan
Currency Euro = 100 cents
Website www.diplomatie.gouv.fr/en/

	130	110	90	50
On wet roads or if full driving licence held for less than 2 years				
	110	100	80	50
If towing below / above 3.5 tonnes gross				
	110/90	100/90	90/80	50

50kph on all roads if fog reduces visibility to less than 50m • Licence will be lost and driver fined for exceeding speed limit by over 40kph

- Compulsory in front seats and, if fitted, in rear
- In rear, 4 or under must have a child safety seat (rear facing if up to 9 months); if 5–10 must use an appropriate restraint system. Under 10 permitted in the front only if rear seats are fully occupied by other under 10s or there are no rear safety belts. In front, if child is in rear-facing child seat, any airbag must be deactivated.
- 0.05%. If towing or with less than 2 years with full driving licence, 0.00% • All drivers/motorcyclists must carry 2 unused breathalysers to French certification standards, showing an NF number.
- Compulsory
- Recommended
- Recommended
- 18
- Use not permitted whilst driving
- LEZ An LEZ operates in the Mont Blanc tunnel
- Dipped headlights compulsory in poor daytime visibility and at all times for motorcycles
- GPS must have fixed speed camera function deactivated; radar-detection equipment is prohibited
- It is compulsory to carry a French-authority-recognised (NF) breathalyser.
- On-the-spot fines imposed
- Tolls on motorways. Electronic tag needed if using automatic tolls.
- Visibility vests must be carried in the passenger compartment; legislation making visibility vests compulsory for motorcyclists and passengers may be reintroduced.
- Winter tyres recommended. Carrying snow chains recommended in winter as these may have to be fitted if driving on snow-covered roads, in accordance with signage.

Germany Deutschland (D)

Area 357,022 sq km (137,846 sq miles)
Population 80,716,000 **Capital** Berlin (6,000,000)
Languages German (official)
Currency Euro = 100 cents
Website www.bundesregierung.de

	*	*	100	50
If towing				
	80	80	80	50

*no limit, 130 kph recommended

- Compulsory
- Under 150 cm and 12 or under must use an appropriate child seat or restraint. In front if child is in rear-facing child seat, airbags must be deactivated.
- 0.05%, 0.0% for drivers 21 or under or with less than two years full licence
- Compulsory
- Compulsory
- Recommended
- Recommended
- 18 (motorbikes: 16 if under 50cc)
- Use permitted only with hands-free kit – also applies to drivers of motorbikes and bicycles
- LEZ More than 60 cities have or are planning LEZs. Proof of compliance needed to acquire sticker. Non-compliant vehicles banned.
- Dipped headlights compulsory in poor weather conditions and tunnels; recommended at other times
- GPS must have fixed speed camera function deactivated; radar detectors prohibited
- Motorcyclists must use dipped headlights at all times; other vehicles must use dipped headlights during poor daytime visibility.
- On-the-spot fines imposed
- Tolls on autobahns for lorries
- Winter tyres compulsory in all winter weather conditions; snow chains recommended

Greece Ellas (GR)

Area 131,957 sq km (50,948 sq miles)
Population 10,816,000
Languages Greek (official)
Capital Athens / Athina (3,758,000)
Currency Euro = 100 cents
Website www.primeminister.gr/english

	120	110	110	50
Motorbikes, and if towing				
	90	70	70	40

- Compulsory in front seats and, if fitted, in rear
- Under 12 or below 135cm must use appropriate child restraint. In front if child is in rear-facing child seat, any airbags must be deactivated.
- 0.05%, 0.00% for drivers with less than 2 years' full licence and motorcyclists
- Compulsory
- Compulsory
- Recommended
- Compulsory
- 18
- Not permitted.
- Dipped headlights compulsory during poor daytime visibility and at all times for motorcycles
- On-the-spot fines imposed
- Radar-detection equipment is prohibited
- Tolls on several newer motorways.

Hungary Magyarország (H)

Area 93,032 sq km (35,919 sq miles)
Population 9,879,000 **Currency** Forint = 100 fillér
Capital Budapest (3,284,000) **Languages** Hungarian (official) **Website** www.kormany.hu/en

	130	110	90	50
If towing				
	80	70	70	50

- Compulsory in front seats and if fitted in rear seats
- Under 150cm and over 3 must be seated in rear and use appropriate child restraint. Under 3 allowed in front only in rear-facing child seat with any airbags deactivated.
- 0.00%
- Compulsory
- Compulsory
- Compulsory
- Recommended
- 17
- Only allowed with a hands-free kit
- LEZ Budapest has vehicle restrictions on days with heavy dust and is planning an LEZ.
- All motorways are toll and operate electronic vignette system with automatic number plate recognition, tickets are available for 4 days, 7 days, 1 month, 1 year
- During the day dipped headlights compulsory outside built-up areas; compulsory at all times for motorcycles
- Electronic vignette system in use for tolls on several motorways
- On-the-spot fines issued
- Snow chains compulsory where conditions dictate
- Visibility vest compulsory

Iceland Ísland (IS)

Area 103,000 sq km (39,768 sq miles)
Population 326,000 **Capital** Reykjavik (209,000)
Languages Icelandic **Currency** Krona = 100 aurar
Website www.government.is/

	n/a	90	80	50

- Compulsory in front and rear seats
- Under 12 or below 150cm not allowed in front seat and must use appropriate child restraint.
- 0.05%
- Compulsory
- Compulsory
- Compulsory
- Compulsory
- 18; 21 to drive a hire car; 25 to hire a jeep
- Only allowed with a hands-free kit
- Dipped headlights compulsory at all times
- Driving off marked roads is forbidden
- Highland roads are not suitable for ordinary cars
- On-the-spot fines imposed
- Winter tyres compulsory c.1 Nov–14 Apr (variable)

Ireland Eire (IRL)

Area 70,273 sq km (27,132 sq miles)
Population 4,593,000 **Capital** Dublin (1,804,000)
Languages Irish, English (both official)
Currency Euro = 100 cents **Website** www.gov.ie/en/

	120	100	80	50
If towing				
	80	80	80	50

- Compulsory where fitted. Driver responsible for ensuring passengers under 17 comply
- Children 3 and under must be in a suitable child restraint system. Airbags must be deactivated if a rear-facing child seat is used in the front. Those under 150 cm and 36 kg must use appropriate child restraint in cars with seatbelts.
- 0.05%, 0.02% for novice and professional drivers
- Compulsory
- Recommended
- Recommended
- Recommended
- 17 (16 for motorbikes up to 125cc; 18 for over 125cc; 18 for lorries; 21 bus/minibus)
- Only allowed with a hands-free kit
- Dipped headlights are compulsory during daylight hours
- Dipped headlights compulsory for motorbikes at all times and in poor visibility for other vehicles
- Driving is on the left
- GPS must have fixed speed camera function deactivated; radar detectors prohibited
- On-the-spot fines imposed
- Tolls are being introduced on some motorways; the M50 Dublin has barrier-free tolling with number-plate recognition.

Italy Italia (I)

Area 301,318 sq km (116,338 sq miles)
Population 60,783,000
Capital Rome / Roma (4,194,000)
Languages Italian (official)
Currency Euro = 100 cents
Website www.italia.it

	130	110	90	50
If towing				
	80	70	70	50
Less than three years with full licence				
	100	90	90	50
When wet				
	100	90	80	50

Some motorways with emergency lanes have speed limit of 150 kph

- Compulsory in front seats and, if fitted, in rear
- Under 12 not allowed in front seats except in child safety seat; children under 3 must have special seat in the back
- 0.05%, but 0.00% for professional drivers or with less than 3 years full licence
- Compulsory
- Recommended
- Compulsory
- Recommended
- 18 (14 for mopeds, 16 up to 125cc, 20 up to 350cc)
- Only allowed with hands-free kit
- LEZ Most northern and several southern regions operate seasonal LEZs and many towns and cities have various schemes that restrict access. There is an LEZ in the Mont Blanc tunnel
- Dipped headlights compulsory outside built-up areas, in tunnels, on motorways and dual carriageways and in poor visibility; compulsory at all times for motorcycles
- On-the-spot fines imposed
- Radar-detection equipment is prohibited
- Snow chains compulsory where signs indicate Nov–April
- Tolls on motorways. Blue lanes accept credit cards; yellow lanes restricted to holders of Telepass pay-toll device.
- Visibility vest compulsory

Kosovo Republika e Kosoves / Republika Kosovo (RKS)

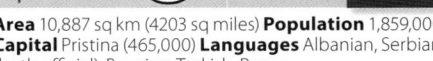

Area 10,887 sq km (4203 sq miles) **Population** 1,859,000
Capital Pristina (465,000) **Languages** Albanian, Serbian (both official), Bosnian, Turkish, Roma
Currency Euro (Serbian dinar in Serb enclaves)
Website www.kryeministri-ks.net/?page?equals?2,1

	120	100	100	60

- Compulsory
- Under 12 must sit in rear seats
- 0.03%, 0.00% for professional, business and commercial drivers
- Compulsory
- Compulsory
- Compulsory
- Compulsory
- 18 (16 for motorbikes less than 125 cc, 14 for mopeds)
- International driving permit, locally purchased third-party insurance (green card is not recognised), documents with proof of ability to cover costs and valid reason for visiting. Visitors from many non-EU countries require a visa.
- Only allowed with hands-free kit
- Dipped headlights compulsory at all times
- Winter tyres or snow chains compulsory in poor winter weather conditions

Latvia Latvija (LV)

Area 64,589 sq km (24,942 sq miles)
Population 1,998,000
Capital Riga (1,018,000)
Languages Latvian (official), Russian
Currency Euro = 100 cents
Website www.mk.gov.lv/en

	90/100	90	90	50
If towing				
	90/100	90	90	50

In residential areas limit is 20kph • If full driving licence held for less than two years, must not exceed 80 kph

- Compulsory in front seats and if fitted in rear
- If under 12 years and 150cm must use child restraint in front and rear seats
- 0.05%, 0.02% with less than 2 years experience
- Compulsory
- Compulsory
- Recommended
- Compulsory
- 18
- Only allowed with hands-free kit
- Dipped headlights must be used at all times all year round
- On-the-spot fines imposed
- Pedestrians have priority
- Visibility vests compulsory
- Winter tyres compulsory for vehicles up to 3.5 tonnes Dec–Feb, but illegal May–Sept

Lithuania Lietuva (LT)

Area 65,200 sq km (25,173 sq miles)
Population 2,944,000
Capital Vilnius (806,000)
Languages Lithuanian (official), Russian, Polish
Currency Litas = 100 centai
Website www.lrvk.lt/en

	130	110	90	50
If towing				
	n/a	70	70	50

In winter speed limits are reduced by 10–20 km/h

- Compulsory in front seats and if fitted in rear seats
- Under 12 not allowed in front seats unless in a child safety seat; under 3 must use appropriate child seat and sit in rear
- 0.04%, 0.02% for those with less than 2 years' full licence
- Compulsory
- Compulsory
- Recommended
- Compulsory
- 18
- Only allowed with a hands-free kit
- Dipped headlights must be used at all times
- On-the-spot fines imposed
- Visibility vest compulsory
- Winter tyres compulsory 10 Nov–1 Apr

Luxembourg (L)

Area 2,586 sq km (998 sq miles)
Population 550,000
Capital Luxembourg (165,000)
Languages Luxembourgian / Letzeburgish (official), French, German
Currency Euro = 100 cents
Website www.visitluxembourg.com

	130/110	90	90	50
If towing				
	90	75	75	50

If full driving licence held for less than two years, must not exceed 75 kph • In 20 km/h zones, pedestrians have right of way.

- Compulsory
- Children under 3 must use an appropriate restraint system. Airbags must be disabled if a rear-facing child seat is used in the front. Children 3 to 18 and / or under 150 cm must use a restraint system appropriate to their size. If over 36kg a seatbelt may be used in the back only
- 0.05%, 0.02 for young drivers, drivers with less than 2 years experience and drivers of taxis and commercial vehicles
- Compulsory
- Compulsory (buses)
- Compulsory
- Compulsory (buses, transport of dangerous goods)
- 18
- Use permitted only with hands-free kit
- Dipped headlights compulsory for motorcyclists and in poor visibility for other vehicles
- On-the-spot fines imposed
- Visibility vest compulsory
- Winter tyres compulsory in winter weather

Macedonia Makedonija (MK)

Area 25,713 sq km (9,927 sq miles)
Population 2,100,000
Capital Skopje (669,000)
Languages Macedonian (official), Albanian
Currency Denar = 100 deni
Website www.vlada.mk/?language=en-gb

	120	100	60	60
Newly qualified drivers				
	100	80	60	60
If towing				
	80	70	50	50

- Compulsory in front seats; compulsory if fitted in rear seats
- Under 12 not allowed in front seats
- 0.05%, 0.00% for business, commercial and professional drivers and with less than 2 years experience
- Compulsory
- Compulsory
- Compulsory
- Recommended; compulsory for LPG vehicles
- 18 (mopeds 16)
- International driving permit; visa
- Use not permitted whilst driving
- Dipped headlights compulsory at all times
- GPS must have fixed speed camera function deactivated; radar detectors prohibited
- Novice drivers may only drive between 11pm and 5am if there is someone over 25 with a valid licence in the vehicle.
- On-the-spot fines imposed
- Tolls apply on many roads
- Visibility vest must be kept in the passenger compartment and worn to leave the vehicle in the dark outside built-up areas
- Winter tyres or snow chains compulsory 15 Nov–15 Mar

Moldova (MD)

Area 33,851 sq km (13,069 sq miles)
Population 3,600,000 **Capital** Chisinau (801,000)
Languages Moldovan / Romanian (official)
Currency Leu = 100 bani **Website** www.moldova.md

	90	90	90	60
If towing or if licence held under 1 year				
	70	70	70	60

- Compulsory in front seats and, if fitted, in rear seats
- Under 12 not allowed in front seats
- 0.00%
- Compulsory Compulsory
- Recommended Compulsory
- 18 (mopeds and motorbikes, 16; vehicles with more than eight passenger places, taxis or towing heavy vehicles, 21)
- International Driving Permit (preferred), visa
- Only allowed with hands-free kit
- ★ Motorcyclists must use dipped headlights at all times
- ★ Winter tyres recommended Nov–Feb

Montenegro Crna Gora (MNE)

Area 14,026 sq km, (5,415 sq miles)
Population 625,000 **Capital** Podgorica (186,000)
Languages Serbian (of the Ijekavian dialect)
Currency Euro = 100 cents
Website www.gov.me/en/homepage

	n/a	100	80	60

80kph speed limit if towing a caravan

- Compulsory in front and rear seats
- Under 12 not allowed in front seats
- 0.05% Compulsory Compulsory
- Compulsory Compulsory
- 18 (16 for motorbikes less than 125cc; 14 for mopeds)
- Prohibited
- ★ An 'eco' tax vignette must be obtained when crossing the border and displayed in the upper right-hand corner of the windscreen
- ★ Dipped headlights must be used at all times
- ★ From mid-Nov to March, driving wheels must be fitted with winter tyres
- ★ On-the-spot fines imposed
- ★ Tolls on some primary roads and in the Sozina tunnel between Lake Skadar and the sea
- ★ Visibility vest compulsory

Netherlands Nederland (NL)

Area 41,526 sq km (16,033 sq miles)
Population 16,820,000 **Currency** Euro = 100 cents
Capital Amsterdam 2,400,000 • administrative capital 's-Gravenhage (The Hague) 1,051,000
Languages Dutch (official), Frisian
Website www.government.nl

	120/100	80/100	80/100	50

- Compulsory
- Under 3 must travel in the back, using an appropriate child restraint; 3-12 or under 135cm must use an appropriate child restraint
- 0.05%, 0.02% with less than 5 years experience or moped riders under 24
- Compulsory Recommended
- Recommended Recommended
- 18
- Only allowed with a hands-free kit
- LEZ About 20 cities operate or are planning LEZs. A national scheme is planned.
- ★ Dipped headlights compulsory for motorcycles and recommended in poor visibility and on open roads for other vehicles.
- ★ On-the-spot fines imposed
- ★ Radar-detection equipment is prohibited

Norway Norge (N)

Area 323,877 sq km (125,049 sq miles)
Population 5,138,000 **Capital** Oslo (1,503,000)
Languages Norwegian (official), Lappish, Finnish
Currency Krone = 100 øre **Website** www.norway.org.uk

	90/100	80	80	30/50
If towing trailer with brakes				
	80	80	80	50
If towing trailer without brakes				
	60	60	60	50

- Compulsory in front seats and, if fitted, in rear
- Children less than 150cm tall must use appropriate child restraint. Children under 4 must use child safety seat or safety restraint (cot)
- 0.01%
- Compulsory Recommended
- Recommended Recommended
- 18 (heavy vehicles 18/21)
- Only allowed with a hands-free kit
- LEZ Planned for Bergen, Oslo and Trondheim
- ★ Dipped headlights must be used at all times
- ★ On-the-spot fines imposed
- ★ Radar-detectors are prohibited
- ★ Tolls apply on some bridges, tunnels and access roads into Bergen, Oslo, Trondheim and Stavangar. Several use electronic fee collection only.
- ★ Visibility vest compulsory
- ★ Winter tyres or summer tyres with snow chains compulsory for snow- or ice-covered roads

Poland Polska (PL)

Area 323,250 sq km (124,807 sq miles)
Population 38,545,000 **Capital** Warsaw / Warszawa (2,666,000) **Languages** Polish (official)
Currency Zloty = 100 groszy **Website** en.polska.pl

Motor-vehicle only roads[1], under/over 3.5 tonnes				
	130[2]/80[2]	110/80	100/80	n/a
Motor-vehicle only roads[1] if towing				
	n/a	80	80	n/a
Other roads, under 3.5 tonnes				
	n/a	100	90	50/60[3]
Other roads, 3.5 tonnes or over				
	n/a	80	70	50/60[3]
Other roads, if towing				
	n/a	60	60	30

[1] Indicated by signs with white car on blue background.
[2] Minimum speed 40 kph. [3] 50 kph 05.00–23.00; 60 kph 23.00–05.00; 20 kph in marked residential areas

- Compulsory in front seats and, if fitted, in rear
- Under 12 not allowed in front seats unless in a child safety seat; in rear seats children under 12 and less than 150 cm must use child safety seat. Rear-facing child seats not permitted in vehicles with airbags.
- 0.02% Compulsory Recommended
- Recommended Compulsory
- 18 (mopeds and motorbikes – 16)
- Only allowed with a hands-free kit
- ★ Dipped headlights compulsory for all vehicles
- ★ On-the-spot fines imposed
- ★ Radar-detection equipment is prohibited
- ★ Visibility vests compulsory for drivers of Polish-registered vehicles

Portugal (P)

Area 88,797 sq km (34,284 sq miles)
Population 10,427,000 **Capital** Lisbon / Lisboa (3,035,000)
Languages Portuguese (official)
Currency Euro = 100 cents
Website www.portugal.gov.pt/en.aspx

	120*	90	90	50
If towing				
	100*	90	80	50

*40kph minimum; 90kph maximum if licence held under 1 year

- Compulsory in front seats; compulsory if fitted in rear seats
- Under 12 and below 150cm must travel in the rear in an appropriate child restraint; rear-facing child seats permitted in front only if airbags deactivated
- 0.05% Compulsory Recommended
- Recommended Recommended
- 18 (motorcycles under 50cc 17)
- MOT certificate for vehicles over 3 years old, photographic proof of identity (e.g. driving licence or passport) must be carried at all times.
- Only allowed with hands-free kit
- LEZ An LEZ prohibits vehicles without catalytic converters from certain parts of Lisbon. There are plans to extend the scheme to the whole of the city
- ★ Dipped headlights compulsory for motorcycles, compulsory for other vehicles in poor visibility and tunnels
- ★ On-the-spot fines imposed
- ★ Radar-detectors prohibited
- ★ Tolls on motorways; do not use green lanes, these are reserved for auto-payment users. Some motorways require an automatic toll device.
- ★ Visibility vest compulsory
- ★ Wearers of spectacles or contact lenses should carry a spare pair

Romania (RO)

Area 238,391 sq km (92,042 sq miles)
Population 20,122,000
Capital Bucharest / Bucuresti (2,272,000)
Languages Romanian (official), Hungarian
Currency Romanian leu = 100 bani
Website www.gov.ro

Cars and motorcycles				
	120/130	100	90	50
Vans				
	110	90	80	50
Motorcycles				
	100	80	80	50

For motor vehicles with trailers or if full driving licence has been held for less than one year, speed limits are 20kph lower than those listed above • Jeep-like vehicles: 70kph outside built-up areas but 60kph in all areas if diesel

- Compulsory
- Under 12 not allowed in front seats
- 0.00% Compulsory
- Compulsory Compulsory
- Compulsory 18
- Only allowed with hands-free kit
- ★ Dipped headlights compulsory outside built-up areas, compulsory everywhere for motorcycles
- ★ Electronic road tax system; price depends on emissions category and length of stay
- ★ It is illegal for vehicles to be dirty
- ★ On-the-spot fines imposed
- ★ Tolls on motorways
- ★ Visibility vest compulsory
- ★ Winter tyres compulsory Nov–Mar if roads are snow- or ice-covered, especially in mountainous areas

Russia Rossiya (RUS)

Area 17,075,000 sq km (6,592,800 sq miles)
Population 143,700,000 **Capital** Moscow / Moskva (11,511,000) **Languages** Russian (official), and many others
Currency Russian ruble = 100 kopeks
Website government.ru/en/

	110	90	90	60
If licence held for under 2 years				
	70	70	70	60

- Compulsory if fitted
- Under 12 permitted in front seat only in an appropriate child restraint
- 0.00% Compulsory Compulsory
- Compulsory Compulsory 18
- International Driving Permit with Russian translation, visa, green card endorsed for Russia, International Certificate for Motor Vehicles
- Only allowed with a hands-free kit
- ★ Dipped headlights compulsory during the day
- ★ On-the-spot fines imposed
- ★ Picking up hitchhikers is prohibited
- ★ Radar detectors/blockers prohibited
- ★ Road tax payable at the border

Serbia Srbija (SRB)

Area 77,474 sq km, 29,913 sq miles
Population 7,187,000 **Capital** Belgrade / Beograd (1,659,000) **Languages** Serbian
Currency Dinar = 100 paras **Website** www.srbija.gov.rs

	120	100	80	60

- Compulsory in front and rear seats
- Age 3–12 must be in rear seats and wear seat belt or appropriate child restraint; under 3 in rear-facing child seat permitted in front only if airbag deactivated
- 0.03%
- Compulsory Compulsory
- Compulsory Compulsory
- 18 (16 for motorbikes less than 125cc; 14 for mopeds)
- International Driving Permit, green card or locally bought third-party insurance
- No legislation
- ★ 3-metre tow bar or rope
- ★ 80km/h speed limit if towing a caravan
- ★ Dipped headlights compulsory
- ★ On-the-spot fines imposed
- ★ Radar detectors prohibited
- ★ Tolls on motorways and some primary roads
- ★ Visibility vest compulsory
- ★ Winter tyres compulsory Nov–Apr for vehicles up to 3.5 tonnes. Carrying snow chains recommended in winter as these may have to be fitted if driving on snow-covered roads, in accordance with signage.

Slovak Republic Slovenska Republika (SK)

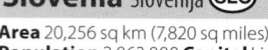

Area 49,012 sq km (18,923 sq miles)
Population 5,416,000 **Capital** Bratislava (660,000)
Languages Slovak (official), Hungarian
Currency Euro = 100 cents
Website www.government.gov.sk

	130	90	90	60

- Compulsory
- Under 12 or below 150cm must be in rear in appropriate child restraint
- 0.0
- Compulsory Compulsory
- Compulsory Recommended
- 18 (15 for mopeds)
- International driving permit, proof of health insurance
- Only allowed with a hands-free kit
- ★ Dipped headlights compulsory at all times
- ★ On-the-spot fines imposed
- ★ Radar-detection equipment is prohibited
- ★ Tow rope recommended
- ★ Vignette required for motorways, car valid for 1 year, 30 days, 7 days; lorry vignettes carry a higher charge.
- ★ Visibility vests compulsory
- ★ Winter tyres compulsory

Slovenia Slovenija (SLO)

Area 20,256 sq km (7,820 sq miles)
Population 2,062,000 **Capital** Ljubljana (275,000)
Languages Slovene **Currency** Euro = 100 cents
Website www.gov.si

	130	90*	90*	50
If towing				
	80	80*	80*	50

*70kph in urban areas

- Compulsory in front seats and, if fitted, in rear
- Under 12 and below 150cm must use appropriate child restraint; babies must use child safety seat
- 0.05%
- Compulsory Compulsory
- Compulsory Recommended
- 18 (motorbikes up to 125cc – 16, up to 350cc – 18)
- Only allowed with hands-free kit
- ★ Dipped headlights must be used at all times
- ★ On-the-spot fines imposed
- ★ Snow chains or winter tyres compulsory mid-Nov to mid-March, and in wintery conditions at other times
- ★ Vignettes valid for variety of periods compulsory for vehicles below 3.5 tonnes for toll roads. Write your vehicle registration number on the vignette before displaying it. For heavier vehicles electronic tolling system applies; several routes are cargo-traffic free during high tourist season.
- ★ Visibility vest compulsory

Spain España (E)

Area 497,548 sq km (192,103 sq miles)
Population 46,704,000 **Capital** Madrid (6,369,000)
Languages Castilian Spanish (official), Catalan, Galician, Basque **Currency** Euro = 100 cents
Website www.lamoncloa.gob.es/home.htm

	110	100	90	50
If towing				
	80	80	70	50

- Compulsory in front seats and if fitted in rear seats
- Under 135cm and below 12 must use appropriate child restraint
- 0.05%, 0.03% if less than 2 years full licence or if vehicle is over 3.5 tonnes or carries more than 9 passengers
- Two compulsory (one for in front, one for behind)
- Recommended
- Compulsory
- Recommended
- 18 (18/21 heavy vehicles; 18 for motorbikes over 125cc; 16 for motorbikes up to 125cc; 14 for mopeds up to 75cc)
- Only allowed with hands-free kit
- ★ Dipped headlights compulsory for motorcycles and in poor daytime visibility for other vehicles.
- ★ It is recommended that spectacles or contact lens wearers carry a spare pair.
- ★ Radar-detection equipment is prohibited
- ★ Snow chains recommended for mountainous areas in winter
- ★ Spare tyre compulsory
- ★ Tolls on motorways
- ★ Visibility vest compulsory

Sweden Sverige (S)

Area 449,964 sq km (173,731 sq miles)
Population 9,658,000 **Capital** Stockholm (2,127,000)
Languages Swedish (official), Finnish
Currency Swedish krona = 100 ore
Website www.sweden.gov.se

	110–120	80	70–100	30–60
If towing trailer with brakes				
	80	80	70	50

- Compulsory in front and rear seats
- Under 16 or below 135cm must use appropriate child restraint; below 140cm may travel in front only if airbag deactivated; rear-facing child seat permitted only if airbag deactivated.
- 0.02%
- Compulsory Recommended
- Recommended Recommended
- 18
- No legislation
- LEZ Gothenberg, Helsingborg, Lund, Malmo, Mölndal and Stockholm have LEZs, progressively prohibiting vehicles 6 or more years old.
- ★ 1 Dec–31 Mar winter tyres, anti-freeze and shovel compulsory
- ★ Dipped headlights must be used at all times
- ★ On-the-spot fines imposed
- ★ Radar-detection equipment is prohibited

Switzerland Schweiz (CH)

Area 41,284 sq km (15,939 sq miles)
Population 8,014,000 **Capital** Bern (356,000)
Languages French, German, Italian, Romansch (all official)
Currency Swiss Franc = 100 centimes / rappen
Website www.admin.ch

	120	80	80	50/30
If towing up to 1 tonne / over 1 tonne				
	80	80	60/80	30/50

- Compulsory in front and, if fitted, in rear
- Up to 12 years and below 150 cm must use an appropriate child restraint. Children 6 and under must sit in the rear.
- 0.05%
- Compulsory
- Recommended
- Recommended
- Recommended
- 18 (mopeds up to 50cc – 16)
- Only allowed with a hands-free kit
- ★ Dipped headlights compulsory
- ★ GPS must have fixed speed camera function deactivated; radar detectors prohibited
- ★ Motorways are all toll and for vehicles below 3.5 tonnes a vignette must be purchased at the border. The vignette is valid for one calendar year. Vehicles over 3.5 tonnes must have an electronic tag for travel on any road.
- ★ On-the-spot fines imposed
- ★ Pedestrians have right of way
- ★ Picking up hitchhikers is prohibited on motorways and main roads
- ★ Spectacles or contact lens wearers must carry a spare pair in their vehicle at all times
- ★ Winter tyres recommended Nov–Mar; snow chains compulsory in designated areas in poor winter weather

Turkey Türkiye (TR)

Area 774,815 sq km (299,156 sq miles)
Population 76,668,000
Capital Ankara (5,045,000)
Languages Turkish (official), Kurdish
Currency New Turkish lira = 100 kurus
Website www.mfa.gov.tr/default.en.mfa

	120	90	90	50
If towing				
	70	70	70	40

- Compulsory in front seats
- Under 150 cm and below 36kg must use suitable child restraint. If above 136 cm may sit in the back without child restraint. Under 3s can only travel in the front in a rear facing seat if the airbag is deactivated. Children 3–12 may not travel in the front seat.
- 0.00%
- Two compulsory (one in front, one behind)
- Compulsory
- Compulsory
- Compulsory
- 18
- International driving permit advised; note that Turkey is in both Europe and Asia, green card/UK insurance that covers whole of Turkey or locally bought insurance, e-visa obtained in advance.
- Prohibited
- ★ Dipped headlights compulsory in daylight hours
- ★ On-the-spot fines imposed
- ★ Several motorways, and the Bosphorus bridges are toll roads
- ★ Tow rope and tool kit must be carried

Ukraine Ukraina (UA)

Area 603,700 sq km (233,088 sq miles)
Population 44,573,000
Capital Kiev / Kyyiv (3,275,000)
Languages Ukrainian (official), Russian
Currency Hryvnia = 100 kopiykas
Website www.kmu.gov.ua/control/en

	130	90	90	60
If towing				
	80	80	80	60

Speed limit in pedestrian zone 20 kph

- Compulsory in front and rear seats
- Under 12 and below 145cm must use an appropriate child restraint and sit in rear
- 0.02% – if use of medication can be proved. Otherwise 0.00%
- Compulsory
- Compulsory
- Optional
- Compulsory
- 18 cars; 16 motorbikes
- International Driving Permit, visa, International Certificate for Motor Vehicles, green card
- No legislation
- ★ A road tax is payable on entry to the country.
- ★ Dipped headlights compulsory in poor daytime visibility
- ★ On-the-spot fines imposed
- ★ Tow rope and tool kit recommended
- ★ Winter tyres compulsory Nov–Apr in snowy conditions

United Kingdom (GB)

Area 241,857 sq km (93,381 sq miles)
Population 63,705,000
Capital London (15,011,000)
Languages English (official), Welsh (also official in Wales), Gaelic
Currency Sterling (pound) = 100 pence
Website www.direct.gov.uk

	112	112	96	48
If towing				
	96	96	80	48

- Compulsory in front seats and if fitted in rear seats
- Under 3 not allowed in front seats except with appropriate restraint, and in rear must use child restraint if available; in front 3–12 or under 135cm must use appropriate child restraint, in rear must use appropriate child restraint (or seat belt if no child restraint is available, e.g. because two occupied restraints prevent fitting of a third).
- 0.08% (may change to 0.05% in Scotland)
- Recommended
- Recommended
- Recommended
- Recommended
- 17 (16 for mopeds)
- Only allowed with hands-free kit
- LEZ London's LEZ operates by number-plate recognition; non-compliant vehicles face hefty daily charges. Foreign-registered vehicles must register.
- ★ Driving is on the left
- ★ On-the-spot fines imposed
- ★ Smoking is banned in all commercial vehicles
- ★ Some toll motorways and bridges

Ski resorts

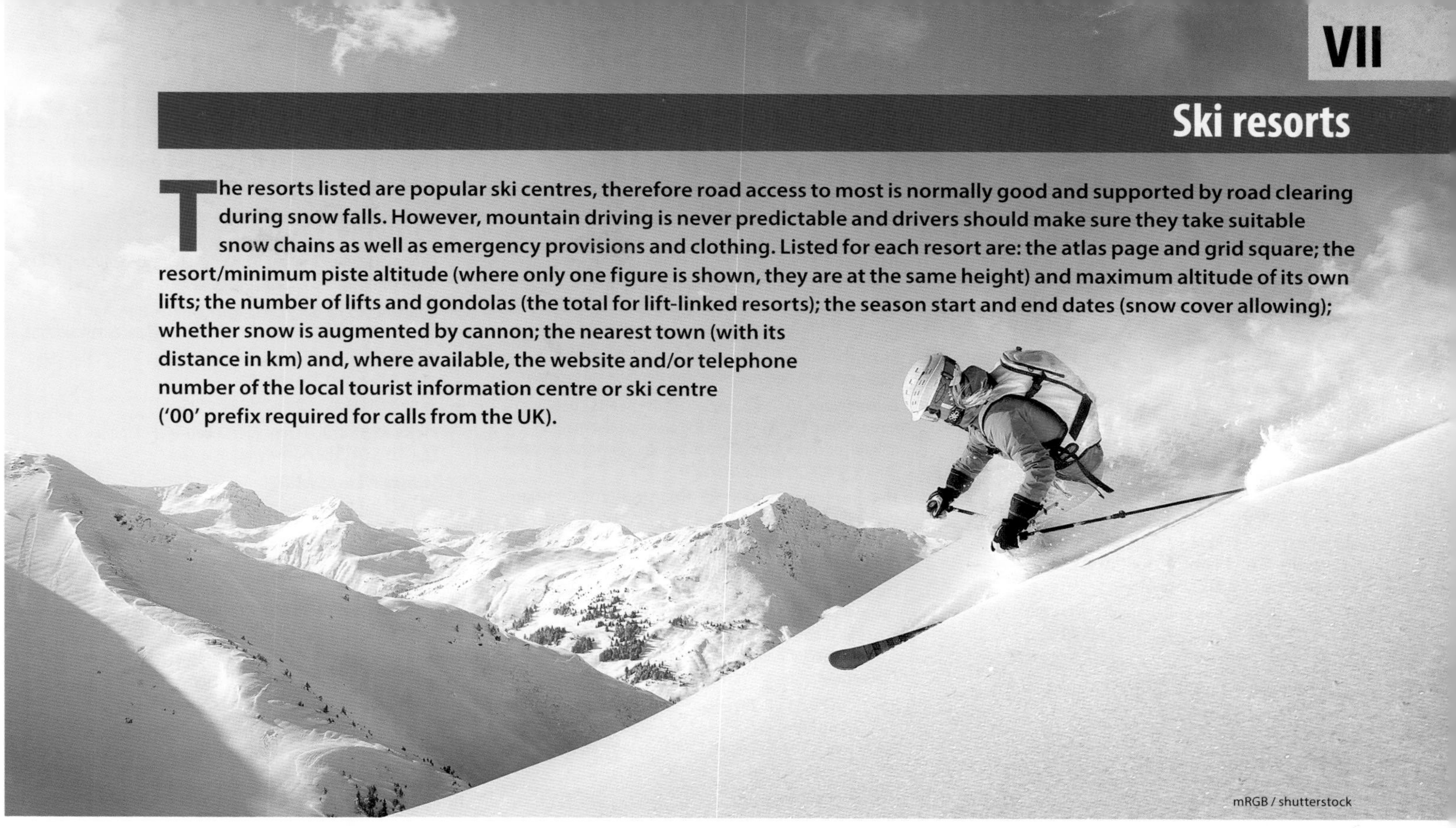

The resorts listed are popular ski centres, therefore road access to most is normally good and supported by road clearing during snow falls. However, mountain driving is never predictable and drivers should make sure they take suitable snow chains as well as emergency provisions and clothing. Listed for each resort are: the atlas page and grid square; the resort/minimum piste altitude (where only one figure is shown, they are at the same height) and maximum altitude of its own lifts; the number of lifts and gondolas (the total for lift-linked resorts); the season start and end dates (snow cover allowing); whether snow is augmented by cannon; the nearest town (with its distance in km) and, where available, the website and/or telephone number of the local tourist information centre or ski centre ('00' prefix required for calls from the UK).

mRGB / shutterstock

The ❄ symbol indicates resorts with snow cannon

Andorra

Pyrenees

Pas de la Casa / Grau Roig 91 A4 ❄ 2050–2640m • 65 lifts • Dec–Apr • Andorra La Vella (30km) www.pasdelacasa-andorra.com • *Access via Envalira Pass (2407m), highest in Pyrenees, snow chains essential.*

Austria

Alps

Bad Gastein 72 A3 ❄ 1050/1100–2700m • 50 lifts • Dec–Mar • St Johann im Pongau (45km) i +43 6432 3393 0 www.gastein.com

Bad Hofgastein 72 A3 ❄ 860–2295m • 50 lifts • Dec–Mar • St Johann im Pongau (40km) i +43 6432 3393 0 www.gastein.com/en/region-orte/bad-hofgastein

Bad Kleinkirchheim 72 B3 ❄ 1070–2310m • 25 lifts • Dec–Mar • Villach (35km) i +43 4240 8212 www.badkleinkirchheim.at

Ehrwald 71 A5 ❄ 1000–2965m • 24 lifts • Dec–Apr • Imst (30km) i +43 5673 2395 www.wetterstein-bahnen.at/en

Innsbruck 71 A6 ❄ 574/850–3200m • 79 lifts • Dec–Apr • Innsbruck i + 43 512 56 2000 www.innsbruck-pauschalen.com • *Motorway normally clear. The motorway through to Italy and through the Arlberg Tunnel are both toll roads.*

Ischgl 71 A5 ❄ 1340/1380–2900m • 42 lifts • Dec–May • Landeck (25km) i +43 50990 100 www.ischgl.com • *Car entry to resort prohibited between 2200hrs and 0600hrs.*

Kaprun 72 A2 ❄ 885/770–3030m, • 53 lifts • Nov–Apr • Zell am See (10km) i +43 6542 770 www.zellamsee-kaprun.com

Kirchberg in Tirol 72 A2 860–2000m • 60 lifts • Nov–Apr • Kitzbühel (6km) i +43 57507 2100 www.kitzbueheler-alpen.com/en • *Easily reached from Munich International Airport (120 km)*

Kitzbühel (Brixen im Thale) 72 A2 ❄ 800/1210–2000m • 60 lifts • Dec–Apr • Wörgl (40km) i +43 57057 2200 www.kitzbueheler-alpen.com/en

Lech/Oberlech 71 A5 ❄ 1450–2810m • 62 lifts • Dec–Apr • Bludenz (50km) i +43 5583 2161 0 www.lechzuers.com • *Roads normally cleared but keep chains accessible because of altitude.*

Mayrhofen 72 A1 ❄ 630–2500m • 75 lifts • Dec–Apr • Jenbach (35km) i +43 5285 6760 www.mayrhofen.at • *Chains rarely required.*

Obertauern 72 A3 ❄ 1740/1640–2350m • 26 lifts • Dec–Apr • Radstadt (20km) i +43 6456 7252 www.obertauern.com • *Roads normally cleared but chain accessibility recommended. Camper vans and caravans not allowed; park these in Radstadt*

Saalbach Hinterglemm 72 A2 ❄ 1030/1100–2100m • 52 lifts • Nov–Apr • Zell am See (19km) i +43 6852 70660 www.saalbach.com • *Both village centres are pedestrianised and there is a good ski bus service during the daytime*

St Anton am Arlberg 71 A5 ❄ 1300–2810m • 84 lifts • Dec–Apr • Innsbruck (104km) i +43 5446 22690 www.stantonamarlberg.com

Schladming 72 A3 ❄ 745–1900m • 88 lifts • Dec–Mar • Schladming i + 43 36 87 233 10 www.schladming-dachstein.at

Serfaus 71 A5 ❄ 1427/1200–2820m • 70 lifts • Dec–Apr • Landeck (30km) i +43 5476 6239 www.serfaus-fiss-ladis.at • *Private vehicles banned from village. Use Dorfbahn Serfaus, an underground funicular which runs on an air cushion.*

Sölden 71 B6 ❄ 1380–3250m • 33 lifts • Sep-Apr (glacier); Nov-Apr (main area) • Imst (50km) i +43 572 000 200 www.soelden.com • *Roads normally cleared but snow chains recommended because of altitude. The route from Italy and the south over the Timmelsjoch via Obergurgl is closed Oct–May and anyone arriving from the south should use the Brenner Pass motorway.*

Zell am See 72 A2 ❄ 750–1950m • 53 lifts • Dec–Mar • Zell am See www.zellamsee-kaprun.com i +43 6542 770 • *Low altitude, so good access and no mountain passes to cross.*

Zell im Zillertal (Zell am Ziller) 72 A1 ❄ 580/930–2410m • 22 lifts • Dec–Apr • Jenbach (25km) i +43 5282 7165–226 www.zillertalarena.com

Zürs 71 A5 ❄ 1720/1700–2450m • 62 lifts • Dec–Apr • Bludenz (30km) i +43 5583 2245 www.lech-zuers.at • *Roads normally cleared but keep chains accessible because of altitude. Village has garage with 24-hour self-service gas/petrol, breakdown service and wheel chains supply.*

France

Alps

Alpe d'Huez 79 A5 ❄ 1860–3330m • 85 lifts • Dec–Apr • Grenoble (63km) i +33 4 76 11 44 44 www.alpedhuez.com • *Snow chains may be required on access road to resort.*

Avoriaz 70 B1 ❄ 1800/1100–2280m • 35 lifts • Dec–May • Morzine (14km) i +33 4 50 74 02 11 www.morzine-avoriaz.com • *Chains may be required for access road from Morzine. Car-free resort, park on edge of village. Horse-drawn sleigh service available.*

Chamonix-Mont-Blanc 70 C1 ❄ 1035–3840m • 49 lifts • Dec–Apr • Martigny (38km) i +33 4 50 53 00 24 www.chamonix.com

Chamrousse 79 A4 ❄ 1700–2250m • 26 lifts • Dec–Apr • Grenoble (30km) i +33 4 76 89 92 65 www.chamrousse.com • *Roads normally cleared, keep chains accessible because of altitude*

Châtel 70 B1 ❄ 1200/1110–2200m • 41 lifts • Dec–Apr • Thonon-Les-Bains (35km) i +33 4 50 73 22 44 http://info.chatel.com/english-version.html

Courchevel 70 C1 ❄ 1750/1300–2470m • 67 lifts • Dec–Apr • Moûtiers (23km) www.courchevel.com • *Roads normally cleared but keep chains accessible. Traffic 'discouraged' within the four resort bases.*

Flaine 70 B1 ❄ 1600–2500m • 26 lifts • Dec–Apr • Cluses (25km) i +33 4 50 90 80 01 www.flaine.com • *Keep chains accessible for D6 from Cluses to Flaine. Car access for depositing luggage and passengers only. 1500-space car park outside resort. Near Sixt-Fer-á-Cheval.*

La Clusaz 69 C6 ❄ 1100–2600m • 55 lifts • Dec–Apr • Annecy (32km) i +33 4 50 32 65 00 www.laclusaz.com • *Roads normally clear but keep chains accessible for final road from Annecy.*

La Plagne 70 C1 ❄ 2500/1250–3250m • 109 lifts • Dec–Apr • Moûtiers (32km) i +33 4 79 09 79 79 www.la-plagne.com • *Ten different centres up to 2100m altitude. Road access via Bozel, Landry or Aime normally cleared. Linked to Les Arcs by cablecar*

Les Arcs 70 C1 ❄ 1600/1200–3230m • 77 lifts • Dec–May • Bourg-St-Maurice (15km) i +33 4 79 07 12 57 www.lesarcs.com • *Four base areas up to 2000 metres; keep chains accessible. Pay parking at edge of each base resort. Linked to La Plagne by cablecar*

Les Carroz d'Araches 70 B1 ❄ 1140–2500m • 80 lifts • Dec–Apr • Cluses (13km) i + 33 4 50 90 00 04 www.lescarroz.com

Les Deux-Alpes 79 B5 ❄ 1650/1300–3600m • 55 lifts • Dec–Apr • Grenoble (75km) i +33 4 76 79 22 00 www.les2alpes.com • *Roads normally cleared, however snow chains recommended for D213 up from valley road (D1091).*

Les Gets 70 B1 ❄ 1170/1000–2000m • 52 lifts • Dec–Apr • Cluses (18km) i +33 4 50 75 80 80 www.lesgets.com

Les Ménuires 69 C6 ❄ 1815/1850–3200m • 40 lifts • Dec–Apr • Moûtiers (27km) i +33 4 00 63 77 www.lesmenuires.com • *Keep chains accessible for D117 from Moûtiers.*

Les Sept Laux Prapoutel 69 C6 ❄ 1350–2400m • 24 lifts • Dec–Apr • Grenoble (38km) i +33 4 76 08 17 86 www.les7laux.com • *Roads normally cleared, however keep chains accessible for mountain road up from the A41 motorway. Near St Sorlin d'Arves.*

Megève 69 C6 ❄ 1100/1050–2350m • 79 lifts • Dec–Apr • Sallanches (12km) i +33 4 50 21 27 28 www.megeve.com • *Horse-drawn sleigh rides available.*

Méribel 69 C6 ❄ 1400/1100–2950m • 61 lifts • Dec–May • Moûtiers (18km) i +33 4 79 08 60 01 www.meribel.net • *Keep chains accessible for 18km to resort on D90 from Moûtiers.*

Morzine 70 B1 ❄ 1000–2460m • 67 lifts, • Dec–Apr • Thonon-Les-Bains (30km) i +33 4 50 74 72 72 www.morzine-avoriaz.com

Pra Loup 79 B5 ❄ 1600/1500–2500m • 53 lifts • Dec–Apr • Barcelonnette (10km) i +33 4 92 84 10 04 www.praloup.com • *Roads normally cleared but chains accessibility recommended.*

Risoul 79 B5 ❄ 1850/1650–2750m • 51 lifts • Dec–Apr • Briançon (40km) i +33 4 92 46 02 60 www.risoul.com • *Keep chains accessible. Near Guillestre. Linked with Vars Les Claux*

St-Gervais Mont-Blanc 70 C1 ❄ 850/1150–2350m • 27 lifts • Dec–Apr • Sallanches (10km) www.st-gervais.com

Serre Chevalier 79 B5 ❄ 1350/1200–2800m • 77 lifts • Dec–Apr • Briançon (10km) i + 33 4 92 24 98 98 www.serre-chevalier.com • *Made up of 13 small villages along the valley road, which is normally cleared.*

Tignes 70 C1 ❄ 2100/1550–3450m • 97 lifts • Jan–Dec • Bourg St Maurice (26km) i +33 4 79 40 04 40 www.tignes.net • *Keep chains accessible because of altitude.*

Val d'Isère 70 C1 ❄ 1850/1550–3450m • 97 lifts • Dec–Apr • Bourg-St-Maurice (30km) i +33 4 79 06 06 60 www.valdisere.com • *Roads normally cleared but keep chains accessible.*

Val Thorens 69 C6 ❄ 2300/1850–3200m • 29 lifts • Dec–Apr • Moûtiers (37km) www.valthorens.com • *Chains essential – highest ski resort in Europe. Obligatory paid parking on edge of resort.*

Valloire 69 C6 ❄ 1430–2600m • 34 lifts • Dec–Apr • Modane (20km) i +33 4 79 59 03 96 www.valloire.net • *Road normally clear up to the Col du Galbier, to the south of the resort, which is closed from 1st November to 1st June. Linked to Valmeinier.*

Valmeinier 69 C6 ❄ 1500–2600m • 34 lifts • Dec–Apr • St Michel de Maurienne (47km) i +33 4 79 59 53 69 www.valmeinier.com • *Access from north on D1006 / D902. Col du Galbier, to the south of the resort closed from 1st November to 1st June. Linked to Valloire.*

Valmorel 69 C6 ❄ 1400–2550m • 90 lifts • Dec–Apr • Moûtiers (15km) i +33 4 79 09 85 55 www.valmorel.com • *Near St Jean-de-Belleville. Linked with ski areas of Doucy-Combelouvière and St François-Longchamp.*

Vars Les Claux 79 B5 ❄ 1850/1650–2750m • 51 lifts • Dec–Apr • Briançon (40km) i +33 4 92 46 51 31 www.vars-ski.com • *Four base resorts up to 1850 metres. Keep chains accessible. Linked with Risoul.*

Villard de Lans 79 A4 ❄ 1050/1160–2170m • 28 lifts • Dec–Apr • Grenoble (32km) i +33 4 76 95 10 38 www.villarddelans.com

Pyrenees

Font-Romeu 91 A5 ❄ 1800/1600–2200m • 25 lifts • Nov–Apr • Perpignan (87km) i +33 4 68 30 68 30 www.font-romeu.fr • *Roads normally cleared but keep chains accessible.*

Saint-Lary Soulan 77 D3 ❄ 830/1650/1700–2515m • 31 lifts • Dec–Mar • Tarbes (75km) i +33 5 62 39 50 81 www.saintlary.com • *Access roads constantly cleared of snow.*

Vosges

La Bresse-Hohneck 60 B2 ❄ 500/900–1350m • 33 lifts • Dec–Mar • Cornimont (6km) i +33 3 29 25 41 29 www.labresse.net

Germany

Alps

Garmisch-Partenkirchen 71 A6 700–2830m • 38 lifts • Dec–Apr • Munich (95km) +49 8821 180 700 www.gapa.de • *Roads usually clear, chains rarely needed.*

Oberaudorf 62 C3 480–1850m • 30 lifts • Dec–Apr • Kufstein (15km) +49 8033 301 20 www.oberaudorf.de • *Motorway normally kept clear. Near Bayrischzell.*

Oberstdorf 71 A5 815m • 26 lifts • Dec–Apr • Sonthofen (15km) +49 8322 7000 http://oberstdorf.de

Rothaargebirge

Winterberg 51 B4 700/620–830m • 19 lifts • Dec–Mar • Brilon (30km) +49 2981 925 00 www.winterberg.de • *Roads usually cleared, chains rarely required.*

Greece

Central Greece

Mount Parnassos: Kelaria-Fterolakka 116 D4 1640–2260m • 14 lifts • Dec–Apr • Amfiklia +30 22340 22694-5 www.parnassos-ski.gr (Greek only)

Mount Parnassos: Gerondovrahos 116 D4 1800–1900m • 14 lifts • Dec–Apr • Amfiklia +30 29444 70371

Peloponnisos

Mount Helmos: Kalavrita Ski Centre 117 D4 1650–2100m • 7 lifts • Dec–Mar • Kalavrita +30 26920 2261 www.kalavrita-ski.gr (Greek only)

Mount Menalo: Ostrakina 117 E4 1500–1600m • 5 lifts • Dec–Mar • Tripoli +30 27960 22227

Macedonia

Mount Falakro: Agio Pneuma 116 A6 1720/1620–2230m • 7 lifts • Dec–Apr • Drama + 30 25210 23691 www.falakro.gr (Greek only)

Mount Vasilitsa: Vasilitsa 116 B3 1750/1800–2113m • 3 lifts • Dec–Mar • Konitsa + 30 24620 26100 www.vasilitsa.com (Greek only)

Mount Vermio: Seli 116 B4 1500–1900m • 8 lifts • Dec–Mar • Kozani + 30 23320 71234 www.seli-ski.gr (in Greek)

Mount Vermio: Tria-Pente Pigadia 116 B3 1420–2005m • 7 lifts • Dec–Mar • Ptolemaida +30 23320 44464 www.3–5pigadia.gr

Mount Verno: Vigla 116 B3 1650–1900m • 5 lifts • Dec–Mar • Florina +30 23850 22354 www.vigla-ski.gr (in Greek)

Mount Vrondous: Lailias 116 A5 1600–1850m • 4 lifts • Dec–Mar • Serres +30 23210 53790

Thessalia

Mount Pilio: Agriolefkes 116 C5 1300–1500m • 4 lifts • Dec–Mar • Volos +30 24280 73719

Italy

Alps

Bardonecchia 79 A5 1312–2750m • 21 lifts • Dec–Apr • Bardonecchia + 39 0122 99137 www.bardonecchiaski.com • *Resort reached through the 11km Frejus tunnel from France, roads normally cleared.*

Bórmio 71 B5 1200/1230–3020m • 24 lifts • Dec–Apr • Tirano (40km) +39 342 902424 www.bormio.com • *Tolls payable in Ponte del Gallo Tunnel, open 0800hrs–2000hrs.*

Breuil-Cervinia 70 C2 2050–3500m • 21 lifts • Jan–Dec • Aosta (54km) +39 166 944311 www.cervinia.it • *Snow chains strongly recommended. Bus from Milan airport.*

Courmayeur 70 C1 1200–2760m • 21 lifts • Dec–Apr • Aosta (40km) +39 165 846658 www.courmayeur-montblanc.com • *Access through the Mont Blanc tunnel from France. Roads constantly cleared.*

Limone Piemonte 80 B1 1000/1050–2050m • 29 lifts • Dec–Apr • Cuneo (27km) + 39 171 925281 www.limonepiemonte.it • *Roads normally cleared, chains rarely required.*

Livigno 71 B5 1800–3000m • 31 lifts • Nov–May • Zernez (CH) (27km) +39 342 052200 www.livigno.com • *Keep chains accessible. The direction of traffic through Munt la Schera Tunnel to/from Zernez is regulated on Saturdays. Check in advance.*

Sestrière 79 B5 2035/1840–2840m • 92 lifts • Dec–Apr • Oulx (22km) +39 122 755444 www.visitsestriere.com • *One of Europe's highest resorts; although roads are normally cleared keep chains accessible.*

Appennines

Roccaraso – Aremogna 103 B7 1285/1240–2140m • 39 lifts • Dec–Apr • Castel di Sangro (7km) +39 864 62210 www.roccaraso.net (in Italian)

Dolomites

Andalo – Fai della Paganella 71 B5 1042/1050/2125m • 19 lifts • Dec–Apr • Trento (40km) +39 461 585836 www.visitdolomitipaganella.it

Arabba 72 B1 1600/1450–2950m • 29 lifts • Dec–Mar • Brunico (45km) +39 436 780019 www.arabba.it • *Roads normally cleared but keep chains accessible.*

Cortina d'Ampezzo 72 B2 1224/1050–2930m • 37 lifts • Dec–Apr • Belluno (72km) +39 436 869086 www.cortina.dolomiti.org • *Access from north on route 51 over the Cimabanche Pass may require chains.*

Corvara (Alta Badia) 72 B1 1568–2500m • 52 lifts • Dec–Apr • Brunico (38km) +39 471 836176 www.altabadia.it • *Roads normally clear but keep chains accessible.*

Madonna di Campiglio 71 B5 1550/1500–2600m • 72 lifts • Dec–Apr • Trento (60km) +39 465 447501 www.campigliodolomiti.it/homepage • *Roads normally cleared but keep chains accessible. Linked to Folgarida and Marilleva.*

Moena di Fassa (Sorte/Ronchi) 72 B1 1184/1450–2520m • 8 lifts • Dec–Apr • Bolzano (40km) +39 462 609770 www.fassa.com

Selva di Val Gardena/Wolkenstein Groden 72 B1 1563/1570–2450m • 84 lifts • Dec–Apr • Bolzano (40km) +39 471 777777 www.valgardena.it • *Roads normally cleared but keep chains accessible.*

Norway

Hemsedal 32 B5 700/640–1450m • 24 lifts • Nov–May • Honefoss (150km) +47 32 055030 www.hemsedal.com • *Be prepared for extreme weather conditions.*

Slovak Republic

Chopok (Jasna-Chopok) 65 B5 900/950–1840m • 17 lifts • Dec–Apr • Jasna +421 907 886644 www.jasna.sk

Donovaly 65 B5 913–1360m • 17 lifts • Nov–Apr • Ruzomberok +421 48 4199900 www.parksnow.sk/zima

Martinské Hole 65 A4 1250/1150–1456m • 8 lifts • Nov–May • Zilina +421 43 430 6000 www.martinky.com (in Slovak only)

Plejsy 65 B6 470–912m • 9 lifts • Dec–Mar • Krompachy +421 53 429 8015 www.plejsy.sk

Strbske Pleso 65 A6 1380–1825m • 7 lifts • Dec–Mar • Poprad +421 917 682 260 www.vt.sk

Slovenia

Julijske Alpe

Kanin (Bovec) 72 B3 460/1600–2389m • 12 lifts • Dec–Apr • Bovec +386 5 384 1919 www.boveckanin.si

Kobla (Bohinj) 72 B3 512/530–1495m • 6 lifts • Dec–Mar • Bohinjska Bistrica +386 4 5747 100 www.bohinj.si/kobla/en/naprave.html

Kranjska Gora 72 B3 800–1210m • 19 lifts • Dec–Mar • Kranjska Gora +386 4 5809 440 www.kranjska-gora.si

Vogel 72 B3 570–1800m • 8 lifts • Dec–Apr • Bohinjska Bistrica +386 4 5729 712 www.vogel.si

Kawiniške Savinjske Alpe

Krvavec 73 B4 1450–1970m • 10 lifts • Dec–Apr • Kranj 386 4 25 25 911 www.rtc-krvavec.si

Pohorje

Rogla 73 B5 1517/1050–1500m • 13 lifts • Dec–Apr • Slovenska Bistrica +386 3 75 77 100 www.rogla.eu

Spain

Pyrenees

Baqueira-Beret/Bonaigua 90 A3 1500–2500m • 33 lifts • Dec–Apr • Vielha (15km) +34 902 415 415 www.baqueira.es • *Roads normally clear but keep chains accessible. Near Salardú.*

Sistema Penibetico

Sierra Nevada 100 B2 2100–3300m • 24 lifts • Dec–May • Granada (32km) +34 902 70 80 90 http://sierranevada.es • *Access road designed to be avalanche safe and is snow cleared.*

Sweden

Idre Fjäll 115 F9 590–890m • 33 lifts • Nov–Apr • Mora (140km) +46 253 41000 www.idrefjall.se • *Be prepared for extreme weather conditions.*

Sälen 34 A5 360m • 100 lifts • Nov–Apr • Malung (70km) +46 771 84 00 00 www.skistar.com/salen • *Be prepared for extreme weather conditions.*

Switzerland

Alps

Adelboden 70 B2 1353m • 55 lifts • Dec–Apr • Frutigen (15km) +41 33 673 80 80 www.adelboden.ch • *Linked with Lenk.*

Arosa 71 B4 1800m • 16 lifts • Dec–Apr • Chur (30km) +41 81 378 70 20 www.arosa.ch (German only) • *Roads cleared but keep chains accessible due to high altitude.*

Crans Montana 70 B2 1500–3000m • 34 lifts • Dec–Apr, Jul-Oct • Sierre (15km) +41 848 22 12 12 www.crans-montana.ch • *Roads normally cleared but keep chains accessible for ascent from Sierre.*

Davos 71 B4 1560/1100–2840m • 38 lifts • Nov–Apr • Davos +41 81 415 21 21 www.davos.ch

Engelberg 70 B3 1000/1050–3020m • 26 lifts • Nov–May • Luzern (39km) +41 41 639 77 77 www.engelberg.ch • *Straight access road normally cleared.*

Flums (Flumserberg) 71 A4 1400/1000–2220m • 17 lifts • Dec–Apr • Buchs (25km) +41 81 720 18 18 www.flumserberg.ch • *Roads normally cleared, but 1000-metre vertical ascent; keep chains accessible.*

Grindelwald 70 B3 1050–2950m • 39 lifts • Dec–Apr • Interlaken (20km) +41 33 854 12 12 www.jungfrauregion.ch

Gstaad – Saanenland 70 B2 1050/950–3000m • 74 lifts • Dec–Apr • Gstaad +41 33 748 81 81 www.gstaad.ch • *Linked to Anzère.*

Klosters 71 B4 1191/1110–2840m • 52 lifts • Dec–Apr • Davos (10km) +41 81 410 20 20 www.klosters.ch • *Roads normally clear but keep chains accessible.*

Leysin 70 B2 2263/1260–2330m • 16 lifts • Dec–Apr • Aigle (6km) +41 24 493 33 00 www.leysin.ch

Mürren 70 B2 1650–2970m • 12 lifts • Dec–Apr • Interlaken (18km) +41 33 856 86 86 www.mymuerren.ch • *No road access. Park in Strechelberg (1500 free places) and take the two-stage cable car.*

Nendaz 70 B2 1365/1400–3300m • 20 lifts • Nov–Apr • Sion (16km) +41 27 289 55 89 www.nendaz.ch • *Roads normally cleared, however keep chains accessible for ascent from Sion. Near Vex.*

Saas-Fee 70 B2 1800–3500m • 23 lifts • Jan–Dec • Brig (35km) +41 27 958 18 58 www.saas-fee.ch • *Roads normally cleared but keep chains accessible because of altitude.*

St Moritz 71 B4 1856/1730–3300m • 24 lifts • Nov–May • Chur (89km) +41 81 837 33 33 www.stmoritz.ch • *Roads normally cleared but keep chains accessible.*

Samnaun 71 B5 1846/1400–2900m • 40 lifts • Dec–May • Scuol (30km) +41 81 861 88 30 www.engadin.com • *Roads normally cleared but keep chains accessible.*

Verbier 70 B2 1500–3330m • 17 lifts • Nov–Apr • Martigny (27km) +41 27 775 38 70 www.verbier.ch • *Roads normally cleared.*

Villars-Gryon 70 B2 1253/1200–2100m • 16 lifts • Dec–Apr, Jun–Jul • Montreux (35km) +41 24 495 32 32 www.villars.ch • *Roads normally cleared but keep chains accessible for ascent from N9. Near Bex.*

Wengen 70 B2 1270–2320m • 39 lifts • Dec–Apr • Interlaken (12km) +41 33 856 85 85 http://wengen.ch • *No road access. Park at Lauterbrunnen and take mountain railway.*

Zermatt 70 B2 1620–3900m • 40 lifts, • all year • Brig (42km) +41 27 966 81 00 www.zermatt.ch • *Cars not permitted in resort, park in Täsch (3km) and take shuttle train.*

Turkey

North Anatolian Mountains

Uludag 118 B4 1770–2320m • 13 lifts • Dec–Mar • Bursa (36km) +90 224 285 21 11 http://skiingturkey.com/resorts/uludag.html

To the best of the Publisher's knowledge the information in this table was correct at the time of going to press. No responsibility can be accepted for any errors or their consequences.

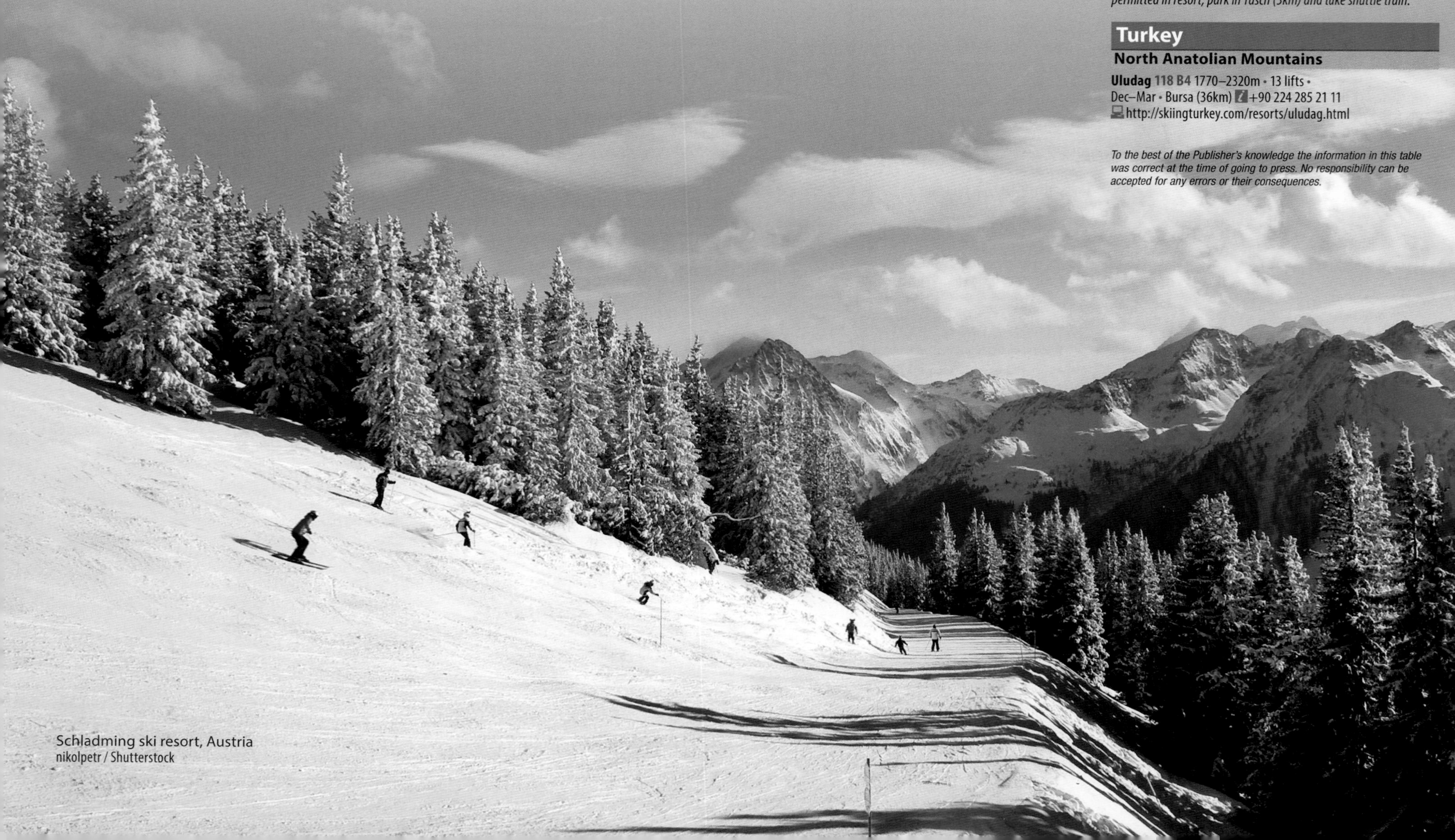

Schladming ski resort, Austria
nikolpetr / Shutterstock

1 : 3 200 000 map pages

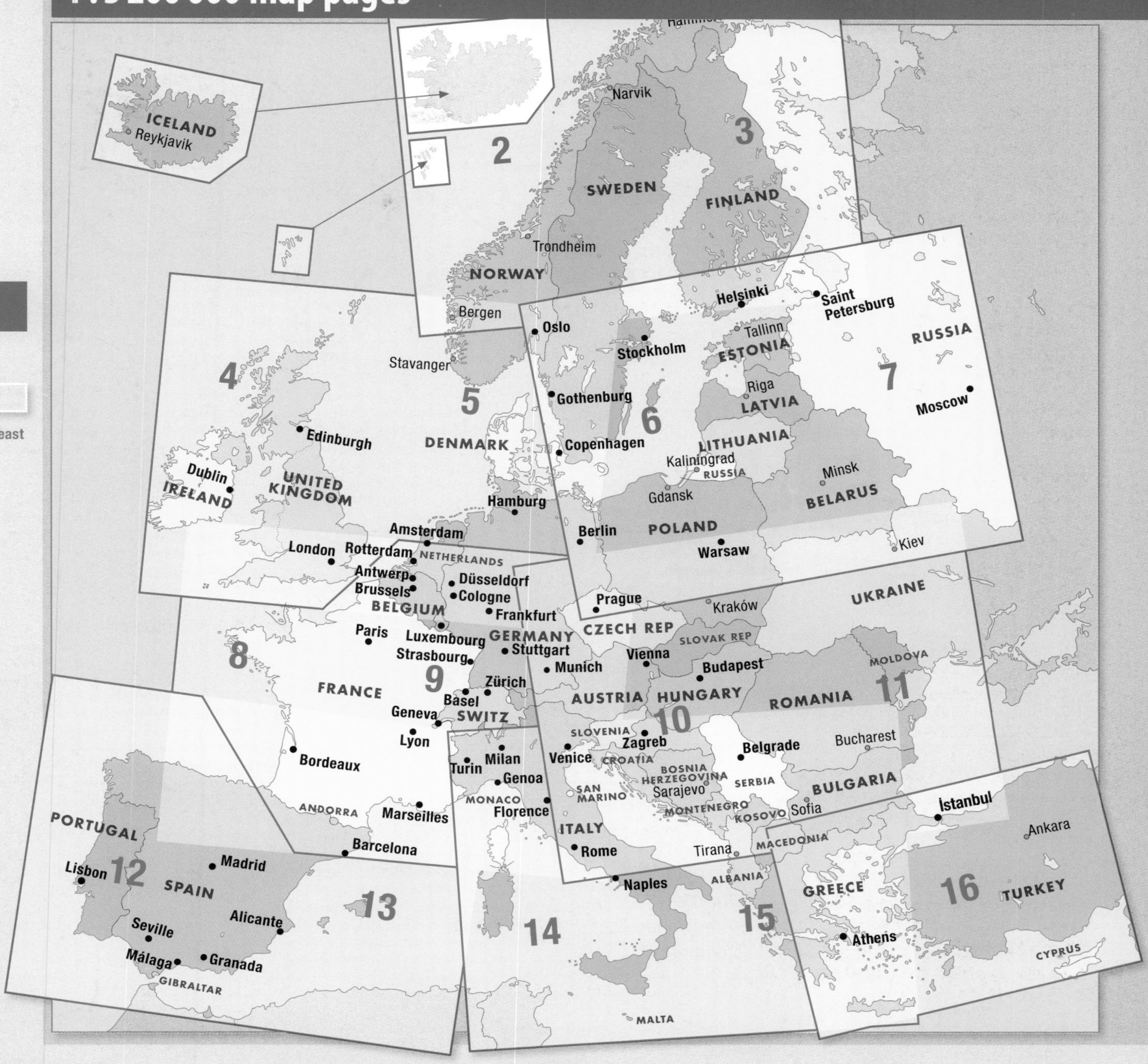

ICELAND
Reykjavik
2
3
Narvik
SWEDEN
FINLAND
Trondheim
NORWAY
Bergen
Oslo
Helsinki
Saint Petersburg
Tallinn
ESTONIA
RUSSIA
Stockholm
Stavanger
4
5
Gothenburg
6
Riga
LATVIA
7
Moscow
Edinburgh
DENMARK
Copenhagen
LITHUANIA
Kaliningrad
RUSSIA
Minsk
Dublin
IRELAND
UNITED KINGDOM
Hamburg
Gdansk
BELARUS
Amsterdam
Berlin
POLAND
London
Rotterdam
NETHERLANDS
Warsaw
Kiev
Antwerp
Brussels
Düsseldorf
Cologne
BELGIUM
Frankfurt
Prague
Kraków
UKRAINE
Paris
Luxembourg
GERMANY
CZECH REP
SLOVAK REP
Strasbourg
Stuttgart
Vienna
8
9
Munich
Budapest
MOLDOVA
FRANCE
Zürich
AUSTRIA
HUNGARY
11
Geneva
Basel
SWITZ
ROMANIA
10
Lyon
SLOVENIA
Zagreb
Belgrade
Bucharest
Milan
Venice
CROATIA
Bordeaux
Turin
Genoa
BOSNIA HERZEGOVINA
SERBIA
SAN MARINO
Sarajevo
BULGARIA
MONACO
Florence
MONTENEGRO
Istanbul
ANDORRA
Marseilles
KOSOVO
Sofia
PORTUGAL
ITALY
Ankara
Barcelona
Rome
Tirana
MACEDONIA
Madrid
Lisbon
12
SPAIN
Naples
ALBANIA
GREECE
16
TURKEY
13
14
15
Alicante
Seville
Athens
Málaga
Granada
CYPRUS
GIBRALTAR
MALTA

Distances

Calais						
548	Dublin					
726	346	Edinburgh				
575	1123	1301	Frankfurt			
1342	477	176	1067	Göteborg		
1189	760	477	1486	485	582	Hamburg

Dublin ➡ Goteborg = 477 km

Distances shown in blue involve at least one ferry journey

	Amsterdam	Athina	Barcelona	Bergen	Berlin	Bruxelles	Bucuresti	Budapest	Calais	Dublin	Edinburgh	Frankfurt	Göteborg	Hamburg	Helsinki	Istanbul	København	Köln	Lisboa	London	Luxembourg	Madrid	Marseille	Milano	Moskva	München	Oslo	Paris	Praha	Roma	Sevilla	Sofiya	Stockholm	Warszawa	Wien
Athina	2945																																		
Barcelona	1505	3192																																	
Bergen	1484	3742	2803																																
Berlin	650	2412	1863	1309																															
Bruxelles	197	2895	1308	1586	764																														
Bucuresti	2245	1219	2644	3037	1707	2181																													
Budapest	1420	1530	1999	2212	882	1358	852																												
Calais	367	3100	1269	1783	956	215	2398	1573																											
Dublin	533	3630	1817	270	1504	763	3021	2196	548																										
Edinburgh	1093	3826	1995	176	1696	941	3124	2299	726	346																									
Frankfurt	441	2499	1313	1508	550	383	1804	979	575	1123	1301																								
Göteborg	1029	3080	2362	819	668	1145	1734	1550	1342	477	176	1067																							
Hamburg	447	2719	1780	1023	286	563	2014	1189	760	477	1486	485	582																						
Helsinki	1560	2539	2338	1063	475	1239	1834	1009	1431	1318	1236	1598	505	1113																					
Istanbul	2756	1145	2990	3653	2223	2706	690	1341	2911	3537	3657	2314	2891	2530	2350																				
København	965	2782	2090	1103	370	1081	2077	1252	1278	752	479	795	284	518	803	2593																			
Köln	256	2684	1376	1427	566	198	1983	1158	390	938	1116	180	986	404	1517	2499	714																		
Lisboa	2331	4460	1268	3723	2869	3141	3917	3222	2069	2617	2795	2400	3282	2700	3817	4342	3014	2339																	
London	480	3200	1387	458	1074	333	2591	1766	118	430	608	693	122	878	1991	3107	1188	508	2187																
Luxembourg	406	2661	1190	1613	749	209	2052	1227	424	972	1150	240	1172	590	1703	2472	900	186	2160	542															
Madrid	1790	3809	617	3183	2364	1600	3262	2622	1528	1634	2254	1930	2742	2160	3276	3589	2473	1798	651	1646	1628														
Marseille	1210	2683	509	2435	1541	1030	2154	1505	1063	1588	1789	1023	1994	1412	2525	2479	1722	1006	1777	1182	822	1126													
Milano	1085	2182	1038	2141	1060	890	1668	992	1072	1620	1798	683	1700	1118	1535	1993	1428	868	2315	1190	679	1655	538												
Moskva	2457	2930	3655	2223	1821	2585	1761	2099	2800	3348	3526	2312	1665	2115	1160	2605	2325	2387	4875	2918	2852	4224	3270	3027											
München	839	2106	1340	1788	594	789	1497	672	994	1524	1720	398	1347	765	1069	1907	969	580	2545	1094	555	2010	1011	473	2305										
Oslo	1347	3372	2680	503	960	1463	2667	1842	1660	773	729	1385	316	900	697	3089	590	1304	3604	1778	1490	3063	2312	2018	1823	1559									
Paris	510	2917	988	1922	1051	320	2307	1482	281	829	1007	591	1481	899	2012	2727	1209	495	1821	399	351	1280	782	857	2903	810	1799								
Praha	950	2067	1750	1675	345	888	1362	537	1097	1635	1816	512	1013	652	770	1878	715	690	2870	1205	753	2329	1399	853	1853	388	1305	1061							
Roma	1691	1140	1385	2706	1502	1520	1904	1263	1678	2226	2404	1289	2265	1683	1977	2237	1993	1474	2653	1796	1285	2002	876	606	3362	918	2583	1389	1309						
Sevilla	2347	4223	1031	3736	2894	2150	3709	3010	2078	2626	2804	2344	3295	2713	3826	4034	3023	2318	401	2196	2178	550	1540	2078	4774	2371	3613	1830	2781	2446					
Sofiya	2206	828	2453	3103	1673	2156	391	790	2361	2891	3087	1764	2341	1980	1800	550	2043	1949	3706	2461	1922	3037	1929	1443	2252	1367	2632	2177	1328	1687	3484				
Stockholm	1393	3418	2726	1063	1006	1509	2713	1888	1673	2254	1069	1431	505	946	167	3185	590	1350	3650	1824	1536	3109	2358	2064	1228	1600	530	1845	1351	2629	3659	2679			
Warszawa	1256	2128	2366	1909	606	1350	1473	648	1542	2110	2268	1136	1274	886	361	1989	956	1152	3480	1680	1345	2960	2015	1469	1245	996	1506	1677	616	1853	3397	1439	1612		
Wien	1168	1772	1856	1970	640	1114	1067	242	1308	1954	2034	731	1308	947	1088	1583	1010	916	3100	1524	993	2473	1353	818	2137	430	1600	1240	295	1126	2876	1033	1646	727	
Zurich	816	2426	1030	1938	863	619	1810	985	804	1352	1530	464	1497	915	2164	2323	1433	589	2296	922	410	1647	699	292	2552	303	1815	592	691	898	2061	1173	1861	1307	743

km

Grænlandssund
Norður-Íshaf
ARCTIC CIRCLE
Grímsey
Raufarhöfn
Horn
Ísafjarðardjúp
Bolungarvík
Ísafjörður
Drangajökull 925
Siglufjörður
Ólafsfjörður
Dalvík
Húsavík
Þórshöfn
Bakkafjörður
Digranes
Arnarfjörður
Glámа 920
Bíldudalur
Hólmavík
Skagaströnd
Blönduós
Sauðárkrókur
Akureyri
Reykjahlíð
Mývatn
Vopnafjörður
Vopnafjörður
Héraðsflói
HIRTSHALS TÓRSHAVN
Glettinganes
Borgarfjörður
Bjargtangar
Hvammstangi
Breiðafjörður
Borðeyri
ÍSLAND
ICELAND
Herðubreið 1682
Seyðisfjörður
Eskifjörður
Reyðarfjörður
Stykkishólmur
Öndverðarnes
Ólafsvík
Snæfellsjökull 1446
Eiríksjökull 1675
1765
Askja
Trölladyngja 1460
Snæfell 1833
Djúpivogur
Borgarnes
Faxaflói
Hvítárvatn
2000
Vatnajökull
Akranes
Geysir
Þórisvatn
Höfn
Stokksnes
Reykjavík
Kópavogur
Þingvallavatn
Keflavík
Hafnarfjörður
Selfoss
Hekla 1491
Öræfajökull 2119
Reykjanes
Þorlákshöfn
Eyrarbakki
Hella
Kirkjubæjarklaustur
Ingólfshöfði
1450
Vestmannaeyjar
Vík
Heimaey
Surtsey
SEYÐISFJÖRÐUR
Føroyar (Danmark)
Færoe Islands (Denmark)
Norðoyar
Slættaratindur 882
Streymoy
Mykines
Klaksvík
Eysturoy
Vágar
Tórshavn
Sandoy
Suðuroy
0 40 80 120 160 200 km
Lofoten
Vesterålen
Andenes
Andøya
Senja
Risøyhamn
Harstad
Langøya
Sortland
Hinnøya
Austvågøy
Stokmarknes
Lødingen
Vestvågøy
Svolvær
Stamsund
Narvik
Bognes
Skarberget
Frostisen 1744
Sørvågen
Moskenesøya
Vestfjorden
Værøy
Røst
Bodø
Saltfjorden
Fauske
Sulitjelma 1913
Vastenjaure
Virihaure
Pieskehaure
ARCTIC CIRCLE
Svartisen 1599
Tomma
Mo i Rana
Nasa 1214
Dønna
Sandnessjøen
Hemnesberget
Korgen
Alsten
Mosjøen
Strimasund
Norra Storfjället 1792
Vega
Røssvatnet
Tärnaby
Brønnøysund
Trofors
Vennesund
Austra
Leka
Vikna
Rørvik
Sorsele
Strömsund
Storuman
Gunnarn
Namsos
Grong
Gäddede
Vilhelmina
Trøndelag
Steinkjer
Snåsavatnet
Åfjord
Follafoss
Frøya
Hitra
Smøla
Frohavet
Fosna
Brekstad
Verdalsøra
Levanger
Stranda
Trondheimsfjorden
Hoting
Strömsund
Trondheim
Heimdal
Stjørdalshalsen
Melhus
Hommelvik
Kristiansund
Hustadvika
Orkanger
Løkken
Støren
Storlien
Duved
Järpen
Åre
Mörsil
Jämtland
Krokom
Östersund
Lit
Storsjön
Sollefteå
Molde
Tingvoll
Sunndalsøra
Ulsberg
Haltdalen
Sylarna 1766
Brunflo
Ålesund
Spjelkavik
Åndalsnes
Oppdal
Kvikne
Brekken
Røros
Funäsdalen
Tännäs
Bräcke
Larsnes
Hareid
Stranda
Ørsta
Volda
Lesjaskog
Lesjaverk
Snøhetta 2286
Hjerkinn
Tynset
Tufsingdalen
Hede
Rätansbyn
Ånge
Måløy
Hellesylt
Grotli
Stryn
Videseter
Dombås
Dovre
Folldal
Alvdal
Sundsvall
Nordfjordeid
Sandane
Olden
Florø
Eikefjord
Naustdal
Førde
Lom
Galdhøpiggen 2469
Skjolden
Skagastølstindane 2403
Idre
Sveg
Ljusdal
Hudiksvall
Iggesund
Vik
Vadheim
Høyanger
Balestrand
Sogndalsfjøra
Sognefjorden
Vangsnes
Kaupanger
Øvre Årdal
Lærdalsøyri
Gudvangen
Flåm
Koppang
Engerdal
Särna
Tretten
Trysil
Bollnäs
Fagernes
Lillehammer
Sälen
Älvdalen
Söderhamn
Ljusne
Hemsedal
Brumunddal
Orsa
Askøy
Ytre Arna
Bergen
Voss
Gol
Gjøvik
Hamar
Elverum
Mora
HIRTSHALS
Nesttun
Os/Osøyro
Norheimsund
Geilo
Nesbyen
Raufoss
Stange
Mjøsa
Sysslebäck
Malungsfors
Malung
Siljan
Rättvik
Gävle
Odda
Brandbu
Sand
Falun
Hofors
Sandviken
Älvkarleby
Skare
Bømlo
Hønefoss
Jevnaker
Eidsvoll
Stöllet
Vansbro
Borlänge
Hedemora
Kongsvinger
Skarnes
NORWAY
SWEDEN
NORGE
SVERIGE

BARENTS SEA
Nordkapp
Magerøya
Honningsvåg
Havøysund
Kjøllefjord
Nordkinn-halvøya
Berlevåg
Båtsfjord
Vardø
Sørøya
Akkarfjord
Porsanger-halvøya
Hammerfest
Kvaløya
Breivikbotn
Loppa
Seiland
Stjernøya
Arnøy
Vanna
Ringvassøy
Kvaløy
Tromsø
Finnsnes
Storfjord
Andselv
Alta
Talvik
Lakselv
Karasjok
Kautokeino
Tana
Varanger-halvøya
Vadsø
Varangerfjorden
Kirkenes
Bjørnevatn
Nikel
Pechenga
Zapolyarnyy
Rybachiy Poluostrov
Utsjoki
Kaamanen
Partakko
Inari
Inarijärvi
Ivalo
Raja Jooseppi
Saariselkä
Polyarnyy
Severomorsk
Murmansk
Kola
Kildinstroy
Murmashi
Teriberka
Kolskiy Zaliv
Kolskiy Kola Poluostrov Peninsula
Olenegorsk
Lovozero
Monchegorsk
Kirovsk
Apatity
Kovdor
Kandalaksha
Polyarnyye Zori
Umba
Olenitsa
Kandalakshskiy Zaliv
Zelenoborskiy
Alakurtti
Kuolayarvi
Salla
Arctic Circle
Loukhi
Ambarnyy
Kestenga
Pongoma
Kalevala
Kem
Voynitsa
Yushkozero
Ozero Kuyto
Kimasozero
Rugozero
Nadvoitsy
Segezha
Reboly
Kuhmo
Sotkamo
Lendery
Padany
Medvezhyegorsk
Finnmark
Lappland
Enontekiö
Muonio
Kittilä
Sodankylä
Pelkosenniemi
Kemijärvi
Vikajärvi
Rovaniemi
Pello
Ylitornio
Tervola
Tornio
Kemi
Simo
Haparanda
Kalix
Övertorneå
Överkalix
Pajala
Kolari
Abisko
Torneträsk
Kiruna
Kebnekaise
Svappavaara
Vittangi
Junosuando
Malmberget
Gällivare
Porjus
Hakkas
Jokkmokk
Kåbdalis
Harads
Morjärv
Boden
Luleå
Gammelstad
Älvsbyn
Arvidsjaur
Arjeplog
Piteå
Norrbotten
Glommersträsk
Jörn
Boliden
Byske
Skellefteå
Skelleftehamn
Bureå
Norsjö
Lycksele
Granö
Vindeln
Ånäset
Vännäs
Umeå
Holmsund
Västerbotten
Mellansel
Örnsköldsvik
Härnösand
Kramfors
Perämeri
Bottenviken
Hailuoto
Haukipudas
Oulu
Muhos
Raahe
Kalajoki
Oulainen
Ylivieska
Nivala
Haapajärvi
Pyhäjärvi
Kiuruvesi
Kokkola
Pietarsaari
Uusikaarlepyy
Raippaluoto
Vaasa
Lapua
Kauhava
Ilmajoki
Seinäjoki
Kurikka
Kauhajoki
Jalasjärvi
Alavus
Kaskinen
Kristiinankaupunki
Pudasjärvi
Taivalkoski
Kuusamo
Suomussalmi
Puolanka
Kajaani
Vuolijoki
Oulujärvi
Iisalmi
Nurmes
Lieksa
Pielinen
Juuka
Siilinjärvi
Juankoski
Kuopio
Kontiolahti
Outokumpu
Joensuu
Eno
Ilomantsi
Liperi
Leppävirta
Varkaus
Pieksämäki
Jyväskylä
Laukaa
Äänekoski
Saarijärvi
Viitasaari
Kyyjärvi
Keuruu
Mänttä
Jämsä
Parkano
Kankaanpää
Pori
Tampere
Nokia
Kangasala
Valkeakoski
Vammala
Huittinen
Rauma
Hämeenlinna
Janakkala
Riihimäki
Hyvinkää
Järvenpää
Kerava
Lahti
Heinola
Kuusankoski
Kouvola
Anjalankoski
Hamina
Kotka
Loviisa
Porvoo
Helsinki
Espoo
Vantaa
Lohja
Karkkila
Forssa
Loimaa
Somero
Salo
Turku
Raisio
Naantali
Uusikaupunki
Parainen
Åland
Mikkeli
Savonlinna
Kitee
Parikkala
Imatra
Ruokolahti
Joutseno
Lappeenranta
Tuohikotti
Kuhmoinen
Päijänne
Saimaa
Vyborg
Primorsk
Sestroretsk
Zelenogorsk
Kronshtadt
Sosnovyy Bor
Sankt-Peterburg
St. Petersburg
Priozersk
Valaam
Sortavala
Pitkyaranta
Vyartsilya
Suoyarvi
Olonets
Svirstroy
Novaya Ladoga
Syasstroy
Volkhov
Ladozhskoye Ozero
Lake Ladoga
Pohjanlahti
Gulf of Bothnia
Bottniska Viken
Selkämeri
Bottenhavet
Rostock
Suomi Finland
Sverige
Geta

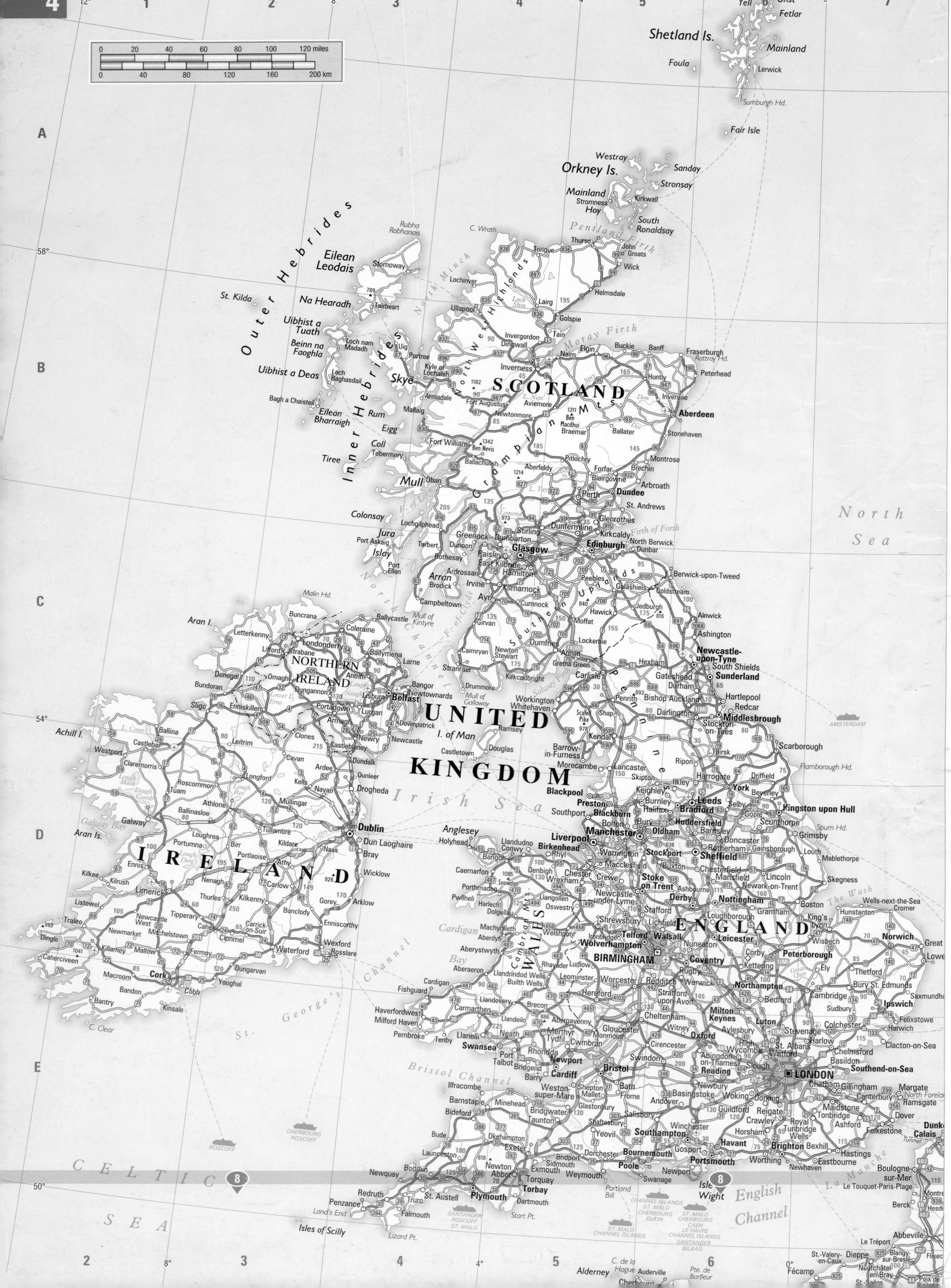
12°
1
2
8°
3
4
4°
5
6
0°
7
0
20
40
60
80
100
120 miles
0
40
80
120
160
200 km
A
B
C
D
E
58°
54°
50°
Shetland Is.
Yell
Unst
Fetlar
Mainland
Foula
Lerwick
Sumburgh Hd.
Fair Isle
Orkney Is.
Westray
Sanday
Stronsay
Mainland
Stromness
Hoy
Kirkwall
South Ronaldsay
Pentland Firth
Thurso
John o' Groats
Wick
Helmsdale
C. Wrath
Rubha Robhanais
Outer Hebrides
Eilean Leodais
Stornoway
St. Kilda
Na Hearadh
Tairbeart
Uibhist a Tuath
Beinn na Faoghla
Loch nam Madadh
Uibhist a Deas
Loch Baghasdail
Bagh a Chaisteil
Eilean Bharraigh
Inner Hebrides
Skye
Portree
Uig
Kyle of Lochalsh
Rum
Eigg
Coll
Tobermory
Tiree
Mull
Oban
Colonsay
Jura
Islay
Port Askaig
Port Ellen
North Minch
North West Highlands
Tongue
Lochinver
Ullapool
Lairg
Loch Shin
Golspie
Tain
Dornoch
Moray Firth
Invergordon
Dingwall
Inverness
Nairn
Elgin
Buckie
Banff
Fraserburgh
Rattray Hd.
Peterhead
Huntly
Inverurie
Aberdeen
Stonehaven
SCOTLAND
Grampian Mts.
Aviemore
Newtonmore
Fort Augustus
L. Ness
Armadale
Mallaig
Fort William
Ben Nevis
Ben Macdhui
Braemar
Ballater
Ballachulish
Pitlochry
Aberfeldy
L. Tay
Forfar
Brechin
Montrose
Blairgowrie
Arbroath
Dundee
Perth
St. Andrews
Glenrothes
Kirkcaldy
Dunfermline
Firth of Forth
North Berwick
Dunbar
Edinburgh
Stirling
L. Lomond
Dumbarton
Greenock
Dunoon
Glasgow
Paisley
East Kilbride
Hamilton
Lochgilphead
Tarbert
Rothesay
Arran
Brodick
Ardrossan
Irvine
Kilmarnock
Ayr
Campbeltown
F. of Clyde
Mull of Kintyre
Cumnock
Girvan
Southern Uplands
Peebles
Galashiels
Coldstream
Berwick-upon-Tweed
Jedburgh
Hawick
Moffat
Lockerbie
Dumfries
Annan
Gretna Green
Newton Stewart
Cairnryan
Stranraer
Kirkcudbright
Solway Firth
Drummore
Mull of Galloway
North Channel
Malin Hd.
Aran I.
Buncrana
Letterkenny
Lifford
Strabane
Londonderry
Coleraine
Ballycastle
Ballymena
Larne
NORTHERN IRELAND
Antrim
Lough Neagh
Bangor
Newtownards
Belfast
Lisburn
Omagh
Dungannon
Donegal
Bundoran
Sligo
Enniskillen
Lower L. Erne
Portadown
Armagh
Lurgan
Downpatrick
Newry
Newcastle
Clones
Castleblaney
Dundalk
Achill I.
Ballina
Castlebar
Westport
Claremorris
Leitrim
Cavan
Ardee
Dunleer
Drogheda
Navan
Kells
Longford
Roscommon
Tuam
Lough Ree
Athlone
Mullingar
Ballinasloe
Galway
Galway Bay
Aran Is.
Tullamore
Kildare
Dublin
Dun Laoghaire
Bray
Naas
Wicklow
Loughrea
Portumna
Lough Derg
Birr
Portlaoise
IRELAND
Ennis
Kilkee
Kilrush
Shannon
Limerick
Nenagh
Thurles
Carlow
Kilkenny
Gorey
Arklow
Listowel
Tralee
Tipperary
Cahir
Carrick-on-Suir
Clonmel
Bunclody
Enniscorthy
Wexford
Rosslare
Waterford
Dingle
Killarney
Newcastle West
Newmarket
Mitchelstown
Mallow
Fermoy
Cahersiveen
Macroom
Cork
Cobh
Youghal
Dungarvan
Bandon
Bantry
Kinsale
C. Clear
Irish Sea
UNITED KINGDOM
I. of Man
Ramsey
Castletown
Douglas
Workington
Whitehaven
Carlisle
Penrith
Scafell Pike
Shap
Kendal
Barrow-in-Furness
Morecambe
Lancaster
Hexham
Newcastle-upon-Tyne
South Shields
Gateshead
Sunderland
Durham
Bishop Auckland
Hartlepool
Redcar
Darlington
Middlesbrough
Stockton-on-Tees
Pennines
Alnwick
Ashington
Scarborough
Flamborough Hd.
Driffield
Ripon
Harrogate
Skipton
York
Beverley
Selby
Kingston upon Hull
Goole
Scunthorpe
Spurn Hd.
Grimsby
Blackpool
Preston
Southport
Blackburn
Burnley
Keighley
Ilkley
Leeds
Bradford
Halifax
Huddersfield
Bolton
Bury
Oldham
Manchester
Liverpool
Birkenhead
Warrington
Stockport
Barnsley
Doncaster
Rotherham
Sheffield
Gainsborough
Louth
Mablethorpe
Anglesey
Holyhead
Llandudno
Conwy
Rhyl
Bangor
Caernarfon
Denbigh
Chester
Wrexham
Crewe
Macclesfield
Buxton
Chesterfield
Mansfield
Newark-on-Trent
Lincoln
Skegness
Porthmadog
Pwllheli
Harlech
Snowdon
Llangollen
Oswestry
Stoke on Trent
Newcastle under-Lyme
Ashbourne
Derby
Nottingham
Grantham
Boston
The Wash
Wells-next-the-Sea
Cromer
Hunstanton
King's Lynn
Norwich
Great Yarmouth
Lowestoft
Wisbech
Cambrian Mts.
WALES
Machynlleth
Aberdyfi
Aberystwyth
Cardigan Bay
Welshpool
Shrewsbury
Telford
Ironbridge
Lichfield
Stafford
Walsall
Wolverhampton
BIRMINGHAM
Nuneaton
Leicester
Loughborough
Coventry
Rugby
Corby
Kettering
Peterborough
Thetford
Ely
ENGLAND
Aberaeron
Rhayader
Llandrindod Wells
Builth Wells
Ludlow
Leominster
Worcester
Redditch
Warwick
Stratford-upon-Avon
Northampton
Bedford
Cambridge
Bury St. Edmunds
Ipswich
Saxmundham
Felixstowe
Harwich
Colchester
Clacton-on-Sea
Fishguard
Cardigan
Haverfordwest
Milford Haven
Pembroke
Tenby
Llanelli
Carmarthen
Llandovery
Llandeilo
Brecon
Abergavenny
Hereford
Cheltenham
Gloucester
Monmouth
Merthyr Tydfil
Cwmbran
Neath
Swansea
Port Talbot
Rhondda
Bridgend
Newport
Cardiff
Barry
Milton Keynes
Luton
Stevenage
Aylesbury
Oxford
Witney
Cirencester
Swindon
Abingdon-on-Thames
High Wycombe
St. Albans
Watford
Harlow
Chelmsford
Basildon
Southend-on-Sea
LONDON
Slough
Reading
Bristol
Bath
Newbury
Chatham
Gillingham
Margate
Ramsgate
North Foreland
Canterbury
Dover
Folkestone
Maidstone
Tonbridge
Ashford
Royal Tunbridge Wells
Crawley
Reigate
Guildford
Woking
Dorking
Basingstoke
Andover
Salisbury
Winchester
Southampton
Horsham
Brighton
Bexhill
Hastings
Eastbourne
Newhaven
Worthing
Havant
Portsmouth
Gosport
Isle of Wight
Newport
Bournemouth
Poole
Swanage
Dorchester
Weymouth
Portland Bill
Bridport
Yeovil
Shaftesbury
Glastonbury
Shepton Mallet
Frome
Bridgwater
Taunton
Weston-super-Mare
Minehead
Bristol Channel
Ilfracombe
Barnstaple
Bideford
Bude
Okehampton
Exeter
Launceston
Sidmouth
Exmouth
Newton Abbot
Torquay
Torbay
Dartmouth
Start Pt.
Plymouth
St. Austell
Bodmin
Newquay
Redruth
Truro
Falmouth
Penzance
Land's End
Lizard Pt.
Isles of Scilly
St. George's Channel
CELTIC SEA
North Sea
AMSTERDAM
ROSCOFF
CHERBOURG ROSCOFF
SANTANDER ROSCOFF ST. MALO
CHANNEL ISLANDS ST. MALO CHERBOURG GIJON
ST. MALO CHERBOURG CAEN LE HAVRE CHANNEL ISLANDS SANTANDER BILBAO
ST. MALO CHANNEL ISLANDS
8
English Channel
La Manche
Tunnel
Dunkerque
Calais
Boulogne-sur-Mer
Le Touquet-Paris-Plage
Montreuil
Hesdin
Berck
Abbeville
Le Tréport
St.-Valery-en-Caux
Dieppe
Blangy-sur-Bresle
Neufchâtel-en-Bray
Fécamp
Alderney
C. de la Hague
Auderville
Pte. de Barfleur
Cherbourg

NORGE
NORWAY
SVERIGE
SWEDEN
DANMARK
DENMARK
DEUTSCHLAND
GERMANY
NEDERLAND
NETHERLANDS
BELGIQUE
BELGIUM
Nordsjøen
Vesterhavet
Nordsee
Noordzee
Skagerrak
Kattegat
Østersøen
Nordfriesische Inseln
Ost-friesische Inseln
Westfriesche Eilanden
Deutsche Bucht
Oslo
Bergen
Stavanger
Kristiansand
Göteborg
Gothenburg
Malmö
KØBENHAVN
COPENHAGEN
Århus
Aalborg
Odense
Kiel
Lübeck
HAMBURG
Bremen
Bremerhaven
Hannover
BERLIN
Rostock
Szczecin
Magdeburg
Leipzig
Dresden
Halle
Braunschweig
Wolfsburg
Kassel
Göttingen
Frankfurt
Würzburg
Nürnberg
Köln
Bonn
Düsseldorf
Essen
Dortmund
Münster
Osnabrück
Bielefeld
AMSTERDAM
ROTTERDAM
's-Gravenhage
The Hague
Utrecht
Groningen
Antwerpen
BRUXELLES
BRUSSELS
Liège
Lille
Namur
Charleroi
Bornholm
(Danmark)
(Denmark)
Sjælland
Fyn
Lolland
Fehmarn
Rügen
Usedom
Helgoland
Jönköping
Örebro
Linköping
Västerås

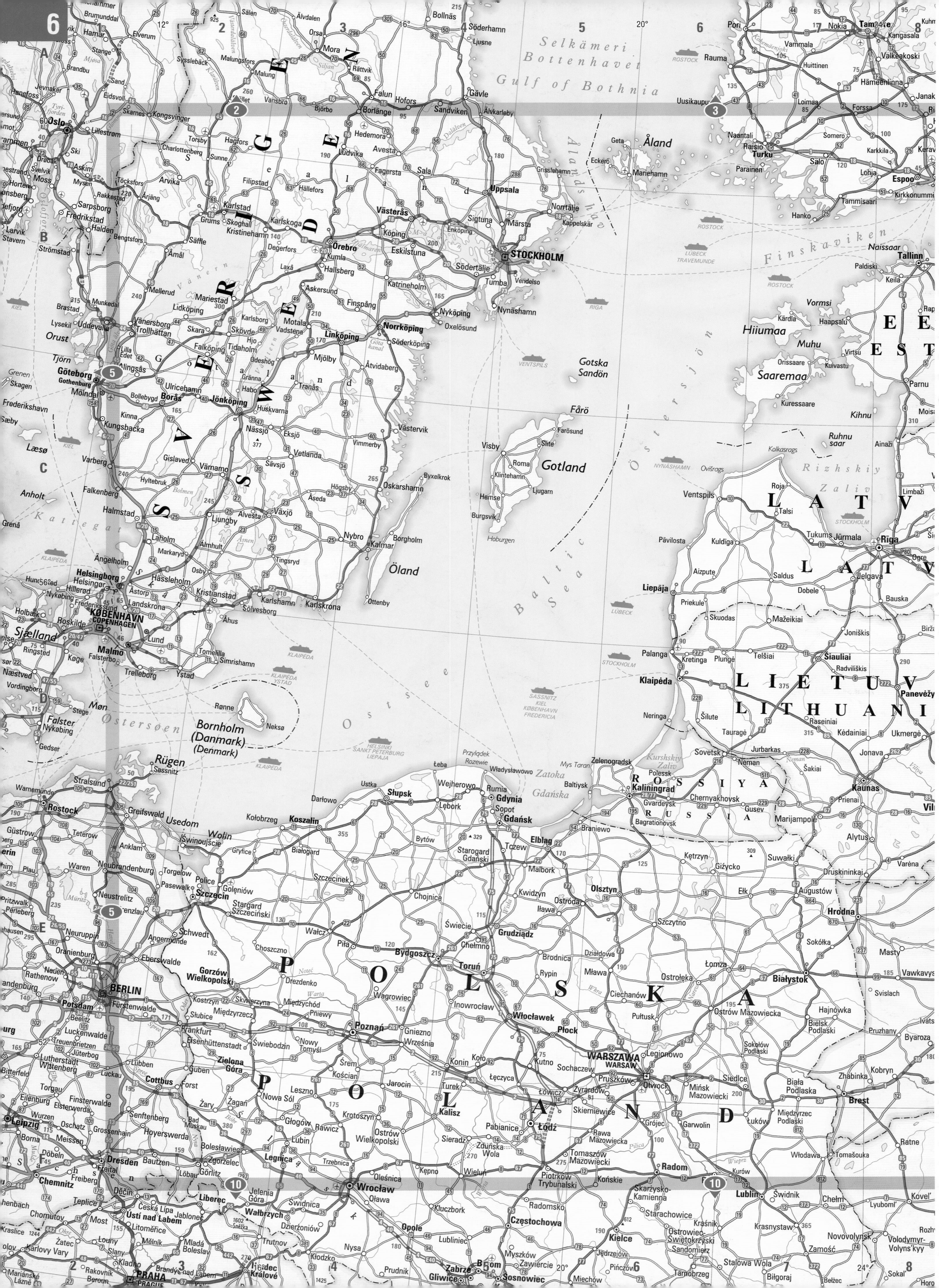

SVERIGE
SWEDEN
POLSKA
POLAND
LIETUVA
LITHUANIA
LATVIJA
EESTI
ROSSIYA
RUSSIA
Selkämeri
Bottenhavet
Gulf of Bothnia
Ålands hav
Finskaviken
Östersjön
Baltic Sea
Ostsee
Østersøen
Kattegat
Rizhskiy Zaliv
Zatoka Gdańska
Kurshskiy Zaliv
Åland
Gotland
Öland
Gotska Sandön
Fårö
Hiiumaa
Saaremaa
Muhu
Vormsi
Kihnu
Ruhnu saar
Bornholm (Danmark) (Denmark)
Rügen
Usedom
Wolin
Sjælland
Falster
Møn
Læsø
Anholt
Orust
Tjörn
Vänern
Vättern
Hjälmaren
Mälaren
STOCKHOLM
Uppsala
Västerås
Örebro
Norrköping
Linköping
Jönköping
Göteborg
Gothenburg
Malmö
Helsingborg
Kalmar
Karlskrona
Visby
Gävle
Falun
Borlänge
Karlstad
Oslo
KØBENHAVN
COPENHAGEN
Helsingør
Turku
Tampere
Espoo
Tallinn
Pärnu
Riga
Jelgava
Liepāja
Ventspils
Klaipėda
Palanga
Šiauliai
Panevėžys
Kaunas
Kaliningrad
Gdańsk
Gdynia
Sopot
Elbląg
Olsztyn
Słupsk
Koszalin
Szczecin
Bydgoszcz
Toruń
Grudziądz
Poznań
Włocławek
Płock
WARSZAWA
WARSAW
Łódź
Radom
Lublin
Białystok
Hrodna
Brest
Kielce
Częstochowa
Wrocław
Opole
Legnica
Zielona Góra
Gorzów Wielkopolski
Kalisz
BERLIN
Potsdam
Rostock
Stralsund
Neubrandenburg
Frankfurt
Cottbus
Dresden
Leipzig
Chemnitz
Liberec
Ústí nad Labem
PRAHA
PRAGUE
Hradec Králové
Zabrze
Gliwice
Bytom
Sosnowiec

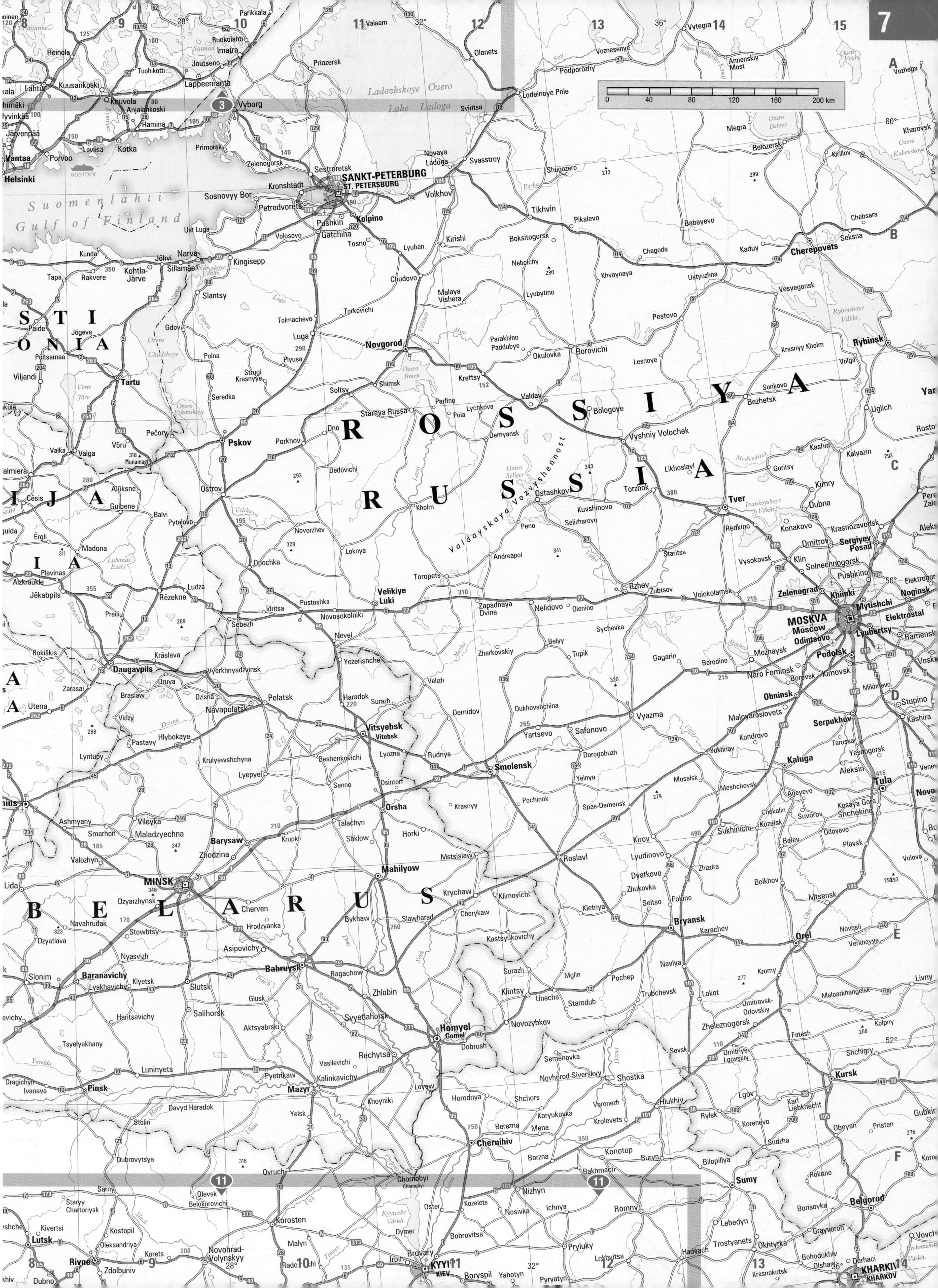

ROSSIYA
RUSSIA
BELARUS
STONIA
Valdayskaya Vozvyshennost
Suomenlahti
Gulf of Finland
Ladozhskoye Ozero
Lake Ladoga
Ozero Chudskoye
Ozero Pskovskoye
Ozero Ilmen
Ozero Seliger
Rybinskoye Vdkhr.
Ivankovskoye Vdkhr.
Kyyivske Vdskh.
0 40 80 120 160 200 km
Helsinki
Vantaa
Porvoo
Lahti
Kouvola
Kotka
Hamina
Imatra
Lappeenranta
Vyborg
Priozersk
Sankt-Peterburg
St. Petersburg
Kronshtadt
Sestroretsk
Zelenogorsk
Sosnovyy Bor
Petrodvorets
Pushkin
Kolpino
Gatchina
Tosno
Lyuban
Kirishi
Volkhov
Novaya Ladoga
Syasstroy
Lodeinoye Pole
Svirtsa
Podporozhy
Olonets
Valaam
Voznesenye
Vytegra
Annenskiy Most
Vozhega
Megra
Belozersk
Kharovsk
Kirillov
Cherepovets
Chebsara
Seksna
Kaduy
Babayevo
Chagoda
Tikhvin
Pikalevo
Boksitogorsk
Shugozero
Ustyuzhna
Vesyegonsk
Khvoynaya
Nebolchy
Lyubytino
Malaya Vishera
Chudovo
Torkovichi
Tolmachevo
Luga
Kingisepp
Narva
Sillamäe
Jõhvi
Kohtla-Järve
Rakvere
Tapa
Kunda
Slantsy
Gdov
Polna
Strugi Krasnyye
Plyusa
Novgorod
Shimsk
Soltsy
Staraya Russa
Parfino
Pola
Lychkova
Demyansk
Krestsy
Okulovka
Parakhino Paddubye
Borovichi
Pestovo
Lesnoye
Valday
Bologoye
Vyshniy Volochek
Bezhetsk
Sonkovo
Krasnyy Kholm
Rybinsk
Uglich
Kashin
Kalyazin
Goritsy
Kimry
Dubna
Konakovo
Tver
Torzhok
Likhoslavl
Ostashkov
Kuvshinovo
Selizharovo
Peno
Andreapol
Toropets
Rzhev
Zubtsov
Staritsa
Volokolamsk
Redkino
Klin
Dmitrov
Sergiyev Posad
Krasnozavodsk
Solnechnogorsk
Vysokovsk
Pushkino
Zelenograd
Khimki
Mytishchi
Noginsk
Elektrostal
MOSKVA
Moscow
Odintsovo
Lyubertsy
Podolsk
Naro Fominsk
Mozhaysk
Borodino
Gagarin
Obninsk
Maloyaroslavets
Serpukhov
Stupino
Kashira
Kaluga
Tula
Aleksin
Tarussa
Yasnogorsk
Shchekino
Kosaya Gora
Odoyevo
Belev
Plavsk
Suvorov
Kozelsk
Sukhinichi
Meshchovsk
Mosalsk
Kondrovo
Yukhnov
Vyazma
Safonovo
Yartsevo
Dorogobuzh
Smolensk
Yelnya
Pochinok
Spas-Demensk
Roslavl
Kirov
Lyudinovo
Zhizdra
Dyatkovo
Bryansk
Karachev
Orel
Mtsensk
Bolkhov
Novosil
Verkhovye
Livny
Kromy
Dmitrovsk-Orlovskiy
Zheleznogorsk
Fatesh
Kursk
Shchigry
Dmitriyev Lgovskiy
Lgov
Kolpny
Maloarkhangelsk
Lokot
Navlya
Sevsk
Trubchevsk
Pochep
Unecha
Starodub
Klintsy
Mglin
Surazh
Novozybkov
Zhukovka
Seltso
Fokino
Kletnya
Pskov
Porkhov
Dno
Dedovichi
Kholm
Loknya
Novorzhev
Opochka
Ostrov
Pytalovo
Pechory
Velikiye Luki
Novosokolniki
Pustoshka
Idritsa
Sebezh
Nevel
Zapadnaya Dvina
Nelidovo
Olenino
Belyy
Tupik
Sychevka
Zharkovskiy
Velizh
Demidov
Dukhovshchina
Rudnya
Krasnyy
Tartu
Võru
Valga
Valka
Viljandi
Põltsamaa
Jõgeva
Paide
Alūksne
Gulbene
Balvi
Madona
Ērgli
Cēsis
Valmiera
Rēzekne
Ludza
Preiļi
Jēkabpils
Aizkraukle
Plavinas
Krāslava
Daugavpils
Rokiškis
Zarasai
Utena
Druya
Braslaw
Dzisna
Vyerkhnyadzvinsk
Polatsk
Navapolatsk
Haradok
Surazh
Vitsyebsk
Vitebsk
Beshenkovichi
Lyozna
Senno
Orsha
Osintorf
Talachyn
Shklow
Horki
Mstsislaw
Krupki
Lyepyel
Krulyewshchyna
Hlybokaye
Pastavy
Vidzy
Lyntupy
Ashmyany
Smarhon
Vileyka
Maladzyechna
Barysaw
Zhodzina
MINSK
Dzyarzhynsk
Valozhyn
Lida
Navahrudak
Dzyatlava
Stowbtsy
Nyasvizh
Baranavichy
Slonim
Lyakhavichy
Klyetsk
Slutsk
Salihorsk
Hantsavichy
Tsyelyakhany
Luninyets
Pinsk
Ivanava
Dragichyn
Stolin
Davyd Haradok
Cherven
Hrodzyanka
Asipovichy
Babruysk
Rahachow
Zhlobin
Bykhaw
Mahilyow
Krychaw
Klimovichi
Cherykaw
Slawharad
Kastsyukovichy
Hlusk
Svyetlahorsk
Aktsyabrski
Homyel
Gomel
Dobrush
Rechytsa
Vasilevichi
Kalinkavichy
Mazyr
Pyetrikaw
Khoyniki
Yelsk
Loyew
Dubrovytsya
Sarny
Olevsk
Ovruch
Chornobyl
Chernobyl
Korosten
Starry Chartoriysk
Belokorovichi
Kostopil
Lutsk
Kivertsi
Rivne
Oleksandriya
Zdolbuniv
Dubno
Korets
Novohrad-Volynskyy
Malyn
Radomyshl
Irpin
Brovary
KYYIV
KIEV
Boryspil
Yahotyn
Pyryatyn
Chernihiv
Horodnya
Shchors
Semenovka
Novhorod-Siverskyy
Shostka
Voronezh
Koryukovka
Mena
Berezna
Krolevets
Hlukhiv
Konotop
Borzna
Buryn
Bakhmach
Nizhyn
Kozelets
Oster
Nosivka
Ichnya
Bobrovitsa
Pryluky
Lokhvytsya
Romny
Hadyach
Lebedyn
Trostyanets
Okhtyrka
Sumy
Bilopillya
Rylsk
Korenevo
Sudzha
Karl Liebknecht
Oboyan
Pristen
Rokitno
Borisovka
Belgorod
Grayvoron
Bohodukhiv
Olshany
Krasnokutsk
Derhaci
KHARKIV
KHARKOV
Gubkin

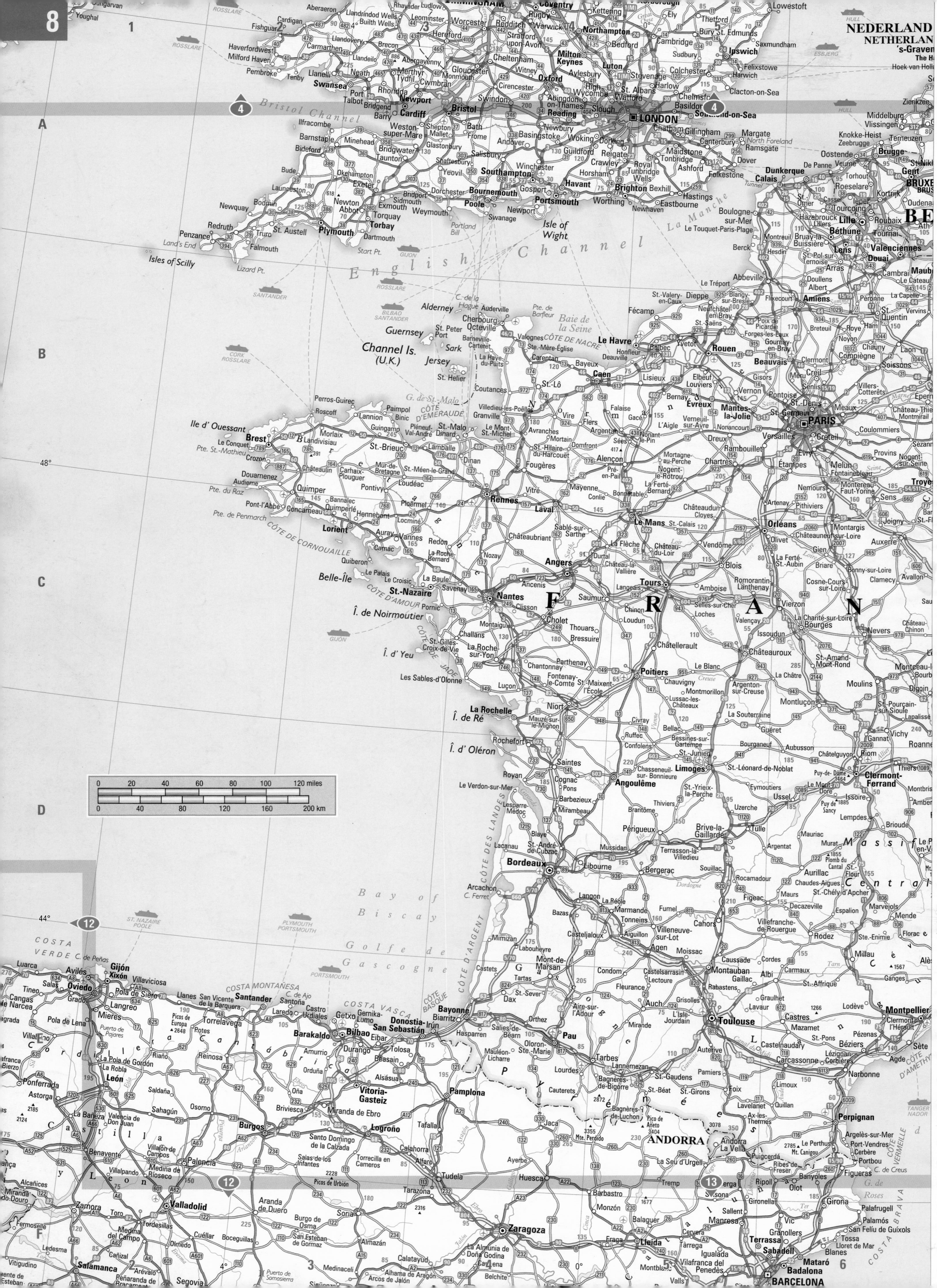
NEDERLAND
NETHERLANDS
LONDON
Bristol Channel
English Channel
La Manche
Channel Is. (U.K.)
Guernsey
Jersey
Alderney
Sark
Isles of Scilly
Isle of Wight
Baie de la Seine
CÔTE DE NACRE
CÔTE D'EMERAUDE
CÔTE DE CORNOUAILLE
CÔTE D'AMOUR
CÔTE DE JADE
CÔTE D'ARGENT
CÔTE DES LANDES
CÔTE BASQUE
COSTA VASCA
COSTA MONTAÑESA
COSTA VERDE
CÔTE VERMEILLE
COSTA BRAVA
CÔTE D'AMETHYSTE
FRANCE
PARIS
Massif Central
Bay of Biscay
Golfe de Gascogne
Pyrénées
ANDORRA
Cantábrica
Castilla y León
Cardiff
Bristol
Plymouth
Southampton
Brighton
Dover
Calais
Dunkerque
Lille
Le Havre
Rouen
Caen
Amiens
Brest
Rennes
Nantes
Le Mans
Orléans
Tours
Angers
Poitiers
Limoges
La Rochelle
Bordeaux
Clermont-Ferrand
Toulouse
Montpellier
Perpignan
Bayonne
Pau
Santander
Bilbao
Donostia-San Sebastián
Oviedo
Gijón
León
Burgos
Vitoria-Gasteiz
Pamplona
Logroño
Valladolid
Zaragoza
Lleida
Barcelona
Salamanca
48°
44°
0°
4°
0 20 40 60 80 100 120 miles
0 40 80 120 160 200 km

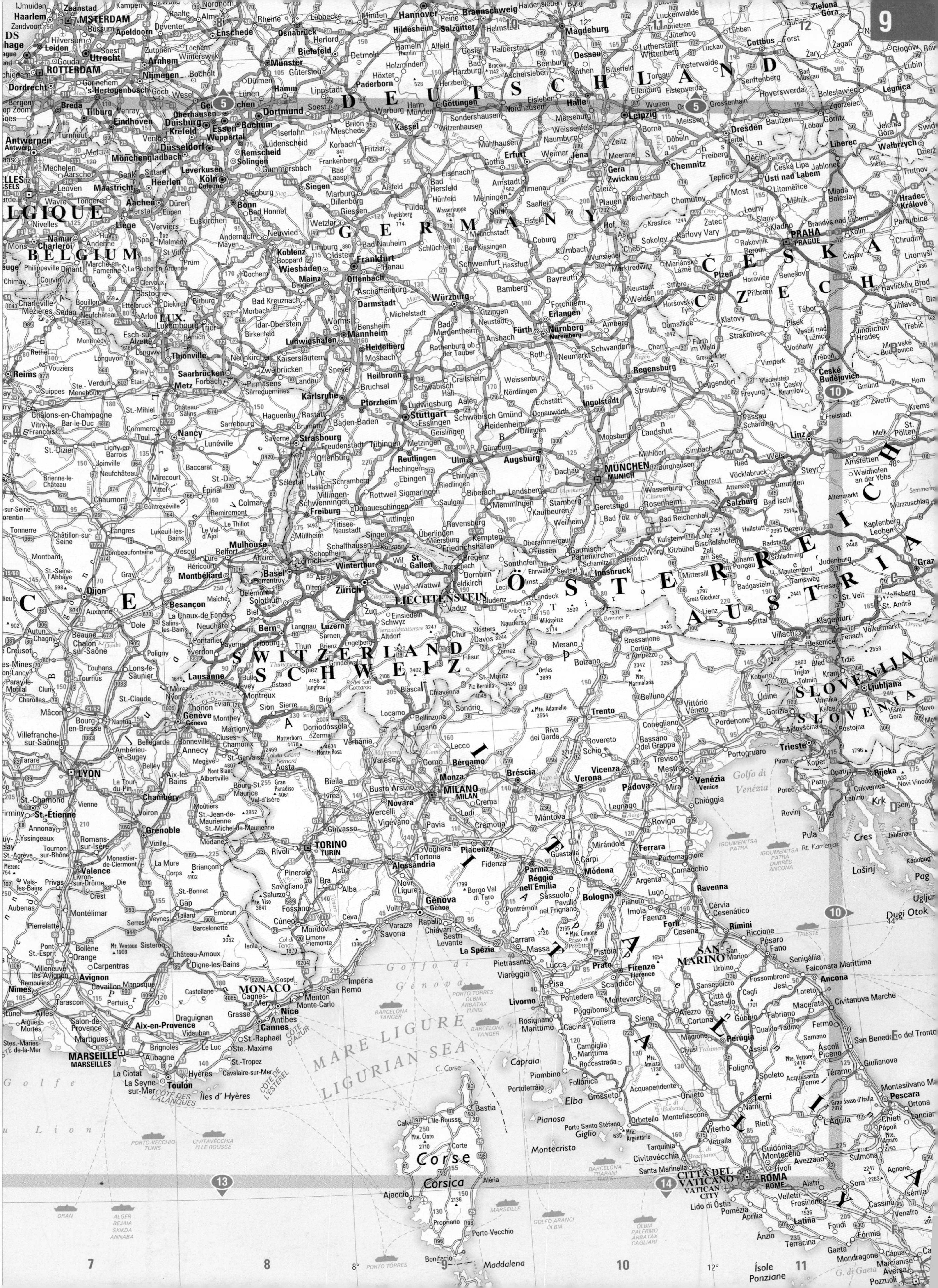
DEUTSCHLAND
GERMANY
BELGIQUE
BELGIUM
LUX.
FRANCE
SWITZERLAND
SCHWEIZ
LIECHTENSTEIN
ÖSTERREICH
AUSTRIA
ČESKÁ
CZECH
SLOVENIJA
SLOVENIA
ITALIA
ITALY
SAN MARINO
MONACO
CITTÀ DEL VATICANO
VATICAN CITY
MARE LIGURE
LIGURIAN SEA
Golfe du Lion
Golfo di Genova
Golfo di Venézia
Corse
Corsica
Elba
AMSTERDAM
ROTTERDAM
Bruxelles
Köln
Frankfurt
Stuttgart
München
Leipzig
Dresden
PRAHA
PRAGUE
Wien
Zürich
Bern
Genève
Lyon
Marseille
MILANO
TORINO
Génova
Venézia
Bologna
Firenze
ROMA
Ljubljana
Trieste
Nice
Innsbruck
Salzburg
Graz
Strasbourg
Dijon
7
8
9
10
11
12
5
10
13
14

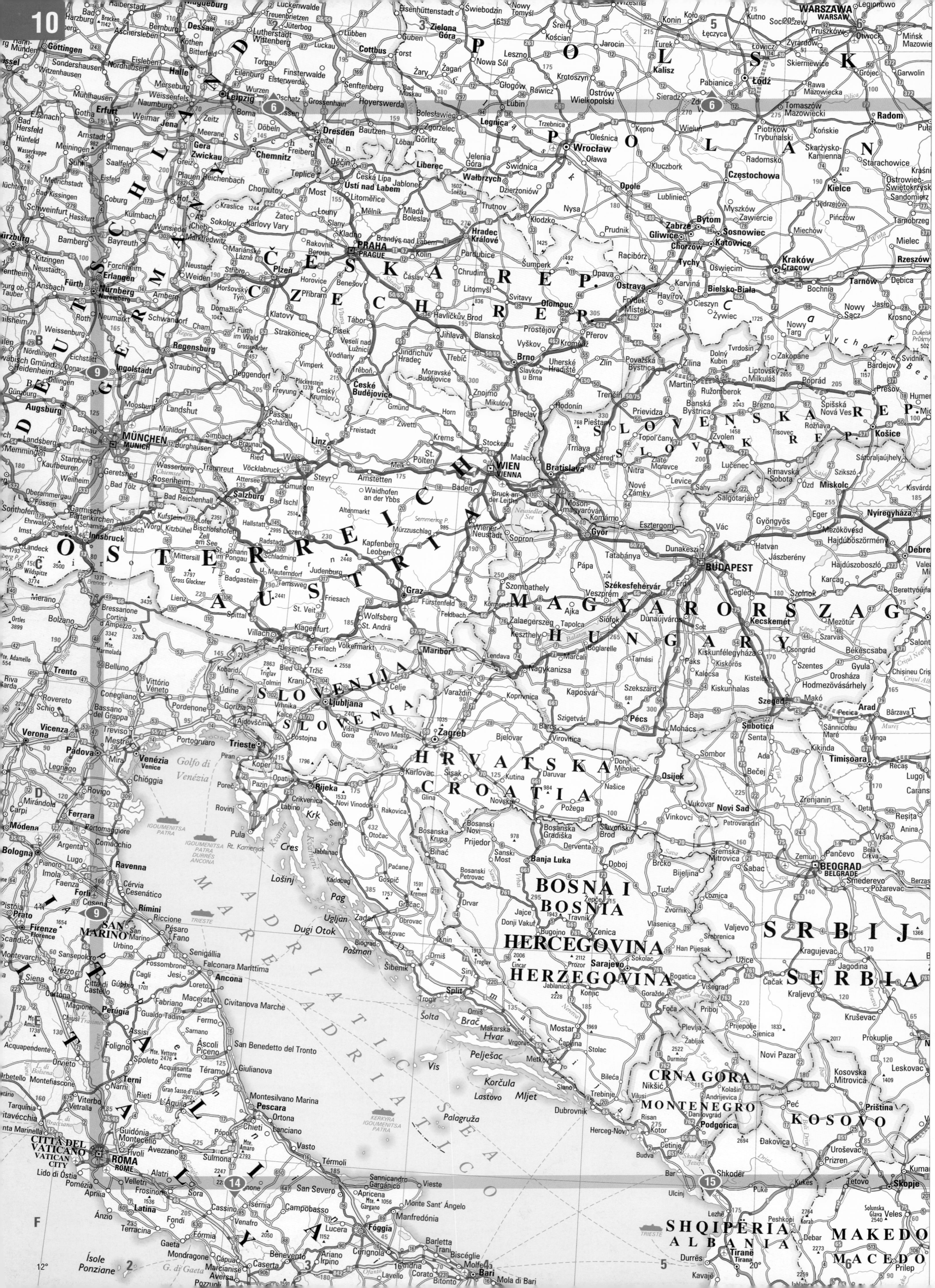
DEUTSCHLAND
GERMANY
POLSKA
POLAND
ČESKÁ REP.
CZECH REP.
SLOVENSKÁ REP.
SLOVAK REP.
ÖSTERREICH
AUSTRIA
MAGYARORSZÁG
HUNGARY
SLOVENIJA
SLOVENIA
HRVATSKA
CROATIA
BOSNA I HERCEGOVINA
BOSNIA HERZEGOVINA
SRBIJA
SERBIA
CRNA GORA
MONTENEGRO
KOSOVO
SHQIPËRIA
ALBANIA
MAKEDO
MACEDO
ITALIA
MARE ADRIATICO
ADRIATIC SEA
Golfo di Venézia
WARSZAWA
WARSAW
Łódź
Wrocław
Kraków
Cracow
Katowice
Poznań
Leipzig
Dresden
Chemnitz
Erfurt
Halle
Nürnberg
Nuremberg
Regensburg
Augsburg
MÜNCHEN
MUNICH
PRAHA
PRAGUE
Plzeň
Brno
Ostrava
Olomouc
České Budějovice
Linz
Salzburg
Innsbruck
Graz
Klagenfurt
WIEN
VIENNA
Bratislava
Košice
Žilina
BUDAPEST
Győr
Debrecen
Szeged
Pécs
Miskolc
Ljubljana
Maribor
Zagreb
Rijeka
Split
Zadar
Dubrovnik
Sarajevo
Banja Luka
Novi Sad
BEOGRAD
BELGRADE
Timişoara
Arad
Podgorica
Priština
Skopje
Tiranë
Tirana
Venézia
Venice
Trieste
Verona
Pádova
Bologna
Firenze
Florence
Ancona
Perúgia
Pescara
ROMA
ROME
CITTÀ DEL VATICANO
VATICAN CITY
SAN MARINO
Bari
Fóggia
Latina

UKRAINA
MOLDOVA
ROMÂNIA
BULGARIYA
BULGARIA
KARA DENIZ
BLACK SEA
Brest
Pinsk
Luninyets
Kobryn
Mazyr
Kalinkavichy
Chernihiv
Konotop
Nizhyn
Chornobyl
Chernobyl
Ovruch
Kovel'
Lublin
Chełm
Zamość
Lutsk
Rivne
Korosten
Zhytomyr
KYYIV
KIEV
Brovary
Boryspil
Fastiv
Bila Tserkva
Pryluky
Lubny
Cherkasy
Kremenchuk
Kremenchuksk Vdskh.
L'viv
Przemyśl
Ternopil
Khmelnytskyy
Vinnytsya
Berdychiv
Uman
Kirovohrad
Oleksandriya
Smila
Zvenyhorodka
Ivano-Frankivsk
Kalush
Stryy
Drohobych
Uzhhorod
Mukacheve
Kamyanets-Podil's'kyy
Chernivtsi
Mohyliv-Podil's'kyy
Balta
Pervomaysk
Kryvyy Rih
Krivoy Rog
Voznesensk
Mykolayiv
Nikolayev
Kherson
ODESA
ODESSA
Illichivsk
Bilhorod-Dnistrovskyy
Chişinău
Kishinev
Tiraspol
Tighina
Bălţi
Soroca
Orhei
Ungheni
Cahul
Comrat
Izmayil
Reni
Kiliya
Tendrovskaya Kosa
Ostriv Dzharylhach
Satu Mare
Baia Mare
Suceava
Botoşani
Iaşi
Bistriţa
Cluj-Napoca
Oradea
Târgu Mureş
Piatra Neamţ
Roman
Bacău
Vaslui
Focşani
Galaţi
Brăila
Tulcea
Sulina
Deva
Alba-Iulia
Sibiu
Braşov
Buzău
Ploieşti
BUCUREŞTI
BUCHAREST
Piteşti
Râmnicu Vâlcea
Târgu-Jiu
Drobeta-Turnu-Severin
Craiova
Slatina
Constanţa
Mangalia
Călăraşi
Slobozia
Giurgiu
Ruse
Dobrich
Varna
Shumen
Pleven
Veliko Tŭrnovo
Gabrovo
Vratsa
Montana
Lom
Vidin
Calafat
SOFIYA
SOFIA
Pernik
Kyustendil
Blagoevgrad
Plovdiv
Stara Zagora
Kazanlŭk
Sliven
Yambol
Burgas
Aytos
Haskovo
Kŭrdzhali
Edirne
Kırklareli
Lüleburgaz
Çorlu
İSTANBUL
İstanbul Boğazı
Zonguldak
Kocaeli
Sakarya
0 40 80 120 160 200 km
7
15
16

0 40 80 120 160 200 km
Bay of Biscay
Golfe de Gascogne
ST. NAZAIRE POOLE
PLYMOUTH PORTSMOUTH
PORTSMOUTH
COSTA VERDE
COSTA MONTAÑESA
COSTA VASCA
C. Ortegal
Ortigueira
Ferrol
A Coruña
Betanzos
Vivero
Ribadeo
Luarca
Avilés
Gijón
Xixón
Villaviciosa
Oviedo
Pola de Siero
Llanes
Santander
Laredo
Castro Urdiales
Bilbao
Donostia
San Sebastián
Eibar
Durango
Tolosa
Santiago de Compostela
Lugo
Mondoñedo
Villalba
Cangas de Narcea
Mieres
Langreo
Torrelavega
Reinosa
Picos de Europa 2648
Cordillera Cantábrica
Vitoria-Gasteiz
Miranda de Ebro
Logroño
Burgos
León
Ponferrada
Astorga
La Bañeza
Sahagún
Palencia
Villafranca del Bierzo
Monforte de Lemos
Pontevedra
Vigo
Ourense
Marín
Redondela
Baiona
Tui
Valença
Caminha
Viana do Castelo
Póvoa de Varzim
Vila do Conde
Braga
Guimarães
Chaves
Bragança
Mirandela
Matosinhos
Porto
Vila Nova de Gaia
Amarante
Peso da Régua
Lamego
Vila Real
Miranda do Douro
Zamora
Toro
Valladolid
Tordesillas
Medina del Campo
Benavente
Castilla y León
Aranda de Duero
Soria
Salamanca
Ávila
Segovia
Aveiro
Viseu
Guarda
Ciudad Rodrigo
Coimbra
Figueira da Foz
Leiria
Covilhã
Castelo Branco
Plasencia
Béjar
MADRID
Leganés
Getafe
Alcalá de Henares
Guadalajara
Toledo
Talavera de la Reina
Aranjuez
Cuenca
P O R T U G A L
E S P A Ñ A
S P A I N
Caldas da Rainha
Peniche
Santarém
Abrantes
Tomar
Cáceres
Trujillo
Mérida
Badajoz
Elvas
Estremoz
Évora
LISBOA
LISBON
Sintra
Cascais
Setúbal
Almada
Barreiro
Montijo
Beja
Sines
Don Benito
Villanueva de la Serena
Ciudad Real
Puertollano
Valdepeñas
Manzanares
Alcázar de San Juan
Castilla-La Mancha
Linares
Jaén
Úbeda
Córdoba
Andújar
Sierra Morena
Sevilla
Seville
Huelva
Faro
Olhão
Tavira
Portimão
Lagos
Sagres
Albufeira
Loulé
Vila Real de Santo António
Ayamonte
Dos Hermanas
Écija
Granada
Málaga
Antequera
Ronda
Marbella
Torremolinos
Fuengirola
Estepona
Almería
Motril
Guadix
Jerez de la Frontera
Cádiz
Sanlúcar de Barrameda
El Puerto de Santa María
San Fernando
Chiclana de la Frontera
Algeciras
Tarifa
La Línea de la Concepción
Gibraltar (U.K.)
COSTA DE LA LUZ
COSTA DEL SOL
G. de Cádiz
Str. of Gibraltar
C. Trafalgar
C. Spartel
Tanger
Tangier
Ceuta (Esp.) (Spain)
Tétouan
Larache
Chechaouen
Ksar el Kebir
Nador
Melilla (Esp.) (Spain)
Alborán
Cap des Trois Fourches
Er Rif
LAS PALMAS DE GRAN CANARIA SANTA CRUZ DE TENERIFE
ISLAS CANARIAS
SÈTE BARCELONA GÉNOVA
MELILLA AL HOCEIMA
MELILLA
MOTRIL MÁLAGA ALMERÍA

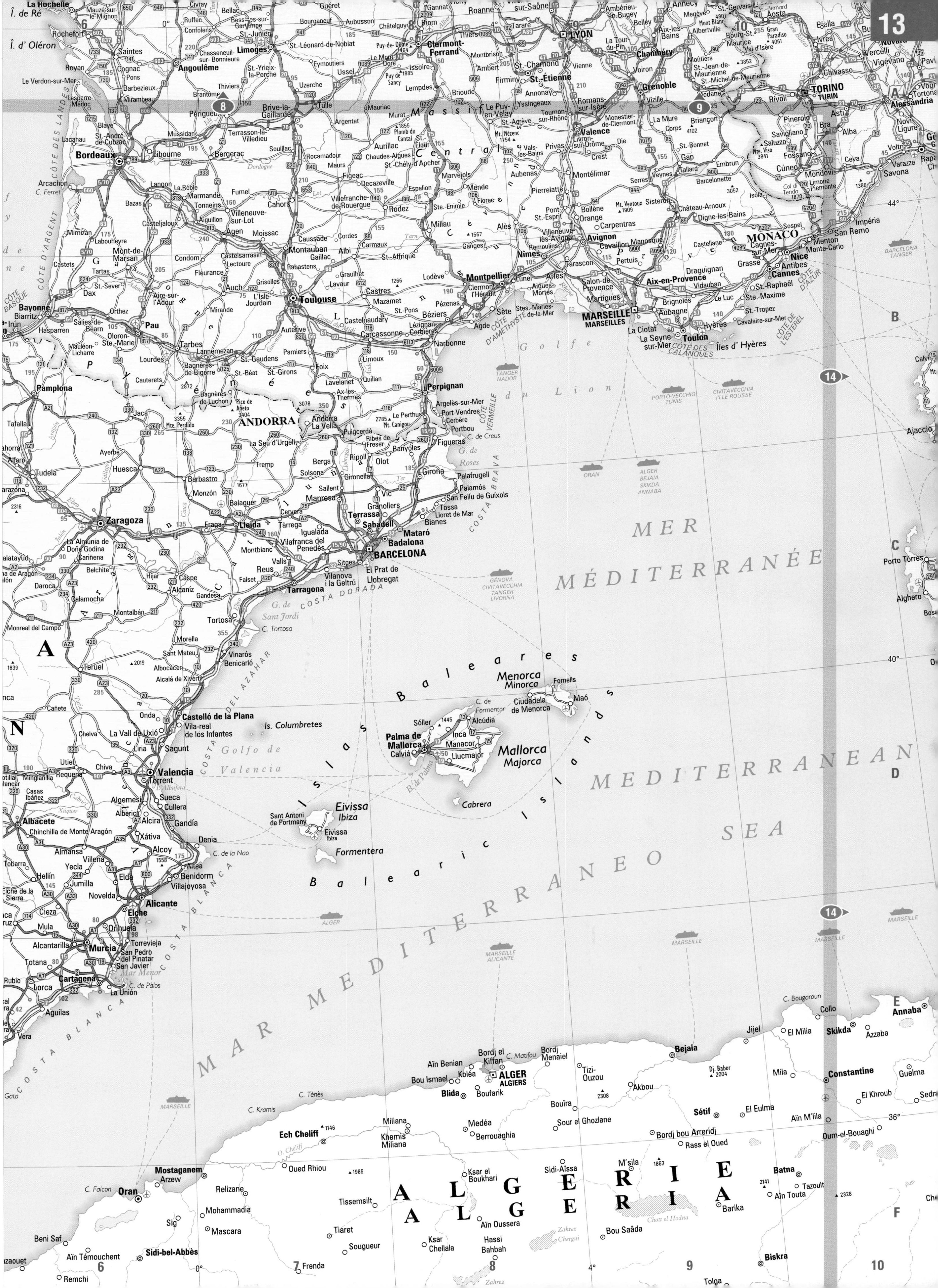
La Rochelle
Î. de Ré
Î. d' Oléron
Rochefort
Royan
Saintes
Cognac
Angoulême
Limoges
Clermont-Ferrand
Roanne
LYON
St.-Étienne
Chambéry
Grenoble
Aosta
TORINO
TURIN
Alessandria
Brive-la-Gaillarde
Tulle
Périgueux
Bordeaux
Libourne
Bergerac
Arcachon
Massif Central
Le Puy-en-Velay
Valence
Gap
Briançon
Cuneo
Savona
Aurillac
Rodez
Cahors
Agen
Montauban
Albi
Millau
Mende
Alès
Nîmes
Avignon
Arles
Montpellier
Aix-en-Provence
MARSEILLE
MARSEILLES
Toulon
Îles d' Hyères
Cannes
Nice
MONACO
San Remo
Menton
Mont-de-Marsan
Dax
Bayonne
Biarritz
Pau
Tarbes
Lourdes
Toulouse
Carcassonne
Béziers
Narbonne
Sète
Perpignan
Foix
ANDORRA
Andorra La Vella
Pamplona
Huesca
Zaragoza
Lleida
Girona
Figueres
Manresa
Terrassa
Sabadell
Mataró
Badalona
BARCELONA
Tarragona
Reus
Tortosa
Teruel
Castelló de la Plana
Sagunt
Valencia
Gandía
Denia
Xàtiva
Albacete
Alicante
Elche
Benidorm
Murcia
Cartagena
Torrevieja
Golfe du Lion
Côte d'Argent
Costa Brava
Costa Dorada
Costa del Azahar
Costa Blanca
Golfo de Valencia
MER MÉDITERRANÉE
MEDITERRANEAN SEA
MAR MEDITERRANEO
Islas Baleares
Balearic Islands
Mallorca
Majorca
Palma de Mallorca
Menorca
Minorca
Maó
Ciutadela de Menorca
Eivissa
Ibiza
Formentera
Cabrera
Is. Columbretes
Alghero
Porto Torres
Ajaccio
ALGERIE
ALGERIA
ALGER
ALGIERS
Blida
Oran
Mostaganem
Sidi-bel-Abbès
Tiaret
Médéa
Bejaia
Sétif
Constantine
Annaba
Skikda
Jijel
Batna
Biskra
Chott el Hodna
14
8
9
A
B
C
D
E
F
6
7
8
9
10
44°
40°
36°
0°
4°

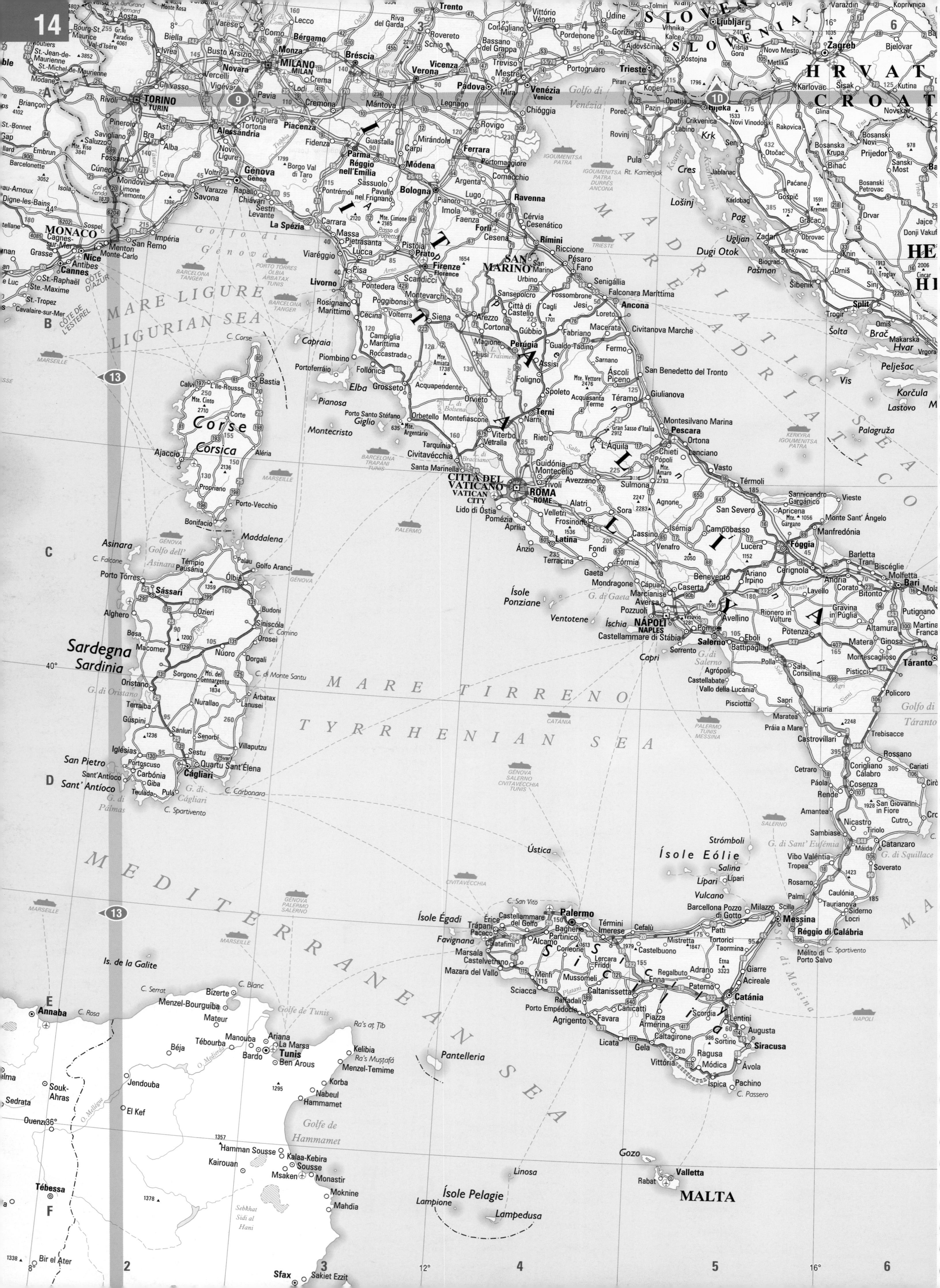

ITALIA
ITALY
SLOVENIJA
SLOVENIA
HRVATSKA
CROATIA
MALTA
Corse
Corsica
Sardegna
Sardinia
Sicilia
MARE LIGURE
LIGURIAN SEA
MARE ADRIATICO
ADRIATIC SEA
MARE TIRRENO
TYRRHENIAN SEA
MEDITERRANEAN SEA
Golfo di Genova
Golfo di Venézia
Torino
Turin
Milano
Milan
Génova
Venézia
Venice
Bologna
Firenze
Florence
Roma
Rome
Città del Vaticano
Vatican City
Nápoli
Naples
Bari
Táranto
Palermo
Catánia
Messina
Réggio di Calábria
Cágliari
Sássari
Ajaccio
Bastia
Monaco
Nice
Cannes
Ljubljana
Zagreb
Rijeka
Split
Zadar
Trieste
Verona
Pádova
Bréscia
Bérgamo
Parma
Módena
Rímini
San Marino
Ancona
Perúgia
Pescara
L'Áquila
Fóggia
Salerno
Cosenza
Catanzaro
Siracusa
Trápani
Tunis
Bizerte
Sousse
Valletta
Gozo
Annaba
Elba
Capri
Íschia
Ísole Eólie
Strómboli
Ísole Égadi
Ústica
Pantelleria
Linosa
Ísole Pelagie
Lampedusa
Capraia
Montecristo
Giglio
Ísole Ponziane
Ventotene
Golfe de Tunis
Golfe de Hammamet
9
10
13
A
B
C
D
E
F
2
3
4
5
6
12°
16°
40°
44°

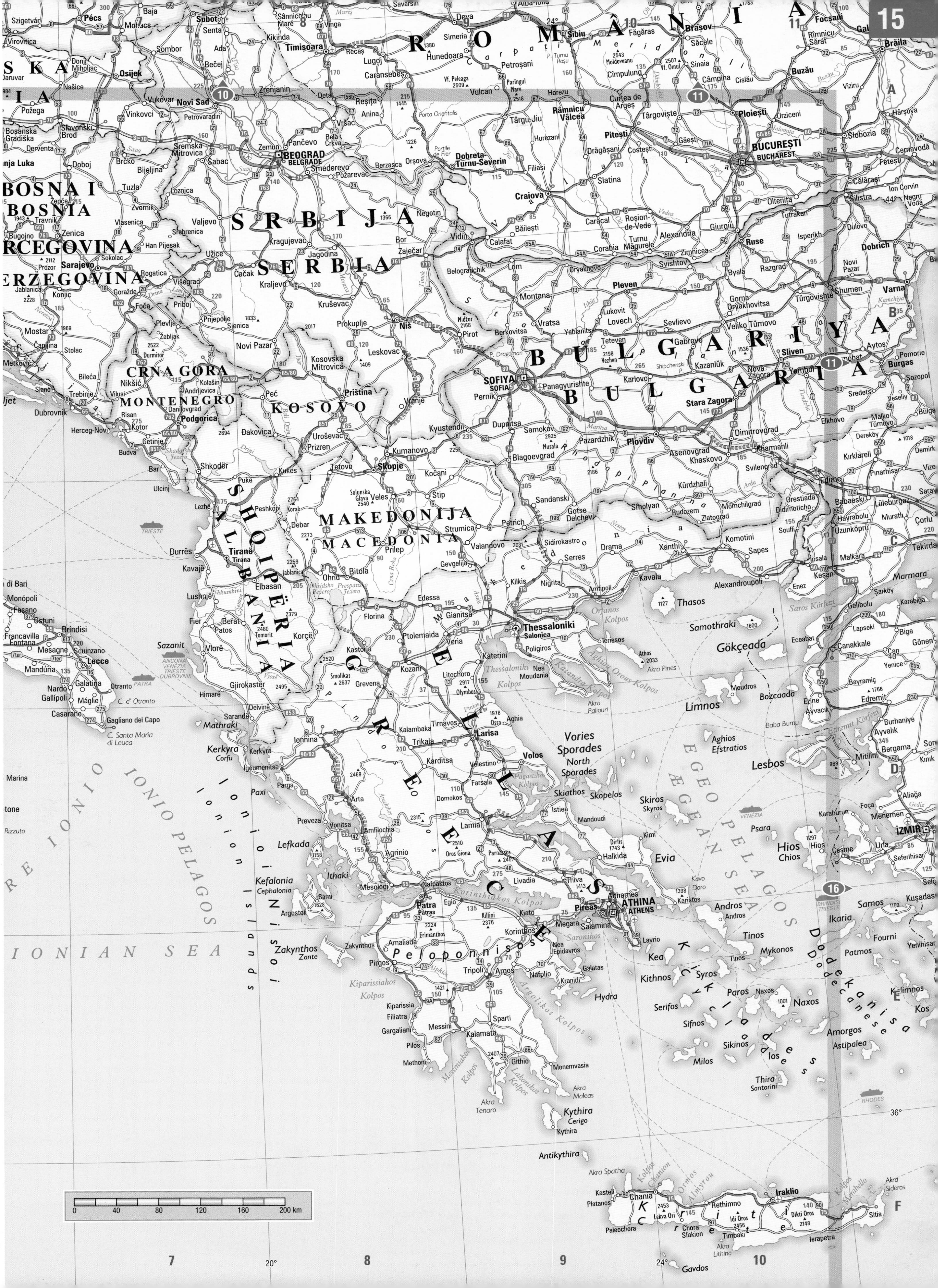
ROMÂNIA
SRBIJA
SERBIA
BOSNA I
BOSNIA
HERCEGOVINA
CRNA GORA
MONTENEGRO
KOSOVO
SHQIPËRIA
ALBANIA
MAKEDONIJA
MACEDONIA
BULGARIYA
BULGARIA
GREECE
Pelopónnisos
IONIAN SEA
Ionion Pelagos
Ionioi Nisoi
Ionian Islands
Aegean Sea
Aigaion Pelagos
Kiklades
Dodekanisa
Dodecanese
Kriti
BUCUREŞTI
BUCHAREST
BEOGRAD
BELGRADE
SOFIYA
SOFIA
Skopje
Tiranë
Tirana
ATHINA
ATHENS
Thessaloniki
Salonica
Sarajevo
Podgorica
Priština
Novi Sad
Niš
Plovdiv
Varna
Burgas
Craiova
Timişoara
Braşov
Ploieşti
Pireas
Patra
Larisa
Volos
Iraklio
Kerkyra
Corfu
Kefalonia
Zakynthos
Lesbos
Limnos
Thasos
Samothraki
Gökçeada
Evia
Hios
Samos
Andros
Tinos
Mykonos
Naxos
Paros
Milos
Thira
Santorini
Kythira
Antikythira
Gavdos
İZMIR
Edirne
Çanakkale
Brindisi
Lecce
Otranto
0
40
80
120
160
200 km
7
8
9
10
20°
24°
36°

TÜRKIYE
TURKEY
GREECE
ELLAS
CYPRUS
ISTANBUL
ANKARA
İZMIR
ATHINA
ATHENS
Thessaloniki
Salonica
Bursa
Eskişehir
Konya
Antalya
Adana
Kayseri
Samsun
Sinop
Zonguldak
Kocaeli
İzmit
Sakarya
Bolu
Kırıkkale
Kütahya
Afyonkarahisar
Isparta
Denizli
Manisa
Balıkesir
Çanakkale
Edirne
Tekirdağ
Plovdiv
Skopje
Larisa
Volos
Pireas
Iraklio
Nicosia
Limassol
Larnaca
Famagusta
Kyrenia
Paphos
Al Lādhiqīyah
Marmara Denizi
Istanbul Boğazı
Saros Körfezi
Edremit Körfezi
Antalya Körfezi
Kerme Körfezi
EGEO PELAGOS
ÆGEAN SEA
Kükladhes
Dodekanisa
Dodecanese
Vories Sporades
North Sporades
Peloponnisos
Kriti
Küre Dağları
Köroğlu Dağları
Toros Dağları
Tahtalı Dağları
Lesbos
Limnos
Gökçeada
Bozcaada
Samothraki
Thasos
Evia
Hios
Chios
Samos
Ikaria
Rhodes
Karpathos
Kasos
Kythira
Cerigo
Antikythira
Gavdos
Andros
Tinos
Mykonos
Naxos
Paros
Syros
Kea
Kithnos
Serifos
Sifnos
Milos
Sikinos
Thira
Santorini
Amorgos
Astipalea
Kos
Kalimnos
Patmos
Fourni
Skiros
Skyros
Skopelos
Skiathos
Psara
Aghios Efstratios
Megiste
Tuz Gölü
Beyşehir Gölü
Eğirdir Gölü
Burdur Gölü
0
40
80
120
160
200 km
24°
28°
32°
36°
40°

Key to road map pages

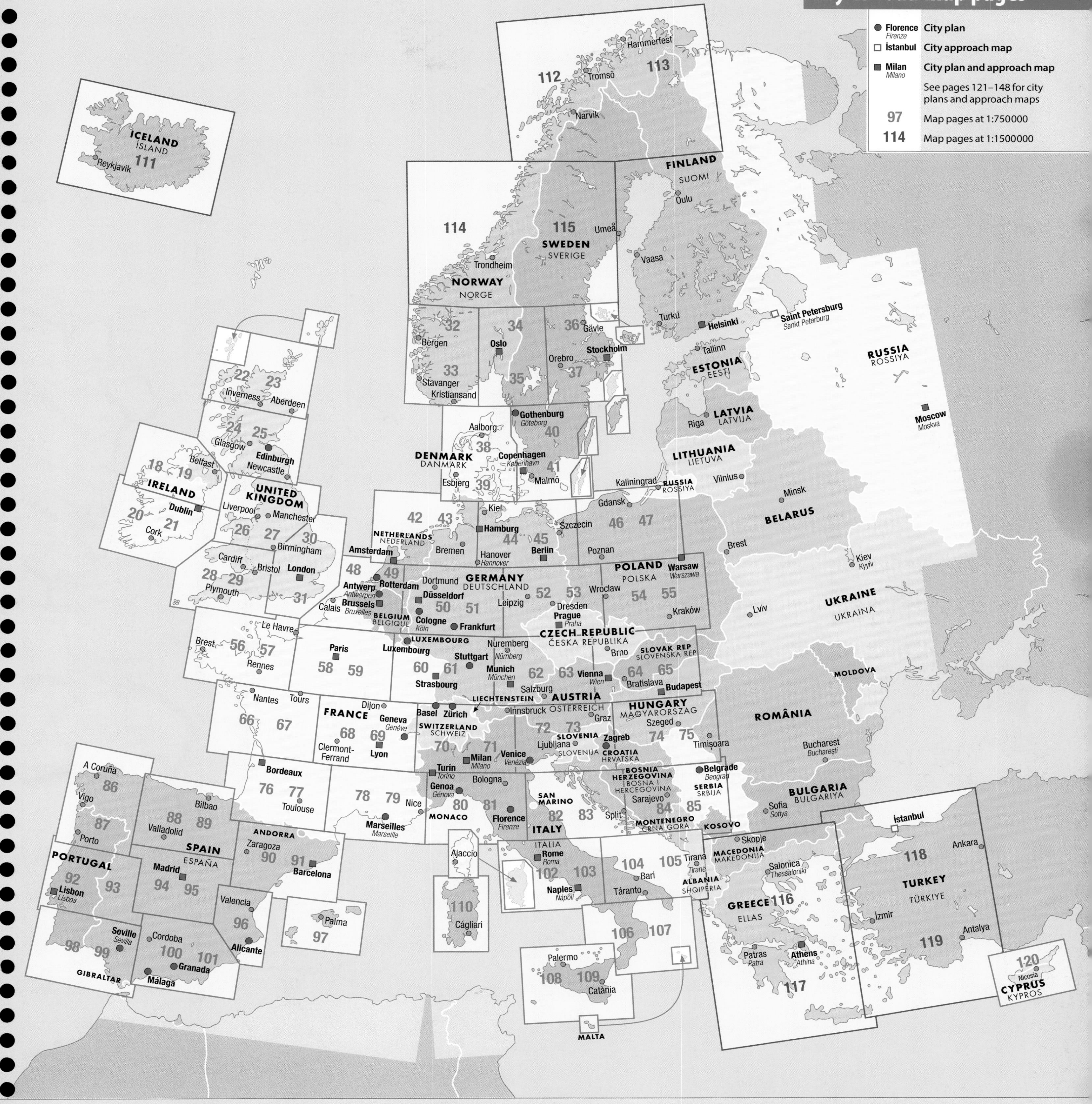

Motorway vignettes

Some countries require you to purchase (and in some cases display) a vignette before using motorways.

In Austria you will need to purchase and display a vignette on the inside of your windscreen. Vignettes are available for purchase at border crossings and petrol stations. More details from **www.austria.info/uk/how-to-get-there/ www.asfinag.at/en/maut/vignette**

In the Czech Republic, you can buy a vignette at the border and also at petrol stations. Make sure you write your vehicle registration number on the vignette before displaying it. The roads without toll are indicated by a traffic sign saying "Bez poplatku".
More details from **www.motorway.cz**

In Hungary a new e-vignette system was introduced in 2008. It is therefore no longer necessary to display the vignette, though you should make doubly sure the information you give on your vehicle is accurate. Vignettes are sold at petrol stations throughout the country. Buy online at **www.motorway.hu**.

In Slovakia, a vignette is also required to be purchased before using the motorways. This is sold in two kinds at the Slovak border and petrol stations. You will need to write your vehicle registration plate on the vignette before displaying it.
More details from **www.slovensko.com**

In Switzerland, you will need to purchase and display a 'vignette' before you drive on the motorway. Bear in mind you will need a separate vignette if you are towing a caravan. Purchase the Swiss vignette in advance from **www.autobahnen.ch**.

11°
1
10°
2
9°
3
0 10 20 30 miles
0 10 20 30 40 50 km
A
B
C
55°
54°
ATLANTIC
OCEAN
Tory I.
Inishbofin
Dunfanaghy
Bloody Foreland
Falcarragh
Inishfree B.
Bunbeg
Errigal 752
Crolly
Derryveagh Mts.
Aran I.
Dunglow
Crohy Hd.
Gweebarra B.
Lettermacaward
Dawros Hd.
Loughros More B.
Glenties
Ardara
444 Slieve Tooey
Glencolumbkille
Blue Stack Mts.
676 Lavagh More
Rossan Pt.
Rathlin O'Birne I.
Slieve League 601
Carrick
Killybegs
Donegal
Carrigan Hd.
Dunkineely
Muckros Hd.
Mc Swyne's Bay
Inver Bay
St. John's Pt.
Ballintra
Donegal Bay
Ballyshannon
Bundoran
Belleek
Inishmurray I.
Kinlough
Lough Melvin
Garrison
Grange
Truskmore 644
Broad Haven
Benwee Hd.
Portacloy
Downpatrick Hd.
Erris Hd.
Lenadoon Pt.
Sligo Bay
Drumcliff
Manorhamilton
Ballycastle
Killala Bay
Easky
Dromore West
Strandhill
Sligo
Belmullet
Mullet Pen.
RATHFRANPARK
Inishcrone
FIBRIS CASTLE
L. Gill
Dromahair
Glenamoy
Killala
MOYNE ABBEY
544 Knockalongy
Ballysadare
Collooney
Dowra
Inishkea North
Bunahowen
Blacksod Bay
Bangor
Drumkeeran
Inishkea South
Nephin Beg Range
Crossmolina
Ballina
Bunnyconnellan
Ballymote
L. Allen
ARDNAREE CHURCH
Moy
Tubbercurry
L. Arrow
Ballycroy
Lough Conn
Mullanys Cross
Keadew
Saddle Hd.
Slievemore 672
Achill Hd.
Keel
Achill I.
806 Nephin
Pontoon
Foxford
L. Key
Boyle
L. Cullin
Charlestown
L. Gara
BOYLE ABBEY
Dooega Hd.
Beltra
Swinford
Carrick-on-Shannon
Mallaranny
Newport
TURLOUGH PARK HOUSE
Bellavary
Ballaghaderreen
Kilkelly
Clew Bay
Castlebar
Clare I.
Knock
139
Westport
Balla
KNOCK SHRINE
CLONALIS HOUSE
Castlerea
Tulsk
Strokestown
Louisburgh
Ballyhaunis
Inishturk
Claremorris
Lough Carra
Ballymoe
Ballindine
Lanesborough
Inishbofin
Inishshark
Partry Mts.
Lough Mask
Roscommon
KYLEMORE ABBEY
Leenaun
Ballinrobe
Kilmaine
Dunmore
Milltown
Glennamaddy
IRELAND
Letterfrack
Maumturk Mts.
Connemara
Maum
Cong
Clare
Athleague
Clifden B.
Clifden
Tuam
Suck
Recess
Lough Corrib
Headford
Moylough
Thomas Street
Ballyconneely
Mountbellew
Slyne Hd.
Oughterard
Screeb
Bertraghboy Bay
Glinsk
Kilkieran
Kilkieran Bay
Moycullen
Claregalway
Ballinasloe
Kilconnell
Athenry
Carraroe
Galway
Oranmore
Inveran
Spiddle
Clarinbridge
Craughwell
TUROE STONE
Laurencetown
Cashla Bay
North Sound
Galway Bay
Loughrea
Black Hd.
Killimor
20
M6

4
5
6
24
26
21
A
B
C
Islay
Port Charlotte
Bridgend
Bowmore
Portnahaven
Ben Bheigeir
Ardbeg
Port Ellen
The Oa
Mull of Oa
DISTILLERIES
Kennacraig
Skipness
Claonaig
SKIPNESS CASTLE
Gigha
Tayinloan
Glenbarr
Saddell
Kilbrannan Sound
Campbeltown
Machrihanish
Southend
Mull of Kintyre
Sanda I.
Lochranza
Pirnmill
North Arran
Goat Fell
Arran
Brodick
Holy I.
Blackwaterfoot
CARN BAN
TORRYLINN CAIRN
Dippen
Kilchattan
ST. BLANE'S CHAPEL
Bute
Millport
West Kilbride
Dalry
Ardrossan
Saltcoats
Irvine
Troon
Prestwick
Firth of Clyde
Larne
Maybole
CULZEAN CASTLE
Kirkoswald
Turnberry
Girvan
Ailsa Craig
Lendalfoot
CARLETON CASTLE
Colmonel
Ballantrae
Cairnryan
Corsewall Pt.
Milleur Pt.
Kirkcolm
Leswalt
Innermessan
Stranraer
GLENLUCE ABBEY
Glenluce
Lochans
Portpatrick
Sandhead
Luce Bay
Port Logan
Drummore
Mull of Galloway
Liverpool
Douglas
Copeland I.
North Channel
Malin Hd.
Glengad Hd.
Trawbreaga B.
Fanad Hd.
Dunaff Hd.
Malin
Carndonagh
Clonmany
Inishowen Peninsula
Slieve Snaght
Inishowen Hd.
Greencastle
Moville
Magilligan
Buncrana
Lough Swilly
Carrickart
Rathmullan
Milford
Lough Foyle
Muff
Rathmelton
Kilmacrenan
Glenveagh
Letterkenny
Eglinton
Derry/Londonderry
Newtown Cunningham
St. Johnstown
Claudy
Dungiven
Limavady
Feeny
Cloghan
Stranorlar
Ballybofey
Lifford
Strabane
Sion Mills
Sperrin Mts.
Sawel
Draperstown
Plumbridge
Gortin
Castlederg
Newtownstewart
Drumquin
Omagh
Mountfield
Pettigo
Dromore
Seskinore
Beragh
Fintona
Kesh
Lower Lough Erne
Irvinestown
CHAMBERED CAIRN
Augher
Clogher
Ballygawley
Aughnacloy
Derrygonnelly
ENNISKILLEN CASTLE
Enniskillen
CASTLE COOLE
Lisbellaw
Fivemiletown
L. Macnean
Belcoo
Upper L. Erne
Maguiresbridge
Lisnaskea
Florence Court
Swanlinbar
Derrylin
Newtownbutler
Clones
Rosslea
Monaghan
Belturbet
Butler's Bridge
Cootehill
Ballinamore
Fenagh
Killashandra
Cavan
Carrigallen
Drumsna
Cloone
Mohill
Bellananagh
Bailieborough
Ballyjamesduff
Kilnaleck
Lough Gowna
Virginia
L. Sheelin
Finnea
L. Ramor
Oldcastle
Granard
Longford
Edgeworthstown
Castlepollard
Killashee
Ballinalack
L. Derravaragh
Keenagh
Ballymahon
L. Owel
Mullingar
Delvin
Lough Ree
Ballymore
Kilcoom
Lough Ennell
Athlone
Moate
Ballynagore
Kilbeggan
Tyrrellspass
CLONMACNOISE
Ferbane
Tullamore
Daingean
Cloghan
Kilcormac
Killeigh
Clonaslee
Portarlington
Rathangan
Kildare
Newbridge
Edenderry
Kinnegad
Clonard
Enfield
Killucan
Rathmolyon
Trim
Athboy
Kells
Crossakiel
Clonmellon
Navan
Slane
NEWGRANGE
Duleek
Drogheda
Julianstown
Termonfeckin
Clogher Hd.
Collon
Dunleer
Ardee
Kingscourt
Bracklin
Carrickmacross
Shercock
Castleblayney
Ballybay
Newbliss
Emyvale
Middletown
Keady
Markethill
Caledon
NAVAN FORT
Armagh
Culleville
Kilcurry
Dundalk
Dundalk Bay
Castlebellingham
Dunany Pt.
Balbriggan
ARDGILLAN CASTLE
Skerries
Naul
TAYTO PARK
Ashbourne
Rush
Lambay I.
Dunshaughlin
Ballivor
NATIONAL SPORTS CAMPUS
Swords
Malahide
Howth Hd.
Dunboyne
Kilcock
Lucan
Celbridge
Clondalkin
Dublin
Dun Laoghaire
Dalkey
Rathcoole
Tallaght
Sallins
Naas
Blessington
Wicklow Mountains
Kippure
Bray
Greystones
Holyhead
Douglas
Holyhead
Liverpool
Grand Canal
Liffey
Barrow
Brosna
Boyne
Coleraine
Portstewart
Downhill
HEZLETT HOUSE
Castlerock
Portrush
DUNLUCE CASTLE
GIANTS CAUSEWAY
Benbane Hd.
Causeway Coast
Bushmills
Ballycastle
BONAMARGY FRIARY
Fair Hd.
Rathlin Island
Knocklayd
Armoy
Dervock
Ballymoney
Mountains of Antrim
Trostan
Cushendall
Antrim Coast
Red B. & Garron Pt.
Glens
Troon
Carnlough
Glenarm
Dunloy
Garvagh
Kilrea
Swatragh
Maghera
Portglenone
Ballymena
Broughshane
Ahoghill
Tobermore
Magherafelt
Randalstown
Kells
Agnews Hill
Larne
Larne Lough
I. Magee
Ballycarry
Whitehead
Ballyclare
Ballynure
Carrickfergus
Greenisland
Belfast Lough
Bangor
Donaghadee
Antrim
Newtownabbey
BELFAST INTERNATIONAL
Moneymore
SPRINGHILL HOUSE
Cookstown
Creeve
Coagh
Lough Neagh
NORTHERN IRELAND
Crumlin
Glenavy
Belfast
GEORGE BEST BELFAST CITY
Holywood
Newtownards
MOUNT STEWART HOUSE
Ballywalter
Comber
Dunmurry
Lisburn
Carryduff
Aghalee
Pomeroy
CASTLE CAULFIELD
Coalisland
Dungannon
Moy
Portadown
Lurgan
Dromore
Hillsborough
Ballygowan
Saintfield
ROWALLANE
Killyleagh
Strangford Lough
Ards Peninsula
Kircubbin
Portavogie
Ballynahinch
INCH ABBEY
Portaferry
Strangford
AUDLEY'S CASTLE
Ballyquintin Pt.
Gilford
Banbridge
Loughbrickland
LEGANANNY DOLMEN
Downpatrick
Clough
Castlewellan
Ardglass
JORDAN'S CASTLE
Lecale Coast
Dundrum
Dundrum Bay
St. John's Pt.
DRUMENA CASHEL
Newcastle
Mourne Mts.
Slieve Donard
Poyntz Pass
Rathfriland
Newtownhamilton
Newry
Ring Of Gullion
Warrenpoint
Mourne
Annalong
Kilkeel
Carlingford
Carlingford Lough
KING JOHN'S CASTLE
Gosford
IRELAND
Calf of Man
55°
54°
7°
6°
5°

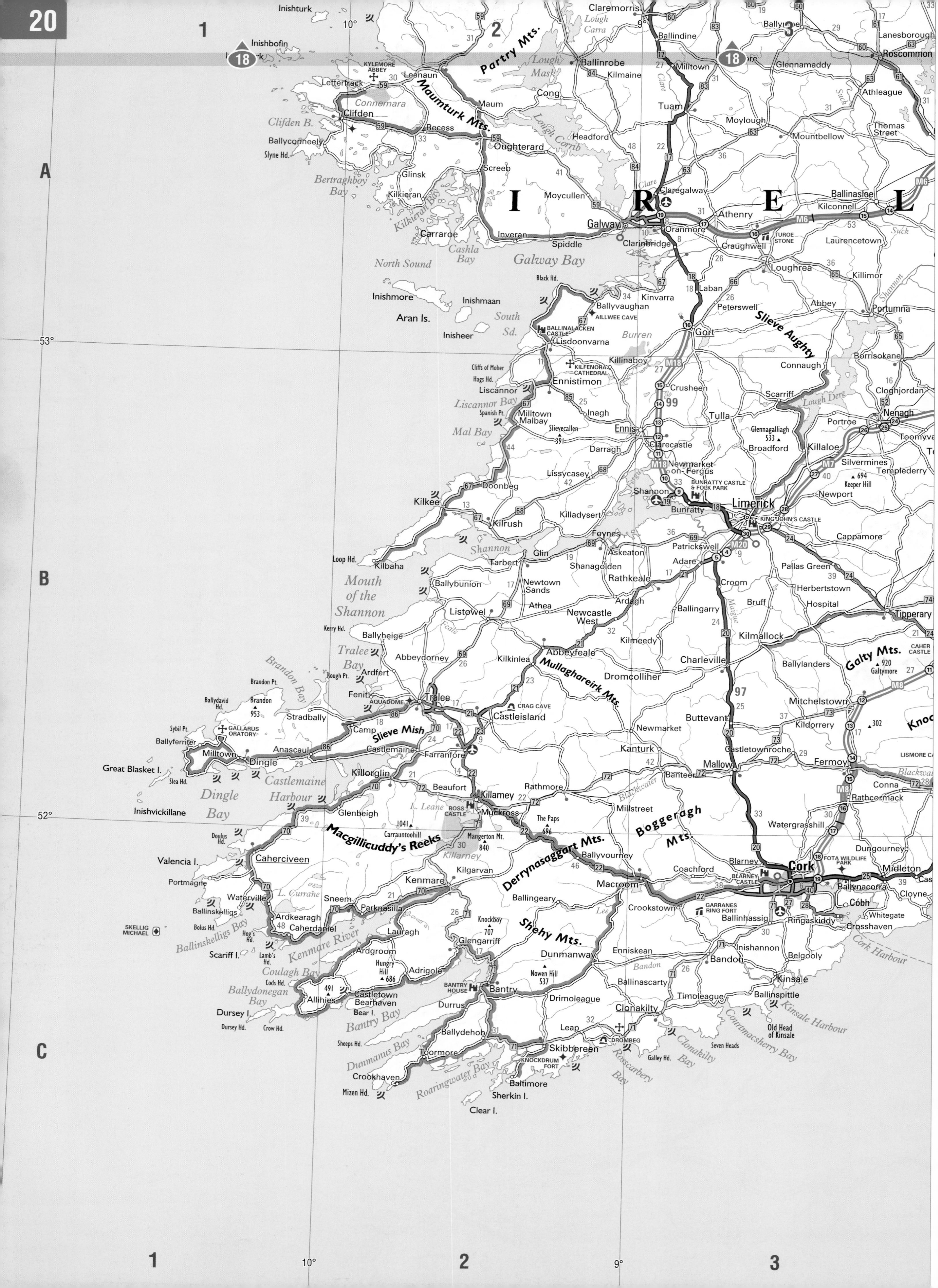
IRELAND
Inishturk
Inishbofin
Claremorris
Partry Mts.
Lough Mask
Ballinrobe
Ballindine
Milltown
Glennamaddy
Roscommon
Lanesborough
Athleague
Kylemore Abbey
Leenaun
Letterfrack
Connemara
Clifden
Clifden B.
Maumturk Mts.
Maum
Cong
Kilmaine
Tuam
Moylough
Mountbellow
Thomas Street
Recess
Ballyconneely
Slyne Hd.
Oughterard
Lough Corrib
Headford
Glinsk
Screeb
Bertraghboy Bay
Kilkieran
Kilkieran Bay
Moycullen
Claregalway
Ballinasloe
Kilconnell
Galway
Athenry
Oranmore
Clarinbridge
Carraroe
Inveran
Spiddle
Cashla Bay
Galway Bay
Turoe Stone
Craughwell
Laurencetown
Loughrea
Killimor
North Sound
Black Hd.
Inishmore
Inishmaan
Aran Is.
Inisheer
South Sd.
Ballyvaughan
Aillwee Cave
Kinvarra
Laban
Peterswell
Abbey
Portumna
Ballinalacken Castle
Lisdoonvarna
Burren
Gort
Slieve Aughty
Cliffs of Moher
Hags Hd.
Kilfenora Cathedral
Killinaboy
Borrisokane
Connaugh
Liscannor
Ennistimon
Crusheen
Scarriff
Lough Derg
Cloghjordan
Liscannor Bay
Spanish Pt.
Milltown Malbay
Inagh
Tulla
Portroe
Nenagh
Mal Bay
Slievecallen 391
Ennis
Glennagalliagh 533
Clarecastle
Broadford
Killaloe
Toomyvara
Darragh
Silvermines
Templederry
Newmarket-on-Fergus
Keeper Hill 694
Lissycasey
Bunratty Castle & Folk Park
Doonbeg
Kilkee
Shannon
Limerick
Newport
Bunratty
Killadysert
King John's Castle
Kilrush
Foynes
Cappamore
Askeaton
Patrickswell
Loop Hd.
Kilbaha
Glin
Tarbert
Shanagolden
Adare
Pallas Green
Mouth of the Shannon
Ballybunion
Newtown Sands
Rathkeale
Croom
Herbertstown
Athea
Ardagh
Bruff
Hospital
Listowel
Newcastle West
Ballingarry
Tipperary
Kerry Hd.
Ballyheigue
Kilmeedy
Kilmallock
Tralee Bay
Abbeydorney
Kilkinlea
Abbeyfeale
Charleville
Ballylanders
Galty Mts.
Galtymore 920
Caher Castle
Rough Pt.
Ardfert
Mullaghareirk Mts.
Dromcolliher
Brandon Pt.
Brandon Bay
Fenit
Aquadome
Tralee
Crag Cave
Castleisland
Mitchelstown
Ballydavid Hd.
Brandon 953
Stradbally
Buttevant
Sybil Pt.
Gallarus Oratory
Camp
Slieve Mish
Newmarket
Kildorrery
Knockmealdown
Ballyferriter
Anascaul
Castlemaine
Farranfore
Kanturk
Castletownroche
Milltown
Dingle
Fermoy
Lismore Castle
Great Blasket I.
Slea Hd.
Killorglin
Castlemaine Harbour
Rathmore
Banteer
Mallow
Conna
Blackwater
Dingle Bay
Beaufort
Killarney
Rathcormack
Inishvickillane
Glenbeigh
L. Leane
Ross Castle
Muckross
The Paps 696
Millstreet
Boggeragh Mts.
Carrauntoohill 1041
Macgillicuddy's Reeks
Mangerton Mt. 840
Watergrasshill
Doulus Hd.
Valencia I.
Caherciveen
Derrynasaggart Mts.
Ballyvourney
Dungourney
Fota Wildlife Park
Blarney
Cork
Midleton
Portmagne
Kilgarvan
Kenmare
Coachford
Blarney Castle
Ballynacorra
Cloyne
Waterville
L. Currane
Sneem
Parknasilla
Macroom
Ballingeary
Crookstown
Garranes Ring Fort
Cóbh
Ballinskelligs
Ardkearagh
Caherdaniel
Ballinhassig
Ringaskiddy
Whitegate
Crosshaven
Skellig Michael
Bolus Hd.
Ballinskelligs Bay
Hog's Hd.
Knockboy 707
Shehy Mts.
Lauragh
Glengarriff
Kenmare River
Scariff I.
Lamb's Hd.
Ardgroom
Dunmanway
Enniskean
Bandon
Innishannon
Belgooly
Cork Harbour
Coulagh Bay
Hungry Hill 686
Adrigole
Nowen Hill 537
Kinsale
Ballydonegan Bay
Allihies
Castletown Bearhaven
Bantry House
Bantry
Ballinascarty
Timoleague
Ballinspittle
Bear I.
Durrus
Drimoleague
Clonakilty
Kinsale Harbour
Dursey I.
Dursey Hd.
Crow Hd.
Bantry Bay
Leap
Drombeg
Clonakilty Bay
Courtmacsherry Bay
Old Head of Kinsale
Seven Heads
Sheeps Hd.
Ballydehob
Skibbereen
Galley Hd.
Dunmanus Bay
Toormore
Knockdrum Fort
Rosscarbery Bay
Crookhaven
Roaringwater Bay
Baltimore
Mizen Hd.
Sherkin I.
Clear I.
53°
52°
10°
9°
1
2
3
A
B
C
18

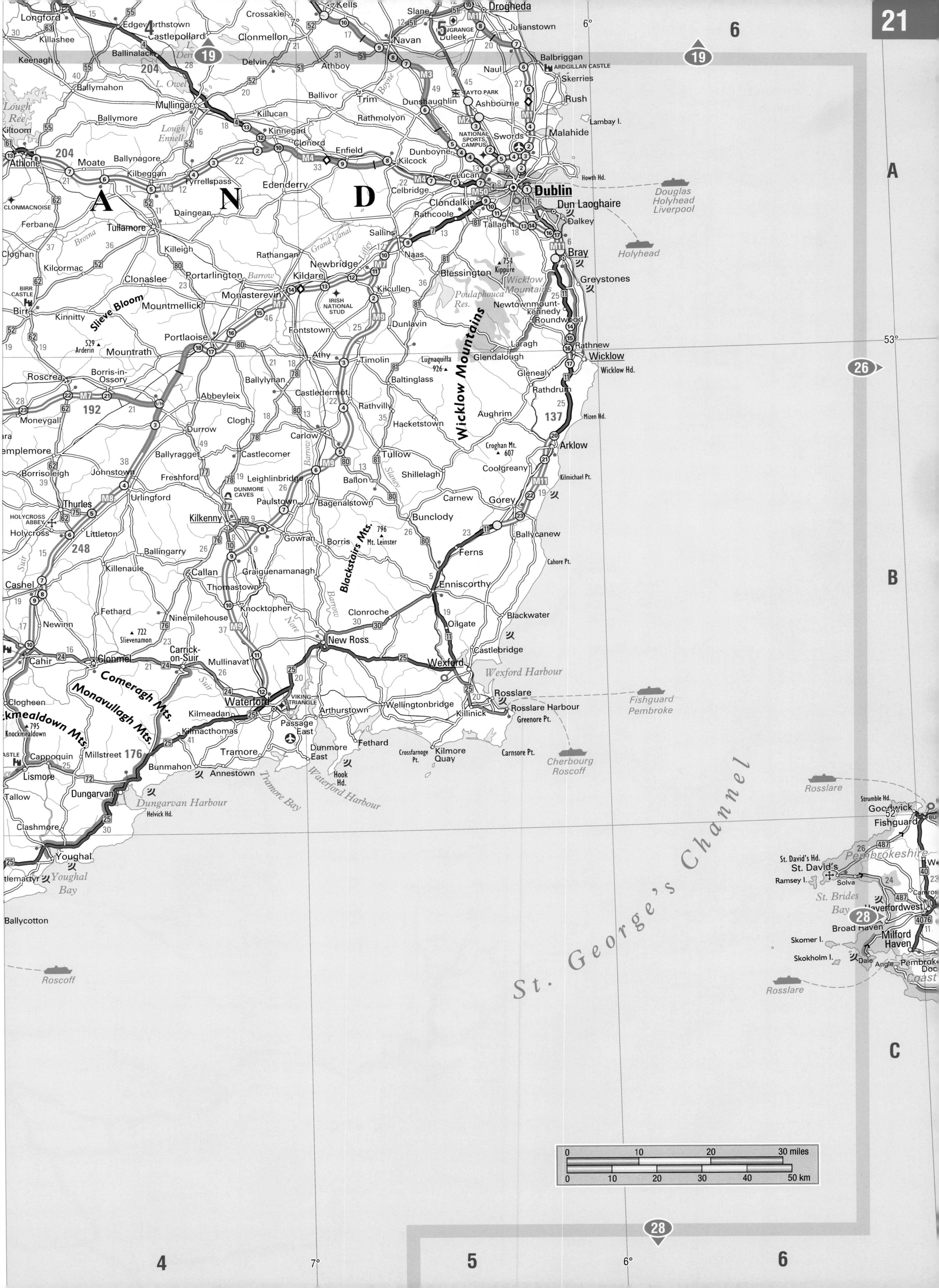
Longford
Edgeworthstown
Crossakiel
Kells
Slane
Drogheda
Julianstown
Castlepollard
Clonmellon
Navan
Duleek
Killashee
Keenagh
Ballinalack
Delvin
Athboy
Balbriggan
Ardgillan Castle
Naul
Skerries
Ballymahon
L. Owel
Ballivor
Trim
Tayto Park
Ashbourne
Rush
Mullingar
Killucan
Dunshaughlin
Lough Ree
Ballymore
Lough Ennell
Kinnegad
Rathmolyon
Lambay I.
Kiltoom
Clonard
National Sports Campus
Swords
Malahide
Athlone
Moate
Ballynagore
Enfield
Dunboyne
Kilbeggan
Kilcock
Tyrrellspass
Edenderry
Celbridge
Lucan
Howth Hd.
Clonmacnoise
Dublin
Douglas
Holyhead
Liverpool
Ferbane
Daingean
Clondalkin
Dun Laoghaire
Tullamore
Rathcoole
Tallaght
Dalkey
Brosna
Grand Canal
Sallins
Cloghan
Killeigh
Rathangan
Naas
Bray
Holyhead
Kilcormac
Newbridge
Blessington
Kippure
Clonaslee
Portarlington
Barrow
Kildare
Greystones
Wicklow Mountains
Birr Castle
Monasterevin
Kilcullen
Poulaphouca Res.
Birr
Slieve Bloom
Mountmellick
Irish National Stud
Newtownmount-kennedy
Kinnitty
Roundwood
Dunlavin
Portlaoise
Fontstown
Wicklow Mountains
Laragh
Arderin
Mountrath
Athy
Rathnew
Glendalough
Wicklow
Timolin
Lugnaquilla
Wicklow Hd.
Roscrea
Borris-in-Ossory
Ballylynan
Baltinglass
Glenealy
Castledermot
Rathdrum
Abbeyleix
Rathvilly
Moneygall
Aughrim
Clogh
Hacketstown
Mizen Hd.
Durrow
Carlow
Templemore
Ballyragget
Castlecomer
Tullow
Arklow
Croghan Mt.
Borrisoleigh
Johnstown
Coolgreany
Freshford
Leighlinbridge
Shillelagh
Ballon
Kilmichael Pt.
Dunmore Caves
Urlingford
Slaney
Carnew
Thurles
Paulstown
Bagenalstown
Gorey
Holycross Abbey
Kilkenny
Bunclody
Holycross
Littleton
Gowran
Borris
Mt. Leinster
Ballycanew
Blackstairs Mts.
Ballingarry
Ferns
Killenaule
Graiguenamanagh
Cahore Pt.
Suir
Callan
Cashel
Thomastown
Enniscorthy
Fethard
Knocktopher
Clonroche
Ninemilehouse
Slievenamon
Blackwater
Newinn
Nore
Oilgate
New Ross
Carrick-on-Suir
Castlebridge
Cahir
Clonmel
Mullinavat
Wexford
Wexford Harbour
Comeragh Mts.
Rosslare
Monavullagh Mts.
Fishguard
Pembroke
Clogheen
Waterford
Viking Triangle
Arthurstown
Wellingtonbridge
Rosslare Harbour
Knockmealdown Mts.
Kilmeadan
Killinick
Knockmealdown
Passage East
Greenore Pt.
Kilmacthomas
Dunmore East
Fethard
Cappoquin
Millstreet
Tramore
Crossfarnoge Pt.
Kilmore Quay
Carnsore Pt.
Cherbourg
Roscoff
Lismore
Bunmahon
Annestown
Hook Hd.
Tramore Bay
Waterford Harbour
Tallow
Dungarvan
Dungarvan Harbour
Helvick Hd.
Rosslare
Strumble Hd.
Goodwick
Fishguard
Clashmore
Youghal
Youghal Bay
Pembrokeshire
St. David's Hd.
St. David's
Solva
Ramsey I.
St. Brides Bay
Haverfordwest
Ballycotton
Broad Haven
Milford Haven
Skomer I.
Skokholm I.
Dale
Angle
Pembroke
Roscoff
St. George's Channel
Rosslare
A N D
A
B
C
4
5
6
6°
7°
53°
52°
19
26
28
0 10 20 30 miles
0 10 20 30 40 50 km

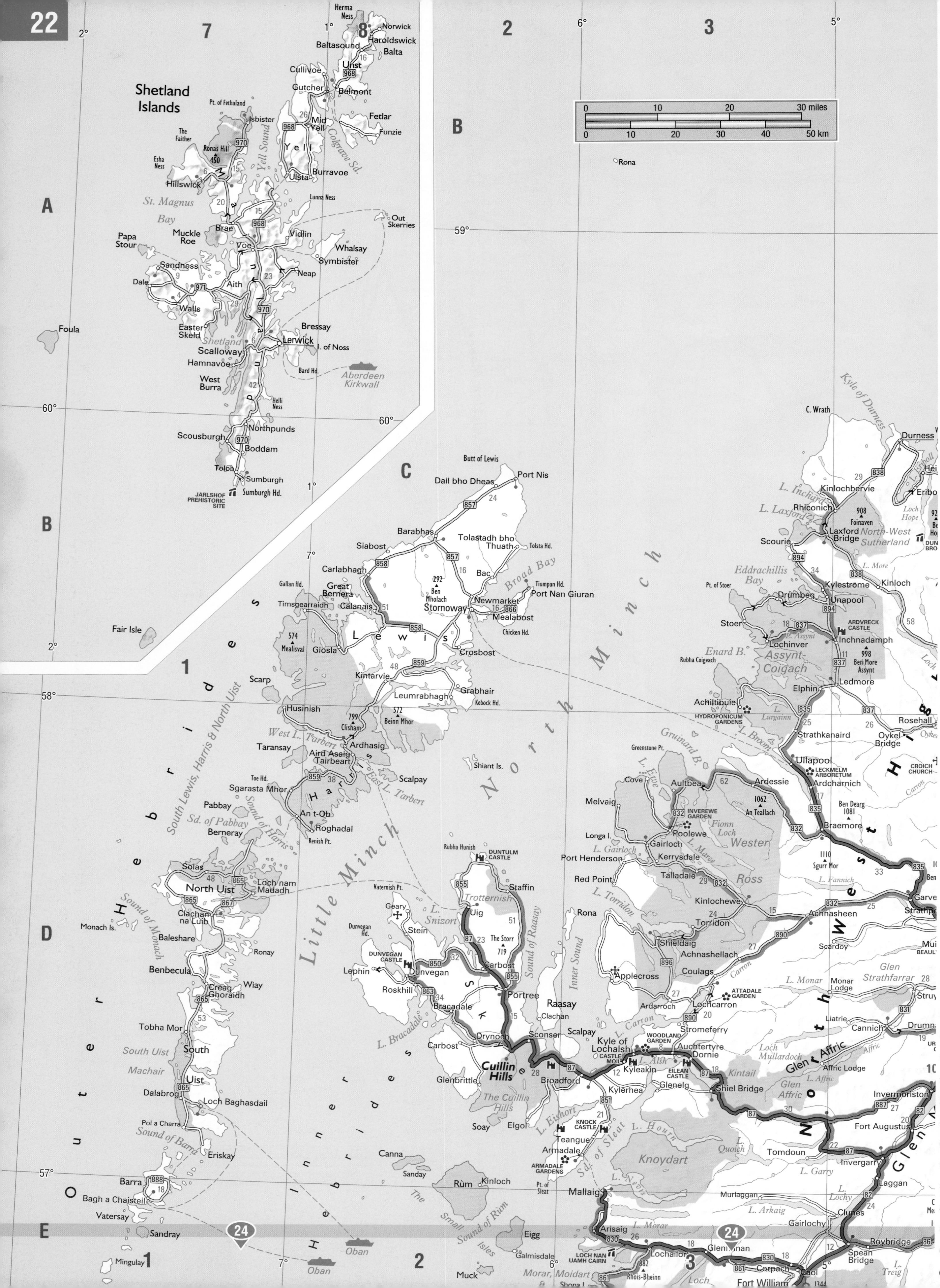

Shetland Islands
Herma Ness
Norwick
Haroldswick
Baltasound
Balta
Unst
Cullivoe
Gutcher
Belmont
Fetlar
Funzie
Mid Yell
Yell
Colgrave Sd.
Yell Sound
Pt. of Fethaland
Isbister
The Faither
Ronas Hill 450
Esha Ness
Hillswick
Ulsta
Burravoe
St. Magnus Bay
Lunna Ness
Out Skerries
Papa Stour
Muckle Roe
Brae
Vidlin
Whalsay
Symbister
Voe
Sandness
Neap
Dale
Aith
Walls
Foula
Bressay
Easter Skeld
Lerwick
I. of Noss
Scalloway
Hamnavoe
Bard Hd.
Aberdeen Kirkwall
West Burra
Helli Ness
Northpunds
Scousburgh
Boddam
Tolob
Sumburgh
Sumburgh Hd.
JARLSHOF PREHISTORIC SITE
Fair Isle
Rona
Butt of Lewis
Port Nis
Dail bho Dheas
Barabhas
Siabost
Tolastadh bho Thuath
Tolsta Hd.
Carlabhagh
Bac
Broad Bay
Gallan Hd.
Great Bernera
Tiumpan Hd.
Port Nan Giuran
Timsgearraidh
Calanais
Stornoway
Newmarket
Mealabost
Chicken Hd.
Mealisval
Giosla
Lewis
Crosbost
Kintarvie
Scarp
Leumrabhagh
Grabhair
Kebock Hd.
Husinish
Clisham
Beinn Mhor
West L. Tarbert
Ardhasig
Taransay
Aird Asaig
Tairbeart
Shiant Is.
Scalpay
East L. Tarbert
Toe Hd.
Sgarasta Mhor
Harris
Pabbay
Sd. of Pabbay
Sound of Harris
An t-Ob
Roghadal
Berneray
Renish Pt.
South Lewis, Harris & North Uist
Outer Hebrides
North Minch
Little Minch
Solas
North Uist
Loch nam Madadh
Sound of Monach
Clachan na Luib
Monach Is.
Baleshare
Ronay
Benbecula
Wiay
Creag Ghoraidh
Tobha Mor
South Uist
Machair
South
Uist
Dalabrog
Loch Baghasdail
Pol a Charra
Sound of Barra
Eriskay
Barra
Bagh a Chaisteil
Vatersay
Sandray
Mingulay
Rubha Hunish
DUNTULM CASTLE
Vaternish Pt.
Staffin
Trotternish
Geary
L. Snizort
Uig
Dunvegan Hd.
Stein
The Storr 719
Sound of Raasay
DUNVEGAN CASTLE
Dunvegan
Carbost
Lephin
Roskhill
Portree
Raasay
Bracadale
Inner Sound
Skye
Clachan
L. Bracadale
Drynoch
Sconser
Scalpay
Carbost
Cuillin Hills
Broadford
Glenbrittle
The Cuillin Hills
Soay
Elgol
Canna
Sanday
Rùm
Kinloch
Inner Hebrides
Sound of Rum
The Small Isles
Eigg
Galmisdale
Muck
Oban
C. Wrath
Kyle of Durness
Durness
L. Eriboll
Kinlochbervie
L. Inchard
Rhiconich
L. Laxford
Foinaven
Loch Hope
Laxford Bridge
North-West Sutherland
Scourie
Eddrachillis Bay
L. More
Kylestrome
Kinloch
Pt. of Stoer
Drumbeg
Unapool
Stoer
ARDVRECK CASTLE
Lochinver
L. Assynt
Inchnadamph
Ben More Assynt
Enard B.
Rubha Coigeach
Assynt-Coigach
Ledmore
Elphin
Achiltibuie
HYDROPONICUM GARDENS
L. Lurgainn
L. Broom
Strathkanaird
Rosehall
Oykel Bridge
Gruinard B.
Greenstone Pt.
Ullapool
LECKMELM ARBORETUM
CROICH CHURCH
Cove
L. Ewe
Aultbea
Ardessie
Ardcharnich
Melvaig
An Teallach
Ben Dearg
INVEREWE GARDEN
Poolewe
Fionn Loch
Braemore
Longa I.
Gairloch
L. Gairloch
Wester Ross
Port Henderson
Kerrysdale
L. Maree
Sgurr Mor
L. Fannich
Red Point
Talladale
Kinlochewe
L. Torridon
Achnasheen
Rona
Torridon
Shieldaig
Achnashellach
Scardoy
Applecross
Coulags
Glen Strathfarrar
L. Monar
Monar Lodge
ATTADALE GARDEN
Ardarroch
Lochcarron
L. Carron
Liatrie
Cannich
Stromeferry
Kyle of Lochalsh
WOODLAND GARDEN
CASTLE MOIL
Auchtertyre
Dornie
L. Alsh
Kyleakin
EILEAN CASTLE
L. Mullardoch
Glen Affric
Affric Lodge
Kintail
Kylerhea
Glenelg
Shiel Bridge
L. Affric
Invermoriston
KNOCK CASTLE
Teangue
L. Eishort
L. Hourn
Fort Augustus
Armadale
ARMADALE GARDENS
Sd. of Sleat
Knoydart
L. Quoich
Tomdoun
Invergarry
Glen More
Pt. of Sleat
L. Garry
Mallaig
L. Nevis
Laggan
Murlaggan
L. Lochy
L. Arkaig
Clunes
Arisaig
L. Morar
Gairlochy
Roybridge
Spean Bridge
LOCH NAN UAMH CAIRN
Lochailort
Glenfinnan
Corpach
Caol
Fort William
Rhois-Bheinn
Morar, Moidart
North West Highlands
Scale: 0 10 20 30 miles; 0 10 20 30 40 50 km

Orkney Islands
Mull Head
Papa Westray
Westray
Pierowall
Midbea
Rapness
Hollandstoun
Dennis Hd.
N. Ronaldsay
The North Sound
Burness
Start Pt.
Sanday
Calfsound
Overbister
Eday
Store
Sanday Sound
Sacquoy Hd.
Wasbister
Eynhallow Sd.
Rousay
Brinyan
Veness
Odie
Aith
Stronsay
Stronsay Firth
Brough Hd.
The Barony
Twatt
Redland
Dounby
Balfour
Shapinsay
Lamb Hd.
SCARA BRAE
MAES HOWE
Hoy & West Mainland
Voy
Finstown
Kirkwall
Mull Head
Mainland
Stromness
Orphir
Gritley
Copinsay
Aberdeen Lerwick
Linksness
Old Man of Hoy
Scrabster
St. Mary's
Scapa Flow
Rose Ness
Burray
Hoy
Flotta
Lyness
Longhope
St. Margaret's Hope
South Ronaldsay
Tor Ness
South Walls
Burwick
Stromness
Pentland Firth
Dunnet Hd.
Stroma
MARY ANN'S COTTAGE
Holborn Hd.
Dunnet B.
Mey
John o' Groats
Duncansby Head
Strathy Pt.
Scrabster
Dunnet
Castletown
Thurso
BUCHOLLY CASTLE
Whiten Hd.
Kyle of Tongue
Dounreay
Melvich
Strathy
Bettyhill
Sordale
Nybster
Keiss
Halkirk
Hastigrow
Tongue
Olgrinmore
Reiss
Noss Hd.
GIRNIGOE CASTLE
Dalhalvaig
Watten
Mybster
Wick
OLD WICK CASTLE
Kyle of Tongue
Loch Loyal
Forsinain
Naver
Thurso
Thrumster
CAIRN OF GET
Ulbster
DORNAIGIL
Achavanich
L. Naver
Lybster
Altnaharra
L. nan Clar
Dunbeath
Latheron
Kinbrace
705 Morven
DUNBEATH CASTLE
961 Meall Nan Con
Strath of Kildonan
Berriedale
Kildonan
CLEARANCE VILLAGE
Ousdale
Helmsdale
Shin
Brora
Sallachy
Lairg
Pittentrail
Brora
Golspie
Inveran
Dornoch Firth
Bonarbridge
Clashmore
Dornoch
Tarbat Ness
Ardgay
Edderton
Dornoch Firth
Portmahomack
Tain
Moray Firth
Fearn
FEARN ABBEY
Balintore
Alness
Kilmuir
Lossiemouth
Alness
Invergordon
Balnabruaich
Burghead
Burghead B.
Spey B.
Findochty
Portknockie
Troup Hd.
Rosehearty
Kinnairds Hd.
Fraserburgh
Inverallochy
Cromarty Firth
Cromarty
Findhorn
Kinloss
Kingston
Elgin
Buckie
Portsoy
Macduff
Banff
PITSLIGO CASTLE
New Aberdour
Rattray Hd.
Crimond
BRODIE CASTLE
Fochabers
Craibstone
Deveron
Strichen
Dingwall
Fortrose
Nairn
Forres
Mulben
Aberchirder
New Pitsligo
Conon Bridge
Ardersier
Auldearn
Kellas
Keith
Turriff
Maud
Mintlaw
Peterhead
North Kessock
Cawdor
CAWDOR CASTLE
Ferness
Rothes
Fortrie
Old Deer
Buchan Ness
Boddam
Beauly
Inverness
Archiestown
Charlestown of Aberlour
Huntly
Methlick
SLAINS CASTLE
Cruden Bay
Dufftown
Ythan
Tarves
Ellon
Dores
Moy
Marypark
Lettoch
Colpy
Insch
Grantown-on-Spey
Tomnavoulin
Oldmeldrum
Newburgh
Kirkwall Lerwick
Loch Ness
Torness
Tomatin
Cabrach
Rhynie
Lumsden
Inverurie
Newmachar
Carrbridge
Tomintoul
Don
Kemnay
Kintore
Dyce
Balmedie
Foyers
Boat of Garten
804 Carn Mor
Ladder Hills
KILDRUMMY CASTLE & GARDEN
Alford
Ordhead
Bridge of Don
Aberdeen
White Bridge
Aviemore
Strathspey
Cairngorms
Strathdon
Westhill
Girdle Ness
Monadhliath Mts.
Avon
CORGARFF CASTLE
1245 Cairn Gorm
871 Morven
Tarland
Cults
942 Carn Ban
Kincraig
Kingussie
Cairngorm Mts.
Torphins
Peterculter
DRUM CASTLE
Portlethen
Newtonmore
Ruthven
1309 Ben Macdhui
Crathie
Ballater
Aboyne
Banchory
Dee
RAEDYKES ROMAN CAMP
Newtonhill
Drumgask
Braemar
Strachan
939 Mt. Keen
Stonehaven
Dee
1154 Lochnagar
DUNNOTTAR CASTLE
L. Laggan
Dalwhinnie
Forest of Atholl
N. Esk
1008 Ben Dearg
1121 Beinn a' Ghlo
Spittle of Glenshee
1067 Glas Maol
Clova
Fettercairn
Inverbervie
Laurencekirk
Marykirk
Johnshaven
1148
Loch
59°
58°
57°
4°
3°
2°

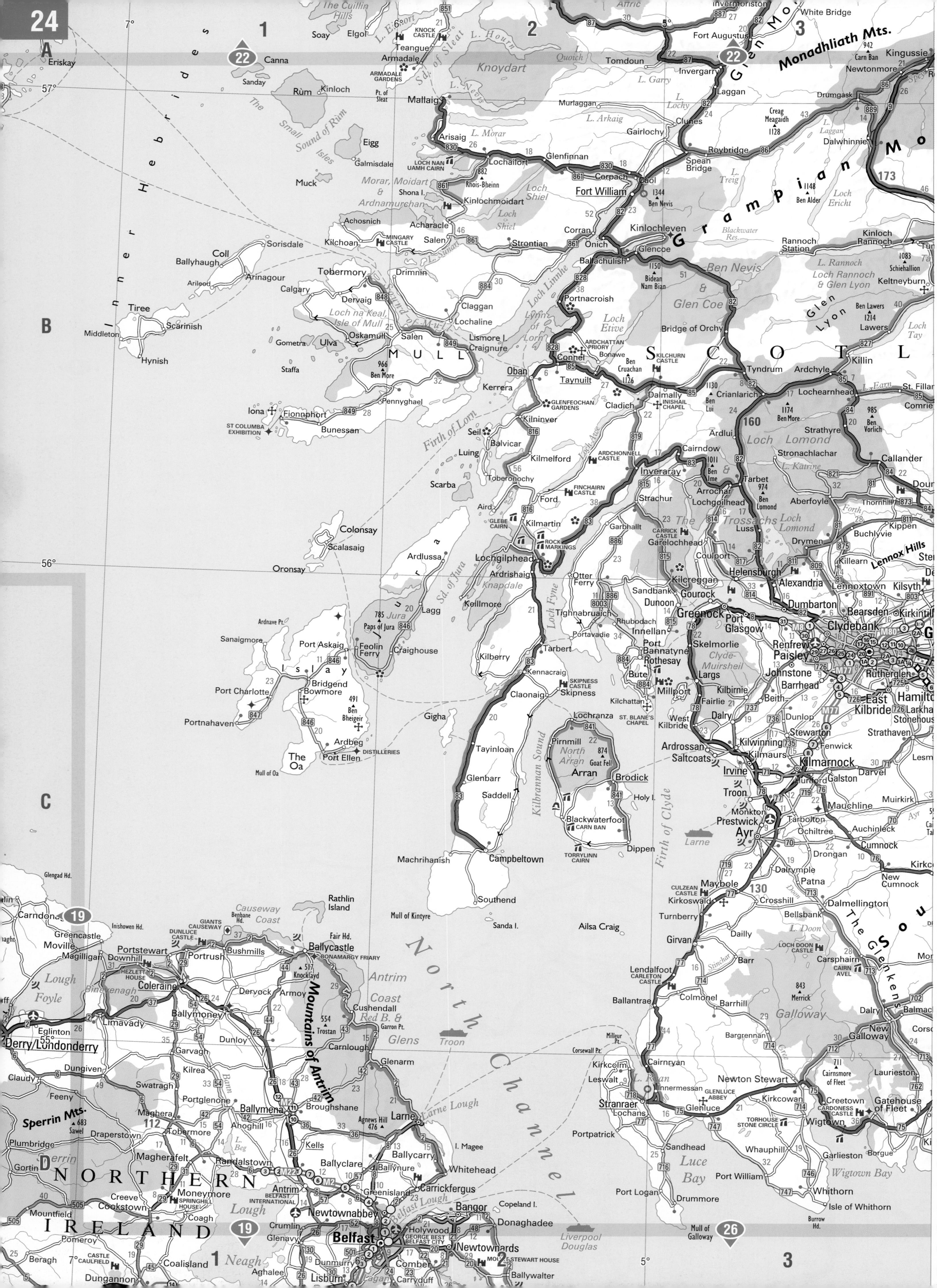
A
B
C
D
1
2
3
22
19
26
Inner Hebrides
Eriskay
Canna
Sanday
Rùm
Kinloch
The Small Isles
Sound of Rùm
Eigg
Muck
Soay
Elgol
The Cuillin Hills
Knock Castle
Teangue
Armadale
Armadale Gardens
Sd. of Sleat
Pt. of Sleat
Mallaig
Knoydart
L. Hourn
L. Nevis
L. Quoich
Tomdoun
L. Garry
Invergarry
Fort Augustus
Invermoriston
White Bridge
Glen Mor
Monadhliath Mts.
Kingussie
Carn Ban
Newtonmore
Laggan
Drumgask
Creag Meagaidh
L. Laggan
Dalwhinnie
L. Lochy
Clunes
Murlaggan
L. Arkaig
Gairlochy
Roybridge
Spean Bridge
Arisaig
L. Morar
Glenfinnan
Loch nan Uamh Cairn
Lochailort
Galmisdale
Rhois-Bheinn
Morar, Moidart & Ardnamurchan
Shona I.
Kinlochmoidart
Corpach
Caol
Fort William
Ben Nevis
Loch Shiel
L. Treig
Ben Alder
Loch Ericht
Grampian Mountains
Achosnich
Acharacle
Kilchoan
Mingary Castle
Salen
Strontian
Corran
Onich
Kinlochleven
Blackwater Res.
Rannoch Station
Kinloch Rannoch
L. Rannoch
Loch Rannoch & Glen Lyon
Schiehallion
Keltneyburn
Glencoe
Ballachulish
Bidean Nam Bian
Ben Nevis & Glen Coe
Coll
Sorisdale
Ballyhaugh
Arinagour
Arileod
Tobermory
Drimnin
Calgary
Dervaig
Tiree
Scarinish
Middleton
Hynish
Gometra
Ulva
Loch na Keal, Isle of Mull
Oskamull
Salen
Sound of Mull
Claggan
Lochaline
Loch Linnhe
Lynn of Lorn
Portnacroish
Loch Etive
Bridge of Orchy
Glen Lyon
Ben Lawers
Lawers
Loch Tay
Mull
Staffa
Ben More
Craignure
Lismore I.
Ardchattan Priory
Connel
Bonawe
Ben Cruachan
Kilchurn Castle
Scotland
Oban
Taynuilt
Tyndrum
Ardchyle
Killin
Kerrera
Iona
Fionnphort
Pennyghael
Bunessan
St Columba Exhibition
Glenfeochan Gardens
Cladich
Dalmally
Inishail Chapel
Crianlarich
Ben Lui
Lochearnhead
L. Earn
St. Fillans
Comrie
Ben Vorlich
Firth of Lorn
Kilninver
Seil
Balvicar
Luing
Kilmelford
Ardchonnell Castle
Loch Awe
Ardlui
Loch Lomond
Stronachlachar
Strathyre
Callander
Scarba
Toberonochy
Inveraray
Cairndow
Ben Ime
Arrochar
Tarbet
L. Katrine
Finchairn Castle
Ford
Strachur
Lochgoilhead
Ben Lomond
Aberfoyle
Thornhill
Aird
Glebe Cairn
Kilmartin
Rock Markings
The Trossachs
Luss
Loch Lomond
Buchlyvie
Kippen
Colonsay
Scalasaig
Garbhallt
Carrick Castle
Garelochhead
Drymen
Lennox Hills
Killearn
Oronsay
Ardlussa
Jura
Sd. of Jura
Lochgilphead
Ardrishaig
Knapdale
Otter Ferry
Coulport
Kilcreggan
Helensburgh
Alexandria
Lennoxtown
Kilsyth
Sandbank
Dunoon
Gourock
Dumbarton
Bearsden
Keillmore
Lagg
Paps of Jura
Loch Fyne
Tighnabruaich
Rhubodach
Greenock
Port Glasgow
Clydebank
Ardnave Pt.
Sanaigmore
Port Askaig
Feolin Ferry
Craighouse
Portavadie
Innellan
Port Bannatyne
Rothesay
Skelmorlie
Renfrew
Paisley
Islay
Bridgend
Bowmore
Tarbert
Kilberry
Kennacraig
Bute
Millport
Clyde-Muirsheil
Largs
Johnstone
Barrhead
Rutherglen
Port Charlotte
Ben Bheigeir
Skipness Castle
Skipness
Claonaig
Kilchattan
Kilbirnie
Fairlie
Beith
East Kilbride
Hamilton
Portnahaven
Gigha
Lochranza
St. Blane's Chapel
West Kilbride
Dalry
Dunlop
Stewarton
Stonehouse
Strathaven
The Oa
Ardbeg
Port Ellen
Distilleries
Mull of Oa
Tayinloan
Pirnmill
North Arran
Goat Fell
Arran
Brodick
Kilbrannan Sound
Ardrossan
Saltcoats
Kilwinning
Kilmaurs
Kilmarnock
Fenwick
Irvine
Troon
Hurlford
Galston
Darvel
Glenbarr
Saddell
Holy I.
Blackwaterfoot
Carn Ban
Torrylinn Cairn
Dippen
Firth of Clyde
Monkton
Prestwick
Ayr
Mauchline
Muirkirk
Tarbolton
Ochiltree
Auchinleck
Cumnock
Drongan
Larne
Machrihanish
Campbeltown
Southend
Mull of Kintyre
Sanda I.
Ailsa Craig
Culzean Castle
Maybole
Dalrymple
Patna
Crosshill
Kirkoswald
Dalmellington
New Cumnock
Turnberry
Bellsbank
L. Doon
Girvan
Dailly
Loch Doon Castle
Carsphairn
The Glenkens
Cairn Avel
Barr
Lendalfoot
Carleton Castle
Merrick
Ballantrae
Colmonel
Barrhill
Galloway
Dalry
Balmaclellan
New Galloway
Bargrennan
Rathlin Island
Causeway Coast
Giants Causeway
Benbane Hd.
Fair Hd.
Ballycastle
Bonamargy Friary
Glengad Hd.
Carndonagh
Inishowen Hd.
Greencastle
Moville
Magilligan
Downhill
Portstewart
Portrush
Bushmills
Dunluce Castle
Hezlett House
Lough Foyle
Binevenagh
Coleraine
Dervock
Armoy
Knocklayd
Antrim Coast
Mountains of Antrim
Cushendall
Red B. & Garron Pt.
Glens
Troon
North Channel
Limavady
Eglinton
Derry/Londonderry
Ballymoney
Dunloy
Trostan
Carnlough
Glenarm
Garvagh
Dungiven
Claudy
Kilrea
Swatragh
Feeny
Portglenone
Ballymena
Broughshane
Agnews Hill
Larne
Larne Lough
Sperrin Mts.
Sawel
Maghera
Tobermore
Draperstown
Ahoghill
Kells
Plumbridge
Magherafelt
Lough Beg
Randalstown
Ballyclare
Ballynure
Ballycarry
I. Magee
Whitehead
Gortin
Northern Ireland
Antrim
Belfast International
Carrickfergus
Greenisland
Newtownabbey
Cookstown
Moneymore
Springhill House
Creeve
Mountfield
Coagh
Lough Neagh
Crumlin
Glenavy
Belfast Lough
Bangor
Copeland I.
Donaghadee
Holywood
George Best Belfast City
Belfast
Newtownards
Mount Stewart House
Ballywalter
Pomeroy
Beragh
Castle Caulfield
Coalisland
Dungannon
Aghalee
Dunmurry
Lisburn
Comber
Carryduff
Liverpool Douglas
Mull of Galloway
Corsewall Pt.
Milleur Pt.
Kirkcolm
Cairnryan
L. Ryan
Leswalt
Innermessan
Stranraer
Lochans
Glenluce Abbey
Glenluce
Newton Stewart
Kirkcowan
Creetown
Cardoness Castle
Gatehouse of Fleet
Cairnsmore of Fleet
Laurieston
Torhouse Stone Circle
Wigtown
Portpatrick
Sandhead
Luce Bay
Whauphill
Garlieston
Wigtown Bay
Port William
Port Logan
Drummore
Whithorn
Isle of Whithorn
Burrow Hd.
57°
56°
55°
7°
6°
5°

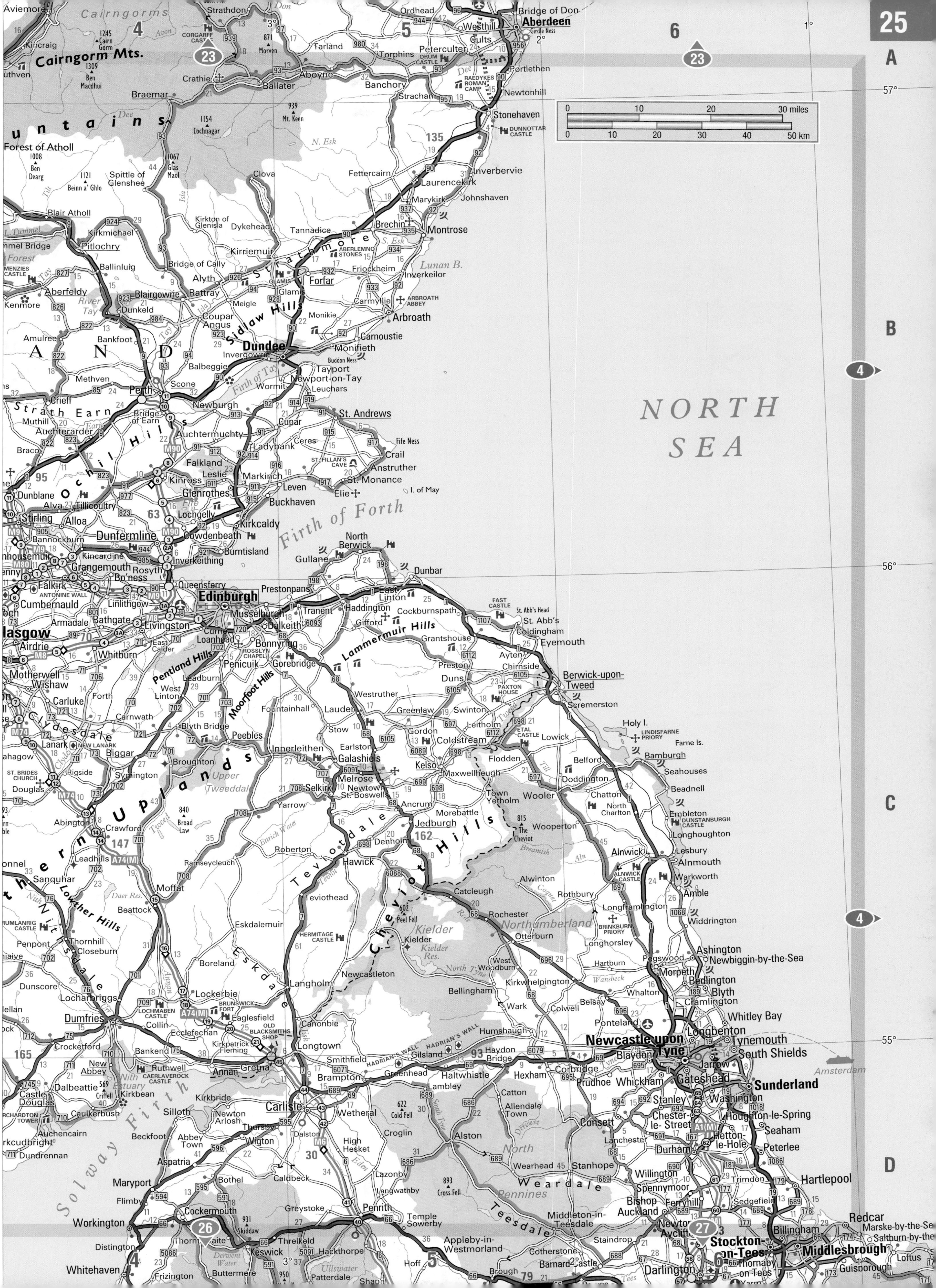
NORTH SEA
Firth of Forth
Firth of Tay
Solway Firth
Cairngorms
Cairngorm Mts.
Sidlaw Hills
Ochil Hills
Strathmore
Strath Earn
Pentland Hills
Moorfoot Hills
Lammermuir Hills
Southern Uplands
Lowther Hills
Cheviot Hills
Teviotdale
Eskdale
Nithsdale
Clydesdale
Upper Tweeddale
Northumberland
Kielder
North Pennines
Weardale
Teesdale
Aviemore
Strathdon
Aberdeen
Bridge of Don
Westhill
Cults
Peterculter
Girdle Ness
Portlethen
Newtonhill
Stonehaven
Dunnottar Castle
Tarland
Torphins
Aboyne
Ballater
Banchory
Crathie
Braemar
Kincraig
Forest of Atholl
Spittle of Glenshee
Clova
Fettercairn
Inverbervie
Laurencekirk
Johnshaven
Marykirk
Brechin
Montrose
Tannadice
Kirriemuir
Forfar
Friockheim
Inverkeilor
Arbroath
Arbroath Abbey
Carnoustie
Monifieth
Dundee
Invergowrie
Tayport
Newport-on-Tay
Wormit
Leuchars
Blair Atholl
Pitlochry
Kirkmichael
Ballinluig
Aberfeldy
Kenmore
Dunkeld
Blairgowrie
Rattray
Alyth
Coupar Angus
Meigle
Glamis
Bridge of Cally
Dykehead
Amulree
Bankfoot
Perth
Scone
Balbeggie
Methven
Crieff
Muthill
Auchterarder
Bridge of Earn
Newburgh
Auchtermuchty
Cupar
St. Andrews
Ceres
Ladybank
Falkland
Leslie
Kinross
Glenrothes
Markinch
Leven
Buckhaven
Crail
Anstruther
St. Monance
Elie
Fife Ness
I. of May
Dunblane
Alva
Tillicoultry
Stirling
Alloa
Dunfermline
Cowdenbeath
Kirkcaldy
Burntisland
Inverkeithing
Rosyth
Grangemouth
Falkirk
Bo'ness
Linlithgow
Queensferry
Edinburgh
Musselburgh
Prestonpans
Tranent
Dalkeith
Bonnyrigg
Penicuik
Gorebridge
Loanhead
Livingston
Bathgate
Armadale
Cumbernauld
Glasgow
Airdrie
Whitburn
Motherwell
Wishaw
Carluke
Lanark
Biggar
Gullane
North Berwick
Dunbar
East Linton
Haddington
Gifford
Cockburnspath
St. Abb's Head
St. Abb's
Coldingham
Eyemouth
Ayton
Chirnside
Duns
Berwick-upon-Tweed
Scremerston
Holy I.
Lindisfarne Priory
Farne Is.
Bamburgh
Seahouses
Beadnell
Embleton
Dunstanburgh Castle
Longhoughton
Lesbury
Alnmouth
Alnwick
Warkworth
Amble
Widdrington
Ashington
Newbiggin-by-the-Sea
Morpeth
Bedlington
Blyth
Cramlington
Whitley Bay
Tynemouth
South Shields
Newcastle upon Tyne
Gateshead
Jarrow
Sunderland
Washington
Houghton-le-Spring
Seaham
Durham
Peterlee
Hartlepool
Stockton-on-Tees
Middlesbrough
Redcar
Darlington
Bishop Auckland
Spennymoor
Lauder
Galashiels
Melrose
Selkirk
Kelso
Coldstream
Jedburgh
Hawick
Peebles
Innerleithen
Moffat
Lockerbie
Langholm
Dumfries
Annan
Gretna
Carlisle
Penrith
Keswick
Cockermouth
Workington
Maryport
Whitehaven
Wigton
Brampton
Haltwhistle
Hexham
Corbridge
Consett
Alston
Wooler
Rothbury
Otterburn
Bellingham
Kielder Res.
The Cheviot
Hadrian's Wall
Amsterdam
Middleton-in-Teesdale
Barnard Castle
Appleby-in-Westmorland
0 10 20 30 miles
0 10 20 30 40 50 km
57°
56°
55°
A
B
C
D
4
5
6
23
26
27

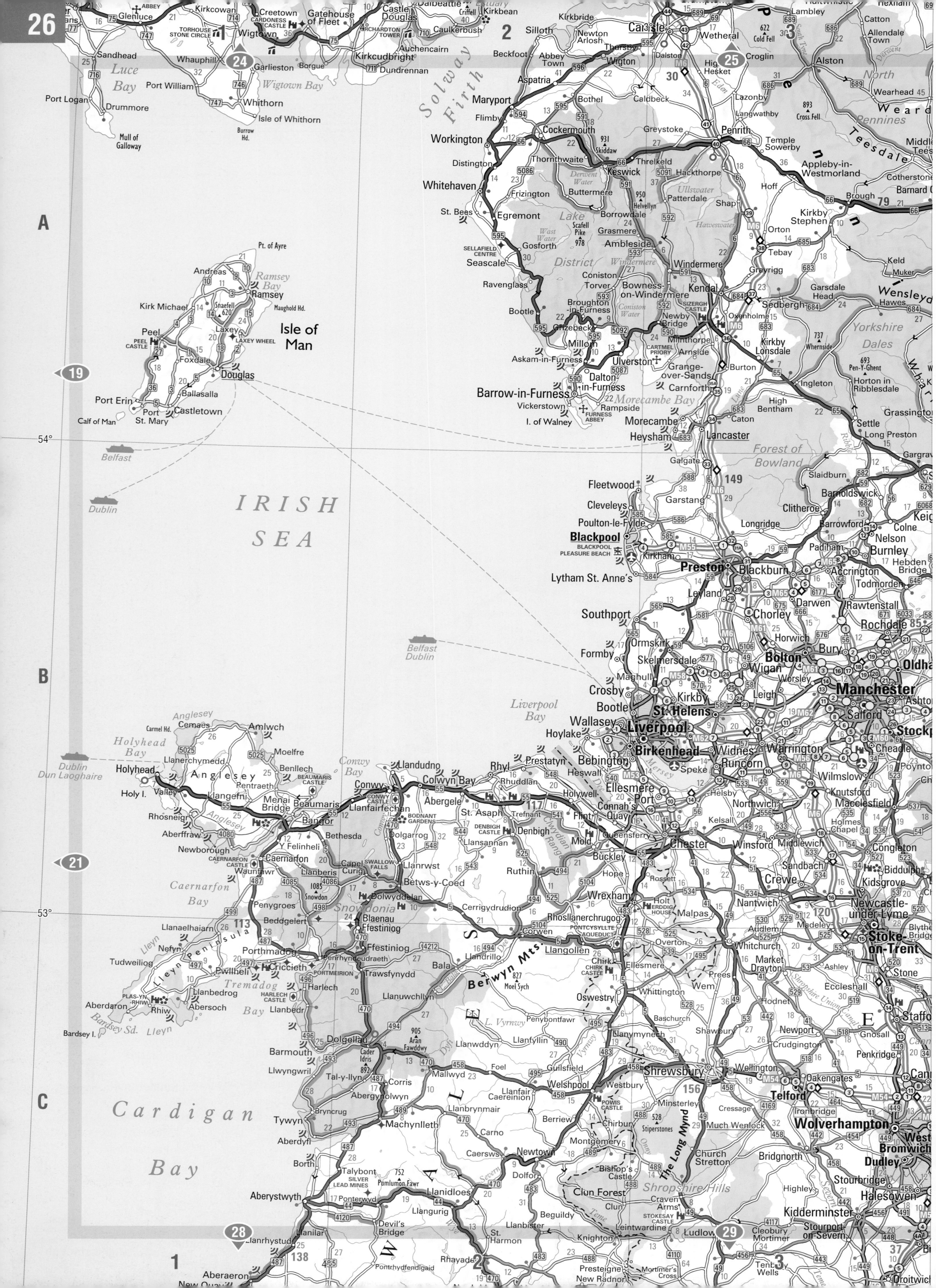

Glenluce
Kirkcowan
Creetown
Gatehouse of Fleet
Castle Douglas
Dalbeattie
Kirkbean
Torhouse Stone Circle
Cardoness Castle
Richardton Tower
Caulkerbush
Wigtown
Sandhead
Whauphill
Garlieston
Borgue
Auchencairn
Kirkcudbright
Dundrennan
Luce Bay
Port William
Wigtown Bay
Port Logan
Drummore
Whithorn
Isle of Whithorn
Burrow Hd.
Mull of Galloway
Silloth
Kirkbride
Newton Arlosh
Carlisle
Wetheral
Lambley
Catton
Allendale Town
Beckfoot
Abbey Town
Thursby
Wigton
Dalston
High Hesket
Croglin
Alston
North Pennines
Aspatria
Solway Firth
Maryport
Bothel
Caldbeck
Lazonby
Langwathby
Cross Fell
Wearhead
Weardale
Flimby
Cockermouth
Greystoke
Penrith
Temple Sowerby
Workington
Skiddaw
Threlkeld
Appleby-in-Westmorland
Teesdale
Distington
Thornthwaite
Keswick
Hackthorpe
Cotherstone
Whitehaven
Derwent Water
Frizington
Buttermere
Ullswater
Patterdale
Helvellyn
Shap
Hoff
Brough
Barnard Castle
St. Bees
Egremont
Lake District
Scafell Pike
Wast Water
Borrowdale
Grasmere
Haweswater
Kirkby Stephen
Orton
Tebay
Sellafield Centre
Gosforth
Ambleside
Seascale
Windermere
Grayrigg
Keld
Muker
Ravenglass
Coniston
Torver
Bowness-on-Windermere
Kendal
Garsdale Head
Hawes
Wensleydale
Bootle
Broughton-in-Furness
Coniston Water
Sizergh Castle
Oxenholme
Sedbergh
Yorkshire Dales
Newby Bridge
Griezbeck
Millom
Lindale
Meathop
Cartmel Priory
Arnside
Kirkby Lonsdale
Whernside
Askam-in-Furness
Ulverston
Grange-over-Sands
Burton
Pen-Y-Ghent
Horton in Ribblesdale
Dalton-in-Furness
Carnforth
Ingleton
Barrow-in-Furness
Morecambe Bay
High Bentham
Vickerstown
Rampside
Furness Abbey
I. of Walney
Morecambe
Caton
Settle
Long Preston
Grassington
Heysham
Lancaster
Forest of Bowland
Galgate
Slaidburn
Gargrave
Fleetwood
Garstang
Barnoldswick
Cleveleys
Clitheroe
Poulton-le-Fylde
Longridge
Barrowford
Colne
Nelson
Blackpool
Blackpool Pleasure Beach
Kirkham
Padiham
Burnley
Preston
Blackburn
Accrington
Hebden Bridge
Lytham St. Anne's
Todmorden
Leyland
Darwen
Rawtenstall
Southport
Chorley
Rochdale
Ormskirk
Horwich
Bury
Formby
Skelmersdale
Bolton
Wigan
Oldham
Maghull
Worsley
Manchester
Crosby
Kirkby
Leigh
Salford
Ashton
Bootle
St. Helens
Wallasey
Liverpool
Stockport
Hoylake
Birkenhead
Widnes
Warrington
Cheadle
Bebington
Runcorn
Speke
Heswall
Ellesmere Port
Wilmslow
Knutsford
Macclesfield
Helsby
Northwich
Holmes Chapel
Congleton
Pt. of Ayre
Andreas
Ramsey Bay
Ramsey
Kirk Michael
Maughold Hd.
Snaefell
Laxey
Laxey Wheel
Isle of Man
Peel
Peel Castle
Foxdale
Douglas
Port Erin
Ballasalla
Port St. Mary
Castletown
Calf of Man
Belfast
Dublin
IRISH SEA
Belfast Dublin
Liverpool Bay
Anglesey
Carmel Hd.
Cemaes
Amlwch
Holyhead Bay
Moelfre
Llanerchymedd
Benllech
Dublin Dun Laoghaire
Holyhead
Pentraeth
Beaumaris Castle
Conwy Bay
Llandudno
Rhyl
Prestatyn
Holy I.
Valley
Llangefni
Menai Bridge
Beaumaris
Conwy
Colwyn Bay
Rhuddlan
Holywell
Rhosneigr
Llanfairfechan
Abergele
St. Asaph
Trefnant
Flint
Connah's Quay
Aberffraw
Bangor
Bodnant Gardens
Denbigh Castle
Denbigh
Queensferry
Newborough
Y Felinheli
Bethesda
Dolgarrog
Llansannan
Mold
Chester
Winsford
Middlewich
Caernarfon Castle
Caernarfon
Llanberis
Capel Curig
Swallow Falls
Llanrwst
Ruthin
Buckley
Hope
Rossett
Crewe
Sandbach
Biddulph
Kidsgrove
Waunfawr
Snowdon
Betws-y-Coed
Dolwyddelan
Wrexham
Holt
Erddig House
Malpas
Nantwich
Caernarfon Bay
Penygroes
Snowdonia
Cerrigydrudion
Rhosllanerchrugog
Newcastle-under-Lyme
Stoke-on-Trent
Blythe Bridge
Llanaelhaiarn
Beddgelert
Blaenau Ffestiniog
Corwen
Pontcysyllte Aqueduct
Audlem
Madeley
Overton
Whitchurch
Lleyn Peninsula
Nefyn
Porthmadog
Ffestiniog
Llandrillo
Llangollen
Market Drayton
Tudweiliog
Penrhyndeudraeth
Chirk
Chirk Castle
Ellesmere
Prees
Ashley
Stone
Pwllheli
Criccieth
Portmeirion
Trawsfynydd
Bala
Berwyn Mts.
Wem
Eccleshall
Tremadog Bay
Harlech
Harlech Castle
Moel Sych
Whittington
Plas-yn-Rhiw
Aberdaron
Rhiw
Llanbedrog
Abersoch
Llanbedr
Llanuwchllyn
Oswestry
Hodnet
Stafford
Bardsey Sd.
Bardsey I.
L. Vyrnwy
Penybontfawr
Baschurch
Newport
Gnosall
Dolgellau
Aran Fawddwy
Llanfyllin
Llanymynech
Shawbury
Barmouth
Cader Idris
Llanwddyn
Crudgington
Penkridge
Llwyngwril
Mallwyd
Foel
Guilsfield
Shrewsbury
Wellington
Oakengates
Telford
Tal-y-llyn
Corris
Llanfair Caereinion
Welshpool
Westbury
Cannock
Cardigan Bay
Aberdyfi
Bryncrug
Tywyn
Abergynolwyn
Machynlleth
Llanbrynmair
Powis Castle
Minsterley
Cressage
Ironbridge
Wolverhampton
Carno
Berriew
Chirbury
Stiperstones
The Long Mynd
Much Wenlock
West Bromwich
Montgomery
Caersws
Newtown
Church Stretton
Bridgnorth
Dudley
Borth
Talybont
Silver Lead Mines
Plynlimon Fawr
Dolfor
Bishop's Castle
Shropshire Hills
Stourbridge
Highley
Halesowen
Aberystwyth
Ponterwyd
Llanidloes
Clun Forest
Clun
Craven Arms
Stokesay Castle
Kidderminster
Llangurig
Beguildy
Llanbister
Leintwardine
Devil's Bridge
Knighton
Ludlow
Cleobury Mortimer
Stourport-on-Severn
Llanrhystud
Llanilar
St. Harmon
Rhayader
Presteigne
Tenbury Wells
Droitwich
Aberaeron
New Quay
Pontrhydfendigaid
New Radnor
Mortimer's Cross
WALES

5
6
A
B
C
0 10 20 30 miles
0 10 20 30 40 50 km
54°
53°
1°
0°
Sunderland
Durham
Hartlepool
Stockton-on-Tees
Middlesbrough
Redcar
Darlington
Whitby
Cleveland Hills
North York Moors
Scarborough
Filey
Flamborough
Bridlington
Bridlington Bay
Yorkshire Wolds
Harrogate
York
Leeds
Bradford
Halifax
Huddersfield
Wakefield
Barnsley
Doncaster
Sheffield
Rotherham
Kingston upon Hull
Beverley
Goole
Scunthorpe
Grimsby
Cleethorpes
Spurn Hd.
Rotterdam
Zeebrugge
Lincolnshire Wolds
Lincoln
Skegness
Chesterfield
Mansfield
Newark-on-Trent
Nottingham
Derby
Grantham
Boston
The Wash
Norfolk Coast
King's Lynn
Loughborough
Leicester
Peterborough
Wisbech
The Fens
Breckland
Thetford
Coventry
BIRMINGHAM
Kettering
Wellingborough
Huntingdon
Ely
ENGLAND

1
2
3
A
B
C
D
6°
5°
4°
52°
51°
50°
21
26
56
Oilgate
Blackwater
Castlebridge
Wexford
Wexford Harbour
Wellingtonbridge
Killinick
Rosslare
Rosslare Harbour
Greenore Pt.
Crossfarnoge Pt.
Kilmore Quay
Carnsore Pt.
Fishguard
Pembroke
Cherbourg
Roscoff
Rosslare
St. George's Channel
Borth
Talybont
Aberystwyth
Devil's Bridge
Llanrhystud
Aberaeron
New Quay
Tregaron
Cambrian Mts.
Llangrannog
Aberporth
Cardigan
St. Dogmaels
Lampeter
Llanwrtyd Wells
W
A
L
Newcastle Emlyn
Llandysul
Llanybydder
Llansawel
Llandovery
Strumble Hd.
Goodwick
Newport
Fishguard
Mynydd Preseli
Pembrokeshire
Greenway
Trelech
St. David's Hd.
St. David's
Ramsey I.
Solva
Wolf's Castle
St. Brides Bay
Haverfordwest
Carmarthen
Llandeilo
Llangadog
Narberth
St. Clears
Cross-Hands
Broad Haven
Skomer I.
Skokholm I.
Milford Haven
Neyland
Coast
Dale
Angle
Pembroke Dock
Pembroke
Saundersfoot
Tenby
Carmarthen Bay
Kidwelly
Burry Port
Llanelli
Gorseinon
Pontardulais
Ammanford
Clydach
Neath
Swansea
Port Talbot
Gowerton
The Mumbles
Rhossili
Gower
Worms Hd.
Port Eynon
Oxwich Pt.
Margam
Swansea Bay
Porthcawl
Manorbier
Caldey I.
St. Govan's Hd.
Rosslare
Bristol Channel
Lundy
Ilfracombe
Lynton
Exmoor
Morte Pt.
Morte Bay
Woolacombe
Croyde
North Devon
Barnstaple or Bideford Bay
Barnstaple
Instow
Appledore
Westward Ho!
Hartland Pt.
Hartland
Clovelly
Bideford
South Molton
Great Torrington
Chulmleigh
Morwenstow
Stibb Cross
Venn Green
Bude Bay
Bude
Stratton
Widemouth
Holsworthy
Poundstock
Okehampton
North Tawton
South Tawton
Cornwall
Boscastle
Tintagel Hd.
Tintagel
Launceston
Delabole
Port Isaac Bay
Port Isaac
Camelford
Brown Willy 419
Dartmoor
Moretonhampstead
Padstow
Trevose Hd.
St. Teath
Bodmin Moor
Tavistock
Wadebridge
St. Issey
Bodmin
Liskeard
Gunnislake
Callington
Yelverton
Buckfastleigh
Ashburton
Newquay
St. Columb Major
Lostwithiel
Saltash
Torpoint
Plymouth
Devonport
Plymstock
Ivybridge
Modbury
South Brent
Perranporth
St. Agnes
St. Austell
St. Blazey
Fowey
Polruan
Polperro
Looe
Whitesand Bay
Charlestown
Mevagissey
Mevagissey Bay
Gorran Haven
Bigbury Bay
Redruth
St. Ives
Carbis Bay
Hayle
Camborne
Truro
Tregony
Veryan
Penryn
St. Mawes
Falmouth
Falmouth Bay
Pendeen
Zennor
St. Just
Marazion
Newlyn
Penzance
Sennen
Land's End
Mousehole
Mount's Bay
Helston
Porthleven
Mullion
St. Keverne
The Manacles
Coverack
Lizard
Lizard Pt.
Isles of Scilly
Tresco
St. Martin's
Hugh Town
St. Mary's
Crow Sound
Wolf Rock
Roscoff
Santander
St Malo
Salcombe
Kingsbridge
Bolt Head
Marlborough

BIRMINGHAM
Coventry
Solihull
Kidderminster
Worcester
Hereford
Gloucester
Cheltenham
Oxford
Northampton
Milton Keynes
Banbury
Stratford-upon-Avon
Warwick
Royal Leamington Spa
Evesham
Cotswolds
Black Mountains
Brecon Beacons
Abergavenny
Monmouth
Merthyr Tydfil
Cwmbran
Newport
Cardiff
Bristol
Bath
Swindon
Reading
High Wycombe
Chiltern Hills
Berkshire Downs
Marlborough Downs
Vale of White Horse
Vale of Pewsey
Salisbury Plain
Hampshire Downs
Basingstoke
Newbury
Andover
Winchester
Salisbury
Southampton
Portsmouth
Havant
Isle of Wight
Newport
Bournemouth
Poole
Dorchester
Weymouth
Yeovil
Taunton
Exeter
Torquay
Bridgwater Bay
Lyme Bay
Weston-super-Mare
Brendon Hills
Blackdown Hills
Polden Hills
North Dorset Downs
South Dorset Downs
Blackmoor Vale
Wiltshire Downs
Cranborne Chase & West
ENGLAND
WALES
Guernsey
Jersey
St. Malo
Gijon
Cherbourg
Bilbao
Santander
Caen
Le Havre
0 10 20 30 miles
0 10 20 30 40 50 km
50°
3°
2°
1°
4
5
6
7
A
B
C
D

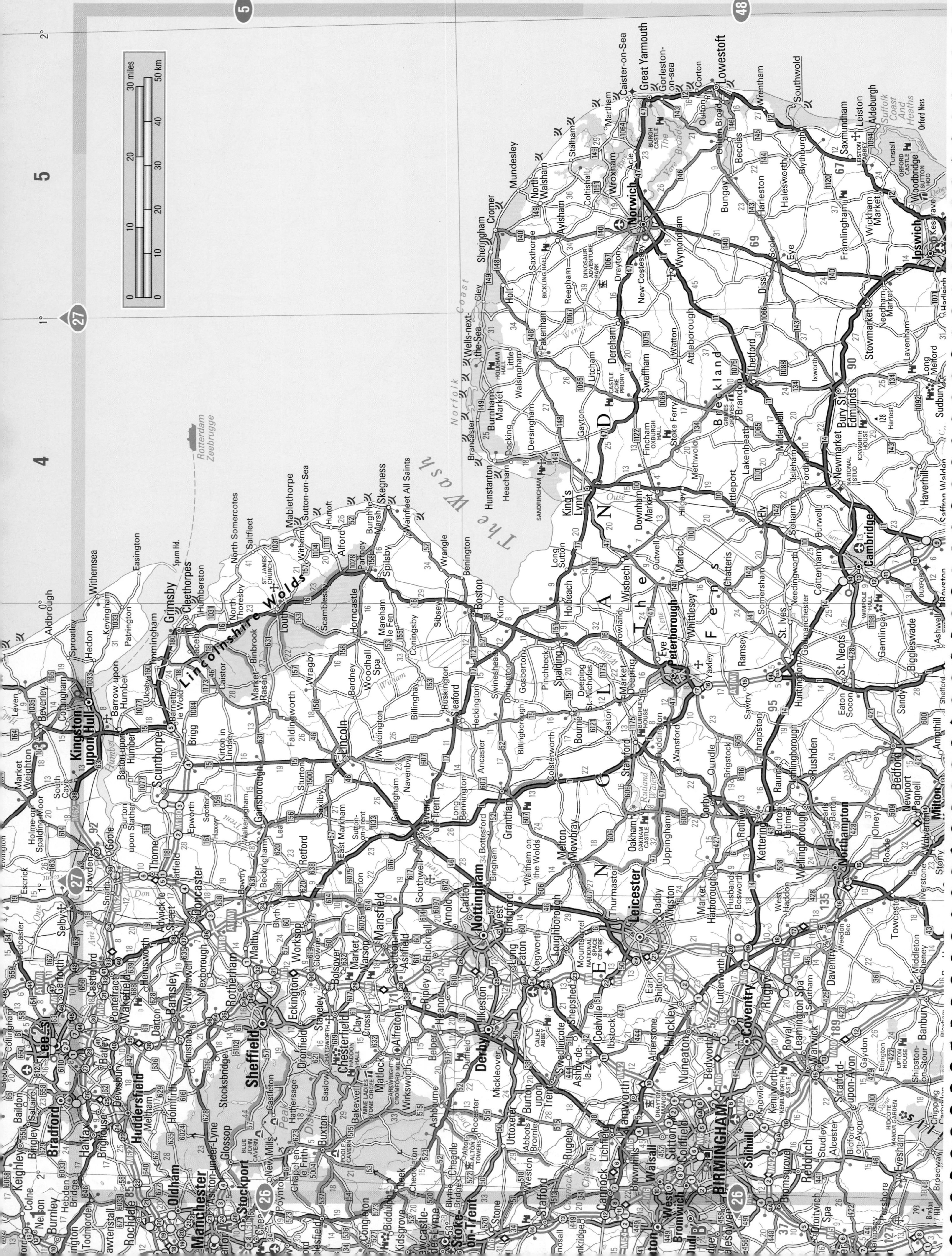
A
B
4
5
5
48
27
26
26
53°
1°
2°
0°
0 10 20 30 miles
0 10 20 30 40 50 km
Rotterdam
Zeebrugge
The Wash
Norfolk Coast
Lincolnshire Wolds
The Fens
ENGLAND
Breckland
The Broads
Peak District
Suffolk Coast And Heaths
Leeds
Bradford
Manchester
Sheffield
Kingston upon Hull
Grimsby
Cleethorpes
Scunthorpe
Doncaster
Lincoln
Nottingham
Derby
Leicester
Coventry
BIRMINGHAM
Norwich
Great Yarmouth
Lowestoft
Ipswich
Cambridge
Peterborough
Northampton
King's Lynn
Boston
Skegness
Mansfield
Chesterfield
Stoke-on-Trent
Wolverhampton
Rugby
Bedford
Huntingdon
Ely
Thetford
Bury St. Edmunds
Newmarket
Cromer
Sheringham
Stockport
Oldham
Huddersfield
Wakefield
Barnsley
Rotherham
Worksop
Newark-on-Trent
Grantham
Stamford
Spalding
Wisbech
Loughborough
Nuneaton
Tamworth
Lichfield
Walsall
Solihull
Kettering
Corby
Wellingborough
Dereham
Swaffham
Fakenham
Wymondham
Diss
Stowmarket

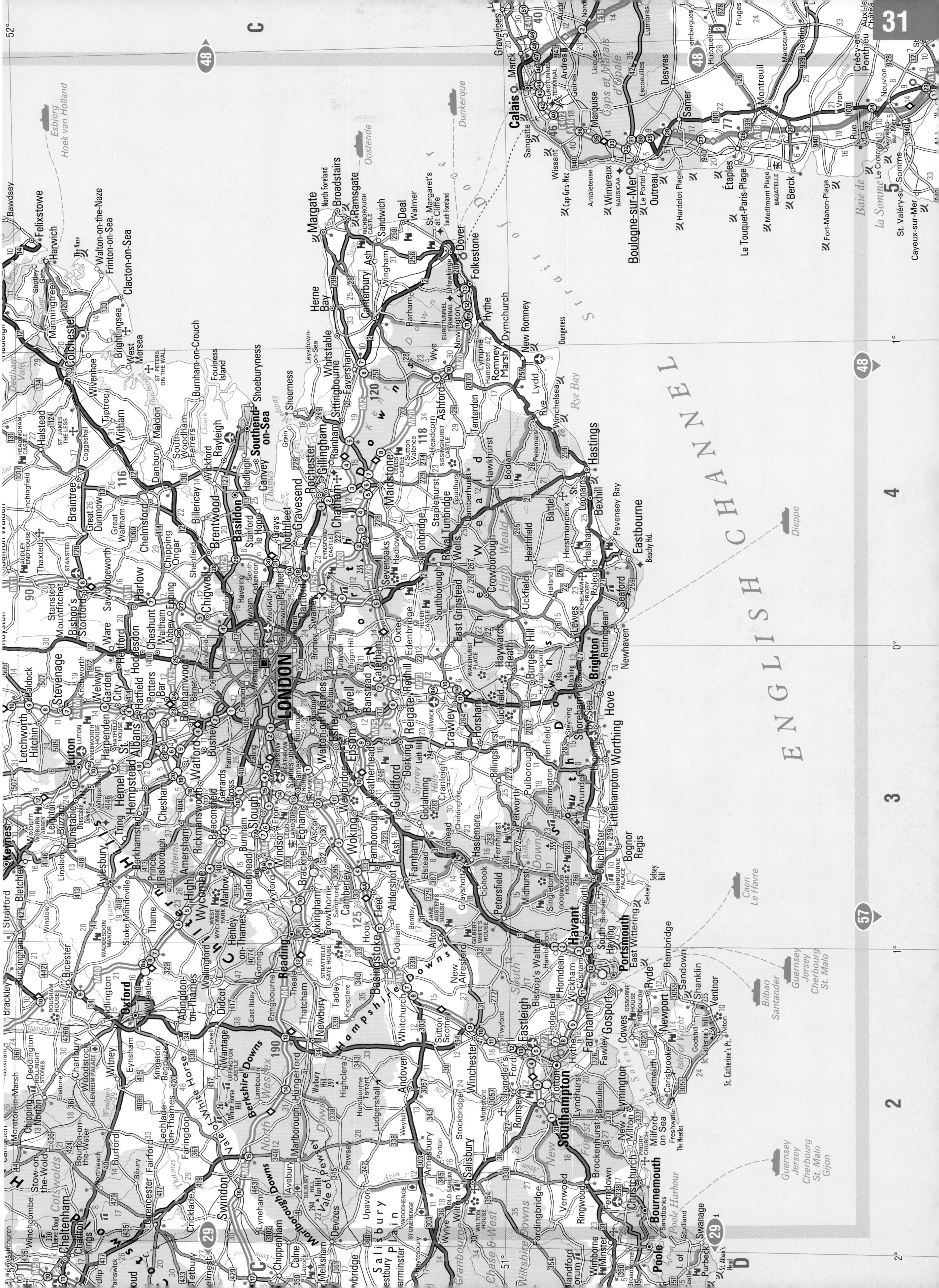
LONDON
ENGLISH CHANNEL
Calais
Boulogne-sur-Mer
Dover
Folkestone
Canterbury
Margate
Ramsgate
Southend-on-Sea
Colchester
Chelmsford
Maidstone
Ashford
Hastings
Eastbourne
Brighton
Worthing
Chichester
Portsmouth
Southampton
Bournemouth
Poole
Salisbury
Winchester
Basingstoke
Reading
Oxford
Swindon
Cheltenham
Luton
Stevenage
Guildford
Crawley
Tunbridge Wells
Dungeness
Newport
Isle of Wight
Dieppe
Caen
Le Havre
Oostende
Dunkerque
Montreuil
Étaples
Le Touquet-Paris-Plage
Berck
Baie de la Somme
Hampshire Downs
Salisbury Plain
Cotswolds
Chiltern Hills
Berkshire Downs
The Weald
North Downs
South Downs
New Forest

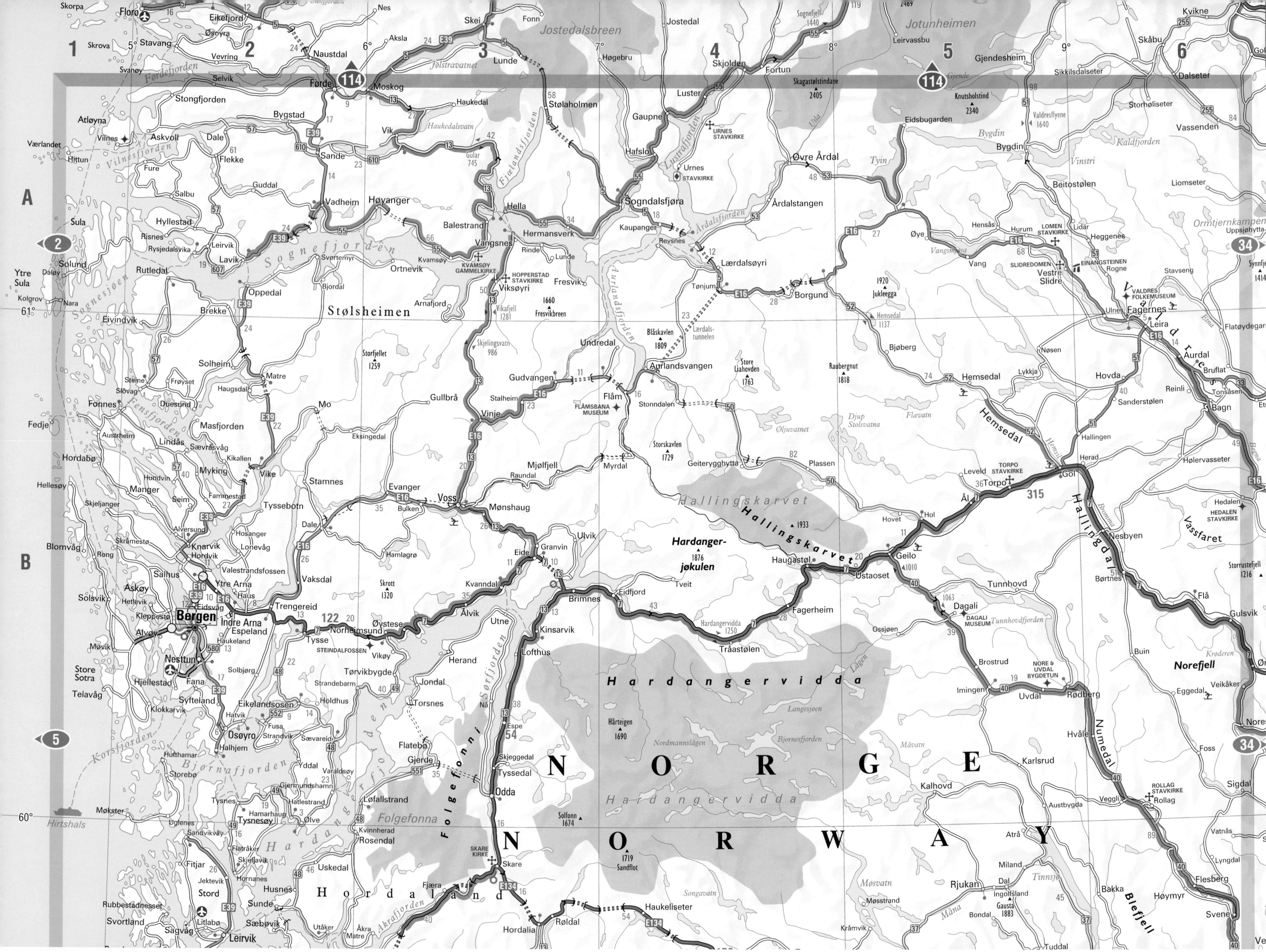
NORGE
NORWAY
Hardangervidda
Hallingskarvet
Hardangerjøkulen
Jostedalsbreen
Jotunheimen
Folgefonna
Folgefonni
Stølsheimen
Hordaland
Hallingdal
Hemsedal
Numedal
Valdres
Norefjell
Blefjell
Vassfaret
Sognefjorden
Hardangerfjorden
Sørfjorden
Aurlandsfjorden
Bjørnafjorden
Bergen
Voss
Odda
Førde
Sogndalsfjøra
Lærdalsøyri
Fagernes
Gol
Geilo
Flåm
Rjukan
Leirvik
Stord
Florø
Nesbyen
Fjærland
Hirtshals

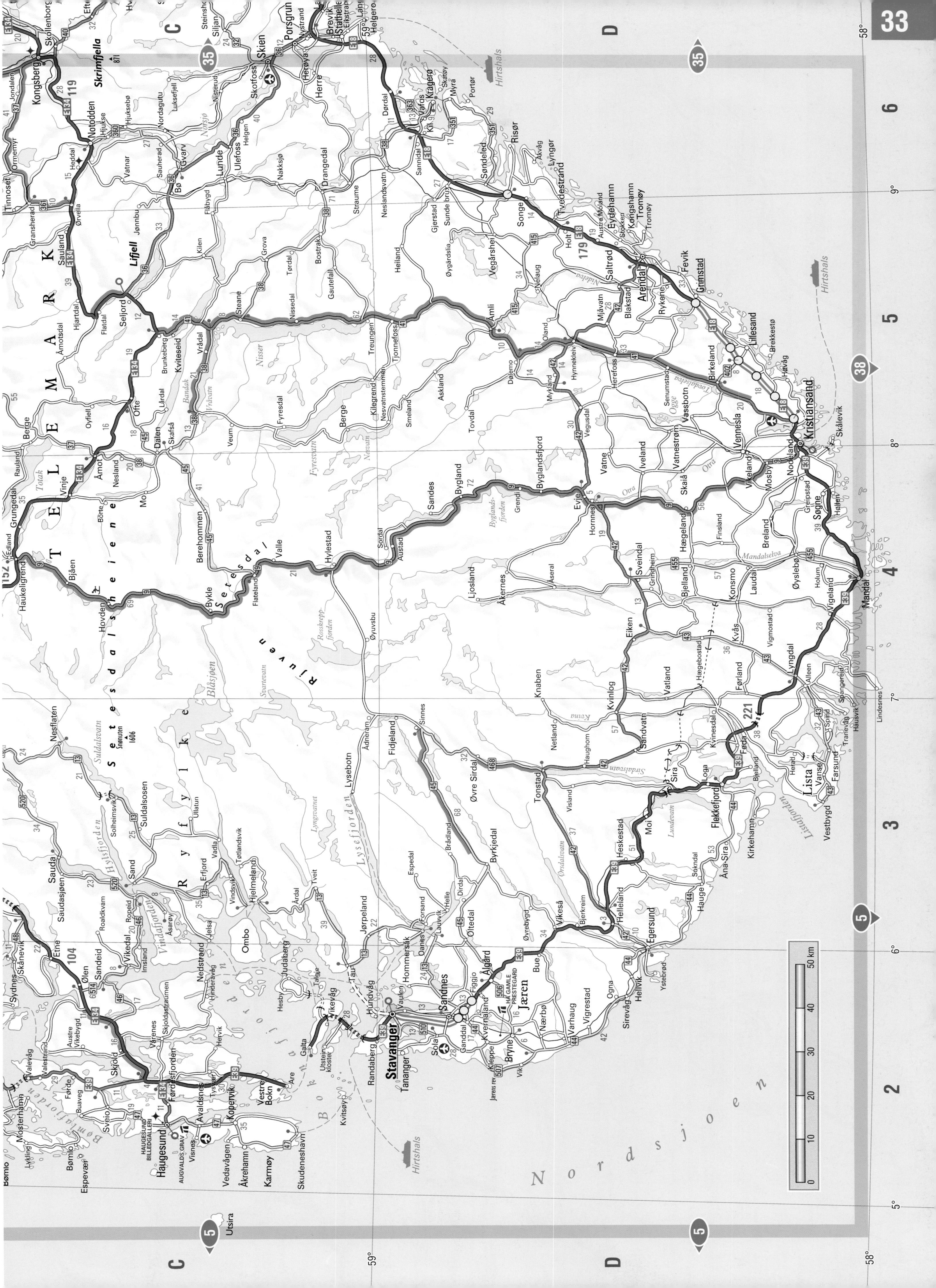
T E L E M A R K
R y f y l k e
S e t e s d a l s h e i e n e
S e t e s d a l
R j u v e n
N o r d s j o e n
B o k n a f j o r d e n
Kongsberg
Notodden
Skien
Porsgrunn
Brevik
Kragerø
Risør
Tvedestrand
Arendal
Grimstad
Lillesand
Kristiansand
Mandal
Lyngdal
Farsund
Flekkefjord
Egersund
Sandnes
Stavanger
Haugesund
Kopervik
Skudeneshavn
Utsira
Sauda
Lysebotn
Bykle
Valle
Evje
Amli
Seljord
Rauland
Haukeligrend
Bø
Lunde
Drangedal
Åmot
Dalen
Vinje
Hovden
Tonstad
Sirdal
Lista
Jæren
Bryne
Ombo
Ølen
Etne
Lindesnes
Skrimfjella
Lifjell
Blåsjøen
Hirtshals
0 10 20 30 40 50 km

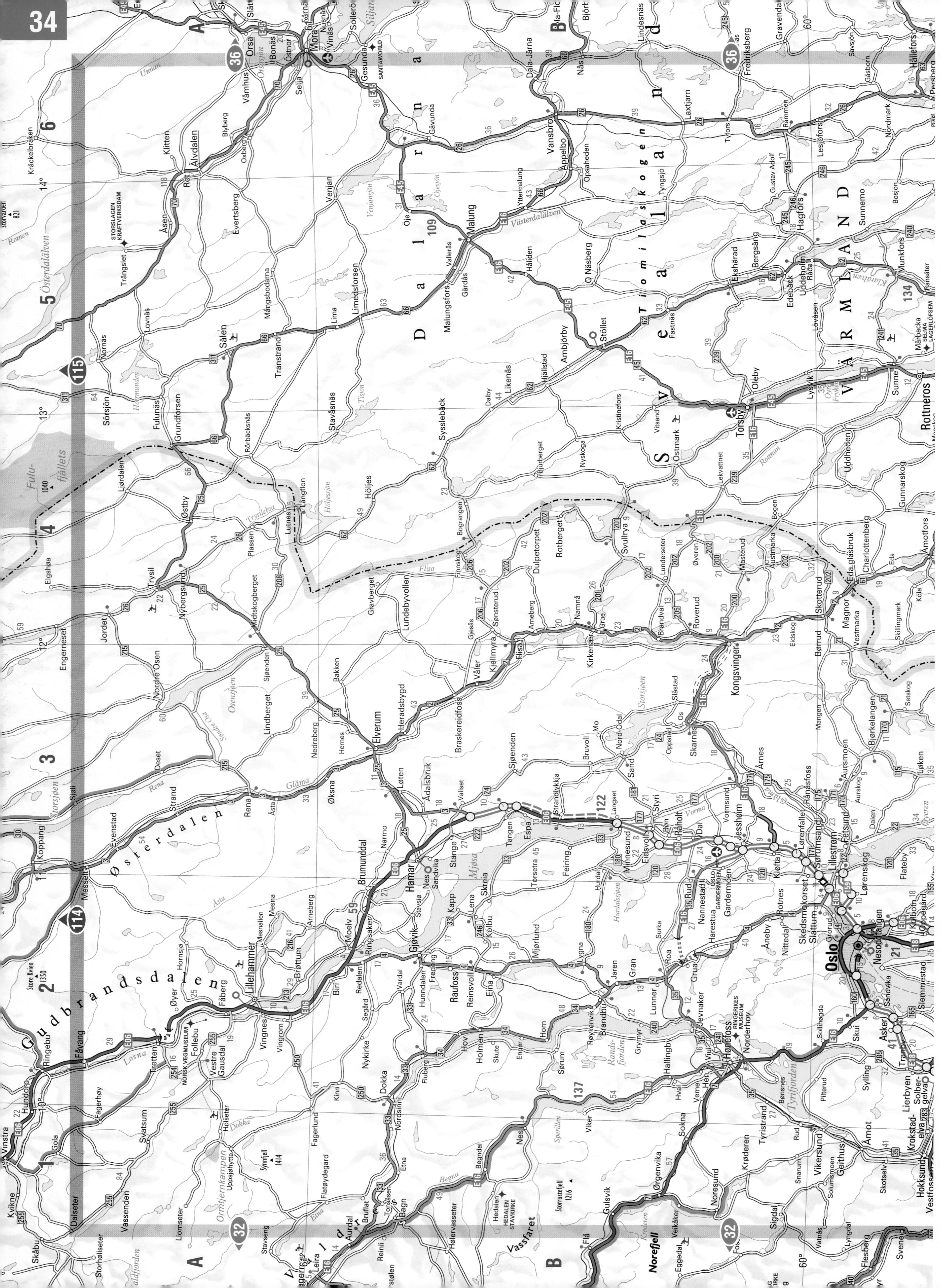
Gudbrandsdalen
Østerdalen
Dalarna
Värmland
Tiomilaskogen
Mjøsa
Oslo
Lillehammer
Hamar
Gjøvik
Elverum
Kongsvinger
Hønefoss
Lillestrøm
Jessheim
Eidsvoll
Asker
Rena
Koppang
Trysil
Sälen
Malung
Mora
Orsa
Älvdalen
Vansbro
Torsby
Hagfors
Sunne
Rottneros
Hällefors
Fåvang
Ringebu
Dokka
Raufoss
Brumunddal
Moelv
Flisa
Charlottenberg
Eda glasbruk
Magnor
Norefjell
Vassfaret
Fulufjällets

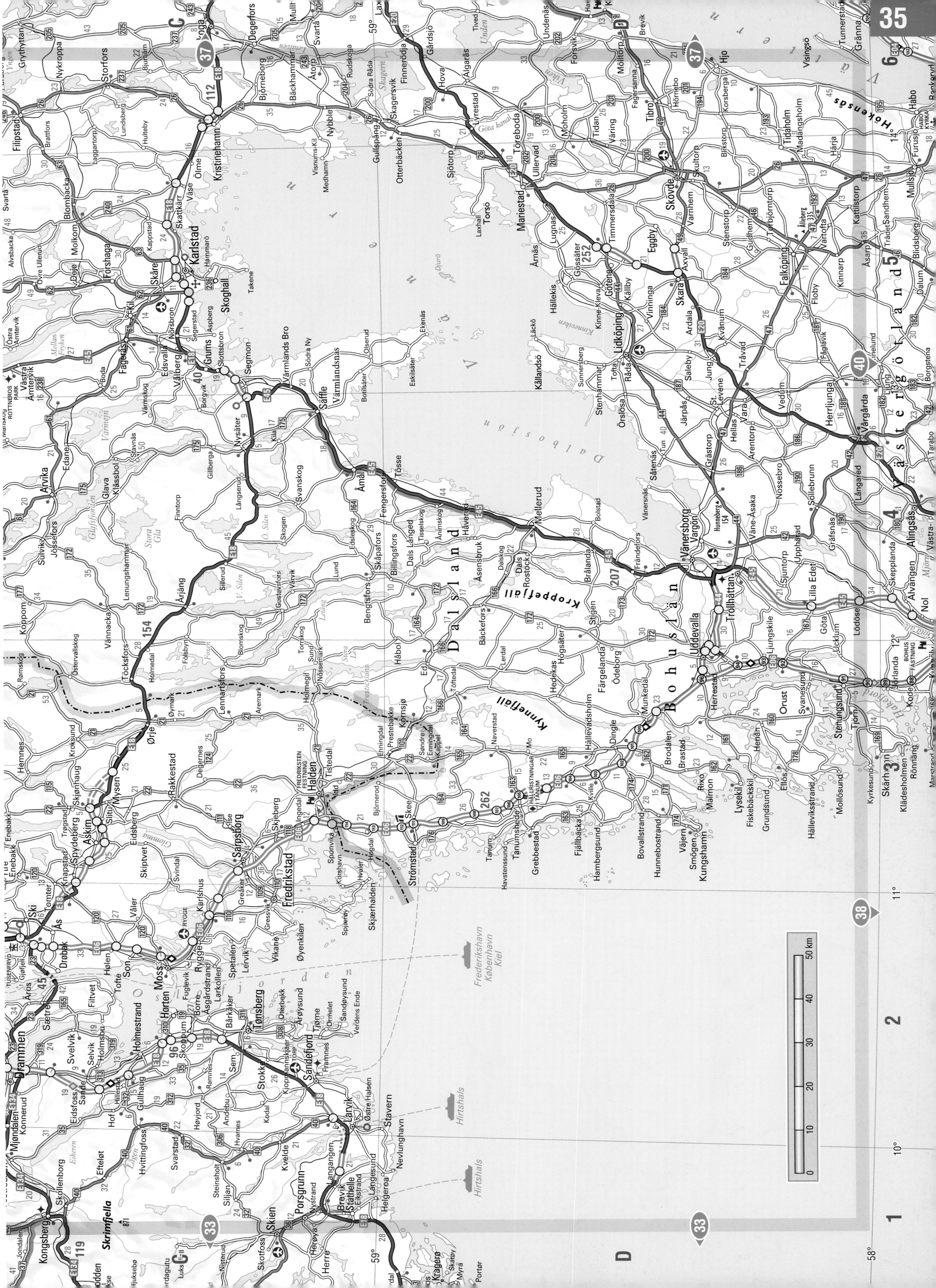
Karlstad
Kristinehamn
Filipstad
Arvika
Säffle
Åmål
Mariestad
Skövde
Lidköping
Skara
Falköping
Vänersborg
Trollhättan
Uddevalla
Alingsås
Strömstad
Halden
Fredrikstad
Sarpsborg
Moss
Horten
Tønsberg
Sandefjord
Larvik
Drammen
Kongsberg
Skien
Porsgrunn
Vänern
Dalbosjön
Dalsland
Bohuslän
Västergötland
Kroppefjäll
Kynnefjäll
Frederikshavn
København
Kiel
Hirtshals
0
10
20
30
40
50 km

Åland (Suomi)
Åland Islands (Finland)
Mariehamn
Jomala
Hammarland
Eckerö
Godby
Saltvik
Sund
Geta
Vårdö
Lumparland
Lemland
Föglö
Kökar
Kumlinge
Seglinge
Sottunga
Enklinge
Delet
Teili
Ålands hav
Kapellskär
Grisslehamn
Turku Helsinki
Bottenhavet
Selkämeri
Öregrundsgrepen
Gävlebukten
Enhammarsfjärden
Gävle
Söderhamn
Sandviken
Falun
Borlänge
Uppsala
Sala
Avesta
Hedemora
Fagersta
Ludvika
Smedjebacken
Säter
Hofors
Bollnäs
Edsbyn
Mora
Orsa
Rättvik
Leksand
Tierp
Östhammar
Öregrund
Norrtälje
Hallstavik
Östervåla
Heby
Söderfors
Skutskär
Ljusne
Gästrikland
Hälsingskogen
Siljan
Dalälven
SVERIGE
SWEDEN
Bottenhavet
0 10 20 30 40 50 km

Västmanland
Närke
Östergötland
Stockholm
Västerås
Eskilstuna
Örebro
Norrköping
Linköping
Nyköping
Södertälje
Motala
Mjölby
Vadstena
Tranås
Gränna
Ödeshög
Karlsborg
Karlskoga
Degerfors
Kumla
Hallsberg
Askersund
Laxå
Lindesberg
Nora
Köping
Arboga
Kungsör
Hallstahammar
Enköping
Strängnäs
Katrineholm
Flen
Finspång
Söderköping
Valdemarsvik
Åtvidaberg
Oxelösund
Trosa
Nynäshamn
Huddinge
Västerhaninge
Vendelsö
Saltsjöbaden
Gustavsberg
Vaxholm
Åkersberga
Täby
Sollentuna
Upplands-Väsby
Märsta
Sigtuna
Bålsta
Knivsta
Mariefred
Gripsholm
Åkers Styckebruk
Gnesta
Järna
Nykvarn
Malmköping
Vingåker
Hjälmaren
Mälaren
Vättern
Roxen
Bråviken
Hålaveden
Tivedens
Kilsbergen
Garphyttan
Gotland
(Sverige)
(Sweden)
Visby
Fårö
Fårösund
Slite
Ljugarn
Hemse
Klintehamn
Burgsvik
Roma
Stånga
Mariehamn
Långnäs
Turku
Helsinki
Tallinn
Riga
Ventspils
Gdansk
Visby
Nynäshamn
Oskarshamn
Norrköpings
Bukten
Krabbfjärden
C
D
E
1
2
3
4
5
6

Skagerrak
Kattegat
Kristiansand
Søgne
Vennesla
Lillesand
Hirtshals
Larvik
Langesund
Kristiansand
Bergen
Stavanger
Tórshavn
Seyðisfjörður
Oslo
Kiel
Skagen
Grenen
Tannis Bugt
Ålbæk Bugt
Frederikshavn
Sæby
Hjørring
Vendsyssel
Brønderslev
Løkken
Jammerbugten
Nørresundby
Aalborg
Limfjorden
Hals
Aalborg Bugt
Himmerland
Hobro
Randers
Mariager Fjord
Randers Fjord
Viborg
Skive
Thisted
Thy
Mors
Nykøbing Mors
Struer
Lemvig
Hanstholm
Vigsø Bugt
Nissum Bredning
Læsø
Læsø Rende
Anholt
Göteborg
Gothenburg
Mölndal
Kungsbacka
Kungälv
Stenungsund
Orust
Tjörn
Alingsås
Lilla Edet
Varberg
Falkenberg
Kungsbackafjord
Hakefjord
0 10 20 30 40 50 km
8° 9° 10° 11° 12°
57° 58°
A B C
1 2 3 4 5
33 35 40 5

DANMARK
Jylland
Sjælland
Fyn
Holstebro
Herning
Silkeborg
Århus
Djursland
Grenaa
Ebeltoft
Skanderborg
Horsens
Vejle
Fredericia
Kolding
Esbjerg
Varde
Ribe
Billund
Haderslev
Aabenraa
Sønderborg
Flensburg
Tønder
Odense
Nyborg
Svendborg
Fåborg
Korsør
Slagelse
Kalundborg
Holbæk
Roskilde
Næstved
Vordingborg
Nakskov
Nykøbing
Lolland
Falster
Langeland
Ærø
Als
Samsø
Sylt
Föhr
Amrum
Rømø
Fanø
Store Bælt
Lille Bælt
Kieler Bucht
Nordfriesische Inseln

S V E R I G E
S W E D E N
Västergötland
Götaland
Småland
Halland
Blekinge
Göteborg
Gothenburg
Borås
Jönköping
Halmstad
Växjö
Kalmar
Öland
Mölndal
Kungsbacka
Kungälv
Alingsås
Lerum
Falköping
Tidaholm
Ulricehamn
Mullsjö
Huskvarna
Gränna
Tranås
Eksjö
Nässjö
Vetlanda
Värnamo
Gislaved
Ljungby
Alvesta
Varberg
Falkenberg
Laholm
Båstad
Markaryd
Älmhult
Lessebo
Emmaboda
Nybro
Hultsfred
Vimmerby
Västervik
Oskarshamn
Mönsterås
Högsby
Kisa
Åtvidaberg
Ödeshög
Mjölby
Hjo
Vättern
Hökensås
Hålaveden
Visingsö
Store Mosse
Bolmen
Åsnen
Kungsbackafjord
Laholmsbukten
Grenaa
57°
58°
A
B
C
35
37
38
41
63
111
134
142
204
210
230

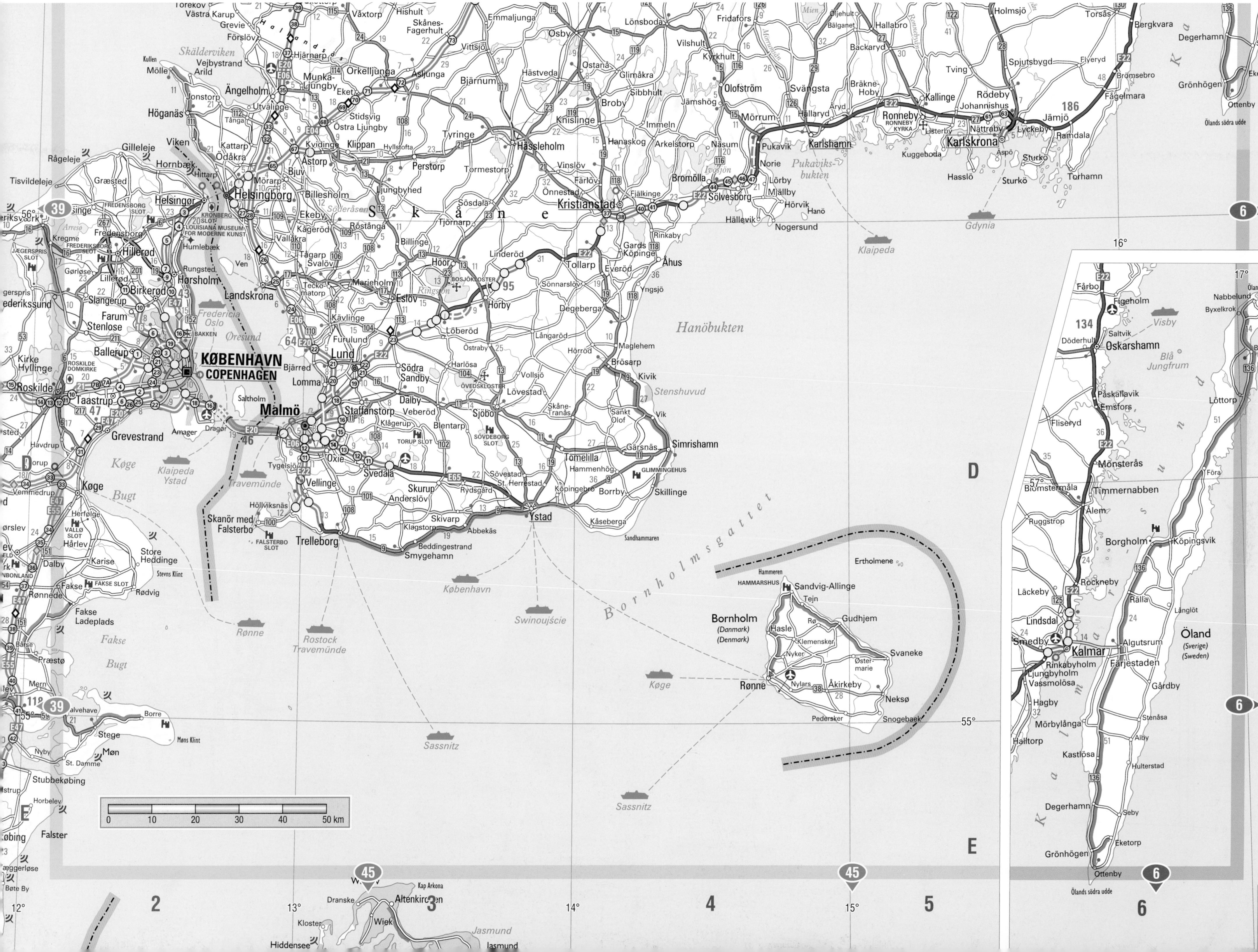

Skåne
København
Copenhagen
Malmö
Helsingborg
Helsingør
Lund
Landskrona
Trelleborg
Ystad
Kristianstad
Karlskrona
Karlshamn
Ronneby
Sölvesborg
Simrishamn
Hässleholm
Ängelholm
Höganäs
Eslöv
Hörby
Sjöbo
Tomelilla
Åhus
Hanöbukten
Bornholm
(Danmark)
(Denmark)
Rønne
Nexø
Svaneke
Gudhjem
Åkirkeby
Hasle
Sandvig-Allinge
Ertholmene
Bornholmsgattet
Öland
(Sverige)
(Sweden)
Kalmar
Färjestaden
Borgholm
Oskarshamn
Mönsterås
Kalmarsund
Køge
Køge Bugt
Roskilde
Hillerød
Falster
Møn
Stege
Fakse
Fakse Bugt
Öresund
Skälderviken
Pukaviksbukten
Gdynia
Klaipeda
Swinoujście
Sassnitz
Rostock
Travemünde
Rønne
Visby
Altenkirchen
Jasmund
Hiddensee
0 10 20 30 40 50 km
56°
55°
57°
12°
13°
14°
15°
16°
17°
B
C
D
E
2
3
4
5
6
7

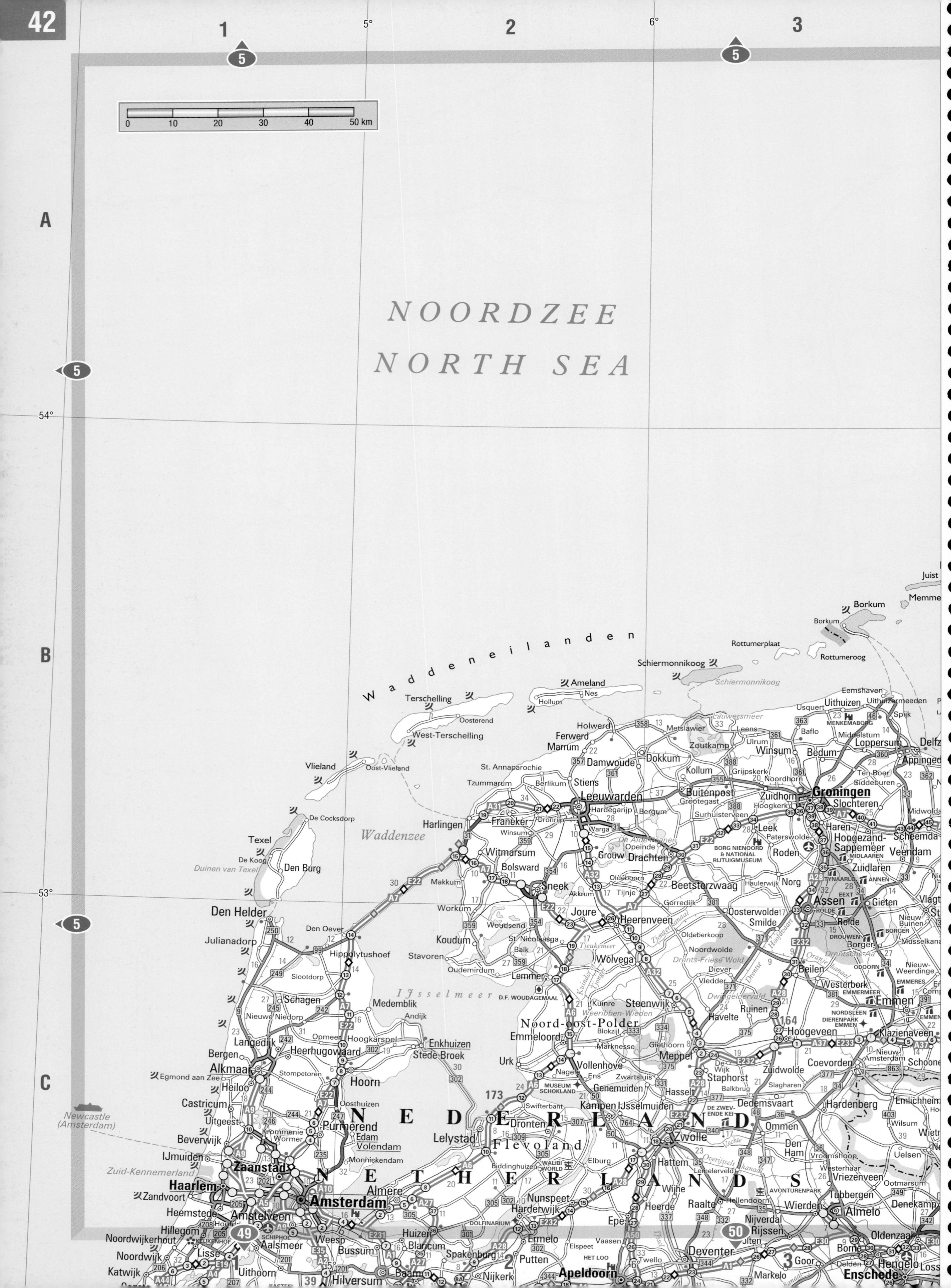

1
2
3
5°
6°
A
B
C
5
0 10 20 30 40 50 km
NOORDZEE
NORTH SEA
54°
53°
Waddeneilanden
Waddenzee
IJsselmeer
NEDERLAND
NETHERLANDS
Flevoland
Noord-oost-Polder
Juist
Memmert
Borkum
Rottumerplaat
Rottumeroog
Schiermonnikoog
Ameland
Nes
Hollum
Terschelling
Oosterend
West-Terschelling
Vlieland
Oost-Vlieland
Texel
De Cocksdorp
De Koog
Den Burg
Duinen van Texel
Den Helder
Julianadorp
Den Oever
Hippolytushoef
Schagen
Medemblik
Andijk
Enkhuizen
Stede Broek
Hoorn
Heerhugowaard
Langedijk
Bergen
Alkmaar
Egmond aan Zee
Heiloo
Castricum
Uitgeest
Beverwijk
IJmuiden
Zaanstad
Purmerend
Edam
Volendam
Monnickendam
Haarlem
Zandvoort
Heemstede
Amsterdam
Amstelveen
Hillegom
Noordwijkerhout
Noordwijk
Katwijk
Lisse
Aalsmeer
Uithoorn
Weesp
Bussum
Hilversum
Huizen
Blaricum
Almere
Lelystad
Dronten
Swifterbant
Urk
Emmeloord
Kampen
IJsselmuiden
Zwolle
Hattem
Heerde
Epe
Nunspeet
Harderwijk
Ermelo
Putten
Nijkerk
Spakenburg
Apeldoorn
Deventer
Raalte
Nijverdal
Rijssen
Wierden
Almelo
Hengelo
Enschede
Oldenzaal
Borne
Goor
Markelo
Ommen
Dedemsvaart
Hardenberg
Coevorden
Hoogeveen
Meppel
Staphorst
Steenwijk
Wolvega
Heerenveen
Joure
Sneek
Bolsward
Harlingen
Franeker
Leeuwarden
Dokkum
Drachten
Groningen
Assen
Emmen
Veendam
Winschoten
Hoogezand-Sappemeer
Delfzijl
Appingedam
Uithuizen
Eemshaven
Lauwersmeer
Newcastle (Amsterdam)
Zuid-Kennemerland
Drents-Friese Wold

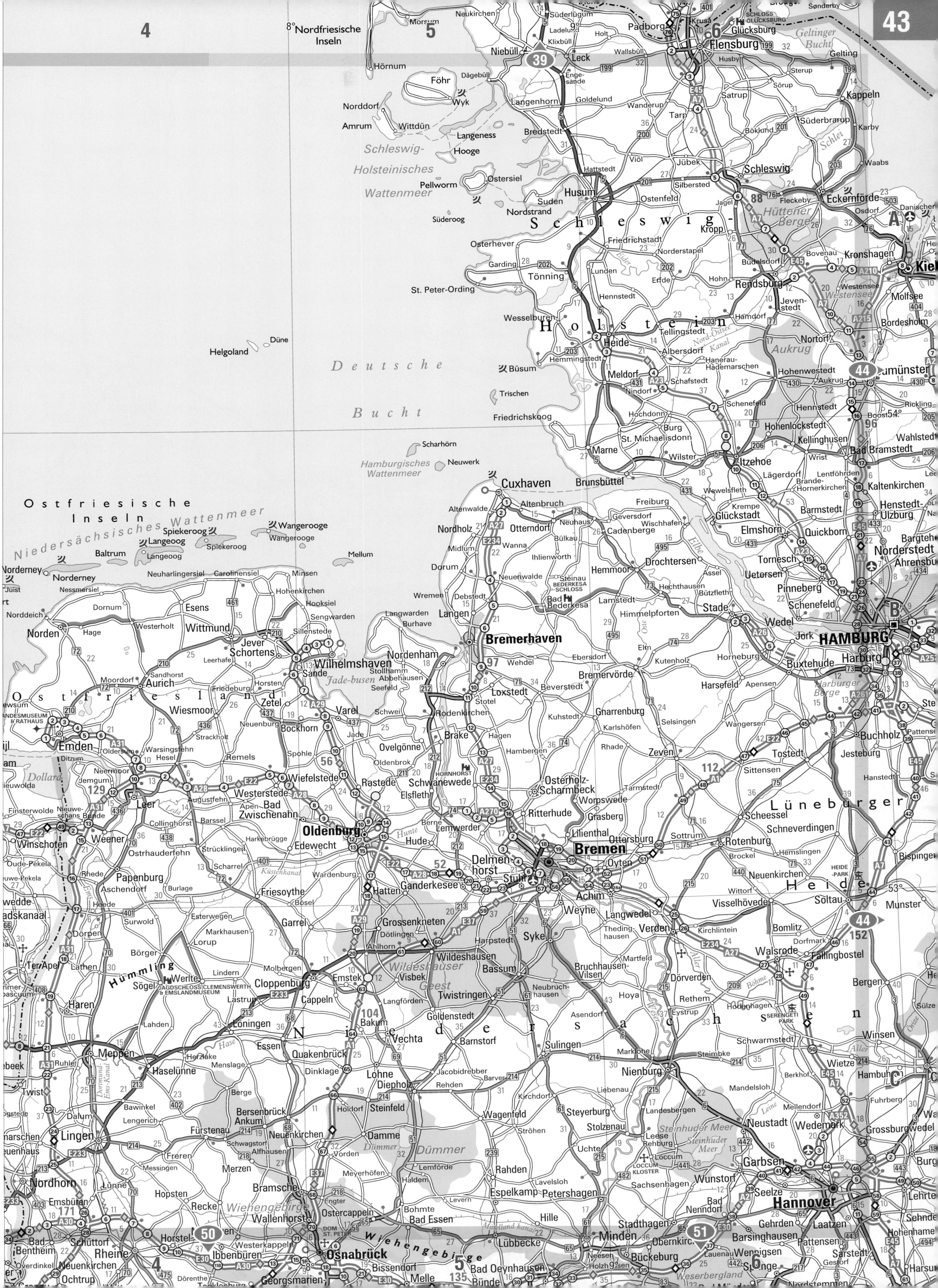

4
5
6
Nordfriesische Inseln
Föhr
Amrum
Wyk
Langeness
Hooge
Pellworm
Süderoog
Schleswig-Holsteinisches Wattenmeer
Niebüll
Leck
Flensburg
Glücksburg
Padborg
Geltinger Bucht
Kappeln
Schleswig
Husum
Eckernförde
Kiel
Kronshagen
Rendsburg
Tönning
St. Peter-Ording
Heide
Meldorf
Büsum
Trischen
Friedrichskoog
Helgoland
Düne
Deutsche Bucht
Schleswig-Holstein
Hohenwestedt
Neumünster
Itzehoe
Marne
Brunsbüttel
Wilster
Glückstadt
Elmshorn
Bad Bramstedt
Kaltenkirchen
Quickborn
Norderstedt
Pinneberg
Wedel
Stade
Hamburg
Harburg
Buxtehude
Scharhörn
Neuwerk
Hamburgisches Wattenmeer
Cuxhaven
Otterndorf
Ostfriesische Inseln
Niedersächsisches Wattenmeer
Wangerooge
Spiekeroog
Langeoog
Baltrum
Norderney
Juist
Mellum
Norden
Esens
Wittmund
Jever
Schortens
Wilhelmshaven
Jade-busen
Aurich
Ostfriesland
Emden
Leer
Papenburg
Varel
Nordenham
Bremerhaven
Brake
Oldenburg
Bad Zwischenahn
Westerstede
Delmenhorst
Bremen
Osterholz-Scharmbeck
Bremervörde
Zeven
Rotenburg
Achim
Verden
Soltau
Lüneburger Heide
Buchholz
Walsrode
Cloppenburg
Vechta
Meppen
Lingen
Nordhorn
Diepholz
Nienburg
Sulingen
Bassum
Syke
Wildeshausen
Niedersachsen
Hümmling
Dümmer
Steinhuder Meer
Wunstorf
Garbsen
Hannover
Minden
Bückeburg
Osnabrück
Rheine
Ibbenbüren
Bad Oeynhausen
Lübbecke
Wiehengebirge
Quakenbrück
Haselünne
Bramsche
Bad Bentheim

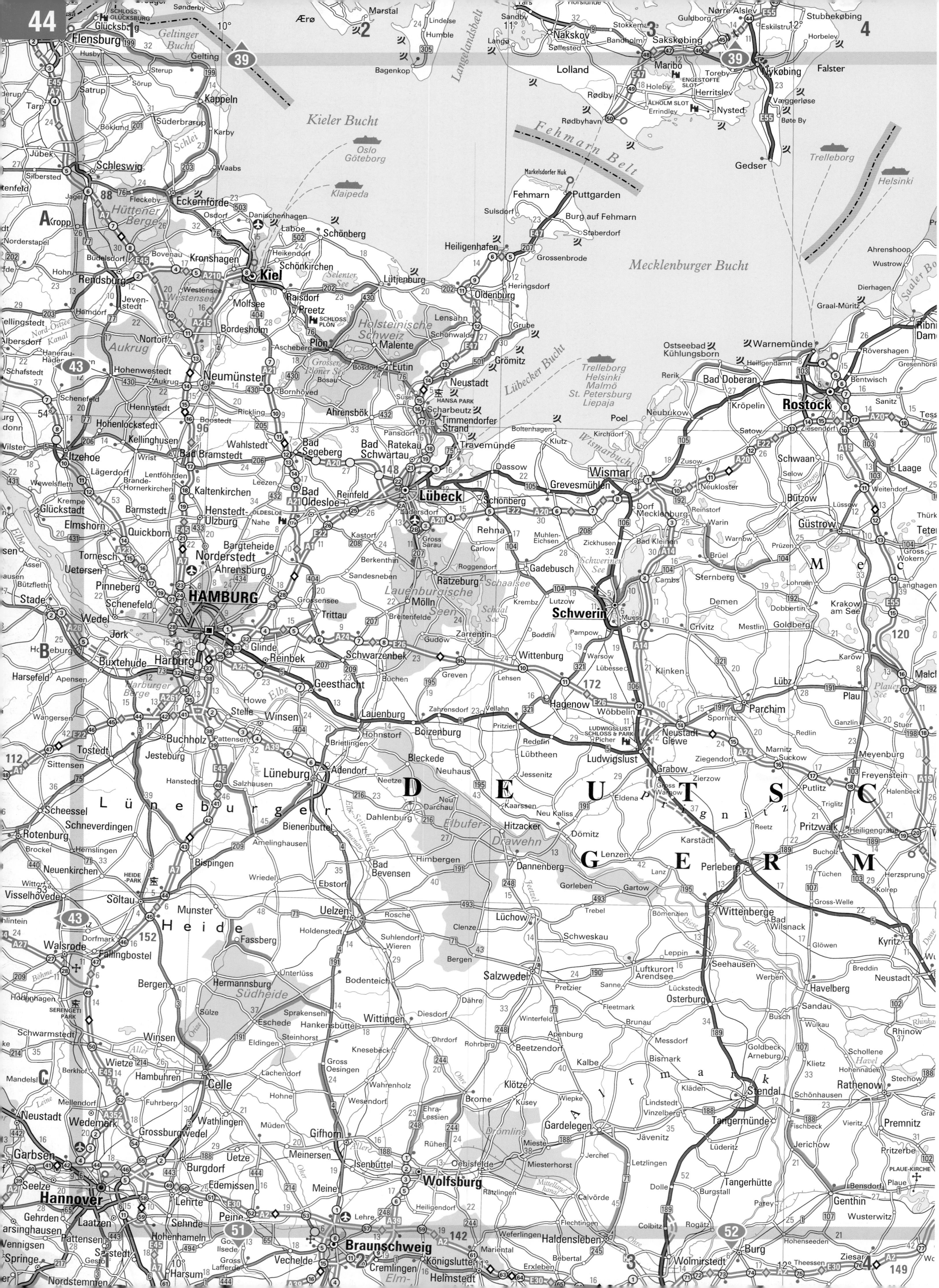
Flensburg
Glücksburg
Schloss Glücksburg
Geltinger Bucht
Kappeln
Schleswig
Schlei
Eckernförde
Hüttener Berge
Rendsburg
Kiel
Kieler Bucht
Oslo
Göteborg
Klaipeda
Ærø
Marstal
Langelandsbelt
Lindelse
Humble
Bagenkop
Nakskov
Lolland
Sakskøbing
Maribo
Rødby
Rødbyhavn
Nykøbing
Falster
Gedser
Stubbekøbing
Fehmarn Belt
Fehmarn
Puttgarden
Burg auf Fehmarn
Heiligenhafen
Oldenburg
Mecklenburger Bucht
Trelleborg
Helsinki
Lübecker Bucht
Trelleborg
Helsinki
Malmö
St. Petersburg
Liepaja
Preetz
Plön
Schloss Plön
Holsteinische Schweiz
Malente
Eutin
Neustadt
Hansa Park
Timmendorfer Strand
Travemünde
Neumünster
Aukrug
Itzehoe
Bad Segeberg
Bad Oldesloe
Lübeck
Wismar
Wismarbucht
Grevesmühlen
Ratzeburg
Schaalsee
Lauenburgische Seen
Mölln
Schwerin
Schweriner See
Rostock
Warnemünde
Kühlungsborn
Bad Doberan
Güstrow
Bützow
Hamburg
Elmshorn
Pinneberg
Wedel
Stade
Buxtehude
Harburg
Harburger Berge
Reinbek
Geesthacht
Lauenburg
Boizenburg
Hagenow
Ludwigslust
Schloss & Park Ludwigslust
Parchim
Lübz
Plau
Neustadt-Glewe
Grabow
Winsen
Buchholz
Lüneburg
Lüneburger Heide
Elbufer-Drawehn
Hitzacker
Dömitz
Dannenberg
Gorleben
Lenzen
Perleberg
Wittenberge
Prignitz
Pritzwalk
Meyenburg
Kyritz
Havelberg
Rotenburg
Soltau
Heide-Park
Munster
Uelzen
Bad Bevensen
Lüchow
Salzwedel
Walsrode
Fallingbostel
Bergen
Südheide
Serengeti Park
Celle
Gifhorn
Wittingen
Altmark
Gardelegen
Stendal
Tangermünde
Rathenow
Drömling
Mittellandkanal
Wolfsburg
Braunschweig
Königslutter
Helmstedt
Haldensleben
Wolmirstedt
Burg
Genthin
Hannover
Lehrte
Peine
Garbsen
Wedemark
Deutschland
Mecklenburg

4
5
6
7
13°
14°
15°
41
46
52
53
A
B
C
0 10 20 30 40 50 km
Trelleborg
Rønne
Klaipeda
Ystad
Wittow
Kap Arkona
Dranske
Altenkirchen
Kloster
Wiek
Hiddensee
Neuendorf
Trent
Rügen
Jasmund
Sagard
Sassnitz
Vorpommersche Boddenlandschaft
Darsser Ort
Zingst
Gingst
Bergen
Binz
Sellin
Hohendorf
Barth
Samtens
Putbus
Göhren
Bodstedt
Stralsund
Garz
Thiessow
Löbnitz
Veglast
Brandshagen
Zudar
Greifswalder Bodden
Richtenberg
Miltzow
Reinberg
Franzburg
Marlow
Grimmen
Greifswald
Lubmin
Peenemünde
Kröslin
Bad Sülze
Tribsees
Kemnitz
Zinnowitz
Koserow
Rakow
Poggendorf
Wolgast
Glewitz
Görmin
Usedom
Loitz
Züssow
Zemitz
Lassan
Bansin
Ahlbeck
Gnoien
Jarmen
Gützkow
Murchin
Świnoujście
Demmin
Tutow
Anklam
Dargun
Jördenstorf
Verchen
Kleines Haff
Stettiner Haff
Zalew Szczeciński
Neukalen
Albinshof
Kummerower See
Abbaue
Burow
Spantekow
Ducherow
Leopoldshagen
Mönkebude
Sarnow
Rathebur
Ueckermünde
Nowe Warpno
Malchin
Eggesin
Altentreptow
Ferdinandshof
Zidorf
Gielow
Reuterstadt Stavenhagen
Brunn
Friedland
Wilhelmsburg
Ahlbeck
Moltzow
Faulenrost
Rosenow
Kittendorf
Torgelow
Hintersee
Schönbeck
Rothemühl
Jatznick
Neubrandenburg
Cölpin
Strasburg
Rothenklempenow
Klein Plasten
Waren
Penzlin
Pasewalk
Löcknitz
Burg Stargard
Woldegk
Wolfshagen
Müritz
Hohenzieritz
Bredenfelde
Görtz
Grambow
Brüssow
Röbel
Möllenbeck
Fürstenwerder
Dedelow
Neustrelitz
Schönermark
Kleptow
Krackow
Vipperow
Feldberg
Prenzlau
Schmölln
Storkow
Penkun
Wesenberg
Triepkendorf
Hardenbeck
Boitzenburg
Wredenhagen
Mirow
Gramzow
Gartz
Hassleben
Lychen
Casekow
Schweinrich
Zechlin
Zechlinerhütte
Fürstenberg
Gerswalde
Wittstock
Schloss Rheinsberg
Stegelitz
Passow
Wallitz
Templin
Milmersdorf
Greiffenberg
Vierraden
Rheinsberg
Hammelspring
Schwedt
Gühlen Glienicke
Dierberg
Gransee
Friedrichswalde
Angermünde
Katerbow
Gross-Dölln
Zehdenick
Krewelin
Joachimsthal
Ziethen
Alt Ruppin
Lindow
Parstein
Neuruppin
Falkenthal
Gross Schönebeck
Herzberg
Löwenberg
Liebenwalde
Oderberg
Hohenwutzen
Wildberg
Wustrau-Altfriesack
Zerpenschleuse
Eberswalde
Nassenheide
Fehrbellin
Sommerfeld
Kremmen
Oranienburg
Biesenthal
Bad Freienwalde
Wandlitz
Heckelberg
Wriezen
Friesack
Königshorst
Velten
Bernau
Steinbeck
Börnicke
Tiefensee
Hohen Neuendorf
Hennigsdorf
Werneuchen
Prötzel
Seefeld
Strausberg
Möthlow
Berge
Nauen
Altlandsberg
Falkensee
Märkische Schweiz
BERLIN
Neuenhagen
Münchebeg
Seelow
Barnewitz
Marzahne
Wachow
Petershagen
Herzfelde
Ketzin
Rüdersdorf
Heinersdorf
Potsdam
Beerfelde
Wust
Gross Kreutz
Erkner
Steinhöfel
Brandenburg
Werder
Teltow
Fürstenwalde
Briesen
Frankfurt
Gross Beeren
Brandenburg (opens 2016)
Michendorf
Blankenfelde
Bad Saarow-Pieskow
Lehnin
Golzow
Klaistow
Ludwigsfelde
Königs Wusterhausen
Storkow
Müllrose
Mittenwalde
Beelitz
Zossen
Wendisch
Lindenberg
Finkenheerd
Brieskow
Ziltendorf
Kołobrzeg
Ustronie Morskie
Mrzeżyno
Dygowo
Niechorze
Rewal
Trzebiatów
Pobierowo
Gościno
Dziwnów
Cerkwica
Gorawino
Międzywodzie
Kamień Pomorski
Świerzno
Rymań
Wolinski
Kolczewo
Rzesznikowo
Międzyzdroje
Gryfice
Mechowo
Lubin
Wolin
Zabrowo
Gołczewo
Płoty
Resko
Rusinowo
Przybiernów
Żabowo
Starogard
Radowo Wielkie
Nowogard
Trzebież
Stepnica
Babigoszcz
Wierzbięcin
Łobez
Siedlice
Jenikow
Dobra
Police
Goleniów
Święta
Węgorzyno
Tanowo
Mosty
Dobra
Lubczyna
Maszewo
Ińsko
Szczecin
Przemocze
Łęczyca
Chociwel
Ciemnik
Stargard Szczeciński
Płonia
Kobylanka
Dobrzany
Kolbacz
Jezioro Miedwie
Suchań
Wapnica
Recz
Dolina Dolnej Odry
Gryfino
Linie
Dolice
Lubiatowo
Choszczno
Kunowo
Pyrzyce
Widuchowo
Banie
Mielęcin
Krzęcin
Pełczyce
Krajnik Dolny
Swobnica
Grzybno
Lipiany
Barlinek
Górzno
Chojna
Piasek
Trzcińsko Zdrój
Myślibórz
Ławy
Przyłęg
Strzelce Krajeńskie
Cedyński
Cedynia
Moryń
Siekierki
Rożańsko
Ściechów
Zwierzyn
Mieszkowice
Barnowko
Kłodawa
Santok
Dębno
Tarnów
Gorzów Wielkopolski
Lipki
Boleszkowice
Witnica
Bogdaniec
Altwein
Neutrebbin
Letschin
Murzynowo
Sarbinowo
Ujście Warty
Kostrzyn
Kietz
Krzeszyce
Skwierzyna
Neuhardenberg
Manschnow
Słońsk
Lubniewice
Górzyca
Ośno Lubuskie
Sulęcin
Międzyrzecz
Lebus
Lisów
Kowalów
Trzemeszno-Lubuskie
Maluszów
Łagowski
Słubice
Rzepin
Boryszyn
Łagów
Jordanowo
Boczów
Torzym
Mostki
Cybinka
Sądów
Debrznica
Toporów
Świebodzin
Węgrzynice

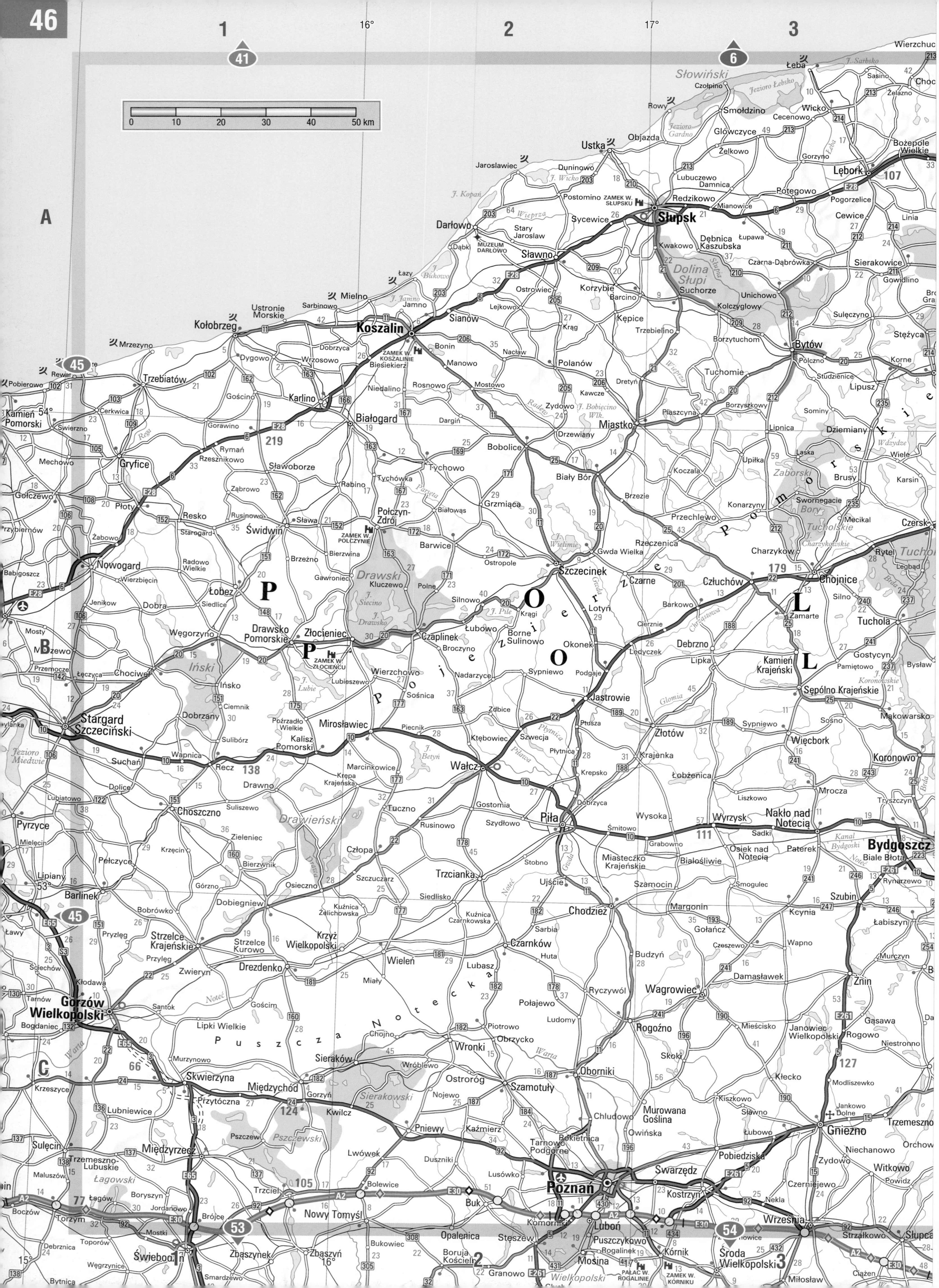

1
2
3
16°
17°
41
6
0 10 20 30 40 50 km
A
B
C
Słowiński
Łeba
J. Sarbsko
Wierzchucino
Czołpino
Jezioro Łebsko
Rowy
Smołdzino
Wicko
Sasino
Choczewo
Żelazno
Cecenowo
Jezioro Gardno
Główczyce
Ustka
Objazda
Żelkowo
Bożepole Wielkie
Gorzyno
Lębork
Jarosławiec
Duninowo
J. Wicko
Lubuczewo
Damnica
J. Kopań
Postomino
ZAMEK W. SŁUPSKU
Redzikowo
Mianowice
Potęgowo
Pogorzelice
Słupsk
Sycewice
Cewice
Linia
Darłowo
Wieprza
Stary Jarosław
MUZEUM DARŁOWO
Dąbki
Sławno
Dębnica Kaszubska
Łupawa
Kwakowo
Czarna-Dąbrówka
Sierakowice
Gowidlino
J. Bukowo
Łazy
Ostrowiec
Korzybie
Dolina Słupi
Suchorze
Unichowo
Kołczygłowy
Mielno
Sarbinowo
J. Jamno
Jamno
Barcino
Ustronie Morskie
Kołobrzeg
Koszalin
Sianów
Lejkowo
Kępice
Trzebielino
Sulęczyno
Stężyca
Kraśnik
Mrzezyno
ZAMEK W. KOSZALINIE
Bonin
Nacław
Borzytuchom
Bytów
Korne
Dobrzyca
Dygowo
Wrzosowo
Biesiekierz
Manowo
Polanów
Rewal
Trzebiatów
Tuchomie
Półczno
Studzienice
Pobierowo
Gościno
Karlino
Niedalino
Rosnowo
Mostowo
Kawcze
Dretyń
Lipusz
Kamień Pomorski
Cerkwica
Białogard
Dargiń
Radew
Zydowo
J. Bobięcino Wlk.
Miastko
Płaszczyna
Borzyszkowy
Sominy
Świerzno
Gorawino
Dzierżęcino
Drzewiany
Lipnica
Dziemiany
Mechowo
Gryfice
Rymań
Rzesznikowo
Bobolice
Tychowo
Laska
Wiele
J. Wdzydze
Sławoborze
Koczała
Upiłka
Zaborski
Brusy
Karsin
Gołczewo
Rabino
Tychówka
Biały Bór
Brzezie
Konarzyny
Swornegacie
Płoty
Resko
Rusinowo
Grzmiąca
Połczyn-Zdrój
Białowąs
Przechlewo
Bory Tucholskie
Mecikal
Przybiernów
Starogard
Świdwin
Sława
ZAMEK W. POŁCZYNIE
Barwice
Rzeczenica
Czersk
Żabowo
Radowo Wielkie
Brzeżno
Bierzwina
J. Wielimie
Gwda Wielka
Charzykowy
J. Charzykowskie
Rytel
Babigoszcz
Nowogard
Wierzbięcin
Gawroniec
Drawski
Kluczewo
Ostropole
Szczecinek
Czarne
Człuchów
Chojnice
Łęgbąd
Łobez
Polne
Silnowo
J. Pile
Kragi
Lotyń
Barkowo
Silno
J. Siecino
Jenikow
Dobra
Siedlice
J. Drawsko
Łubowo
Borne Sulinowo
Zamarte
Tuchola
Węgorzyno
Drawsko Pomorskie
Złocieniec
Czaplinek
Broczyno
Cierznie
Okonek
Debrzno
Gostycyn
Mosty
ZAMEK W. ZŁOCIEŃCU
Lędyczek
Kamień Krajeński
Pamiętowo
Bysław
Przemocze
Łęczyca
Chociwel
Iński
Wierzchowo
Lubieszewo
Nadarzyce
Sypniewo
Podgaje
Lipka
J. Koronowskie
Ińsko
J. Lubie
Sośnica
Jastrowie
Glomia
Sępólno Krajeńskie
Ciemnik
Zdbice
Dobrzany
Stargard Szczeciński
Pożrzadło Wielkie
Mirosławiec
Piecnik
Szwecja
Płytnica
Ptusza
Złotów
Sypniewo
Sośno
Mąkowarsko
Jezioro Miedwie
Sulibórz
Kalisz Pomorski
Kłębowiec
Więcbork
Suchań
Wapnica
J. Betyń
Piława
Krajenka
Koronowo
Recz
Marcinkowice
Wałcz
Krępsko
Łobżenica
Dolice
Drawno
Krępa Krajeńska
Liszkowo
Mrocza
Tryszczyn
Lubiatowo
Choszczno
Suliszewo
Tuczno
Gostomia
Dobrzyca
Wysoka
Wyrzysk
Nakło nad Notecią
Drawieński
Rusinowo
Szydłowo
Piła
Śmiłowo
Grabowno
Sadki
Osiek nad Notecią
Paterek
Bydgoszcz
Białe Błota
Kanał Bydgoski
Pyrzyce
Zieleniec
Krzęcin
Mielęcin
Bierzwnik
Człopa
Drawa
Stobno
Miasteczko Krajeńskie
Białośliwie
Rynarzewo
Pełczyce
Szczuczarz
Trzcianka
Ujście
Lipiany
Barlinek
Górzno
Osieczno
Siedlisko
Noteć
Szamocin
Smogulec
Szubin
Dobiegniew
Kuźnica Żelichowska
Kuźnica Czarnkowska
Chodzież
Margonin
Kcynia
Bobrówko
Gołańcz
Łabiszyn
Ławy
Przyłęg
Strzelce Krajeńskie
Strzelce Kurowo
Krzyż Wielkopolski
Sarbia
Czeszewo
Wapno
Ściechów
Zwierzyn
Drezdenko
Wieleń
Czarnków
Huta
Budzyń
Murczyn
Kłodawa
Miały
Lubasz
Damasławek
Żnin
Tarnów
Gorzów Wielkopolski
Santok
Gościm
Połajewo
Ryczywół
Wągrowiec
Bogdaniec
Lipki Wielkie
Ludomy
Mieścisko
Janowiec Wielkopolski
Gąsawa
Rogowo
Puszcza Notecka
Chojno
Piotrowo
Obrzycko
Rogoźno
Niestronno
Murzynowo
Sieraków
Wronki
Warta
Skoki
Wróblewo
Kłecko
Skwierzyna
Międzychód
Ostroróg
Szamotuły
Oborniki
Modliszewko
Krzeszyce
Przytoczna
Gorzyń
Sierakowski
Nojewo
Kiszkowo
Sławno
Jankowo Dolne
Trzemeszno
Lubniewice
Kwilcz
Chludowo
Murowana Goślina
Pniewy
Kaźmierz
Owińska
Łubowo
Gniezno
Sulęcin
Pszczew
Pszczewski
Rokietnica
Tarnowo Podgórne
Orchowo
Trzemeszno-Lubuskie
Międzyrzecz
Lwówek
Duszniki
Pobiedziska
Niechanowo
Maluszów
Łagowski
Lusówko
Swarzędz
Zydowo
Witkowo
Powidz
Łagów
Trzciel
Bolewice
Poznań
Kostrzyn
Czerniejewo
Boryszyn
Jordanowo
Buk
Nekla
Boczów
Torzym
Brójce
Nowy Tomyśl
Komorniki
Luboń
Września
Mostki
Opalenica
Stęszew
Puszczykowo
Rogalinek
Środa Wielkopolski
Strzałkowo
Słupca
Toporów
Debrznica
Świebodzin
Zbąszynek
Zbąszyń
Bukowiec
Boruja Kościelna
Kórnik
Mosina
Granowo
Ciążeń
Miłosław
Węgrzynice
Smardzewo
Bytnica
Wielkopolski
PAŁAC W. ROGALINIE
ZAMEK W. KÓRNIKU
Pojezierze Pomorskie
Pojezierze Drawskie
Pomorskie
Pojezierze Krajeńskie

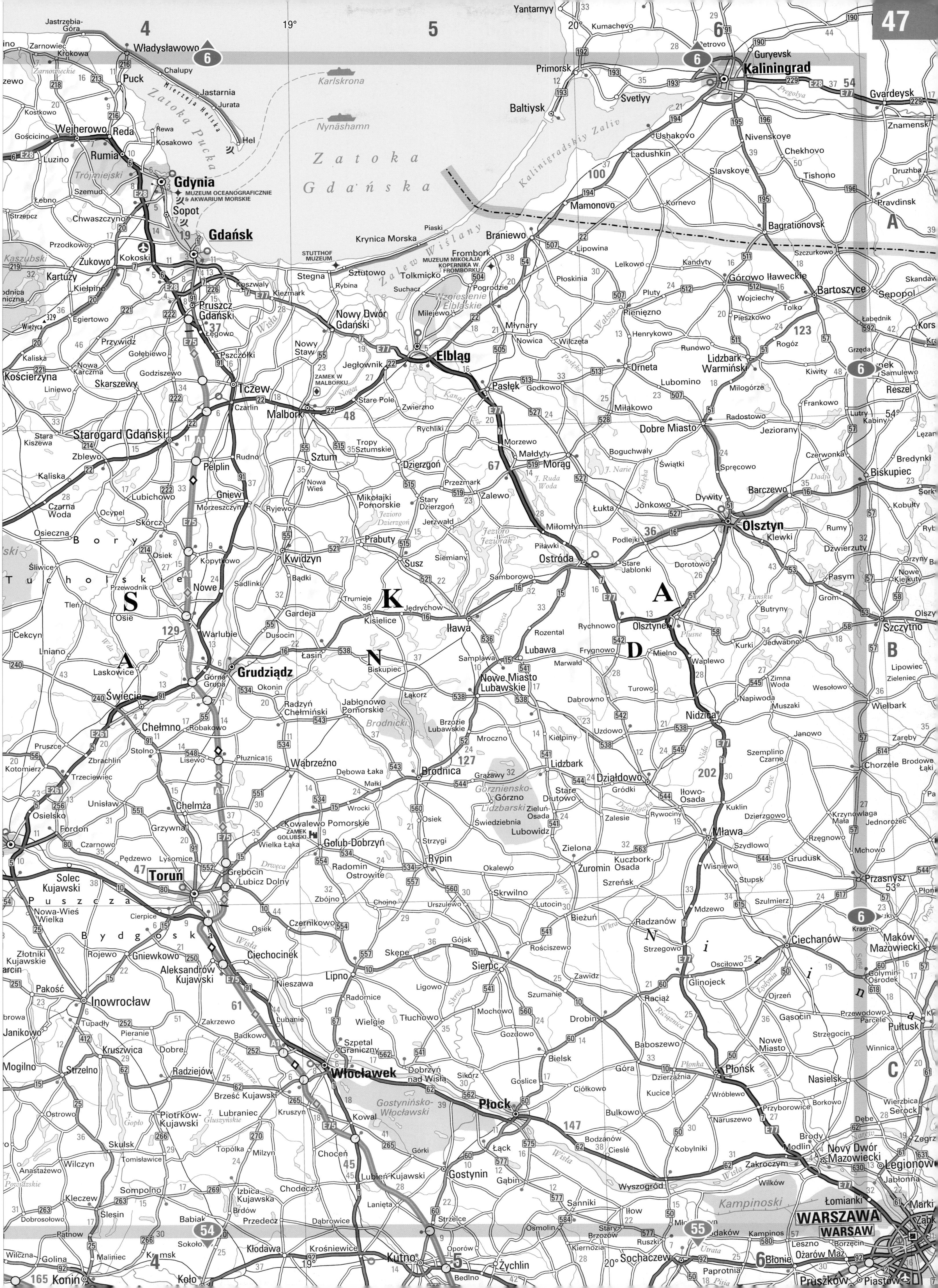

4
5
6
19°
20°
54°
53°
A
B
C
Zatoka Gdańska
Zatoka Pucka
Mierzeja Helska
Zalew Wiślany
Kaliningradskiy Zaliv
Karlskrona
Nynäshamn
Jastrzębia-Góra
Władysławowo
Żarnowiec
Krokowa
Puck
Chałupy
Jastarnia
Jurata
Hel
Wejherowo
Reda
Rewa
Kosakowo
Rumia
Luzino
Gościcino
Kostkowo
Gdynia
MUZEUM OCEANOGRAFICZNE & AKWARIUM MORSKIE
Sopot
Gdańsk
Trójmiejski
Szemud
Łebno
Chwaszczyno
Strzepcz
Przodkowo
Żukowo
Kokoszki
Kaszubski
Kartuzy
Kiełpino
Egiertowo
Wieżyca
Przywidz
Kaliska
Kościerzyna
Nowa Karczma
Liniewo
Skarszewy
Gołębiewo
Godziszewo
Pruszcz Gdański
Łęgowo
Pszczółki
Koszwały
Kiezmark
Stegna
Sztutowo
Rybina
STUTTHOF MUZEUM
Krynica Morska
Piaski
Nowy Dwór Gdański
Nowy Staw
Tczew
Czarlin
Malbork
ZAMEK W MALBORKU
Nogat
Stare Pole
Jegłownik
Elbląg
Milejewo
Tolkmicko
Suchacz
Frombork
MUZEUM MIKOŁAJA KOPERNIKA W FROMBORKU
Pogrodzie
Wzniesienie Elbląskie
Braniewo
Starogard Gdański
Stara Kiszewa
Zblewo
Kaliska
Pelplin
Rudno
Gniew
Morzeszczyn
Lubichowo
Czarna Woda
Ocypel
Skórcz
Osieczna
Bory Tucholskie
Osiek
Kopytkowo
Nowe
Przewodnik
Osie
Tleń
Śliwice
Warlubie
Cekcyn
Lniano
Laskowice
Świecie
Grudziądz
Górna Grupa
Chełmno
Robakowo
Pruszcz
Zbrachlin
Kotomierz
Trzeciewiec
Stolno
Lisewo
Płużnica
Unisław
Chełmża
Osielsko
Fordon
Czarnowo
Grzywna
Pędzewo
Łysomice
Toruń
Solec Kujawski
Puszcza Bydgoska
Nowa-Wieś Wielka
Cierpice
Złotniki Kujawskie
Rojewo
Gniewkowo
Aleksandrów Kujawski
Ciechocinek
Inowrocław
Pakość
Janikowo
Tupadły
Pieranie
Kruszwica
Mogilno
Strzelno
Radziejów
Brześć Kujawski
Piotrków Kujawski
Gopło
Lubraniec
Jezioro Głuszyńskie
Ostrowo
Skulsk
Wilczyn
Anastazewo
Powidzkie
Sompolno
Tomisławice
Topólka
Izbica Kujawska
Bródw
Kleczew
Ślesin
Dobrosołowo
Golina
Konin
Patnow
Maliniec
Wilczna
Babiak
Przedecz
Chodecz
Kłodawa
Sokoło
Krośniewice
Kutno
Kramsk
Koło
Sztum
Tropy Sztumskie
Nowa Wieś
Dzierzgoń
Mikołajki Pomorskie
Jezioro Dzierzgoń
Ryjewo
Stary Dzierzgoń
Przezmark
Zalewo
Jerzwałd
Kwidzyn
Prabuty
Susz
Siemiany
Sadlinki
Bądki
Gardeja
Trumieje
Kisielice
Jędrychowo
Iława
Dusocin
Łasin
Biskupiec
Okonin
Radzyń Chełmiński
Jabłonowo Pomorskie
Brodnicki
Łąkorz
Wąbrzeźno
Dębowa Łąka
Małki
Brodnica
Grążawy
Brzozie Lubawskie
Mroczno
Wrocki
Kowalewo Pomorskie
ZAMEK GOLUBSKI
Wielka Łąka
Golub-Dobrzyń
Radomin
Ostrowite
Zbójno
Rypin
Osiek
Strzygi
Okalewo
Chojno
Urszulewo
Skrwilno
Czernikowo
Osiek
Nieszawa
Lipno
Skępe
Gójsk
Sierpc
Radomice
Wielgie
Tłuchowo
Ligowo
Mochowo
Szpetal Graniczny
Włocławek
Dobrzyń nad Wisłą
Sikórz
Lubanie
Badkowo
Zakrzewo
Dobre
Gostynińsko-Włocławski
Kruszyn
Kowal
Choceń
Lubień Kujawski
Łanięta
Dąbrowice
Gostynin
Łąck
Gąbin
Strzelce
Oporów
Żychlin
Bedlno
Płock
Goślice
Bielsk
Gozdowo
Drobin
Zawidz
Szumanie
Raciąż
Glinojeck
Baboszewo
Dzierzążnia
Kucice
Płońsk
Wróblewo
Naruszewo
Bulkowo
Bodzanów
Ciesle
Kobylniki
Wyszogród
Sanniki
Iłow
Stary Brzozów
Ruszki
Młodzieszyn
Kiernozia
Sochaczew
Paprotnia
Kampinoski
Kampinos
Leszno
Błonie
Ożarów Maz.
Pruszków
Piastów
Zakroczym
Modlin
Nowy Dwór Mazowiecki
Legionowo
Jabłonna
Łomianki
Marki
WARSZAWA
WARSAW
Wilków
Brody
Dębe
Serock
Wierzbica
Borkowo
Przyborowice
Nasielsk
Winnica
Strzegocin
Pułtusk
Przewodowo Parcele
Gąsocin
Nowe Miasto
Ojrzeń
Sońsk
Gołymin-Ośrodek
Maków Mazowiecki
Krasne
Ciechanów
Opinogóra
Oscisłowo
Strzegowo
Radzanów
Mdzewo
Szulmierz
Stupsk
Przasnysz
Grudusk
Szydłowo
Rzęgnowo
Mchowo
Wiśniewo
Mława
Iłowo-Osada
Kuklin
Dzierzgowo
Krzynowłoga Mała
Jednorożec
Chorzele
Brodowe Łąki
Szemplino Czarne
Janowo
Zaręby
Wielbark
Muszaki
Napiwoda
Nidzica
Zimna Woda
Wesołowo
Lipowiec
Zieleniec
Szczytno
Jedwabno
Kurki
Butryny
Grom
Pasym
Dźwierzuty
Rumy
Klewki
Olsztyn
Dywity
Barczewo
Biskupiec
Kobułty
Sorkwity
Purda
Stawiguda
Olsztynek
Mielno
Waplewo
Pluśne
Turowo
Uzdowo
Działdowo
Gródki
Rywociny
Kielpiny
Lidzbark
Górzno
Górznieńsko-Lidzbarski
Stare Dłutowo
Zieluń-Osada
Świedziebnia
Lubowidz
Zalesie
Zielona
Żuromin
Kuczbork-Osada
Szreńsk
Lutocin
Bieżuń
Rościszewo
Nowe Miasto Lubawskie
Lubawa
Samplawa
Frygnowo
Marwałd
Rychnowo
Rozental
Dąbrówno
Ostróda
Piławki
Samborowo
Stare Jabłonki
Dorotowo
Podlejki
Gietrzwałd
Miłomłyn
Łukta
Jonkowo
Morąg
Małdyty
Morzewo
Boguchwały
Świątki
Jezioro Jeziorak
Jezioro Narie
Ruda Woda
Pasłęk
Godkowo
Rychliki
Zwierzno
Kanał Elbląski
Młynary
Nowica
Wilczęta
Płoskinia
Orneta
Lubomino
Miłakowo
Dobre Miasto
Radostowo
Jeziorany
Sprecowo
Lidzbark Warmiński
Kiwity
Milogórze
Frankowo
Reszel
Samulewo
Kabiny
Lutry
Łężany
Czerwonka
Bredynki
Runowo
Henrykowo
Pieniężno
Pluty
Wojciechy
Pieszkowo
Rogóż
Tolko
Bartoszyce
Sępopol
Łabędnik
Skandawa
Korsze
Grzęda
Kandyty
Górowo Iławeckie
Lelkowo
Lipowina
Szczurkowo
Mamonovo
Kornevo
Bagrationovsk
Pravdinsk
Druzhba
Tishono
Chekhovo
Nivenskoye
Slavskoye
Ladushkin
Ushakovo
Baltiysk
Primorsk
Svetlyy
Kaliningrad
Pregolya
Guryevsk
Petrovo
Kumachevo
Yantarnyy
Gvardeysk
Znamensk

Lowestoft
Thetford
Cambridge
Newmarket
Bury St Edmunds
Ipswich
Felixstowe
Harwich
Colchester
Chelmsford
Clacton-on-Sea
Southend-on-Sea
LONDON
Gravesend
Rochester
Gillingham
Chatham
Maidstone
Canterbury
Margate
Broadstairs
Ramsgate
Dover
Folkestone
Ashford
Hastings
Eastbourne
Lewes
Esbjerg
Hoek van Holland
Strait of Dover
Dieppe
Newhaven
Hull
Calais
Dunkerque
Oostende
Boulogne-sur-Mer
St. Omer
Le Touquet-Paris-Plage
Montreuil
Béthune
Lens
Arras
Abbeville
Amiens
Baie de la Somme
Caps et Marais d'Opale
North Downs
The Weald
Picardie
0 10 20 30 miles
0 10 20 30 40 50 km

4
5
6
42
49
Haarlem
Amsterdam
Zaanstad
Almere
Zandvoort
Amstelveen
Hilversum
Amersfoort
Apeldoorn
Leiden
'S-Gravenhage
The Hague
Zoetermeer
Gouda
Utrecht
Delft
Rotterdam
Schiedam
Dordrecht
Nieuwegein
Arnhem
Nijmegen
Ede
Hull
Harwich
Hoek van Holland
Spijkenisse
Gorinchem
Oss
's-Hertogenbosch
Breda
Tilburg
Eindhoven
Helmond
Roosendaal
Bergen op Zoom
Middelburg
Vlissingen
Goes
Zierikzee
Terneuzen
Antwerpen
Antwerp
Brugge
Gent
Ghent
Sint Niklaas
Mechelen
Leuven
Hasselt
Genk
Maastricht
Liège
Bruxelles
Brussels
Aalst
Kortrijk
Mouscron
Roubaix
Tournai
Mons
La Louvière
Charleroi
Namur
Valenciennes
Douai
Cambrai
Maubeuge
St. Quentin
Dinant
Huy
Seraing
Bastogne
Roermond
Venray
Sittard
Weert
Turnhout
Herentals
Wavre
Waterloo
Nivelles
BELGIQUE
BELGIUM
Zeeuws Vlaanderen
Oosterschelde
Westerschelde
Ardennes
Avesnois
Thiérache
Plaines de l'Escaut
50
59

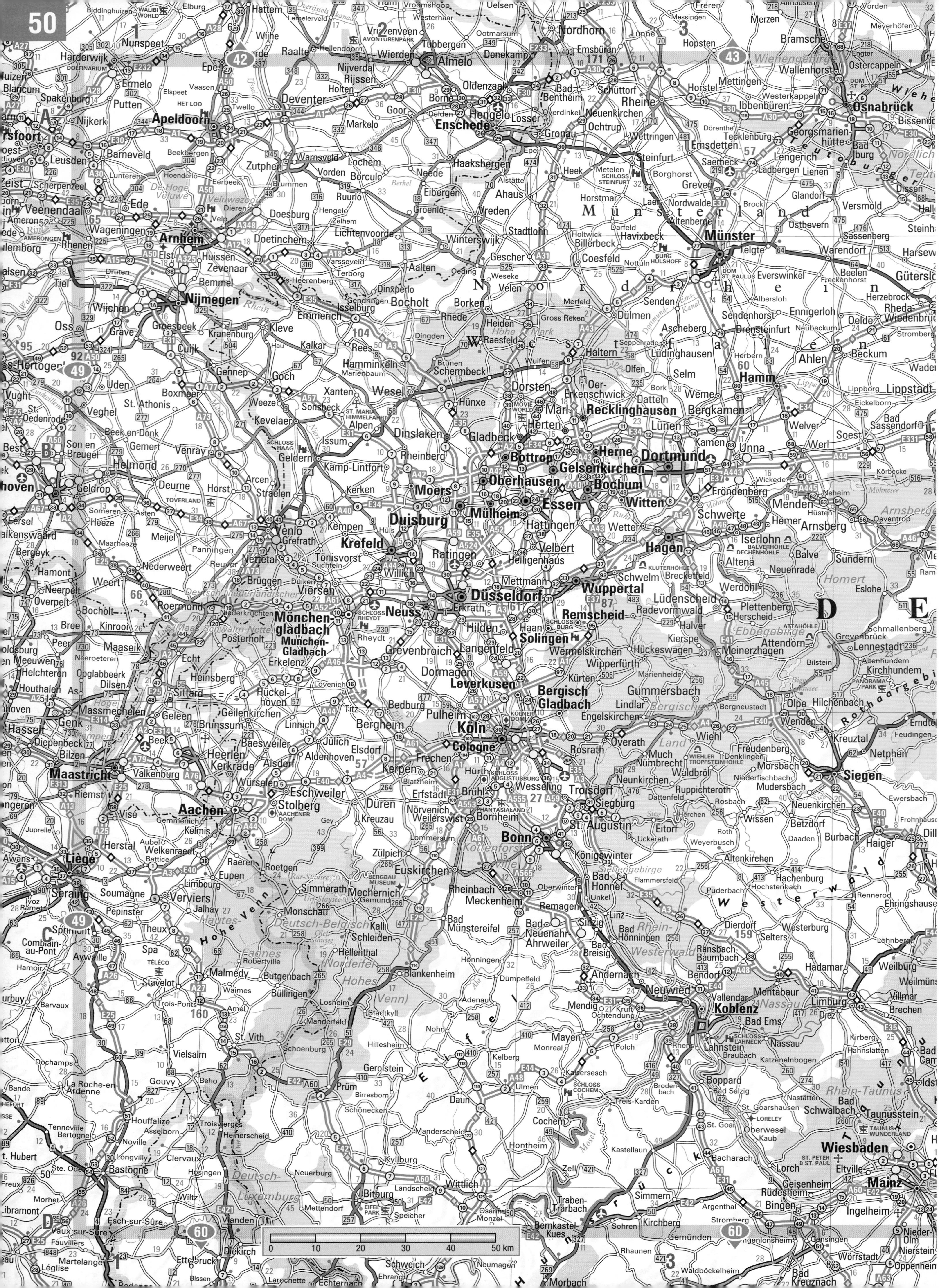

Apeldoorn
Arnhem
Nijmegen
Almelo
Hengelo
Enschede
Nordhorn
Rheine
Osnabrück
Münster
Münsterland
Nordrhein-Westfalen
Recklinghausen
Dortmund
Gelsenkirchen
Bochum
Herne
Bottrop
Oberhausen
Essen
Mülheim
Duisburg
Moers
Krefeld
Venlo
Düsseldorf
Wuppertal
Remscheid
Solingen
Hagen
Neuss
Mönchengladbach
Leverkusen
Bergisch Gladbach
Köln
Cologne
Aachen
Maastricht
Liège
Bonn
Siegen
Koblenz
Wiesbaden
Mainz
Hamm
Eifel
Westerwald
Hunsrück
Rothaargebirge
Teutoburger Wald
0 10 20 30 40 50 km

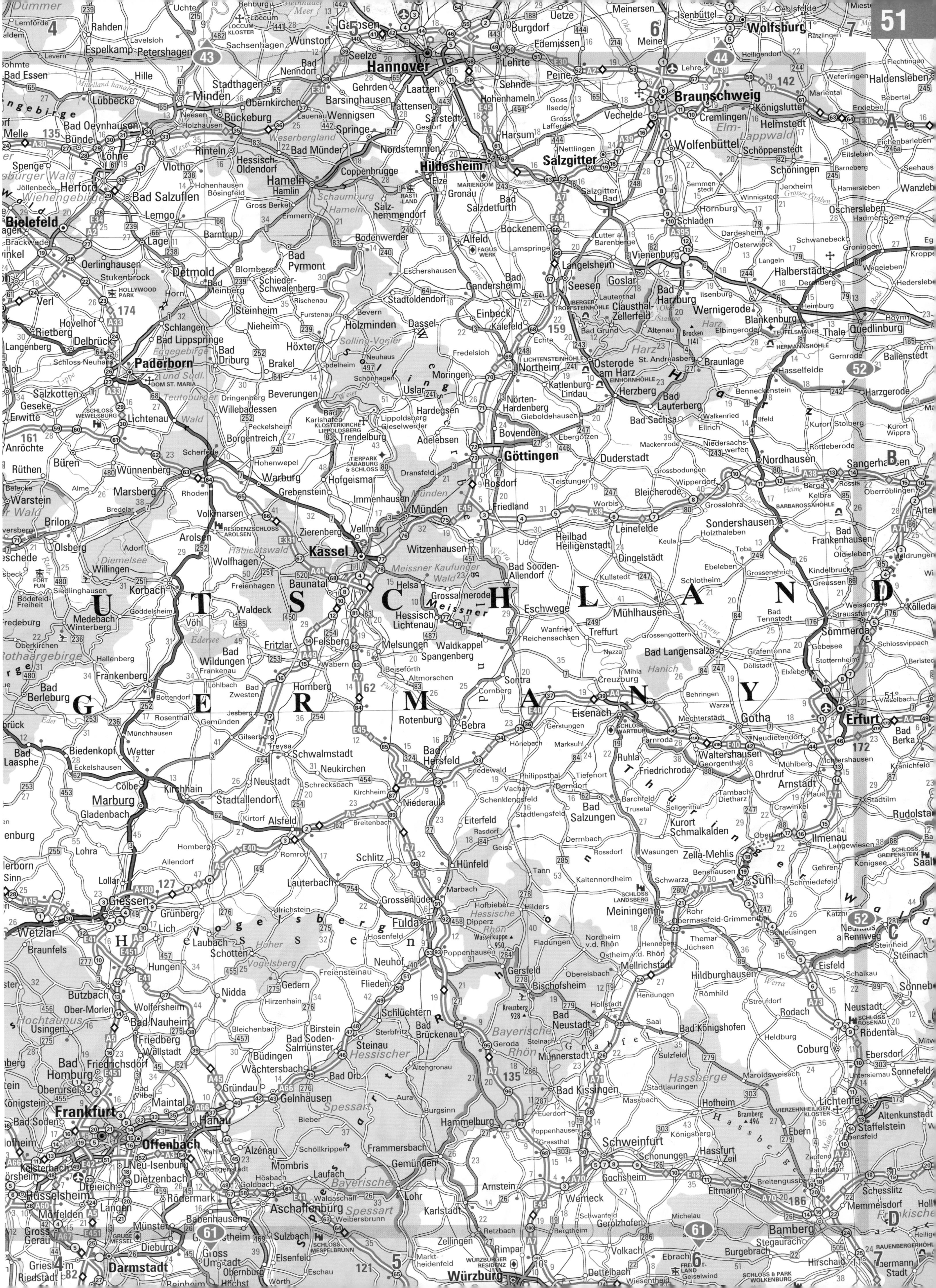

Hannover
Braunschweig
Wolfsburg
Hildesheim
Salzgitter
Wolfenbüttel
Bielefeld
Herford
Minden
Hameln
Detmold
Paderborn
Göttingen
Kassel
Nordhausen
Halberstadt
Quedlinburg
Wernigerode
Goslar
Northeim
Einbeck
Holzminden
Höxter
Marburg
Giessen
Wetzlar
Fulda
Bad Hersfeld
Eisenach
Gotha
Erfurt
Mühlhausen
Sömmerda
Arnstadt
Suhl
Meiningen
Bad Kissingen
Schweinfurt
Würzburg
Bamberg
Coburg
Lichtenfels
Frankfurt
Offenbach
Hanau
Darmstadt
Aschaffenburg
Bad Homburg
Friedberg
Gelnhausen
Schlüchtern
Hammelburg
Gemünden
Lohr
Karlstadt
Hassfurt
Rüsselsheim
D E U T S C H L A N D
G E R M A N Y
Harz
Vogelsberg
Spessart
Rhön
Thüringer Wald

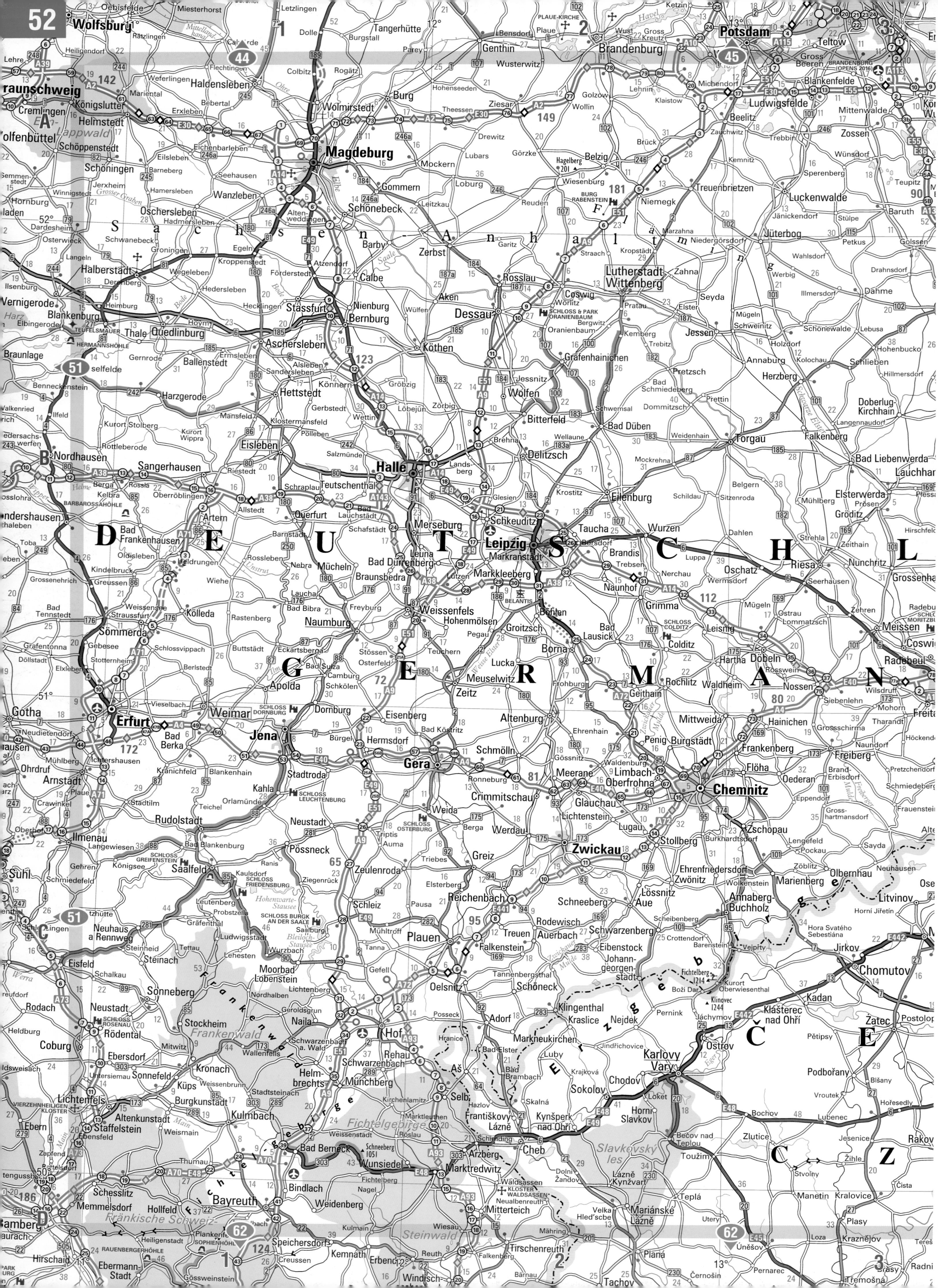

Wolfsburg
Potsdam
Brandenburg
Magdeburg
Braunschweig
Halberstadt
Wernigerode
Quedlinburg
Dessau
Lutherstadt Wittenberg
Halle
Leipzig
Torgau
Riesa
Meissen
Nordhausen
Erfurt
Weimar
Jena
Gera
Zwickau
Chemnitz
Plauen
Hof
Bayreuth
Coburg
Karlovy Vary
Chomutov
Sachsen-Anhalt
Fläming
Erzgebirge
Frankenwald
Fichtelgebirge
Thüringer Wald
DEUTSCHLAND
GERMANY
ČESKÁ REPUBLIKA
CZ

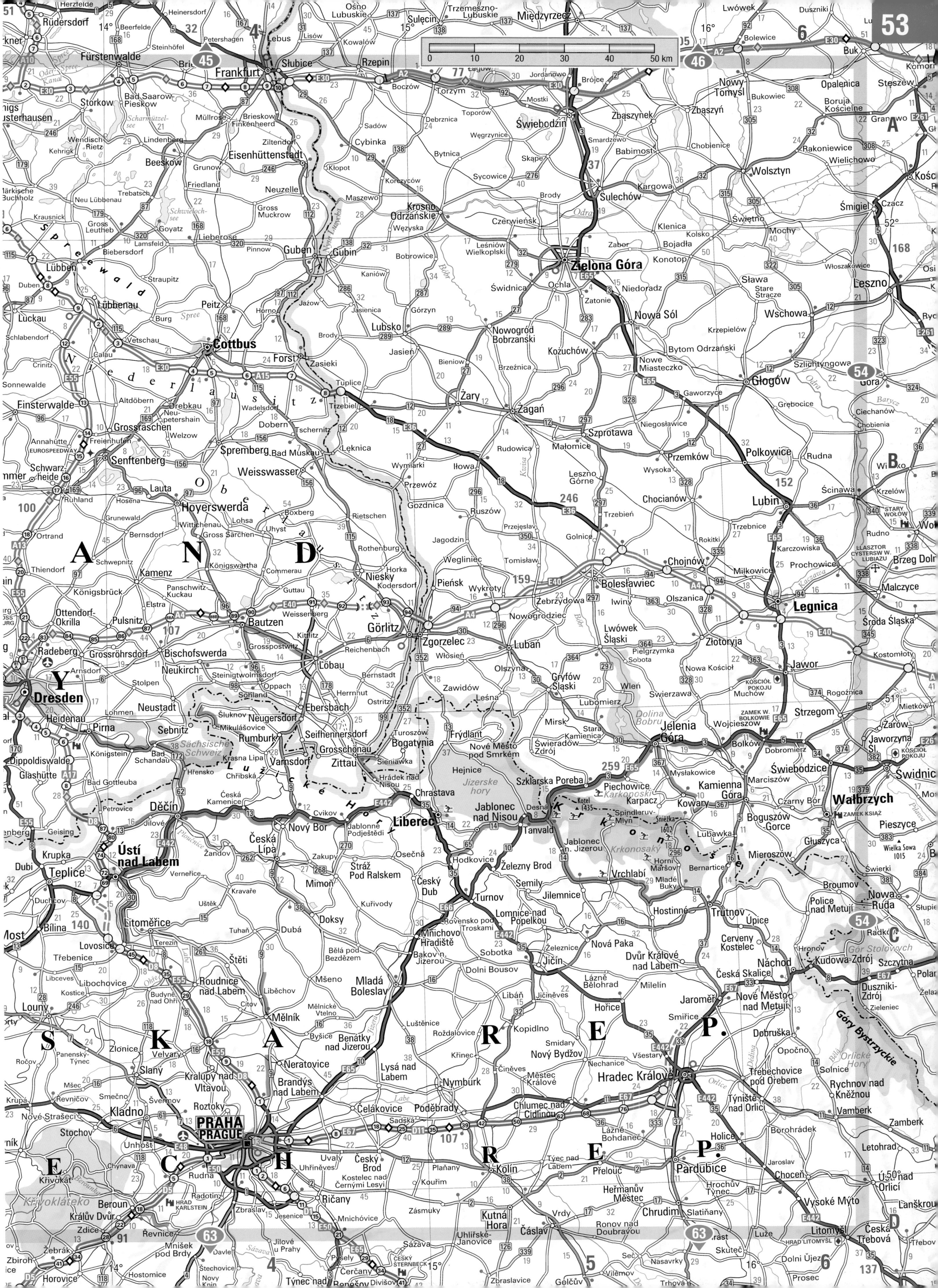
Frankfurt
Słubice
Fürstenwalde
Eisenhüttenstadt
Guben
Gubin
Cottbus
Forst
Lübben
Lübbenau
Spremberg
Senftenberg
Hoyerswerda
Weisswasser
Bautzen
Görlitz
Zgorzelec
Löbau
Zittau
Dresden
Pirna
Děčín
Ústí nad Labem
Teplice
Liberec
Jablonec nad Nisou
Turnov
Mladá Boleslav
Mělník
Kladno
PRAHA
PRAGUE
Kolín
Pardubice
Hradec Králové
Jaroměř
Náchod
Trutnov
Vrchlabí
Jelenia Góra
Wałbrzych
Świdnica
Legnica
Lubin
Głogów
Bolesławiec
Lubań
Żary
Żagań
Zielona Góra
Nowa Sól
Świebodzin
Sulechów
Krosno Odrzańskie
Leszno
Wolsztyn
Nowy Tomyśl
Chrudim
Čáslav
Kutná Hora
Beroun
Litomyšl
Česká Třebová
Vysoké Mýto
Ústí nad Orlicí
Kudowa-Zdrój
Polkowice
Chojnów
Jawor
Strzegom
A N D
Y
S K A
R E P.
Č E C H
R E P.
Spreewald
Niederlausitz
Oberlausitz
Lužické Hory
Jizerské hory
Krkonoše
Góry Bystrzyckie
0 10 20 30 40 50 km

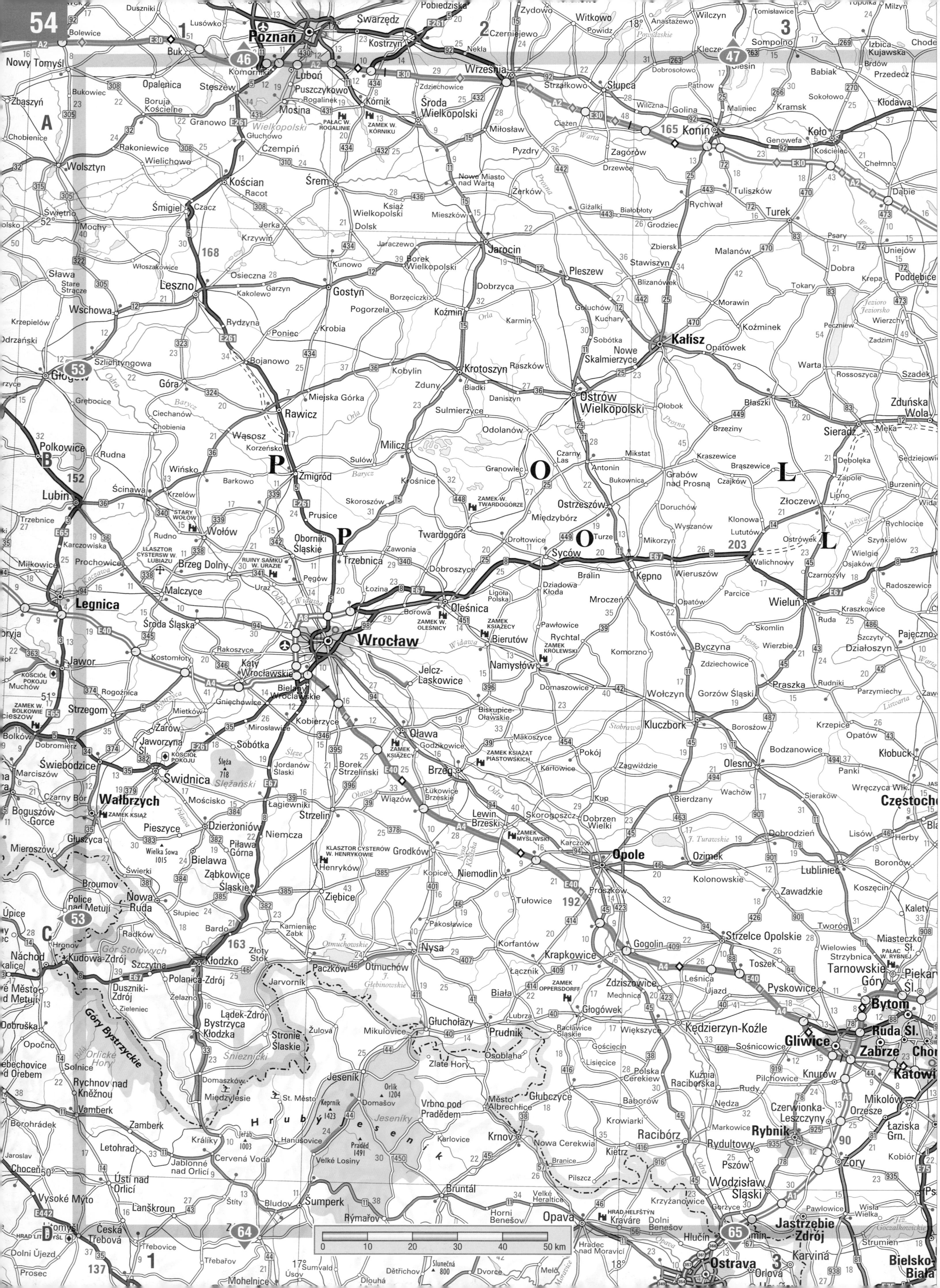
Poznań
Swarzędz
Kostrzyn
Września
Nekla
Czerniejewo
Buk
Nowy Tomyśl
Komorniki
Luboń
Puszczykowo
Kórnik
Środa Wielkopolski
Mosina
Stęszew
Opalenica
Zbąszyń
Wolsztyn
Grodzisk
Kościan
Śmigiel
Czempiń
Śrem
Gostyń
Leszno
Wschowa
Głogów
Rawicz
Jarocin
Pleszew
Krotoszyn
Kalisz
Ostrów Wielkopolski
Konin
Koło
Turek
Słupca
Kłodawa
Sieradz
Zduńska Wola
Złoczew
Wieluń
Kępno
Syców
Oleśnica
Milicz
Trzebnica
Oborniki Śląskie
Wołów
Lubin
Legnica
Polkowice
Jawor
Środa Śląska
Wrocław
Oława
Brzeg
Namysłów
Kluczbork
Olesno
Opole
Strzelce Opolskie
Kędzierzyn-Koźle
Gliwice
Zabrze
Bytom
Ruda Śl.
Katowice
Rybnik
Żory
Jastrzębie Zdrój
Wodzisław Śląski
Racibórz
Głubczyce
Prudnik
Nysa
Krapkowice
Strzelin
Ziębice
Ząbkowice Śląskie
Dzierżoniów
Świdnica
Wałbrzych
Świebodzice
Strzegom
Kłodzko
Nowa Ruda
Bielawa
Kudowa-Zdrój
Polanica-Zdrój
Duszniki-Zdrój
Bystrzyca Kłodzka
Lądek-Zdrój
Stronie Śląskie
Głuchołazy
Paczków
Otmuchów
Grodków
Niemodlin
Lubliniec
Częstochowa
Tarnowskie Góry
Pyskowice
Mikołów
Orzesze
Knurów
Czerwionka-Leszczyny
Ostrava
Opava
Krnov
Bruntál
Šumperk
Jeseník
Náchod
Hronov
Broumov
Vamberk
Rychnov nad Kněžnou
Králíky
Lanškroun
Česká Třebová
Ústí nad Orlicí
Vysoké Mýto
Choceň
Karviná
Bielsko-Biała
Hlučín
Kravaře
P O L S K A
Hrubý Jeseník
Góry Bystrzyckie
Góry Stołowe
Odra
Warta
Prosna
Barycz
Widawa
E30
E40
E261
E67
E65
A1
A2
A4
A8
46
47
53
64
65
0 10 20 30 40 50 km

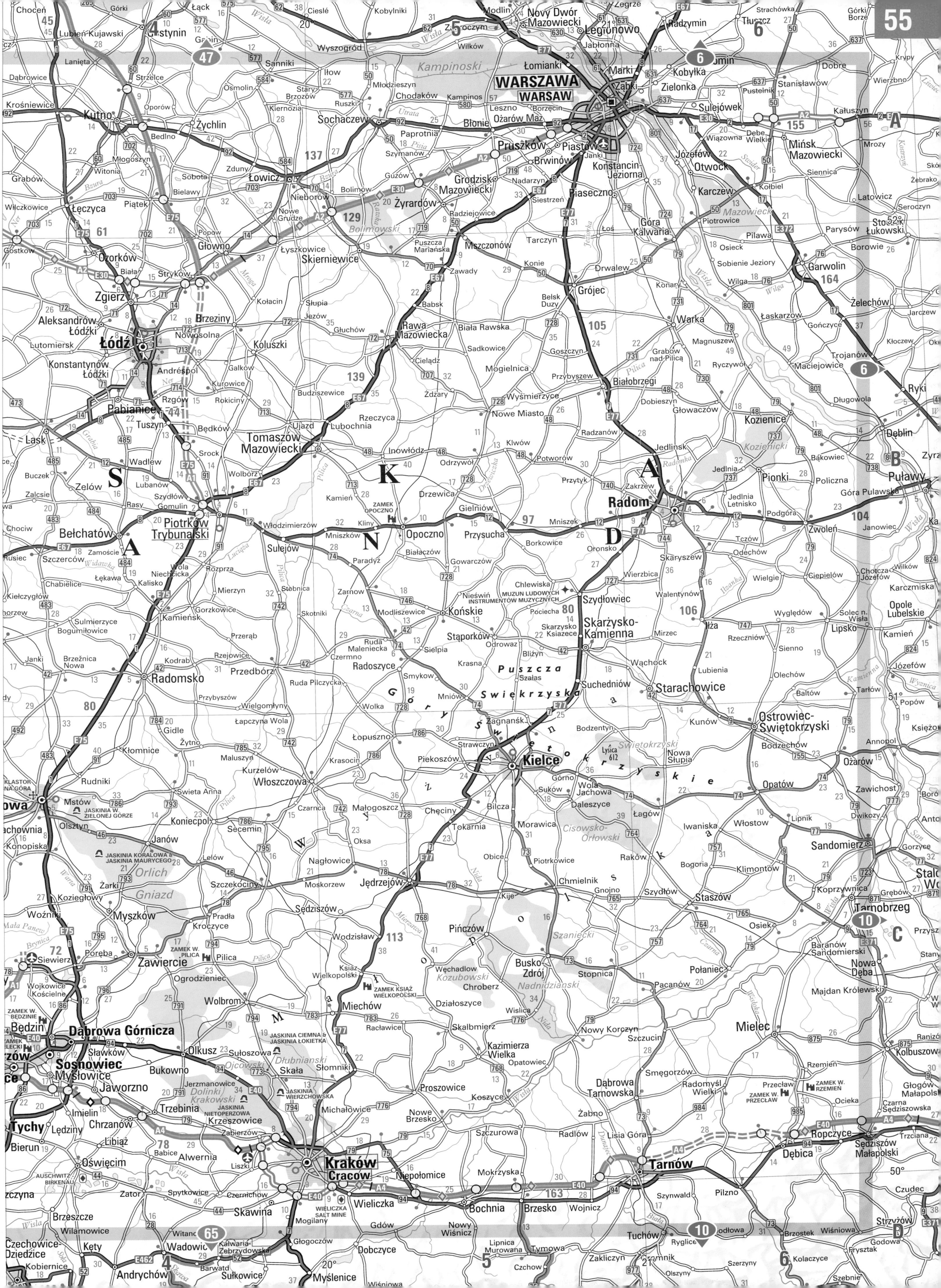

WARSZAWA
WARSAW
Kampinoski
Nowy Dwór Mazowiecki
Legionowo
Modlin
Radzymin
Tłuszcz
Łomianki
Marki
Ząbki
Kobyłka
Zielonka
Sulejówek
Pruszków
Piastów
Błonie
Ożarów Maz.
Brwinów
Grodzisk Mazowiecki
Żyrardów
Sochaczew
Łowicz
Nieborów
Kutno
Łęczyca
Żychlin
Gostynin
Płock
Wyszogród
Mińsk Mazowiecki
Kałuszyn
Józefów
Otwock
Karczew
Konstancin-Jeziorna
Piaseczno
Góra Kalwaria
Garwolin
Żelechów
Łaskarzew
Ryki
Dęblin
Puławy
Łódź
Zgierz
Ozorków
Głowno
Stryków
Brzeziny
Koluszki
Aleksandrów Łódzki
Konstantynów Łódzki
Pabianice
Łask
Tuszyn
Andrespol
Rzgów
Skierniewice
Bolimowski
Rawa Mazowiecka
Biała Rawska
Mszczonów
Grójec
Warka
Białobrzegi
Mogielnica
Nowe Miasto
Tomaszów Mazowiecki
Inowłódz
Piotrków Trybunalski
Bełchatów
Opoczno
Przysucha
Radom
Kozienice
Kozienicki
Pionki
Zwoleń
Szydłowiec
Skarżysko-Kamienna
Końskie
Stąporków
Suchedniów
Starachowice
Iłża
Lipsko
Ostrowiec Świętokrzyski
Opatów
Ożarów
Sandomierz
Tarnobrzeg
Kielce
Chęciny
Góry Świętokrzyskie
Puszcza Świętokrzyska
Świętokrzyski
Nowa Słupia
Łysica 612
Jędrzejów
Włoszczowa
Radomsko
Przedbórz
Sulejów
Koniecpol
Częstochowa
Myszków
Zawiercie
Pilica
Wolbrom
Olkusz
Miechów
Busko Zdrój
Pińczów
Chmielnik
Staszów
Połaniec
Mielec
Kolbuszowa
Dąbrowa Tarnowska
Tarnów
Dębica
Ropczyce
Sędziszów Małopolski
Bochnia
Brzesko
Wieliczka
Niepołomice
Kraków
Cracow
Skawina
Krzeszowice
Chrzanów
Trzebinia
Jaworzno
Mysłowice
Sosnowiec
Dąbrowa Górnicza
Będzin
Tychy
Oświęcim
Kęty
Wadowice
Andrychów
Myślenice
Kalwaria Zebrzydowska
Dobczyce
Lipnica Murowana
Zakliczyn
Pilzno
Czechowice-Dziedzice
Wyżyna Małopolska
Wyżyna Kielecka
Nida
Wisła
Pilica
Radomka
Pilawa
Kazimierza Wielka
Proszowice
Słomniki
Skała
Ojcowski
Cisowsko-Orłowski
Szaniecki
Nadnidziański
Kozubowski
Dłubniański
Orlich
Gniazd
Zamek Opoczno
Zamek Książ Wielkopolski
Zamek w Pilica
Zamek w Będzinie
Zamek w Rzemień
Zamek w Przecław
Jaskinia Ciemna & Jaskinia Łokietka
Jaskinia Wierzchowska
Jaskinia Nietoperzowa
Jaskinia w Zielonej Górze
Jaskinia Koralowa & Jaskinia Maurycego
Wieliczka Salt Mine
Auschwitz-Birkenau
Muzeum Ludowych Instrumentów Muzycznych
Klasztor Jasna Góra
A1
A2
A4
E30
E40
E67
E75
E77
E371
E372
E462
S
K
A
N
D
A
B
C
D
5
6
4
47
65
10
50°
51°
52°
20°
21°

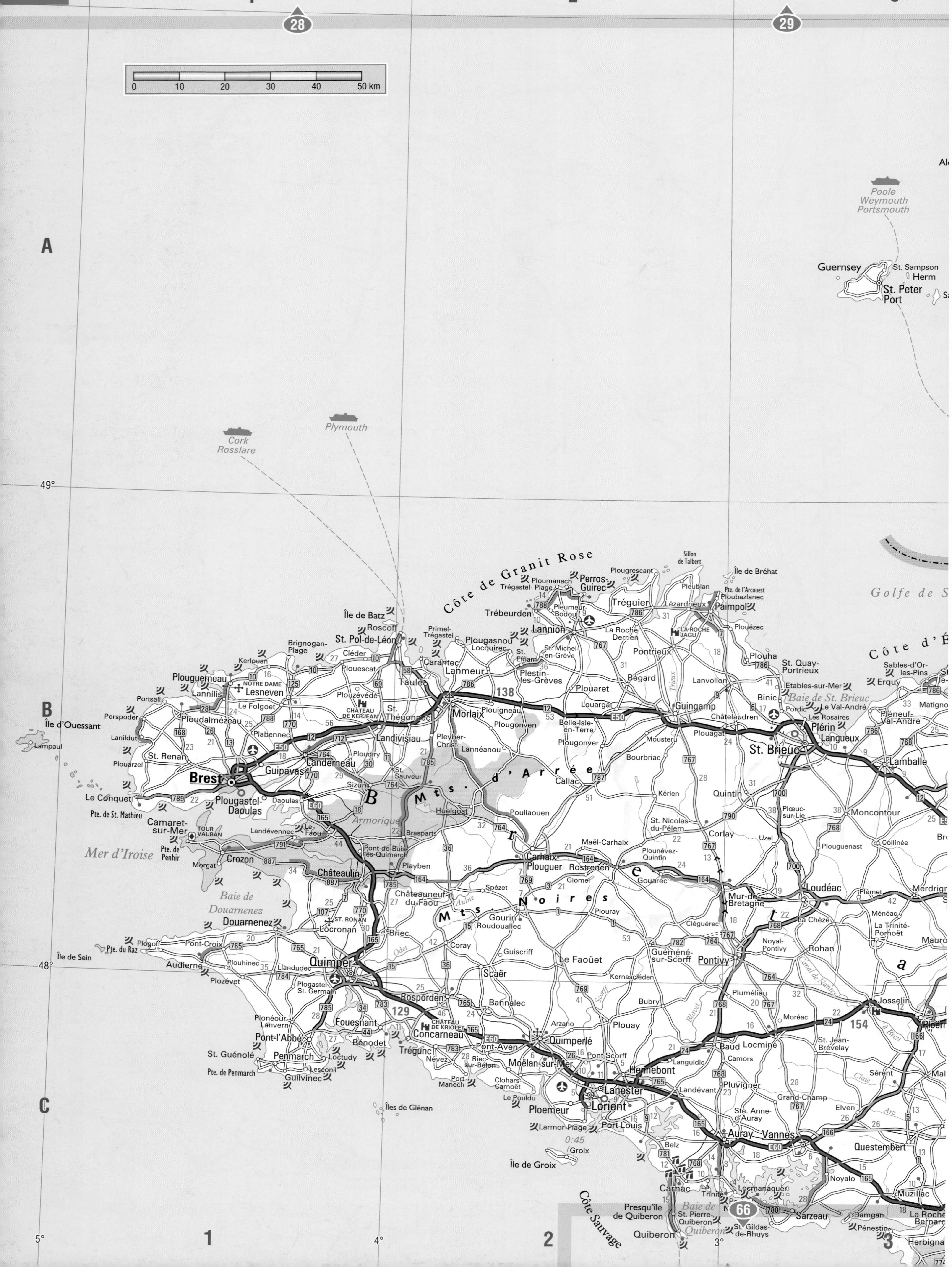

5°
1
4°
2
3°
3
28
29
0
10
20
30
40
50 km
A
B
C
49°
48°
Poole
Weymouth
Portsmouth
Guernsey
St. Sampson
Herm
St. Peter Port
Cork
Rosslare
Plymouth
Golfe de S
Côte de Granit Rose
Côte d'É
Sillon de Talbert
Île de Bréhat
Plougrescant
Pleubian
Pte. de l'Arcouest
Ploubazlanec
Paimpol
Lézardrieux
Tréguier
Perros-Guirec
Ploumanac'h
Trégastel-Plage
Pleumeur-Bodou
Trébeurden
Lannion
La Roche Derrien
LA ROCHE JAGU
Plouézec
Île de Batz
Roscoff
St. Pol-de-Léon
Primel-Trégastel
Plougasnou
Locquirec
St. Michel-en-Grève
St. Efflam
Plestin-les-Grèves
Pontrieux
Plouha
St. Quay-Portrieux
Sables-d'Or-les-Pins
Erquy
Brignogan-Plage
Cléder
Plouescat
Kerlouan
Plouguerneau
NOTRE DAME
Lesneven
Lannilis
Le Folgoet
Plouzévédé
CHÂTEAU DE KERJEAN
Carantec
Taulé
Lanmeur
Morlaix
St. Thégonnec
Plouigneau
Plougonven
Plouaret
Bégard
Lanvollon
Etables-sur-Mer
Binic
Baie de St. Brieuc
Le Val-André
Pordic
Les Rosaires
Pléneuf-Val-André
Matignon
Guingamp
Louargat
Belle-Isle-en-Terre
Châtelaudren
Plouagat
Plérin
Langueux
St. Brieuc
Lamballe
Portsall
Porspoder
Ploudalmézeau
Île d'Ouessant
Lampaul
Lanildut
Plabennec
Landivisiau
Plouvorn
Pleyber-Christ
Lannéanou
Plougonver
Mousteru
Bourbriac
St. Renan
Plouarzel
Brest
Guipavas
Landerneau
Ploudiry
St. Sauveur
Sizun
Mts. d'Arrée
Callac
Quintin
Moncontour
Le Conquet
Pte. de St. Mathieu
Plougastel-Daoulas
Daoulas
Huelgoat
Poullaouen
Kérien
Plœuc-sur-Lie
Camaret-sur-Mer
TOUR VAUBAN
Landévennec
Le Faou
Armorique
Brasparts
St. Nicolas-du-Pélem
Corlay
Uzel
Mer d'Iroise
Pte. de Penhir
Crozon
Morgat
Pont-de-Buis-lès-Quimerch
Carhaix-Plouguer
Maël-Carhaix
Plounévez-Quintin
Rostrenen
Plouguenast
Collinée
Châteaulin
Playben
Glomel
Gouarec
Loudéac
Plémet
Merdrignac
Baie de Douarnenez
Châteauneuf-du-Faou
Aulne
Spézet
Mts. Noires
Mur-de-Bretagne
La Chèze
Ménéac
La Trinité-Porhoët
Douarnenez
ST. RONAN
Locronan
Briec
Gourin
Roudouallec
Plouray
Cléguérec
Noyal-Pontivy
Rohan
Mauron
Île de Sein
Pte. du Raz
Plogoff
Pont-Croix
Audierne
Plouhinec
Quimper
Odet
Coray
Guiscriff
Le Faouët
Guémené-sur-Scorff
Pontivy
Canal de Nantes
Plozévet
Landudec
Plogastel-St. Germain
Scaër
Kernascléden
Rosporden
Bannalec
Bubry
Pluméliau
Josselin
Ploërmel
Plonéour-Lanvern
Fouesnant
CHÂTEAU DE KRIOLET
Concarneau
Arzano
Plouay
Moréac
Pont-l'Abbé
Bénodet
Trégunc
Névez
Pont-Aven
Riec-sur-Bélon
Quimperlé
Pont Scorff
Baud
Locminé
St. Jean-Brévelay
Sérent
St. Guénolé
Pte. de Penmarch
Penmarch
Loctudy
Lesconil
Guilvinec
Moëlan-sur-Mer
Port Manech
Clohars-Carnoët
Le Pouldu
Hennebont
Languidic
Camors
Pluvigner
Îles de Glénan
Ploemeur
Lanester
Lorient
Landévant
Grand-Champ
Elven
Larmor-Plage
Port Louis
Ste. Anne-d'Auray
Auray
Vannes
Questembert
0:45
Groix
Île de Groix
Belz
Carnac
La Trinité
Locmariaquer
Noyalo
Muzillac
Côte Sauvage
Presqu'île de Quiberon
Baie de St. Pierre-Quiberon
Quiberon
Sarzeau
St. Gildas-de-Rhuys
Damgan
Pénestin
La Roche Bernard
Herbignac
66
E50
E60
138
129
154

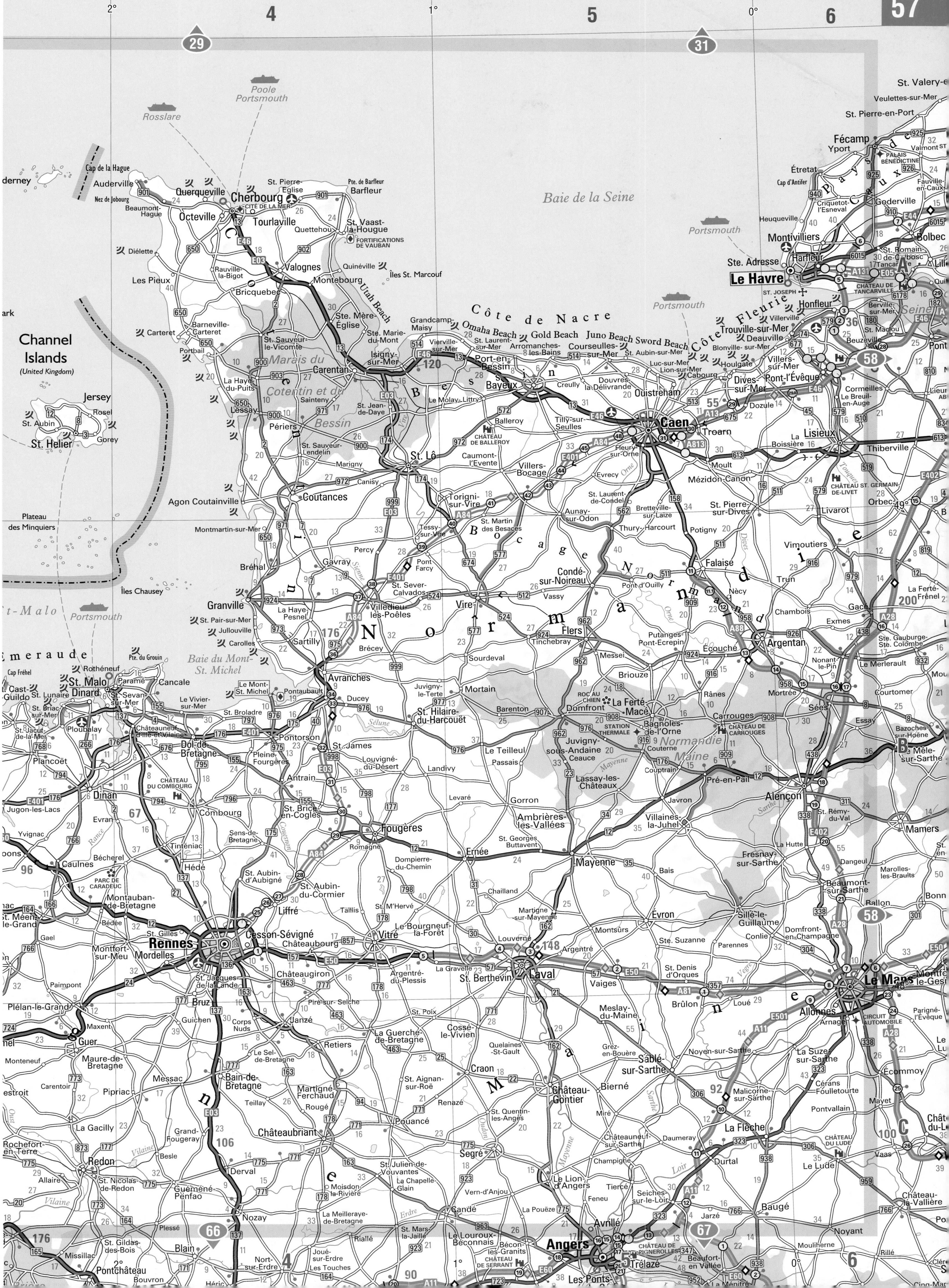

Baie de la Seine
Channel Islands
(United Kingdom)
Jersey
St. Helier
St. Aubin
Gorey
Rosel
Plateau des Minquiers
Îles Chausey
Cap de la Hague
Auderville
Querqueville
Cherbourg
Octeville
Tourlaville
Barfleur
St. Vaast-la-Hougue
Valognes
Les Pieux
Bricquebec
Montebourg
Utah Beach
Omaha Beach
Gold Beach
Juno Beach
Sword Beach
Côte de Nacre
Côte Fleurie
Pays de Caux
Carentan
Isigny-sur-Mer
Bayeux
Caen
Ouistreham
Lessay
Périers
St. Lô
Coutances
Granville
Avranches
Villedieu-les-Poêles
Vire
Flers
Falaise
Argentan
Lisieux
Le Havre
Honfleur
Fécamp
Étretat
Trouville-sur-Mer
Deauville
Cabourg
Bessin
Marais du Cotentin et du Bessin
Bocage
Normandie
St. Malo
Dinard
Cancale
Mont-St. Michel
Baie du Mont-St. Michel
Dinan
Dol-de-Bretagne
Pontorson
Fougères
Vitré
Rennes
Cesson-Sévigné
Laval
Mayenne
Domfront
Bagnoles-de-l'Orne
Alençon
Sées
Mamers
Le Mans
Sablé-sur-Sarthe
Château-Gontier
La Flèche
Segré
Châteaubriant
Redon
Angers
Maine
Portsmouth
Poole Portsmouth
Rosslare
Côte d'Émeraude

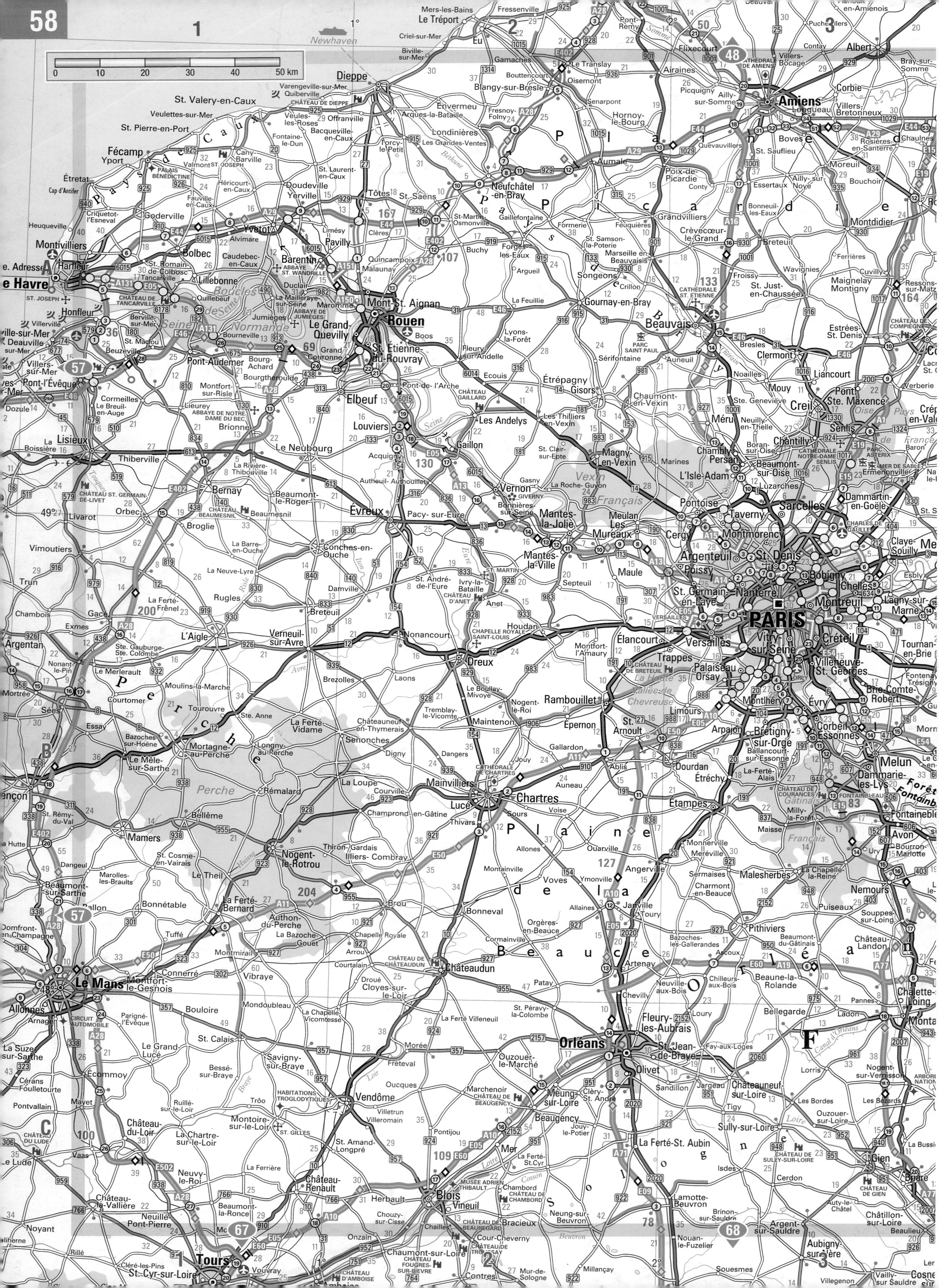

1
2
3
Newhaven
0 10 20 30 40 50 km
Le Tréport
Dieppe
Fécamp
Le Havre
Honfleur
Rouen
Amiens
Beauvais
Évreux
Lisieux
Bernay
Vernon
Mantes-la-Jolie
Pontoise
Cergy
St. Denis
PARIS
Versailles
Créteil
Évry
Melun
Dreux
Chartres
Rambouillet
Étampes
Alençon
Le Mans
Mamers
Nogent-le-Rotrou
Châteaudun
Vendôme
Orléans
Blois
Tours
Gien
Montargis
Pithiviers
Fontainebleau
Creil
Senlis
Compiègne
Clermont
Gisors
Les Andelys
Louviers
Elbeuf
Yvetot
Bolbec
Étretat
Montivilliers
Neufchâtel-en-Bray
Aumale
Montdidier
Albert
Chantilly
Sarcelles
Argenteuil
Montreuil
Poissy
Nanterre
St. Germain-en-Laye
Vitry-sur-Seine
Trappes
Palaiseau
Orsay
Limours
Arpajon
Corbeil-Essonnes
Nemours
Malesherbes
Mortagne-au-Perche
L'Aigle
Verneuil-sur-Avre
Argentan
Sées
La Ferté-Bernard
Bellême
Perche
Pays de Caux
Pays de Bray
Picardie
Vexin Français
Plaine de la Beauce
Sologne
Orléanais
Boucles de la Seine Normande
Forêt de Fontainebleau
Gâtinais Français
Chevreuse

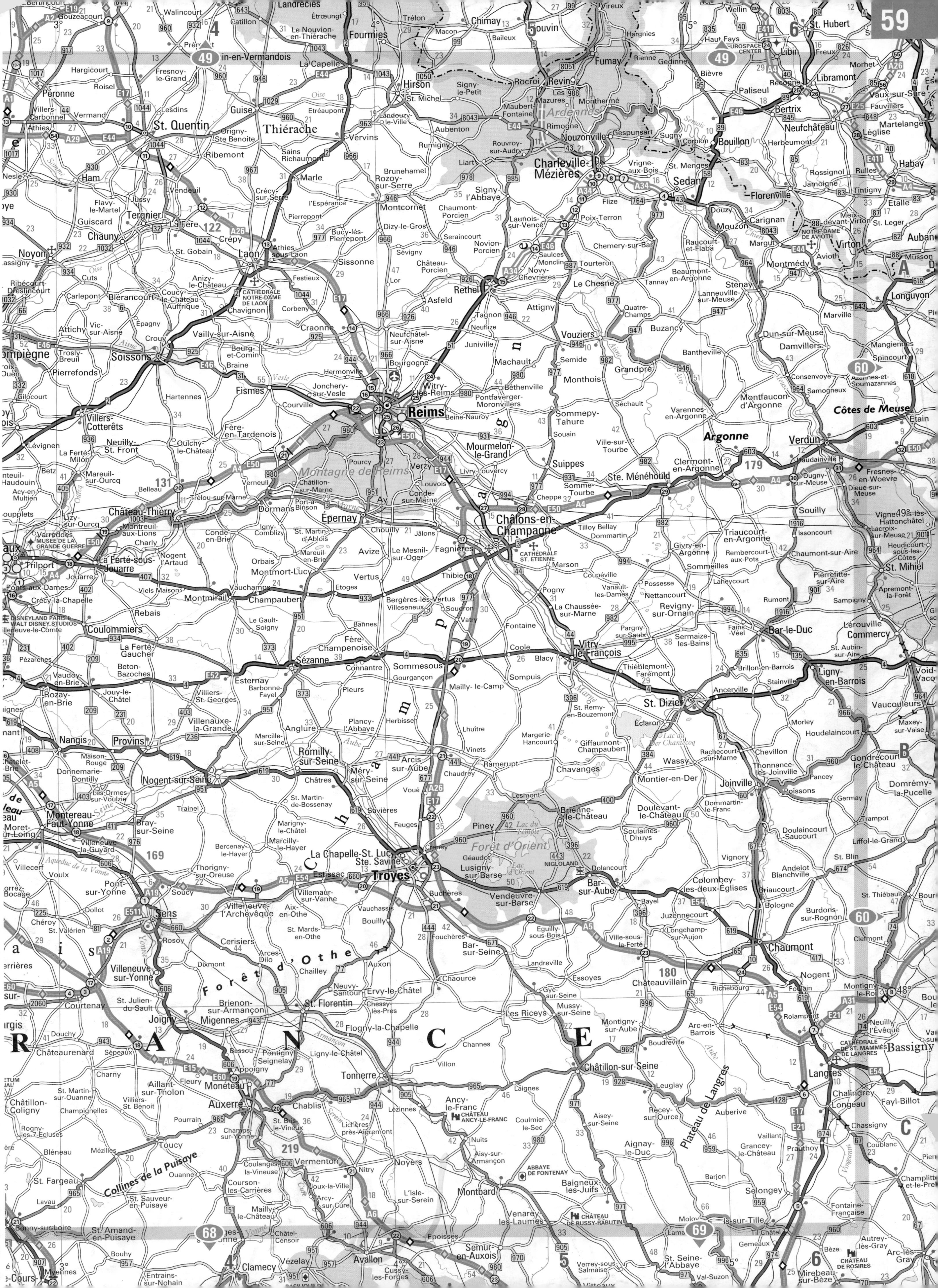

St. Quentin
Thiérache
Guise
Hirson
Vervins
Laon
Soissons
Reims
Montagne de Reims
Épernay
Châlons-en-Champagne
Charleville-Mézières
Sedan
Rethel
Vouziers
Argonne
Verdun
Ste. Ménehould
Vitry-le-François
St. Dizier
Bar-le-Duc
Commercy
St. Mihiel
Côtes de Meuse
Château-Thierry
Coulommiers
Provins
Sézanne
Nogent-sur-Seine
Romilly-sur-Seine
Troyes
Forêt d'Orient
Lac d'Orient
Bar-sur-Aube
Chaumont
Joinville
Langres
Sens
Joigny
Auxerre
Tonnerre
Châtillon-sur-Seine
Montbard
Avallon
Clamecy
Forêt d'Othe
Collines de la Puisaye
Plateau de Langres
Noyon
Compiègne
Ardennes
Fumay
Revin
Rocroi
Bouillon
Libramont
Neufchâteau
Virton
Longuyon
Montmédy
Stenay
Montereau-Fault-Yonne
Villeneuve-sur-Yonne
St. Florentin
Brienne-le-Château
Chablis
Semur-en-Auxois
Vendeuvre-sur-Barse
FRANCE

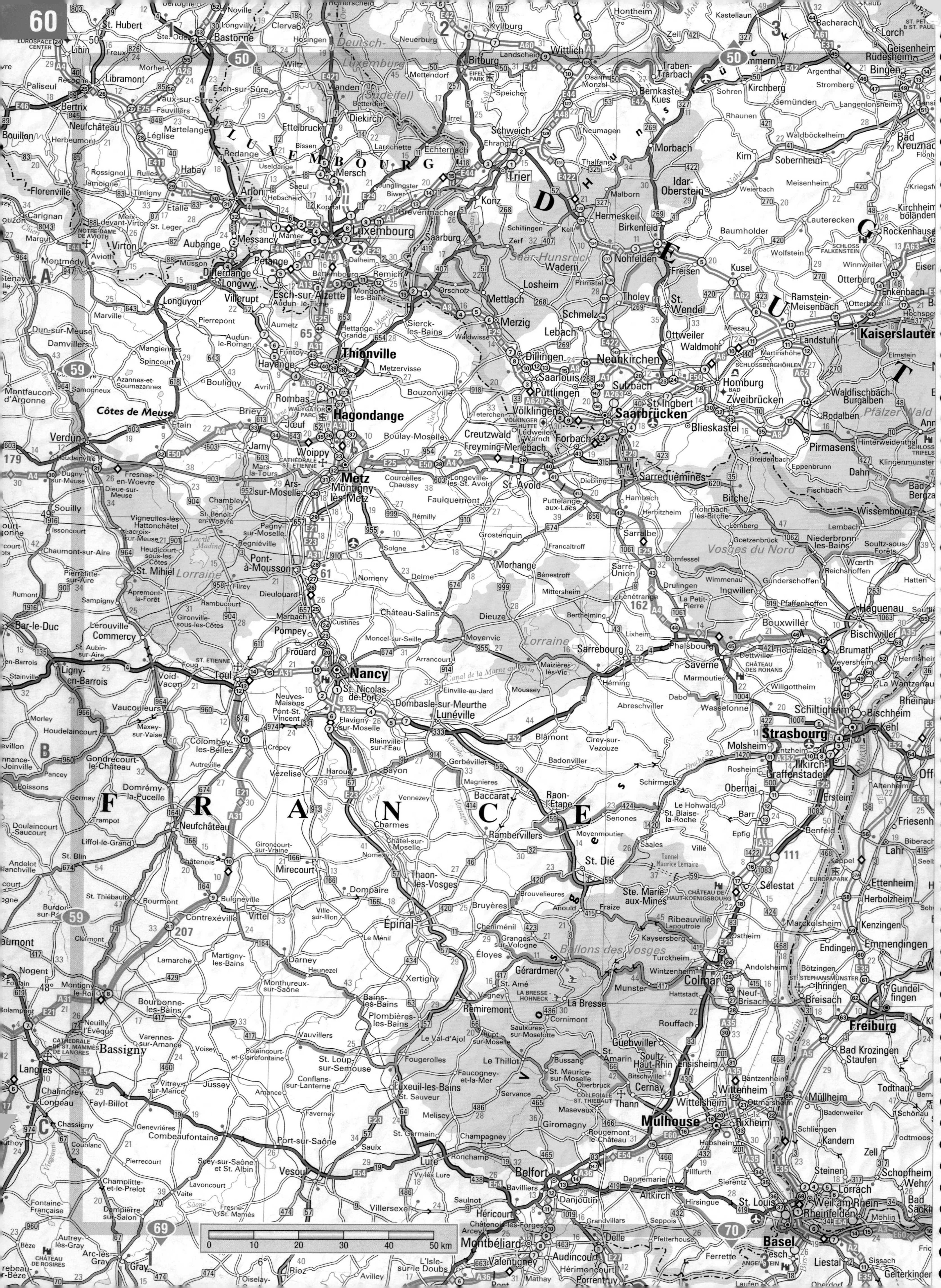
LUXEMBOURG
D E U T
F R A N C E
Luxembourg
Thionville
Hagondange
Metz
Nancy
Saarbrücken
Kaiserslautern
Strasbourg
Freiburg
Mulhouse
Basel
Colmar
Épinal
Belfort
Trier
Bitburg
Wittlich
Arlon
Bastogne
Verdun
Toul
Lunéville
St. Dié
Saverne
Haguenau
Sarreguemines
Sarrebourg
Forbach
Völklingen
Saarlouis
Merzig
Neunkirchen
Homburg
Zweibrücken
Pirmasens
Bad Kreuznach
Bingen
Rüdesheim
Idar-Oberstein
Longwy
Esch-sur-Alzette
Differdange
Neufchâteau
Vesoul
Lure
Montbéliard
Remiremont
Gérardmer
Lahr
Offenburg
Kehl
Lörrach
Weil am Rhein
Rheinfelden
Langres
Bar-le-Duc
Commercy
St. Mihiel
Pont-à-Mousson
Côtes de Meuse
Vosges du Nord
Ballons des Vosges
Lorraine
Pfälzer Wald
Saar-Hunsrück
Deutsch-Luxemburg
(Südeifel)
0 10 20 30 40 50 km

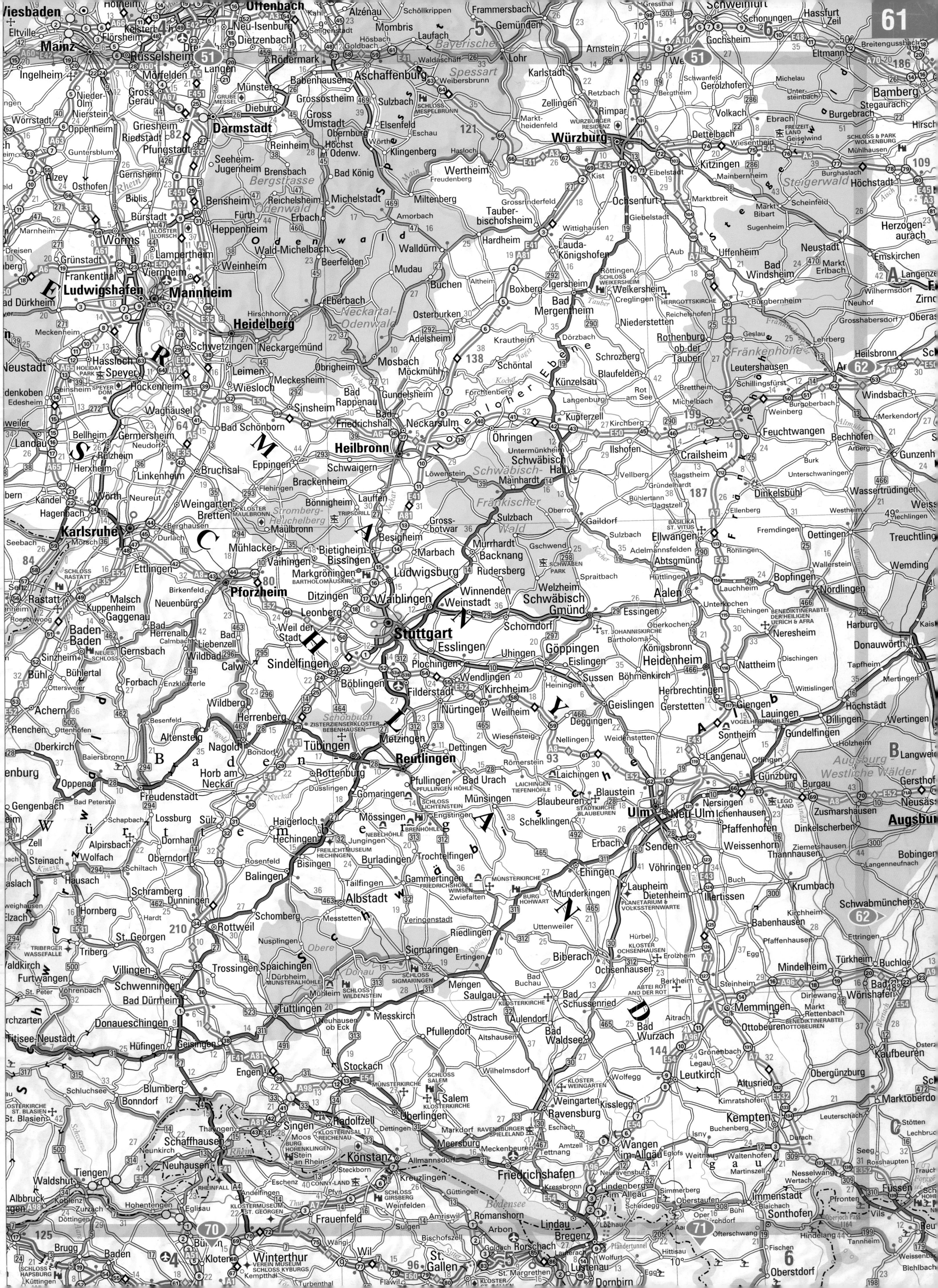
Wiesbaden
Offenbach
Mainz
Rüsselsheim
Aschaffenburg
Darmstadt
Würzburg
Schweinfurt
Bamberg
Kitzingen
Wertheim
Miltenberg
Worms
Mannheim
Ludwigshafen
Heidelberg
Speyer
Tauberbischofsheim
Bad Mergentheim
Rothenburg ob der Tauber
Ansbach
Heilbronn
Schwäbisch Hall
Crailsheim
Dinkelsbühl
Karlsruhe
Pforzheim
Ludwigsburg
Stuttgart
Esslingen
Schwäbisch Gmünd
Aalen
Nördlingen
Baden-Baden
Göppingen
Heidenheim
Tübingen
Reutlingen
Ulm
Neu-Ulm
Günzburg
Augsburg
Freudenstadt
Rottweil
Balingen
Albstadt
Sigmaringen
Biberach
Memmingen
Villingen
Schwenningen
Donaueschingen
Tuttlingen
Kempten
Ravensburg
Friedrichshafen
Konstanz
Singen
Schaffhausen
Lindau
Bregenz
Winterthur
St. Gallen
Füssen
Oberstdorf
Spessart
Odenwald
Bergstrasse
Steigerwald
Frankenhöhe
Hohenloher Ebene
Schwäbische Alb
Schwarzwald
Baden-Württemberg
Bodensee
Allgäu

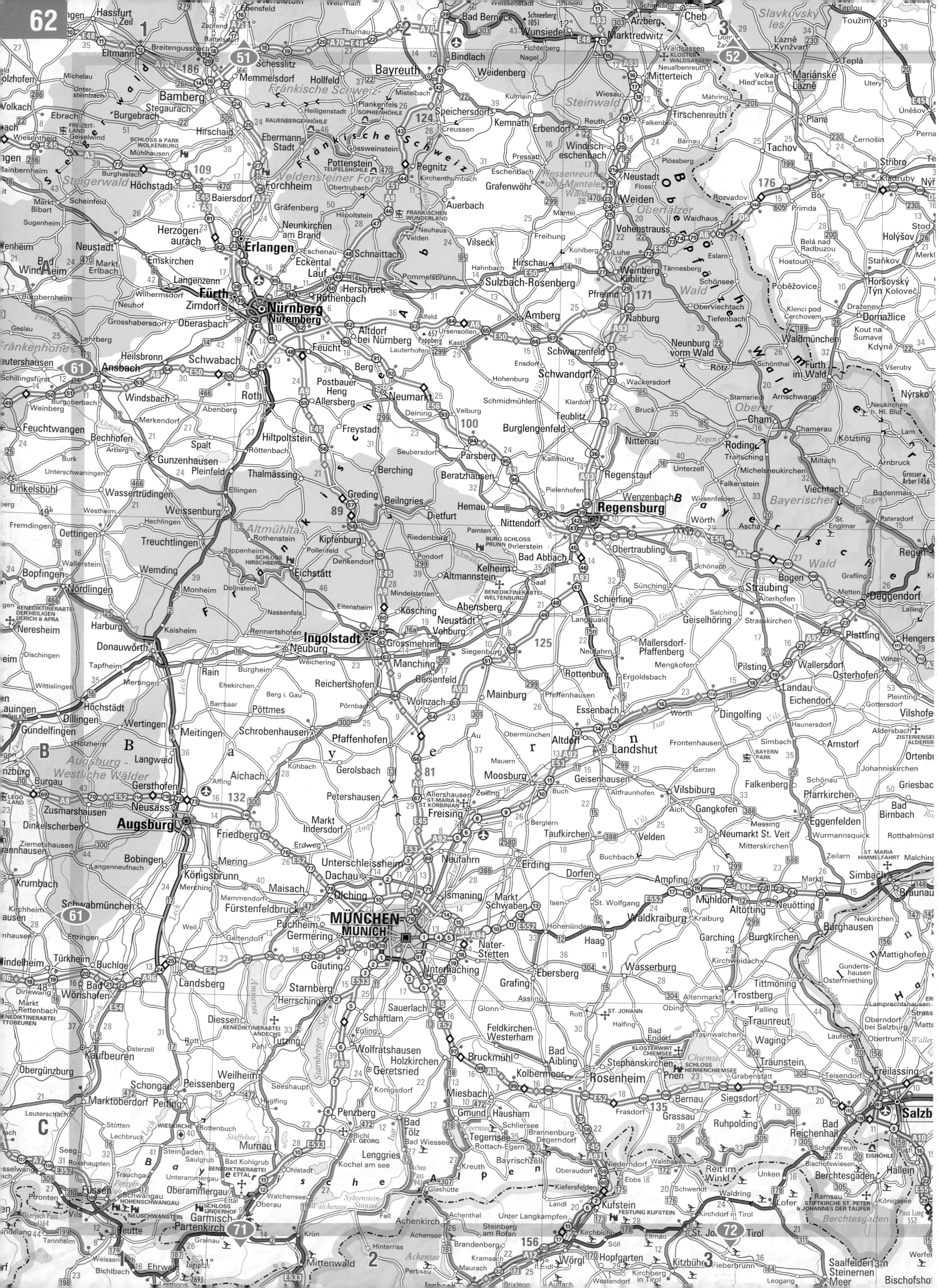

Bamberg
Bayreuth
Erlangen
Fürth
Nürnberg
Nuremberg
Ansbach
Schwabach
Amberg
Weiden
Regensburg
Ingolstadt
Kelheim
Straubing
Deggendorf
Landshut
Freising
Augsburg
MÜNCHEN
MUNICH
Rosenheim
Kufstein
Salzb
Garmisch-Partenkirch
Füssen
Kaufbeuren
Landsberg
Donauwörth
Nördlingen
Weissenburg
Eichstätt
Neumarkt
Cham
Marktredwitz
Wunsiedel
Cheb
Mariánské Lázně
Tachov
Domažlice
Fränkische Schweiz
Steigerwald
Oberpfälzer Wald
Bayerischer Wald
Fränkische Alb
Bayerische Alpen
Chiemsee

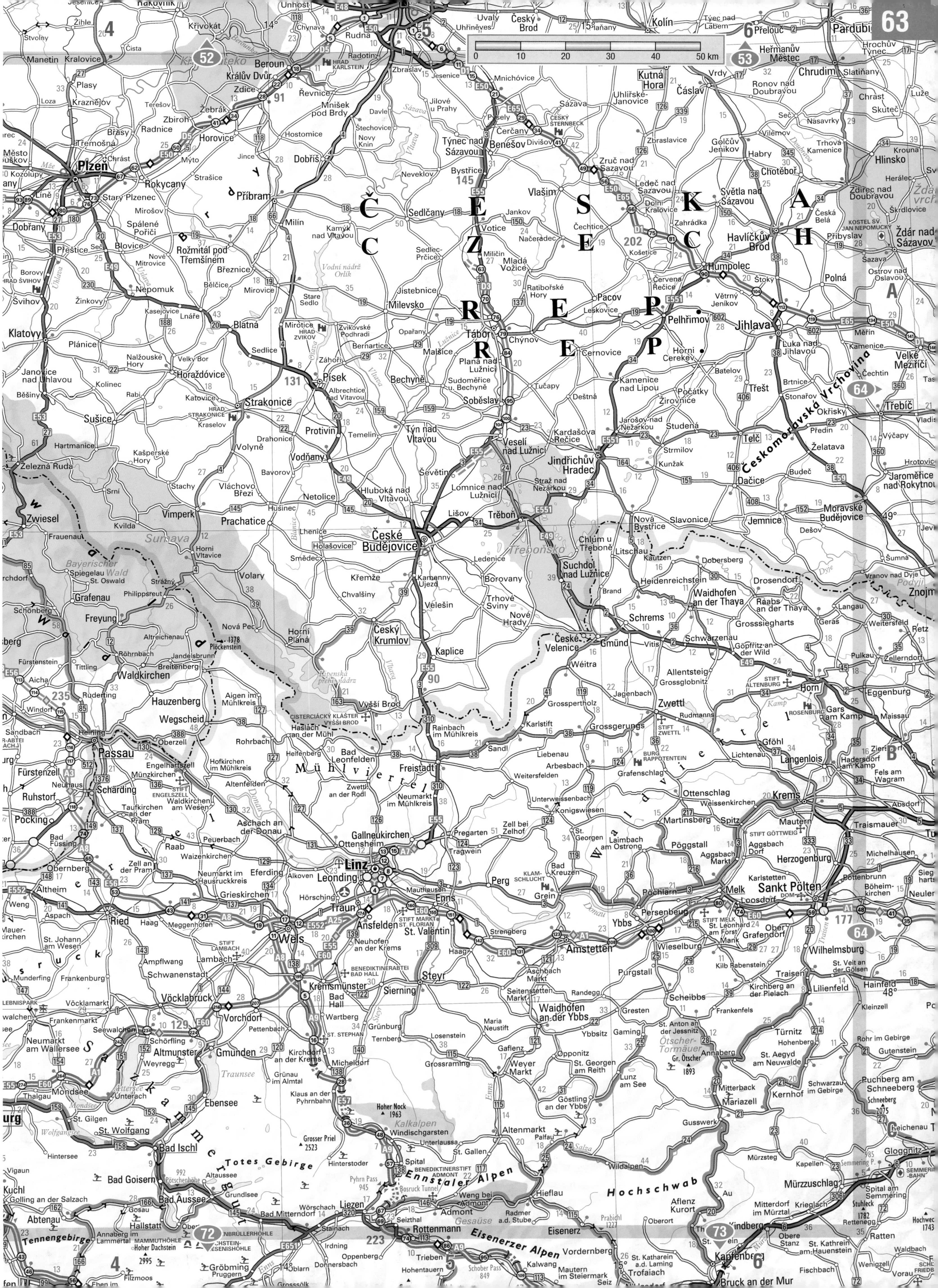

0 10 20 30 40 50 km
52
53
64
72
73
Č E S K Á
C Z E C H
R E P U B L I C
R E P.
Praha
Kolín
Pardubice
Beroun
Králův Dvůr
Rakovník
Křivoklát
Kutná Hora
Čáslav
Chrudim
Přelouč
Heřmanův Městec
Plzeň
Rokycany
Horovice
Příbram
Dobříš
Benešov
Týnec nad Sázavou
Vlašim
Sedlčany
Votice
Zruč nad Sázavou
Ledeč nad Sázavou
Havlíčkův Brod
Chotěboř
Hlinsko
Humpolec
Pelhřimov
Jihlava
Žďár nad Sázavou
Velké Meziříčí
Třebíč
Tábor
Milevsko
Písek
Strakonice
Klatovy
Sušice
Horažďovice
Blatná
Nepomuk
Přeštice
Dobřany
Stod
Pacov
Kamenice nad Lipou
Počátky
Třešť
Telč
Dačice
Jindřichův Hradec
Veselí nad Lužnicí
Soběslav
Bechyně
Týn nad Vltavou
Vodňany
Protivín
Hluboká nad Vltavou
České Budějovice
Třeboň
Lišov
Suchdol nad Lužnicí
České Velenice
Nové Hrady
Trhové Sviny
Kaplice
Český Krumlov
Horní Planá
Vyšší Brod
Prachatice
Vimperk
Netolice
Volary
Železná Ruda
Zwiesel
Grafenau
Freyung
Waldkirchen
Passau
Schärding
Ried
Wels
Linz
Leonding
Traun
Ansfelden
Enns
St. Valentin
Steyr
Amstetten
Ybbs
Melk
Krems
Sankt Pölten
Herzogenburg
Gmünd
Zwettl
Horn
Waidhofen an der Thaya
Schrems
Langenlois
Freistadt
Gallneukirchen
Vöcklabruck
Gmunden
Bad Ischl
Bad Aussee
Liezen
Rottenmann
Eisenerz
Mariazell
Kapfenberg
Bruck an der Mur
Waidhofen an der Ybbs
Lilienfeld
Traisen
Znojmo
Moravské Budějovice
Jemnice
Mühlviertel
Waldviertel
Salzkammergut
Totes Gebirge
Ennstaler Alpen
Eisenerzer Alpen
Hochschwab
Českomoravská Vrchovina
Šumava
Bayerischer Wald
Třeboňsko
Brdy
Vltava
Donau

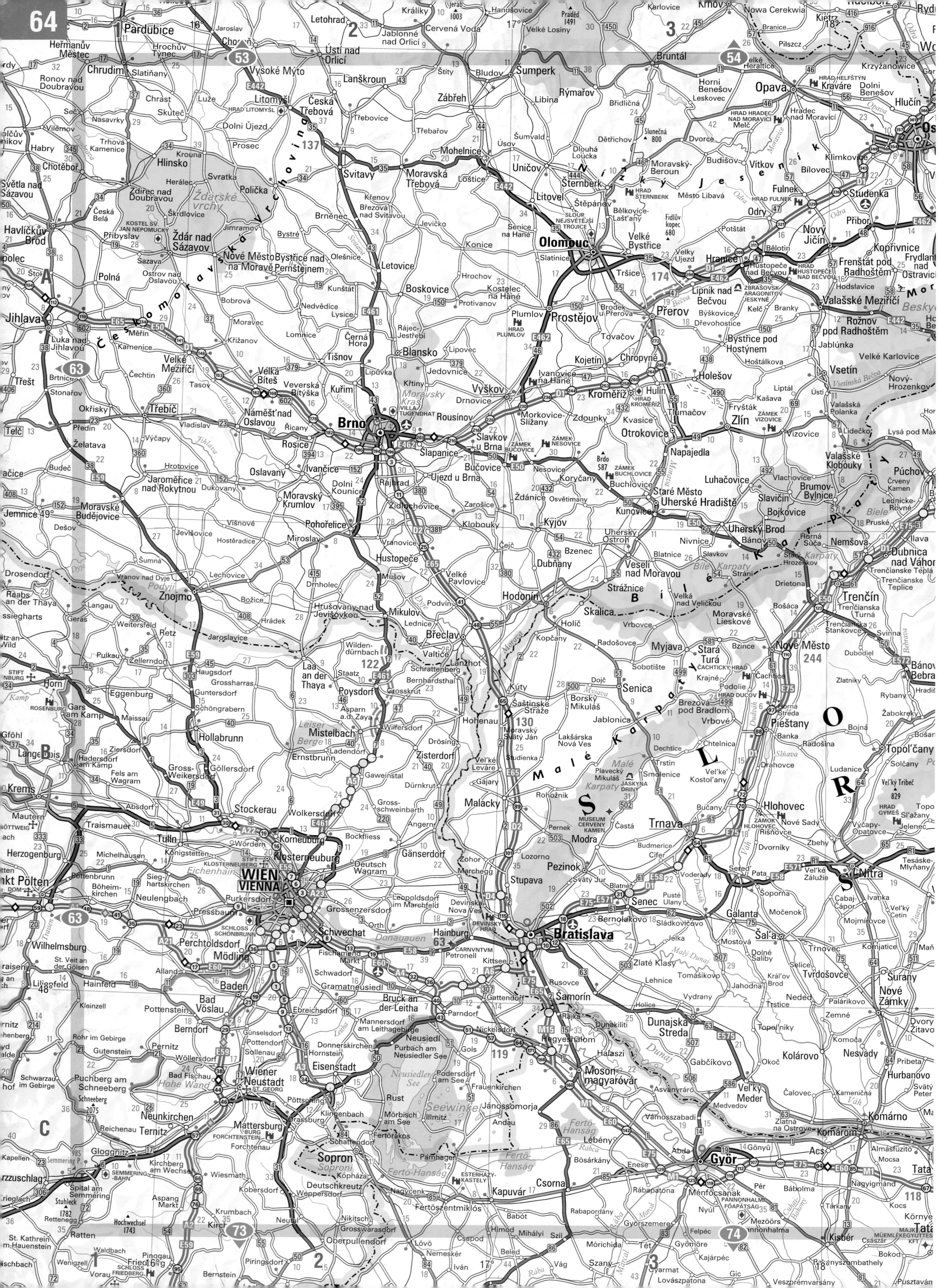
Pardubice
Chrudim
Vysoké Mýto
Litomyšl
Česká Třebová
Ústí nad Orlicí
Lanškroun
Šumperk
Bruntál
Krnov
Opava
Ostrava
Hlučín
Zábřeh
Mohelnice
Uničov
Šternberk
Litovel
Olomouc
Přerov
Hranice
Nový Jičín
Kopřivnice
Frenštát pod Radhoštěm
Valašské Meziříčí
Rožnov pod Radhoštěm
Vsetín
Bystřice pod Hostýnem
Holešov
Zlín
Kroměříž
Prostějov
Vyškov
Boskovice
Blansko
Svitavy
Moravská Třebová
Polička
Hlinsko
Žďár nad Sázavou
Havlíčkův Brod
Jihlava
Velké Meziříčí
Třebíč
Nové Město na Moravě
Bystřice nad Pernštejnem
Tišnov
Brno
Slavkov u Brna
Bučovice
Kyjov
Hodonín
Břeclav
Mikulov
Znojmo
Moravský Krumlov
Hustopeče
Veselí nad Moravou
Uherské Hradiště
Uherský Brod
Trenčín
Nové Mesto
Piešťany
Trnava
Senica
Skalica
Myjava
Malacky
Pezinok
Bratislava
Senec
Galanta
Šaľa
Nitra
Nové Zámky
Komárno
Dunajská Streda
Šamorín
Mosonmagyaróvár
Győr
Tata
Sopron
Eisenstadt
Neusiedl
Wiener Neustadt
Baden
Mödling
WIEN VIENNA
Schwechat
Tulln
Krems
Sankt Pölten
Stockerau
Korneuburg
Klosterneuburg
Hollabrunn
Mistelbach
Laa an der Thaya
Horn
Neunkirchen
Mattersburg
Českomoravská Vrchovina
Nízký Jeseník
Bílé Karpaty
Malé Karpaty
Moravský Kras
Žďárské vrchy
Neusiedler See
Fertő
Hanság
Seewinkel
Podyjí
SLOVAKIA
Dunaj
Donauauen
53
54
63
73
74
1
2
3
A
B
C

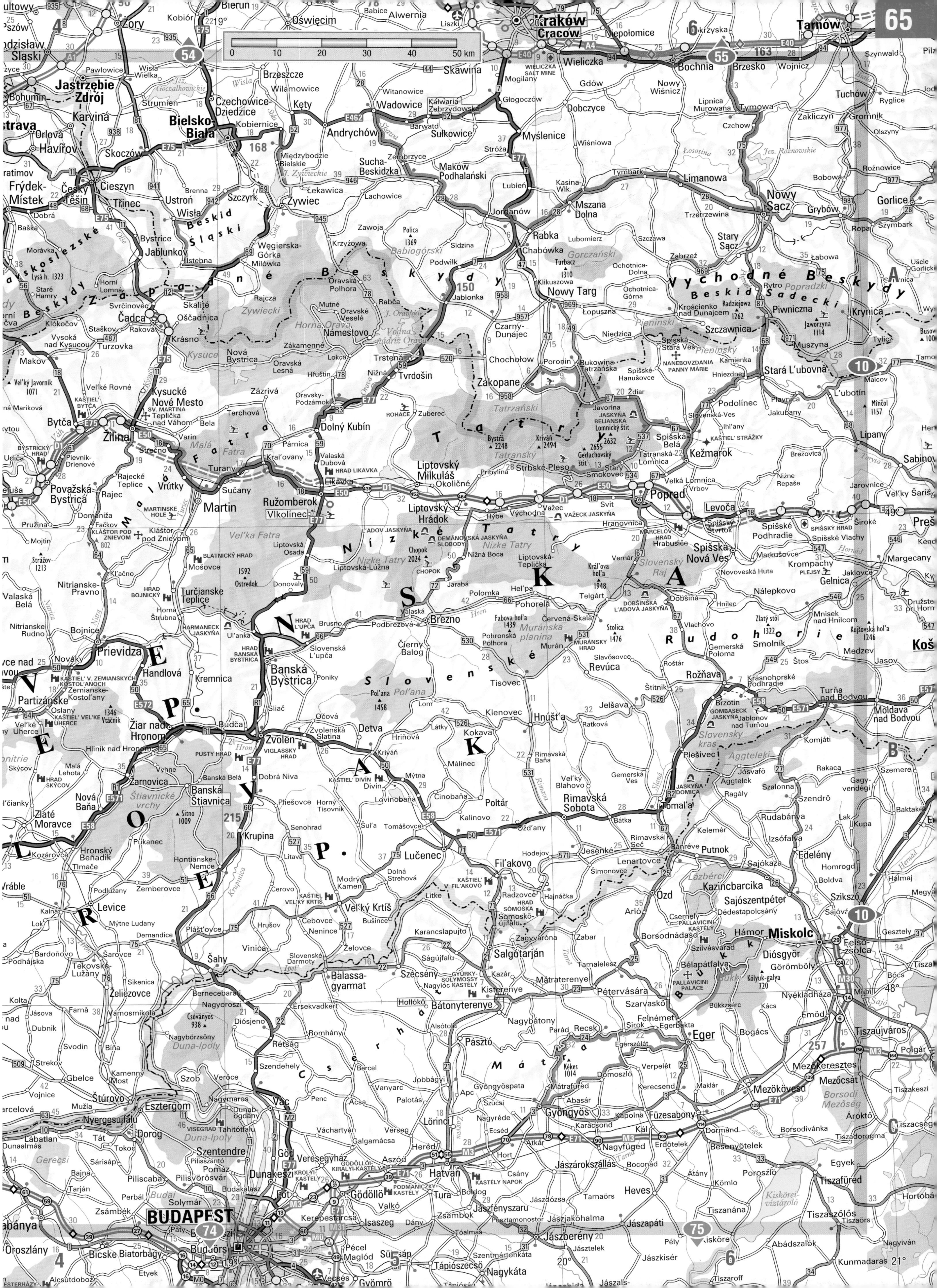
Kraków
Cracow
Tarnów
Wieliczka
WIELICZKA SALT MINE
Bochnia
Brzesko
Oświęcim
Bielsko-Biała
Jastrzębie Zdrój
Karviná
Havířov
Ostrava
Frýdek-Místek
Český Těšin
Cieszyn
Żywiec
Wadowice
Andrychów
Myślenice
Limanowa
Nowy Sącz
Nowy Targ
Zakopane
Rabka
Beskid Śląski
Beskidy
Západné Beskydy
Východné Beskydy
Beskid Sądecki
Krynica
Stará L'ubovňa
Čadca
Žilina
Martin
Ružomberok
Dolný Kubín
Liptovský Mikuláš
Poprad
Kežmarok
Levoča
Spišská Nová Ves
Tatry
Nízke Tatry
Malá Fatra
Veľká Fatra
Slovenský Raj
Rudohorie
Slovenské
SLOVENSKÁ
Prievidza
Banská Bystrica
Brezno
Zvolen
Banská Štiavnica
Žiar nad Hronom
Levice
Lučenec
Rimavská Sobota
Rožňava
Košice
Miskolc
Eger
Gyöngyös
Salgótarján
Balassagyarmat
Vác
Esztergom
Szentendre
Gödöllő
Hatvan
BUDAPEST
Budaörs
Jászberény
Mezőkövesd
Tiszaújváros
Mátra
Cserhát
Bükk
Aggteleki
EUROPA
EUROPA
0 10 20 30 40 50 km
54
55
74
75
4
5
6
A
B
C
10

Auray
Vannes
Questembert
Rochefort-en-Terre
Redon
Châteaubriant
Segré
Belz
Carnac
La Trinité
Locmariaquer
Port-Navalo
Sarzeau
Muzillac
Noyalo
Presqu'île de Quiberon
St. Pierre-Quiberon
Quiberon
Baie de Quiberon
St. Gildas-de-Rhuys
Côte Sauvage
Sauzon
Le Palais
Bangor
Locmaria
Belle-Île
Île de Houat
Île de Hœdic
Damgan
Pénestin
La Roche-Bernard
Herbignac
Missillac
Pontchâteau
Bouvron
Blain
St. Nicolas-de-Redon
Guémené-Penfao
Plessé
St. Gildas-des-Bois
Derval
Nozay
Nort-sur-Erdre
Héric
Joué-sur-Erdre
Les Touches
La Meilleraye-de-Bretagne
Riallé
St. Julien-de-Vouvantes
La Chapelle-Glain
Candé
Vern-d'Anjou
St. Mars-la-Jaille
Le Louroux-Béconnais
Bécon-les-Granits
Château de Serrant
Ingrandes
Varades
Ancenis
Ligné
Oudon
Liré
Montjean-sur-Loire
St. Florent-le-Vieil
Piriac-sur-Mer
La Turballe
St. Lyphard
Brière
St. Joachim
Montoir-de-Bretagne
Trignac
Guérande
La Baule-Escoublac
Le Croisic
Pte. du Croisic
Le Pouliguen
Pornichet
St. Nazaire
Donges
Savenay
Le Temple-de-Bretagne
La Chapelle-sur-Erdre
Carquefou
Orvault
Nantes
Côte d'Amour
Paimboeuf
St. Brevin-les-Pins
St. Michel-Chef-Chef
St. Père-en-Retz
St. Etienne-de-Montluc
Couëron
St. Herblain
Le Pellerin
Bouguenais
Bouaye
Rezé
Vertou
St. Laurent-des-Autels
Le Loroux-Bottereau
Champtoceaux
Montrevault
St. Pierre-Montlimart
Beaupréau
Gesté
Jallais
Vallet
Le May-sur-Èvre
Gijón
Pte. de St. Gildas
Préfailles
Pornic
La Bernerie-en-Retz
Baie de Bourgneuf
Bourgneuf-en-Retz
Arthon-en-Retz
Lac de Grand-Lieu
Pont St. Martin
St. Philbert-de-Grand-Lieu
Aigrefeuille-sur-Maine
Clisson
Château de Clisson
Montfaucon
Cholet
Torfou
Machecoul
Noirmoutier-en-l'Île
La Guérinière
Île de Noirmoutier
Barbâtre
Beauvoir-sur-Mer
Bouin
La Barre-de-Monts
Vieillevigne
Rocheservière
La Garnache
Touvois
Montaigu
La Bruffière
La Gaubretière
Mortagne-sur-Sèvre
St. Laurent-sur-Sèvre
Chavagnes-en-Paillers
Puy du Fou
Mauléon
Challans
St. Christophe-du-Ligneron
Legé
Les Lucs-sur-Boulogne
St. Fulgent
Les Herbiers
St. Michel-Mont-Mercure
Côte de Jade
St. Jean-de-Monts
Port-Joinville
Île d'Yeu
Palluau
Le Poiré-sur-Vie
Les Essarts
Belleville-sur-Vie
Aizenay
St. Hilaire-de-Riez
St. Gilles-Croix-de-Vie
Beaulieu-sous-la-Roche
La Ferrière
La Roche-sur-Yon
La Chaize-le-Vicomte
Chantonnay
Mouilleron-en-Pareds
Pouzauges
La Châtaigneraie
La Chaize-Giraud
Brem-sur-Mer
La Mothe-Achard
Aubigny
Bournezeau
La Caillère
Ste. Hermine
Nieul-le-Dolent
Mareuil-sur-Lay
Olonne-sur-Mer
Château-d'Olonne
Les Sables-d'Olonne
Moutiers-les-Mauxfaits
Ste. Gemme-la-Plaine
Talmont-St. Hilaire
Jard-sur-Mer
Longeville-sur-Mer
Angles
Luçon
Nalliers
Triaize
Chaillé-les-Marais
Maillezais
Marais
La Tranche-sur-Mer
L'Aiguillon-sur-Mer
St. Michel-en-l'Herm
Marans
Pertuis Breton
F
Ars-en-Ré
St. Martin-de-Ré
Île de Ré
La Flotte
Nieul-sur-Mer
Nuaillé-d'Aunis
Dompierre-sur-Mer
La Rochelle
Rivedoux-Plage
Aigrefeuille-d'Aunis
Angoulins
Pertuis d'Antioche
Châtelaillon-Plage
Muron
St. Denis-d'Oléron
Île d'Aix
St. Georges-d'Oléron
Fouras
Rochefort
Tonnay-Charente
St. Pierre-d'Oléron
Port-des-Barques
Le Château-d'Oléron
La Cotinière
Île d'Oléron
Brouage
Bourcefranc-le-Chapus
St. Agnant
St. Trojan-les-Bains
Marennes
Pertuis de Maumusson
Ronce-les-Bains
St. Porchaire
La Tremblade
Cadeuil
La Palmyre
Pte. de la Coubre
Saujon
St. Palais-sur-Mer
Royan
St. Georges-de-Didonne
Cozes
Pte. de Grave
Meschers-sur-Gironde
Le Verdon-sur-Mer
Talmont-sur-Gironde
Soulac-sur-Mer
Gironde
Mortagne-sur-Gironde
St. Vivien-de-Médoc
Montalivet-les-Bains
Vendays-Montalivet
Lesparre-Médoc
Hourtin-Plage
Cissac-Médoc
Hourtin
Étang d'Hourtin-Carcans
St. Laurent-Médoc
Fort Médoc
Carcans-Plage
Carcans
Listrac-Médoc
56
57
76
47°
46°
3°
2°
1°
A
B
C
1
2
3
0
10
20
30
40
50 km

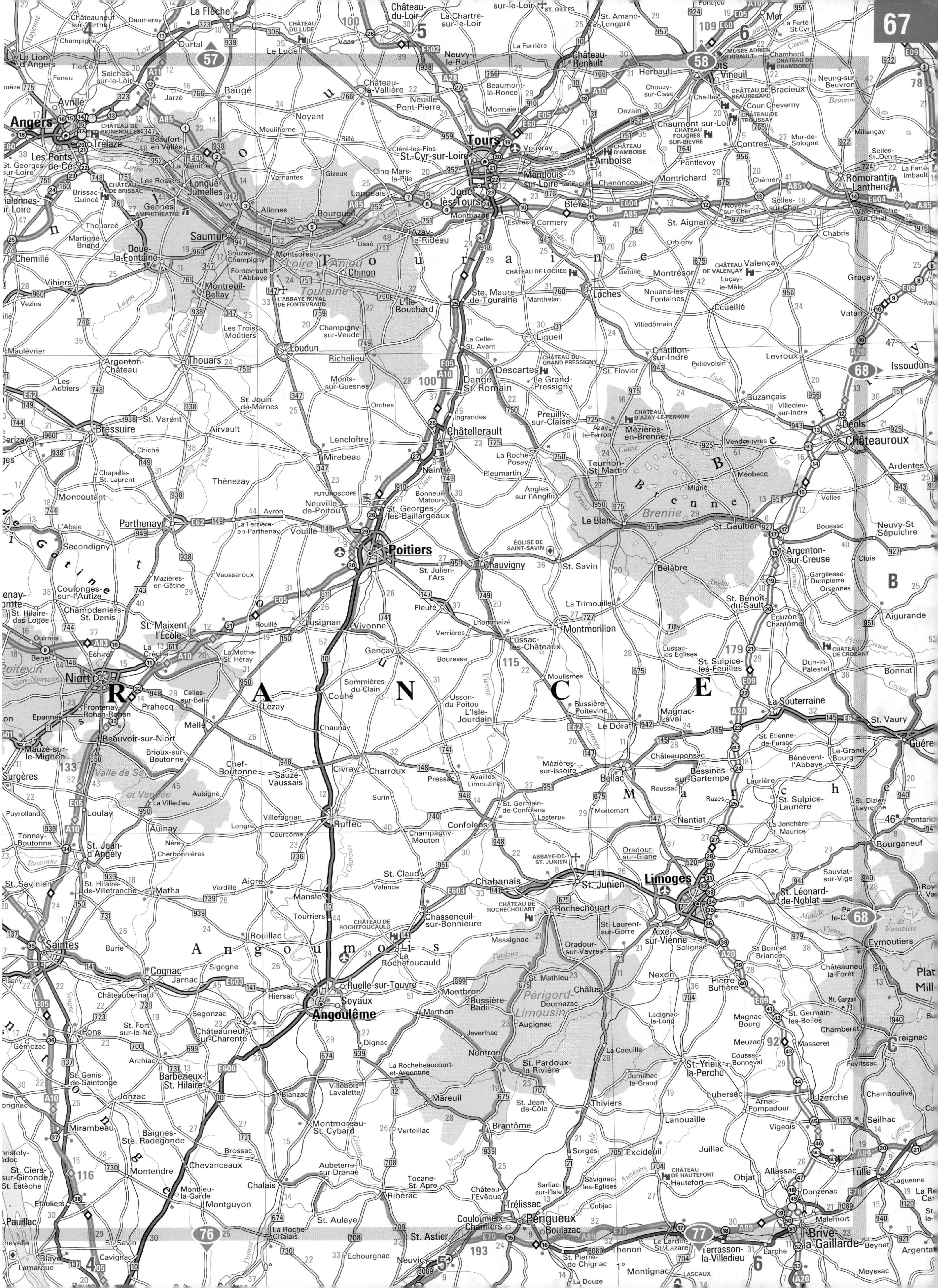

Château-du-Loir
La Chartre-sur-le-Loir
La Flèche
Durtal
Le Lude
Châteauneuf-sur-Sarthe
Champigné
Le Lion-d'Angers
Tiercé
Feneu
Seiches-sur-le-Loir
Baugé
Jarzé
Avrillé
Angers
Trélazé
Les Ponts-de-Cé
St. Georges-sur-Loire
Château de Pignerolles
Beaufort-en-Vallée
La Ménitré
Longué-Jumelles
Les Rosiers
Gennes
Amphithéâtre
Brissac-Quincé
Château de Brissac
Noyant
Mouliherne
Vernantes
Gizeux
Allones
Bourgueil
Saumur
Doué-la-Fontaine
Thouarcé
Martigné-Briand
Chemillé
Vihiers
Vezins
Montsoreau
Souzay-Champigny
Fontevrault-l'Abbaye
L'Abbaye Royal de Fontevraud
Loire Anjou Touraine
Chinon
Montreuil-Bellay
Les Trois-Moûtiers
Loudun
Richelieu
Thouars
Argenton-Château
Les Aubiers
Bressuire
St. Varent
Airvault
Chiché
Chapelle-St. Laurent
Moncoutant
Parthenay
L'Absie
Secondigny
Gâtine
Vasseroux
Mazières-en-Gâtine
Coulonges-sur-l'Autize
Champdeniers-St. Denis
St. Hilaire-des-Loges
Oulmes
Benet
Niort
Echiré
St. Maixent-l'École
La Crèche
La Mothe-St. Héray
Rouillé
Lusignan
Vivonne
Poitevin
Sèvre-Niortaise
Frontenay-Rohan-Rohan
Epannes
Mauzé-sur-le-Mignon
Beauvoir-sur-Niort
Prahecq
Celles-sur-Belle
Melle
Brioux-sur-Boutonne
Surgères
Valle de Sèvre et Vendée
Aubigné
La Villedieu
Loulay
Puyrolland
Tonnay-Boutonne
St. Jean-d'Angély
Aulnay
Néré
Cherbonnières
St. Savinien
St. Hilaire-de-Villefranche
Matha
Saintes
Burie
Cognac
Jarnac
Châteaubernard
Segonzac
Pons
St. Fort-sur-le-Né
Archiac
Gémozac
St. Genis-de-Saintonge
Jonzac
Barbezieux-St. Hilaire
Mirambeau
Baignes-Ste. Radegonde
Brossac
Montendre
Chevanceaux
St. Ciers-sur-Gironde
St. Estèphe
Pauillac
Etauliers
Blaye
Cavignac
St. Savin
Montlieu-la-Garde
Montguyon
Chalais
La Roche-Chalais
Angoumois
Rouillac
Angoulême
Soyaux
Ruelle-sur-Touvre
Hiersac
Châteauneuf-sur-Charente
Dignac
La Rochefoucauld
Château de Rochefoucauld
Montbron
Marthon
Blanzac
Villebois-Lavalette
Montmoreau-St. Cybard
Aubeterre-sur-Dronne
Ribérac
Verteillac
Tocane-St. Apre
St. Aulaye
St. Astier
Echourgnac
Neuvic
Mansle
Aigre
Tourriers
Villefagnan
Ruffec
Courcôme
Civray
Charroux
Sauzé-Vaussais
Chef-Boutonne
Couhé
Chaunay
Lezay
Sommières-du-Clain
Gençay
Usson-du-Poitou
L'Isle-Jourdain
Availles-Limouzine
Pressac
Confolens
Champagny-Mouton
St. Claud
Valence
Chasseneuil-sur-Bonnieure
Chabanais
St. Junien
Abbaye de St. Junien
Rochechouart
Château de Rochechouart
Massignac
Périgord-Limousin
Bussière-Badil
Nontron
Javerlhac
Augignac
Dournazac
Châlus
St. Mathieu
Oradour-sur-Vayres
St. Pardoux-la-Rivière
Mareuil
Brantôme
La Rochebeaucourt-et-Argentine
St. Jean-de-Côle
Thiviers
Château-l'Evêque
Périgueux
Coulounieix-Chamiers
Boulazac
Trélissac
Sorges
Excideuil
Savignac-les-Eglises
Sarliac-sur-l'Isle
Cubjac
Château de Hautefort
Hautefort
Juillac
Objat
Lanouaille
Jumilhac-le-Grand
La Coquille
St. Yrieix-la-Perche
Lubersac
Arnac-Pompadour
Vigeois
Uzerche
Allassac
Donzenac
Tulle
Brive-la-Gaillarde
Malemort
Larche
Terrasson-la-Villedieu
Le Lardin-St. Lazare
St. Pierre-de-Chignac
Thenon
Montignac
Lascaux
La Douze
Meyssac
Beynat
Argentat
Laguenne
Seilhac
Chamboulive
Limoges
Aixe-sur-Vienne
Solignac
Nexon
Pierre-Buffière
Ladignac-le-Long
Magnac-Bourg
Meuzac
Masseret
Coussac-Bonneval
St. Germain-les-Belles
Chamberet
Treignac
Eymoutiers
St Bonnet Briance
Châteauneuf-la-Forêt
Mt. Gargan
St. Léonard-de-Noblat
Sauviat-sur-Vige
Ambazac
La Jonchère-St. Maurice
Bourganeuf
St. Laurent-sur-Gorre
Oradour-sur-Glane
Nantiat
Razès
Roussac
Mortemart
St. Germain-de-Confolens
Lesterps
Bellac
Mézières-sur-Issoire
Le Dorat
Magnac-Laval
Châteauponsac
Bessines-sur-Gartempe
Laurière
St. Sulpice-Laurière
St. Etienne-de-Fursac
Bénévent-l'Abbaye
Le-Grand-Bourg
La Souterraine
St. Vaury
Guéret
St. Dizier-Leyrenne
Marche
Bussière-Poitevine
Moulismes
Lussac-les-Châteaux
L'hommaizé
Montmorillon
La Trimouille
Lussac-les-Eglises
St. Sulpice-les-Feuilles
Dun-le-Palestel
Château de Crozant
Bonnat
Aigurande
Eguzon-Chantôme
St. Benoît-du-Sault
Tilly
Gargilesse-Dampierre
Orsennes
Cluis
Argenton-sur-Creuse
Neuvy-St. Sépulchre
Bouesse
Bélâbre
St. Savin
Eglise de Saint-Savin
Chauvigny
St. Julien-l'Ars
Fleuré
Verrières
Bouresse
Poitiers
Vouillé
Ayron
La Ferrière-en-Parthenay
Neuville-de-Poitou
Futuroscope
St. Georges-lès-Baillargeaux
Bonneuil-Matours
Naintré
Châtellerault
Ingrandes
Dangé-St. Romain
Descartes
Le Grand-Pressigny
Château du Grand Pressigny
La Roche-Posay
Pleumartin
Angles sur l'Anglin
Preuilly-sur-Claise
Azay-le-Ferron
Château d'Azay-le-Ferron
Mézières-en-Brenne
Tournon-St. Martin
Le Blanc
Brenne
St.-Gaultier
Migné
Méobecq
Vendœuvres
Déols
Châteauroux
Ardentes
Velles
Buzançais
Villedieu-sur-Indre
Levroux
Pellevoisin
Châtillon-sur-Indre
St. Flovier
Ligueil
La Celle-St. Avant
Ste. Maure-de-Touraine
Manthelan
Loches
Villedômain
Nouans-les-Fontaines
Ecueillé
Montrésor
Genillé
Château de Loches
Château de Valençay
Valençay
Luçay-le-Mâle
Vatan
Graçay
Issoudun
Mirebeau
Thénezay
Lencloître
Orches
Monts-sur-Guesnes
St. Jouin-de-Marnes
Champigny-sur-Veude
L'Ile-Bouchard
Usse
Azay-le-Rideau
Montbazon
Esvres
Cormery
Joué-lès-Tours
Tours
St. Cyr-sur-Loire
Cléré-les-Pins
Cinq-Mars-la-Pile
Langeais
Rillé
Château-la-Vallière
Neuillé-Pont-Pierre
Beaumont-la-Ronce
Monnaie
Vouvray
Montlouis-sur-Loire
La Croix
Bléré
Chenonceaux
Amboise
Château d'Amboise
Neuvy-le-Roi
Château-Renault
Vaas
Château du Lude
La Ferrière
St. Amand-Longpré
Herbault
Onzain
Chouzy-sur-Cisse
Chaumont-sur-Loire
Château Fougres-sur-Bievre
Pontlevoy
Montrichard
St. Aignan
Orbigny
Noyers-sur-Cher
Selles-sur-Cher
Châtillon
Chémery
Contres
Mur-de-Sologne
Cour-Cheverny
Château de Troussay
Château de Beauregard
Bracieux
Chailles
Blois
Vineuil
Musée Adrien Thibault
Chambord
Château de Chambord
Mer
La Ferté-St.Cyr
Neung-sur-Beuvron
Millançay
Romorantin-Lanthenay
Villefranche-sur-Cher
Selles-St. Denis
La Ferté-Imbault
Chabris
Gracay
Touraine
Anjou
FRANCE
Berry
Limousin

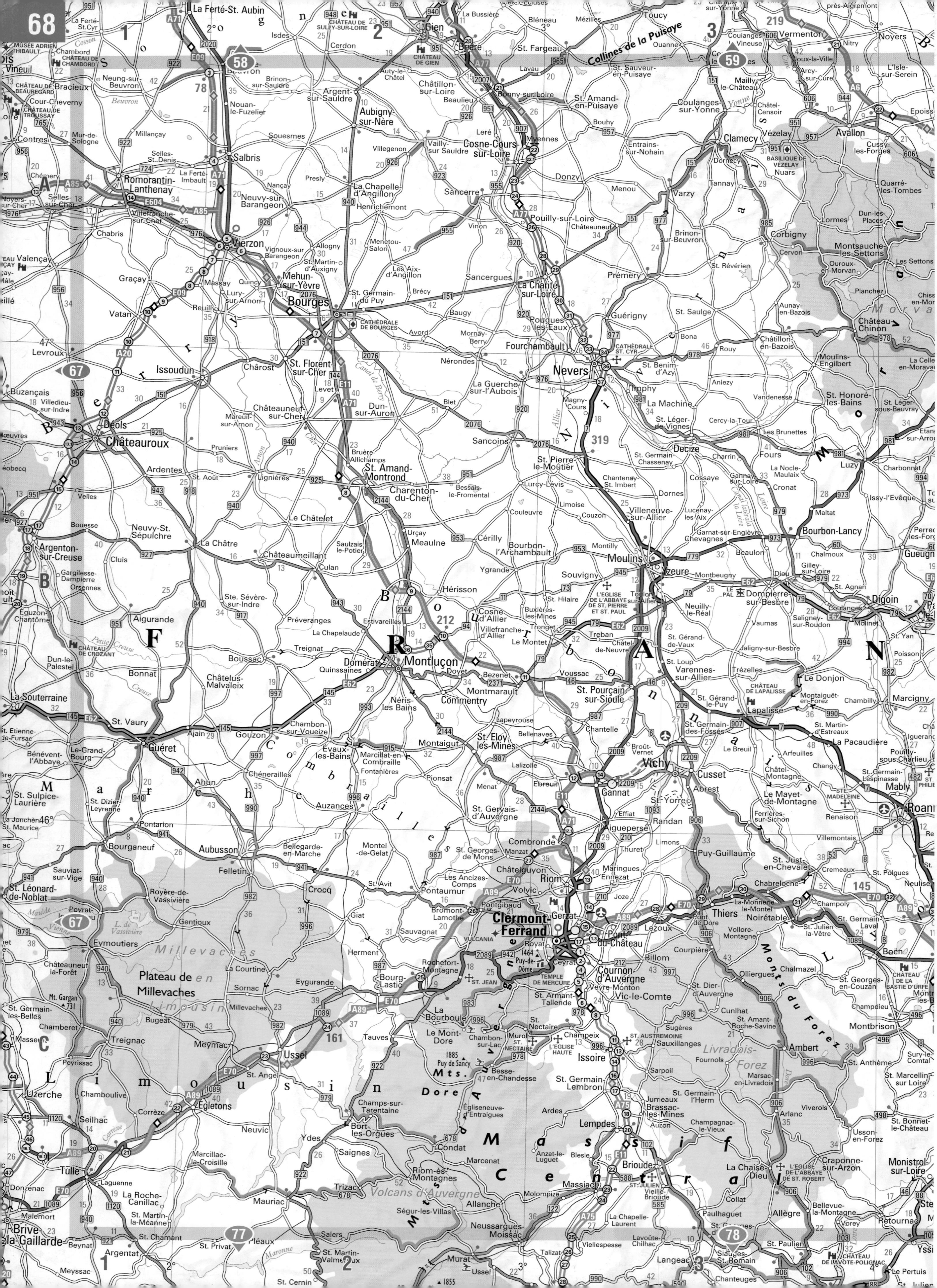

La Ferté-St. Aubin
Gien
Briare
Toucy
Bléneau
St. Fargeau
Collines de la Puisaye
Coulanges-Vineuse
Vermenton
Noyers
Beuvron
Cerdon
Isdes
Chambord
Château de Chambord
Neung-sur-Beuvron
Brinon-sur-Sauldre
Argent-sur-Sauldre
Aubigny-sur-Nère
Châtillon-sur-Loire
Bonny-sur-Loire
St. Sauveur-en-Puisaye
St. Amand-en-Puisaye
Coulanges-sur-Yonne
Mailly-le-Château
Cour-Cheverny
Nouan-le-Fuzelier
Souesmes
Cosne-Cours-sur-Loire
Myennes
Entrains-sur-Nohain
Clamecy
Vézelay
Avallon
Contres
Salbris
Romorantin-Lanthenay
La Ferté-Imbault
Neuvy-sur-Barangeon
Presly
La Chapelle-d'Angillon
Henrichemont
Sancerre
Donzy
Menou
Varzy
Tannay
Quarré-les-Tombes
Vierzon
Vignoux-sur-Barangeon
Allogny
Menetou-Salon
Vinon
Pouilly-sur-Loire
Brinon-sur-Beuvron
Corbigny
Lormes
Montsauche-les-Settons
Valençay
Graçay
Massay
Mehun-sur-Yèvre
Les Aix-d'Angillon
Sancergues
La Charité-sur-Loire
Prémery
St. Révérien
Vatan
Bourges
Cathédrale de Bourges
Baugy
Pouques-les-Eaux
Guérigny
St. Saulge
Château-Chinon
Levroux
Issoudun
Chârost
St. Florent-sur-Cher
Avord
Nérondes
Fourchambault
Nevers
Cathédrale St. Cyr
St. Benin-d'Azy
Châtillon-en-Bazois
Moulins-Engilbert
Buzançais
Déols
Châteauroux
Châteauneuf-sur-Cher
Levet
Dun-sur-Auron
La Guerche-sur-l'Aubois
Magny-Cours
Imphy
La Machine
St. Léger-de-Vignes
Decize
St. Honoré-les-Bains
Luzy
Ardentes
Lignières
St. Amand-Montrond
Charenton-du-Cher
Bessais-le-Fromental
Sancoins
St. Pierre-le-Moûtier
Lurcy-Lévis
Chantenay-St. Imbert
Dornes
Cossaye
Cronat
Issy-l'Evêque
Velles
Neuvy-St. Sépulchre
Le Châtelet
Urçay
Meaulne
Cérilly
Bourbon-l'Archambault
Villeneuve-sur-Allier
Bourbon-Lancy
Argenton-sur-Creuse
La Châtre
Châteaumeillant
Culan
Ygrande
Souvigny
Moulins
Yzeure
Chevagnes
Beaulon
Dompierre-sur-Besbre
Digoin
Gueugnon
Eguzon-Chantôme
Aigurande
Ste. Sévère-sur-Indre
Préveranges
Hérisson
Cosne-d'Allier
Buxières-les-Mines
L'Eglise de l'Abbaye de St. Pierre et St. Paul
Neuilly-le-Réal
Château de Crozant
Boussac
Treignat
Domérat
Montluçon
Quinssaines
Villefranche-d'Allier
Le Montet
Treban
St. Gérand-de-Vaux
Jaligny-sur-Besbre
Dun-le-Palestel
Bonnat
Châtelus-Malvaleix
Néris-les-Bains
Commentry
Montmarault
Bezenet
Doyet
Voussac
St. Pourçain-sur-Sioule
Varennes-sur-Allier
Château de Lapalisse
Lapalisse
Le Donjon
Marcigny
La Souterraine
St. Vaury
Guéret
Ajain
Gouzon
Chambon-sur-Voueize
Evaux-les-Bains
Montaigut
St. Eloy-les-Mines
Chantelle
Vichy
Cusset
La Pacaudière
Bénévent-l'Abbaye
Le-Grand-Bourg
Chénerailles
Marcillat-en-Combraille
Pionsat
Menat
Gannat
St. Yorre
Le Mayet-de-Montagne
Mably
Roanne
St. Sulpice-Laurière
St. Dizier-Leyrenne
Ahun
Auzances
St. Gervais-d'Auvergne
Aigueperse
Randan
Renaison
Pontarion
Bourganeuf
Aubusson
Bellegarde-en-Marche
Montel-de-Gelat
Combronde
Riom
Châtelguyon
Volvic
Puy-Guillaume
St. Just-en-Chevalet
St. Léonard-de-Noblat
Felletin
Crocq
Pontaumur
Pontgibaud
Clermont-Ferrand
Vulcania
Royat
Puy-de-Dôme
Pont-du-Château
Lezoux
Thiers
Noirétable
Boën
Eymoutiers
Plateau de Millevaches
Millevaches
Limousin
La Courtine
Herment
Rochefort-Montagne
Cournon-d'Auvergne
Billom
Courpière
Monts du Forez
Mt. Gargan
Bugeat
Sornac
Eygurande
Bourg-Lastic
La Bourboule
Le Mont-Dore
Chambon-sur-Lac
Murol
St. Nectaire
Champeix
Vic-le-Comte
Issoire
Sauxillanges
Livradois-Forez
Ambert
Montbrison
Treignac
Meymac
Ussel
Tauves
Puy de Sancy
Mts. Dore
Besse-en-Chandesse
St. Germain-Lembron
Sarpoil
Uzerche
Egletons
Neuvic
Bort-les-Orgues
Champs-sur-Tarentaine
Condat
Ardes
Lempdes
Brassac-les-Mines
Arlanc
Saignes
Marcenat
Anzat-le-Luguet
Blesle
Brioude
La Chaise-Dieu
Craponne-sur-Arzon
Tulle
Laguenne
La Roche-Canillac
Riom-ès-Montagnes
Volcans d'Auvergne
Mauriac
Allanche
Massiac
Paulhaguet
Allègre
Monistrol-sur-Loire
Brive-la-Gaillarde
Argentat
Pleaux
St. Privat
Salers
Ségur-les-Villas
Neussargues-Moissac
Langeac
Retournac
Yssingeaux
Massif Central
Berry
Bourbonnais
Combrailles
Morvan
Nivernais

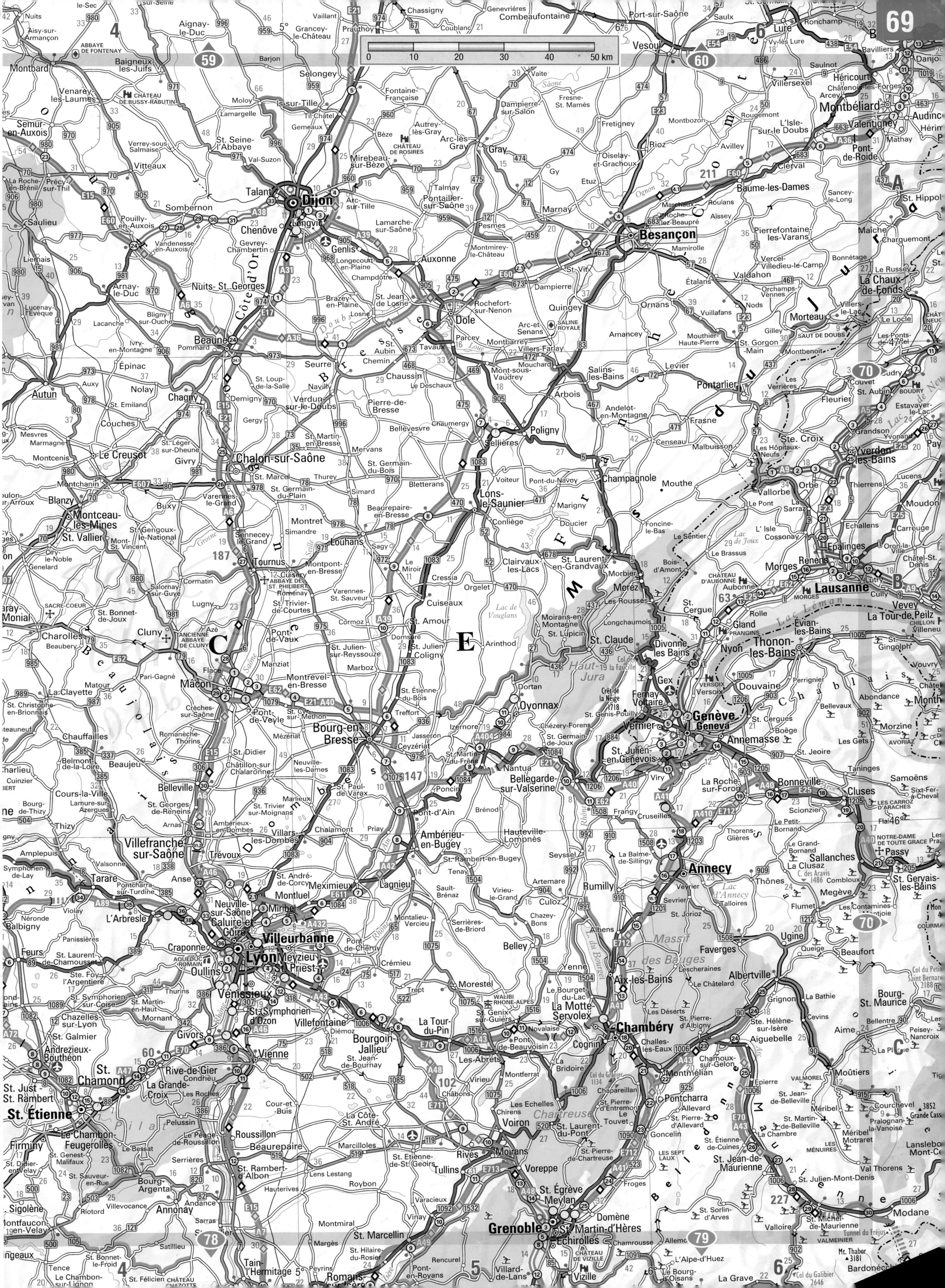

0 10 20 30 40 50 km
59
60
70
78
79
Dijon
Besançon
Montbéliard
Lausanne
Genève
Geneva
Lyon
Villeurbanne
Grenoble
Chambéry
Annecy
St. Étienne
Chalon-sur-Saône
Mâcon
Bourg-en-Bresse
Lons-le-Saunier
Dole
Beaune
Vesoul
Pontarlier
Neuchâtel
Yverdon-les-Bains
Morges
Nyon
Thonon-les-Bains
Évian-les-Bains
Annemasse
Bonneville
Cluses
Sallanches
Albertville
Aix-les-Bains
Vienne
Voiron
Romans-sur-Isère
Villefranche-sur-Saône
Oyonnax
St. Claude
Bellegarde-sur-Valserine
Belley
Bourgoin-Jallieu
Le Creusot
Montceau-les-Mines
Autun
Tournus
Louhans
Cluny
Charolles
Paray-le-Monial
Poligny
Arbois
Salins-les-Bains
Gray
Auxonne
Nuits-St-Georges
Semur-en-Auxois
Montbard
Saulieu
Vitteaux
Is-sur-Tille
Baume-les-Dames
Lure
Héricourt
Morteau
La Chaux-de-Fonds
Le Locle
Valence
Tain-l'Hermitage
Annonay
Rive-de-Gier
Givors
Vénissieux
Meyzieu
St. Priest
Oullins
Tarare
Montluel
Ambérieu-en-Bugey
Nantua
St. Genis-Pouilly
Ferney-Voltaire
Gex
Divonne-les-Bains
Rumilly
Faverges
Ugine
Megève
St. Gervais-les-Bains
Moûtiers
Bourg-St. Maurice
St. Jean-de-Maurienne
Modane
Montmélian
Pontcharra
Vizille
Échirolles
St. Martin-d'Hères
Meylan
St. Égrève
Voreppe
Moirans
Rives
La Tour-du-Pin
Villefontaine
Côte d'Or
Bresse
Dombes
Beaujolais
Jura
Monts du Jura
Franche-Comté
Lac Léman
Lac de Vouglans
Massif des Bauges
Chartreuse
Belledonne
Maurienne
Pilat
Chablais
Haut-Jura
Lac d'Annecy
Lac du Bourget
A
B
C
E
4
5
6

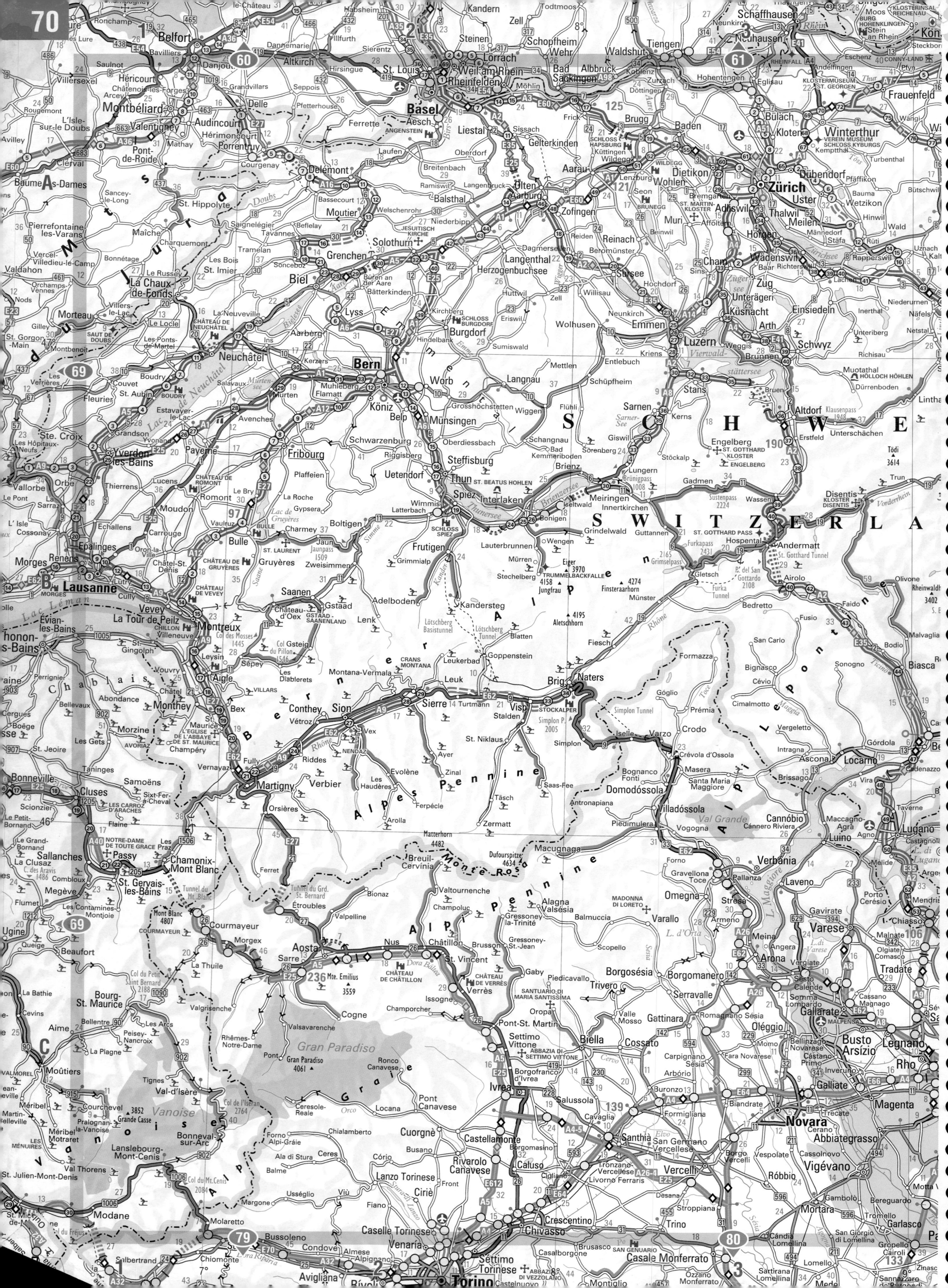
Belfort
Montbéliard
Basel
Lörrach
Schaffhausen
Winterthur
Zürich
Frauenfeld
Baden
Aarau
Delémont
Solothurn
Biel
Grenchen
La Chaux-de-Fonds
Neuchâtel
Bern
Burgdorf
Luzern
Zug
Schwyz
Altdorf
Fribourg
Thun
Interlaken
Spiez
Yverdon-les-Bains
Lausanne
Vevey
Montreux
Lac Léman
Thonon-les-Bains
Évian-les-Bains
Aigle
Monthey
Martigny
Sion
Sierre
Visp
Brig
Zermatt
Matterhorn 4482
Jungfrau 4158
Eiger 3970
Finsteraarhorn 4274
Aletschhorn 4195
SCHWEIZ
SWITZERLAND
Berner Alpen
Alpes Pennines
Alpi Pennine
Alpi Lepontine
Monte Rosa
Domodóssola
Locarno
Lugano
Bellinzona
Biasca
Airolo
Andermatt
Chamonix-Mont Blanc
Mont Blanc 4807
Courmayeur
Aosta
Gran Paradiso 4061
Vanoise
Alpi Graie
Ivrea
Biella
Novara
Vercelli
Varese
Gallarate
Busto Arsízio
Legnano
Rho
Magenta
Vigévano
Verbania
Arona
Borgomanero
Chivasso
Torino
Casale Monferrato
Modane
Bourg-St. Maurice
Sallanches
Cluses
Bonneville
Jura
Doubs

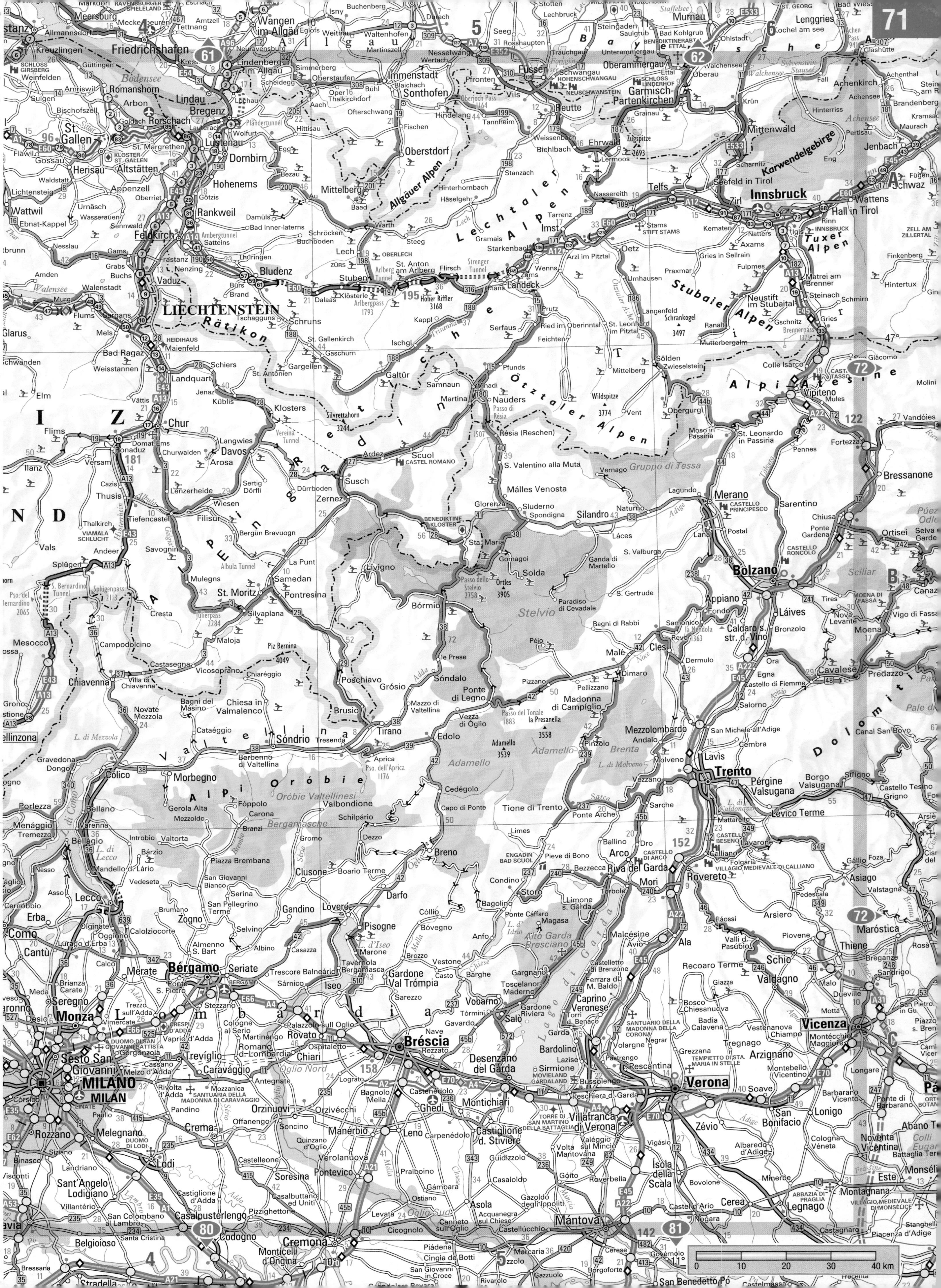

Meersburg
Friedrichshafen
Wangen im Allgäu
Isny
Allgäu
Bayerische
Murnau
Lenggries
Kochel am see
Tettnang
Lindenberg im Allgäu
Immenstadt
Sonthofen
Füssen
Oberammergau
Garmisch-Partenkirchen
Bodensee
Romanshorn
Lindau
Bregenz
Rorschach
St. Gallen
Herisau
Appenzell
Altstätten
Lustenau
Dornbirn
Hohenems
Oberstdorf
Mittelberg
Allgäuer Alpen
Reutte
Ehrwald
Zugspitze 2693
Mittenwald
Karwendelgebirge
Jenbach
Schwaz
Seefeld in Tirol
Telfs
Innsbruck
Hall in Tirol
Wattens
Lechtaler Alpen
Imst
Landeck
Tuxer Alpen
Stubaier Alpen
Rankweil
Feldkirch
Vaduz
LIECHTENSTEIN
Bludenz
Lech
Warth
St. Anton am Arlberg
Arlbergpass 1793
Hoher Riffler 3168
Schruns
Rätikon
Ischgl
Galtür
Serfaus
Ötztaler Alpen
Wildspitze 3774
Sölden
Obergurgl
Längenfeld
Schrankogel 3497
Matrei am Brenner
Steinach
Gries
Brennerpass 1375
Vipiteno
Alpi Atesine
Walensee
Sargans
Bad Ragaz
Maienfeld
Landquart
Klosters
Silvrettahorn 3244
Davos
Arosa
Chur
Flims
Ilanz
Thusis
Splügen
Lenzerheide
Scuol
Susch
Zernez
Nauders
Passo di Resia
Résia (Reschen)
S. Valentino alla Muta
Málles Venosta
Glorenza
Silandro
Merano
Gruppo di Tessa
St. Leonardo in Passiria
Fortezza
Bressanone
Samedan
St. Moritz
Silvaplana
Pontresina
Maloja
Piz Bernina 4049
Livigno
Bórmio
Passo dello Stelvio 2758
Ortles 3905
Solda
Stelvio
Poschiavo
Tirano
Sóndalo
Ponte di Legno
Passo del Tonale 1883
La Presanella 3558
Madonna di Campiglio
Cles
Malè
Bolzano
Appiano
Ortisei
Sciliar
Cavalese
Dolomiti
Mesocco
Chiavenna
Bellinzona
Sóndrio
Valtellina
Morbegno
Colico
Alpi Orobie
Edolo
Adamello 3539
Adamello
Brenta
Mezzolombardo
Lavis
Trento
Pérgine Valsugana
Levico Terme
Rovereto
Riva del Garda
Arco
Mori
Ala
Schio
Asiago
Maróstica
Thiene
Valdagno
Vicenza
Lago di Como
Bellagio
Menaggio
Lecco
Como
Cantù
Erba
Breno
Lóvere
Clusone
Darfo
Pisogne
L. d'Iseo
Iseo
Gardone Val Trómpia
Bérgamo
Seriate
Monza
Seregno
Lombardia
MILANO
MILAN
Sesto San Giovanni
Rozzano
Melegnano
Lodi
Sant'Angelo Lodigiano
Casalpusterlengo
Codogno
Crema
Treviglio
Caravàggio
Chiari
Rovato
Bréscia
Ghedi
Montichiari
Manérbio
Orzinuovi
Salò
Lago di Garda
Desenzano del Garda
Sirmione
Peschiera d. Garda
Bardolino
Garda
Malcésine
Verona
Villafranca di Verona
Soave
San Bonifacio
Lonigo
Legnago
Este
Mántova
Castiglione d. Stiviere
Asola
Cremona
Monticelli d'Ongina
Pavia
Stradella
San Benedetto Po
0 10 20 30 40 km

Innsbruck
Hall in Tirol
Schwaz
Jenbach
Wörgl
Kufstein
Kitzbühel
St. Johann in Tirol
Lofer
Berchtesgaden
Hallein
Bad Ischl
Bad Goisern
Bad Aussee
Hallstatt
Kuchl
Abtenau
Tennengebirge
Werfen
Bischofshofen
Saalfelden am Steinernen Meer
Zell am See
Mittersill
St. Johann im Pongau
Radstadt
Schladming
Gröbming
Bad Hofgastein
Bad Gastein
Tamsweg
St. Michael im Lungau
Mittenwald
Karwendelgebirge
Mayrhofen
Zillertaler Alpen
Kitzbüheler Alpen
Tuxer Alpen
Hohe Tauern
Grossvenediger 3674
Grossglockner 3797
Heiligenblut
Matrei in Osttirol
Lienz
Spittal an der Drau
Villach
Arnoldstein
Tarvisio
Hermagor
Kötschach
Gailtaler Alpen
Karnische Hochalpen
Julijske Alpe
Triglav 2864
Bovec
Kobarid
Tolmin
ÖSTERREICH
ITALIA
Vipiteno
Brunico
Dobbiaco
Bressanone
Ortisei
Cortina d'Ampezzo
Dolomiti
Pieve di Cadore
Belluno
Feltre
Agordo
Cavalese
Moena
Tolmezzo
Gemona del Friuli
Udine
Cividale del Friuli
Gorizia
Nova Gorica
Palmanova
Monfalcone
Trieste
Koper
Piran
Umag
Poreč
Rovinj
Pordenone
Sacile
Conegliano
Vittório Véneto
Treviso
Bassano del Grappa
Castelfranco Véneto
Vicenza
Pádova
Mestre
Venézia Venice
Chióggia
Rovigo
Portogruaro
Latisana
Lignano Sabbiadoro
Grado
Cáorle
Jésolo
San Donà di Piave
Golfo di Venézia
G. di Trieste
Igoumenitsa Patra
Igoumenitsa Patra Durrës Ancona
0 10 20 30 40 50 km
62
63
71
82
1
2
3
12°
13°

Hochschwab
Eisenerzer Alpen
Seckauer Alpen
Gleinalpe
Wölzer Tauern
Ennstaler Alpen
Graz
Bruck an der Mur
Leoben
Kapfenberg
Judenburg
Knittelfeld
Wolfsberg
Deutschlandsberg
Klagenfurt
St. Veit an der Glan
Völkermarkt
Villach
Szombathely
Maribor
Ptuj
Murska Sobota
Celje
Velenje
Ljubljana
Kranj
Novo Mesto
Kamnik
Pohorje
Kamniske in Savinjske Alpe
Karawanken
Bohor
Gorjanci
Žumberak-Samoborsko gorje
Medvednica
Ivanšćica
Kalnik
Petrova Gora
Zrinska Gora
Velika Kapela
Zagreb
Karlovac
Rijeka
Opatija
Varaždin
Čakovec
Sisak
Velika Gorica
Samobor
Zaprešić
Ogulin
Delnice
Kočevje
Postojna
Logatec
Vrhnika
Jesenice
Bled
SLOVENIJA
SLOVENIA
HRVATSKA
CROATIA

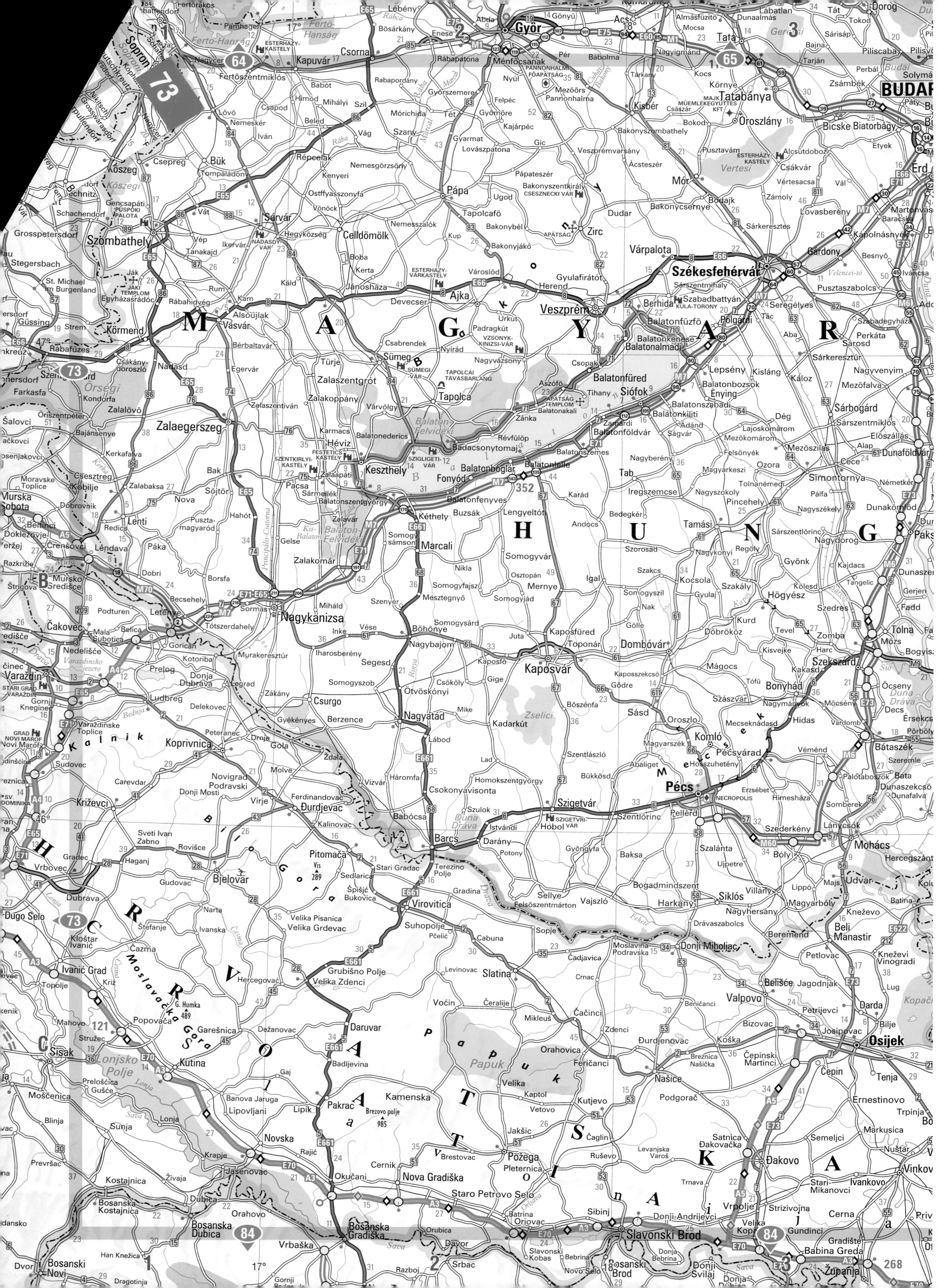

MAGYARORSZÁG
HUNGARY
HRVATSKA
SLAVONIJA
Sopron
Fertőd
Kapuvár
Csorna
Győr
Ménfőcsanak
Pannonhalma
Tata
Tatabánya
Oroszlány
Budapest
Bicske
Biatorbágy
Érd
Kisbér
Mór
Pápa
Zirc
Várpalota
Székesfehérvár
Veszprém
Ajka
Devecser
Jánosháza
Celldömölk
Sárvár
Szombathely
Kőszeg
Bük
Körmend
Vasvár
Szentgotthárd
Zalaegerszeg
Lenti
Sümeg
Tapolca
Zalaszentgrót
Hévíz
Keszthely
Fonyód
Balatonboglár
Balatonfüred
Tihany
Siófok
Balatonalmádi
Balatonfűzfő
Polgárdi
Enying
Lepsény
Gárdony
Velencei-tó
Ercsi
Adony
Dunaújváros
Sárbogárd
Simontornya
Paks
Tamási
Marcali
Nagykanizsa
Letenye
Kaposvár
Dombóvár
Szekszárd
Tolna
Bonyhád
Komló
Pécs
Pécsvárad
Szigetvár
Barcs
Nagyatád
Csurgó
Siklós
Harkány
Mohács
Bóly
Bátaszék
Baja
Čakovec
Varaždin
Koprivnica
Križevci
Bjelovar
Đurđevac
Virovitica
Slatina
Daruvar
Pakrac
Kutina
Novska
Sisak
Ivanić Grad
Dugo Selo
Vrbovec
Garešnica
Požega
Nova Gradiška
Okučani
Slavonski Brod
Đakovo
Osijek
Našice
Valpovo
Beli Manastir
Vinkovci
Županja
Bosanska Gradiška
Bosanska Dubica
Bosanski Brod
Bosanski Novi
Balaton
Papuk
Bilo Gora
Moslavačka Gora
Mecsek
Bakony
Vértes
Gerecse
Dráva
Duna
Sáva
73
64
65
84
268

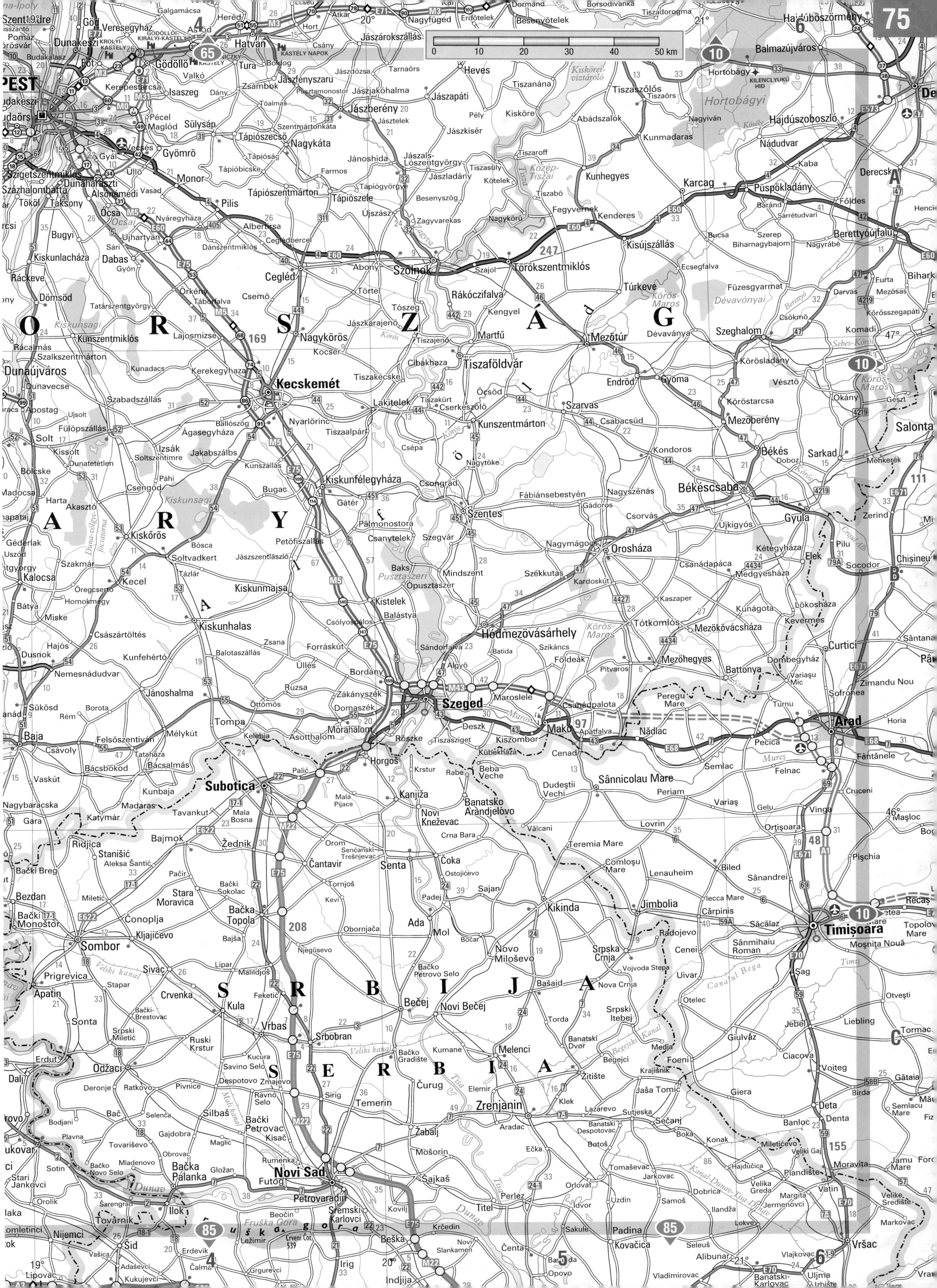

O R S Z Á G
A R Y
Ö f l d
S R B I J A
S E R B I A
Kecskemét
Szeged
Subotica
Novi Sad
Szolnok
Cegléd
Békéscsaba
Hódmezővásárhely
Kiskunfélegyháza
Kiskunhalas
Arad
Timișoara
Zrenjanin
Kikinda
Sombor
Bačka Topola
Senta
Makó
Orosháza
Szentes
Csongrád
Gyula
Mezőtúr
Karcag
Kunhegyes
Törökszentmiklós
Kisújszállás
Nagykőrös
Jászberény
Gödöllő
Hatvan
Dunakeszi
Gyömrő
Monor
Pilis
Dabas
Ráckeve
Kunszentmiklós
Dunaújváros
Kalocsa
Baja
Kiskőrös
Kecel
Kiskunmajsa
Kistelek
Mórahalom
Tompa
Jánoshalma
Szarvas
Gyoma
Endrőd
Tiszaföldvár
Martfű
Kunszentmárton
Mezőkovácsháza
Battonya
Mezőhegyes
Tótkomlós
Püspökladány
Berettyóújfalu
Hajdúszoboszló
Szeghalom
Hortobágy
Hortobágyi
Kiskunsági
Pusztaszeri
Kanjiža
Horgoš
Čantavir
Bečej
Novi Bečej
Kula
Vrbas
Srbobran
Temerin
Odžaci
Apatin
Bačka Palanka
Titel
Beška
Indjija
Irig
Šid
Ilok
Vukovar
Kovačica
Vršac
Jimbolia
Sânnicolau Mare
Nădlac
Pecica
Salonta
Deta
Fruška Gora
Dunav
Tisza
Maros
Mureș
Körös
0 10 20 30 40 50 km

Golfe de Gascogne
Bay of Biscay
Côte des Landes
Côte d'Argent
Côte Basque
Landes de Gascogne
Aquitaine
Gascogne
Béarn
Pays Basque
Pirineos Occidentales
Pyrénées
Bigorre
Bordeaux
Mérignac
Pessac
Arcachon
Biscarrosse
Mimizan
Mont-de-Marsan
Dax
Bayonne
Biarritz
Anglet
Hendaye
Irun
Donostia-San Sebastián
Pamplona
Pau
Tarbes
Lourdes
Oloron-Ste. Marie
Orthez
Aire-sur-l'Adour
Langon
Libourne
Marmande
Roquefort
Hossegor
Capbreton
St. Jean-de-Luz
St. Jean-Pied-de-Port
Mauléon-Licharre
Tolosa
Estella
Jaca
0 10 20 30 40 50 km
45°
44°
2°
1°
0°
A
B
C
D
1
2
66
67
89
90

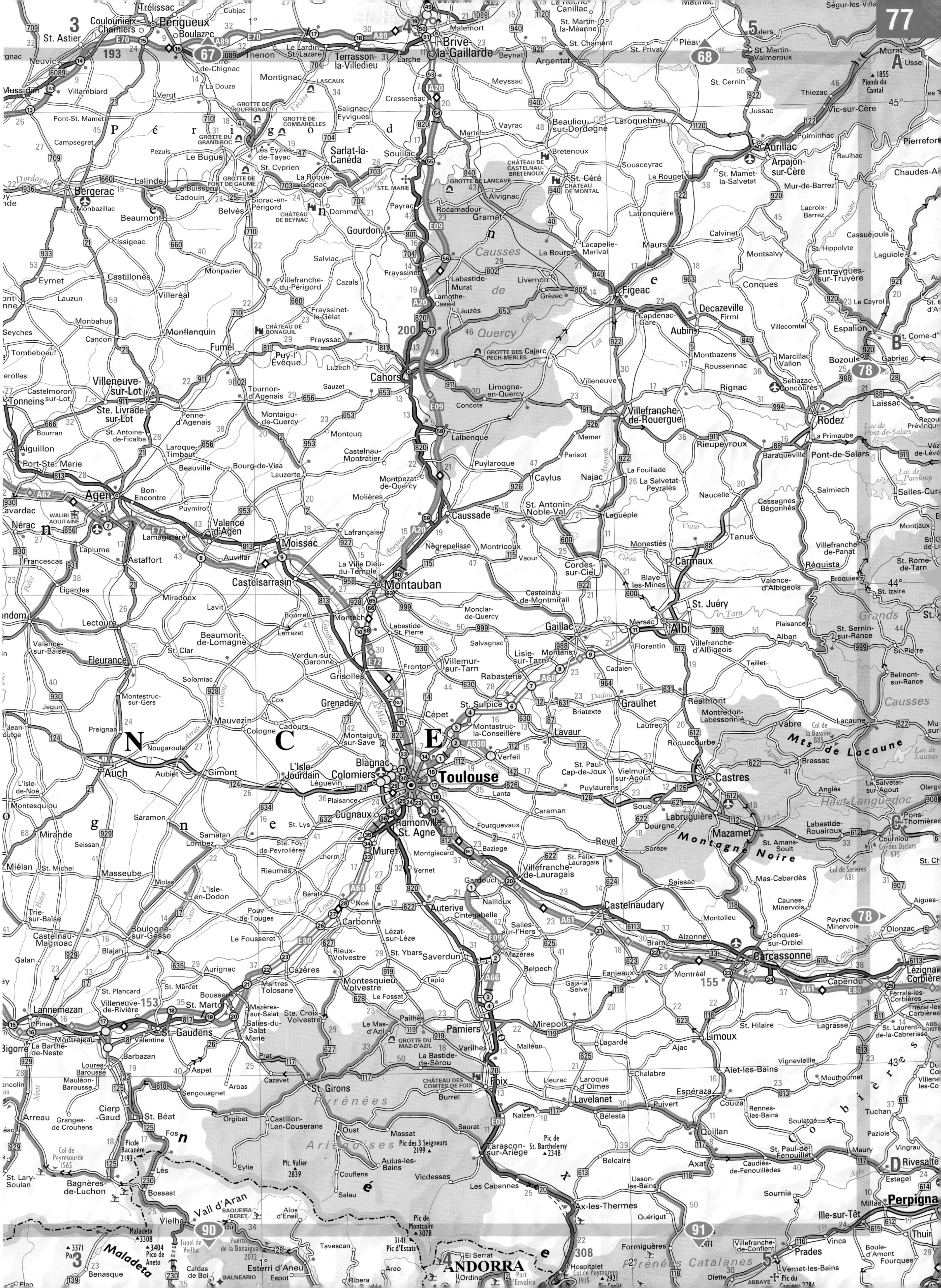
Périgueux
Brive-la-Gaillarde
Terrasson-la-Villedieu
Bergerac
Sarlat-la-Canéda
Les Eyzies-de-Tayac
Le Bugue
Gourdon
Rocamadour
Gramat
Figeac
Aurillac
Arpajon-sur-Cère
Decazeville
Villeneuve-sur-Lot
Fumel
Cahors
Causses de Quercy
Villefranche-de-Rouergue
Rodez
Agen
Valence-d'Agen
Moissac
Castelsarrasin
Montauban
Caussade
Carmaux
Albi
Gaillac
Castres
Mazamet
Lectoure
Fleurance
Auch
L'Isle-Jourdain
Blagnac
Colomiers
Toulouse
Muret
Castelnaudary
Carcassonne
Montagne Noire
Mts de Lacaune
Saint-Gaudens
Lannemezan
Pamiers
Foix
Mirepoix
Limoux
Quillan
St. Girons
Pyrénées Ariégoises
Tarascon-sur-Ariège
Ax-les-Thermes
Bagnères-de-Luchon
Vielha
Andorra
Prades
Perpignan
Corbières
Grands Causses
Haut-Languedoc
Pyrénées Catalanes
Maladeta

Massif Central
Volcans d'Auvergne
Mts. d'Aubrac
Mts. de la Margeride
Mts. du Velay
Causse-Méjean
Causse du Larzac
Grands Causses
Cévennes
Garrigues
Mts. de Lacaune
Haut-Languedoc
Corbières
Monts d'Ardèche
Camargue
Alpilles
La Crau
F R A
Côte d'Améthyste
Côte Vermeille
Golfe du Lion
Golfe d'Aigues-Mortes
Étang de Vaccarès
Étang de Leucate
Étang de Vic
Méditerranée
Narbonnaise
Tanger
Nador
Oran
Alger
Annaba
Bejaia
Skikda
Aurillac
Arpajon-sur-Cère
St. Flour
Murat
Le Puy-en-Velay
Yssingeaux
Tournon-sur-Rhône
Valence
Privas
Aubenas
Montélimar
Rodez
Millau
Mende
Marvejols
Florac
Alès
Nîmes
Avignon
Arles
Montpellier
Sète
Agde
Béziers
Narbonne
Perpignan
Lodève
Pézenas
Lunel
Uzès
Orange
Bollène
Tarascon
Beaucaire
Istres
Miramas
Fos-sur-Mer
Port-de-Bouc
Aigues-Mortes
La Grande-Motte
Stes. Maries-de-la-Mer
Frontignan
Leucate
Rivesaltes
Elne
St. Cyprien
Argelès-sur-Mer
Port-la-Nouvelle
Sigean
Gruissan
Lézignan-Corbières
Espalion
Laguiole
Chaudes-Aigues
St. Chély-d'Apcher
Langogne
Pradelles
Villefort
Les Vans
Joyeuse
Largentière
Bagnols-sur-Cèze
Pont-St. Esprit
Le Vigan
Ganges
St. Affrique
Sévérac-le-Château
Bédarieux
Clermont-l'Hérault
Gignac
Lamastre
Le Cheylard
La Voulte-sur-Rhône
Pierrelatte
Villeneuve-lès-Avignon
Sorgues
Châteaurenard
St. Rémy-de-Provence
St. Gilles
Vauvert
Sommières
Anduze
Ledignan
Quissac

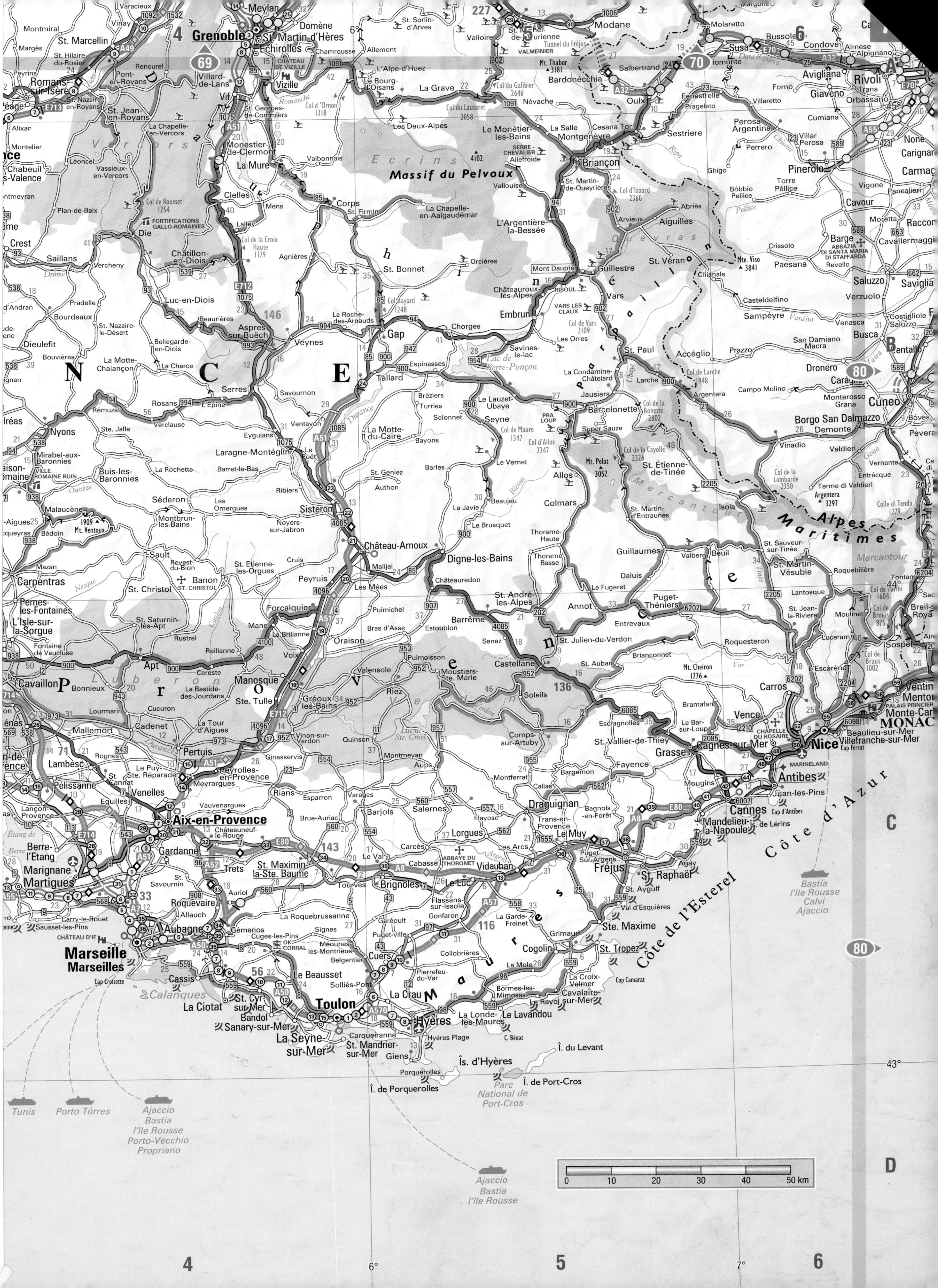

Grenoble
Meylan
Domène
St. Martin-d'Hères
Echirolles
St. Marcellin
Vinay
Montmiral
Romans-sur-Isère
St. Jean-en-Royans
Pont-en-Royans
Villard-de-Lans
Vif
Vizille
Chamrousse
Allemont
L'Alpe-d'Huez
Le Bourg-d'Oisans
La Grave
St. Sorlin-d'Arves
Valloire
St. Michel-de-Maurienne
Modane
Tunnel du Fréjus
Mt. Thabor 3181
Bardonécchia
Salbertrand
Oulx
Susa
Bussoleno
Condove
Almese
Alpignano
Avigliana
Rivoli
Giaveno
Orbassano
Forno
Trana
Villaretto
Fenestrelle
Pragelato
Sestriere
Cesana Tor.
Montgenèvre
La Salle
Névache
Col du Galibier 2646
Col du Lautaret 2058
Le Monêtier-les-Bains
Serre-Chevalier
Ailefroide
Briançon
Les Deux-Alpes
Col d'Ornon 1318
St. Georges-de-Commiers
Monestier-de-Clermont
La Mure
Valbonnais
Ecrins
Massif du Pelvoux
4102
Vallouise
St. Martin-de-Queyrières
Col d'Izoard 2360
L'Argentière-la-Bessée
Arvieux
Aiguilles
Abriès
Queyras
Mte. Viso 3841
Chianale
St. Véran
Guillestre
Mont Dauphin
Risoul
Vars
Col de Vars 2109
Châteauroux-les-Alpes
Embrun
Les Orres
Savines-le-lac
Lac de Serre-Ponçon
Chorges
Gap
Tallard
Espinasses
Perosa Argentina
Villar Perosa
Perrero
Pinerolo
Torre Pellice
Bóbbio Pellice
Ghigo
Cavour
Vigone
Pancalieri
None
Carignano
Carmagnola
Barge
Abbazia di Santa Maria di Staffarda
Revello
Paesana
Crissolo
Moretta
Racconigi
Cavallermaggiore
Saluzzo
Savigliano
Verzuolo
Costigliole Saluzzo
Venasca
Busca
Casteldelfino
Sampéyre
Dronero
Caraglio
Cuneo
Borgo San Dalmazzo
Demonte
Vinadio
Valdieri
Vernante
Entracque
Terme di Valdieri
Argentera 3297
Colle di Tenda 1279
Acceglio
Prazzo
San Damiano Macra
Campo Molino
Monterosso Grana
Col de Larche 1948
Argentera
Larche
St. Paul
La Condamine-Châtelard
Jausiers
Barcelonette
Col de la Bonette 2802
Pra Loup
Super Sauze
Col d'Allos 2247
Allos
Mt. Pelat 3052
Col de la Cayolle 2326
St. Étienne-de-Tinée
Isola
Mercantour
Alpes Maritimes
St. Martin-d'Entraunes
Colmars
Le Lauzet-Ubaye
Seyne
Col de Maure 1347
Le Vernet
Beaujeu
La Javie
Le Brusquet
Digne-les-Bains
Thorame-Haute
Thorame-Basse
Guillaumes
Valberg
Beuil
Daluis
St. Sauveur-sur-Tinée
St. Martin-Vésubie
Roquebillière
Lantosque
Le Fugeret
Annot
Puget-Théniers
Entrevaux
St. André-les-Alpes
Barrême
St. Julien-du-Verdon
Castellane
Moustiers-Ste. Marie
Mt. Cheiron 1776
Roquesteron
Briançonnet
St. Auban
L'Escarène
Sospel
Luceram
Col de Turini 1604
Col de Brouis 875
Col de Braus 1002
Breil-sur-Roya
Moulinet
St. Jean-la-Riviere
Carros
Vence
Bramafan
Le Bar-sur-Loup
Escragnolles
St. Vallier-de-Thiey
Grasse
Cagnes-sur-Mer
Nice
Villefranche-sur-Mer
Beaulieu-sur-Mer
Monte-Carlo
Monaco
Menton
Ventimiglia
Cap Ferrat
Antibes
Juan-les-Pins
Cannes
Cap d'Antibes
Mandelieu-la-Napoule
Îs. de Lérins
Marineland
Mougins
Fayence
Bargemon
Callas
Montferrat
Draguignan
Comps-sur-Artuby
Soleils
Bagnols-en-Forêt
Le Muy
Trans-en-Provence
Les Arcs
Vidauban
Fréjus
St. Raphaël
Agay
Puget-sur-Argens
St. Aygulf
Val d'Esquières
Ste. Maxime
Grimaud
St. Tropez
Cogolin
La Garde-Freinet
Côte de l'Esterel
Côte d'Azur
Cap Camarat
La Croix-Valmer
Cavalaire-sur-Mer
Rayol
La Mole
Collobrières
Bormes-les-Mimosas
Le Lavandou
La Londe-les-Maures
C. Bénat
Hyères
Hyères Plage
Carqueiranne
Îs. d'Hyères
Î. du Levant
Î. de Port-Cros
Parc National de Port-Cros
Î. de Porquerolles
Porquerolles
Giens
Toulon
La Seyne-sur-Mer
St. Mandrier-sur-Mer
Sanary-sur-Mer
Bandol
St. Cyr-sur-Mer
La Ciotat
Cassis
Calanques
Cap Croisette
Marseille
Marseilles
Château d'If
Aubagne
Gémenos
Cuges-les-Pins
Le Beausset
Solliès-Pont
La Crau
Cuers
Pierrefeu-du-Var
Puget-ville
Méounes-les-Montrieux
Belgentier
Signes
Garéoult
Gonfaron
Flassans-sur-Issole
Le Luc
Brignoles
Tourves
St. Maximin-la-Ste. Baume
La Roquebrussanne
Carcès
Cabasse
Abbaye du Thoronet
Lorgues
Flayosc
Salernes
Barjols
Varages
Rians
Esparron
Brue-Auriac
Trets
Auriol
Roquevaire
Gardanne
Aix-en-Provence
Châteauneuf-le-Rouge
Vauvenargues
Meyrargues
Peyrolles-en-Provence
Le Puy-Ste. Réparade
Venelles
Eguilles
St. Cannat
Pélissanne
Lançon-Provence
Berre-l'Etang
Marignane
Martigues
Carry-le-Rouet
Sausset-les-Pins
Lambesc
Rognes
Mallemort
Pertuis
Cadenet
La Tour d'Aigues
Cucuron
Lourmarin
Cavaillon
Bonnieux
Cereste
Apt
Luberon
La Bastide-des-Jourdans
Manosque
Gréoux-les-Bains
Ste. Tulle
Vinon-sur-Verdon
Quinson
Montmeyan
Aups
Riez
Valensole
Puimoisson
Ginasservis
Oraison
La Brillanne
Volx
Mane
Forcalquier
Reillanne
Rustrel
St. Saturnin-lès-Apt
L'Isle-sur-la-Sorgue
Fontaine de Vaucluse
Pernes-les-Fontaines
Carpentras
Mazan
Sault
Banon
St. Christol
Revest-du-Bion
St. Etienne-les-Orgues
Cruis
Peyruis
Les Mées
Puimichel
Bras d'Asse
Estoublon
Châteauredon
Château-Arnoux
Malijai
Sisteron
Noyers-sur-Jabron
Ribiers
Authon
St. Geniez
Barles
Bayons
La Motte-du-Caire
Le Poët
Laragne-Montéglin
Eyguians
Ventavon
Savournon
Serres
L'Epine
Rosans
Rémuzat
Verclause
Nyons
Ste. Jalle
Mirabel-aux-Baronnies
Buis-les-Baronnies
La Rochette
Barret-le-Bas
Séderon
Les Omergues
Montbrun-les-Bains
Mt. Ventoux 1909
Malaucène
Bédoin
Vaison-la-Romaine
Veynes
Aspres-sur-Buëch
Bellegarde-en-Diois
La Motte-Chalançon
La Charce
Luc-en-Diois
Beaurières
St. Nazaire-le-Désert
Bourdeaux
Dieulefit
Bouvières
Pradelle
Châtillon-en-Diois
Die
Col de la Croix Haute 1179
Lalley
Clelles
Mens
Corps
St. Firmin
La Chapelle-en-Valgaudémar
Agnières
St. Bonnet
Orcières
La Roche-des-Arnauds
Col Bayard 1248
Col de Rousset 1254
Fortifications Gallo-Romaines
La Chapelle-en-Vercors
Vassieux-en-Vercors
Vercors
Léoncel
Chabeuil
Plan-de-Baix
Crest
Saillans
Vercheny
Dauphiné
Provence
France
0 10 20 30 40 50 km
Tunis
Porto Tórres
Ajaccio Bastia l'Ile Rousse Porto-Vecchio Propriano
Ajaccio Bastia l'Ile Rousse
Bastia l'Ile Rousse Calvi Ajaccio
43°
44°
6°
7°

79
Torino
Turin
Caselle Torinese
Venaria
Settimo Torinese
Rívoli
Avigliana
Giaveno
Orbassano
Moncalieri
Chieri
Pinerolo
Carignano
Carmagnola
Poirino
Villastellone
Cavour
Racconigi
Savigliano
Saluzzo
Barge
Revello
Paesana
Mte. Viso 3841
Crissolo
Verzuolo
Busca
Fossano
Cuneo
Caráglio
Centallo
Bra
Alba
Cherasco
Dogliani
Carrù
Mondovì
Ceva
Borgo San Dalmazzo
Demonte
Vinadio
Valdieri
Entràcque
Vernante
Limone Piemonte
Colle di Tenda
Tende
Alpes Maritimes
Mercantour
St. Martin-Vésubie
St. Sauveur-sur-Tinée
Lantosque
Roquebilière
Fontan
Saorge
Breil-sur-Roya
Sospel
Sospel
L'Escarène
Carros
Nice
Villefranche-sur-Mer
Beaulieu-sur-Mer
Monte-Carlo
MONACO
Menton
Ventimiglia
Bordighera
San Remo
Tággia
Riva Lígure
Impéria
Diano Marina
Alássio
Laiguéglia
Albenga
Loano
Pietra Ligure
Finale Lígure
Noli
Spotorno
Vado Lígure
Savona
Albisola Marina
Celle Ligure
Varazze
Arenzano
Voltri
Pegli
Génova
Genoa
Nervi
Recco
Camogli
Santa Margherita Ligure
Portofino
Rapallo
Chiávari
Lavagna
Sestri Levante
Monéglia
Déiva Marina
Lévanto
Monterosso al Mare
Vernazza
Golfo di Génova
Riviera di Ponente
Riviera di Levante
Côte d'Azur
Antibes
Juan-les-Pins
Cap d'Antibes
MARE LIGURE
LIGURIAN SEA
Asti
Alessándria
Casale Monferrato
Valenza
Tortona
Novi Lígure
Serravalle Scrivia
Gavi
Ovada
Acqui Terme
Nizza Monferrato
Canelli
Busalla
Voghera
Stradella
Broni
Casteggio
Pavia
Mortara
Garlasco
Vercelli
Trino
Crescentino
Chivasso
Varzi
Bóbbio
Torriglia
Appennino Ligure
Piemonte
Liguria
Barcelona Tanger
Palermo Tunis
Olbia Porto Tórres Arbatax
Bastia
Bastia Calvi
Bastia l'Ile Rousse Calvi Ajaccio
Nice Savona
Nice Marseille
C. Corse
Ersa
Rogliano
Macinaggio
Pino
Luri
Santa Severa
Marine de Sisco
Nonza
Brando
Erbalunga
G. de St. Florent
St. Florent
Patrimonio
San-Martino-di-Lota
Ville-di-Pietrabugno
Bastia
Oletta
Biguglia
Santo-Pietro-di Tenda
l'Île-Rousse
Belgodere
Murato
44°
43°
8°
A
B
C
D
1
2
3
0 10 20 30 40 50 km

Cremona
Mántova
Legnago
Rovigo
Parma
Réggio nell'Emília
Módena
Carpi
Ferrara
Bologna
Ímola
Faenza
Forlì
Cesena
Lugo
Ravenna
Fidenza
Salsomaggiore Terme
Pontrémoli
Aulla
La Spézia
Carrara
Massa
Lucca
Pistóia
Prato
Firenze
Florence
Pisa
Livorno
Viaréggio
Empoli
Siena
Arezzo
Grosseto
Piombino
Portoferráio
Elba
Cécina
Poggibonsi
Montevarchi
Cortona
Chiusi
Orvieto
Capraia
Gorgona
Appennino
Tosco
Emiliano
Romagna
Toscana
Colline Metallifere
Maremma
Alpi Apuane
Canale di Piombino
Arcipelago Toscano
Parco Nazionale dell'Arcipélago Toscano
Golfo Aranci Ólbia
Bastia
Barcelona Tanger
Marseille Toulon Nice Génova Savona Livorno
L. Trasimeno
L. di Bolsena
Mte. Cimone 2165
Mte. Amiata 1738

1
2
13°
14°
12°
Cavarzere
Adria
Rosolina Mare
72
Loreo
Rovinj
Vrsar
Bale
Barbariga
Vodnjan
Brijuni
Brionski
Pula
PULA ANTIČKO NALAZIŠTE
Premantura
Medulin
Rt. Kamenjak
Labin
Plomin
Rabac
Barban
Raša
Žminj
Svetvinčenat
Kanfanar
ISTARSKA
Marčana
Koromačno
Kvarner
Martinšćica
Unije
Nerezine
Susak
Brestova
Porozina
Dragozetići
Taglio di Po
Contarina
Ariano nel Polésine
Ca'Pisani
Porto Tolle
Scardovari
Delta del Po
Foci del Po
Mésola
Iolanda di Savoia
Copparo
Crespino
Polesella
45°
Codigoro
Pomposa
ABBAZIA DI POMPOSA
Tresigallo
Massa Fiscáglia
Lagosanto
Migliarino
Lido di Volano
Lido delle Nazioni
Lido di Pomposa
Lido degli Scacchi
Porto Garibaldi
Lido degli Estensi
Portomaggiore
Comácchio
Valli di Comácchio
Consándolo
Longastrino
DUOMO DI SAN NICOLÒ
Lavezzola
Conselice
San Alberto
Alfonsine
Mezzano
Massa Lombarda
Marina Romea
Marina di Ravenna
Punta Marina
Lugo
Bagnacavallo
Ravenna
Russi
MIRABILANDIA
Lido di Classe
Lido di Savio
Milano Marittima
Cérvia
Savio
Pinerella
Faenza
Forlì
Forlimpopoli
Cesenático
Gatteo a Mare
Bellária
Igea Marina
ITALIA IN MINIATURA
Viserba
Savignano sul Rubicone
Bertinoro
Méldola
Cesena
Predáppio
Modigliana
Castrocaro Terme
Santarcángelo di Romagna
Rímini
FIABILANDIA
Miramare
Riccione
Cattólica
STA. MARIA DELLE LACRIME
Rocca San Casciano
Civitella di Romagna
Galeata
Mercato Saraceno
Sogliano al Rubicone
Ránchio
Santa Sofia
Sársina
SAN MARINO
San Marino
Talamello
San Leo
Novafeltria
Pésaro
Morciano di Romagna
Saludécio
Mercatino Conca
San Piero in Bagno
Sant'Agata Feltria
Pennabilli
Bagno di Romagna
Macerata Féltria
Badia Pratáglia
Carpegna
Sassocorvaro
Fano
Montécchio
Mombaróccio
Marotta
Urbino
Saltara
Calcinelli
Fossombrone
San Costanzo
Mondolfo
Senigállia
Sestino
Badia Tedalda
Pieve S. Stefano
Lunano
Borgo Pace
Urbánia
Monte Porzio
Sant'Angelo in Vado
Mondavio
Corinaldo
Marzocca
Rocca Priora
Falconara Marittima
Ancona
Zadar
Chiaravalle
Ostra
San Marcello
Cónero
SAN PIETRO
Camerano
Sirolo
Numana
VILLAGGIO MEDIEVALE DI SIROLO
Igoumenitsa
Patra
Split
Starigrad
Durrës
Zadar
Trieste
Piobbico
Apécchio
Sansepolcro
San Giustino
Anghiari
Subbiano
Arezzo
Cagli
Pérgola
San Lorenzo in Campo
Arcévia
Montecarotto
Móie
Jesi
Agugliano
Ósimo
Castelfidardo
Loreto
Porto Recanati
Città di Castello
Pietralunga
Cantiano
SAN GIOVANNI BATTISTA
Mte. Cátria
SAN FRANCESCO DI SASSOFERRATO
GROTTA DI FRASSASSI
Serra S. Quírico
Cupramontana
Filottrano
Cíngoli
Montefano
Recanati
Porto Potenza Picena
Potenza Picena
Montecassiano
Scheggia
Sassoferrato
Monte Cucco
Gúbbio
Fabriano
Sigillo
Apiro
Cerreto d'Esi
Umbértide
Castiglion Fiorentino
Cortona
Foiano della Chiana
Macerata
Civitanova Alta
Civitanova Marche
Tréia
Passo di Tréia
SAN CLAUDIO AL CHIENTI
Sforzacosta
Porto Sant'Elpídio
Mercatale
Tuoro sul Trasimeno
Passignano sul Trasimeno
L. Trasimeno
Magione
Castiglione del Lago
Pozzuolo
Fossato di Vico
Branca
Scritto
Casa Castalda
Gualdo Tadino
Matélica
San Severino Marche
Tolentino
Corridónia
Montegranaro
Sant'Elpídio a Mare
Lido di Fermo
Porto San Giórgio
Castelraimondo
Serrapetrona
Camerino
Abbadia di Fiastra
ABBAZIA DI CHIARAVALLE DI FIASTRA
Mogliano
Caldarola
San Ginésio
Montegiórgio
Fermo
Pióraco
Piccione
Valfabbrica
Nocera Umbra
Ponte Felcino
Perúgia
Ponte San Giovanni
Bastia
Assisi
Monte Subásio
Mte. Pennino 1571
Serravalle di Chienti
Múccia
Servigliano
Monterubbiano
Pedaso
Chiusi
Mugnano
Tavernelle
Bettona
Cannara
Spello
Valtopina
Colfiorito
Pieve Torina
Sarnano
Santa Vittória in Matenano
Montalto d. Marche
Ripatransone
Cupra Maríttima
Grottammare
San Benedetto del Tronto
Città della Pieve
Piegaro
Monteleone d'Orvieto
Cerqueto
Marsciano
Deruta
Casalina
Bevagna
Foligno
Casenove
Appennino
Bolognola
Amándola
Montefortino
MADONNA DEL PIANO
Comunanza
Rotella
Offida
Acquaviva Picena
Porto d'Áscoli
Martinsicuro
Collepepe
San Venanzo
Fratta Todina
Bastardo
Montefalco
Trevi
Sellano
Visso
Castelsantángelo
Monte Sibillini
Montemónaco
Áscoli Piceno
Mte. Vettore 2476
Balzo
Arquata del Tronto
Sant'Egídio alla Vibrata
Nereto
Alba Adriática
Tortoreto Lido
Civitella di Tronto
Giulianova
Mosciano Sant'Angelo
Piazze
San Casciano dei Bagni
Ficulle
Tévere
Prodo
Todi
Massa Martana
San Giácomo
Spoleto
Piedipaterno
Triponzo
Nórcia
Serravalle
Acquasanta Terme
Valle Castellana
Campli
Téramo
CATTEDRALE DI SAN BERNARDO
Notaresco
Roseto degli Abruzzi
Pineto
Acquapendente
Orvieto
Capretta
San Lorenzo Nuovo
Bolsena
L. di Bolsena
Bagnorégio
Baschi
Acquasparta
Montecastrilli
102
DUOMO DI SANTA MARIA ASSUNTA
Guardea
Amélia
San Gémini Fonte
Terni
Cáscia
Accúmoli
Gran Sasso e Monti della Laga
Amatrice
Roccapassa
Montório al Vomano
Monteleone di Spoleto
Civita
Ferentillo
Montefranco
CENTRO NAZIONALE DI CANOTTAGGIO
Leonessa
Montefiascone
Atri
Silvi Marina
103
MARE ADRIATICO
Romagna
Appennino
Umbro-Marchigiano
Monte Falterona
Campigna
Bibbiena
Rássina
Casentino
Poppi
Subbiano
Ville
Palazzo del Pero
Trestina
Niccone
Camporeggiano
Riguttino
Anghiari
VILLAGGIO MEDIEVALE DI SUBBIANO

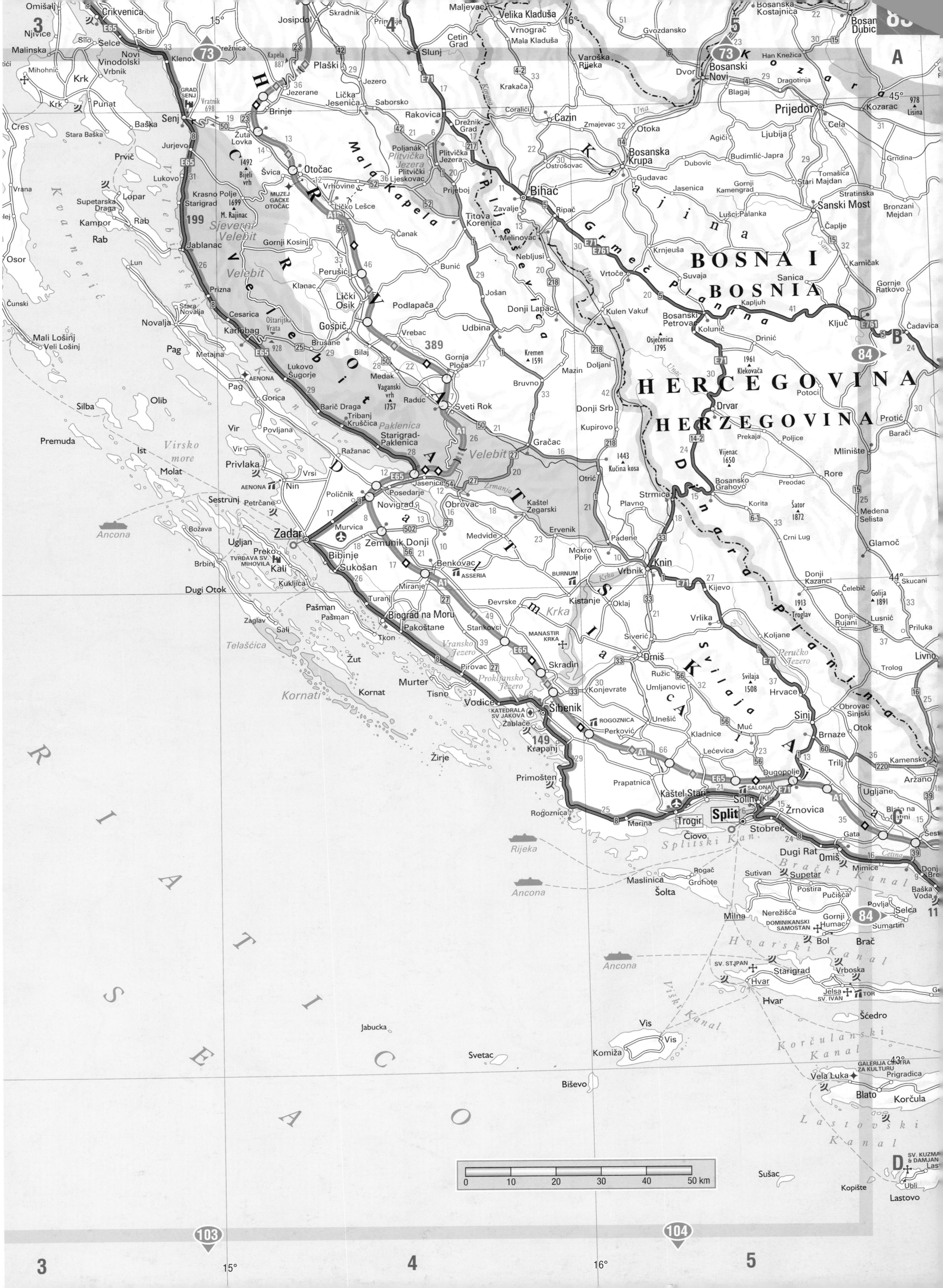

HRVATSKA
CROATIA
BOSNA I
BOSNIA
HERCEGOVINA
HERZEGOVINA
DALMACIJA
Kvarnerić
Krajina
Grmeč Planina
Mala Kapela
Velebit
Sjeverni Velebit
Paklenica
Plitvička Jezera
Kanal
Virsko more
Kornati
Telašćica
Splitski Kan.
Brački Kanal
Hvarski Kanal
Viški Kanal
Korčulanski Kanal
Lastovski Kanal
Dinara Planina
Svilaja
Krka
Una
Cetina
Zrmanja
Vransko Jezero
Prokljansko Jezero
Peručko Jezero
MARE ADRIATICO
ADRIATIC SEA
Ancona
Rijeka
Crikvenica
Novi Vinodolski
Krk
Senj
Otočac
Slunj
Cetin Grad
Velika Kladuša
Cazin
Bihać
Bosanski Novi
Prijedor
Bosanska Krupa
Sanski Most
Ključ
Bosanski Petrovac
Drvar
Titova Korenica
Gospić
Karlobag
Pag
Novalja
Rab
Mali Lošinj
Veli Lošinj
Cres
Zadar
Nin
Obrovac
Benkovac
Biograd na Moru
Gračac
Knin
Drniš
Šibenik
Vodice
Primošten
Trogir
Split
Solin
Kaštel-Stari
Omiš
Sinj
Trilj
Vrlika
Livno
Glamoč
Šolta
Milna
Supetar
Bol
Brač
Hvar
Jelsa
Vis
Komiža
Biševo
Svetac
Jabucka
Sušac
Vela Luka
Blato
Korčula
Lastovo
Kopište
Ubli
Dugi Otok
Pašman
Ugljan
Molat
Silba
Olib
Premuda
Ist
Murter
Žirje
Kornat
Žut
Zmajevac
Drežnik-Grad
Plitvički Ljeskovac
Udbina
Donji Lapac
Kulen Vakuf
Strmica
Bosansko Grahovo
Kistanje
Skradin
Stankovci
Novigrad
Posedarje
Jasenice
Starigrad-Paklenica
Lukovo Šugorje
Brinje
Ogulin
Plaški
Saborsko
Rakovica
Udbina
Medak
Sveti Rok
Gornja Ploča
Perušić
Lički Osik
Kapela
Vratnik
Krasno Polje
Jablanac
Stara Novalja
Cesarica
Prizna
E65
E71
E761
A1
0 10 20 30 40 50 km
15°
16°
45°
44°
43°
73
84
103
104
199
149
389
3
4
5
A
B
C
D

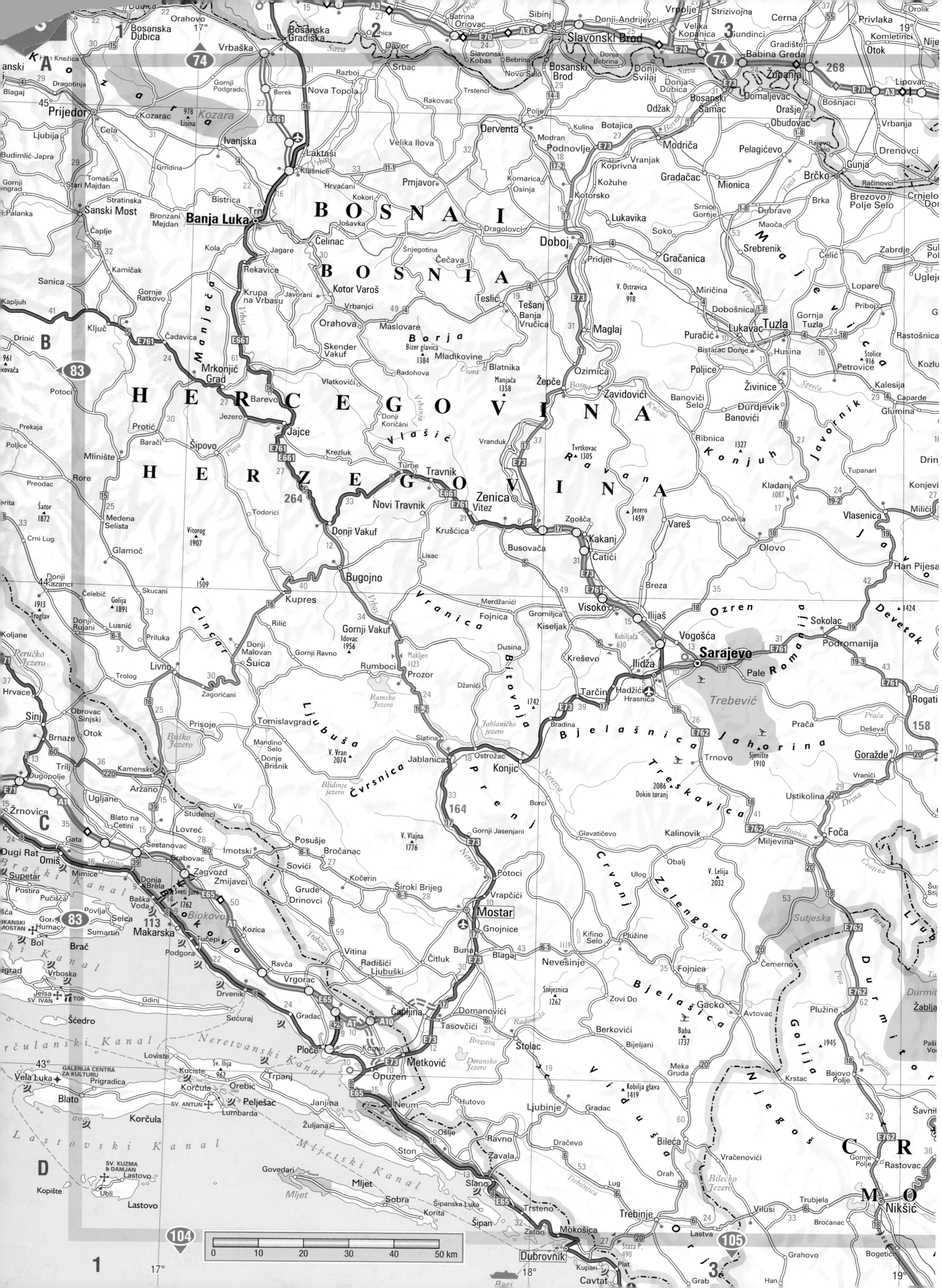

BOSNA I
BOSNIA
HERCEGOVINA
HERZEGOVINA
Banja Luka
Sarajevo
Mostar
Zenica
Tuzla
Doboj
Slavonski Brod
Bosanski Brod
Bosanska Gradiška
Bosanska Dubica
Prijedor
Sanski Most
Ključ
Mrkonjić Grad
Jajce
Travnik
Novi Travnik
Donji Vakuf
Bugojno
Kupres
Livno
Tomislavgrad
Gornji Vakuf
Prozor
Jablanica
Konjic
Visoko
Kakanj
Vareš
Olovo
Kladanj
Vlasenica
Sokolac
Pale
Goražde
Foča
Kalinovik
Trnovo
Nevesinje
Gacko
Bileća
Trebinje
Ljubinje
Stolac
Čapljina
Metković
Ploče
Opuzen
Neum
Dubrovnik
Cavtat
Makarska
Omiš
Sinj
Imotski
Vrgorac
Široki Brijeg
Ljubuški
Čitluk
Posušje
Grude
Derventa
Modriča
Gradačac
Brčko
Županja
Orašje
Prnjavor
Teslić
Tešanj
Maglaj
Žepce
Zavidovići
Lukavac
Živinice
Banovići
Gračanica
Srebrenik
Kotor Varoš
Čelinac
Laktaši
Šipovo
Glamoč
Ilidža
Ilijaš
Vogošća
Kiseljak
Fojnica
Busovača
Vitez
Kreševo
Tarčin
Hadžići
Nikšić
Ozren
Romanija
Jahorina
Treskavica
Bjelašnica
Prenj
Čvrsnica
Ljubuša
Vranica
Vlašić
Borja
Konjuh
Javornik
Majevica
Zelengora
Crvanj
Bjelašica
Vidusa
Golija
Njegoš
Durmitor
Biokovo
Kozara
Cincar
Manjača
Trebević
Sutjeska
Neretvanski Kanal
Mljetski Kanal
Lastovski Kanal
Brač
Korčula
Pelješac
Mljet
Lastovo
Vela Luka
Blato
Orebić
Ston
Slano
Trsteno
Sava
Bosna
Neretva
Drina
Vrbas
Una
CRNA GORA
0 10 20 30 40 50 km
74
83
104
105
113
158
164
264
268

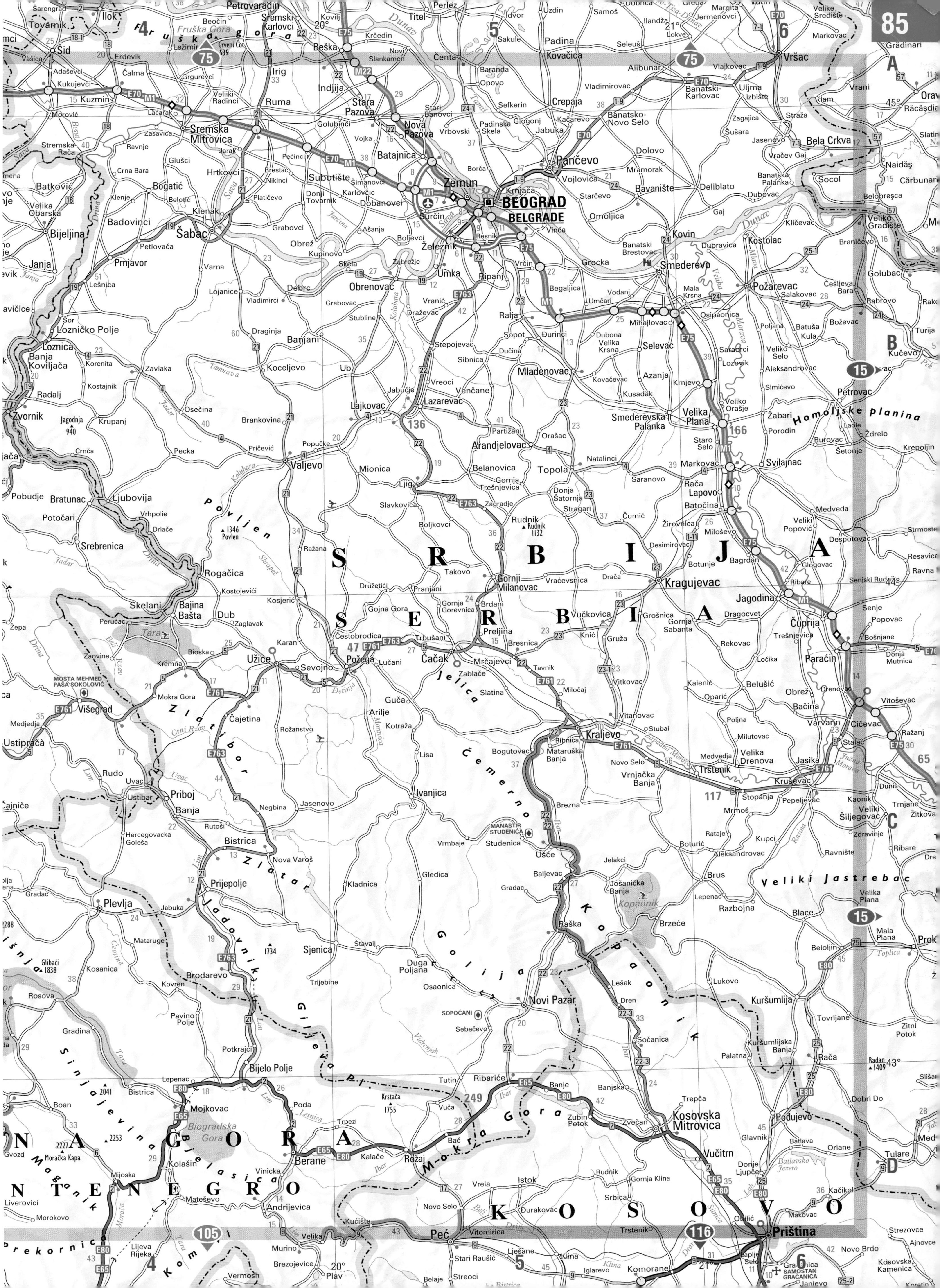
SRBIJA
SERBIA
BEOGRAD
BELGRADE
Zemun
Pančevo
Novi Sad
Petrovaradin
Sremski Karlovci
Fruška Gora
Šid
Sremska Mitrovica
Ruma
Indjija
Stara Pazova
Nova Pazova
Batajnica
Surčin
Vršac
Bela Crkva
Kovačica
Alibunar
Šabac
Bijeljina
Zvornik
Loznica
Banja Koviljača
Obrenovac
Smederevo
Kovin
Požarevac
Kostolac
Veliko Gradište
Mladenovac
Smederevska Palanka
Velika Plana
Lazarevac
Valjevo
Arandjelovac
Topola
Kragujevac
Jagodina
Ćuprija
Paraćin
Svilajnac
Despotovac
Homoljske planina
Povljen
Ljubovija
Srebrenica
Bajina Bašta
Užice
Požega
Čačak
Gornji Milanovac
Kraljevo
Vrnjačka Banja
Trstenik
Kruševac
Višegrad
Zlatibor
Čajetina
Priboj
Prijepolje
Nova Varoš
Zlatar
Ivanjica
Čemerno
Jelica
Plevlja
Sjenica
Golija
Novi Pazar
Raška
Kopaonik
Brus
Blace
Veliki Jastrebac
Kuršumlija
Prokuplje
Bijelo Polje
Mojkovac
Biogradska Gora
Bjelasica
Berane
Rožaj
Kolašin
Andrijevica
Mokra Gora
Kosovska Mitrovica
Vučitrn
Podujevo
Priština
Peć
Gračanica
CRNA GORA
MONTENEGRO
KOSOVO
E70
E75
E761
E763
E65
E80
M1
75
15
105
116
45°
44°
43°
21°
20°
A
B
C
D
4
5
6

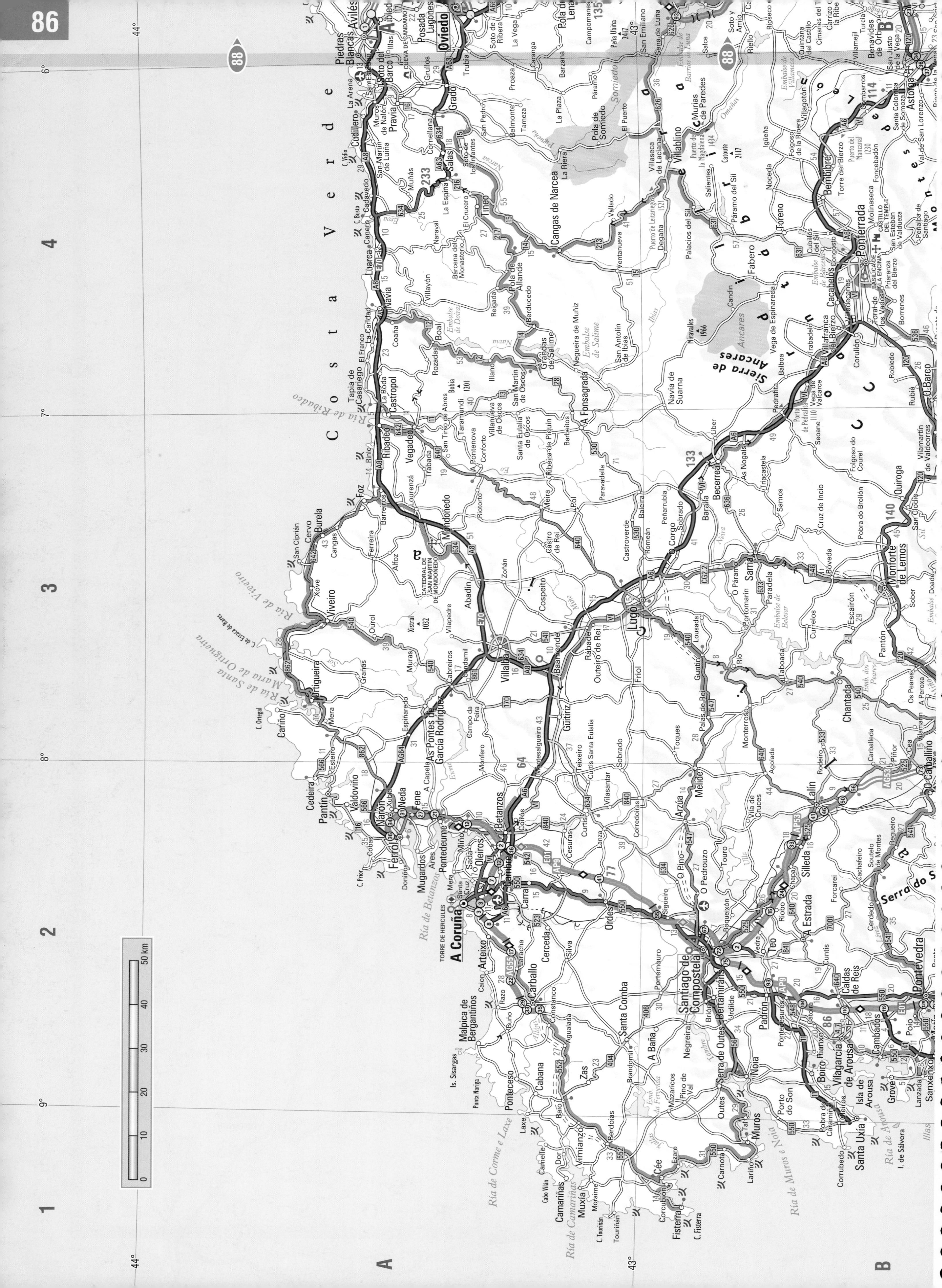
Costa Verde
Ría de Ribadeo
Ría de Viveiro
Ría de Santa María de Ortigueira
Ría de Betanzos
Ría de Corme e Laxe
Ría de Camariñas
Ría de Muros e Noia
Ría de Arousa
Sierra de Ancares
A Coruña
Ferrol
Santiago de Compostela
Lugo
Oviedo
Pontevedra
Ponferrada
Astorga
Monforte de Lemos
O Barco
Villablino
Cangas de Narcea
Tineo
Luarca
Navia
Ribadeo
Foz
Burela
Viveiro
Ortigueira
Cariño
Cedeira
Betanzos
As Pontes de García Rodríguez
Vilalba
Mondoñedo
Guitiriz
Melide
Arzúa
Ordes
Carballo
Arteixo
Malpica de Bergantiños
Ponteceso
Cabana
Zas
Santa Comba
Camariñas
Muxía
Fisterra
C. Fisterra
Cée
Corcubión
Muros
Noia
Padrón
Boiro
Ribeira
Vilagarcía de Arousa
Cambados
Caldas de Reis
A Estrada
Silleda
Lalín
Chantada
Sarria
Becerreá
Vegadeo
Castropol
Tapia de Casariego
Grado
Pravia
Avilés
Piedras Blancas
Villafranca del Bierzo
Bembibre
Quiroga
O Carballiño
Grove
Sanxenxo
Isla de Arousa
Santa Uxía
Corrubedo
Torre de Hércules
Catedral de San Martín de Mondoñedo
Cueva de Candamo
Basílica de la Encina
Castillo del Temple
C. Ortegal
C. de Estaca de Bares
C. Prior
C. Vidío
C. Busto
Cabo Vilán
Punta Nariga
Is. Sisargas
I. de Sálvora
1
2
3
4
A
B
44°
43°
6°
7°
8°
9°
0
10
20
30
40
50 km
88
114
140

Costa Verde
Vigo
Ourense
Porto
Vila Nova de Gaia
Braga
Guimarães
Viana do Castelo
Póvoa de Varzim
Vila do Conde
Matosinhos
Maia
Aveiro
Viseu
Lamego
Peso da Régua
Vila Real
Chaves
Bragança
Mirandela
Macedo de Cavaleiros
Miranda do Douro
Ciudad Rodrigo
Guarda
Trancoso
Amarante
Penafiel
Valongo
Gondomar
Espinho
Ovar
Estarreja
Ílhavo
Águeda
Oliveira de Azeméis
Santa Maria da Feira
São João da Madeira
Barcelos
Vila Nova de Famalicão
Santo Tirso
Fafe
Felgueiras
Ponte de Lima
Arcos de Valdevez
Monção
Valença
Tui
Caminha
A Guarda
Baiona
Redondela
Ponteareas
Ribadavia
Celanova
Xinzo de Limia
Allariz
Verín
A Gudiña
Puebla de Sanabria
Mombuey
Montalegre
Boticas
Vila Pouca de Aguiar
Murça
Vinhais
Torre de Moncorvo
Vila Nova de Foz Côa
Freixo de Espada à Cinta
Mogadouro
Alfândega da Fé
Vimioso
Figueira de Castelo Rodrigo
Pinhel
Vilar Formoso
Fuentes de Oñoro
Mangualde
Celorico da Beira
São Pedro do Sul
Vouzela
Castelo de Paiva
Arouca
Serra do Gerês
Serra da Peneda
Serra do Barroso
Serra de Alvão
Serra do Marão
Serra de Nogueira
Serra Gralheira
Serra de Queixa
Sierra Cabrera
Sierra de la Culebra
Sa. do Eixe
La Sanabria
Montezinho
Douro
Internacional
Arribes del Duero
Embalse de Almendra
Lago de Sanabria
Baixa Limia-Sierra do Xurés
Ría de Pontevedra
Ría de Vigo
Ría de Aveiro
Atlánticas
Galicia
42°
41°
9°
C
D
1
2
3
4
87

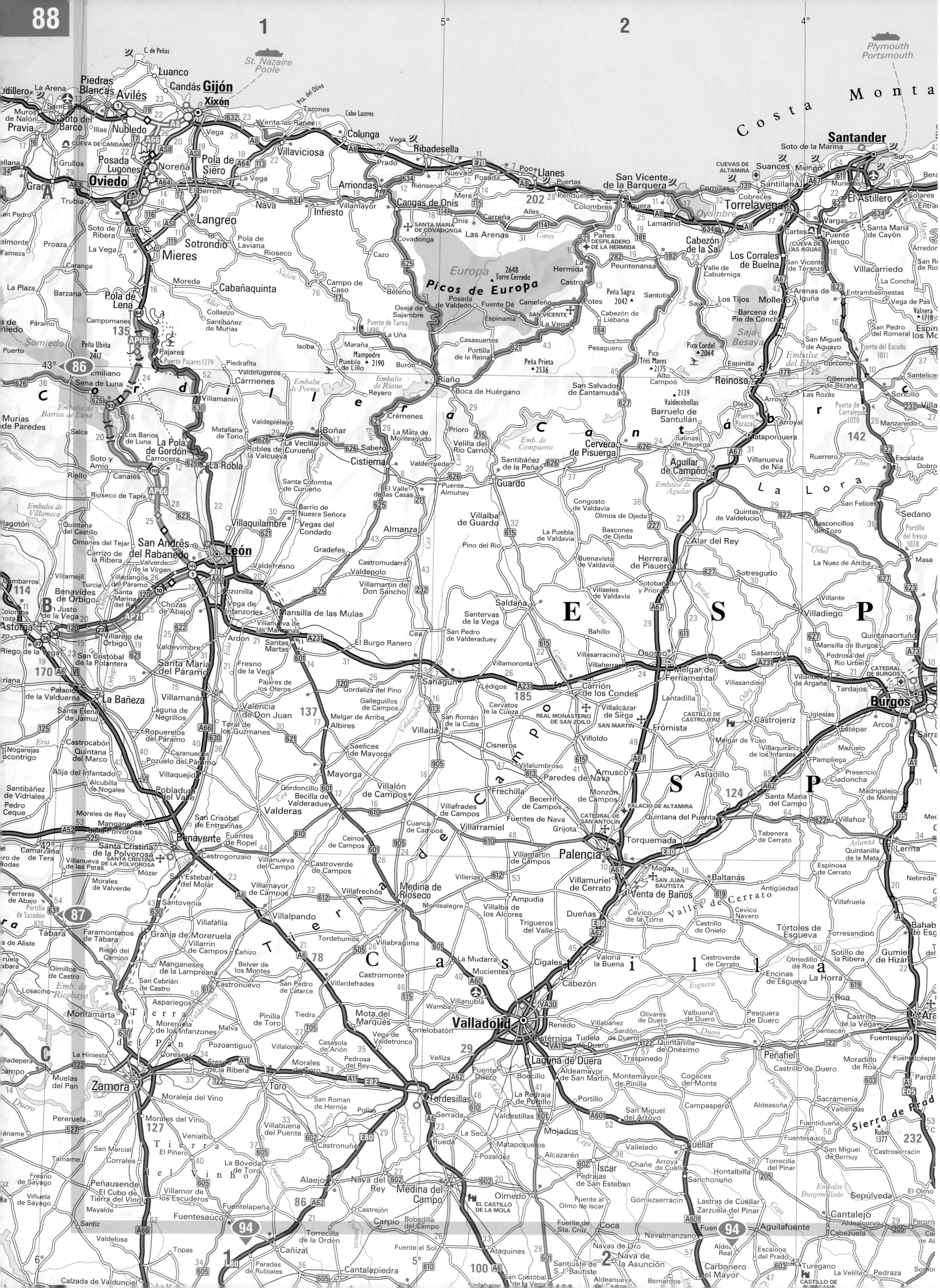
Costa Montañesa
Cordillera Cantábrica
Picos de Europa
Tierra de Campos
La Lora
Valles de Cerrato
Tierra del Pan
Tierra del Vino
Sierra de Prado
ESPAÑA
Castilla
St. Nazaire Poole
Plymouth Portsmouth
Gijón
Xixón
Avilés
Oviedo
Santander
Torrelavega
Llanes
Ribadesella
Cangas de Onís
Mieres
Langreo
Potes
Reinosa
Riaño
León
Astorga
La Bañeza
Benavente
Zamora
Toro
Tordesillas
Valladolid
Medina del Campo
Medina de Rioseco
Palencia
Burgos
Aguilar de Campóo
Cervera de Pisuerga
Guardo
Saldaña
Sahagún
Carrión de los Condes
Osorno
Melgar de Fernamental
Frómista
Astudillo
Villadiego
Castrojeriz
Dueñas
Venta de Baños
Baltanás
Peñafiel
Cuéllar
Íscar
Olmedo
Portillo
Lerma
Aranda de Duero
Sepúlveda
Cantalejo
Coca
Mansilla de las Mulas
Valencia de Don Juan
Mayorga
Villalón de Campos
Villalpando
Cistierna
Boñar
La Robla
La Pola de Gordón
Villamanín
Sahagún
2648 Torre Cerredo
2536 Peña Prieta
1490 Puerto de Tarna
1379 Puerto Pajares
A8
A66
A67
A6
A62
A231
A11
A601
A60
E70
E80
E82
E05
AP66
AP71
86
87
94
1
2
5°
4°
43°
42°
A
B
C

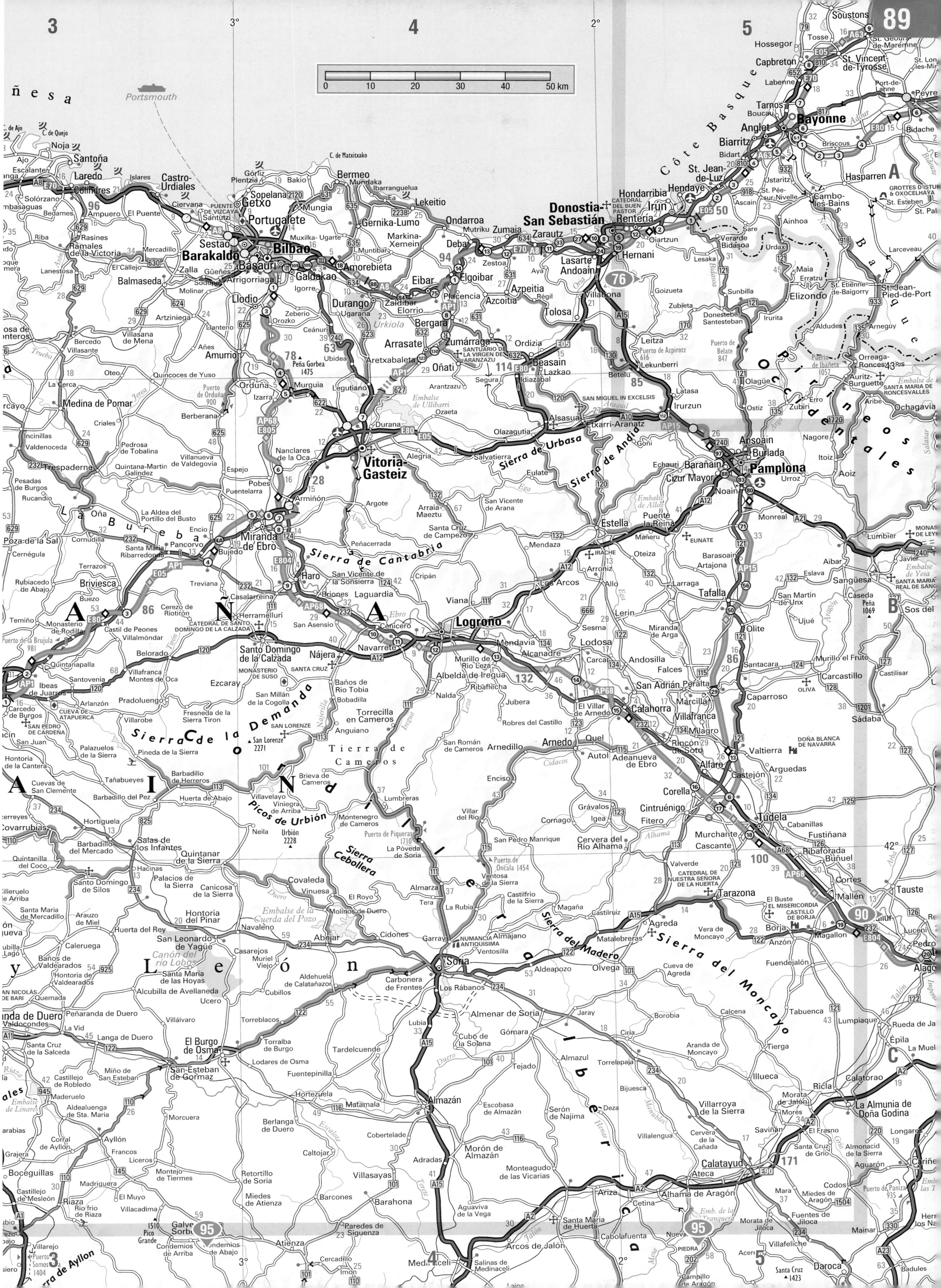

3
4
5
3°
2°
0 10 20 30 40 50 km
Portsmouth
ñesa
Côte Basque
Pays Basque
Pirineos Occidentales
Sierra de Urbasa
Sierra de Andía
Sierra de Cantabria
La Bureba
Sierra de la Demanda
Tierra de Cameros
Picos de Urbión
Sierra Cebollera
Sierra del Madero
Sierra del Moncayo
Castilla y León
Aragón
Cordillera Ibérica
Bilbao
Barakaldo
Getxo
Portugalete
Vitoria-Gasteiz
Donostia-San Sebastián
Bayonne
Biarritz
Anglet
Hendaye
Irún
Pamplona
Logroño
Miranda de Ebro
Haro
Calahorra
Tudela
Tarazona
Soria
Almazán
Calatayud
Burgos
Estella
Tafalla
Alfaro
Ágreda
El Burgo de Osma
San Leonardo de Yagüe
Medinaceli
Santo Domingo de la Calzada
Nájera
Briviesca
Medina de Pomar
Castro-Urdiales
Laredo
Santoña
Durango
Eibar
Arrasate
Zumárraga
Tolosa
Hernani
Rentería
Zarautz
Beasain
Alsasua
Elizondo
St.-Jean-de-Luz
St.-Jean-Pied-de-Port
Hasparren
Sangüesa
Ejea
Borja
Mallén
Épila
La Almunia de Doña Godina
Ateca
Daroca
Aranda de Duero
Ayllón
Berlanga de Duero
Atienza
Peña Gorbea 1475
San Lorenzo 2271
Urbión 2228
Embalse de Ullíbarri
Embalse de la Cuerda del Pozo
Cañón del río Lobos
Ebro
Duero
A
B
C

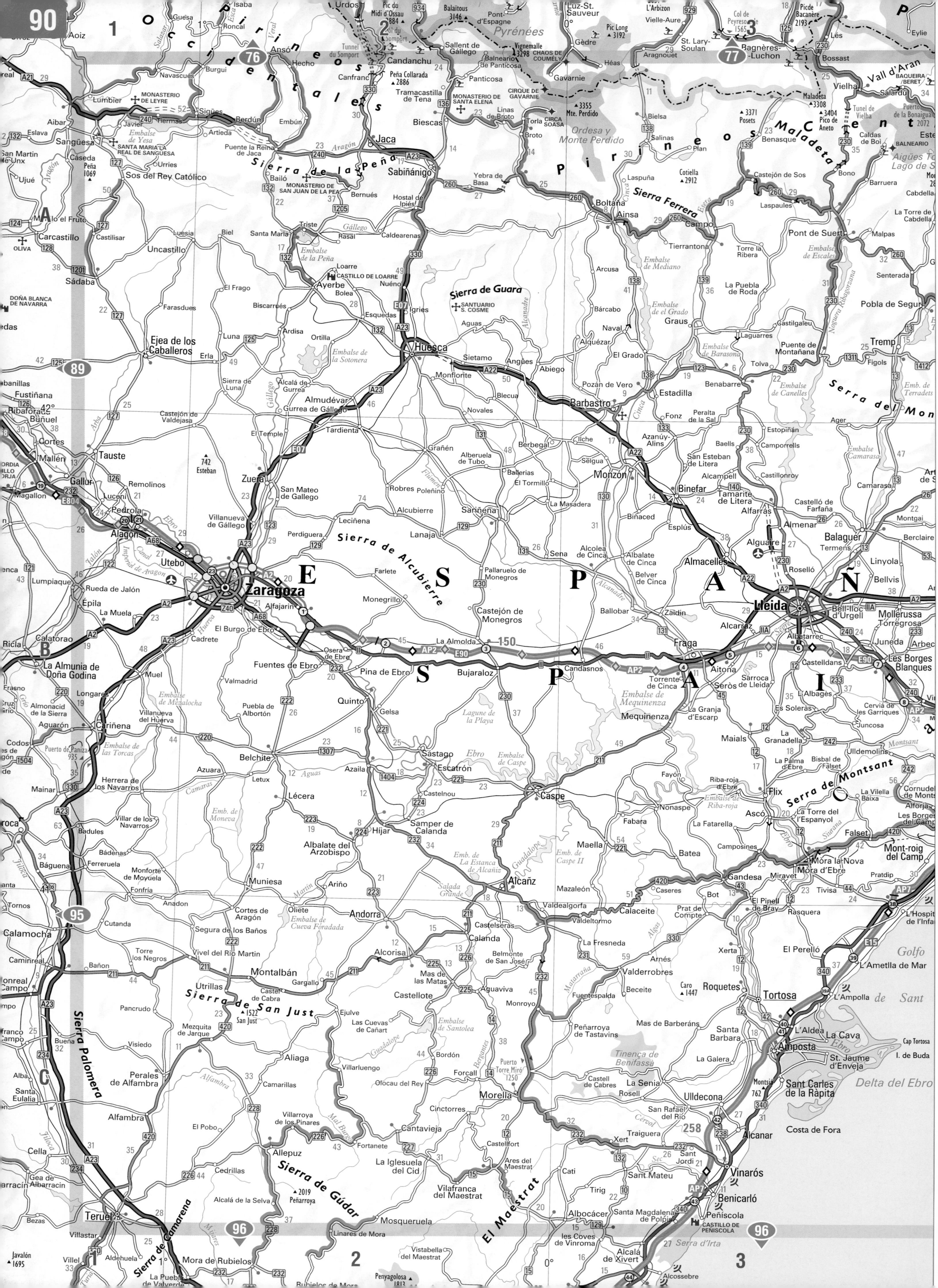
Pirineos Occidentales
Pirineos Centrales
Pyrénées
Sierra de la Peña
Sierra Ferrera
Sierra de Guara
Sierra de Alcubierre
Serra del Montsec
Serra de Montsant
Sierra Palomera
Sierra de San Just
Sierra de Gúdar
Sierra de Camarena
El Maestrat
ESPAÑA
ESPAÑA
Zaragoza
Huesca
Lleida
Teruel
Jaca
Sabiñánigo
Barbastro
Monzón
Binéfar
Fraga
Caspe
Alcañiz
Tortosa
Amposta
Vinaròs
Benicarló
Peñíscola
Morella
Ejea de los Caballeros
Tauste
Alagón
Utebo
Calatayud
La Almunia de Doña Godina
Cariñena
Belchite
Calamocha
Montalbán
Andorra
Alcorisa
Calanda
Híjar
Quinto
Pina de Ebro
Bujaraloz
Candasnos
Mequinenza
Sariñena
Almudévar
Zuera
Ayerbe
Graus
Boltaña
Aínsa
Benabarre
Tremp
Balaguer
Alcarràs
Les Borges Blanques
Flix
Móra d'Ebre
Gandesa
Valderrobres
Alcanar
Sant Carles de la Ràpita
Ulldecona
L'Ametlla de Mar
Delta del Ebro
Golfo de Sant Jordi
Vall d'Aran
Vielha
Bagnères-Luchon
Ordesa y Monte Perdido
Embalse de Mequinenza
Embalse de Caspe
76
77
89
95
96
96
1
2
3
1
2
3
A
B
C

4
5
6
77
78
97
A
B
C
N
42°
41°
2°
3°
Ariégoises
Pyrénées Catalanes
Roussillon
Côte Vermeille
Cerdaña
Pirineos Orientales
Serra del Cadí
Cadí Moixeró
Mts. Albères
Golfo de Roses
Costa Brava
Costa Dorada
ANDORRA
Andorra la Vella
Encamp
Ordino
Les Escaldes
St. Julià de Loria
Port d'Envalira
Pas de la Casa/Grau Roig
El Serrat
Tarascon-sur-Ariège
St. Barthelemy 2348
Pic des 3 Seigneurs 2199
Aulus-les-Bains
Mt. Valier 2839
Couflens
Vicdessos
Salau
Cabannes
Ax-les-Thermes
Belcaire
Usson-les-Bains
Quérigut
Quillan
Axat
St. Paul-de-Fenouillet
Caudiès-de-Fenouillèdes
Paziols
Maury
Vingrau
Rivesaltes
Estagel
Sournia
Millas
Perpignan
Ille-sur-Têt
Thuir
Vinca
Prades
Villefranche-de-Conflent
Vernet-les-Bains
Pic du Canigou 2784
Abbaye St. Martin-du-Canigou
Olette
Madrès 2471
Formiguères
Mont-Louis
Font-Romeu
Fontpédrouse
Col de la Perche 1579
Saillagouse
Llívia
Ur
Bourg-Madame
Puigcerdà
Puigmal 2910
Pic de Montcalm 3078
Pic d'Estats 3141
L'Hospitalet
Col de Puymorens 1915
Pic Carlit 2921
Amélie-les-Bains-Palalda
Arles-sur-Tech
Céret
Le Boulou
Le Perthus
Prats-de-Mollo-la-Preste
La Preste
Elne
Argelès-sur-Mer
Port-Vendres
Banyuls-sur-Mer
Cerbère
Cap Béar
St. Cyprien
Canet-Plage
Alenya
St. Laurent-de-la-Salanque
Port-Barcarès
Salses-le-Château
Forteresse de Salses
Étang de Leucate
Cathédrale Ste. Eulalie-et-Ste. Julie
Boule-d'Amont
Fourques
Portbou
Colera
El Port de Llançà
Llançà
El Port de la Selva
C. de Creus
Cadaqués
Roses
Figueres
Museo Dalí
Castelló d'Empúries
Vilajuïga
Serra de Rodes
Santa Maria de Castello d'Empuries
Perelada
Mollet de Perelada
Garriguella
La Jonquera
Espolla
Maçanet de Cabrenys
Albanyà
Pont de Molins
Cabanelles
Sadernes
Sant Pere Pescador
Viladamat
L'Escala
Ampurias
Colomers
Verges
Torroella de Montgrí
Estartit
Parlavà
Pals
Begur
Cap de Begur
Aiguablava
Tamariu
Llafranc
Calella
Palafrugell
La Bisbal d'Empordà
Calonge
Palamós
Platja d'Aro
S'Agaro
Sant Antoni de Calonge
Sant Feliu de Guíxols
Llagostera
Canyet de Mar
Tossa de Mar
Lloret de Mar
Water World
Blanes
Tordera
Castillo de Sant Joan
Malgrat de Mar
Pineda de Mar
Calella
Canet de Mar
Arenys de Mar
Arenys de Munt
Mataró
Vilassar de Mar
Premià de Mar
El Masnou
Badalona
Santa Coloma de Gramenet
BARCELONA
L'Hospitalet de Llobregat
El Prat de Llobregat
Gavà
Castelldefels
Sant Boi de Llobregat
Molins de Rei
Sant Feliu
Rubí
Martorell
Terrassa
Sabadell
Granollers
Cardedeu
La Garriga
Caldes de Montbui
Argentona
Castellar del Vallès
Sant Llorenç del Munt y l'Obac
Sant Feliu de Codines
Sant Celoni
Montseny
El Montseny 1709
Breda
Hostalric
Sils
Caldas de Malavella
Cassà de la Selva
Girona
Salt
Sarrià de Ter
Anglès
Banyoles
Besalú
Olot
Castellfollit de la Roca
Santa Pau
Mieres
Sant Martí de Llemaná
Amer
Les Planes d'Hostoles
Santa Maria de Corco
Roda de Ter
Vilanova de Sau
Sant Hilari Sacalm
Espinelves
Santa Coloma de Farners
Arbúcies
Viladrau
Taradell
Vic
Manlleu
Torelló
Sant Quirze de Besora
Ripoll
Monasterio de Santa Maria de Ripoll
Sant Joan de les Abadesses
Sant Pau de Seguries
Camprodón
Molló
Setcases
Sant Jaume de Queralbs
Queralbs
Ribes de Freser
La Molina
Bellver de Cerdanya
Montella
Lles
Queixans
La Seu d'Urgell
Adrall
Pallerols
La Farga de Moles
Sort
Llavorsí
Llessui
Ribera de Cardós
Areo
Tavescan
Alos d'Ensil
Espot
Els Castells
Noves de Segre
Organyà
Garganta de Organyà
Coll de Nargó
Boixols
Alinyà
Sant Llorenç de Morunys
Emb. d'Oliana
Graho de la Grande
Oliana
Lladurs
Castellar de la Ribera
Bassella
Solsona
Navès
Emb. de Sant Ponç
Cardona
La Serra
Ponts
Agramunt
Torà
Castellfollit de Riubregos
Guisona
Calaf
St. Pere Sallavinera
La Manresana dels Prats
Sant Ramon
Cervera
Tàrrega
Verdú
Bellpuig d'Urgell
Ciutadilla
Vallfogona de Riucorb
Sant Martí de Maldà
Belltall
La Fulioala
Igualada
Sta. Margarida de Montbui
Capellades
Santa Coloma de Queralt
La Llacuna
Rocafort de Queralt
Sarral
Solivella
Monasterio de Poblet
Espluga de Francolí
Montblanc
Prades
El Pla de Santa Maria
Vila-Rodona
Stas Creus
Valls
Alcover
La Selva del Camp
Constantí
Reus
Vilaseca
Cambrils
Salou
C. de Salou
Universal Mediterranea
Tarragona
Aqueducte
Anfiteatro de Gaià
Roda de Bara
La Riera de Gaià
La Villa del Moro
Tamarit de Mar
Castillo Tamarit de Mar
Torredembarra
Coma-ruga
Calafell
El Vendrell
Aquapark
Rodonà
Cubelles
Vilanova i la Geltrú
Sitges
l'Arboç
Castellet
Sant Jaume dels Domenys
El Pont d'Armentera
Vilafranca del Penedès
Sant Martí Sarroca
St. Pere de Riudebitlles
St. Sadurní d'Anoia
Gelida
Piera
Esparreguera
Olesa de Montserrat
Monistrol de Montserrat
Monasterio de Montserrat
Montserrat 1236
Castellbell i el Vilar
Castellolí
Jorba
St. Vicenç de Castellet
Manresa
Navarcles
Castellterçol
Sant Llorenç Savall
Calders
Centelles
Moià
Artés
Sallent
Súria
Santpedor
Callús
Balsareny
Avinyó
L'Estany
Tona
Navás
Puig Reig
Olost
Sant Feliu Sasserra
Sant Hipòlit de Voltregà
Sant Agustí de Lluçanès
Gironella
Berga
Avià
L'Espunyola
Llinars
Cercs
Borredà
Palmerola
La Pobla de Lillet
Guardiola de Berguedà
Baga
Tunel del Cadí
Begues
Génova
Civitavécchia
Livorno
Maó
Palma de Mallorca
Eivissa
Tanger
Jordi
0
10
20
30
40
50 km

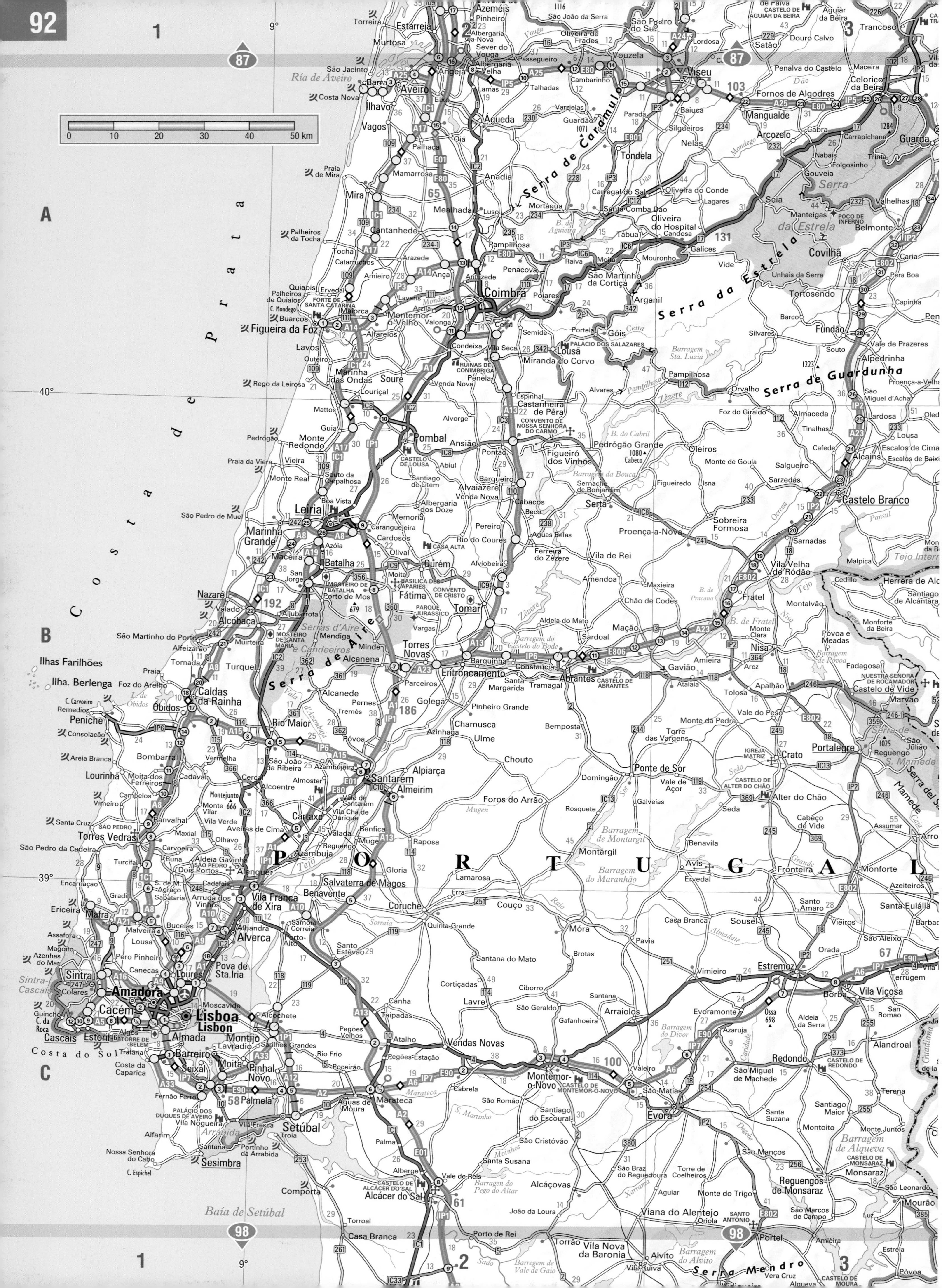
1
2
3
A
B
C
87
98
0 10 20 30 40 50 km
9°
40°
39°
Costa de Prata
Ría de Aveiro
Costa do Sol
Baía de Setúbal
PORTUGAL
Serra do Caramulo
Serra da Estrela
Serra de Guardunha
Serra de Aire
Serras d'Aire e Candeeiros
Serra Mendro
Serra de S. Mamede
Ilhas Farilhões
Ilha. Berlenga
Torreira
Estarreja
Azeméis
São João da Serra
São Pedro do Sul
Castelo de Aguiar da Beira
Aguiar da Beira
Trancoso
Murtosa
Oliveira de Frades
Vouzela
Lordosa
Sátão
Douro Calvo
São Jacinto
Albergaria-a-Velha
Angeja
Sever do Vouga
Passegueiro
Viseu
Penalva do Castelo
Maceira
Celorico da Beira
Barra
Aveiro
Costa Nova
Ílhavo
Eixo
Lamas
Talhadas
Cambarinho
Fornos de Algodres
Mangualde
Vagos
Águeda
Varzielas
Guardão
Parada
Silgueiros
Nelas
Baiuca
Arcozelo
Cabra
Carrapichana
Guarda
Palhaça
Oiã
Tondela
Nabais
Folgosinho
Trinta
Praia de Mira
Mamarrosa
Anadia
Gouveia
Mira
Mealhada
Luso
Carregal do Sal
Oliveira do Conde
Lagares
Mortágua
Santa Comba Dão
Oliveira do Hospital
Seia
Manteigas
Poço de Inferno
Valhelhas
Belmonte
Palheiros da Tocha
Cantanhede
Tocha
Catarruchos
Arazede
Pampilhosa
Tábua
Candosa
Galices
Covilhã
Caria
Anca
Penacova
Raiva
Mouronho
São Martinho da Cortiça
Vide
Unhais da Serra
Pera Boa
Quiaios
Palheiros de Quiaios
Ervedal
Amieiro
Antuzede
Coimbra
Poiares
Arganil
Tortosendo
Forte de Santa Catarina
C. Mondego
Buarcos
Figueira da Foz
Maiorca
Lavariz
Montemor-o-Velho
Arzila
Valonga
Alfarelos
Ceira
Semide
Capinha
Barco
Fundão
Silvares
Lavos
Outeiro
Condeixa
Vila Seca
Portela
Góis
Palácio dos Salazares
Lousã
Barragem Sta. Luzia
Souto
Vale de Prazeres
Alpedrinha
Ruínas de Conímbriga
Miranda do Corvo
Penela
Pampilhosa
Marinha das Ondas
Soure
Rego da Leirosa
Louriçal
Venda Nova
Espinhal
Castanheira de Pêra
Alvares
Orvalho
Proença-a-Velha
São Miguel d'Acha
Mattos
Guia
Alvorge
Convento de Nossa Senhora do Carmo
Foz do Giraldo
Almaceda
Lardosa
Pedrógão
Monte Redondo
Pombal
Ansião
Pontão
Figueiró dos Vinhos
Pedrógão Grande
B. do Cabril
Oleiros
Tinhalhas
Lousa
Cafede
Escalos de Cima
Escalos de Baixo
Alcains
Praia da Vieira
Vieira
Castelo de Lousa
Abiul
Monte de Goula
Salgueiro
Monte Real
Souto da Carpalhosa
Santiago de Litém
Barqueiro
Alvaiázere
Barragem da Bouça
Sernache de Bonjardim
Figueiredo
Isna
Sarzedas
Castelo Branco
São Pedro de Muel
Boa Vista
Leiria
Albergaria dos Doze
Cabaços
Beco
Sertã
Sobreira Formosa
Ponsul
Marinha Grande
Caranguejeira
Memória
Pereiro
Proença-a-Nova
Sarnadas
Cardosos
Rio do Couros
Águas Belas
Maceira
Azóia
Olival
Casa Alta
Ferreira do Zêzere
Vila de Rei
Malpica
Tejo Internacional
Batalha
Ourém
Alvioberia
San Jorge
Mosteiro de Batalha
Basílica dos Apareies
Fátima
Convento de Cristo
Maxieira
Vila Velha de Ródão
Cedillo
Herrera de Alcántara
Santiago de Alcántara
Nazaré
Porto de Mos
Tomar
Parque Jurássico
Amendoa
Chão de Codes
B. de Pracana
Fratel
Valado
Alcobaça
Aljubarrota
Vargas
Montalvão
Monforte da Beira
São Martinho do Porto
Mosteiro de Santa Maria
Muirteira
Mendiga
Minde
Aldeia do Mato
Sardoal
Mação
Barragem do Castelo do Bode
B. de Fratel
Monte Clara
Nisa
Póvoa e Meadas
Alfeizarão
Tornada
Turquel
Torres Novas
Alcanena
Barquinha
Constância
Entroncamento
Abrantes
Castelo de Abrantes
Gavião
Amieira
Arez
Barragem de Póvoa
Fadagosa
Praia
Foz do Arelho
Caldas da Rainha
Óbidos
L. de Óbidos
C. Carvoeiro
Remedios
Peniche
Consolação
Alcanede
Pernes
Tremés
Parceiros
Golegã
Santa Margarida
Tramagal
Atalaia
Tolosa
Apalhão
Nuestra Señora de Rocamador
Castelo de Vide
Marvão
Rio Maior
Pinheiro Grande
Chamusca
Bemposta
Vale do Peso
Monte da Pedra
Torre das Vargens
Portalegre
Reguengo
São Julião
Serra de S. Mamede
Areia Branca
Bombarral
Azinhaga
Ulme
Póvoa
Vermelha
Alpiarça
Chouto
Igreja Matriz
Crato
Lourinhã
Moita dos Ferreiros
Cadaval
São João da Ribeira
Azambujeira
Santarém
Ponte de Sor
Vale de Açor
Domingão
Castelo de Alter do Chão
Alter do Chão
Campelos
Vimeiro
Montejunto
Monte Vilar
Alcoentre
Almoster
Almeirim
Vale de Santarém
Foros do Arrão
Galveias
Seda
Cabeço de Vide
Santa Cruz
São Pedro
Ranvalhal
Maxial
Vila Verde
Cartaxo
Vila Chã de Ourique
Benfica
Rosquete
Mugen
Assumar
Torres Vedras
Olhavo
Aveiras de Cima
Valada
Muge
Raposa
Barragem de Montargil
Benavila
São Pedro da Cadeira
Carvoeira
Runa
Aldeia Gavinha
Reguengo
Azambuja
Montargil
Avis
Turcifal
Dois Portos
Alenquer
Gloria
Barragem do Maranhão
Ervedal
Fronteira
Monforte
Arronches
Encarnação
S. de M. Agraço
Sapataria
Cadafais
Salvaterra de Magos
Lamarosa
Gradil
Arruda dos Vinhos
Vila Franca de Xira
Benavente
Azeiteiros
Ericeira
Mafra
Coruche
Erra
Couço
Santo Amaro
Santa Eulália
Barbacena
Malveira
Bucelas
Alhandra
Samora Correia
Quinta Grande
Casa Branca
Sousel
Vieiros
Assafora
Lousã
Alverca
Porto Alto
Móra
Pavia
São Aleixo
Magoito
Azenhas do Mar
Pero Pinheiro
Póvoa de Sta. Iria
Santo Estêvão
Brotas
Orada
Sintra
Colares
Canecas
Loures
Santana do Mato
Vimieiro
Estremoz
Terrugem
Sintra-Cascais
Amadora
Cortiçadas
Ciborro
Borba
Vila Viçosa
Guincho
C. da Roca
Cacém
Moscavide
Lisboa
Lisbon
Alcochete
Canha
Taipadas
Lavre
São Geraldo
Santana
Arraiolos
Gafanhoeira
Evoramonte
Ossa
San Romão
Aldeia da Serra
Cascais
Estoril
Algés
Torre de Belém
Almada
Montijo
Samouco
Pegões Velhos
Atalho
Vendas Novas
Barragem do Divor
Azaruja
Alandroal
Trafaria
Lavradio
Barreiro
Moita
Pegões Estação
Rio Frio
Poceirão
Montemor-o-Novo
Valério
São Matias
Redondo
Castelo de Redondo
Costa da Caparica
Seixal
Pinhal Novo
Cabrela
São Miguel de Machede
Terena
Fernão Ferro
Palmela
Marateca
São Romão
Castelo de Montemor-o-Novo
Palácio dos Duques de Aveiro
Vila Nogueira
Águas de Moura
Santiago do Escoural
Évora
Santa Suzana
Santiago Maior
Alfarim
Vila Fresca
Setúbal
Arrábida
Troia
Palma
São Martinho
Montoito
Monte Juntos
Barragem de Alqueva
Nossa Senhora do Cabo
Santana
Portinho da Arrábida
São Cristóvão
São Manços
C. Espichel
Sesimbra
Moinhos
Santa Susana
São Braz do Regedoura
Torre de Coelheiros
Castelo de Monsaraz
Monsaraz
Reguengos de Monsaraz
Alberge
Vale de Reis
Castelo de Alcácer do Sal
Barragen do Pego do Altar
Alcáçovas
Aguiar
Monte do Trigo
São Leonardo
Comporta
Alcácer do Sal
Xarrama
Mourão
João da Loura
Viana do Alentejo
Oriola
Santo António
São Marcos de Campo
Luz
Torroal
Casa Branca
Porto de Rei
Portel
Amieira
Estrela
Torrão
Vila Nova da Baronia
Barragem do Alvito
Alvito
Vila Ruiva
Barragem de Vale de Gaio
Sado
Vera Cruz
Alqueva
Póvoa
Castelo de Moura

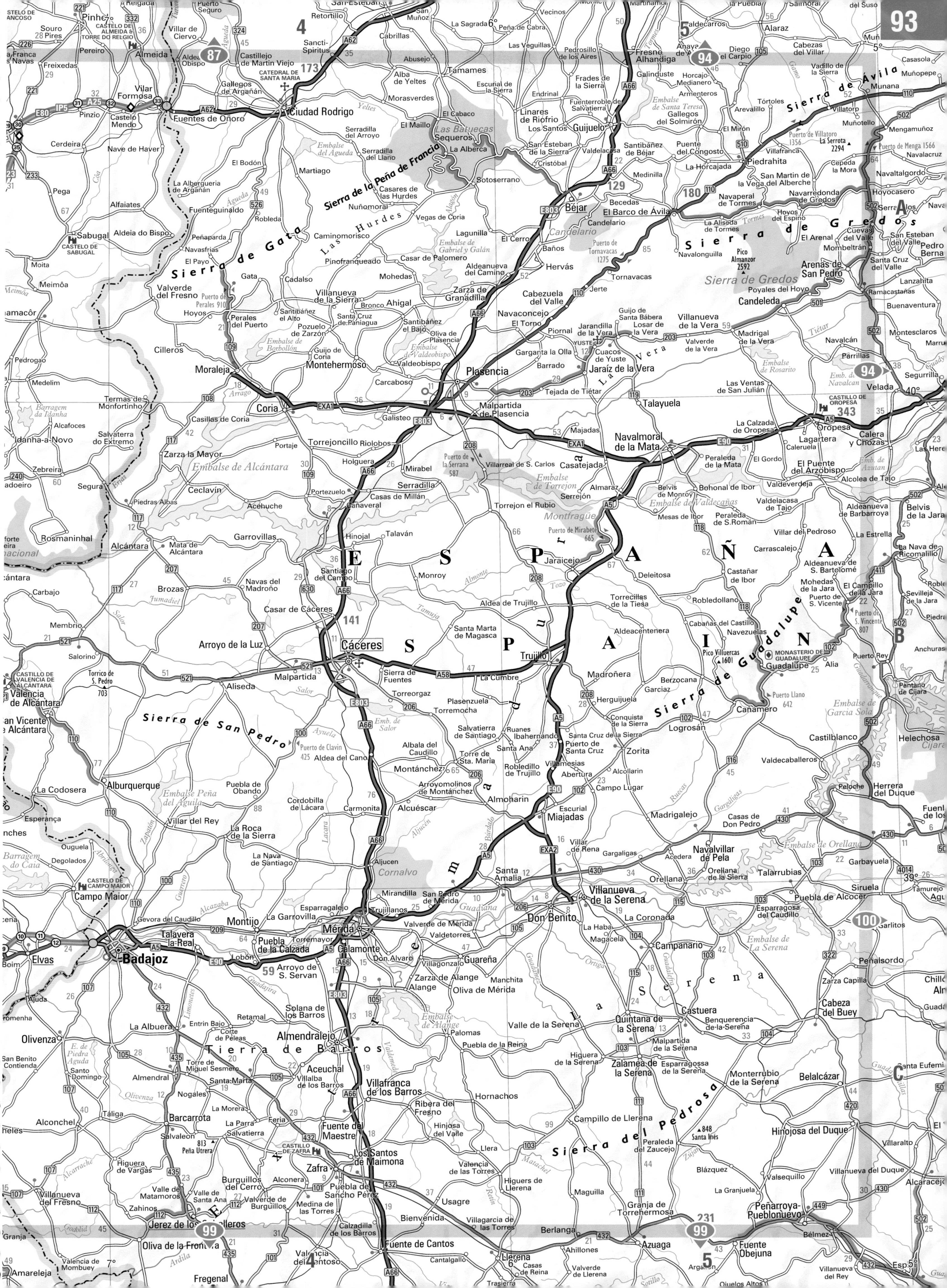
ESPAÑA
Sierra de Gata
Sierra de la Peña de Francia
Sierra de Gredos
Sierra de Ávila
Sierra de San Pedro
Sierra de Guadalupe
Sierra del Pedrosa
Tierra de Barros
La Serena
La Vera
Las Hurdes
Ciudad Rodrigo
Fuentes de Oñoro
Almeida
Castelo Mendo
Vilar Formosa
Sabugal
Béjar
El Barco de Ávila
Guijuelo
Piedrahita
Arenas de San Pedro
Candeleda
Plasencia
Jaraíz de la Vera
Moraleja
Coria
Navalmoral de la Mata
Oropesa
Talayuela
Alcántara
Cáceres
Trujillo
Guadalupe
Valencia de Alcántara
Alburquerque
Miajadas
Campo Maior
Elvas
Badajoz
Mérida
Montijo
Don Benito
Villanueva de la Serena
Almendralejo
Olivenza
Zafra
Los Santos de Maimona
Jerez de los Caballeros
Fuente de Cantos
Llerena
Azuaga
Castuera
Cabeza del Buey
Peñarroya-Pueblonuevo
Fuente Obejuna
Herrera del Duque
Embalse de Alcántara
Embalse de Orellana
Embalse de La Serena
Embalse de García Sola
Monfragüe
Cornalvo
Pico Almanzor 2592
Puerto de Tornavacas 1275
Puerto de Miravete 665
Puerto de Clavin 425
Pico Villuercas 1601
Monasterio de Guadalupe
Castelo de Sabugal
Castillo de Oropesa
Castelo de Campo Maior
Castillo de Zafra
Castillo de Valencia de Alcántara
Catedral de Santa María
A5
A66
E803
E90
EXA1
EXA2
A58
A62
E80
A25
IP5
87
94
99
100
4
5
A
B
C

Salamanca
Medina del Campo
Olmedo
Cuéllar
Sepúlveda
Segovia
Sierra de Guadarrama
Arévalo
Ávila
Sierra de Ávila
Peñaranda de Bracamonte
Alba de Tormes
Béjar
El Barco de Ávila
Piedrahita
Sierra de Gredos
Arenas de San Pedro
Candeleda
Collado Villalba
Colmenar Viejo
El Escorial
San Lorenzo de El Escorial
Guadarrama
Alcobendas
Las Rozas
Majadahonda
Pozuelo de Alarcón
Alcorcón
Móstoles
Getafe
Fuenlabrada
Parla
Navalcarnero
Illescas
San Martín de Valdeiglesias
Toledo
Torrijos
Talavera de la Reina
Oropesa
Navalmoral de la Mata
Jaraíz de la Vera
Plasencia
Trujillo
Guadalupe
Sierra de Guadalupe
Montes de Toledo
Sierra del Chorito
Sierra de la Calderina
Los Yébenes
Orgaz
Mora
Sonseca
Malagón
Ciudad Real
Miguelturra
Almagro
Piedrabuena
Herrera del Duque
Fuenlabrada de los Montes
Navalvillar de Pela
Villanueva de la Serena
Don Benito
Campanario
Puebla de Alcocer
Siruela
Talarrubias
Orellana la Vieja
Logrosán
Zorita
E
S
P
0 10 20 30 40 50 km

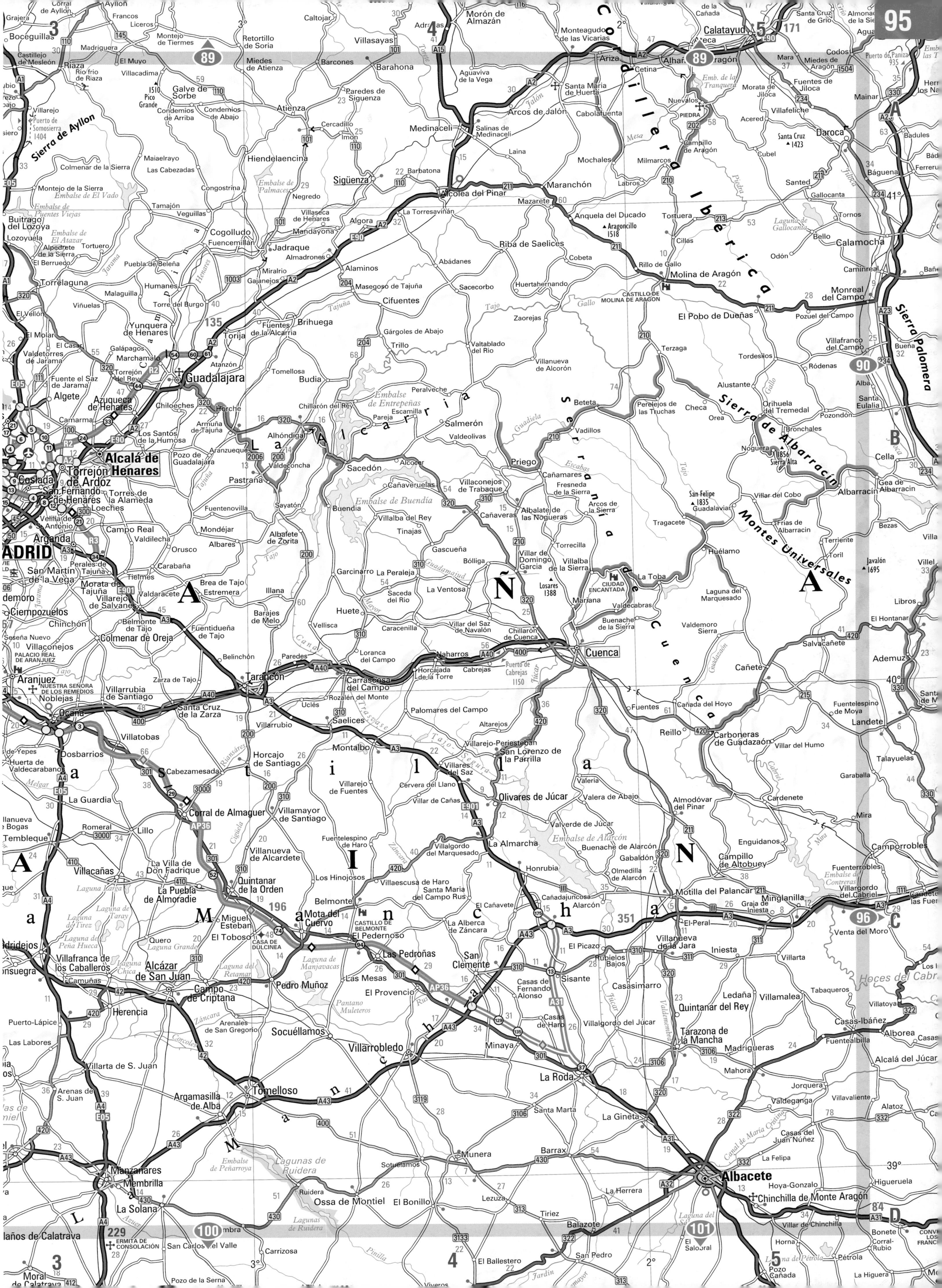
Sierra de Ayllon
Boceguillas
Riaza
Atienza
Medinaceli
Morón de Almazán
Calatayud
Ariza
Daroca
Cordillera Ibérica
Sigüenza
Alcolea del Pinar
Maranchón
Molina de Aragón
Monreal del Campo
Calamocha
Sierra Palomera
Buitrago del Lozoya
Jadraque
Cogolludo
Torrelaguna
Cifuentes
Brihuega
Torija
Guadalajara
Alcalá de Henares
Torrejón de Ardoz
Coslada
San Fernando de Henares
Arganda
Madrid
Chinchón
Aranjuez
Colmenar de Oreja
Pastrana
Sacedón
Embalse de Entrepeñas
Embalse de Buendía
Buendía
Priego
Beteta
Serranía de Cuenca
Sierra de Albarracín
Albarracín
Montes Universales
Ciudad Encantada
Cuenca
Huete
Tarancón
Ocaña
Carrascosa del Campo
Saelices
Uclés
Montalbo
Olivares de Júcar
Embalse de Alarcón
Motilla del Palancar
Minglanilla
Quintanar de la Orden
Corral de Almaguer
Mota del Cuervo
El Toboso
Belmonte
Las Pedroñas
San Clemente
Madridejos
Alcázar de San Juan
Campo de Criptana
Pedro Muñoz
Socuéllamos
Villarrobledo
Minaya
La Roda
Tomelloso
Argamasilla de Alba
Manzanares
Membrilla
La Solana
Lagunas de Ruidera
Ossa de Montiel
Munera
Albacete
Chinchilla de Monte Aragón
Casas-Ibáñez
Tarazona de la Mancha
Quintanar del Rey
Iniesta
Hoces del Cabriel
La Mancha
Castilla-La Mancha

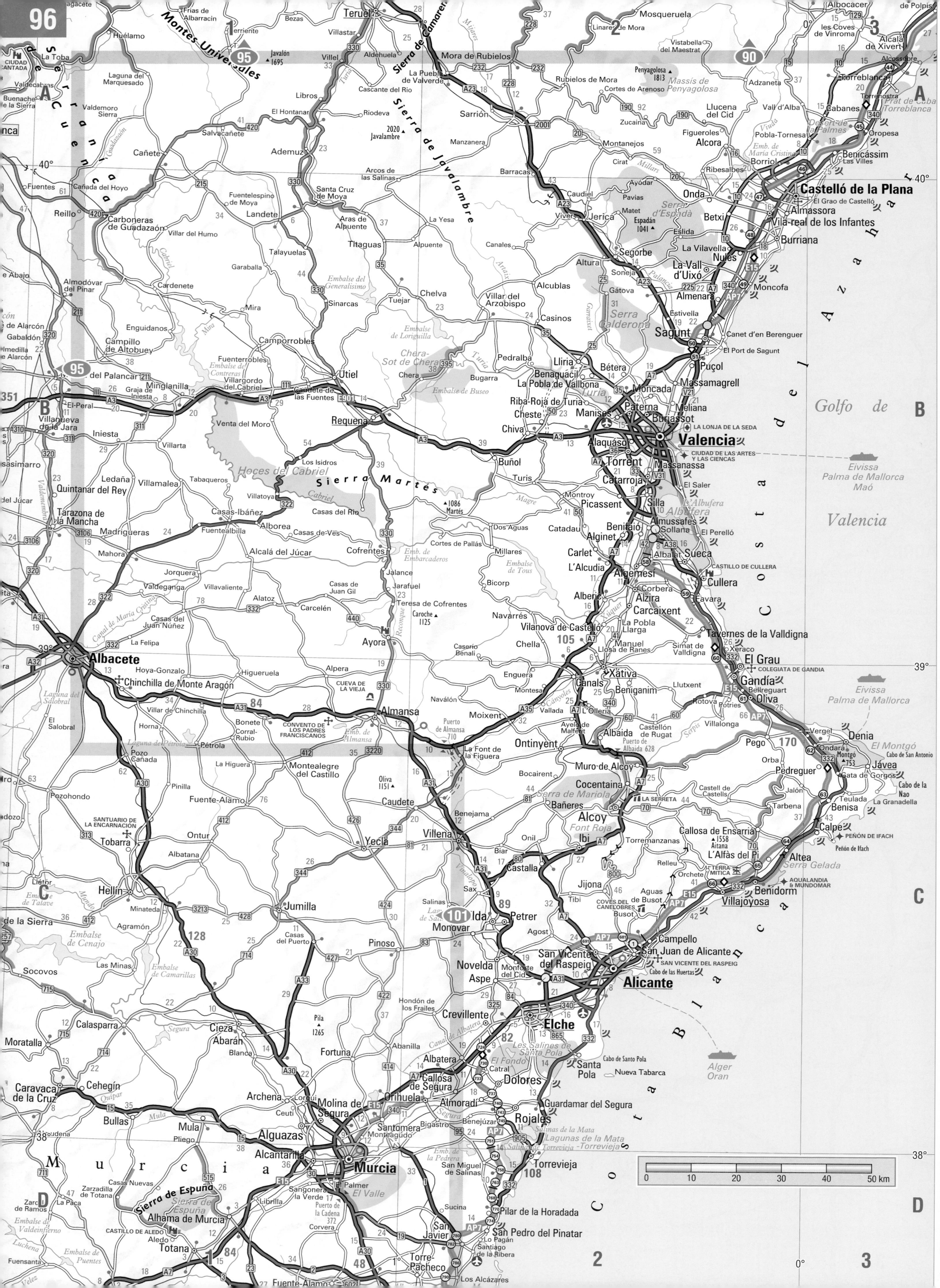

Teruel
Mosqueruela
Albocàcer
Montes Universales
Serranía de Cuenca
Sierra de Camarena
Sierra de Javalambre
Frías de Albarracín
Huélamo
La Toba
Javalón 1695
Villel
Aldehuela
Mora de Rubielos
La Puebla de Valverde
Rubielos de Mora
Penyagolosa 1813
Massís de Penyagolosa
Cortes de Arenoso
Vistabella del Maestrat
Linares de Mora
les Coves de Vinromà
Alcalà de Xivert
Alcossebre
Torreblanca
Adzaneta
Laguna del Marquesado
Valdecabras
Buenache de la Sierra
Cascante del Río
Libros
Sarrión
Valdemoro Sierra
El Hontanar
Riodeva
2020 Javalambre
Zucaina
Llucena del Cid
Vall d'Alba
Cabanes
Torrenostra
Prat de Cabanes Torreblanca
Desert de les Palmes
Oropesa
Benicàssim
Las Villes
Salvacañete
Cañete
Ademuz
Manzanera
Montanejos
Figueroles
Alcora
Pobla-Tornesa
Borriol
Emb. de María Cristina
Arcos de las Salinas
Barracas
Cirat
Ribesalbes
Fuentes
Cañada del Hoyo
Reillo
Fuentelespino de Moya
Santa Cruz de Moya
Caudiel
Ayódar
Pavías
Onda
Castelló de la Plana
El Grao de Castelló
Almassora
Vila-real de los Infantes
Burriana
Carboneras de Guadazaón
Villar del Humo
Landete
Aras de Alpuente
La Yesa
Matet
Espadán 1041
Serra d'Espadà
Jérica
Viver
Betxi
Eslida
Talayuelas
Titaguas
Alpuente
Canales
Segorbe
La Vilavella
Nules
Garaballa
Emblase del Generalísimo
Altura
Soneja
La Vall d'Uixó
Moncofa
Almodóvar del Pinar
Cardenete
Chelva
Villar del Arzobispo
Alcublas
Gátova
Almenara
Tuéjar
Sinarcas
Mira
Enguídanos
Embalse de Loriguilla
Casinos
Serra Calderona
Estivella
Sagunt
Canet d'en Berenguer
El Port de Sagunt
Gabaldón
Campillo de Altobuey
Camporrobles
Chera-Sot de Chera
Chera
Pedralba
Bugarra
Llíria
Bétera
Puçol
Benaguacil
La Pobla de Vallbona
Massamagrell
Fuenterrobles
Villargordo del Cabriel
Embalse de Contreras
Utiel
Minglanilla
Graja de Iniesta
Caudete de las Fuentes
Embalse de Buseo
Riba-Roja de Turia
Moncada
Paterna
Meliana
Burjassot
Golfo de Valencia
El Peral
Villanueva de la Jara
Iniesta
Venta del Moro
Requena
Cheste
Manises
Chiva
Valencia
La Lonja de la Seda
Ciudad de las Artes y las Ciencias
Alaquàs
Torrent
Massanassa
Villarta
Los Isidros
Buñol
Turís
Catarroja
El Saler
Eivissa Palma de Mallorca Maó
Hoces del Cabriel
Sierra Martés
Ledaña
Villamalea
Tabaqueros
Quintanar del Rey
Villatoya
1086 Martés
Montroy
Picassent
L'Albufera
Silla
Tarazona de la Mancha
Casas-Ibáñez
Casas del Río
Madrigueras
Fuentealbilla
Alborea
Casas de Ves
Dos Aguas
Catadau
Benifaió
Almussafes
Sollana
El Perelló
Mahora
Alcalá del Júcar
Cofrentes
Emb. de Embarcaderos
Cortes de Pallás
Millares
Carlet
Alginet
Sueca
Albalat
Jorquera
Jalance
Embalse de Tous
L'Alcudia
Algemesí
Castillo de Cullera
Cullera
Valdeganga
Villavaliente
Casas de Juan Gil
Jarafuel
Bicorp
Alberic
Corbera
Favara
Alatoz
Carcelén
Teresa de Cofrentes
Alzira
Carcaixent
Canal de María Cristina
Casas del Juan Núñez
Caroche 1125
Navarrés
La Pobla Llarga
Vilanova de Castelló
Tavernes de la Valldigna
La Felipa
Ayora
Caserío Benali
Chella
Manuel
Llosa de Ranes
Simat de Valldigna
Xeraco
Albacete
Hoya-Gonzalo
Higueruela
Alpera
El Grau
Colegiata de Gandia
Chinchilla de Monte Aragón
Cueva de la Vieja
Enguera
Xàtiva
Canals
Montesa
Llutxent
Gandía
Bellreguart
Oliva
Laguna del Salobral
Villar de Chinchilla
Navalón
Moixent
Vallada
L'Olleria
Beniganim
Rotova
Potries
El Salobral
Horna
Bonete
Corral-Rubio
Convento de los Padres Franciscanos
Almansa
Emb. de Almansa
Puerto de Almansa 710
Ayelo de Malferit
Albaida
Castellón de Rugat
Villalonga
Vergel
Dénia
Laguna del Pétrola
Pétrola
Pozo Cañada
La Font de la Figuera
Ontinyent
Puerto de Albaida 628
Pego
Ondara
El Montgó
Montgó 753
Cabo de San Antonio
Jávea
La Higuera
Montealegre del Castillo
Muro de Alcoy
Orba
Pedreguer
Gata de Gorgos
Cabo de la Nao
Oliva 1151
Bocairent
Cocentaina
Castell de Castells
Pinilla
Fuente-Álamo
Caudete
Serra de Mariola
La Serreta
Jalón
Teulada
La Granadella
Pozohondo
Benejama
Bañeres
Alcoy
Tarbena
Benisa
Santuario de la Encarnación
Font Roja
Callosa de Ensarrià
Calpe
Peñón de Ifach
Tobarra
Ontur
Yecla
Villena
Onil
Ibi
Torremanzanas
Aitana 1558
L'Alfàs del Pi
Albatana
Biar
Castalla
Relleu
Terra Mítica
Altea
Serra Gelada
Liétor
Hellín
Emb. de Talave
Jumilla
Sax
Jijona
Orcheta
Aqualandia & Mundomar
Benidorm
Minateda
Salinas
Laguna de Salinas
Monóvar
Elda
Petrer
Tibi
Coves del Canelobres
Aguas de Busot
Busot
Villajoyosa
de la Sierra
Agramón
Embalse de Cenajo
Casas del Puerto
Pinoso
Agost
Campello
San Vicente del Raspeig
San Juan de Alicante
San Vicente del Raspeig
Cabo de las Huertas
Socovos
Las Minas
Embalse de Camarillas
Novelda
Aspe
Monforte del Cid
Alicante
Hondón de los Frailes
Crevillente
Elche
Calasparra
Cieza
Abarán
Pila 1265
Canal de Albatera
Moratalla
Blanca
Fortuna
Abanilla
Les Salines de Santa Pola
El Fondo
Cabo de Santo Pola
Santa Pola
Nueva Tabarca
Alger Oran
Caravaca de la Cruz
Cehegín
Archena
Lorquí
Albatera
Callosa de Segura
Catral
Dolores
Bullas
Ceuti
Molina de Segura
Orihuela
Almoradí
Guardamar del Segura
Mula
Pliego
Alguazas
Santomera
Monteagudo
Bigastro
Benejúzar
Rojales
Salinas de la Mata
Lagunas de la Mata - Torrevieja
Salinas de Torrevieja
Alcantarilla
Murcia
Emb. de la Pedrera
San Miguel de Salinas
Torrevieja
Murcia
Costa Blanca
Costa del Azahar
Sierra de Espuña
Casas Nuevas
Zarzadilla de Totana
La Paca
Zarcilla de Ramos
Sangonera la Verde
El Palmer
El Valle
Puerto de la Cadena 372
Librilla
Corvera
Sucina
Pilar de la Horadada
Embalse de Valdeinfierno
Alhama de Murcia
Castillo de Aledo
Aledo
Totana
San Javier
San Pedro del Pinatar
Lo Pagán
Santiago de la Ribera
Embalse de Puentes
Torre-Pacheco
Fuensanta
Fuente-Álamo
Los Alcázares
0 10 20 30 40 50 km

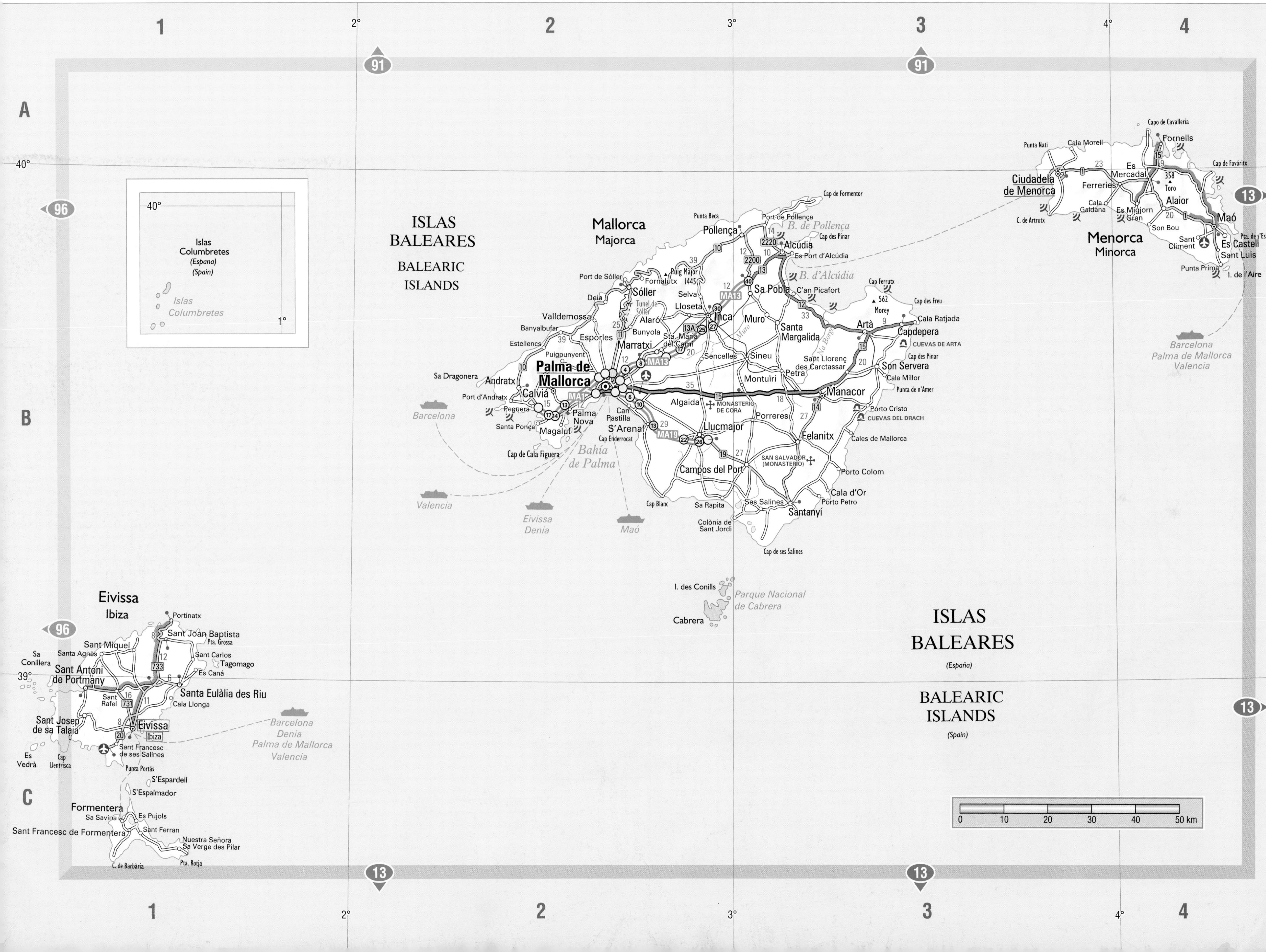
ISLAS BALEARES
BALEARIC ISLANDS
ISLAS BALEARES (España)
BALEARIC ISLANDS (Spain)
Islas Columbretes (Espana) (Spain)
Islas Columbretes
Mallorca
Majorca
Menorca
Minorca
Eivissa
Ibiza
Formentera
Palma de Mallorca
Pollença
Port de Pollença
B. de Pollença
Cap de Formentor
Punta Beca
Cap des Pinar
Alcúdia
Es Port d'Alcúdia
B. d'Alcúdia
Sa Pobla
C'an Picafort
Port de Sóller
Sóller
Fornalutx
Puig Major 1445
Deià
Valldemossa
Banyalbufar
Estellencs
Esporles
Puigpunyent
Bunyola
Alaró
Selva
Lloseta
Inca
Muro
Santa Margalida
Marratxi
Sta. Maria del Camí
Sencelles
Sineu
Montuïri
Petra
Sant Llorenç des Carctassar
Artà
Capdepera
Cala Ratjada
Cap des Freu
Cap Ferrutx
Morey
Cuevas de Arta
Son Servera
Cala Millor
Punta de n'Amer
Manacor
Porto Cristo
Cuevas del Drach
Cales de Mallorca
Sa Dragonera
Andratx
Port d'Andratx
Calvià
Peguera
Santa Ponça
Magaluf
Palma Nova
Cap de Cala Figuera
Bahía de Palma
Can Pastilla
S'Arenal
Cap Enderrocat
Algaida
Monasterio de Cora
Llucmajor
Porreres
Felanitx
Campos del Port
San Salvador (Monasterio)
Porto Colom
Cala d'Or
Porto Petro
Santanyí
Ses Salines
Sa Rapita
Colònia de Sant Jordi
Cap Blanc
Cap de ses Salines
I. des Conills
Cabrera
Parque Nacional de Cabrera
Barcelona
Valencia
Eivissa Denia
Maó
Capo de Cavalleria
Fornells
Punta Nati
Cala Morell
Ciudadela de Menorca
C. de Artrutx
Ferreries
Cala Galdana
Es Mercadal
Toro
Es Migjorn Gran
Alaior
Son Bou
Sant Climent
Cap de Favàritx
Pta. de s'Esperó
Es Castell
Sant Luis
Punta Prima
I. de l'Aire
Barcelona Palma de Mallorca Valencia
Portinatx
Sant Joan Baptista
Pta. Grossa
Sant Miquel
Santa Agnès
Sa Conillera
Sant Antoni de Portmany
Sant Carlos
Tagomago
Es Caná
Santa Eulàlia des Riu
Cala Llonga
Sant Rafel
Sant Josep de sa Talaia
Es Vedrà
Cap Llentrisca
Sant Francesc de ses Salines
Punta Portás
S'Espardell
S'Espalmador
Barcelona Denia Palma de Mallorca Valencia
Sa Savina
Es Pujols
Sant Ferran
Sant Francesc de Formentera
Nuestra Señora Sa Verge des Pilar
C. de Barbària
Pta. Rotja
0 10 20 30 40 50 km

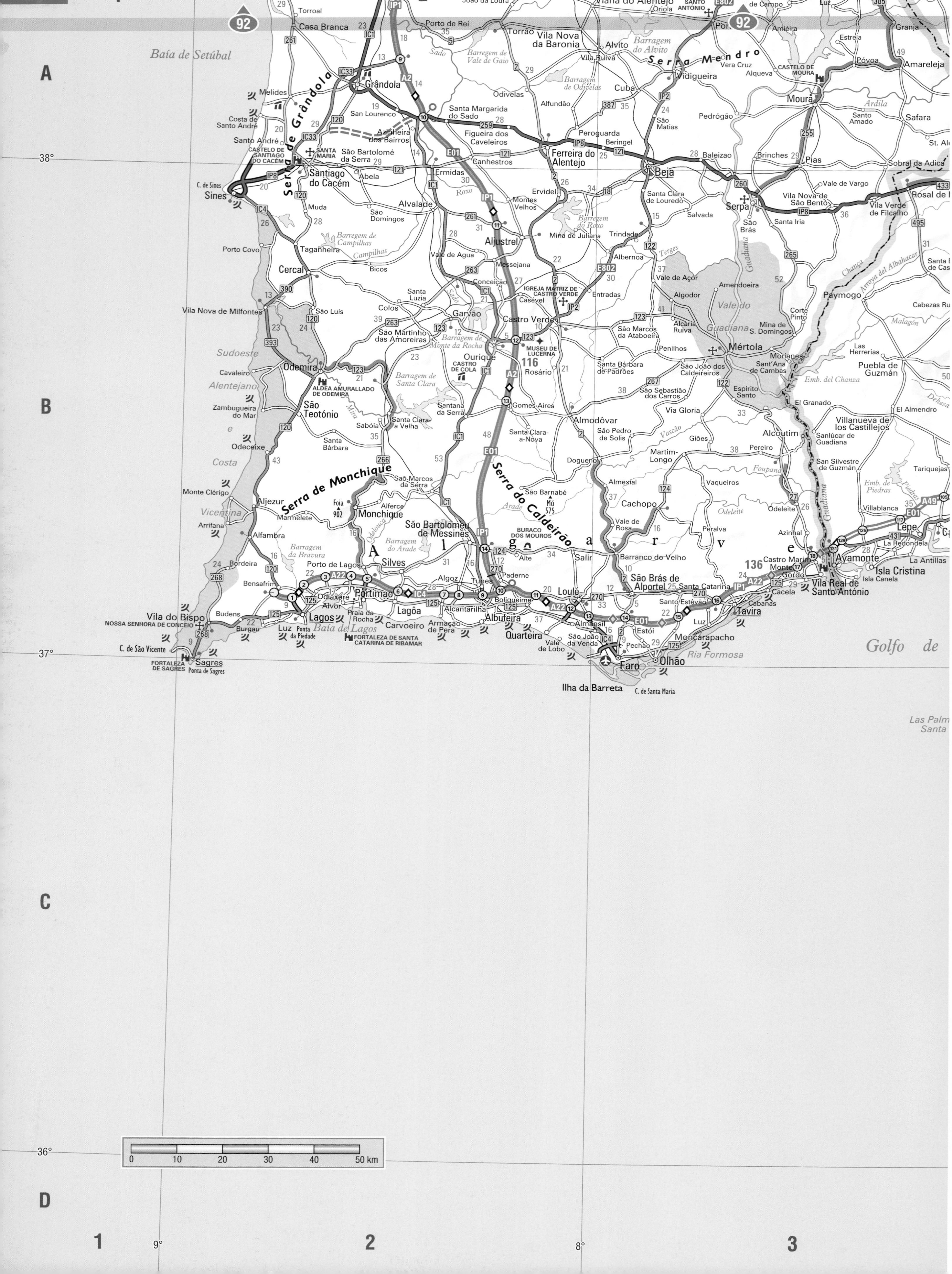

Baía de Setúbal
Comporta
Alcácer do Sal
Alcáçovas
Aguiar
Monte do Trigo
de Monsaraz
São Leonardo
Mourão
Torroal
Casa Branca
Porto de Rei
Torrão
Vila Nova da Baronia
Alvito
Barragem do Alvito
Viana do Alentejo
Oriola
Santo António
São Marcos de Campo
Luz
Granja
Estrela
Amieira
Serra Mendro
Vera Cruz
Alqueva
Castelo de Moura
Póvoa
Amareleja
Melides
Grândola
Serra de Grândola
Costa de Santo André
Santo André
Castelo de Santiago do Cacém
Santa Maria
São Bartolomeu da Serra
San Lourenco
Azinheira dos Bairros
Santa Margarida do Sado
Figueira dos Caveleiros
Odivelas
Barragem de Odivelas
Alfundão
Cuba
Vila Ruiva
Vidigueira
Pedrógão
Moura
Santo Amado
Safara
Ardila
Peroguarda
Beringel
Ferreira do Alentejo
Canhestros
Beja
Baleizao
Brinches
Pias
Sobral da Adiça
Vale de Vargo
Vila Nova de São Bento
Rosal de la Frontera
Vila Verde de Ficalho
Serpa
São Brás
Santa Iria
Salvada
Santa Clara de Louredo
C. de Sines
Sines
Santiago do Cacém
Abela
Ermidas
Roxo
Montes Velhos
Ervidel
Barragem do Roxo
Mina de Juliana
Trindade
Albernoa
Terges
Alvalade
São Domingos
Muda
Barragem de Campilhas
Taganheira
Campilhas
Porto Covo
Cercal
Bicos
Vale de Agua
Aljustrel
Messejana
Conceição
Igreja Matriz de Castro Verde
Casével
Castro Verde
Entradas
Vale de Açor
Algodor
Amendoeira
Guadiana
Corte Pinto
Paymogo
Cabezas Rubias
Malagón
Chança
Arroyo del Albahacar
Vila Nova de Milfontes
São Luis
Colos
Santa Luzia
Garvão
São Martinho das Amoreiras
Barragem de Monte da Rocha
Ourique
Museu de Lucerna
Castro de Cola
Rosário
São Marcos da Ataboeira
Alcaria Ruiva
Mina de S. Domingos
Mértola
Penilhos
Sudoeste
Alentejano
Costa
Vicentina
Cavaleiro
Odemira
Aldea Amurallado de Odemira
Zambugueira do Mar
São Teotónio
Mira
Barragem de Santa Clara
Santana da Serra
Santa Clara-a-Velha
Sabóia
Gomes Aires
Santa Bárbara de Padrões
São João dos Caldeireiros
Moriones
Sant'Ana de Cambas
Las Herrerías
Puebla de Guzmán
Emb. del Chanza
São Sebastião dos Carros
Espirito Santo
Via Gloria
El Granado
El Almendro
Odeceixe
Santa Bárbara
Santa Clara-a-Nova
Almodôvar
São Pedro de Solis
Vascão
Martim-Longo
Gióes
Alcoutim
Villanueva de los Castillejos
Sanlúcar de Guadiana
Pereiro
Foupana
San Silvestre de Guzmán
Tariquejas
Serra de Monchique
São Marcos da Serra
Serra do Caldeirão
Doguenos
Almexial
Vaqueiros
Emb. de Piedras
Monte Clérigo
Aljezur
Foia 902
Monchique
Alferce
Marmelete
Arade
São Barnabé
Mú 575
Cachopo
Odeleite
Villablanca
Arrifana
São Bartolomeu de Messines
Buraco dos Mouros
Vale de Rosa
Peralva
Azinhal
Lepe
Alfambra
Barragem da Bravura
Barragem do Arade
Algarve
Alte
Salir
Barranco do Velho
Castro Marim
Ayamonte
La Redondela
Bordeira
Porto de Lagos
Silves
Algoz
Tunes
Paderne
Loulé
São Brás de Alportel
Monte Gordo
Vila Real de Santo António
Isla Cristina
La Antillas
Isla Canela
Bensafrim
Portimão
Odiáxere
Alvor
Lagôa
Alcantarilha
Boliqueime
Santa Catarina
Cacela
Cabanas
Tavira
Santo Estêvão
Vila do Bispo
Nossa Senhora de Conceiò
Budens
Burgau
Luz
Lagos
Ponta da Piedade
Baía de Lagos
Praia da Rocha
Fortaleza de Santa Catarina de Ribamar
Carvoeiro
Armação de Pera
Albufeira
Quarteira
Almansil
Vale de Lobo
São João da Venda
Estói
Pechão
Moncarapacho
Ria Formosa
Golfo de
C. de São Vicente
Fortaleza de Sagres
Sagres
Ponta de Sagres
Faro
Olhão
Ilha da Barreta
C. de Santa Maria
Las Palmas
Santa
0
10
20
30
40
50 km
A
B
C
D
1
2
3
9°
8°
38°
37°
36°

Jerez de los Caballeros
Burguillos del Cerro
Alconera
Puebla de Sancho Pérez
Usagre
Higuera de Llerena
Maguilla
Granja de Torrehermosa
La Granjuela
Valsequillo
Peñarroya-Pueblonuevo
Alcaracejos
Oliva de la Frontera
Valencia del Ventoso
Calzadilla de los Barros
Fuente de Cantos
Bienvenida
Villagarcia de las Torres
Berlanga
Azuaga
Llerena
Ahillones
Fuente Obejuna
Bélmez
Espiel
Fregenal de la Sierra
Higuera la Real
Bodonal de la Sierra
Montemolín
Casas de Reina
Trasierra
Valverde de Llerena
Fuente del Arco
Argallón
Ojuelos Altos
Sierra de los Santos
Villaharta
Barrancos
Encinasola
Segura de León
Calera de León
Monesterio
Pallares
Puebla del Maestre
Guadalcanal
Malcocinado
La Cardanchosa
Embalse de Puente Nuevo
Villaviciosa de Córdoba
Cumbres Mayores
Cumbres de S. Bartolomé
Fuentes de León
Cabeza la Vaca
Tentudía
Sierra Morena
Picos de Aroche
La Contienda
Sierra de Aracena y Picas
Hinojales
Cañaveral de León
Arroyomolinos de León
Hoya de Santa María
Embalse de El Pintado
Alanís
San Nicolás del Puerto
San Calixto
La Nava
Valdelarco
Cala
El Real de la Jara
Sierra Norte de Sevilla
La Purísima Concepción
Sierra de Hornachuelos
Santa María de Trassierra
Aroche
Cortegana
Galaroza
Jabugo
Aracena
Sierra de Aracena
Alájar
Corteconcepción
Puerto Moral
Embalse de Aracena
Santa Olalla
Almadén de la Plata
Santa María de Consolación
Cazalla de la Sierra
Las Navas de la Concepción
Embalse del Retortillo
Embalse del Bembézar
Constantina
La Quintera
Hornachuelos
Embalse de la Breña
Almodóvar del Río
Almonaster la Real
Higuera de la Sierra
Zufre
El Pedroso
La Puebla de los Infantes
Posadas
San Telmo
Andalucía
Campofrío
Embalse de la Minilla
Embalse de Cala
El Ronquillo
Peñaflor
Guadalquivir
Guadalcázar
Fuente Palmera
La Carlota
El Cerro de Andévalo
Valdeflores
La Aulaga
El Campillo
Nerva
Minas de Riotinto
El Castillo de las Guardas
Castilblanco de los Arroyos
Villanueva del Río y Minas
Palma del Río
Lora del Río
Zalamea la Real
El Madroño
El Alamo
Cantillana
Villaverde del Río
Villanueva del Río
Alcolea del Río
Calañas
El Garrobo
Las Pajanosas
Burguillos
Tocina
La Campana
Cañada Rosal
Écija
Santaella
Valverde del Camino
Berrocal
Brenes
La Luisiana
Tharsis
Alosno
Gerena
Guillena
Alcalá del Río
Fuentes de Andalucía
Aznalcóllar
Necrópolis Romana
La Rinconada
Carmona
San Bartolomé de la Torre
Ciudad Antiquísima de Itálica
La Algaba
Dolmen de Soto
La Palma del Condado
Santiponce
Sevilla
Seville
El Viso del Alcor
Marinaleda
Gibraleón
Trigueros
Castillo de Niebla
Villalba del Alcor
Paterna del Campo
Escacena del Campo
Olivares
Camas
Mairena del Alcor
Marchena
Beas
Niebla
Manzanilla
Sanlúcar la Mayor
Castilleja
Alcalá de Guadaira
La Lantejuela
El Rubio
Villarrasa
Carrión
Benacazón
Bormujos
Bollullos
Gelves
Paradas
Bollullos par del Condado
Mairena del Aljarafe
Alcázar de Alcalá de Guadaira
El Arahal
Osuna
Bonares
Lucena
Rociana del Condado
Pilas
Aznalcázar
Coria del Río
Dos Hermanas
Gilena
Aguadulce
Aljaraque
Monasterio de Santa Clara
Moguer
Hinojos
La Puebla del Río
La Puebla de Cazalla
La Roda de Andalucía
Cartaya
Huelva
Monasterio de Santa María de la Rábida
Almonte
Villamanrique de la Condesa
El Rompido
Palos de la Frontera
Utrera
Punta Umbría
Isla de Saltes
Mazagón
Los Palacios y Villafranca
Los Morales
Morón de la Frontera
Sierra de Yeguas
Martín de la Jara
Los Corrales
El Rocío
Villafranco del Guadalquivir
Entorno de Doñana
El Coronil
El Saucejo
Queipo
Embalse de la Torre del Águila
Villanueva de S. Juan
Cádiz
Parque Nacional de Doñana
Montellano
Torre de la Higuera
Las Cabezas de San Juan
Almargen
Teba
Coripe
La Encarnación
Pruna
Castillo de Olvera
Olvera
Cañete la Real
Lebrija
Puerto Serrano
Alcalá del Valle
Las Palmas de Gran Canaria
Santa Cruz de Tenerife
Costa de la Luz
Algodonales
Trebujena
El Cuervo
Espera
Villamartín
Zahara
El Gastor
Setenil
Ardales
Cuevas del Becerro
Embalse de Zahara
El Burgo
Sanlúcar de Barrameda
Bonanza
Bornos
Prado del Rey
Grazalema
Arriate
Chipiona
Arcos de la Frontera
Embalse de Bornos
El Bosque
Sierra de Grazalema
Benaocaz
Benaoján
Cueva de la Pileta
Ronda
Castillo de Ronda
Yunquera
Jerez de la Frontera
Embalse de los Hurones
Serranía de Ronda
Sierra de las Nieves
Tolox
La Barca de la Florida
Algar
Ubrique
Jimera de Líbar
Embalse de Guadalcacín
Cortes de la Frontera
Rota
Laguna de Medina
Garcisobaco
El Puerto de Santa María
Jubrique
Istán
Bahía de Cádiz
Algatocín
Benarrabá
Puerto Real
Baños de Gigonza
El Comenar
Sierra Bermeja
Paterna de Rivera
Gaucín
Medina Sidonia
Alcalá de los Gazules
Castillo de Jimena de la Frontera
Casares
San Pedro
Chiclana de la Frontera
San Fernando
Los Alcornocales
Jimena de la Frontera
Estepona
Embalse de Barbate
Sancti-Petri
Manilva
San Martín del Tesorillo
La Barrosa
Campano
Benalup
Castellar de la Frontera
Castillo de Castellar Viejo
Almoraima
San Enrique
Embalse de Celemín
Guadiaro
Cabo Roche
Conil de la Frontera
Embalse de Palmones
Charco-Redondo
San Roque
Arrecife
Las Palmas de Gran Canaria
Santa Cruz de Tenerife
Santa Cruz de la Palma
Vejer de la Frontera
Castillo Árabe
La Línea de la Concepción
Los Caños de Meca
Los Barrios
Puente Mayorga
C. Trafalgar
Barbate
Algeciras
Gibraltar (U.K.)
Pta. de Europa
Zahara de los Atunes
Castillo de Almadrabas
Facinas
Bahía de Algeciras
Baelo Claudia
Castillo de Guzmán el Bueno
Tarifa
Punta Marroquí
Tanger
Strait of Gibraltar
Ceuta (España) (Spain)
Ksar es Seghir
Tanger
Souk Tleta
38°
37°
36°
7°
6°
5°
A
B
C
D
4
5

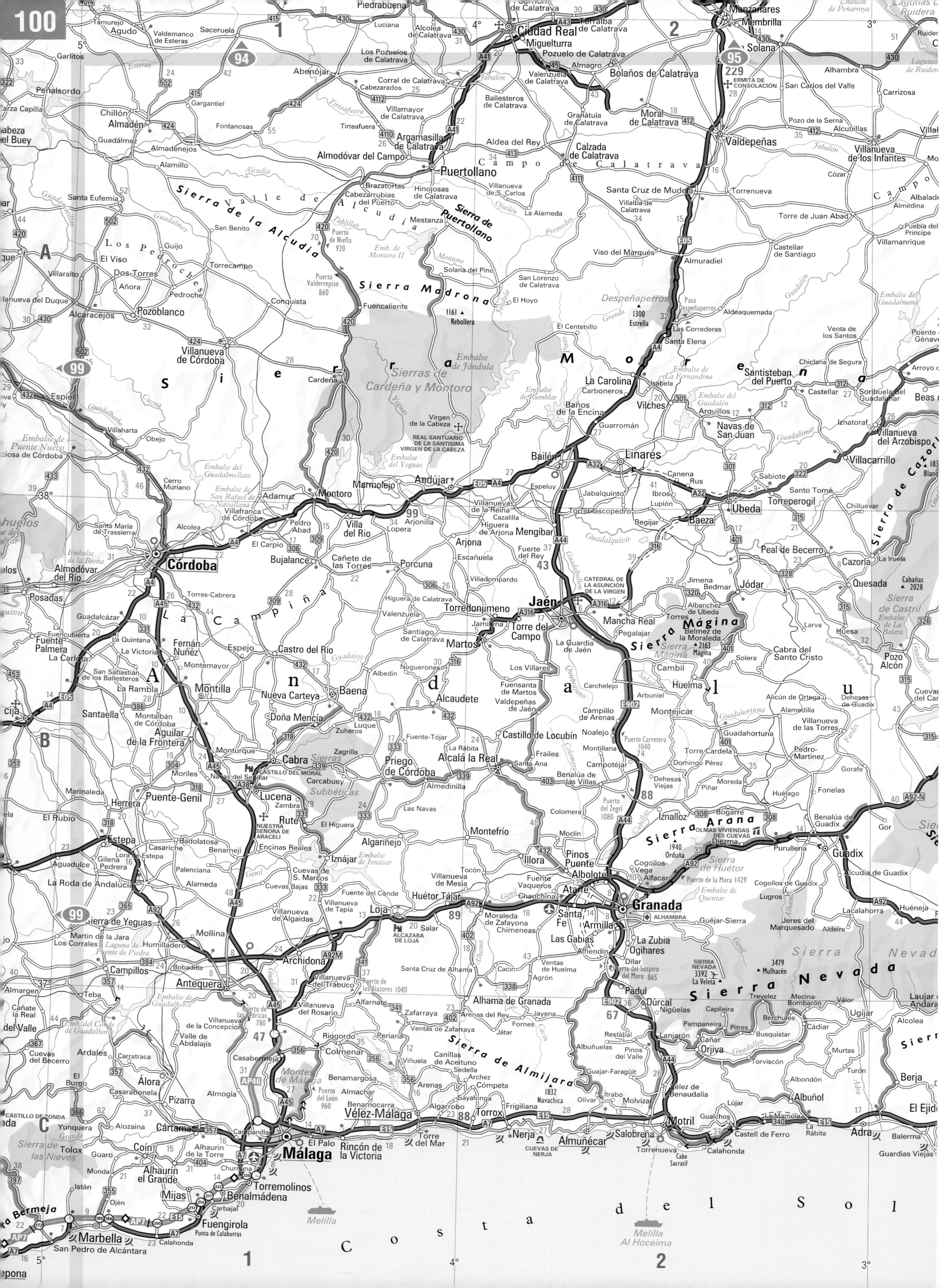

Piedrabuena
Tamurejo
Agudo
Valdemanco de Esteras
Saceruela
Luciana
Alcolea de Calatrava
Ciudad Real
Miguelturra
Torralba de Calatrava
Manzanares
Membrilla
Solana
Lagunas de Ruidera
Garlitos
Peñalsordo
Abenójar
Corral de Calatrava
Cabezarados
Pozuelo de Calatrava
Almagro
Valenzuela de Calatrava
Bolaños de Calatrava
Ermita de Consolación
San Carlos del Valle
Alhambra
Carrizosa
Zarza Capilla
Chillón
Almadén
Gargantiel
Tirteafuera
Villamayor de Calatrava
Ballesteros de Calatrava
Granátula de Calatrava
Moral de Calatrava
Pozo de la Serna
Alcubillas
Cabeza del Buey
Guadalmez
Almadenejos
Fontanosas
Argamasilla de Calatrava
Almodóvar del Campo
Aldea del Rey
Calzada de Calatrava
Valdepeñas
Villanueva de los Infantes
Alamillo
Puertollano
Campo de Calatrava
Cózar
Santa Eufemia
Valle de Alcudia
Brazatortas
Cabezarrubias del Puerto
Hinojosas de Calatrava
Villanueva de San Carlos
Santa Cruz de Mudela
Torrenueva
Campo
Albaladejo
Almedina
Sierra de la Alcudia
Sierra de Puertollano
Mestanza
La Alameda
Villalba de Calatrava
Torre de Juan Abad
San Benito
Puerto de Niefla 920
Emb. de Montoro II
Los Pedroches
Guijo
El Viso
Dos Torres
Añora
Torrecampo
Villaralto
Pedroche
Solana del Pino
Viso del Marqués
Almuradiel
Castellar de Santiago
Villamanrique
Puebla del Príncipe
Puerto Valderrepiso 860
Sierra Madrona
San Lorenzo de Calatrava
El Hoyo
Despeñaperros
Paso Despeñaperros
Aldeaquemada
Villanueva del Duque
Pozoblanco
Conquista
Fuencaliente
1161 Rebollera
1300 Estrella
Alcaracejos
El Centenillo
Las Correderas
Santa Elena
Venta de los Santos
Embalse del Guadalmena
Villanueva de Córdoba
Sierras de Cardeña y Montoro
Embalse de Jándula
Sierra Morena
La Carolina
Carboneros
Isabela
Embalse de La Fernandina
Santisteban del Puerto
Chiclana de Segura
Castellar
Sorihuela del Guadalimar
Arroyo del Ojanco
Beas de Segura
Cardeña
Espiel
Embalse de Rumblar
Baños de la Encina
Vilches
Embalse del Guadalén
Arquillos
Navas de San Juan
Villahartа
Obejo
Virgen de la Cabeza
Real Santuario de la Santísima Virgen de la Cabeza
Guarromán
Iznatoraf
Villanueva del Arzobispo
Embalse de Puente Nuevo
Hinojosa de Córdoba
Embalse del Guadalmellato
Embalse del Yeguas
Bailén
Linares
Villacarrillo
Cerro Muriano
Embalse de San Rafael de Navallana
Marmolejo
Andújar
Espeluy
Canena
Rus
Sabiote
Santo Tomé
Adamuz
Montoro
Villanueva de la Reina
Jabalquinto
Ibros
Lupión
Úbeda
Torreperogil
Chilluevar
Sierra de Cazorla
Villafranca de Córdoba
Cazalilla
Torreblascopedro
Begíjar
Baeza
Alcolea
Pedro Abad
Villa del Río
Lopera
Arjonilla
Higuera de Arjona
Mengíbar
Santa María de Trassierra
El Carpio
Arjona
Fuerte del Rey
Peal de Becerro
Cazorla
La Iruela
Embalse de la Breña
Córdoba
Bujalance
Cañete de las Torres
Porcuna
Escañuela
Jimena
Bedmar
Jódar
Quesada
Cabañas 2028
Almodóvar del Río
Villadompardo
Catedral de la Asunción de la Virgen
Posadas
Torres-Cabrera
La Campiña
Higuera de Calatrava
Torredonjimeno
Jaén
Albanchez de Úbeda
Sierra de Castril
Guadalcázar
Valenzuela
Jamilena
Torre del Campo
Mancha Real
Torres
Pegalajar
Sierra Mágina
Belmez de la Moraleda
2163 Mágina
Larva
Huesa
Embalse de La Bolera
Fuente Palmera
La Carlota
Fuencubierta
La Quintana
La Victoria
Fernán Núñez
Espejo
Castro del Río
Santiago de Calatrava
Martos
La Guardia de Jaén
Cabra del Santo Cristo
Pozo Alcón
San Sebastián de los Ballesteros
Montemayor
Noguerones
Los Villares
Cambil
Solera
Écija
La Rambla
Montilla
Albendín
Baena
Alcaudete
Fuensanta de Martos
Valdepeñas de Jaén
Carchelejo
Arbuniel
Huelma
Alicún de Ortega
Dehesas de Guadix
Santaella
Nueva Carteya
Montalbán de Córdoba
Doña Mencía
Zuheros
Luque
Campillo de Arenas
Montejícar
Alamedilla
Villanueva de las Torres
Aguilar de la Frontera
Fuente-Tójar
La Rábita
Castillo de Locubín
Noalejo
Puerto Carretero 1040
Guadahortuna
Monturque
Zagrilla
Cabra
Priego de Córdoba
Alcalá la Real
Frailes
Montillana
Torre Cardela
Pedro-Martínez
Moriles
Castillo del Moral
Carcabuey
Navas del Selpillar
Sierras Subbéticas
Santa Ana
Campotéjar
Domingo Pérez
Benalúa de las Villas
Gorafe
Marinaleda
Puente-Genil
Lucena
Zambra
Almedinilla
Dehesas Viejas
Piñar
Moreda
Huélago
Fonelas
Herrera
Las Navas
Colomera
Puerto del Zegrí 1080
Iznalloz
Bogarre
Benalúa de Guadix
El Rubio
Rute
Nuestra Señora de Araceli
El Higuera
Montefrío
Sierra Arana
Cuevas del Campo
Olmas Viviendas de las Cuevas
Diezma
Purullena
Guadix
Gor
Estepa
Casariche
Badolatosa
Benamejí
Encinas Reales
Algarinejo
Moclín
Íllora
Pinos Puente
1940 Orduña
Cogollos-Vega
Sierra de Huétor
Puerto de la Mora 1429
Alcudia de Guadix
Gilena
Lora de Estepa
Pedrera
Aguadulce
Palenciana
Iznájar
Embalse de Iznájar
Cuevas de S. Marcos
Tocón
Albolote
Alfacar
Embalse de Quéntar
Cogollos de Guadix
Lugros
La Roda de Andalucía
Alameda
Cuevas Bajas
Villanueva de Mesia
Fuente Vaqueros
Atarfe
Chauchina
Granada
Alhambra
Guéjar-Sierra
Lacalahorra
Huéneja
Fuente de Piedra
Fuente del Conde
Villanueva de Tapia
Huétor Tájar
Loja
Alcazaba de Loja
Salar
Moraleda de Zafayona
Chimeneas
Santa Fe
Armilla
Jeres del Marquesado
Aldeire
Sierra de Yeguas
Villanueva de Algaidas
Martín de la Jara
Los Corrales
Laguna de Fuente de Piedra
Humilladero
Mollina
Archidona
Las Gabias
La Zubia
Ogíjares
Alhendín
Dílar
Puerto del Suspiro del Moro 865
Sierra Nevada
3479 Mulhacén
3392 La Veleta
Campillos
Bobadilla
Antequera
Villanueva del Trabuco
Puerto de los Alazores 1040
Santa Cruz del Alhama
Cacín
Ventas de Huelma
Agrón
Padul
Almargen
Teba
Embalse de Guadalhorce
Puerto de las Pedrizas 780
Villanueva del Rosario
Alfarnate
Zafarraya
Alhama de Granada
Jayena
Dúrcal
Nigüelas
Trevélez
Mecina-Bombarón
Válor
Laujar de Andarax
Cañete la Real
Emb. del Conde de Guadalhorce
Villanueva de la Concepción
Ventas de Zafarraya
Arenas del Rey
Fornes
Játar
Capileira
Pampaneira
Bérchules
Ugíjar
Alcolea
Almáchar
Valle de Abdalajís
Riogordo
Colmenar
Periana
Sierra de Almijara
Restábal
Lanjarón
Pitres
Busquístar
Cádiar
Ardales
Carratraca
Cuevas del Becerro
Casabermeja
Viñuela
Canillas de Aceituno
Sedella
Albuñuelas
Pinos del Valle
Cáñar
Órgiva
Murtas
Torvizcón
El Burgo
Montes de Málaga
Benamargosa
Archez
Cómpeta
1832 Navachica
Guajar-Faragüit
Turón
Álora
Casarabonela
Almogía
Puerto del León 960
Arenas
Sayalonga
Ítrabo
Molvízar
Vélez de Benaudalla
Albondón
Albuñol
Berja
Pizarra
Benamocarra
Algarrobo
Torrox
Frigiliana
Olivar
Lújar
Castillo de Ronda
Yunquera
Alozaina
Cártama
Vélez-Málaga
Motril
Gualchos
La Mamola
El Ejido
Sierra de las Nieves
Tolox
Campanillas
El Palo
Rincón de la Victoria
Torre del Mar
Nerja
Cuevas de Nerja
Almuñécar
Salobreña
Torrenueva
Cabo Sacratif
Calahonda
Castell de Ferro
La Rábita
Adra
Balerma
Guardias Viejas
Guaro
Coín
Alhaurín de la Torre
Málaga
Monda
Alhaurín el Grande
Churriana
Torremolinos
Istán
Ojén
Mijas
Benalmádena
Sierra Bermeja
Carbajal
Fuengirola
Punta de Calaburras
Marbella
San Pedro de Alcántara
Calahonda
Estepona
Costa del Sol
Melilla
Melilla Al Hoceima

Albacete
Chinchilla de Monte Aragón
Almansa
Hellín
Tobarra
Jumilla
Yecla
Villena
Caudete
Ontinyent
Alcoy
Ibi
Castalla
Elda
Petrer
Monóvar
Novelda
Aspe
San Vicente del Raspeig
Elche
Crevillente
Santa Pola
Pinoso
Callosa de Segura
Orihuela
Almoradí
Dolores
Rojales
Guardamar del Segura
Torrevieja
Pilar de la Horadada
San Pedro del Pinatar
San Javier
Torre-Pacheco
Los Alcázares
Mar Menor
Cartagena
La Unión
Cabo de Palos
Escombreras
Mazarrón
Puerto de Mazarrón
Golfo de Mazarrón
Águilas
Cabo Cope
Lorca
Totana
Alhama de Murcia
Sierra de Espuña
Murcia
Molina de Segura
Alcantarilla
Alguazas
Archena
Cieza
Abarán
Fortuna
Mula
Bullas
Cehegín
Caravaca de la Cruz
Calasparra
Moratalla
Sierra de Taibilla
Nerpio
Yeste
Elche de la Sierra
Socovos
Letur
Sierra de Alcaraz
Alcaraz
Riopar
Sierra de Segura
Sierras de Cazorla Segura y Las Villas
Puebla de Don Fadrique
Huéscar
Castril
Orce
Galera
Cúllar
Baza
Caniles
Sierra de Baza
Sierra de María
María
Velez Blanco
Vélez Rubio
Puerto Lumbreras
Sierra de las Estancias
Huércal-Overa
Albox
Olula del Río
Serón
Tíjola
Macael
Cuevas del Almanzora
Vera
Garrucha
Mojacar
Sierra de los Filabres
Sierra Cabrera
Sorbas
Tabernas
Sierra Alhamilla
Carboneras
Níjar
Sierra de Gádor
Almería
Golfo de Almería
Roquetas de Mar
La Mojonera
Vícar
Sierra del Cabo de Gata
Cabo de Gata
San José
Melilla
Murcia
Andalucía
0 10 20 30 40 50 km
A
B
C
3
4
5
2°
1°
37°
38°

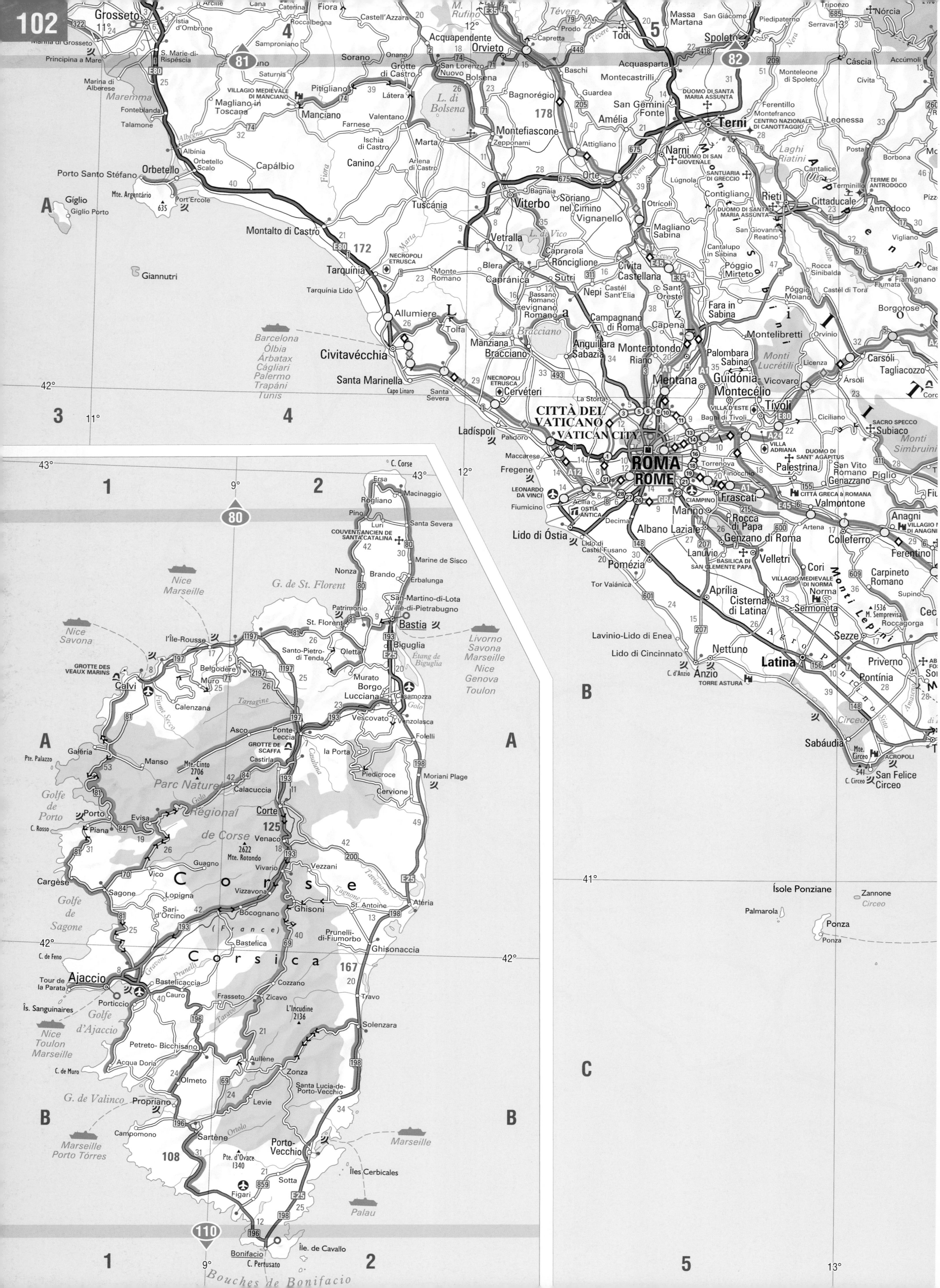
Grosseto
Orvieto
Todi
Spoleto
Terni
Rieti
Viterbo
Tuscánia
Montalto di Castro
Tarquínia
Civitavécchia
Santa Marinella
Cerveteri
Bracciano
Ladíspoli
Fiumicino
Lido di Óstia
CITTÀ DEL VATICANO
VATICAN CITY
ROMA
ROME
Frascati
Tívoli
Guidónia Montecélio
Mentana
Monterotondo
Palestrina
Subiaco
Valmontone
Colleferro
Anagni
Ferentino
Velletri
Albano Laziale
Genzano di Roma
Pomézia
Aprília
Cisterna di Latina
Latina
Sezze
Priverno
Pontínia
Sabáudia
San Felice Circeo
Anzio
Nettuno
Ísole Ponziane
Ponza
Palmarola
Zannone
Orbetello
Porto Santo Stéfano
Gíglio
Giannutri
L. di Bolsena
L. di Bracciano
Monti Lepini
Barcelona
Ólbia
Árbatax
Cágliari
Palermo
Trapáni
Tunis
Corse
Corsica
(France)
Bastia
Calvi
Ajaccio
Corte
Porto-Vecchio
Bonifacio
Sartène
Propriano
Porto
Cargèse
L'Île-Rousse
St. Florent
Ghisonaccia
Solenzara
Aléria
Parc Naturel Régional de Corse
Mte. Cinto 2706
Mte. Rotondo 2622
L'Incudine 2136
Golfe de Porto
Golfe de Sagone
Golfe d'Ajaccio
G. de Valinco
G. de St. Florent
Bouches de Bonifacio
Nice
Marseille
Savona
Livorno
Genova
Toulon
Porto Tórres
Palau
Îles Cerbicales
Île. de Cavallo
C. Corse
C. Pertusato
A
B
C
1
2
3
4
5

104
6
7
8
14°
15°
82
83
104
106
0 10 20 30 40 50 km
A
B
C
42°
41°
Gran Sasso e Monti della Laga
Gran Sasso d'Itália
Corno Grande 2912
Téramo
Notaresco
Giulianova
Roseto degli Abruzzi
Pineto
Silvi Marina
Atri
Città Sant'Angelo
Montesilvano
Pescara
Francavilla al Mare
Spoltore
Penne
Pianella
Chieti
Ortona
Lido Riccio
San Vito Chietino
Fossacésia
Lanciano
Guardiagrele
Casalbordino
Vasto
San Salvo Marina
San Salvo
Térmoli
Campomarino
Trémiti
Pianosa
Lago di Lésina
Lésina
Poggio Imperiale
Sannicandro Gargánico
Apricena
San Marco in Lámis
San Severo
Torremaggiore
Lucera
Fóggia
Tróia
Orsara di Púglia
Orta Nova
Áscoli Satriano
Candela
L'Aquila
Amatrice
Montório al Vomano
Isola del Gr. Sasso d'Itália
Castél del Monte
Capestrano
Pópoli
Sulmona
Prátola Peligna
Celano
Avezzano
Magliano de'Marsi
Mte. Velino 2487
Sirento Velino
Pescina
Scanno
Maiella
Mte. Amaro 2793
Atessa
Cásoli
Gissi
Montenero di Bisáccia
Guglionesi
Larino
Castelmáuro
Trivento
Agnone
Capracotta
Castèl di Sangro
Roccaraso
Pescocostanzo
Pescasséroli
Abruzzo
Sora
Isola del Liri
Frosinone
Cassino
Pontecorvo
Isérnia
Venafro
Campobasso
Bojano
Monti del Matese
Monti d. Sánnio
Piedimonte Matese
Morcone
Benevento
Ariano Irpino
Grottaminarda
Avellino
Caserta
Cápua
Teano
Sessa Aurunca
Minturno
Fórmia
Gaeta
Terracina
Sperlonga
Fondi
Monti Aurunci
Monti Ausoni
Golfo di Gaeta
Mondragone
Castél Volturno
Aversa
Giugliano in Campania
Afragola
Acerra
Nola
Pozzuoli
NÁPOLI
NAPLES
Bácoli
Prócida
Íschia
Ventoténe
Torre del Greco
Torre Annunziata
Castellammare di Stábia
Vesúvio 1281
Pompei
Nocera Inferiore
Cava de'Tirreni
Salerno
Sorrento
Massa Lubrense
Capri
Anacapri
Positano
Amalfi
Golfo di Nápoli
Golfo di Salerno
Battipáglia
Éboli
Paestum
Capáccio
Agrópoli
Castellabate
Roccadáspide
Monti Picentini
Montella
Lioni
Calitri
Bisáccia
Melfi
Muro Lucano
Bella
Avigliano
Potenza
Polla
Sala Consilina
Teggiano
Vallo della Lucánia
Vallo di Diano
Cilento
Buonabitácolo
Cágliari
Palermo Tunis Messina
Catánia
Palermo Strómboli Ginostra Panarea Lípari Vulcano Milazzo

1
2
3
A
B
C
16°
17°
42°
83
84
103
106
107
0 10 20 30 40 50 km
Kopište
Ubli
Lastovo
Mljet
Sobra
Palagruža
(Hrvatska)
(Croatia)
Pianosa
Trémiti
MARE ADRIATICO
Dubrovnik
Bar
Durrës
Kerkyra
Igoumenitsa
Patra
Rodi Gargánico
Peschici
Ischitella
Lago di Lésina
Lago di Varano
Lésina
Vico del Gargano
Vieste
Carpino
Testa del Gargano
Poggio Imperiale
Sannicandro Gargánico
Cagnano Varano
Apricena
Gargano
Pugnochiuso
San Marco in Lámis
Mte. Calvo
1055
Báia delle Zágare
Mattinata
San Severo
Rignano Gargánico
San Giovanni Rotondo
Monte Sant'Angelo
Manfredónia
Lido di Siponto
Golfo di Manfredónia
Lucera
Fóggia
Améndola
Zapponeta
Salina di Margherita di Savóia
Carapelle
Tróia
Giardinetto Vecchio
Orta Nova
Trinitápoli
Margherita di Savóia
CANNAE ANTICA
Barletta
Castelluccio de' Sáuri
San Ferdinando di Púglia
Trani
Stornara
Ofanto
Cerignola
Andria
Bisceglie
Bovino
Deliceto
Áscoli Satriano
Canosa di Púglia
Molfetta
Giovinazzo
Monteleone di Púglia
Accadia
Corato
Santo Spirito
Sant'Agata di Púglia
Candela
Terlizzi
Bari
Rocchetta S. António
Posta Piana
Minervino Murge
Ruvo di Púglia
Bitonto
Lacedónia
Invaso Diga Locone
CASTEL DEL MONTE
Palo del Colle
Modugno
Triggiano
Mola di Bari
Bisaccia
Lavello
Bitetto
Sannicandro di Bari
Capurso
Noicáttaro
Vallata
Melfi
Montemilone
Alta Murgia
Grumo Áppula
Adelfia
Rutigliano
Aquilónia
1326
M. Vúlture
Rapolla
Venosa
Spinazzola
Toritto
Casamássima
Polignano a Mare
Monópoli
Andretta
Rionero in Vúlture
Conversano
Calitri
Ripacándida
Palazzo San Gervásio
Acquaviva delle Fonti
Turi
GROTTA DI CASTELLANA
Castellana Grotte
PARCO ARCHEOLOGICO DI EGNAZIA
Savelletri
Teora
Ruvo del Monte
Atella
L. di Serra di Corvo
Cassano delle Murge
Sammichele di Bari
Pescopagano
Forenza
CASTELLO DI LAGOPESOLE
Genzano di Lucánia
Gravina in Púglia
Altamura
Putignano
Fasano
Torre Canne
Laviano
San Fele
Pso. d. Crocelle 1136
Acerenza
Bradano
Gióia del Colle
Noci
Rosa Marina
Villanova
Muro Lucano
Bella
Avigliano
Pietragalla
Oppido Lucano
Santéramo in Colle
Alberobello
Locorotondo
Ostuni
Ruoti
Cancellara
Irsina
Cisternino
Vaglio Basilicata
Tolve
Martina Franca
Carovigno
San Gregorio Magno
Picerno
Matera
Buccino
Potenza
Tricárico
Grassano
Móttola
Céglie Messápica
San Vito dei Normanni
Vietri di Potenza
Tito
Caggiano
Trivigno
L. di S. Giuliano
Laterza
Castellaneta
Crispiano
Villa Castelli
Auletta
GROTTA DELL'ANGELO
Salandrella
Gróttole
Miglionico
Ginosa
Palagiano
Massafra
Francavilla Fontana
Mte. Alburno
1742
Pso. Croce d. Scrivano 1143
Anzi
Garaguso
Salandra
Montemésola
Grottáglie
Polla
Pomárico
Montescaglioso
Cilento e Vallo di Diano
Brienza
Accettura
San Máuro Forte
Lido Azzurro
Oria
Corleto Monforte
Calvello
Laurenzana
Ferrandina
Táranto
Torre Santa Susanna
Sala Consilina
Márscico Nuovo
Basento
Castellaneta Marina
Chéradi
San Giórgio Iónico
Monteparano
Fragagnano
Sella di Conza
Sella d. Corticato 1026
San Rufo
M. Volturino 1836
Corleto Perticara
Stigliano
Marina di Ginosa
Bernalda
Talsano
Lizzano
Sava
Teggiano
Cirigliano
Pisticci
PARCO ARCHEOLOGICO METAPONTO
Pulsano
Manduria
Torricella
Laurino
Padula
CERTOSA DI SAN LORENZO
Viggiano
Sauro
Cavone
Lido di Metaponto
Lido Silvana
Avetrana
Mte. Cervati 1898
Montesano sulla Marcellana
Montemurro
Missanello
Montalbano Iónico
Maruggio
Vallo della Lucánia
Buonabitácolo
Sella Cessuta 1040
Spinoso
GRUMENTUM ANTICA
Agri
SANTUARIO SANTA MARIA D'ANGLONA
Lido di Scanzano
Scanzano Jónico
1705
Casalbuono
Sanza
San Arcángelo
SAN FRANCESCO
L. di Monte Cotugno
Tursi
M. Sacro o Gelbison
Rofrano
San Chírico Raparo
Colobraro
Policoro
Mte. Sirino 2005
Roccanova
Sinni
Montano Antilia
Castelsaraceno
Rotondella
Lido di Policoro
Torre Orsáia
Lagonegro
Chiaromonte
Senise
Lucano
Appennino
E55
E45
E90
E842
E843
E847
A3
A14

CRNA GORA
MONTENEGRO
SHQIPËRIA
ALBANIA
ADRIATICO
MARE ADRIATICO
Prekornica
Orjen
Prokletije
Rumija
Lovćen
Skadarsko Jezero
Liqeni i Shkodrës
Dubrovnik
Cavtat
Čilipi
Gruda
Zaton
Mokošica
Trebinje
Šipan
Herceg-Novi
Igalo
Bijela
Risan
Perast
Tivat
Kotor
Dobrota
Budva
Sveti Stefan
Petrovac
Sutomore
Bar
Stari Bar
Ulcinj
Sveti Nikola
Cetinje
Podgorica
Danilovgrad
Nikšić
Virpazar
Tuzi
Golubovci
Rt Oštra
Boka Kotorska
Bari
Ancona
Trieste
Kerkyra
Igoumenitsa
Sami
Patra
Han i Hotit
Koplik
Shkodër
Velipojë
Shëngjin
Lezhë
Gjiri i Drinit
Milot
Laç
Mamuras
Gjiri i Rodonit
Kepi i Rodonit
Gjiri i Lalzit
Bishti i Pallës
Fushë-Krujë
Krujë
Vorë
Tiranë
Tirana
Durrës
Shijak
Gjiri i Durrësit
Kavajë
Kala e Turrës
Rrogozhinë
Peqin
Elbasan
Cërrik
Divjakë
Lushnjë
Myzeqe
Karavastasë
Fier
Patos
Levan
Ballsh
Berat
Kuçovë
Novoselë
Selenicë
Vlorë
Gjiri i Vlorës
Kaninë
Sazanit
Kep i Gjuhës
Karaburun
Orikum
Mali i Gribës
Malakaster
Dukat
Bregdet
Dhërmi
Himarë
Tepelenë
Memaliaj
Puke
Fushë Arrëz
Bajram Curri
Tropojë
Fierzë
Burrel
Krrabë
Gramsh
Brindisi
Torre Guaceto
Mesagne
Latiano
San Pietro Vernotico
Cellino S. Marco
Squinzano
Trepuzzi
Surbo
Lecce
Campi Salentina
Guagnano
S. Dónaci
Érchie
San Pancrazio Salentino
Sálice Salentino
Véglie
Leverano
Copertino
Porto Cesáreo
Monteroni di Lecce
San Cesário di Lecce
Léquile
Vérnole
Melendugno
San Foca
Torre dell'Orso
Calimera
Martano
Galatina
Soleto
Galatone
Nardò
Otranto
San Cataldo
Casa l'Abate
Torchiarolo
Abbazia Santa Maria di Cerrate
19°
20°
42°
41°
84
85
107
116
A
B
C
4
5

1
2
3
A
B
C
D
103
104
14
109
40°
39°
38°
15°
16°
Agrópoli
Capaccio
Ogliastro Cilento
Cilento
Felitto
Teggiano
Laurino
Stio
Vallo di Diano
Padula
Certosa di San Lorenzo
Montesano sulla Marcellana
Viggiano
Montemurro
Pisticci
Craco
Montalbano Iónico
San Marco
Castellabate
Punta Licosa
Ogliastro Marina
Montecórice
Póllica
Acciaroli
Velia
Ascea
Fasana
Vallo della Lucánia
Mte. Sacro o Gelbison
Mte. Cervati 1898
Buonabitácolo
Ceraso
Rofrano
Montano Antilia
Sanza
Casalbuono
Torre Orsáia
Pisciotta
Foria
Palinuro
C. Palinuro
Mte. Bulgheria 1225
Camerota
San Giovanni a Piro
Sapri
Lagonegro
Mte. Sirino 2005
Moliterno
Grumentum Antica
Spinoso
San Arcángelo
San Chirico Raparo
Roccanova
Castelsaraceno
Chiaromonte
Senise
Noépoli
Tursi
Policoro
Colobraro
Rotondella
Nova Siri
Rocca Imperiale
Oriolo
Montegiordano Marina
Santuario Santa Maria d'Anglona
Scanzano
Lido di
Rivello
Latrónico
Episcopia
Francavilla in Sinni
Lauria
Castelluccio Inferiore
San Severino Lucano
Pollino
Golfo di Policastro
Maratea
Tórtora
Rotonda
Viggianello
Mte. Pollino 2248
Terranova di Pollino
Amendolara
Albidona
Marina di Amendolara
Práia a Mare
Capo Scalea
Scalea
Papasídero
Mormanno
Morano Cálabro
Cherchiara di Calábria
San Lorenzo Bellizzi
Trebisacce
Santa Doménica Talao
Orsomarso
Castrovillari
Cassano allo Iónio
Lungro
Verbicaro
Cirella
Diamante
Buonvicino
Czo.d. Pellegrino 1987
Firmo
Altomonte
Sibari
Spezzano Albanese
Pso d. Scalone 740
San Sosti
Roggiano Gravina
Terranova
Tarsia di Sibari
Belvedere Maríttimo
Sant'Ágata di Ésaro
Monastero di Santa Maria del Patire
Corigliano Cálabro
Rossano
San Demétrio Corone
Sangineto Lido
Fagnano Castello
San Marco Argentano
Bisignano
Acri
Sila Greca
Cropalati
Cetraro
Marina di Acquappesa
Rota Greca
Luzzi
Abbazia di Sambucina
Longobucco
Bocchigliero
Montalto Uffugo
Fuscaldo
San Francesco di Páola
Páola
San Fili
Rose
L. di Cecita
Sila Grande
Camigliatello Silano
Rende
Cosenza
San Lúcido
Spezzano della Sila
Botte Donato 1928
Lorica
Torremezzo di Falconara
Carolei
Fiumefreddo Brúzio
M. Cocuzzo 1541
Aprigliano
C. d'Ascione 1384
La Sila
L. Arvo
L. Ampollino
Lago
Rogliano
Parenti
Amantea
Petília Policastro
Scigliano
Aiello Cálabro
Soveria Mannelli
Cóiraci
M. Femminamorta 1723
Sila Piccola
Villaggio Mancuso
Nocera Terinese
Pso. di Acquabona 1020
Decollatura
Carlópoli
Taverna
Platania
Serrastretta
Gizzeria
Sersale
Capo Súvero
Nicastro
Tiriolo
Sambiase
Gizzeria Lido
Sant'Eufemia Lamezia
Catanzaro
Golfo di Sant'Eufémia
Máida
Curinga
Girifalco
Catanzaro Marina
Bórgia
Lido di Squillace
Squillace
Pta. d. Staletti
Filadélfia
Briático
Pizzo
Tropea
Vibo Valéntia
Olivadi
Soverato
Chiaravalle Centrale
C. Vaticano
M. Poro 710
Ióppolo
Mileto
Simbário
Soriano Cálabro
Santuario di Santa Maria nel Bosco
Serra San Bruno
Badolato
Nicótera
Golfo di Gióia
Marchesale
M. Pecoraro 1423
Dinami
Mongiana
Guardavalle
Rosarno
Laureana di Borrello
Pso. di Pietra Spada 1335
Stilo
Pso. Croce Ferrata 1110
Fabrizia
Gióia Táuro
Políistena
Cinquefrondi
Pta. Stilo
Monasterace Marina
Caulónia
Capo Barbi
Palmi
Taurianova
Cittanova
Seminara
Grotteria
Gioiosa Iónica
Mámmola
Bagnara Cálabra
Oppido Mamertina
Roccella Iónica
Marina di Gioiosa Iónica
Torre Faro
Scilla
Santa Eufémia d'Aspromonte
Gerace
Siderno
Villa San Giovanni
Delianuova
Platì
Locri Antica
Locri
Ardore
Réggio di Calábria
Laganadi
Gambárie
Montalto (M. Cocuzza) 1955
San Luca
Careri
Bovalino Marina
Sella Entrata 1408
Aspromonte
Cardeto
Bianco
Pta. di Péllaro
Montebello Iónico
Bagaladi
Staíti
Lazzaro
Bova
Bova Marina
Brancaleone Marina
Mélito di Porto Salvo
C. Spartivento
Nápoli
Strómboli
Basiluzzo
Panarea
Ísole Eólie
Filicudi
Malfa
Salina
Canneto
Lípari
Vulcano
Salerno
Capo di Milazzo
Golfo di Milazzo
Spartà
Villafranca Tirrena
Mortelle
Milazzo
Spadafora
Capo Calavá
Golfo di Patti
Gioiosa Marea
C. d'Orlando
Brolo
Barcellona-Pozzo di Gotto
Messina
Rometta
Santa Lucia del Mela
Naso
Patti
Falcone
Castroreale
Str. di Messina
Sant'Ágata Militello
Città di Tyndaris
Mazzarrà S. Andrea
Monti Peloritani
M. Poverello 1279
Alcara li Fusi
Longi
Ucria
San Piero Patti
Scaletta Zanclea
San Fratello
Tortorici
Montalbano Elicona
Novara di Sicília
Mandanici
Floresta
Ali Terme
Roccalumera
Monti Nébrodi
Plla. d'Zoppo 1264
Antillo
Plla. Mandrazzi 1125
M. Soro 1847
Santa Doménica Vittória
Santa Teresa di Riva
Francavilla di Sicília
Randazzo
Castiglione di Sicília
Capizzi
L. di Ancipa
Cesarò
Passopisciaro
Linguaglossa
Taormina
Giardini Naxos
Troina
Maletto
Etna
Piedimonte Etneo
Bronte
Fiumefreddo di Sicília

Marina di Ginosa
PARCO ARCHEOLOGICO METAPONTO
Lido di Metaponto
Talsano
Pulsano
Silvana
Lizzano
Sava
Mandúria
Torricella
Avetrana
Marúggio
San Pancrazio Salentino
Guagnano
Trepuzzi
Sálice Salentino
Campi Salentina
Véglie
Surbo
Lecce
San Cataldo
Monteroni di Lecce
Leverano
Léquile
San Cesário di Lecce
Vérnole
San Foca
Melendugno
Torre dell'Orso
Copertino
Porto Cesáreo
Calimera
Martano
Soleto
Galatina
Nardò
Galàtone
Otranto
C. d'Otranto
Santa Maria al Bagno
Cutrofiano
Máglie
Uggiano la Chiesa
Gallípoli
Alézio
Collepasso
Poggiardo
Sant'Andrea
Parábita
Nociglia
Santa Cesárea Terme
GROTTA DI ROMANELLI & ZINZULUSA
Casarano
Diso
Castro
Ruffano
Taviano
Miggiano
Rácale
Taurisano
Tricase
Ugento
Presicce
Alessano
Marina di Nováglie
Gagliano del Capo
Castrignano del Capo
Marina di Léuca
C. Santa Maria di Léuca
Golfo di Táranto
Scanzano
Jónico
Policoro
C. Trionto
Crosia
Cariati
Pta. Fiume Nicá
Campana
Crúcoli
Pta. Alice
Cirò
Cirò Marina
Umbriático
San Nicola dell'Alto
Stróngoli
Giovanni in Fiore
Vitravo
Neto
Cotronei
Santa Severina
Roccabernarda
Scandale
Crotone
Mesoraca
Petronà
C. Colonna
Cutro
Crópani
Ísola di Capo Rizzuto
Botricello
C. Rizzuto
MARE IONIO
IONIAN SEA
14° 30'
Gozo
San Dimitri Pt
Pozzallo
Victoria (Rabat)
Mgarr
Comino
36°
San Pawl il-Bahar
Mellieha
Sliema
Mosta
Valletta
Birkirkara
Rabat
Paola
MALTA
Birzebbugia
Benghisa Pt
Filfla
0 10 20 30 40 50 km
104
105
116
117
15
A
B
C
D
4
5
40°
39°
38°
17°
18°
19°

12°
13°
1
2
14
A
B
C
0 10 20 30 40 50 km
Ústica
Nápoli
Génova
Salerno
Civitavécchia
Cágliari
Tunis
Civitavécchia
Cágliari
Tunis
Pantelleria
Golfo di Castellammare
Golfo di Términi Imerese
C. San Vito
San Vito lo Capo
C. Gallo
Isola delle Fémmine
Mondello
Terrasini
Carini
Capaci
Palermo
Monreale
Santa Maria Nuova
Montelepre
Ficarazzi
Bagheria
Balestrate
Partinico
Altofonte
Casteldáccia
Misilmeri
Trabia
Términi Imerese
Campofelice di Roccella
Caccamo
Pizzolungo
Érice
Trápani
Valdérice
Castellammare del Golfo
M. Spàragio 1110
Scopello
Lévanzo
Ísole Égadi
Maréttimo
Favignana
Paceco
Fulgatore
Rilievo
Stagnone
Tempio Greco di Segesta
Calatafimi
Vita
Álcamo
San Cipirello
San Giuseppe Jato
Piana degli Albanesi
Bolognetta
Marineo
Villafrati
Ciminna
Cerda
Camporeale
Case Romana
Marsala
Matarocco
Salemi
Gibellina Nuova
Santa Ninfa
Partanna
Val di Mazara
Roccamena
Corleone
Mezzojuso
Rca. Busambra 1613
Vicari
Roccapalumba
Caltavuturo
Montemaggiore Belsito
Ália
Salaparuta
Campofiorito
Bisacquino
Prizzi
Lercara Friddi
Valledolmo
Strasatti
Mazara del Vallo
Castelvetrano
Campobello di Mazara
Granitola-Torretta
C. Granitola
Città Greca di Selinunte
Marinella
Menfi
Santa Margherita di Belice
Sambuca di Sicília
Pila. Misilbesi 295
L. Aráncio
Chiusa Sclafani
San Carlo
Palazzo Adriano
Bivona
Santo Stéfano Quisquina
M. Cammarata 1578
Cammarata
Vallelunga Pratameno
Villalba
Mussomeli
Marianópoli
Castello di Chiaromonte
Búrgio
Caltabellotta
Alessándria della Rocca
Cianciana
Ribera
Casteltérmini
Campofranco
San Biágio Plátani
C. S. Marco
Sciacca
Cattólica Eraclea
Montallegro
Raffadali
Aragona
Montedoro
Racalmuto
Serradifalco
Heraclea Minoa
Siciliana
Agrigento
Porto Empédocle
Canicattì
Castrofilippo
Favara
Naro
Camastra
Palma di Montechiaro
Canale di Sicilia
Strait of Sicily
Linosa
Lampedusa
Trápani
Pantelleria
Pantelleria (Italia) (Italy)
836
36°
Porto Empédocle
Linosa
Ísole Pelágie (Italia) (Italy)
Lampione
Lampedusa
37°
38°

3
4
5
15°
16°
106
Nápoli
Strómboli
Basiluzzo
Panarea
Salerno
Filicudi
Alicudi
Malfa
Salina
Ísole Eólie
Canneto
Lípari
Vulcano
Golfo di Milazzo
Capo di Milazzo
Milazzo
Villafranca Tirrena
Spadafora
Spartà
Torre Faro
Mortelle
Messina
Rometta
Santa Lucia del Mela
Golfo di Patti
Capo Calavá
Gioiosa Marea
Brolo
C. d'Orlando
Naso
Patti
Barcellona-Pozzo di Gotto
Falcone
CITTÀ DI TYNDARIS
San Piero Patti
Mazzarrà S. Andrea
Castroreale
M. Poverello 1279
Monti Peloritani
Sant'Ágata Militello
Alcara il Fusi
Longi
Ucria
Tortorici
San Fratello
Cefalù
Santo Stéfano di Camastra
Caronia
Tusa
Castelbuono
Monti Nébrodi
Nébrodi
M. Soro 1847
Floresta
Plla. d'Zoppo 1264
Montalbano Elicona
Novara di Sicília
Mandanici
Antillo
Ali Terme
Roccalumera
Scaletta Zanclea
Santa Teresa di Riva
Plla. Mandrazzi 1125
Francavilla di Sicília
Castiglione di Sicília
Linguaglossa
Taormina
Giardini Naxos
Mistretta
Plla Femmina Morta 1524
Santa Doménica Vittória
Randazzo
Passopisciaro
Etna
Piedimonte Etneo
Fiumefreddo di Sicília
Máscali
Riposto
Giarre
Maletto
Bronte
Etna 3323
ETNA
CASTELLO DI ADRANO
Cesarò
Capizzi
Colle del Contrasto 1107
L. di Ancipa
Troina
Cerami
Gangi
Sperlinga
Geraci Siculo
Petralia Sottana
Pzo. Carbonara 1979
Pella. Madonnuzza 1147
Nicosia
Gagliano Castelferrato
L. di Pozzillo
Alimena
Adrano
Biancavilla
Zafferana Etnea
Nicolosi
Trecastagni
Acireale
Aci Catena
Aci Castello
Regalbuto
Centúripe
Agira
Ássoro
Leonforte
Calascibetta
Villarosa
Plla di Recattivo 832
Enna
Pergusa
Caltanissetta
Santa Maria di Licodia
Belpasso
Paternò
Catenanuova
Misterbianco
Catánia
Golfo di Catánia
Valguarnera Caropepe
Plla Grottacalda 647
Raddusa
Castel di Iúdica
Gerbini
Pietraperzia
Aidone
Piazza Armerina
Barrafranca
VILLA ROMANA DEL CASALE
Mazzarino
Sommatino
Riesi
Ramacca
Palagonía
Lago di Lentini
Mirabella Imbáccari
San Michele di Ganzaria
Scordia
Lentini
Militello in Val di Catánia
Capo S. Croce
Augusta
Golfo di Augusta
Villasmundo
Caltagirone
Grammichele
Mineo
Francofonte
Melilli
Priolo Gargallo
Butera
Niscemi
Vizzini
Licodia Eubea
Buccheri
Sortino
Monti Iblei
M. Lauro 986
Monterosso Almo
Ferla
Solarino
Florídia
Siracusa
San Pietro
Giarratana
Palazzolo Acréide
Canicattini Bagni
C. Murro di Porco
Cassibile
Falconara
Gela
Golfo di Gela
Acate
Chiaramonte Gulfi
Vittória
Cómiso
Ragusa
Noto
Avola
Golfo di Noto
Scoglitti
Santa Croce Camerina
Módica
Rosolini
ELORO ANTICA
C. Scarámia
Marina di Ragusa
Donnalucata
Scicli
Íspica
Marzamemi
Sampieri
Pozzallo
Pachino
C. Passero
Portopalo di C. Passero
Valletta
Briático
Pizzo
Vibo Valéntia
Tropea
C. Vaticano
M. Poro 710
Mileto
Soriano Cálabro
Simbário
Ióppolo
Nicótera
Marchesale
Cropane Micone
Dinami
Golfo di Gióia
Rosarno
Laureana di Borrello
Fabrizia
Pso. Croce Ferrata
Gióia Táuro
Cinquefrondi
Polístena
Capo Barbi
Palmi
Taurianova
Seminara
Cittanova
Mámmola
Grotteria
Bagnara Cálabra
Óppido Mamertina
Scilla
Santa Eufémia d'Aspromonte
Gerace
Villa San Giovanni
Delianuova
Platì
LOCRI ANTICA
Locri
Laganadi
Aspromonte
Montalto (M. Cocuzza) 1955
Ardore
Gambárie
San Luca
Sella Entrata 1408
Réggio di Calábria
Str. di Messina
Cardeto
Bianco
Pta. di Péllaro
Montebello Iónico
Bagaladi
Staiti
Lazzaro
Bova
Bova Marina
Brancaleone Marina
Mélito di Porto Salvo
C. Spartivento
A
B
C
14
37°
38°

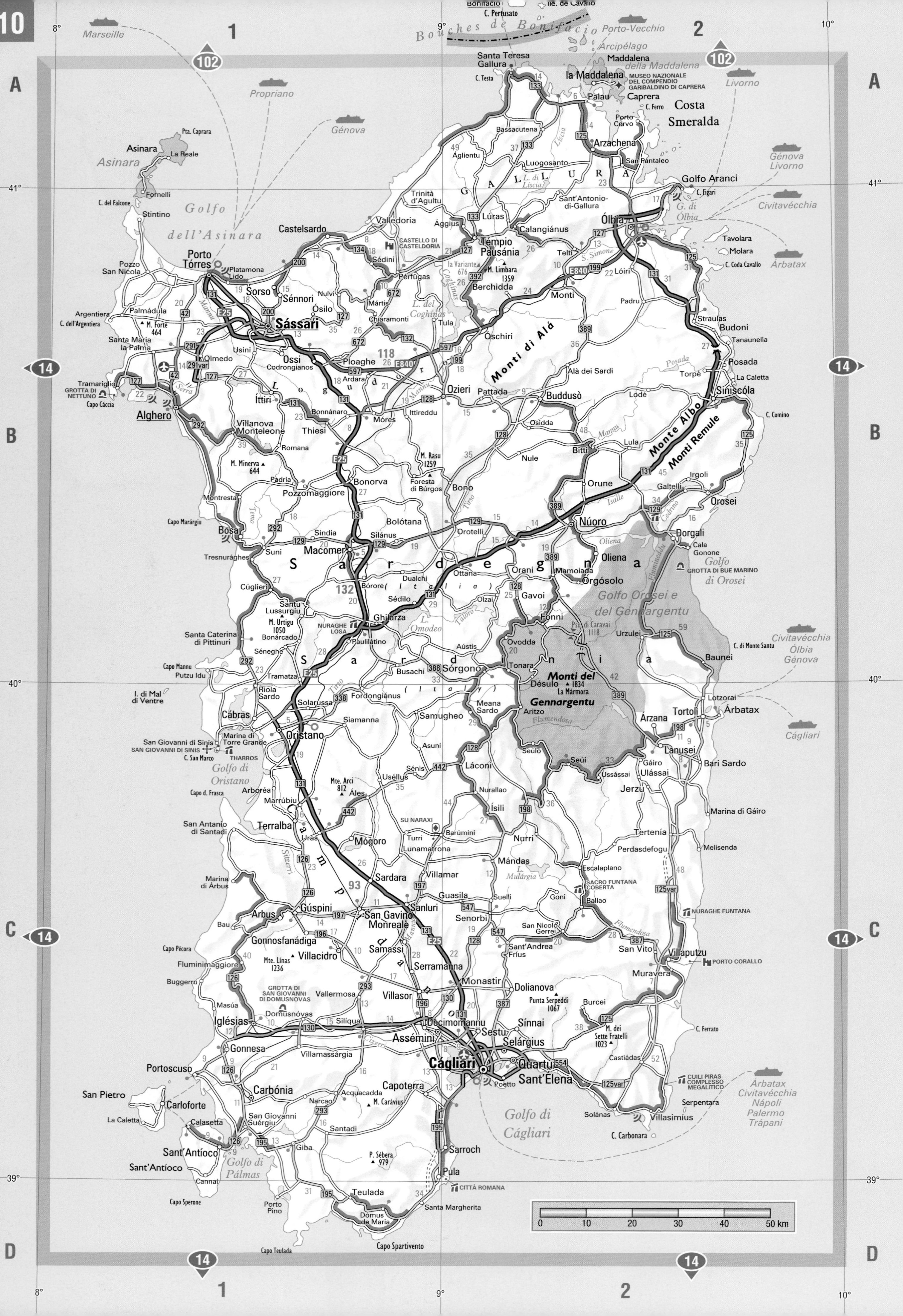

Bonifacio
C. Pertusato
Bouches de Bonifacio
Porto-Vecchio
Arcipélago
Maddalena
della Maddalena
Marseille
Propriano
Génova
Livorno
Génova
Livorno
Civitavécchia
Árbatax
Civitavécchia
Ólbia
Génova
Cágliari
Árbatax
Civitavécchia
Nápoli
Palermo
Trápani
102
14
Santa Teresa Gallura
C. Testa
la Maddalena
MUSEO NAZIONALE DEL COMPENDIO GARIBALDINO DI CAPRERA
Palau
Caprera
C. Ferro
Costa Smeralda
Porto Cervo
Arzachena
San Pantaleo
Bassacutena
Aglientu
Luogosanto
L. di Liscia
G A L L U R A
Golfo Aranci
C. Figari
G. di Ólbia
Ólbia
Sant'Antonio-di-Gallura
Trinità d'Agultu
Valledoria
Ággius
Lúras
Calangiánus
Tempio Pausánia
M. Limbara 1359
Berchidda
Telti
S. Simone
Lóiri
Tavolara
Molara
C. Coda Cavallo
Castelsardo
CASTELLO DI CASTELDORIA
Sédini
Pérfugas
L. del Coghinas
Monti
Padru
Asinara
Pta. Caprara
La Reale
Fornelli
C. del Falcone
Stintino
Golfo dell'Asinara
Porto Tórres
Platamona Lido
Pozzo San Nicola
Sorso
Sénnori
Nulvi
Mártis
Ósilo
Chiaramonti
Tula
Oschiri
Monti di Alá
Straulas
Budoni
Tanaunella
Posada
La Caletta
Torpè
Siniscóla
Argentiera
C. dell'Argentiera
Palmádula
M. Forte 464
Sássari
Santa Maria la Palma
Olmedo
Usini
Ossi
Codrongianos
Ploaghe
Ardara
L o g u d o r o
Ozieri
Pattada
Alà dei Sardi
Lodè
Buddusò
Tramariglio
GROTTA DI NETTUNO
Capo Cáccia
Alghero
Íttiri
Bonnánaro
Móres
Ittireddu
Osidda
Monte Albo
Monti Remule
C. Comino
Villanova Monteleone
Thiesi
Romana
M. Rasu 1259
Bitti
Lula
M. Minerva 644
Padria
Pozzomaggiore
Bonorva
Foresta di Búrgos
Bono
Nule
Orune
Irgoli
Galtellì
Orosei
Montresta
Capo Marárgiu
Bosa
Sindia
Bolótana
Orotelli
Núoro
Dorgali
Cala Gonone
GROTTA DI BUE MARINO
Golfo di Orosei
Tresnurághes
Suni
Macomer
Silánus
Oliena
Orgósolo
Mamoiada
Orani
S a r d e g n a
Cúglieri
Dualchi
Bórore
Ottana
Sédilo
Gavoi
Olzai
Golfo Orosei e del Gennargentu
Santu Lussurgiu
M. Urtigu 1050
Bonárcado
NURAGHE LOSA
Ghilarza
L. Omodeo
Fonni
Pso. di Caravai 1118
Urzulei
Santa Caterina di Pittinuri
Paulilátino
Seneghe
Ovodda
Tonara
Áustis
Baunei
C. di Monte Santu
Capo Mannu
Putzu Idu
Tramatza
Busachi
Sórgono
Monti del Gennargentu
Désulo
1834 La Mármora
I. di Mal di Ventre
Riola Sardo
Solarussa
Fordongiánus
Meana Sardo
Aritzo
Flumendosa
Lotzorai
Tortolì
Árbatax
Cábras
Siamanna
Samugheo
Árzana
San Giovanni di Sinis
SAN GIOVANNI DI SINIS
Marina di Torre Grande
Oristano
THARROS
C. San Marco
Golfo di Oristano
Asuni
Seulo
Lanusei
Bari Sardo
Sénis
Láconi
Seúi
Gáiro
Ussássai
Ulássai
Capo d. Frasca
Arboréa
Mte. Arci 812
Usellus
Áles
Nurallao
Jerzu
Marrúbiu
Ísili
Marina di Gáiro
San Antonio di Santadi
Terralba
SU NARAXI
Barúmini
Turri
Lunamatrona
Nurri
Tertenía
Uras
Mógoro
Perdasdefogu
Melisenda
Campidano
Mándas
L. Mulárgia
Escalaplano
Sardara
Villamar
SACRO FUNTANA COBERTA
Ballao
Goni
Marina di Árbus
Guasila
Suelli
NURAGHE FUNTANA
Arbus
Gúspini
San Gavino Monreale
Sanluri
Senorbì
San Nicolò Gerrei
Flumendosa
Bau
Gonnosfanádiga
Samassi
Sant'Andrea Frius
San Vito
Villaputzu
PORTO CORALLO
Capo Pécora
Fluminimaggiore
Mte. Línas 1236
Villacidro
Serramanna
Muravera
Buggerru
GROTTA DI SAN GIOVANNI DI DOMUSNOVAS
Vallermosa
Villasor
Monastir
Dolianova
Punta Serpeddì 1067
Burcei
Masúa
Domusnóvas
Iglésias
Siliqua
Decimomannu
Sestu
Sínnai
M. dei Sette Fratelli 1023
C. Ferrato
Gonnesa
Assémini
Selárgius
Villamassárgia
Cágliari
Quartu
Sant'Elena
Castiádas
Portoscuso
Poetto
CUILI PIRAS COMPLESSO MEGALITICO
Capoterra
Carbónia
Acquacadda
M. Carávius
Narcao
Golfo di Cágliari
Serpentara
San Pietro
Carloforte
San Giovanni Suérgiu
Solánas
Villasimius
La Caletta
Calasetta
Santadi
C. Carbonara
Sant'Antíoco
Giba
Sarroch
P. Sébera 979
Sant'Antíoco
Golfo di Pálmas
Cannai
Pula
CITTÀ ROMANA
Capo Sperone
Porto Pino
Teulada
Santa Margherita
Domus de Maria
Capo Spartivento
Capo Teulada
0 10 20 30 40 50 km
A
B
C
D
1
2
8°
9°
10°
41°
40°
39°

ÍSLAND
ICELAND
Vatnajökull
Hofsjökull 1765
Langjökull
Eiríksjökull 1675
Mýrdals-
jökull
Eyjafjallajökull 1666
Drangajökull 925
Snæfellsjökull
Ódáðahraun
Tröllaskagi
Gláma
Skeiðarársandur
Hvannadalshnúkur 2119
Herðubreið 1682
Snæfell 1833
Hekla 1491
Bláfjall 1222
Hrafnagil 1538
1460 Trölladyngja
LAKAGIGAR
Reykjavík
Kópavogur
Hafnarfjörður
Keflavík
Njarðvík
Hafnir
Reykjanes
Grindavík
Þorlákshöfn
Hveragerði
Selfoss
Eyrarbakki
Stokkseyri
Þykkvibær
Hella
Hvolsvöllur
Holt
Vík
Dyrhólaey
Landeyjahöfn
Vestmannaeyjar
Heimaey
Surtsey
Kirkjubæjarklaustur
Búland
Langholt
Skaftafell
Ingólfshöfði
Höfn
Nesjahverfi
Stokksnes
Gerði
Djúpivogur
Berufjörður
Breiðdalsvík
Stöðvarfjörður
Fáskrúðsfjörður
Reyðarfjörður
Eskifjörður
Neskaupstaður
Seyðisfjörður
Egilsstaðir
Hallormsstaður
Valþjófsstaður
Bakkagerði
Glettinganes
Tórshavn
Hirtshals
Húsey
Sleðbrjótur
Vopnafjörður
Bakkafjörður
Digranes
Þórshöfn
Hlíð
Fontur
Svalbarð
Raufarhöfn
Kópasker
Ásbyrgi
Húsavík
Laxamýri
Laugar
Reykjahlíð
Mývatn
Grímsstaðir
Möðrudalur
Mýri
Akureyri
Saurbær
Grenivík
Björg
Dalvík
Hauganes
Ólafsfjörður
Siglufjörður
Hofsós
Hólar
Sauðárkrókur
Varmahlíð
Goðdalir
Hrun
Hvammur
Skagaströnd
Blönduós
Tjörn
Hvammstangi
Laugarbakki
Borðeyri
Óspakseyri
Hólmavík
Drangsnes
Árnes
Munaðarnes
Ögur
Unaðsdalur
Ísafjörður
Bolungarvík
Súðavík
Flateyri
Suðureyri
Þingeyri
Hrafnseyri
Sjónfríð
Selárdalur
Bíldudalur
Tálknafjörður
Patreksfjörður
Brjánslækur
Ásgarður
Bjargtangar
Reykhólar
Saurbær
Skarð
Staðarfell
Búðardalur
Stykkishólmur
Grundarfjörður
Ólafsvík
Hellissandur
Öndverðarnes
Hellnar
Kolbeinsstaðir
Varmaland
Húsafell
Reykholt
Borgarnes
Hvanneyri
Saurbær
Akranes
Mosfellsbær
Þingvellir
Laugarvatn
Geysir
Reykholt
Flúðir
Laugarás
Grímsey
Horn
Straumnes
Breiðafjörður
Faxaflói
Borgarfjörður
Húnaflói
Skagafjörður
Eyjafjörður
Skjálfandi
Öxarfjörður
Þistilfjörður
Bakkaflói
Vopnafjörður
Héraðsflói
Ísafjarðardjúp
Arnarfjörður
Blöndulón
Hvítárvatn
Þórisvatn
Þingvallavatn
ARCTIC CIRCLE
A
B
C
D
1
2
3
4
5
6
7
8
9
10
11
12
66°30'
66°
64°
14°
16°
18°
20°
22°
24°
0
20
40
60
80
100 km

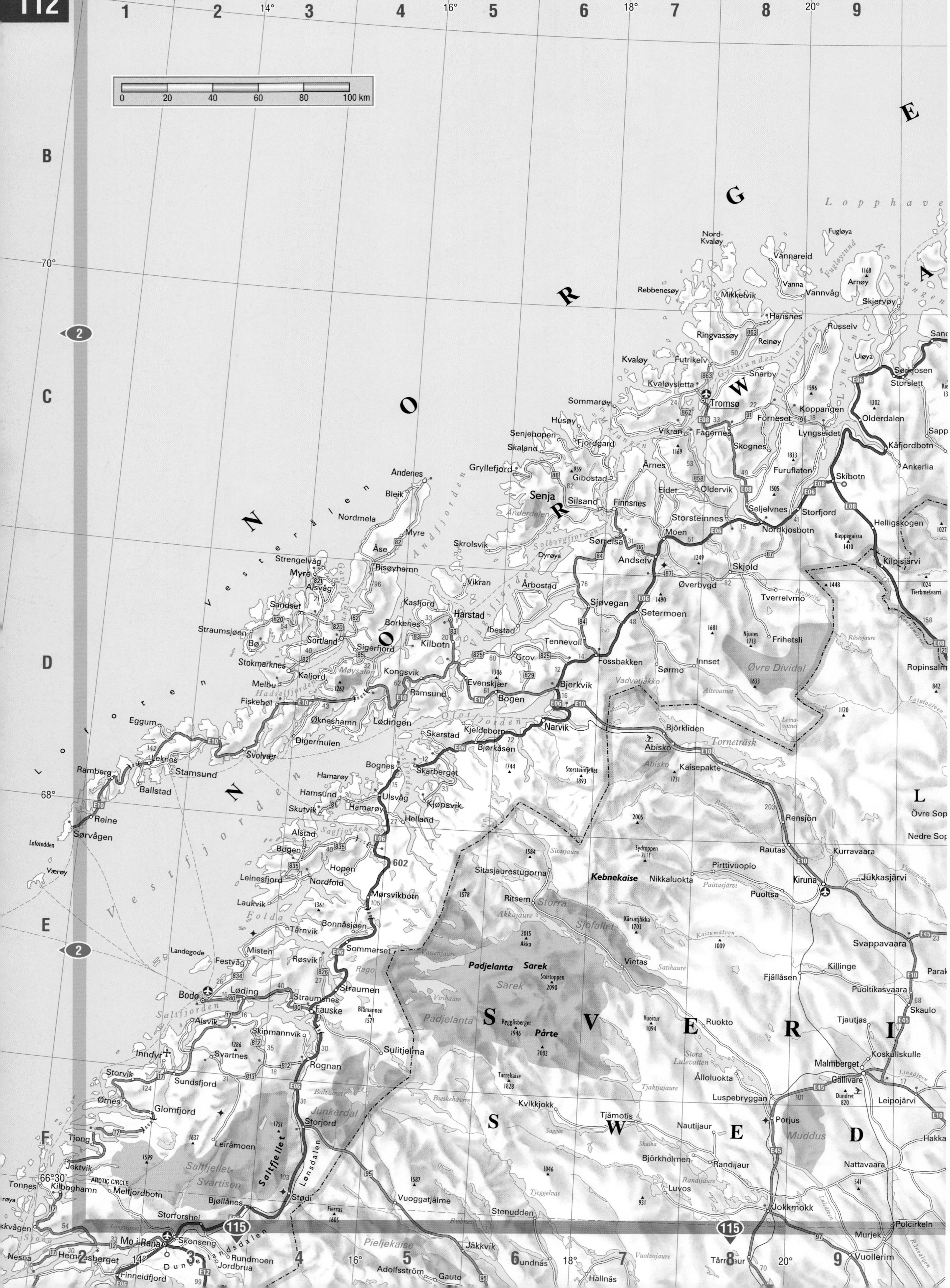

1
2
14°
3
4
16°
5
6
18°
7
8
20°
9
0
20
40
60
80
100 km
B
C
D
E
F
70°
68°
66°30'
2
ARCTIC CIRCLE
N O R G E
N O R W A Y
S V E R I G E
S W E D E N
L
Lopphavet
Kvænangen
Vesterålen
Lofoten
Vestfjorden
Andfjorden
Malangen
Ullsfjorden
Lyngen
Ofotfjorden
Tysfjorden
Sagfjorden
Folda
Saltfjorden
Hadselfjorden
Gavlfjorden
Solbergfjorden
Vågsfjorden
Grøtsundet
Fugløysund
Torneträsk
Rautasjaure
Kaitumälven
Sitasjaure
Vastenjaure
Virihaure
Akkajaure
Storra
Lulevatten
Sjöfallet
Stora Lulevatten
Satihaure
Tjaktjajaure
Saggat
Tjeggelvas
Riebnes
Randijaure
Vuolvojaure
Pieljekaise
Langvatnet
Balvatnet
Bieskehavrre
Nord-Kvaløy
Fugløya
Vannareid
Vanna
Vannvåg
Arnøy
1168
Skjervøy
Rebbenesøy
Mikkelvik
Hansnes
Ringvassøy
Reinøy
Russelv
Kvaløy
Futrikelv
Snarby
Uløya
Sørkjosen
Storslett
Kvaløysletta
Tromsø
Sommarøy
Husøy
Senjehopen
Skaland
Fjordgard
Vikran
Fagernes
Forneset
Koppangen
Lyngseidet
Olderdalen
Kåfjordbotn
Ankerlia
Skognes
Furuflaten
Skibotn
Gryllefjord
Gibostad
Årnes
Eidet
Oldervik
Senja
Silsand
Finnsnes
Seljelvnes
Storfjord
Helligskogen
Storsteinnes
Moen
Nordkjosbotn
Anderdalen
Andenes
Bleik
Nordmela
Myre
Åse
Skrolsvik
Sørreisa
Dyrøya
Andselv
Skjold
Kilpisjärvi
Strengelvåg
Myre
Alsvåg
Bisøyhamn
Vikran
Årbostad
Øverbygd
Tverrelvmo
Sandset
Kasfjord
Harstad
Sjøvegan
Setermoen
Straumsjøen
Borkenes
Ibestad
Bø
Sortland
Kilbotn
Tennevoll
Frihetsli
Øvre Dividal
Stokmarknes
Sigerfjord
Grov
Fossbakken
Innset
Sørmo
Ropinsalmi
Melbu
Kaljord
Møysalen
Kongsvik
Evenskjær
Bjerkvik
Fiskebøl
Ramsund
Bogen
Vadvetjåkko
Altevatnet
Eggum
Økneshamn
Lødingen
Narvik
Björkliden
Skarstad
Kjeldebotn
Digermulen
Bjørkåsen
Abisko
Svolvær
Leknes
Stamsund
Kaisepakte
Ramberg
Ballstad
Bognes
Skarberget
Storsteinfjellet
1893
Hamarøy
Hamsund
Ulsvåg
Kjøpsvik
Skutvik
Hamarøy
Helland
Rensjön
Reine
Sørvågen
Lofotodden
Værøy
Alstad
Bogen
Sydtoppen
2111
Rautas
Kurravaara
Hopen
Leinesfjord
Nordfold
Sitasjaurestugorna
Kebnekaise
Nikkaluokta
Pirttivuopio
Paittasjärvi
Kiruna
Jukkasjärvi
Laukvik
Mørsvikbotn
Ritsem
Puoltsa
Kårsatjåkka
1703
Tårnvik
Bonnåsjøen
Akka
2015
Svappavaara
Landegode
Misten
Sommarset
Padjelanta
Sarek
Stortoppen
2090
Vietas
Killinge
Festvåg
Røsvik
Rago
Fjällåsen
Parak
Bodø
Løding
Straumen
Puoltikasvaara
Straumsnes
Fauske
Blåmannen
1571
Skaulo
Alsvik
Ryggåsberget
1946
Pårte
2002
Vuoitur
1094
Ruokto
Tjautjas
Skipmannvik
Koskullskulle
Inndyr
Svartnes
Sulitjelma
Malmberget
Rognan
Gällivare
Storvik
Sundsfjord
Tarrekaise
1828
Ålloluokta
Leipojärvi
Ørnes
Luspebryggan
Dundret
820
Glomfjord
Kvikkjokk
Tjåmotis
Porjus
Muddus
Storjord
Junkerdal
Saltfjellet
Tjong
Nautijaur
Leiråmoen
Hakka
Jektvik
Saltfjellet-Svartisen
Lønsdalen
Björkholmen
Randijaur
Nattavaara
Tonnes
Kilboghamn
Melfjordbotn
Luvos
Bjøllånes
Stødi
Vuoggatjålme
Fierras
1605
Storforshei
Stenudden
Jokkmokk
Polcirkeln
Mo i Rana
Skonseng
Dunderlandsdalen
Jäkkvik
Murjek
Nesna
Hemnesberget
Rundmoen
Jordbrua
Gundnäs
Tårrajaur
Vuollerim
Finneidfjord
Adolfsström
Gauto
Hällnäs
Luleälven
Råneälven
Linaälven
Vittangiälven
Lainioälven
Rostaelva
Råstojaure
Öyre Soppero
Nedre Soppero
Sandvåg
Tierbmešvarri
Sappen
Leina-vatnet
E6
E8
E10
E12
E45
E06
E08
115
602

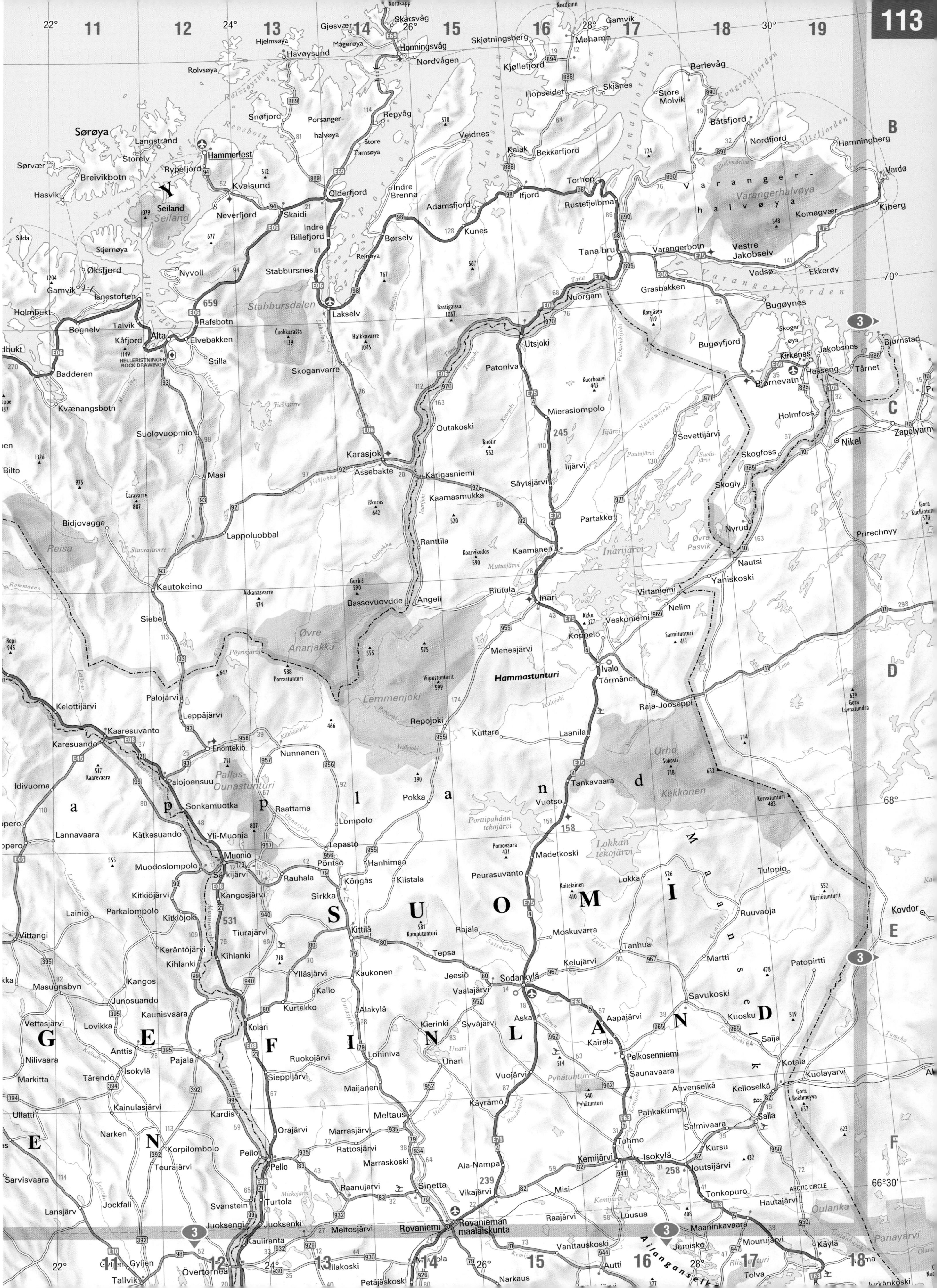

11
12
13
14
15
16
17
18
19
22°
24°
26°
28°
30°
B
C
D
E
F
70°
68°
66°30'
Nordkapp
Skarsvåg
Gjesvær
Hjelmsøya
Magerøya
Honningsvåg
Havøysund
Nordvågen
Rolvsøya
Nordkinn
Gamvik
Mehamn
Skjøtningsberg
Kjøllefjord
Hopseidet
Skjånes
Berlevåg
Store Molvik
Båtsfjord
Nordfjord
Hamningberg
Vardø
Sørøya
Langstrand
Hammerfest
Storelv
Sørvær
Breivikbotn
Hasvik
Rypefjord
Kvalsund
Seiland
Neverfjord
Skaidi
Snøfjord
Porsanger-halvøya
Repvåg
Store Tamsøya
Veidnes
Kalak
Bekkarfjord
Torhop
Ifjord
Rustefjelbma
Varanger-halvøya
Komagvær
Kiberg
Olderfjord
Indre Brenna
Adamsfjord
Kunes
Indre Billefjord
Børselv
Reinøya
Tana bru
Varangerbotn
Vestre Jakobselv
Vadsø
Ekkerøy
Silda
Stjernøya
Øksfjord
Nyvoll
Stabbursnes
Gamvik
Isnestoften
Holmbukt
Stabbursdalen
Lakselv
Rastigaissa 1067
Nuorgam
Grasbakken
Bugøynes
Bognelv
Talvik
Kåfjord
Alta
Rafsbotn
Elvebakken
Stilla
HELLERISTNINGER ROCK DRAWINGS
Čuokkarašša 1139
Halkkavarre 1045
Utsjoki
Korgåsen 419
Bugøyfjord
Skogerøya
Bjørnstad
Kirkenes
Jakobsnes
Hesseng
Tårnet
Bjørnevatn
Badderen
Skoganvarre
Patoniva
Kuorboaivi 443
Kværangsbotn
Mieraslompolo
Holmfoss
Zapolyarny
Outakoski
Sevettijärvi
Nikel
Suoloyuopmio
Karasjok
Ruotir 552
Skogfoss
Bilto
Masi
Assebakte
Karigasniemi
Iijärvi
Säytsjärvi
Skogly
Čaravarre 887
Kaamasmukka
Iškuras 642
Partakko
Nyrud
Bidjovagge
Lappoluobbal
Ranttila
Koarvikodds 590
Kaamanen
Inarijärvi
Øvre Pasvik
Prirechnyy
Reisa
Nautsi
Yaniskoski
Kautokeino
Gurbiš 590
Akkanasvarre 474
Bassevuovdde
Angeli
Riutula
Inari
Virtaniemi
Nelim
Siebe
Akku 327
Veskoniemi
Koppelo
Sarmitunturi 411
Ropi 945
Øvre Anarjakka
Menesjärvi
Ivalo
Törmänen
Hammastunturi
Porrastunturi 588
Viipustunturit 599
Palojärvi
Lemmenjoki
Raja-Jooseppi
Kelottijärvi
Leppäjärvi
Repojoki
Kaaresuvanto
Karesuando
Enontekiö
Kuttara
Laanila
Nunnanen
Urho Kekkonen
Sokosti 718
Idivuoma
Palojoensuu
Pallas-Ounastunturi
Tankavaara
Korvatunturi 483
Sonkamuotka
Raattama
Pokka
Vuotso
Lompolo
Porttipahdan tekojärvi
Lannavaara
Kätkesuando
Yli-Muonio
Tepasto
Pomovaara 421
Madetkoski
Lokkan tekojärvi
Muonio
Muodoslompolo
Särkijärvi
Pöntsö
Hanhimaa
Rauhala
Köngäs
Kiistala
Peurasuvanto
Lokka
Tulppio
Kitkiöjärvi
Kangosjärvi
Sirkka
Koitelainen 410
Värriötunturit 552
Lainio
Parkalompolo
Kitkiöjoki
Kittilä
Kumputunturi 581
Kovdor
Ruuvaoja
Vittangi
Tiurajärvi
Rajala
Moskuvarra
Tanhua
Kerantöjärvi
Kihlanki
Tepsa
Martti
Patopirtti
Yllasjärvi
Kaukonen
Jeesiö
Sodankylä
Kelujärvi
Masugnsbyn
Kangos
Kallo
Vaalajärvi
Junosuando
Kaunisvaara
Kurtakko
Alakylä
Savukoski
Vettasjärvi
Lovikka
Kolari
Kierinki
Syväjärvi
Aska
Aapajärvi
Kuosku
Saija
Anttis
Pajala
Lohiniva
Unari
Kairala
Pelkosenniemi
Nilivaara
Isokylä
Ruokojärvi
Kotala
Markitta
Tärendö
Sieppijärvi
Vuojärvi
Saunavaara
Kuolayarvi
Maijanen
Pyhätunturi 540
Ahvenselkä
Kelloselkä
Gora Rokhmoyva 657
Ullatti
Kainulasjärvi
Kardis
Käyrämö
Pahkakumpu
Salla
Meltaus
Salmivaara
Narken
Korpilombolo
Orajärvi
Marrasjärvi
Rattosjärvi
Tohmo
Kursu
Teurajärvi
Pello
Marraskoski
Ala-Nampa
Kemijärvi
Isokylä
Joutsijärvi
Sarvisvaara
Raanujärvi
Sinetta
Vikajärvi
Misi
ARCTIC CIRCLE
Tonkopuro
Hautajärvi
Oulanka
Lansjärv
Jockfall
Svanstein
Turtola
Juoksengi
Juoksenki
Rovaniemi
Rovaniemen maalaiskunta
Raajärvi
Luusua
Maaninkavaara
Meltosjärvi
Kauliranta
Vanttauskoski
Jumisko
Mourujärvi
Käylä
Panayarvi
Gyljen
Tallvik
Övertorneå
Ellakoski
Petäjäskoski
Narkaus
Autti
Tolva
SUOMI
FINLAND
Lappland

1
2
3
4
5
6
7
8
A
B
C
D
E
F
6°
8°
10°
12°
66°
64°
0
20
40
60
80
100 km
N O R S K E H A V E T
N O R W E G I A N
S E A
Trænfjorden
Dønna
Sandnes
Silvalen
Tjøtta
Gladstad
Vega
Anndalsvåge
Brønnøysund
Berg
Vik
Vennesund
Bindalsfjorden
Holm
Leka
Lyngsnes
Sjølstad
Fold
Valøy
Vikna
Rørvik
Kolvereid
Salsbruket
Abelvær
Lund
Foldfjorden
Jøa
Salen
Folda
Utvorda
Høylandet
Lauvsnes
Namsos
Overhalla
Tøttdal
Jøssund
Bangsund
Osen
Sjøåsen
Namdalseid
Hofstad
Kvam
Velde
Harsvik
Malm
Snåsavatnet
Steinkjer
Follafoss
Ratvika
Åfjord
Beitstadfjorden
Gaulstad
Fosna
Sparbu
Lysøysund
Straumen
Verrabotn
Mosvik
Røra
Verdalsøra
Nes
Botngård
Uthaug
Levanger
Vuku
Brekstad
Leksvik
Skogn
Frohavet
Frøya
Sistranda
Titran
Hitra
Fillan
Agdenes
Årnset
Frosta
Markabygd
Sandvika
Sandstad
Åsen
Veidholmen
Lensvik
Vanviken
Trondheimsfjorden
Skatval
Stjørdalshalsen
Dyrnes
Smøla
Forsnes
Trondheimsleia
Heim
Snillfjord
Trondheim
Malvik
Hegra
Gudå
Meråker
Edøy
Heimdal
Skarvan Og Roltdalen
Storlien
Gullstein
Aure
Kyrksæterøra
Orkanger
Melhus
Stordal
Tustna
Kristiansund
Aresvika
Vinje
Selbusjøen
Mebonden
Fongen
Bremsnes
Lundamo
Hennset
Halsa
Storås
Løkken
Averøya
Åsskard
Meldal
Rindal
Mo
Hustad
Hustadvika
Bud
Eide
Støren
Tydal
Essandsjøen
Elnesvågen
Tingvoll
Surnadalsøra
Soknedal
Haltdalen
Gossa
Batnfjordsøra
Kvenna
Singsås
Stugudal
Nordøyane
Molde
Hjelset
Eidsvåg
Todal
Trollheimen
Rennebu
Berkåk
Budal
Otterøya
Hessdalen
Reitan
Brattvåg
Vestnes
Romsdalsfjorden
Åfarnes
Sunndalsøra
Storli
Ulsberg
Forollhogna
Såtåhaugen
Søvik
Eresfjord
Brekken
Tomra
Isfjorden
Løvset
Kvikne
Røros
Søreyane
Ålesund
Sjøholt
Andalsnes
Oppdal
Os
Storvigelen
Spjelkavik
Tresfjord
Voll
Gjøra
Hareid
Sykkylven
Stordal
Eikesdal
Storfjorden
Dovrefjell-Sunndalsfjella
Drivstua
Settalsjøia
Tolga
Sørvika
Ulsteinvik
Festøy
Stranda
Verma
Romsdalen
Vartdal
Sylte
Larsnes
Narbuvollen
Stadhavet
Ørsta
Eidsdal
Lesjaskog
Dovrefjell
Leikanger
Pyttegga
Tynset
Tufsingdalen
Femundsmarka
Folkestad
Volda
Tafjord
Hjerkinn
Holøydal
Sildegapet
Selje
Storfjorden
Hellesylt
Lora
Reinheimen
Fokstua
Dovre
Folldal
Femunden
Raudeberg
Åheim
Djupvasshytta
Tylldal
Elgå
Måløy
Totland
Nyseter
Dombås
Alvdal
Gutulia
Stårheim
Hornindal
Grotli
Bremanger
Isane
Stryn
Videseter
Pollfoss
Barkald
Nordfjordeid
Kalvåg
Innvik
Ålfotbreen
Lodalskåpa
Sotaseter
Bismo
Vågåvatn
Vågåmo
Neset
Øvre Rendal
Drevsjø
Midtgulen
Svelgen
Sandane
Olden
Lom
Rondslottet
Byrkjelo
Jostedalsbreen
Hyen
Lalm
Otta
Rondane
Enden
Florø
Eikefjord
Nordstedalsseter
Bøverdal
Glittertind
Randsverk
Sjoa
Storfjellseter
Atna
Ytre Rendal
Østerhogna
Stavang
Skei
Jostedal
Kvam
Åsheim
Engerdal
Naustdal
Stongfjorden
Skjolden
Leirvassbu
Skåbu
Vinstra
Hundorp
Ringebu
Koppang
Bygstad
Førde
Moskog
Jotunheimen

Mo i Rana
Skonseng
Rundmoen
Jordbrua
Hemnesberget
Finneidfjord
Korgen
Bredviken
Vilasund
Mosjøen
Hemavan
Tärnaby
Hattfjelldal
Trofors
Laksfors
Børgefjell
Majavatn
Smalåsen
Namsskogan
Røyrvik
Brekkvasselv
Kongsmoen
Skorovatn
Grong
Snåsa
Gäddede
Nordli
Jormvattnet
Hotagsfjällen
Hotagen
Sösjöfjällen
Jämtland
Duved
Åre
Järpen
Krokom
Östersund
Brunflo
Anarisfjällen
Svenstavik
Funäsdalen
Hede
Vemdalen
Härjedalen
Sveg
Lillhärdal
Särna
Idre
Ammarnäs
Arjeplog
Sorsele
Storuman
Stensele
Vilhelmina
Dorotea
Åsele
Strömsund
Hammerdal
Västerbotten
Lycksele
Umeå
Vännäs
Bjurholm
Nordmaling
Örnsköldsvik
Ångermanland
Sollefteå
Kramfors
Härnösand
Medelpad
Timrå
Sundsvall
Ljusdal
Hudiksvall
Iggesund
Hälsingland
Malå
Arvidsjaur
Norsjö
Boliden
Gävleborg
SWEDEN

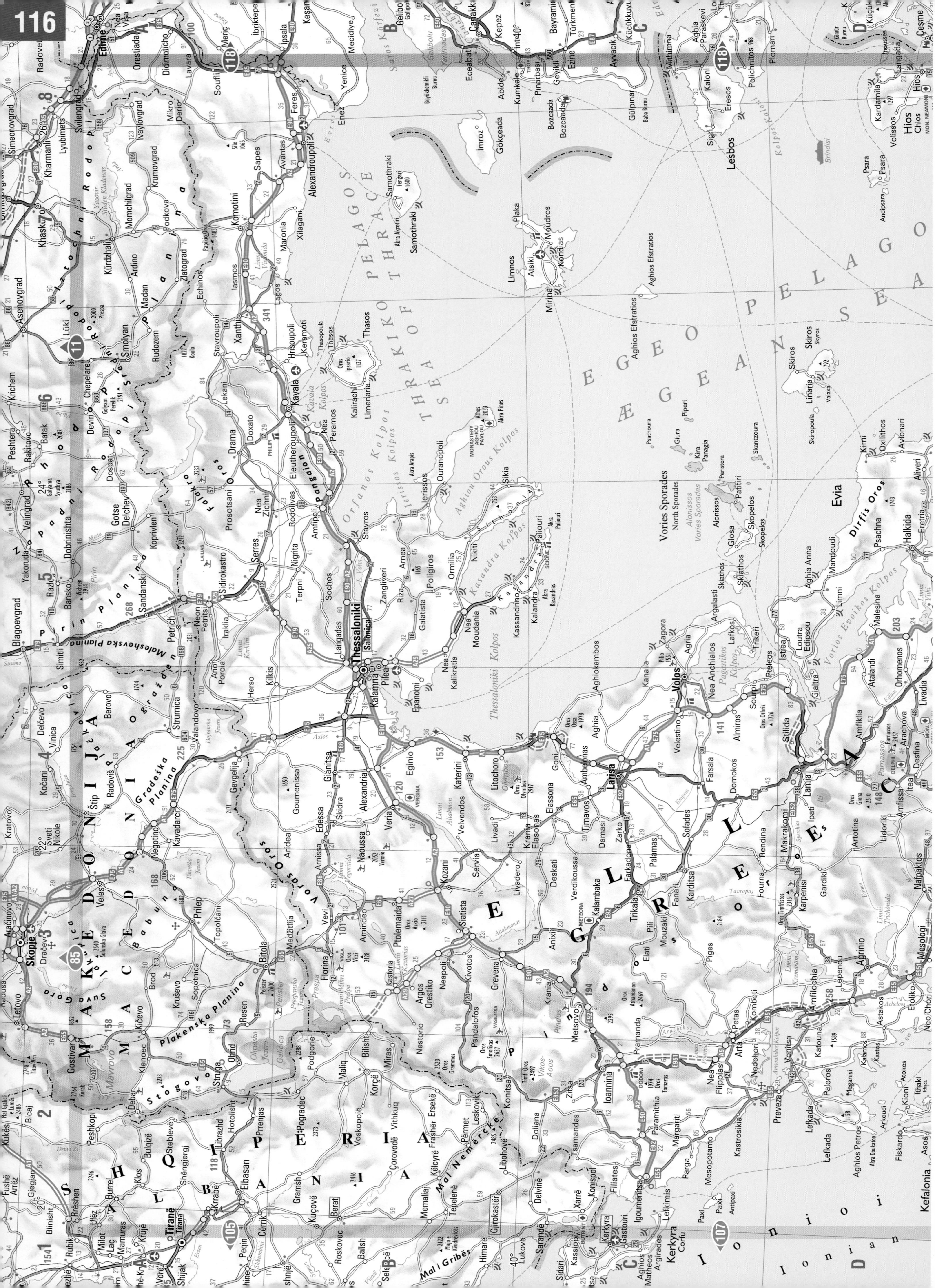
MAKEDONIJA
MACEDONIA
SHQIPERIA
ALBANIA
ELLADA
GREECE
EGEO PELAGOS
AEGEAN SEA
THRAKIKO PELAGOS
THRACE SEA
Ionio
Ionian
Thessaloniki
Skopje
Tiranë
Larisa
Volos
Ioannina
Kavala
Alexandroupoli
Edirne
Lesbos
Evia
Limnos
Samothraki
Thasos
Vories Sporades
North Sporades
Kerkyra
Corfu
Kefalonia
Lefkada
Skiros
Hios

IONIO PELAGOS
IONION SEA
MIRTOO PELAGOS
MIRTOO SEA
KRITIKO PELAGOS
SEA OF CRETE
Kiklades
Cyclades
Ionian Islands
Kriti
Crete
Korinthiakos Kolpos
Gulf of Corinth
Patraikos Kolpos
Saronikos Kolpos
Argolikos Kolpos
Messiniakos Kolpos
Lakonikos Kolpos
Kiparissiakos Kolpos
Kolpos Kissamos
Kolpos Chanion
Ormos Almyrou
Kolpos Mirabello
Kolpos Mesara
Notios Evoikos Kolpos
Parnonas Oros
Taygetos Oros
Psiloritis Oros
Ochi Oros
ATHINA
ATHENS
Pireas
Piraeus
Glifada
Elefsina
Acharnes
Kiffisia
Marathonas
Nea Makri
Rafina
Markopoulo
Keratea
Lavrio
Megara
Salamina
Thiva
Thebes
Korinthos
Corinth
Patra
Patras
Egio
Pirgos
Olympia
Tripoli
Argos
Nafplio
Mikines
Megalopoli
Kalamata
Sparti
Sparta
Githio
Monemvasia
Neapoli
Areopoli
Kythira
Zakynthos
Zante
Cephalonia
Argostoli
Ithaki
Andros
Tinos
Mykonos
Syros
Ermoupoli
Naxos
Paros
Milos
Thira
Santorini
Amorgos
Ios
Folegandros
Serifos
Kithnos
Kea
Sifnos
Kimolos
Anafi
Ikaria
Astipalea
Chania
Iraklio
Heraklion
Rethimno
Aghios Nikolaos
Sitia
Ierapetra
Gavdos
E 15
119
E
F
G
H
2
3
4
5
6
7
20°
22°
24°
26°
36°
38°
0
20
40
60
80
100 km

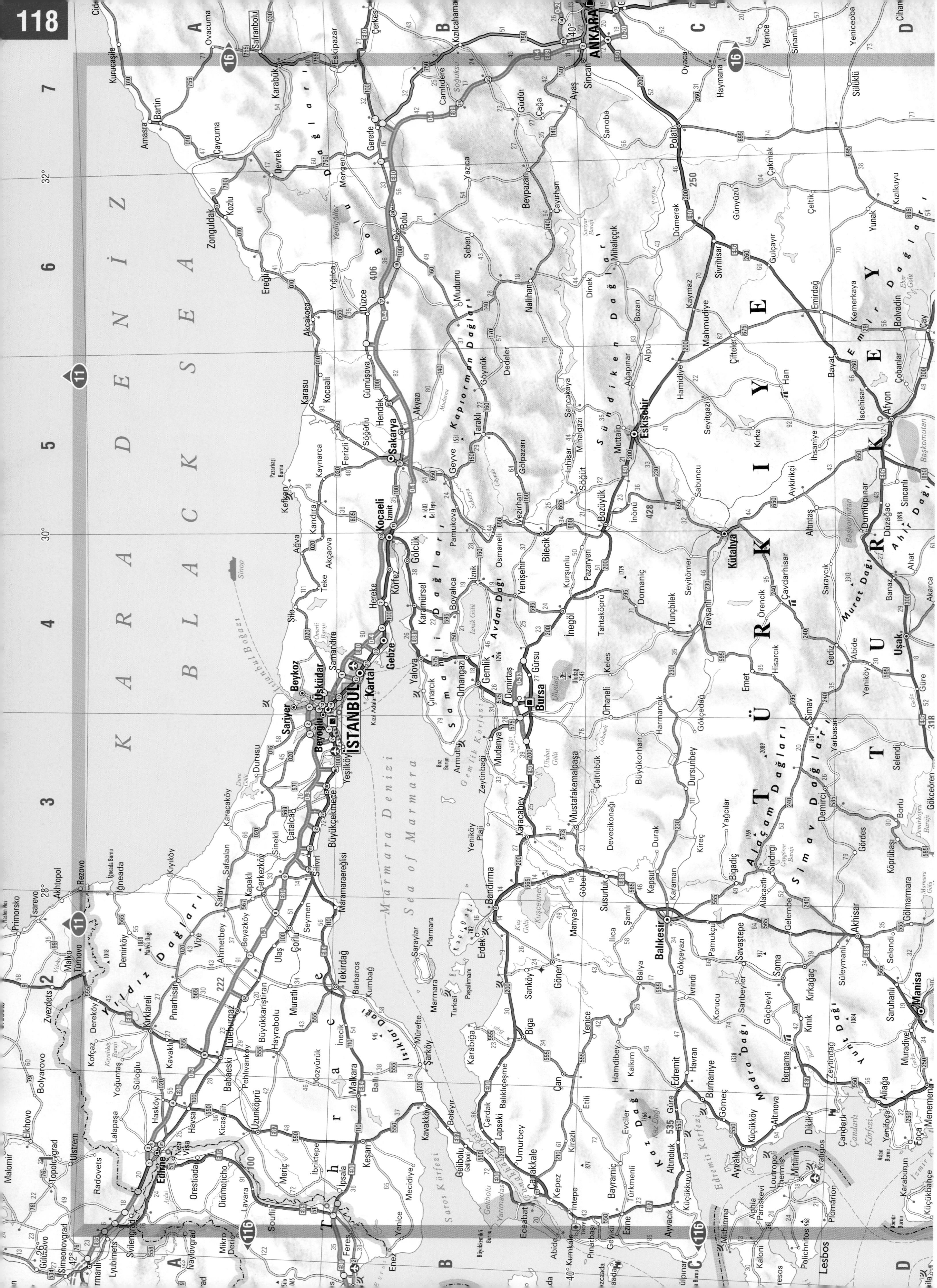
KARADENİZ
BLACK SEA
Marmara Denizi
Sea of Marmara
TÜRKİYE
TURKEY
Thrace
İSTANBUL
ANKARA
Bursa
Eskişehir
Kocaeli
Sakarya
Balıkesir
Manisa
Kütahya
Edirne
Çanakkale
Tekirdağ
Zonguldak
Bolu
Düzce
Afyon
Uşak
Bilecik
Kırklareli
Karabük
Bartın
Lesbos
Saros Körfezi
Edremit Körfezi
Gemlik Körfezi
Köroğlu Dağları
Bolu Dağları
Sündiken Dağları
Simav Dağları
Yıldız Dağları
Madra Dağı
Kaz Dağı
Uludağ
Murat Dağı
Emir Dağları
Samanlı Dağları
Kapıdağ
Işıklar Dağı
Alaçam Dağları
Avdan Dağı
Kapıorman Dağları
Yunt Dağı
Ahır Dağı

İZMIR
Aydın
Denizli
Isparta
Burdur
Antalya
Konya
Muğla
Marmaris
Bodrum
Fethiye
Alanya
Manavgat
Rhodes
Kos
Samos
Karpathos
Kasos
Ikaria
Patmos
Leros
Kalimnos
Tilos
Simi
Halki
Astipalea
Boz Dağları
Aydın Dağları
Gölgeli Dağları
Kavak Dağı
Akdağları
Bey Dağları
Katrancı Dağı
Söğüt Dağı
Barla Dağı
Kumalar Dağı
Çatma Dağı
Kuşadası Körfezi
Güllük Körfezi
Gökova Körfezi
Fethiye Körfezi
Antalya Körfezi
Finike Körfezi
Stenon Karpathos
Stenon Kasos
Dodecanese
Dodekanisa
AK DENİZ
MEDITERRANEAN SEA
0 20 40 60 80 100 km

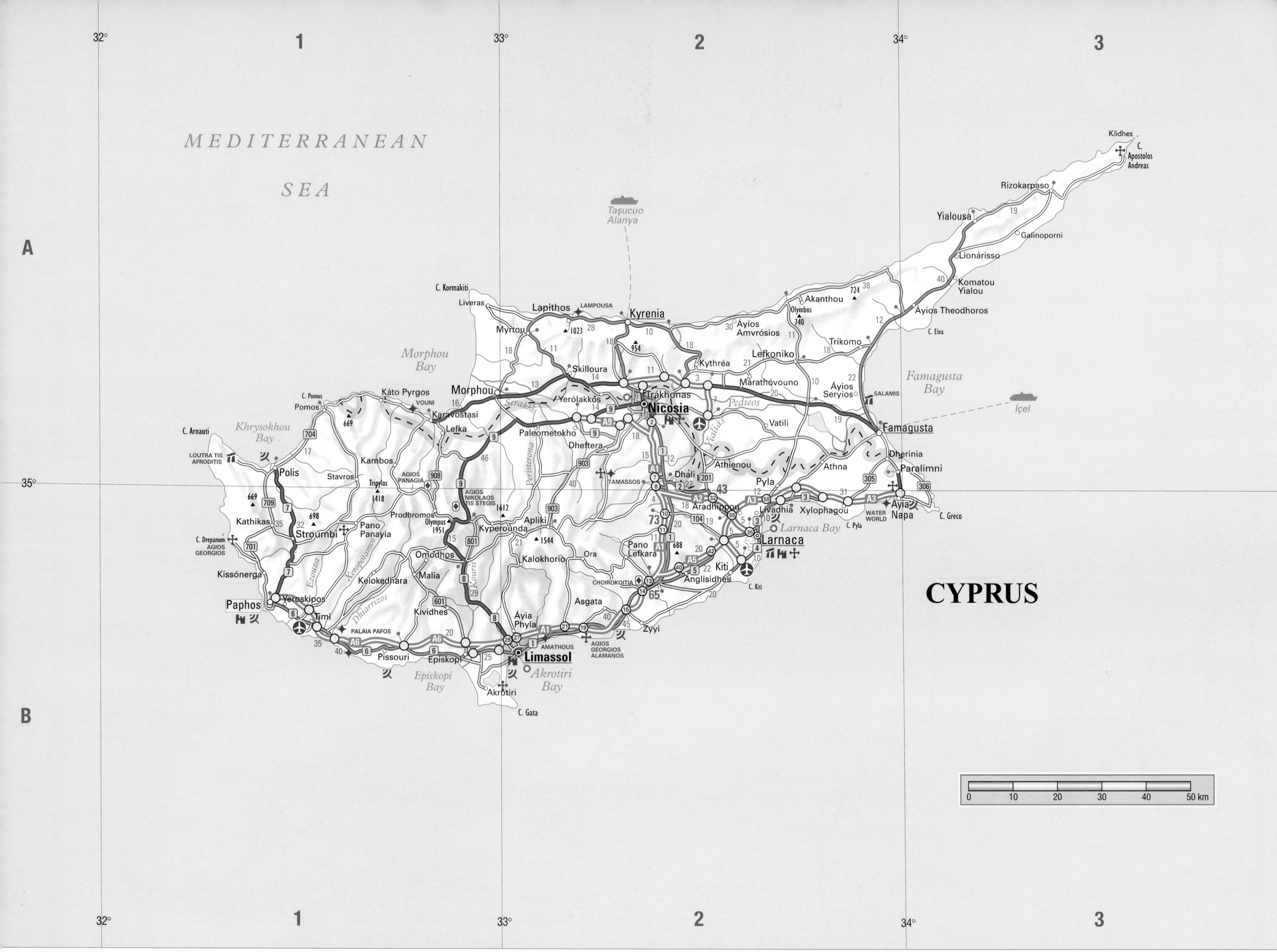
CYPRUS
MEDITERRANEAN SEA
Nicosia
Famagusta
Kyrenia
Larnaca
Limassol
Paphos
Morphou
Polis
Lapithos
Myrtou
Liveras
C. Kormakiti
Skilloura
Yerólakkos
Trákhonas
Kythréa
Lefkoniko
Marathóvouno
Áyios Amvrósios
Akanthou
Trikomo
Áyios Seryios
Vatili
Athienou
Athna
Dherinia
Paralimni
Ayia Napa
C. Greco
Xylophagou
Livadhia
Pyla
Aradhippou
Dhali
Kiti
Anglisidhes
Pano Lefkara
Ora
Kalokhorio
Asgata
Zyyi
Áyia Phyla
Akrotiri
C. Gata
Episkopi
Pissouri
Kividhes
Malia
Omodhos
Kelokedhara
Prodhromos
Kyperounda
Apliki
Pano Panayia
Stroumbi
Stavros
Kambos
Káto Pyrgos
Karavostasi
Lefka
Paleometokho
Dheftera
Pomos
C. Pomos
C. Arnauti
Kathikas
Kissónerga
Yeroskipos
Timi
C. Drepanum
Rizokarpaso
Yialousa
Galinoporni
Lionárisso
Komatou Yialou
Áyios Theodhoros
C. Elea
Klidhes
C. Apostolos Andreas
Morphou Bay
Khrysokhou Bay
Famagusta Bay
Larnaca Bay
Akrotiri Bay
Episkopi Bay
Taşucuo Alanya
İçel
C. Pyla
C. Kiti
LOUTRA TIS AFRODITIS
AGIOS GEORGIOS
PALAIA PAFOS
AGIOS GEORGIOS ALAMANOS
AMATHOUS
CHOIROKOITIA
TAMASSOS
AGIOS NIKOLAOS TIS STEGIS
AGIOS PANAGIA
VOUNI
SALAMIS
LAMPOUSA
WATER WORLD
Olympus 1951
Olymbos 740
Pedieos
Yialias
Serakhis
Peristerona
Kouris
Xeropotamos
Dhiarrizos
Ezousa
32°
33°
34°
35°
1
2
3
A
B
0
10
20
30
40
50 km

City plans • Plans de villes
Stadtpläne • Piante di città

Motorway	Autoroute
Major through route	Route principale majeur
Through route	Route principale
Secondary road	Route secondaire
Dual carriageway	Chaussées séparées
Other road	Autre route
Tunnel	Tunnel
Limited access / pedestrian road	Rue réglementée / rue piétonne
One-way street	Sens unique
Parking	Parc de stationnement
Motorway number (A7)	Numéro d'autoroute
National road number (447)	Numéro de route nationale
European road number (E45)	Numéro de route européenne
Destination (GENT)	Destination
Car ferry	Bac passant les autos
Railway	Chemin de fer
Rail/bus station	Gare/gare routière
Underground, metro station	Station de métro
Cable car	Téléférique
Abbey, cathedral	Abbaye, cathédrale
Church of interest	Église intéressante
Synagogue	Synagogue
Hospital	Hôpital
Police station (POL)	Police
Post office	Bureau de poste
Tourist information	Office de tourisme
Place of interest (Theatre)	Autre curiosité

Autobahn	Autostrada
Hauptstrecke	Strada di grande communicazione
Schnellstrasse	Strada d'importanza regionale
Nebenstrasse	Strada d'interesse locale
Zweispurig Schnellstrasse	Strada a carreggiate doppie
Nebenstrecke	Altra strada
Tunnel	Galleria stradale
Beschränkter Zugang/ Fussgängerzone	Strada pedonale / a accesso limitato
Einbahnstrasse	Senso unico
Parkplatz	Parcheggio
Autobahnnummer (A7)	Numero di autostrada
Nationalstrassen-nummer (447)	Numero di strada nazionale
Europäische Strassennummer (E45)	Numero di strada europea
Ziel (GENT)	Destinazione
Autofähre	Traghetto automobili
Eisenbahn	Ferrovia
Bahnhof / Busstation	Stazione ferrovia / pullman
U-Bahnstation	Metropolitano
Drahtseilbahn	Funivia
Abtei, Kloster, Kathedrale	Abbazia, duomo
Interessante Kirche	Chiesa da vedere
Synagoge	Sinagoga
Krankenhaus	Ospedale
Polizeiwache (POL)	Polizia
Postamt	Ufficio postale
Informationsbüro	Ufficio informazioni turistiche
Sonstige Sehenswürdigkeit (Theatre)	Luogo da vedere

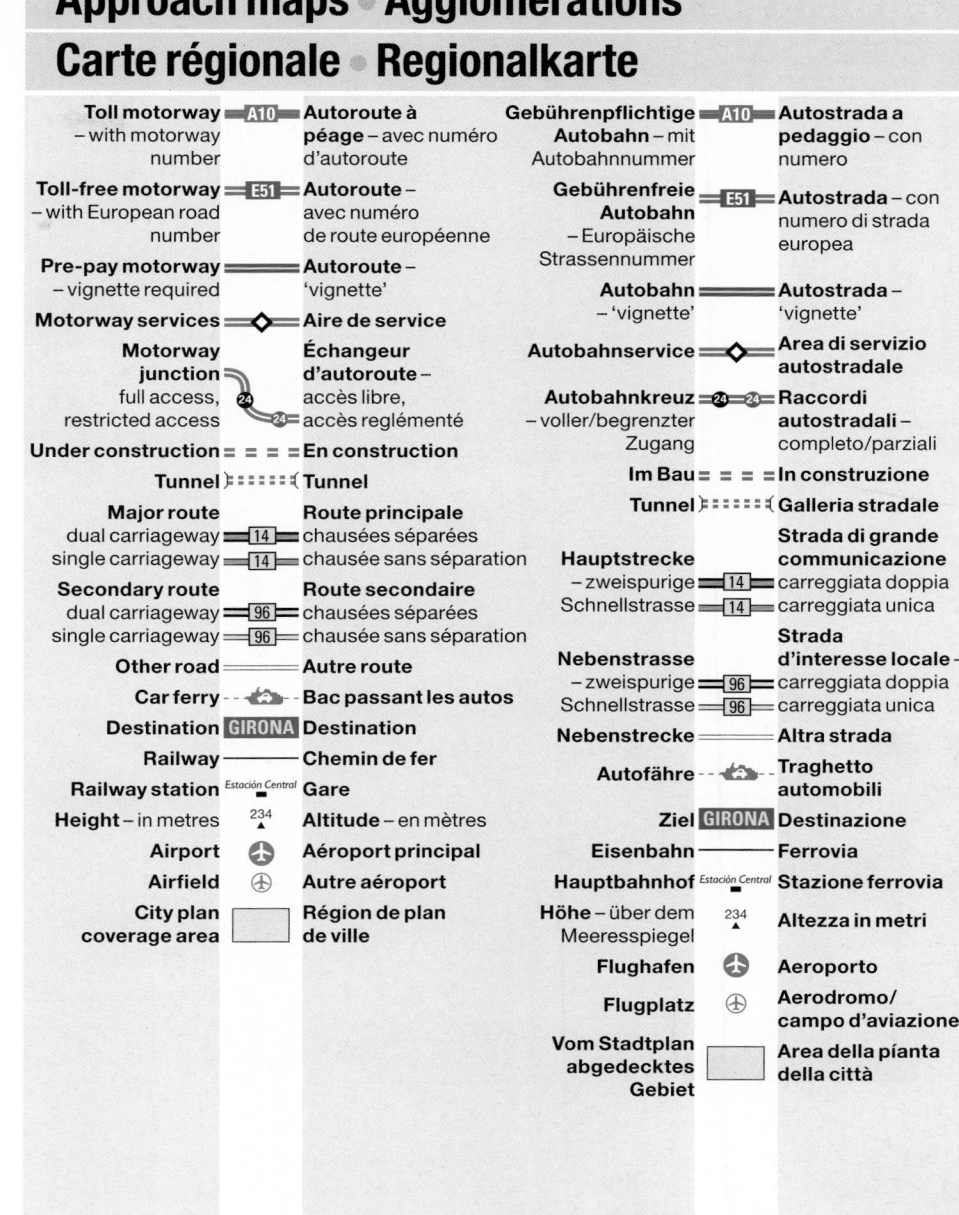

Approach maps • Agglomérations
Carte régionale • Regionalkarte

Toll motorway – with motorway number (A10)	Autoroute à péage – avec numéro d'autoroute
Toll-free motorway – with European road number (E51)	Autoroute – avec numéro de route européenne
Pre-pay motorway – vignette required	Autoroute – 'vignette'
Motorway services	Aire de service
Motorway junction full access, restricted access (24)	Échangeur d'autoroute – accès libre, accès reglémenté
Under construction	En construction
Tunnel	Tunnel
Major route dual carriageway / single carriageway (14)	Route principale chausées séparées / chaussée sans séparation
Secondary route dual carriageway / single carriageway (96)	Route secondaire chausées séparées / chaussée sans séparation
Other road	Autre route
Car ferry	Bac passant les autos
Destination (GIRONA)	Destination
Railway	Chemin de fer
Railway station (Estación Central)	Gare
Height – in metres (234)	Altitude – en mètres
Airport	Aéroport principal
Airfield	Autre aéroport
City plan coverage area	Région de plan de ville

Gebührenpflichtige Autobahn – mit Autobahnnummer (A10)	Autostrada a pedaggio – con numero
Gebührenfreie Autobahn – Europäische Strassennummer (E51)	Autostrada – con numero di strada europea
Autobahn – 'vignette'	Autostrada – 'vignette'
Autobahnservice	Area di servizio autostradale
Autobahnkreuz – voller/begrenzter Zugang (24)	Raccordi autostradali – completo/parziali
Im Bau	In construzione
Tunnel	Galleria stradale
Hauptstrecke – zweispurige / Schnellstrasse (14)	Strada di grande communicazione carreggiata doppia / carreggiata unica
Nebenstrasse – zweispurige / Schnellstrasse (96)	Strada d'interesse locale – carreggiata doppia / carreggiata unica
Nebenstrecke	Altra strada
Autofähre	Traghetto automobili
Ziel (GIRONA)	Destinazione
Eisenbahn	Ferrovia
Hauptbahnhof (Estación Central)	Stazione ferrovia
Höhe – über dem Meeresspiegel (234)	Altezza in metri
Flughafen	Aeroporto
Flugplatz	Aerodromo/ campo d'aviazione
Vom Stadtplan abgedecktes Gebiet	Area della pianta della città

Alicante

0 km 0,5

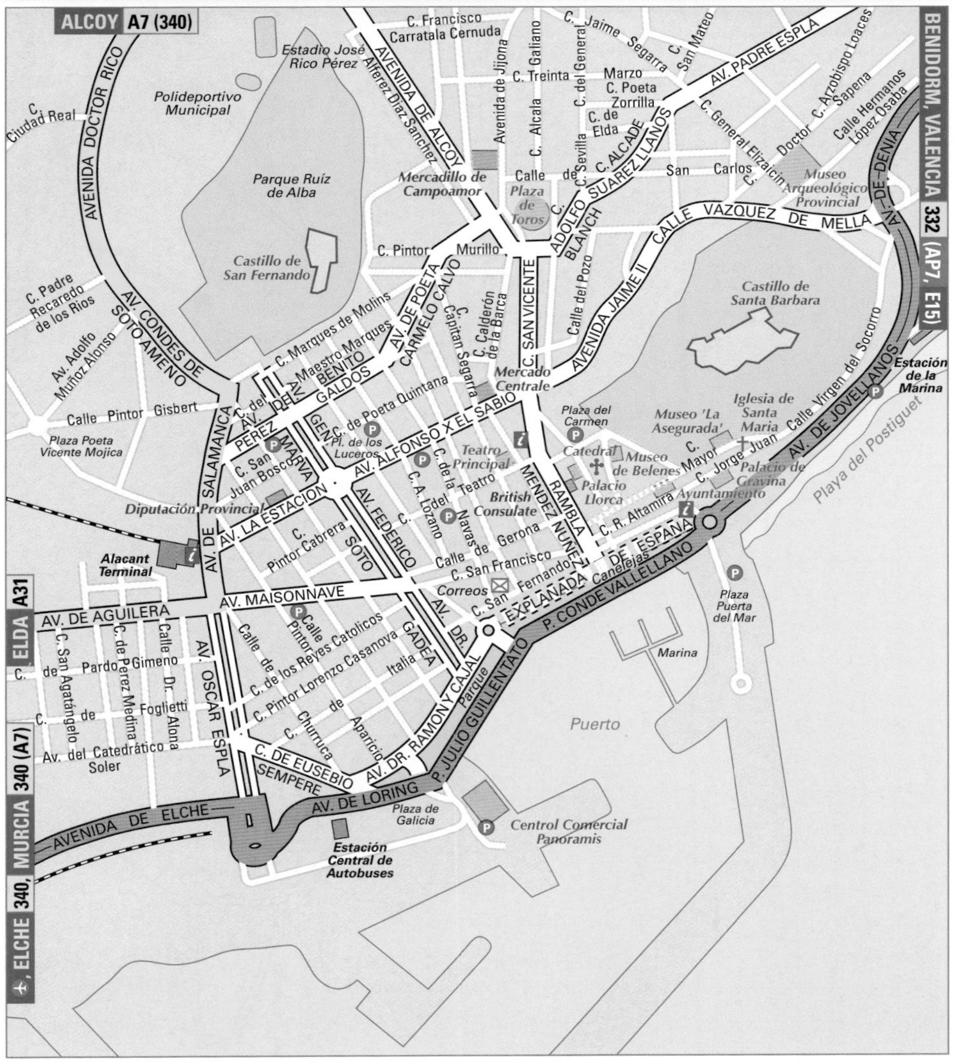

Antwerpen Antwerp

0 km 1

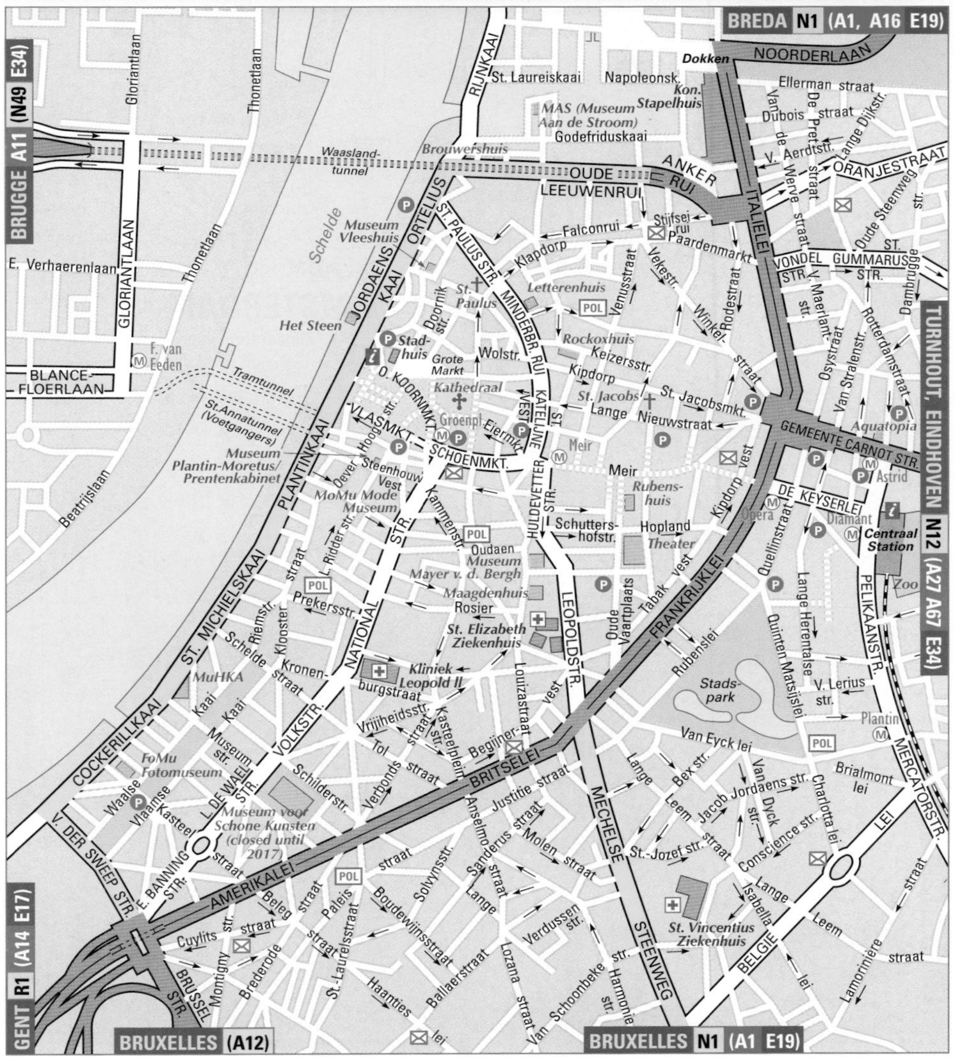

Amsterdam

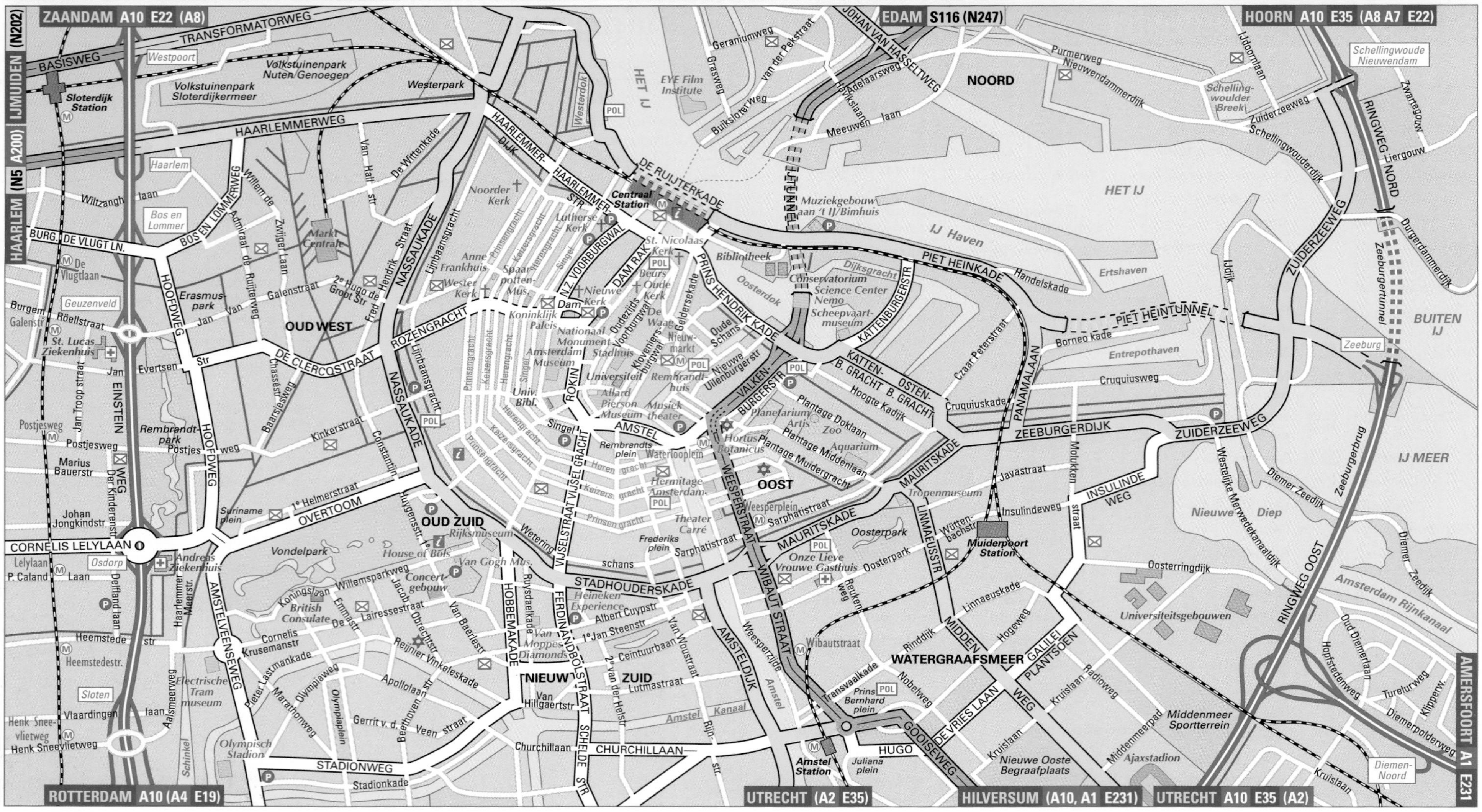

Amsterdam

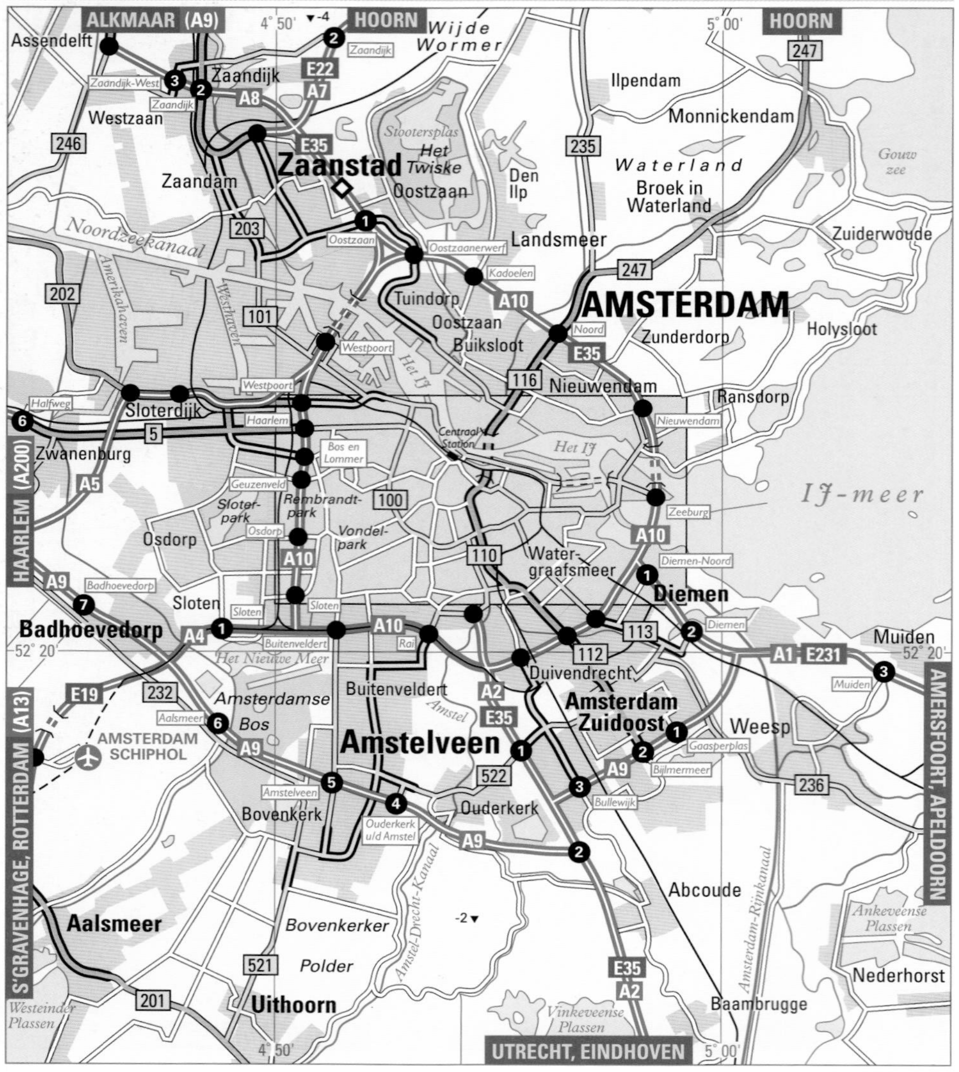

Athina Athens

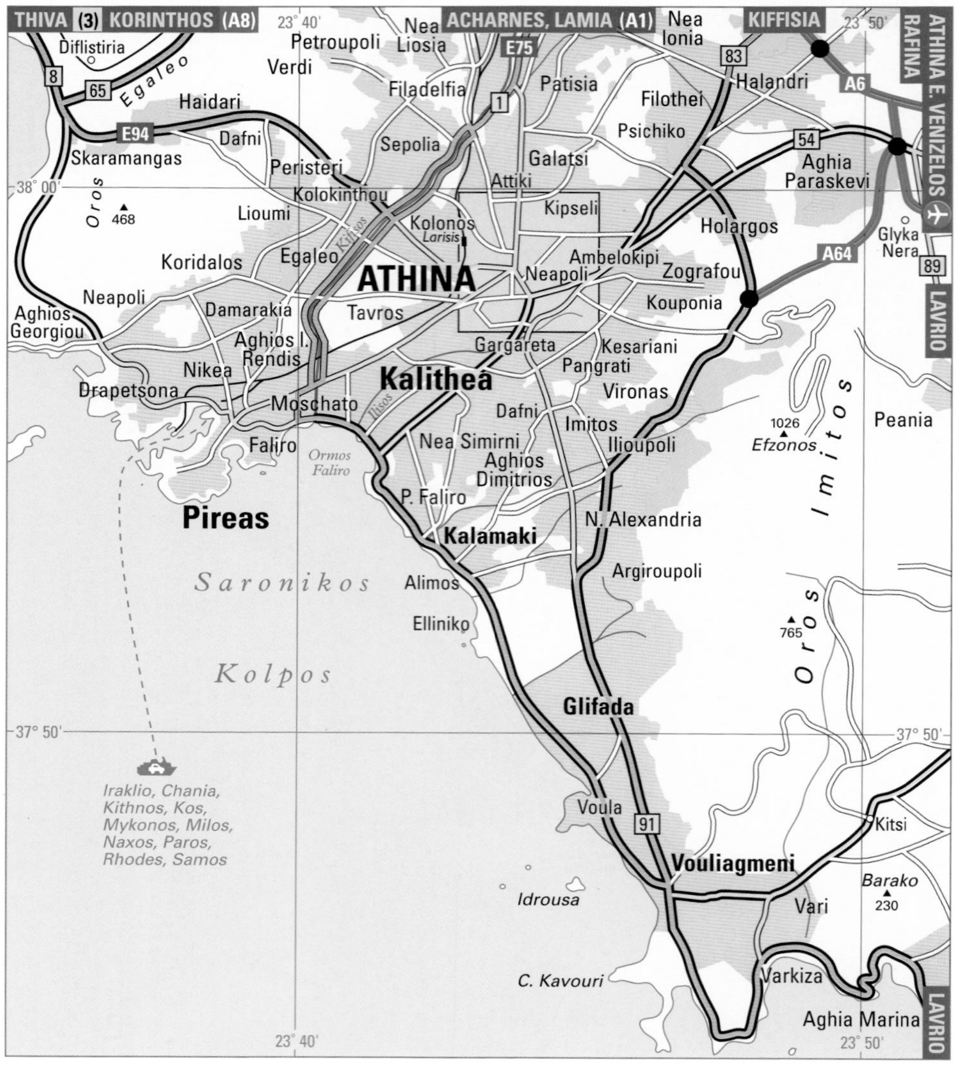

Athina Athens

0 km 1

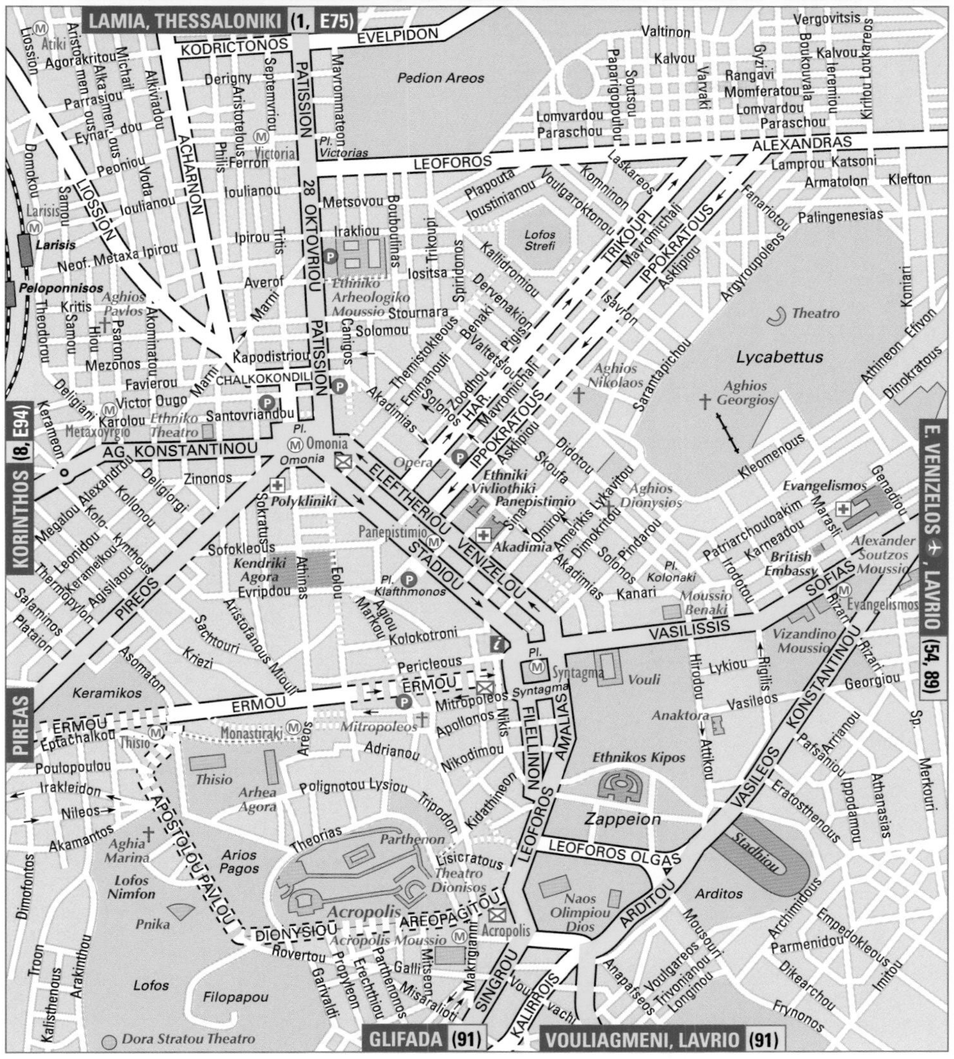

Basel

0 km 0.5

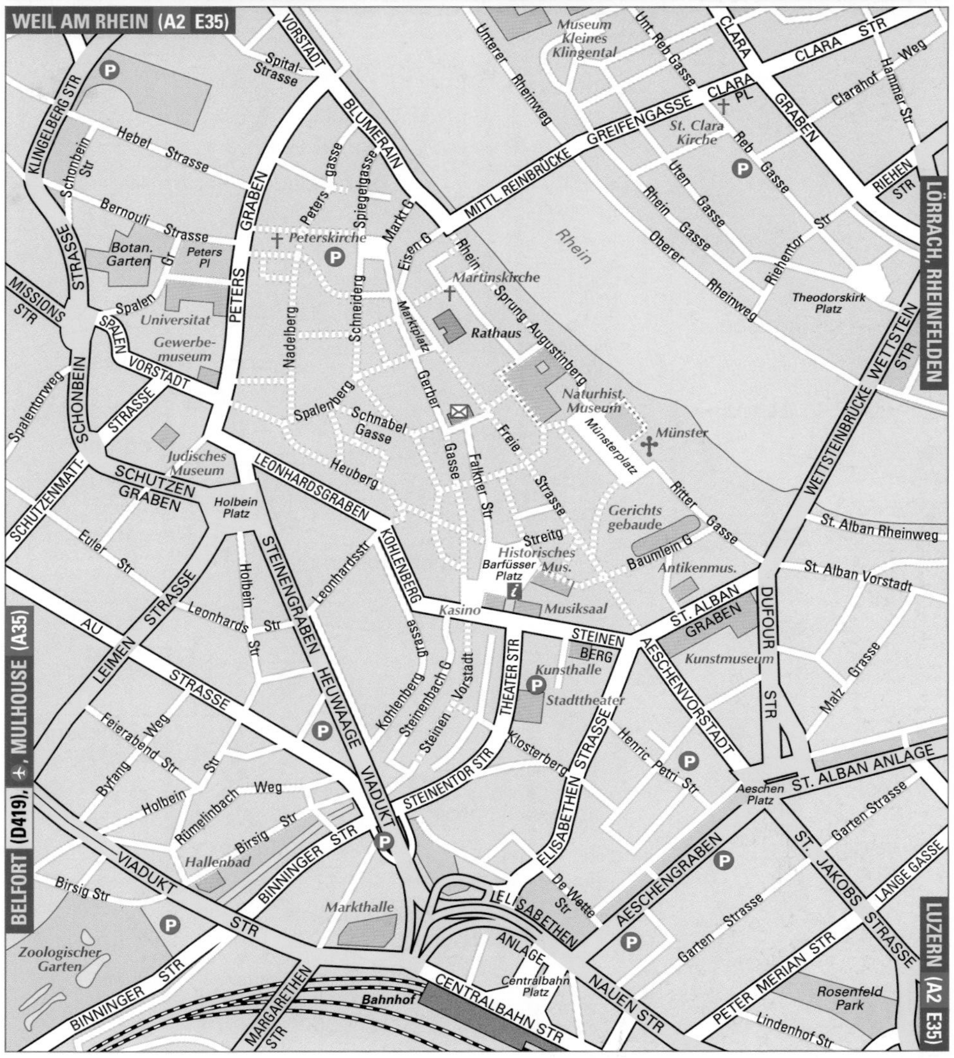

Barcelona

0 km 5

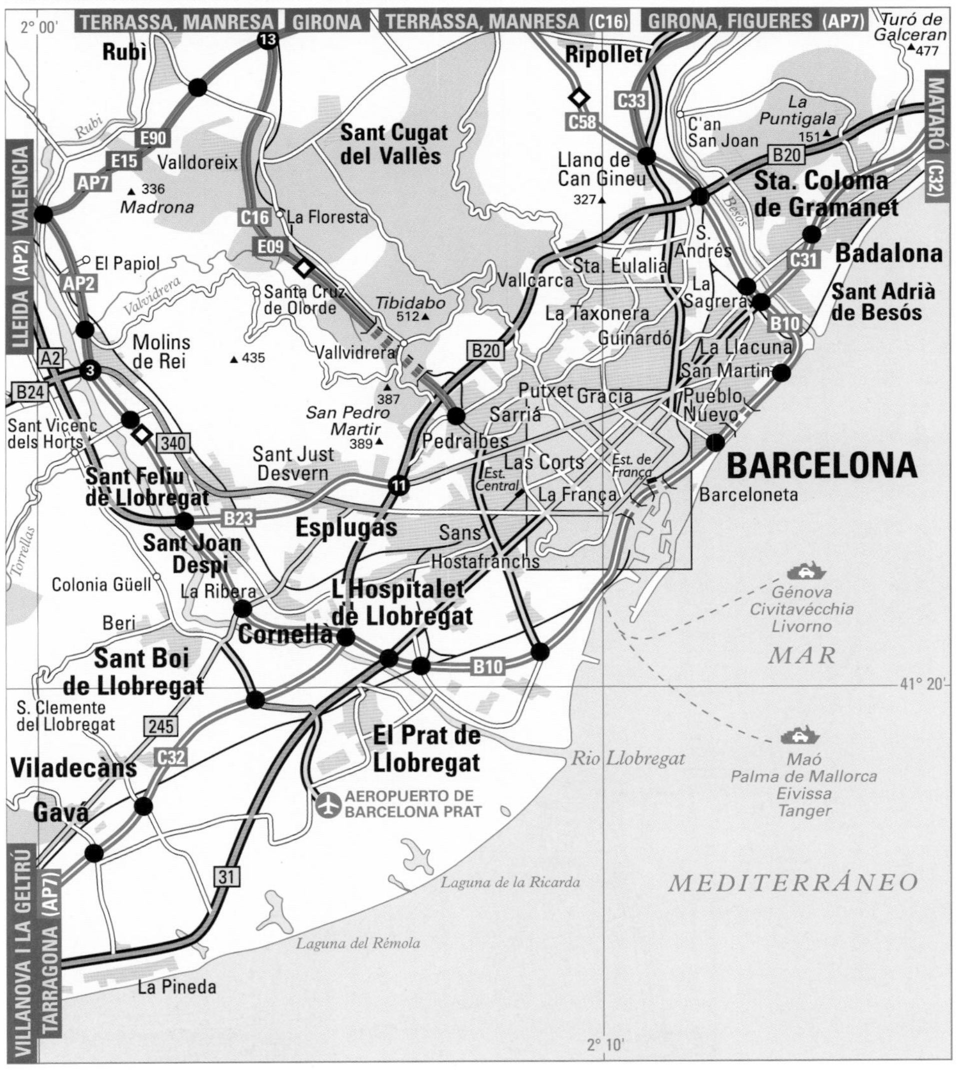

Barcelona

0 km 1

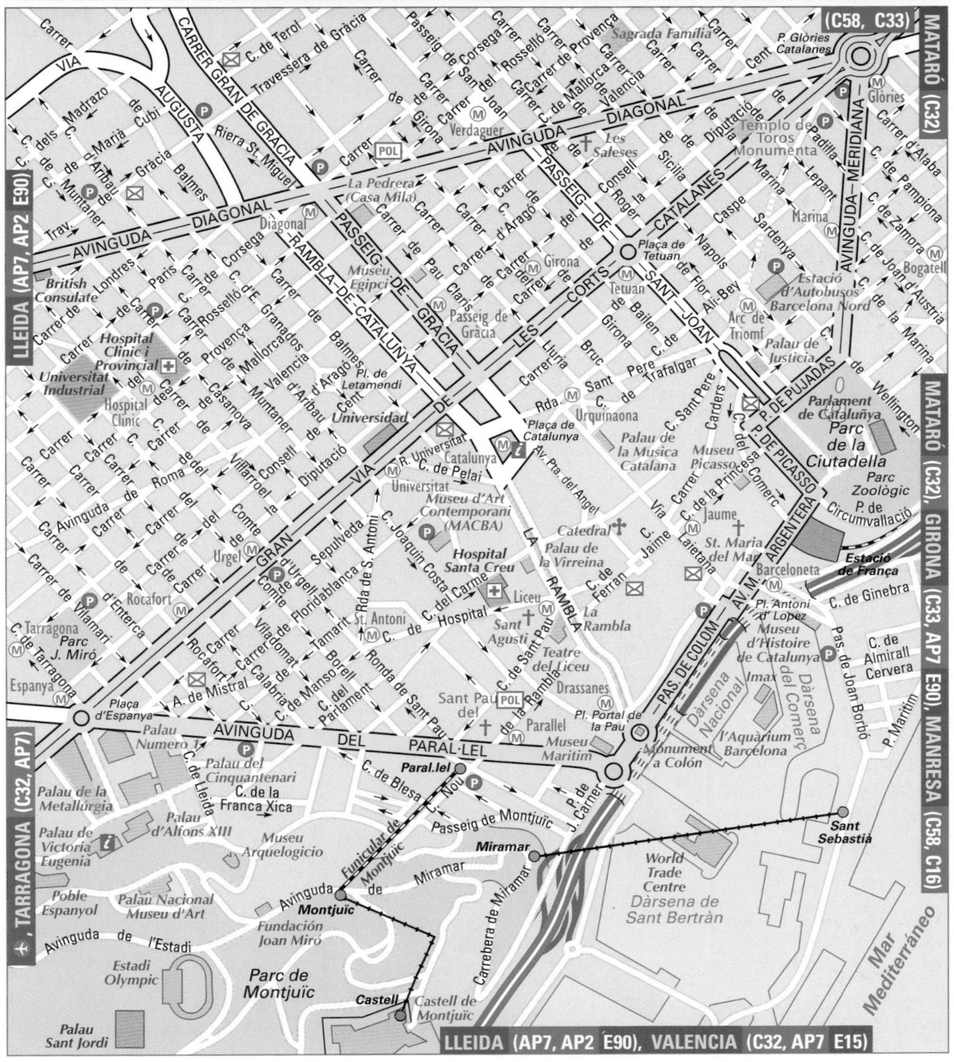

Berlin

0 km 5

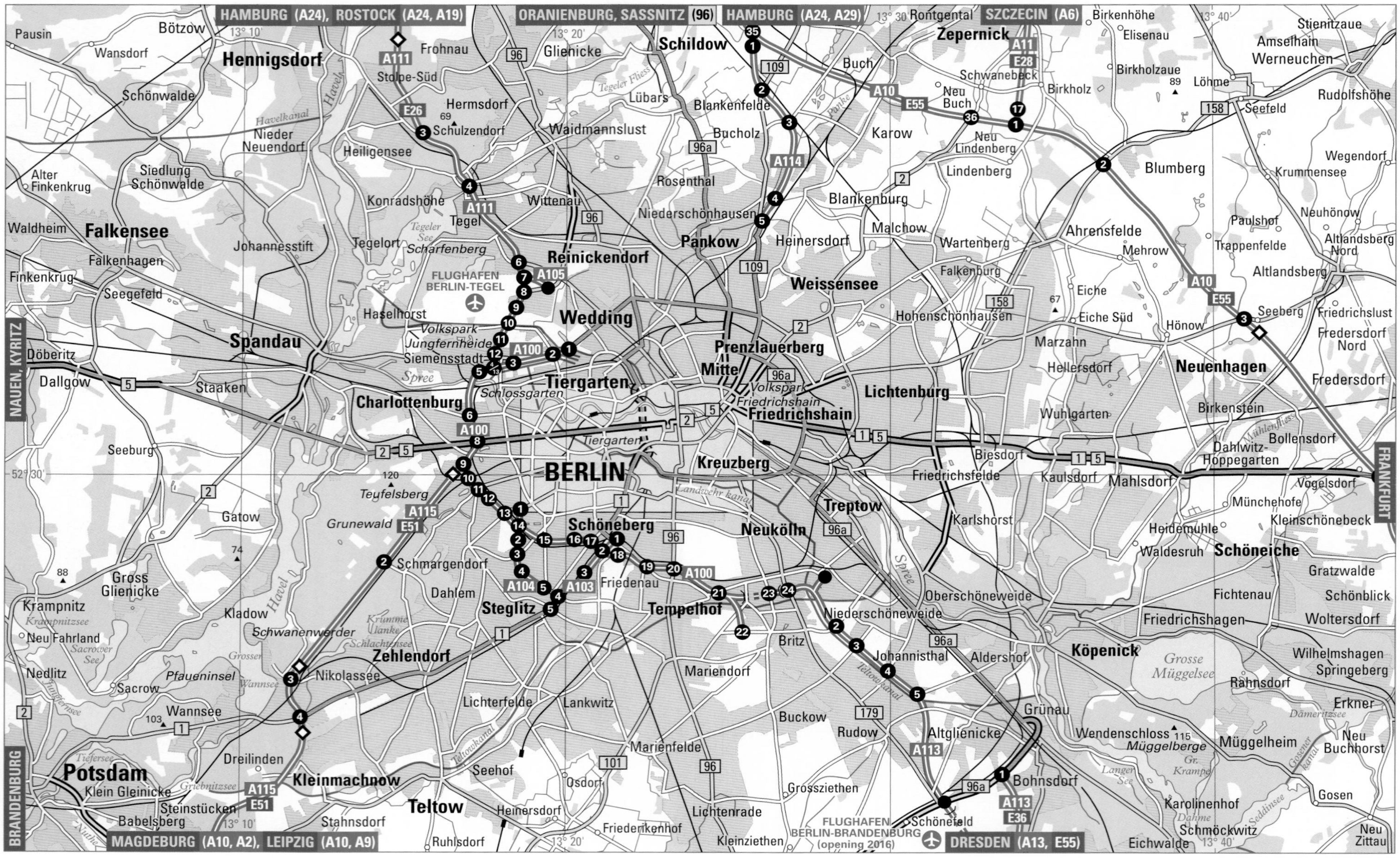
HAMBURG (A24), ROSTOCK (A24, A19)
ORANIENBURG, SASSNITZ (96)
HAMBURG (A24, A29)
SZCZECIN (A6)
NAUEN, KYRITZ
BRANDENBURG
FRANKFURT
MAGDEBURG (A10, A2), LEIPZIG (A10, A9)
DRESDEN (A13, E55)
Hennigsdorf
Falkensee
Spandau
Charlottenburg
Tiergarten
Wedding
Reinickendorf
Pankow
Weissensee
Prenzlauer Berg
Mitte
Friedrichshain
Lichtenburg
Kreuzberg
BERLIN
Neukölln
Treptow
Schöneberg
Steglitz
Zehlendorf
Tempelhof
Köpenick
Neuenhagen
Zepernick
Schildow
Potsdam
Kleinmachnow
Teltow
Blumberg
FLUGHAFEN BERLIN-TEGEL
FLUGHAFEN BERLIN-BRANDENBURG (opening 2016)

Berlin

0 km 1

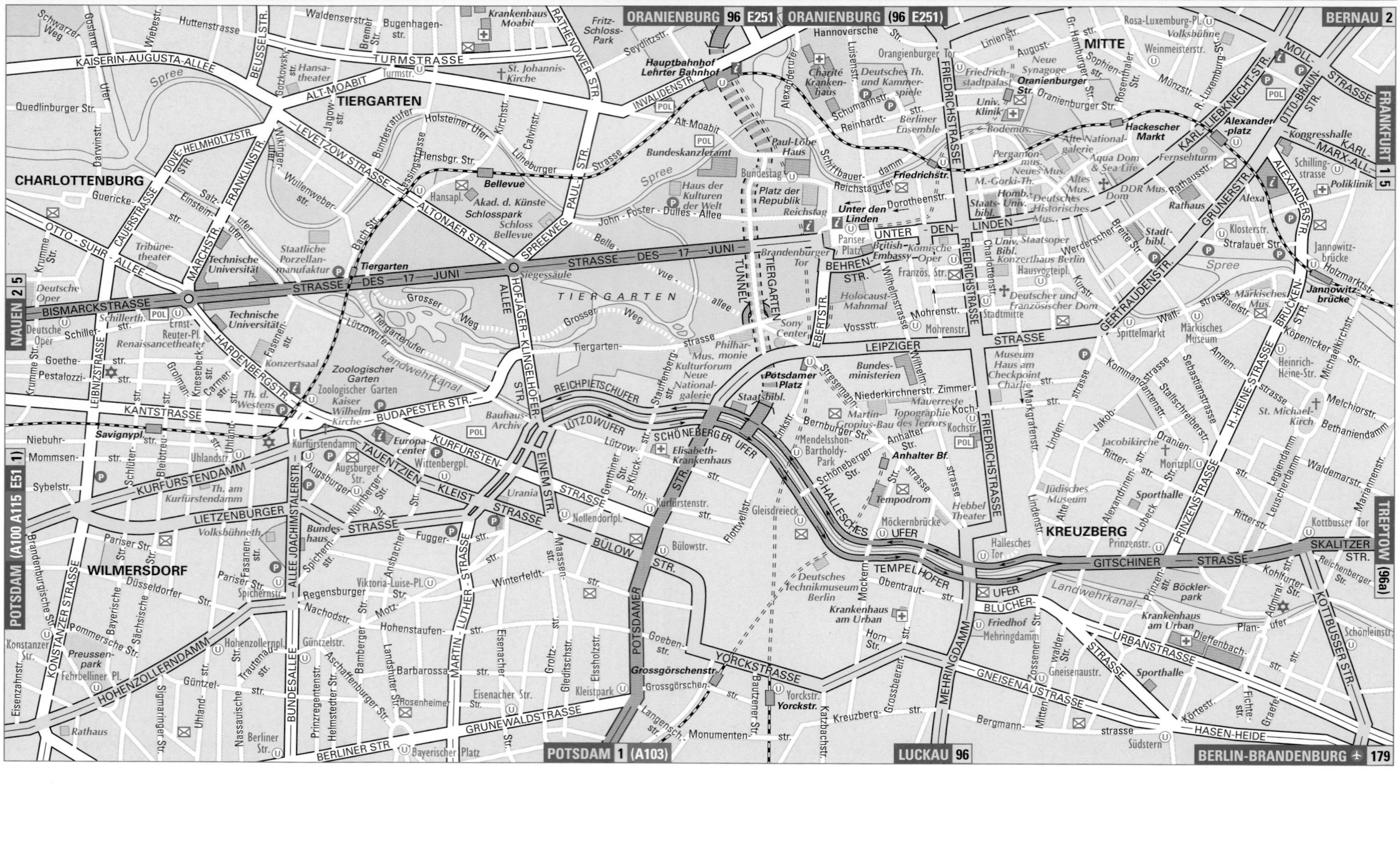
ORANIENBURG 96 E251
ORANIENBURG (96 E251)
BERNAU 2
FRANKFURT 1 5
TREPTOW (96a)
NAUEN 2 5
POTSDAM (A100 A115 E51 1)
POTSDAM 1 (A103)
LUCKAU 96
BERLIN-BRANDENBURG 179
TIERGARTEN
CHARLOTTENBURG
MITTE
KREUZBERG
WILMERSDORF
Hauptbahnhof Lehrter Bahnhof
Bundeskanzleramt
Reichstag
Brandenburger Tor
Unter den Linden
Alexanderplatz
Potsdamer Platz
Kurfürstendamm
Zoologischer Garten
Anhalter Bf.
Friedrichstr.
STRASSE DES 17. JUNI

Beograd Belgrade

0 km 1

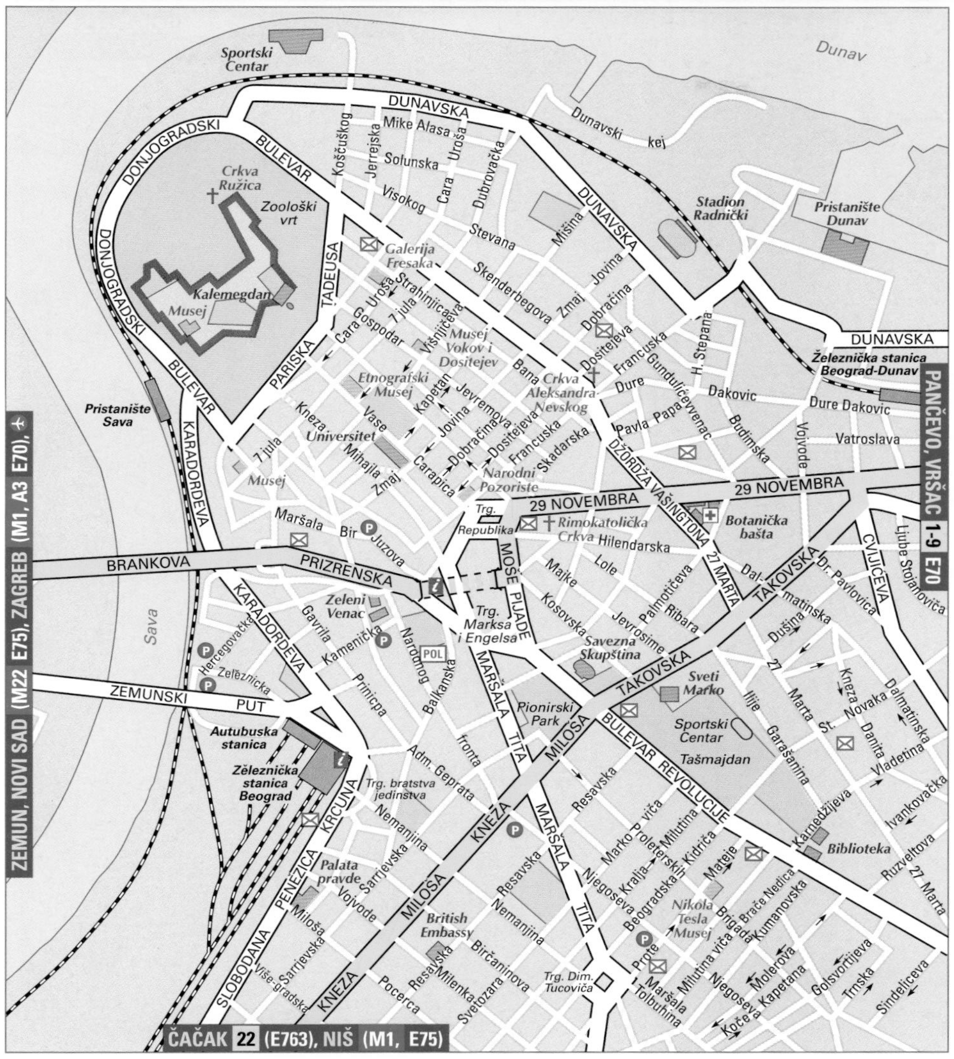

Bruxelles Brussels

0 km 5

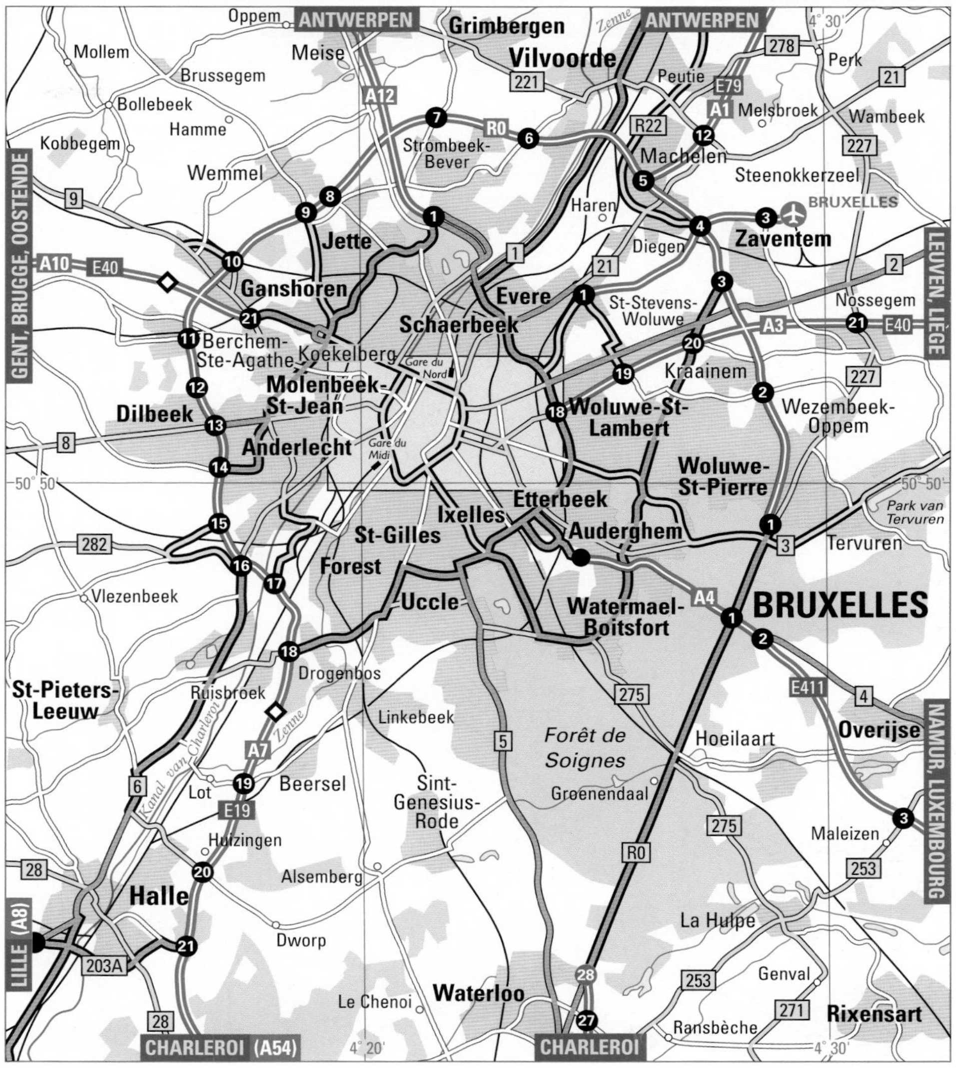

Bordeaux

0 km 5

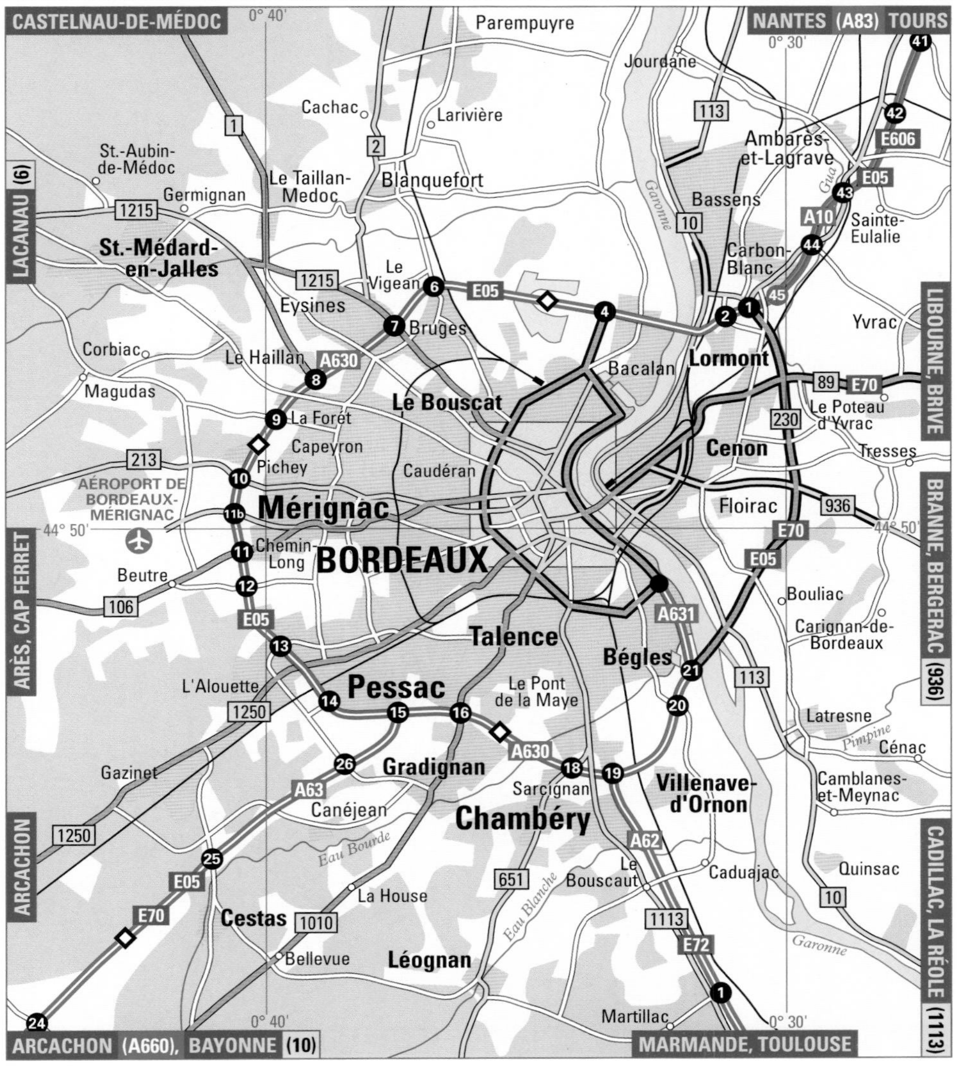

Bordeaux

0 km 1

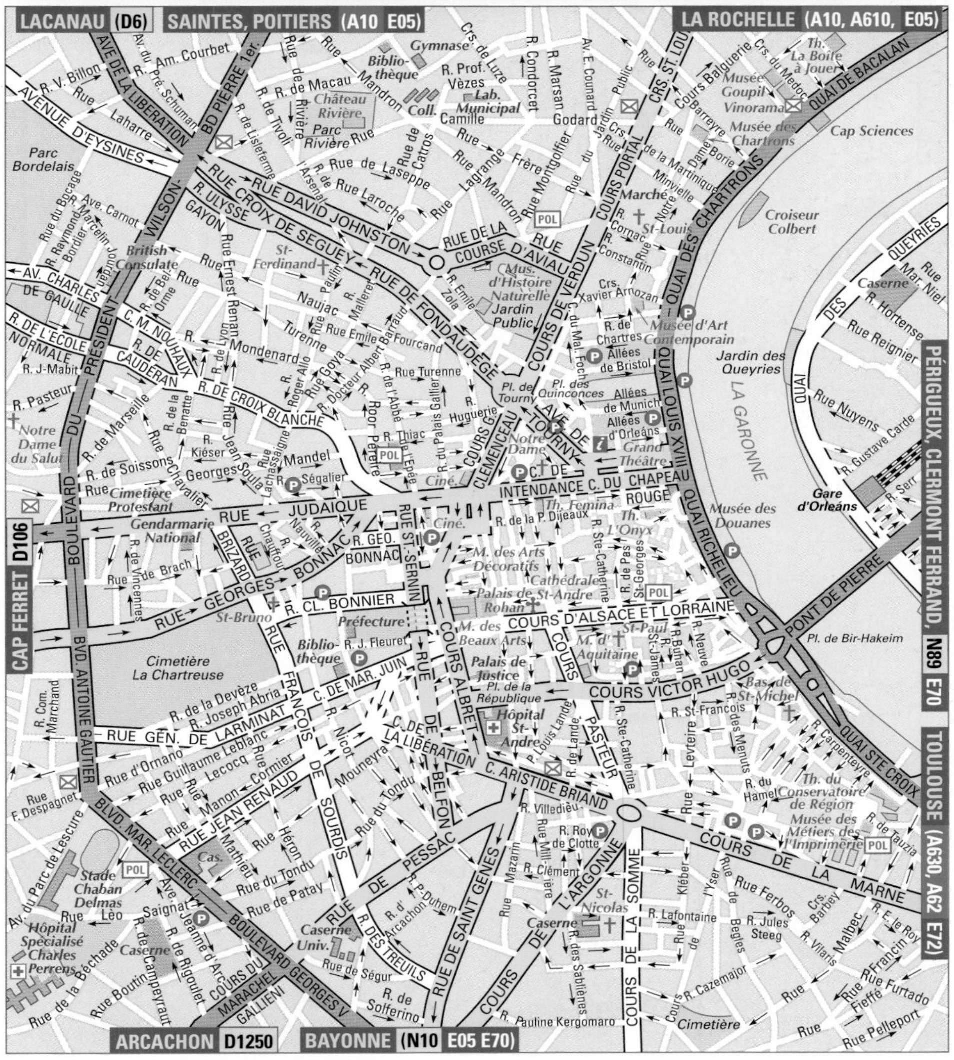

Bruxelles Brussels

0 km 1

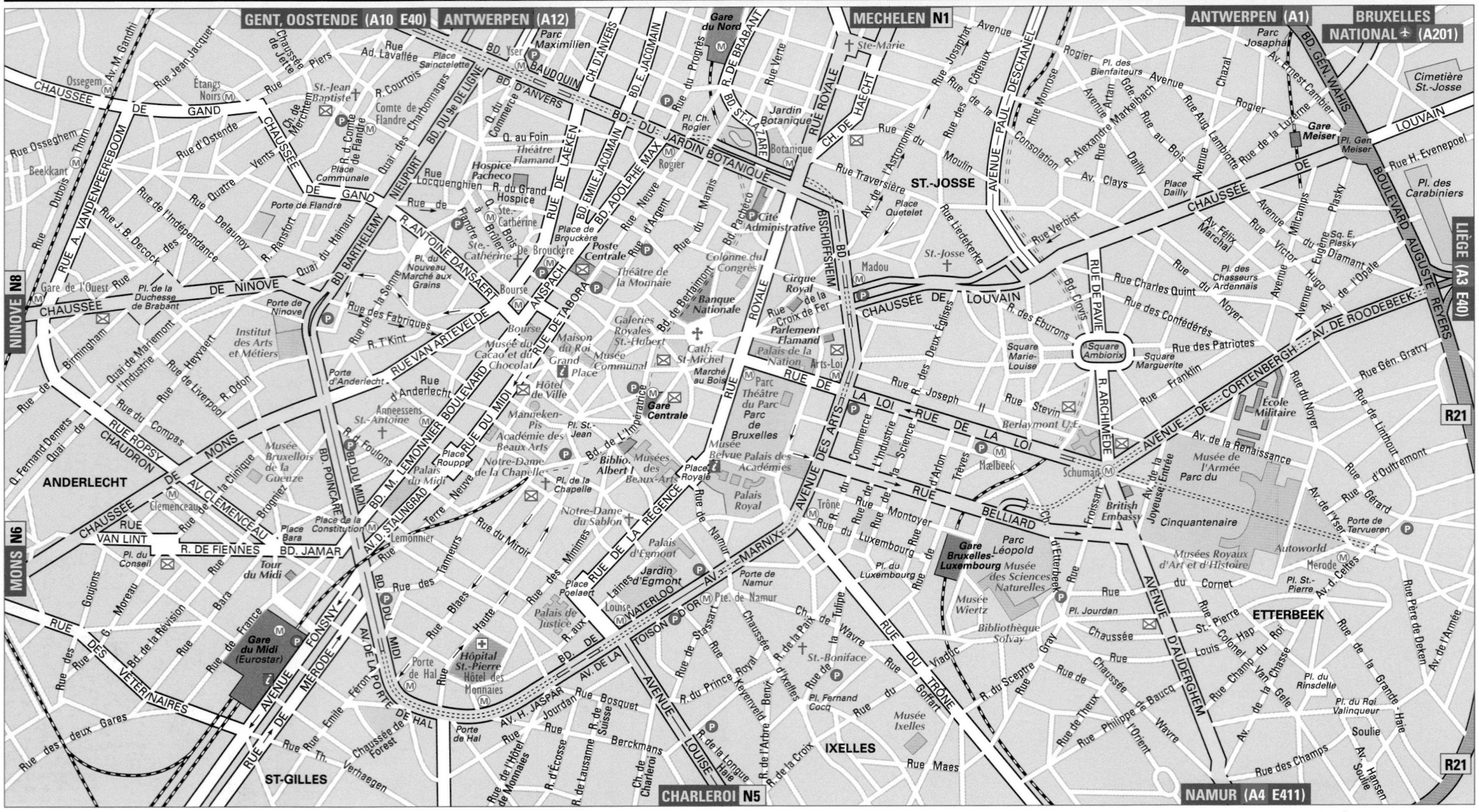

Budapest

0 km 5

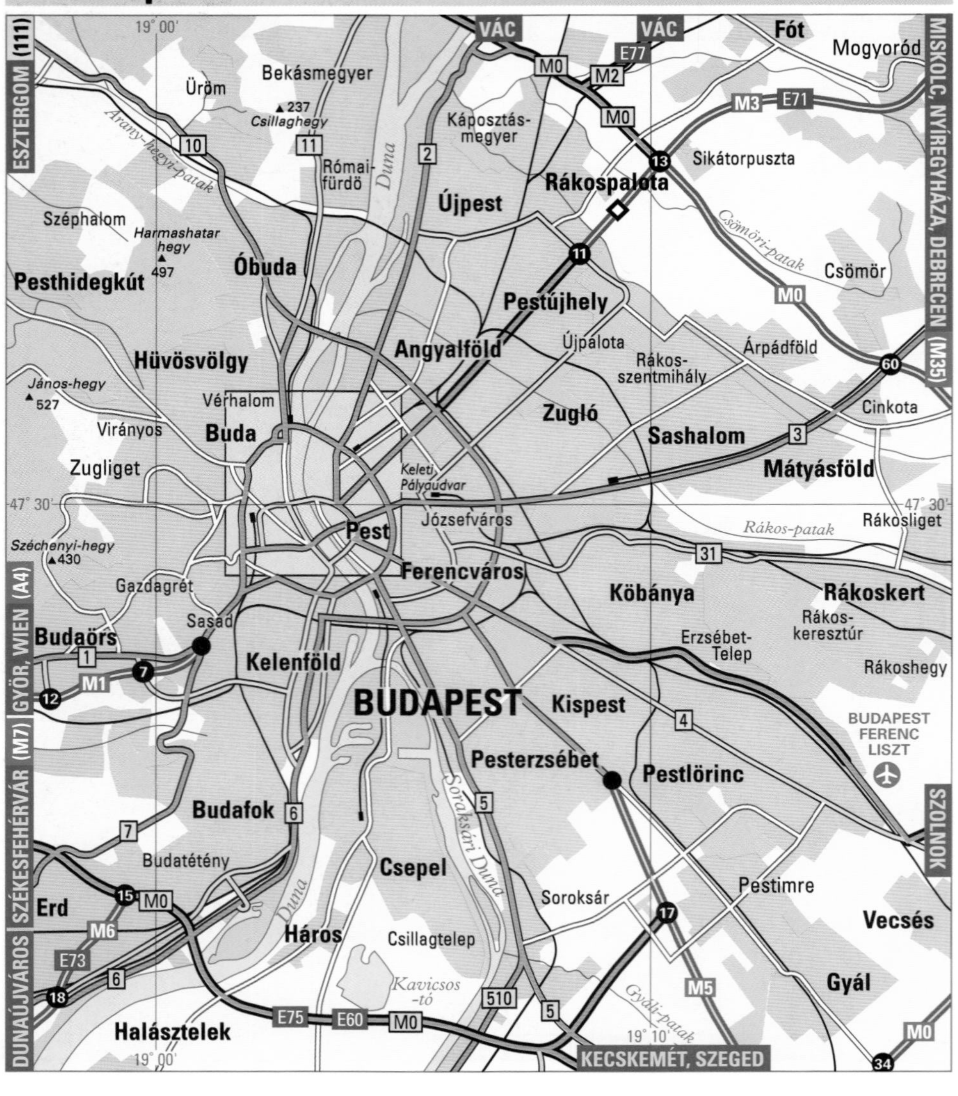

Budapest

0 km 1

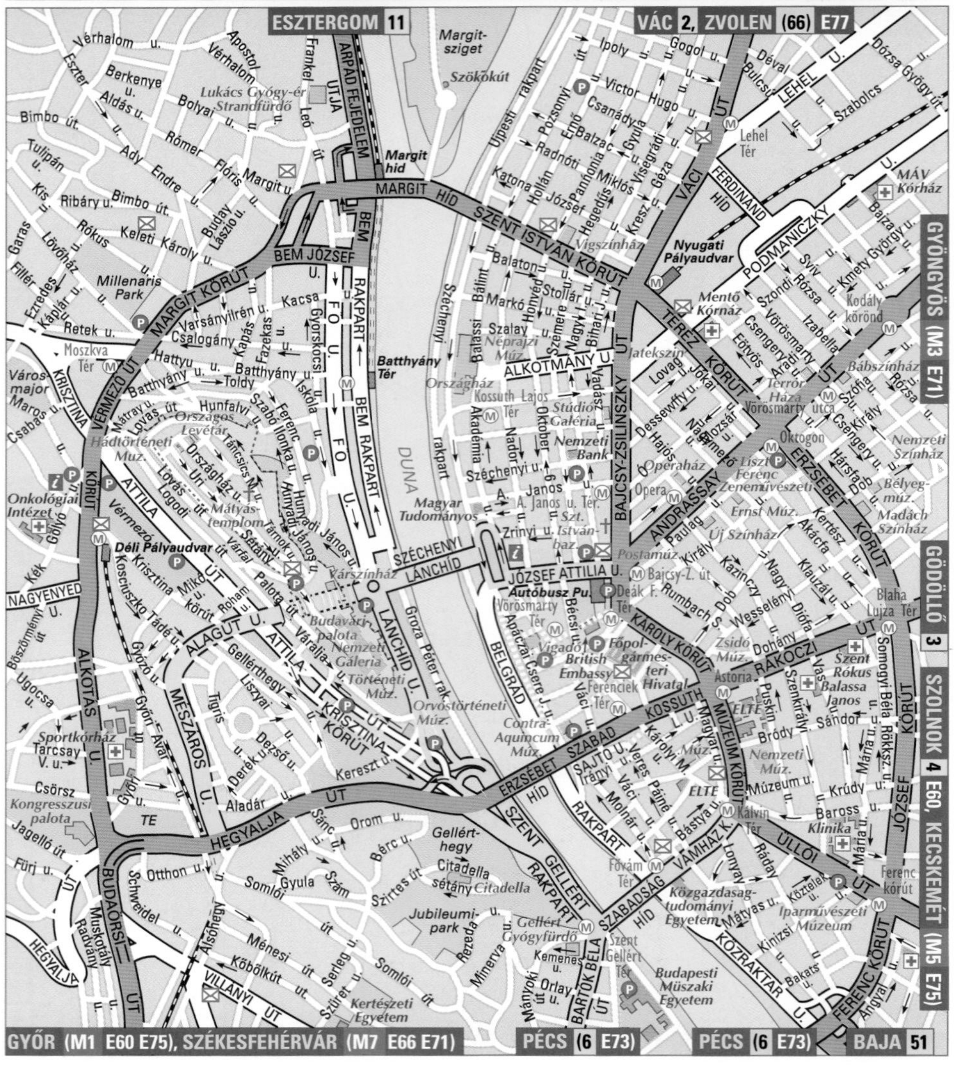

Dublin

0 km 5

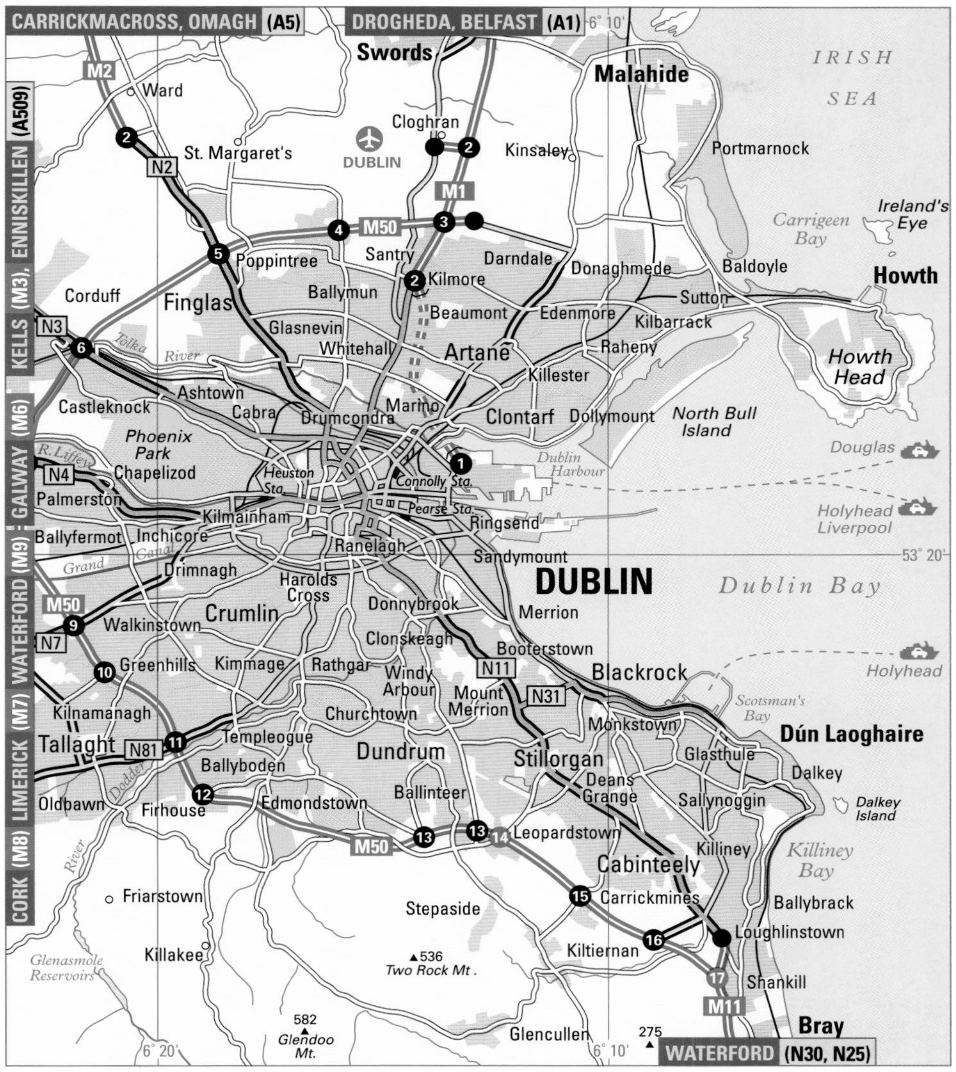

Dublin

0 km 0.5

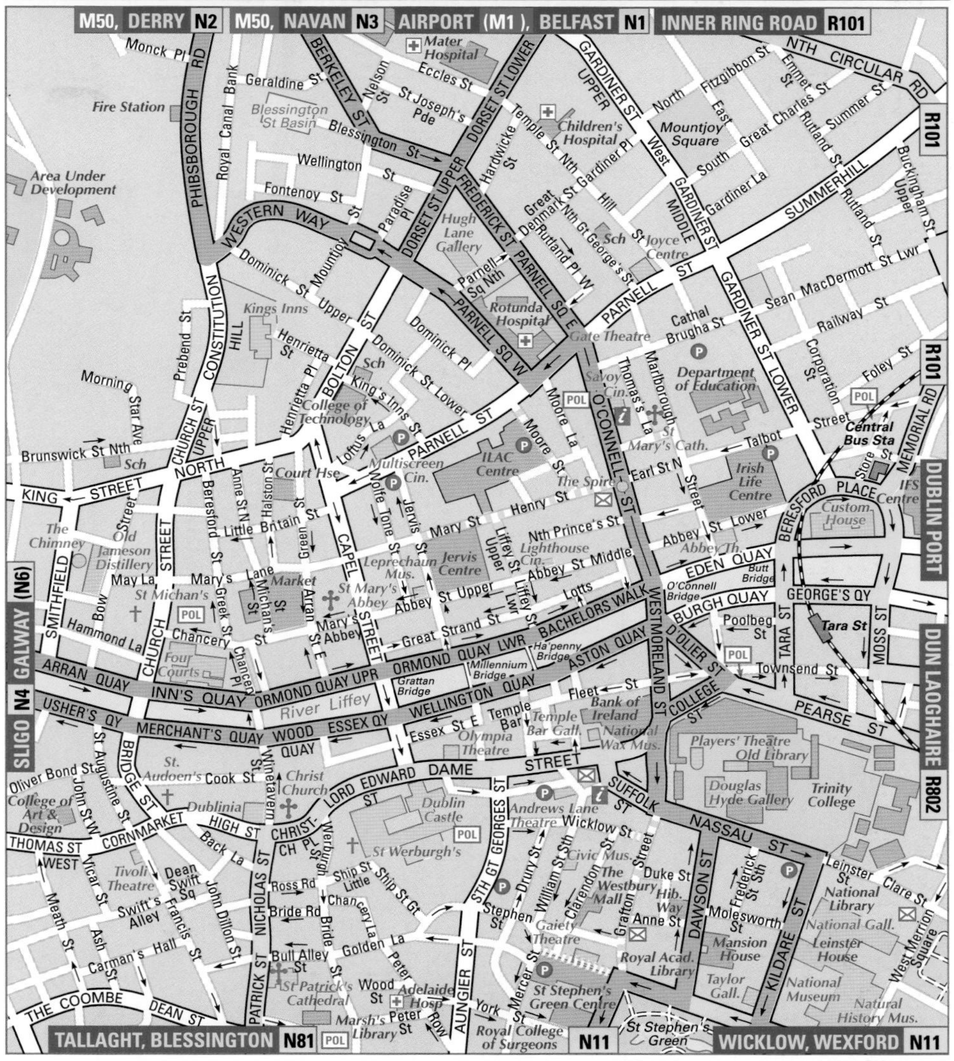

Düsseldorf

0 km 0.5

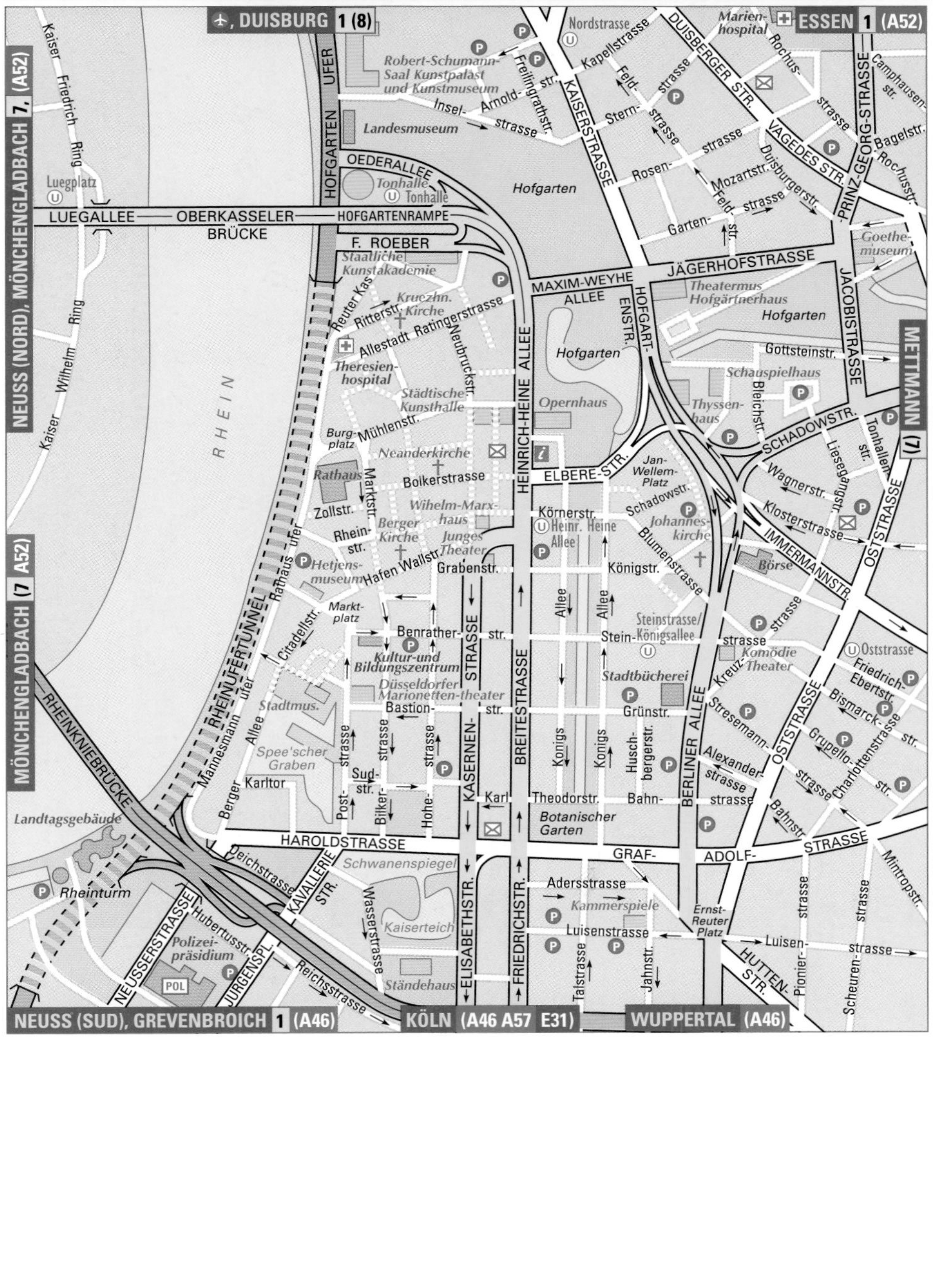

Edinburgh

0 km 0.5

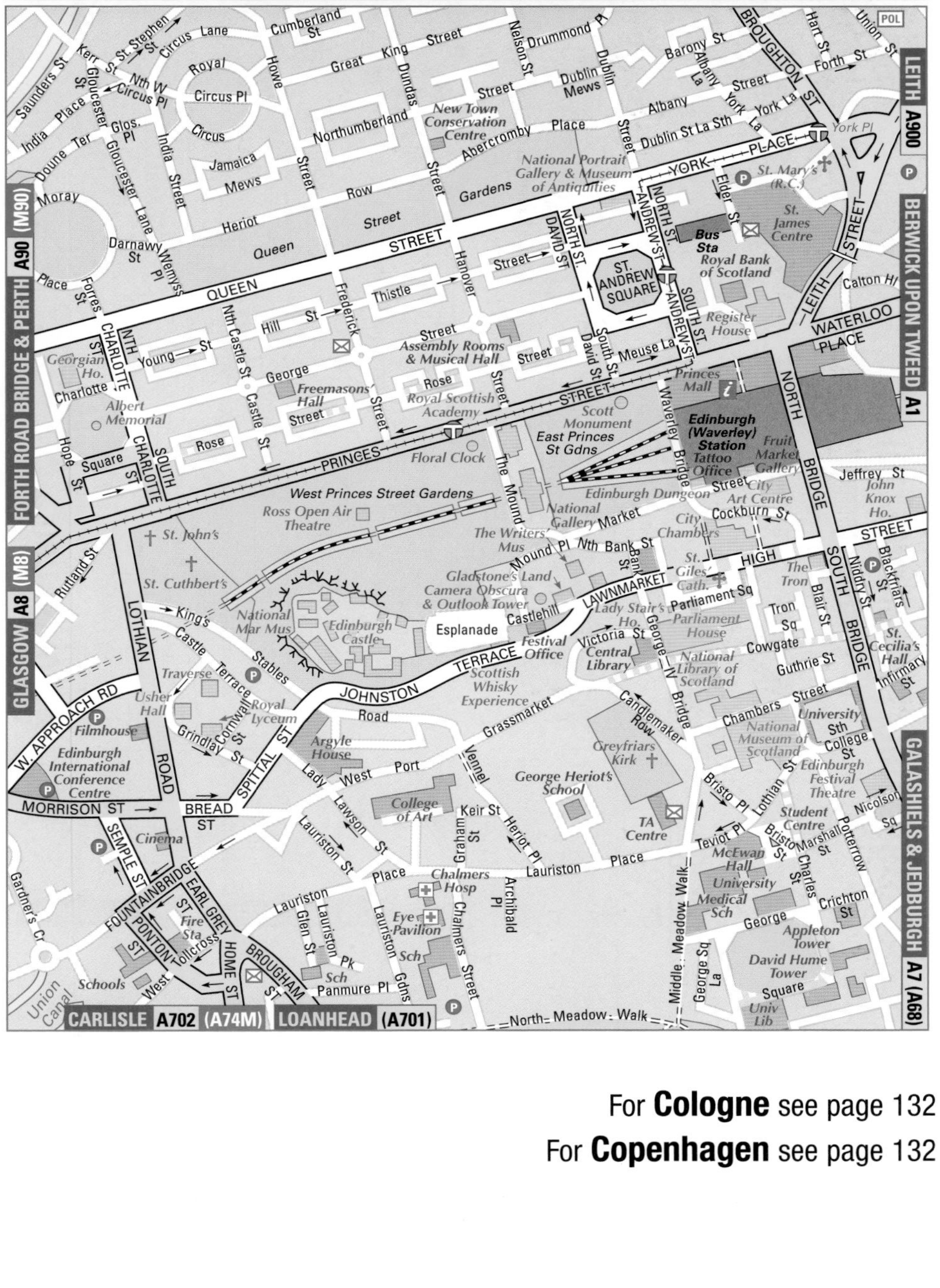

For **Cologne** see page 132
For **Copenhagen** see page 132

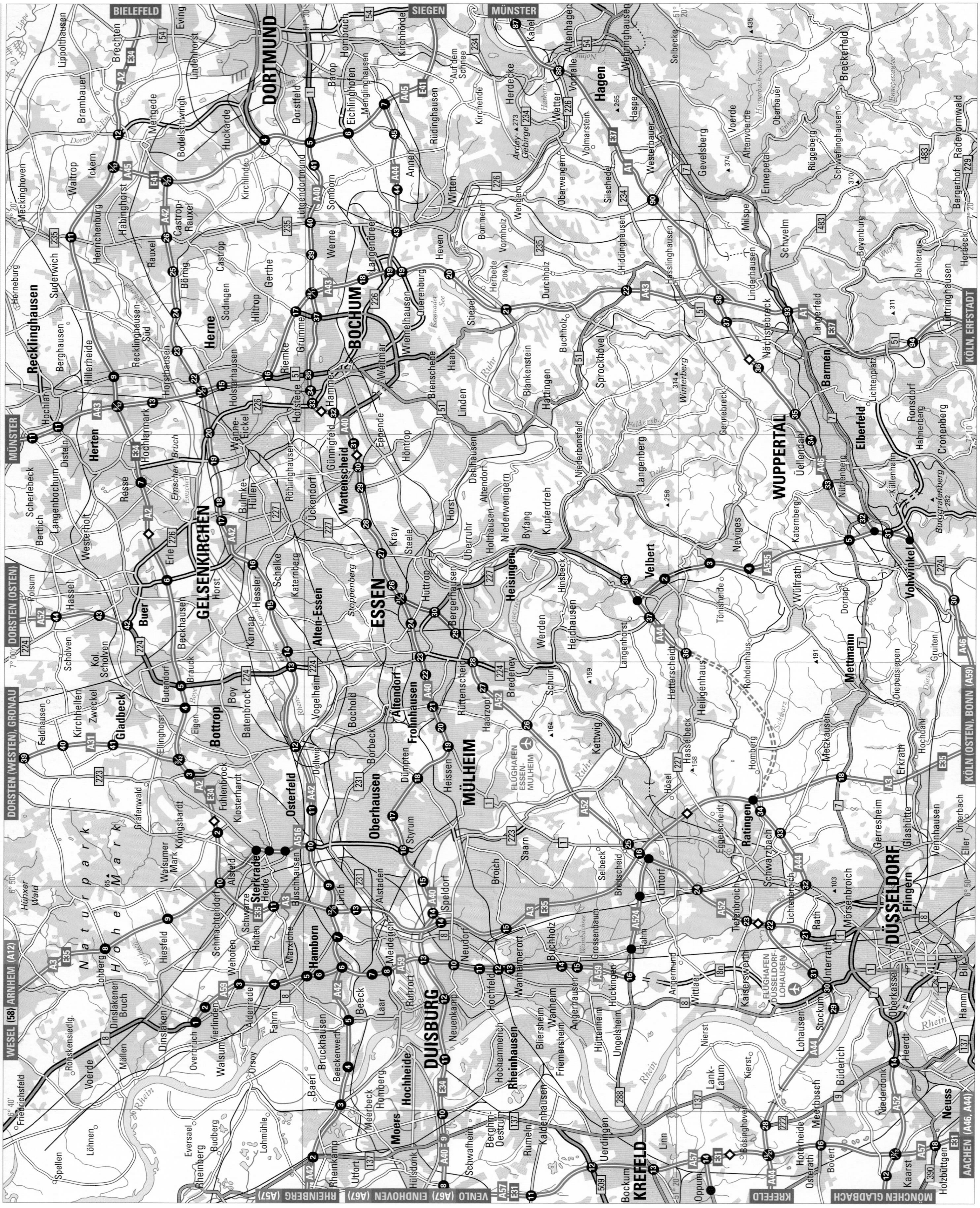
Düsseldorf (Ruhrgebiet)
DORTMUND
BOCHUM
GELSENKIRCHEN
ESSEN
MÜLHEIM
DUISBURG
Oberhausen
WUPPERTAL
DÜSSELDORF
KREFELD
Recklinghausen
Herne
Herten
Bottrop
Gladbeck
Hagen
Velbert
Ratingen
Mettmann
Neuss
Moers
Wattenscheid
Witten
Hattingen
Barmen
Elberfeld
Vohwinkel
BIELEFELD
MÜNSTER
SIEGEN
KÖLN, ERFSTADT
KÖLN (OSTEN), BONN (A59)
MÖNCHEN GLADBACH
AACHEN (A46, A44)
KREFELD
VENLO (A57)
EINDHOVEN (A67)
RHEINBERG (A57)
WESEL (58) ARNHEIM (A12)
DORSTEN (WESTEN), GRONAU
DORSTEN (OSTEN)
km
0
5

Firenze Florence

0 km 1

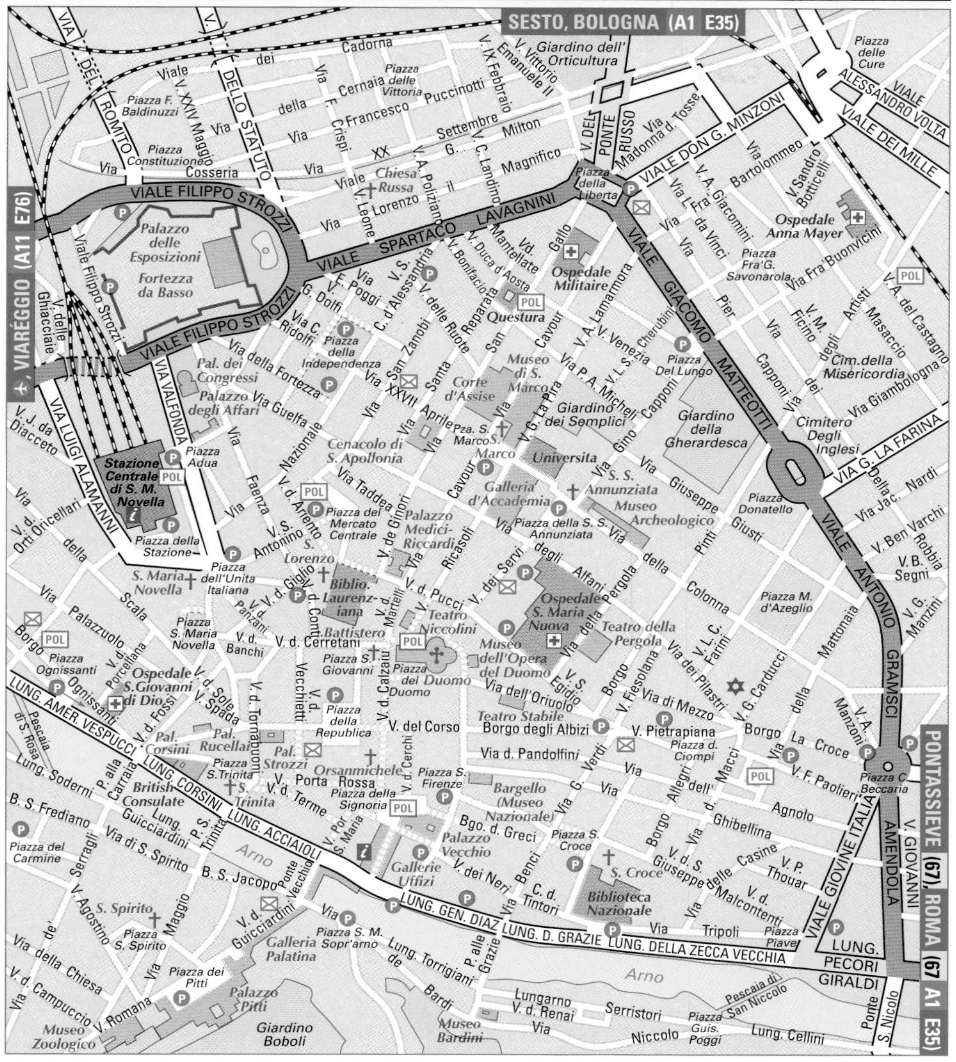

Frankfurt

0 km 0,5

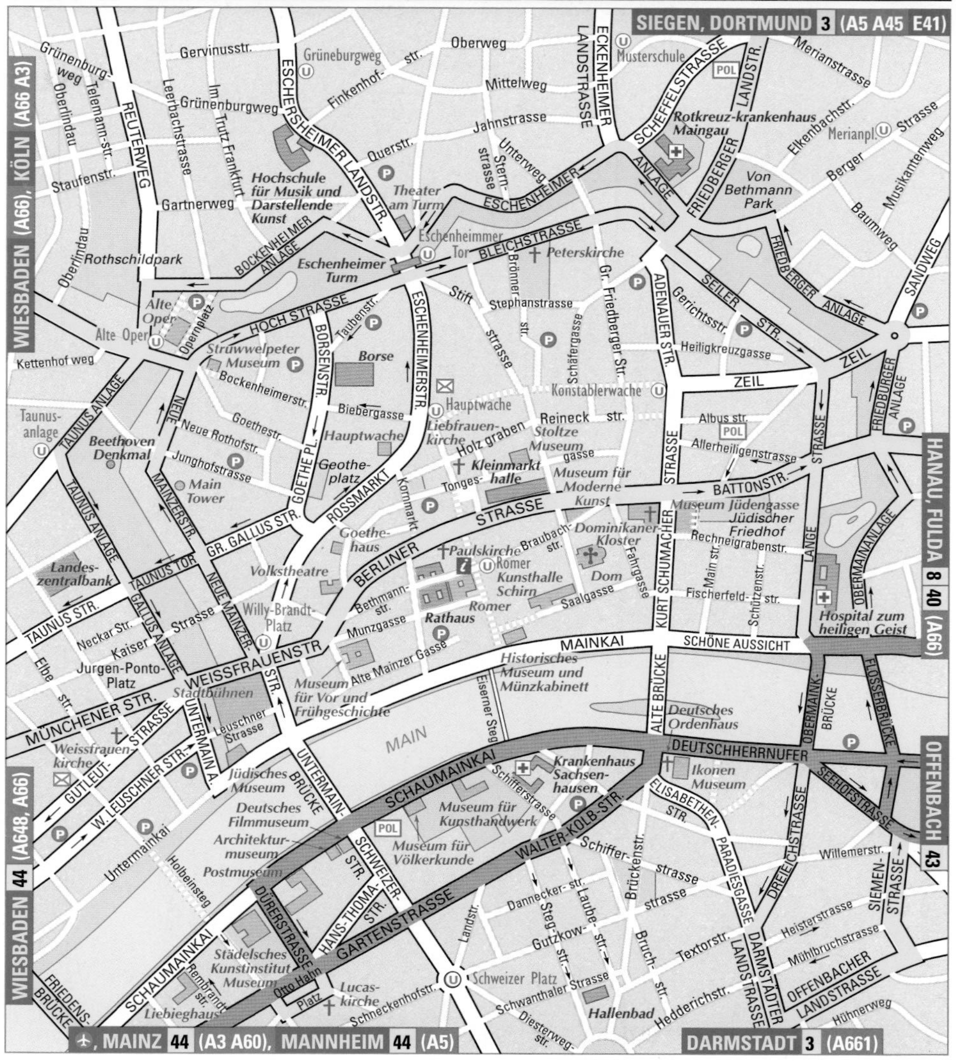

Genève Geneva

0 km 1

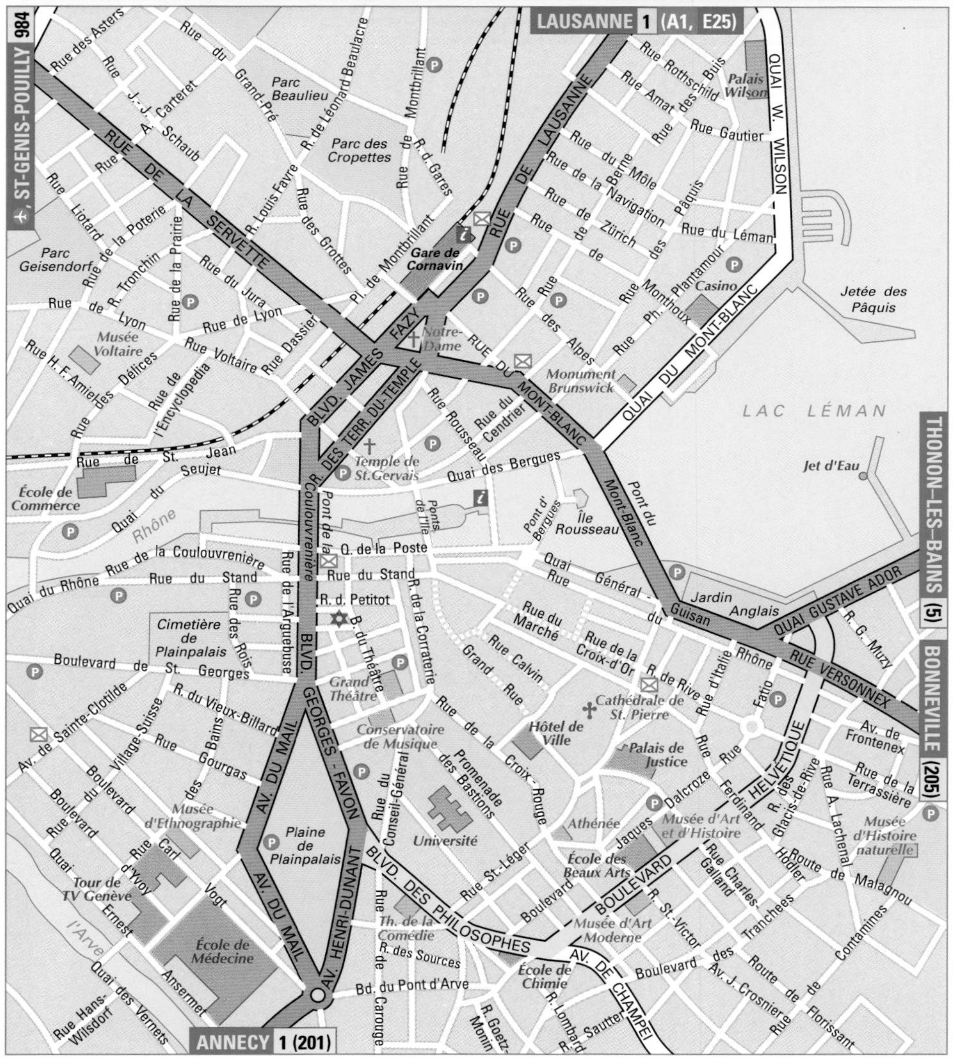

Génova Genoa

0 km 1

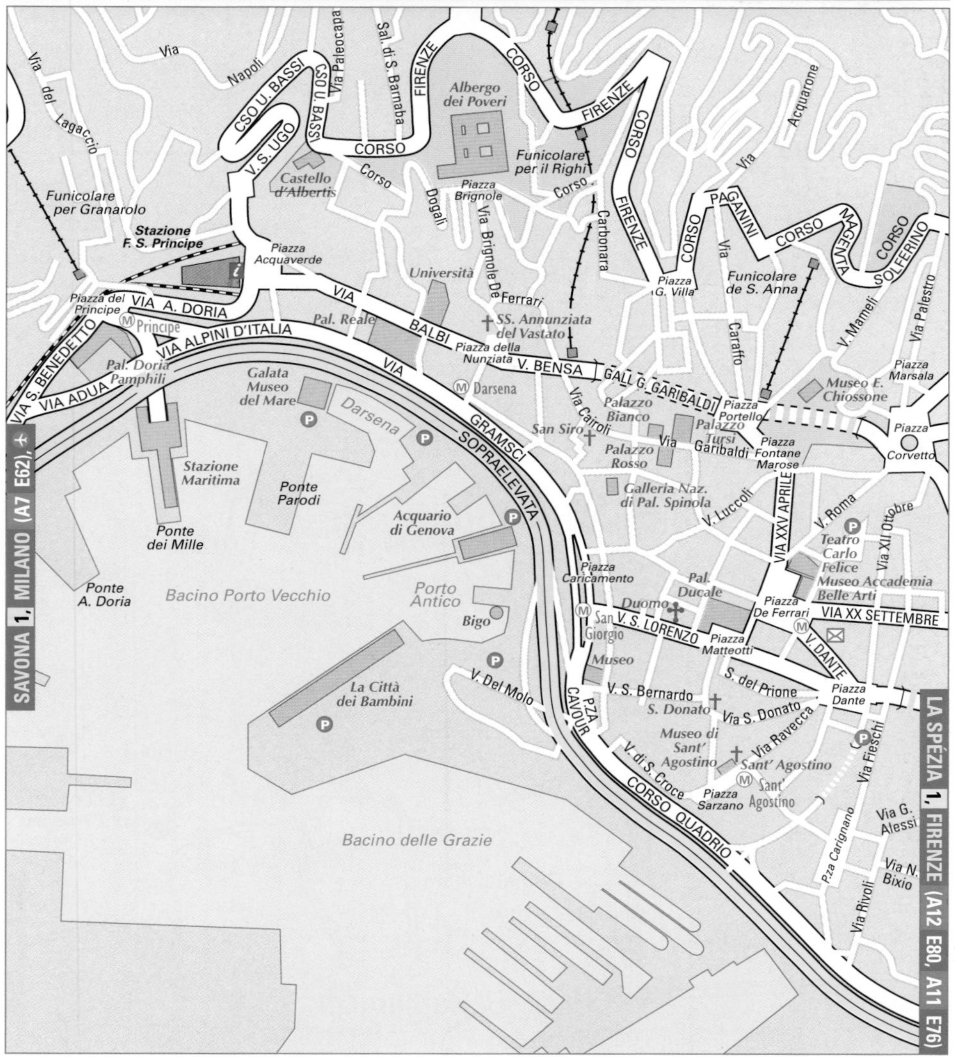

Granada

0 km 0.5

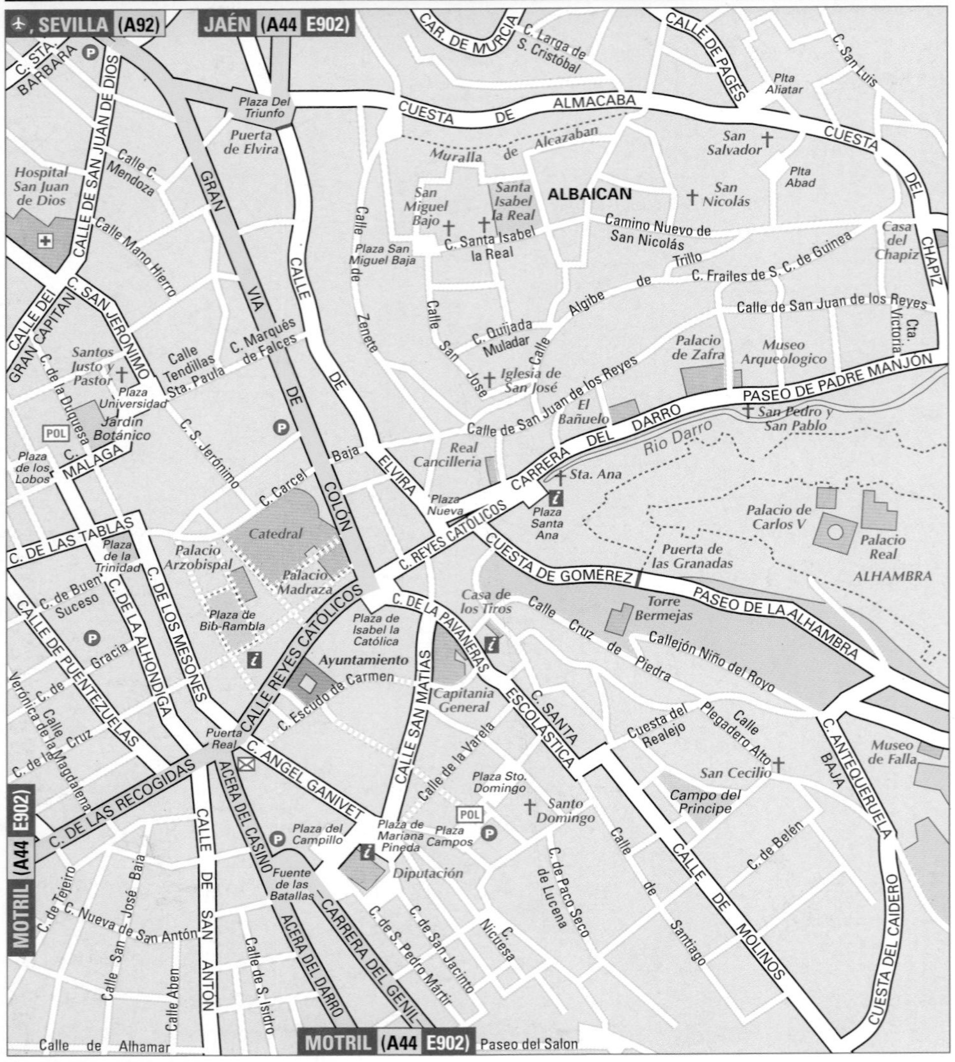

Göteborg Gothenburg

0 km 1

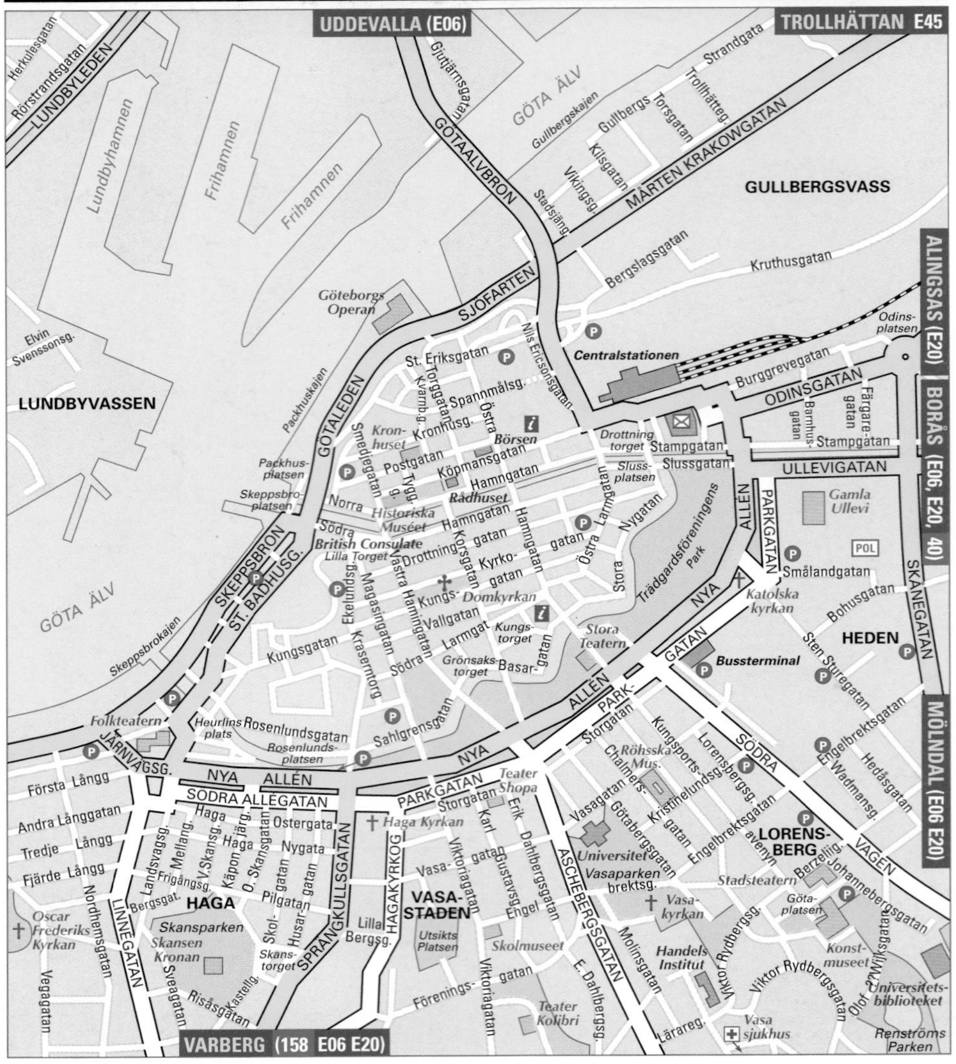

Hamburg

0 km 5

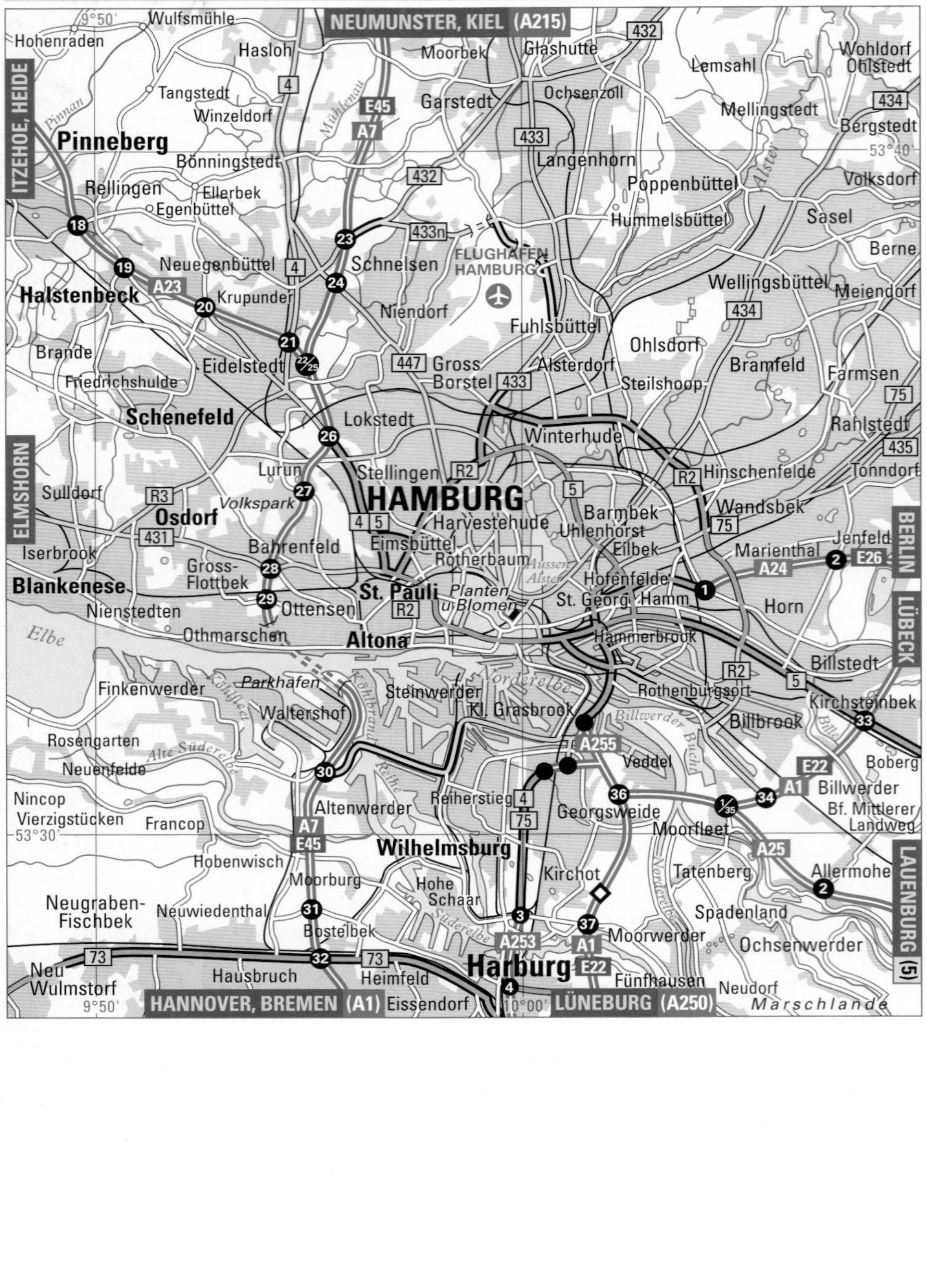

Hamburg

0 km 1

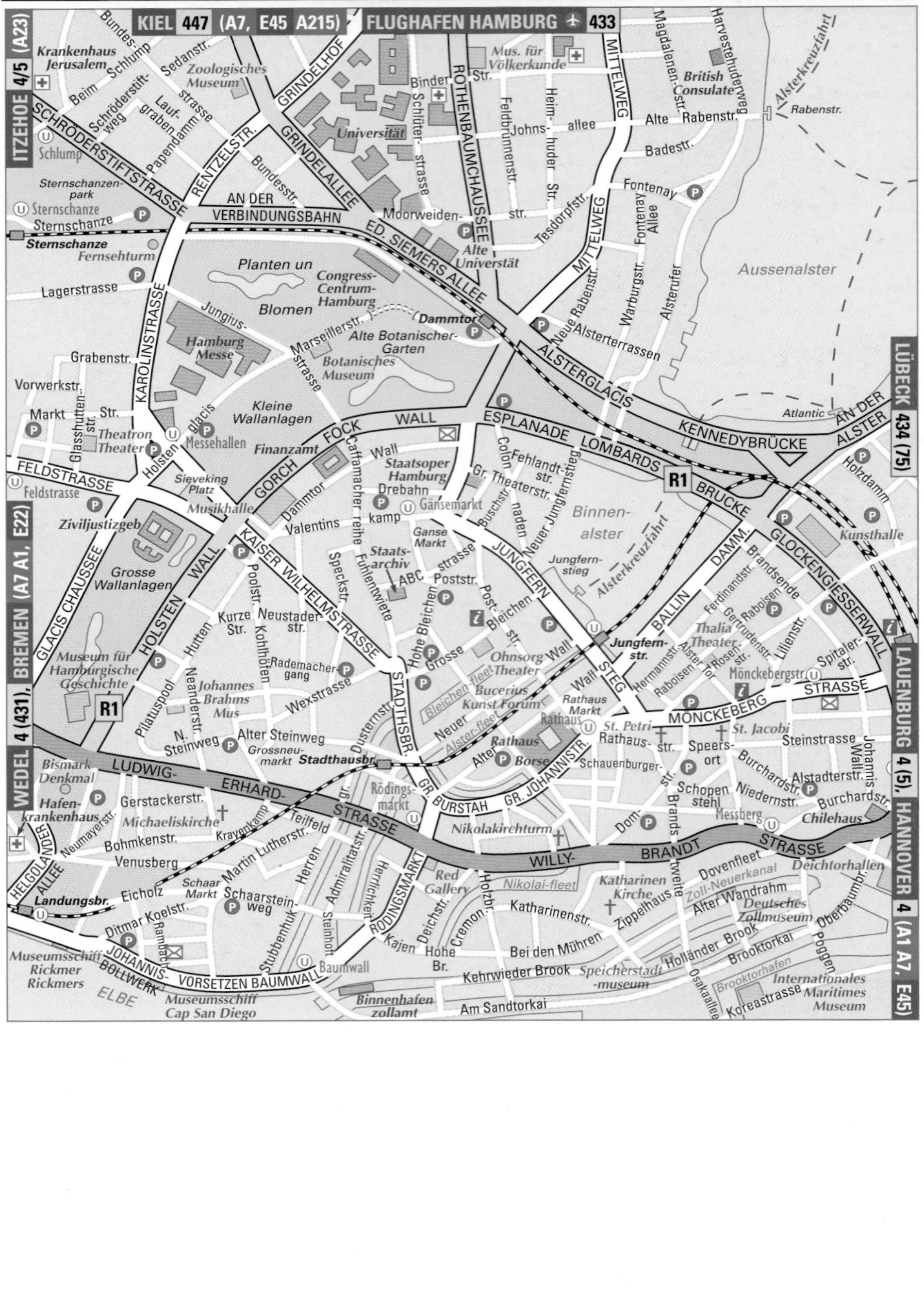

Helsinki

0 km 1

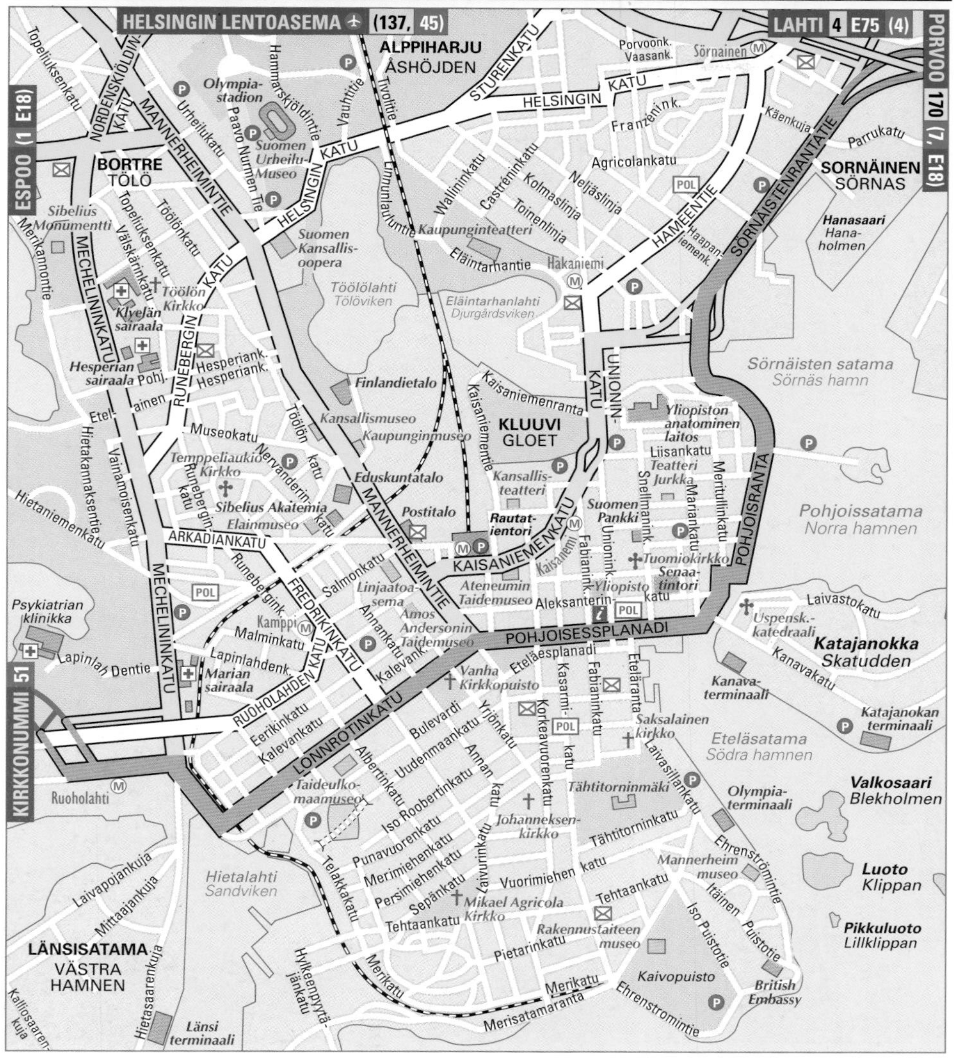

İstanbul

0 km 5

Helsinki

0 km 10

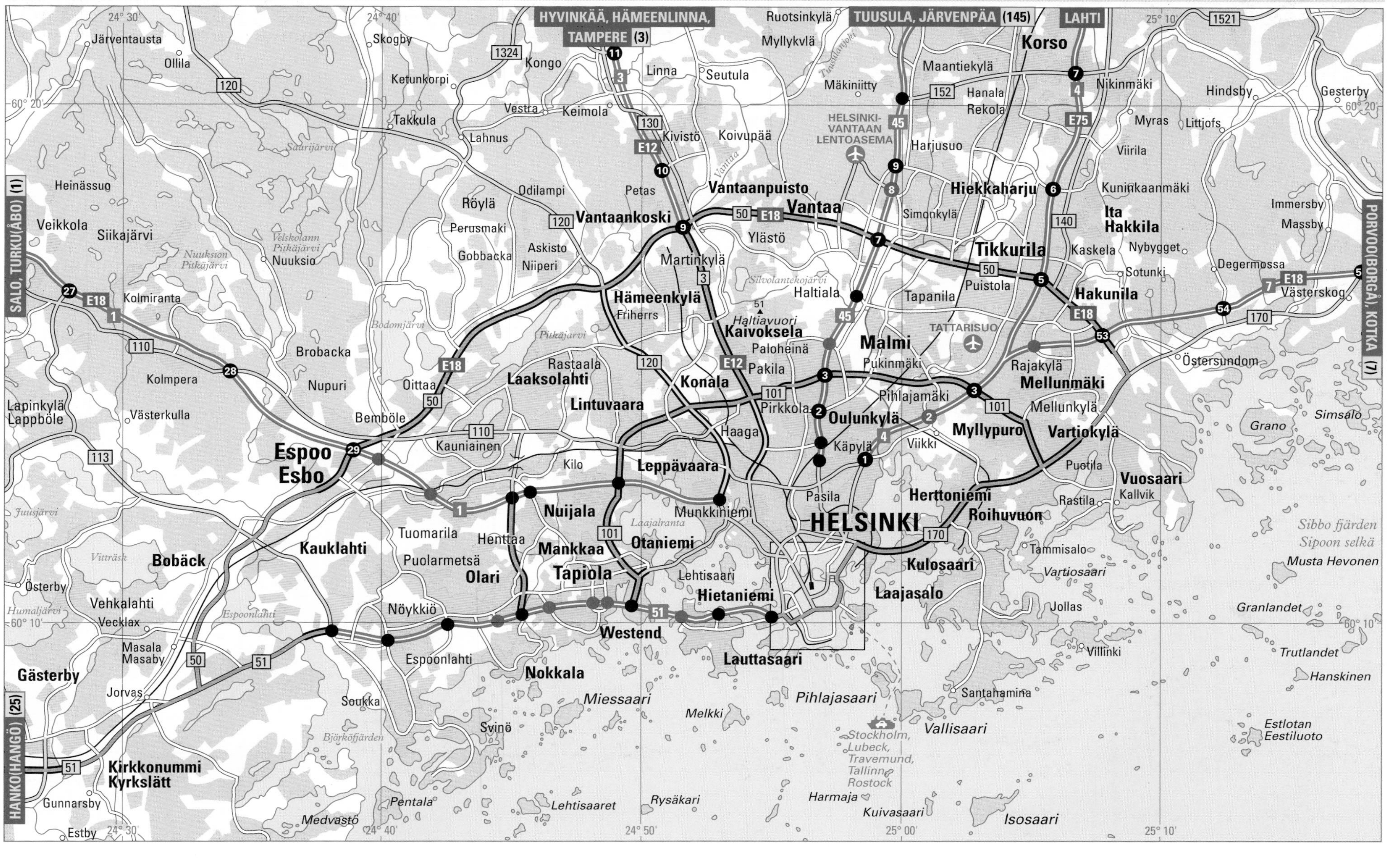

København Copenhagen

0 km 5

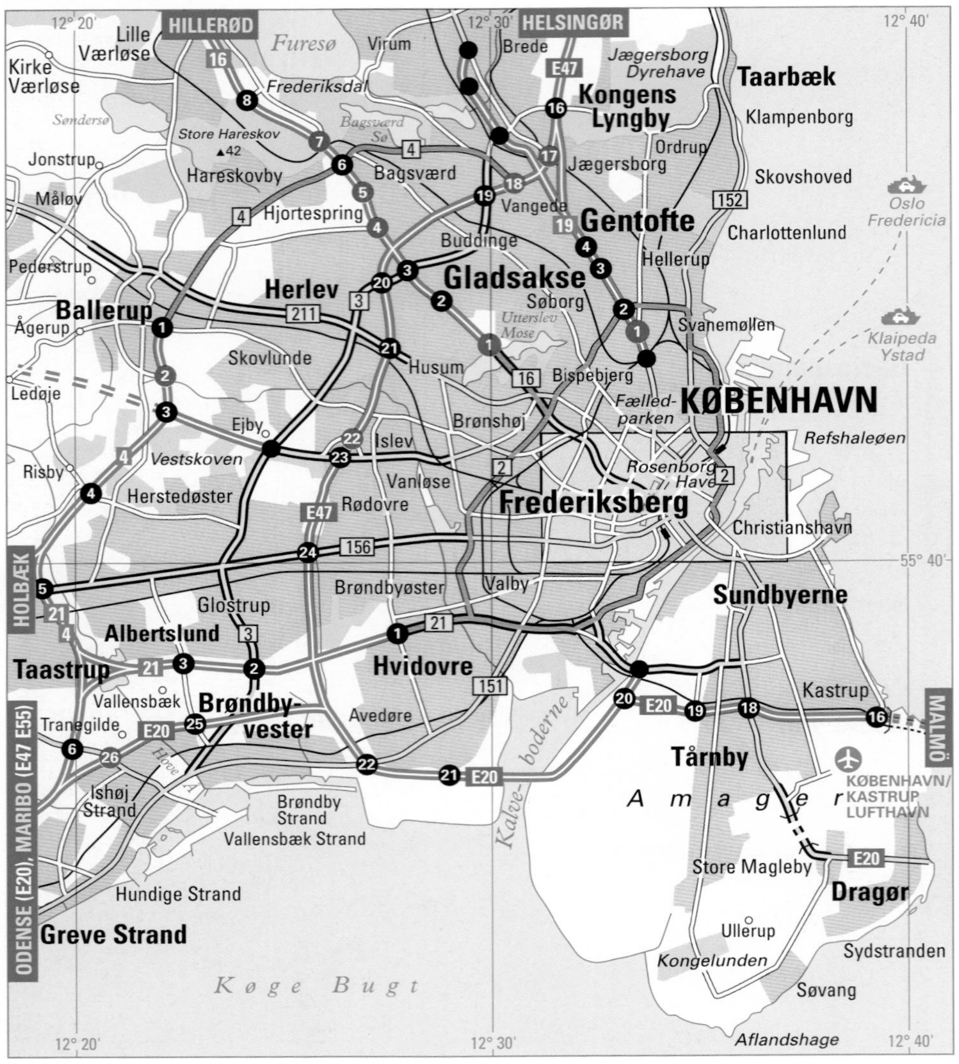

Köln Cologne

0 km 1

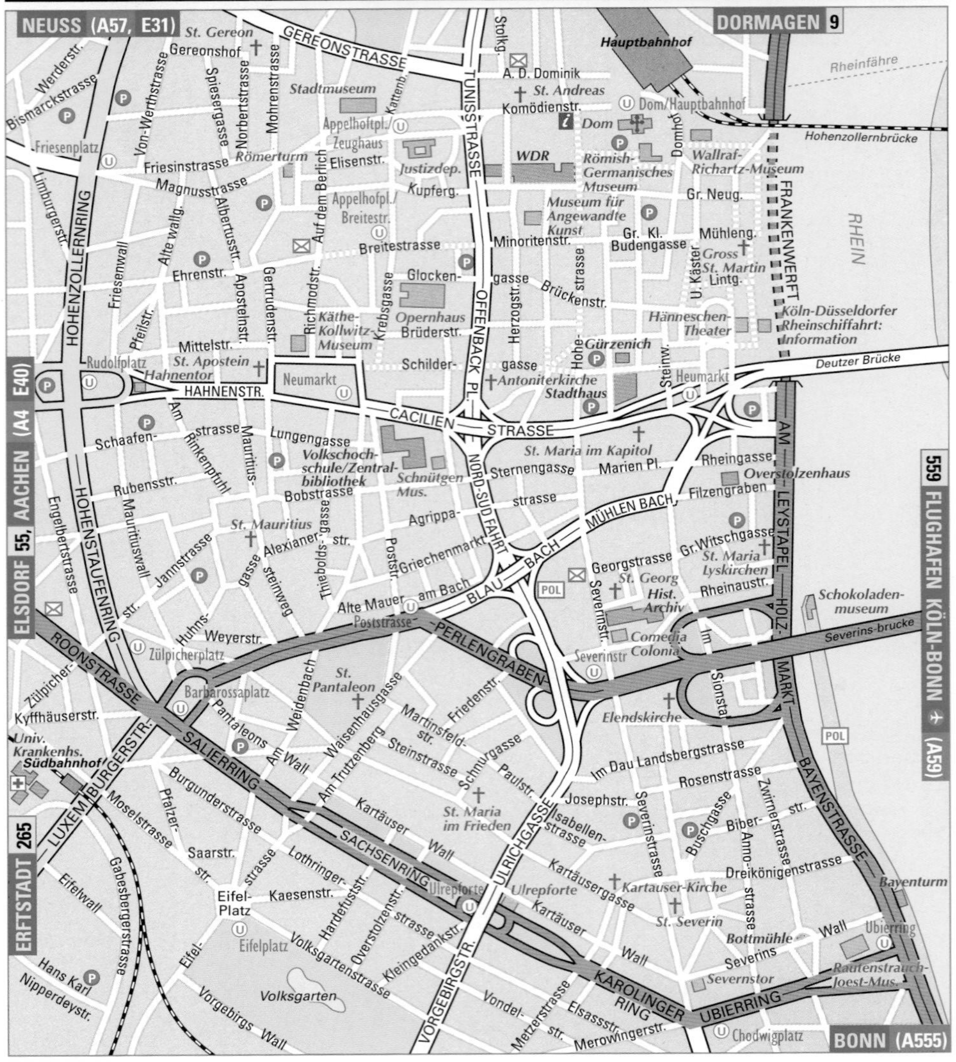

København Copenhagen

0 km 1

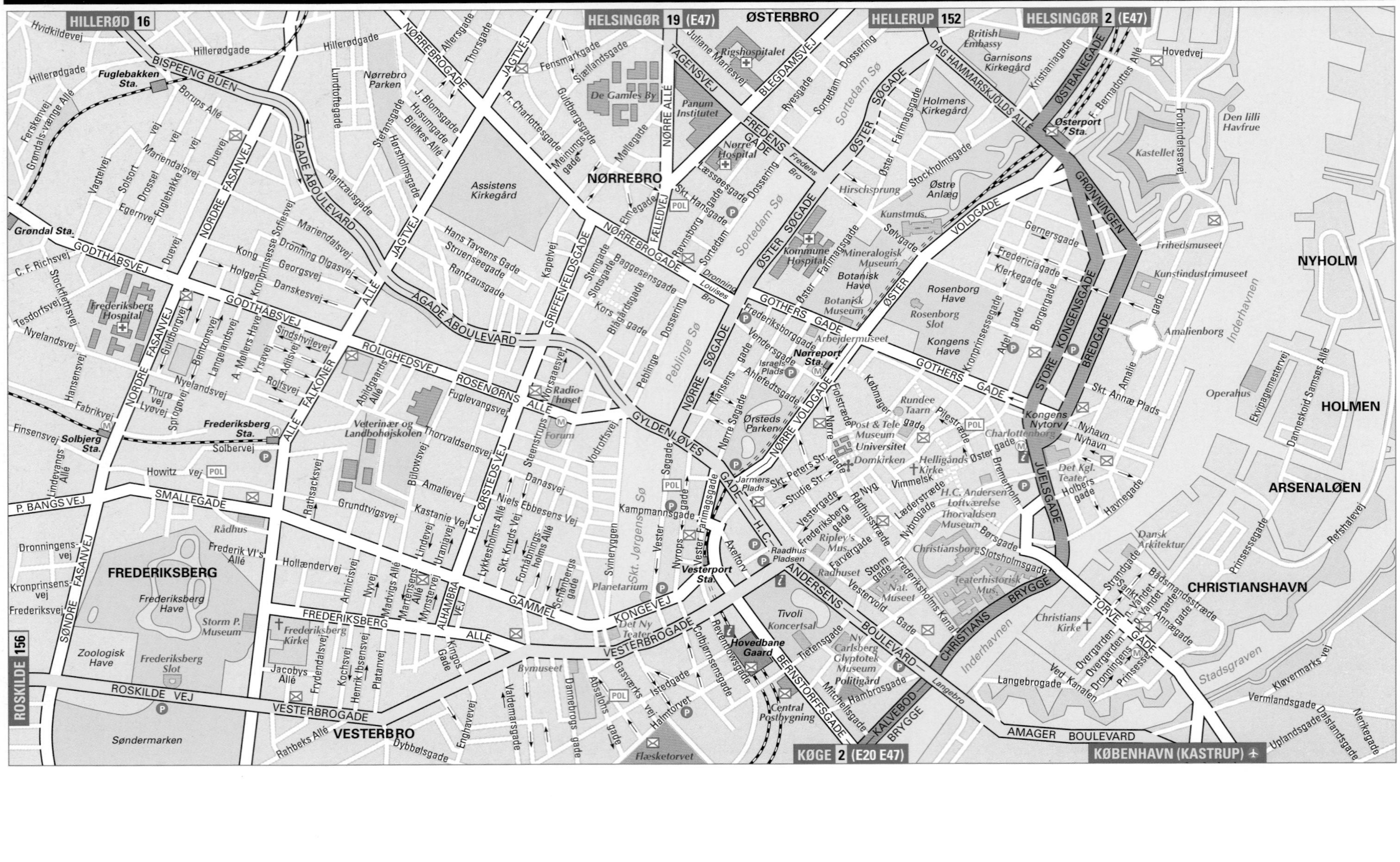

Lisboa Lisbon

0 km 5

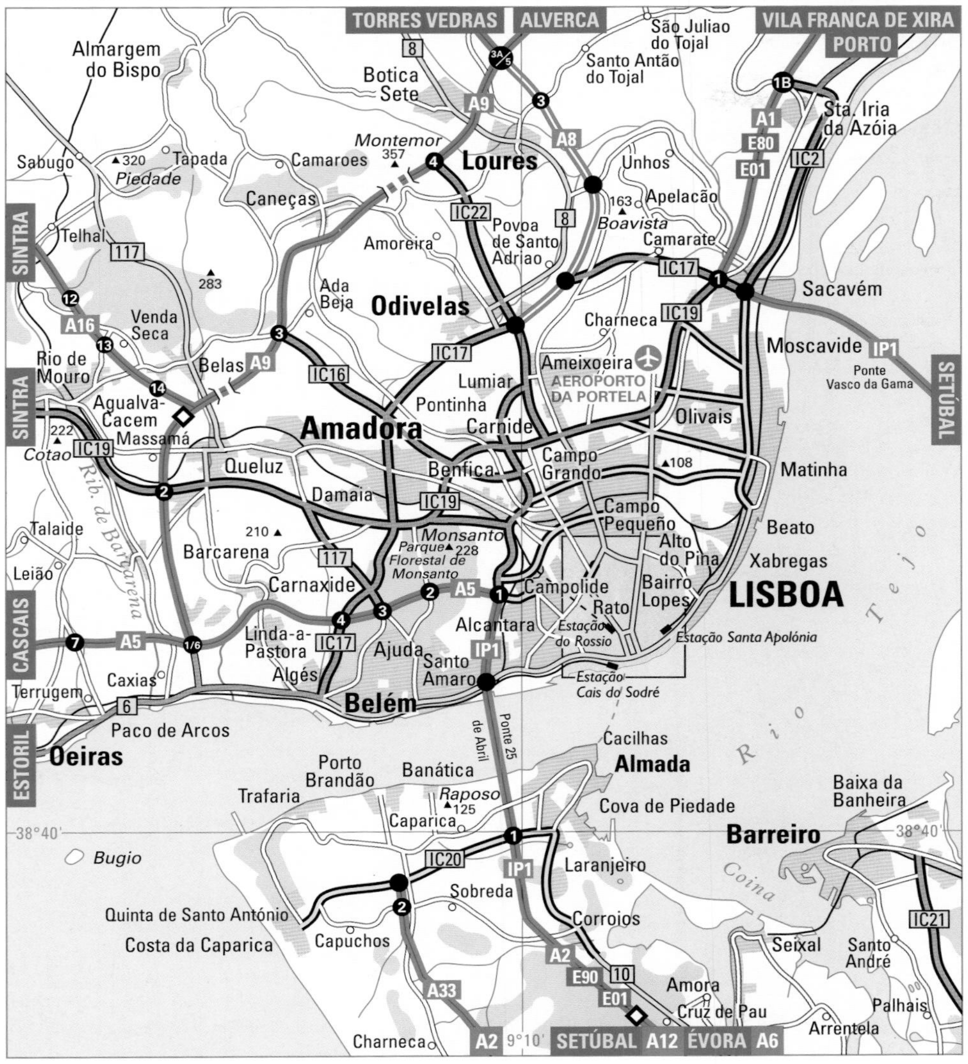

Lisboa Lisbon

0 km 1

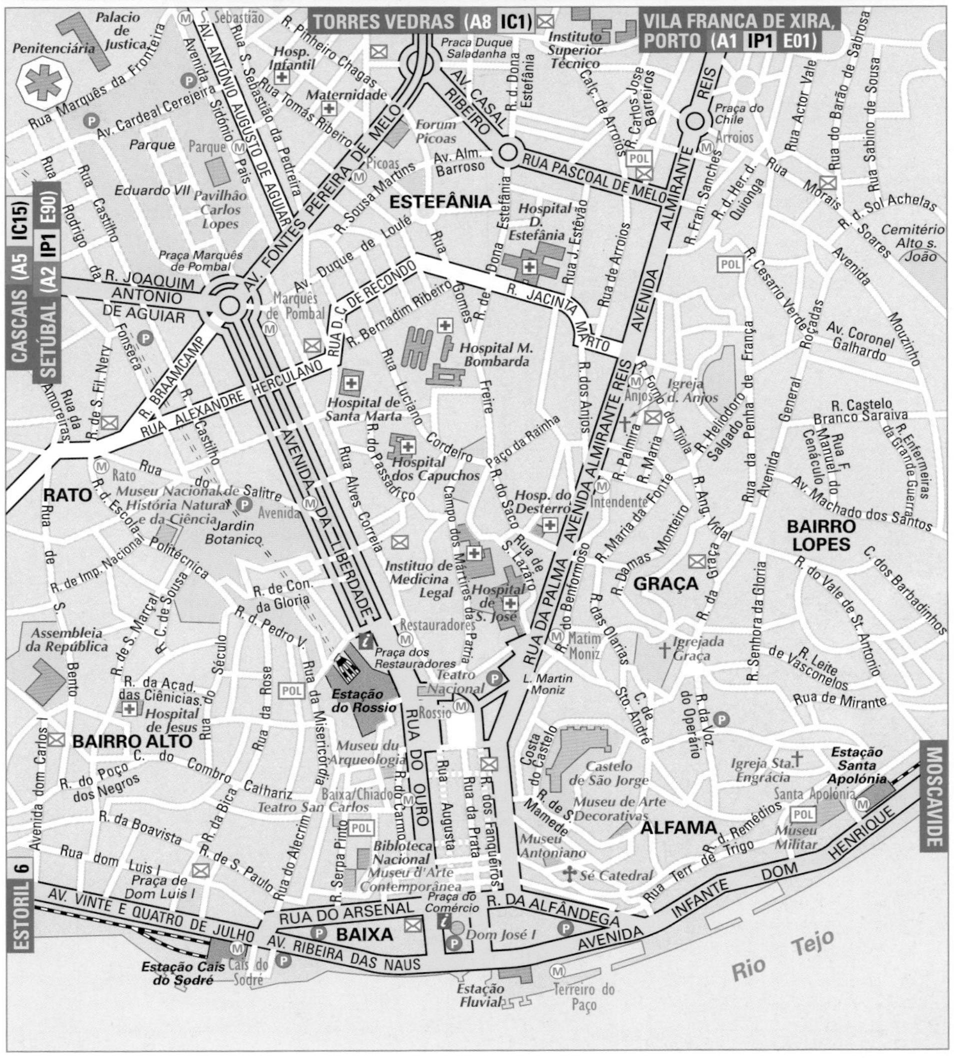

London

0 km 2

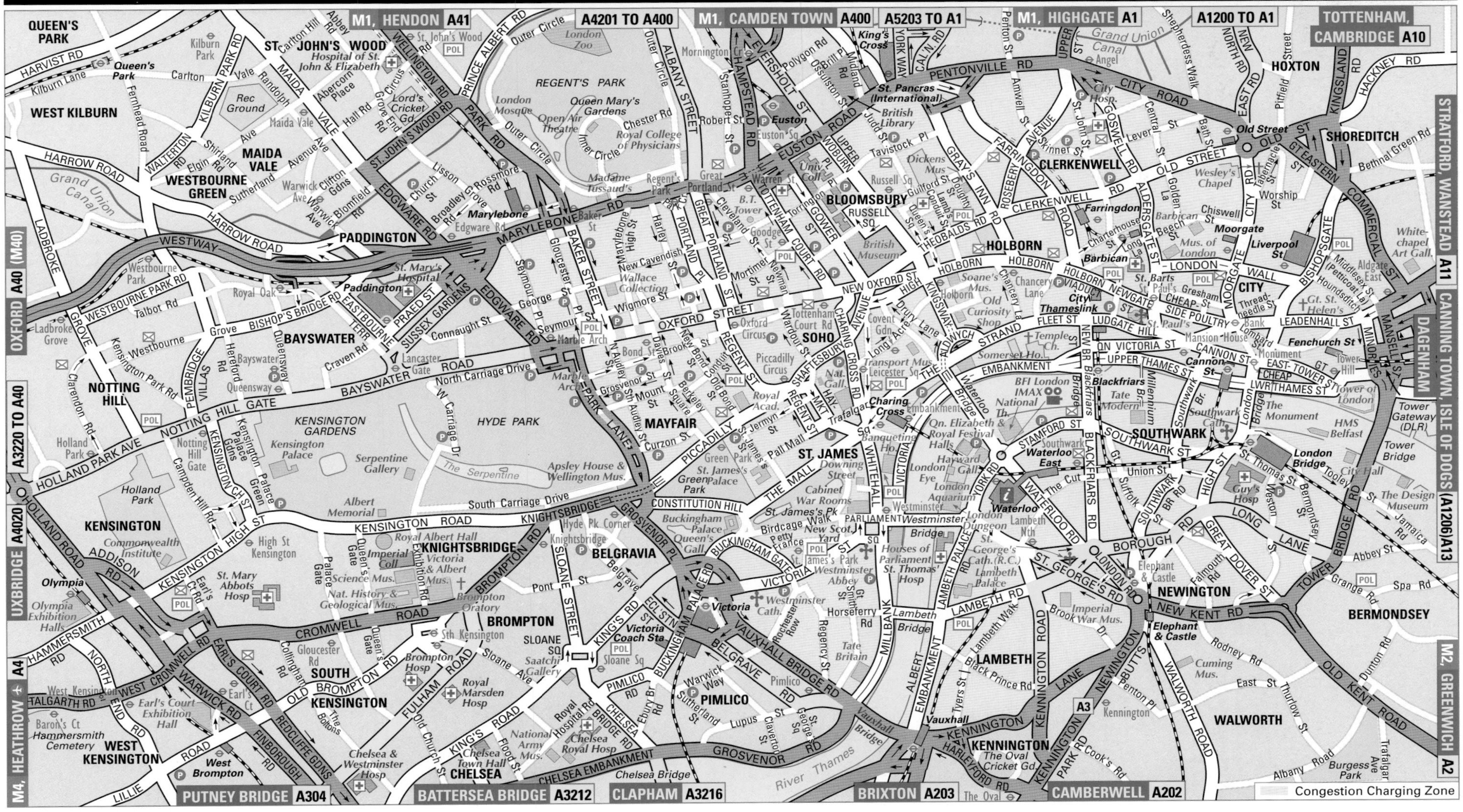

London

0 km 10

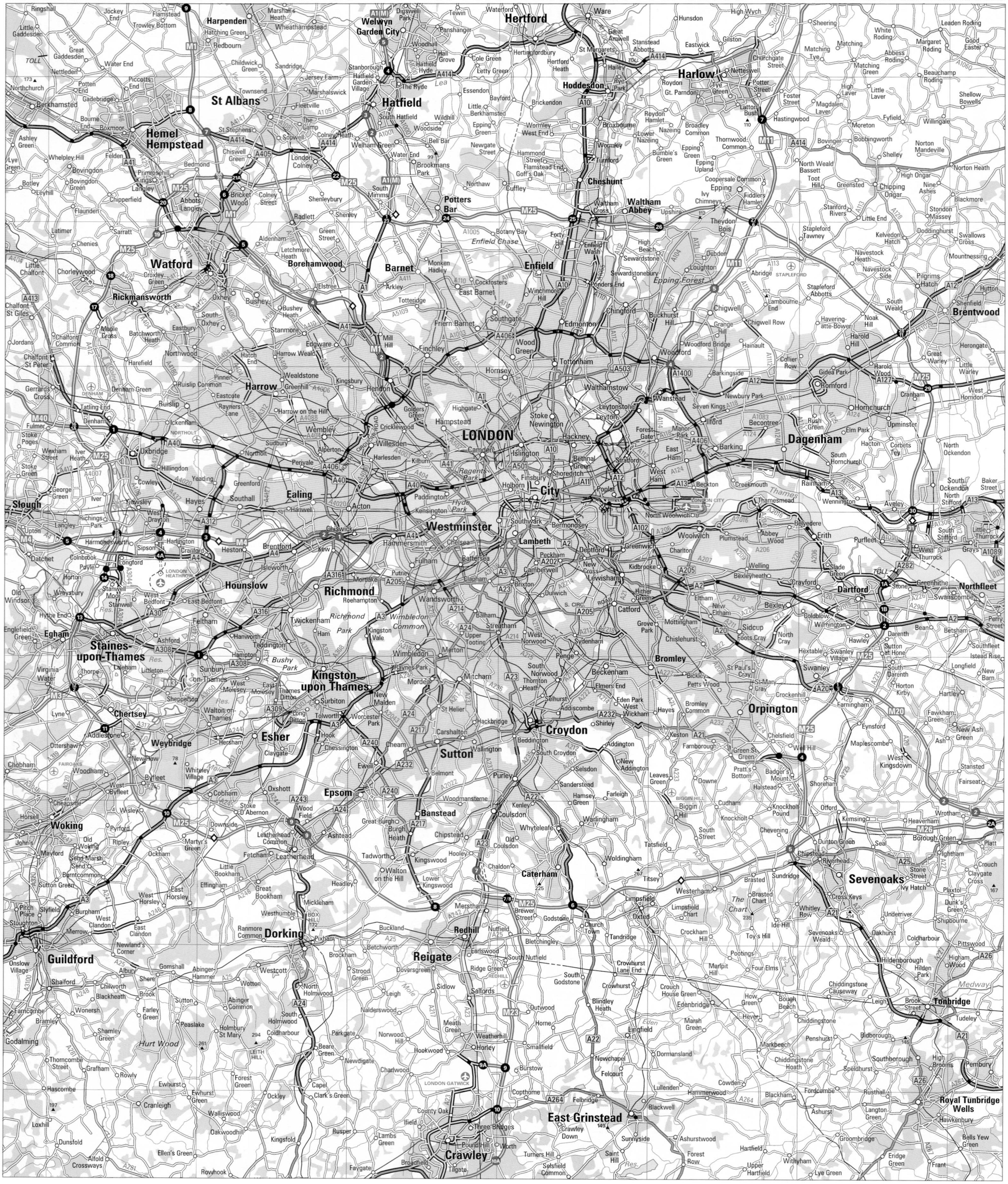

Lyon

0 km 5

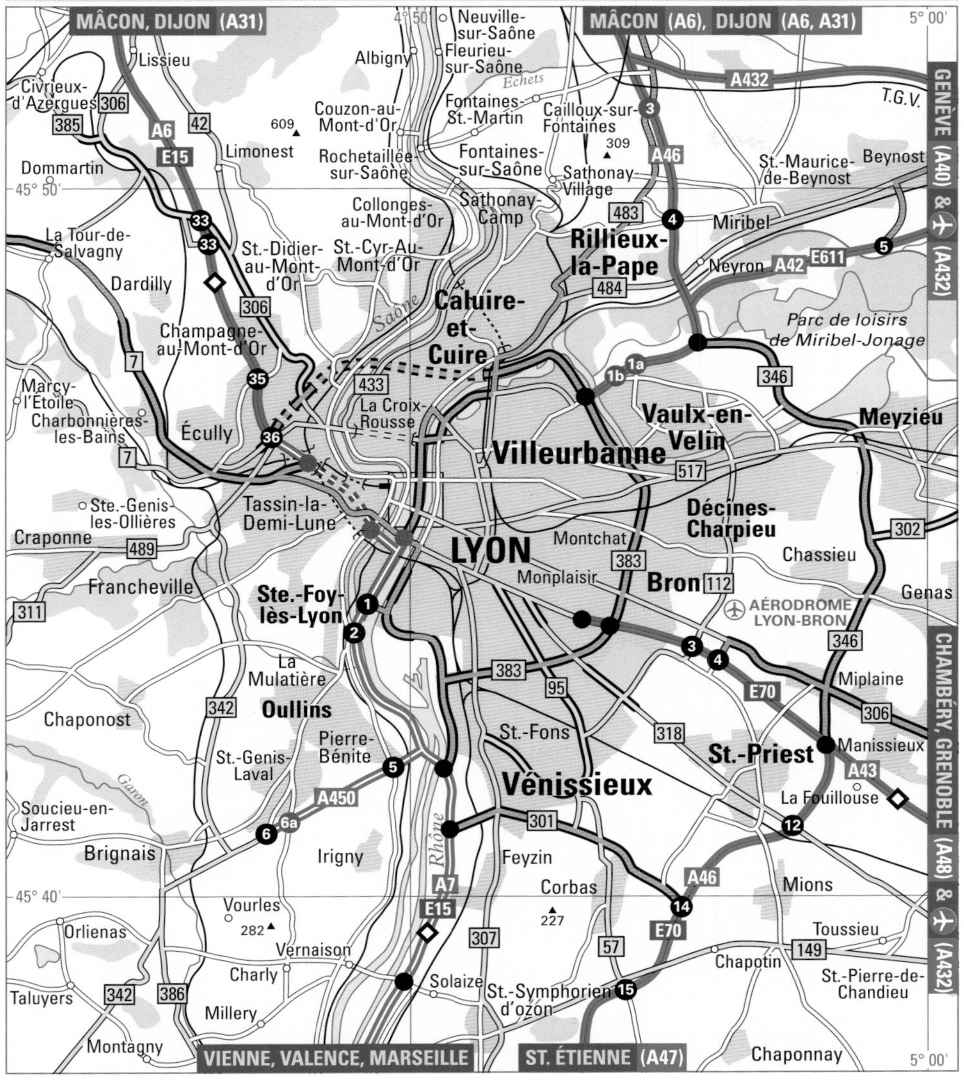

Lyon

0 km 1

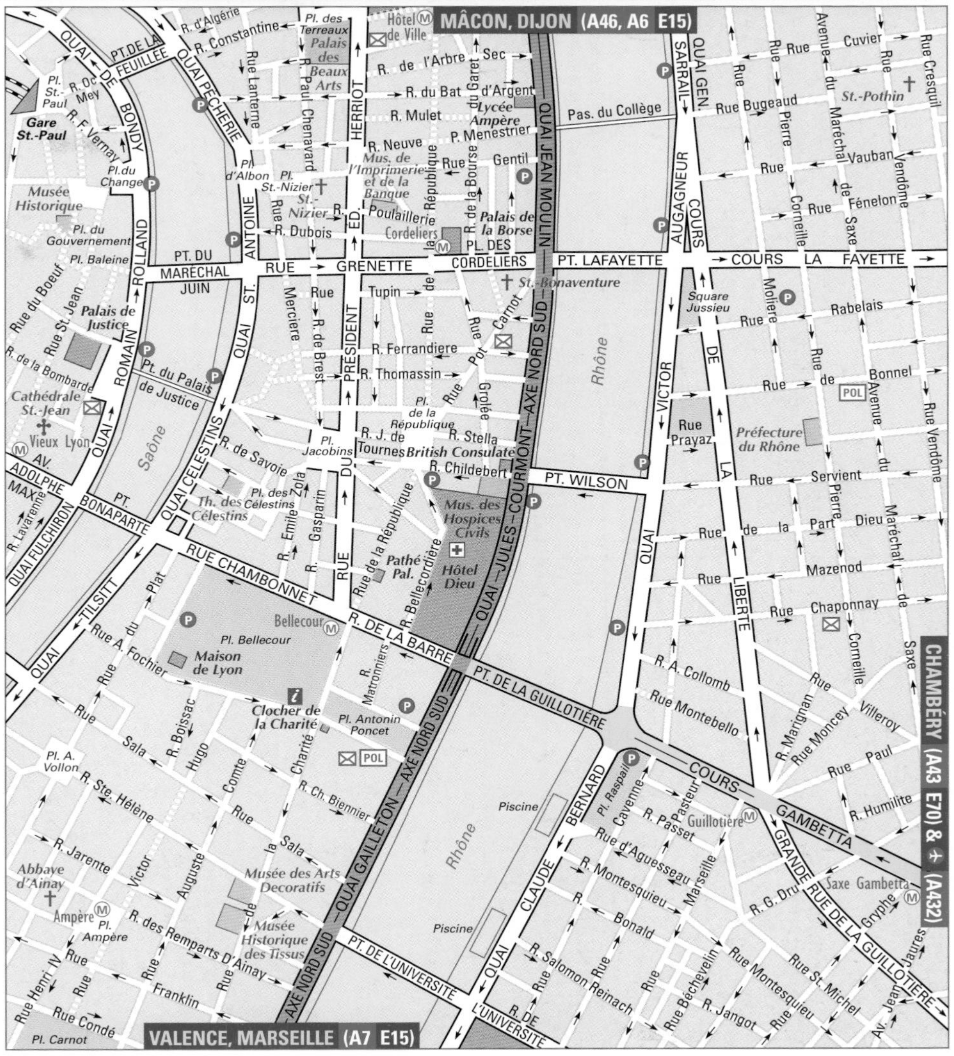

Luxembourg

0 km 0.5

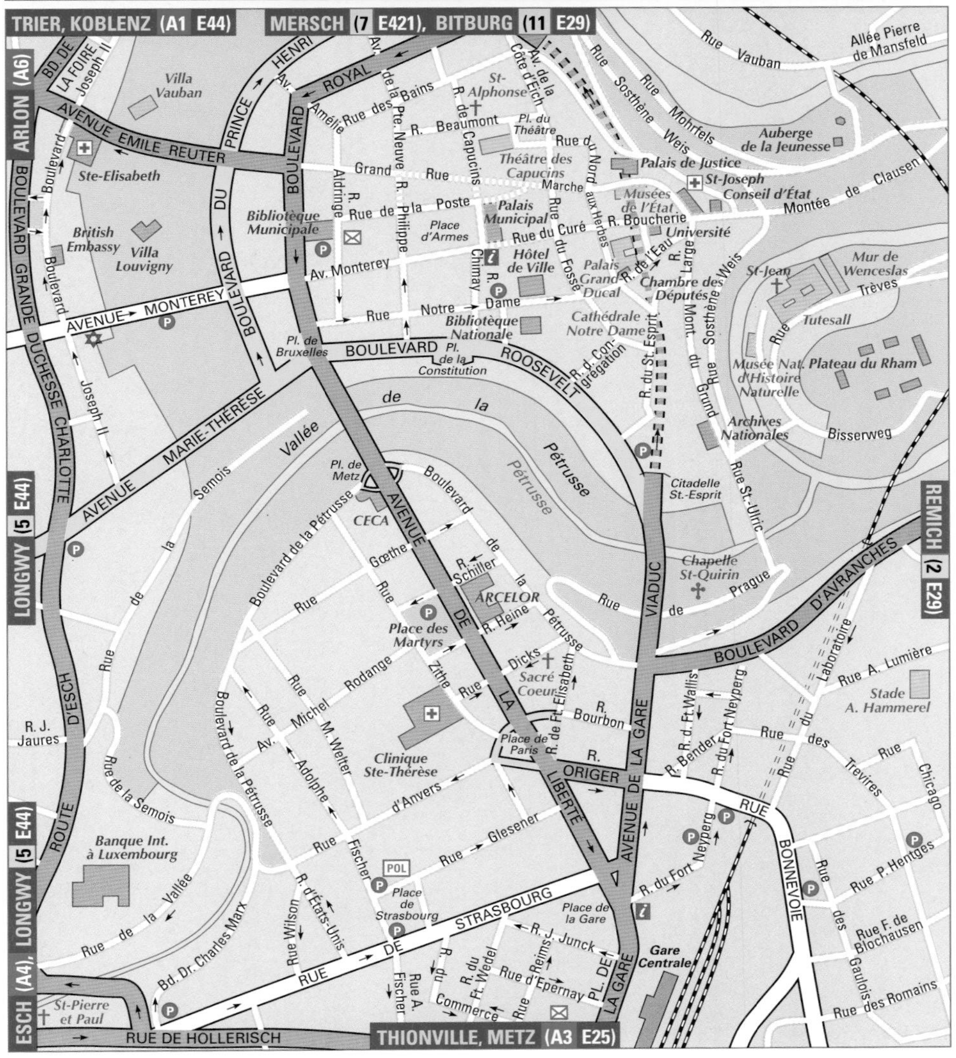

Madrid

0 km 5

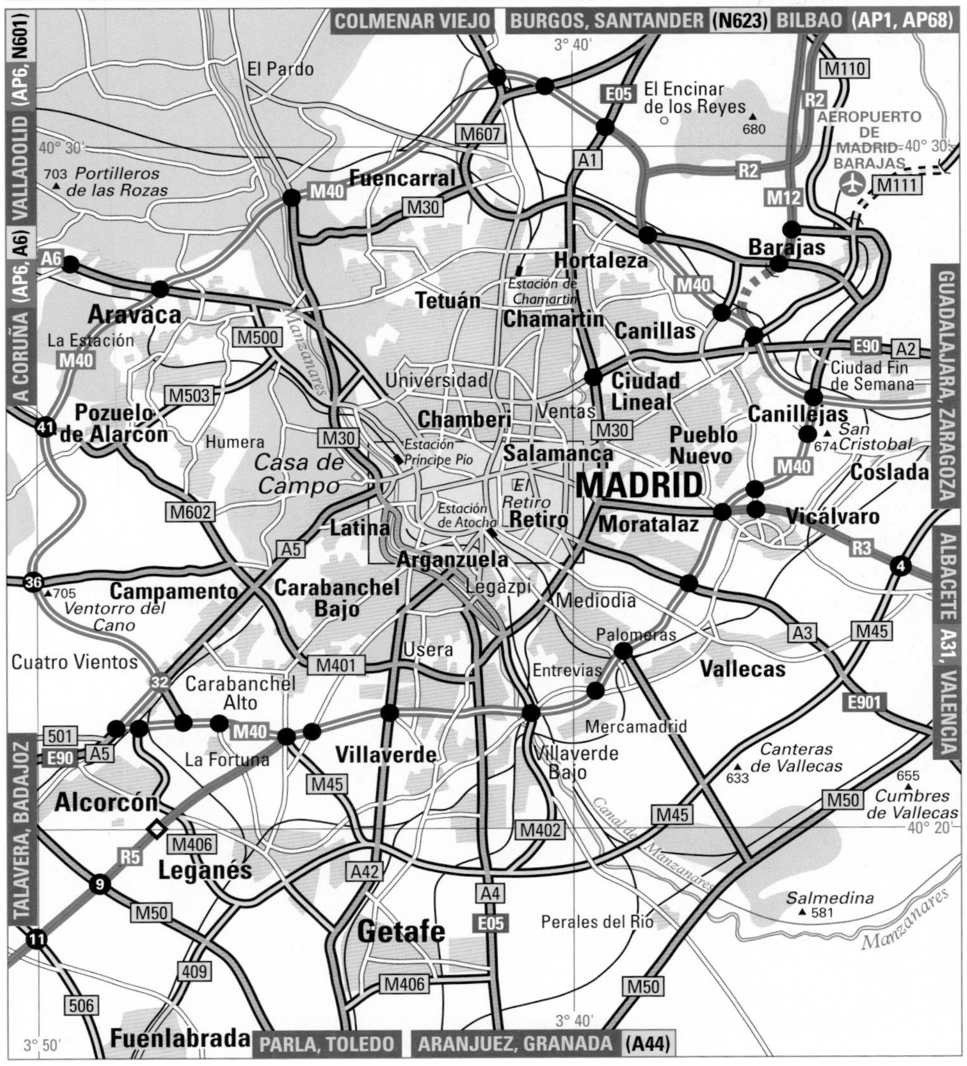

Madrid

0 km 1

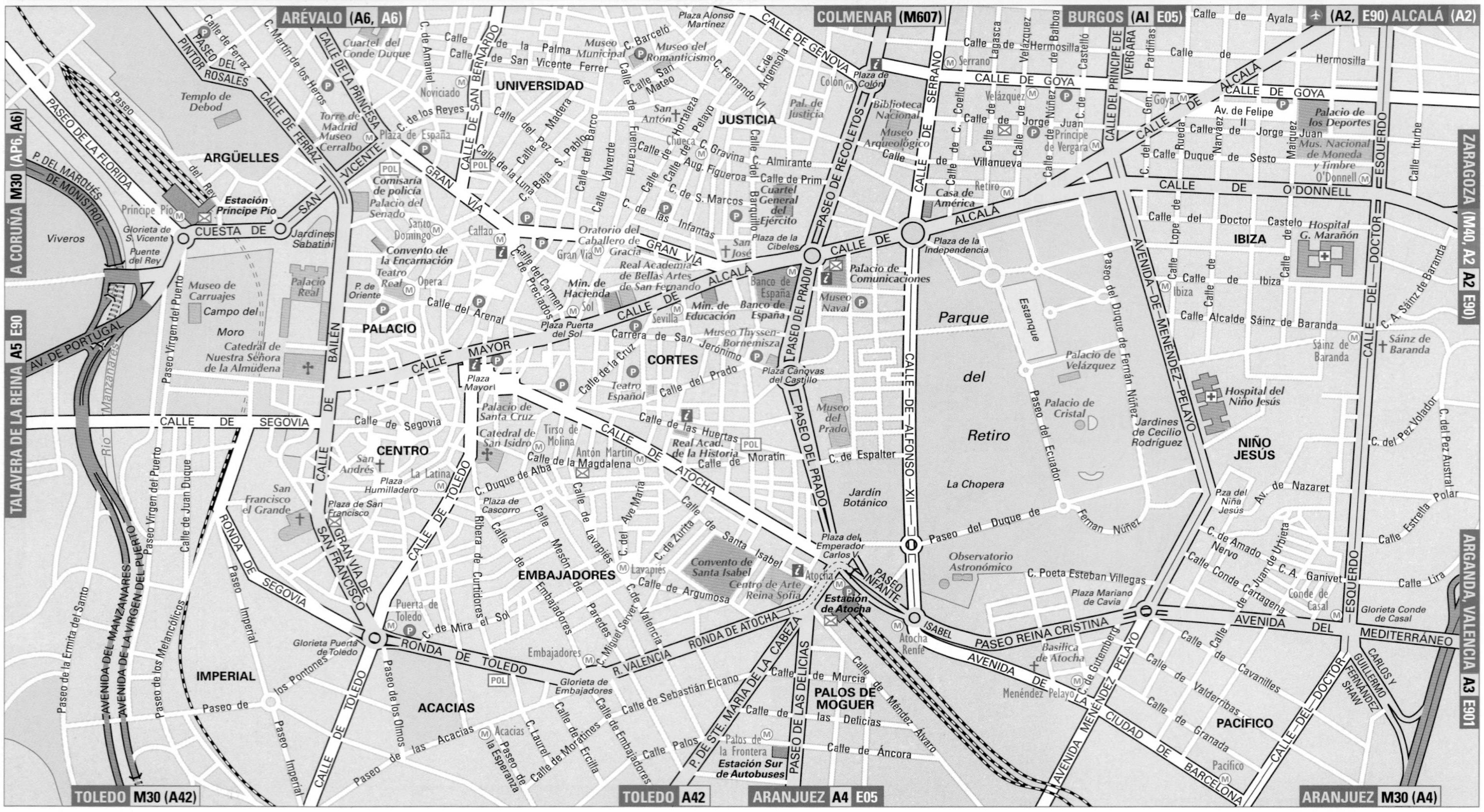

Málaga

0 km 0.5

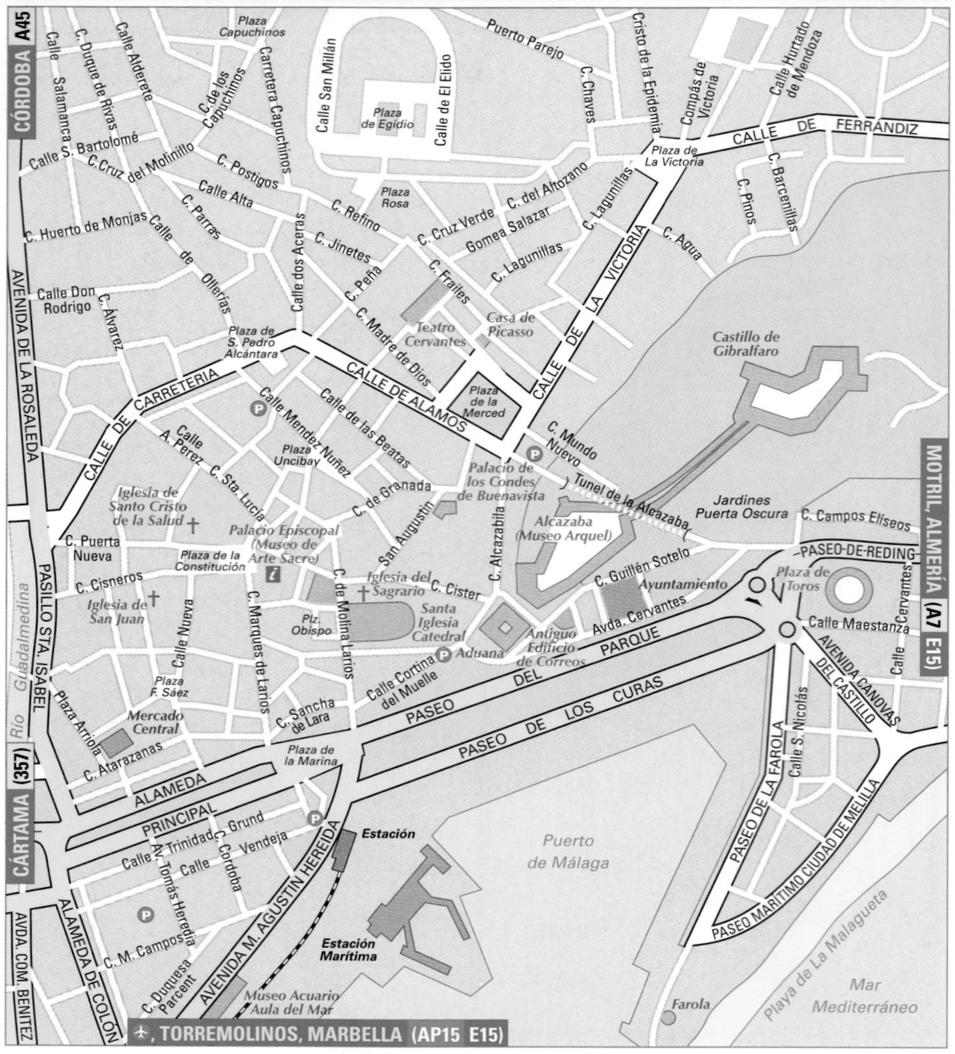

Marseille Marseilles

0 km 0,5

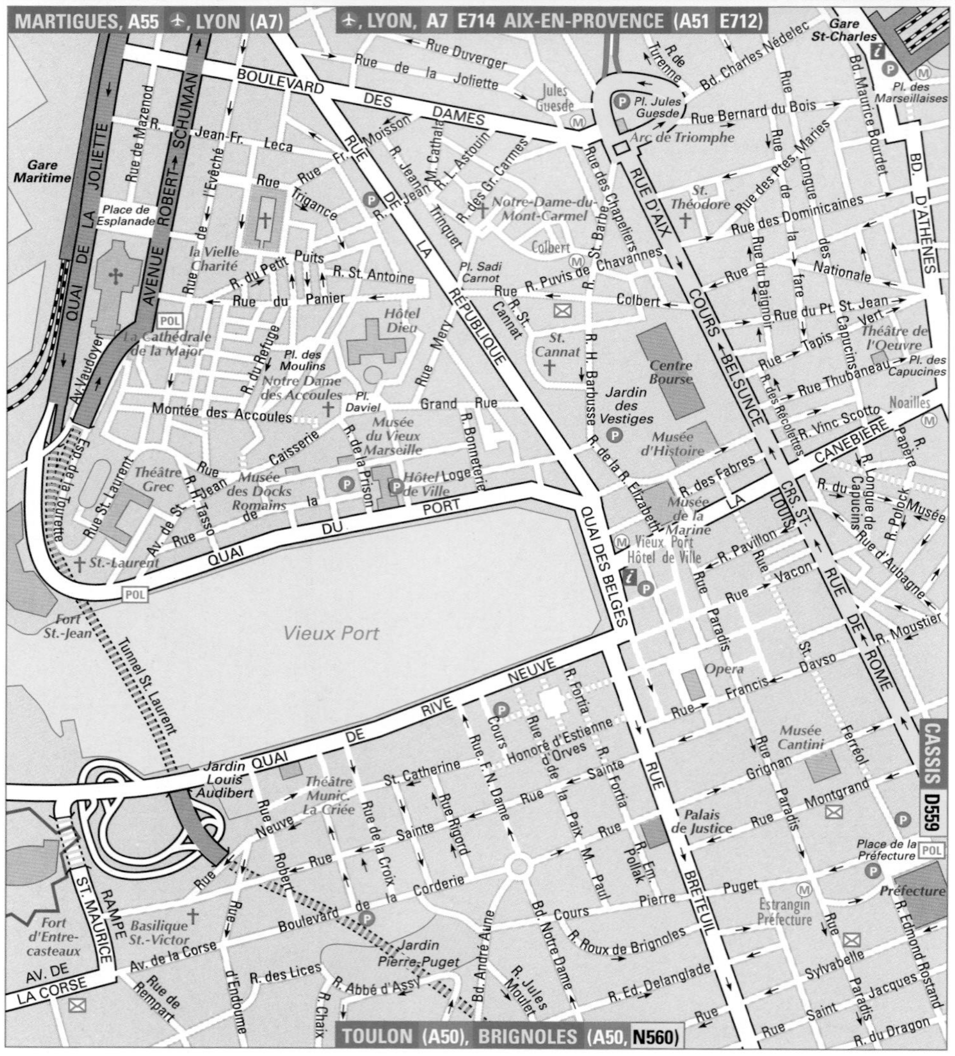

Milano

0 km 5

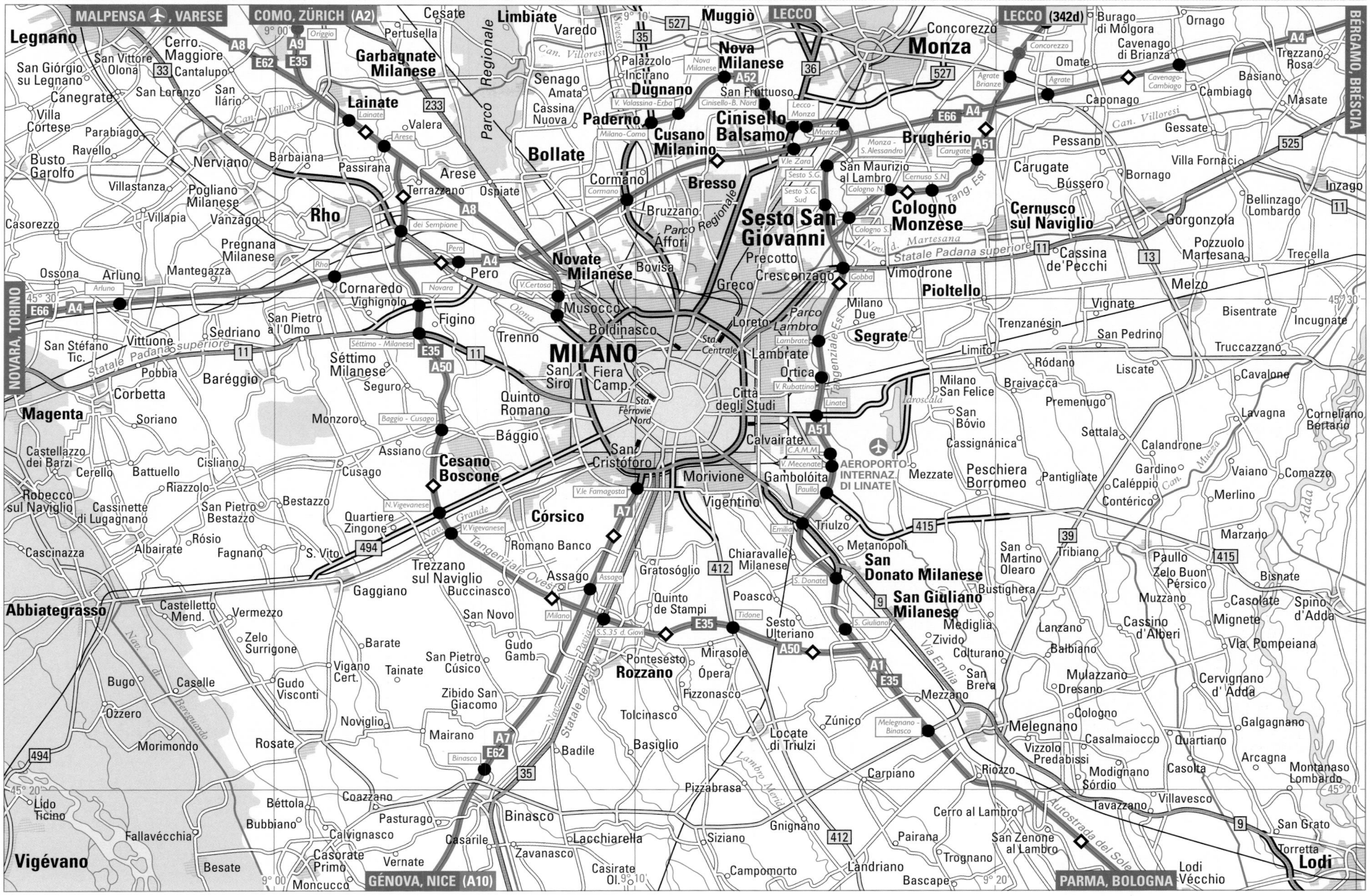

MALPENSA, VARESE
COMO, ZÜRICH (A2)
LECCO
LECCO (342d)
BERGAMO, BRESCIA
NOVARA, TORINO
GÉNOVA, NICE (A10)
PARMA, BOLOGNA
Legnano
Cerro Maggiore
Garbagnate Milanese
Limbiate
Varedo
Muggiò
Monza
Concorezzo
Nova Milanese
Lainate
Bollate
Paderno
Dugnano
Cusano Milanino
Cinisello Balsamo
Brughério
Rho
Arese
Bresso
Sesto San Giovanni
Cologno Monzese
Cernusco sul Naviglio
Novate Milanese
Pero
Vimodrone
Pioltello
Segrate
MILANO
Magenta
Cesano Boscone
Córsico
Trezzano sul Naviglio
Assago
San Donato Milanese
San Giuliano Milanese
Rozzano
Abbiategrasso
Melegnano
Binasco
Vigévano
Lodi
AEROPORTO INTERNAZ. DI LINATE

Milano Milan

0 km 1

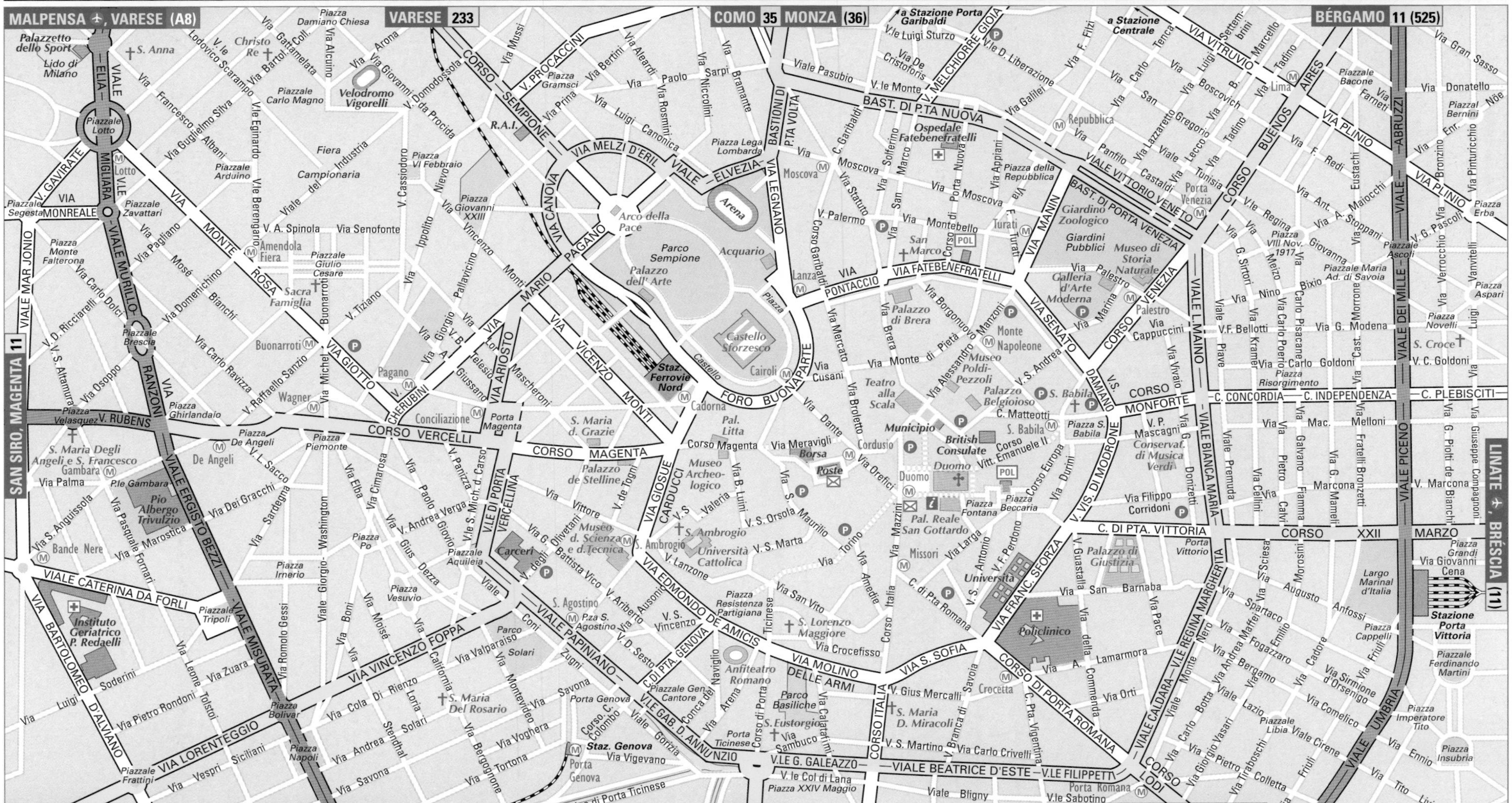

MALPENSA, VARESE (A8)
VARESE 233
COMO 35 MONZA (36)
BÉRGAMO 11 (525)
SAN SIRO, MAGENTA 11
LINATE, BRESCIA (11)
ABBIATEGRASSO 494
GÉNOVA (A7 E62)
PAVIA 35
LODI 9 PARMA (A51, A1)
Arena
Parco Sempione
Castello Sforzesco
Staz. Ferrovie Nord
Duomo
Stazione Porta Vittoria
Policlinico
Università Cattolica
Staz. Genova

Moskva Moscow

0 km 5

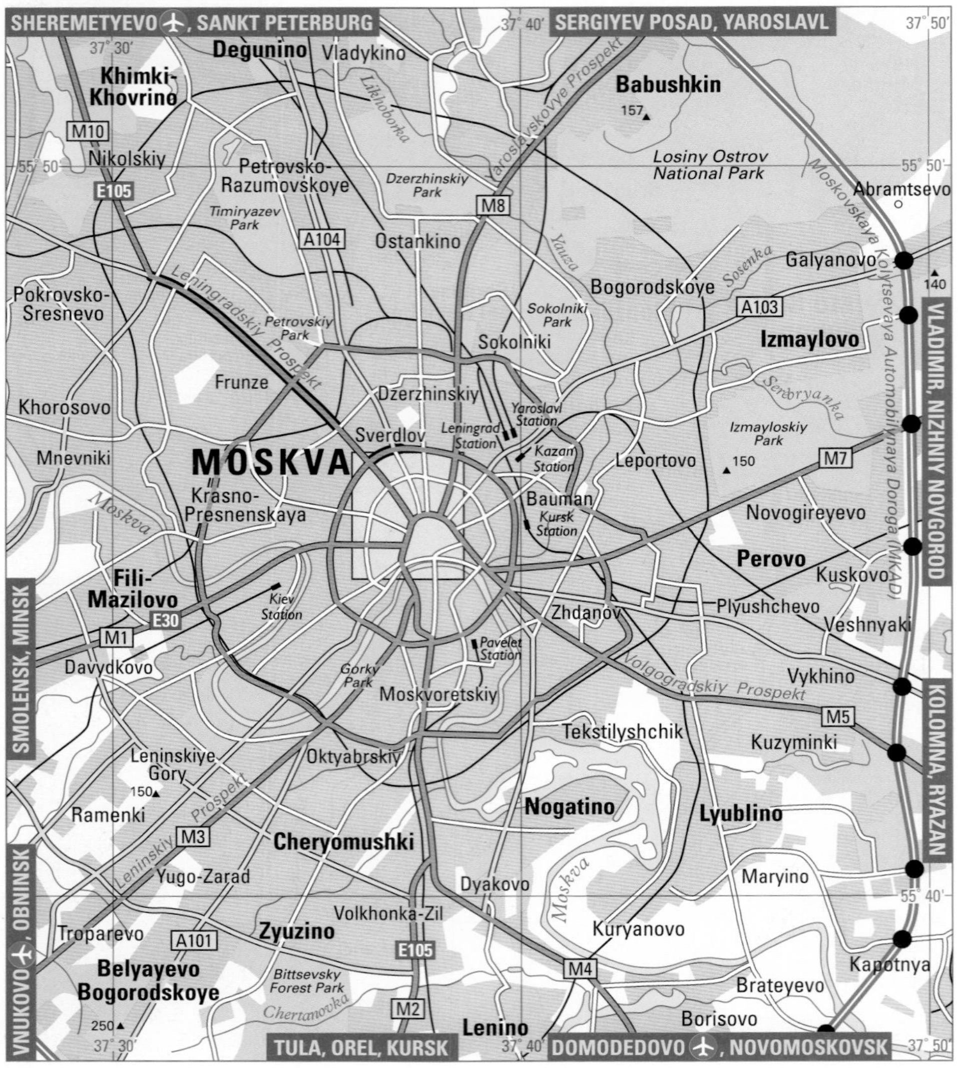

Moskva

0 km 1

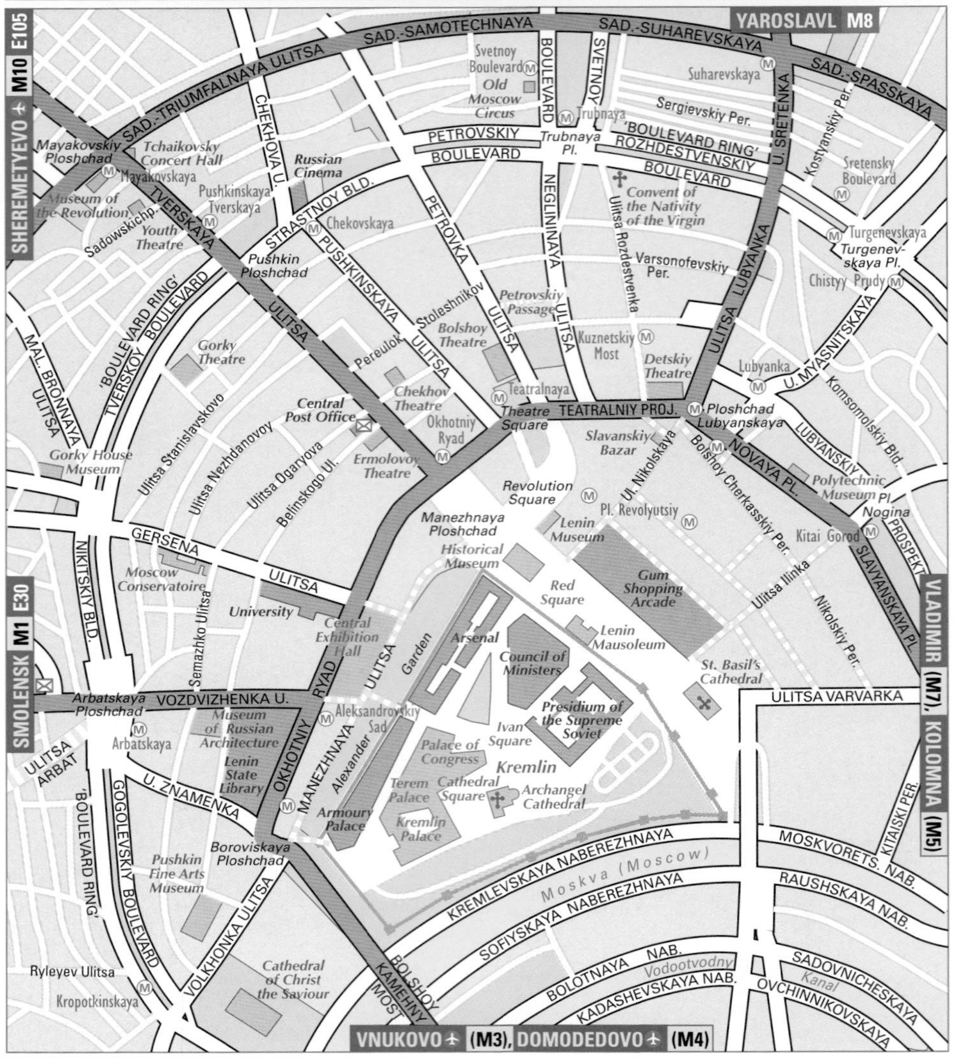

München Munich

0 km 5

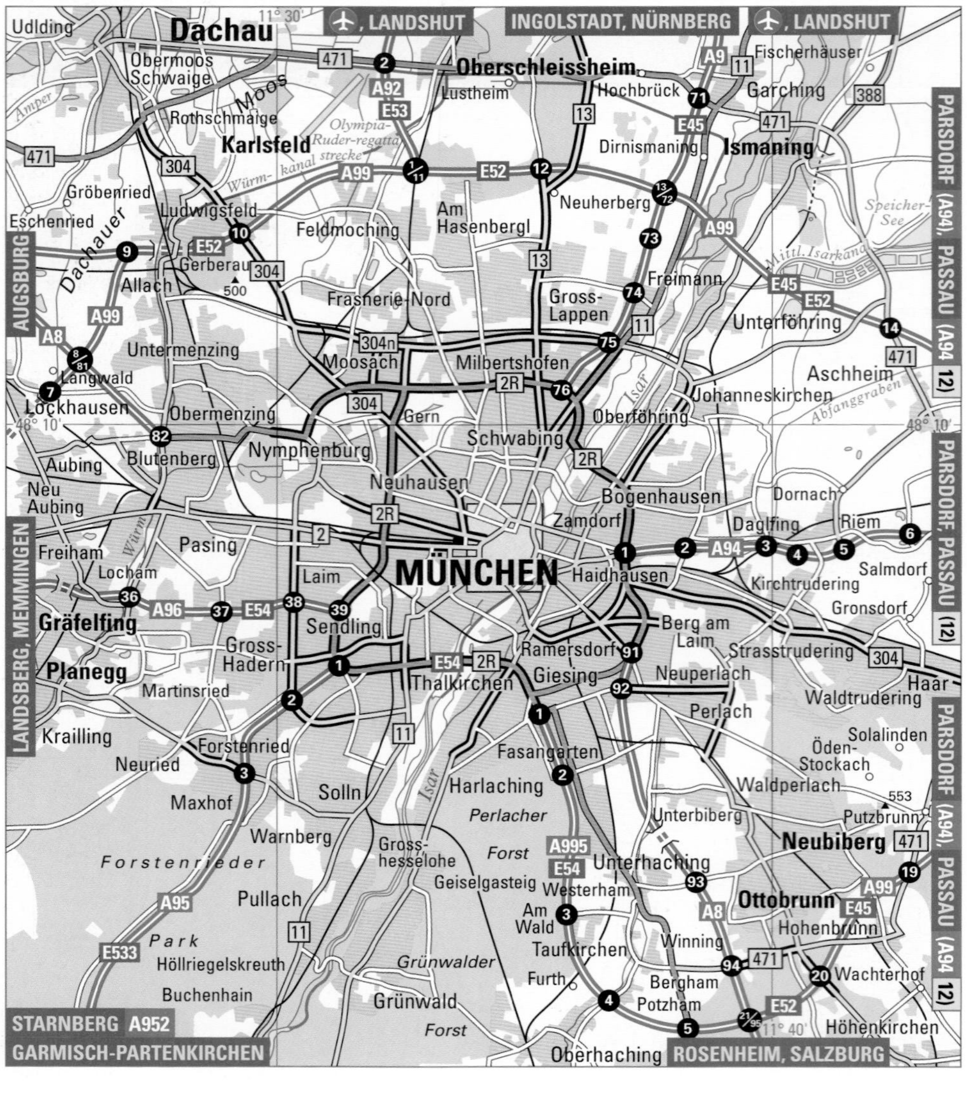

München Munich

0 km 1

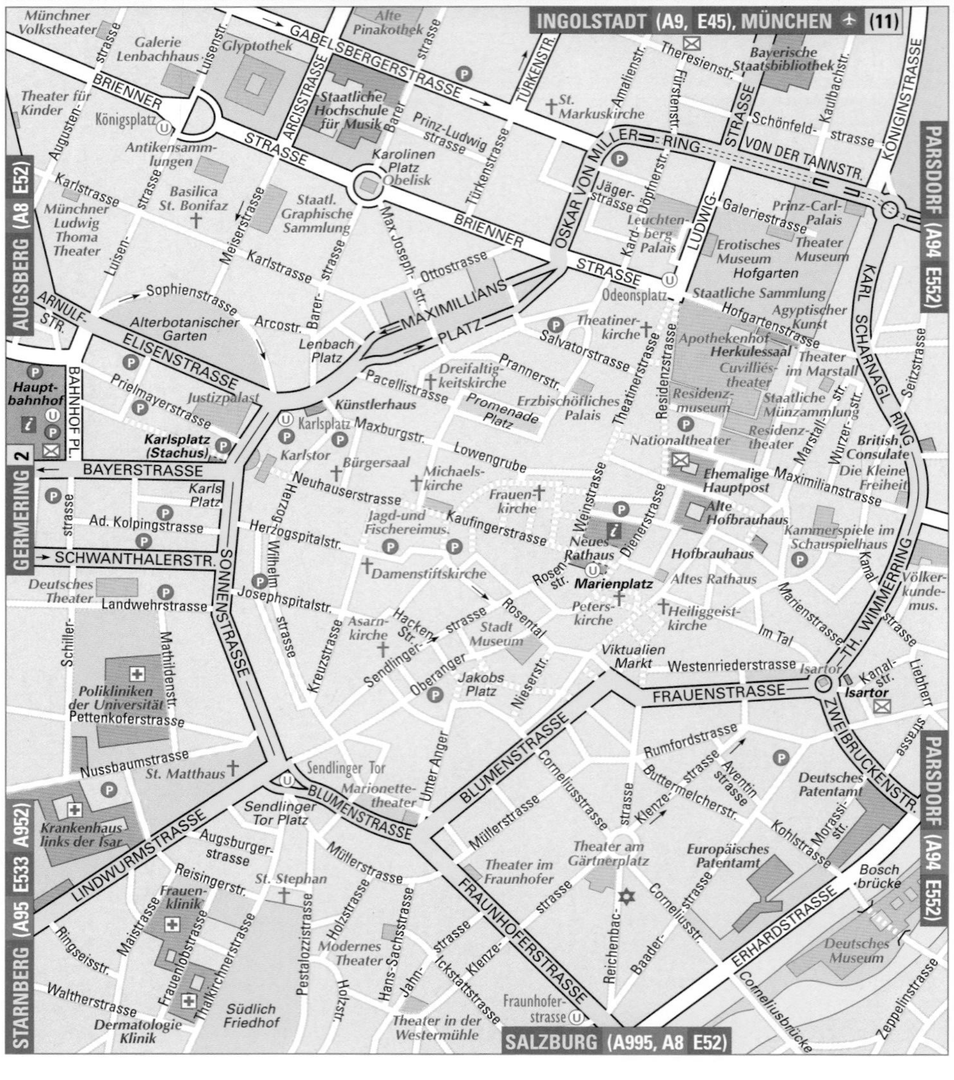

Nápoli Naples

0 km 5

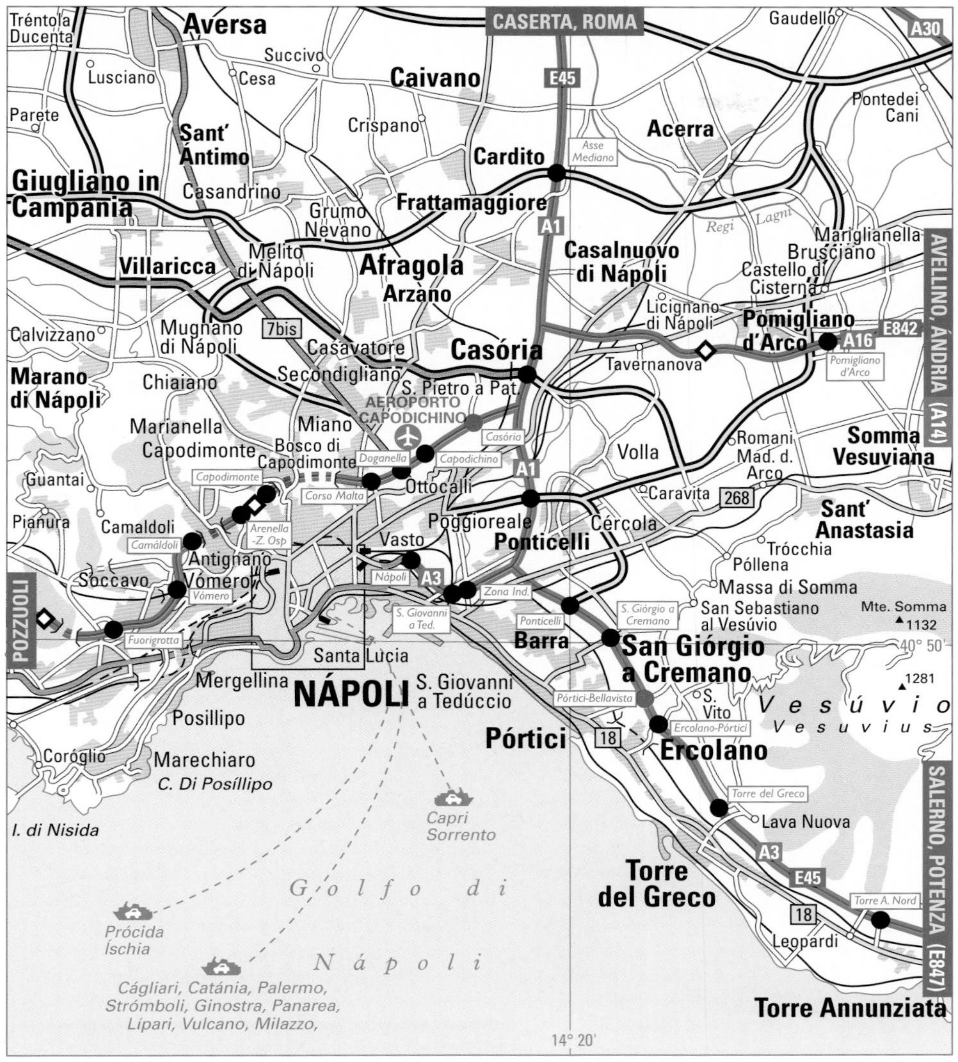

Nápoli Naples

0 km 1

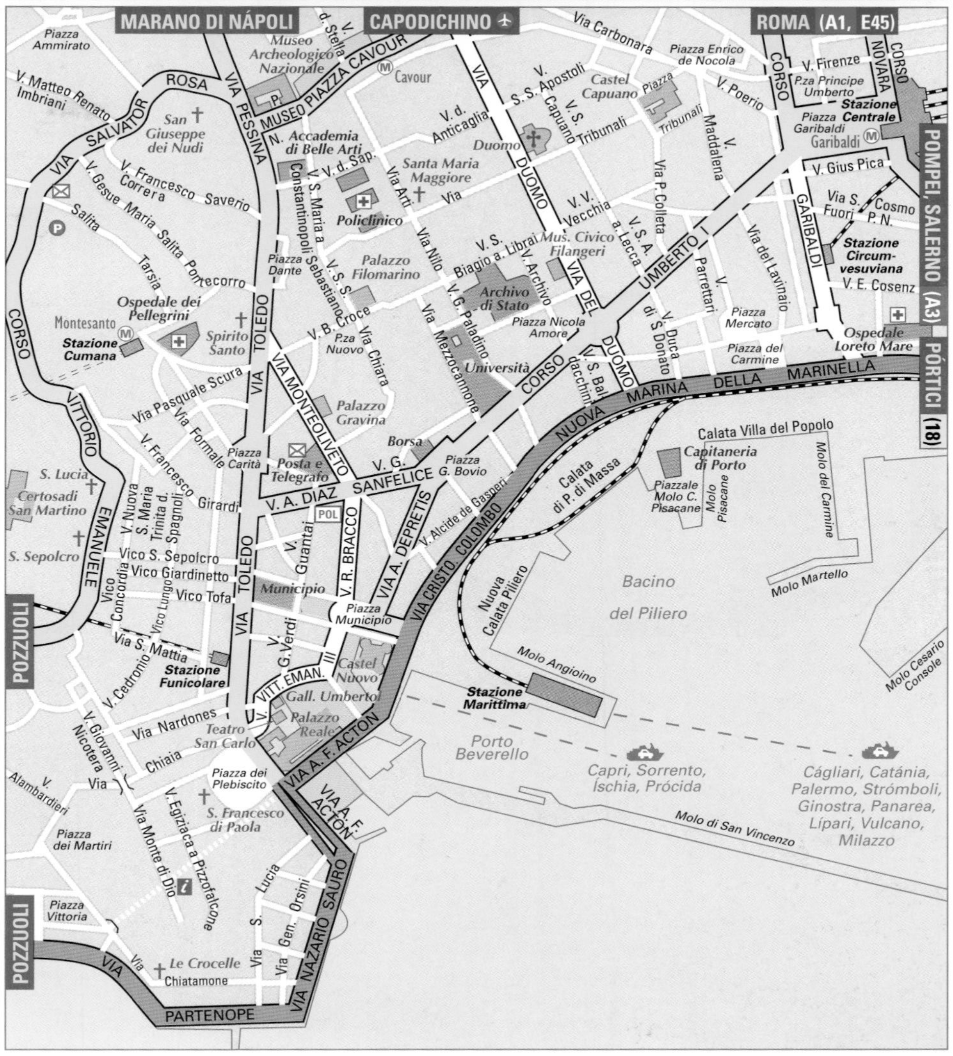

Oslo

0 km 5

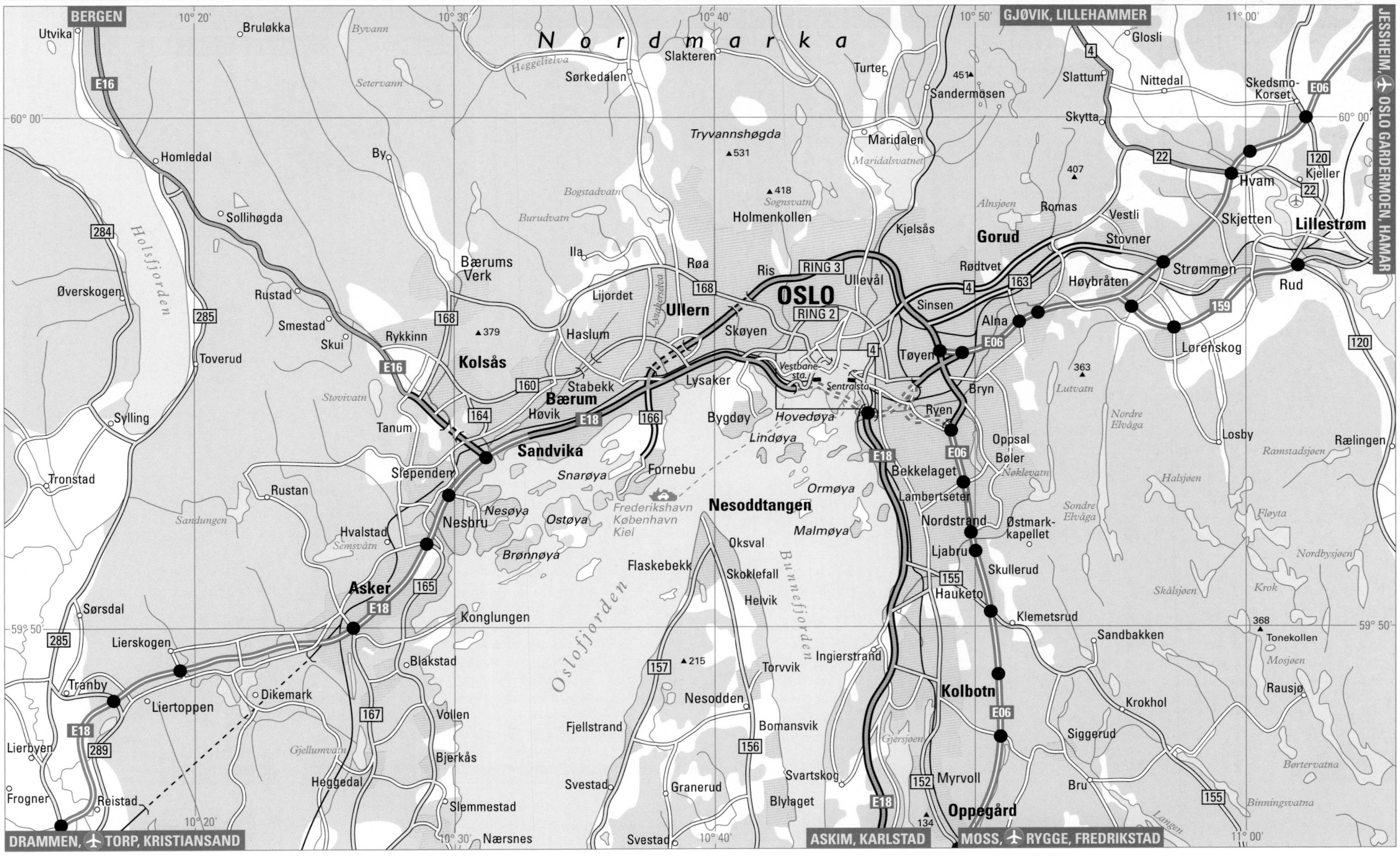

Oslo

0 km 0.5

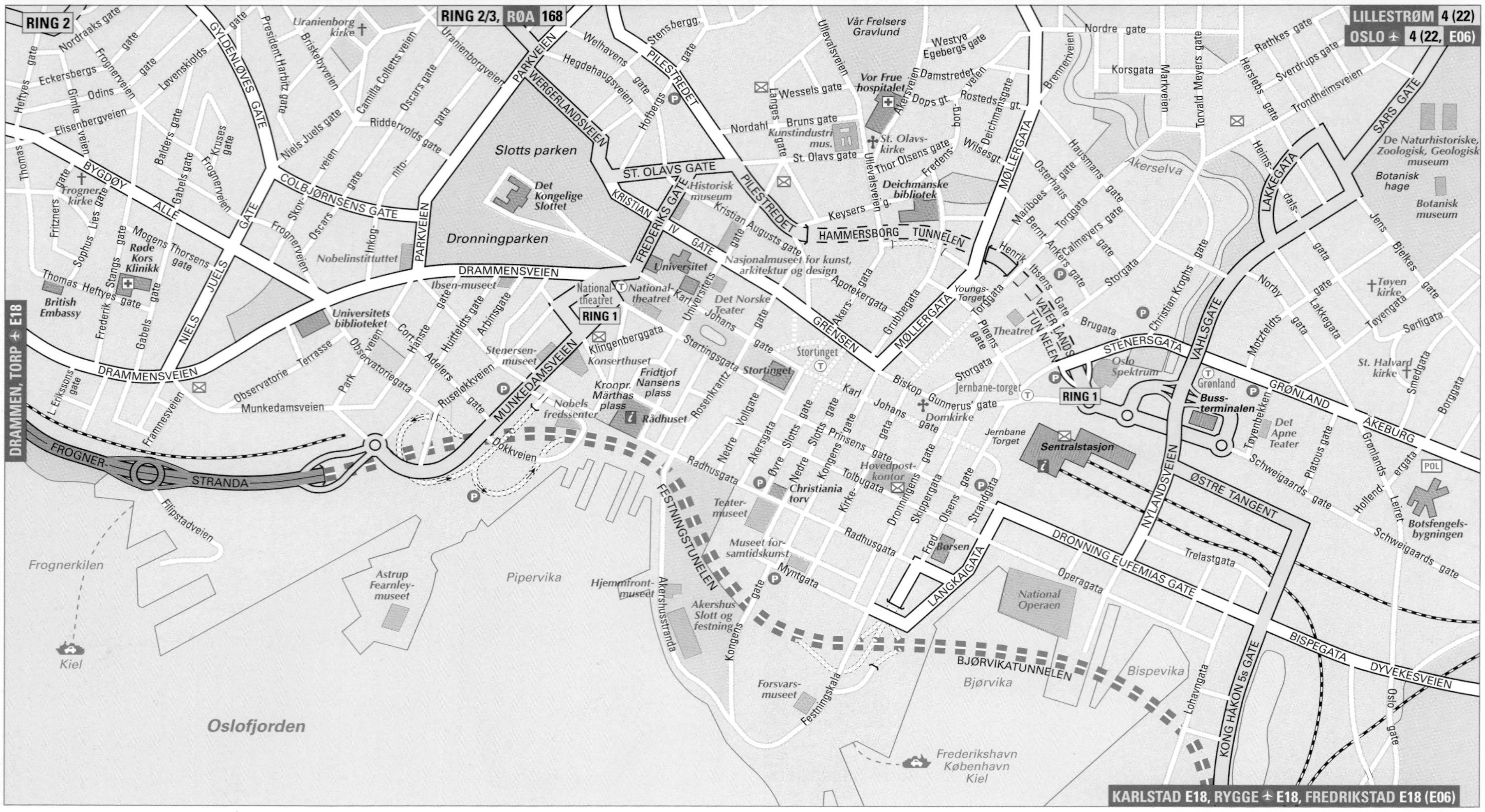
RING 2
RING 2/3, ROA 168
LILLESTRØM 4 (22)
OSLO ✈ 4 (22, E06)
DRAMMEN, TORP ✈ E18
KARLSTAD E18, RYGGE ✈ E18, FREDRIKSTAD E18 (E06)
RING 1
Slotts parken
Det Kongelige Slottet
Dronningparken
DRAMMENSVEIEN
BYGDØY ALLÉ
PARKVEIEN
ST. OLAVS GATE
HAMMERSBORG TUNNELEN
Nasjonalmuseet for kunst, arkitektur og design
Universitet
Nationaltheatret
Stortinget
Rådhuset
Oslo Spektrum
Sentralstasjon
Buss-terminalen
Akershus Slott og festning
National Operaen
Bjørvika
BJØRVIKATUNNELEN
Bispevika
Pipervika
Frognerkilen
Oslofjorden
Kiel
Frederikshavn København Kiel
FESTNINGSTUNNELEN
Deichmanske bibliotek
Vår Frelsers Gravlund
Akerselva
Botanisk hage
Botanisk museum
Botsfengels-bygningen
GRØNLAND
DRONNING EUFEMIAS GATE
KONG HÅKON 5s GATE
DYVEKESVEIEN
BISPEGATA
ØSTRE TANGENT

Paris

0 km 1

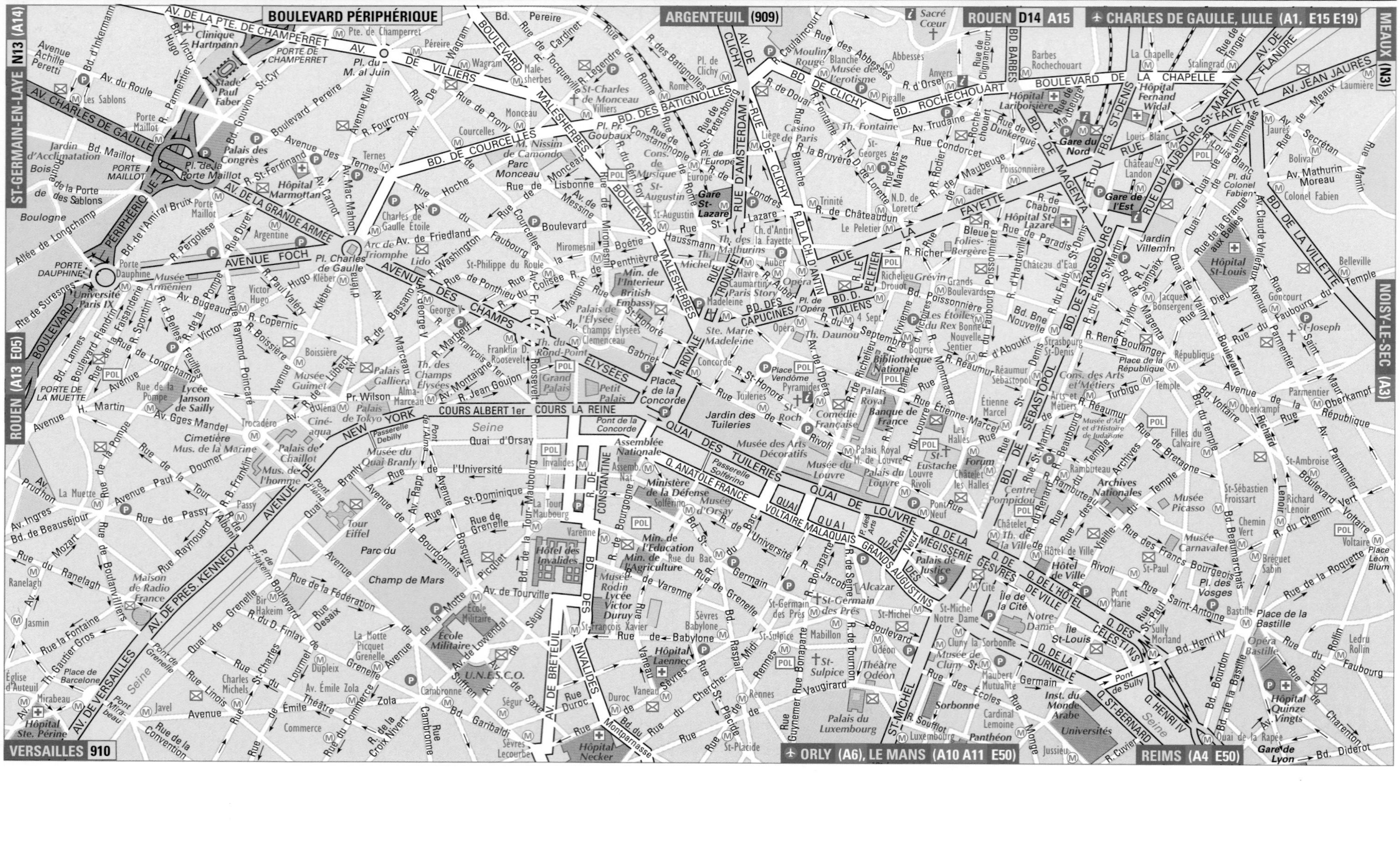
BOULEVARD PÉRIPHÉRIQUE
ARGENTEUIL (909)
ROUEN D14 A15
✈ CHARLES DE GAULLE, LILLE (A1, E15 E19)
MEAUX (N3)
ST-GERMAIN-EN-LAYE N13 (A14)
ROUEN (A13 E05)
NOISY-LE-SEC (A3)
VERSAILLES 910
✈ ORLY (A6), LE MANS (A10 A11 E50)
REIMS (A4 E50)
AV. CHARLES DE GAULLE
AVENUE FOCH
AVENUE DES CHAMPS ELYSÉES
Arc de Triomphe
Seine
Tour Eiffel
Champ de Mars
Hôtel des Invalides
Musée d'Orsay
Jardin des Tuileries
Musée du Louvre
QUAI DES TUILERIES
QUAI DU LOUVRE
Gare St-Lazare
Gare du Nord
Gare de l'Est
Gare de Lyon
Notre Dame
Centre Pompidou
Panthéon
Palais du Luxembourg
Sorbonne
BOULEVARD DE LA CHAPELLE
BD. DE CLICHY
BD. DE COURCELLES
BD. DES BATIGNOLLES
BOULEVARD MALESHERBES
BD. DE STRASBOURG
BD. DE SÉBASTOPOL
Place de la Concorde
Place de la Bastille
Jardin Villemin
Opéra
Madeleine
Moulin Rouge
Sacré Cœur
U.N.E.S.C.O.
École Militaire
Universite Paris IX

Paris

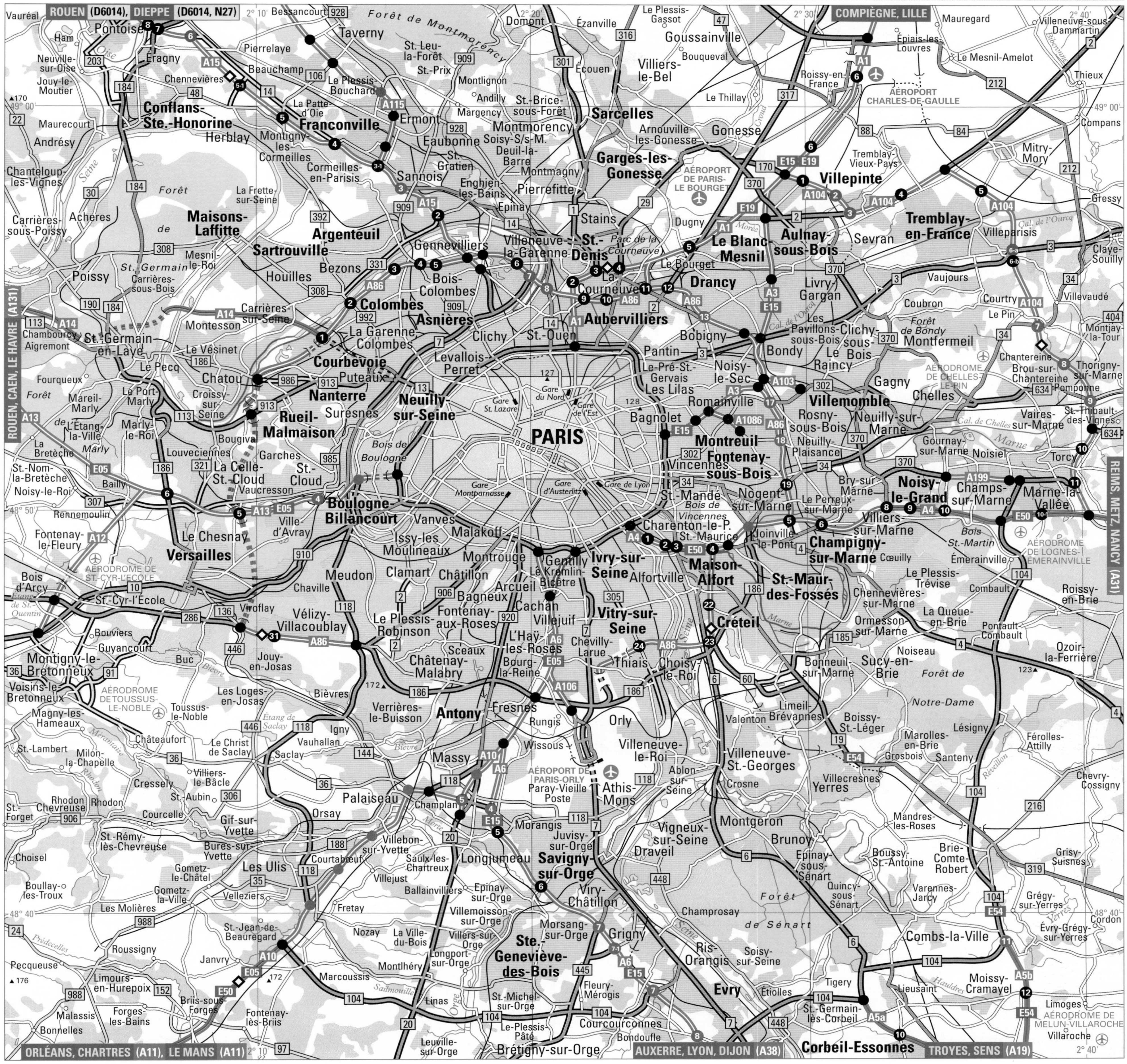

0 km 5
ROUEN (D6014), DIEPPE (D6014, N27)
COMPIÈGNE, LILLE
ROUEN, CAEN, LE HAVRE (A13)
REIMS, METZ, NANCY (A31)
ORLÉANS, CHARTRES (A11), LE MANS (A11)
AUXERRE, LYON, DIJON (A38)
TROYES, SENS (A19)
PARIS
Pontoise
Taverny
Forêt de Montmorency
Conflans-Ste.-Honorine
Franconville
Herblay
Ermont
Eaubonne
Montmorency
Sarcelles
Goussainville
Villiers-le-Bel
Garges-lès-Gonesse
Gonesse
AÉROPORT CHARLES-DE-GAULLE
AÉROPORT DE PARIS-LE BOURGET
Roissy-en-France
Villepinte
Tremblay-en-France
Aulnay-sous-Bois
Le Blanc-Mesnil
Sevran
Villeparisis
Drancy
Bobigny
Livry-Gargan
Clichy-sous-Bois
Montfermeil
Bondy
Le Raincy
Gagny
Chelles
Villemomble
Neuilly-sur-Marne
Rosny-sous-Bois
Noisy-le-Sec
Romainville
Pantin
Bagnolet
Montreuil
Fontenay-sous-Bois
Vincennes
St.-Mandé
Nogent-sur-Marne
Noisy-le-Grand
Champs-sur-Marne
Marne-la-Vallée
Torcy
Maisons-Laffitte
Sartrouville
Argenteuil
Gennevilliers
Villeneuve-la-Garenne
St.-Denis
Stains
Aubervilliers
La Courneuve
Le Bourget
Colombes
Bois-Colombes
Asnières
Clichy
St.-Ouen
Levallois-Perret
Courbevoie
Puteaux
Nanterre
Neuilly-sur-Seine
Suresnes
Rueil-Malmaison
Chatou
St.-Germain-en-Laye
Poissy
Houilles
Bezons
Le Vésinet
Montesson
Bougival
Louveciennes
La Celle-St.-Cloud
St.-Cloud
Garches
Vaucresson
Boulogne-Billancourt
Issy-les-Moulineaux
Vanves
Malakoff
Montrouge
Clamart
Meudon
Châtillon
Bagneux
Arcueil
Gentilly
Le Kremlin-Bicêtre
Ivry-sur-Seine
Vitry-sur-Seine
Villejuif
Cachan
L'Haÿ-les-Roses
Fontenay-aux-Roses
Le Plessis-Robinson
Sceaux
Bourg-la-Reine
Châtenay-Malabry
Antony
Fresnes
Thiais
Choisy-le-Roi
Alfortville
Maisons-Alfort
Charenton-le-P.
St.-Maurice
Joinville-le-Pont
Créteil
St.-Maur-des-Fossés
Champigny-sur-Marne
Villiers-sur-Marne
Chennevières-sur-Marne
Sucy-en-Brie
Boissy-St.-Léger
Villeneuve-St.-Georges
Valenton
Limeil-Brévannes
Orly
Villeneuve-le-Roi
Rungis
AÉROPORT DE PARIS-ORLY
Athis-Mons
Paray-Vieille-Poste
Juvisy-sur-Orge
Savigny-sur-Orge
Viry-Châtillon
Grigny
Ris-Orangis
Evry
Corbeil-Essonnes
Draveil
Vigneux-sur-Seine
Montgeron
Brunoy
Yerres
Ste.-Geneviève-des-Bois
Brétigny-sur-Orge
Longjumeau
Massy
Palaiseau
Orsay
Les Ulis
Gif-sur-Yvette
Versailles
Le Chesnay
Vélizy-Villacoublay
Viroflay
Chaville
Ville-d'Avray
St.-Cyr-l'École
Montigny-le-Bretonneux
Bois d'Arcy
Jouy-en-Josas
Bièvres
Igny
Saclay
Combs-la-Ville
Moissy-Cramayel
Lieusaint
Ozoir-la-Ferrière
Roissy-en-Brie
Pontault-Combault
Forêt de Notre-Dame
Forêt de Sénart
Bois de Boulogne
Bois de Vincennes
Gare du Nord
Gare de l'Est
Gare St. Lazare
Gare Montparnasse
Gare d'Austerlitz
Gare de Lyon
AÉRODROME DE ST.-CYR-L'ÉCOLE
AÉRODROME DE TOUSSUS-LE-NOBLE
AÉRODROME DE CHELLES-LE PIN
AÉRODROME DE LOGNES-ÉMERAINVILLE
AÉRODROME DE MELUN-VILLAROCHE

Praha Prague

0 km 5

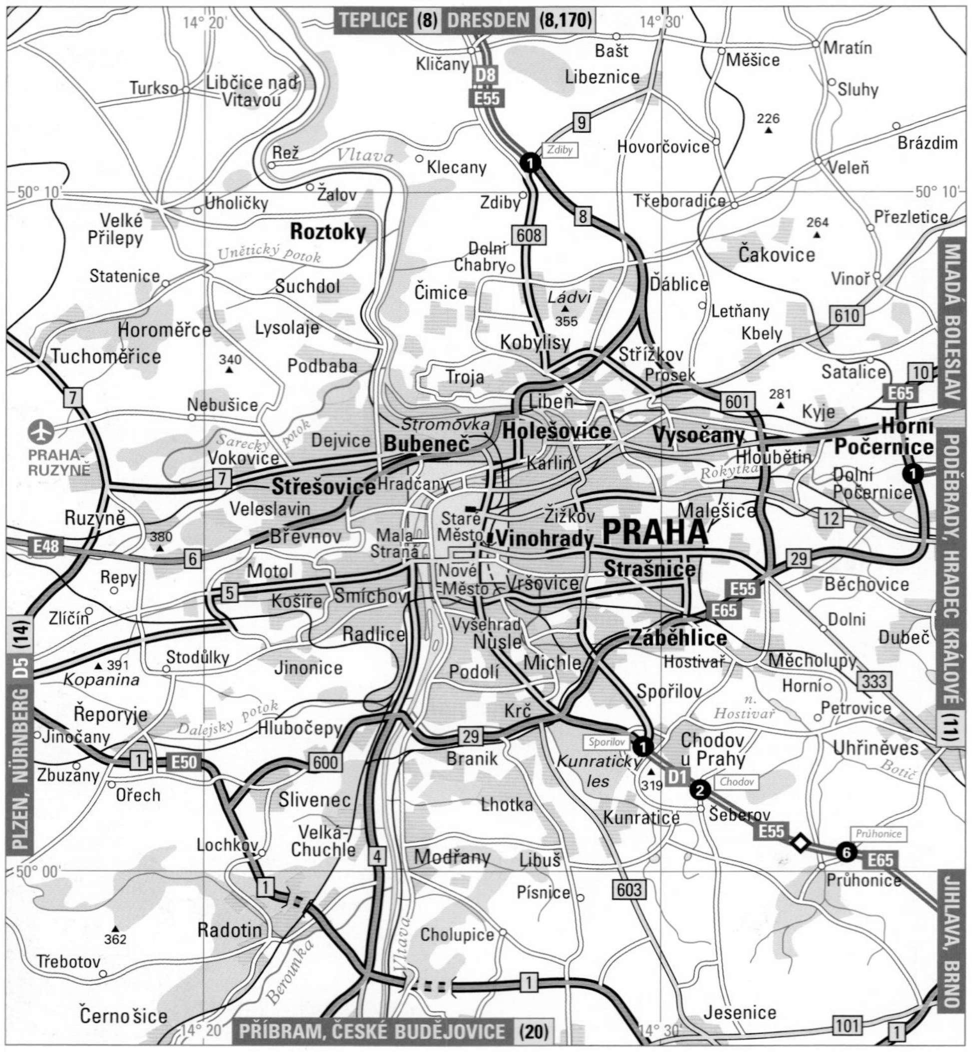

Praha Prague

0 km 1

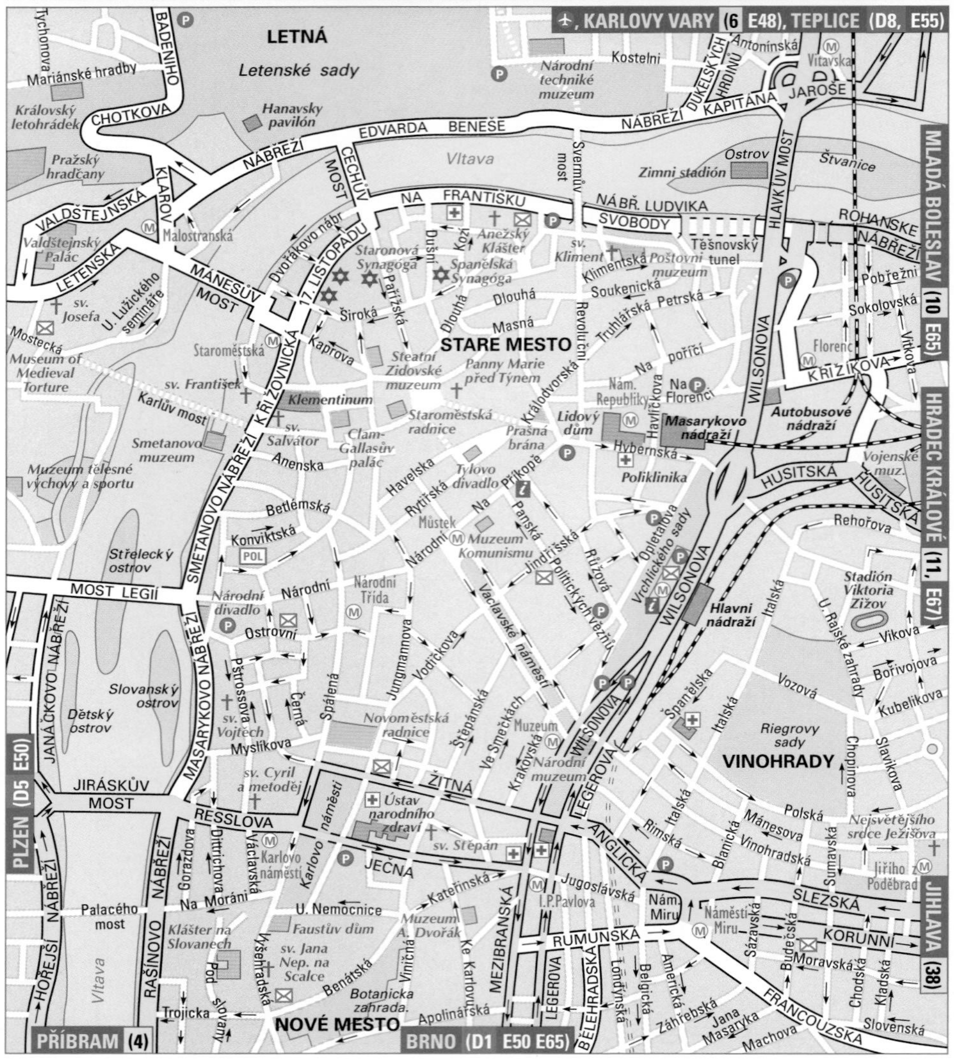

Rotterdam

0 km 1

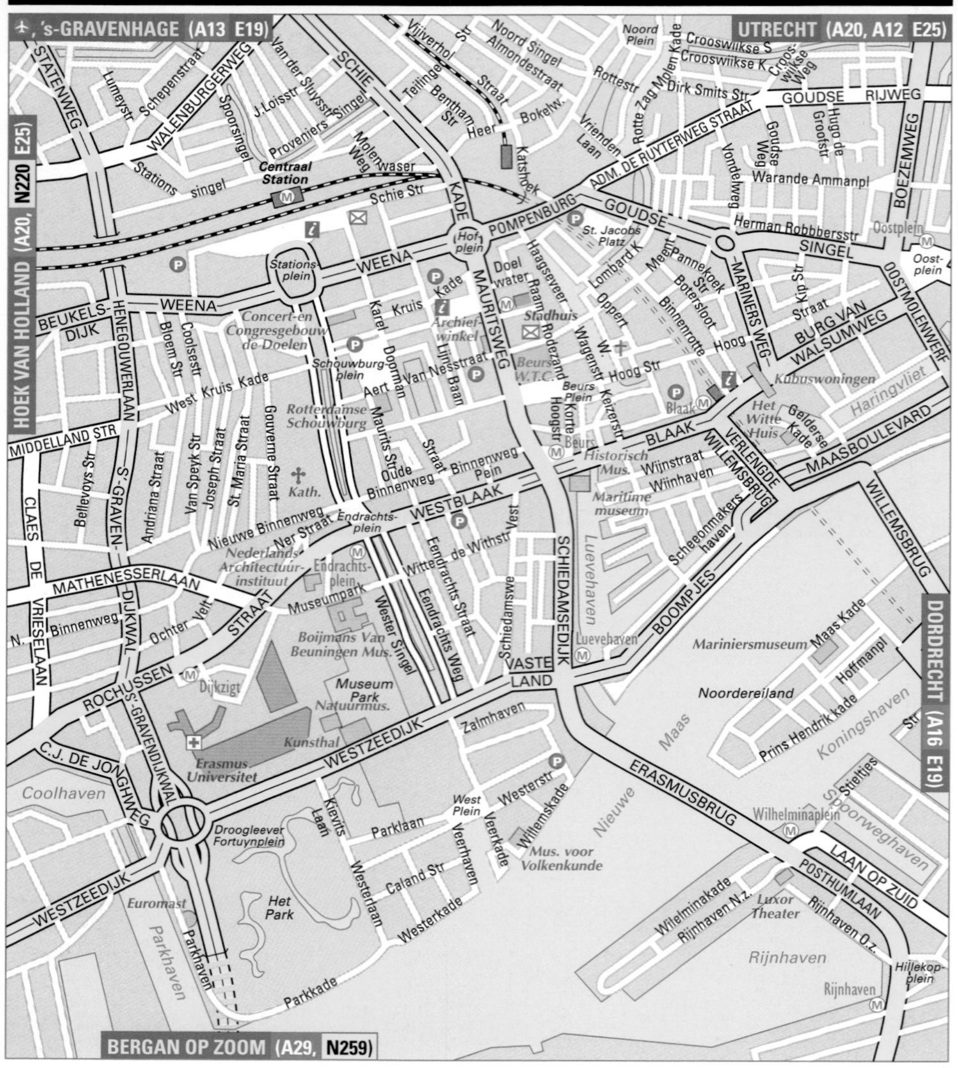

Sankt-Peterburg St. Petersburg

0 km 5

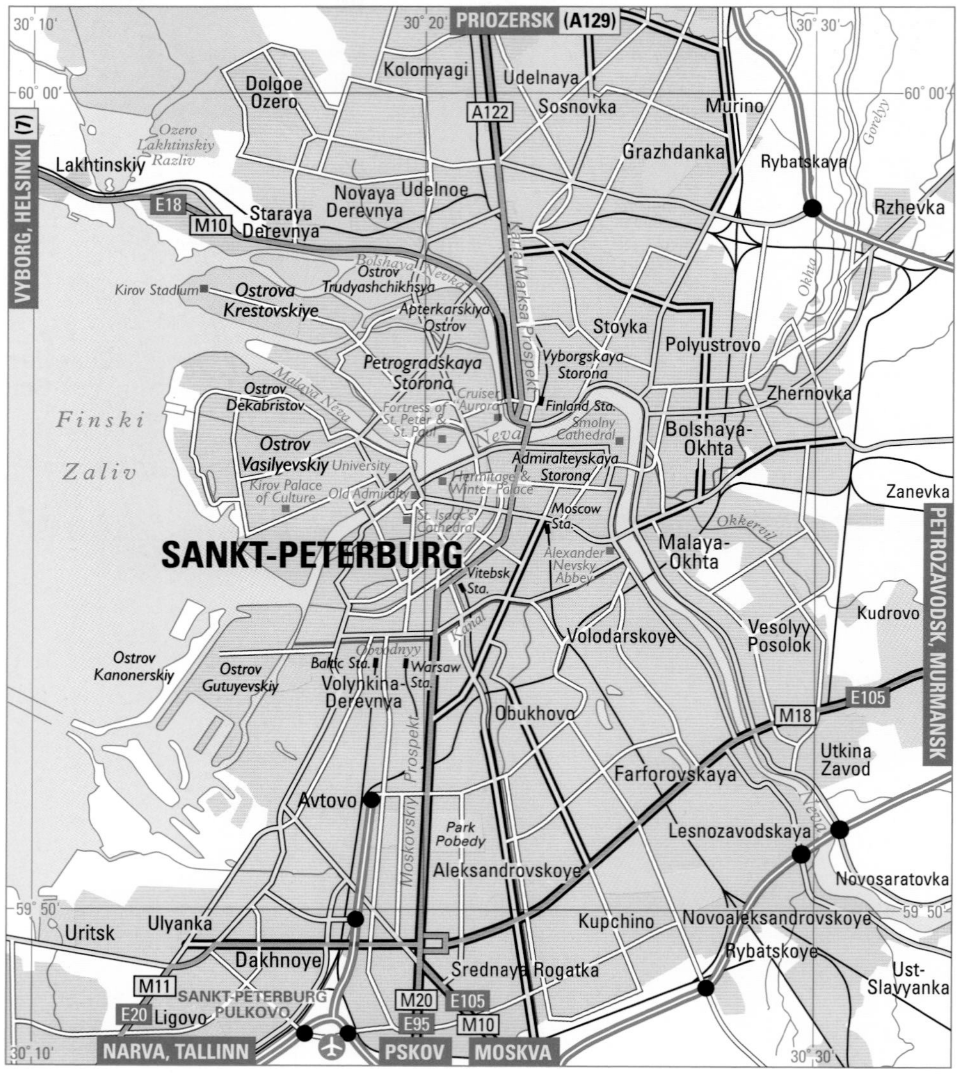

For **Rome** see page 143

Roma Rome

0 km 5

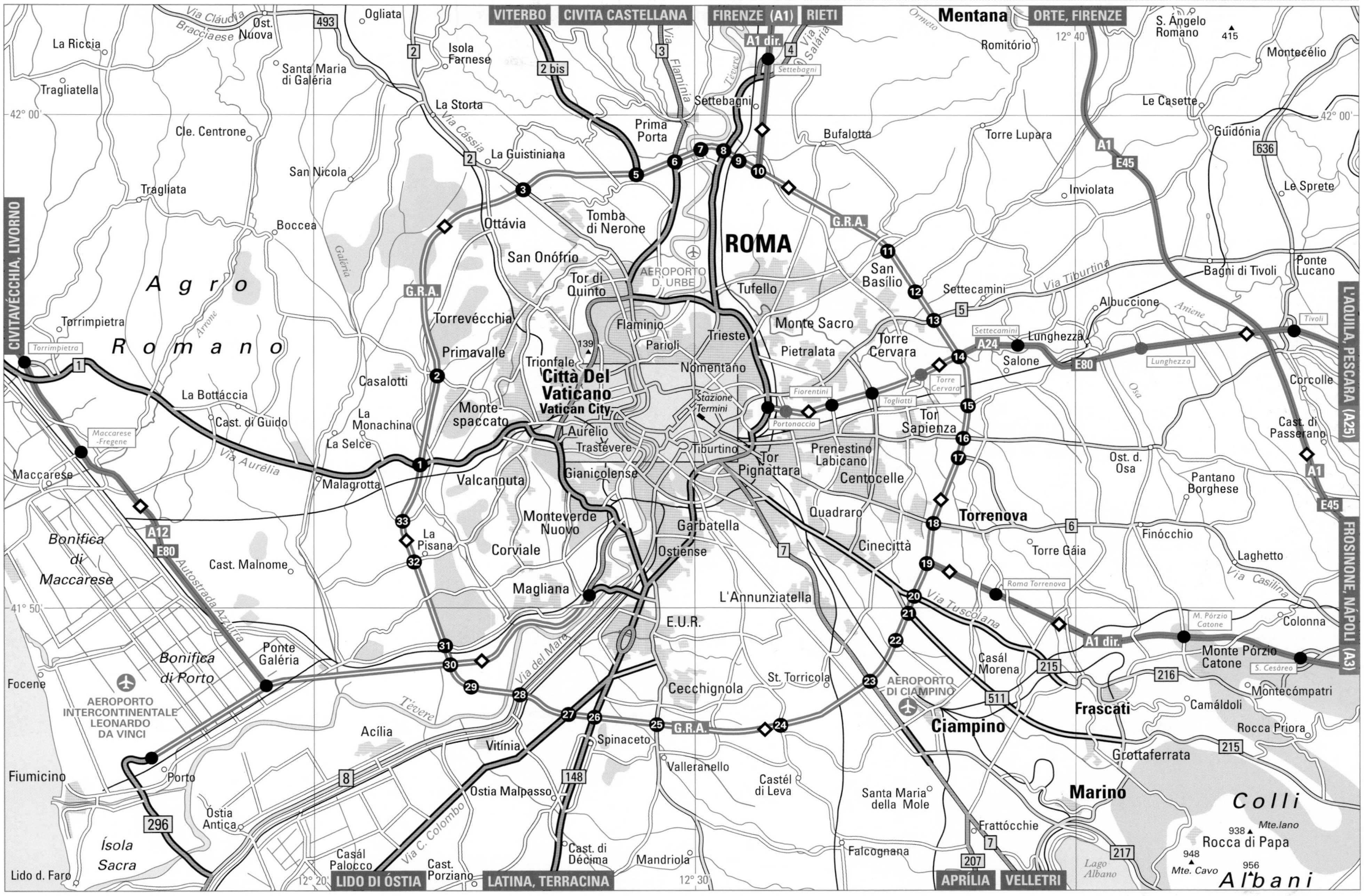

VITERBO
CIVITA CASTELLANA
FIRENZE (A1)
RIETI
Mentana
ORTE, FIRENZE
S. Àngelo Romano
415
Montecèlio
Ogliata
Ost. Nuova
493
La Riccia
Isola Farnese
2 bis
A1 dir.
Settebagni
Romitório
12° 40'
Santa Maria di Galéria
Tragliatella
42° 00'
La Storta
Prima Porta
Le Casette
Guidónia
636
Cle. Centrone
La Guistiniana
Bufalotta
Torre Lupara
A1
E45
San Nicola
Tragliata
Tomba di Nerone
Inviolata
Le Sprete
Boccea
Ottàvia
G.R.A.
ROMA
Agro Romano
San Onófrio
Tor di Quinto
AEROPORTO D' URBE
San Basilio
Ponte Lucano
Bagni di Tivoli
CIVITAVÉCCHIA, LIVORNO
Torrimpietra
Torrevécchia
Tufello
Settecamini
Albuccione
L'AQUILA, PESCARA (A25)
Flaminio
Parioli
Monte Sacro
Lunghezza
Primavalle
Trionfale
Trieste
Pietralata
Torre Cervara
A24
Salone
Città Del Vaticano
Vatican City
Nomentano
E80
Corcolle
Casalotti
Stazione Termini
La Bottáccia
Monte-spaccato
Tor Sapienza
Cast. di Guido
La Monachina
Aurèlio
Trastevere
Cast. di Passerano
La Selce
Tiburtino
Tor Pignattara
Prenestino Labicano
Ost. d. Osa
Maccarese
Via Aurèlia
Gianicolense
Valcannuta
Centocelle
Pantano Borghese
Malagrotta
Quadraro
Torrenova
A12
Bonifica di Maccarese
La Pisana
Monteverde Nuovo
Garbatella
Finócchio
Corviale
Ostiense
Torre Gáia
Laghetto
Cast. Malnome
Cinecittà
FROSINONE, NAPOLI (A3)
Magliana
L'Annunziatella
Via Casilina
41° 50'
E.U.R.
Colonna
Bonifica di Porto
Ponte Galéria
Casál Morena
Monte Pòrzio Catone
Focene
St. Torricola
AEROPORTO DI CIAMPINO
Montecómpatri
AEROPORTO INTERCONTINENTALE LEONARDO DA VINCI
Cecchignola
Frascati
Camáldoli
Acília
Ciampino
Rocca Priora
Vitínia
Spinaceto
Grottaferrata
Fiumicino
Porto
Vallerànello
Castél di Leva
Santa Maria della Mole
Marino
Ostia Malpasso
Colli Albani
Ostia Antica
Frattócchie
Mte.Iano
Rocca di Papa
Ìsola Sacra
Cast. di Décima
Falcognana
Casál Palocco
Mandriola
Lago Albano
Mte. Cavo
Lido d. Faro
Cast. Porziano
LIDO DI OSTIA
LATINA, TERRACINA
12° 30'
APRILIA
VELLETRI

Roma Rome

0 km 1

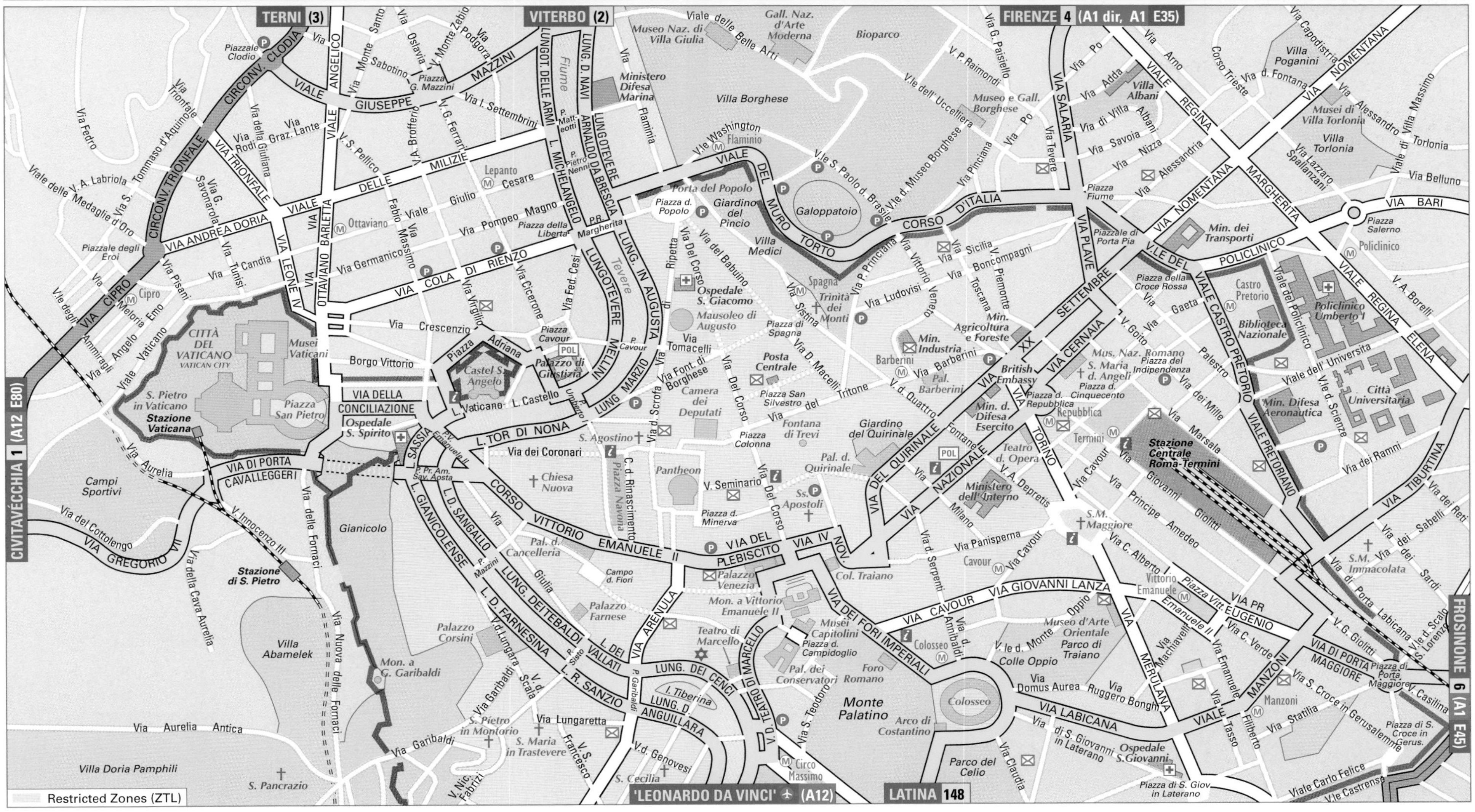

TERNI (3)
VITERBO (2)
FIRENZE 4 (A1 dir, A1 E35)
Museo Naz. di Villa Giulia
Gall. Naz. d'Arte Moderna
Bioparco
Villa Borghese
Ministero Difesa Marina
Villa Poganini
Villa Torlonia
Villa Albani
Museo e Gall. Borghese
Piazzale Clodio
Piazza G. Mazzini
VIALE GIUSEPPE MAZZINI
VIALE DELLE MILIZIE
Lepanto
Flaminio
Galoppatoio
Villa Medici
Porta del Popolo
Piazza d. Popolo
Giardino del Pincio
CORSO D'ITALIA
VIA NOMENTANA
Piazza Fiume
VIALE REGINA MARGHERITA
VIA BARI
Policlinico
Ottaviano
Piazzale degli Eroi
VIA ANDREA DORIA
VIA COLA DI RIENZO
Piazza della Libertà
Spagna
Trinità dei Monti
Barberini
Min. dei Trasporti
VIALE CASTRO PRETORIO
Policlinico Umberto I
Città Universitaria
Cipro
CITTÀ DEL VATICANO
VATICAN CITY
Musei Vaticani
Borgo Vittorio
Castel S. Angelo
Piazza Cavour
Mausoleo di Augusto
Min. Agricoltura e Foreste
British Embassy
Biblioteca Nazionale
Min. Difesa Aeronautica
S. Pietro in Vaticano
Piazza San Pietro
Stazione Vaticana
VIA DELLA CONCILIAZIONE
Ospedale S. Spirito
Posta Centrale
Camera dei Deputati
Piazza Colonna
Fontana di Trevi
Giardino del Quirinale
Repubblica
Termini
Stazione Centrale Roma-Termini
CIVITAVÉCCHIA 1 (A12 E80)
Campi Sportivi
VIA DI PORTA CAVALLEGGERI
Pantheon
Chiesa Nuova
Teatro d. Opera
Ministero dell'Interno
S.M. Maggiore
Gianicolo
CORSO VITTORIO EMANUELE II
VIA DEL PLEBISCITO
Palazzo Venezia
Col. Traiano
Vittorio Emanuele
Stazione di S. Pietro
Campo d. Fiori
Palazzo Farnese
Mon. a Vittorio Emanuele II
VIA DEI FORI IMPERIALI
VIA CAVOUR
VIA GIOVANNI LANZA
Museo d'Arte Orientale
Parco di Traiano
S.M. Immacolata
Villa Abamelek
Palazzo Corsini
Teatro di Marcello
Musei Capitolini
Colosseo
Colle Oppio
Domus Aurea
Manzoni
FROSINONE 6 (A1 E45)
Mon. a G. Garibaldi
LUNG. DEI CENCI
I. Tiberina
Foro Romano
Monte Palatino
Arco di Costantino
VIA LABICANA
Piazza di S. Croce in Gerus.
S. Pietro in Montorio
S. Maria in Trastevere
Via Aurelia Antica
Villa Doria Pamphili
S. Pancrazio
Circo Massimo
Parco del Celio
Ospedale S. Giovanni
Piazza di S. Giov. in Laterano
'LEONARDO DA VINCI' (A12)
LATINA 148
Restricted Zones (ZTL)

Sevilla Seville

0 km 0.5

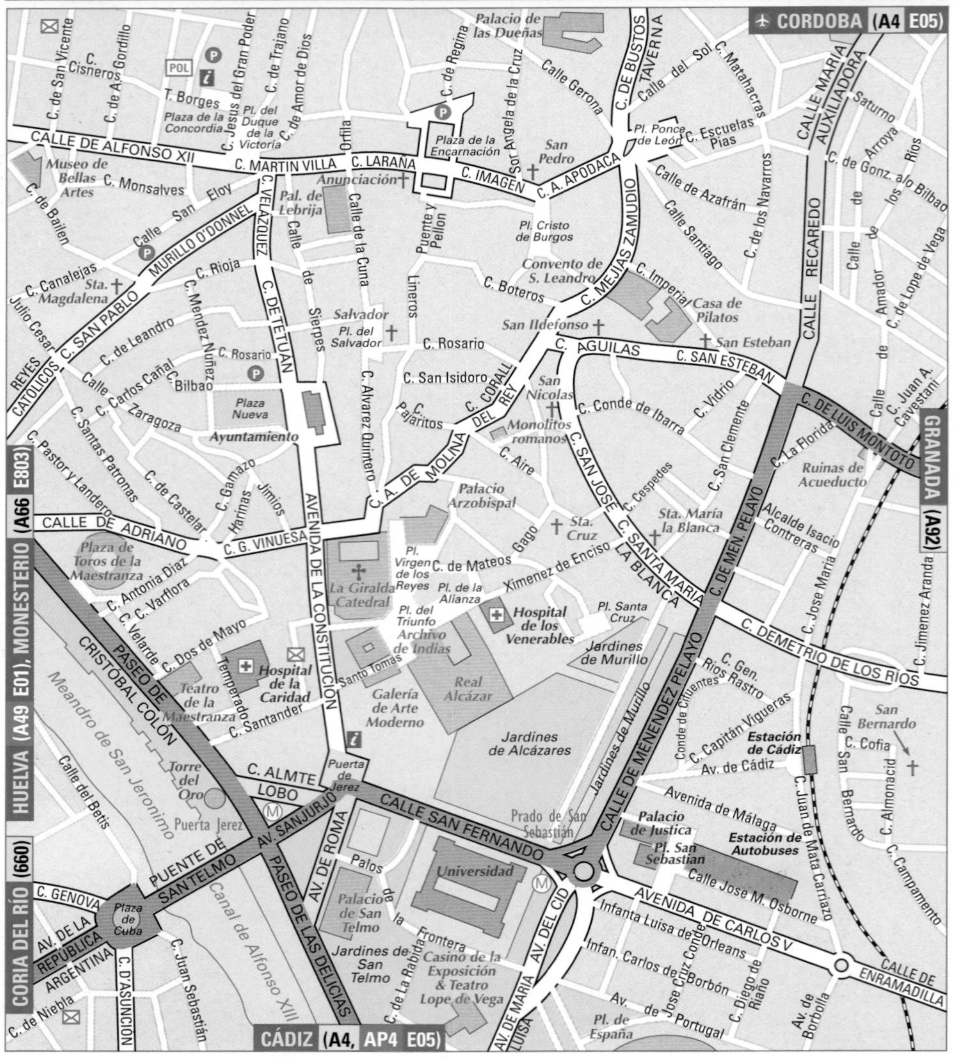

Stuttgart

0 km 0.5

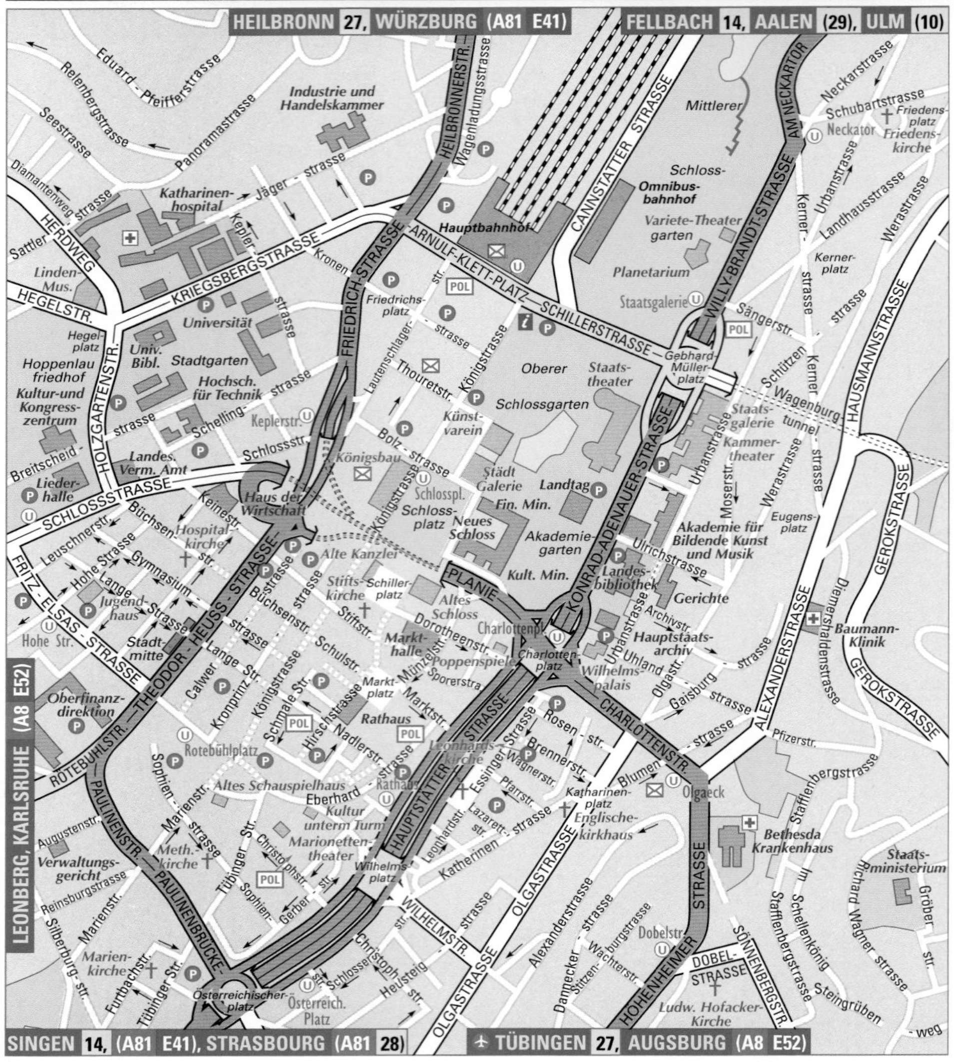

Strasbourg

0 km 5

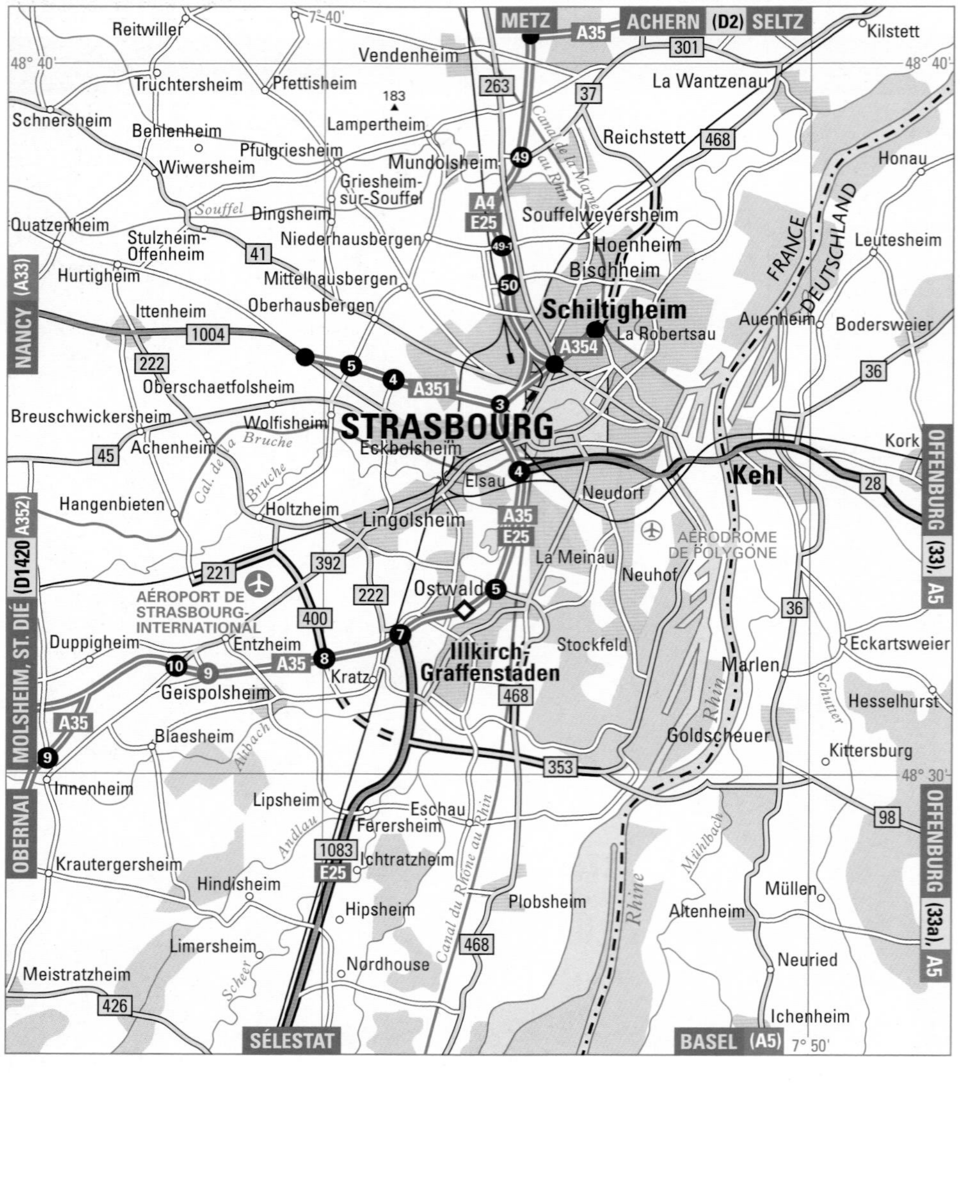

Strasbourg

0 km 0.5

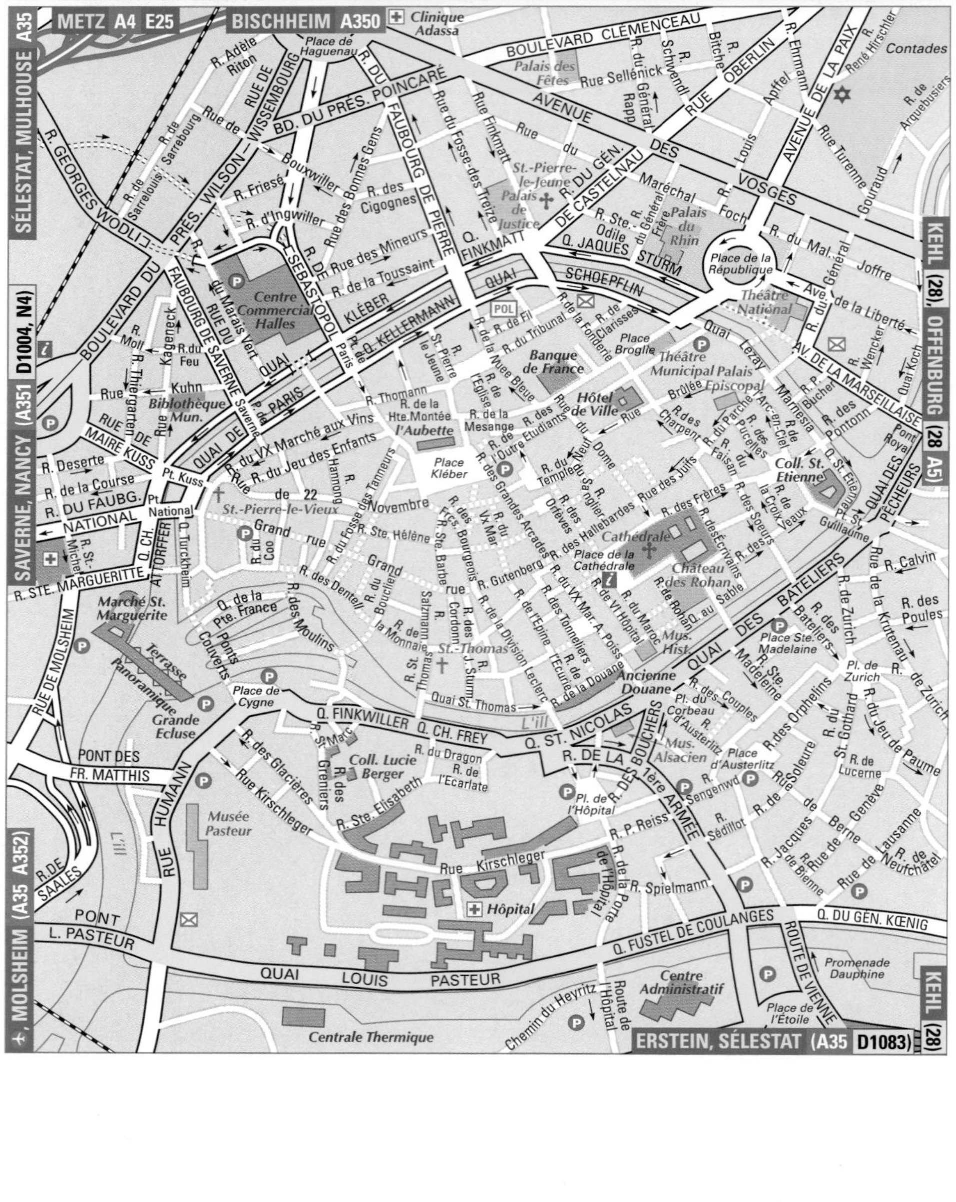

Stockholm

0 km 5

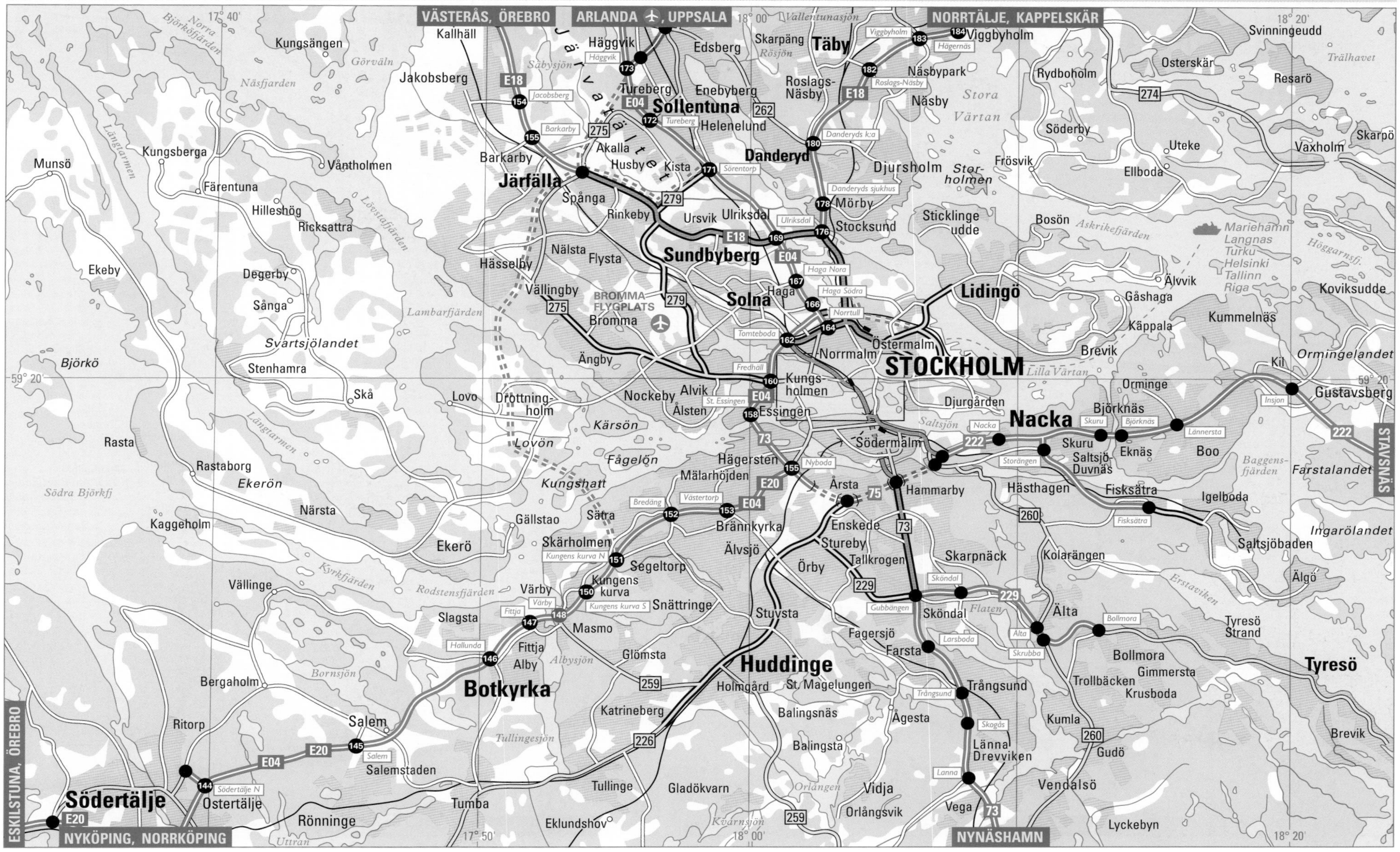
VÄSTERÅS, ÖREBRO
ARLANDA, UPPSALA
NORRTÄLJE, KAPPELSKÄR
ESKILSTUNA, ÖREBRO
NYKÖPING, NORRKÖPING
NYNÄSHAMN
STAVSNÄS
Kungsängen
Jakobsberg
Kallhäll
Häggvik
Edsberg
Täby
Viggbyholm
Svinningeudd
Tureberg
Sollentuna
Enebyberg
Roslags-Näsby
Näsbypark
Rydboholm
Österskär
Resarö
Barkarby
Akalla
Helenelund
Danderyd
Djursholm
Stora Värtan
Söderby
Uteke
Vaxholm
Munsö
Kungsberga
Vänthofmen
Järfälla
Husby
Kista
Spånga
Färentuna
Hilleshög
Ricksattra
Rinkeby
Ursvik
Ulriksdal
Mörby
Stocksund
Sticklinge udde
Bosön
Frösvik
Ellboda
Storholmen
Ekeby
Nälsta
Hässelby
Flysta
Sundbyberg
Degerby
Sånga
Vällingby
BROMMA FLYGPLATS
Bromma
Solna
Haga
Lidingö
Älvvik
Gåshaga
Koviksudde
Kummelnäs
Käppala
Svartsjölandet
Björkö
Stenhamra
Ängby
Östermalm
Norrmalm
STOCKHOLM
Brevik
Orminge
Ormingelandet
Kil
Gustavsberg
Skå
Lovö
Drottningholm
Nockeby
Alvik
Ålsten
Kungsholmen
Essingen
Djurgården
Nacka
Björknäs
Rasta
Kärsön
Fågelön
Hägersten
Södermalm
Skuru
Saltsjö-Duvnäs
Eknäs
Boo
Farstalandet
Rastaborg
Ekerön
Kungshatt
Mälarhöjden
Årsta
Hammarby
Hästhagen
Fisksätra
Igelboda
Närsta
Gällstao
Sätra
Bränkyrka
Enskede
Kaggeholm
Ekerö
Skärholmen
Älvsjö
Stureby
Tallkrogen
Örby
Skarpnäck
Kolarängen
Saltsjöbaden
Ingarölandet
Vällinge
Värby
Segeltorp
Kungens kurva
Snättringe
Älgö
Slagsta
Masmo
Stuvsta
Sköndal
Älta
Tyresö Strand
Fittja
Alby
Glömsta
Fagersjö
Farsta
Bollmora
Gimmersta
Tyresö
Bergaholm
Botkyrka
Huddinge
Holmgård
St. Magelungen
Trollbäcken
Krusboda
Trångsund
Salem
Katrineberg
Balingsnäs
Ågesta
Kumla
Brevik
Ritorp
Balingsta
Länna
Drevviken
Gudö
Salemstaden
Södertälje
Östertälje
Tullinge
Gladökvarn
Vidja
Orlångsvik
Vendalsö
Rönninge
Tumba
Eklundshov
Vega
Lyckebyn
E18
E04
E20
222
229
259
260
262
274
275
279
226
73
75

Stockholm

0 km 1

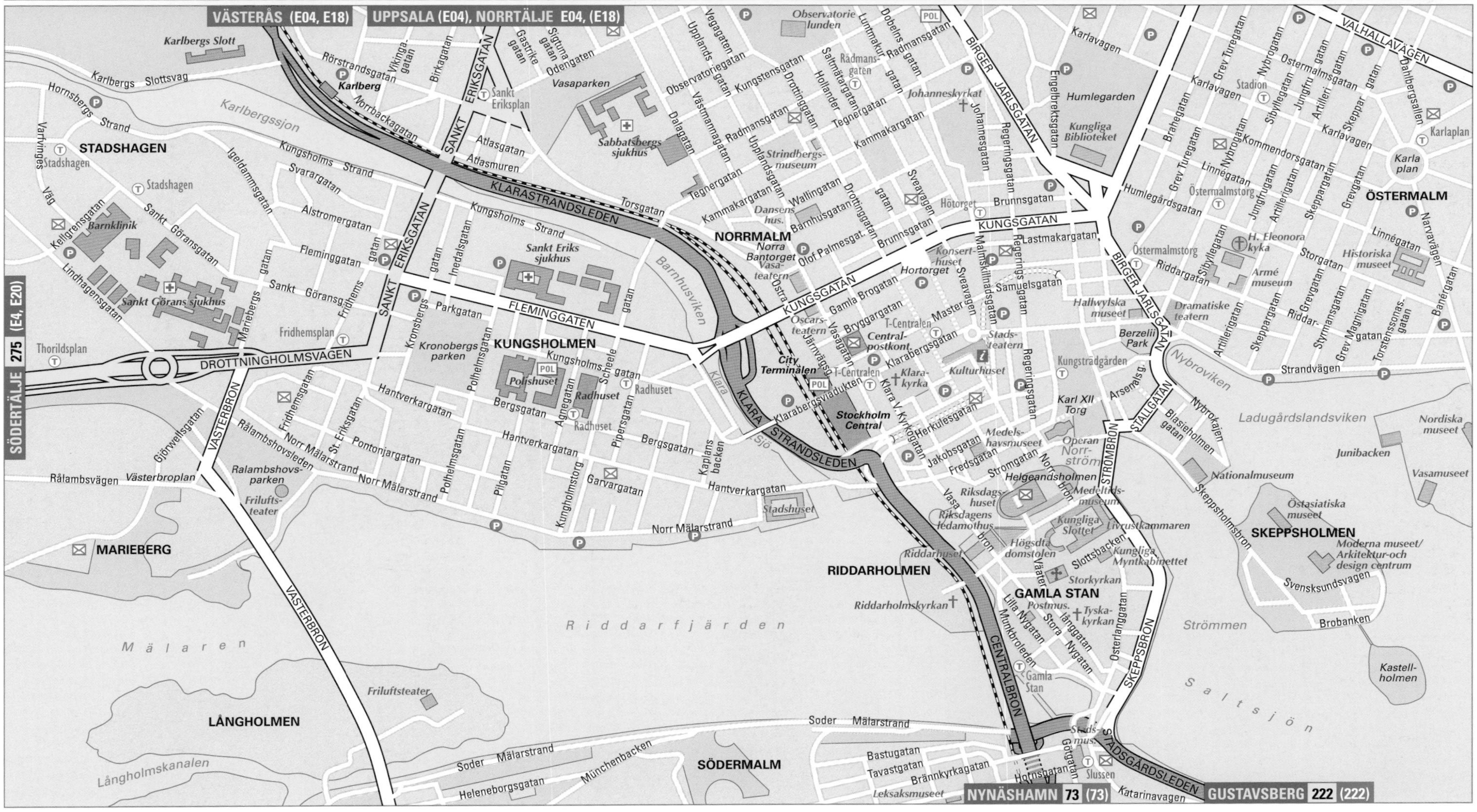
VÄSTERÅS (E04, E18)
UPPSALA (E04), NORRTÄLJE E04, (E18)
SÖDERTÄLJE 275 (E4, E20)
NYNÄSHAMN 73 (73)
GUSTAVSBERG 222 (222)
Karlbergs Slott
Karlberg
STADSHAGEN
Sankt Eriksplan
Vasaparken
Observatorielunden
Johanneskyrkat
Humlegården
Kungliga Biblioteket
Stadion
Karla plan
ÖSTERMALM
Sabbatsbergs sjukhus
Strindbergsmuseum
Barnklinik
Sankt Eriks sjukhus
Sankt Görans sjukhus
Fridhemsplan
Thorildsplan
DROTTNINGHOLMSVÄGEN
KUNGSHOLMEN
Kronobergsparken
Polishuset
Radhuset
NORRMALM
Norra Bantorget
Konserthuset
Hötorget
Kulturhuset
Hallwylska museet
Berzelii Park
Dramatiska teatern
Historiska museet
Armémuseum
Karl XII Torg
Kungsträdgården
Operan
Norrström
Stockholm Central
City Terminalen
Centralpostkont
Klara kyrka
Medelhavsmuseet
Helgeandsholmen
Riksdagshuset
Medeltidsmuseum
Kungliga Slottet
Livrustkammaren
Storkyrkan
Tyska kyrkan
GAMLA STAN
Riddarholmskyrkan
RIDDARHOLMEN
Nationalmuseum
SKEPPSHOLMEN
Moderna museet/ Arkitektur-och design centrum
Östasiatiska museet
Ladugårdslandsviken
Nordiska museet
Junibacken
Vasamuseet
Strömmen
Kastellholmen
Saltsjön
Riddarfjärden
Mälaren
MARIEBERG
Rålambshovsparken
Friluftsteater
Stadshuset
LÅNGHOLMEN
Långholmskanalen
SÖDERMALM
Slussen
VÄSTERBRON
CENTRALBRON
STRÖMBRON
SKEPPSBRON
KLARASTRANDSLEDEN
BIRGER JARLSGATAN
KUNGSGATAN
FLEMINGGATAN
SANKT ERIKSGATAN
VALHALLAVÄGEN
STADSGÅRDSLEDEN
Norr Mälarstrand
Söder Mälarstrand
Hantverkargatan
Strandvägen
Karlavägen
Kungsholms Strand
Rålambsvägen
Västerbroplan

Torino Turin

0 km 5

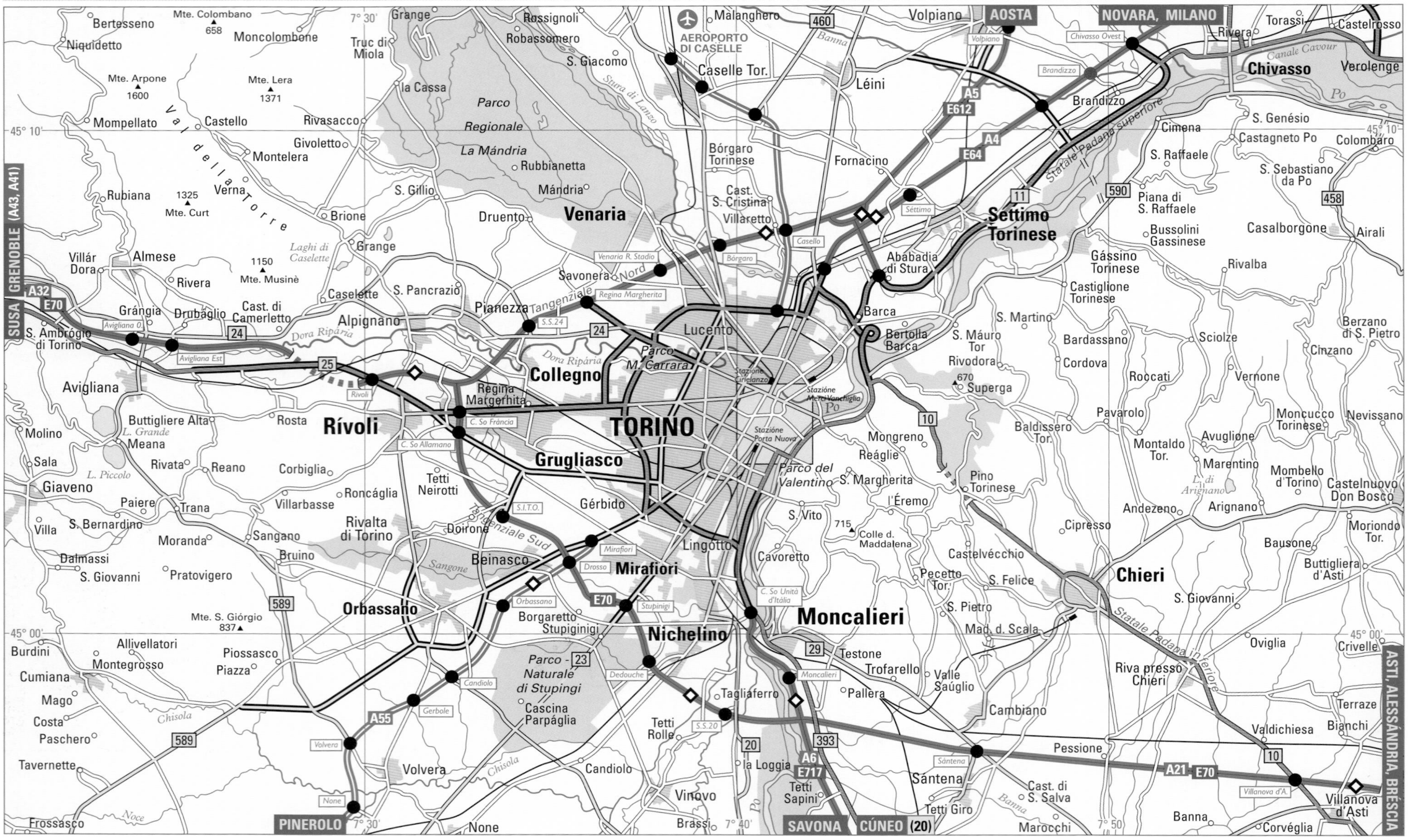

Venézia Venice

0 km 0.5

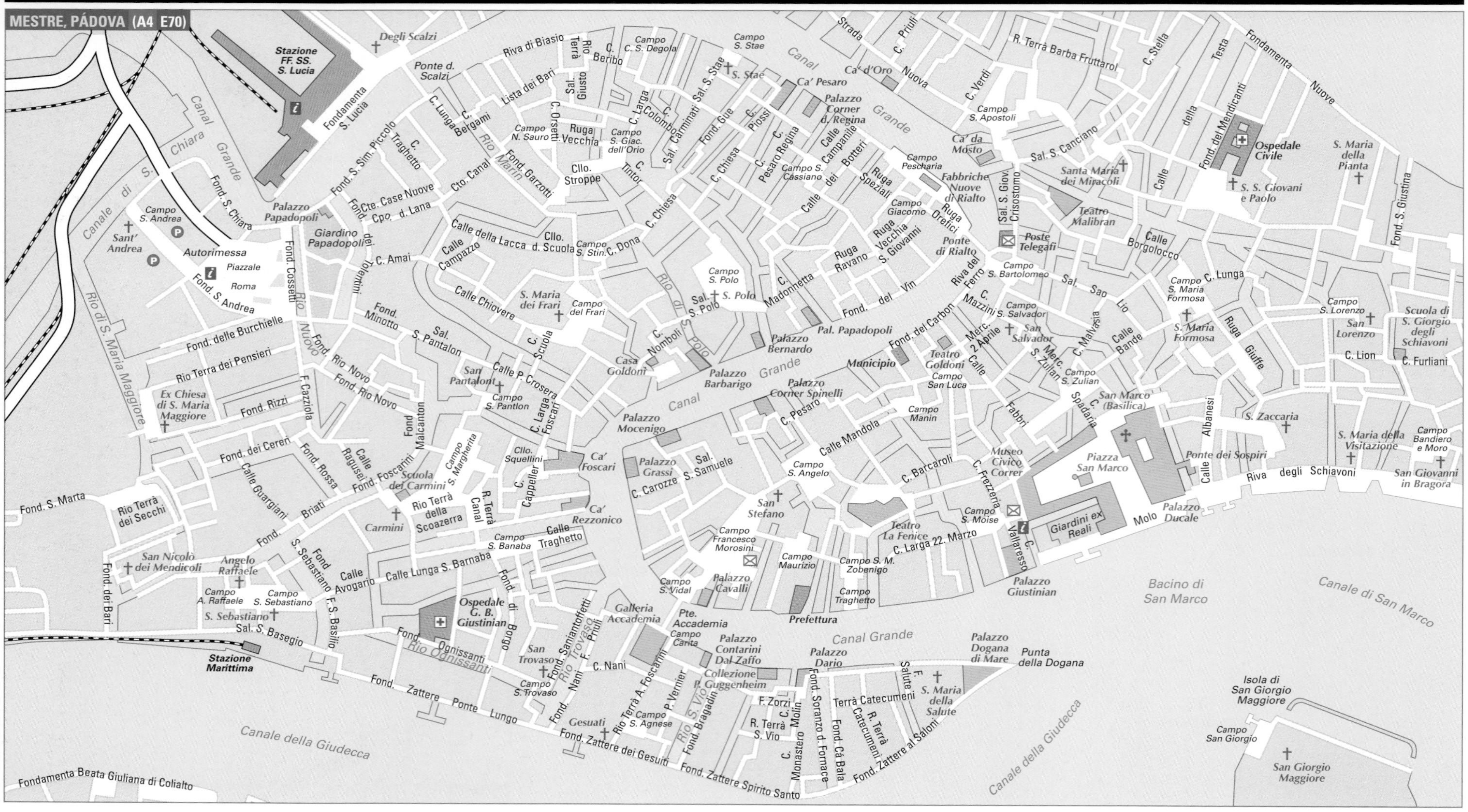

Torino Turin

0 km 1

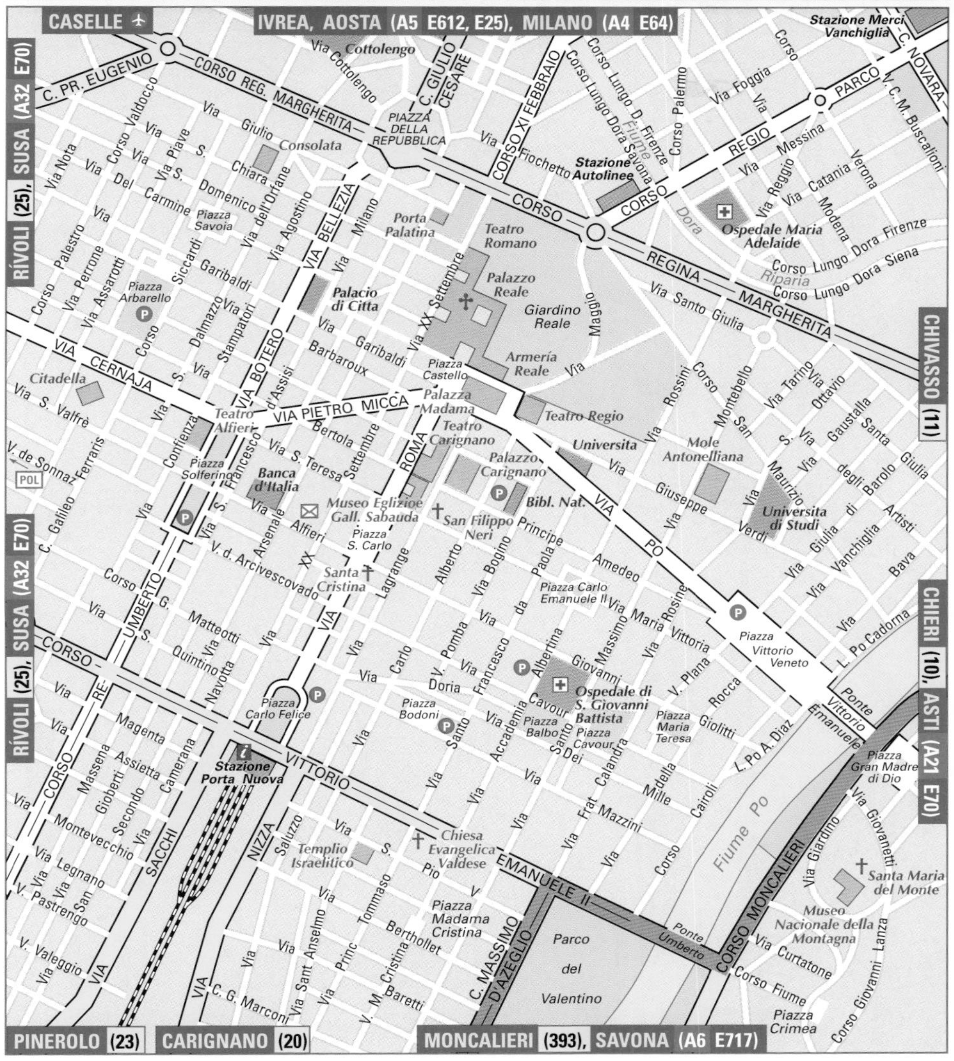

Wien Vienna

0 km 5

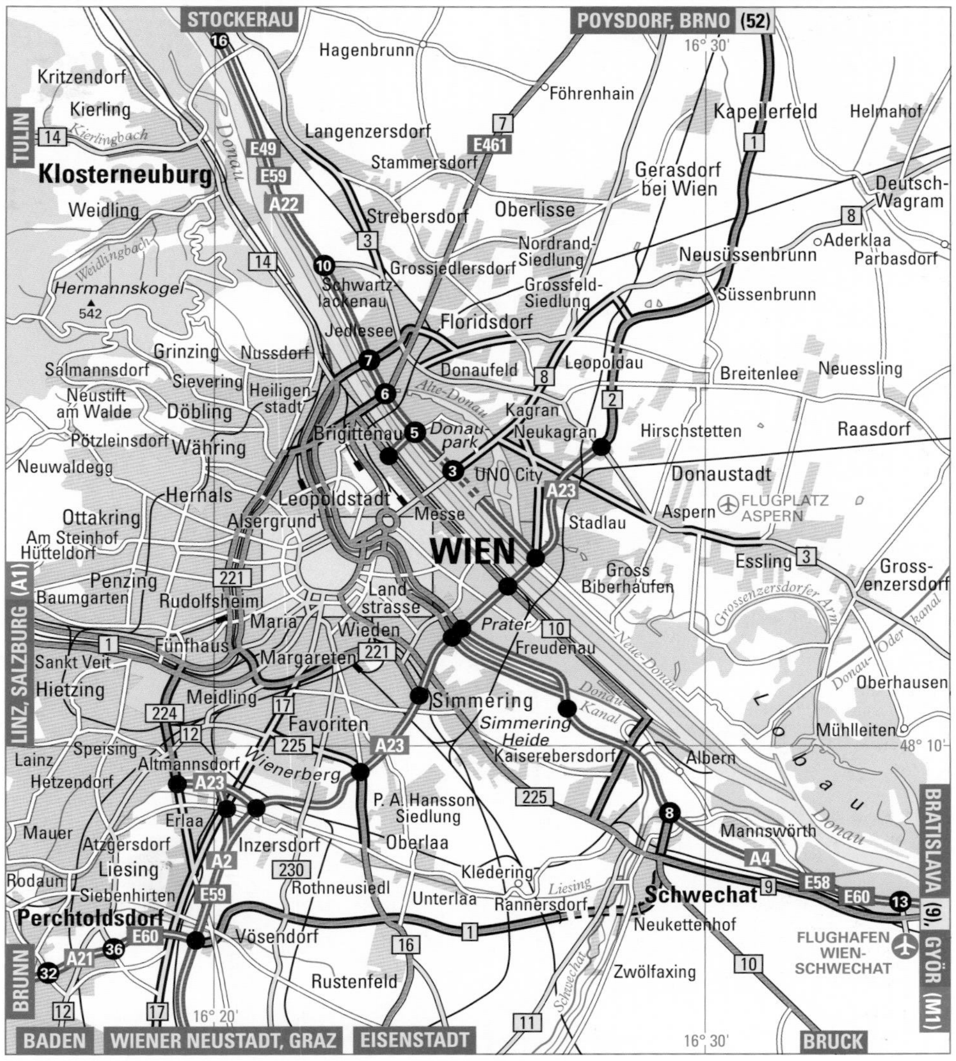

Warszawa Warsaw

0 km 5

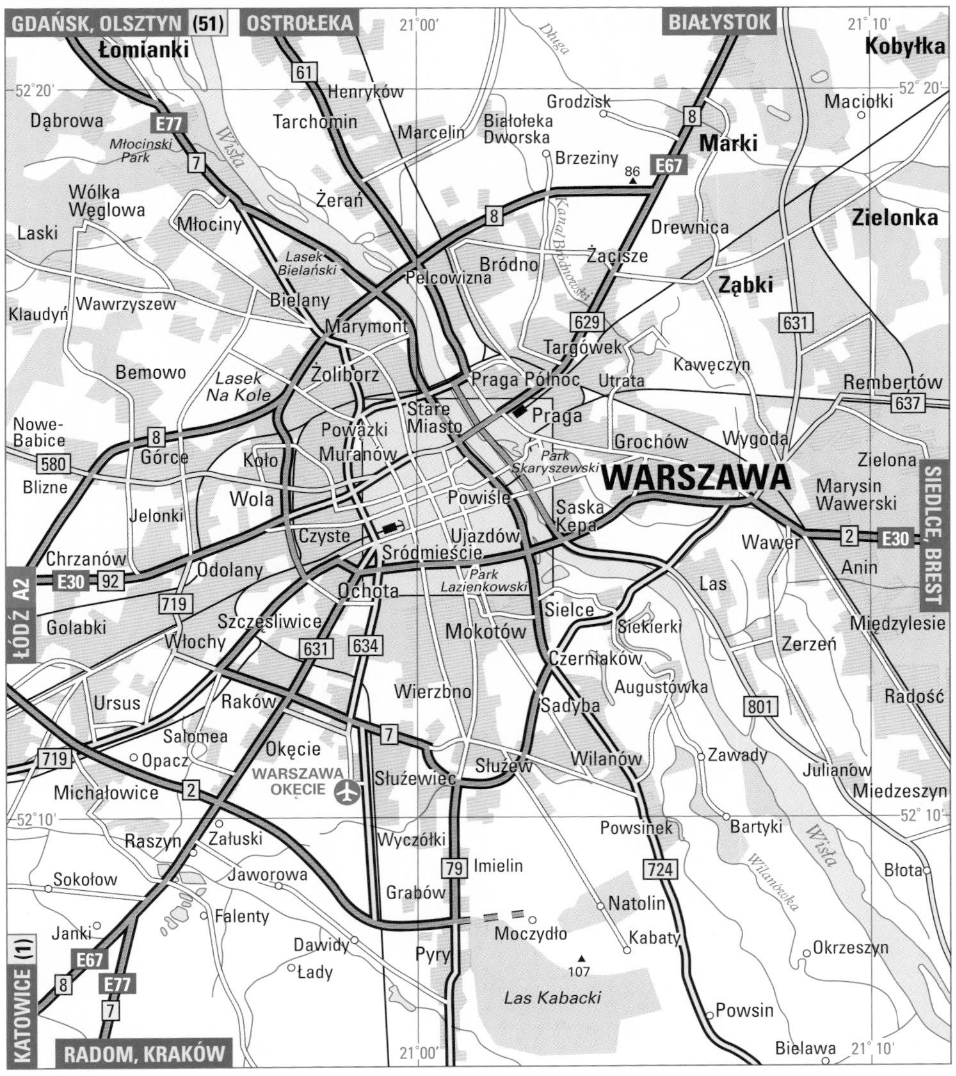

Warszawa Warsaw

0 km 1

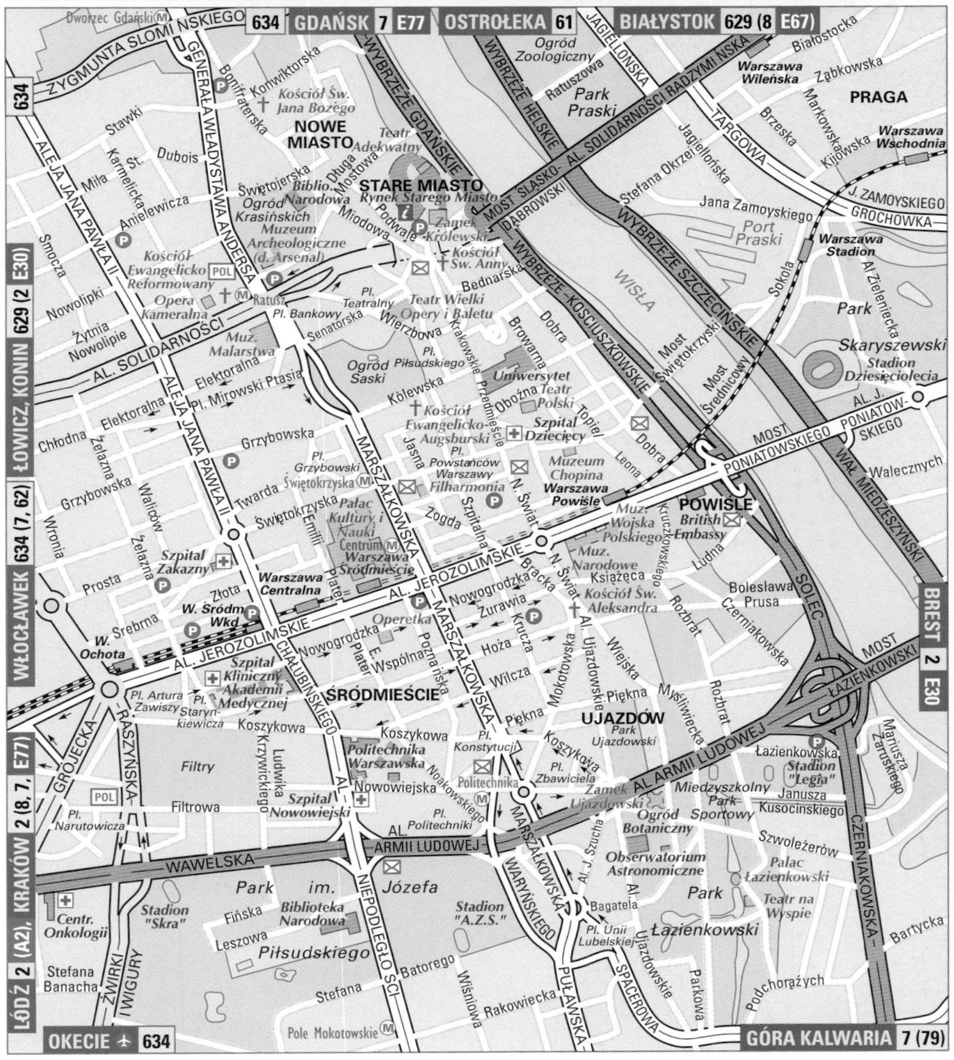

Wien Vienna

0 km 1

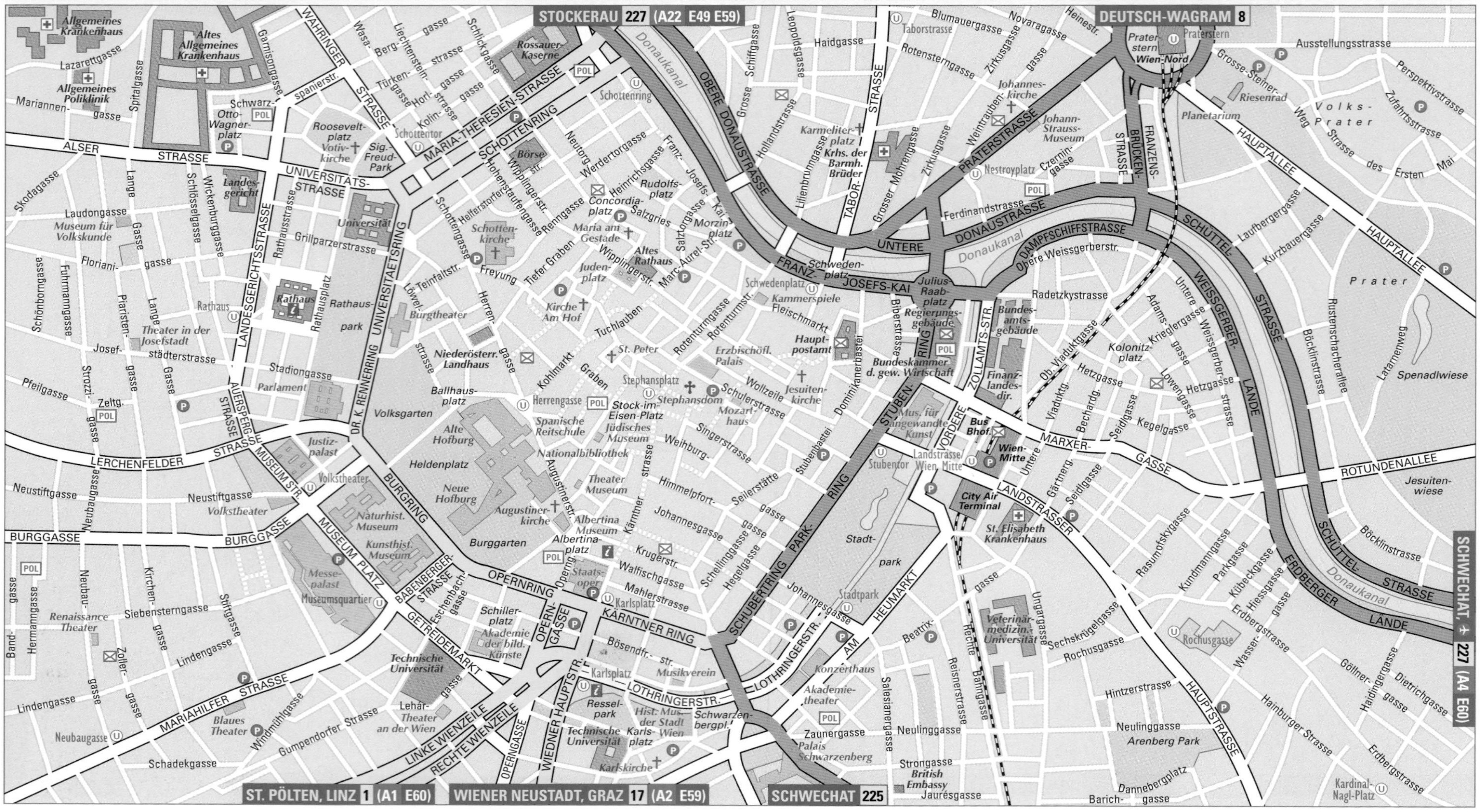

Zagreb

0 km 0.5

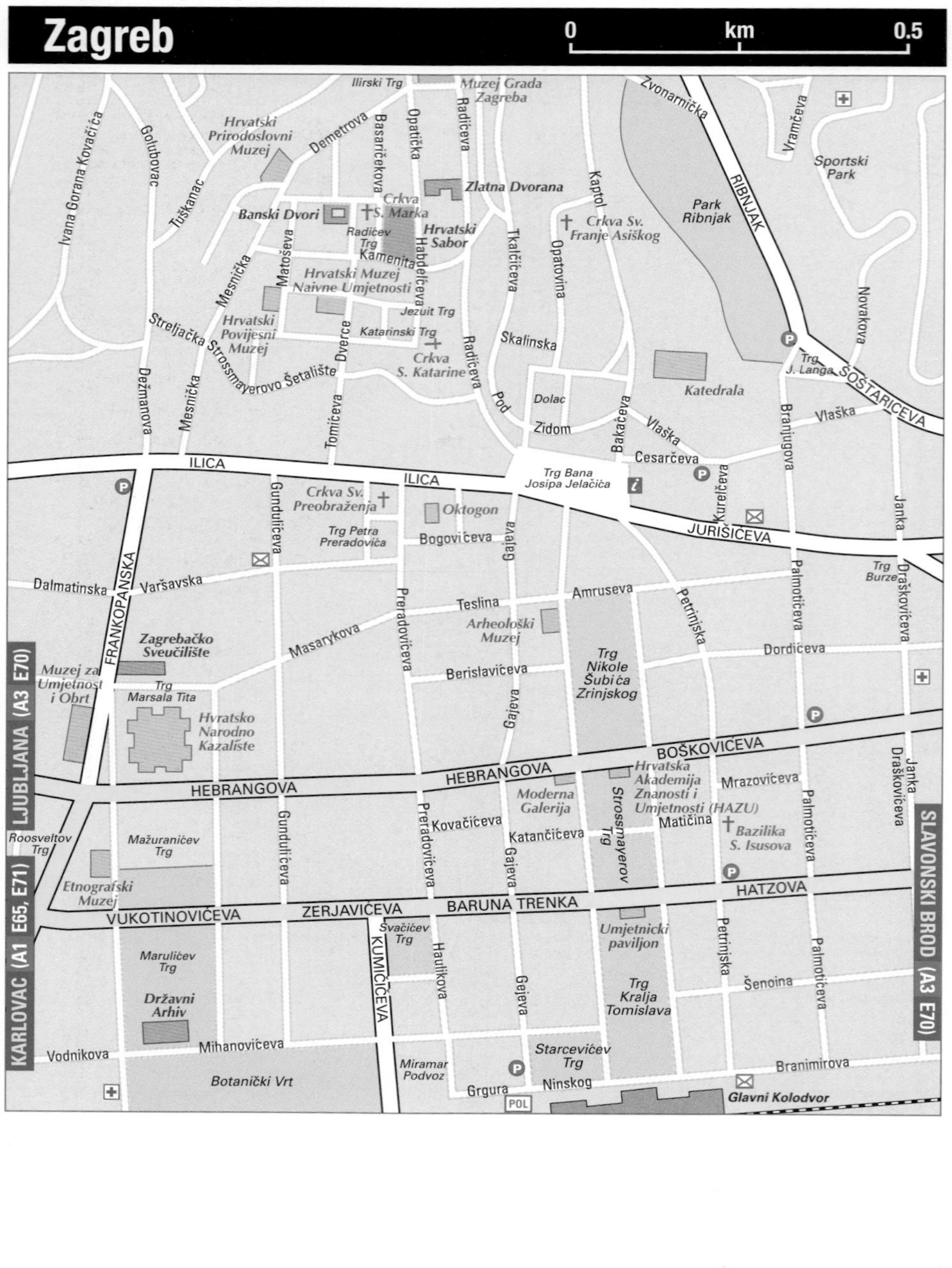

Zürich

0 km 0.5

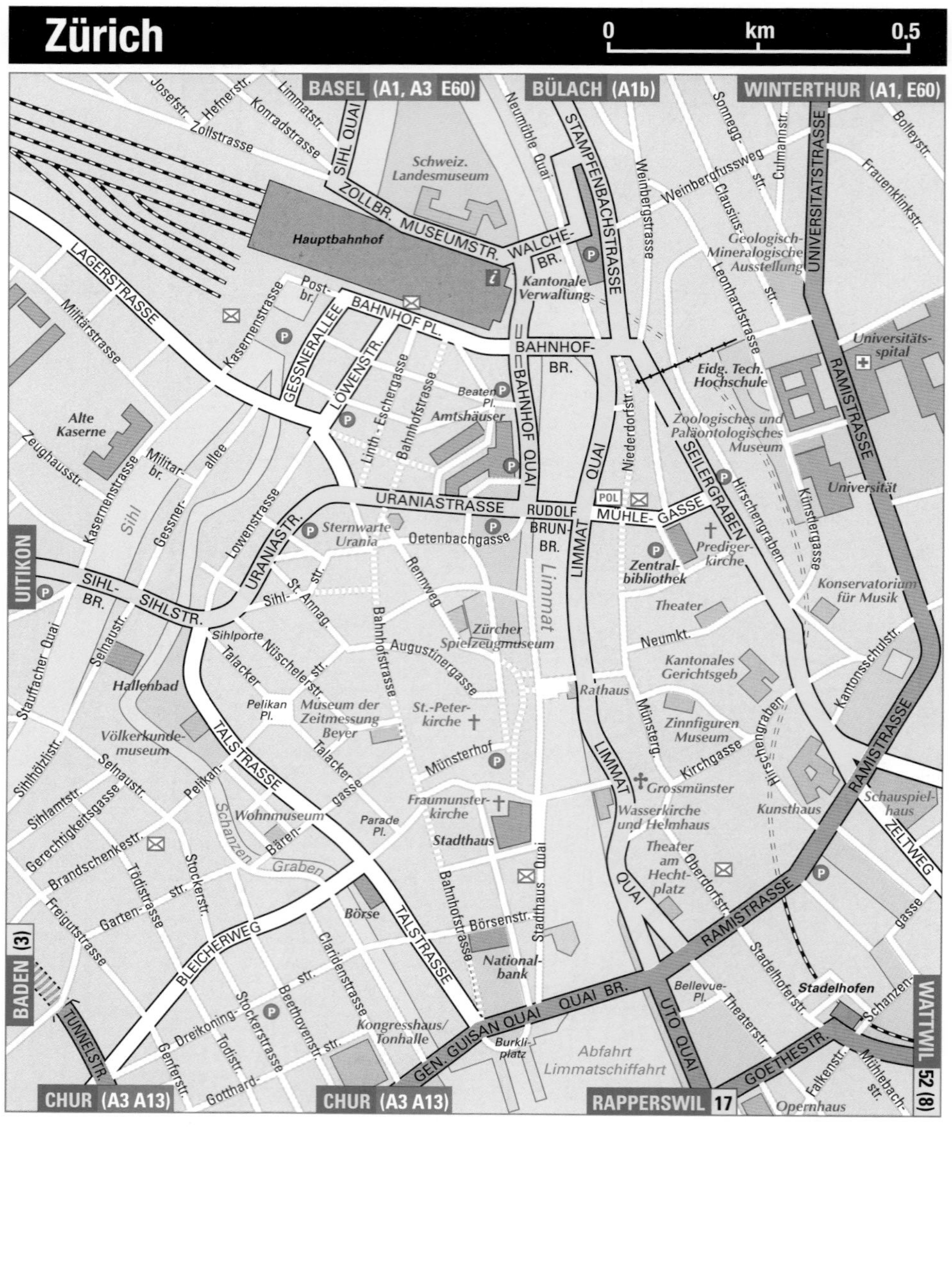

A	Austria	Autriche	Österreich	Austria
AL	Albania	Albanie	Albanien	Albania
AND	Andorra	Andorre	Andorra	Andorra
B	Belgium	Belgique	Belgien	Belgio
BG	Bulgaria	Bulgarie	Bulgarien	Bulgaria
BIH	Bosnia-Herzegovin	Bosnia-Herzegovine	Bosnien-Herzegowina	Bosnia-Herzegovina
BY	Belarus	Belarus	Weissrussland	Bielorussia
CH	Switzerland	Suisse	Schweiz	Svizzera
CY	Cyprus	Chypre	Zypern	Cipro
CZ	Czech Republic	République Tchèque	Tschechische Republik	Repubblica Ceca
D	Germany	Allemagne	Deutschland	Germania
DK	Denmark	Danemark	Dänemark	Danimarca
E	Spain	Espagne	Spanien	Spagna
EST	Estonia	Estonie	Estland	Estonia
F	France	France	Frankreich	Francia
FIN	Finland	Finlande	Finnland	Finlandia
FL	Liechtenstein	Liechtenstein	Liechtenstein	Liechtenstein
FO	Faeroe Islands	Îles Féroé	Färoër-Inseln	Isole Faroe
GB	United Kingdom	Royaume Uni	Grossbritannien und Nordirland	Regno Unito
GBZ	Gibraltar	Gibraltar	Gibraltar	Gibilterra
GR	Greece	Grèce	Greichenland	Grecia
H	Hungary	Hongrie	Ungarn	Ungheria
HR	Croatia	Croatie	Kroatien	Croazia
I	Italy	Italie	Italien	Italia
IRL	Ireland	Irlande	Irland	Irlanda
IS	Iceland	Islande	Island	Islanda
KOS	Kosovo	Kosovo	Kosovo	Kosovo
L	Luxembourg	Luxembourg	Luxemburg	Lussemburgo
LT	Lithuania	Lituanie	Litauen	Lituania
LV	Latvia	Lettonie	Lettland	Lettonia
M	Malta	Malte	Malta	Malta
MC	Monaco	Monaco	Monaco	Monaco
MD	Moldova	Moldavie	Moldawien	Moldavia
MK	Macedonia	Macédoine	Makedonien	Macedonia
MNE	Montenegro	Monténégro	Montenegro	Montenegro
N	Norway	Norvège	Norwegen	Norvegia
NL	Netherlands	Pays-Bas	Niederlande	Paesi Bassi
P	Portugal	Portugal	Portugal	Portogallo
PL	Poland	Pologne	Polen	Polonia
RO	Romania	Roumanie	Rumanien	Romania
RSM	San Marino	Saint-Marin	San Marino	San Marino
RUS	Russia	Russie	Russland	Russia
S	Sweden	Suède	Schweden	Svezia
SK	Slovak Republic	République Slovaque	Slowak Republik	Repubblica Slovacca
SLO	Slovenia	Slovénie	Slowenien	Slovenia
SRB	Serbia	Serbie	Serbien	Serbia
TR	Turkey	Turquie	Türkei	Turchia
UA	Ukraine	Ukraine	Ukraine	Ucraina

A

Aab–Als

Aabenraa DK 39 D2
Aabybro DK 38 B2
Aach D 71 A4
Aachen D 50 C2
Aalborg DK 38 B2
Aalen D 61 B6
Aalestrup DK 38 C2
Aalsmeer NL 49 A5
Aalst B 49 C5
Aalten NL 50 B2
Aalter B 49 B4
Äänekoski FIN 3 E26
Aapajärvi FIN 113 E16
Ağapınar TR 118 C5
Aarau CH 70 A3
Aarberg CH 70 A2
Aarburg CH 70 A2
Aardenburg NL 49 B4
Aars DK 38 C2
Aarschot B 49 C5
Aarup DK 39 D3
Aba H 74 A3
Abádanes E 95 B4
Abades E 94 B2
Abadin E 86 A3
Abádszalók H 75 A5
Abaliget H 74 B3
Abana TR 16 A7
A Baña E 86 B2
Abanilla E 101 A4
Abano Terme I 72 C1
Abarán E 101 A4
Abasár H 65 C6
Abbadia San Salvatore I 81 D5
Abbaue D 45 B5
Abbehausen D 43 B5
Abbekäs S 41 D3
Abbeville F 48 C2
Abbey IRL 20 A3
Abbeydorney IRL 20 B2
Abbeyfeale IRL 20 B2
Abbeyleix IRL 21 B4
Abbey Town GB 25 D4
Abbiategrasso I 70 C3
Abborrträsk S 115 B16
Abbots Bromley GB 27 C4
Abbotsbury GB 29 C5
Abda H 64 C3
Abejar E 89 C4
Abela P 98 B2
Abelvær N 114 C8
Abenberg D 62 A1
Abenójar E 100 A1
Abensberg D 62 B2
Aberaeron GB 28 A3
Abercarn GB 29 B4
Aberchirder GB 23 D6
Aberdare GB 29 B4
Aberdaron GB 26 C1
Aberdeen GB 23 D6
Aberdulais GB 28 B4
Aberdyfi GB 26 C1
Aberfeldy GB 25 B4
Aberffraw GB 26 B1
Aberfoyle GB 24 B3
Abergavenny GB 29 B4
Abergele GB 26 B2
Abergynolwyn GB 26 C2
Aberporth GB 28 A3
Abersoch GB 26 C1
Abertillery GB 29 B4
Abertura E 93 B5
Aberystwyth GB 26 C1
Abetone I 81 B4
Abfaltersbach A 72 B2
Abide
  Çanakkale TR 118 B1
  Kütahya TR 118 D4
Abiego E 90 A2
Abild DK 39 E1
Abingdon-on-Thames GB 31 C2
Abington GB 25 C4
Abisko S 112 D7
Abiul P 92 B2
Abla E 101 B3
Ablis F 58 B2
A Bola E 87 B3
Abondance F 70 B1
Abony H 75 A5
Aboyne GB 23 D6
Abrantes P 92 B2
Abreiro P 87 C3
Abreschviller F 60 B3
Abrest F 68 B3
Abriès F 79 B5
Abrud RO 11 C7
Absdorf A 64 B1
Abtenau A 72 A3
Abtsgmünd D 61 B5
Abusejo E 93 A4
Åby
  Kronoberg S 40 B4
  Östergötland S 37 D3
Åbyggeby S 36 B4
Åbytorp S 37 C2
A Cañiza E 87 B2
A Capela E 86 A2
Acate I 109 B3
Accadía I 103 B8
Accéglio I 79 B5
Accettura I 104 C2
Acciaroli I 106 A2
Accous F 76 D2
Accrington GB 26 B3
Accúmoli I 82 D2
Acedera E 93 B5
Acehuche E 93 B4
Acered E 95 A5
Acerenza I 104 C1
Acerno I 103 C8
Acerra I 103 C7
Aceuchal E 93 C4
Acharacle GB 24 B2
Acharnes GR 117 D5
Achavanich GB 23 C5
Achene B 49 C6
Achenkirch A 72 A1
Achensee A 72 A1
Achenthal A 72 A1
Achentrias GR 117 H7
Achern D 61 B4
Acheux-en-Amienois F 48 C3
Achiltibuie GB 22 C3
Achim D 43 B6
Achladokambos GR 117 E4
Achnasheen GB 22 D3
Achnashellach GB 22 D3
Achosnich GB 24 B1
Aci Castello I 109 B4
Aci Catena I 109 B4
Acilia I 102 B5
Acıpayam TR 119 E4
Acireale I 109 B4
Acle GB 30 B5
A Coruña E 86 A2
Acquacadda I 110 C1
Acqua Doria F 102 B1
Acquanegra sul Chiese I 71 C5
Acquapendente I 81 D5
Acquasanta Terme I 82 D2
Acquasparta I 102 A5
Acquaviva I 81 C5
Acquaviva delle Fonti I 104 C2
Acquaviva Picena I 82 D2
Acquigny F 58 A2
Ácqui Terme I 80 B2
Acri I 106 B3
Acs H 64 C4
Acsa H 65 C5
Ácsteszér H 74 A2
Acy-en-Multien F 59 A3
Ada SRB 75 C5
Adak S 115 B15
Ådalsbruk N 34 B3
Adamas GR 117 F6
Adamsfjord N 113 B15
Adamuz E 100 A1
Adana TR 16 C7
Ádánd H 74 B3
Adanero E 94 B2
Adare IRL 20 B3
Adaševci SRB 85 A4
Adeanueva de Ebro E 89 B5
Adelboden CH 70 B2
Adelebsen D 51 B5
Adélfia I 104 B2
Adelmannsfelden D 61 B6
Adelsheim D 61 A5
Adelsö S 37 C4
Ademuz E 96 A1
Adenau D 50 C2
Adendorf D 44 B2
Adinkerke B 48 B3
Adjud RO 11 C9
Adliswil CH 70 A3
Admont A 63 C5
Ådneram N 33 C3
Adolfsström S 115 A13
Adony H 74 A3
Adorf
  Hessen D 51 B4
  Sachsen D 52 C2
Adra E 100 C2
Adradas E 89 C4
Adrall E 91 A4
Adrano I 109 B3
Ádria I 82 A1
Adrigole IRL 20 C2
Adwick le Street GB 27 B4
Adzaneta E 96 A2
Aesch CH 70 A2
A Estrada E 86 B2
Afandou GR 119 F3
Åfarnes N 114 E4
Affing D 62 B1
Affoltern CH 70 A3
Affric Lodge GB 22 D3
Åfjord N 114 D7
Aflenz Kurort A 73 A5
A Fonsagrada E 86 A3
Afragóla I 103 C7
Afritz A 72 B3
Afyon TR 118 D5
Ágasegyháza H 75 B4
Agay F 79 C5
Agazzano I 80 B3
Agde F 78 C2
Agdenes N 114 D6
Agen F 77 B3
Ager E 90 B3
Agerbæk DK 39 D1
Agerskov DK 39 D2
Ageyevo RUS 7 D14
Agger DK 38 C1
Aggersund DK 38 B2
Äggius I 110 B2
Aggsbach Dorf A 63 B6
Aggsbach Markt A 63 B6
Aggtelek H 65 B6
Aghalee GB 19 B5
Aghia GR 116 C4
Aghia Anna GR 116 D5
Aghia Galini GR 117 G6
Aghia Marina GR 119 G1
Aghia Paraskevi GR 118 C1
Aghia Pelagia GR 117 F4
Aghia Triada GR 117 E3
Aghiokambos GR 116 C4
Aghios Efstratios GR 116 C6
Aghios Kirikos GR 119 E1
Aghios Matheos GR 116 C1
Aghios Mironas GR 117 G7
Aghios Nikolaos GR 117 G7
Aghios Petros GR 116 D2
Aghio Theodori GR 117 E5
Agiči BIH 83 B5
Agira I 109 B3
Aglientu I 110 A2
Agnières F 79 B4
Agno CH 70 C3
Agnone I 103 B7
Agolada E 86 B2
Agon Coutainville F 57 A4
Ágordo I 72 B2
Agost E 96 C2
Agramón E 101 A4
Agramunt E 91 B4
Agreda E 89 C5
Agria GR 116 C5
Agrigento I 108 B2
Agrinio GR 116 D3
Agrón E 100 B2
Agrópoli I 103 C7
Aguadulce
  Almería E 101 C3
  Sevilla E 100 B1
Agualada E 86 A2
Agua Longa P 87 C2
A Guarda E 87 C2
Aguarón E 89 C5
Aguas E 90 A2
Aguas Belas P 92 B2
Aguas de Busot E 96 C2
Aguas de Moura P 92 C2
Águas Frias P 87 C3
Aguas Santas P 87 C2
Aguaviva E 90 C2
Aguaviva de la Vega E 89 C4
A Gudiña E 87 B3
Agudo E 94 D2
Águeda P 92 A2
Aguessac F 78 B2
Agugliano I 82 C2
Aguiar P 92 C3
Aguiàr da Beira P 87 D3
Aguilafuente E 94 A2
Aguilar de Campóo E 88 B2
Aguilar de la Frontera E 100 B1
Aguilas E 101 B4
Agunnaryd S 40 C4
Ahat TR 118 D4
Ahaus D 50 A2
Åheim N 114 E2
Ahigal E 93 A4
Ahigal de Villarino E 87 C4
Ahillones E 99 A5
Ahlbeck
  Mecklenburg-Vorpommern D 45 B6
  Mecklenburg-Vorpommern D 45 B6
Ahlen D 50 B3
Ahlhorn D 43 C5
Ahmetbey TR 118 A2
Ahmetler TR 119 D4
Ahmetli TR 119 D2
Ahoghill GB 19 B5
Ahrensbök D 44 A2
Ahrensburg D 44 B2
Ahrenshoop D 44 A4
Ahun F 68 B2
Åhus S 41 D4
Ahvenselkä FIN 113 F17
Aibar E 89 B5
Aich D 62 B3
Aicha D 63 B4
Aichach D 62 B2
Aidone I 109 B3
Aiello Cálabro I 106 B3
Aigen im Mühlkreis A 63 B4
Aigle CH 70 B1
Aignan F 76 C3
Aignay-le-Duc F 59 C5
Aigre F 67 C5
Aigrefeuille-d'Aunis F 66 B4
Aigrefeuille-sur-Maine F 66 A3
Aiguablava E 91 B6
Aiguebelle F 69 C6
Aigueperse F 68 B3
Aigues-Mortes F 78 C3
Aigues-Vives F 78 C1
Aiguilles F 79 B5
Aiguillon F 77 B3
Aigurande F 68 B1
Ailefroide F 79 B5
Aillant-sur-Tholon F 59 C4
Ailly-sur-Noye F 58 A3
Ailly-sur-Somme F 58 A3
Aimargues F 78 C3
Aime F 69 C6
Ainaži LV 6 C8
Ainet A 72 B2
Ainhoa F 76 C1
Ainsa E 90 A3
Airaines F 48 D2
Aird GB 24 B2
Aird Asaig Tairbeart GB 22 D2
Airdrie GB 25 C4
Aire-sur-l'Adour F 76 C2
Aire-sur-la-Lys F 48 C3
Airole I 80 C1
Airolo CH 70 B3
Airvault F 67 B4
Aisey-sur-Seine F 59 C5
Aïssey F 69 A6
Aisy-sur-Armançon F 59 C5
Aiterhofen D 62 B3
Aith
  Orkney GB 23 B6
  Shetland GB 22 A7
Aitona E 90 B3
Aitrach D 61 C6
Aiud RO 11 C7
Aix-en-Othe F 59 B4
Aix-en-Provence F 79 C4
Aixe-sur-Vienne F 67 C6
Aix-les-Bains F 69 C5
Aizenay F 66 B3
Aizkraukle LV 7 C8
Aizpute LV 6 C6
Ajac F 77 C5
Ajaccio F 102 B1
Ajain F 68 B1
Ajaureforsen S 115 B12
Ajdovščina SLO 72 C3
Ajka H 74 A2
Ajo E 89 A3
Ajofrin E 94 C3
Ajuda P 93 C3
Akanthou CY 120 A2
Akarca TR 118 D4
Akasztó H 75 B4
Akçakoca TR 118 A6
Akçaova TR 118 A4
Akçay TR 119 F4
Aken D 52 B2
Åkerby S 36 B4
Åkernes N 33 D4
Åkersberga S 37 C5
Åkers Styckebruk S 37 C4
Åkervik N 115 B10
Akhisar TR 118 D2
Åkirkeby DK 41 D4
Akköy TR 119 E2
Akkrum NL 42 B2
Akören TR 119 E7
Åkra N 32 C3
Akranes IS 111 C3
Åkrehamn N 33 C2
Akrotiri CY 120 B1
Aksaray TR 16 B7
Akşehir TR 119 D6
Akseki TR 119 E6
Aksla N 32 A3
Aksu TR 119 F5
Aktsyabrski BY 7 E10
Akureyri IS 111 B7
Åkvåg N 33 D6
Akyazı TR 118 B5
Ål N 32 B5
Ala I 71 C6
Alaca TR 16 A7
Alacaatlı TR 118 C3
Alaçam TR 16 A7
Alaçatı TR 119 D1
Alàdei Sardi I 110 B2
Ala di Stura I 70 C2
Alaejos E 88 C1
Alagna Valsésia I 70 C2
Alagón E 90 B1
Alaior E 97 B4
Alájar E 99 B4
Alakurtti RUS 3 C29
Alakylä FIN 113 E13
Alameda E 100 B1
Alameda de la Sagra E 94 B3
Alamedilla E 100 B2
Alamillo E 100 A1
Alaminos E 95 B4
Ala-Nampa FIN 113 F15
Alanäs S 115 C12
Alandroal P 92 C3
Alange E 93 C4
Alanís E 99 A5
Alanno I 103 A6
Ålansbro S 115 E14
Alanya TR 119 F7
Alap H 74 B3
Alaquáso E 96 B2
Alaraz E 94 B1
Alarcón E 95 C4
Alar del Rey E 88 B2
Alaró E 97 B2
Alaşehir TR 119 D3
Alássio I 80 B2
Ağlasun TR 119 E5
Alatoz E 96 B1
Alatri I 103 B6
Alavus FIN 3 E25
Alba
  E 95 B5
  I 80 B2
Alba Adriática I 82 D2
Albacete E 95 D5
Alba de Tormes E 94 B1
Alba de Yeltes E 93 A4
Albaida E 96 C2
Alba-Iulia RO 11 C7
Albæk DK 38 B3
Albaladejo E 101 A3
Albala del Caudillo E 93 B4
Albalat E 96 B2
Albalate de Cinca E 90 B3
Albalate del Arzobispo E 90 B2
Albalate de las Nogueras E 95 B4
Albalete de Zorita E 95 B4
Alban F 77 C5
Albánchez E 101 B3
Albanchez de Ubeda E 100 B2
Albano Laziale I 102 B5
Albanyà E 91 A5
Albaredo d'Adige I 71 C6
Albares E 95 B3
Albarracín E 95 B5
Albatana E 101 A4
Albatarrec E 90 B3
Albatera E 101 A5
Albbruck D 61 C4
Albedin E 100 B1
Albelda de Iregua E 89 B4
Albenga I 80 B2
Albens F 69 C5
Ålberga
  Södermanland S 37 C3
  Södermanland S 37 D3
Albergaria-a-Nova P 87 D2
Albergaria-a-Velha P 92 A2
Albergaria dos Doze P 92 B2
Alberge P 92 C2
Alberic E 96 B2
Albernoa P 98 B3
Alberobello I 104 C3
Alberoni I 72 C2
Albersdorf D 43 A6
Albersloh D 50 B3
Albert F 48 C3
Albertirsa H 75 A4
Albertville F 69 C6
Alberuela de Tubo E 90 B2
Albi F 77 C5
Albidona I 106 B3
Albínia I 102 A4
Albino I 71 C4
Albinshof D 45 B5
Albires E 88 B1
Albisola Marina I 80 B2
Albocácer E 90 C3
Albolote E 100 B2
Albondón E 100 C2
Alborea E 96 B1
Albox E 101 B3
Albrechtice nad Vitavou CZ 63 A5
Albstadt D 61 B5
Albufeira P 98 B2
Albuñol E 100 C2
Albuñuelas E 100 C2
Alburquerque E 93 B3
Alby
  Öland S 41 C6
  Västernorrland S 115 E12
Alcácer do Sal P 92 C2
Alcáçovas P 92 C2
Alcadozo E 101 A4
Alcafoces P 93 B3
Alcains P 92 B3
Alcaláde Guadaira E 99 B5
Alcaláde Gurrea E 90 A2
Alcaláde Henares E 95 B3
Alcaláde la Selva E 90 C2
Alcaládel Júcar E 96 B1
Alcaláde los Gazules E 99 C5
Alcaládel Río E 99 B5
Alcaládel Valle E 99 C5
Alcaláde Xivert E 90 C3
Alcalála Real E 100 B2
Álcamo I 108 B1
Alcampell E 90 B3
Alcanadre E 89 B4
Alcanar E 90 C3
Alcanede P 92 B2
Alcanena P 92 B2
Alcañices E 87 C4
Alcántara E 93 B4
Alcantarilha P 98 B2
Alcantarilla E 101 B4
Alcañiz E 90 B2
Alcaracejos E 100 A1
Alcara il Fusi I 109 A3
Alcaraz E 101 A3
Alcaria Ruiva P 98 B3
Alcarraz E 90 B3
Alcaudete E 100 B1
Alcaudete de la Jara E 94 C2
Alcázar de San Juan E 95 C3
Alcazarén E 88 C2
Alcester GB 29 A6
Alcoba E 94 C2
Alcobaça P 92 B1
Alcobendas E 94 B3
Alcocer E 95 B4
Alcochete P 92 C2
Alcoentre P 92 B2
Alcolea
  Almería E 100 C3
  Córdoba E 100 B1
Alcolea de Calatrava E 94 D2
Alcolea de Cinca E 90 B3
Alcolea del Pinar E 95 A4
Alcolea del Rio E 99 B5
Alcolea de Tajo E 93 B5
Alcollarin E 93 B5
Alconchel E 93 C3
Alconera E 93 C4
Alcontar E 101 B3
Alcora E 96 A2
Alcorcón E 94 B3
Alcorisa E 90 C2
Alcossebre E 96 A3
Alcoutim P 98 B3
Alcover E 91 B4
Alcoy E 96 C2
Alcsútdoboz H 74 A3
Alcubierre E 90 B2
Alcubilla de Avellaneda E 89 C3
Alcubilla de Nogales E 88 B1
Alcubillas E 100 A2
Alcublas E 96 B2
Alcúdia E 97 B3
Alcudia de Guadix E 100 B2
Alcuéscar E 93 B4
Aldbrough GB 27 B5
Aldeacentenera E 93 B5
Aldeadávila de la Ribera E 87 C4
Aldea del Cano E 93 B4
Aldea del Fresno E 94 B2
Aldea del Obispo E 87 D4
Aldea del Rey E 100 A2
Alde de Trujillo E 93 B5
Aldealcorvo E 94 A3
Aldealuenga de Santa Maria E 89 C3
Aldeamayor de San Martin E 88 C2
Aldeanueva de Barbarroya E 94 C1
Aldeanueva del Camino E 93 A5
Aldeanueva del Codonal E 94 A2
Aldeanueva de San Bartolomé E 94 C1
Aldeapozo E 89 C4
Aldeaquemada E 100 A2
Aldea Real E 94 A2
Aldearrubia E 94 A1
Aldeaseca de la Frontera E 94 B1
Aldeasoña E 88 C2
Aldeatejada E 94 B1
Aldeavieja E 94 B2
Aldeburgh GB 30 B5
Aldehuela E 96 A1
Aldehuela de Calatañazor E 89 C4
Aldeia da Serra P 92 C3
Aldeia do Bispo P 93 A4
Aldeia do Mato P 92 B2
Aldeia Gavinha P 92 B1
Aldeire E 100 B2
Aldenhoven D 50 C2
Aldersbach D 62 B4
Aldershot GB 31 C3
Aldudes F 76 C1
Åled S 40 C2
Aledo E 101 B4
Alegria E 89 B4
Aleksandrovac
  Srbija SRB 85 B6
  Srbija SRB 85 C6
Aleksandrów Kujawski PL 47 C4
Aleksandrów Łódźki PL 55 B4
Aleksa Šantić SRB 75 C4
Aleksin RUS 7 D14
Ålem S 40 C6
Alençon F 57 B6
Alenquer P 92 B1
Alenya F 91 A5
Aléria F 102 A2
Alès F 78 B3
Áles I 110 C1
Alessándria I 80 B2
Alessándria della Rocca I 108 B2
Alessano I 107 B5
Ålesund N 114 E3
Alet-les-Bains F 77 D5
Alexandria
  GB 24 C3
  GR 116 B4
  RO 11 E8
Alexandroupoli GR 116 B7
Aleyrac F 78 B3
Alézio I 107 A5
Alfacar E 100 B2
Alfaiates P 93 A4
Alfajarin E 90 B2
Alfambra
  E 90 C1
  P 98 B2
Alfândega da Fé P 87 C4
Alfarela de Jafes P 87 C3
Alfarelos P 92 A2
Alfarim P 92 C1
Alfarnate E 100 C1
Alfaro E 89 B5
Alfarrás E 90 B3
Alfaz del Pi E 96 C2
Alfedena I 103 B7
Alfeizarão P 92 B1
Alfeld
  Bayern D 62 A2
  Niedersachsen D 51 B5
Alfena P 87 C2
Alferce P 98 B2
Alfhausen D 43 C4
Alfonsine I 81 B6
Alford
  Aberdeenshire GB 23 D6
  Lincolnshire GB 27 B6
Alforja E 90 B3
Alfoz E 86 A3
Alfreton GB 27 B4
Alfta S 36 A3
Alfundão P 98 A2
Algaida E 97 B2
Algar E 99 C5
Älgarås S 35 D6
Ålgård N 33 D2
Algarinejo E 100 B1
Algarrobo E 100 C1
Algatocin E 99 C5
Algeciras E 99 C5
Algemesí E 96 B2
Algés P 92 C1
Algete E 95 B3
Alghero I 110 B1
Älghult S 40 B5
Alginet E 96 B2
Algodonales E 99 C5
Algodor
  E 94 C3
  P 98 B3
Algora E 95 B4
Algoso P 87 C4
Algoz P 98 B2
Älgsjö S 115 C14
Alguaire E 90 B3
Alguazas E 101 A4
Algutsrum S 41 C6
Algyö H 75 B5
Alhama de Almería E 101 C3
Alhama de Aragón E 89 C5
Alhama de Granada E 100 C2
Alhama de Murcia E 101 B4
Alhambra E 100 A2
Alhandra P 92 C1
Alhaurin de la Torre E 100 C1
Alhaurín el Grande E 100 C1
Alhendin E 100 B2
Alhóndiga E 95 B4
Alia E 93 B5
Ália I 108 B2
Aliağa TR 118 D1
Aliaga E 90 C2
Alibunar SRB 85 A5
Alicante E 96 C2
Alicún de Ortega E 100 B2
Alife I 103 B7
Alija del Infantado E 88 B1
Alijó P 87 C3
Alimena I 109 B3
Alingsås S 40 B2
Alinyà E 91 A4
Aliseda E 93 B4
Ali Terme I 109 A4
Aliveri GR 116 D6
Alixan F 79 B4
Aljaraque E 99 B3
Aljezur P 98 B2
Aljorra E 101 B4
Aljubarrota P 92 B2
Aljucen E 93 B4
Aljustrel P 98 B2
Alken B 49 C6
Alkmaar NL 42 C1
Alkoven A 63 B5
Allaines F 58 B2
Allaire F 57 C3
Allanche F 68 C2
Alland A 64 B2
Allariz E 87 B3
Allassac F 67 C6
Allauch F 79 C4
Alleen N 33 D4
Allègre F 68 C3
Allemont F 69 C6
Allendale Town GB 25 D5
Allendorf D 51 C4
Allentsteig A 63 B6
Allepuz E 90 C2
Allersberg D 62 A2
Allershausen D 62 B2
Alles E 88 A2
Allevard F 69 C6
Allgunnen S 40 B5
Allihies IRL 20 C1
Allingåbro DK 38 C3
Allmannsdorf D 61 C5
Allo E 89 B4
Alloa GB 25 B4
Allogny F 68 A2
Ålloluokta S 112 E8
Allones
  Eure et Loire F 58 B2
  Maine-et-Loire F 67 A5
Allonnes F 57 C6
Allons F 76 B2
Allos F 79 B5
Allstedt D 52 B1
Alltwalis GB 28 B3
Allumiere I 102 A4
Almaceda P 92 B3
Almacelles E 90 B3
Almachar E 100 C1
Almada P 92 C1
Almadén E 100 A1
Almadén de la Plata E 99 B4
Almadenejos E 100 A1
Almadrones E 95 B4
Almagro E 100 A2
Almajano E 89 C4
Almansa E 96 C1
Almansil P 98 B2
Almanza E 88 B1
Almaraz E 93 B5
Almargen E 99 C5
Almarza E 89 C4
Almásfüzitő H 64 C4
Almassora E 96 B2
Almazán E 89 C4
Almazul E 89 C4
Alme D 51 B4
Almedina E 100 A3
Almedinilla E 100 B1
Almeida
  E 87 C4
  P 93 A4
Almeirim P 92 B2
Almelo NL 42 C3
Almenar E 90 B3
Almenara E 96 B2
Almenar de Soria E 89 C4
Almendra P 87 D3
Almendral E 93 C4
Almendral de la Cañada E 94 B2
Almendralejo E 93 C4
Almenno San Bartolomeo I 71 C4
Almere NL 42 C2
Almería E 101 C3
Almerimar E 101 C3
Almese I 70 C2
Almexial P 98 B3
Älmhult S 40 C4
Almiropotamos GR 117 D6
Almiros GR 116 C4
Almodôvar P 98 B2
Almodóvar del Campo E 100 A1
Almodóvar del Pinar E 95 C5
Almodóvar del Río E 99 B5
Almofala P 87 D3
Almogia E 100 C1
Almoharin E 93 B4
Almonacid de la Sierra E 89 C5
Almonacid de Toledo E 94 C3
Almonaster la Real E 99 B4
Almondsbury GB 29 B5
Almonte E 99 B4
Almoradí E 101 A5
Almoraima E 99 C5
Almorox E 94 B2
Almoster P 92 B2
Almsele S 115 C14
Älmsta S 36 C5
Almudena E 101 A4
Almudévar E 90 A2
Almuñécar E 100 C2
Almunge S 36 C5
Almuradiel E 100 A2
Almussafes E 96 B2
Almvik S 40 B6
Alness GB 23 D4
Alnmouth GB 25 C6
Alnwick GB 25 C6
Åloppe S 36 C4
Álora E 100 C1
Alos d'Ensil E 91 A4
Alosno E 99 B3
Alozaina E 100 C1
Alpbach A 72 A1
Alpedrete de la Sierra E 95 B3
Alpedrinha P 92 A3
Alpen D 50 B2
Alpera E 96 C1
Alphen aan de Rijn NL 49 A5
Alpiarça P 92 B2
Alpignano I 70 C2
Alpirsbach D 61 B4
Alpu TR 118 C5
Alpuente E 96 B1
Alqueva P 98 A3
Alquézar E 90 A3
Als DK 38 C3
Alsasua E 89 B4
Alsdorf D 50 C2
Alselv DK 39 D1
Alsfeld D 51 C5
Alsike S 36 C4
Alskog S 37 E5
Alsleben D 52 B1
Alsónémedi H 75 A4
Alsótold H 65 C5

Alsóújlak H 74 A1
Alstad N 112 E4
Alstätte D 50 A2
Alsterbro S 40 C5
Alstermo S 40 C5
Alston GB 25 D5
Alsvåg N 112 D4
Alsvik N 112 E3
Alta N 113 C12
Älta S 37 C5
Altamura I 104 C2
Altarejos E 95 C4
Altaussee A 63 C4
Altavilla Irpina I 103 B7
Altavilla Silentina I 103 C8
Altdöbern D 53 B4
Altdorf
CH 70 B3
D 62 B3
Altdorf bei Nürnberg
D 62 A2
Alte P 98 B2
Altea E 96 C2
Altedo I 81 B5
Altena D 50 B3
Altenau D 51 B6
Altenberg D 53 C3
Altenberge D 50 A3
Altenbruch D 43 B5
Altenburg D 52 C2
Altenfelden A 63 B4
Altengronau D 51 C5
Altenheim D 60 B3
Altenhundem D 50 B4
Altenkirchen
Mecklenburg-Vorpommern D 45 A5
Radom D 50 C3
Altenkunstadt D 52 C1
Altenmarkt
A 63 C5
D 62 B3
Altenmarkt im Pongall
A 72 A3
Altensteig D 61 B4
Altentreptow D 45 B5
Altenwalde D 43 B5
Alten-weddingen D 52 A1
Alter do Chão P 92 B3
Altfraunhofen D 62 B3
Altheim
A 63 B4
D 61 A5
Althofen A 73 B4
Altınoluk TR 118 C1
Altınova TR 118 C1
Altıntaş TR 118 C5
Altınyaka TR 119 F5
Altınyayla TR 119 E4
Altkirch F 60 C3
Altlandsberg D 45 C5
Altlewin D 45 C6
Altmannstein D 62 B2
Altmorschen D 51 B5
Altmunster A 63 C4
Altnaharra GB 23 C4
Alto Campoó E 88 A2
Altofonte I 108 A2
Altomonte I 106 B3
Alton
Hampshire GB 31 C3
Staffordshire GB 27 C4
Altopáscio I 81 C4
Altötting D 62 B3
Altreichenau D 63 B4
Alt Ruppin D 45 C4
Altshausen D 61 C5
Altstätten CH 71 A4
Altura E 96 B2
Altusried D 61 C6
Alūksne LV 7 C9
Alunda S 36 B5
Alustante E 95 B5
Alva GB 25 B4
Alvaiázere P 92 B2
Alvalade P 98 B2
Älvängen S 38 B5
Alvarenga P 87 D2
Alvares P 92 A2
Alvdal N 114 E7
Älvdalen S 34 A6
Alverca P 92 C1
Alversund N 32 B2
Alvesta S 40 C4
Alvignac F 77 B4
Alvignano I 103 B7
Ålvik N 32 B3
Alvik S 36 B1
Alvimare F 58 A1
Alviobeira P 92 B2
Alvito P 98 A3
Älvkarleby S 36 B4
Älvkarleöbruk S 36 B4
Alvor P 98 B2
Alvorge P 92 B2
Alvøy N 32 B2
Älvros S 115 E11
Alvsbacka S 35 C5
Älvsbyn S 3 D24
Älvsered S 40 B2
Alwernia PL 55 C4
Alwinton GB 25 C5
Alyth GB 25 B4
Alytus LT 6 D8
Alzénau D 51 C5
Alzey D 61 A4
Alzira E 96 B2
Alzonne F 77 C5
Amadora P 92 C1
Åmål S 35 C4
Amalfi I 103 C7
Amaliada GR 117 E3
Amance F 60 C2
Amancey F 69 A6
Amándola I 82 D2
Amantea I 106 B3
Amarante P 87 C2
Amareleja P 98 A3
Amares P 87 C2
Amaseno I 103 B6
Amasra TR 118 A7
Amasya TR 16 A8
Amatrice I 103 A6
Amay B 49 C6
Ambarnyy RUS 3 D30
Ambazac F 67 C6
Ambelonas GR 116 C4
Amberg D 62 A2
Ambérieu-en-Bugey
F 69 C5
Ambérieux-en-Dombes
F 69 B4
Ambert F 68 C3
Ambés F 76 A2
Ambjörby S 34 B5
Ambjörnarp S 40 B3
Amble GB 25 C6
Ambleside GB 26 A3
Ambleteuse F 48 C2
Amboise F 67 A5
Ambrières-les-Vallées
F 57 B5
Amden CH 71 A4
Amel B 50 C2
Amélia I 102 A5
Amélie-les-Bains-Palalda
F 91 A5
Amelinghausen D 44 B2
Amendoa P 92 B2
Amendoeira P 98 B3
Améndola I 104 B1
Amendolara I 106 B3
Amer E 91 A5
A Merca E 87 B3
Amerongen NL 49 A6
Amersfoort NL 49 A6
Amersham GB 31 C3
Amesbury GB 29 B6
Amfiklia GR 116 D4
Amfilochia GR 116 D3
Amfipoli GR 116 B5
Amfissa GR 116 D4
Amièira P 98 A3
Amieira P 92 B3
Amieiro P 92 A2
Amiens F 58 A3
Amindeo GR 116 B3
Åminne S 40 B3
Åmli N 33 D5
Amlwch GB 26 B1
Ammanford GB 28 B4
Ammarnäs S 115 B13
Åmmeberg S 37 D1
Amorbach D 61 A5
Amorebieta E 89 A4
Amorgos GR 117 F7
Amorosa P 87 C2
Amorosi I 103 B7
Åmot
Buskerud N 34 C1
Telemark N 33 C4
S 36 B3
Åmotfors S 34 C4
Åmotsdal N 33 C5
Amou F 76 C2
Ampezzo I 72 B2
Ampfing D 62 B3
Ampflwang A 63 B4
Amplepuis F 69 C4
Amposta E 90 C3
Ampthill GB 30 B3
Ampudia E 88 C2
Ampuero E 89 A3
Amriswil CH 71 A4
Åmsele S 115 C16
Amstelveen NL 49 A5
Amsterdam NL 42 C1
Amstetten A 63 B5
Amtzell D 61 C5
Amulree GB 25 B4
Amurrio E 89 A4
Amusco E 88 B2
Anacapri I 103 C7
Anadia P 92 A2
Anadon E 90 C1
Anafi GR 117 F7
Anagni I 102 B6
Anamur TR 16 C6
Ananyiv UA 11 C10
Anascaul IRL 20 B1
Ånäset S 3 D24
Åna-Sira N 33 D3
Anastaźewo PL 47 C4
Anaya de Alba E 94 B1
Ança P 92 A2
Ancaster GB 27 C5
Ancede P 87 C2
Ancenis F 66 A3
Ancerville F 59 B6
Anchuras E 94 C2
Ancona I 82 C2
Ancora P 87 C2
Ancrum GB 25 C5
Ancy-le-Franc F 59 C5
Andalo I 71 B5
Åndalsnes N 114 E4
Andance F 69 C4
Andau A 64 C3
Andebu N 35 C2
Andeer CH 71 B4
Andelfingen CH 61 C4
Andelot-Blanchville F 59 B6
Andelot-en-Montagne
F 69 B5
Andenes N 112 C5
Andenne B 49 C6
Anderlues B 49 C5
Andermatt CH 70 B3
Andernach D 50 C3
Andernos-les-Bains F 76 B1
Anderslöv S 41 D3
Anderstorp S 40 B3
Andijk NL 42 C2
Andoain E 89 A4
Andocs H 74 B2
Andolsheim F 60 B3
Andorra E 90 C2
Andorra La Vella AND 91 A4
Andosilla E 89 B5
Andover GB 31 C2
Andratx E 97 B2
Andreapol RUS 7 C12
Andreas GB 26 A1
Andréspol PL 55 B4
Andrest F 76 C3
Andretta I 103 C8
Andrezieux-Bouthéon
F 69 C4
Ándria I 104 B2
Andrijevica MNE 85 D4
Andritsena GR 117 E3
Andros GR 117 E6
Andrychów PL 65 A5
Andselv N 112 C7
Andújar E 100 A1
Anduze F 78 B2
Åneby N 34 B2
Aneby S 40 B4
Añes E 89 A3
Anet F 58 B2
Anfo I 71 C5
Ang S 40 B4
Anga S 37 E5
Angaïs F 76 C2
Änge S 115 D11
Ånge S 115 E12
Angeja P 92 A2
Ängelholm S 41 C2
Angeli FIN 113 D14
Ängelsberg S 36 C3
Anger A 73 A5
Angera I 70 C3
Angermünde D 45 B6
Angern A 64 B2
Angers F 67 A4
Angerville F 58 B3
Anghiari I 82 C1
Angle GB 28 B2
Anglès E 91 B5
Anglés F 77 C5
Angles F 66 B3
Anglesola E 91 B4
Angles sur l'Anglin F 67 B5
Anglet F 76 C1
Anglisidhes CY 120 B2
Anglure F 59 B4
Angoulême F 67 C5
Angoulins F 66 B3
Angsö S 37 C3
Angueira P 87 C4
Angües E 90 A2
Anguiano E 89 B4
Anguillara Sabazia I 102 A5
Anguillara Véneta I 72 C1
Anhée B 49 C5
Anholt DK 38 C4
Aniane F 78 C2
Aniche F 49 C4
Ånimskog S 35 D4
Anina RO 10 D6
Anixi GR 116 C3
Anizy-le-Château F 59 A4
Anjalankoski FIN 3 F27
Anjan S 115 D9
Ankara TR 118 C7
Ankaran SLO 72 C3
Ankarsrum S 40 B6
Ankerlia N 112 C9
Anklam D 45 B5
Ankum D 43 C4
Anlauftal A 72 A3
Anlezy F 68 B3
Ånn S 115 D9
Annaberg A 63 C6
Annaberg-Buchholz
D 52 C3
Annaberg im Lammertal
A 72 A3
Annaburg D 52 B3
Annahütte D 53 B3
Annalong GB 19 B6
Annan GB 25 D4
Anndalsvågen N 115 B9
Anneberg
Halland S 38 B5
Jönköping S 40 B4
Annecy F 69 C6
Annelund S 40 B3
Annemasse F 69 B6
Annenskiy Most RUS 7 A14
Annerstad S 40 C3
Annestown IRL 21 B4
Annevoie-Rouillon B 49 C5
Annonay F 69 C4
Annot F 79 C5
Annweiler D 60 A3
Ano Poroia GR 116 A5
Añora E 100 A1
Ano Siros GR 117 E6
Anould F 60 B2
Anquela del Ducado
E 95 B4
Anröchte D 51 B4
Ans DK 39 C2
Ansager DK 39 D1
Ansbach D 62 A1
Anse F 69 C4
Anseroeul B 49 C4
Ansfelden A 63 B5
Ansião P 92 B2
Ansó E 76 D2
Ansoain E 76 D1
Anstruther GB 25 B5
Antalya TR 119 F5
Antas E 101 B4
Antegnate I 71 C4
Antequera E 100 B1
Anterselva di Mezzo I 72 B2
Antibes F 79 C6
Antigüedad E 88 C2
Antillo I 109 B4
Antirio GR 117 D3
An t-Ob GB 22 D1
Antoing B 49 C4
Antonin PL 54 B2
Antrain F 57 B4
Antrim GB 19 B5
Antrodoco I 102 A6
Antronapiana I 70 B3
Anttis S 113 E11
Antuzede P 92 A2
Antwerp = Antwerpen
B 49 B5
Antwerpen = Antwerp
B 49 B5
Anversa d'Abruzzi I 103 B6
Anvin F 48 C3
Anzat-le-Luguet F 68 C3
Anzi I 104 C1
Ánzio I 102 B5
Anzola d'Emilia I 81 B5
Anzón E 89 C5
Aoiz E 76 D1
Aosta I 70 C2
Apalhão P 92 B3
Apátfalva H 75 B5
Apatin SRB 75 C4
Apatity RUS 3 C30
Apc H 65 C5
Apécchio I 82 C1
Apeldoorn NL 50 A1
Apen D 43 B4
Apenburg D 44 C3
Apensen D 43 B6
A Peroxa E 86 B3
Apiro I 82 C2
Apliki CY 120 B2
Apolda D 52 B1
Apolonia GR 117 F6
A Pontenova E 86 A3
Apostag H 75 B3
Äppelbo S 34 B6
Appennino I 82 D2
Appenzell CH 71 A4
Appiano I 71 B6
Appingedam NL 42 B3
Appleby-in-Westmorland
GB 26 A3
Applecross GB 22 D3
Appledore GB 28 B3
Appoigny F 59 C4
Apremont-la-Forêt F 60 B1
Aprica I 71 B5
Apricena I 103 B8
Aprigliano I 106 B3
Aprília I 102 B5
Apt F 79 C4
Apúlia P 87 C2
Aquiléia I 72 C3
Aquilónia I 103 C8
Aquino I 103 B6
Ar S 37 E5
Arabayona E 94 A1
Arabba I 72 B1
Araç TR 16 A6
Aracena E 99 B4
Arachova GR 116 D4
Arad RO 75 B6
Aradac SRB 75 C5
Aradhippou CY 120 B2
Aragnouet F 76 D3
Aragona I 108 B2
Aramits F 76 C2
Aramon F 78 C3
Aranda de Duero E 88 C3
Aranda de Moncayo
E 89 C5
Arandjelovac SRB 85 B5
Aranjuez E 95 B3
Arantzazu E 89 B4
Aranzueque E 95 B3
Aras de Alpuente E 96 B1
Arauzo de Miel E 89 C3
Arazede P 92 A2
Arbas F 77 D3
Árbatax I 110 C2
Arbeca E 90 B3
Arberg D 62 A1
Arbesbach A 63 B5
Arboga S 37 C2
Arbois F 69 B5
Arbon CH 71 A4
Arboréa I 110 C1
Arbório I 70 C3
Årbostad N 112 D6
Arbrå S 36 A3
Arbroath GB 25 B5
Arbùcies E 91 B5
Arbuniel E 100 B2
Arbus I 110 C1
Arcachon F 76 B1
Arce I 103 B6
Arcen NL 50 B2
Arc-en-Barrois F 59 C5
Arces-Dilo F 59 B4
Arc-et-Senans F 69 A5
Arcévia I 82 C1
Arcey F 70 A1
Archanes GR 117 G7
Archangelos GR 119 F3
Archena E 101 A4
Archez E 100 C2
Archiac F 67 C4
Archidona E 100 B1
Archiestown GB 23 D5
Archivel E 101 A4
Arcidosso I 81 D5
Arcille I 81 D5
Arcis-sur-Aube F 59 B5
Arc-lès-Gray F 69 A5
Arco I 71 C5
Arcones E 94 A3
Arcos E 88 B3
Arcos de Jalón E 95 A4
Arcos de la Frontera
E 99 C5
Arcos de la Sierra E 95 B4
Arcos de las Salinas
E 96 B1
Arcos de Valdevez P 87 C2
Arcozelo P 92 A3
Arc-sur-Tille F 69 A5
Arcusa E 90 A3
Arcy-sur-Cure F 59 C4
Ardagh IRL 20 B2
Årdal N 33 C3
Ardala S 35 D5
Ardales E 100 C1
Årdalstangen N 32 A4
Ardara
I 110 B1
IRL 18 B3
Ardarroch GB 22 D3
Ardbeg GB 24 C1
Ardcharnich GB 22 D3
Ardchyle GB 24 B3
Ardee IRL 19 C5
Arden DK 38 C2
Ardentes F 68 B1
Ardenza I 81 C4
Ardersier GB 23 D4
Ardes F 68 C3
Ardessie GB 22 D3
Ardez CH 71 B5
Ardfert IRL 20 B2
Ardgay GB 23 D4
Ardglass GB 19 B6
Ardgroom IRL 20 C2
Ardhasig GB 22 D2
Ardino BG 116 A7
Ardisa E 90 A2
Ardkearagh IRL 20 C1
Ardlui GB 24 B3
Ardlussa GB 24 B2
Ardón E 88 B1
Ardooie B 49 C4
Ardore I 106 C3
Ardre S 37 E5
Ardres F 48 C2
Ardrishaig GB 24 B2
Ardrossan GB 24 C3
Are N 33 C2
Åre S 115 D10
Areia Branca P 92 B1
Aremark N 35 C3
Arenales de San Gregorio
E 95 C3
Arenas E 100 C1
Arenas de Iguña E 88 A2
Arenas del Rey E 100 C2
Arenas de San Juan
E 95 C3
Arenas de San Pedro
E 94 B1
Arendal N 33 D5
Arendonk B 49 B6
Arengosse F 76 B2
Arentorp S 35 D4
Arenys de Mar E 91 B5
Arenys de Munt E 91 B5
Arenzano I 80 B2
Areo E 91 A4
Areopoli GR 117 F4
Ares E 86 A2
Arès F 76 B1
Ares del Maestrat E 90 C2
Aresvika N 114 D5
Arette F 76 C2
Aretxabaleta E 89 A4
Arevalillo E 93 A5
Arévalo E 94 A2
Arez P 92 B3
Arezzo I 81 C5
Arfeuilles F 68 B3
Argalasti GR 116 C5
Argallón E 99 A5
Argamasilla de Alba
E 95 C3
Argamasilla de Calatrava
E 100 A1
Arganda E 95 B3
Arganil P 92 A2
Argasion GR 117 E2
Argegno I 71 C4
Argelès-Gazost F 76 C2
Argelès-sur-Mer F 91 A6
Argenta I 81 B5
Argentan F 57 B5
Argentat F 77 A4
Argentera I 79 B5
Argenteuil F 58 B3
Argenthal D 50 D3
Argentiera I 110 B1
Argentona E 91 B5
Argenton-Château F 67 B4
Argenton-sur-Creuse
F 67 B6
Argentré F 57 B5
Argentré-du-Plessis
F 57 B4
Argent-sur-Sauldre F 68 A2
Argirades GR 116 C1
Argıthanı TR 119 D6
Argos GR 117 E4
Argos Orestiko GR 116 B3
Argostoli GR 117 D2
Argote E 89 B4
Arguedas E 89 B5
Argueil F 58 A2
Arholma S 36 C6
Århus DK 39 C3
Ariano Irpino I 103 B8
Ariano nel Polésine I 82 B1
Aribe E 76 D1
Aridea GR 116 B4
Arienzo I 103 B7
Arild S 41 C2
Arileod GB 24 B1
Arilje SRB 85 C5
Arinagour GB 24 B1
Ariño E 90 B2
Arinthod F 69 B5
Arisaig GB 24 B2
Arisgotas E 94 C3
Aritzo I 110 C2
Ariza E 89 C4
Årjäng S 35 C4
Arjeplog S 115 A14
Arjona E 100 B1
Arjonilla E 100 B1
Arkasa GR 119 G2
Arkelstorp S 41 C4
Arklow IRL 21 B5
Arkösund S 37 D3
Ärla S 37 C3
Arlanc F 68 C3
Arlanzón E 89 B3
Arlebosc F 78 A3
Arlena di Castro I 102 A4
Arles F 78 C3
Arles-sur-Tech F 91 A5
Arló H 65 B6
Arlon B 60 A1
Armação de Pera P 98 B2
Armadale
Highland GB 22 D3
West Lothian GB 25 C4
Armagh GB 19 B5
Armamar P 87 C3
Armenistis GR 117 E8
Armeno I 70 C3
Armenteros E 93 A5
Armentières F 48 C3
Armilla E 100 B2
Armiñón E 89 B4
Armoy GB 19 A5
Armuña de Tajuña E 95 B3
Armutlu
Bursa TR 118 B3
İzmir TR 119 D2
Arnac-Pompadour F 67 C6
Arnafjord N 32 A3
Arnage F 57 C6
Arnas F 69 B4
Årnäs S 35 D5
Arnay-le-Duc F 69 A4
Arnborg DK 39 C2
Arnbruck D 62 A3
Arnea GR 116 B5
Arneberg
Hedmark N 34 A2
Hedmark N 34 B4
Arneburg D 44 C4
Arnedillo E 89 B4
Arnedo E 89 B4
Arneguy F 76 C1
Arnés E 90 C3
Árnes IS 111 A4
Årnes
Akershus N 34 B3
Troms N 112 C7
Arnfels A 73 B5
Arnhem NL 50 B1
Arnissa GR 116 B3
Arno S 37 D4
Arnold GB 27 B4
Arnoldstein A 72 B3
Arnsberg D 50 B4
Arnschwang D 62 A3
Arnsdorf D 53 B3
Årnset N 114 D6
Arnside GB 26 A3
Arnstadt D 51 C6
Arnstein D 51 D5
Arnstorf D 62 B3
Arnum DK 39 D1
Aroche E 99 B4
Arolla CH 70 B2
Arolsen D 51 B5
Arona I 70 C3
Äros N 35 C2
Arosa
CH 71 B4
P 87 C2
Ærøskøbing DK 39 E3
Arøsund DK 39 D2
Arouca P 87 D2
Årøysund N 35 C2
Arpajon F 58 B3
Arpajon-sur-Cère F 77 B5
Arpino I 103 B6
Arquata del Tronto I 82 D2
Arques F 48 C3
Arques-la-Bataille F 58 A2
Arquillos E 100 A2
Arraia-Maeztu E 89 B4
Arraiolos P 92 C2
Arrancourt F 60 B2
Arras F 48 C3
Arrasate E 89 A4
Årre DK 39 D1
Arreau F 77 D3
Arredondo E 89 A3
Arrens-Marsous F 76 D2
Arriate E 99 C5
Arrifana P 98 B2
Arrigorriaga E 89 A4
Arriondas E 88 A1
Arroba de los Montes
E 94 C2
Arrochar GB 24 B3
Arromanches-les-Bains
F 57 A5
Arronches P 92 B3
Arroniz E 89 B4
Arrou F 58 B2
Arroya E 88 B2
Arroya de Cuéllar E 88 C2
Arroyal E 88 B2
Arroyo de la Luz E 93 B4
Arroyo del Ojanco E 100 A3
Arroyo de San Servan
E 93 C4
Arroyomolinos de León
E 99 A4
Arroyomolinos de Montánchez E 93 B4
Arruda dos Vinhos P 92 C1
Arsac F 76 B2
Ars-en-Ré F 66 B3
Arsiè I 72 C1
Arsiero I 71 C6
Årslev DK 39 D3
Ársoli I 102 A6
Ars-sur-Moselle F 60 A2
Årsunda S 36 B3
Artà E 97 B3
Arta GR 116 C3
Artajona E 89 B5
Artegna I 72 B3
Arteixo E 86 A2
Artemare F 69 C5
Arten I 72 B1
Artena I 102 B5
Artenay F 58 B2
Artern D 52 B1
Artés E 91 B4
Artesa de Segre E 91 B4
Arth CH 70 A3
Arthez-de-Béarn F 76 C2
Arthon-en-Retz F 66 A3
Arthurstown IRL 21 B5
Artieda E 90 A2
Artix F 76 C2
Artotina GR 116 D4
Artsyz UA 11 C10
Artziniega E 89 A3
A Rúa E 87 B3
Arudy F 76 C2
Arundel GB 31 D3
Arveyres F 76 B2
Arvidsjaur S 115 B16
Arvieux F 79 B5
Arvika S 35 C4
Åryd
Blekinge S 41 C5
Kronoberg S 40 C4
Arzachena I 110 A2
Arzacq-Arraziguet F 76 C2
Árzana I 110 C2
Arzano F 56 C2
Aržano HR 84 C1
Arzberg D 52 C2
Arzignano I 71 C6
Arzila P 92 A2
Arzl im Pitztal A 71 A5
Arzúa E 86 B2
As B 49 B6
Aš CZ 52 C2
Ås N 35 C2
Åsa S 40 B2
Asaa DK 38 B3
Aşağıçiğil TR 119 D6
Ašanja SRB 85 B5
Åsarna S 115 E11
Åsarøy N 33 C3
Åsarp S 40 A3
Asasp F 76 C2
Åsbro S 37 C2
Åsby S 40 B2
Asby S 40 B5
Asbygri IS 111 A9
Ascain F 76 C1
Ascea I 106 A2
Ascha D 62 A3
Aschach an der Donau
A 63 B5
Aschaffenburg D 51 D5
Aschbach Markt A 63 B5
Ascheberg
Nordrhein-Westfalen D 50 B3
Schleswig-Holstein D 44 A2
Aschendorf D 43 B4
Aschersleben D 52 B1
Asciano I 81 C5
Ascó E 90 B3
Asco F 102 A2
Áscoli Piceno I 82 D2
Áscoli Satriano I 104 B1
Ascona CH 70 B3
Ascot GB 31 C3
Ascoux F 58 B3
Åse N 112 C4
Åseda S 40 B5
Åsele S 115 C14
Åsen
N 114 D8
S 34 A5
Asendorf D 43 C6
Asenovgrad BG 11 E8
Åsensbruk S 35 D4
Åseral N 33 D4
Asfeld F 59 A5
Åsgårdstrand N 35 C2
Ásgarður IS 111 B1
Asgate CY 120 B2
Ash
Kent GB 31 C5
Surrey GB 31 C3
Åshammar S 36 B3
Ashbourne
GB 27 B4
IRL 21 A5
Ashburton GB 28 C4
Ashby-de-la-Zouch
GB 27 C4
Ashchurch GB 29 B5
Åsheim N 114 F8
Ashford GB 31 C4
Ashington GB 25 C6
Ashley GB 26 C3
Ashmyany BY 7 D8
Ashton Under Lyne
GB 26 B3
Ashwell GB 30 B3
Asiago I 71 C6
Asipovichy BY 7 E10
Aska FIN 113 E15
Askam-in-Furness
GB 26 A2
Askeaton IRL 20 B3
Asker N 34 C2
Askersund S 37 D1
Åskilje S 115 C14
Askim N 35 C3
Askland N 33 D5
Äsköping S 37 C3
Askvoll N 32 A2
Åsljunga S 41 C3
Asnæs DK 39 D4
As Neves E 87 B2
As Nogaís E 86 B3
Ásola I 71 C5
Asolo I 72 C1
Asos GR 116 D2
Asotthalom H 75 B4
Aspach A 63 B4
Aspang Markt A 64 C2
Aspariegos E 88 C1
Asparn an der Zaya A 64 B2
Aspatria GB 26 A2
Aspberg S 35 C5
Aspe E 101 A5
Aspet F 77 C3
Äspö S 41 C5
As Pontes de García Rodríguez E 86 A3
Aspres-sur-Buëch F 79 B4
Aspsele S 115 D15
Assafora P 92 C1
Asse B 49 C5
Assebakte N 113 C14
Assel D 43 B6
Asselborn L 50 C1
Assémini I 110 C1
Assen NL 42 C3
Assenede B 49 B4
Assens
Aarhus Amt. DK 38 C3
Fyns Amt. DK 39 D2
Assesse B 49 C6
Assisi I 82 C1
Åsskard N 114 D5
Assling D 62 C3
Asso I 71 C4
Asson F 76 C2
Ássoro I 109 B3
Assumar P 92 B3
Åsta N 34 A3
Astaffort F 77 B3
Astakos GR 116 D3
Asten NL 50 B1
Asti I 80 B2
Astipalea GR 119 F1
Astorga E 86 B4
Åstorp S 41 C2
Åsträsk S 115 C16
Astudillo E 88 B2
Asuni I 110 C1
Asványráró H 64 C3
Aszód H 65 C5
Aszófö H 74 B2
Atabey TR 119 E5
Atalaia P 92 B3
Atalandi GR 116 D4
Atalho P 92 C2
Átány H 65 C6
Atanzón E 95 B3
Ataquines E 94 A2
Atarfe E 100 B2
Atça TR 119 E3
Ateca E 89 C5
A Teixeira E 87 B3
Atella I 104 C1
Atessa I 103 A7
Ath B 49 C4
Athboy IRL 19 C5
Athea IRL 20 B2
Athenry IRL 20 A3
Athens = Athina GR 117 E5
Atherstone GB 27 C4
Athienou CY 120 A2
Athies F 59 A3
Athies-sous-Laon F 59 A4
Athina = Athens GR 117 E5
Athleague IRL 20 A3
Athlone IRL 21 A4
Athna CY 120 A2
Athy IRL 21 B5
Atienza E 95 A4
Atina I 103 B6
Atkár H 65 C5
Atlantı TR 119 D7
Atna N 114 F7
Åtorp S 35 C6
Atrå N 32 C5
Ätran S 40 B2
Atri I 103 A6
Atripalda I 103 C7
Atsiki GR 116 C7
Attendorn D 50 B3
Attichy F 59 A4
Attigliano I 102 A5
Attigny F 59 A5
Attleborough GB 30 B5
Åtvidaberg S 37 D2
Atzendorf D 52 B1
Au
Steiermark A 63 C6
Vorarlberg A 71 A4
Bayern D 62 B2
Bayern D 62 C2
Aub D 61 A6
Aubagne F 79 C4
Aubange B 60 A1
Aubel B 50 C1
Aubenas F 78 B3
Aubenton F 59 A5
Auberive F 59 C6
Aubeterre-sur-Dronne
F 67 C5
Aubiet F 77 C3
Aubigné F 67 B4
Aubigny F 66 B3
Aubigny-au-Bac F 49 C4
Aubigny-en-Artois F 48 C3
Aubigny-sur-Nère F 68 A2
Aubin F 77 B5
Aubonne CH 69 B6
Aubrac F 78 B1
Aubusson F 68 C2
Auch F 77 C3
Auchencairn GB 25 D4
Auchinleck GB 24 C3
Auchterarder GB 25 B4
Auchtermuchty GB 25 B4
Auchtertyre GB 22 D3
Auchy-au-Bois F 48 C3
Audenge F 76 B1
Auderville F 57 A4
Audierne F 56 B1
Audincourt F 70 A1
Audlem GB 26 C3
Audruicq F 48 C3
Audun-le-Roman F 60 A1
Audun-le-Tiche F 60 A1
Aue
Nordrhein-Westfalen D 50 B4
Sachsen D 52 C2
Auerbach
Bayern D 62 A2
Sachsen D 52 C2
Auffach A 72 A2
Augher GB 19 B4
Aughnacloy GB 19 B5
Aughrim IRL 21 B5
Augignac F 67 C5
Augsburg D 62 B1
Augusta I 109 B4
Augusten-borg DK 39 E2
Augustfehn D 43 B4
Augustów PL 6 E7
Aukrug D 44 A1
Auktsjaur S 115 B16
Auldearn GB 23 D5
Aulendorf D 61 C5
Auletta I 103 C8
Aulla I 81 B3
Aullène F 102 B2
Aulnay F 67 B4
Aulnoye-Aymeries F 49 C4
Ault F 48 C2
Aultbea GB 22 D3
Aulum DK 39 C1
Aulus-les-Bains F 77 D4
Auma D 52 C1
Aumale F 58 A2
Aumetz F 60 A1
Aumont-Aubrac F 78 B2
Aunay-en-Bazois F 68 A3
Aunay-sur-Odon F 57 A5
Aune N 115 C10
Auneau F 58 B2
Auneuil F 58 A2
Auning DK 39 C3
Aunsetra N 115 C9
Aups F 79 C5
Aura D 51 C5
Auray F 56 C3
Aurdal N 32 B6
Aure N 114 D5
Aurich D 43 B4
Aurignac F 77 C3
Aurillac F 77 B5
Auriol F 79 C4
Auritz-Burguette E 76 D1
Aurlandsvangen N 32 B4
Auronzo di Cadore I 72 B2
Auros F 76 B2
Auroux F 78 B2
Aurskog N 34 C3
Aursmoen N 34 C3
Ausónia I 103 B6
Ausservillgraton A 72 B2
Austad N 33 D4
Austbygda N 32 B5
Aústis I 110 B2
Austmarka N 34 B4
Austre Moland N 33 D5
Austre Vikebygd N 33 C2
Austrheim N 32 B1
Auterive F 77 C4
Autheuil-Authouillet
F 58 A2
Authon F 79 B5
Authon-du-Perche F 58 B1
Autol E 89 B5
Autreville F 60 B1
Autrey-lès-Gray F 69 A5
Autun F 69 B4
Auty-le-Châtel F 58 C3
Auvelais B 49 C5
Auvillar F 77 B3
Auxerre F 59 C4
Auxi-le-Château F 48 C3
Auxon F 59 B4
Auxonne F 69 A5
Auxy F 69 B4
Auzances F 68 B2
Auzon F 68 C3
Ağva TR 118 A4
Availles-Limouzine F 67 B5
Avaldsnes N 33 C2
Avallon F 68 A3
Avantas GR 116 B7
Avaviken S 115 B15
Avebury GB 29 B6
A Veiga E 87 B3
Aveiras de Cima P 92 B2
Aveiro P 92 A2
Avelgem B 49 C4
Avellino I 103 C7
Avenches CH 70 B2
A-Ver-o-Mar P 87 C2
Aversa I 103 C7
Avesnes-le-Comte F 48 C3
Avesnes-sur-Helpe F 49 C4
Avesta S 36 B3
Avetrana I 105 C3
Avezzano I 103 A6
Avià E 91 A4
Aviano I 72 B2
Aviemore GB 23 D5
Avigliana I 80 A1
Avigliano I 104 C1
Avignon F 78 C3
Ávila E 94 B2
Avilés E 88 A1
Avilley F 69 A6
Avintes P 87 C2
Avinyo E 91 B4
Àvio I 71 C5
Avioth F 59 A6
Avis P 92 B3
Avize F 59 B5
Avlonari GR 116 D6
Ávola I 109 C4
Avon F 58 B3
Avonmouth GB 29 B5
Avord F 68 A2
Avranches F 57 B4
Avril F 60 A1
Avrillé F 67 A4
Avtovac BIH 84 C3
Awans B 49 C6
Axams A 71 A6
Axat F 77 D5
Axbridge GB 29 B5
Axel NL 49 B4
Ax-les-Thermes F 77 D4
Axmarby S 36 B4
Axmarsbruk S 36 A4
Axminster GB 29 C4
Axvall S 35 D5
Ay F 59 A5
Aya E 89 A4
Ayamonte E 98 B3
Ayancık TR 16 A7
Ayaş TR 118 B7
Aydın TR 119 E2
Ayelo de Malferit E 96 C2
Ayer CH 70 B2
Ayerbe E 90 A2
Ayette F 48 C3
Áyia Napa CY 120 B2
Áyia Phyla CY 120 B2
Áyios Amvrósios
CY 120 A2
Áyios Seryios CY 120 A2
Áyios Theodhoros
CY 120 A3
Aykirikçi TR 118 C5
Aylesbury GB 31 C3
Ayllón E 89 C3
Aylsham GB 30 B5
Ayna E 101 A3
Ayódar E 96 B2
Ayora E 96 B1
Ayr GB 24 C3
Ayrancı TR 16 C6
Ayrancılar TR 119 D2
Ayron F 67 B5
Aysgarth GB 27 A4
Ayton GB 25 C5
Aytos BG 11 E9
Ayvacık TR 118 C1
Ayvalık TR 118 C1
Aywaille B 49 C6
Azaila E 90 B2
Azambuja P 92 B2
Azambujeira P 92 B2
Azanja SRB 85 B5
Azannes-et-Soumazannes
F 60 A1
Azanúy-Alins E 90 B3
Azaruja P 92 C3
Azay-le-Ferron F 67 B6
Azay-le-Rideau F 67 A5
Azcoitia E 89 A4
Azé F 69 B4
Azeiteiros P 92 B3
Azenhas do Mar P 92 C1
Azinhaga P 92 B2
Azinhal P 98 B3
Azinheira dos Bairros
P 98 A2
Aznalcázar E 99 B4
Aznalcóllar E 99 B4
Azóia P 92 B2
Azpeitia E 89 A4
Azuaga E 99 A5
Azuara E 90 B2
Azuqueca de Henares
E 95 B3
Azur F 76 C1
Azzano Décimo I 72 C2

B

Baad A 71 A5
Baamonde E 86 A3
Baar CH 70 A3
Bağarasi TR 119 E2
Baarle-Nassau B 49 B5
Baarn NL 49 A6
Babadağ TR 119 E3
Babadag RO 11 D10
Babaeski TR 118 A2
Babayevo RUS 7 B13
Babenhausen
Bayern D 61 B6
Hessen D 51 D4
Babiak PL 54 A3
Babice PL 55 C4
Babigoszcz PL 45 B6
Babimost PL 53 A5
Babina Greda HR 84 A3
Babócsa H 74 B2
Bábolma H 64 C3
Baborów PL 54 C2
Baboszewo PL 47 C6
Babót H 64 C3
Babruysk BY 7 E10
Babsk PL 55 B5
Bac GB 22 C2
Bač
MNE 85 D5
SRB 75 C4
Bacares E 101 B3
Bacău RO 11 C9
Baccarat F 60 B2
Bacharach D 50 C3
Bačina SRB 85 C6
Backa S 36 B2
Bačka Palanka SRB 75 C4
Backaryd S 41 C5
Bačka Topola SRB 75 C4
Backe S 115 D13
Bäckebo S 40 C6
Bäckefors S 35 D4
Bäckhammar S 35 C6
Bački Breg SRB 75 C3
Bački-Brestovac SRB 75 C4
Bački Monoštor SRB 75 C3
Bački Petrovac SRB 75 C4
Bački Sokolac SRB 75 C4
Backnang D 61 B5
Bačko Gradište SRB 75 C5
Bačko Novo Selo
SRB 75 C4
Bačko Petrovo Selo
SRB 75 C5
Bácoli I 103 C7
Bacqueville-en-Caux
F 58 A2
Bácsalmás H 75 B4
Bácsbokod H 75 B4
Bad Abbach D 62 B3
Badacsonytomaj H 74 B2
Bad Aibling D 62 C3
Badajoz E 93 C4
Badalona E 91 B5
Badalucco I 80 C1
Bad Aussee A 63 C4
Bad Bederkesa D 43 B5
Bad Bentheim D 50 A3
Bad Bergzabern D 60 A3
Bad Berka D 52 C1
Bad Berleburg D 51 B4
Bad Berneck D 52 C1
Bad Bevensen D 44 B2
Bad Bibra D 52 B1
Bad Birnbach D 62 B4
Bad Blankenburg D 52 C1
Bad Bleiberg A 72 B3
Bad Brambach D 52 C2
Bad Bramstedt D 44 B1
Bad Breisig D 50 C3
Bad Brückenau D 51 C5
Bad Buchau D 61 B5
Bad Camberg D 50 C4
Badderen N 113 C11
Bad Doberan D 44 A3
Bad Driburg D 51 B5
Bad Düben D 52 B2
Bad Dürkheim D 61 A4
Bad Dürrenberg D 52 B2
Bad Dürrheim D 61 B4
Bad Elster D 52 C2
Bad Ems D 50 C3
Baden
A 64 B2
CH 70 A3
Bádenas E 90 B1
Baden-Baden D 61 B4
Bad Endorf D 62 C3
Badenweiler D 60 C3
Baderna HR 72 C3
Bad Essen D 50 A4
Bad Fischau A 64 C2
Bad Frankenhausen
D 52 B1
Bad Freienwalde D 45 C6
Bad Friedrichshall D 61 A5
Bad Füssing D 63 B4
Bad Gandersheim D 51 B6
Bad Gastein A 72 A3
Bad Gleichenberg A 73 B5
Bad Goisern A 63 C4
Bad Gottleuba D 53 C3
Bad Grund D 51 B6
Bad Hall A 63 B5
Bad Harzburg D 51 B6
Bad Herrenalb D 61 B4
Bad Hersfeld D 51 C5
Bad Hofgastein A 72 A3
Bad Homburg D 51 C4
Bad Honnef D 50 C3
Bad Hönningen D 50 C3
Badia Calavena I 71 C6
Badia Polésine I 81 A5
Badia Pratáglia I 81 C5
Badia Tedalda I 82 C1
Bad Iburg D 50 A4
Bad Innerlaterns A 71 A4
Bad Ischl A 63 C4
Bad Karlshafen D 51 B5
Bad Kemmeriboden
CH 70 B2
Bądki PL 47 B4
Bad Kissingen D 51 C6
Bad Kleinen D 44 B3
Bad Kohlgrub D 62 C2
Bad König D 61 A5
Bad Königshofen D 51 C6
Bad Köstritz D 52 C2
Badkowo PL 47 C4
Bad Kreuzen A 63 B5

Bad Kreuznach D 60 A3
Bad Krozingen D 60 C3
Bad Laasphe D 51 C4
Bad Langensalza D 51 B6
Bad Lauchstädt D 52 B1
Bad Lausick D 52 B2
Bad Lauterberg D 51 B6
Bad Leonfelden A 63 B5
Bad Liebenwerda D 52 B3
Bad Liebenzell D 61 B4
Bad Lippspringe D 51 B4
Badljevina HR 74 C2
Bad Meinberg D 51 B4
Bad Mergentheim D 61 A5
Bad Mitterndorf A 72 A3
Bad Münder D 51 A5
Bad Münstereifel D 50 C2
Bad Muskau D 53 B4
Bad Nauheim D 51 C4
Bad Nenndorf D 43 C6
Bad Neuenahr-Ahrweiler
D 50 C3
Bad Neustadt D 51 C6
Bad Oeynhausen D 51 A4
Badolato I 106 C3
Badolatosa E 100 B1
Bad Oldesloe D 44 B2
Badonviller F 60 B2
Bad Orb D 51 C5
Badovinci SRB 85 B4
Bad Peterstal D 61 B4
Bad Pyrmont D 51 B5
Bad Radkersburg A 73 B5
Bad Ragaz CH 71 B4
Bad Rappenau D 61 A5
Bad Reichenhall D 62 C3
Bad Saarow-Pieskow
D 53 A4
Bad Sachsa D 51 B6
Bad Säckingen D 70 A2
Bad Salzdetfurth D 51 A6
Bad Salzig D 50 C3
Bad Salzuflen D 51 A4
Bad Salzungen D 51 C6
Bad Sankt Leonhard
A 73 B4
Bad Sassendorf D 50 B4
Bad Schandau D 53 C4
Bad Schmiedeberg D 52 B2
Bad Schönborn D 61 A4
Bad Schussenried D 61 B5
Bad Schwalbach D 50 C4
Bad Schwartau D 44 B2
Bad Segeberg D 44 B2
Bad Soden D 51 C4
Bad Soden-Salmünster
D 51 C5
Bad Sooden-Allendorf
D 51 B5
Bad Sulza D 52 B1
Bad Sülze D 45 A4
Bad Tatzmannsdorf A 73 A6
Bad Tennstedt D 51 B6
Bad Tölz D 62 C2
Badules E 90 B1
Bad Urach D 61 B5
Bad Vellach A 73 B4
Bad Vilbel D 51 C4
Bad Vöslau A 64 C2
Bad Waldsee D 61 C5
Bad Wiessee D 62 C2
Bad Wildungen D 51 B5
Bad Wilsnack D 44 C3
Bad Windsheim D 61 A6
Bad Wörishafen D 62 B1
Bad Wurzach D 61 C5
Bad Zwesten D 51 B5
Bad Zwischenahn D 43 B5
Baells E 90 B3
Baena E 100 B1
Baesweiler D 50 C2
Baeza E 100 B2
Baflo NL 42 B3
Bafra TR 16 A7
Baga E 91 A4
Bagaladi I 106 C2
Bagenkop DK 39 E3
Baggetorp S 37 C3
Bagh a Chaisteil GB 22 E1
Bagheria I 108 A2
Bagn N 32 B6
Bagnacavallo I 81 B5
Bagnáia I 102 A5
Bagnara Cálabra I 106 C2
Bagnasco I 80 B1
Bagnères-de-Bigorre
F 76 C3
Bagnères-de-Luchon
F 77 D3
Bagni del Másino I 71 B4
Bagni di Lucca I 81 B4
Bagni di Rabbi I 71 B5
Bagni di Tivoli I 102 B5
Bagno di Romagna I 81 C5
Bagnoles-de-l'Orne F 57 B5
Bagnoli dei Trigno I 103 B7
Bagnoli di Sopra I 72 C1
Bagnoli Irpino I 103 C8
Bagnolo Mella I 71 C5
Bagnols-en-Forêt F 79 C5
Bagnols-sur-Cèze F 78 B3
Bagnorégio I 102 A5
Bagolino I 71 C5
Bagrationovsk RUS 47 A6
Bagrdan SRB 85 B6
Báguena E 95 A5
Bahabón de Esgueva
E 88 C3
Bahillo E 88 B2
Báia delle Zágare I 104 B2
Báia Domizia I 103 B6
Baia Mare RO 11 C7
Baiano I 103 C7
Baião P 87 C2
Baiersbronn D 61 B4
Baiersdorf D 62 A2
Baignes-Ste Radegonde
F 67 C4
Baigneux-les-Juifs F 59 C5
Baildon GB 27 B4
Bailén E 100 A2
Băileşti RO 11 D7
Baileux B 49 C5
Bailieborough IRL 19 C5
Bailleul F 48 C3
Baillonville B 49 C6
Bailó E 90 A2
Bain-de-Bretagne F 57 C4
Bains F 78 A2
Bains-les-Bains F 60 B2
Bainton GB 27 B5
Baio E 86 A2
Baiona E 87 B2
Bais F 57 B5
Baiso I 81 B4
Baiuca P 92 A3
Baja H 75 B3
Bajánsenye H 73 B6
Bajina Bašta SRB 85 C4
Bajmok SRB 75 C4
Bajna H 65 C4
Bajovo Polje MNE 84 C3
Bajram Curri AL 105 A6
Bajša SRB 75 C4
Bajzë AL 105 A5
Bak H 74 B1
Bakar HR 73 C4
Bakewell GB 27 B4
Bakhmach UA 7 F12
Bakio E 89 A4
Bakırdağı TR 16 B7
Bakka N 32 C6
Bakkafjörður IS 111 A11
Bakkagerði IS 111 B12
Bække DK 39 D2
Bakken N 34 B3
Baklan TR 119 E4
Bækmarksbro DK 39 C1
Bakonybél H 74 A2
Bakonycsernye H 74 A3
Bakonyjákó H 74 A2
Bakonyszentkirály H 74 A2
Bakonyszombathely
H 74 A2
Bakov nad Jizerou
CZ 53 C4
Bąkowiec PL 55 B6
Baks H 75 B5
Baksa H 74 C3
Bakum D 43 C5
Bala GB 26 C2
Bâlâ TR 16 B6
Balaguer E 90 B3
Balassagyarmat H 65 B5
Balástya H 75 B5
Balatonakali H 74 B2
Balatonalmádi H 74 A3
Balatonboglár H 74 B2
Balatonbozsok H 74 B3
Balatonederics H 74 B2
Balatonfenyves H 74 B2
Balatonföldvár H 74 B2
Balatonfüred H 74 B2
Balatonfüzfő H 74 A3
Balatonkenese H 74 A3
Balatonkiliti H 74 B3
Balatonlelle H 74 B2
Balatonszabadi H 74 B3
Balatonszemes H 74 B2
Balatonszentgyörgy
H 74 B2
Balazote E 101 A3
Balbeggie GB 25 B4
Balbigny F 69 C4
Balboa E 86 B4
Balbriggan IRL 19 C5
Balchik BG 11 E10
Balçova TR 119 D2
Baldock GB 31 C3
Bale HR 82 A2
Baleira E 86 A3
Baleizao P 98 A3
Balen B 49 B6
Balerma E 100 C3
Balestrand N 32 A3
Balestrate I 108 A2
Balfour GB 23 B6
Bälganet S 41 C5
Balıkesir TR 118 C2
Balıklıçeşme TR 118 B2
Bälinge S 36 C4
Balingen D 61 B4
Balingsta S 36 C4
Balintore GB 23 D5
Balizac F 76 B2
Baljevac SRB 85 C5
Balk NL 42 C2
Balkbrug NL 42 C3
Balla IRL 18 C2
Ballachulish GB 24 B2
Ballaghaderreen IRL 18 C3
Ballancourt-sur-Essonne
F 58 B3
Ballantrae GB 24 C3
Ballao I 110 C2
Ballasalla GB 26 A1
Ballater GB 23 D5
Ballen DK 39 D3
Ballenstedt D 52 B1
Ballerias E 90 B2
Balleroy F 57 A5
Ballerup DK 41 D2
Ballesteros de Calatrava
E 100 A2
Ballı TR 118 B2
Ballina IRL 18 B2
Ballinalack IRL 19 C4
Ballinamore IRL 19 B4
Ballinascarty IRL 20 C3
Ballinasloe IRL 20 A3
Ballindine IRL 18 C3
Balling DK 38 C1
Ballingarry
Limerick IRL 20 B3
Tipperary IRL 21 B4
Ballingeary IRL 20 C2
Ballinhassig IRL 20 C3
Ballinluig GB 25 B4
Ballino I 71 C5
Ballinrobe IRL 18 C2
Ballinskelligs IRL 20 C1
Ballinspittle IRL 20 C3
Ballintra IRL 18 B3
Ballivor IRL 21 A5
Ballobar E 90 B3
Ballon
F 58 B1
IRL 21 B5
Ballószög H 75 B4
Ballsh AL 105 C5
Ballstad N 112 D2
Ballum DK 39 D1
Ballybay IRL 19 B5
Ballybofey IRL 19 B4
Ballybunion IRL 20 B2
Ballycanew IRL 21 B5
Ballycarry GB 19 B6
Ballycastle
GB 19 A5
IRL 18 B2
Ballyclare GB 19 B6
Ballyconneely IRL 18 C1
Ballycotton IRL 20 C3
Ballycroy IRL 18 B2
Ballydehob IRL 20 C2
Ballyferriter IRL 20 B1
Ballygawley GB 19 B4
Ballygowan GB 19 B6
Ballyhaunis IRL 18 C3
Ballyheige IRL 20 B2
Ballyjamesduff IRL 19 C4
Ballylanders IRL 20 B3
Ballylynan IRL 21 B4
Ballymahon IRL 21 A4
Ballymena GB 19 B5
Ballymoe IRL 18 C3
Ballymoney GB 19 A5
Ballymore IRL 21 A4
Ballymote IRL 18 B3
Ballynacorra IRL 20 C3
Ballynagore IRL 21 A4
Ballynahinch GB 19 B6
Ballynure GB 19 B6
Ballyragget IRL 21 B4
Ballysadare IRL 18 B3
Ballyshannon IRL 18 B3
Ballyvaughan IRL 20 A2
Ballyvourney IRL 20 C2
Ballywalter GB 19 B6
Balmaclellan GB 24 C3
Balmaseda E 89 A3
Balme I 70 C2
Balmedie GB 23 D6
Balmuccia I 70 C3
Balna-paling GB 23 D4
Balneario de Panticosa
E 76 D2
Balotaszállás H 75 B4
Balsa P 87 C3
Balsareny E 91 B4
Balsorano-Nuovo I 103 B6
Bålsta S 37 C4
Balsthal CH 70 A2
Balta UA 11 B10
Baltanás E 88 C2
Baltar E 87 C3
Baltasound GB 22 A8
Bălţi MD 11 C9
Baltimore IRL 20 C2
Baltinglass IRL 21 B5
Baltiysk RUS 47 A5
Baltów PL 55 B6
Balugães P 87 C2
Bælum DK 38 C3
Balve D 50 B3
Balvi LV 7 C9
Balvicar GB 24 B2
Balya TR 118 C2
Balzo I 82 D2
Bamberg D 62 A1
Bamburgh GB 25 C6
Banatska Palanka
SRB 85 B6
Banatski Brestovac
SRB 85 B5
Banatski Despotovac
SRB 75 C5
Banatski Dvor SRB 75 C5
Banatski-Karlovac
SRB 85 A6
Banatsko Arandjelovo
SRB 75 B5
Banatsko-Novo Selo
SRB 85 B5
Banaz TR 118 D4
Banbridge GB 19 B5
Banbury GB 30 B2
Banchory GB 23 D6
Bande
B 49 C6
E 87 B3
Bandholm DK 39 E4
Bandırma TR 118 B2
Bandol F 79 C4
Bandon IRL 20 C3
Bañeres E 96 C2
Banff GB 23 D6
Bangor
F 66 A1
Down GB 19 B6
Gwynedd GB 26 B1
IRL 18 B2
Bangsund N 114 C8
Banie PL 45 B6
Banja SRB 85 C4
Banja Koviljača SRB 85 B4
Banjaloka SLO 73 C4
Banja Luka BIH 84 B2
Banjani SRB 85 B4
Banja Vručica BIH 84 B2
Banje KOS 85 D5
Banjska KOS 85 D5
Banka SK 64 B3
Bankekind S 37 D2
Bankend GB 25 C4
Bankeryd S 40 B4
Bankfoot GB 25 B4
Banloc RO 75 C6
Bannalec F 56 C2
Bannes F 59 B4
Bannockburn GB 25 B4
Bañobárez E 87 D4
Bañon E 90 C1
Banon F 79 B4
Baños E 93 A5
Baños de Gigonza E 99 C5
Baños de la Encina
E 100 A2
Baños de Molgas E 87 B3
Baños de Rio Tobia
E 89 B4
Baños de Valdearados
E 89 C3
Bánov CZ 64 B3
Bánova Jaruga HR 74 C1
Bánovce nad Bebravou
SK 64 B4
Banovići BIH 84 B3
Banoviči Selo BIH 84 B3
Bánréve H 65 B6
Bansin D 45 B6
Banská Belá SK 65 B4
Banská Bystrica SK 65 B5
Banská Štiavnica SK 65 B4
Banstead GB 31 C3
Banteer IRL 20 B3
Bantheville F 59 A6
Bantry IRL 20 C2
Bantzenheim F 60 C3
Banyalbufar E 97 B2
Banyoles E 91 A5
Banyuls-sur-Mer F 91 A6
Bapaume F 48 C3
Bar
MNE 105 A5
UA 11 B9
Barabhas GB 22 C2
Barači BIH 84 B1
Baracs H 74 B3
Baracska H 74 A3
Barahona E 89 C4
Barajes de Melo E 95 B4
Barakaldo E 89 A4
Baralla E 86 B3
Barañain E 76 D1
Baranavichy BY 7 E9
Báránd H 75 A6
Baranda SRB 85 A5
Baranello I 103 B7
Baranów Sandomierski
PL 55 C6
Baraqueville F 77 B5
Barasoain E 89 B5
Barbacena P 92 C3
Barbadás E 87 B3
Barbadillo E 94 B1
Barbadillo de Herreros
E 89 B3
Barbadillo del Mercado
E 89 B3
Barbadillo del Pez E 89 B3
Barban HR 82 A3
Barbarano Vicento I 71 C6
Barbariga HR 82 B2
Barbaros TR 118 B2
Barbastro E 90 A3
Barbate E 99 C5
Barbatona E 95 A4
Barbâtre F 66 B2
Barbazan F 77 C3
Barbeitos E 86 A3
Barbentane F 78 C3
Barberino di Mugello
I 81 B5
Barbezieux-St Hilaire
F 67 C4
Barbonne-Fayel F 59 B4
Barbotan-les-Thermes
F 76 C2
Barby D 52 B1
Barcabo E 90 A3
Barca de Alva P 87 C4
Barcarrota E 93 C4
Barcellona-Pozzo di Gotto
I 109 A4
Barcelona E 91 B5
Barcelonette F 79 B5
Barcelos P 87 C2
Bárcena del Monasterio
E 86 A4
Barcena de Pie de
Concha E 88 A2
Barchfeld D 51 C6
Barcin PL 46 C3
Barcino PL 46 A2
Bárcis I 72 B2
Barco P 92 A3
Barcones E 89 C4
Barcs H 74 C2
Barcus F 76 C2
Barczewo PL 47 B6
Bardejov SK 10 B6
Bårdesø DK 39 D3
Bardi I 81 B3
Bardney GB 27 B5
Bardo PL 54 C1
Bardolino I 71 C5
Bardonécchia I 79 A5
Bardoňovo SK 65 B4
Barèges F 76 D3
Barenstein D 52 C3
Barentin F 58 A1
Barenton F 57 B5
Barevo BIH 84 B2
Barfleur F 57 A4
Barga I 81 B4
Bargas E 94 C2
Barge I 79 B6
Bargemon F 79 C5
Barghe I 71 C5
Bargoed GB 29 B4
Bargrennan GB 24 C3
Bargteheide D 44 B2
Barham GB 31 C5
Bari I 104 B2
Barič Draga HR 83 B4
Barilović HR 73 C5
Bari Sardo I 110 C2
Barisciano I 103 A6
Barjac F 78 B3
Barjols F 79 C4
Barjon F 59 C5
Bårkåker N 35 C2
Barkald N 114 F7
Barkowo
Dolnośląskie PL 54 B1
Pomorskie PL 46 B3
Bârlad RO 11 C9
Bar-le-Duc F 59 B6
Barles F 79 B5
Barletta I 104 B2
Barlinek PL 45 C7
Barmouth GB 26 C1
Barmstedt D 43 B6
Barnard Castle GB 27 A4
Barnarp S 40 B4
Bärnau D 62 A3
Bärnbach A 73 A5
Barneberg D 52 A1
Barnenitz D 45 C4
Barnet GB 31 C3
Barnetby le Wold GB 27 B5
Barneveld NL 49 A6
Barneville-Carteret F 57 A4
Barnoldswick GB 26 B3
Barnowko PL 45 C6
Barnsley GB 27 B4
Barnstädt D 52 B1
Barnstaple GB 28 B3
Barnstorf D 43 C5
Barntrup D 51 B5
Baron F 58 A3
Baronissi I 103 C7
Barqueiro P 92 B2
Barquinha P 92 B2
Barr
F 60 B3
GB 24 C3
Barra P 92 A2
Barracas E 96 A2
Barraco E 94 B2
Barrado E 93 A5
Barrafranca I 109 B3
Barranco do Velho P 98 B3
Barrancos P 99 A4
Barrax E 95 C4
Barrbaar D 62 B1
Barre-des-Cevennes
F 78 B2
Barreiro P 92 C1
Barreiros E 86 A3
Barrême F 79 C5
Barret-le-Bas F 79 B4
Barrhead GB 24 C3
Barrhill GB 24 C3
Barrio de Nuesra Señora
E 88 B1
Barrowford GB 26 B3
Barrow-in-Furness
GB 26 A2
Barrow upon Humber
GB 27 B5
Barruecopardo E 87 C4
Barruelo de Santullán
E 88 B2
Barruera E 90 A3
Barry GB 29 B4
Bårse DK 39 D4
Barsinghausen D 51 A5
Barssel D 43 B4
Bar-sur-Aube F 59 B5
Bar-sur-Seine F 59 B5
Barth D 45 A4
Bartholomä D 61 B5
Bartin TR 118 A7
Barton upon Humber
GB 27 B5
Bartoszyce PL 47 A6
Barúmini I 110 C1
Baruth D 52 A3
Barvaux B 49 C6
Barver D 43 C5
Barwatd PL 65 A5
Barwice PL 46 B2
Barysaw BY 7 D10
Barzana E 88 A1
Bârzava RO 10 C6
Bárzio I 71 C4
Bas E 91 A5
Bašaid SRB 75 C5
Basaluzzo I 80 B2
Basarabeasca MD 11 C10
Basauri E 89 A4
Baschi I 82 D1
Baschurch GB 26 C3
Basconcillos del Tozo
E 88 B3
Bascones de Ojeda E 88 B2
Basécles B 49 C4
Basel CH 70 A2
Basélice I 103 B7
Basildon GB 31 C4
Basingstoke GB 31 C2
Baška
CZ 65 A4
HR 83 B3
Baška Voda HR 84 C1
Bäsksjö S 115 C14
Baslow GB 27 B4
Başmakçı TR 119 E5
Basovizza I 72 C3
Bassacutena I 110 A2
Bassano del Grappa I 72 C1
Bassano Romano I 102 A5
Bassecourt CH 70 A2
Bassella E 91 A4
Bassevuovdde N 113 D14
Bassou F 59 C4
Bassoues F 76 C3
Bassum D 43 C5
Båstad S 40 C2
Bastardo I 82 D1
Bastelica F 102 A2
Bastelicaccia F 102 B1
Bastia
F 102 A2
I 82 C1
Bastogne B 50 C1
Baston GB 30 B3
Bastuträsk S 115 C17
Bata H 74 B3
Batajnica SRB 85 B5
Batalha P 92 B2
Bátaszék H 74 B3
Batea E 90 B3
Batelov CZ 63 A6
Bath GB 29 B5
Bathgate GB 25 C4
Batida H 75 B5
Batignano I 81 D5
Batina HR 74 C3
Bátka SK 65 B6
Batković BIH 85 B4
Batlava KOS 85 D6
Batley GB 27 B4
Batnfjordsøra N 114 E4
Batočina SRB 85 B6
Bátonyterenye H 65 C5
Batsi GR 117 E6
Båtsfjord N 113 B18
Battaglia Terme I 72 C1
Bätterkinden CH 70 A2
Battice B 50 C1
Battipáglia I 103 C7
Battle GB 31 D4
Battonya H 75 B6
Batuša SRB 85 B6
Bátya H 75 B3
Bau I 110 C1
Baud F 56 C2
Baudour B 49 C4
Baugé F 67 A4
Baugy F 68 A2
Bauma CH 70 A3
Baume-les-Dames F 69 A6
Baumholder D 60 A3
Baunatal D 51 B5
Baunei I 110 B2
Bauska LV 6 C8
Bautzen D 53 B4
Bavanište SRB 85 B5
Bavay F 49 C4
Bavilliers F 60 C2
Bavorov CZ 63 A5
Bawdsey GB 31 B5
Bawinkel D 43 C4
Bawtry GB 27 B4
Bayat TR 118 D5
Bayel F 59 B5
Bayeux F 57 A5
Bayındır TR 119 D2
Bayon F 60 B2
Bayonne F 76 C1
Bayons F 79 B5
Bayramiç TR 118 C1
Bayreuth D 52 D1
Bayrischzell D 62 C3
Baza E 101 B3
Bazas F 76 B2
Baziege F 77 C4
Bazoches-les-Gallerandes
F 58 B3
Bazoches-sur-Hoëne
F 58 B1
Bazzano I 81 B5
Beaconsfield GB 31 C3
Beade E 87 B2
Beadnell GB 25 C6
Beaminster GB 29 C5
Bearsden GB 24 C3
Beas E 99 B4
Beasain E 89 A4
Beas de Segura E 100 A3
Beattock GB 25 C4
Beaubery F 69 B4
Beaucaire F 78 C3
Beaufort
F 69 C6
IRL 20 B2
Beaufort-en Vallée F 67 A4
Beaugency F 58 C2
Beaujeu
Alpes-de-Haute-Provence F 79 B5
Rhône F 69 B4
Beaulac F 76 B2
Beaulieu
F 68 A2
GB 31 D2
Beaulieu-sous-la-Roche
F 66 B3
Beaulieu-sur-Dordogne
F 77 B4
Beaulieu-sur-Mer F 80 C1
Beaulon F 68 B3
Beauly GB 23 D4
Beaumaris GB 26 B1
Beaumesnil F 58 A1
Beaumetz-lès-Loges
F 48 C3
Beaumont
B 49 C5
F 77 B3
Beaumont-de-Lomagne
F 77 C3
Beaumont-du-Gâtinais
F 58 B3
Beaumont-en-Argonne
F 59 A6
Beaumont-Hague F 57 A4
Beaumont-la-Ronce
F 58 C1
Beaumont-le-Roger F 58 A1
Beaumont-sur-Oise F 58 A3
Beaumont-sur-Sarthe
F 57 B6
Beaune F 69 A4
Beaune-la-Rolande F 58 B3
Beaupréau F 66 A4
Beauraing B 49 C5
Beaurepaire F 69 C5
Beaurepaire-en-Bresse
F 69 B5
Beaurières F 79 B4
Beauvais F 58 A3
Beauval F 48 C3
Beauville F 77 B3
Beauvoir-sur-Mer F 66 B2
Beauvoir-sur-Niort F 67 B4
Beba Veche RO 75 B5
Bebertal D 52 A1
Bebington GB 26 B2
Bebra D 51 C5
Bebrina HR 84 A2
Beccles GB 30 B5
Becedas E 93 A5
Beceite E 90 C3
Bečej SRB 75 C5
Becerreá E 86 B3
Becerril de Campos E 88 B2
Bécherel F 57 B4
Bechhofen D 61 A6
Bechyně CZ 63 A5
Bečići MNE 105 A4
Becilla de Valderaduey
E 88 B1
Beckfoot GB 25 D4
Beckingham GB 27 B5
Beckum D 50 B4
Beco P 92 B2
Bécon-les-Granits F 66 A4
Bečov nad Teplou CZ 52 C2
Becsehely H 74 B1
Bedale GB 27 A4
Bedames E 89 A3
Bédar E 101 B4
Bédarieux F 78 C2
Bédarrides F 78 B3
Bedburg D 50 C2
Beddgelert GB 26 B1
Beddingestrand S 41 D3
Bédée F 57 B4
Bedegkér H 74 B3
Beden TR 119 F7
Bedford GB 30 B3
Będków PL 55 B4
Bedlington GB 25 C6
Bedlno PL 55 A4
Bedmar E 100 B2
Bédoin F 79 B4
Bedónia I 80 B3
Bedretto CH 70 B3
Bedsted DK 38 C1
Bedum NL 42 B3
Bedwas GB 29 B4
Bedworth GB 30 B2
Będzin PL 55 C4
Beekbergen NL 50 A1
Beek en Donk NL 49 B6
Beelen D 50 B4
Beelitz D 52 A2
Beer GB 29 C4
Beerfelde D 45 C6
Beerfelden D 61 A4
Beernem B 49 B4
Beeskow D 53 A4
Beetsterzwaag NL 42 B3
Beetzendorf D 44 C3
Beflelay CH 70 A2
Begaljica SRB 85 B5
Bégard F 56 B2
Begejci SRB 75 C5
Begijar E 100 B2
Begijnendijk B 49 B5
Begndal N 34 B1
Begues E 91 B4
Beguildy GB 26 C2
Begur E 91 B6
Beho B 50 C1
Behringen D 51 B6
Beilen NL 42 C3
Beilngries D 62 A2
Beine-Nauroy F 59 A5
Beinwil CH 70 A3
Beiseförth D 51 B5
Beith GB 24 C3
Beitostølen N 32 A5
Beiuş RO 11 C7
Beja P 98 A3
Béjar E 93 A5
Bekçiler TR 119 F4
Békés H 75 B6
Békéscsaba H 75 B6
Bekilli TR 119 D4
Bekkarfjord N 113 B16
Bela SK 65 A4
Bélâbre F 67 B6
Bela Crkva SRB 85 B6
Belalcázar E 93 C5
Bělánad Radbuzou
CZ 62 A3
Belanovica SRB 85 B5
Bélapátfalva H 65 B6
Bělápod Bezdězem
CZ 53 C4
Belcaire F 77 D4
Bełchatów PL 55 B4
Belchite E 90 B2
Bělčice CZ 63 A4
Belcoo GB 19 B4
Belecke D 51 B4
Beled H 74 A2
Belej HR 83 B3
Beleño E 88 A1
Bélesta F 77 D4
Belev RUS 7 E14
Belevi TR 119 D2
Belfast GB 19 B6
Belford GB 25 C6
Belfort F 60 C2
Belgentier F 79 C4
Belgern D 52 B3
Belgioioso I 71 C4
Belgodère F 102 A2
Belgooly IRL 20 C3
Belgorod RUS 7 F14
Belgrade = Beograd
SRB 85 B5
Belhade F 76 B2
Belica HR 74 B1
Beli Manastir HR 74 C3
Belin-Béliet F 76 B2
Belinchón E 95 B3
Belišće HR 74 C3
Bělkovice-Lašťany
CZ 64 A3
Bella I 104 C1
Bellac F 67 B6
Bellágio I 71 C4
Bellananagh IRL 19 C4
Bellano I 71 B4
Bellária I 82 B1
Bellavary IRL 18 C2
Belleau F 59 A4
Belleek GB 18 B3
Bellegarde
Gard F 78 C3
Loiret F 58 C3
Bellegarde-en-Diois F 79 B4
Bellegarde-en-Marche
F 68 C2
Bellegarde-sur-Valserine
F 69 B5
Belle-Isle-en-Terre F 56 B2
Bellême F 58 B1
Bellenaves F 68 B3
Bellentre F 70 C1
Bellevaux F 69 B6
Bellevesvre F 69 B5
Belleville F 69 B4
Belleville-sur-Vie F 66 B3
Bellevue-la-Montagne
F 68 C3
Belley F 69 C5
Bellheim D 61 A4
Bellinge DK 39 D3
Bellingham GB 25 C5
Bellinzago Novarese
I 70 C3
Bellinzona CH 70 B4
Bell-lloc d'Urgell E 90 B3
Bello E 95 B5
Bellpuig d'Urgell E 91 B4
Bellreguart E 96 C2
Bellsbank GB 24 C3
Belltall E 91 B4
Belluno I 72 B2
Bellver de Cerdanya
E 91 A4
Bellvis E 90 B3
Bélmez E 93 C5
Belmez de la Moraleda
E 100 B2
Belmont GB 22 A8
Belmont-de-la-Loire F 69 B4
Belmonte
Asturias E 86 A4
Cuenca E 95 C4
P 92 A3
Belmonte de San José
E 90 C2
Belmonte de Tajo E 95 B3
Belmont-sur-Rance F 78 C1
Belmullet IRL 18 B2
Belobreşca RO 85 B6
Beloeil B 49 C4
Belogradchik BG 11 E7
Belokorovichi UA 11 A10
Beloljin SRB 85 C6
Belorado E 89 B3
Belotič SRB 85 B4
Bělotin CZ 64 A3
Belozersk RUS 7 B14
Belp CH 70 B2
Belpasso I 109 B3
Belpech F 77 C4
Belper GB 27 B4
Belsay GB 25 C6
Belsh AL 105 C5
Belsk Duzy PL 55 B5
Beltinci SLO 73 B6
Beltra IRL 18 C2
Belturbet IRL 19 B4
Beluša SK 64 A4
Belušić SRB 85 C6
Belvedere Marittimo
I 106 B2
Belver de Cinca E 90 B3
Belver de los Montes
E 88 C1
Belvès F 77 B3
Belvezet F 78 B2
Belvis de la Jara E 94 C2
Belvis de Monroy E 93 B5
Belyy RUS 7 D12
Belz F 56 C2
Bełżec PL 11 A7
Belzig D 52 A2
Bembibre E 86 B4
Bembridge GB 31 D2
Bemmel NL 50 B1
Bemposta
Bragança P 87 C4
Santarém P 92 B2
Benabarre E 90 A3
Benacazón E 99 B4
Benaguacil E 96 B2
Benahadux E 101 C3
Benalmádena E 100 C1
Benalúa de Guadix
E 100 B2
Benalúa de las Villas
E 100 B2
Benalup E 99 C5
Benamargosa E 100 C1
Benamaurel E 101 B3
Benameji E 100 B1
Benamocarra E 100 C1
Benaocaz E 99 C5
Benaoján E 99 C5
Benarrabá E 99 C5
Benasque E 90 A3
Benátky nad Jizerou
CZ 53 C4
Benavente
E 88 B1
P 92 C2
Benavides de Órbigo
E 88 B1
Benavila P 92 B3
Bendorf D 50 C3
Benedikt SLO 73 B5
Benejama E 101 A5
Benejúzar E 101 A5
Benešov CZ 63 A5
Bénestroff F 60 B2
Benet F 67 B4
Bene Vagienna I 80 B1
Bénévent-l'Abbaye F 67 B6
Benevento I 103 B7
Benfeld F 60 B3
Benfica P 92 B2
Bengtsfors S 35 C4
Bengtsheden S 36 B2
Beničanci HR 74 C3
Benicarló E 90 C3
Benicássim E 96 A3
Benidorm E 96 C2
Benifaió E 96 B2
Beniganim E 96 C2
Benington GB 27 B6
Benisa E 96 C3
Benkovac HR 83 B4
Benllech GB 26 B1
Benneckenstein D 51 B6
Bénodet F 56 C1
Benquerencia de la
Serena E 93 C5
Bensafrim P 98 B2
Bensdorf D 44 C4
Benshausen D 51 C6
Bensheim D 61 A4
Bentley GB 31 C3
Bentwisch D 44 A4
Beočin SRB 75 C4
Beograd = Belgrade
SRB 85 B5
Beragh GB 19 B4
Berane MNE 85 D4
Beranga E 89 A3
Berat AL 105 C5
Bérat F 77 C4
Beratzhausen D 62 A2
Bérbaltavár H 74 A1
Berbegal E 90 B2
Berbenno di Valtellina
I 71 B4
Berberana E 89 B3
Bercedo E 89 A3
Bercel H 65 C5
Bercenay-le-Hayer F 59 B4
Berceto I 81 B3
Berchem B 49 C4
Berchidda I 110 B2
Berching D 62 A2
Berchtesgaden D 62 C4
Bérchules E 100 C2
Bercianos de Aliste E 87 C4
Berck F 48 C2
Berclaire d'Urgell E 90 B3
Berdoias E 86 A1
Berducedo E 86 A4
Berdún E 90 A2
Berdychiv UA 11 B10
Bere Alston GB 28 C3
Bereguardo I 70 C4
Berehommen N 33 C4
Berehove UA 11 B7
Berek BIH 84 A2
Beremend H 74 C3
Bere Regis GB 29 C5
Berestechko UA 11 A8
Berettyóújfalu H 10 C6
Berezhany UA 11 B8
Berezivka UA 11 C11
Berezna UA 7 F11
Berg
D 62 A2
N 114 B9
S 37 D3
Berga
Sachsen-Anhalt D 51 B7
Thüringen D 52 C2
E 91 A4
S 40 B6
Bergama TR 118 C2
Bérgamo I 71 C4
Bergara E 89 A4
Bergby S 36 B4
Berge
Brandenburg D 45 C4
Niedersachsen D 43 C4
Telemark N 33 C5
Telemark N 33 C5
Bergeforsen S 115 E14
Bergen
Mecklenburg-Vorpommern D 45 A5
Niedersachsen D 44 C1
Niedersachsen D 44 C2
N 32 B2
NL 42 C1
Bergen op Zoom NL 49 B5
Bergerac F 77 B3
Bergères-lés-Vertus
F 59 B5
Bergeyk NL 49 B6
Berghausen D 61 B4
Bergheim D 50 C2
Berghem S 40 B2
Berg im Gau D 62 B2
Bergisch Gladbach D 50 C3
Bergkamen D 50 B3
Bergkvara S 41 C6
Berglern D 62 B2
Bergneustadt D 50 B3
Bergsäng S 34 B5
Bergshamra S 37 C5
Bergsjö S 115 F14
Bergs slussar S 37 D2
Bergtheim D 61 A6
Bergues F 48 C3
Bergum NL 42 B2
Bergün Bravuogn CH 71 B4
Bergwitz D 52 B2
Berhida H 74 A3
Beringel P 98 A3
Beringen B 49 B6
Berja E 100 C3
Berkåk N 114 E7
Berkeley GB 29 B5
Berkenthin D 44 B2
Berkhamsted GB 31 C3
Berkheim D 61 B6
Berkhof D 43 C6
Berkovići BIH 84 C3
Berkovitsa BG 11 E7
Berlanga E 99 A5
Berlanga de Duero E 89 C4
Berlevåg N 113 B18
Berlikum NL 42 B2
Berlin D 45 C5
Berlstedt D 52 B1
Bermeo E 89 A4
Bermillo de Sayago E 87 C4
Bern CH 70 B2
Bernalda I 104 C2
Bernardos E 94 A2
Bernartice
Jihočeský CZ 63 A5
Vychodočeský CZ 53 C5
Bernau
Baden-Württemberg D 61 C4
Bayern D 62 C3
Brandenburg D 45 C5
Bernaville F 48 C3
Bernay F 58 A1
Bernburg D 52 B1
Berndorf A 64 C2
Berne D 43 B5
Bernecebarati H 65 B4
Bernhardsthal A 64 B2
Bernkastel-Kues D 60 A3
Bernolakovo SK 64 B3
Bernsdorf D 53 B4
Bernstadt D 53 B4
Bernstein A 73 A6
Bernués E 90 A2
Beromünster CH 70 A3
Beroun CZ 53 D4
Berovo MK 116 A4
Berre-l'Etang F 79 C4
Berriedale GB 23 C5
Berriew GB 26 C2
Berrocal E 99 B4
Bersenbrück D 43 C4
Bershad' UA 11 B10
Bertamirans E 86 B2
Berthåga S 36 C4
Berthelming F 60 B2
Bertincourt F 48 C3
Bertinoro I 82 B1
Bertogne B 49 C6
Bertrix B 59 A6
Berufjörður IS 111 C11
Berville-sur-Mer F 58 A1
Berwick-upon-Tweed
GB 25 C5
Berzasca RO 10 D6
Berzence H 74 B2
Berzocana E 93 B5
Besalú E 91 A5
Besançon F 69 A6
Besenfeld D 61 B4
Besenyőtelek H 65 C6
Besenyszög H 75 A5
Beshenkovichi BY 7 D10
Besigheim D 61 B5
Běšiny CZ 63 A4
Beška SRB 75 C5
Beşkonak TR 119 E6
Besle F 57 C4
Besnyö H 74 A3
Bessais-le-Fromental
F 68 B2
Bessan F 78 C2
Besse-en-Chandesse
F 68 C2
Bessèges F 78 B3
Bessé-sur-Braye F 58 C1
Bessines-sur-Gartempe
F 67 B6
Best NL 49 B6
Bestorp S 37 D2
Betanzos E 86 A2
Betelu E 76 C1
Bétera E 96 B2
Beteta E 95 B4
Béthenville F 59 A5
Bethesda GB 26 B1
Béthune F 48 C3
Beton-Bazoches F 59 B4
Bettembourg L 60 A2
Betterdorf L 60 A2
Bettna S 37 D3
Béttola I 80 B3
Bettona I 82 C1
Bettyhill GB 23 C4
Betws-y-Coed GB 26 B2
Betxi E 96 B2
Betz F 59 A3
Betzdorf D 50 C3
Beuil F 79 B5
Beulah GB 29 A4
Beuzeville F 58 A1
Bevagna I 82 D1
Bevens-bruk S 37 C2
Beveren B 49 B5
Beverley GB 27 B5
Bevern D 51 B5
Beverstedt D 43 B5
Beverungen D 51 B5
Beverwijk NL 42 C1
Bex CH 70 B2
Bexhill GB 31 D4
Beyazköy TR 118 A2
Beychevelle F 76 A2
Beydağ TR 119 D3
Beyeğaç TR 119 E3
Beykoz TR 118 A4
Beynat F 68 C1
Beyoğlu TR 118 A4
Beypazarı TR 118 B6
Beyşehir TR 119 E6
Bezas E 95 B5
Bezau A 71 A4
Bezdan SRB 75 C3
Bèze F 69 A5
Bezenet F 68 B2
Bezhetsk RUS 7 C14
Béziers F 78 C2
Bezzecca I 71 C5
Biadki PL 54 B2
Biała
Łódzkie PL 55 B4
Opolskie PL 54 C2
Białaczów PL 55 B5
Biała Podlaska PL 6 E7
Biała Rawska PL 55 B5
Biale Błota PL 46 B3
Białobloty PL 54 A2
Białobrzegi PL 55 B5
Białogard PL 46 B1
Białośliwie PL 46 B3
Białowąs PL 46 B2
Biały Bór PL 46 B2
Białystok PL 6 E7
Biancavilla I 109 B3
Bianco I 106 C3
Biandrate I 70 C3
Biar E 101 A5
Biarritz F 76 C1
Bias F 76 B1
Biasca CH 70 B3
Biatorbágy H 74 A3
Bibbiena I 81 C5
Bibbona I 81 C4
Biberach
Baden-Württemberg D 61 B4
Baden-Württemberg D 61 B5
Bibinje HR 83 B4
Bibione I 72 C3
Biblis D 61 A4
Bibury GB 29 B6
Biccari I 103 B8
Bicester GB 31 C2
Bichl D 62 C2
Bichlbach A 71 A5
Bicorp E 96 B2
Bicos P 98 B2
Bicske H 74 A3
Bidache F 76 C1
Bidart F 76 C1
Biddinghuizen NL 42 C2
Biddulph GB 26 B3
Bideford GB 28 B3
Bidford-on-Avon GB 29 A6
Bidjovagge N 113 C11
Bie S 37 C3
Bieber D 51 C5
Biebersdorf D 53 B3
Biedenkopf D 51 C4
Biel
CH 70 A2
E 90 A2
Bielany Wroclawskie
PL 54 B1
Bielawa PL 54 C1
Bielawy PL 55 A4
Bielefeld D 51 A4
Biella I 70 C3
Bielsa E 90 A3
Bielsk PL 47 C5
Bielsko-Biała PL 65 A5
Bielsk Podlaski PL 6 E7
Bienenbuttel D 44 B2
Bieniow PL 53 B5
Bienservida E 101 A3
Bienvenida E 93 C4
Bierdzany PL 54 C3
Bierné F 57 C5
Biersted DK 38 B2
Bierun PL 55 C4
Bierutów PL 54 B2
Bierwart B 49 C6
Bierzwina PL 46 B1
Bierzwnik PL 46 B1
Biescas E 90 A2
Biesenthal D 45 C5

Biesiekierz PL 46 A2
Bietigheim-Bissingen D 61 B5
Bièvre B 49 D6
Bieżuń PL 47 C5
Biga TR 118 B2
Bigadiç TR 118 C3
Biganos F 76 B2
Bigas P 87 D3
Bigastro E 101 A5
Bigbury GB 28 C4
Biggar GB 25 C4
Biggin Hill GB 31 C4
Biggleswade GB 30 B3
Bignasco CH 70 B3
Biguglia F 102 A2
Bihać BIH 83 B4
Biharnagybajom H 75 A6
Bijela MNE 105 A4
Bijeljani BIH 84 C3
Bijeljina BIH 85 B4
Bijelo Polje MNE 85 C4
Bijuesca E 89 C5
Bilaj HR 83 B4
Bila Tserkva UA 11 B11
Bilbao E 89 A4
Bilcza PL 55 C5
Bildudalur IS 111 B2
Bileća BIH 84 D3
Bilecik TR 118 B4
Biled RO 75 C5
Biłgoraj PL 11 A7
Bilhorod-Dnistrovskyy UA 11 C11
Bílina CZ 53 C3
Bilisht AL 116 B2
Bilje HR 74 C3
Billdal S 38 B4
Billerbeck D 50 B3
Billericay GB 31 C4
Billesholm S 41 C2
Billingborough GB 30 B3
Billinge S 41 D3
Billingham GB 27 A4
Billinghay GB 27 B5
Billingsfors S 35 D4
Billingshurst GB 31 C3
Billom F 68 C3
Billsta S 115 D15
Billund DK 39 D2
Bílopillya UA 7 F13
Bílovec CZ 64 A4
Bilstein D 50 B4
Bilthoven NL 49 A6
Bilto N 112 C10
Bilzen B 49 C6
Bíňa SK 65 C4
Binaced E 90 B3
Binasco I 71 C4
Binbrook GB 27 B5
Binche B 49 C5
Bindlach D 52 D1
Bindslev DK 38 B3
Binefar E 90 B3
Bingen D 50 D3
Bingham GB 27 C5
Bingley GB 27 B4
Bingsjö S 36 A2
Binic F 56 B3
Binz D 45 A5
Bioče MNE 105 A5
Biograd na Moru HR 83 C4
Bionaz I 70 C2
Bioska SRB 85 C4
Birda RO 75 C6
Birdlip GB 29 B5
Biri N 34 B2
Birkeland N 33 D5
Birkenfeld
Baden-Württemberg D 61 B4
Rheinland-Pfalz D 60 A3
Birkenhead GB 26 B2
Birkerød DK 41 D2
Birkfeld A 73 A5
Birkirkara M 107 C5
Birmingham GB 27 C4
Birr IRL 21 A4
Birresborn D 50 C2
Birstein D 51 C5
Biržai LT 6 C8
Birzebbugia M 107 C5
Bisáccia I 103 B8
Bisacquino I 108 B2
Bisbal de Falset E 90 B3
Biscarosse F 76 B1
Biscarosse Plage F 76 B1
Biscarrués E 90 A2
Biscéglie I 104 B2
Bischheim F 60 B3
Bischofsheim D 51 C5
Bischofshofen A 72 A3
Bischofswerda D 53 B4
Bischofswiesen D 62 C3
Bischofszell CH 71 A4
Bischwiller F 60 B3
Bisenti I 103 A6
Bishop Auckland GB 27 A4
Bishop's Castle GB 26 C3
Bishops Lydeard GB 29 B4
Bishop's Stortford GB 31 C4
Bishop's Waltham GB 31 D2
Bisignano I 106 B3
Bisingen D 61 B4
Biskupice-Oławskie PL 54 B2
Biskupiec PL 47 B5
Bismark D 44 C3
Bismo N 114 F5
Bispgården S 115 D13
Bispingen D 44 B1
Bissen L 60 A2
Bissendorf D 50 A4
Bisserup DK 39 D4
Bistango I 80 B2
Bistarac Donje BIH 84 B3
Bistrica
BIH 84 B2
MNE 85 D4
SRB 85 C4
Bistrica ob Sotli SLO 73 B5
Bistrița RO 11 C8
Bisztynek PL 47 A6
Bitburg D 50 D2
Bitche F 60 A3
Bitetto I 104 B2
Bitola MK 116 A3
Bitonto I 104 B2
Bitschwiller F 60 C3
Bitterfeld D 52 B2
Bitti I 110 B2
Biville-sur-Mer F 48 D2
Bivona I 108 B2
Biwer L 60 A2
Bizeljsko SLO 73 B5
Bizovac HR 74 C3
Bjåen N 33 C4
Bjärnum S 41 C3
Bjärred S 41 D3
Bjästa S 115 D15
Bjelland
Vest-Agder N 33 D3
Vest-Agder N 33 D4
Bjelovar HR 74 C1
Bjerkreim N 33 D3
Bjerkvik N 112 D6
Bjerreby DK 39 E3
Bjerregrav DK 38 C2
Bjerringbro DK 39 C2
Bjøberg N 32 B5
Bjøllånes N 112 F3
Björbo S 36 B1
Bjordal N 32 A2
Björg IS 111 B8
Bjørkåsen N 112 D5
Björke
Gävleborg S 36 B4
Björke *continued*
Östergötland S 37 D2
Bjørkelangen N 34 C3
Björketorp S 40 B2
Björkholmen S 112 F8
Björkliden S 112 D7
Björklinge S 36 B4
Björko S 36 C6
Björkö S 38 B4
Björköby S 40 B4
Björkvik S 37 D3
Bjørn N 115 A9
Björna S 115 D15
Björneborg S 35 C6
Björnerod S 35 C3
Bjørnevatn N 113 C18
Björnlunda S 37 C4
Bjørnstad N 113 C19
Björsäter S 37 D3
Bjurberget S 34 B4
Bjurholm S 115 D16
Bjursås S 36 B2
Bjurtjärn S 35 C6
Bjuv S 41 C2
Blace SRB 85 C6
Blachownia PL 54 C3
Blackburn GB 26 B3
Blackpool GB 26 B2
Blackstad S 40 B6
Blackwater IRL 21 B5
Blackwaterfoot GB 24 C2
Blacy F 59 B5
Bladåker S 36 B5
Blaenau Ffestiniog GB 26 C2
Blaenavon GB 29 B4
Blaengarw GB 29 B4
Blagaj
BIH 83 A5
BIH 84 C2
Blagdon GB 29 B5
Blagnac F 77 C4
Blagoevgrad BG 11 E7
Blaichach D 61 C6
Blain F 66 A3
Blainville-sur-l'Eau F 60 B2
Blair Atholl GB 25 B4
Blairgowrie GB 25 B4
Blajan F 77 C3
Blakeney GB 29 B5
Blakstad N 33 D5
Blâmont F 60 B2
Blanca E 101 A4
Blancos E 87 C3
Blandford Forum GB 29 C5
Blanes E 91 B5
Blangy-sur-Bresle F 58 A2
Blankaholm S 40 B6
Blankenberge B 49 B4
Blankenburg D 51 B6
Blankenfelde D 45 C5
Blankenhain D 52 C1
Blankenheim D 50 C2
Blanquefort F 76 B2
Blansko CZ 64 A2
Blanzac F 67 C5
Blanzy F 69 B4
Blaricum NL 49 A6
Blarney IRL 20 C3
Blascomillán E 94 B1
Blascosancho E 94 B2
Błaszki PL 54 B3
Blatná CZ 63 A4
Blatné SK 64 B3
Blatnice CZ 64 B3
Blatnika BIH 84 B2
Blato HR 84 D1
Blato na Cetini HR 84 C1
Blatten CH 70 B2
Blattnicksele S 115 B14
Blatzheim D 50 C2
Blaubeuren D 61 B5
Blaufelden D 61 A5
Blaustein D 61 B5
Blaydon GB 25 D6
Blaye F 76 A2
Blaye-les-Mines F 77 B5
Blázquez E 93 C5
Bleckede D 44 B2
Blecua E 90 A2
Bled SLO 73 B4
Bleiburg A 73 B4
Bleichenbach D 51 C5
Bleicherode D 51 B6
Bleik N 112 C4
Bleikvassli N 115 B10
Bléneau F 59 C3
Blentarp S 41 D3
Blera I 102 A5
Blérancourt F 59 A4
Bléré F 67 A5
Blesle F 68 C3
Blessington IRL 21 A5
Blet F 68 B2
Bletchley GB 31 C3
Bletterans F 69 B5
Blidö S 37 C5
Blidsberg S 40 B3
Blieskastel D 60 A3
Bligny-sur-Ouche F 69 A4
Blikstorp S 35 D6
Blinisht AL 105 B6
Blinja HR 73 C6
Blizanówek PL 54 B3
Bliżyn PL 55 B5
Blois F 58 C2
Blokhus DK 38 B2
Blokzijl NL 42 C2
Blombacka S 35 C5
Blomberg D 51 B5
Blomskog S 35 C4
Blomstermåla S 40 C6
Blomvåg N 32 B1
Blönduós IS 111 B5
Błonie PL 55 A5
Blonville-sur-Mer F 57 A6
Blötberget S 36 B2
Blovice CZ 63 A4
Bloxham GB 31 B2
Blšany CZ 52 C3
Bludenz A 71 A4
Bludov CZ 64 A2
Blumberg D 61 C4
Blyberg S 34 A6
Blyth
Northumberland GB 25 C6
Nottinghamshire GB 27 B4
Blyth Bridge GB 25 C4
Blythburgh GB 30 B5
Blythe Bridge GB 26 C3
Bø
Nordland N 112 D3
Telemark N 33 C6
Boal E 86 A4
Boan MNE 85 D4
Boario Terme I 71 C5
Boat of Garten GB 23 D5
Boa Vista P 92 B2
Boğazkale TR 16 A7
Boğazlıyan TR 16 B7
Boba H 74 A2
Bobadilla
Logroño E 89 B4
Málaga E 100 B1
Bobadilla del Campo E 94 A1
Bobadilla del Monte E 94 B3
Bóbbio I 80 B3
Bóbbio Pellice I 79 B6
Bobigny F 58 B3
Bobingen D 62 B1
Böblingen D 61 B5
Bobolice PL 46 B2
Boboras E 87 B2
Bobowa PL 65 A6
Bobrinets UA 11 B12
Bobrová CZ 64 A2
Bobrovitsa UA 11 A11
Bobrowice PL 53 B5
Bobrówko PL 46 C1
Boca de Huérgano E 88 B2
Bocairent E 96 C2
Bočar SRB 75 C5
Bocchigliero I 106 B3
Boceguillas E 89 C3
Bochnia PL 55 D5
Bocholt
B 49 B6
D 50 B2
Bochov CZ 52 C3
Bochum D 50 B3
Bockara S 40 B6
Bockenem D 51 A6
Bockfliess A 64 B2
Bockhorn D 43 B5
Bočna SLO 73 B4
Bocognano F 102 A2
Boconád H 65 C6
Boczów PL 45 C6
Boda S 36 A2
Böda S 41 B7
Boda
Stockholm S 36 B5
Värmland S 35 C5
Västernorrland S 115 E13
Bodafors S 40 B4
Boda Glasbruk S 40 C5
Bodajk H 74 A3
Boddam
Aberdeenshire GB 23 D7
Shetland GB 22 B7
Boddin D 44 B3
Bödefeld-Freiheit D 51 B4
Boden S 3 D24
Bodenmais D 62 A4
Bodenteich D 44 C2
Bodenwerder D 51 B5
Bodiam GB 31 C4
Bodinnick GB 28 C3
Bodio CH 70 B3
Bodjani SRB 75 C4
Bodmin GB 28 C3
Bodø N 112 E3
Bodonal de la Sierra E 99 A4
Bodrum TR 119 E2
Bodstedt D 45 A4
Bodzanów PL 47 C6
Bodzanowice PL 54 C3
Bodzechów PL 55 C6
Bodzentyn PL 55 C5
Boecillo E 88 C2
Boëge F 69 B6
Boën F 68 C3
Bogács H 65 C6
Bogadmindszent H 74 C3
Bogajo E 87 D4
Bogarra E 101 A3
Bogarre E 100 B2
Bogatić SRB 85 B4
Bogatynia PL 53 C4
Bogdaniec PL 45 C7
Bogë AL 105 A5
Boge S 37 E5
Bogen
D 62 B3
Nordland N 112 D5
Nordland N 112 E4
S 34 B4
Bogense DK 39 D3
Bogetići MNE 84 D3
Bognanco Fonti I 70 B3
Bognelv N 113 B11
Bognes N 112 D5
Bogno CH 70 B4
Bognor Regis GB 31 D3
Bogoria PL 55 C6
Bograngen S 34 B4
Boguchwaly PL 47 B6
Bogumiłowice PL 55 B4
Boguslav UA 11 B11
Boguszów-Gorce PL 53 C6
Bogutovac SRB 85 C5
Bogyiszló H 74 B3
Bohain-en-Vermandois F 49 D4
Böheimkirchen A 64 B1
Bohinjska Bistrica SLO 72 B3
Böhlen D 52 B2
Böhmenkirch D 61 B5
Bohmte D 43 C5
Bohonal de Ibor E 93 B5
Böhönye H 74 B2
Bohumin CZ 65 A4
Boiro E 86 B2
Bois-d'Amont F 69 B6
Boisseron F 78 C3
Boitzenburg D 45 B5
Boixols E 91 A4
Boizenburg D 44 B2
Bojadła PL 53 B5
Bojano I 103 B7
Bojanowo PL 54 B1
Bøjden DK 39 D3
Bojkovice CZ 64 A3
Bojná SK 64 B4
Bojnice SK 65 B4
Boka SRB 75 C5
Böklund D 43 A6
Bokod H 74 A3
Böksholm S 40 B4
Boksitogorsk RUS 7 B12
Bol HR 83 C5
Bolaños de Calatrava E 100 A2
Bolayır TR 118 B1
Bolbec F 58 A1
Bölcske H 75 B3
Bolderslev DK 39 E2
Boldog H 65 C5
Boldva H 65 B6
Bolea E 90 A2
Bolekhiv UA 11 B7
Bolesławiec PL 53 B5
Boleszkowice PL 45 C6
Bolewice PL 46 C2
Bólgheri I 81 C4
Bolhrad UA 11 D10
Boliden S 3 D24
Bolimów PL 55 A5
Boliqueime P 98 B2
Boljevci SRB 85 B5
Boljkovci SRB 85 B5
Bolkhov RUS 7 E14
Bolków PL 53 C6
Bollebygd S 40 B2
Bollène F 78 B3
Bólliga E 95 B4
Bollnäs S 36 A3
Bollstabruk S 115 E14
Bollullos E 99 B4
Bollullos par del Condado E 99 B4
Bologna I 81 B5
Bologne F 59 B6
Bolognetta I 108 B2
Bolognola I 82 D2
Bologoye RUS 7 C13
Bolótana I 110 B1
Bolsena I 102 A4
Bolshaya Vradiyevka UA 11 C11
Bolsover GB 27 B4
Bolstad S 35 D4
Bolsward NL 42 B2
Boltaña E 90 A3
Boltenhagen D 44 B3
Boltigen CH 70 B2
Bolton GB 26 B3
Bolu TR 118 B6
Bolungarvík IS 111 A2
Bolvadin TR 118 D6
Bóly H 74 C3
Bolzaneto I 80 B2
Bolzano I 71 B6
Bomba I 103 A7
Bombarral P 92 B1
Bömenzien D 44 C3
Bomlitz D 43 C6
Bømlo N 33 C2
Bøn N 34 B3
Bona F 68 A3
Bonaduz CH 71 B4
Bonanza E 99 C4
Boñar E 88 B1
Bonarbridge GB 23 D4
Bonárcado I 110 B1
Bonares E 99 B4
Bonäs S 36 A1
Bonassola I 80 B3
Bonawe GB 24 B2
Bondal N 32 C5
Bondeno I 81 B5
Bondorf D 61 B4
Bondstorp S 40 B3
Bon-Encontre F 77 B3
Bo'ness GB 25 B4
Bonete E 101 A4
Bonifacio F 102 B2
Bonigen CH 70 B2
Bonin PL 46 A2
Bonn D 50 C3
Bonnánaro I 110 B1
Bonnåsjøen N 112 E4
Bonnat F 68 B1
Bonndorf D 61 C4
Bonnétable F 58 B1
Bonnétage F 70 A1
Bonneuil-les-Eaux F 58 A3
Bonneuil-Matours F 67 B5
Bonneval F 58 B2
Bonneval-sur-Arc F 70 C2
Bonneville F 69 B6
Bonnières-sur-Seine F 58 A2
Bonnieux F 79 C4
Bönnigheim D 61 A5
Bonnyrigg GB 25 C4
Bonny-sur-Loire F 68 A2
Bono
E 90 A3
I 110 B2
Bonorva I 110 B1
Bønsnes N 34 B2
Bonyhád H 74 B3
Boom B 49 B5
Boos F 58 A2
Boostedt D 44 A2
Bootle
Cumbria GB 26 A2
Merseyside GB 26 B2
Bopfingen D 61 B6
Boppard D 50 C3
Boqueixón E 86 B2
Bor
CZ 62 A3
S 40 B4
SRB 11 D7
TR 16 C7
Boran-sur-Oise F 58 A3
Borås S 40 B2
Borba P 92 C3
Borbona I 102 A6
Borča SRB 85 B5
Borci BIH 84 C3
Borculo NL 50 A2
Bordány H 75 B4
Bordeaux F 76 B2
Bordeira P 98 B2
Bordesholm D 44 A2
Borðeyri IS 111 B4
Bordighera I 80 C1
Bording DK 39 C2
Bordón E 90 C2
Bore I 81 B3
Borehamwood GB 31 C3
Borek Strzeliński PL 54 C2
Borek Wielkopolski PL 54 B2
Boreland GB 25 C4
Borello I 82 B1
Borensberg S 37 D2
Borgafjäll S 115 C12
Borgarnes IS 111 C4
Borgentreich D 51 B5
Börger D 43 C4
Borger NL 42 C3
Borggård S 37 D2
Borghamn S 37 D1
Borghetta di Vara I 81 B3
Borghetto d'Arróscia I 80 B1
Borghetto Santo Spirito I 80 B2
Borgholm S 41 C6
Borghorst D 50 A3
Bórgia I 106 C3
Borgloon B 49 C6
Børglum DK 38 B2
Borgo F 102 A2
Borgo alla Collina I 81 C5
Borgo a Mozzano I 81 C4
Borgoforte I 81 A4
Borgofranco d'Ivrea I 70 C2
Borgomanero I 70 C3
Borgomasino I 70 C2
Borgonovo Val Tidone I 80 A3
Borgo Pace I 82 C1
Borgorose I 102 A6
Borgo San Dalmazzo I 80 B1
Borgo San Lorenzo I 81 C5
Borgosésia I 70 C3
Borgo Val di Taro I 81 B3
Borgo Valsugana I 71 B6
Borgo Vercelli I 70 C3
Borgstena S 40 B3
Borgue GB 24 D3
Borgund N 32 A4
Borgvik S 35 C4
Borisovka RUS 7 F14
Borja E 89 C5
Bork D 50 B3
Borken D 50 B2
Borkenes N 112 D5
Børkop DK 39 D2
Borkowice PL 55 B5
Borkowo PL 47 C6
Borkum D 42 B3
Borlänge S 36 B2
Borlu TR 118 D3
Bormes-les-Mimosas F 79 C5
Bormio I 71 B5
Bormujos E 99 B4
Borna D 52 B2
Borne NL 50 A2
Bornes P 87 C3
Borne Sulinowo PL 46 B2
Bornheim D 50 C2
Bornhöved D 44 A2
Börnicke D 45 C4
Bornos E 99 C5
Borobia E 89 C5
Borodino RUS 7 D13
Borohrádek CZ 53 C6
Boronów PL 54 C3
Bórore I 110 B1
Borosźow PL 54 C3
Borota H 75 B4
Boroughbridge GB 27 A4
Borovany CZ 63 B5
Borovichi RUS 7 B12
Borovnica SLO 73 C4
Borovo HR 75 C3
Borovsk RUS 7 D14
Borovy CZ 63 A4
Borowa PL 54 B2
Borowie PL 55 B6
Borox E 94 B3
Borrby S 41 D4
Borre
DK 41 E2
N 35 C2
Borredá E 91 A4
Borrenes E 86 B4
Borriol E 96 A2
Borris
DK 39 D1
IRL 21 B5
Borris-in-Ossory IRL 21 B4
Borrisokane IRL 20 B3
Borrisoleigh IRL 21 B4
Borrowdale GB 26 A2
Børrud N 34 C4
Borşa RO 11 C8
Borsdorf D 52 B2
Børselv N 113 B14
Borsfa H 74 B1
Borský Mikuláš SK 64 B3
Borsodivánka H 65 C6
Borsodnádasd H 65 B6
Börte N 33 C4
Borth GB 26 C1
Bort-les-Orgues F 68 C2
Börtnan S 115 E10
Børtnes N 32 B6
Boruja Kościelne PL 54 A1
Borup DK 39 D4
Boryslav UA 11 B7
Boryspil UA 11 A11
Boryszyn PL 46 C1
Borzęciczki PL 54 B2
Borzęcin PL 55 C5
Borzna UA 7 F12
Borzonasca I 80 B3
Borzyszkowy PL 46 A3
Borzytuchom PL 46 A3
Bosa I 110 B1
Bošáca SK 64 B3
Bosanci HR 73 C5
Bosanska Dubica BIH 74 C1
Bosanska Gradiška BIH 74 C2
Bosanska Kostajnica BIH 74 C1
Bosanska Krupa BIH 83 B5
Bosanski Brod BIH 84 A2
Bosanski Novi BIH 83 A5
Bosanski Petrovac BIH 83 B5
Bosanski Šamac BIH 84 A3
Bosansko Grahovo BIH 83 B5
Bošany SK 64 B4
Bösárkány H 64 C3
Bosau D 44 A2
Bósca H 75 B4
Boscastle GB 28 C3
Bosco I 80 B2
Bosco Chiesanuova I 71 C6
Bösdorf D 44 A2
Bösel D 43 B4
Bosham GB 31 D3
Bösingfeld D 51 A5
Bosjön S 34 C5
Boskoop NL 49 A5
Boskovice CZ 64 A2
Bošnjaci HR 84 A3
Bošnjane SRB 85 C6
Bossast E 77 D3
Bossolasco I 80 B2
Boštanj SLO 73 B5
Boston GB 27 C5
Bostrak N 33 C5
Böszénfa H 74 B2
Bot E 90 B3
Botajica BIH 84 B3
Bøte By DK 44 A3
Bothel GB 26 A2
Boticas P 87 C3
Botilsäter S 35 C5
Botngård N 114 D6
Botoš SRB 75 C5
Botoşani RO 11 C9
Botricello I 107 C3
Bottendorf D 51 B4
Bottesford GB 27 C5
Bottnaryd S 40 B3
Bottrop D 50 B2
Botunje SRB 85 B6
Boturić SRB 85 C5
Bötzingen D 60 B3
Bouaye F 66 A3
Bouça P 87 C3
Boucau F 76 C1
Bouchain F 49 C4
Bouchoir F 58 A3
Boudreville F 59 C5
Boudry CH 70 B1
Bouesse F 68 B1
Bouguenais F 66 A3
Bouhy F 68 A3
Bouillargues F 78 C3
Bouillon B 59 A6
Bouilly F 59 B4
Bouin F 66 B3
Boulay-Moselle F 60 A2
Boulazac F 67 C5
Boule-d'Amont F 91 A5
Bouligny F 60 A1
Boulogne-sur-Gesse F 77 C3
Boulogne-sur-Mer F 48 C2
Bouloire F 58 C1
Bouquemaison F 48 C3
Bourbon-Lancy F 68 B3
Bourbon-l'Archambault F 68 B3
Bourbonne-les-Bains F 60 C1
Bourbourg F 48 C3
Bourbriac F 56 B2
Bourcefranc-le-Chapus F 66 C3
Bourdeaux F 79 B4
Bouresse F 67 B5
Bourg F 76 A2
Bourg-Achard F 58 A1
Bourganeuf F 68 C1
Bourg-Argental F 69 C4
Bourg-de-Péage F 79 A4
Bourg-de-Thizy F 69 B4
Bourg-de-Visa F 77 B3
Bourg-en-Bresse F 69 B5
Bourges F 68 A2
Bourg-et-Comin F 59 A4
Bourg-Lastic F 68 C2
Bourg-Madame F 91 A4
Bourgneuf-en-Retz F 66 A3
Bourgogne F 59 A5
Bourgoin-Jallieu F 69 C5
Bourg-St Andéol F 78 B3
Bourg-St Maurice F 70 C1
Bourgtheroulde F 58 A1
Bourgueil F 67 A5
Bourmont F 60 B1
Bourne GB 30 B3
Bournemouth GB 29 C6
Bourneville F 58 A1
Bournezeau F 66 B3
Bourran F 77 B3
Bourret F 77 C4
Bourron-Marlotte F 58 B3
Bourton-on-The-Water GB 29 B6
Boussac F 68 B2
Boussens F 77 C3
Boutersem B 49 C5
Bouttencourt F 48 D2
Bouvières F 79 B4
Bouvron F 66 A3
Bouxwiller F 60 B3
Bouzas E 87 B2
Bouzonville F 60 A2
Bova I 106 D2
Bovalino Marina I 106 C3
Bovallstrand S 35 D3
Bova Marina I 106 D2
Bovec SLO 72 B3
Bóveda E 86 B3
Bóvegno I 71 C5
Bovenau D 44 A1
Bovenden D 51 B5
Bøverdal N 114 F5
Boves F 58 A3
Bóves I 80 B1
Bovey Tracey GB 28 C4
Bovino I 103 B8
Bøvlingbjerg DK 38 C1
Bovolenta I 72 C1
Bovolone I 71 C6
Bowes GB 27 A4
Bowmore GB 24 C1
Bowness-on-Windermere GB 26 A3
Box GB 29 B5
Boxberg
Baden-Württemberg D 61 A5
Sachsen D 53 B4
Boxholm S 37 D2
Boxmeer NL 50 B1
Boxtel NL 49 B6
Boyabat TR 16 A7
Boyalıca TR 118 B4
Boyle IRL 18 C3
Bozan TR 118 C6
Božava HR 83 B3
Bozburun TR 119 F3
Bozcaada TR 116 C8
Bozdoğan TR 119 E3
Bożepole Wielkie PL 46 A3
Boževac SRB 85 B6
Božice CZ 64 B2
Boži Dar CZ 52 C2
Bozkır TR 119 E7
Bozouls F 78 B1
Bozova TR 119 E5
Bozüyük TR 118 C5
Bózzolo I 81 A4
Bra I 80 B1
Braås S 40 B5
Brabrand DK 39 C3
Bracadale GB 22 D2
Bracciano I 102 A5
Bracieux F 67 A6
Bräcke S 115 E12
Brackenheim D 61 A5
Brackley GB 30 B2
Bracklin IRL 19 C5
Bracknell GB 31 C3
Brackwede D 51 B4
Braco GB 25 B4
Brad RO 11 C7
Bradford GB 27 B4
Bradford on Avon GB 29 B5
Bradina BIH 84 C3
Brådland N 33 D3
Brædstrup DK 39 D2
Brae GB 22 A7
Braemar GB 23 D5
Braemore GB 22 D3
Braga P 87 C2
Bragança P 87 C4
Brăila RO 11 D9
Braine F 59 A4
Braine-le-Comte B 49 C5
Braintree GB 31 C4
Braives B 49 C6
Brake D 43 B5
Brakel
B 49 C4
D 51 B5
Bråkne-Hoby S 41 C5
Brålanda S 35 D4
Bralin PL 54 B2
Brallo di Pregola I 80 B3
Bram F 77 C5
Bramafan F 79 C5
Bramberg am Wildkogel A 72 A2
Bramdrupdam DK 39 D2
Bramming DK 39 D1
Brampton GB 25 D5
Bramsche D 43 C4
Branca I 82 C1
Brancaleone Marina I 106 D3
Brancaster GB 30 B4
Brand
Nieder Östereich A 63 B6
Vorarlberg A 71 A4
Brandbu N 34 B2
Brande DK 39 D2
Brande-Hornerkirchen D 43 B6
Brandenberg A 72 A1
Brandenburg D 45 C4
Brand-Erbisdorf D 52 C3
Brandis D 52 B2
Brando F 102 A2
Brandomil E 86 A2
Brandon GB 30 B4
Brandshagen D 45 A5
Brandval N 34 B4
Brandýs nad Labem CZ 53 C4
Branice PL 54 C2
Braniewo PL 47 A5
Branik SLO 72 C3
Brankovina SRB 85 B4
Branky CZ 64 A3
Branne F 76 B2
Brannenburg-Degerndorf D 62 C3
Brantôme F 67 C5
Branzi I 71 B4
Bras d'Asse F 79 C5
Braskereidfoss N 34 B3
Braslaw BY 7 D9
Brașov RO 11 D8
Brasparts F 56 B2
Brassac F 77 C5
Brassac-les-Mines F 68 C3
Brasschaat B 49 B5
Brastad S 35 D3
Břasy CZ 63 A4
Brąszewice PL 54 B3
Bratislava SK 64 B3
Brattfors S 35 C6
Brattvåg N 114 E3
Bratunac BIH 85 B4
Braubach D 50 C3
Braunau A 62 B4
Braunfels D 51 C4
Braunlage D 51 B6
Braunsbedra D 52 B1
Braunschweig D 51 A6
Bray IRL 21 A5
Bray Dunes F 48 B3
Bray-sur-Seine F 59 B4
Bray-sur-Somme F 48 D3
Brazatortas E 100 A1
Brazey-en-Plaine F 69 A5
Brbinj HR 83 B4
Brčko BIH 84 B3
Brdani SRB 85 C5
Brdów PL 47 C4
Brea de Tajo E 95 B3
Brécey F 57 B4
Brechin GB 25 B5
Brecht B 49 B5
Brecketfeld D 50 B3
Břeclav CZ 64 B2
Brecon GB 29 B4
Brécy F 68 A2
Breda
E 91 B5
NL 49 B5
Bredaryd S 40 B3
Bredbyn S 115 D15
Breddin D 44 C4
Bredebro DK 39 D1
Bredelar D 51 B4
Bredenfelde D 45 B5
Bredsjö S 36 C1
Bredstedt D 43 A5
Bredsten DK 39 D2
Bredträsk S 115 D15
Bredviken S 115 A11
Bree B 49 B6
Bregana HR 73 C5
Breganze I 72 C1
Bregenz A 71 A4
Bréhal F 57 B4
Brehna D 52 B2
Breiðdalsvík IS 111 C11
Breidenbach F 60 A3
Breil-sur-Roya F 80 C1
Breisach D 60 B3
Breitenbach
CH 70 A2
Breitenbach *continued*
D 51 C5
Breitenberg D 63 B4
Breitenfelde D 44 B2
Breitengussbach D 51 D6
Breivikbotn N 113 B11
Brejning DK 39 D2
Brekke N 32 A2
Brekken N 114 E8
Brekkestø N 33 D5
Brekkvasselv N 115 C10
Brekstad N 114 D6
Breland N 33 D4
Bremanger N 114 F1
Bremen D 43 B5
Bremerhaven D 43 B5
Bremervörde D 43 B6
Bremgarten CH 70 A3
Bremsnes N 114 D4
Brem-sur-Mer F 66 B3
Brenderup DK 39 D2
Brenes E 99 B5
Brengova SLO 73 B5
Brenna PL 65 A4
Breno I 71 C5
Brénod F 69 B5
Brensbach D 61 A4
Brentwood GB 31 C4
Brescello I 81 B4
Bréscia I 71 C5
Breskens NL 49 B4
Bresles F 58 A3
Bresnica SRB 85 C5
Bressana I 80 A3
Bressanone I 72 B1
Bressuire F 67 B4
Brest
BY 6 E7
F 56 B1
HR 72 C3
Brestač SRB 85 B4
Brestanica SLO 73 B5
Brestova HR 82 A3
Brestovac HR 74 C2
Bretenoux F 77 B4
Breteuil
Eure F 58 B1
Oise F 58 A3
Brétigny-sur-Orge F 58 B3
Bretten D 61 A4
Bretteville-sur-Laize F 57 A5
Brettheim D 61 A6
Breuil-Cervinia I 70 C2
Breukelen NL 49 A6
Brevik
N 35 C1
Stockholm S 37 C5
Västra Götaland S 37 D1
Breza BIH 84 B3
Brežice SLO 73 C5
Bréziers F 79 B5
Breznica HR 73 B6
Breznica Našička HR 74 C3
Březnice CZ 63 A4
Brezno SK 65 B5
Brezolles F 58 B2
Březová nad Svitavou CZ 64 A2
Brezová pod Bradlom SK 64 B3
Brezovica
SK 65 A6
SLO 73 B4
Brezovo Polje Selo BIH 84 B3
Briançon F 79 B5
Brianconnet F 79 C5
Briare F 58 C3
Briatexte F 77 C4
Briático I 106 C3
Briaucourt F 59 B6
Bribir HR 73 C4
Bricquebec F 57 A4
Bridgend
Argyll & Bute GB 24 C1
Bridgend GB 29 B4
Bridge of Cally GB 25 B4
Bridge of Don GB 23 D6
Bridge of Earn GB 25 B4
Bridge of Orchy GB 24 B3
Bridgnorth GB 26 C3
Bridgwater GB 29 B5
Břidličná CZ 64 A3
Bridlington GB 27 A5
Bridport GB 29 C5
Briec F 56 B1
Brie-Comte-Robert F 58 B3
Brienne-le-Château F 59 B5
Brienon-sur-Armançon F 59 C4
Brienz CH 70 B3
Brienza I 104 C1
Briesen D 45 C6
Brieskow Finkenheerd D 53 A4
Brietlingen D 44 B2
Brieva de Cameros E 89 B4
Briey F 60 A1
Brig CH 70 B3
Brigg GB 27 B5
Brighouse GB 27 B4
Brightlingsea GB 31 C5
Brighton GB 31 D3
Brignogan-Plage F 56 B1
Brignoles F 79 C5
Brigstock GB 30 B3
Brihuega E 95 B4
Brijuni HR 82 B2
Brillon-en-Barrois F 59 B6
Brilon D 51 B4
Brimnes N 32 B3
Brinches P 98 A3
Brindisi I 105 C3
Brinje HR 83 A4
Brinon-sur-Beuvron F 68 A3
Brinon-sur-Sauldre F 68 A2
Brinyan GB 23 B5
Brión E 86 B2
Briones E 89 B4
Brionne F 58 A1
Brioude F 68 C3
Brioux-sur-Boutonne F 67 B4
Briouze F 57 B5
Briscous F 76 C1
Brisighella I 81 B5
Brissac-Quincé F 67 A4
Brissago CH 70 B3
Bristol GB 29 B5
Brive-la-Gaillarde F 67 C6
Briviesca E 89 B3
Brixham GB 29 C4
Brixlegg A 72 A1
Brjánslækur IS 111 B2
Brka BIH 84 B3
Brnaze HR 83 C5
Brněnec CZ 64 A2
Brno CZ 64 A2
Bro S 37 C4
Broadclyst GB 29 C4
Broadford
GB 22 D3
IRL 20 B3
Broad Haven GB 28 B2
Broadstairs GB 31 C5
Broadstone GB 29 C5
Broadway GB 29 A6
Broager DK 39 E2
Broaryd S 40 B3
Broby S 41 C4
Brobyværk DK 39 D3
Bročanac BIH 84 C2
Bročanac MNE 84 D3
Brocas F 76 B2
Brock D 50 A3
Brockel D 43 B6
Brockenhurst GB 31 D2
Broczyno PL 46 B2
Brod MK 116 A3
Brodalen S 35 D3
Brodarevo SRB 85 C4
Broddbo S 36 C3
Brodek u Přerova CZ 64 A3
Broden-bach D 50 C3
Brodick GB 24 C2
Brod na Kupi HR 73 C4
Brodnica PL 47 B5
Brodnica Graniczna PL 47 A4
Brody
Lubuskie PL 53 B5
Lubuskie PL 53 B4
Mazowieckie PL 47 C6
UA 11 A8
Broglie F 58 B1
Brójce PL 53 A5
Brokind S 37 D2
Brolo I 109 A3
Brome D 44 C2
Bromley GB 31 C4
Bromölla S 41 C4
Bromont-Lamothe F 68 C2
Brömsebro S 41 C5
Bromsgrove GB 29 A5
Bromyard GB 29 A5
Bronchales E 95 B5
Bronco E 93 A4
Brønderslev DK 38 B2
Broni I 80 A3
Brønnøysund N 114 B9
Brøns DK 39 D1
Bronte I 109 B3
Bronzani Mejdan BIH 84 B1
Bronzolo I 71 B6
Broons F 57 B3
Broquies F 78 B1
Brora GB 23 C5
Brørup DK 39 D2
Brösarp S 41 D4
Brossac F 67 C4
Brostrud N 32 B5
Brotas P 92 C2
Brötjärna S 36 B2
Broto E 90 A2
Brottby S 37 C5
Brøttum N 34 A2
Brou F 58 B2
Brouage F 66 C3
Brough GB 26 A3
Broughshane GB 19 B5
Broughton GB 25 C4
Broughton-in-Furness GB 26 A2
Broumov CZ 53 C6
Broût-Vernet F 68 B3
Brouvelieures F 60 B2
Brouwershaven NL 49 B4
Brovary UA 11 A11
Brovst DK 38 B2
Brownhills GB 27 C4
Brozas E 93 B4
Brozzo I 71 C5
Brtnice CZ 63 A6
Brtonigla HR 72 C3
Bruay-la-Buissière F 48 C3
Bruchhausen-Vilsen D 43 C6
Bruchsal D 61 A4
Bruck D 62 A3
Brück D 52 A2
Bruck an der Grossglocknerstrasse A 72 A2
Bruck an der Leitha A 64 B2
Bruck an der Mur A 73 A5
Brückl A 73 B4
Bruckmühl D 62 C2
Brue-Auriac F 79 C4
Brüel D 44 B3
Bruen CH 70 B3
Bruère-Allichamps F 68 B2
Bruff IRL 20 B3
Bruflat N 32 B6
Brugg CH 70 A3
Brugge B 49 B4
Brüggen D 50 B2
Brühl D 50 C2
Bruinisse NL 49 B5
Brûlon F 57 C5
Brumano I 71 C4
Brumath F 60 B3
Brummen NL 50 A2
Brumov-Bylnice CZ 64 A4
Brumunddal N 34 B2
Brunau D 44 C3
Brunehamel F 59 A5
Brünen D 50 B2
Brunete E 94 B2
Brunflo S 115 D11
Brunico I 72 B1
Brunkeberg N 33 C5
Brunn D 45 B5
Brunnen CH 70 B3
Brunsbüttel D 43 B6
Brunssum NL 50 C1
Bruntál CZ 54 D2
Brus SRB 85 C6
Brušane HR 83 B4
Brusasco I 70 C3
Brusio CH 71 B5
Brusno SK 65 B5
Brusque F 78 C1
Brussels = Bruxelles B 49 C5
Brusson I 70 C2
Brüssow D 45 B6
Brusy PL 46 B3
Bruton GB 29 B5
Bruvno HR 83 B4
Bruvoll N 34 B3
Bruxelles = Brussels B 49 C5
Bruyères F 60 B2
Bruz F 57 B4
Bruzaholm S 40 B5
Brwinów PL 55 A5
Brynamman GB 28 B4
Bryncrug GB 26 C1
Bryne N 33 D2
Brynmawr GB 29 B4
Bryrup DK 39 C2
Brzeće SRB 85 C5
Brzeg PL 54 C2
Brzeg Dolny PL 54 B1
Brześć Kujawski PL 47 C4
Brzesko PL 55 D5
Brzeszcze PL 55 D4
Brzezie PL 46 B2
Brzeziny
Łódzkie PL 55 B4
Wielkopolskie PL 54 B3
Brzeźnica PL 53 B5
Brzeźnica Nowa PL 55 B4
Brzeźno PL 46 B1
Brzotín SK 65 B6
Brzozie Lubawskie PL 47 B5
Bua S 40 B2
Buarcos P 92 A2
Buaveg N 33 C2
Bubbio I 80 B2
Bubry F 56 C2
Buca TR 119 D2
Bucak TR 119 E5
Bučany SK 64 B3
Buccheri I 109 B3
Buccino I 103 C8
Bucelas P 92 C1
Buch
Bayern D 61 B6
Bayern D 62 B3
Buchach UA 11 B8
Bucharest = București RO 11 D9
Buchbach D 62 B3
Buchboden A 71 A4
Buchen D 61 A5
Büchen D 44 B2
Buchenberg D 61 C6

Buchères F 59 B5
Buchholz D 44 B1
Buchloe D 62 B1
Buchlovice CZ 64 A3
Buchlyvie GB 24 B3
Bucholz D 44 B4
Buchs CH 71 A4
Buchy F 58 A2
Bückeburg D 51 A5
Buckfastleigh GB 28 C4
Buckhaven GB 25 B4
Buckie GB 23 D6
Buckingham GB 31 B3
Buckley GB 26 B2
Bückwitz D 44 C4
Bučovice CZ 64 A3
Bucsa H 75 A6
București = Bucharest RO 11 D9
Bucy-lés-Pierrepont F 59 A4
Buczek PL 55 B4
Bud N 114 E3
Budakalasz H 65 C5
Budakeszi H 75 A3
Budal N 114 E7
Budaörs H 75 A3
Budapest H 75 A4
Búðardalur IS 111 B4
Budča SK 65 B5
Buddusò I 110 B2
Bude GB 28 C3
Budeč CZ 63 A6
Büdelsdorf D 43 A6
Budens P 98 B2
Budia E 95 B4
Budimlić-Japra BIH 83 B5
Büdingen D 51 C5
Budinšćina HR 73 B6
Budišov CZ 64 A3
Budleigh Salterton GB 29 C4
Budmerice SK 64 B3
Budoni I 110 B2
Búdrio I 81 B5
Budva MNE 105 A4
Budyně nad Ohří CZ 53 C4
Budziszewice PL 55 B4
Budzyń PL 46 C2
Bue N 33 D2
Bueña E 95 B5
Buenache de Alarcón E 95 C4
Buenache de la Sierra E 95 B5
Buenaventura E 94 B2
Buenavista de Valdavia E 88 B2
Buendia E 95 B4
Bueu E 87 B2
Buezo E 89 B3
Bugac H 75 B4
Bugarra E 96 B2
Bugeat F 68 C1
Buggerru I 110 C1
Bugojno BIH 84 B2
Bugøyfjord N 113 C18
Bugøynes N 113 C18
Bugyi H 75 A4
Buharkent TR 119 E3
Bühl
Baden-Württemberg D 61 B4
Bayern D 61 C6
Bühlertal D 61 B4
Bühlertann D 61 A5
Buia I 72 B3
Builth Wells GB 29 A4
Buin N 32 B6
Buis-les-Baronnies F 79 B4
Buitenpost NL 42 B3
Buitrago del Lozoya E 94 B3
Bujalance E 100 B1
Bujaraloz E 90 B2
Buje HR 72 C3
Bujedo E 89 B3
Bük H 74 A1
Buk PL 46 C2
Bükkösd H 74 B2
Bükkzsérc H 65 C6
Bukovci SLO 73 B5
Bukowiec PL 53 A6
Bukowina Tatrzańska PL 65 A6
Bukownica PL 54 B3
Bukowno PL 55 C4
Bülach CH 70 A3
Búland IS 111 D7
Buldan TR 119 D3
Bulgari BG 11 E9
Bulgnéville F 60 B1
Bulgurca TR 119 D2
Bülkau D 43 B5
Bulken N 32 B3
Bulkowo PL 47 C6
Bullas E 101 A4
Bulle CH 70 B2
Büllingen B 50 C2
Bulqizë AL 116 A2
Buna BIH 84 C2
Bunahowen IRL 18 B2
Bunbeg IRL 18 A3
Bunclody IRL 21 B5
Buncrana IRL 19 A4
Bunde D 43 B4
Bünde D 51 A4
Bundoran IRL 18 B3
Bunessan GB 24 B1
Bungay GB 30 B5
Bunge S 37 E6
Bunić HR 83 B4
Bunmahon IRL 21 B4
Bunnyconnellan IRL 18 B2
Buño E 86 A2
Buñol E 96 B2
Bunratty IRL 20 B3
Bunsbeek B 49 C5
Buñuel E 89 C5
Bünyan TR 16 B7
Bunyola E 97 B2
Buonabitácolo I 104 C1
Buonalbergo I 103 B7
Buonconvento I 81 C5
Buonvicino I 106 B2
Burano I 72 C2
Burbach D 50 C4
Burcei I 110 C2
Burdons-sur-Rognon F 59 B6
Burdur TR 119 E5
Bureå S 3 D24
Burela E 86 A3
Büren D 51 B4
Büren an der Aare CH 70 A2
Burford GB 29 B6
Burg
Cottbus D 53 B4
Magdeburg D 52 A1
Schleswig-Holstein D 43 B6
Burgas BG 11 E9
Burgau
A 73 A6
D 61 B6
P 98 B2
Burg auf Fehmarn D 44 A3
Burgbernheim D 61 A6
Burgdorf
CH 70 A2
D 44 C2
Burgebrach D 62 A1
Bürgel D 52 C1
Burgess Hill GB 31 D3
Burghaslach D 61 A6
Burghausen D 62 B3
Burghead GB 23 D5
Burgheim D 62 B2
Burgh le Marsh GB 27 B6
Búrgio I 108 B2
Burgkirchen D 62 B3
Burgkunstadt D 52 C1
Burglengenfeld D 62 A3
Burgo P 87 D2
Burgoberbach D 61 A6
Burgohondo E 94 B2
Burgos E 88 B3
Burgsinn D 51 C5
Burgstädt D 52 C2
Burgstall D 44 C3
Burg Stargard D 45 B5
Burgsvik S 37 E5
Burgui E 76 D2
Burguillos E 99 B5
Burguillos del Cerro E 93 C4
Burguillos de Toledo E 94 C3
Burhaniye TR 118 C1
Burhave D 43 B5
Burie F 67 C4
Burjassot E 96 B2
Burk D 61 A6
Burkhardtsdorf D 52 C2
Burlada E 76 D1
Burladingen D 61 B5
Burlage D 43 B4
Burness GB 23 B6
Burnham GB 31 C3
Burnham Market GB 30 B4
Burnham-on-Crouch GB 31 C4
Burnham-on-Sea GB 29 B5
Burniston GB 27 A5
Burnley GB 26 B3
Burntisland GB 25 B4
Burón E 88 A1
Buronzo I 70 C3
Burovac SRB 85 B6
Burow D 45 B5
Burravoe GB 22 A7
Burrel AL 105 B6
Burret F 77 D4
Burriana E 96 B2
Burry Port GB 28 B3
Bürs A 71 A4
Bursa TR 118 B4
Burseryd S 40 B3
Bürstadt D 61 A4
Burton Agnes GB 27 A5
Burton Bradstock GB 29 C5
Burton Latimer GB 30 B3
Burton upon Stather GB 27 B5
Burton upon Trent GB 27 C4
Burujón E 94 C2
Burwell GB 30 B4
Burwick GB 23 C6
Bury GB 26 B3
Buryn UA 7 F12
Bury St Edmunds GB 30 B4
Burzenin PL 54 B3
Busachi I 110 B1
Busalla I 80 B2
Busana I 81 B4
Busano I 70 C2
Busca I 80 B1
Busch D 44 C3
Buševec HR 73 C6
Bushat AL 105 B5
Bushey GB 31 C3
Bushmills GB 19 A5
Bušince SK 65 B5
Buskhyttan S 37 D3
Busko-Zdrój PL 55 C5
Busot E 96 C2
Busovača BIH 84 B2
Busquistar E 100 C2
Bussang F 60 C2
Busseto I 81 B4
Bussière-Badil F 67 C5
Bussière-Poitevine F 67 B5
Bussolengo I 71 C5
Bussoleno I 70 C2
Bussum NL 49 A6
Busto Arsizio I 70 C3
Büsum D 43 A5
Butera I 109 B3
Butgenbach B 50 C2
Butler's Bridge IRL 19 B4
Butryny PL 47 B6
Bütschwil CH 70 A4
Buttermere GB 26 A2
Buttevant IRL 20 B3
Buttle S 37 E5
Buttstädt D 52 B1
Butzbach D 51 C4
Bützfleth D 43 B6
Bützow D 44 B3
Buxières-les-Mines F 68 B2
Buxtehude D 43 B6
Buxton GB 27 B4
Buxy F 69 B4
Büyükçekmece TR 118 A3
Büyükkariştiran TR 118 A2
Büyükorhan TR 118 C3
Buzançais F 67 B6
Buzancy F 59 A5
Buzău RO 11 D9
Buzet HR 72 C3
Buzsák H 74 B2
Buzy F 76 C2
By S 36 B3
Byala BG 11 E8
Byaroza BY 6 E8
Byczyna PL 54 B3
Bydalen S 115 D10
Bydgoszcz PL 47 B4
Bygdin N 32 A5
Bygland N 33 D4
Byglandsfjord N 33 D4
Bygstad N 32 A2
Bykhaw BY 7 E11
Bykle N 33 C4
Bylderup-Bov DK 39 E2
Byrkjedal N 33 D3
Byrkjelo N 114 F3
Byrum DK 38 B3
Byšice CZ 53 C4
Byske S 3 D24
Býškovice CZ 64 A3
Bysław PL 46 B3
Bystré CZ 64 A2
Bystřice CZ 63 A5
Bystrice CZ 65 A4
Bystřice nad Pernštejnem CZ 64 A2
Bystřice pod Hostýnem CZ 64 A3
Bystrzyca Kłodzka PL 54 C1
Bytča SK 65 A4
Bytnica PL 53 A5
Bytom PL 54 C3
Bytom Odrzański PL 53 B5
Bytów PL 46 A3
Byxelkrok S 41 B7
Bzenec CZ 64 B3
Bzince SK 64 B3

C

Çağa TR 118 B7
Cabaços P 92 B2
Cabaj-Čápor SK 64 B4
Cabana E 86 A2
Cabanac-et-Villagrains F 76 B2
Cabañaquinta E 88 A1
Cabanas P 98 B3
Cabañas del Castillo E 93 B5
Cabañas de Yepes E 95 C3
Cabanelles E 91 A5
Cabanes E 96 A3
Cabanillas E 89 B5
Čabar HR 73 C4
Cabasse F 79 C5
Cabdella E 91 A4
Cabeceiras de Basto P 87 C2
Cabeço de Vide P 92 B3
Cabella Ligure I 80 B3
Cabeza del Buey E 93 C5
Cabeza la Vaca E 99 A4
Cabezamesada E 95 C3
Cabezarados E 100 A1
Cabezarrubias del Puerto E 100 A1
Cabezas del Villar E 94 B1
Cabezas Rubias E 98 B3
Cabezón E 88 C2
Cabezón de la Sal E 88 A2
Cabezón de Liébana E 88 A2
Cabezuela E 94 A3
Cabezuela del Valle E 93 A5
Cabo de Gata E 101 C3
Cabo de Palos E 101 B5
Cabolafuente E 95 A4
Cabourg F 57 A5
Cabra
E 100 B1
P 92 A3
Cabrach GB 23 D5
Cabra del Santo Cristo E 100 B2
Cábras I 110 C1
Cabreiro P 87 C2
Cabreiros E 86 A3
Cabrejas E 95 B4
Cabrela P 92 C2
Cabrillas E 87 D4
Cabuna HR 74 C2
Cacabelos E 86 B4
Čačak SRB 85 C5
Cáccamo I 108 B2
Caccuri I 107 B3
Cacela P 98 B3
Cacém P 92 C1
Cáceres E 93 B4
Cachafeiro E 86 B2
Cachopo P 98 B3
Čachtice SK 64 B3
Cacin E 100 B2
Čačinci HR 74 C2
Cadafais P 92 C1
Cadalen F 77 C5
Cadalso E 93 A4
Cadaqués E 91 A6
Cadaval P 92 B1
Cadavedo E 86 A4
Čadavica BIH 84 B1
Čadca SK 65 A4
Cadéac F 77 D3
Cadelbosco di Sopra I 81 B4
Cadenazzo CH 70 B3
Cadenberge D 43 B6
Cadenet F 79 C4
Cadeuil F 66 C4
Cádiar E 100 C2
Cadillac F 76 B2
Cádiz E 99 C4
Čadjavica HR 74 C2
Cadouin F 77 B3
Cadours F 77 C4
Cadrete E 90 B2
Caen F 57 A5
Caerleon GB 29 B5
Caernarfon GB 26 B1
Caerphilly GB 29 B4
Caersws GB 26 C2
Cafede P 92 B3
Caggiano I 104 C1
Cagli I 82 C1
Cágliari I 110 C2
Čaglin HR 74 C2
Cagnano Varano I 104 B1
Cagnes-sur-Mer F 79 C6
Caher IRL 21 B4
Caherciveen IRL 20 C1
Caherdaniel IRL 20 C1
Cahors F 77 B4
Cahul MD 11 D10
Caiazzo I 103 B7
Caion E 86 A2
Cairndow GB 24 B3
Cairnryan GB 24 D2
Cairo Montenotte I 80 B2
Caister-on-Sea GB 30 B5
Caistor GB 27 B5
Caivano I 103 C7
Cajarc F 77 B4
Čajetina SRB 85 C4
Čajniče BIH 84 C4
Çakırlar TR 119 F5
Çakmak TR 118 C6
Čakovec HR 73 B6
Çakran AL 105 C5
Çal TR 119 D4
Cala E 99 B4
Calabritto I 103 C8
Calaceite E 90 C3
Calacuccia F 102 A2
Cala d'Or E 97 B3
Calaf E 91 B4
Calafat RO 11 D7
Calafell E 91 B4
Cala Galdana E 97 B3
Cala Gonone I 110 B2
Calahonda
Granada E 100 C2
Málaga E 100 C1
Calahorra E 89 B5
Calais F 48 C2
Cala Llonga E 97 C1
Calalzo di Cadore I 72 B2
Cala Millor E 97 B3
Calamocha E 95 B5
Calamonte E 93 C4
Cala Morell E 97 A3
Calanais GB 22 C2
Calañas E 99 B4
Calanda E 90 C2
Calangiánus I 110 B2
Călărași RO 11 D9
Cala Ratjada E 97 B3
Calascibetta I 109 B3
Calasetta I 110 C1
Calasparra E 101 A4
Calatafimi I 108 B1
Calatayud E 89 C5
Calatorao E 89 C5
Calau D 53 B3
Calbe D 52 B1
Calcena E 89 C5
Calcinelli I 82 C1
Calco I 71 C4
Caldaro sulla strada del Vino I 71 B6
Caldas da Rainha P 92 B1
Caldas de Boi E 90 A3
Caldas de Malavella E 91 B5
Caldas de Reis E 86 B2
Caldas de San Jorge P 87 D2
Caldas de Vizela P 87 C2
Caldaso de los Vidrios E 94 B2
Caldbeck GB 26 A2
Caldearenas E 90 A2
Caldelas P 87 C2
Calders E 91 B4
Caldes de Montbui E 91 B5
Caldicot GB 29 B5
Caldirola I 80 B3
Caledon GB 19 B5
Calella
Barcelona E 91 B5
Girona E 91 B6
Calenzana F 102 A1
Calera de León E 99 A4
Calera y Chozas E 94 C2
Caleruega E 89 C3
Caleruela E 93 B5
Cales de Mallorca E 97 B3
Calestano I 81 B4
Calfsound GB 23 B6
Calgary GB 24 B1
Calimera I 105 C4
Calitri I 103 C8
Calizzano I 80 B2
Callac F 56 B2
Callan IRL 21 B4
Callander GB 24 B3
Callas F 79 C5
Calliano
Piemonte I 80 A2
Trentino Alto Adige I 71 C6
Callington GB 28 C3
Callosa de Ensarriá E 96 C2
Callosa de Segura E 101 A5
Callús E 91 B4
Čalma SRB 85 A4
Calmbach D 61 B4
Calne GB 29 B6
Calolziocorte I 71 C4
Calonge E 91 B6
Čalovec SK 64 C3
Calpe E 96 C3
Caltabellotta I 108 B2
Caltagirone I 109 B3
Caltanissetta I 109 B3
Caltavuturo I 108 B2
Çaltılıbük TR 118 C3
Caltojar E 89 C4
Caluire-et-Cuire F 69 C4
Caluso I 70 C2
Calvello I 104 C1
Calvi F 102 A1
Calviá E 97 B2
Calvinet F 77 B5
Calvisson F 78 C3
Calvörde D 44 C3
Calw D 61 B4
Calzada de Calatrava E 100 A2
Calzada de Valdunciel E 94 A1
Calzadilla de los Barros E 93 C4
Cam GB 29 B5
Camaiore I 81 C4
Camarasa E 90 B3
Camarena E 94 B2
Camarès F 78 C1
Camaret-sur-Aigues F 78 B3
Camaret-sur-Mer F 56 B1
Camarillas E 90 C2
Camariñas E 86 A1
Camarma E 95 B3
Camarzana de Tera E 87 B4
Camas E 99 B4
Camastra I 108 B2
Cambados E 86 B2
Cambarinho P 92 A2
Camberley GB 31 C3
Cambil E 100 B2
Cambligeu F 48 C3
Cambo-les-Bains F 76 C1
Camborne GB 28 C2
Cambrai F 49 C4
Cambre E 86 A2
Cambridge GB 30 B4
Cambrils E 91 B4
Cambs D 44 B3
Camburg D 52 B1
Camden GB 31 C3
Cameleño E 88 A2
Camelford GB 28 C3
Çameli TR 119 E4
Camelle E 86 A1
Camerano I 82 C2
Camerino I 82 C2
Camerota I 106 A2
Camigliatello Silano I 106 B3
Caminha P 87 C2
Caminomorisco E 93 A4
Caminreal E 95 B5
Camisano Vicentino I 72 C1
Camlidere TR 118 B7
Cammarata I 108 B2
Camogli I 80 B3
Camors F 56 C3
Camp IRL 20 B2
Campagna I 103 C8
Campagnano di Roma I 102 A5
Campagnático I 81 D5
Campan F 76 C3
Campana I 107 B3
Campanario E 93 C5
Campanillas E 100 C1
Campano E 99 C4
Campaspero E 88 C2
Campbeltown GB 24 C2
Campello E 96 C2
Campelos P 92 B1
Campi Bisénzio I 81 C5
Campico López E 101 B4
Campíglia Marittima I 81 C4
Campillo de Altobuey E 95 C5
Campillo de Aragón E 95 A5
Campillo de Arenas E 100 B2
Campillo de Llerena E 93 C5
Campillos E 100 B1
Câmpina RO 11 D8
Campi Salentina I 105 C4
Campli I 82 D2
Campo E 90 A3
Campobasso I 103 B7
Campobello di Licata I 108 B2
Campobello di Mazara I 108 B1
Campo da Feira E 86 A3
Campodársego I 72 C1
Campo de Bacerros E 87 B3
Campo de Caso E 88 A1
Campo de Criptana E 95 C3
Campodolcino I 71 B4
Campofelice di Roccella I 108 B2
Campofiorito I 108 B2
Campofórmido I 72 B3
Campofranco I 108 B2
Campofrio E 99 B4
Campogalliano I 81 B4
Campo Ligure I 80 B2
Campolongo I 72 B2
Campo Lugar E 93 B5
Campo Maior P 93 B3
Campomanes E 88 A1
Campomarino I 103 B8
Campo Molino I 79 B6
Campomono F 102 B1
Campo Real E 95 B3
Camporeale I 108 B2
Camporeggiano I 82 C1
Camporrells E 90 B3
Camporrobles E 96 B1
Campos P 87 C3
Camposa P 87 C2
Camposampiero I 72 C1
Camposanto I 81 B5
Campos del Port E 97 B3
Camposines E 90 B3
Campotéjar E 100 B2
Campotosto I 103 A6
Campo Túres I 72 B1
Camprodon E 91 A5
Campsegret F 77 B3
Camrose GB 28 B2
Camuñas E 95 C3
Çamyolu TR 119 F7
Çan TR 118 B2
Cana I 81 D5
Cañada del Hoyo E 95 C5
Cañadajuncosa E 95 C4
Cañada Rosal E 99 B5
Čanak HR 83 B4
Çanakkale TR 118 B1
Canale I 80 B1
Canales
Asturias E 88 B1
Castellón de la Plana E 96 B2
Canals E 96 C2
Canal San Bovo I 72 B1
Cañamares E 95 B4
Cañamero E 93 B5
Cañar E 100 C2
Cañate la Real E 99 C5
Cañaveral E 93 B4
Cañaveral de León E 99 A4
Cañaveras E 95 B4
Cañaveruelas E 95 B4
Canazei I 72 B1
Cancale F 57 B4
Cancellara I 104 C1
Cancello ed Arnone I 103 B7
Cancon F 77 B3
Canda E 87 B4
Candamil E 86 A3
Candanchu E 76 D2
Çandarlı TR 118 D1
Candas E 88 A1
Candasnos E 90 B3
Candé F 66 A3
Candela I 104 B1
Candelario E 93 A5
Candeleda E 93 A5
Cándia Lomellina I 70 C3
Candide Casamazzagno I 72 B2
Candin E 86 B4
Candosa P 92 A3
Canecas P 92 C1
Canelli I 80 B2
Canena E 100 A2
Canencia E 94 B3
Canero E 86 A4
Canet F 78 C2
Canet de Mar E 91 B5
Canet d'en Berenguer E 96 B2
Cañete E 95 B5
Cañete de las Torres E 100 B1
Canet-Plage F 91 A6
Canfranc E 76 D2
Cangas
Lugo E 86 A3
Pontevedra E 87 B2
Cangas de Narcea E 86 A4
Cangas de Onís E 88 A1
Canha P 92 C2
Canhestros P 98 A2
Canicattì I 108 B2
Canicattini Bagni I 109 B4
Canicosa de la Sierra E 89 C3
Caniles E 101 B3
Canillas de Aceituno E 100 C1
Canino I 102 A4
Canisy F 57 A4
Cañizal E 94 A1
Cañizo E 88 C1
Canjáyar E 101 C3
Çankırı TR 16 A6
Cannai I 110 C1
Cannara I 82 C1
Cánnero Riviera I 70 B3
Cannes F 79 C6
Canneto
Sicilia I 106 C1
Toscana I 81 C4
Canneto sull'Oglio I 71 C5
Cannich GB 22 D4
Cannóbio I 70 B3
Cannock GB 26 C3
Canonbie GB 25 C5
Canosa di Púglia I 104 B2
Can Pastilla E 97 B2
C'an Picafort E 97 B3
Cantalapiedra E 94 A1
Cantalejo E 94 A3
Cantalgallo E 99 A4
Cantalice I 102 A5
Cantalpino E 94 A1
Cantalupo in Sabina I 102 A5
Cantanhede P 92 A2
Cantavieja E 90 C2
Čantavir SRB 75 C4
Canterbury GB 31 C5
Cantiano I 82 C1
Cantillana E 99 B5
Cantiveros E 94 B2
Cantoria E 101 B3
Cantù I 71 C4
Canvey GB 31 C4
Cany-Barville F 58 A1
Canyet de Mar E 91 B5
Caol GB 24 B2
Cáorle I 72 C2
Caorso I 81 A3
Capáccio I 103 C8
Capaci I 108 A2
Capálbio I 102 A4
Capánnori I 81 C4
Caparde BIH 84 B3
Caparroso E 89 B5
Capbreton F 76 C1
Capdenac-Gare F 77 B5
Capdepera E 97 B3
Cap-de-Pin F 76 B2
Capel Curig GB 26 B2
Capellades E 91 B4
Capena I 102 A5
Capendu F 77 C5
Capestang F 78 C2
Capestrano I 103 A6
Cap Ferret F 76 B1
Capileira E 100 C2
Capinha P 92 A3
Ca'Pisani I 82 B1
Capistrello I 103 B6
Capizzi I 109 B3
Čaplje BIH 83 B5
Čapljina BIH 84 C2
Capo di Ponte I 71 B5
Caposile I 72 C2
Capoterra I 110 C1
Cappamore IRL 20 B3
Cappeln D 43 C5
Cappoquin IRL 21 B4
Capracotta I 103 B7
Capránica I 102 A5
Caprarola I 102 A5
Capretta I 82 D1
Capri I 103 C7
Capriati a Volturno I 103 B7
Caprino Veronese I 71 C5
Captieux F 76 B2
Cápua I 103 B7
Capurso I 104 B2
Capvern F 77 C3
Carabaña E 95 B3
Carabias E 88 C3
Caracal RO 11 D8
Caracenilla E 95 B4
Caráglio I 80 B1
Caraman F 77 C4
Caramánico Terme I 103 A7
Caranga E 86 A4
Caranguejeira P 92 B2
Caransebeș RO 11 D7
Carantec F 56 B2
Carapelle I 104 B1
Carasco I 80 B3
Carate Brianza I 71 C4
Caravaca de la Cruz E 101 A4
Caravággio I 71 C4
Carbajal E 100 C1
Carbajo E 93 B3
Carballeda E 86 B3
Carballeda de Avia E 87 B2
Carballo E 86 A2
Carbis Bay GB 28 C2
Carbon-Blanc F 76 B2
Carbonera de Frentes E 89 C4
Carboneras E 101 C4
Carboneras de Guadazaón E 95 C5
Carbonero el Mayor E 94 A2
Carboneros E 100 A2
Carbonin I 72 B2
Carbonne F 77 C4
Carbost
Highland GB 22 D2
Highland GB 22 D2
Carcaboso E 93 A4
Carcabuey E 100 B1
Carcaixent E 96 B2
Carcans F 76 A1
Carcans-Plage F 76 A1
Carção P 87 C4
Carcar E 89 B5
Cárcare I 80 B2
Carcassonne F 77 C5
Carcastillo E 89 B5
Carcedo de Burgos E 89 B3
Carcelén E 96 B1
Carcès F 79 C5
Carchelejo E 100 B2
Çardak
Çanakkale TR 118 B1
Denizli TR 119 E4
Cardedeu E 91 B5
Cardeña E 100 A1
Cardenete E 95 C5
Cardeñosa E 94 B2
Cardeto I 109 A4
Cardiff GB 29 B4
Cardigan GB 28 A3
Cardona E 91 B4
Cardosos P 92 B2
Carei RO 11 C7
Carentan F 57 A4
Carentoir F 57 C3
Careri I 106 C3
Carevdar HR 74 B1
Cargèse F 102 A1
Carhaix-Plouguer F 56 B2
Caria P 92 A3
Cariati I 107 B3
Carignan F 59 A6
Carignano I 80 B1
Cariñena E 90 B1
Carini I 108 A2
Cariño E 86 A3
Carinola I 103 B6
Carisbrooke GB 31 D2
Carlabhagh GB 22 C2
Carlepont F 59 A4
Carlet E 96 B2
Carlingford IRL 19 B5
Carlisle GB 25 D5
Carloforte I 110 C1
Carlópoli I 106 B3
Carlow
D 44 B2
IRL 21 B5
Carlton GB 27 C4
Carluke GB 25 C4
Carmagnola I 80 B1
Carmarthen GB 28 B3
Carmaux F 77 B5
Carmena E 94 C2
Cármenes E 88 B1
Carmine I 80 B1
Carmona E 99 B5
Carmonita E 93 B4
Carmyllie GB 25 B5
Carnac F 56 C2
Carndonagh IRL 19 A4
Carnew IRL 21 B5
Carnforth GB 26 A3
Cárnia I 72 B3
Carnlough GB 19 B6
Carno GB 26 C2
Carnon Plage F 78 C2
Carnota E 86 B1
Carnoustie GB 25 B5
Carnwath GB 25 C4
Carolei I 106 B3
Carolinensiel D 43 B4
Carolles F 57 B4
Carona I 71 B4
Caronia I 109 A3
Carovigno I 104 C3
Carovilli I 103 B7
Carpaneto Piacentino I 81 B3
Carpegna I 82 C1
Carpenédolo I 71 C5
Carpentras F 79 B4
Carpi I 81 B4
Carpignano Sésia I 70 C3
Carpineti I 81 B4
Carpineto Romano I 102 B6
Cărpinis RO 75 C5
Carpino I 104 B1
Carpinone I 103 B7
Carpio E 94 A1
Carquefou F 66 A3
Carqueiranne F 79 C5
Carral E 86 A2
Carranque E 94 B3
Carrapichana P 92 A3
Carrara I 81 B4
Carraroe IRL 20 A2
Carrascalejo E 93 B5
Carrascosa del Campo E 95 B4
Carratraca E 100 C1
Carrazeda de Ansiães P 87 C3
Carrazedo de Montenegro P 87 C3
Carrbridge GB 23 D5
Carregal do Sal P 92 A2
Carreña E 88 A2
Carrick IRL 18 B3
Carrickart IRL 19 A4
Carrickfergus GB 19 B6
Carrickmacross IRL 19 C5
Carrick-on-Shannon IRL 18 C3
Carrick-on-Suir IRL 21 B4
Carrigallen IRL 19 C4
Carrión E 99 B4
Carrión de Calatrava E 94 C3
Carrión de los Condes E 88 B2
Carrizo de la Ribera E 88 B1
Carrizosa E 100 A3
Carro F 79 C4
Carrocera E 88 B1
Carros F 79 C6
Carrouge CH 70 B1
Carrouges F 57 B5
Carrù I 80 B1
Carryduff GB 19 B6
Carry-le-Rouet F 79 C4
Carsòli I 102 A6
Carsphairn GB 24 C3
Cartagena E 101 B5
Cártama E 100 C1
Cartaxo P 92 B2
Cartaya E 98 B3
Carteret F 57 A4
Cartes E 88 A2
Carúnchio I 103 B7
Carviçães P 87 C4
Carvin F 48 C3
Carvoeira P 92 B1
Carvoeiro P 98 B2
Casabermeja E 100 C1
Casa Branca
Portalegre P 92 C3
Setúbal P 98 A2
Casacalenda I 103 B7
Casa Castalda I 82 C1
Casaio E 87 B4
Casa l'Abate I 105 C4
Casalarreina E 89 B4
Casalbordino I 103 A7
Casalborgone I 70 C2
Casalbuono I 104 C1
Casalbuttano ed Uniti I 71 C4
Casàl di Principe I 103 B7
Casalécchio di Reno I 81 B5
Casale Monferrato I 70 C3
Casalina I 82 D1
Casalmaggiore I 81 B4
Casalnuovo Monterotaro I 103 B8
Casaloldo I 71 C5
Casalpusterlengo I 71 C4
Casamássima I 104 C2
Casamicciola Terme I 103 C6
Casamozza F 102 A2
Casarabonela E 100 C1
Casarano I 107 A5
Casar de Cáceres E 93 B4
Casar de Palomero E 93 A4
Casarejos E 89 C3
Casares E 99 C5
Casares de las Hurdes E 93 A4
Casariche E 100 B1
Casarrubios del Monte E 94 B2
Casas de Don Pedro E 93 B5
Casas de Fernando Alonso E 95 C4
Casas de Haro E 95 C4
Casas de Juan Gil E 96 B1
Casas del Juan Núñez E 95 C5
Casas del Puerto E 101 A4
Casas del Rio E 96 B1
Casas de Millán E 93 B4
Casas de Reina E 99 A5
Casas de Ves E 96 B1
Casas-Ibáñez E 96 B1
Casasimarro E 95 C4
Casas Nuevas E 101 B4
Casasola E 94 B2
Casasola de Arión E 88 C1
Casasuertes E 88 A2
Casatejada E 93 B5
Casavieja E 94 B2
Casazza I 71 C4
Cascais P 92 C1
Cascante E 89 C5
Cascante del Rio E 96 A1
Cáscia I 82 D2
Casciana Terme I 81 C4
Cáscina I 81 C4
Cáseda E 89 B5
Casekow D 45 B6
Casella I 80 B3
Caselle Torinese I 70 C2
Casemurate I 82 B1
Casenove I 82 D1
Caseres E 90 B3
Caserio Benali E 96 B2
Caserta I 103 B7
Casével P 98 B2
Cashel IRL 21 B4
Casillas E 94 B2
Casillas de Coria E 93 B4
Casina I 81 B4
Casinos E 96 B2
Čáslav CZ 63 A6
Cásola Valsénio I 81 B5
Cásole d'Elsa I 81 C5
Cásoli I 103 A7
Casória I 103 C7
Caspe E 90 B2
Cassà de la Selva E 91 B5
Cassagnas F 78 B2
Cassagnes-Bégonhès F 77 B5
Cassano allo Iónio I 106 B3
Cassano d'Adda I 71 C4
Cassano delle Murge I 104 C2
Cassano Magnago I 70 C3
Cassano Spinola I 80 B2
Cassel F 48 C3
Cassibile I 109 C4
Cassine I 80 B2
Cassino I 103 B6
Cassis F 79 C4
Cassolnovo I 70 C3
Cassuéjouls F 78 B1
Castá SK 64 B3
Castagnaro I 71 C6
Castagneto Carducci I 81 C4
Castagnola CH 70 B3
Castalla E 96 C2
Castañar de Ibor E 93 B5
Castanheira de Pêra P 92 A2
Cástano Primo I 70 C3
Castasegna CH 71 B4
Castéggio I 80 A3
Casteição P 87 D3
Castejón E 89 B5
Castejón de Monegros E 90 B2
Castejón de Sos E 90 A3
Castejón de Valdejasa E 90 B2
Castèl Baronia I 103 B8
Castel Bolognese I 81 B5
Castelbuono I 109 B3
Casteldáccia I 108 A2
Castel d'Aiano I 81 B4
Castel d'Ario I 71 C5
Castel de Cabra E 90 C2
Casteldelfino I 79 B6
Castél del Monte I 103 A6
Castel del Piano I 81 D5
Castel di Iúdica I 109 B3
Castel di Rio I 81 B5
Castèl di Sangro I 103 B7
Castél di Tora I 102 A5
Castelfidardo I 82 C2
Castelfiorentino I 81 C4
Castelforte I 103 B6
Castelfranco Emília I 81 B5
Castelfranco in Miscano I 103 B8
Castelfranco Véneto I 72 C1
Castèl Frentano I 103 A7
Casteljaloux F 76 B3
Castellabate I 103 C7
Castellammare del Golfo I 108 A1
Castellammare di Stábia I 103 C7
Castellamonte I 70 C2
Castellana Grotte I 104 C3
Castellane F 79 C5
Castellaneta I 104 C2
Castellaneta Marina I 104 C2
Castellar E 100 A2
Castellarano I 81 B4
Castellar de la Frontera E 99 C5
Castellar de la Ribera E 91 A4
Castellar del Vallès E 91 B5
Castellar de Santiago E 100 A2
Castell Arquato I 81 B3
Castell'Azzara I 81 D5
Castellbell i Villar E 91 B4
Castelldans E 90 B3
Castell de Cabres E 90 C3
Castell de Castells E 96 C2
Castelldefels E 91 B4
Castell de Ferro E 100 C2
Castelleone I 71 C4
Castellet E 91 B4
Castelletto di Brenzone I 71 C5
Castellfollit de la Roca E 91 A5
Castellfollit de Riubregos E 91 B4
Castellfort E 90 C2
Castellina in Chianti I 81 C5
Castellina Marittima I 81 C4
Castellóde Farfaña E 90 B3
Castellóde la Plana E 96 B2
Castello d'Empùries E 91 A6
Castello di Fiemme I 71 B6
Castellolí E 91 B4
Castellón de Rugat E 96 C2
Castellote E 90 C2
Castello Tesino I 72 B1
Castellterçol E 91 B5
Castellúcchio I 71 C5
Castellúccio de'Sáuri I 103 B8
Castelluccio Inferiore I 106 B2
Castelmassa I 81 A5
Castelmáuro I 103 B7
Castelmoron-sur-Lot F 77 B3
Castelnaudary F 77 C4
Castelnau-de-Médoc F 76 A2
Castelnau-de-Montmirail F 77 C4
Castelnau-Magnoac F 77 C3
Castelnau-Montratier F 77 B4
Castelnou E 90 B2
Castelnovo ne'Monti I 81 B4
Castelnuovo Berardenga I 81 C5
Castelnuovo della Dàunia I 103 B8
Castelnuovo di Garfagnana I 81 B4
Castelnuovo di Val di Cécina I 81 C4
Castelnuovo Don Bosco I 80 A1
Castelnuovo Scrivia I 80 B2
Castelo Branco
Bragança P 87 C4
Castelo Branco P 92 B3
Castelo de Paiva P 87 C2
Castelo de Vide P 92 B3
Castelo do Neiva P 87 C2
Castelo Mendo P 93 A4
Castelraimondo I 82 C2
Castel San Gimignano I 81 C5
Castèl San Giovanni I 80 A3
Castèl San Pietro Terme I 81 B5
Castelsantángelo I 82 D2
Castél Sant'Elia I 102 A5
Castelsaraceno I 106 A2
Castelsardo I 110 B1
Castelsarrasin F 77 B4
Castelserás E 90 C2
Casteltérmini I 108 B2
Castelvecchio Subéquo I 103 A6
Castelvetrano I 108 B1
Castél Volturno I 103 B6
Castenédolo I 71 C5
Castets F 76 C1
Castiádas I 110 C2
Castiglioncello I 81 C4
Castiglione I 102 A6
Castiglione Chiavarese I 80 B3
Castiglione d'Adda I 71 C4
Castiglione dei Pepoli I 81 B5
Castiglione del Lago I 81 C6
Castiglione della Pescáia I 81 D4
Castiglione delle Stiviere I 71 C5
Castiglione di Sicília I 109 B4
Castiglione d'Órcia I 81 C5
Castiglione Messer Marino I 103 B7
Castiglione Messer Raimondo I 103 A6
Castiglion Fibocchi I 81 C5
Castiglion Fiorentino I 81 C5
Castilblanco E 94 C1
Castilblanco de los Arroyos E 99 B5
Castil de Peones E 89 B3
Castilfrío de la Sierra E 89 C4
Castilgaleu E 90 A3
Castilisar E 90 A1
Castilleja E 99 B4
Castillejar E 101 B3
Castillejo de Martin Viejo E 93 A4
Castillejo de Mesleón E 89 C3
Castillejo de Robledo E 89 C3
Castillo de Bayuela E 94 B2
Castillo de Locubín E 100 B2
Castillonès F 77 B3
Castillon-la-Bataille F 76 B2
Castillon-Len-Couserans F 77 D4
Castillonroy E 90 B3
Castilruiz E 89 C4
Castione CH 70 B4
Castions di Strada I 72 C3
Castirla F 102 A2
Castlebar IRL 18 C2
Castlebellingham IRL 19 C5
Castleblaney IRL 19 B5
Castlebridge IRL 21 B5
Castle Cary GB 29 B5
Castlecomer IRL 21 B4
Castlederg GB 19 B4
Castledermot IRL 21 B5
Castle Douglas GB 25 D4
Castleford GB 27 B4
Castleisland IRL 20 B2
Castlemaine IRL 20 B2
Castlemartyr IRL 20 C3
Castlepollard IRL 19 C4
Castlerea IRL 18 C3
Castleton GB 27 B4
Castletown
Highland GB 23 C5
Isle of Man GB 26 A1
Castletown Bearhaven IRL 20 C2
Castletownroche IRL 20 B3
Castlewellan GB 19 B6
Casto I 71 C5
Castrejón E 88 C1
Castrelo del Valle E 87 B3
Castres F 77 C5
Castricum NL 42 C1
Castries F 78 C2
Castrignano del Capo I 107 B5
Castril E 101 B3
Castrillo de Duero E 88 C3
Castrillo de la Vega E 88 C3
Castrillo de Onielo E 88 C2
Castro
E 88 A2
I 107 A5
Castrocabón E 88 B1
Castro-Caldelas E 87 B3
Castrocaro Terme I 81 B5
Castrocontrigo E 87 B4
Castro Daire P 87 D3
Castro dei Volsci I 103 B6
Castro del Río E 100 B1

Castro de Rey E 86 A3
Castrofilippo I 108 B2
Castrogonzaio E 88 B1
Castrojeriz E 88 B2
Castro Laboreiro P 87 B2
Castro Marim P 98 B3
Castromonte E 88 C1
Castromudarra E 88 B1
Castronuevo E 88 C1
Castronuño E 88 C1
Castropol E 86 A3
Castroreale I 109 A4
Castroserracin E 88 C3
Castro-Urdiales E 89 A3
Castroverde E 86 A3
Castro Verde P 98 B2
Castroverde de Campos E 88 C1
Castroverde de Cerrato E 88 C2
Castrovillari I 106 B3
Castuera E 93 C5
Catadau E 96 B2
Cataéggio I 71 B4
Çatalca TR 118 A3
Catallar TR 119 F5
Çatalzeytin TR 16 A7
Catánia I 109 B4
Catanzaro I 106 C3
Catanzaro Marina I 106 C3
Catarroja E 96 B2
Catarruchos P 92 A2
Catcleugh GB 25 C5
Catenanuova I 109 B3
Caterham GB 31 C3
Çati E 90 C3
Čatići BIH 84 B3
Catignano I 103 A6
Catillon F 49 C4
Catoira E 86 B2
Caton GB 26 A3
Catral E 101 A5
Catterick GB 27 A4
Cattólica I 82 C1
Cattólica Eraclea I 108 B2
Catton GB 25 D5
Caudebec-en-Caux F 58 A1
Caudete E 101 A5
Caudete de las Fuentes E 96 B1
Caudiel E 96 B2
Caudiès-de-Fenouillèdes F 77 D5
Caudry F 49 C4
Caulkerbush GB 25 D4
Caulnes F 57 B3
Caulónia I 106 C3
Caumont-l'Evente F 57 A5
Caunes-Minervois F 77 C5
Cauro F 102 B1
Caussade F 77 B4
Causse-de-la-Selle F 78 C2
Cauterets F 76 D2
Cava de Tirreni I 103 C7
Cavaglia I 70 C3
Cavaillon F 79 C4
Cavalaire-sur-Mer F 79 C5
Cavaleiro P 98 B2
Cavalese I 71 B6
Cavallermaggiore I 80 B1
Cavallino I 72 C2
Cavan IRL 19 C4
Cavàrzere I 72 C2
Çavdarhisar TR 118 C4
Çavdır TR 119 E4
Cavernães P 87 D3
Cavezzo I 81 B5
Cavignac F 76 A2
Čavle HR 73 C4
Cavo I 81 D4
Cavour I 80 B1
Cavtat HR 84 D3
Cawdor GB 23 D5
Çay TR 118 D6
Çaycuma TR 118 A7
Cayeux-sur-Mer F 48 C2
Cayiralan TR 16 B7
Çayırhan TR 118 B6
Caylus F 77 B4
Cayres F 78 B2
Cazalilla E 100 B2
Cazalla de la Sierra E 99 B5
Cazals F 77 B4
Cazanuecos E 88 B1
Cazaubon F 76 C2
Cazaux F 76 B1
Cazavet F 77 C4
Cazères F 77 C4
Cazin BIH 83 B4
Cazis CH 71 B4
Čazma HR 74 C1
Cazo E 88 A1
Cazorla E 100 B3
Cazouls-lès-Béziers F 78 C2
Cea
León E 88 B1
Orense E 86 B3
Ceánuri E 89 A4
Ceauce F 57 B5
Čebolla E 94 C2
Čebovce SK 65 B5
Cebreros E 94 B2
Čečava BIH 84 B2
Ceccano I 103 B6
Cece H 74 B3
Cecenowo PL 46 A3
Čechtice CZ 63 A6
Čechtín CZ 64 A1
Cécina I 81 C4
Ceclavín E 93 B4
Cedégolo I 71 B5
Cedeira E 86 A2
Cedillo E 92 B3
Cedillo del Condado E 94 B3
Cedrillas E 90 C2
Cedynia PL 45 C6
Cée E 86 B1
Cefalù I 109 A3
Céggia I 72 C2
Cegléd H 75 A4
Ceglédbercel H 75 A4
Céglie Messápica I 104 C3
Cehegín E 101 A4
Ceilhes-et-Rocozels F 78 C2
Ceinos de Campos E 88 B1
Ceira P 92 A2
Čejč CZ 64 B2
Cekcyn PL 47 B4
Cela BIH 83 B5
Čelákovice CZ 53 C4
Celano I 103 A6
Celanova E 87 B3
Celbridge IRL 21 A5
Čelebić BIH 83 C5
Celenza Valfortore I 103 B7
Čelić BIH 84 B3
Čelinac BIH 84 B2
Celje SLO 73 B5
Cella E 95 B5
Celldömölk H 74 A2
Celle D 44 C2
Celle Ligure I 80 B2
Celles B 49 C5
Celles-sur-Belle F 67 B4
Cellino San Marco I 105 C3
Celorico da Beira P 92 A3
Celorico de Basto P 87 C2
Çeltik TR 118 C6
Çeltikçi TR 119 E5
Cemaes GB 26 B1
Cembra I 71 B6
Čemerno BIH 84 C3
Cenad RO 75 B5
Cencenighe Agordino I 72 B1
Cenei RO 75 C5
Ceneselli I 81 A5
Cenicero E 89 B4
Cenicientos E 94 B2
Censeau F 69 B6
Čenta SRB 85 A5
Centallo I 80 B1
Centelles E 91 B5
Cento I 81 B5
Centuripe I 109 B3
Cepeda la Mora E 94 B1
Cépet F 77 C4
Čepin HR 74 C3
Čepinski Martinci HR 74 C3
Cepovan SLO 72 B3
Ceprano I 103 B6
Čeralije HR 74 C2
Cerami I 109 B3
Cerano I 70 C3
Cérans Foulletourte F 57 C6
Ceraso I 106 A2
Cerbaia I 81 C5
Cerbère F 91 A6
Cercadillo E 95 A4
Cercal
Lisboa P 92 B1
Setúbal P 98 B2
Čerčany CZ 63 A5
Cerceda E 94 B3
Cercedilla E 94 B2
Cercemaggiore I 103 B7
Cercs E 91 A4
Cercy-la-Tour F 68 B3
Cerda I 108 B2
Cerdedo E 86 B2
Cerdeira P 93 A3
Cerdon F 58 C3
Cerea I 71 C6
Ceres
GB 25 B5
I 70 C2
Cerese I 81 A4
Ceresole-Reale I 70 C2
Cereste F 79 C4
Céret F 91 A5
Cerezo de Abajo E 95 A3
Cerezo de Riotirón E 89 B3
Cerfontaine B 49 C5
Cergy F 58 A3
Cerignola I 104 B1
Cérilly F 68 B2
Cerisiers F 59 B4
Cerizay F 67 B4
Çerkeş TR 16 A6
Çerkezköy TR 118 A3
Cerkije SLO 73 B4
Cerknica SLO 73 C4
Cerkno SLO 72 B3
Cerkwica PL 45 A7
Çermë-Proshkë AL 105 B5
Černá HR 74 C3
Černá Hora CZ 64 A2
Cernavodă RO 11 D10
Cernay F 60 C3
Cerne Abbas GB 29 C5
Cernégula E 89 B3
Černik HR 74 C2
Cernobbio I 70 C4
Černošín CZ 62 A3
Cernovice CZ 63 A5
Cérons F 76 B2
Cerovlje HR 73 C4
Cerovo SK 65 B5
Cerqueto I 82 D1
Cerralbo E 87 D4
Cerreto d'Esi I 82 C1
Cerreto Sannita I 103 B7
Cerrigydrudion GB 26 B2
Cërrik AL 105 B5
Cerro Muriano E 100 A1
Certaldo I 81 C5
Certosa di Pésio I 80 B1
Cerva P 87 C3
Cervaro I 103 B6
Cervatos de la Cueza E 88 B2
Červena Řečice CZ 63 A6
Červená-Skala SK 65 B6
Červená Voda CZ 54 C1
Cerveny Kostelec CZ 53 C6
Cervera E 91 B4
Cervera de la Cañada E 89 C5
Cervera del Llano E 95 C4
Cervera del Río Alhama E 89 B5
Cervera de Pisuerga E 88 B2
Cervéteri I 102 B5
Cérvia I 82 B1
Cerviàde les Garriques E 90 B3
Cervignano del Friuli I 72 C3
Cervinara I 103 B7
Cervione F 102 A2
Cervo E 86 A3
Cervon F 68 A3
Cesana Torinese I 79 B5
Cesarica HR 83 B4
Cesarò I 109 B3
Cesena I 82 B1
Cesenático I 82 B1
Cēsis LV 7 C8
Česká Belá CZ 63 A6
Česká Kamenice CZ 53 C4
Česká Lípa CZ 53 C4
Česká Třebová CZ 64 A2
České Budějovice CZ 63 B5
České Velenice CZ 63 B5
Český Brod CZ 53 C4
Český Dub CZ 53 C4
Český Krumlov CZ 63 B5
Český Těšín CZ 65 A4
Ćešljeva Bara SRB 85 B6
Çeşme TR 119 D1
Cessenon F 78 C2
Cesson-Sévigné F 57 B4
Cestas F 76 B2
Čestobrodica SRB 85 C5
Cesuras E 86 A2
Cetina E 89 C5
Cetin Grad HR 73 C5
Cetinje MNE 105 A4
Cetraro I 106 B2
Ceuta E 99 D5
Ceuti E 101 A4
Ceva I 80 B2
Cevico de la Torre E 88 C2
Cevico Navero E 88 C2
Cevins F 69 C6
Cévio CH 70 B3
Çevizli TR 119 E6
Čevo MNE 105 A4
Cewice PL 46 A3
Ceyhan TR 16 C7
Çeylan TR 119 F4
Ceyrat F 68 C3
Ceyzériat F 69 B5
Chaam NL 49 B5
Chabanais F 67 C5
Chabeuil F 79 B4
Chabielice PL 55 B4
Chablis F 59 C4
Châbons F 69 C5
Chabówka PL 65 A5
Chabreloche F 68 C3
Chabris F 67 A6
Chagford GB 28 C4
Chagny F 69 B4
Chagoda RUS 7 B13
Chaherrero E 94 B2
Chailland F 57 B5
Chaillé-les-Marais F 66 B3
Chailles F 67 A6
Chailley F 59 B4
Chalabre F 77 D5
Chalais F 67 C5
Chalamont F 69 C5
Châlette-sur-Loing F 58 B3
Chalindrey F 59 C6
Challacombe GB 28 B4
Challans F 66 B3
Challes-les-Eaux F 69 C5
Chalmazel F 68 C3
Chalmoux F 68 B3
Chalonnes-sur-Loire F 66 A4
Châlons-en-Champagne F 59 B5
Chalon-sur-Saône F 69 B4
Chalupy PL 47 A4
Châlus F 67 C5
Cham
CH 70 A3
D 62 A3
Chamberet F 68 C1
Chambéry F 69 C5
Chambilly F 68 B4
Chambley F 60 A1
Chambly F 58 A3
Chambois F 57 B6
Chambon-sur-Lac F 68 C2
Chambon-sur-Voueize F 68 B2
Chambord F 58 C2
Chamborigaud F 78 B2
Chamboulive F 68 C1
Chamerau D 62 A3
Chamonix-Mont Blanc F 70 C1
Chamoux-sur-Gelon F 69 C6
Champagnac-le-Vieux F 68 C3
Champagney F 60 C2
Champagnole F 69 B5
Champagny-Mouton F 67 B5
Champaubert F 59 B4
Champdeniers-St Denis F 67 B4
Champdieu F 68 C4
Champdôtre F 69 A5
Champeix F 68 C3
Champéry CH 70 B1
Champigne F 57 C5
Champignelles F 59 C4
Champigny-sur-Veude F 67 A5
Champlitte-et-le-Prelot F 60 C1
Champoluc I 70 C2
Champoly F 68 C3
Champorcher I 70 C2
Champrond-en-Gâtine F 58 B2
Champs-sur-Tarentaine F 68 C2
Champs-sur-Yonne F 59 C4
Champtoceaux F 66 A3
Chamrousse F 69 C5
Chamusca P 92 B2
Chanac F 78 B2
Chanaleilles F 78 B2
Chandler's Ford GB 31 D2
Chandra GR 117 G8
Chandrexa de Queixa E 87 B3
Chañe E 88 C2
Changy F 68 B3
Chania GR 117 G6
Channes F 59 C5
Chantada E 86 B3
Chantelle F 68 B3
Chantenay-St Imbert F 68 B3
Chanteuges F 78 A2
Chantilly F 58 A3
Chantonnay F 66 B3
Chão de Codes P 92 B2
Chaource F 59 B5
Chapa E 86 B2
Chapareillan F 69 C5
Chapel en le Frith GB 27 B4
Chapelle Royale F 58 B2
Chapelle-St Laurent F 67 B4
Charbonnat F 68 B4
Chard GB 29 C5
Charenton-du-Cher F 68 B2
Charlbury GB 31 C2
Charleroi B 49 C5
Charlestown
GB 28 C3
IRL 18 C3
Charlestown of Aberlour GB 23 D5
Charleville IRL 20 B3
Charleville-Mézières F 59 A5
Charlieu F 68 B4
Charlottenberg S 34 C4
Charlton Kings GB 29 B5
Charly F 59 B4
Charmes F 60 B2
Charmes-sur-Rhône F 78 B3
Charmey CH 70 B2
Charminster GB 29 C5
Charmont-en-Beauce F 58 B3
Charny F 59 C4
Charolles F 69 B4
Chârost F 68 B2
Charquemont F 70 A1
Charrin F 68 B3
Charroux F 67 B5
Chartres F 58 B2
Charzykow PL 46 B3
Chasseneuil-sur-Bonnieure F 67 C5
Chassigny F 59 C6
Château-Arnoux F 79 B5
Châteaubernard F 67 C4
Châteaubourg F 57 B4
Châteaubriant F 57 C4
Château-Chinon F 68 A3
Château-d'Oex CH 70 B2
Château-d'Olonne F 66 B3
Château-du-Loir F 58 C1
Châteaudun F 58 B2
Châteaugiron F 57 B4
Château-Gontier F 57 C5
Château-Landon F 58 B3
Château-la-Vallière F 67 A5
Château-l'Evêque F 67 C5
Châteaulin F 56 B1
Châteaumeillant F 68 B2
Châteauneuf
Nièvre F 68 A3
Saône-et-Loire F 69 B4
Châteauneuf-de-Randon F 78 B2
Châteauneuf-d'Ille-et-Vilaine F 57 B4
Châteauneuf-du-Faou F 56 B2
Châteauneuf-du-Pape F 78 B3
Châteauneuf-en-Thymerais F 58 B2
Châteauneuf la-Forêt F 67 C6
Châteauneuf-le-Rouge F 79 C4
Châteauneuf-sur-Charente F 67 C4
Châteauneuf-sur-Cher F 68 B2
Châteauneuf-sur-Loire F 58 C3
Châteauneuf-sur-Sarthe F 57 C5
Châteauponsac F 67 B6
Château-Porcien F 59 A5
Châteauredon F 79 B5
Châteaurenard
Bouches du Rhône F 78 C3
Loiret F 59 C3
Château-Renault F 58 C1
Châteauroux F 68 B1
Châteauroux-les-Alpes F 79 B5
Château-Salins F 60 B2
Château-Thierry F 59 A4
Châteauvillain F 59 B5
Châtel F 70 B1
Châtelaillon-Plage F 66 B3
Châtelaudren F 56 B3
Châtel-Censoir F 68 A3
Châtel-de-Neuvre F 68 B3
Châtelet B 49 C5
Châtelguyon F 68 C3
Châtellerault F 67 B5
Châtel-Montagne F 68 B3
Châtel-St Denis CH 70 B1
Châtel-sur-Moselle F 60 B2
Châtelus-Malvaleix F 68 B2
Châtenois F 60 B1
Châtenois-les-Forges F 70 A1
Chatham GB 31 C4
Châtillon I 70 C2
Châtillon-Coligny F 59 C3
Châtillon-en-Bazois F 68 A3
Châtillon-en-Diois F 79 B4
Châtillon-sur Chalaronne F 69 B4
Châtillon-sur-Indre F 67 B6
Châtillon-sur-Loire F 58 C3
Châtillon-sur-Marne F 59 A4
Châtillon-sur-Seine F 59 C5
Châtres F 59 B4
Chatteris GB 30 B4
Chatton GB 25 C6
Chauchina E 100 B2
Chaudes-Aigues F 78 B2
Chaudrey F 59 B5
Chauffailles F 69 B4
Chaulnes F 58 A3
Chaument Gistoux B 49 C5
Chaumergy F 69 B5
Chaumont F 59 B6
Chaumont-en-Vexin F 58 A2
Chaumont-Porcien F 59 A5
Chaumont-sur-Aire F 59 B6
Chaumont-sur-Loire F 67 A6
Chaunay F 67 B5
Chauny F 59 A4
Chaussin F 69 B5
Chauvigny F 67 B5
Chavagnes-en-Paillers F 66 B3
Chavanges F 59 B5
Chaves P 87 C3
Chavignon F 59 A4
Chazelles-sur-Lyon F 69 C4
Chazey-Bons F 69 C5
Cheadle
Greater Manchester GB 26 B3
Staffordshire GB 27 C4
Cheb CZ 52 C2
Chebsara RUS 7 B15
Checa E 95 B5
Chęciny PL 55 C5
Cheddar GB 29 B5
Cheddleton GB 26 B3
Chef-Boutonne F 67 B4
Chekalin RUS 7 D14
Chekhovo RUS 47 A6
Cheles E 93 C3
Chella E 96 B2
Chelles F 58 B3
Chełm PL 11 A7
Chełmno
Kujawsko-Pomorskie PL 47 B4
Wielkopolskie PL 54 A3
Chelmsford GB 31 C4
Chełmża PL 47 B4
Cheltenham GB 29 B5
Chelva E 96 B1
Chémery F 67 A6
Chemery-sur-Bar F 59 A5
Chemillé F 67 A4
Chemin F 69 B5
Chemnitz D 52 C2
Chénerailles F 68 B2
Cheniménil F 60 B2
Chenonceaux F 67 A6
Chenôve F 69 A4
Chepelare BG 116 A6
Chepstow GB 29 B5
Chera E 96 B2
Cherasco I 80 B1
Cherbonnières F 67 C4
Cherbourg F 57 A4
Cherchiara di Calàbria I 106 B3
Cherepovets RUS 7 B14
Cherkasy UA 11 B12
Chernihiv UA 7 F11
Chernivtsi UA 11 B8
Chernobyl = Chornobyl UA 7 F11
Chernyakhovsk RUS 6 D6
Chéroy F 59 B3
Cherven BY 7 E10
Chervonohrad UA 11 A8
Cherykaw BY 7 E11
Chesham GB 31 C3
Cheshunt GB 31 C3
Chessy-lès-Pres F 59 B4
Cheste E 96 B2
Chester GB 26 B3
Chesterfield GB 27 B4
Chester-le-Street GB 25 D6
Chevagnes F 68 B3
Chevanceaux F 67 C4
Chevillon F 59 B6
Chevilly F 58 B2
Chew Magna GB 29 B5
Chézery-Forens F 69 B5
Chialamberto I 70 C2
Chiampo I 71 C6
Chianale I 79 B6
Chianciano Terme I 81 C5
Chiaramonte Gulfi I 109 B3
Chiaramonti I 110 B1
Chiaravalle I 82 C2
Chiaravalle Centrale I 106 C3
Chiaréggio I 71 B4
Chiari I 71 C4
Chiaromonte I 106 A3
Chiasso CH 70 C4
Chiávari I 80 B3
Chiavenna I 71 B4
Chiché F 67 B4
Chichester GB 31 D3
Chiclana de la Frontera E 99 C4
Chiclana de Segura E 100 A2
Chiddingfold GB 31 C3
Chieri I 80 A1
Chiesa in Valmalenco I 71 B4
Chieti I 103 A7
Chieti Scalo I 103 A7
Chiéuti I 103 B8
Chigirin UA 11 B12
Chigwell GB 31 C4
Chiliomodi GR 117 E4
Chillarón de Cuenca E 95 B4
Chillarón del Rey E 95 B4
Chilleurs-aux-Bois F 58 B3
Chillón E 100 A1
Chilluévar E 100 B2
Chiloeches E 95 B3
Chimay B 49 C5
Chimeneas E 100 B2
Chinchilla de Monte Aragón E 96 C1
Chinchón E 95 B3
Chingford GB 31 C4
Chinon F 67 A5
Chióggia I 72 C2
Chiomonte I 79 A5
Chipiona E 99 C4
Chippenham GB 29 B5
Chipping Campden GB 29 A6
Chipping Norton GB 31 C2
Chipping Ongar GB 31 C4
Chipping Sodbury GB 29 B5
Chirac F 78 B2
Chirbury GB 26 C2
Chirens F 69 C5
Chirivel E 101 B3
Chirk GB 26 C2
Chirnside GB 25 C5
Chişinău = Khisinev MD 11 C10
Chişineu Criş RO 10 C6
Chissey-en-Morvan F 69 A4
Chiusa I 71 B6
Chiusa di Pésio I 80 B1
Chiusaforte I 72 B3
Chiusa Scláfani I 108 B2
Chiusi I 81 C5
Chiva E 96 B2
Chivasso I 70 C2
Chlewiska PL 55 B5
Chludowo PL 46 C2
Chlumec nad Cidlinou CZ 53 C5
Chlum u Třeboně CZ 63 B5
Chmielnik PL 55 C5
Chobienia PL 54 B1
Chobienice PL 53 A5
Choceň CZ 53 D6
Choceń PL 47 C5
Chochołow PL 65 A5
Chocianów PL 53 B5
Chociw PL 55 B4
Chociwel PL 46 B1
Choczewo PL 46 A3
Chodaków PL 55 A5
Chodecz PL 47 C5
Chodov CZ 52 C2
Chodzież PL 46 C2
Chojna PL 45 C6
Chojnice PL 46 B3
Chojno
Kujawsko-Pomorskie PL 47 C5
Wielkopolskie PL 46 C2
Chojnów PL 53 B5
Cholet F 66 A4
Chomérac F 78 B3
Chomutov CZ 52 C3
Chop UA 11 B7
Chora GR 117 E3
Chora Sfakion GR 117 G6
Chorges F 79 B5
Chorley GB 26 B3
Chornobyl = Chernobyl UA 7 F11
Chortkiv UA 11 B8
Chorzew PL 54 B3
Chorzów PL 54 C3
Choszczno PL 46 B1
Chotcza-Józefów PL 55 B6
Chotěboř CZ 63 A6
Chouilly F 59 A5
Chouto P 92 B2
Chouzy-sur-Cisse F 67 A6
Chozas de Abajo E 88 B1
Chrast CZ 64 A1
Chrást CZ 63 A4
Chrastava CZ 53 C4
Chřibská CZ 53 C4
Christchurch GB 29 C6
Christiansfeld DK 39 D2
Chroberz PL 55 C5
Chropyně CZ 64 A3
Chrudim CZ 53 D5
Chrzanów PL 55 C4
Chtelnica SK 64 B3
Chudovo RUS 7 B11
Chueca E 94 C3
Chulmleigh GB 28 C4
Chur CH 71 B4
Church Stretton GB 26 C3
Churriana E 100 C1
Churwalden CH 71 B4
Chvalšiny CZ 63 B5
Chwaszczyno PL 47 A4
Chynava CZ 53 C4
Chýnov CZ 63 A5
Ciacova RO 75 C6
Ciadîr-Lunga MD 11 C10
Ciadoncha E 88 B3
Cianciana I 108 B2
Ciano d'Enza I 81 B4
Ciążen PL 54 A2
Cibakhaza H 75 B5
Ciborro P 92 C2
Cicagna I 80 B3
Cicciano I 103 C7
Cičevac SRB 85 C6
Ciciliano I 102 B5
Cicognolo I 71 C5
Cidadelhe P 87 D3
Cide TR 16 A6
Cidones E 89 C4
Ciechanów
Dolnośląskie PL 54 B1
Mazowieckie PL 47 C6
Ciechocinek PL 47 C4
Cielądz PL 55 B5
Ciemnik PL 46 B1
Ciempozuelos E 95 B3
Ciepielów PL 55 B6
Čierny Balog SK 65 B5
Cierp-Gaud F 77 D3
Cierpice PL 47 C4
Ciervana E 89 A3
Cierznie PL 46 B3
Cieslé PL 47 C6
Cieszyn PL 65 A4
Cieutat F 76 C3
Cieza E 101 A4
Cifer SK 64 B3
Çifteler TR 118 C6
Cifuentes E 95 B4
Cigales E 88 C2
Cigliano I 70 C3
Cihanbeyli TR 16 B6
Cilipi HR 105 A4
Cillas E 95 B5
Cilleros E 93 A4
Cilleruelo de Arriba E 88 C3
Cilleruelo de Bezana E 88 B3
Cimalmotto CH 70 B3
Cimanes del Tejar E 88 B1
Ciminna I 108 B2
Cimişlia MD 11 C10
Cimoláis I 72 B2
Cîmpulung RO 11 D8
Çınarcık TR 118 B4
Cinctorres E 90 C2
Cinderford GB 29 B5
Çine TR 119 E3
Činěves CZ 53 C5
Ciney B 49 C6
Cinfães P 87 C2
Cingia de' Botti I 81 A4
Cingoli I 82 C2
Cinigiano I 81 D5
Cinobaňa SK 65 B5
Cinq-Mars-la-Pile F 67 A5
Cinquefrondi I 106 C3
Cintegabelle F 77 C4
Cintruénigo E 89 B5
Ciółkowo PL 47 C5
Ciperez E 87 D4
Cirat E 96 A2
Cirella I 106 B2
Cirencester GB 29 B6
Cirey-sur-Vezouze F 60 B2
Ciria E 89 C5
Ciriè I 70 C2
Cirigliano I 104 C2
Cirò I 107 B4
Cirò Marina I 107 B4
Ciry-le-Noble F 69 B4
Cislău RO 11 D9
Cismon del Grappa I 72 C1
Cisneros E 88 B2
Cissac-Médoc F 66 C4
Čista CZ 52 C3
Cisterna di Latina I 102 B5
Cistérniga E 88 C2
Cisternino I 104 C3
Cistierna E 88 B1
Čitluk BIH 84 C2
Čitov CZ 53 C4
Cittadella I 72 C1
Cittàdella Pieve I 81 D6
Cittàdel Vaticano = Vatican City I 102 B5
Cittàdi Castello I 82 C1
Cittaducale I 102 A5
Cittanova I 106 C3
Città Sant'Angelo I 103 A7
Ciudadela de Menorca E 97 B3
Ciudad Real E 94 D3
Ciudad Rodrigo E 93 A4
Ciutadilla E 91 B4
Cividale del Friuli I 72 B3
Civita I 102 A6
Civita Castellana I 102 A5
Civitanova Alta I 82 C2
Civitanova Marche I 82 C2
Civitavécchia I 102 A4
Civitella di Romagna I 81 B5
Civitella di Tronto I 82 D2
Civitella Roveto I 103 B6
Civray F 67 B5
Çivril TR 119 D4
Cizur Mayor E 76 D1
Clabhach GB 24 B1
Clachan GB 22 D2
Clachan na Luib GB 22 D1
Clacton-on-Sea GB 31 C5
Cladich GB 24 B2
Claggan GB 24 B2
Clairvaux-les-Lacs F 69 B5
Clamecy F 68 A3
Claonaig GB 24 C2
Clarecastle IRL 20 B3
Claregalway IRL 20 A3
Claremorris IRL 18 C2
Clarinbridge IRL 20 A3
Clashmore
GB 23 D4
IRL 21 B4
Claudy GB 19 B4
Clausthal-Zellerfeld D 51 B6
Cláut I 72 B2
Clay Cross GB 27 B4
Claye-Souilly F 58 B3
Cléder F 56 B1
Cleethorpes GB 27 B5
Clefmont F 60 B1
Cléguérec F 56 B2
Clelles F 79 B4
Clenze D 44 C2
Cleobury Mortimer GB 29 A5
Cléon-d'Andran F 78 B3
Cléré-les-Pins F 67 A5
Clères F 58 A2
Clermont F 58 A3
Clermont-en-Argonne F 59 A6
Clermont-Ferrand F 68 C3
Clermont-l'Hérault F 78 C2
Clerval F 69 A6
Clervaux L 50 C2
Cléry-St André F 58 C2
Cles I 71 B6
Clevedon GB 29 B5
Cleveleys GB 26 B2
Cley GB 30 B5
Clifden IRL 18 C1
Clifford GB 29 A4
Clisson F 66 A3
Clitheroe GB 26 B3
Clogh IRL 21 B4
Cloghan
Donegal IRL 19 B4
Offaly IRL 21 A4
Clogheen IRL 21 B4
Clogher GB 19 B4
Cloghjordan IRL 20 B3
Clohars-Carnoët F 56 C2
Clonakilty IRL 20 C3
Clonaslee IRL 21 A4
Clondalkin IRL 21 A5
Clones IRL 19 B4
Clonmany IRL 19 A4
Clonmel IRL 21 B4
Clonmellon IRL 19 C4
Clonord IRL 21 A4
Clonroche IRL 21 B5
Cloone IRL 19 C4
Cloppenburg D 43 C5
Closeburn GB 25 C4
Clough GB 19 B6
Clova GB 25 B4
Clovelly GB 28 C3
Clowne GB 27 B4
Cloyes-sur-le-Loir F 58 C2
Cloyne IRL 20 C3
Cluis F 68 B1
Cluj-Napoca RO 11 C7
Clun GB 26 C2
Clunes GB 24 B3
Cluny F 69 B4
Cluses F 69 B6
Clusone I 71 C4
Clydach GB 28 B4
Clydebank GB 24 C3
Coachford IRL 20 C3
Coagh GB 19 B5
Coalisland GB 19 B5
Coalville GB 27 C4
Coaña E 86 A4
Çobanlar TR 118 D5
Cobas E 86 A2
Cobertelade E 89 C4
Cobeta E 95 B4
Cóbh IRL 20 C3
Cobreces E 88 A2
Coburg D 51 C6
Coca E 94 A2
Cocentaina E 96 C2
Cochem D 50 C3
Cockburnspath GB 25 C5
Cockermouth GB 26 A2
Codigoro I 82 B1
Codogno I 71 C4
Codos E 89 C5
Codróipo I 72 C2
Codrongianos I 110 B1
Coelhoso P 87 C4
Coesfeld D 50 B3
Coevorden NL 42 C3
Cofrentes E 96 B1
Cogeces del Monte E 88 C2
Coggeshall GB 31 C4
Cognac F 67 C4
Cogne I 70 C2
Cognin F 69 C5
Cogolin F 79 C5
Cogollos de Guadix E 100 B2
Cogollos-Vega E 100 B2
Cogolludo E 95 B3
Coimbra P 92 A2
Coín E 100 C1
Coirós E 86 A2
Čoka SRB 75 C5
Col SLO 73 C4
Colares P 92 C1
Cölbe D 51 C4
Colbitz D 52 A1
Colchester GB 31 C4
Coldingham GB 25 C5
Colditz D 52 B2
Coldstream GB 25 C5
Colebrooke GB 28 C4
Colera E 91 A6
Coleraine GB 19 A5
Colfiorito I 82 C1
Cólico I 71 B4
Coligny F 69 B5
Colindres E 89 A3
Collado-Mediano E 94 B2
Collado Villalba E 94 B3
Collagna I 81 B4
Collanzo E 88 A1
Collat F 68 C3
Coll de Nargó E 91 A4
Collécchio I 81 B4
Colledimezzo I 103 B7
Colle di Val d'Elsa I 81 C5
Colleferro I 102 B6
Colle Isarco I 71 B6
Collelongo I 103 B6
Collepasso I 107 A5
Collepepe I 82 D1
Collesalvetti I 81 C4
Colle Sannita I 103 B7
Collesano I 108 B2
Colli a Volturno I 103 B7
Collin GB 25 C4
Collinée F 56 B3
Collingham
Nottinghamshire GB 27 B5
West Yorkshire GB 27 B4
Collinghorst D 43 B4
Cóllio I 71 C5
Collobrières F 79 C5
Collon IRL 19 C5
Collooney IRL 18 B3
Colmar F 60 B3
Colmars F 79 B5
Colmenar E 100 C1
Colmenar de la Sierra E 95 A3
Colmenar de Oreja E 95 B3
Colmenar Viejo E 94 B3
Colmonel GB 24 C3
Colne GB 26 B3
Colobraro I 106 A3
Cologna Véneta I 71 C6
Cologne = Köln D 50 C2
Cologne F 77 C3
Cologne al Serio I 71 C4
Colombey-les-Belles F 60 B1
Colombey-les-deux-Églises F 59 B5
Colombres E 88 A2
Colomera E 100 B2
Colomers E 91 A5
Colomiers F 77 C4
Colònia de Sant Jordi E 97 B3
Colorno I 81 B4
Colos P 98 B2
Cölpin D 45 B5
Colpy GB 23 D6
Colsterworth GB 30 B3
Coltishall GB 30 B5
Colunga E 88 A1
Colwell GB 25 C5
Colwyn Bay GB 26 B2
Colyford GB 29 C4
Comácchio I 82 B1
Coma-ruga E 91 B4
Combarros E 86 B4
Combeaufontaine F 60 C1
Comber GB 19 B6
Comblain-au-Pont B 49 C6
Combloux F 70 C1
Combourg F 57 B4
Combronde F 68 C3
Comeglians I 72 B2
Comillas E 88 A2
Comines F 49 C4
Cómiso I 109 C3
Comloşu Mare RO 75 C5
Commensacq F 76 B2
Commentry F 68 B2
Commerau D 53 B4
Commercy F 60 B1
Como I 71 C4
Cómpeta E 100 C2
Compiègne F 58 A3
Comporta P 92 C2
Comps-sur-Artuby F 79 C5
Comrat MD 11 C10
Comrie GB 25 B4
Comunanza I 82 D2
Cona
Emilia Romagna I 81 B5
Veneto I 72 C2
Concarneau F 56 C2
Conceição P 98 B2
Conches-en-Ouche F 58 B1
Concordia Sagittária I 72 C2
Concordia sulla Sécchia I 81 B4
Concots F 77 B4
Condat F 68 C2
Condé-en-Brie F 59 B4
Condeixa P 92 A2
Condemios de Abajo E 95 A3
Condemios de Arriba E 95 A3
Condé-sur-l'Escaut F 49 C4
Condé-sur-Marne F 59 A5
Condé-sur-Noireau F 57 B5
Condino I 71 C5
Condom F 77 C3
Condove I 70 C2
Condrieu F 69 C4
Conegliano I 72 C2
Conflans-sur-Lanterne F 60 C2
Confolens F 67 B5
Conforto E 86 A3
Cong IRL 18 C2
Congleton GB 26 B3
Congosto E 86 B4
Congosto de Valdavia E 88 B2
Congostrina E 95 A3
Conil de la Frontera E 99 C4
Coningsby GB 27 B5
Coniston GB 26 A2
Conlie F 57 B5
Conliège F 69 B5
Conna IRL 20 B3
Connah's Quay GB 26 B2
Connantre F 59 B4
Connaugh IRL 20 B3
Connaux F 78 B3
Connel GB 24 B2
Connerré F 58 B1
Cononbridge GB 23 D4
Čonoplja SRB 75 C4
Conques F 77 B5
Conques-sur-Orbiel F 77 C5
Conquista E 100 A1
Conquista de la Sierra E 93 B5
Consándolo I 81 B5
Consélice I 81 B5
Conselve I 72 C1
Consenvoye F 59 A6
Consett GB 25 D6
Consolação P 92 B1
Constancia P 92 B2
Constanco E 86 A2
Constanța RO 11 D10
Constanti E 91 B4
Constantina E 99 B5
Consuegra E 95 C3
Consuma I 81 C5
Contarina I 82 A1
Contay F 48 D3
Conthey CH 70 B2
Contigliano I 102 A5
Contis-Plage F 76 B1
Contrada I 103 C7
Contres F 67 A6
Contrexéville F 60 B1
Controne I 103 C8
Contursi Termi I 103 C8
Conty F 58 A3
Conversano I 104 C3
Conwy GB 26 B2
Cookstown GB 19 B5
Coole F 59 B5
Coolgreany IRL 21 B5
Cooneen GB 19 B4
Cootehill IRL 19 B4
Cope E 101 B4
Copenhagen = København DK 41 D2
Copertino I 105 C4
Copparo I 81 B5
Coppenbrugge D 51 A5
Corabia RO 11 E8
Córaci I 106 B3
Coralići BIH 83 B4
Corato I 104 B2
Coray F 56 B2
Corbeil-Essonnes F 58 B3
Corbeny F 59 A4
Corbera E 96 B2
Corbie F 58 A3
Corbigny F 68 A3
Corbion B 59 A5
Corbridge GB 25 D5
Corby GB 30 B3
Corconte E 88 A3
Corcubión E 86 B1
Corcumello I 103 A6
Cordenòns I 72 C2
Cordes-sur-Ciel F 77 B4
Córdoba E 100 B1
Cordobilla de Lácara E 93 B4
Cordovado I 72 C2
Corella E 89 B5
Coreses E 88 C1
Corfe Castle GB 29 C5
Corga de Lobão P 87 D2
Cori I 102 B5
Coria E 93 B4
Coria del Río E 99 B4
Corigliano Cálabro I 106 B3
Corinaldo I 82 C1
Corinth = Korinthos GR 117 E4
Cório I 70 C2
Coripe E 99 C5
Cork IRL 20 C3
Corlay F 56 B2
Corleone I 108 B2
Corleto Monforte I 103 C8
Corleto Perticara I 104 C2
Çorlu TR 118 A2
Cormainville F 58 B2
Cormatin F 69 B4
Cormeilles F 58 A1
Cormery F 67 A5
Cormons I 72 C3
Cormoz F 69 B5
Cornago E 89 B4
Cornberg D 51 B5
Cornellana E 86 A4
Cornești MD 11 C10
Corniglio I 81 B4
Cornimont F 60 C2
Corniolo I 81 C5
Cornudella de Montsant E 90 B3
Cornudilla E 89 B3
Cornus F 78 C2
Çorovodë AL 116 B2
Corpach GB 24 B2
Corps F 79 B4
Corps Nuds F 57 C4
Corral de Almaguer E 95 C3
Corral de Ayllon E 89 C3
Corral de Calatrava E 100 A1
Corrales E 88 C1
Corral-Rubio E 101 A4
Corran GB 24 B2
Corredoiras E 86 A2
Correggio I 81 B4
Corrèze F 68 C1
Corridónia I 82 C2
Corris GB 26 C2
Corrubedo E 86 B1
Córsico I 71 C4
Corsock GB 25 C4
Corte F 102 A2
Corteconcepción E 99 B4
Corte de Peleas E 93 C4
Cortegaca P 87 D2
Cortegada E 87 B2
Cortegana E 99 B4
Cortemaggiore I 81 B3
Cortemilia I 80 B2
Corte Pinto P 98 B3
Cortes E 89 C5
Cortes de Aragón E 90 C2
Cortes de Arenoso E 96 A2
Cortes de Baza E 101 B3
Cortes de la Frontera E 99 C5
Cortes de Pallás E 96 B2
Cortiçadas P 92 C2
Cortico P 87 C3
Cortijo de Arriba E 94 C2
Cortijos Nuevos E 101 A3
Cortina d'Ampezzo I 72 B2
Corton GB 30 B5
Cortona I 81 C5
Coruche P 92 C2
Corullón E 86 B4
Çorum TR 16 A7
Corvara in Badia I 72 B1
Corvera E 101 B4
Corwen GB 26 C2
Cosenza I 106 B3
Cosham GB 31 D2
Coslada E 95 B3
Cosne-Cours-sur-Loire F 68 A2
Cosne d'Allier F 68 B2
Cospeito E 86 A3
Cossato I 70 C3
Cossaye F 68 B3
Cossé-le-Vivien F 57 C5
Cossonay CH 69 B6
Costa da Caparica P 92 C1
Costa de Santo André P 98 A2
Costalpino I 81 C5
Costa Nova P 92 A2
Costaros F 78 B2
Costești RO 11 D8
Costigliole d'Asti I 80 B2
Costigliole Saluzzo I 80 B1
Coswig
Sachsen D 52 B3
Sachsen-Anhalt D 52 B2
Cotherstone GB 27 A4
Cotronei I 107 B3
Cottbus D 53 B4
Cottenham GB 30 B4
Cottingham GB 27 B5
Coublanc F 60 C1
Couches F 69 B4
Couço P 92 C2
Coucouron F 78 B2
Coucy-le-Château-Auffrique F 59 A4
Couëron F 66 A3
Couflens F 77 D4
Couhé F 67 B5
Couiza F 77 D5
Coulags GB 22 D3
Coulanges F 68 B3
Coulanges-la-Vineuse F 59 C4
Coulanges-sur-Yonne F 68 A3
Couleuvre F 68 B2
Coulmier-le-Sec F 59 C5
Coulommiers F 59 B4
Coulonges-sur-l'Autize F 67 B4
Coulounieix-Chamiers F 67 C5
Coulport GB 24 B3
Coupar Angus GB 25 B4
Coupéville F 59 B5

Couptrain F 57 B5
Coura P 87 C2
Courcelles B 49 C5
Courcelles-Chaussy F 60 A2
Courchevel F 70 C1
Cour-Cheverny F 67 A6
Courcôme F 67 C5
Courçon F 66 B4
Cour-et-Buis F 69 C4
Courgenay CH 70 A2
Courmayeur I 70 C1
Courniou F 78 C1
Cournon d'Auvergne F 68 C3
Cournonterral F 78 C2
Courpière F 68 C3
Coursan F 78 C2
Courseulles-sur-Mer F 57 A5
Cours-la-Ville F 69 B4
Courson-les-Carrières F 59 C4
Courtalain F 58 B2
Courtenay F 59 B4
Courtomer F 58 B1
Courville
Eure-et-Loire F 58 B2
Marne F 59 A4
Coussac-Bonneval F 67 C6
Coutances F 57 A4
Couterne F 57 B5
Coutras F 76 A2
Couvet CH 70 B1
Couvin B 49 C5
Couzon F 68 B3
Covadonga E 88 A1
Covaleda E 89 C4
Covarrubias E 89 B3
Covas P 87 C2
Cove GB 22 D3
Coventry GB 30 B2
Coverack GB 28 C2
Covigliáio I 81 B5
Covilhã P 92 A3
Cowbridge GB 29 B4
Cowdenbeath GB 25 B4
Cowes GB 31 D2
Cox F 77 C4
Cózar E 100 A2
Cozes F 66 C4
Cozzano F 102 B2
Craco I 104 C2
Cracow = Kraków PL 55 C4
Craibstone GB 23 D6
Craighouse GB 24 C2
Craignure GB 24 B2
Crail GB 25 B5
Crailsheim D 61 A6
Craiova RO 11 D7
Cramlington GB 25 C6
Cranleigh GB 31 C3
Craon F 57 C5
Craonne F 59 A4
Craponne F 69 C4
Craponne-sur-Arzon F 68 C3
Crathie GB 23 D5
Crato P 92 B3
Craughwell IRL 20 A3
Craven Arms GB 26 C3
Crawford GB 25 C4
Crawinkel D 51 C6
Crawley GB 31 C3
Creag Ghoraidh GB 22 D1
Crecente E 87 B2
Crèches-sur-Saône F 69 B4
Crécy-en-Ponthieu F 48 C2
Crécy-la-Chapelle F 59 B3
Crécy-sur-Serre F 59 A4
Crediton GB 29 C4
Creeslough IRL 19 A4
Creetown GB 24 D3
Creeve GB 19 B5
Creglingen D 61 A6
Creil F 58 A3
Creissels F 78 B2
Crema I 71 C4
Cremeaux F 68 C3
Crémenes E 88 B1
Crémieu F 69 C5
Cremlingen D 51 A6
Cremona I 81 A4
Creney F 59 B5
Črenšovci SLO 73 B6
Créon F 76 B2
Crepaja SRB 85 A5
Crépey F 60 B1
Crépy F 59 A4
Crépy-en-Valois F 59 A3
Cres HR 83 B3
Crescentino I 70 C3
Crespino I 81 B5
Crespos E 94 B2
Cressage GB 26 C3
Cressensac F 77 A4
Cressia F 69 B5
Crest F 79 B4
Cresta CH 71 B4
Créteil F 58 B3
Creully F 57 A5
Creussen D 62 A2
Creutzwald F 60 A2
Creuzburg D 51 B6
Crevalcore I 81 B5
Crèvecoeur-le-Grand F 58 A3
Crevillente E 101 A5
Crévola d'Ossola I 70 B3
Crewe GB 26 B3
Crewkerne GB 29 C5
Criales E 89 B3
Crianlarich GB 24 B3
Criccieth GB 26 C1
Crickhowell GB 29 B4
Cricklade GB 29 B6
Crieff GB 25 B4
Criel-sur-Mer F 48 C2
Crikvenica HR 73 C4
Crillon F 58 A2
Crimmitschau D 52 C2
Crimond GB 23 D7
Crinitz D 53 B3
Cripán E 89 B4
Criquetot-l'Esneval F 57 A6
Crispiano I 104 C3
Crissolo I 79 B6
Cristóbal E 93 A5
Crivitz D 44 B3
Črna SLO 73 B4
Crna Bara
Srbija SRB 85 B4
Vojvodina SRB 75 C5
Crnac HR 74 C2
Crnča SRB 85 B4
Crni Lug
BIH 83 B5
HR 73 C4
Črni Vrh SLO 73 C4
Crnjelovo Donje BIH 85 B4
Črnomelj SLO 73 C5
Crocketford GB 25 C4
Crocq F 68 C2
Crodo I 70 B3
Croglin GB 25 D5
Crolly IRL 18 A3
Cromarty GB 23 D4
Cromer GB 30 B5
Cronat F 68 B3
Crookhaven IRL 20 C2
Crookstown IRL 20 C3
Croom IRL 20 B3
Cropalati I 106 B3
Crópani I 107 C3
Crosbost GB 22 C2
Crosby GB 26 B2
Crosía I 106 B3
Crossakiel IRL 19 C4
Cross-Hands GB 28 B3
Crosshaven IRL 20 C3
Crosshill GB 24 C3
Crossmolina IRL 18 B2
Crotone I 107 B4
Crottendorf D 52 C2
Crouy F 59 A4
Crowborough GB 31 C4
Crowland GB 30 B3
Crowthorne GB 31 C3
Croyde GB 28 B3
Croydon GB 31 C3
Crozon F 56 B1
Cruas F 78 B3
Cruceni RO 75 B6
Crúcoli I 107 B4
Cruden Bay GB 23 D7
Crudgington GB 26 C3
Cruis F 79 B4
Crumlin GB 19 B5
Cruseilles F 69 B6
Crusheen IRL 20 B3
Cruz de Incio E 86 B3
Crvenka SRB 75 C4
Červeny Kamen SK 64 A4
Csabacsüd H 75 B5
Csabrendek H 74 A2
Csákánydoroszló H 74 B1
Csákvár H 74 A3
Csanádapáca H 75 B5
Csanádpalota H 75 B5
Csány H 65 C5
Csanytelek H 75 B5
Csapod H 74 A1
Császár H 74 A3
Császártöltés H 75 B4
Csávoly H 75 B4
Csemő H 75 A4
Csengöd H 75 B4
Csépa H 75 B5
Csepreg H 74 A1
Cserkeszölö H 75 B5
Csernely H 65 B6
Csesztreg H 74 B1
Csökmő H 75 A6
Csököly H 74 B2
Csokonyavisonta H 74 B2
Csólyospálos H 75 B4
Csongrád H 75 B5
Csopak H 74 B2
Csorna H 64 C3
Csorvás H 75 B5
Csurgo H 74 B2
Cuacos de Yuste E 93 A5
Cualedro E 87 C3
Cuanca de Campos E 88 B1
Cuba P 98 A3
Cubel E 95 A5
Cubelles E 91 B4
Cubillos E 89 C4
Cubillos del Sil E 86 B4
Cubjac F 67 C5
Cubo de la Solana E 89 C4
Çubuk TR 16 A6
Cuckfield GB 31 C3
Cucuron F 79 C4
Cudillero E 86 A4
Cuéllar E 88 C2
Cuenca E 95 B4
Cuers F 79 C5
Cuerva E 94 C2
Cueva de Agreda E 89 C5
Cuevas Bajas E 100 B1
Cuevas del Almanzora E 101 B4
Cuevas del Becerro E 99 C5
Cuevas del Campo E 100 B3
Cuevas del Valle E 94 B1
Cuevas de San Clemente E 89 B3
Cuevas de San Marcos E 100 B1
Cuges-les-Pins F 79 C4
Cúglieri I 110 B1
Cugnaux F 77 C4
Cuijk NL 50 B1
Cuinzier F 69 B4
Cuiseaux F 69 B5
Cuisery F 69 B5
Culan F 68 B2
Culemborg NL 49 B6
Cúllar E 101 B3
Cullaville GB 19 B5
Cullera E 96 B2
Cullivoe GB 22 A7
Cullompton GB 29 C4
Cully CH 70 B1
Culoz F 69 C5
Cults GB 23 D6
Cumbernauld GB 25 C4
Cumbres de San Bartolomé E 99 A4
Cumbres Mayores E 99 A4
Cumiana I 80 B1
Čumić SRB 85 B5
Cumnock GB 24 C3
Çumra TR 16 C6
Cúneo I 80 B1
Cunlhat F 68 C3
Čunski HR 83 B3
Cuntis E 86 B2
Cuorgnè I 70 C2
Cupar GB 25 B4
Cupello I 103 A7
Cupra Marittima I 82 C2
Cupramontana I 82 C2
Ćuprija SRB 85 C6
Curinga I 106 C3
Currelos E 86 B3
Currie GB 25 C4
Curtea de Argeş RO 11 D8
Curtici RO 75 B6
Curtis E 86 A2
Curtis Santa Eulalia E 86 A2
Čurug SRB 75 C5
Cusano Mutri I 103 B7
Cushendall GB 19 A5
Cusset F 68 B3
Cussy-les-Forges F 68 A4
Custines F 60 B2
Cutanda E 90 C1
Cutro I 107 B3
Cutrofiano I 107 A5
Cuts F 59 A4
Cuvilly F 58 A3
Cuxhaven D 43 B5
Cvikov CZ 53 C4
Cwmbran GB 29 B4
Cybinka PL 53 A4
Czacz PL 54 A1
Czajków PL 54 B3
Czaplinek PL 46 B2
Czarlin PL 47 A4
Czarna-Dąbrówka PL 46 A3
Czarna Woda PL 47 B4
Czarnca PL 55 C4
Czarne PL 46 B2
Czarnków PL 46 C2
Czarnowo PL 47 B4
Czarnozyly PL 54 B3
Czarny Bór PL 53 C6
Czarny-Dunajec PL 65 A5
Czarny Las PL 54 B2
Czchow PL 65 A6
Czechowice-Dziedzice PL 65 A4
Czempiń PL 54 A1
Czermno PL 55 B5
Czernichow PL 55 D4
Czerniejewo PL 46 C3
Czernikowo PL 47 C4
Czersk PL 46 B3
Czerwieńsk PL 53 A5
Czerwionka-Leszczyny PL 54 C3
Czerwonka PL 47 B6
Częstochowa PL 55 C4
Czeszewo PL 46 C3
Człopa PL 46 B2
Człuchów PL 46 B3
Czołpino PL 46 A3

D

Dağ TR 119 E5
Daaden D 50 C3
Dabas H 75 A4
Dąbie PL 54 A3
Dąbki PL 46 A2
Dabo F 60 B3
Dabrowa PL 46 C3
Dąbrowa Górnicza PL 55 C4
Dąbrowa Tarnowska PL 55 C5
Dąbrowice PL 55 A4
Dabrowno PL 47 B6
Dachau D 62 B2
Dačice CZ 63 A6
Daday TR 16 A6
Dagali N 32 B5
Dägebüll D 39 E1
Dagmersellen CH 70 A2
Dahlen D 52 B2
Dahlenburg D 44 B2
Dahme D 52 B3
Dahn D 60 A3
Dähre D 44 C2
Daikanvik S 115 B13
Dail bho Dheas GB 22 C2
Dailly GB 24 C3
Daimiel E 95 C3
Daingean IRL 21 A4
Đakovica KOS 10 E6
Đakovo HR 74 C3
Dal
Akershus N 34 B3
Telemark N 32 C5
Dalaas A 71 A5
Dalabrog GB 22 D1
Dala-Floda S 36 B1
Dala-Husby S 36 B2
Dala-Järna S 36 B1
Dalaman TR 119 F3
Dalarö S 37 C5
Dalbeattie GB 25 D4
Dalby
DK 39 D3
Skåne S 41 D3
Uppsala S 37 C4
Värmland S 34 B4
Dale
Pembrokeshire GB 28 B2
Shetland GB 22 A7
Hordaland N 32 B2
Sogn og Fjordane N 32 A2
Dalen
Akershus N 34 C3
Telemark N 33 C5
Daleszyce PL 55 C5
Dalhalvaig GB 23 C5
Dalheim L 60 A2
Dalhem S 37 E5
Dalias E 100 C3
Dalj HR 75 C3
Dalkeith GB 25 C4
Dalkey IRL 21 A5
Dalmally GB 24 B3
Dalmellington GB 24 C3
Dalmose DK 39 D4
Daløy N 32 A1
Dalry
Dumfries & Galloway GB 24 C3
North Ayrshire GB 24 C3
Dalrymple GB 24 C3
Dalseter N 32 A6
Dalsjöfors S 40 B3
Dalskog S 35 D4
Dals Långed S 35 D4
Dals Rostock S 35 D4
Dalston GB 25 D5
Dalstorp S 40 B3
Dalton-in-Furness GB 26 A2
Daluis F 79 B5
Dalum
D 43 C4
S 40 B3
Dalvík IS 111 B7
Dalwhinnie GB 24 B3
Dalyan TR 119 F3
Damasi GR 116 C4
Damasławek PL 46 C3
Damazan F 76 B3
Damës AL 105 C5
Damgan F 56 C3
Dammarie-les-Lys F 58 B3
Dammartin-en-Goële F 58 A3
Damme D 43 C5
Damnica PL 46 A3
Dampierre F 69 A5
Dampierre-sur-Salon F 69 A5
Damüls A 71 A4
Damville F 58 B2
Damvillers F 59 A6
Damwoude NL 42 B2
Danasjö S 115 B13
Danbury GB 31 C4
Dångebo S 40 C5
Dangers F 58 B2
Dangé-St Romain F 67 B5
Dangeul F 58 B1
Danilovgrad MNE 105 A5
Danischenhagen D 44 A2
Daniszyn PL 54 B2
Danjoutin F 60 C2
Dannas S 40 B3
Dannemarie F 60 C3
Dannemora S 36 B4
Dannenberg D 44 B3
Dánszentmiklós H 75 A4
Dány H 75 A4
Daoulas F 56 B1
Darabani RO 11 B9
Darány H 74 C2
Darda HR 74 C3
Dardesheim D 51 B6
Darfeld D 50 A3
Darfo I 71 C5
Dargiń PL 46 A2
Dargun D 45 B4
Darlington GB 27 A4
Darłowo PL 46 A2
Darmstadt D 61 A4
Darney F 60 B2
Daroca E 95 A5
Darque P 87 C2
Darragh IRL 20 B2
Dartford GB 31 C4
Dartington GB 28 C4
Dartmouth GB 29 C4
Darton GB 27 B4
Daruvar HR 74 C2
Darvas H 75 A6
Darvel GB 24 C3
Darwen GB 26 B3
Dassel D 51 B5
Dassow D 44 B2
Datça TR 119 F2
Datteln D 50 B3
Dattenfeld D 50 C3
Daugard DK 39 D2
Daugavpils LV 7 D9
Daumeray F 57 C5
Daun D 50 C2
Daventry GB 30 B2
Davle CZ 63 A5
Davor HR 84 A2
Davos CH 71 B4
Davutlar TR 119 E2
Davyd Haradok BY 7 E9
Dawlish GB 29 C4
Dax F 76 C1
Dazkırı TR 119 E4
Deal GB 31 C5
Deauville F 57 A6
Deba E 89 A4
Debar MK 116 A2
Debe Wielkie PL 55 A6
Dębica PL 55 C6
Dębnica Kaszubska PL 46 A3
Dębno PL 45 C6
Dęboleka PL 54 B3
Dębowa Łaka PL 47 B5
Debrc SRB 85 B4
Debrecen H 10 C6
Debrznica PL 53 A5
Debrzno PL 46 B3
Debstedt D 43 B5
Decazeville F 77 B5
Dechtice SK 64 B3
Decima I 102 B5
Decimomannu I 110 C1
Děčín CZ 53 C4
Decize F 68 B3
De Cocksdorp NL 42 B1
Decollatura I 106 B3
Decs H 74 B3
Dedaj AL 105 A5
Deddington GB 31 C2
Dedeler TR 118 B5
Dedelow D 45 B5
Dedemli TR 119 E7
Dedemsvaart NL 42 C3
Dédestapolcsány H 65 B6
Dedovichi RUS 7 C10
Deeping St Nicholas GB 30 B3
Dég H 74 B3
Degaña E 86 B4
Degeberga S 41 D4
Degerby FIN 36 B7
Degerfors S 37 C1
Degerhamn S 41 C6
Degernes N 35 C3
Deggendorf D 62 B3
Deggingen D 61 B5
Dego I 80 B2
Degolados P 93 B3
De Haan B 49 B4
Dehesas de Guadix E 100 B2
Dehesas Viejas E 100 B2
Deia E 97 B2
Deining D 62 A2
Deinze B 49 C4
Déiva Marina I 80 B3
Dej RO 11 C7
Deje S 35 C5
De Koog NL 42 B1
Delabole GB 28 C3
Delary S 40 C3
Delbrück D 51 B4
Delden NL 50 A2
Deleitosa E 93 B5
Delekovec HR 74 B1
Delémont CH 70 A2
Delft NL 49 A5
Delfzijl NL 42 B3
Délia I 108 B2
Delianuova I 106 C2
Deliblato SRB 85 B6
Delice TR 16 B6
Deliceto I 103 B8
Delitzsch D 52 B2
Dellach A 72 B3
Delle F 70 A2
Delme F 60 B2
Delmen-horst D 43 B5
Delnice HR 73 C4
Delsbo S 115 F13
Delvin IRL 19 C4
Delvinë AL 116 C2
Demandice SK 65 B4
Demen D 44 B3
Demidov RUS 7 D11
Demigny F 69 B4
Demirci TR 118 C3
Demirköy TR 118 A2
Demirtaş TR 118 B4
Demmin D 45 B5
Demonte I 79 B6
Demyansk RUS 7 C12
Denain F 49 C4
Denbigh GB 26 B2
Den Burg NL 42 B1
Dender-monde B 49 B5
Denekamp NL 42 C3
Den Ham NL 42 C3
Den Helder NL 42 C1
Denholm GB 25 C5
Denia E 96 C3
Denizli TR 119 E4
Denkendorf D 62 B2
Denklingen D 50 C3
Denny GB 25 B4
Den Oever NL 42 C2
Denta RO 75 C6
Déols F 68 B1
De Panne B 48 B3
Derbent TR 119 D3
Derby GB 27 C4
Dereköy TR 118 A2
Derenberg D 51 B6
Derinkuyu TR 16 B7
Dermbach D 51 C6
Dermulo I 71 B6
Deronje SRB 75 C4
Derrygonnelly GB 19 B4
Derrylin GB 19 B4
Derry/Londonderry GB 19 B4
Dersingham GB 30 B4
Deruta I 82 D1
Dervaig GB 24 B1
Derval F 57 C4
Derveni GR 117 D4
Derventa BIH 84 B2
Dervock GB 19 A5
Desana I 70 C3
Descartes F 67 B5
Desenzano del Garda I 71 C5
Deset N 34 A3
Deševa BIH 84 C3
Desfina GR 116 D4
Desimirovac SRB 85 B5
Désio I 71 C4
Deskati GR 116 C3
Deskle SLO 72 B3
Desná CZ 53 C5
Dešov CZ 63 B6
Despotovac SRB 85 B6
Despotovo SRB 75 C4
Dessau D 52 B2
Deštná CZ 63 A5
Destriana E 87 B4
Désulo I 110 B2
Desvres F 48 C2
Deszk H 75 B5
Deta RO 75 C6
Detmold D 51 B4
Dětřichov CZ 64 A3
Dettelbach D 61 A6
Dettingen
Baden-Württemberg D 61 B5
Baden-Württemberg D 61 C5
Dettwiller F 60 B3
Detva SK 65 B5
Deurne NL 50 B1
Deutschkreutz A 64 C2
Deutschlandsberg A 73 B5
Deutsch Wagram A 64 B2
Deva RO 11 D7
Dévaványa H 75 A5
Devecikonağı TR 118 C3
Devecser H 74 A2
Develi TR 16 B7
Deventer NL 50 A2
Devil's Bridge GB 28 A4
Devin BG 116 A6
Devinska Nova Ves SK 64 B2
Devizes GB 29 B6
Devonport GB 28 C3
Devrek TR 118 A6
Devrekâni TR 16 A6
Đevrske HR 83 C4
De Wijk NL 42 C3
Dewsbury GB 27 B4
Deza E 89 C4
Dežanovac HR 74 C2
Dezzo I 71 C5
Dhali CY 120 A2
Dheftera CY 120 A2
Dherinia CY 120 A2
Dhërmi AL 105 C5
Diamante I 106 B2
Dianalund DK 39 D4
Diano d'Alba I 80 B2
Diano Marina I 80 C2
Dicomano I 81 C5
Didcot GB 31 C2
Didimoticho GR 118 A1
Die F 79 B4
Diebling F 60 A2
Dieburg D 61 A4
Diego del Carpio E 93 A5
Diekirch L 60 A2
Diélette F 57 A4
Diémoz F 69 C5
Dienten am Hochkönig A 72 A2
Diepenbeck B 49 C6
Diepholz D 43 C5
Dieppe F 58 A2
Dierberg D 45 B4
Dierdorf D 50 C3
Dieren NL 50 A2
Dierhagen D 44 A4
Diesdorf D 44 C2
Diessen D 62 C2
Diest B 49 C6
Dietenheim D 61 B6
Dietfurt D 62 A2
Dietikon CH 70 A3
Dietzenbach D 51 C4
Dieue-sur-Meuse F 60 A1
Dieulefit F 79 B4
Dieulouard F 60 B2
Dieuze F 60 B2
Diever NL 42 C3
Diez D 50 C4
Diezma E 100 B2
Differdange L 60 A1
Digermulen N 112 D4
Dignac F 67 C5
Dignano I 72 B2
Digne-les-Bains F 79 B5
Digny F 58 B2
Digoin F 68 B3
Dijon F 69 A5
Dikanäs S 115 B13
Dikili TR 118 C1
Diksmuide B 48 B3
Dilar E 100 B2
Dillenburg D 50 C4
Dillingen
Bayern D 61 B6
Saarland D 60 A2
Dilsen B 50 B1
Dimaro I 71 B5
Dimitrovgrad BG 11 E8
Dimitsana GR 117 E4
Dinami I 106 C3
Dinan F 57 B3
Dinant B 49 C5
Dinar TR 119 D5
Dinard F 57 B3
Dinek TR 118 C6
Dingden D 50 B2
Dingelstädt D 51 B6
Dingle
IRL 20 B1
S 35 D3
Dingolfing D 62 B3
Dingtuna S 37 C3
Dingwall GB 23 D4
Dinkelsbühl D 61 A6
Dinkelscherben D 62 B1
Dinklage D 43 C5
Dinslaken D 50 B2
Dinxperlo NL 50 B2
Diö S 40 C4
Diósgyör H 65 B6
Diósjeno H 65 C5
Diou F 68 B3
Dippen GB 24 C2
Dipperz D 51 C5
Dippoldiswalde D 53 C3
Dirdal N 33 D3
Dirksland NL 49 B5
Dirlewang D 61 C6
Dischingen D 61 B6
Disentis CH 70 B3
Diso I 107 A5
Diss GB 30 B5
Dissen D 50 A4
Distington GB 26 A2
Ditzingen D 61 B5
Ditzum D 43 B4
Divača SLO 72 C3
Dives-sur-Mer F 57 A5
Divín SK 65 B5
Divion F 48 C3
Divišov CZ 63 A5
Divjakë AL 105 C5
Divonne les Bains F 69 B6
Dixmont F 59 B4
Dizy-le-Gros F 59 A5
Djúpivogur IS 111 C11
Djupvasshytta N 114 E4
Djura S 36 B1
Djurås S 36 B2
Djurmo S 36 B2
Djursdala S 40 B5
Dlouhá Loucka CZ 64 A3
Długowola PL 55 B6
Dmitriyev Lgovskiy RUS 7 E13
Dmitrov RUS 7 C14
Dmitrovsk-Orlovskiy RUS 7 E13
Dno RUS 7 C10
Doade E 86 B3
Doğanhisar TR 119 D6
Dobanovci SRB 85 B5
Dobbertin D 44 B4
Dobbiaco I 72 B2
Dobczyce PL 65 A6
Dobele LV 6 C7
Döbeln D 52 B3
Doberlug-Kirchhain D 52 B3
Dobern D 53 B4
Dobersberg A 63 B6
Dobiegniew PL 46 C1
Dobieszyn PL 55 B6
Doboj BIH 84 B3
Dobošnica BIH 84 B3
Doboz H 75 B6
Dobrá CZ 65 A4
Dobra
Wielkopolskie PL 54 B3
Zachodnio-Pomorskie PL 45 B6
Zachodnio-Pomorskie PL 45 B7
Dobrá Niva SK 65 B5
Dobřany CZ 63 A4
Dobre
Kujawsko-Pomorskie PL 47 C4
Mazowieckie PL 55 A6
Dobre Miasto PL 47 B6
Dobreta-Turnu-Severin RO 11 D7
Dobri H 74 B1
Dobrica SRB 75 C5
Dobrich BG 11 E9
Dobri Do SRB 85 D6
Dobříš CZ 63 A5
Dobro E 89 B3
Dobrodzień PL 54 C3
Döbrököz H 74 B3
Dobromierz PL 53 C6
Dobrosołowo PL 47 C4
Dobroszyce PL 54 B2
Dobrota MNE 105 A4
Dobrovnik SLO 73 B6
Dobrush BY 7 E11
Dobruška CZ 53 C6
Dobrzany PL 46 B1
Dobrzen Wielki PL 54 C2
Dobrzyca
Wielkopolskie PL 46 B2
Wielkopolskie PL 54 B2
Zachodnio-Pomorskie PL 46 A1
Dobrzyńad Wisłą PL 47 C5
Dobšiná SK 65 B6
Dobwalls GB 28 C3
Dochamps B 49 C6
Docking GB 30 B4
Docksta S 115 D15
Doddington GB 25 C5
Döderhult S 40 B6
Doesburg NL 50 A2
Doetinchem NL 50 B2
Dogliani I 80 B1
Dogueno P 98 B3
Doische B 49 C5
Dois Portos P 92 B1
Dojč SK 64 B3
Dokka N 34 B2
Dokkedal DK 38 C3
Dokkum NL 42 B2
Dokležovje SLO 73 B6
Doksy CZ 53 C4
Dokuz TR 119 D7
Dolancourt F 59 B5
Dolceácqua I 80 C1
Dol-de-Bretagne F 57 B4
Dole F 69 A5
Dølemo N 33 D5
Dolenja vas SLO 73 C4
Dolenjske Toplice SLO 73 C5
Dolfor GB 26 C2
Dolgarrog GB 26 B2
Dolgellau GB 26 C2
Doliana GR 116 C2
Dolianova I 110 C2
Dolice PL 45 B7
Doljani HR 83 B5
Döllach im Mölltal A 72 B2
Dolle D 44 C3
Dollnstein D 62 B2
Dollot F 59 B4
Döllstadt D 51 B6
Dolná Strehová SK 65 B5
Dolné Saliby SK 64 B3
Dolni Benešov CZ 64 A4
Dolni Bousov CZ 53 C5
Dolni Kounice CZ 64 A2
Dolni Kralovice CZ 63 A6
Dolni Újezd CZ 64 A2
Dolni Žandov CZ 52 C2
Dolný Kubín SK 65 A5
Dolo I 72 C2
Dolores E 96 C2
Dolovo SRB 85 B5
Dölsach A 72 B2
Dolsk PL 54 B2
Dolwyddelan GB 26 B2
Dolynska UA 11 B12
Domaljevac BIH 84 A3
Domaniç TR 118 C4
Domaniža SK 65 A4
Domanovići BIH 84 C2
Domašov CZ 54 C2
Domaszék H 75 B4
Domaszków PL 54 C1
Domaszowice PL 54 B2
Domat-Ems CH 71 B4
Domažlice CZ 62 A3
Dombås N 114 E6
Dombasle-sur-Meurthe F 60 B2
Dombegyház H 75 B6
Dombóvár H 74 B3
Domène F 69 C5
Domérat F 68 B2
Domfessel F 60 B3
Domfront F 57 B5
Domfront-en-Champagne F 57 B6
Domingão P 92 B2
Domingo Pérez
Granada E 100 B2
Toledo E 94 C2
Dömitz D 44 B3
Dommartin F 59 B5
Dommartin-le-Franc F 59 B5
Domme F 77 B4
Dommitzsch D 52 B2
Domodóssola I 70 B3
Domokos GR 116 C4
Domoszló H 65 C6
Dompaire F 60 B2
Dompierre-du-Chemin F 57 B4
Dompierre-sur-Besbre F 68 B3
Dompierre-sur-Mer F 66 B3
Domrémy-la-Pucelle F 60 B1
Dömsöd H 75 A4
Domsure F 69 B5
Dómus de Maria I 110 D1
Domusnóvas I 110 C1
Domvena GR 117 D4
Domžale SLO 73 B4
Donado E 87 B4
Donaghadee GB 19 B6
Don Alvaro E 93 C4
Doña Mencía E 100 B1
Donaueschingen D 61 C4
Donauwörth D 62 B1
Don Benito E 93 C5
Doncaster GB 27 B4
Donegal IRL 18 B3
Donestebe-Santesteban E 76 C1
Donges F 66 A2
Dongo I 71 B4
Donington GB 30 B3
Doniños E 86 A2
Donja Bebrina HR 84 A3
Donja Brela HR 84 C1
Donja Dubica BIH 84 A3
Donja Dubrava HR 74 B1
Donja Kupčina HR 73 C5
Donja Mutnica SRB 85 C6
Donja Šatornja SRB 85 B5
Donja Stubica HR 73 C5
Donje Brišnik BIH 84 C2
Donje Ljupče KOS 85 D6
Donje Stative HR 73 C5
Donji-Andrijevci HR 74 C3
Donji Kazanci BIH 83 C5
Donji Koričáni BIH 84 B2
Donji Lapac HR 83 B4
Donji Malovan BIH 84 C2
Donji Miholjac HR 74 C3
Donji Mosti HR 74 B1
Donji Poloj HR 73 C5
Donji-Rujani BIH 83 C5
Donji Srb HR 83 B5
Donji Svilaj BIH 84 A3
Donji Tovarnik SRB 85 B4
Donji Vakuf BIH 84 B2
Donnalucata I 109 C3
Donnemarie-Dontilly F 59 B4
Donnersbach A 73 A4
Donnersbachwald A 73 A4
Donnerskirchen A 64 C2
Donorático I 81 C4
Donostia-San Sebastián E 76 C1
Donovaly SK 65 B5
Donzenac F 67 C6
Donzère F 78 B3
Donzy F 68 A3
Doonbeg IRL 20 B2
Doorn NL 49 A6
Dor E 86 A1
Dorchester GB 29 C5
Dørdal N 33 D6
Dordrecht NL 49 B5
Dörenthe D 50 A3
Dores GB 23 D4
Dorfen D 62 B3
Dorfgastein A 72 A3
Dorfmark D 43 C6
Dorf Mecklenburg D 44 B3
Dorgali I 110 B2
Dorking GB 31 C3
Dormagen D 50 B2
Dormánd H 65 C6
Dormans F 59 A4
Dornava SLO 73 B5
Dornbirn A 71 A4
Dornburg D 52 B1
Dorndorf D 51 C6
Dornecy F 68 A3
Dornes F 68 B3
Dornhan D 61 B4
Dornie GB 22 D3
Dornoch GB 23 D4
Dornum D 43 B4
Dorog H 65 C4
Dorogobuzh RUS 7 D12
Dorohoi RO 11 C9
Dorotea S 115 C13
Dorotowo PL 47 B6
Dörpen D 43 C4
Dorsten D 50 B2
Dortan F 69 B5
Dortmund D 50 B3
Doruchów PL 54 B3
Dorum D 43 B5
Dörverden D 43 C6
Dörzbach D 61 A5
Dos Aguas E 96 B2
Dosbarrios E 95 C3
Döşemealtı TR 119 E5
Dos Hermanas E 99 B5
Dospat BG 116 A6
Dos-Torres E 100 A1
Dötlingen D 43 C5
Dottignies B 49 C4
Döttingen CH 70 A3
Douai F 49 C4
Douarnenez F 56 B1
Douchy F 59 C4
Douchy-les-Mines F 49 C4
Doucier F 69 B5
Doudeville F 58 A1
Doué-la-Fontaine F 67 A4
Douglas
Isle of Man GB 26 A1
South Lanarkshire GB 25 C4
Doulaincourt-Saucourt F 59 B6
Doulevant-le-Château F 59 B5
Doullens F 48 C3
Dounby GB 23 B5
Doune GB 24 B3
Dounreay GB 23 C5
Dour B 49 C4
Dourdan F 58 B3
Dourgne F 77 C5
Dournazac F 67 C5
Douro Calvo P 87 D3
Douvaine F 69 B6
Douvres-la-Délivrande F 57 A5
Douzy F 59 A6
Dover GB 31 C5
Dovje SLO 72 B3
Dovre N 114 F6
Downham Market GB 30 B4
Downhill GB 19 A5
Downpatrick GB 19 B6
Dowra IRL 18 B3
Doxato GR 116 A6
Doyet F 68 B2
Dozule F 57 A5
Drača SRB 85 B5
Dračevo BIH 84 D3
Drachten NL 42 B3
Draga SLO 73 C4
Drăgăşani RO 11 D8
Dragatuš SLO 73 C5
Dragichyn BY 7 E8
Draginja SRB 85 B4
Dragobi AL 105 A5
Dragocvet SRB 85 C6
Dragolovci BIH 84 B2
Dragoni I 103 B7
Dragør DK 41 D2
Dragotina HR 73 C6
Dragotinja BIH 83 A5
Dragozetići HR 82 A3
Draguignan F 79 C5
Drahnsdorf D 52 B3
Drahonice CZ 63 A5
Drahovce SK 64 B3
Drama GR 116 A6
Drammen N 35 C2
Drangedal N 33 C6
Drangsnes IS 111 B4
Dransfeld D 51 B5
Dranske D 45 A5
Draperstown GB 19 B5
Drassburg A 64 C2
Drávaszabolcs H 74 C3
Dravograd SLO 73 B5
Drawno PL 46 B1
Drawsko Pomorskie PL 46 B1
Drayton GB 30 B5
Draženov CZ 62 A3
Draževac SRB 85 B5
Dražice HR 73 C4
Drebkau D 53 B4
Dreieich D 51 C4
Dreisen D 61 A4
Dren KOS 85 C5
Drenovac SRB 85 C6
Drenovci HR 84 B3
Drensteinfurt D 50 B3
Dresden D 53 B3
Dretyń PL 46 A2
Dreux F 58 B2
Dřevohostice CZ 64 A3
Drevsjø N 114 F9
Drewitz D 52 A2
Drezdenko PL 46 C1
Drežnica HR 83 A4
Drežnik-Grad HR 83 B4
Drietona SK 64 B3
Driffield GB 27 A5
Drimnin GB 24 B2
Drimoleague IRL 20 C2
Dringenberg D 51 B5
Drinić BIH 83 B5
Drinjača BIH 85 B4
Drinovci BIH 84 C2
Driopida GR 117 E6
Drivstua N 114 E6
Drlače SRB 85 B4
Drnholec CZ 64 B2
Drniš HR 83 C5
Drnje HR 74 B1
Drnovice CZ 64 A2
Dro I 71 C5
Drøbak N 35 C2
Drobin PL 47 C6
Drochia MD 11 B9
Drochtersen D 43 B6
Drogheda IRL 19 C5
Drohobych UA 11 B7
Droitwich Spa GB 29 A5
Drołtowice PL 54 B2
Dromahair IRL 18 B3
Dromcolliher IRL 20 B3
Dromore
Down GB 19 B5
Tyrone GB 19 B4
Dromore West IRL 18 B3
Dronero I 79 B6
Dronfield GB 27 B4
Drongan GB 24 C3
Dronninglund DK 38 B3
Dronrijp NL 42 B2
Dronten NL 42 C2
Drosendorf A 63 B6
Drösing A 64 B2
Drottningholm S 37 C4
Droué F 58 B2
Drulingen F 60 B3
Drumbeg GB 22 C3
Drumcliff IRL 18 B3
Drumgask GB 23 D4
Drumkeeran IRL 18 B3
Drummore GB 24 D3
Drumnadrochit GB 23 D4
Drumquin GB 19 B4
Drumshanbo IRL 18 B3
Drumsna IRL 19 C4
Drunen NL 49 B6
Druskininkai LT 6 D7
Druten NL 49 B6
Druya BY 7 D9
Družetići SRB 85 B5
Drvar BIH 83 B5
Drvenik HR 84 C2
Drwalew PL 55 B6
Drymen GB 24 B3
Drynoch GB 22 D2
Drzewce PL 54 A2
Drzewiany PL 46 B2
Drzewica PL 55 B5
Dualchi I 110 B1
Duas Igrejas P 87 C4
Dub SRB 85 C4
Dubá CZ 53 C4
Dubăsari MD 11 C10
Duben D 53 B3
Dübendorf CH 70 A3
Dubi CZ 53 C3
Dubica HR 74 C1
Dublin IRL 21 A5
Dubna RUS 7 C14
Dubňany CZ 64 B3
Dubnica nad Váhom SK 64 B4
Dubnik SK 65 C4
Dubno UA 11 A8
Dubodiel SK 64 B4
Dubona SRB 85 B5
Dubovac SRB 85 B6
Dubovic BIH 83 B5
Dubranec HR 73 C5
Dubrava HR 74 C1
Dubrave BIH 84 B3
Dubravica
HR 73 C5
SRB 85 B6
Dubrovnik HR 84 D3
Dubrovytsya UA 7 F9
Ducey F 57 B4
Duchcov CZ 53 C3
Ducherow D 45 B5
Dučina SRB 85 B5
Duclair F 58 A1
Dudar H 74 A2
Duddington GB 30 B3
Duderstadt D 51 B6
Dudeştii Vechi RO 75 B5
Dudley GB 26 C3
Dueñas E 88 C2
Duesund N 32 B2
Dueville I 72 C1
Duffel B 49 B5
Duffield GB 27 C4
Dufftown GB 23 D5
Duga Poljana SRB 85 C5
Duga Resa HR 73 C5
Dugi Rat HR 83 C5
Dugny-sur-Meuse F 59 A6
Dugopolje HR 83 C5
Dugo Selo HR 73 C6
Duino I 72 C3
Duisburg D 50 B2
Dukat AL 105 C5
Dukhovshchina RUS 7 D12
Dukovany CZ 64 A2
Duleek IRL 19 C5
Dülken D 50 B2
Dülmen D 50 B3
Dulovo BG 11 E9
Dulpetorpet N 34 B4
Dulverton GB 29 B4
Dumbarton GB 24 C3
Dümerek TR 118 C6
Dumfries GB 25 C4
Dumlupınar TR 118 D4
Dümpelfeld D 50 C2
Dunaalmás H 65 C4
Dunabogdány H 65 C5
Dunafalva H 74 B3
Dunaföldvár H 74 B3
Dunaharaszti H 75 A4
Dunajská Streda SK 64 C3
Dunakeszi H 65 C5
Dunakiliti H 64 C3
Dunakömlöd H 74 B3
Dunapataj H 75 B3
Dunaszekcsö H 74 B3
Dunaszentgyorgy H 74 B3
Dunatetétlen H 75 B4
Dunaújváros H 74 B3
Dunavecse H 75 B3
Dunbar GB 25 B5
Dunbeath GB 23 C5
Dunblane GB 25 B4
Dunboyne IRL 21 A5
Dundalk IRL 19 B5
Dundee GB 25 B5
Dundrennan GB 25 D4
Dundrum GB 19 B6
Dunfanaghy IRL 19 A4
Dunfermline GB 25 B4
Dungannon GB 19 B5
Dungarvan IRL 21 B4
Dungiven GB 19 B5
Dunglow IRL 18 B3
Dungourney IRL 20 C3
Duninowo PL 46 A2
Đunis SRB 85 C6
Dunkeld GB 25 B4
Dunker S 37 C3
Dunkerque = Dunkirk F 48 B3
Dunkineely IRL 18 B3
Dunkirk = Dunkerque F 48 B3
Dun Laoghaire IRL 21 A5
Dunlavin IRL 21 A5
Dunleer IRL 19 C5
Dun-le-Palestel F 67 B6
Dun-les-Places F 68 A4
Dunlop GB 24 C3
Dunloy GB 19 A5
Dunmanway IRL 20 C2
Dunmore IRL 18 C3
Dunmore East IRL 21 B5
Dunmurry GB 19 B5
Dunnet GB 23 C5
Dunningen D 61 B4
Dunoon GB 24 C3
Duns GB 25 C5
Dunscore GB 25 C4
Dunsford GB 28 C4
Dunshaughlin IRL 21 A5
Dunstable GB 31 C3
Dunster GB 29 B4
Dun-sur-Auron F 68 B2
Dun-sur-Meuse F 59 A6
Dunvegan GB 22 D2
Duplek SLO 73 B5
Dupnitsa BG 11 E7
Durağan TR 16 A7
Durach D 61 C6
Durak TR 118 C3
Đurakovac KOS 85 D5
Durana E 89 B4
Durance F 76 B3
Durango E 89 A4
Durankulak BG 11 E10
Duras F 76 B3
Durban-Corbières F 78 D1
Dürbheim D 61 B4
Durbuy B 49 C6
Dúrcal E 100 C2
Đurdjenovac HR 74 C3
Đurdjevac HR 74 B2

Đurdjevik BIH 84 B3
Düren D 50 C2
Durham GB 25 D6
Đurinci SRB 85 B5
Durlach D 61 B4
Đurmanec HR 73 B5
Durness GB 22 C4
Dürnkrut A 64 B2
Dürrboden CH 71 B4
Dürrenboden CH 70 B3
Durrës AL 105 B5
Durrow IRL 21 B4
Durrus IRL 20 C2
Dursunbey TR 118 C3
Durtal F 57 C5
Durup DK 38 C1
Durusu TR 118 A3
Dusina BIH 84 C2
Dusnok H 75 B3
Dusocin PL 47 B4
Düsseldorf D 50 B2
Dusslingen D 61 B5
Duszniki PL 46 C2
Duszniki-Zdrój PL 54 C1
Dutovlje SLO 72 C3
Duvebo S 40 A4
Duved S 115 D9
Düzağac TR 118 D5
Düzce TR 118 B6
Dvärsätt S 115 D11
Dvor HR 83 A5
Dvorce CZ 64 A3
Dvorníky SK 64 B3
Dvory nad Žitavou SK 64 C4
Dvůr Královénad Labem CZ 53 C5
Dyatkovo RUS 7 E13
Dybvad DK 38 B3
Dyce GB 23 D6
Dygowo PL 46 A1
Dykehead GB 25 B4
Dymchurch GB 31 C5
Dymer UA 11 A11
Dyrnes N 114 D4
Dywity PL 47 B6
Džanići BIH 84 C2
Dziadowa Kłoda PL 54 B2
Działdowo PL 47 B6
Działoszyce PL 55 C5
Działoszyn PL 54 B3
Dziemiany PL 46 A3
Dzierząźnia PL 47 C6
Dzierzgoń PL 47 B5
Dzierzgowo PL 47 B6
Dzierżoniów PL 54 C1
Dzisna BY 7 D10
Dziwnów PL 45 A6
Dzyarzhynsk BY 7 E9
Dzyatlava BY 7 E8

E

Ea E 89 A4
Eaglesfield GB 25 C4
Ealing GB 31 C3
Eardisley GB 29 A4
Earls Barton GB 30 B3
Earl Shilton GB 30 B2
Earlston GB 25 C5
Easington GB 27 B6
Easky IRL 18 B3
Eastbourne GB 31 D4
East Calder GB 25 C4
East Dereham GB 30 B4
Easter Skeld GB 22 A7
East Grinstead GB 31 C4
East Ilsley GB 31 C2
East Kilbride GB 24 C3
Eastleigh GB 31 D2
East Linton GB 25 C5
East Markham GB 27 B5
Easton GB 29 C5
East Wittering GB 31 D3
Eaton Socon GB 30 B3
Eaux-Bonnes F 76 D2
Eauze F 76 C3
Ebberup DK 39 D2
Ebbs A 62 C3
Ebbw Vale GB 29 B4
Ebeleben D 51 B6
Ebeltoft DK 39 C3
Ebene Reichenau A 72 B3
Eben im Pongau A 72 A3
Ebensee A 63 C4
Ebensfeld D 51 C6
Eberbach D 61 A4
Ebergötzen D 51 B6
Ebermann-Stadt D 62 A2
Ebern D 51 C6
Eberndorf A 73 B4
Ebersbach D 53 B4
Ebersberg D 62 B2
Ebersdorf
Bayern D 52 C1
Niedersachsen D 43 B6
Eberstein A 73 B4
Eberswalde D 45 C5
Ebnat-Kappel CH 71 A4
Éboli I 103 C8
Ebrach D 61 A6
Ebreichsdorf A 64 C2
Ebreuil F 68 B3
Ebstorf D 44 B2
Ecclefechan GB 25 C4
Eccleshall GB 26 C3
Eceabat TR 118 B1
Echallens CH 69 B6
Echauri E 76 D1
Echinos GR 116 A7
Échiré F 67 B4
Échirolles F 69 C5
Echourgnac F 76 A3
Echt NL 50 B1
Echte D 51 B6
Echternach L 60 A2
Ecija E 99 B5
Ečka SRB 75 C5
Eckartsberga D 52 B1
Eckelshausen D 51 C4
Eckental D 62 A2
Eckernförde D 44 A1
Eckerö FIN 36 B6
Eckington GB 27 B4
Éclaron F 59 B5
Écommoy F 58 C1
Écouché F 57 B5
Ecouis F 58 A2
Ecséd H 65 C5
Ecsegfalva H 75 A5
Écueillé F 67 A6
Ed S 35 D3
Eda S 34 C4
Eda glasbruk S 34 C4
Edam NL 42 C2
Edane S 35 C4
Edderton GB 23 D4
Ede NL 49 A6
Edebäck S 34 B5
Edebo S 36 B5
Edelény H 65 B6
Edelschrott A 73 A5
Edemissen D 44 C2
Edenbridge GB 31 C4
Edenderry IRL 21 A4
Edenkoben D 61 A4
Edesheim D 61 A4
Edessa GR 116 B4
Edewecht D 43 B4
Edgeworthstown IRL 19 C4
Edinburgh GB 25 C4
Edineţ MD 11 B9
Edirne TR 118 A1
Edland N 33 C4
Edolo I 71 B5
Edøy N 114 D5
Edremit TR 118 C2
Edsbro S 36 C5
Edsbruk S 40 A6
Edsbyn S 36 A2
Edsele S 115 D13
Edsleskog S 35 C4
Edsvalla S 35 C5
Eekloo B 49 B4
Eemshaven NL 42 B3
Eerbeek NL 50 A2
Eersel NL 49 B6
Eferding A 63 B5
Effiat F 68 B3
Efteløt N 35 C1
Egeln D 52 B1
Eger H 65 C6
Egerbakta H 65 C6
Egernsund DK 39 E2
Egersund N 33 D3
Egerszólát H 65 C6
Egervár H 74 B1
Egg
A 71 A4
D 61 B6
Eggby S 35 D5
Eggedal N 32 B6
Eggenburg A 64 B1
Eggenfelden D 62 B3
Eggesin D 45 B6
Eggum N 112 D2
Egham GB 31 C3
Éghezée B 49 C5
Egiertowo PL 47 A4
Egilsstaðir IS 111 B11
Egina GR 117 E5
Eginio GR 116 B4
Egio GR 117 D4
Égletons F 68 C2
Egling D 62 C2
Eglinton GB 19 A4
Eglisau CH 61 C4
Égliseneuve-d'Entraigues F 68 C2
Eglofs D 61 C5
Egmond aan Zee NL 42 C1
Egna I 71 B6
Egosthena GR 117 D5
Egremont GB 26 A2
Egtved DK 39 D2
Eguilles F 79 C4
Eguilly-sous-Bois F 59 B5
Éguzon-Chantôme F 67 B6
Egyek H 65 C6
Egyházasrádóc H 74 A1
Ehekirchen D 62 B2
Ehingen D 61 B5
Ehra-Lessien D 44 C2
Ehrang D 60 A2
Ehrenfriedersdorf D 52 C2
Ehrenhain D 52 C2
Ehrenhausen A 73 B5
Ehringshausen D 51 C4
Ehrwald A 71 A5
Eibar E 89 A4
Eibelstadt D 61 A6
Eibenstock D 52 C2
Eibergen NL 50 A2
Eibiswald A 73 B5
Eichenbarleben D 52 A1
Eichendorf D 62 B3
Eichstätt D 62 B2
Eickelborn D 50 B4
Eide
Hordaland N 32 B3
Møre og Romsdal N 114 E4
Eidet N 112 C7
Eidfjord N 32 B4
Eidsberg N 35 C3
Eidsbugarden N 32 A5
Eidsdal N 114 E4
Eidsfoss N 35 C2
Eidskog N 34 B4
Eidsvåg
Hordaland N 32 B2
Møre og Romsdal N 114 E5
Eidsvoll N 34 B3
Eikefjord N 114 F2
Eikelandsosen N 32 B2
Eiken N 33 D4
Eikesdal N 114 E5
Eikstrand N 35 C1
Eilenburg D 52 B2
Eilsleben D 52 A1
Eina N 34 B2
Einbeck D 51 B5
Eindhoven NL 49 B6
Einsiedeln CH 70 A3
Einville-au-Jard F 60 B2
Eisenach D 51 C6
Eisenberg
Rheinland-Pfalz D 61 A4
Thüringen D 52 C1
Eisenerz A 73 A4
Eisenhüttenstadt D 53 A4
Eisenkappel A 73 B4
Eisenstadt A 64 C2
Eisentratten A 72 B3
Eisfeld D 51 C6
Eisleben D 52 B1
Eislingen D 61 B5
Eitensheim D 62 B2
Eiterfeld D 51 C5
Eitorf D 50 C3
Eivindvik N 32 B2
Eivissa = Ibiza E 97 C1
Eixo P 92 A2
Ejby DK 39 D2
Ejea de los Caballeros E 90 A1
Ejstrupholm DK 39 D2
Ejulve E 90 C2
Eke B 49 C4
Ekeby
Gotland S 37 E5
Skåne S 41 D2
Uppsala S 36 B5
Ekeby-Almby S 37 C2
Ekenäs S 35 D5
Ekenässjön S 40 B5
Ekerö S 37 C4
Eket S 41 C3
Eketorp S 41 C6
Ekevik S 40 A6
Ekkerøy N 113 B19
Ekshärad S 34 B5
Eksingedal N 32 B2
Eksjö S 40 B4
Eksta S 37 E5
Ekträsk S 115 C16
El Alamo
Madrid E 94 B3
Sevilla E 99 B4
El Algar E 101 B5
El Almendro E 98 B3
El Alquián E 101 C3
Élancourt F 58 B2
El Arahal E 99 B5
El Arenal E 94 B1
El Arguellite E 101 A3
Elassona GR 116 C4
El Astillero E 88 A3
Elati GR 116 C3
Żelazno PL 54 C1
El Ballestero E 101 A3
El Barco de Ávila E 93 A5
Elbasan AL 116 A2
El Berrón E 88 A1
El Berrueco E 95 B3
Elbeuf F 58 A1
Elbingerode D 51 B6
Elbląg PL 47 A5
El Bodón E 93 A4
El Bonillo E 95 D4
El Bosque E 99 C5
El Bullaque E 94 C2
Elburg NL 42 C2
El Burgo E 100 C1
El Burgo de Ebro E 90 B2
El Burgo de Osma E 89 C3
El Burgo Ranero E 88 B1
El Buste E 89 C5
El Cabaco E 93 A4
El Callejo E 89 A3
El Campillo E 99 B4
El Campillo de la Jara E 94 C1
El Cañavete E 95 C4
El Carpio E 100 B1
El Carpio de Tajo E 94 C2
El Casar E 95 B3
El Casar de Escalona E 94 B2
El Castillo de las Guardas E 99 B4
El Centenillo E 100 A2
El Cerro E 93 A5
El Cerro de Andévalo E 99 B4
Elche E 96 C2
Elche de la Sierra E 101 A3
Elchingen D 61 B6
El Comenar E 99 C5
El Coronil E 99 B5
El Crucero E 86 A4
El Cubo de Tierra del Vino E 88 C1
El Cuervo E 99 C4
Elda E 101 A5
Eldena D 44 B3
Eldingen D 44 C2
Elefsina GR 117 D5
El Ejido E 101 C3
Elek H 75 B6
Elemir SRB 75 C5
El Escorial E 94 B2
El Espinar E 94 B2
Eleutheroupoli GR 116 B6
El Frago E 90 A2
El Franco E 86 A4
El Frasno E 89 C5
Elgå N 114 E8
El Garrobo E 99 B4
El Gastor E 99 C5
Elgin GB 23 D5
Elgoibar E 89 A4
Elgol GB 22 D2
El Gordo E 93 B5
El Grado E 90 A3
El Granado E 98 B3
El Grao de Castelló E 96 B3
El Grau E 96 C2
Elgshøa N 34 A4
El Higuera E 100 B1
El Hijate E 101 B3
El Hontanar E 96 A1
El Hoyo E 100 A2
Elie GB 25 B5
Elizondo E 76 C1
Ełk PL 6 E7
Elkhovo BG 11 E9
Ellenberg D 61 A6
Ellesmere GB 26 C3
Ellesmere Port GB 26 B3
Ellezelles B 49 C4
Ellingen D 62 A1
Ellmau A 72 A2
Ellon GB 23 D6
Ellös S 35 D3
Ellrich D 51 B6
Ellwangen D 61 B6
Elm
CH 71 B4
D 43 B6
Elmadağ TR 16 B6
El Madroño E 99 B4
El Maillo E 93 A4
Elmalı TR 119 F4
El Masnou E 91 B5
El Mirón E 93 A5
El Molar E 95 B3
El Molinillo E 94 C2
El Morell E 91 B4
Elmshorn D 43 B6
Elmstein D 60 A3
El Muyo E 89 C3
Elne F 91 A5
Elnesvågen N 114 E4
El Olmo E 88 C3
Elorrio E 89 A4
Elöszállás H 74 B3
Elouda GR 117 G7
Éloyes F 60 B2
El Palo E 100 C1
El Pardo E 94 B3
El Payo E 93 A4
El Pedernoso E 95 C4
El Pedroso E 99 B5
El Peral E 95 C5
El Perelló
Tarragona E 90 C3
Valencia E 96 B2
Elphin GB 22 C3
El Picazo E 95 C4
El Pinell de Bray E 90 B3
El Piñero E 88 C1
El Pla de Santa Maria E 91 B4
El Pobo E 90 C2
El Pobo de Dueñas E 95 B5
El Pont d'Armentera E 91 B4
El Port de la Selva E 91 A6
El Port de Llançà E 91 A6
El Port de Sagunt E 96 B2
El Prat de Llobregat E 91 B5
El Provencio E 95 C4
El Puente E 89 A3
El Puente del Arzobispo E 93 B5
El Puerto E 86 A4
El Puerto de Santa María E 99 C4
El Real de la Jara E 99 B4
El Real de San Vincente E 94 B2
El Robledo E 94 C2
El Rocio E 99 B4
El Rompido E 99 B3
El Ronquillo E 99 B4
El Royo E 89 C4
El Rubio E 100 B1
El Sabinar E 101 A3
El Saler E 96 B2
El Salobral E 101 A4
El Saucejo E 99 B5
Els Castells E 91 A4
Elsdorf D 50 C2
Elsenfeld D 61 A5
El Serrat AND 91 A4
Elsfleth D 43 B5
Elspeet NL 50 A1
Elst NL 50 B1
Elstead GB 31 C3
Elster D 52 B2
Elsterberg D 52 C2
Elsterwerda D 52 B3
Elstra D 53 B4
El Temple E 90 B2
El Tiemblo E 94 B2
Eltmann D 51 D6
El Toboso E 95 C4
El Tormillo E 90 B2
El Torno E 93 A5
Eltville D 50 C4
El Valle de las Casas E 88 B1
Elvas P 93 C3
Elvebakken N 113 C12
El Vellón E 95 B3
Elven F 56 C3
El Vendrell E 91 B4
Elverum N 34 B3
El Villar de Arnedo E 89 B4
Elvington GB 27 B5
El Viso E 100 A1
El Viso del Alcor E 99 B5
Elxleben D 51 B6
Ely GB 30 B4
Elzach D 61 B4
Elze D 51 A5
Emådalen S 36 A1
Embleton GB 25 C6
Embonas GR 119 F2
Embrun F 79 B5
Embún E 90 A2
Emden D 43 B4
Emecik TR 119 F2
Emet TR 118 C4
Emirdağ TR 118 C6
Emlichheim D 42 C3
Emmaboda S 40 C5
Emmaljunga S 41 C3
Emmeloord NL 42 C2
Emmen
CH 70 A3
NL 42 C3
Emmendingen D 60 B3
Emmer-Compascuum NL 43 C4
Emmerich D 50 B2
Emmern D 51 A5
Emöd H 65 C6
Émpoli I 81 C4
Emsbüren D 43 C4
Emsdetten D 50 A3
Emsfors S 40 B6
Emskirchen D 62 A1
Emstek D 43 C5
Emsworth GB 31 D3
Emyvale IRL 19 B5
Enafors S 115 D9
Enånger S 115 F14
Encamp AND 91 A4
Encarnaçao P 92 C1
Encinas de Abajo E 94 B1
Encinas de Esgueva E 88 C2
Encinasola E 99 A4
Encinas Reales E 100 B1
Encio E 89 B3
Enciso E 89 B4
Enden N 114 F7
Endingen D 60 B3
Endrinal E 93 A5
Endröd H 75 B5
Enebakk N 34 C3
Eneryda S 40 C4
Enese H 64 C3
Enez TR 116 B8
Enfield IRL 21 A5
Eng A 72 A1
Engelberg CH 70 B3
Engelhartszell A 63 B4
Engelskirchen D 50 C3
Engen D 61 C4
Enger N 34 B2
Engerdal N 114 F8
Engerneset N 34 A4
Enge-sande D 39 E1
Engesvang DK 39 C2
Enghien B 49 C5
Engstingen D 61 B5
Engter D 43 C5
Enguera E 96 C2
Enguidanos E 95 C5
Enkenbach D 60 A3
Enkhuizen NL 42 C2
Enklinge FIN 36 B7
Enköping S 37 C4
Enna I 109 B3
Ennezat F 68 C3
Ennigerloh D 50 B4
Enningdal N 35 D3
Ennis IRL 20 B3
Enniscorthy IRL 21 B5
Enniskean IRL 20 C3
Enniskillen GB 19 B4
Ennistimon IRL 20 B2
Enns A 63 B5
Eno FIN 3 E29
Enontekiö FIN 113 D12
Ens NL 42 C2
Enschede NL 50 A2
Ensdorf D 62 A2
Ensisheim F 60 C3
Enstaberga S 37 D3
Enstone GB 31 C2
Entlebuch CH 70 A3
Entrácque I 80 B1
Entradas P 98 B2
Entrains-sur-Nohain F 68 A3
Entrambasaguas E 88 A3
Entrambasmestas E 88 A3
Entraygues-sur-Truyère F 77 B5
Entre-os-Rios P 87 C2
Entrevaux F 79 C5
Entrin Bajo E 93 C4
Entroncamento P 92 B2
Entzheim F 60 B3
Envermeu F 58 A2
Enviken S 36 B2
Enying H 74 B3
Enzingerboden A 72 A2
Enzklösterle D 61 B4
Épagny F 59 A4
Epalinges CH 70 B1
Epannes F 67 B4
Epanomi GR 116 B4
Epe
D 50 A3
NL 42 C2
Épernay F 59 A4
Épernon F 58 B2
Epfig F 60 B3
Epierre F 69 C6
Épila E 90 B1
Épinac F 69 B4
Épinal F 60 B2
Episcopia I 106 A3
Episkopi CY 120 B1
Epitalio GR 117 E3
Epoisses F 69 A4
Eppenbrunn D 60 A3
Eppendorf D 52 C3
Epping GB 31 C4
Eppingen D 61 A4
Epsom GB 31 C3
Epworth GB 27 B5
Eraclea I 72 C2
Eraclea Mare I 72 C2
Erba I 71 C4
Erbach
Baden-Württemberg D 61 B5
Hessen D 61 A4
Erbalunga F 102 A2
Erbendorf D 62 A3
Érchie I 105 C3
Ercolano I 103 C7
Ercsi H 74 A3
Érd H 74 A3
Erdek TR 118 B2
Erdemli TR 16 C7
Erdevik SRB 85 A4
Erding D 62 B2
Erdötelek H 65 C6
Erdut HR 75 C4
Erdweg D 62 B2
Ereğli
Konya TR 16 C7
Zonguldak TR 118 A6
Erenkaya TR 119 E7
Eresfjord N 114 E5
Eresos GR 116 C7
Eretria GR 116 D5
Erfde D 43 A6
Erfjord N 33 C3
Erfstadt D 50 C2
Erfurt D 52 C1
Ērgli LV 7 C8
Ergoldsbach D 62 B3
Eriboll GB 22 C4
Érice I 108 A1
Ericeira P 92 C1
Eğridir TR 119 E5
Eriksberg S 115 B12
Eriksmåla S 40 C5
Eringsboda S 40 C5
Eriswil CH 70 A2
Erithres GR 117 D5
Erkelenz D 50 B2
Erkner D 45 C5
Erkrath D 50 B2
Erla E 90 A2
Erlangen D 62 A2
Erli I 80 B2
Erlsbach A 72 B2
Ermelo NL 49 A6
Ermenak TR 16 C6
Ermenonville F 58 A3
Ermezinde P 87 C2
Ermidas P 98 A2
Ermioni GR 117 E5
Ermoupoli GR 117 E6
Ermsleben D 52 B1
Erndtebrück D 50 C4
Ernée F 57 B5
Ernestinovo HR 74 C3
Ernstbrunn A 64 B2
Erolzheim D 61 B6
Erquelinnes B 49 C5
Erquy F 56 B3
Erra P 92 C2
Erratzu E 76 C1
Errindlev DK 44 A3
Erro E 76 D1
Ersa F 102 A2
Érsekcsanád H 75 B3
Ersekë AL 116 B2
Érsekvadkert H 65 C5
Erstein F 60 B3
Erstfeld CH 70 B3
Ertebølle DK 38 C2
Ertingen D 61 B5
Ervedal
Coimbra P 92 A2
Portalegre P 92 B3
Ervenik HR 83 B4
Ervidel P 98 B2
Ervy-le-Châtel F 59 B4
Erwitte D 51 B4
Erxleben D 52 A1
Erzsébet H 74 B3
Esbjerg DK 39 D1
Esbly F 58 B3
Escacena del Campo E 99 B4
Escairón E 86 B3
Escalada E 88 B3
Escalante E 89 A3
Escalaplano I 110 C2
Escalona E 94 B2
Escalona del Prado E 94 A2
Escalonilla E 94 C2
Escalos de Baixo P 92 B3
Escalos de Cima P 92 B3
Escamilla E 95 B4
Es Caná E 97 B1
Escañuela E 100 B1
Es Castell E 97 B4
Escatrón E 90 B2
Eschach D 61 C5
Eschau D 61 A5
Eschede D 44 C2
Eschenau D 62 A2
Eschenbach D 62 A2
Eschenz CH 61 C4
Eschershausen D 51 B5
Esch-sur-Alzette L 60 A1
Esch-sur-Sûre L 60 A1
Eschwege D 51 B6
Eschweiler D 50 C2
Escobasa de Almazán E 89 C4
Escoeuilles F 48 C2
Escombreras E 101 B5
Escos F 76 C1
Escource F 76 B1
Escragnolles F 79 C5
Escrick GB 27 B4
Escurial E 93 B5
Escurial de la Sierra E 93 A5
Esens D 43 B4
Esgos E 87 B3
Esher GB 31 C3
Eskdalemuir GB 25 C4
Eskifjörður IS 111 B12
Eskilhem S 37 E5
Eskilsäter S 35 D5
Eskilstrup DK 39 E4
Eskilstuna S 37 C3
Eskipazar TR 118 B7
Eskişehir TR 118 C5
Eslarn D 62 A3
Eslava E 89 B5
Eslida E 96 B2
Eslohe D 50 B4
Eslöv S 41 D3
Eşme TR 119 D3
Es Mercadal E 97 B4
Es Migjorn Gran E 97 B4
Espa N 34 B3
Espalion F 78 B1
Esparragalejo E 93 C4
Esparragosa del Caudillo E 93 C5
Esparragossa de la Serena E 93 C5
Esparreguera E 91 B4
Esparron F 79 C4
Espe N 32 B3
Espedal N 33 D3
Espejo
Alava E 89 B3
Córdoba E 100 B1
Espeland N 32 B2
Espelkamp D 43 C5
Espeluche F 78 B3
Espeluy E 100 A2
Espera E 99 C5
Esperança P 93 B3
Espéraza F 77 D5
Espéria I 103 B6
Espevær N 33 C2
Espiel E 99 A5
Espinama E 88 A2
Espiñaredo E 86 A3
Espinasses F 79 B5
Espinelves E 91 B5
Espinhal P 92 A2
Espinho P 87 C2
Espinilla E 88 A2
Espinosa de Cerrato E 88 C3
Espinosa de los Monteros E 89 A3
Espinoso del Rey E 94 C2
Espirito Santo P 98 B3
Espluga de Francolí E 91 B4
Esplús E 90 B3
Espolla E 91 A5
Espoo FIN 6 A8
Esporles E 97 B2
Es Port d'Alcúdia E 97 B3
Esposende P 87 C2
Espot E 91 A4
Es Pujols E 97 C1
Esquedas E 90 A2
Esquivias E 94 B3
Essay F 57 B6
Essen
B 49 B5
Niedersachsen D 43 C4
Nordrhein-Westfalen D 50 B3
Essenbach D 62 B3
Essertaux F 58 A3
Essingen D 61 B6
Esslingen D 61 B5
Es Soleràs E 90 B3
Essoyes F 59 B5
Estacas E 87 B2
Estadilla E 90 A3
Estagel F 78 D1
Estaires F 48 C3
Estang F 76 C2
Estarreja P 87 D2
Estartit E 91 A6
Estavayer-le-Lac CH 70 B1
Este I 72 C1
Esteiro E 86 A2
Estela P 87 C2
Estella E 89 B4
Estellencs E 97 B2
Estepa E 100 B1
Estépar E 88 B3
Estepona E 99 C5
Esternay F 59 B4
Esterri d'Aneu E 91 A4
Esterwegen D 43 C4
Estissac F 59 B4
Estivadas E 87 B3
Estivareilles F 68 B2
Estivella E 96 B2
Estói P 98 B3
Estopiñán E 90 B3
Estoril P 92 C1
Estoublon F 79 C5
Estrée-Blanche F 48 C3
Estrées-St Denis F 58 A3
Estrela P 98 A3
Estremera E 95 B3
Estremoz P 92 C3
Estuna S 36 C5
Esyres F 67 A5
Esztergom H 65 C4
Étables-sur-Mer F 56 B3
Étain F 60 A1
Étalans F 69 A6
Étalle B 60 A1
Étampes F 58 B3
Étang-sur-Arroux F 69 B4
Étaples F 48 C2
Étauliers F 67 C4
Etili TR 118 C1
Etna N 34 B1
Etne N 33 C2
Étoges F 59 B4
Etoliko GR 116 D3
Eton GB 31 C3
Étréaupont F 59 A4
Étréchy F 58 B3
Étrépagny F 58 A2
Étretat F 57 A6
Étroeungt F 49 C4
Étroubles I 70 C2
Ettal D 62 C2
Ettelbruck L 60 A2
Etten NL 49 B5
Ettenheim D 60 B3
Ettington GB 29 A6
Ettlingen D 61 B4
Ettringen D 62 B1
Étuz F 69 A5
Etxarri-Aranatz E 89 B4
Etyek H 74 A3
Eu F 48 C2
Euerdorf D 51 C6
Eulate E 89 B4
Eupen B 50 C2
Europoort NL 49 B5
Euskirchen D 50 C2
Eutin D 44 A2
Evanger N 32 B3
Évaux-les-Bains F 68 B2
Evciler
Afyon TR 119 D4
Çanakkale TR 118 C1
Evenskjær N 112 D5
Evenstad N 34 A3
Evercreech GB 29 B5
Evergem B 49 B4
Everöd S 41 D4
Eversberg D 51 B4
Everswinkel D 50 B3
Evertsberg S 34 A5
Evesham GB 29 A6
Évian-les-Bains F 69 B6
Evisa F 102 A1
Evje N 33 D4
Evolène CH 70 B2
Évora P 92 C3
Evoramonte P 92 C3
Evran F 57 B4
Evrecy F 57 A5
Évreux F 58 A2
Évron F 57 B5
Évry F 58 B3
Ewell GB 31 C3
Ewersbach D 50 C4
Excideuil F 67 C6
Exeter GB 29 C4
Exmes F 57 B6
Exminster GB 29 C4
Exmouth GB 29 C4
Eydehamn N 33 D5
Eye
Peterborough GB 30 B3
Suffolk GB 30 B5
Eyemouth GB 25 C5
Eyguians F 79 B4
Eyguières F 79 C4
Eygurande F 68 C2
Eylie F 77 D3
Eymet F 77 B3
Eymoutiers F 68 C1
Eynsham GB 31 C2
Eyrarbakki IS 111 D4
Eystrup D 43 C6
Ezaro E 86 B1
Ezcaray E 89 B4
Ezcároz E 76 D1
Ezine TR 118 C1
Ezmoriz P 87 D2

F

Fabara E 90 B3
Fábbrico I 81 B4
Fåberg N 34 A2
Fabero E 86 B4
Fábiánsebestyén H 75 B5
Fåborg DK 39 D3
Fabrègues F 78 C2
Fabriano I 82 C1
Fabrizia I 106 C3
Facha P 87 C2
Facinas E 99 C5
Fačkov SK 65 A4
Fadagosa P 92 B3
Fadd H 74 B3
Faédis I 72 B3
Faenza I 81 B5
Fafe P 87 C2
Fagagna I 72 B3
Făgăras RO 11 D8
Fågelberget S 115 C11
Fågelfors S 40 B5
Fågelmara S 41 C5
Fågelsta S 37 D2
Fagerås S 35 C5
Fagerheim N 32 B4
Fagerhøy N 34 A1
Fagerhult S 40 B5
Fagerlund N 34 B2
Fagernes
Oppland N 32 B6
Troms N 112 C8
Fagersanna S 35 D6
Fagersta S 36 B2
Fåglavik S 35 D5
Fagnano Castello I 106 B3
Fagnières F 59 B5
Faido CH 70 B3
Fains-Véel F 59 B6
Fairford GB 29 B6
Fairlie GB 24 C3
Fajsz H 74 B3
Fakenham GB 30 B4
Fåker S 115 D11
Fakse DK 39 D5
Fakse Ladeplads DK 41 D2
Falaise F 57 B5
Falcade I 72 B1
Falcarragh IRL 18 A3
Falces E 89 B5
Fălciu RO 11 C10
Falconara I 109 B3
Falconara Maríttima I 82 C2
Falcone I 109 A4
Faldingworth GB 27 B5
Falerum S 37 D3
Făleşti MD 11 C9
Falkenberg
Bayern D 62 A3
Bayern D 62 B3
Brandenburg D 52 B3
S 40 C2
Falkensee D 45 C5
Falkenstein
Bayern D 62 A3
Sachsen D 52 C2
Falkenthal D 45 C5
Falkirk GB 25 B4
Falkland GB 25 B4
Falköping S 35 D5
Fall D 62 C2
Falla S 37 D2
Fallingbostel D 43 C6
Falmouth GB 28 C2
Falset E 90 B3
Fălticeni RO 11 C9
Falun S 36 B2
Famagusta CY 120 A2
Fammestad N 32 B2
Fana N 32 B2
Fanano I 81 B4
Fanari GR 116 C3
Fanjeaux F 77 C5
Fano I 82 C2
Fântânele RO 75 B6
Fara in Sabina I 102 A5
Faramontanos de Tábara E 88 C1
Fara Novarese I 70 C3
Farasdues E 90 A1
Fårbo S 40 B6
Fareham GB 31 D2
Färentuna S 37 C4
Färgelanda S 35 D3
Färila S 115 F12
Faringdon GB 31 C2
Faringe S 36 C5
Farini I 80 B3
Fariza E 87 C4
Färjestaden S 41 C6
Farkadona GR 116 C4
Farkasfa H 73 B6
Farlete E 90 B2
Färlöv S 41 C4
Farmos H 75 A4
Farnă SK 65 C4
Färnäs S 36 B1
Farnborough GB 31 C3
Farnese I 102 A4
Farnham GB 31 C3
Farnroda D 51 C6
Faro P 98 B3
Fåro S 37 E6
Fårösund S 37 E6
Farra d'Alpago I 72 B2
Farranfore IRL 20 B2
Farre DK 39 C2
Farsala GR 116 C4
Farsø DK 38 C2
Farsund N 33 D3
Farum DK 41 D2
Fårup DK 38 C2
Fasana I 103 C8
Fasano I 104 C3
Fáskrúðsfjörður IS 111 C11
Fassberg D 44 C2
Fastiv UA 11 A10
Fastnäs S 34 B5
Fatesh RUS 7 E13
Fátima P 92 B2
Fatmomakke S 115 B12
Fättjaur S 115 B12
Faucogney-et-la-Mer F 60 C2
Fauguerolles F 76 B3
Faulenrost D 45 B4
Faulquemont F 60 A2
Fauquembergues F 48 C3
Fauske N 112 E4
Fauville-en-Caux F 58 A1
Fauvillers B 60 A1
Fåvang N 34 A2
Favara
E 96 B2
I 108 B2
Faverges F 69 C6
Faverney F 60 C2
Faversham GB 31 C4
Favignana I 108 B1
Fawley GB 31 D2
Fay-aux-Loges F 58 C3
Fayence F 79 C5
Fayet F 78 C1
Fayl-Billot F 60 C1
Fayón E 90 B3
Fearn GB 23 D5
Fécamp F 58 A1
Feda N 33 D3
Fedje N 32 B1
Feeny GB 19 B4
Fegen S 40 B3
Fegyvernek H 75 A5
Fehrbellin D 45 C4
Fehring A 73 B6
Feichten A 71 A5
Feiring N 34 B3
Feistritz im Rosental A 73 B4
Feke TR 16 C7
Feketić SRB 75 C4
Felanitx E 97 B3
Feld am See A 72 B3
Feldbach A 73 B5
Feldberg D 45 B5
Feldkirch A 71 A4
Feldkirchen in Kärnten A 73 B4
Feldkirchen-Westerham D 62 C2
Felgueiras P 87 C2
Felitto I 103 C8
Félix E 101 C3
Felixstowe GB 31 C5
Felizzano I 80 B2
Felletin F 68 C2
Fellingsbro S 37 C2
Felnac RO 75 B6
Felnémet H 65 C6
Felpéc H 74 A2
Fels am Wagram A 64 B1
Felsberg D 51 B5
Felsönyék H 74 B3
Felsöszentiván H 75 B4
Felsöszentmárton H 74 C2
Felsözsolca H 65 B6
Felsted DK 39 E2
Feltre I 72 B1
Femsjö S 40 C3
Fenagh IRL 19 B4
Fene E 86 A2
Fenestrelle I 79 A6
Fénétrange F 60 B3
Feneu F 57 C5
Fengersfors S 35 D4
Fenit IRL 20 B2
Fensmark DK 39 D4
Fenwick GB 24 C3
Feolin Ferry GB 24 C1
Ferbane IRL 21 A4
Ferdinandovac HR 74 B2
Ferdinandshof D 45 B5
Fère-Champenoise F 59 B4
Fère-en-Tardenois F 59 A4
Ferentillo I 102 A5
Ferentino I 103 B6
Feres GR 116 B8
Feria E 93 C4
Feričanci HR 74 C2
Ferizli TR 118 B5
Ferla I 109 B3
Ferlach A 73 B4
Ferleiten A 72 A2
Fermil P 87 C3
Fermo I 82 C2
Fermoselle E 87 C4
Fermoy IRL 20 B3
Fernancabellero E 94 C3
Fernán Nuñéz E 100 B1
Fernán Peréz E 101 C3
Fernão Ferro P 92 C1
Fernay-Voltaire F 69 B6
Ferndown GB 29 C6
Ferness GB 23 D5
Fernhurst GB 31 C3
Ferns IRL 21 B5
Ferpécle CH 70 B2
Ferrals-les-Corbières F 78 C1
Ferrandina I 104 C2
Ferrara I 81 B5
Ferrara di Monte Baldo I 71 C5
Ferreira E 86 A3
Ferreira do Alentejo P 98 A2
Ferreira do Zêzere P 92 B2
Ferreras de Abajo E 87 C4
Ferreras de Arriba E 87 C4
Ferreries E 97 B4
Ferreruela E 90 B1
Ferreruela de Tabara E 87 C4
Ferret CH 70 C2
Ferrette F 70 A2
Ferriere I 80 B3
Ferrière-la-Grande F 49 C4
Ferrières
Hautes-Pyrénées F 76 C2
Loiret F 58 B3
Oise F 58 A3
Ferrières-sur-Sichon F 68 B3
Ferrol E 86 A2
Ferryhill GB 27 A4
Fertörakos H 64 C2
Fertöszentmiklós H 64 C2
Ferwerd NL 42 B2
Festieux F 59 A4
Festøy N 114 E3
Festvåg N 112 E3
Feteşti RO 11 D9
Fethard
Tipperary IRL 21 B4
Wexford IRL 21 B5
Fethiye TR 119 F4
Fetsund N 34 C3
Fettercairn GB 25 B5
Feucht D 62 A2
Feuchtwangen D 61 A6
Feudingen D 50 C4
Feuges F 59 B5
Feuquières F 58 A2
Feurs F 69 C4
Fevik N 33 D5
Ffestiniog GB 26 C2
Fiamignano I 102 A6
Fiano I 70 C2
Ficarazzi I 108 A2
Ficarolo I 81 B5
Fichtelberg D 52 C1
Ficulle I 82 D1
Fidenza I 81 B4
Fidjeland N 33 D3
Fieberbrunn A 72 A2
Fier AL 105 C5
Fiera di Primiero I 72 B1
Fierzë AL 105 A6
Fiesch CH 70 B3
Fiesso Umbertiano I 81 B5
Figari F 102 B2
Figeac F 77 B5
Figeholm S 40 B6
Figgjo N 33 D2
Figline Valdarno I 81 C5
Figols E 90 A3
Figueira da Foz P 92 A2
Figueira de Castelo Rodrigo P 87 D4
Figueira dos Caveleiros P 98 A2
Figueiredo P 92 B3
Figueiredo de Alva P 87 D3
Figueiródos Vinhos P 92 B2
Figueres E 91 A5
Figueroles E 96 A2
Figueruela de Arriba E 87 C4
Filadélfia I 106 C3
Fil'akovo SK 65 B5
Filderstadt D 61 B5
Filey GB 27 A5
Filiaşi RO 11 D7
Filiates GR 116 C2
Filiatra GR 117 E3
Filipstad S 35 C6
Filisur CH 71 B4
Fillan N 114 D5
Filotio GR 117 E7
Filottrano I 82 C2
Filskov DK 39 D2
Filton GB 29 B5
Filtvet N 35 C2
Filzmoos A 72 A3
Finale Emília I 81 B5
Finale Ligure I 80 B2
Fiñana E 101 B3
Finby FIN 36 B7
Fincham GB 30 B4
Finchingfield GB 31 C4
Findhorn GB 23 D5
Findochty GB 23 D6
Finike TR 119 F5
Finkenberg A 72 A1
Finnea IRL 19 C4
Finneidfjord N 115 A10
Finnerödja S 37 D1
Finnskog N 34 B4
Finnsnes N 112 C7
Finntorp S 35 C4
Finócchio I 102 B5
Finsjö S 40 B6
Finsland N 33 D4
Finspång S 37 D2
Finsterwalde D 53 B3
Finsterwolde NL 43 B4
Finstown GB 23 B5
Fintona GB 19 B4
Fionnphort GB 24 B1
Fiorenzuola d'Arda I 81 B3
Firenze = Florence I 81 C5
Firenzuola I 81 B5
Firmi F 77 B5
Firminy F 69 C4
Firmo I 106 B3
Fischamend Markt A 64 B2
Fischbach
A 73 A5
D 60 A3
Fischbeck D 44 C4
Fischen D 71 A5
Fishbourne GB 31 D2
Fishguard GB 28 B3
Fiskardo GR 116 D2
Fiskebäckskil S 35 D3
Fiskebøl N 112 D3
Fismes F 59 A4
Fisterra E 86 B1
Fitero E 89 B5
Fitjar N 32 C2
Fiuggi I 102 B6
Fiumata I 102 A6
Fiumefreddo Brúzio I 106 B3
Fiumefreddo di Sicilia I 109 B4
Fiumicino I 102 B5
Fivemiletown GB 19 B4
Fivizzano I 81 B4
Fjälkinge S 41 C4
Fjällåsen S 112 E9
Fjällbacka S 35 D3
Fjæra N 32 C3
Fjärdhundra S 36 C3
Fjellerup DK 38 C3
Fjerritslev DK 38 B2
Fjordgard N 112 C6
Fjugesta S 37 C1
Flå N 32 B6
Flåbygd N 33 C5

Flaça E 91 A5
Flace F 69 B4
Fladungen D 51 C6
Flaine F 70 B1
Flaka FIN 36 B7
Flåm N 32 B4
Flamatt CH 70 B2
Flamborough GB 27 A5
Flammersfeld D 50 C3
Flassans-sur-Issole F 79 C5
Flatdal N 33 C5
Flatebø N 32 B3
Flateby N 34 C3
Flateland N 33 C4
Flateyri IS 111 A2
Flatøydegard N 32 B6
Flatråker N 32 C2
Flattach A 72 B3
Flatvarp S 37 E3
Flauenskjold DK 38 B3
Flavigny-sur-Moselle
F 60 B2
Flavy-le-Martel F 59 A4
Flawil CH 71 A4
Flayosc F 79 C5
Flechtingen D 44 C3
Fleckeby D 44 A1
Fleet GB 31 C3
Fleetmark D 44 C3
Fleetwood GB 26 B2
Flehingen D 61 A4
Flekke N 32 A2
Flekkefjord N 33 D3
Flen S 37 C3
Flensburg D 39 E2
Fleringe S 37 E5
Flerohopp S 40 C5
Flers F 57 B5
Flesberg N 32 C6
Fleurance F 77 C3
Fleuré F 67 B5
Fleurier CH 69 B6
Fleurus B 49 C5
Fleury
Hérault F 78 C2
Yonne F 59 C4
Fleury-les-Aubrais F 58 C2
Fleury-sur-Andelle F 58 A2
Fleury-sur-Orne F 57 A5
Flieden D 51 C5
Flimby GB 26 A2
Flims CH 71 B4
Flines-lèz-Raches F 49 C4
Flint GB 26 B2
Flirey F 60 B1
Flirsch A 71 A5
Flisa N 34 B4
Flisby S 40 B4
Fliseryd S 40 B6
Flix E 90 B3
Flixecourt F 48 C3
Flize F 59 A5
Flobecq B 49 C4
Floby S 35 D5
Floda S 40 B2
Flodden GB 25 C5
Flogny-la-Chapelle F 59 C4
Flöha D 52 C3
Flonheim D 61 A4
Florac F 78 B2
Floreffe B 49 C5
Florence = Firenze I 81 C5
Florennes B 49 C5
Florensac F 78 C2
Florentin F 77 C5
Florenville B 59 A6
Flores de Avila E 94 B1
Floresta I 109 B3
Floreşti MD 11 C10
Florídia I 109 B4
Florina GR 116 B3
Florø N 114 F2
Flörsheim D 51 C4
Floss D 62 A3
Fluberg N 34 B2
Flúðir IS 111 C5
Flühli CH 70 B3
Flumet F 69 C6
Fluminimaggiore I 110 C1
Flums CH 71 A4
Flyeryd S 41 C5
Flygsfors S 40 C5
Foča BIH 84 C3
Foça TR 118 D1
Fochabers GB 23 D5
Focşani RO 11 D9
Foel GB 26 C2
Foeni RO 75 C5
Fogdö S 37 C3
Fóggia I 104 B1
Foglianise I 103 B7
Föglö FIN 36 B7
Fohnsdorf A 73 A4
Foiano della Chiana I 81 C5
Foix F 77 D4
Fojnica
BIH 84 C2
BIH 84 C3
Fokino RUS 7 E13
Fokstua N 114 E6
Földeák H 75 B5
Foldereid N 114 C9
Főldes H 75 A6
Folegandros GR 117 F6
Folelli F 102 A2
Folgaria I 71 C6
Folgosinho P 92 A3
Folgoso de la Ribera
E 86 B4
Folgoso do Courel E 86 B3
Foligno I 82 D1
Folkärna S 36 B3
Folkestad N 114 E3
Folkestone GB 31 C5
Follafoss N 114 D8
Folldal N 114 E6
Follebu N 34 A2
Follina I 72 C2
Föllinge S 115 D11
Follónica I 81 D4
Fölsbyn S 35 C4
Foncebadón E 86 B4
Foncine-le-Bas F 69 B6
Fondevila E 87 C2
Fondi I 103 B6
Fondo I 71 B6
Fonelas E 100 B2
Fonfría
Teruel E 90 C1
Zamora E 87 C4
Fonnes N 32 B1
Fonni I 110 B2
Fontaine F 59 B5
Fontainebleau F 58 B3
Fontaine de Vaucluse
F 79 C4
Fontaine-Française F 69 A5
Fontaine-le-Dun F 58 A1
Fontan F 80 B1
Fontanarejo E 94 C2
Fontane I 80 B1
Fontanélice I 81 B5
Fontanières F 68 B2
Fontanosas E 100 A1
Fonteblanda I 102 A4
Fontenay-le-Comte F 66 B4
Fontenay-Trésigny F 59 B3
Fontevrault-l'Abbaye
F 67 A5
Fontiveros E 94 B2
Fontoy F 60 A1
Fontpédrouse F 91 A5
Font-Romeu F 91 A5
Fontstown IRL 21 A5
Fonyód H 74 B2
Fonz E 90 A3
Fonzaso I 72 B1
Fóppolo I 71 B4
Föra S 41 B6
Forbach
D 61 B4
F 60 A2
Forcall E 90 C2
Forcalquier F 79 C4
Forcarei E 86 B2
Forchheim D 62 A2
Forchtenau A 64 C2
Forchtenberg D 61 A5
Ford GB 24 B2
Førde
Hordaland N 33 C2
Sogn og Fjordane N 32 A2
Förderstedt D 52 B1
Førdesfjorden N 33 C2
Fordham GB 30 B4
Fordingbridge GB 29 C6
Fordon PL 47 B4
Fordongiánus I 110 C1
Forenza I 104 C1
Foresta di Búrgos I 110 B1
Forfar GB 25 B5
Forges-les-Eaux F 58 A2
Foria I 106 A2
Forio I 103 C6
Forjães P 87 C2
Førland N 33 D4
Forlì I 81 B6
Forlimpopoli I 82 B1
Formazza I 70 B3
Formby GB 26 B2
Formerie F 58 A2
Fórmia I 103 B6
Formígine I 81 B4
Formigliana I 70 C3
Formiguères F 91 A5
Fornalutx E 97 B2
Fornåsa S 37 D2
Fornelli I 110 B1
Fornells E 97 A4
Fornelos de Montes
E 87 B2
Fornes E 100 C2
Forneset N 112 C8
Forni Avoltri I 72 B2
Forni di Sopra I 72 B2
Forni di Sotto I 72 B2
Forno
Piemonte I 70 C3
Piemonte I 79 A6
Forno Alpi-Gráie I 70 C2
Forno di Zoldo I 72 B2
Fornos de Algodres
P 92 A3
Fornovo di Taro I 81 B4
Foros do Arrão P 92 B2
Forráskút H 75 B4
Forres GB 23 D5
Forriolo E 87 B3
Fors S 36 B3
Forsand N 33 D3
Forsbacka S 36 B3
Forserum S 40 B4
Forshaga S 35 C5
Forsheda S 40 B3
Forsinain GB 23 C5
Førslev DK 39 D4
Förslöv S 41 C2
Forsmark
Uppsala S 36 B5
Västerbotten S 115 B12
Forsmo S 115 D14
Forsnäs S 115 A15
Forsnes N 114 D5
Forssa FIN 3 F25
Forssjöbruk S 37 D3
Forst D 53 B4
Forsvik S 37 D1
Fortanete E 90 C2
Fort Augustus GB 22 D4
Forte dei Marmi I 81 C4
Fortezza I 72 B1
Forth GB 25 C4
Fort-Mahon-Plage F 48 C2
Fortrie GB 23 D6
Fortrose GB 23 D4
Fortun N 32 A4
Fortuna E 101 A4
Fortuneswell GB 29 C5
Fort William GB 24 B2
Forvik N 115 B9
Fos F 77 D3
Fosdinovo I 81 B4
Foss N 32 B6
Fossacésia I 103 A7
Fossano I 80 B1
Fossato di Vico I 82 C1
Fossbakken N 112 D6
Fosse-la-Ville B 49 C5
Fossombrone I 82 C1
Fos-sur-Mer F 78 C3
Fot H 65 C5
Fouchères F 59 B5
Fouesnant F 56 C1
Foug F 60 B1
Fougères F 57 B4
Fougerolles F 60 C2
Foulain F 59 B6
Fountainhall GB 25 C5
Fouras F 66 C3
Fourchambault F 68 A3
Fourmies F 49 C5
Fourna GR 116 C3
Fournels F 78 B2
Fourni GR 119 E1
Fournols F 68 C3
Fourques F 91 A5
Fourquevaux F 77 C4
Fours F 68 B3
Fowey GB 28 C3
Foxdale GB 26 A1
Foxford IRL 18 C2
Foyers GB 23 D4
Foynes IRL 20 B2
Foz E 86 A3
Foza I 72 C1
Foz do Arelho P 92 B1
Foz do Giraldo P 92 B3
Frabosa Soprana I 80 B1
Frades de la Sierra E 93 A5
Fraga E 90 B3
Fragagnano I 104 C3
Frailes E 100 B2
Fraire B 49 C5
Fraize F 60 B2
Framlingham GB 30 B5
Frammersbach D 51 C5
Framnes N 35 C2
França P 87 C4
Francaltroff F 60 B2
Francavilla al Mare I 103 A7
Francavilla di Sicília
I 109 B4
Francavilla Fontana
I 104 C3
Francavilla in Sinni I 106 A3
Francescas F 77 B3
Franco P 87 C3
Francofonte I 109 B3
Francos E 89 C3
Frändefors S 35 D4
Franeker NL 42 B2
Frangy F 69 B5
Frankenau D 51 B4
Frankenberg
Hessen D 51 B4
Sachsen D 52 C3
Frankenburg A 63 B4
Frankenfels A 63 C6
Frankenmarkt A 63 C4
Frankenthal D 61 A4
Frankfurt
Brandenburg D 45 C6
Hessen D 51 C4
Frankowo PL 47 A6
Frankrike S 115 D10
Fränsta S 115 E13
Františkovy Lázně
CZ 52 C2
Franzburg D 45 A4
Frascati I 102 B5
Frasdorf D 62 C3
Fraserburgh GB 23 D6
Frashër AL 116 B2
Frasne F 69 B6
Frasnes-lez-Anvaing
B 49 C4
Frasseto F 102 B2
Frastanz A 71 A4
Fratel P 92 B3
Fratta Todina I 82 D1
Frauenau D 63 B4
Frauenfeld CH 70 A3
Frauenkirchen A 64 C2
Frauenstein D 52 C3
Frauental A 73 B5
Frayssinet F 77 B4
Frayssinet-le-Gélat F 77 B4
Frechas P 87 C3
Frechen D 50 C2
Frechilla E 88 B2
Freckenhorst D 50 B3
Fredeburg D 50 B4
Fredelsloh D 51 B5
Fredeng N 34 B2
Fredensborg DK 41 D2
Fredericia DK 39 D2
Frederiks DK 39 C2
Frederikshavn DK 38 B3
Frederikssund DK 39 D5
Frederiksværk DK 39 D5
Fredrika S 115 C15
Fredriksberg S 34 B6
Fredriksdal S 40 B4
Fredrikstad N 35 C2
Fregenal de la Sierra
E 99 A4
Fregene I 102 B5
Freiberg D 52 C3
Freiburg
Baden-Württemberg
D 60 C3
Niedersachsen D 43 B6
Freienhagen D 51 B5
Freienhufen D 53 B3
Freiensteinau D 51 C5
Freihung D 62 A2
Freilassing D 62 C3
Freisen D 60 A3
Freising D 62 B2
Freistadt A 63 B5
Freital D 52 B3
Freixedas P 93 A3
Freixo de Espada à Cinta
P 87 C4
Fréjus F 79 C5
Fremdingen D 61 B6
Frenštát pod Radhoštěm
CZ 64 A4
Freren D 43 C4
Freshford IRL 21 B4
Freshwater GB 31 D2
Fresnay-sur-Sarthe F 57 B6
Fresneda de la Sierra
E 95 B4
Fresneda de la Sierra
Tiron E 89 B3
Fresnedillas E 94 B2
Fresnes-en-Woevre F 60 A1
Fresne-St Mamès F 69 A5
Fresno Alhandiga E 94 B1
Fresno de la Ribera E 88 C1
Fresno de la Vega E 88 B1
Fresno de Sayago E 87 C5
Fresnoy-Folny F 58 A2
Fresnoy-le-Grand F 59 A4
Fressenville F 48 C2
Fresvik N 32 A3
Fréteval F 58 C2
Fretigney F 69 A5
Freudenberg
Baden-Württemberg
D 61 A5
Nordrhein-Westfalen
D 50 C3
Freudenstadt D 61 B4
Freux B 49 D6
Frévent F 48 C3
Freyburg D 52 B1
Freyenstein D 44 B4
Freyming-Merlebach
F 60 A2
Freystadt D 62 A2
Freyung D 63 B4
Frias de Albarracin E 95 B5
Fribourg CH 70 B2
Frick CH 70 A3
Fridafors S 41 C4
Fridaythorpe GB 27 A5
Friedberg
A 73 A6
Bayern D 62 B1
Hessen D 51 C4
Friedeburg D 43 B4
Friedewald D 51 C5
Friedland
Brandenburg D 53 A4
Mecklenburg-Vorpommern D 45 B5
Niedersachsen D 51 B5
Friedrichroda D 51 C6
Friedrichsdorf D 51 C4
Friedrichshafen D 61 C5
Friedrichskoog D 43 A5
Friedrichstadt D 43 A6
Friedrichswalde D 45 B5
Friesach A 73 B4
Friesack D 45 C4
Friesenheim D 60 B3
Friesoythe D 43 B4
Friggesund S 115 F13
Frigiliana E 100 C2
Frihetsli N 112 D8
Frillesås S 40 B2
Frinnaryd S 40 B4
Frinton-on-Sea GB 31 C5
Friockheim GB 25 B5
Friol E 86 A3
Fristad S 40 B2
Fritsla S 40 B2
Fritzlar D 51 B5
Frizington GB 26 A2
Frödinge S 40 B6
Froges F 69 C5
Frohburg D 52 B2
Frohnhausen D 50 C4
Frohnleiten A 73 A5
Froissy F 58 A3
Frombork PL 47 A5
Frome GB 29 B5
Frómista E 88 B2
Fröndenberg D 50 B3
Fronsac F 76 B2
Front I 70 C2
Fronteira P 92 B3
Frontenay-Rohan-Rohan
F 67 B4
Frontenhausen D 62 B3
Frontignan F 78 C2
Fronton F 77 C4
Fröseke S 40 C5
Frosinone I 103 B6
Frosolone I 103 B7
Frosta N 114 D7
Frøstrup DK 38 B1
Frosunda S 37 C5
Frouard F 60 B2
Frövi S 37 C2
Frøyset N 32 B2
Fruges F 48 C3
Frutigen CH 70 B2
Frýdek-Místek CZ 65 A4
Frýdlant CZ 53 C5
Frydlant nad Ostravicí
CZ 65 A4
Frygnowo PL 47 B6
Fryšták CZ 64 A3
Fucécchio I 81 C4
Fuencaliente
Ciudad Real E 94 C3
Ciudad Real E 100 A1
Fuencemillán E 95 B3
Fuendejalón E 89 C5
Fuengirola E 100 C1
Fuenlabrada E 94 B3
Fuenlabrada de los
Montes E 94 C2
Fuensalida E 94 B2
Fuensanta E 101 B4
Fuensanta de Martos
E 100 B2
Fuente-Alamo E 101 A4
Fuente-Álamo de Murcia
E 101 B4
Fuentealbilla E 96 B1
Fuente al Olmo de Iscar
E 88 C2
Fuentecén E 88 C3
Fuente Dé E 88 A2
Fuente de Cantos E 99 A4
Fuente del Arco E 99 A5
Fuente del Conde E 100 B1
Fuente del Maestre E 93 C4
Fuente de Santa Cruz
E 94 A2
Fuente el Fresno E 94 C3
Fuente el Saz de Jarama
E 95 B3
Fuente el Sol E 94 A2
Fuenteguinaldo E 93 A4
Fuentelapeña E 88 C1
Fuentelcésped E 89 C3
Fuentelespino de Haro
E 95 C4
Fuentelespino de Moya
E 95 C5
Fuentenovilla E 95 B3
Fuente Obejuna E 99 A5
Fuente Palmera E 99 B5
Fuentepelayo E 94 A2
Fuentepinilla E 89 C4
Fuenterroble de
Salvatierra E 93 A5
Fuenterrobles E 96 B1
Fuentes E 95 C4
Fuentesauco E 88 C2
Fuentesaúco E 94 A1
Fuentes de Andalucía
E 99 B5
Fuentes de Ebro E 90 B2
Fuentes de Jiloca E 89 C5
Fuentes de la Alcarria
E 95 B4
Fuentes de León E 99 A4
Fuentes de Nava E 88 B2
Fuentes de Oñoro E 93 A4
Fuentes de Ropel E 88 B1
Fuentespalda E 90 C3
Fuentespina E 88 C3
Fuente-Tójar E 100 B1
Fuente Vaqueros E 100 B2
Fuentidueña E 88 C3
Fuentidueña de Tajo
E 95 B3
Fuerte del Rey E 100 B2
Fügen A 72 A1
Fuglebjerg DK 39 D4
Fuglevik N 35 C2
Fuhrberg D 44 C1
Fulda D 51 C5
Fulgatore I 108 B1
Fully CH 70 B2
Fulnek CZ 64 A3
Fülöpszállás H 75 B4
Fulpmes A 71 A6
Fulunäs S 34 A5
Fumay F 49 D5
Fumel F 77 B3
Funäsdalen S 115 E9
Fundão P 92 A3
Funzie GB 22 A8
Furadouro P 87 D2
Fure N 32 A2
Fürstenau D 43 C4
Furstenau D 51 B5
Fürstenberg D 45 B5
Fürstenfeld A 73 A6
Fürstenfeldbruck D 62 B2
Fürstenstein D 63 B4
Fürstenwalde D 45 C6
Fürstenwerder D 45 B5
Fürstenzell D 63 B4
Fürth
Bayern D 62 A1
Hessen D 61 A4
Furth im Wald D 62 A3
Furtwangen D 61 B4
Furuby S 40 C5
Furudal S 36 A2
Furuflaten N 112 C9
Furulund S 41 D3
Furusjö S 40 B3
Fusa N 32 B2
Fuscaldo I 106 B3
Fusch an der
Grossglocknerstrasse
A 72 A2
Fushë Arrëz AL 105 A6
Fushë-Krujë AL 105 B5
Fusina I 72 C2
Fusio CH 70 B3
Füssen D 62 C1
Fustiñana E 89 B5
Futog SRB 75 C4
Futrikelv N 112 C8
Füzesabony H 65 C6
Füzesgyarmat H 75 A6
Fužine HR 73 C4
Fyllinge S 40 C2
Fynshav DK 39 E2
Fyresdal N 33 C5

G

Gaaldorf A 73 A4
Gabaldón E 95 C5
Gabarret F 76 C3
Gabčíkovo SK 64 C3
Gąbin PL 47 C5
Gabriac F 78 B1
Gabrovo BG 11 E8
Gaby I 70 C2
Gacé F 58 B1
Gacko BIH 84 C3
Gäddede S 115 C11
Gadebusch D 44 B3
Gadmen CH 70 B3
Gádor E 101 C3
Gádoros H 75 B5
Gael F 57 B3
Găeşti RO 11 D8
Gaeta I 103 B6
Gafanhoeira P 92 C2
Gaflenz A 63 C5
Gagarin RUS 7 D13
Gaggenau D 61 B4
Gagliano Castelferrato
I 109 B3
Gagliano del Capo I 107 B5
Gagnet S 36 B2
Gaibanella I 81 B5
Gaildorf D 61 B5
Gaillac F 77 C4
Gaillefontaine F 58 A2
Gaillon F 58 A2
Gainsborough GB 27 B5
Gairloch GB 22 D3
Gairlochy GB 24 B3
Gáiro I 110 C2
Gaj
HR 74 C2
SRB 85 B6
Gaja-la-Selve F 77 C4
Gajanejos E 95 B4
Gajary SK 64 B2
Gajdobra SRB 75 C4
Galan F 77 C3
Galanta SK 64 B3
Galapagar E 94 B2
Galápagos E 95 B3
Galaroza E 99 B4
Galashiels GB 25 C5
Galatas GR 117 E5
Galaţi RO 11 D10
Galatina I 107 A5
Galatista GR 116 B5
Galátone I 107 A5
Galaxidi GR 117 D4
Galdakao E 89 A4
Galeata I 81 C5
Galende E 87 B4
Galera E 101 B3
Galéria F 102 A1
Galgamácsa H 65 C5
Galgate GB 26 B3
Galgon F 76 B2
Galices P 92 A3
Galinduste E 93 A5
Galinoporni CY 120 A3
Galisteo E 93 B4
Galków PL 55 B4
Gallarate I 70 C3
Gallardon F 58 B2
Gallegos de Argañán
E 93 A4
Gallegos del Solmirón
E 93 A5
Galleguillos de Campos
E 88 B1
Galleno I 81 C4
Galliate I 70 C3
Gallicano I 81 B4
Gállio I 72 C1
Gallipoli = Gelibolu
TR 118 B1
Gallípoli I 107 A4
Gällivare S 112 E9
Gallizien A 73 B4
Gallneukirchen A 63 B5
Gällö S 115 E12
Gallocanta E 95 B5
Gällstad S 40 B3
Gallur E 90 B1
Galmisdale GB 24 B1
Galmpton GB 29 C4
Galston GB 24 C3
Galta N 33 C2
Galtelli I 110 B2
Galten DK 39 C2
Galtür A 71 B5
Galve de Sorbe E 95 A3
Galveias P 92 B2
Gálvez E 94 C2
Galway IRL 20 A2
Gamaches F 48 D2
Gámbara I 71 C5
Gambárie I 106 C2
Gambassi Terme I 81 C4
Gambatesa I 103 B7
Gambolò I 70 C3
Gaming A 63 C6
Gamla Uppsala S 36 C4
Gamleby S 40 B6
Gamlingay GB 30 B3
Gammelgarn S 37 E5
Gammelstad S 3 D25
Gammertingen D 61 B5
Gams CH 71 A4
Gamvik
Finnmark N 113 A17
Finnmark N 113 B11
Gan F 76 C2
Gáname E 87 C4
Ganda di Martello I 71 B5
Gandarela P 87 C2
Ganddal N 33 D2
Ganderkesee D 43 B5
Gandesa E 90 B3
Gandía E 96 C2
Gandino I 71 C4
Gandrup DK 38 B3
Ganges F 78 C2
Gånghester S 40 B3
Gangi I 109 B3
Gangkofen D 62 B3
Gannat F 68 B3
Gannay-sur-Loire F 68 B3
Gänserdorf A 64 B2
Ganzlin D 44 B4
Gap F 79 B5
Gara H 75 B4
Garaballa E 96 B1
Garaguso I 104 C2
Garbayuela E 94 C1
Garbhallt GB 24 B2
Garbsen D 43 C6
Garching D 62 B3
Garciaz E 93 B5
Garcihernández E 94 B1
Garcillán E 94 B2
Garcinarro E 95 B4
Garcisobaco E 99 C5
Garda I 71 C5
Gardanne F 79 C4
Gärdås S 34 B5
Gårdby S 41 C6
Gardeja PL 47 B4
Gardelegen D 44 C3
Gardermoen N 34 B3
Gardiki GR 116 D3
Garding D 43 A5
Gardone Riviera I 71 C5
Gardone Val Trómpia
I 71 C5
Gárdony H 74 A3
Gardouch F 77 C4
Gårdsjö S 37 D1
Gårdskär S 36 B4
Gards Köpinge S 41 D4
Garein F 76 B2
Garelochhead GB 24 B3
Garéoult F 79 C5
Garešnica HR 74 C1
Garéssio I 80 B2
Garforth GB 27 B4
Gargaliani GR 117 E3
Gargaligas E 93 B5
Gargallo E 90 C2
Garganta la Olla E 93 A5
Gargantiel E 100 A1
Gargellen A 71 B4
Gargilesse-Dampierre
F 67 B6
Gargnano I 71 C5
Gargnäs S 115 B14
Gárgoles de Abajo E 95 B4
Gargrave GB 26 B3
Garitz D 52 B2
Garlasco I 70 C3
Garlieston GB 24 D3
Garlin F 76 C2
Garlitos E 94 D1
Garmisch-Partenkirchen
D 71 A6
Garnat-sur-Engièvre
F 68 B3
Garpenberg S 36 B3
Garphyttan S 37 C1
Garray E 89 C4
Garrel D 43 C5
Garriguella E 91 A6
Garrison GB 18 B3
Garrovillas E 93 B4
Garrucha E 101 B4
Gars-am-Kamp A 63 B6
Garsås S 36 B1
Garsdale Head GB 26 A3
Gärsnäs S 41 D4
Garstang GB 26 B3
Gartow D 44 B3
Gartz D 45 B6
Gærum DK 38 B3
Garvagh GB 19 B5
Garvão P 98 B2
Garve GB 22 D4
Garwolin PL 55 B6
Garz D 45 A5
Garzyn PL 54 B1
Gąsawa PL 46 C3
Gåsborn S 34 C6
Gaschurn A 71 B5
Gascueña E 95 B4
Gasny F 58 A2
Gąsocin PL 47 C6
Gastes F 76 B1
Gastouni GR 117 E3
Gastouri GR 116 C1
Gata
E 93 A4
HR 83 C5
Gata de Gorgos E 96 C3
Gatchina RUS 7 B11
Gatehouse of Fleet
GB 24 D3
Gátér H 75 B4
Gateshead GB 25 D6
Gátova E 96 B2
Gattendorf A 64 B2
Gatteo a Mare I 82 B1
Gattinara I 70 C3
Gattorna I 80 B3
Gaucín E 99 C5
Gaulstad N 114 D9
Gaupne N 32 A4
Gautefall N 33 C5
Gauting D 62 B2
Gauto S 115 A13
Gava E 91 B5
Gavardo I 71 C5
Gavarnie F 76 D2
Gavi I 80 B2
Gavião P 92 B3
Gavirate I 70 C3
Gävle S 36 B4
Gavoi I 110 B2
Gavorrano I 81 D4
Gavray F 57 B4
Gavrio GR 117 E6
Gävunda S 34 B6
Gaweinstal A 64 B2
Gaworzyce PL 53 B5
Gawroniec PL 46 B2
Gaydon GB 30 B2
Gayton GB 30 B4
Gazipaşa TR 119 F7
Gazoldo degli Ippoliti
I 71 C5
Gazzuolo I 81 A4
Gbelce SK 65 C4
Gdańsk PL 47 A4
Gdinj HR 84 C1
Gdov RUS 7 B9
Gdów PL 65 A6
Gdynia PL 47 A4
Gea de Albarracin E 95 B5
Geary GB 22 D2
Géaudot F 59 B5
Geaune F 76 C2
Gebesee D 51 B6
Gebiz TR 119 E5
Gebze TR 118 B4
Géderlak H 75 B3
Gedern D 51 C5
Gedinne B 49 D5
Gediz TR 118 D4
Gèdre F 76 D3
Gedser DK 44 A3
Gedsted DK 38 C2
Geel B 49 B5
Geesthacht D 44 B2
Geetbets B 49 C6
Gefell D 52 C1
Gehrden D 51 A5
Gehren D 52 C1
Geilenkirchen D 50 C2
Geilo N 32 B5
Geinsheim D 61 A4
Geisa D 51 C5
Geiselhöring D 62 B3
Geiselwind D 61 A6
Geisenfeld D 62 B2
Geisenhausen D 62 B3
Geisenheim D 50 D4
Geising D 53 C3
Geisingen D 61 C4
Geislingen D 61 B5
Geistthal A 73 A5
Geiterygghytta N 32 B4
Geithain D 52 B2
Geithus N 34 C1
Gela I 109 B3
Geldermalsen NL 49 B6
Geldern D 50 B2
Geldrop NL 49 B6
Geleen NL 50 C1
Gelembe TR 118 C2
Gelendost TR 119 D6
Gelibolu = Gallipoli
TR 118 B1
Gelida E 91 B4
Gelnhausen D 51 C5
Gelnica SK 65 B6
Gelsa E 90 B2
Gelse H 74 B1
Gelsenkirchen D 50 B3
Gelsted DK 39 D2
Geltendorf D 62 B2
Gelterkinden CH 70 A2
Gelting D 39 E2
Gelu RO 75 B6
Gelves E 99 B4
Gembloux B 49 C5
Gemeaux F 69 A5
Gémenos F 79 C4
Gemerská Poloma
SK 65 B6
Gemerská Ves SK 65 B6
Gemert NL 50 B1
Gemla S 40 C4
Gemlik TR 118 B4
Gemmenich B 50 C1
Gemona del Friuli I 72 B3
Gémozac F 67 C4
Gemund D 50 C2
Gemünden
Bayern D 51 C5
Hessen D 51 C4
Rheinland-Pfalz D 60 A3
Genappe B 49 C5
Génave E 101 A3
Genazzano I 102 B5
Gençay F 67 B5
Gencsapáti H 74 A1
Gendringen NL 50 B2
Genelard F 69 B4
Genemuiden NL 42 C3
Generalski Stol HR 73 C5
Geneva = Genève CH 69 B6
Genevad S 40 C3
Genève = Geneva CH 69 B6
Genevriéres F 60 C1
Gengenbach D 61 B4
Genillé F 67 A6
Genk B 49 C6
Genlis F 69 A5
Gennep NL 50 B1
Genner DK 39 D2
Gennes F 67 A4
Genoa = Génova I 80 B2
Genola I 80 B1
Génova = Genoa I 80 B2
Genowefa PL 54 A3
Gensingen D 60 A3
Gent = Ghent B 49 B4
Genthin D 44 C4
Gentioux F 68 C1
Genzano di Lucánia
I 104 C2
Genzano di Roma I 102 B5
Georgenthal D 51 C6
Georgsmarienhütte D 50 A4
Gera D 52 C2
Geraards-bergen B 49 C4
Gerace I 106 C3
Geraci Sículo I 109 B3
Geraki GR 117 F4
Gérardmer F 60 B2
Geras A 63 B6
Gerbéviller F 60 B2
Gerbini I 109 B3
Gerbstedt D 52 B1
Gerði IS 111 C9
Gerede TR 118 B7
Gerena E 99 B4
Geretsried D 62 C2
Gérgal E 101 B3
Gergy F 69 B4
Gerindote E 94 C2
Gerjen H 74 B3
Gerlos A 72 A2
Germay F 59 B6
Germencik TR 119 E2
Germering D 62 B2
Germersheim D 61 A4
Gërneç AL 105 C5
Gernika-Lumo E 89 A4
Gernrode D 52 B1
Gernsbach D 61 B4
Gernsheim D 61 A4
Geroda D 51 C5
Gerola Alta I 71 B4
Geroldsgrun D 52 C1
Gerolsbach D 62 B2
Gerolstein D 50 C2
Gerolzhofen D 61 A6
Gerovo HR 73 C4
Gerpinnes B 49 C5
Gerrards Cross GB 31 C3
Gerri de la Sal E 91 A4
Gersfeld D 51 C5
Gerstetten D 61 B6
Gersthofen D 62 B1
Gerstungen D 51 C6
Gerswalde D 45 B5
Gerzat F 68 C3
Gerze TR 16 A7
Gerzen D 62 B3
Gescher D 50 B3
Geseke D 51 B4
Geslau D 61 A6
Gespunsart F 59 A5
Gesté F 66 A3
Gestorf D 51 A5
Gesualda I 103 C8
Gesunda S 36 B1
Geta FIN 36 B6
Getafe E 94 B3
Getinge S 40 C2
Getxo E 89 A4
Geversdorf D 43 B6
Gevgelija MK 116 A4
Gevora del Caudillo
E 93 C4
Gevrey-Chambertin F 69 A4
Gex F 69 B6
Gey D 50 C2
Geyikli TR 118 C1
Geysir IS 111 C5
Geyve TR 118 B5
Gföhl A 63 B6
Ghedi I 71 C5
Ghent = Gent B 49 B4
Gheorgheni RO 11 C8
Ghigo I 79 B6
Ghilarza I 110 B1
Ghisonaccia F 102 A2
Ghisoni F 102 A2
Gialtra GR 116 D4
Gianitsa GR 116 B4
Giardinetto Vécchio
I 103 B8
Giardini Naxos I 109 B4
Giarratana I 109 B3
Giarre I 109 B4
Giat F 68 C2
Giaveno I 80 A1
Giazza I 71 C6
Giba I 110 C1
Gibellina Nuova I 108 B1
Gibostad N 112 C7
Gibraleón E 99 B4
Gibraltar GBZ 99 C5
Gic H 74 A2
Gideå S 115 D16
Gideåkroken S 115 C14
Gidle PL 55 C4
Giebelstadt D 61 A5
Gieboldehausen D 51 B6
Gielniów PL 55 B5
Gielow D 45 B4
Gien F 58 C3
Giengen D 61 B6
Giens F 79 C5
Giera RO 75 C5
Gieselwerder D 51 B5
Giessen D 51 C4
Gieten NL 42 B3
Giethoorn NL 42 C3
Giffaumont-Champaubert
F 59 B5
Gifford GB 25 C5
Gifhorn D 44 C2
Gige H 74 B2
Giglio Porto I 102 A3
Gignac F 78 C2
Gijón = Xixón E 88 A1
Gilena E 100 B1
Gilford GB 19 B5
Gillberga S 35 C4
Gilleleje DK 41 C2
Gilley F 69 A6
Gilley-sur-Loire F 68 B3
Gillingham
Dorset GB 29 B5
Medway GB 31 C4
Gilocourt F 59 A3
Gilserberg D 51 C5
Gilsland GB 25 D5
Gilze NL 49 B5
Gimåt S 115 D15
Gimo S 36 B5
Gimont F 77 C3
Ginasservis F 79 C4
Gingelom B 49 C6
Gingst D 45 A5
Ginosa I 104 C2
Ginzling A 72 A1
Giões P 98 B3
Gióia dei Marsi I 103 B6
Gióia del Colle I 104 C2
Gióia Sannitica I 103 B7
Gióia Táuro I 106 C2
Gioiosa Iónica I 106 C3
Gioiosa Marea I 109 A3
Giosla GB 22 C2
Giovinazzo I 104 B2
Girifalco I 106 C3
Giromagny F 60 C2
Girona E 91 B5
Gironcourt-sur-Vraine
F 60 B1
Gironella E 91 A4
Gironville-sous-les-Côtes
F 60 B1
Girvan GB 24 C3
Gislaved S 40 B3
Gislev DK 39 D3
Gisors F 58 A2
Gissi I 103 A7
Gistad S 37 D2
Gistel B 48 B3
Gistrup DK 38 C3
Giswil CH 70 B3
Githio GR 117 F4
Giugliano in Campania
I 103 C7
Giulianova I 82 D2
Giulvăz RO 75 C5
Giurgiu RO 11 E8
Give DK 39 D2
Givet F 49 C5
Givors F 69 C4
Givry
B 49 C5
F 69 B4
Givry-en-Argonne F 59 B5
Givskud DK 39 D2
Giźalki PL 54 A2
Gizeux F 67 A5
Giżycko PL 6 D6
Gizzeria I 106 C3
Gizzeria Lido I 106 C3
Gjedved DK 39 D2
Gjegjan AL 105 B6
Gjendesheim N 32 A5
Gjerde N 32 B3
Gjerlev DK 38 C3
Gjermundshamn N 32 B2
Gjerrild DK 38 C3
Gjerstad N 33 D6
Gjesås N 34 B4
Gjesvær N 113 A14
Gjirokastër AL 116 B2
Gjøfjell N 35 C2
Gjøl DK 38 B2
Gjøra N 114 E6
Gjøvik N 34 B2
Gladbeck D 50 B2
Gladenbach D 51 C4
Gladstad N 114 B8
Glamis GB 25 B5
Glamoč BIH 84 B1
Glamsbjerg DK 39 D3
Gland CH 69 B6
Glandorf D 50 A3
Glanegg A 73 B4
Glanshammar S 37 C2
Glarus CH 70 A4
Glasgow GB 24 C3
Glashütte
Bayern D 62 C2
Sachsen D 53 C3
Glastonbury GB 29 B5
Glatzau A 73 B5
Glauchau D 52 C2
Glava S 35 C4
Glavatičevo BIH 84 C3
Glavičice BIH 85 B4
Glavnik KOS 85 D6
Gledica SRB 85 C5
Glein
A 73 A4
N 115 A9
Gleinstätten A 73 B5
Gleisdorf A 73 A5
Glenamoy IRL 18 B2
Glenarm GB 19 B6
Glenavy GB 19 B5
Glenbarr GB 24 C2
Glenbeigh IRL 20 B2
Glenbrittle GB 22 D2
Glencoe GB 24 B2
Glencolumbkille IRL 18 B3
Glendalough IRL 21 A5
Glenealy IRL 21 B5
Glenelg GB 22 D3
Glenfinnan GB 24 B2
Glengarriff IRL 20 C2
Glenluce GB 24 D3
Glennamaddy IRL 18 C3
Glenrothes GB 25 B4
Glenties IRL 18 B3
Glesborg DK 38 C3
Glesien D 52 B2
Gletsch CH 70 B3
Glewitz D 45 A4
Glifada GR 117 E5
Glimåkra S 41 C4
Glin IRL 20 B2
Glina HR 73 C6
Glinde D 44 B2
Glinojeck PL 47 C6
Glinsk IRL 20 A2
Gliwice PL 54 C3
Glödnitz A 73 B4
Gloggnitz A 64 C1
Głogoczów PL 65 A5
Glogonj SRB 85 B5
Glogovac SRB 85 B6
Głogów PL 53 B6
Głogówek PL 54 C2
Glomel F 56 B2
Glomfjord N 112 F2
Glommen S 40 C2
Glommersträsk S 115 B16
Glonn D 62 C2
Glorenza I 71 B5
Gloria P 92 B2
Glosa GR 116 C5
Glossop GB 27 B4
Gloucester GB 29 B5
Głowaczów PL 55 B6
Główczyce PL 46 A3
Glöwen D 44 C4
Głowno PL 55 B4
Gložan SRB 75 C4
Głubczyce PL 54 C2
Głuchołazy PL 54 C2
Głuchów PL 55 B5
Głuchowo PL 54 A1
Glücksburg D 39 E2
Glückstadt D 43 B6
Glumina BIH 84 B4
Glumsø DK 39 D4
Glušci SRB 85 B4
Glusk BY 7 E10
Głuszyca PL 53 C6
Glyngøre DK 38 C1
Glyn Neath GB 29 B4
Gmünd
Karnten A 72 B3
Nieder Östereich A 63 B5
Gmund D 62 C2
Gmunden A 63 C4
Gnarp S 115 E14
Gnarrenburg D 43 B6
Gnesau A 72 B3
Gnesta S 37 C4
Gnięchowice PL 54 B1
Gniew PL 47 B4
Gniewkowo PL 47 C4
Gniezno PL 46 C3
Gnoien D 45 B4
Gnojnice BIH 84 C2
Gnojno PL 55 C5
Gnosall GB 26 C3
Gnosjö S 40 B3
Göbel TR 118 B3
Göçbeyli TR 118 C2
Goch D 50 B2
Gochsheim D 51 C6
Göd H 65 C5
Godalming GB 31 C3
Godby FIN 36 B6
Goðdalir IS 111 B6
Goddelsheim D 51 B4
Gódega di Sant'Urbano
I 72 C2
Godegård S 37 D2
Godelheim D 51 B5
Goderville F 58 A1
Godiasco I 80 B3
Godič SLO 73 B4
Godkowo PL 47 A5
Godmanchester GB 30 B3
Gödöllö H 65 C5
Gödre H 74 B2
Godshill GB 31 D2
Godzikowice PL 54 C2
Godziszewo PL 47 A4
Goes NL 49 B4
Goetzenbrück F 60 B3
Góglio I 70 B3
Gogolin PL 54 C3
Göhren D 45 A5
Goirle NL 49 B6
Góis P 92 A2
Góito I 71 C5
Goizueta E 76 C1
Gojna Gora SRB 85 C5
Gójsk PL 47 C5
Gökçedağ TR 118 C3
Gökçen TR 119 D2
Gökçeören TR 119 D3
Gökçeyazı TR 118 C2
Göktepe TR 119 E3
Gol N 32 B5
Gola
HR 74 B2
N 34 A1
Gołańcz PL 46 C3
Gölbaşı TR 16 B6
Gölby FIN 36 B6
Gölcük
Kocaeli TR 118 B4
Niğde TR 16 B7
Golčův Jenikov CZ 63 A6
Gołczewo PL 45 B6
Goldach CH 71 A4
Goldbach D 51 C5
Goldbeck D 44 C3
Goldberg D 44 B4
Goldelund D 43 A6

Goldenstedt D 43 C5
Gołębiewo PL 47 A4
Golegã P 92 B2
Goleniów PL 45 B6
Golfo Aranci I 110 B2
Gölhisar TR 119 E4
Golina PL 54 A3
Gölle H 74 B3
Göllersdorf A 64 B2
Golling an der Salzach
A 63 C4
Gölmarmara TR 118 D2
Golnice PL 53 B5
Golnik SLO 73 B4
Gölova TR 119 F5
Gölpazarı TR 118 B5
Gols A 64 C2
Golspie GB 23 D5
Golssen D 52 B3
Golubac SRB 85 B6
Golub-Dobrzyń PL 47 B5
Golubinci SRB 85 B5
Golubovci MNE 105 A5
Goluchów PL 54 B2
Golzow D 52 A2
Gomagoi I 71 B5
Gómara E 89 C4
Gomaringen D 61 B5
Gömbe TR 119 F4
Gömeç TR 118 C1
Gomel = Homyel BY 7 E11
Gomes Aires P 98 B2
Gómezserracin E 88 C2
Gommern D 52 A1
Gomulin PL 55 B4
Gonäs S 36 B2
Goncelin F 69 C5
Gończyce PL 55 B6
Gondomar
E 87 B2
P 87 C2
Gondrecourt-le-Château
F 60 B1
Gondrin F 76 C3
Gönen
Balıkesir TR 118 B2
İsparta TR 119 E5
Gonfaron F 79 C5
Goñi E 76 D1
Goni
GR 116 C4
I 110 C2
Gonnesa I 110 C1
Gonnosfanádiga I 110 C1
Gönyü H 64 C3
Gonzaga I 81 B4
Goodrich GB 29 B5
Goodwick GB 28 A2
Gooik B 49 C5
Goole GB 27 B5
Goor NL 50 A2
Göpfritz an der Wild
A 63 B6
Goppenstein CH 70 B2
Göppingen D 61 B5
Gor E 100 B3
Góra
Dolnośląskie PL 54 B1
Mazowieckie PL 47 C6
Gorafe E 100 B2
Góra Kalwaria PL 55 B6
Gorawino PL 46 B1
Goražde BIH 84 C3
Gordaliza del Pino E 88 B1
Gördes TR 118 D3
Gørding DK 39 D1
Górdola CH 70 B3
Gordon GB 25 C5
Gordoncillo E 88 B1
Gorebridge GB 25 C4
Gorenja Vas SLO 73 B4
Gorenje Jelenje HR 73 C4
Gorey
GB 57 A3
IRL 21 B5
Gorgonzola I 71 C4
Gorica HR 83 B4
Gorican HR 74 B1
Gorinchem NL 49 B5
Goring GB 31 C2
Goritsy RUS 7 C14
Göritz D 45 B5
Gorízia I 72 C3
Górki PL 47 C5
Gorleben D 44 B3
Gorleston-on-sea GB 30 B5
Gørlev DK 39 D4
Görlitz D 53 B4
Górliz E 89 A4
Görmin D 45 B5
Górna Grupa PL 47 B4
Gorna Oryakhovitsa
BG 11 E8
Gornja Gorevnica
SRB 85 C5
Gornja Klina KOS 85 D5
Gornja Ploča HR 83 B4
Gornja Radgona SLO 73 B5
Gornja Sabanta SRB 85 C6
Gornja Trešnjevica
SRB 85 B5
Gornja Tuzla BIH 84 B3
Gornje Polje MNE 84 D3
Gornje Ratkovo BIH 84 B1
Gornji Grad SLO 73 B4
Gornji Humac HR 83 C5
Gornji Jasenjani BIH 84 C2
Gornji Kamengrad
BIH 83 B5
Gornji Kneginec HR 73 B6
Gornji Kokoti MNE 105 A5
Gornji Kosinj HR 83 B4
Gornji Milanovac
SRB 85 B5
Gornji Podgradci BIH 84 A2
Gornji Ravno BIH 84 C2
Gornji Sjenicak HR 73 C5
Gornji Vakuf BIH 84 C2
Górno PL 55 C5
Görömböly H 65 B6
Górowo Iławeckie
PL 47 A6
Gorran Haven GB 28 C3
Gorredijk NL 42 B3
Gorron F 57 B5
Gorseinon GB 28 B3
Gort IRL 20 A3
Gortin GB 19 B4
Görzke D 52 A2
Gorzkowice PL 55 B4
Górzno
Kujawsko-Pomorskie
PL 47 B5
Zachodnio-Pomorskie
PL 46 B1
Gorzów Śląski PL 54 B3
Gorzów Wielkopolski
PL 45 C7
Górzyca PL 45 C6
Gorzyce PL 54 D3
Górzyn PL 53 B4
Gorzyń PL 46 C1
Gorzyno PL 46 A3
Gosaldo I 72 B1
Gosau A 63 C4
Gosberton GB 30 B3
Gościcino PL 47 A4
Gościęcin PL 54 C3
Gościm PL 46 C1
Gościno PL 46 A1
Gosdorf A 73 B5
Gosforth GB 26 A2
Goslar D 51 B6
Goslice PL 47 C5
Gospič HR 83 B4
Gosport GB 31 D2
Gössäter S 35 D5
Gossau CH 71 A4
Goss Ilsede D 51 A6
Gössnitz D 52 C2
Gössweinstein D 62 A2
Gostimë AL 105 C6
Gostkow PL 55 B4
Göstling an der Ybbs
A 63 C5
Gostomia PL 46 B2
Gostycyn PL 46 B3
Gostyń PL 54 B2
Gostynin PL 47 C5
Goszczyn PL 55 B5
Göta S 35 D4
Göteborg = Gothenburg
S 38 B4
Götene S 35 D5
Gotha D 51 C6
Gothem S 37 E5
Gothenburg = Göteborg
S 38 B4
Gotse Delchev BG 116 A5
Gottersdorf D 62 B3
Göttingen D 51 B5
Gottne S 115 D15
Götzis A 71 A4
Gouarec F 56 B2
Gouda NL 49 A5
Goudhurst GB 31 C4
Goumenissa GR 116 B4
Goura GR 117 E4
Gourdon F 77 B4
Gourgançon F 59 B5
Gourin F 56 B2
Gournay-en-Bray F 58 A2
Gourock GB 24 C3
Gouveia P 92 A3
Gouvy B 50 C1
Gouzeacourt F 49 C4
Gouzon F 68 B2
Govedari HR 84 D2
Govérnolo I 81 A4
Gowarczów PL 55 B5
Gowerton GB 28 B3
Gowidlino PL 46 A3
Gowran IRL 21 B4
Goyatz D 53 A4
Göynük
TR 118 B5
Antalya TR 119 F5
Gozdnica PL 53 B5
Gozdowo PL 47 C5
Gozee B 49 C5
Graal-Müritz D 44 A4
Grab BIH 84 D3
Grabenstätt D 62 C3
Grabhair GB 22 C2
Gråbo S 38 B5
Grabovac
HR 84 C1
SRB 85 B5
Grabovci SRB 85 B4
Grabow D 44 B3
Grabów PL 55 A4
Grabow nad Pilicą PL 55 B6
Grabów nad Prosną
PL 54 B3
Grabowno PL 46 B3
Grabs CH 71 A4
Gračac HR 83 B4
Gračanica
BIH 84 B3
KOS 85 D6
Graçay F 68 A1
Gracen AL 105 B5
Grad SLO 73 B6
Gradac
BIH 84 D3
HR 84 C2
MNE 85 C4
SRB 85 C5
Gradačac BIH 84 B3
Gradec HR 74 C1
Gradefes E 88 B1
Grades A 73 B4
Gradil P 92 C1
Gradina
HR 74 C2
MNE 85 C4
Gradisca d'Isonzo I 72 C3
Gradište HR 74 C3
Grado
E 86 A4
I 72 C3
Grafenau D 63 B4
Gräfenberg D 62 A2
Gräfenhainichen D 52 B2
Grafenschlag A 63 B6
Grafenstein A 73 B4
Gräfenthal D 52 C1
Grafentonna D 51 B6
Grafenwöhr D 62 A2
Grafing D 62 B2
Grafling D 62 B3
Gräfsnäs S 40 A2
Gragnano I 103 C7
Grahovo
MNE 84 D3
SLO 72 B3
Graiguenamanagh
IRL 21 B5
Grain GB 31 C4
Grainau D 71 A6
Graja de Iniesta E 95 C5
Grajera E 89 C3
Gram DK 39 D2
Gramais A 71 A5
Gramat F 77 B4
Gramatneusiedl A 64 B2
Grambow D 45 B6
Grammichele I 109 B3
Gramsh AL 116 B2
Gramzow D 45 B6
Gran N 34 B2
Granada E 100 B2
Granard IRL 19 C4
Grañas E 86 A3
Granátula de Calatrava
E 100 A2
Grancey-le-Château
F 59 C6
Grandas de Salime E 86 A4
Grandcamp-Maisy F 57 A4
Grand-Champ F 56 C3
Grand Couronne F 58 A2
Grand-Fougeray F 57 C4
Grândola P 98 A2
Grandpré F 59 A5
Grandrieu
B 49 C5
F 78 B2
Grandson CH 70 B1
Grandvillars F 70 A1
Grandvilliers F 58 A2
Grañén E 90 B2
Grangärde S 36 B1
Grange IRL 18 B3
Grangemouth GB 25 B4
Grange-over-Sands
GB 26 A3
Grängesberg S 36 B1
Granges-de Crouhens
F 77 D3
Granges-sur-Vologne
F 60 B2
Gräningen D 44 C4
Granitola-Torretta I 108 B1
Granja
Évora P 98 A3
Porto P 87 C2
Granja de Moreruela
E 88 C1
Granja de Torrehermosa
E 93 C5
Gränna S 40 A4
Grannäs
Västerbotten S 115 B13
Västerbotten S 115 B14
Granö S 115 C16
Granollers E 91 B5
Granowiec PL 54 B2
Granowo PL 54 A1
Gransee D 45 B5
Gransherad N 33 C6
Grantham GB 27 C5
Grantown-on-Spey
GB 23 D5
Grantshouse GB 25 C5
Granville F 57 B4
Granvin N 32 B3
Grærup Strand DK 39 D1
Gräsås S 40 C2
Grasbakken N 113 B17
Grasberg D 43 B6
Grasmere GB 26 A2
Gräsmyr S 115 D16
Grasö S 36 B5
Grassano I 104 C2
Grassau D 62 C3
Grasse F 79 C5
Grassington GB 27 A4
Græsted DK 41 C2
Gråsten DK 39 E2
Grästorp S 35 D4
Gratkorn A 73 A5
Gråträsk S 115 B16
Gratwein A 73 A5
Graulhet F 77 C4
Graus E 90 A3
Grávalos E 89 B5
Gravberget N 34 B4
Grave NL 50 B1
Gravedona I 71 B4
Gravelines F 48 B3
Gravellona Toce I 70 C3
Gravendal S 36 B1
Gravens DK 39 D2
Gravesend GB 31 C4
Graveson F 78 C3
Gravina in Púglia I 104 C2
Gray F 69 A5
Grayrigg GB 26 A3
Grays GB 31 C4
Grayshott GB 31 C3
Grayvoron RUS 7 F13
Graz A 73 A5
Grazalema E 99 C5
Grążawy PL 47 B5
Grazzano Visconti I 80 B3
Greåker N 35 C3
Great Dunmow GB 31 C4
Great Malvern GB 29 A5
Great Torrington GB 28 C3
Great Waltham GB 31 C4
Great Yarmouth GB 30 B5
Grebbestad S 35 D3
Grebenstein D 51 B5
Grębocice PL 53 B6
Grębocin PL 47 B4
Greding D 62 A2
Gredstedbro DK 39 D1
Greencastle IRL 19 A4
Greenhead GB 25 D5
Greenisland GB 19 B6
Greenlaw GB 25 C5
Greenock GB 24 C3
Greenway GB 28 B3
Greenwich GB 31 C4
Grefrath D 50 B2
Greifenburg A 72 B3
Greiffenberg D 45 B5
Greifswald D 45 A5
Grein A 63 B5
Greipstad N 33 D4
Greiz D 52 C2
Grenaa DK 39 C3
Grenade F 77 C4
Grenade-sur-l'Adour
F 76 C2
Grenchen CH 70 A2
Grendi N 33 D4
Grenivík IS 111 B7
Grenoble F 69 C5
Gréoux-les-Bains F 79 C4
Gresenhorst D 44 A4
Gressoney-la-Trinité
I 70 C2
Gressoney-St-Jean I 70 C2
Gressthal D 51 C6
Gressvik N 35 C2
Gresten A 63 C6
Gretna GB 25 D4
Greussen D 51 B6
Greve in Chianti I 81 C5
Greven
Mecklenburg-
Vorpommern D 44 B2
Nordrhein-Westfalen
D 50 A3
Grevena GR 116 B3
Grevenbroich D 50 B2
Grevenbrück D 50 B4
Grevenmacher L 60 A2
Grevesmühlen D 44 B3
Grevestrand DK 41 D2
Grevie S 41 C2
Greystoke GB 26 A3
Greystones IRL 21 A5
Grez-Doiceau B 49 C5
Grèzec F 77 B4
Grez-en-Bouère F 57 C5
Grezzana I 71 C6
Grgar SLO 72 B3
Grgurevci SRB 85 A4
Gries A 71 A6
Griesbach D 63 B4
Griesheim D 61 A4
Gries in Sellrain A 71 A6
Grieskirchen A 63 B4
Griffen A 73 B4
Grignan F 78 B3
Grignano I 72 C3
Grigno I 72 B1
Grignols F 76 B2
Grignon F 69 C6
Grijota E 88 B2
Grijpskerk NL 42 B3
Gril AL 105 A5
Grillby S 37 C4
Grimaud F 79 C5
Grimbergen B 49 C5
Grimma D 52 B2
Grimmen D 45 A5
Grimmialp CH 70 B2
Grimsås S 40 B3
Grimsby GB 27 B5
Grimslöv S 40 C4
Grímsstaðir IS 111 B9
Grimstad N 33 D5
Grimstorp S 40 B4
Grindavík IS 111 D3
Grindelwald CH 70 B3
Grindheim N 33 D4
Grindsted DK 39 D1
Griñón E 94 B3
Gripenberg S 40 B4
Gripsholm S 37 C4
Grisolles F 77 C4
Grisslehamn S 36 B5
Gritley GB 23 C6
Grizebeck GB 26 A2
Grndina BIH 84 B1
Gröbming A 72 A3
Gröbzig D 52 B1
Grocka SRB 85 B5
Gröditz D 52 B3
Gródki PL 47 B6
Grodków PL 54 C2
Grodziec PL 54 A3
Grodzisk Mazowiecki
PL 55 A5
Groenlo NL 50 A2
Groesbeek NL 50 B1
Grohote HR 83 C5
Groitzsch D 52 B2
Groix F 56 C2
Grójec PL 55 B5
Grom PL 47 B6
Gromiljca BIH 84 C3
Grömitz D 44 A2
Gromnik PL 65 A6
Gromo I 71 C4
Gronau
Niedersachsen D 51 A5
Nordrhein-Westfalen
D 50 A3
Grønbjerg DK 39 C1
Grönenbach D 61 C6
Grong N 114 C9
Grönhögen S 41 C6
Groningen
D 52 B1
NL 42 B3
Grønnestrand DK 38 B2
Grono CH 71 B4
Grönskåra S 40 B5
Grootegast NL 42 B3
Gropello Cairoli I 70 C3
Grorud N 34 C2
Grósio I 71 B5
Grošnica SRB 85 C5
Grossalmerode D 51 B5
Grossarl A 72 A3
Gross Beeren D 45 C5
Gross Berkel D 51 A5
Grossbodungen D 51 B6
Gross-botwar D 61 B5
Grossburgwedel D 44 C1
Grosschönau D 53 C4
Gross-Dölln D 45 B5
Grossenbrode D 44 A3
Grossenehrich D 51 B6
Grossengottern D 51 B6
Grossenhain D 52 B3
Grossenkneten D 43 C5
Grossenlüder D 51 C5
Grossensee D 44 B2
Grossenzersdorf A 64 B2
Grosseto I 81 D5
Gross-Gerau D 61 A4
Grossgerungs A 63 B5
Grossglobnitz A 63 B6
Grosshabersdorf D 62 A1
Grossharras A 64 B2
Grosshartmansdorf
D 52 C3
Grosshöchstetten
CH 70 B2
Gross Kreutz D 45 C4
Grosskrut A 64 B2
Gross Lafferde D 51 A6
Gross Leutheb D 53 A4
Grosslohra D 51 B6
Grossmehring D 62 B2
Gross Muckrow D 53 A4
Gross Oesingen D 44 C2
Grossostheim D 61 A5
Grosspertholz A 63 B5
Grosspetersdorf A 73 A6
Grosspostwitz D 53 B4
Grossraming A 63 C5
Grossräschen D 53 B4
Gross Reken D 50 B3
Grossrinderfeld D 61 A5
Grossröhrsdorf D 53 B4
Gross Sarau D 44 B2
Gross Särchen D 53 B4
Grossschirma D 52 C3
Gross Schönebeck D 45 C5
Grossschweinbarth A 64 B2
Grosssiegharts A 63 B6
Grosssölk A 72 A3
Gross Umstadt D 61 A4
Grosswarasdorf A 74 A1
Gross Warnow D 44 B3
Gross-Weikersdorf A 64 B1
Gross-Welle D 44 B4
Grosswilfersdorf A 73 A5
Gross Wokern D 44 B4
Grostenquin F 60 B2
Grosuplje SLO 73 C4
Grotli N 114 E4
Grötlingbo S 37 E5
Grottáglie I 104 C3
Grottaminarda I 103 B8
Grottammare I 82 D2
Grotte di Castro I 81 D5
Grotteria I 106 C3
Gróttole I 104 C2
Grouw NL 42 B2
Grov N 112 D6
Grova N 33 C5
Grove E 86 B2
Grua N 34 B2
Grube D 44 A3
Grubišno Polje HR 74 C2
Gruda HR 105 A4
Grude BIH 84 C2
Grudusk PL 47 B6
Grudziądz PL 47 B4
Grue N 34 B4
Gruissan F 78 C2
Grullos E 86 A4
Grumo Áppula I 104 B2
Grums S 35 C5
Grünau im Almtal A 63 C4
Grünberg D 51 C4
Grünburg A 63 C5
Grundarfjörður IS 111 C2
Gründau D 51 C5
Gründelhardt D 61 A5
Grundforsen S 34 A4
Grundlsee A 63 C4
Grundsund S 35 D3
Grunewald D 53 B3
Grungedal N 33 C4
Grunow D 53 A4
Grünstadt D 61 A4
Gruvberget S 36 A3
Gruyères CH 70 B2
Gruža SRB 85 C5
Grybów PL 65 A6
Grycksbo S 36 B2
Gryfice PL 45 B7
Gryfino PL 45 B6
Gryfów Śląski PL 53 B5
Gryllefjord N 112 C6
Grymyr N 34 B2
Gryt S 37 D3
Grytgöl S 37 D2
Grythyttan S 37 C1
Grytnäs S 37 D4
Grzmiąca PL 46 B2
Grzybno PL 45 B6
Grzywna PL 47 B4
Gschnitz A 71 A6
Gschwend D 61 B5
Gstaad CH 70 B2
Gsteig CH 70 B2
Guadahortuna E 100 B2
Guadalajara E 95 B3
Guadalaviar E 95 B5
Guadalcanal E 99 A5
Guadalcázar E 100 B1
Guadalix de la Sierra
E 94 B3
Guadálmez E 100 A1
Guadalupe E 93 B5
Guadamur E 94 C2
Guadarrama E 94 B2
Guadiaro E 99 C5
Guadix E 100 B2
Guagnano I 105 C3
Guagno F 102 A1
Guajar-Faragüit E 100 C2
Gualchos E 100 C2
Gualdo Tadino I 82 C1
Gualtieri I 81 B4
Guarcino I 103 B6
Guarda P 92 A3
Guardamar del Segura
E 96 C2
Guardão P 92 A2
Guardavalle I 106 C3
Guardea I 102 A5
Guárdia I 103 C8
Guardiagrele I 103 A7
Guardiarégia I 103 B7
Guárdia Sanframondi
I 103 B7
Guardias Viejas E 100 C3
Guardiola de Bergueda
E 91 A4
Guardo E 88 B2
Guareña E 93 C4
Guaro E 100 C1
Guarromán E 100 A2
Guasila I 110 C2
Guastalla I 81 B4
Gubbhögen S 115 C12
Gúbbio I 82 C1
Guben D 53 B4
Gubin PL 53 B4
Guča SRB 85 C5
Gudå N 114 D8
Gudavac BIH 83 B5
Guddal N 32 A2
Güderup DK 39 E2
Gudhem S 35 D5
Gudhjem DK 41 D4
Gudovac HR 74 C1
Gudow D 44 B2
Güdüı TR 118 B7
Gudvangen N 32 B3
Guebwiller F 60 C3
Guéjar-Sierra E 100 B2
Guéméné-Penfao F 57 C4
Guéméné-sur-Scorff
F 56 B2
Güeñes E 89 A3
Guer F 57 C3
Guérande F 66 A2
Guéret F 68 B1
Guérigny F 68 A3
Guesa E 76 D1
Gueugnon F 68 B4
Guglionesi I 103 B7
Gühlen Glienicke D 45 B4
Guia P 92 B2
Guichen F 57 C4
Guidizzolo I 71 C5
Guidónia-Montecélio
I 102 B5
Guiglia I 81 B4
Guignes F 58 B3
Guijo E 100 A1
Guijo de Coria E 93 A4
Guijo de Santa Bábera
E 93 A5
Guijuelo E 93 A5
Guildford GB 31 C3
Guillaumes F 79 B5
Guillena E 99 B4
Guillestre F 79 B5
Guillos F 76 B2
Guilsfield GB 26 C2
Guilvinec F 56 C1
Guimarães P 87 C2
Guincho P 92 C1
Guînes F 48 C2
Guingamp F 56 B2
Guipavas F 56 B1
Guisborough GB 27 A4
Guiscard F 59 A4
Guiscriff F 56 B2
Guise F 59 A4
Guisona E 91 B4
Guitiriz E 86 A3
Guîtres F 76 A2
Gujan-Mestras F 76 B1
Gulbene LV 7 C9
Gulçayır TR 118 C6
Guldborg DK 39 E4
Gullabo S 40 C5
Gullane GB 25 B5
Gullbrå N 32 B3
Gullbrandstorp S 40 C2
Gulleråsen S 36 A2
Gullhaug N 35 C2
Gullringen S 40 B5
Gullspång S 35 D6
Gullstein N 114 D5
Güllük TR 119 E2
Gülnar TR 16 C6
Gülpınar TR 116 C8
Gülşehir TR 16 B7
Gulsvik N 34 B1
Gumiel de Hizán E 88 C3
Gummersbach D 50 B3
Gümüldür TR 119 D2
Gümüşhaciköy TR 16 A7
Gümüşova TR 118 B5
Gundelfingen D 61 B6
Gundel-fingen D 60 B3
Gundelsheim D 61 A5
Gunderschoffen F 60 B3
Gundertshausen A 62 B3
Gundinci HR 74 C3
Gündoğmuş TR 119 F7
Güney
Burdur TR 119 E4
Denizli TR 119 D4
Gunja HR 84 B3
Günlüce TR 119 F3
Gunnarn S 115 B14
Gunnarskog S 34 C4
Gunnebo S 40 B6
Gunnislake GB 28 C3
Günselsdorf A 64 C2
Guntersblum D 61 A4
Guntersdorf A 64 B2
Guntin E 86 B3
Günyüzü TR 118 C6
Günzburg D 61 B6
Gunzenhausen D 62 A1
Güre
Balıkesir TR 118 C1
Uşak TR 118 D4
Gurk A 73 B4
Gurrea de Gállego E 90 A2
Gürsu TR 118 B4
Gušće HR 74 C1
Gusev RUS 6 D7
Gusinje MNE 105 A5
Gusmar AL 105 C5
Gúspini I 110 C1
Gusselby S 37 C2
Güssing A 73 A6
Gusswerk A 63 C6
Gustav Adolf S 34 B5
Gustavsberg S 37 C5
Gustavsfors S 35 C4
Güstrow D 44 B4
Gusum S 37 D3
Gutcher GB 22 A7
Gutenstein A 64 C1
Gütersloh D 51 B4
Guttannen CH 70 B3
Guttaring A 73 B4
Guttau D 53 B4
Güttingen CH 61 C5
Gützkow D 45 B5
Guzów PL 55 A5
Gvardeysk RUS 6 D6
Gvarv N 33 C6
Gvozd MNE 85 D4
Gvozdansko HR 73 C6
Gwda Wielka PL 46 B2
Gwennap GB 28 C2
Gy F 69 A5
Gyál H 75 A4
Gyarmat H 74 A2
Gyékényes H 74 B2
Gyé-sur-Seine F 59 B5
Gylling DK 39 D3
Gyoma H 75 B5
Gyömöre H 74 A2
Gyömrö H 75 A4
Gyón H 75 A4
Gyöngyfa H 74 C2
Gyöngyös H 65 C5
Gyöngyöspata H 65 C5
Gyönk H 74 B3
Györ H 64 C3
Györszemere H 74 A2
Gypsera CH 70 B2
Gysinge S 36 B3
Gyttorp S 37 C1
Gyula H 75 B6
Gyulafirátót H 74 A2
Gyulaj H 74 B3

H

Haacht B 49 C5
Haag
Nieder Östereich A 63 B5
Ober Östereich A 63 B4
D 62 B3
Haaksbergen NL 50 A2
Haamstede NL 49 B4
Haan D 50 B3
Haapajärvi FIN 3 E26
Haapsalu EST 6 B7
Haarlem NL 42 C1
Habas F 76 C2
Habay B 60 A1
Habo S 40 B4
Håbol S 35 D4
Habry CZ 63 A6
Habsheim F 60 C3
Hachenburg D 50 C3
Hacıbektaş TR 16 B7
Hacılar TR 16 B7
Hacinas E 89 C3
Hackås S 115 E11
Hacketstown IRL 21 B5
Hackthorpe GB 26 A3
Hadamar D 50 C4
Hädanberg S 115 D15
Haddington GB 25 C5
Hadersdorf am Kamp
A 63 B6
Haderslev DK 39 D2
Haderup DK 39 C1
Hadım TR 119 F7
Hadleigh
Essex GB 31 C4
Suffolk GB 30 B4
Hadlow GB 31 C4
Hadmersleben D 52 A1
Hadsten DK 39 C3
Hadsund DK 38 C3
Hadyach UA 7 F13
Hadžići BIH 84 C3
Hafnarfjörður IS 111 C4
Hafnir IS 111 D3
Hafslo N 32 A4
Haganj HR 74 C1
Hagby S 40 C6
Hage D 43 B4
Hægebostad N 33 D4
Hægeland N 33 D4
Hagen
Niedersachsen D 43 B5
Nordrhein-Westfalen
D 50 B3
Hagenbach D 61 A4
Hagenow D 44 B3
Hagetmau F 76 C2
Hagfors S 34 B5
Häggenås S 115 D11
Hagondange F 60 A2
Hagsta S 36 B4
Haguenau F 60 B3
Hahnbach D 62 A2
Hahnslätten D 50 C4
Hahót H 74 B1
Haiger D 50 C4
Haigerloch D 61 B4
Hailsham GB 31 D4
Hainburg A 64 B2
Hainfeld A 64 B1
Hainichen D 52 C3
Hajdúböszörmény H 10 C6
Hajdučica SRB 75 C5
Hajdúszoboszló H 75 A6
Hajnáčka SK 65 B5
Hajnówka PL 6 E7
Hajós H 75 B4
Håkafot S 115 C11
Hakkas S 113 F10
Håksberg S 36 B2
Halaszi H 64 C3
Halberstadt D 52 B1
Halberton GB 29 C4
Hald Ege DK 39 C2
Haldem D 43 C5
Halden N 35 C3
Haldensleben D 52 A1
Halenbeck D 44 B4
Halesowen GB 26 C3
Halesworth GB 30 B5
Halfing D 62 C3
Halhjem N 32 B2
Håliden S 34 B5
Halifax GB 27 B4
Häljelöt S 37 D3
Halkida GR 116 D5
Halkirk GB 23 C5
Hall S 37 E5
Hälla S 115 D14
Hallabro S 41 C5
Hällabrottet S 37 C2
Halland GB 31 D4
Hällaryd S 41 C4
Hallaryd S 40 C3
Hällberga S 37 C3
Hällbybrunn S 37 C3
Halle
B 49 C5
Nordrhein-Westfalen
D 51 A4
Sachsen-Anhalt D 52 B1
Hålleberga S 40 C5
Hällefors S 36 C1
Hälleforsnäs S 37 C3
Hallein A 62 C4
Hällekis S 35 D5
Hallen S 115 D11
Hållen S 36 B4
Hallenberg D 51 B4
Hällestad S 37 D2
Hällevadsholm S 35 D3
Hällevik S 41 C4
Hälleviksstrand S 35 D3
Hallingby N 34 B2
Hallingeberg S 40 B6
Hallingen N 32 B6
Hall in Tirol A 71 A6
Hällnäs S 115 A15
Hållnäs S 36 B4
Hällnäs S 115 C16
Hallormsstaður IS 111 B11
Hallsberg S 37 C2
Hållsta S 37 C3
Hallstahammar S 37 C3
Hallstatt A 72 A3
Hallstavik S 36 B5
Halltorp S 40 C6
Halluin F 49 C4
Hallviken S 115 D12
Hallworthy GB 28 C3
Halmstad S 40 C2
Hals DK 38 B3
Halsa N 114 D5
Halstead GB 31 C4
Haltdalen N 114 E8
Haltern D 50 B3
Haltwhistle GB 25 D5
Halvarsgårdarna S 36 B2
Halver D 50 B3
Halvrimmen DK 38 B2
Ham F 59 A4
Hamar N 34 B3
Hamarhaug N 32 B2
Hamarøy N 112 D4
Hambach F 60 A3
Hambergen D 43 B5
Hambergsund S 35 D3
Hambledon GB 31 D2
Hambuhren D 44 C1
Hamburg D 44 B2
Hamdibey TR 118 C2
Hamdorf D 43 A6
Hämeenlinna FIN 3 F26
Hameln = Hamlin D 51 A5
Hamersleben D 52 A1
Hamidiye TR 118 C5
Hamilton GB 24 C3
Hamina FIN 7 A9
Hamlagrø N 32 B3
Hamlin = Hameln D 51 A5
Hamm D 50 B3
Hammar S 37 D1
Hammarland FIN 36 B6
Hammarö S 35 C5
Hammarstrand S 115 D13
Hamme B 49 B5
Hammel DK 39 C2
Hammelburg D 51 C5
Hammelspring D 45 B5
Hammenhög S 41 D4
Hammerdal S 115 D12
Hammerfest N 113 B12
Hammershøj DK 38 C2
Hammerum DK 39 C2
Hamminkeln D 50 B2
Hamnavoe GB 22 A7
Hamneda S 40 C3
Hamningberg N 113 B19
Hamoir B 49 C6
Hamont B 49 B6
Hámor H 65 B6
Hamra
Gävleborg S 115 F12
Gotland S 37 F5
Hamrångefjärden S 36 B4
Hamstreet GB 31 C4
Hamsund N 112 D4
Han
MNE 84 D3
TR 118 C5
Hanaskog S 41 C4
Hanau D 51 C4
Händelöp S 40 B6
Handlová SK 65 B4
Hanerau-Hademarschen
D 43 A6
Hånger S 40 B3
Hanhimaa FIN 113 E14
Han i Hotit AL 105 A5
Hanken S 37 D1
Hankensbüttel D 44 C2
Han Knežica BIH 83 A5
Hanko FIN 6 B7
Hannover D 43 C6
Hannut B 49 C6
Han Pijesak BIH 84 B3
Hansnes N 112 C8
Hanstedt D 44 B2
Hanstholm DK 38 B1
Hantsavichy BY 7 E9
Hanušovice CZ 54 C1
Haparanda S 3 D26
Haradok BY 7 D10
Harads S 3 C24
Häradsbäck S 40 C4
Häradsbygden S 36 B2
Harbo S 36 B4
Harboør DK 38 C1
Harburg
Bayern D 62 B1
Hamburg D 44 B1
Hårby DK 39 D3
Harc H 74 B3
Hardegarijp NL 42 B2
Hardegsen D 51 B5
Hardelot Plage F 48 C2
Hardenbeck D 45 B5
Hardenberg NL 42 C3
Harderwijk NL 42 C2
Hardheim D 61 A5
Hardt D 61 B4
Hareid N 114 E3
Haren
D 43 C4
NL 42 B3
Harestua N 34 B2
Harfleur F 57 A6
Harg S 36 B5
Hargicourt F 49 D4
Hargnies F 49 C5
Hargshamn S 36 B5
Härja S 40 A3
Harkány H 74 C3
Härkeberga S 37 C4
Harkebrügge D 43 B4
Harlech GB 26 C1
Harleston GB 30 B5
Hårlev DK 41 D2
Harlingen NL 42 B2
Harlösa S 41 D3
Harlow GB 31 C4
Harmancık TR 118 C4
Harmånger S 115 F14
Härnevi S 37 C4
Härnösand S 115 E14
Haro E 89 B4
Haroldswick GB 22 A8
Háromfa H 74 B2
Haroué F 60 B2
Harpenden GB 31 C3
Harplinge S 40 C2
Harpstedt D 43 C5
Harrogate GB 27 A4
Harrow GB 31 C3
Härryda S 40 B2
Harsefeld D 43 B6
Harsewinkel D 50 B4
Hârşova RO 11 D9
Harstad N 112 D5
Harsum D 51 A5
Harsvik N 114 C7
Harta H 75 B4
Hartberg A 73 A5
Hartburn GB 25 C6
Hartennes F 59 A4
Hartest GB 30 B4
Hartha D 52 B2
Hartland GB 28 C3
Hartlepool GB 27 A4
Hartmanice CZ 63 A4
Hartmannsdorf A 73 A5
Harvassdal N 115 B11
Harwell GB 31 C2
Harwich GB 31 C5
Harzgerode D 52 B1
Häselgehr A 71 A5
Haselünne D 43 C4
Hasköy TR 118 A1
Haslach D 61 B4
Haslach an der Mühl
A 63 B5
Hasle DK 41 D4
Haslemere GB 31 C3
Haslev DK 39 D4
Hasloch D 61 A5
Hasparren F 76 C1
Hassela S 115 E13
Hasselfelde D 51 B6
Hasselfors S 37 C1
Hasselt
B 49 C6
NL 42 C3
Hassfurt D 51 C6
Hassleben D 45 B5
Hässleholm S 41 C3
Hasslö S 41 C5
Hassloch D 61 A4
Hästbo S 36 B4
Hastersboda FIN 36 B7
Hästholmen S 37 D1
Hastière-Lavaux B 49 C5
Hastigrow GB 23 C5
Hastings GB 31 D4
Hästveda S 41 C3
Hasvik N 113 B11
Hatfield
Hertfordshire GB 31 C3
South Yorkshire GB 27 B5
Hatherleigh GB 28 C3
Hathersage GB 27 B4
Hatlestrand N 32 B2
Hattem NL 42 C3
Hatten
D 43 B5
F 60 B3
Hattfjelldal N 115 B10
Hatting DK 39 D2
Hattingen D 50 B3
Hattstadt F 60 B3
Hattstedt D 43 A6
Hatvan H 65 C5
Hatvik N 32 B2
Hau D 50 B2
Haudainville F 59 A6
Hauganes IS 111 B7
Haugastøl N 32 B4
Hauge N 33 D3
Haugesund N 33 C2
Haughom N 33 D3
Haugsdal N 32 B2
Haugsdorf A 64 B2
Haukedal N 32 A3
Haukeland N 32 B2
Haukeligrend N 33 C4
Haukeliseter N 32 C4
Haukipudas FIN 3 D26
Haulerwijk NL 42 B3
Haunersdorf D 62 B3
Haus N 32 B2
Hausach D 61 B4
Hausham D 62 C2
Hausmannstätten A 73 B5
Hausvik N 33 D3
Hautajärvi FIN 113 F18
Hautefort F 67 C6
Hauterives F 69 C5
Hauteville-Lompnès
F 69 C5
Haut-Fays B 49 C6
Hautmont F 49 C4
Hautrage B 49 C4
Hauzenberg D 63 B4
Havant GB 31 D3
Havdhem S 37 E5
Havdrup DK 39 D5
Havelange B 49 C6
Havelberg D 44 C4
Havelte NL 42 C3
Haverfordwest GB 28 B3
Haverhill GB 30 B4
Havering GB 31 C4
Håverud S 35 D4
Havířov CZ 65 A4
Havixbeck D 50 B3
Havlíčkův Brod CZ 63 A6
Havndal DK 38 C3
Havneby DK 39 D1
Havnebyen DK 39 D4
Havnsø DK 39 D4
Havøysund N 113 A13
Havran TR 118 C2
Havrebjerg DK 39 D4
Havsa TR 118 A1
Havstenssund S 35 D3
Havza TR 16 A7
Hawes GB 26 A3
Hawick GB 25 C5
Hawkhurst GB 31 C4
Hawkinge GB 31 C5
Haxey GB 27 B5
Hayange F 60 A2
Haydarlı TR 119 D5
Haydon Bridge GB 25 D5
Hayle GB 28 C2
Haymana TR 118 C7
Hay-on-Wye GB 29 A4
Hayrabolu TR 118 A2
Haysyn UA 11 B10
Hayvoron UA 11 B10
Haywards Heath GB 31 D3
Hazebrouck F 48 C3
Hazlov CZ 52 C2
Heacham GB 30 B4
Headcorn GB 31 C4
Headford IRL 20 A2
Heanor GB 27 B4
Héas F 76 D3
Heathfield GB 31 D4
Hebden Bridge GB 26 B3
Heberg S 40 C2
Heby S 36 C3
Hechingen D 61 B4
Hechlingen D 62 B1
Hecho E 76 D2
Hechtel B 49 B6
Hechthausen D 43 B6
Heckelberg D 45 C5
Heckington GB 27 C5
Hecklingen D 52 B1
Hed S 37 C2
Hedalen N 34 B1
Hedared S 40 B2
Heddal N 33 C6
Hédé F 57 B4
Hede S 115 E10
Hedekas S 35 D3
Hedemora S 36 B2
Hedensted DK 39 D2
Hedersleben D 52 B1
Hedesunda S 36 B4
Hedge End GB 31 D2
Hedon GB 27 B5
Heede D 43 C4
Heek D 50 A3
Heemstede NL 42 C1
Heerde NL 42 C3
Heerenveen NL 42 C2
Heerhugowaard NL 42 C1
Heerlen NL 50 C1
Heeze NL 49 B6
Heggenes N 32 A6
Hegra N 114 D8
Hegyeshalom H 64 C3
Hegyközség H 74 A1
Heia N 114 C9
Heide D 43 A6
Heidelberg D 61 A4
Heiden D 50 B2
Heidenau D 53 C3
Heidenheim D 61 B6
Heidenreichstein A 63 B6
Heikendorf D 44 A2
Heilam GB 22 C4
Heiland N 33 D5
Heilbad Heiligenstadt
D 51 B6
Heilbronn D 61 A5
Heiligenblut A 72 A2
Heiligendamn D 44 A3
Heiligendorf D 44 C2
Heiligengrabe D 44 B4
Heiligenhafen D 44 A2
Heiligenhaus D 50 B2
Heiligenkreuz A 73 B6
Heiligenstadt D 62 A2
Heiloo NL 42 C1
Heilsbronn D 62 A1
Heim N 114 D6
Heimburg D 51 B6
Heimdal N 114 D7
Heinerscheid L 50 C2
Heinersdorf D 45 C6
Heining D 63 B4
Heiningen D 61 B5
Heinola FIN 3 F27
Heinsberg D 50 B2
Heist-op-den-Berg B 49 B5
Hejde S 37 E5
Hejdeby S 37 E5
Hejls DK 39 D2
Hejnice CZ 53 C5
Hel PL 47 A4
Helchteren B 49 B6
Heldburg D 51 C6
Heldrungen D 52 B1
Helechosa E 94 C2
Helensburgh GB 24 B3
Helfenberg A 63 B5
Helgen N 33 C6
Helgeroa N 35 D1
Hella
IS 111 D5
N 32 A3
Helland N 112 D5
Hellas S 35 D4
Helle N 33 D3
Helleland N 33 D3
Hellendoorn NL 42 C3
Hellenthal D 50 C2
Hellesøy N 32 B1
Hellesylt N 114 E3
Hellevoetsluis NL 49 B5
Helligskogen N 112 C9
Hellín E 101 A4
Hellissandur IS 111 C2
Hellnar IS 111 C2
Hellum DK 38 B3
Hellvi S 37 E5
Hellvik N 33 D2
Helm-brechts D 52 C1
Helmond NL 49 B6
Helmsdale GB 23 C5

Helmsley GB 27 A4
Helmstedt D 51 A6
Hel'pa SK 65 B5
Helsa D 51 B5
Helsby GB 26 B3
Helsingborg S 41 C2
Helsinge DK 41 C2
Helsingør DK 41 C2
Helsinki FIN 6 A8
Helston GB 28 C2
Hemau D 62 A2
Hemavan S 115 B12
Hemel Hempstead
GB 31 C3
Hemer D 50 B3
Héming F 60 B2
Hemmet DK 39 D1
Hemmingstedt D 43 A6
Hemmoor D 43 B6
Hemnes N 35 C3
Hemnesberget N . . . 115 A10
Hemse S 37 E5
Hemsedal N 32 B5
Hemslingen D 43 B6
Hemsworth GB 27 B4
Hen N 34 B2
Henån S 35 D3
Hendaye F 76 C1
Hendek TR 118 B5
Hendungen D 51 C6
Henfield GB 31 D3
Hengelo
Gelderland NL 50 A2
Overijssel NL 50 A2
Hengersberg D 62 B4
Hengoed GB 29 B4
Hénin-Beaumont F . . . 48 C3
Henley-on-Thames
GB 31 C3
Hennan S 115 E12
Henneberg D 51 C6
Hennebont F 56 C2
Henne Strand DK 39 D1
Hennigsdorf D 45 C5
Hennset N 114 D5
Hennstedt
Schleswig-Holstein
D 43 A6
Schleswig-Holstein D . 43 A6
Henrichemont F 68 A2
Henryków PL 54 C2
Henrykowo PL 47 A6
Hensås N 32 A5
Henstedt-Ulzburg D . . 44 B1
Heppenheim D 61 A4
Herad
Buskerud N 32 B6
Vest-Agder N 33 D3
Heradsbygd N 34 B3
Heraklion = Iraklio
GR 117 G7
Herálec CZ 64 A2
Herand N 32 B3
Herbault F 58 C2
Herbern D 50 B3
Herbertstown IRL 20 B3
Herbeumont B 59 A6
Herbignac F 66 A2
Herbisse F 59 B5
Herbitzheim F 60 A3
Herbolzheim D 60 B3
Herborn D 50 C4
Herbrechtingen D 61 B6
Herby PL 54 C3
Herceg-Novi MNE . . . 105 A4
Hercegovać HR 74 C2
Hercegovacka Goleša
SRB 85 C4
Hercegszántó H 75 C3
Herchen D 50 C3
Heréd H 65 C5
Hereford GB 29 A5
Herefoss N 33 D5
Hereke TR 118 B4
Herencia E 95 C3
Herend H 74 A2
Herent B 49 C5
Herentals B 49 B5
Hérépian F 78 C2
Herfølge DK 41 D2
Herford D 51 A4
Herguijuela E 93 B5
Héric F 66 A3
Héricourt F 60 C2
Héricourt-en-Caux F . . 58 A1
Hérimoncourt F 70 A1
Heringsdorf D 44 A3
Herisau CH 71 A4
Hérisson F 68 B2
Herk-de-Stad B 49 C6
Herlufmagle DK 39 D4
Hermagor A 72 B3
Hermannsburg D 44 C2
Hermansverk N 32 A3
Heřmanův Městec
CZ 53 D5
Herment F 68 C2
Hermeskeil D 60 A2
Hermisende E 87 C4
Hermonville F 59 A4
Hermsdorf D 52 C1
Hernani E 76 C1
Hernansancho E 94 B2
Herne D 50 B3
Herne Bay GB 31 C5
Hernes N 34 B3
Herning DK 39 C1
Herøya N 35 C1
Herramelluri E 89 B3
Herräng S 36 B5
Herre N 33 C6
Herrenberg D 61 B4
Herrera E 100 B1
Herrera de Alcántara
E 92 B3
Herrera del Duque E . . 94 C1
Herrera de los Navarros
E 90 B1
Herrera de Pisuerga
E 88 B2
Herreros del Suso E . . 94 B1
Herrestad S 35 D3
Herrhamra S 37 D4
Herritslev DK 44 A3
Herrlisheim F 60 B3
Herrljunga S 40 A3
Herrnhut D 53 B4
Herrsching D 62 B2
Hersbruck D 62 A2
Hersby S 37 C5
Herscheid D 50 B3
Herselt B 49 B5
Herso GR 116 A4
Herstal B 49 C6
Herstmonceux GB 31 D4
Herten D 50 B3
Hertford GB 31 C3
Hervás E 93 A5
Hervik N 33 C2
Herxheim D 61 A4
Herzberg
Brandenburg D 45 C4
Brandenburg D 52 B3
Niedersachsen D 51 B6
Herzebrock D 50 B4
Herzfelde D 45 C5
Herzlake D 43 C4
Herzogen-aurach D . . . 62 A1
Herzogenbuchsee CH . . 70 A2
Herzogenburg A 63 B6
Herzsprung D 44 B4
Hesby N 33 C2
Hesdin F 48 C3
Hesel D 43 B4
Heskestad N 33 D3
Hessdalen N 114 E8
Hesselager DK 39 D3
Hesseng N 113 C18
Hessisch Lichtenau
D 51 B5
Hessisch-Oldendorf
D 51 A5
Hestra S 40 B3
Heswall GB 26 B2
Hetlevik N 32 B2
Hettange-Grande F . . . 60 A2
Hetton-le-Hole GB 25 D6
Hettstedt D 52 B1
Heuchin F 48 C3
Heudicourt-sous-les-
Côtes F 60 B1
Heunezel F 60 B2
Heuqueville F 57 A6
Heves H 65 C6
Héviz H 74 B2
Hexham GB 25 D5
Heysham GB 26 A3
Heytesbury GB 29 B5
Hidas H 74 B3
Hieflau A 63 C5
Hiendelaencina E 95 A4
Hiersac F 67 C5
High Bentham GB 26 A3
Highclere GB 31 C2
High Hesket GB 25 D5
Highley GB 26 C3
High Wycombe GB 31 C3
Higuera de Arjona E . 100 B2
Higuera de Calatrava
E 100 B1
Higuera de la Serena
E 93 C5
Higuera de la Sierra
E 99 B4
Higuera de Vargas E . . 93 C4
Higuera la Real E 99 A4
Higuers de Llerena E . . 93 C4
Higuerulea E 96 C1
Híjar E 90 B2
Hilchenbach D 50 B4
Hildburghausen D 51 C6
Hilden D 50 B2
Hilders D 51 C5
Hildesheim D 51 A5
Hilgay GB 30 B4
Hillared S 40 B3
Hille D 51 A4
Hillegom NL 49 A5
Hillerød DK 41 D2
Hillerstorp S 40 B3
Hillesheim D 50 C2
Hillestad N 35 C2
Hillmersdorf D 52 B3
Hillsborough GB 19 B5
Hillswick GB 22 A7
Hilpoltstein D 62 A2
Hiltpoltstein D 62 A2
Hilvarenbeek NL 49 B6
Hilversum NL 49 A6
Himarë AL 116 B1
Himbergen D 44 B2
Himesháza H 74 B3
Himmelberg A 73 B4
Himmelpforten D 43 B6
Himód H 74 A2
Hinckley GB 30 B2
Hindås S 40 B2
Hindelang D 71 A5
Hindelbank CH 70 A2
Hinderavåg N 33 C2
Hindhead GB 31 C3
Hinjosa del Valle E . . . 93 C4
Hinnerup DK 39 C3
Hinneryd S 40 C3
Hinojal E 93 B4
Hinojales E 99 B4
Hinojos E 99 B4
Hinojosa del Duque E . 93 C5
Hinojosas de Calatrava
E 100 A1
Hinterhornbach A 71 A5
Hinterriss A 71 A6
Hintersee
A 63 C4
D 45 B6
Hinterstoder A 63 C5
Hintertux A 72 A1
Hinterweidenthal D . . . 60 A3
Hinwil CH 70 A3
Hios GR 116 D8
Hippolytushoef NL 42 C1
Hirschaid D 62 A1
Hirschau D 62 A2
Hirschfeld D 52 B3
Hirschhorn D 61 A4
Hirsingue F 60 C3
Hirson F 59 A5
Hirtshals DK 38 B2
Hirzenhain D 51 C5
Hisarcık TR 118 C4
Hishult S 41 C3
Hitchin GB 31 C3
Hitra N 114 D5
Hittarp S 41 C2
Hittisau A 71 A4
Hittun N 32 A1
Hitzacker D 44 B3
Hjallerup DK 38 B3
Hjällstad S 34 B5
Hjältevad S 40 B5
Hjärnarp S 41 C2
Hjartdal N 33 C5
Hjellestad N 32 B2
Hjelmeland N 33 C3
Hjelset N 114 E4
Hjerkinn N 114 E6
Hjerm DK 38 C1
Hjerpsted DK 39 D1
Hjerting DK 39 D1
Hjo S 35 D6
Hjordkær DK 39 D2
Hjørring DK 38 B2
Hjorted S 40 B6
Hjortkvarn S 37 D2
Hjortnäs S 36 B1
Hjortsberga S 40 C4
Hjukse N 33 C6
Hjuksebø N 33 C6
Hjulsjö S 36 C1
Hlinik nad Hronom
SK 65 B4
Hlinsko CZ 64 A1
Hlío IS 111 A10
Hlohovec SK 64 B3
Hlubokánad Vltavou
CZ 63 A5
Hlučín CZ 64 A4
Hlukhiv UA 7 F12
Hlyboka UA 11 B8
Hlybokaye BY 7 D9
Hniezdne SK 65 A6
Hnilec SK 65 B6
Hnúšťa SK 65 B5
Hobol H 74 B2
Hobro DK 38 C2
Hobscheid L 60 A1
Hocalar TR 119 D4
Hochdonn D 43 A6
Hochdorf CH 70 A3
Hochfelden F 60 B3
Hochspeyer D 60 A3
Höchstädt D 61 B6
Höchstadt D 62 A1
Hochstenbach D 50 C3
Höchst im Odenwald
D 61 A5
Höckendorf D 52 C3
Hockenheim D 61 A4
Hoddesdon GB 31 C3
Hodejov SK 65 B5
Hodenhagen D 43 C6
Hodkovice CZ 53 C5
Hódmezővásárhely
H 75 B5
Hodnet GB 26 C3
Hodonín CZ 64 B3
Hodslavice CZ 64 A4
Hoedekenskerke NL . . . 49 B4
Hoegaarden B 49 C5
Hoek van Holland NL . . 49 B5
Hoenderlo NL 50 A1
Hof
D 52 C1
N 35 C2
Hofbieber D 51 C5
Hoff GB 26 A3
Hofgeismar D 51 B5
Hofheim
Bayern D 51 C6
Hessen D 51 C4
Hofkirchen im Mühlkreis
A 63 B4
Höfn IS 111 C10
Hofors S 36 B3
Hofsós IS 111 B6
Hofstad N 114 C7
Höganäs S 41 C2
Högbo S 36 B3
Hogdal S 35 C3
Høgebru N 32 A4
Högfors S 36 C2
Högklint S 37 E5
Högsäter S 35 D4
Högsby S 40 B6
Högsjö S 37 C2
Hogstad S 37 D2
Högyész H 74 B3
Hohenau A 64 B2
Hohenberg A 63 C6
Hohenbucko D 52 B3
Hohenburg D 62 A2
Hohendorf D 45 A4
Hohenems A 71 A4
Hohenhameln D 51 A6
Hohenhausen D 51 A4
Hohenkirchen D 43 B4
Hohenlinden D 62 B2
Hohenlockstedt D 43 B6
Hohenmölsen D 52 B2
Hohennauen D 44 C4
Hohen Neuendorf D . . . 45 C5
Hohenseeden D 52 A2
Hohentauern A 73 A4
Hohentengen D 70 A3
Hohenwepel D 51 B5
Hohenwestedt D 43 A6
Hohenwutzen D 45 C6
Hohenzieritz D 45 B5
Hohn D 43 A6
Hohne D 44 C2
Hohnstorf D 44 B2
Højer DK 39 E1
Højslev Stby DK 38 C2
Hok S 40 B4
Hökerum S 40 B3
Hökhuvud S 36 B5
Hokksund N 34 C1
Hökön S 40 C4
Hol N 32 B5
Hola Pristan UA 11 C12
Hólar IS 111 B6
Holašovice CZ 63 B5
Holbæk
Aarhus Amt. DK 38 C3
Vestsjællands Amt.
DK 39 D4
Holbeach GB 30 B4
Holdenstedt D 44 C2
Holdhus N 32 B2
Holdorf D 43 C5
Holeby DK 44 A3
Hølen N 35 C2
Hølervasseter N 32 B6
Holešov CZ 64 A3
Holguera E 93 B4
Holíč SK 64 B3
Holice
CZ 53 C5
SK 64 C3
Höljes S 34 B4
Hollabrunn A 64 B2
Hollandstoun GB 23 B6
Høllen N 33 D4
Hollfeld D 52 D1
Hollókő H 65 C5
Hollstadt D 51 C6
Hollum NL 42 B2
Höllviksnäs S 41 D2
Holm N 114 B9
Hólmavík IS 111 B4
Holmbukt N 113 B10
Holmedal S 35 C3
Holmegil N 35 C3
Holmen N 34 B2
Holme-on-Spalding-Moor
GB 27 B5
Holmes Chapel GB . . . 26 B3
Holmestrand N 35 C2
Holmfirth GB 27 B4
Holmfoss N 113 C19
Holmsbu N 35 C2
Holmsjö S 41 C5
Holmsund S 3 E24
Holmsveden S 36 A3
Holmudden S 37 E6
Hölö S 37 C4
Holøydal N 114 E8
Holsbybrunn S 40 B5
Holseter N 34 A1
Holsljunga S 40 B2
Holstebro DK 39 C1
Holsted DK 39 D1
Holsworthy GB 28 C3
Holt
D 39 E2
Norfolk GB 30 B5
Wrexham GB 26 B3
IS 111 D6
N 33 D5
Holten NL 50 A2
Holtwick D 50 A3
Holum N 33 D4
Holwerd NL 42 B2
Holycross IRL 21 B4
Holyhead GB 26 B1
Holýšov CZ 62 A4
Holywell GB 26 B2
Holywood GB 19 B6
Holzdorf D 52 B3
Holzhausen D 51 A4
Holzheim D 61 B6
Holzkirchen D 62 C2
Holzminden D 51 B5
Holzthaleben D 51 B6
Homberg
Hessen D 51 B5
Hessen D 51 C5
Homburg D 60 A3
Hommelstø N 115 B9
Hommersåk N 33 D2
Homokmegy H 75 B4
Homokszentgyörgy
H 74 B2
Homrogd H 65 B6
Homyel = Gomel BY . . . 7 E11
Honaz TR 119 E4
Hondarribia E 76 C1
Hondón de los Frailes
E 101 A5
Hondschoote F 48 C3
Hönebach D 51 C5
Hønefoss N 34 B2
Honfleur F 57 A6
Høng DK 39 D4
Honiton GB 29 C4
Hönningen D 50 C2
Honningsvåg N 113 B14
Hönö S 38 B4
Honrubia E 95 C4
Hontalbilla E 88 C2
Hontheim D 50 C2
Hontianske-Nemce
SK 65 B4
Hontoria de la Cantera
E 88 B3
Hontoria del Pinar E . . 89 C3
Hontoria de Valdearados
E 89 C3
Hoofddorp NL 49 A5
Hoogerheide NL 49 B5
Hoogeveen NL 42 C3
Hoogezand-Sappemeer
NL 42 B3
Hoogkarspel NL 42 C2
Hoogkerk NL 42 B3
Hoogstede D 42 C3
Hoogstraten B 49 B5
Hook GB 31 C3
Hooksiel D 43 B5
Höör S 41 D3
Hoorn NL 42 C2
Hope GB 26 B2
Hopen N 112 E4
Hope under Dinmore
GB 29 A5
Hopfgarten A 72 A2
Hopfgarten in Defereggen
A 72 B2
Hopseidet N 113 B16
Hopsten D 43 C4
Hoptrup DK 39 D2
Hora Svatého Sebestiána
CZ 52 C3
Horažďovice CZ 63 A4
Horb am Neckar D 61 B4
Horbelev DK 39 E5
Hørby DK 38 B3
Hörby S 41 D3
Horcajada de la Torre
E 95 B4
Horcajo de los Montes
E 94 C2
Horcajo de Santiago
E 95 C3
Horcajo-Medianero E . . 93 A5
Horche E 95 B3
Horda S 40 B4
Hordabø N 32 B1
Hordalia N 32 C3
Hordvik N 32 B2
Hořesedly CZ 52 C3
Horezu RO 11 D8
Horgen CH 70 A3
Horgoš SRB 75 B4
Hořice CZ 53 C5
Horjul SLO 73 B4
Horka D 53 B4
Hörken S 36 B1
Horki BY 7 D11
Hörle S 40 B4
Horn
A 63 B6
D 51 B4
N 34 B2
S 40 B5
Horna E 101 A4
Hornachos E 93 C4
Hornachuelos E 99 B5
Horná Mariková SK . . . 64 A4
Hornanes N 32 C2
Horná Streda SK 64 B3
Horná Štrubna SK 65 B4
Horná Súča SK 64 B3
Hornbæk
Aarhus Amt. DK 38 C2
Frederiksværk DK 41 C2
Hornberg D 61 B4
Hornburg D 51 A6
Horncastle GB 27 B5
Horndal S 36 B3
Horndean GB 31 D2
Horne
Fyns Amt. DK 39 D3
Ribe Amt. DK 39 D1
Hörnebo S 35 D6
Horneburg D 43 B6
Hörnefors S 115 D16
Horní Bečva CZ 64 A4
Horni Benešov CZ 64 A3
Horni Cerekev CZ 63 A6
Horní Jiřetín CZ 52 C3
Horní Lomná CZ 65 A4
Horní Maršov CZ 53 C5
Hornindal N 114 F3
Hørning DK 39 C3
Hörningsholm S 37 C4
Horní Planá CZ 63 B5
Horni Slavkov CZ 52 C2
Horni Vltavice CZ 63 B4
Hornnes N 33 D4
Hornoy D 53 B4
Hornos E 101 A3
Hornoy-le-Bourg F 58 A2
Hornsea GB 27 B5
Hornsjø N 34 A2
Hornslet DK 39 C3
Hornstein A 64 C2
Hörnum D 39 E1
Hornum DK 38 C2
Horný Tisovník SK 65 B5
Horodenka UA 11 B8
Horodnya UA 7 F11
Horodok
Khmelnytskyy UA 11 B9
Lviv UA 11 B7
Horodyshche UA 11 B11
Horokhiv UA 11 A8
Horovice CZ 63 A4
Horred S 40 B2
Hörröd S 41 D4
Hörsching A 63 B5
Horsens DK 39 D2
Horsham GB 31 C3
Hørsholm DK 41 D2
Horslunde DK 39 E4
Horšovský Týn CZ 62 A3
Horst NL 50 B2
Horstel D 50 A3
Horstmar D 50 A3
Hort H 65 C5
Horta P 87 C3
Horten N 35 C2
Hortezuela E 89 C4
Hortiguela E 89 B3
Hortobágy H 75 A6
Horton in Ribblesdale
GB 26 A3
Hørve DK 39 D4
Hörvik S 41 C4
Horwich GB 26 B3
Hosanger N 32 B2
Hösbach D 51 C5
Hosena D 53 B4
Hosenfeld D 51 C5
Hosingen L 50 C2
Hospental CH 70 B3
Hospital IRL 20 B3
Hossegor F 76 C1
Hosszuhetény H 74 B3
Hostal de Ipiés E 90 A2
Hošťálkova CZ 64 A3
Hostalric E 91 B5
Hostens F 76 B2
Hostěradice CZ 64 B2
Hostinné CZ 53 C5
Hostomice CZ 63 A5
Hostouň CZ 62 A3
Hotagen S 115 D11
Hoting S 115 C13
Hotolisht AL 116 A2
Hotton B 49 C6
Houdain F 48 C3
Houdan F 58 B2
Houdelaincourt F 60 B1
Houeillès F 76 B3
Houffalize B 50 C1
Houghton-le-Spring
GB 25 D6
Houlberg DK 39 C2
Houlgate F 57 A5
Hounslow GB 31 C3
Hourtin F 66 C3
Hourtin-Plage F 66 C3
Houthalen B 49 B6
Houyet B 49 C5
Hov
DK 39 D3
N 34 B2
Hova S 35 D6
Høvåg N 33 D5
Hovborg DK 39 D1
Hovda N 32 B6
Hovden N 33 C4
Hove GB 31 D3
Hovedgård DK 39 D2
Hovelhof D 51 B4
Hoven DK 39 D1
Hovet N 32 B5
Hovingham GB 27 A5
Hovmantorp S 40 C5
Hovsta S 37 C2
Howden GB 27 B5
Howe D 44 B2
Höxter D 51 B5
Hoya D 43 C6
Hoya de Santa Maria
E 99 B4
Hoya-Gonzalo E 95 D5
Høyanger N 32 A3
Hoyerswerda D 53 B4
Høyjord N 35 C2
Hoylake GB 26 B2
Høylandet N 114 C9
Hoym D 52 B1
Høymyr N 32 C6
Hoyocasero E 94 B2
Hoyo de Manzanares
E 94 B3
Hoyo de Pinares E 94 B2
Hoyos E 93 A4
Hoyos del Espino E . . . 93 A5
Hrabusiče SK 65 B6
Hradec Králové CZ 53 C5
Hradec nad Moravicí
CZ 64 A3
Hrádek CZ 64 B2
Hrádek nad Nisou CZ . . 53 C4
Hradište SK 65 B4
Hrafnagil IS 111 B7
Hrafnseyri IS 111 B2
Hranice
Severomoravský
CZ 64 A3
Západočeský CZ 52 C2
Hranovnica SK 65 B6
Hrasnica BIH 84 C3
Hrastnik SLO 73 B5
Hřebenka UA 11 A12
Hřensko CZ 53 C4
Hriňová SK 65 B5
Hrisoupoli GR 116 B6
Hrochov CZ 64 A2
Hrochův Tynec CZ 53 D5
Hrodna BY 6 E7
Hrodzyanka BY 7 E10
Hronov CZ 53 C6
Hronský Beňadik SK . . . 65 B4
Hrotovice CZ 64 A2
Hrtkovci SRB 85 B4
Hrun IS 111 A5
Hrušov SK 65 B5
Hrušovany nad
Jevišovkou CZ 64 B2
Hřuštín SK 65 A5
Hrvaćani BIH 84 B2
Hrvace HR 83 C5
Hrymayliv UA 11 B9
Huben A 72 B2
Hückel-hoven D 50 B2
Hückeswagen D 50 B3
Hucknall GB 27 B4
Hucqueliers F 48 C2
Huddersfield GB 27 B4
Huddinge S 37 C4
Huddunge S 36 B3
Hude D 43 B5
Hudiksvall S 115 F14
Huélago E 100 B2
Huélamo E 95 B5
Huelgoat F 56 B2
Huelma E 100 B2
Huelva E 99 B4
Huéneja E 100 B3
Huércal de Almeria
E 101 C3
Huércal-Overa E 101 B4
Huerta de Abajo E 89 B3
Huerta del Rey E 89 C3
Huerta de
Valdecarabanos E . . . 95 C3
Huertahernando E 95 B4
Huesa E 100 B2
Huesca E 90 A2
Huéscar E 101 B3
Huete E 95 B4
Huétor Tájar E 100 B1
Hüfingen D 61 C4
Hufthamar N 32 B2
Hugh Town GB 28 D1
Huglfing D 62 C2
Huissen NL 50 B1
Huittinen FIN 3 F25
Huizen NL 49 A6
Hulin CZ 64 A3
Hüls D 50 B2
Hulsig DK 38 B3
Hulst NL 49 B5
Hult S 40 B5
Hulta S 40 A6
Hulteby S 35 C6
Hulterstad S 41 C6
Hultsfred S 40 B5
Humanes E 95 B3
Humberston GB 27 B5
Humble DK 39 E3
Humenné SK 10 B6
Humilladero E 100 B1
Humlebæk DK 41 D2
Humlum DK 38 C1
Hummelsta S 37 C3
Humpolec CZ 63 A6
Humshaugh GB 25 C5
Hundåla N 115 B9
Hundested DK 39 D4
Hundvåg N 33 C2
Hundvin N 32 B2
Hunedoara RO 11 D7
Hünfeld D 51 C5
Hungen D 51 C4
Hungerford GB 31 C2
Hunndalen N 34 B2
Hunnebostrand S 35 D3
Hunstanton GB 30 B4
Huntingdon GB 30 B3
Huntley GB 29 B5
Huntly GB 23 D6
Hünxe D 50 B2
Hurbanovo SK 64 C4
Hürbel D 61 B5
Hurdal N 34 B3
Hurezani RO 11 D7
Hurlford GB 24 C3
Hurstbourne Tarrant
GB 31 C2
Hurstpierpoint GB 31 D3
Hürth D 50 C2
Hurum N 32 A5
Hurup DK 38 C1
Húsafell IS 111 C5
Húsavík IS 111 A8
Husbands Bosworth
GB 30 B2
Husby
D 39 E2
DK 39 C1
Husey IS 111 B11
Huşi RO 11 C10
Husina BIH 84 B3
Husinec CZ 63 A4
Husinish GB 22 D1
Huskvarna S 40 B4
Husnes N 32 C2
Husøy N 112 C6
Hustad N 114 E4
Hüsten D 50 B3
Hustopeče CZ 64 B2
Hustopeče nad Bečvou
CZ 64 A3
Husum
D 43 A6
S 115 D16
Husvika N 115 B9
Huta PL 46 C2
Hutovo BIH 84 D2
Hüttenberg A 73 B4
Hüttlingen D 61 B6
Huttoft GB 27 B6
Hutton Cranswick GB . . 27 B5
Hüttschlag A 72 A3
Huttwil CH 70 A2
Huy B 49 C6
Hüyük TR 119 E6
Hval N 34 B2
Hvåle N 32 B6
Hvaler N 35 C3
Hvalpsund DK 38 C2
Hvammstangi IS 111 B5
Hvammur IS 111 B6
Hvanneyri IS 111 C4
Hvar HR 83 C5
Hvarnes N 35 C1
Hveragerði IS 111 D4
Hvidbjerg DK 38 C1
Hvide Sande DK 39 D1
Hvittingfoss N 35 C2
Hvolsvöllur IS 111 D5
Hybe SK 65 A5
Hycklinge S 40 B5
Hydra GR 117 E5
Hyen N 114 F2
Hyères F 79 C5
Hyères Plage F 79 C5
Hylestad N 33 C4
Hylke DK 39 D2
Hyllestad N 32 A2
Hyllstofta S 41 C3
Hyltebruk S 40 B3
Hynish GB 24 B1
Hynnekleiv N 33 D5
Hythe
Hampshire GB 31 D2
Kent GB 31 C5
Hyvinkää FIN 3 F26

I

Iam RO 85 A6
Iaşi RO 11 C9
Iasmos GR 116 A7
Ibahernando E 93 B5
Iballë AL 105 A5
Ibarranguelua E 89 A4
Ibbenbüren D 50 A3
Ibeas de Juarros E 89 B3
Ibestad N 112 D6
Ibi E 96 C2
Ibiza = Eivissa E 97 C1
İbradı TR 119 E6
İbriktepe TR 118 A1
Ibros E 100 A2
Ibstock GB 27 C4
İçel TR 16 C7
Ichenhausen D 61 B6
Ichnya UA 11 A12
Ichtegem B 49 B4
Ichtershausen D 51 C6
Idanha-a-Novo P 93 B3
Idar-Oberstein D 60 A3
Idd N 35 C3
Idiazábal E 89 B4
Idivuoma S 113 D10
Idkerberget S 36 B2
Idön S 36 B5
Idre S 115 F9
Idrija SLO 73 C4
Idritsa RUS 7 C10
Idstein D 50 C4
Idvor SRB 75 C5
Iecca Mare RO 75 C5
Ielsi I 103 B7
Ieper = Ypres B 48 C3
Ierapetra GR 117 G7
Ierissos GR 116 B5
Ifjord N 113 B16
Ig SLO 73 C4
Igal H 74 B2
Igea E 89 B4
Igea Marina I 82 B1
Igelfors S 37 D2
Igersheim D 61 A5
Iggesund S 115 F14
Iglarevo KOS 85 D5
Iglesias E 88 B3
Iglesias I 110 C1
Igls A 71 A6
Igny-Comblizy F 59 A4
Igorre E 89 A4
Igoumenitsa GR 116 C2
Igries E 90 A2
Igualada E 91 B4
Igüeña E 86 B4
Iguerande F 68 B4
Iharosberény H 74 B2
Ihl'any SK 65 A6
Ihlienworth D 43 B5
Ihringen D 60 B3
Ihrlerstein D 62 B2
İhsaniye TR 118 C5
Ii FIN 3 D26
Iijärvi FIN 113 C16
Iisalmi FIN 3 E27
IJmuiden NL 42 C1
IJsselmuiden NL 42 C2
IJzendijke NL 49 B4
Ikast DK 39 C2
Ikervár H 74 A1
Ilandža SRB 75 C5
Ilanz CH 71 B4
Ilava SK 64 B4
Iława PL 47 B5
il Castagno I 81 C4
Ilche E 90 B3
Ilchester GB 29 C5
Ilfeld D 51 B6
Ilfracombe GB 28 B3
Ilgaz TR 16 A6
Ilgın TR 119 D6
Ílhavo P 92 A2
Ilica TR 118 C2
Ilidža BIH 84 C3
Ilijaš BIH 84 C3
Ilirska Bistrica SLO . . . 73 C4
Ilkeston GB 27 C4
Ilkley GB 27 B4
Illana E 95 B4
Illano E 86 A4
Illar E 101 C3
Illas E 88 A1
Illats F 76 B2
Illertissen D 61 B6
Illescas E 94 B3
Ille-sur-Têt F 91 A5
Illfurth F 60 C3
Illichivsk UA 11 C11
Illiers-Combray F 58 B2
Illkirch-Graffenstaden
F 60 B3
Illmersdorf D 52 B3
Illmitz A 64 C2
Íllora E 100 B2
Illueca E 89 C5
Ilmajoki FIN 3 E25
Ilmenau D 51 C6
Ilminster GB 29 C5
Ilok HR 75 C4
Ilomantsi FIN 3 E29
Iłow PL 47 C6
Iłowa PL 53 B5
Iłowo-Osada PL 47 B6
Ilsenburg D 51 B6
Ilshofen D 61 A5
Ilz A 73 A5
Iłża PL 55 B6
Imatra FIN 3 F28
Imielin PL 55 C4
Imingen N 32 B5
Immeln S 41 C4
Immenhausen D 51 B5
Immenstadt D 61 C6
Immingham GB 27 B5
Ímola I 81 B5
Imon E 95 A4
Imotski HR 84 C2
Impéria I 80 C2
Imphy F 68 B3
İmroz TR 116 B7
Imsland N 33 C2
Imst A 71 A5
Inagh IRL 20 B2
Inari FIN 113 D15
Inca E 97 B2
Inchnadamph GB 22 C4
Incinillas E 89 B3
Indal S 115 E14
Indija SRB 85 A5
Indre Arna N 32 B2
Indre Billefjord N . . . 113 B14
Indre Brenna N 113 B14
İğneada TR 118 A2
İnebolu TR 16 A6
İnecik TR 118 B2
İnegöl TR 118 B4
Inerthal CH 70 A3
Infiesto E 88 A1
Ingatorp S 40 B5
Ingedal N 35 C3
Ingelheim D 50 D4
Ingelmunster B 49 C4
Ingelstad S 40 C4
Ingleton GB 26 A3
Ingolfsland N 32 C5
Ingolstadt D 62 B2
Ingrandes
Maine-et-Loire F 66 A4
Vienne F 67 B5
Ingwiller F 60 B3
Inhisar TR 118 B5
Inhulec UA 11 C12
Iniesta E 95 C5
Inishannon IRL 20 C3
Inishcrone IRL 18 B2
Inke H 74 B2
Innellan GB 24 C3
Innerleithen GB 25 C4
Innermessan GB 24 D3
Innertkirchen CH 70 B3
Innervillgraten A 72 B2
Innsbruck A 71 A6
Innset N 112 D7
Innvik N 114 F3
İnönü TR 118 C5
Inowłodz PL 55 B5
Inowrocław PL 47 C4
Ins CH 70 A2
Insch GB 23 D6
Insjön S 36 B2
Ińsko PL 46 B1
Instow GB 28 B3
İntepe TR 118 B1
Interlaken CH 70 B2
Intragna CH 70 B3
Introbio I 71 C4
Inverallochy GB 23 D7
Inveran
GB 23 D4
IRL 20 A2
Inveraray GB 24 B2
Inverbervie GB 25 B5
Invergarry GB 22 D4
Invergordon GB 23 D4
Invergowrie GB 25 B4
Inverkeilor GB 25 B5
Inverkeithing GB 25 B4
Invermoriston GB 23 D4
Inverness GB 23 D4
Inveruno I 70 C3
Inverurie GB 23 D6
Ioannina GR 116 C2
Iolanda di Savoia I 81 B5
Ion Corvin RO 11 D9
Iòppolo I 106 C2
Ios GR 117 F7
Ipati GR 116 D4
İpsala TR 118 B1
Ipswich GB 30 B5
Iraklia GR 116 A5
Iraklio = Heraklion
GR 117 G7
Irdning A 73 A4
Iregszemcse H 74 B3
Irgoli I 110 B2
Irig SRB 85 A4
Ironbridge GB 26 C3
Irpin UA 11 A11
Irrel D 60 A2
Irsina I 104 C2
Irsta S 37 C3
Irthlingborough GB . . . 30 B3
Iruela E 87 B4
Irún E 76 C1
Irurita E 76 C1
Irurzun E 76 D1
Irvine GB 24 C3
Irvinestown GB 19 B4
Isaba E 76 D2
Isabela E 100 A2
Ísafjörður IS 111 A2
Isane N 114 F2
Isaszeg H 75 A4
İsbister GB 22 A7
İscar E 88 C2
İscehisar TR 118 D5
Ischgl A 71 A5
Íschia I 103 C6
Ischia di Castro I 102 A4
Ischitella I 104 B1
Isdes F 58 C3
Ise N 35 C3
Iselle I 70 B3
Iseltwald CH 70 B2
Isen D 62 B3
Isenbüttel D 44 C2
Iseo I 71 C5
Iserlohn D 50 B3
Isernia I 103 B7
Isfjorden N 114 E4
Ishëm AL 105 B5
Isigny-sur-Mer F 57 A4
Işıklı TR 119 D4
Ísili I 110 C2
İskilip TR 16 A7
Isla Canela E 98 B3
Isla Cristina E 98 B3
Islares E 89 A3
Isleham GB 30 B4
Isle of Whithorn GB . . . 24 D3
Ismaning D 62 B2
Isna P 92 B3
Isnestoften N 113 B11
Isny D 61 C6
Isoba E 88 A1
Isokylä
FIN 113 F16
S 113 E11
Isola F 79 B6
Isola d'Asti I 80 B2
Isola del Gran Sasso
d'Itália I 103 A6
Ísola della Scala I 71 C6
Isola delle Fémmine
I 108 A2
Ísola del Liri I 103 B6
Ísola di Capo Rizzuto
I 107 C4
Isona E 91 A4
Ispagnac F 78 B2
Isparta TR 119 E5
Isperikh BG 11 E9
Íspica I 109 C3
Isselburg D 50 B2
Issigeac F 77 B3
Issogne I 70 C2
Issoire F 68 C3
Issoncourt F 59 B6
Issoudun F 68 B2
Issum D 50 B2
Is-sur-Tille F 69 A5
Issy-l'Evêque F 68 B3
İstán E 100 C1
İstanbul TR 118 A3
İstebna PL 65 A4
Ístia d'Ombrone I 81 D5
Istiea GR 116 D5
Istok KOS 85 D5
Istres F 78 C3
Istvándi H 74 B2
Itea GR 116 D4
Ithaki GR 117 D2
Itoiz E 76 D1
Ítrabo E 100 C2
Itri I 103 B6
Ittireddu I 110 B1
Íttiri I 110 B1
Itzehoe D 43 B6
Ivalo FIN 113 D16
Iván H 74 A1
Ivanava BY 7 E8
Ivančice CZ 64 A2
Ivančna Gorica SLO . . . 73 C4
Iváncsa H 74 A3
Ivanec HR 73 B6
Ivanić Grad HR 73 C6
Ivanjica SRB 85 C5
Ivanjska BIH 84 B2
Ivanka SK 64 B4
Ivankovo HR 74 C3
Ivano-Frankivsk UA . . . 11 B8
Ivanovice na Hané
CZ 64 A3
Ivanska HR 74 C1
Ivatsevichy BY 7 E8
Ivaylovgrad BG 116 A8
Iveland N 33 D4
Ivoz Ramet B 49 C6
Ivrea I 70 C2
İvrindi TR 118 C2
Ivry-en-Montagne F . . . 69 A4
Ivry-la-Bataille F 58 B2
Ivybridge GB 28 C4
Iwaniska PL 55 C6
Iwiny PL 53 B5
Iwuy F 49 C4
Ixworth GB 30 B4
Izarra E 89 B4
Izbica Kujawska PL . . . 47 C4
Izbište SRB 85 A6
Izeda P 87 C4
Izegem B 49 C4
Izernore F 69 B5
Izmayil UA 11 D10
İzmir TR 119 D2
İzmit = Kocaeli TR . . . 118 B4
Iznájar E 100 B1
Iznalloz E 100 B2
Iznatoraf E 100 A2
İznik TR 118 B4
Izola SLO 72 C3
Izsák H 75 B4
Izsófalva H 65 B6
Izyaslav UA 11 A9

J

Jabalquinto E 100 A2
Jablanac HR 83 B3
Jablanica BIH 84 C2
Jablonec nad Jizerou
CZ 53 C5
Jablonec nad Nisou
CZ 53 C5
Jablonica SK 64 B3
Jablonka PL 65 A5
Jabłonna PL 55 A5
Jablonnénad Orlicí
CZ 54 C1
Jablonne Podještědí
CZ 53 C4
Jablonov nad Turňou
SK 65 B6
Jabłonowo Pomorskie
PL 47 B5
Jablúnka CZ 64 A3
Jablunkov CZ 65 A4
Jabučje SRB 85 B5
Jabugo E 99 B4
Jabuka
Srbija SRB 85 C4
Vojvodina SRB 85 B5
Jabukovac HR 73 C6
Jaca E 90 A2
Jáchymov CZ 52 C2
Jacobidrebber D 43 C5
Jade D 43 B5
Jäderfors S 36 B3
Jädraås S 36 B3
Jadraque E 95 B4
Jaén E 100 B2
Jagare BIH 84 B2
Jagel D 43 A6
Jagenbach A 63 B6
Jægerspris DK 39 D4
Jagodina SRB 85 C6
Jagodnjak HR 74 C3
Jagodzin PL 53 B5
Jagstheim D 61 A6
Jagstzell D 61 A6
Jahodna SK 64 B3
Jajce BIH 84 B2
Ják H 74 A1
Jakabszálbs H 75 B4
Jäkkvik S 115 A14
Jaklovce SK 65 B6
Jakobsnes N 113 C19
Jakovlje HR 73 C5
Jakšic HR 74 C2
Jakubany SK 65 A6
Jalance E 96 B1
Jalasjärvi FIN 3 E25
Jalhay B 50 C1
Jaligny-sur-Besbre F . . 68 B3
Jallais F 66 A4
Jalón E 96 C2
Jâlons F 59 B5
Jamena SRB 84 B4
Jamilena E 100 B2
Jämjö S 41 C5
Jamnička Kiselica
HR 73 C5
Jamno PL 46 A2
Jamoigne B 59 A6
Jämsä FIN 3 F26
Jämshög S 41 C4
Janakkala FIN 3 F26
Jandelsbrunn D 63 B4
Jänickendorf D 52 A3
Janikowo PL 47 C4
Janja BIH 85 B4
Janjina HR 84 D2
Janki
Łódzkie PL 55 B4
Mazowieckie PL 55 A5
Jankov CZ 63 A5
Jankowo Dolne PL 46 C3
Jánoshalma H 75 B4
Jánosháza H 74 A2
Jánoshida H 75 A5
Jánossomorja H 64 C3
Janovice nad Uhlavou
CZ 63 A4
Janów PL 55 C4
Janowiec Wielkopolski
PL 46 C3
Janowo PL 47 B6
Jänsmässholmen
S 115 D10
Janville F 58 B2
Janzé F 57 C4
Jarabá SK 65 B5
Jaraczewo PL 54 B2
Jarafuel E 96 B1
Jaraicejo E 93 B5
Jaraíz de la Vera E . . . 93 A5
Jarak SRB 85 B4
Jarandilla de la Vera
E 93 A5
Jaray E 89 C4
Järbo S 36 B3
Jard-sur-Mer F 66 B3
Jaren N 34 B2
Jargeau F 58 C3
Jarkovac SRB 75 C5
Järlåsa S 36 C4
Jarmen D 45 B5
Järna S 37 C4
Jarnac F 67 C4
Järnäs S 115 D16
Järnforsen S 40 B5

Jarny F 60 A1
Jarocin PL 54 B2
Jaroměř CZ 53 C5
Jaroměřice nad Rokytnou CZ 64 A1
Jaroslav CZ 53 C6
Jaroslavice CZ 64 B2
Jarosław PL 11 A7
Jaroslawiec PL 46 A2
Jarošov nad Nežarkou CZ 63 A6
Järpås S 35 D4
Järpen S 115 D10
Jarrow GB 25 D6
Järso FIN 36 B6
Järvenpää FIN 7 A8
Jarvorník CZ 54 C1
Järvsö S 115 F13
Jarzé F 67 A4
Jaša Tomic SRB 75 C5
Jasenak HR 73 C5
Jasenica BIH 83 B5
Jasenice HR 83 B4
Jasenovac HR 74 C1
Jasenovo
Srbija SRB 85 C4
Vojvodina SRB 85 B6
Jasień PL 53 B5
Jasienica PL 53 B4
Jasika SRB 85 C6
Jasło PL 10 B6
Jásova SK 65 C4
Jasseron F 69 B5
Jastarnia PL 47 A4
Jastrebarsko HR 73 C5
Jastrowie PL 46 B2
Jastrzębia-Góra PL 47 A4
Jastrzębie Zdrój PL 54 D3
Jászals-Lószentgyörgy H 75 A5
Jászapáti H 75 A5
Jászárokszállás H 65 C5
Jászberény H 75 A4
Jászdózsa H 65 C6
Jászfényszaru H 75 A4
Jászjakóhalma H 75 A5
Jászkarajenö H 75 A5
Jászkisér H 75 A5
Jászladány H 75 A5
Jászszentlászló H 75 B4
Jásztelek H 75 A5
Játar E 100 C2
Jättendal S 115 F14
Jatznick D 45 B5
Jaun CH 70 B2
Jausiers F 79 B5
Jávea E 96 C3
Jävenitz D 44 C3
Javerlhac F 67 C5
Javier E 90 A1
Javorani BIH 84 B2
Javorina SK 65 A6
Javron F 57 B5
Jawor PL 53 B6
Jaworzno PL 55 C4
Jaworzyna Śl. PL 54 C1
Jayena E 100 C2
Jażow PL 53 B4
Jebel RO 75 C6
Jebjerg DK 38 C2
Jedburgh GB 25 C5
Jedlinsk PL 55 B6
Jedlnia PL 55 B6
Jedlnia Letnisko PL 55 B6
Jedovnice CZ 64 A2
Jędrychow PL 47 B5
Jędrzejów PL 55 C5
Jedwabno PL 47 B6
Jeesiö FIN 113 E15
Jegłownik PL 47 A5
Jegun F 77 C3
Jēkabpils LV 7 C8
Jektevik N 32 C2
Jektvik N 112 F2
Jelakci SRB 85 C5
Jelcz-Laskowice PL 54 B2
Jelenec SK 64 B4
Jelenia Góra PL 53 C5
Jelgava LV 6 C7
Jelka SK 64 B3
Jelling DK 39 D2
Jels DK 39 D2
Jelsa
HR 83 C5
N 33 C3
Jelšava SK 65 B6
Jemgum D 43 B4
Jemnice CZ 63 A6
Jena D 52 C1
Jenaz CH 71 B4
Jenbach A 72 A1
Jenikow PL 45 B7
Jennersdorf A 73 B6
Jenny S 40 B6
Jerchel D 44 C3
Jeres del Marquesado E 100 B2
Jerez de la Frontera E 99 C4
Jerez de los Caballeros E 99 A4
Jerica E 96 B2
Jerichow D 44 C4
Jerka PL 54 A1
Jermenovci SRB 75 C6
Jerslev DK 38 B3
Jerte E 93 A5
Jerup DK 38 B3
Jerxheim D 51 A6
Jerzmanowice PL 55 C4
Jerzu I 110 C2
Jerzwałd PL 47 B5
Jesberg D 51 C5
Jesenice
Středočeský CZ 52 C3
Středočeský CZ 53 D4
SLO 73 B4
Jeseník CZ 54 C2
Jesenké SK 65 B6
Jesi I 82 C2
Jésolo I 72 C2
Jessen D 52 B2
Jessenitz D 44 B3
Jessheim N 34 B3
Jessnitz D 52 B2
Jesteburg D 44 B1
Jeumont F 49 C5
Jeven-stedt D 43 A6
Jever D 43 B4
Jevíčko CZ 64 A2
Jevišovice CZ 64 B1
Jevnaker N 34 B2
Jezerane HR 83 A4
Jezero
BIH 84 B2
HR 83 A4
Jeziorany PL 47 B6
Jezów PL 55 B4
Jičín CZ 53 C5
Jičiněves CZ 53 C5
Jihlava CZ 63 A6
Jijona E 96 C2
Jilemnice CZ 53 C5
Jilové CZ 53 C4
Jilovéu Prahy CZ 63 A5
Jimbolia RO 75 C5
Jimena E 100 B2
Jimena de la Frontera E 99 C5
Jimera de Libar E 99 C5
Jimramov CZ 64 A2
Jince CZ 63 A4
Jindřichovice CZ 52 C2
Jindřichův Hradec CZ 63 A6
Jirkov CZ 52 C3
Jistebnice CZ 63 A5
Joachimsthal D 45 C5
João da Loura P 92 C2
Jobbágyi H 65 C5
Jochberg A 72 A2
Jockfall S 113 F11
Jódar E 100 B2
Jodoigne B 49 C5
Joensuu FIN 3 E28
Joesjö S 115 B11
Joeuf F 60 A1
Jõgeva EST 7 B9
Johanngeorgenstadt D 52 C2
Johannishus S 41 C5
Johanniskirchen D 62 B3
Johansfors S 40 C5
John o'Groats GB 23 C5
Johnshaven GB 25 B5
Johnstone GB 24 C3
Johnstown IRL 21 B4
Jõhvi EST 7 B9
Joigny F 59 C4
Joinville F 59 B6
Jokkmokk S 112 F8
Jöllenbeck D 51 A4
Jomala FIN 36 B6
Jönåker S 37 D3
Jonava LT 6 D8
Jonchery-sur-Vesle F 59 A4
Jondal N 32 B3
Jondalen N 33 C6
Joniškis LT 6 C7
Jönköping S 40 B4
Jonkowo PL 47 B6
Jønnbu N 33 C6
Jonsberg S 37 D3
Jonsered S 38 B5
Jonstorp S 41 C2
Jonzac F 67 C4
Jorba E 91 B4
Jordanów PL 65 A5
Jordanowo PL 46 C1
Jordanów Ślaski PL 54 C1
Jordbro S 37 C5
Jordbrua N 115 A11
Jördenstorf D 45 B4
Jordet N 34 A4
Jordøse DK 39 D3
Jork D 43 B6
Jörlanda S 38 B4
Jormlien S 115 C10
Jormvattnet S 115 C11
Jörn S 115 B17
Jørpeland N 33 C3
Jorquera E 96 B1
Jošan HR 83 B4
Jošanička Banja SRB 85 C5
Jošavka BIH 84 B2
Josipdol HR 73 C5
Josipovac HR 74 C3
Jössefors S 35 C4
Josselin F 56 C3
Jøssund N 114 C7
Jostedal N 114 F4
Jósvafö H 65 B6
Jou P 87 C3
Jouarre F 59 B4
Joué-lès-Tours F 67 A5
Joué-sur-Erdre F 66 A3
Joure NL 42 C2
Joutseno FIN 3 F28
Joutsijärvi FIN 113 F16
Joux-la-Ville F 59 C4
Jouy F 58 B2
Jouy-le-Châtel F 59 B4
Jouy-le-Potier F 58 C2
Joyeuse F 78 B3
Joze F 68 C3
Józefów PL 55 A6
Juankoski FIN 3 E28
Juan-les-Pins F 79 C6
Juban AL 105 A5
Jübek D 43 A6
Jubera E 89 B4
Jubrique E 99 C5
Jüchsen D 51 C6
Judaberg N 33 C2
Judenburg A 73 A4
Juelsminde DK 39 D3
Jugon-les-Lacs F 56 B3
Juillac F 67 C6
Juillan F 76 C3
Juist D 43 B4
Jukkasjärvi S 112 E9
Jule N 115 C10
Julianadorp NL 42 C1
Julianstown IRL 19 C5
Jülich D 50 C2
Jullouville F 57 B4
Jumeaux F 68 C3
Jumièges F 58 A1
Jumilhac-le-Grand F 67 C6
Jumilla E 101 A4
Juncosa E 90 B3
Juneda E 90 B3
Jung S 35 D5
Jungingen D 61 B5
Junglingster L 60 A2
Juniville F 59 A5
Junosuando S 113 E11
Junqueira P 87 C3
Junsele S 115 D13
Juoksengi S 113 F12
Juoksenki FIN 113 F12
Juprelle B 49 C6
Jurata PL 47 A4
Jurbarkas LT 6 D7
Jurjevo HR 83 B3
Jūrmala LV 6 C7
Juromenha P 93 C3
Jursla S 37 D3
Jussac F 77 B5
Jussey F 60 C1
Jussy F 59 A4
Juta H 74 B2
Jüterbog D 52 B3
Juuka FIN 3 E28
Juvigny-le-Terte F 57 B4
Juvigny-sous-Andaine F 57 B5
Juzennecourt F 59 B5
Jyderup DK 39 D4
Jyväskylä FIN 3 E26

K

Kaamanen FIN 113 C16
Kaamasmukka FIN 113 C15
Kaaresuvanto FIN 113 D11
Kaarssen D 44 B3
Kaatscheuvel NL 49 B6
Kaba H 75 A6
Kåbdalis S 115 A17
Kačarevo SRB 85 B5
Kačikol KOS 85 D6
Kács H 65 C6
Kadan CZ 52 C3
Kadarkút H 74 B2
Kadınhanı TR 119 D7
Kaduy RUS 7 B14
Kåfalla S 37 C2
Kåfjord N 113 C12
Kåfjordbotn N 112 C9
Kågeröd S 41 D3
Kahl D 51 C5
Kahla D 52 C1
Kainach bei Voitsberg A 73 A5
Kaindorf A 73 A5
Kainulasjärvi S 113 F11
Kairala FIN 113 E16
Kaisepakte S 112 D8
Kaisersesch D 50 C3
Kaiserslautern D 60 A3
Kaisheim D 62 B1
Kajaani FIN 3 D27
Kajárpéc H 74 A2
Kajdacs H 74 B3
Kakanj BIH 84 B3
Kakasd H 74 B3
Kaklik TR 119 E4
Kakolewo PL 54 B1
Kál H 65 C6
Kalače MNE 85 D5
Kalajoki FIN 3 D25
Kalak N 113 B16
Kalamata GR 117 E4
Kalambaka GR 116 C3
Kalamria GR 116 B4
Kalandra GR 116 C5
Kälarne S 115 E13
Kalavrita GR 117 D4
Kalbe D 44 C3
Kalce SLO 73 C4
Káld H 74 A2
Kale
Antalya TR 119 F4
Denizli TR 119 E3
Kalecik TR 16 A6
Kalefeld D 51 B6
Kalenić SRB 85 C5
Kalesija BIH 84 B3
Kalety PL 54 C3
Kalevala RUS 3 D29
Kalhovd N 32 B5
Kalí HR 83 B4
Kalimnos GR 119 F2
Kaliningrad RUS 47 A6
Kalinkavichy BY 7 E10
Kalinovac HR 74 B2
Kalinovik BIH 84 C3
Kalinovo SK 65 B5
Kalirachi GR 116 B6
Kaliska
Pomorskie PL 47 A4
Pomorskie PL 47 B4
Kalisko PL 55 B4
Kalisz PL 54 B3
Kalisz Pomorski PL 46 B1
Kalix S 3 D25
Kaljord N 112 D4
Kalkan TR 119 F4
Kalkar D 50 B2
Kalkım TR 118 C2
Kall
D 50 C2
S 115 D10
Källby S 35 D5
Kållered S 38 B5
Kållerstad S 40 B3
Kallinge S 41 C5
Kallmeti i Madh AL 105 B5
Kallmünz D 62 A2
Kallo FIN 113 E13
Kallsedet S 115 D9
Källvik S 37 D4
Kalmar S 40 C6
Kalmthout B 49 B5
Kalná SK 65 B4
Kalocsa H 75 B3
Kalokhorio CY 120 B2
Kalo Nero GR 117 E3
Kaloni GR 116 C8
Káloz H 74 B3
Kals A 72 A2
Kalsdorf A 73 B5
Kaltbrunn CH 70 A4
Kaltenbach A 72 A1
Kaltenkirchen D 44 B1
Kaltennordheim D 51 C6
Kaluga RUS 7 D14
Kalundborg DK 39 D4
Kalush UA 11 B8
Kałuszyn PL 55 A6
Kalv S 40 B3
Kalvåg N 114 F1
Kalvehave DK 41 D2
Kalwang A 73 A4
Kalwaria-Zebrzydowska PL 65 A5
Kalyazin RUS 7 C14
Kam H 74 A1
Kaman TR 16 B6
Kamares GR 117 F6
Kambos CY 120 A1
Kamen D 50 B3
Kamenice CZ 64 A1
Kamenice nad Lipou CZ 63 A6
Kameničná SK 64 C4
Kamenný Most SK 65 C4
Kamenny Ujezd CZ 63 B5
Kamenska HR 74 C2
Kamensko HR 84 C1
Kamenz D 53 B4
Kamičak BIH 84 B1
Kamień PL 55 B5
Kamieniec Zabk PL 54 C1
Kamienka SK 65 A6
Kamień Krajeński PL 46 B3
Kamienna Góra PL 53 C6
Kamień Pomorski PL 45 B6
Kamieńsk PL 55 B4
Kaminka UA 11 B12
Kamiros Skala GR 119 F2
Kamnik SLO 73 B4
Kampen NL 42 C2
Kampinos PL 55 A5
Kamp-Lintfort D 50 B2
Kampor HR 83 B3
Kamyanets-Podil's'kyy UA 11 B9
Kamyanka-Buz'ka UA 11 A8
Kamýk nad Vltavou CZ 63 A5
Kanal SLO 72 B3
Kanalia GR 116 C4
Kandalaksha RUS 3 C30
Kandanos GR 117 G5
Kandel D 61 A4
Kandern D 60 C3
Kandersteg CH 70 B2
Kandila GR 117 E4
Kandıra TR 118 A5
Kandyty PL 47 A6
Kanfanar HR 82 A2
Kangasala FIN 3 F26
Kangos S 113 E11
Kangosjärvi FIN 113 E12
Kaninë AL 105 C5
Kaniów PL 53 B4
Kanjiža SRB 75 B5
Kankaanpää FIN 3 F25
Kannus FIN 3 E25
Kanturk IRL 20 B3
Kaonik SRB 85 C6
Kapaklı TR 118 A2
Kapellen
A 63 C6
B 49 B5
Kapellskär S 37 C6
Kapfenberg A 73 A5
Kapfenstein A 73 B5
Kaplice CZ 63 B5
Kapljuh BIH 83 B5
Kápolna H 65 C6
Kápolnásnyék H 74 A3
Kaposfö H 74 B2
Kaposfüred H 74 B2
Kaposszekcsö H 74 B3
Kaposvár H 74 B2
Kapp N 34 B2
Kappel D 60 B3
Kappeln D 44 A1
Kappelshamn S 37 E5
Kappl A 71 A5
Kappstad S 35 C5
Kaprun A 72 A2
Kaptol HR 74 C2
Kapuvár H 64 C3
Karaadilli TR 119 D5
Karabiğa TR 118 B2
Karabük TR 118 A7
Karaburun TR 118 D1
Karacabey TR 118 B3
Karacaköy TR 118 A3
Karacaören TR 119 D5
Karacasu TR 119 E3
Karachev RUS 7 E13
Karácsond H 65 C6
Karád H 74 B2
Karahallı TR 119 D4
Karaisali TR 16 C7
Karaman
Balıkesir TR 118 C3
Karaman *continued*
Karaman TR 16 C6
Karamanlı TR 119 E4
Karamürsel TR 118 B4
Karan SRB 85 C4
Karancslapujto H 65 B5
Karaova TR 119 E2
Karapınar TR 16 C6
Karasjok N 113 C14
Karasu TR 118 A5
Karataş
Adana TR 16 C7
Manisa TR 119 D3
Karatoprak TR 119 E2
Karavostasi CY 120 A1
Karbenning S 36 B3
Kårberg S 37 D1
Kårböle S 115 F12
Karbunara AL 105 C5
Karby
D 44 A1
DK 38 C1
Kårby S 40 B6
Karby S 37 C5
Karcag H 75 A5
Karczew PL 55 A6
Karczów PL 54 C2
Karczowiska PL 53 B6
Kardamena GR 119 F2
Kardamila GR 116 D8
Kardamili GR 117 F4
Kardašova Rečice CZ 63 A5
Kardis S 113 F12
Karditsa GR 116 C3
Kärdla EST 6 B7
Kardoskút H 75 B5
Karesuando S 113 D11
Kargı TR 16 A7
Kargowa PL 53 A5
Karigasniemi FIN 113 C14
Karise DK 41 D2
Karistos GR 117 D6
Karkkila FIN 6 A8
Karlholmsbruk S 36 B4
Karlino PL 46 A1
Karl Liebknecht RUS 7 F13
Karlobag HR 83 B4
Karlovac HR 73 C5
Karlovasi GR 119 E1
Karlovčic SRB 85 B5
Karlovice CZ 54 C2
Karlovo BG 11 E8
Karlovy Vary CZ 52 C2
Karłowice PL 54 C2
Karlsborg S 37 D1
Karlshamn S 41 C4
Karlshöfen D 43 B6
Karlshus N 35 C2
Karlskoga S 37 C1
Karlskrona S 41 C5
Karlsrud N 32 B5
Karlsruhe D 61 A4
Karlstad S 35 C5
Karlstadt D 51 D5
Karlstetten A 63 B6
Karlstift A 63 B5
Karlstorp S 40 B5
Karmacs H 74 B2
Karmin PL 54 B2
Kärna S 38 B4
Karnobat BG 11 E9
Karojba HR 72 C3
Karow D 44 B4
Karpacz PL 53 C5
Karpathos GR 119 G2
Karpenisi GR 116 D3
Karpuzlu TR 119 E2
Kärrbo S 37 C3
Karrebaeksminde DK 39 D4
Karshult S 40 B3
Karsin PL 46 B3
Kårsta S 37 C5
Karstädt D 44 B3
Kartal TR 118 B4
Kartitsch A 72 B2
Kartuzy PL 47 A4
Karup DK 39 C2
Karviná CZ 65 A4
Kås DK 38 B2
Kaş TR 119 F4
Kasaba TR 119 F4
Kašava CZ 64 A3
Kåseberga S 41 D4
Kasejovice CZ 63 A4
Kasfjord N 112 D5
Kashin RUS 7 C14
Kašina HR 73 C6
Kasina-Wielka PL 65 A6
Kaskinen FIN 3 E24
Kašperské Hory CZ 63 A4
Kassandrino GR 116 B5
Kassel D 51 B5
Kassiopi GR 116 C1
Kastamonu TR 16 A6
Kastav HR 73 C4
Kasteli GR 117 G5
Kastellaun D 50 C3
Kastelli GR 117 G7
Kaštel-Stari HR 83 C5
Kaštel Zegarski HR 83 B4
Kasterlee B 49 B5
Kastl D 62 A2
Kastlösa S 41 C6
Kastorf D 44 B2
Kastoria GR 116 B3
Kastorio GR 117 E4
Kastraki GR 117 F7
Kastrosikia GR 116 C2
Kastsyukovichy BY 7 E12
Kaszaper H 75 B5
Katakolo GR 117 E3
Katapola GR 117 F7
Katastari GR 117 E2
Katerbow D 45 C4
Katerini GR 116 B4
Kathikas CY 120 B1
Kätkesuando S 113 D12
Katlenburg-Lindau D 51 B6
Kato Achaia GR 117 D3
Káto Pyrgos CY 120 A1
Katouna GR 116 D3
Katovice CZ 63 A4
Katowice PL 55 C4
Katrineberg S 36 A3
Katrineholm S 37 D3
Kattarp S 41 C2
Kattavia GR 119 G2
Katthammarsvik S 37 E5
Kattilstorp S 40 A3
Katwijk NL 49 A5
Katymár H 75 B4
Kąty Wrocławskie PL 54 B1
Katzenelnbogen D 50 C3
Katzhütte D 52 C1
Kaub D 50 C3
Kaufbeuren D 62 C1
Kauhajoki FIN 3 E25
Kauhava FIN 3 E25
Kaukonen FIN 113 E13
Kaulsdorf D 52 C1
Kaunas LT 6 D7
Kaunisvaara S 113 E12
Kaupanger N 32 A4
Kautokeino N 113 C12
Kautzen A 63 B6
Kavadarci MK 116 A4
Kavajë AL 105 B5
Kavakköy TR 118 B1
Kavaklı TR 118 A2
Kavaklıdere TR 119 E3
Kavala GR 116 B6
Kavarna BG 11 E10
Kävlinge S 41 D3
Kawcze PL 46 A2
Kaxås S 115 D10
Kaxholmen S 40 B4
Kaymakçı TR 119 D3
Kaymaz TR 118 C6
Kaynarca TR 118 A5
Käyrämö FIN 113 F15
Kayseri TR 16 B7
Kaysersberg F 60 B3
Kazanlŭk BG 11 E8
Kazár H 65 B5
Kazimierza Wielka PL 55 C5
Kazincbarcika H 65 B6
Kaźmierz PL 46 C2
Kcynia PL 46 B3
Kdyně CZ 62 A4
Kea GR 117 E6
Keadew IRL 18 B3
Keady GB 19 B5
Kecel H 75 B4
Keçiborlu TR 119 E5
Kecskemét H 75 B4
Kėdainiai LT 6 D7
Kędzierzyn-Koźle PL 54 C3
Keel IRL 18 C1
Keenagh IRL 19 C4
Keerbergen B 49 B5
Kefalos GR 119 F1
Kefken TR 118 A5
Keflavík IS 111 C3
Kegworth GB 27 C4
Kehl D 60 B3
Kehrigk D 53 A3
Keighley GB 27 B4
Keila EST 6 B8
Keillmore GB 24 C2
Keiss GB 23 C5
Keith GB 23 D6
Kelberg D 50 C2
Kelbra D 51 B7
Kelč CZ 64 A3
Kelchsau A 72 A2
Këlcyrë AL 116 B2
Keld GB 26 A3
Kelebia H 75 B4
Kelekçi TR 119 E4
Kelemér H 65 B6
Keles TR 118 C4
Kelheim D 62 B2
Kell D 60 A2
Kellas GB 23 D5
Kellinghusen D 43 B6
Kelloselkä FIN 113 F17
Kells
GB 19 B5
IRL 19 C5
Kelmis B 50 C2
Kelokedhara CY 120 B1
Kelottijärvi FIN 113 D11
Kelsall GB 26 B3
Kelso GB 25 C5
Kelsterbach D 51 C4
Keltneyburn GB 24 B3
Kelujärvi FIN 113 E16
Kemaliye TR 119 D3
Kemalpaşa TR 119 D2
Kematen A 71 A6
Kemberg D 52 B2
Kemer
Antalya TR 119 F5
Burdur TR 119 E5
Muğla TR 119 F4
Kemerkaya TR 118 D6
Kemeten A 73 A6
Kemi FIN 3 D26
Kemijärvi FIN 113 F16
Kemnath D 62 A2
Kemnay GB 23 D6
Kemnitz
Brandenburg D 52 A2
Mecklenburg-Vorpommern D 45 A5
Kempen D 50 B2
Kempsey GB 29 A5
Kempten D 61 C6
Kemptthal CH 70 A3
Kendal GB 26 A3
Kenderes H 75 A5
Kengyel H 75 A5
Kenilworth GB 30 B2
Kenmare IRL 20 C2
Kenmore GB 25 B4
Kennacraig GB 24 C2
Kenyeri H 74 A2
Kenzingen D 60 B3
Kepez TR 118 B1
Kępice PL 46 A2
Kępno PL 54 B3
Kepsut TR 118 C3
Keramoti GR 116 B6
Keräntöjärvi S 113 E12
Keratea GR 117 E5
Kerava FIN 7 A8
Kerecsend H 65 C6
Kerekegyhaza H 75 B4
Kerepestarcsa H 75 A4
Keri GR 117 E2
Kérien F 56 B2
Kerkafalva H 74 B1
Kerken D 50 B2
Kerkrade NL 50 C2
Kerkyra GR 116 C1
Kerlouan F 56 B1
Kernascléden F 56 B2
Kernhof A 63 C6
Kerns CH 70 B3
Kerpen D 50 C2
Kerrysdale GB 22 D3
Kerta H 74 A2
Kerteminde DK 39 D3
Kerzers CH 70 B2
Keşan TR 118 B1
Kesgrave GB 30 B5
Kesh GB 19 B4
Keskin TR 16 B6
Kesselfall A 72 A2
Kestenga RUS 3 D29
Keswick GB 26 A2
Keszthely H 74 B2
Kétegyháza H 75 B6
Kéthely H 74 B2
Kętrzyn PL 6 D6
Kettering GB 30 B3
Kettlewell GB 26 A3
Kęty PL 65 A5
Ketzin D 45 C4
Keula D 51 B6
Keuruu FIN 3 E26
Kevelaer D 50 B2
Kevermes H 75 B6
Kevi SRB 75 C4
Keyingham GB 27 B5
Keynsham GB 29 B5
Kežmarok SK 65 A6
Kharmanli BG 11 F8
Khaskovo BG 11 F8
Kherson UA 11 C12
Khimki RUS 7 D14
Khisinev = Chişinău MD 11 C10
Khmelnik UA 11 B9
Khmelnytskyy UA 11 B9
Khodoriv UA 11 B8
Kholm RUS 7 C11
Khorol UA 11 B12
Khotyn UA 11 B9
Khoyniki BY 7 F10
Khust UA 11 B7
Khvoynaya RUS 7 B13
Kiato GR 117 D4
Kibæk DK 39 C1
Kiberg N 113 B19
Kicasalih TR 118 A1
Kičevo MK 116 A2
Kidderminster GB 26 C3
Kidlington GB 31 C2
Kidsgrove GB 26 B3
Kidwelly GB 28 B3
Kiefersfelden D 62 C3
Kiel D 44 A2
Kielce PL 55 C5
Kiełczygłów PL 54 B4
Kielder GB 25 C5
Kiełpino PL 47 A4
Kielpiny PL 47 B5
Kierinki FIN 113 E14
Kiernozia PL 55 A4
Kierspe D 50 B3
Kietrz PL 54 C3
Kietz D 45 C6
Kiev = Kyyiv UA 11 A11
Kiezmark PL 47 A4
Kiffisia GR 117 D5
Kifino Selo BIH 84 C3
Kihlanki
FIN 113 E12
S 113 E12
Kiistala FIN 113 E14
Kije PL 55 C5
Kijevo HR 83 C5
Kikallen N 32 B2
Kikinda SRB 75 C5
Kil
N 33 D6
Örebro S 37 C2
Värmland S 35 C5
Kila S 35 C4
Kilafors S 36 A3
Kilbaha IRL 20 B2
Kilbeggan IRL 21 A4
Kilberry GB 24 C2
Kilbirnie GB 24 C3
Kilboghamn N 112 F2
Kilbotn N 112 D5
Kilb Rabenstein A 63 B6
Kilchattan GB 24 C2
Kilchoan GB 24 B1
Kilcock IRL 21 A5
Kilconnell IRL 20 A3
Kilcormac IRL 21 A4
Kilcreggan GB 24 C3
Kilcullen IRL 21 A5
Kilcurry IRL 19 B5
Kildare IRL 21 A5
Kildinstroy RUS 3 B30
Kildonan GB 23 C5
Kildorrery IRL 20 B3
Kilegrend N 33 C5
Kilen N 33 C5
Kilgarvan IRL 20 C2
Kiliya UA 11 D10
Kilkee IRL 20 B2
Kilkeel GB 19 B5
Kilkelly IRL 18 C3
Kilkenny IRL 21 B4
Kilkieran IRL 20 A2
Kilkinlea IRL 20 B2
Kilkis GR 116 A4
Kill IRL 21 B4
Killadysert IRL 20 B2
Killala IRL 18 B2
Killaloe IRL 20 B3
Killarney IRL 20 B2
Killashandra IRL 19 B4
Killashee IRL 19 C4
Killearn GB 24 B3
Killeberg S 40 C4
Killeigh IRL 21 A4
Killenaule IRL 21 B4
Killimor IRL 20 A3
Killin GB 24 B3
Killinaboy IRL 20 B2
Killinge S 112 E9
Killinick IRL 21 B5
Killorglin IRL 20 B2
Killucan IRL 21 A4
Killybegs IRL 18 B3
Killyleagh GB 19 B6
Kilmacrenan IRL 19 A4
Kilmacthomas IRL 21 B4
Kilmaine IRL 18 C2
Kilmallock IRL 20 B3
Kilmarnock GB 24 C3
Kilmartin GB 24 B2
Kilmaurs GB 24 C3
Kilmeadan IRL 21 B4
Kilmeedy IRL 20 B3
Kilmelford GB 24 B2
Kilmore Quay IRL 21 B5
Kilmuir GB 23 D4
Kilnaleck IRL 19 C4
Kilninver GB 24 B2
Kilpisjärvi FIN 112 C9
Kilrea GB 19 B5
Kilrush IRL 20 B2
Kilsmo S 37 C2
Kilsyth GB 24 C3
Kiltoom IRL 20 A3
Kilwinning GB 24 C3
Kimasozero RUS 3 D29
Kimi GR 116 D6
Kimolos GR 117 F6
Kimovsk RUS 7 D14
Kimratshofen D 61 C6
Kimry RUS 7 C14
Kimstad S 37 D2
Kinbrace GB 23 C5
Kincardine GB 25 B4
Kincraig GB 23 D5
Kindberg A 73 A5
Kindelbruck D 52 B1
Kingarrow IRL 18 B3
Kingisepp RUS 7 B10
Kingsbridge GB 28 C4
Kingsclere GB 31 C2
Kingscourt IRL 19 C5
King's Lynn GB 30 B4
Kingsteignton GB 29 C4
Kingston
Greater London GB 31 C3
Moray GB 23 D5
Kingston Bagpuize GB 31 C2
Kingston upon Hull GB 27 B5
Kingswear GB 29 C4
Kingswood GB 29 B5
Kington GB 29 A4
Kingussie GB 23 D4
Kınık
Antalya TR 119 F4
İzmir TR 118 C2
Kinloch
Highland GB 22 C4
Highland GB 22 D2
Kinlochbervie GB 22 C3
Kinlochewe GB 22 D3
Kinlochleven GB 24 B3
Kinlochmoidart GB 24 B2
Kinloch Rannoch GB 24 B3
Kinloss GB 23 D5
Kinlough IRL 18 B3
Kinn N 34 B2
Kinna S 40 B2
Kinnared S 40 B3
Kinnarp S 40 A3
Kinnegad IRL 21 A4
Kinne-Kleva S 35 D5
Kinnitty IRL 21 A4
Kinrooi B 50 B1
Kinross GB 25 B4
Kinsale IRL 20 C3
Kinsarvik N 32 B3
Kintarvie GB 22 C2
Kintore GB 23 D6
Kinvarra IRL 20 A3
Kioni GR 116 D2
Kiparissia GR 117 E3
Kipfenburg D 62 B2
Kippen GB 24 B3
Kiraz TR 119 D3
Kirazlı TR 118 B1
Kirberg D 50 C4
Kirchbach in Steiermark A 73 B5
Kirchberg
CH 70 A2
Baden-Württemberg D 61 A5
Rheinland-Pfalz D 60 A3
Kirchberg am Wechsel A 64 C1
Kirchberg an der Pielach A 63 B6
Kirchberg in Tirol A 72 A2
Kirchbichl A 72 A2
Kirchdorf
Bayern D 63 B4
Mecklenburg-Vorpommern D 44 B3
Niedersachsen D 43 C5
Kirchdorf an der Krems A 63 C5
Kirchdorf in Tirol A 72 A2
Kirchenlamitz D 52 C1
Kirchenthumbach D 62 A2
Kirchhain D 51 C4
Kirchheim
Baden-Württemberg D 61 B5
Bayern D 61 B6
Hessen D 51 C5
Kirchheimbolanden D 61 A4
Kirchhundem D 50 B4
Kirchlintein D 43 C6
Kirchschlag A 73 A6
Kirchweidach D 62 B3
Kirchzarten D 60 C3
Kircubbin GB 19 B6
Kireç TR 118 C3
Kırıkkale TR 16 B6
Kirillov RUS 7 B15
Kirishi RUS 7 B12
Kırka TR 118 C5
Kırkağaç TR 118 C2
Kirkbean GB 25 D4
Kirkbride GB 25 D4
Kirkby GB 26 B3
Kirkby Lonsdale GB 26 A3
Kirkby Malzeard GB 27 A4
Kirkbymoorside GB 27 A5
Kirkby Stephen GB 26 A3
Kirkcaldy GB 25 B4
Kirkcolm GB 24 D2
Kirkconnel GB 24 C3
Kirkcowan GB 24 D3
Kirkcudbright GB 24 D3
Kirkehamn N 33 D3
Kirke Hyllinge DK 39 D4
Kirkenær N 34 B4
Kirkenes N 113 C19
Kirkham GB 26 B3
Kirkintilloch GB 24 C3
Kirkjubæjarklaustur IS 111 D7
Kirkkonummi FIN 6 A8
Kırklareli TR 118 A2
Kirkmichael GB 25 B4
Kirk Michael GB 26 A1
Kirkoswald GB 24 C3
Kirkpatrick Fleming GB 25 C4
Kirkton of Glenisla GB 25 B4
Kirkwall GB 23 C6
Kirkwhelpington GB 25 C6
Kirn D 60 A3
Kiro AL 105 A5
Kirov RUS 7 D13
Kirovohrad UA 11 B12
Kirovsk RUS 3 C30
Kirriemuir GB 25 B5
Kırşehir TR 16 B7
Kirton GB 30 B3
Kirton in Lindsey GB 27 B5
Kirtorf D 51 C5
Kiruna S 112 E9
Kisa S 40 B5
Kisač SRB 75 C4
Kisbér H 74 A3
Kiseljak BIH 84 C3
Kisielice PL 47 B5
Kisköre H 75 A5
Kiskőrös H 75 B4
Kiskunfélegyháza H 75 B4
Kiskunhalas H 75 B4
Kiskunlacháza H 75 A3
Kiskunmajsa H 75 B4
Kisláng H 74 B3
Kisslegg D 61 C5
Kissolt H 75 B4
Kissónerga CY 120 B1
Kist D 61 A5
Kistanje HR 83 C4
Kistelek H 75 B4
Kisterenye H 65 B5
Kisújszállás H 75 A5
Kisvárda H 11 B7
Kisvejke H 74 B3
Kiszkowo PL 46 C3
Kiszombor H 75 B5
Kitee FIN 3 E29
Kithnos GR 117 E6
Kiti CY 120 B2
Kitkiöjärvi S 113 E12
Kitkiöjoki S 113 E12
Kittelfjäll S 115 B12
Kittendorf D 45 B4
Kittilä FIN 113 E13
Kittlitz D 53 B4
Kittsee A 64 B3
Kitzbühel A 72 A2
Kitzingen D 61 A6
Kiuruvesi FIN 3 E27
Kivertsi UA 11 A8
Kividhes CY 120 B1
Kivik S 41 D4
Kivotos GR 116 B3
Kiwity PL 47 A6
Kıyıköy TR 118 A3
Kızılcabölük TR 119 E4
Kızılcadağ TR 119 E4
Kızılcahamam TR 16 A6
Kızılırmak TR 16 A6
Kızılkaya TR 119 E5
Kızılkuyu TR 118 D6
Kızılören
Afyon TR 119 D5
Konya TR 119 E7
Kjeldebotn N 112 D5
Kjellerup DK 39 C2
Kjellmyra N 34 B4
Kjøllefjord N 113 B16
Kjopmannskjaer N 35 C2
Kjøpsvik N 112 D5
Kl'ačno SK 65 B4
Kladanj BIH 84 B3
Kläden D 44 C3
Klädesholmen S 38 B4
Kladnica SRB 85 C5
Kladnice HR 83 C5
Kladno CZ 53 C4
Kladruby CZ 62 A3
Klagenfurt A 73 B4
Klågerup S 41 D3
Klagstorp S 41 D3
Klaipėda LT 6 D6
Klaistow D 52 A2
Klaksvík FO 2 E10
Klana HR 73 C4
Klanac HR 83 B4
Klanjec HR 73 B5
Klardorf D 62 A3
Klarup DK 38 B3
Klašnice BIH 84 B2
Klässbol S 35 C4
Klášterec nad Ohří CZ 52 C3
Kláštor pod Znievom SK 65 B4
Klatovy CZ 63 A4
Klaus an der Pyhrnbahn A 63 C5
Klazienaveen NL 42 C3
Kłecko PL 46 C3
Kleczew PL 47 C4
Klein Plasten D 45 B4
Klein Sankt Paul A 73 B4
Kleinsölk A 72 A3
Kleinzell A 64 C1
Klejtrup DK 38 C2
Klek SRB 75 C5
Klemensker DK 41 D4
Klenak SRB 85 B4
Klenci pod Cerchovem CZ 62 A3
Klenica PL 53 B5
Klenje SRB 85 B4
Klenoec MK 116 A2
Klenovec SK 65 B5
Klenovica HR 83 A3
Klenovnik HR 73 B6
Kleppe N 33 D2
Kleppestø N 32 B2
Kleptow D 45 B5
Kletnya RUS 7 E12
Kleve D 50 B2
Klevshult S 40 B4
Klewki PL 47 B6
Kličevac SRB 85 B6
Kliening A 73 B4
Klietz D 44 C4
Klikuszowa PL 65 A5
Klimkovice CZ 64 A4
Klimontów PL 55 C6
Klimovichi BY 7 E11
Klimpfjäll S 115 B11
Klin RUS 7 C14
Klina KOS 85 D5
Klinča Sela HR 73 C5
Klingenbach A 64 C2
Klingenberg D 61 A5
Klingenmunster D 61 A4
Klingenthal D 52 C2
Klinken D 44 B3
Klintehamn S 37 E5
Klintsy RUS 7 E12
Kliny PL 55 B5
Kliplev DK 39 E2
Klippan S 41 C3
Klis HR 83 C5
Klitmøller DK 38 B1
Klitten S 34 A6
Klixbüll D 39 E1
Kljajićevo SRB 75 C4
Ključ BIH 83 B5
Klobouky CZ 64 B2
Kłobuck PL 54 C3
Klockestrand S 115 E14
Kłodawa
Lubuskie PL 45 C7
Wielkopolskie PL 54 A3
Kłodzko PL 54 C1
Kløfta N 34 B3
Klokkarvik N 32 B2
Klokkerholm DK 38 B3
Klokočov SK 65 A4
Kłomnice PL 55 C4
Klonowa PL 54 B3
Kloosterzande NL 49 B5
Kłopot PL 53 A4
Klos AL 116 A2
Kloštar Ivanić HR 73 C6
Kloster
D 45 A5
DK 39 C1
Klösterle A 71 A5
Klostermansfeld D 52 B1
Klosterneuburg A 64 B2
Klosters CH 71 B4
Kloten CH 70 A3
Klötze D 44 C3
Klövsjö S 115 E11
Kluczbork PL 54 C3
Kluczewo PL 46 B2
Kluisbergen B 49 C4
Klundert NL 49 B5
Klutz D 44 B3
Klwów PL 55 B5
Klyetsk BY 7 E9
Knaben N 33 D3
Knaften S 115 C15
Knapstad N 35 C3
Knäred S 40 C3
Knaresborough GB 27 A4
Knarvik N 32 B2
Knebel DK 39 C3
Knebworth GB 31 C3
Knesebeck D 44 C2
Knesselare B 49 B4
Knežak SLO 73 C4
Kneževi Vinogradi HR 74 C3
Kneževo HR 74 C3
Knić SRB 85 C5
Knighton GB 29 A4
Knin HR 83 B5
Knislinge S 41 C4
Knittelfeld A 73 A4
Knivsta S 37 C4
Knock IRL 18 C3
Knocktopher IRL 21 B4
Knokke-Heist B 49 B4
Knowle GB 30 B2
Knurów PL 54 C3
Knutby S 36 C5
Knutsford GB 26 B3
Kobarid SLO 72 B3
København = Copenhagen DK 41 D2
Kobenz A 73 A4
Kobersdorf A 64 C2
Kobiernice PL 65 A5
Kobierzyce PL 54 C1
Kobilje SLO 73 B6
Kobiór PL 54 C3
Koblenz
CH 61 C4
D 50 C3
Kobryn BY 6 E8
Kobylanka PL 45 B6
Kobylin PL 54 B2
Kobyłka PL 55 A6
Kobylniki PL 47 C6
Kocaali TR 118 A5
Kocaaliler TR 119 E5
Kocaeli = İzmit TR 118 B4
Kočani MK 11 F7
Koçarlı TR 119 E2
Koceljevo SRB 85 B4
Kočerin BIH 84 C2
Kočevje SLO 73 C4
Kočevska Reka SLO 73 C4
Kochel am see D 62 C2
Kocs H 64 C4
Kocsér H 75 A4
Kocsola H 74 B3
Koczala PL 46 B3
Kodal N 35 C2
Kode S 38 B4
Kodersdorf D 53 B4
Kodrab PL 55 B4
Koekelare B 48 B3
Kofçaz TR 118 A2
Köflach A 73 A5
Køge DK 41 D2
Kohlberg D 62 A3
Kohtla-Järve EST 7 B9
Köinge S 40 B2
Kojetín CZ 64 A3
Kökar FIN 36 C7
Kokava SK 65 B5
Kokkola FIN 3 E25
Kokori BIH 84 B2
Kokoski PL 47 A4
Koksijde B 48 B3
Kola
BIH 84 B2
RUS 3 B30
Köla S 34 C4
Kołacin PL 55 B4
Kolari FIN 113 E12
Kolárovo SK 64 C3
Kolašin MNE 85 D4
Kolbäck S 37 C3
Kolbacz PL 45 B6
Kolbeinsstaðir IS 111 C3
Kolbermoor D 62 C3
Kołbiel PL 55 A6
Kolbnitz A 72 B3
Kolbotn N 34 C2
Kolbu N 34 B2
Kolby Kås DK 39 D3
Kolczewo PL 45 B6
Kolczyglowy PL 46 A3
Kolding DK 39 D2
Kölesd H 74 B3
Kolgrov N 32 A1
Kolín CZ 53 C5
Kolind DK 39 C3
Kolinec CZ 63 A4
Koljane HR 83 C5
Kølkær DK 39 C2
Kölleda D 52 B1
Kollum NL 42 B3

Köln = Cologne D 50 C2
Koło PL 54 A3
Kołobrzeg PL 46 A1
Kolochau D 52 B3
Kolomyya UA 11 B8
Kolonje AL 105 C5
Kolonowskie PL 54 C3
Koloveč CZ 62 A4
Kolpino RUS 7 B11
Kolpny RUS 7 E14
Kolrep D 44 B4
Kölsillre S 115 E12
Kolsko PL 53 B5
Kolsva S 37 C2
Kolta SK 65 B4
Kolunič BIH 83 B5
Koluszki PL 55 B4
Kolut SRB 75 C3
Kolvereid N 114 C8
Kølvrå DK 39 C2
Komagvær N 113 B19
Koman AL 105 A5
Komarica BIH 84 B2
Komárno SK 64 C4
Komárom H 64 C4
Komatou Yialou CY 120 A3
Komboti GR 116 C3
Komen SLO 72 C3
Komin HR 84 C2
Komiža HR 83 C5
Komjáti H 65 B6
Komjatice SK 64 B4
Komletinci HR 75 C3
Komló H 74 B3
Kömlo H 65 C6
Komoča SK 64 C4
Komorane KOS 85 D5
Komorniki PL 54 A1
Komorzno PL 54 B3
Komotini GR 116 A7
Konak SRB 75 C5
Konakovo RUS 7 C14
Konary PL 55 B6
Konarzyny PL 46 B3
Kondias GR 116 C7
Kondorfa H 73 B6
Kondoros H 75 B5
Kondrovo RUS 7 D13
Køng DK 39 D4
Konga S 40 C5
Köngäs FIN 113 E13
Kongerslev DK 38 C3
Kongsberg N 35 C1
Kongshamn N 33 D5
Kongsmark DK 39 D1
Kongsmoen N 115 C9
Kongsvik N 112 D5
Kongsvinger N 34 B4
Konice CZ 64 A2
Konie PL 55 B5
Koniecpol PL 55 C4
Königsberg D 51 C6
Königsbronn D 61 B6
Königsbrück D 53 B3
Königsbrunn D 62 B1
Konigsdorf D 62 C2
Königsee D 52 C1
Königshorst D 45 C4
Königslutter D 51 A6
Königssee D 62 C3
Königstein
Hessen D 51 C4
Sachsen D 53 C4
Königstetten A 64 B2
Königswartha D 53 B4
Konigswiesen A 63 B5
Königswinter D 50 C3
Königs Wusterhausen
D 52 A3
Konin PL 54 A3
Konispol AL 116 C2
Konitsa GR 116 B2
Köniz CH 70 B2
Konjevići BIH 85 B4
Konjevrate HR 83 C5
Konjic BIH 84 C2
Konjščina HR 73 B6
Könnern D 52 B1
Konnerud N 35 C2
Konopiska PL 54 C3
Konotop
PL 53 B5
UA 7 F12
Końskie PL 55 B5
Konsmo N 33 D4
Konstancin-Jeziorna
PL 55 A6
Konstantynów Łódźki
PL 55 B4
Konstanz D 61 C5
Kontich B 49 B5
Kontiolahti FIN 3 E28
Konya TR 119 E7
Konz D 60 A2
Kópasker IS 111 A9
Kópavogur IS 111 C4
Kopčany SK 64 B3
Koper SLO 72 C3
Kopervik N 33 C2
Kópháza H 64 C2
Kopice PL 54 C2
Kopidlno CZ 53 C5
Köping S 37 C2
Köpingebro S 41 D3
Köpingsvik S 41 C6
Koplik AL 105 A5
Köpmanholmen S 115 D15
Koppang N 34 A3
Koppangen N 112 C9
Kopparberg S 36 C1
Koppelo FIN 113 D16
Koppom S 35 C4
Koprivlen BG 116 A5
Koprivna BIH 84 B3
Koprivnica HR 74 B1
Kopřivnice CZ 64 A4
Köprübaşı TR 118 D3
Koprzywnica PL 55 C6
Kopstal L 60 A2
Kopychyntsi UA 11 B8
Kopytkowo PL 47 B4
Korbach D 51 B4
Körbecke D 50 B4
Korçë AL 116 B2
Korčula HR 84 D2
Korczyców PL 53 A4
Korenevo RUS 7 F13
Korenita SRB 85 B4
Korets UA 11 A9
Korfantów PL 54 C2
Körfez TR 118 B4
Korgen N 115 A10
Korinth DK 39 D3
Korinthos = Corinth
GR 117 E4
Korita
BIH 83 B5
HR 84 D2
Korithi GR 117 E2
Korkuteli TR 119 E5
Körmend H 74 A1
Korne PL 46 A3
Korneuburg A 64 B2
Kornevo RUS 47 A6
Kórnik PL 54 A2
Kornsjø N 35 D3
Környe H 74 A3
Koromačno HR 82 B3
Koroni GR 117 F3
Koronos GR 117 E7
Koronowo PL 46 B3
Körösladány H 75 B6
Köröstarcsa H 75 B6
Korosten UA 11 A10
Korostyshev UA 11 A10
Korpilombolo S 113 F12
Korsberga
Jönköping S 40 B5
Skaraborg S 35 D6
Korshavn N 35 C2
Korskrogen S 115 F12
Korsnäs S 36 B2
Korsør DK 39 D4
Korsun Shevchenkovskiy
UA 11 B11
Kortrijk B 49 C4
Korucu TR 118 C2
Koryčany CZ 64 A3
Koryukovka UA 7 F12
Korzeńsko PL 54 B1
Korzybie PL 46 A2
Kos GR 119 F2
Kosakowo PL 47 A4
Kosanica MNE 85 C4
Kosaya Gora RUS 7 D14
Kösching D 62 B2
Kościan PL 54 A1
Kościelec PL 54 A3
Kościerzyna PL 46 A3
Koserow D 45 A5
Košetice CZ 63 A6
Košice SK 10 B6
Kosjerić SRB 85 C4
Koška HR 74 C3
Koskullskulle S 112 E9
Kosovska Mitrovica
KOS 85 D5
Kosta S 40 C5
Kostajnica HR 74 C1
Kostajnik SRB 85 B4
Kostanica MNE 105 A5
Kostanjevica SLO 73 C5
Kostelec nad Černými
Lesy CZ 53 D4
Kostelec na Hané CZ 64 A3
Kostice CZ 53 C3
Kostkowo PL 47 A4
Kostojevići SRB 85 B4
Kostolac SRB 85 B6
Kostomłoty PL 54 B1
Kostopil UA 11 A9
Kostów PL 54 B3
Kostrzyn
Lubuskie PL 45 C6
Wielkopolskie PL 46 C3
Koszalin PL 46 A2
Koszęcin PL 54 C3
Köszeg H 74 A1
Koszwaly PL 47 A4
Koszyce PL 55 C5
Kot SLO 73 C5
Kotala FIN 113 E17
Kotë AL 105 C5
Kötelek H 75 A5
Köthen D 52 B1
Kotka FIN 7 A9
Kotomierz PL 47 B4
Kotor MNE 105 A4
Kotoriba HR 74 B1
Kotorsko BIH 84 B3
Kotor Varoš BIH 84 B2
Kotovsk UA 11 C10
Kotraža SRB 85 C5
Kotronas GR 117 F4
Kötschach A 72 B2
Kötzting D 62 A3
Koudum NL 42 C2
Kouřim CZ 53 C4
Kout na Šumave CZ 62 A4
Kouvola FIN 3 F27
Kovačevac SRB 85 B5
Kovačica SRB 85 A5
Kovdor RUS 3 C29
Kovel' UA 11 A8
Kovilj SRB 75 C5
Kovin SRB 85 B5
Kovren MNE 85 C4
Kowal PL 47 C5
Kowalewo Pomorskie
PL 47 B4
Kowalów PL 45 C6
Kowary PL 53 C5
Köyceğiz TR 119 F3
Kozan TR 16 C7
Kozani GR 116 B3
Kozarac
BIH 84 B1
HR 73 C5
Kozárovce SK 65 B4
Kozelets UA 11 A11
Kozelsk RUS 7 D13
Kozica HR 84 C2
Koziegłowy PL 55 C4
Kozienice PL 55 B6
Kozina SLO 72 C3
Kozje SLO 73 B5
Kozlu TR 118 A6
Kozluk BIH 85 B4
Koźmin PL 54 B2
Koźminek PL 54 B3
Kozolupy CZ 63 A4
Kożuchów PL 53 B5
Kožuhe BIH 84 B3
Kozyatyn UA 11 B10
Kozyürük TR 118 A1
Krackow D 45 B6
Kraddsele S 115 B13
Krąg PL 46 A2
Kragenæs DK 39 E4
Kragerø N 33 D6
Krągi PL 46 B2
Kragujevac SRB 85 B5
Kraiburg D 62 B3
Krajenka PL 46 B2
Krajišnik SRB 75 C5
Krajková CZ 52 C2
Krajné SK 64 B3
Krajnik Dolny PL 45 B6
Krakača BIH 83 A4
Kräklingbo S 37 E5
Kraków = Cracow PL 55 C4
Krakow am See D 44 B4
Králíky CZ 54 C1
Kraljevica HR 73 C4
Kraljevo SRB 85 C5
Kral'ovany SK 65 A5
Král'ov Brod SK 64 B3
Kralovice CZ 52 D3
Kralupy nad Vltavou
CZ 53 C4
Králův Dvůr CZ 63 A5
Kramfors S 115 E14
Kramsach A 72 A1
Kramsk PL 54 A3
Kråmvik N 32 C5
Kranenburg D 50 B2
Krania GR 116 C3
Krania Elasonas GR 116 C4
Kranichfeld D 52 C1
Kranidi GR 117 E5
Kranj SLO 73 B4
Kranjska Gora SLO 72 B3
Krapanj HR 83 C4
Krapina HR 73 B5
Krapje HR 74 C1
Krapkowice PL 54 C2
Kraselov CZ 63 A4
Krašić HR 73 C5
Krāslava LV 7 D9
Kraslice CZ 52 C2
Krasna PL 55 B5
Krasna Lipa CZ 53 C4
Kraśnik PL 11 A7
Krašnja SLO 73 B4
Krásno SK 65 A4
Krásnohorské Podhradie
SK 65 B6
Krasno Polje HR 83 B4
Krasnozavodsk RUS 7 C15
Krasnystaw PL 11 A7
Krasnyy RUS 7 D11
Krasnyy Kholm RUS 7 B14
Krasocin PL 55 C5
Kraszewice PL 54 B3
Kraszkowice PL 54 B3
Kratigos GR 118 C1
Kraubath A 73 A4
Krausnick D 53 A3
Krautheim D 61 A5
Kravaře CZ 53 C4
Kraváre CZ 64 A4
Kravarsko HR 73 C6
Kraznějov CZ 63 A4
Krčedin SRB 75 C5
Kŭrdzhali BG 116 A7
Krefeld D 50 B2
Kregme DK 39 D5
Krembz D 44 B3
Kremenchuk UA 11 B12
Kremenets UA 11 A8
Kremmen D 45 C5
Kremna SRB 85 C4
Kremnica SK 65 B4
Krempe D 43 B6
Krems A 63 B6
Kremsbrücke A 72 B3
Kremsmünster A 63 B5
Křemže CZ 63 B5
Křenov CZ 64 A2
Krepa PL 54 B3
Krępa Krajeńska PL 46 B2
Krepsko PL 46 B2
Kreševo BIH 84 C3
Kressbronn D 61 C5
Krestena GR 117 E3
Kretinga LT 6 D6
Krettsy RUS 7 B12
Kreuth D 62 C2
Kreuzau D 50 C2
Kreuzlingen CH 61 C5
Kreuztal D 50 C3
Krewelin D 45 C5
Krezluk BIH 84 B2
Krieglach A 73 A5
Kriegsfeld D 60 A3
Kriens CH 70 A3
Krimml A 72 A2
Krimpen aan de IJssel
NL 49 B5
Křinec CZ 53 C5
Kristdala S 40 B6
Kristiansand N 33 D5
Kristianstad S 41 C4
Kristiansund N 114 D4
Kristiinankaupunki
FIN 3 E24
Kristinefors S 34 B4
Kristinehamn S 35 C6
Kriváň SK 65 B5
Křivokát CZ 53 C3
Krivoy Rog = Kryvyy Rih
UA 11 C12
Kriź HR 74 C1
Křižanov CZ 64 A2
Križevci HR 74 B1
Krk HR 83 A3
Krka SLO 73 C4
Krnjača SRB 85 B5
Krnjak HR 73 C5
Krnjeuša BIH 83 B5
Krnjevo SRB 85 B6
Krnov CZ 54 C2
Krobia PL 54 B1
Kroczyce PL 55 C4
Krøderen N 34 B1
Krokees GR 117 F4
Krokek S 37 D3
Krokom S 115 D11
Krokowa PL 47 A4
Krokstad-elva N 34 C1
Kroksund N 35 C3
Krolevets UA 7 F12
Kroměříž CZ 64 A3
Krommenie NL 42 C1
Krompachy SK 65 B6
Kromy RUS 7 E13
Kronach D 52 C1
Kronshagen D 44 A2
Kronshtadt RUS 7 B10
Kröpelin D 44 A3
Kropp D 43 A6
Kroppenstedt D 52 B1
Kropstädt D 52 B2
Krościenko nad
Dunajcem PL 65 A6
Kröslin D 45 A5
Krośnice PL 54 B2
Krośniewice PL 55 A4
Krosno PL 10 B6
Krosno Odrzańskie
PL 53 A5
Krostitz D 52 B2
Krotoszyn PL 54 B2
Krottendorf A 73 A5
Krouna CZ 64 A2
Krowiarki PL 54 C3
Krrabë AL 105 B5
Kršan HR 73 C4
Krško SLO 73 C5
Krstac MNE 84 C3
Krstur SRB 75 B5
Křtiny CZ 64 A2
Kruft D 50 C3
Kruishoutem B 49 C4
Krujë AL 105 B5
Krulyewshchyna BY 7 D9
Krumbach
A 73 A6
D 61 B6
Krumovgrad BG 116 A7
Krün D 71 A6
Krupá CZ 53 C3
Krupa na Vrbasu BIH 84 B2
Krupanj SRB 85 B4
Krupina SK 65 B5
Krupka CZ 53 C3
Krupki BY 7 D10
Kruså DK 39 E2
Krušćica BIH 84 B2
Kruševac SRB 85 C6
Kruševo MK 116 A3
Kruszwica PL 47 C4
Kruszyn PL 47 C5
Krute MNE 105 A5
Krychaw BY 7 E11
Krynica PL 65 A6
Krynica Morska PL 47 A5
Kryvyy Rih = Krivoy Rog
UA 11 C12
Krzęcin PL 46 B1
Krzelów PL 54 B1
Krzepice PL 54 C3
Krzepielów PL 53 B6
Krzeszowice PL 55 C4
Krzeszyce PL 45 C7
Krzynowlaga Mała
PL 47 B6
Krzywiń PL 54 B1
Krzyżanowice PL 54 D3
Krzyżowa PL 65 A5
Krzyż Wielkopolski
PL 46 C2
Ksiaz Wielkopolski
PL 55 C5
Książ Wielkopolski
PL 54 A2
Ktębowiec PL 46 B2
Kübekháza H 75 B5
Küblis CH 71 B4
Kuç AL 105 C5
Kuchary PL 54 B2
Kuchl A 63 C4
Kucice PL 47 C6
Kuciste HR 84 D2
Kućište KOS 85 D5
Kuçovë AL 105 C5
Küçükbahçe TR 118 D1
Küçükköy TR 118 C1
Küçükkuyu TR 118 C1
Kucura SRB 75 C4
Kuczbork-Osada PL 47 B6
Kuddby S 37 D3
Kudowa-Zdrój PL 53 C6
Kufstein A 62 C3
Kuggeboda S 41 C5
Kuggörana S 115 F14
Kühbach D 62 B2
Kuhmo FIN 3 D28
Kuhmoinen FIN 3 F26
Kuhnsdorf A 73 B4
Kuhstedt D 43 B5
Kuinre NL 42 C2
Kuivastu EST 6 B7
Kukës AL 10 E6
Kuklin PL 47 B6
Kukljica HR 83 B4
Kukujevci SRB 85 A4
Kula
Srbija SRB 85 B6
Vojvodina SRB 75 C4
TR 119 D3
Kuldīga LV 6 C6
Kulen Vakuf BIH 83 B5
Kulina BIH 84 B3
Kullstedt D 51 B6
Kulmain D 62 A2
Kulmbach D 52 C1
Kulu TR 16 B6
Kumafşarı TR 119 E4
Kumane SRB 75 C5
Kumanovo MK 10 E6
Kumbağ TR 118 B2
Kumdanlı TR 119 D5
Kumkale TR 118 C1
Kumla S 37 C2
Kumlakyrkby S 36 C3
Kumlinge FIN 36 B7
Kumluca TR 119 F5
Kumrovec HR 73 B5
Kunadacs H 75 B4
Kunágota H 75 B6
Kunbaja H 75 B4
Kunda EST 7 B9
Kundl A 72 A1
Kunes N 113 B15
Kunfehértó H 75 B4
Kungälv S 38 B4
Kungsängen S 37 C4
Kungsäter S 40 B2
Kungsbacka S 38 B5
Kungsgården S 36 B3
Kungshamn S 35 D3
Kungs-Husby S 37 C4
Kungsör S 37 C3
Kunhegyes H 75 A5
Kunmadaras H 75 A5
Kunovice CZ 64 A3
Kunów PL 55 C6
Kunowo
Wielkopolskie PL 54 B2
Zachodnio-Pomorskie
PL 45 B6
Kunštát CZ 64 A2
Kunszállás H 75 B4
Kunszentmárton H 75 B5
Kunszentmiklós H 75 A4
Kunžak CZ 63 A6
Künzelsau D 61 A5
Kuolayarvi RUS 113 F18
Kuopio FIN 3 E27
Kuosku FIN 113 E17
Kup
H 74 A2
PL 54 C2
Kupa H 65 B6
Kupari HR 84 D3
Kupci SRB 85 C6
Kupferzell D 61 A5
Kupinec HR 73 C5
Kupinečki Kraljevac
HR 73 C5
Kupinovo SRB 85 B5
Kupirovo HR 83 B5
Kupjak HR 73 C4
Kuppenheim D 61 B4
Kupres BIH 84 C2
Küps D 52 C1
Kurbnesh AL 105 B6
Kurd H 74 B3
Küre TR 16 A6
Kuressaare EST 6 B7
Kurikka FIN 3 E25
Kuřim CZ 64 A2
Kuřivody CZ 53 C4
Kurki PL 47 B6
Kurort Oberwiesenthal
D 52 C2
Kurort Schmalkalden
D 51 C6
Kurort Stolberg D 51 B6
Kurort Wippra D 52 B1
Kurów PL 11 A7
Kurowice PL 55 B4
Kurravaara S 112 E9
Kursk RUS 7 F14
Kursu FIN 113 F17
Kuršumlija SRB 85 C6
Kuršumlijska Banja
SRB 85 C6
Kurşunlu
Bursa TR 118 B4
Çankırı TR 16 A6
Kurtakko FIN 113 E13
Kürten D 50 B3
Kurucaşile TR 16 A6
Kurzelów PL 55 C4
Kusadak SRB 85 B5
Kuşadası TR 119 E2
Kusel D 60 A3
Kusey D 44 C3
Küsnacht CH 70 A3
Kütahya TR 118 C4
Kutenholz D 43 B6
Kutina HR 74 C1
Kutjevo HR 74 C2
Kutná Hora CZ 53 D5
Kutno PL 55 A4
Kuttara FIN 113 D15
Küttingen CH 70 A3
Kúty SK 64 B3
Kuusamo FIN 3 D28
Kuusankoski FIN 3 F27
Kuvshinovo RUS 7 C13
Kuyucak TR 119 E3
Kuzmin SRB 85 A4
Kuźnia Raciborska
PL 54 C3
Kuźnica Czarnkowska
PL 46 C2
Kuźnica Żelichowska
PL 46 C2
Kvaløysletta N 112 C7
Kvalsund N 113 B12
Kvam
Nord-Trøndelag N 114 C8
Oppland N 114 F6
Kvamsøy N 32 A3
Kvænangsbotn N 113 C11
Kvanndal N 32 B3
Kvänum S 35 D5
Kværndrup DK 39 D3
Kvås N 33 D4
Kvasice CZ 64 A3
Kvelde N 35 C1
Kvenna N 114 E5
Kvernaland N 33 D2
Kvibille S 40 C2
Kvicksund S 37 C3
Kvidinge S 41 C3
Kvikkjokk S 112 F6
Kvikne N 114 E7
Kvilda CZ 63 A4
Kville S 35 D3
Kvillsfors S 40 B5
Kvinesdal N 33 D3
Kvinlog N 33 D3
Kvinnherad N 32 C3
Kvissel DK 38 B3
Kvissleby S 115 E14
Kviteseid N 33 C5
Kvitsøy N 33 C2
Kwakowo PL 46 A3
Kwidzyn PL 47 B4
Kwilcz PL 46 C2
Kyjov CZ 64 B3
Kyleakin GB 22 D3
Kyle of Lochalsh GB 22 D3
Kylerhea GB 22 D3
Kylestrome GB 22 C3
Kyllburg D 50 C2
Kyllini GR 117 E3
Kynšperk nad Ohří
CZ 52 C2
Kyperounda CY 120 B1
Kyrenia CY 120 A2
Kyritz D 44 C4
Kyrkesund S 38 A4
Kyrkhult S 41 C4
Kyrksæterøra N 114 D6
Kysucké Nové Mesto
SK 65 A4
Kythira GR 117 F4
Kythréa CY 120 A2
Kyustendil BG 11 E7
Kyyiv = Kiev UA 11 A11
Kyyjärvi FIN 3 E26

L

Laa an der Thaya A 64 B2
La Adrada E 94 B2
Laage D 44 B4
La Alameda E 100 A2
La Alberca E 93 A4
La Alberca de Záncara
E 95 C4
La Alberguería de
Argañán E 93 A4
La Albuera E 93 C4
La Aldea del Portillo del
Busto E 89 B3
La Algaba E 99 B4
La Aliseda de Tormes
E 93 A5
La Almarcha E 95 C4
La Almolda E 90 B2
La Almunia de Doña
Godina E 89 C5
Laanila FIN 113 D16
La Antillas E 98 B3
La Arena E 86 A4
Laatzen D 51 A5
La Aulaga E 99 B4
La Balme-de-Sillingy
F 69 C6
Laban IRL 20 A3
La Bañeza E 88 B1
La Barca de la Florida
E 99 C5
La Barre-de-Monts F 66 B2
La Barre-en-Ouche F 58 B1
La Barrosa E 99 C4
La Barthe-de-Neste F 77 C3
La Bassée F 48 C3
La Bastide-de-Sèrou
F 77 C4
La Bastide-des-Jourdans
F 79 C4
Labastide-Murat F 77 B4
La Bastide-Puylaurent
F 78 B2
Labastide-Rouairoux
F 77 C5
Labastide-St Pierre F 77 C4
La Bathie F 69 C6
Lábatlan H 65 C4
La Baule-Escoublac
F 66 A2
La Bazoche-Gouet F 58 B1
La Bégude-de-Mazenc
F 78 B3
Labenne F 76 C1
La Bernerie-en-Retz F 66 A2
Labin HR 82 A3
La Bisbal d'Empordà
E 91 B6
Łabiszyn PL 46 C3
Lablachère F 78 B3
Lábod H 74 B2
Laboe D 44 A2
La Boissière F 57 A6
Labouheyre F 76 B2
La Bourboule F 68 C2
La Bóveda de Toro E 88 C1
Łabowa PL 65 A6
La Brède F 76 B2
La Bresse F 60 B2
La Bridoire F 69 C5
La Brillanne F 79 C4
Labrit F 76 B2
Labros E 95 A5
La Bruffière F 66 A3
Labruguière F 77 C5
Labrujo P 87 C2
L'Absie F 67 B4
La Bussière F 58 C3
Laç AL 105 B5
La Caillère F 66 B4
Lacalahorra E 100 B2
La Caletta
Cágliari I 110 C1
Núoro I 110 B2
La Calmette F 78 C3
La Calzada de Oropesa
E 93 B5
La Campana E 99 B5
La Cañada E 94 B2
Lacanau F 76 B1
Lacanau-Océan F 76 A1
Lacanche F 69 A4
La Canourgue F 78 B2
La Capelle F 49 D4
Lacapelle-Marival F 77 B4
Laćarak SRB 85 A4
La Cardanchosa E 99 A5
La Caridad E 86 A4
La Carlota E 100 B1
La Carolina E 100 A2
Lacaune F 78 C1
La Cava E 90 C3
La Cavalerie F 78 B2
Laceby GB 27 B5
Lacedónia I 103 B8
La Celle-en-Moravan
F 69 A4
La Celle-St Avant F 67 A5
La Cerca E 89 B3
Láces I 71 B5
La Chaise-Dieu F 68 C3
La Chaize-Giraud F 66 B3
La Chaize-le-Vicomte
F 66 B3
La Chambre F 69 C6
Lachania GR 119 G2
La Chapelaude F 68 B2
La Chapelle-d'Angillon
F 68 A2
La Chapelle-en-
Aalgaudémar F 79 B5
La Chapelle-en-Vercors
F 79 B4
La Chapelle-Glain F 57 C4
La Chapelle-la-Reine
F 58 B3
La Chapelle-Laurent
F 68 C3
La Chapelle-St Luc F 59 B5
La Chapelle-sur-Erdre
F 66 A3
La Chapelle-Vicomtesse
F 58 C2
La Charce F 79 B4
La Charité-sur-Loire
F 68 A3
La Chartre-sur-le-Loir
F 58 C1
La Châtaigneraie F 67 B4
La Châtre F 68 B1
La Chaussée-sur-Marne
F 59 B5
La Chaux-de-Fonds
CH 70 A1
Lachen CH 70 A3
Lachendorf D 44 C2
La Cheppe F 59 A5
La Chèze F 56 B3
Lachowice PL 65 A5
La Ciotat F 79 C4
Łąck PL 47 C5
Läckeby S 40 C6
Läckö S 35 D5
La Clayette F 69 B4
La Clusaz F 69 C6
Lacock GB 29 B5
La Codosera E 93 B3
La Concha E 88 A3
La Condamine-Châtelard
F 79 B5
Láconi I 110 C2
La Contienda E 99 A4
La Coquille F 67 C5
La Coronada E 93 C5
La Côte-St André F 69 C5
La Cotinière F 66 C3
La Courtine F 68 C2
Lacq F 76 C2
La Crau F 79 C5
La Crèche F 67 B4
La Croix F 67 A5
Lacroix-Barrez F 77 B5
Lacroix-St Ouen F 58 A3
Lacroix-sur-Meuse F 60 B1
La Croix-Valmer F 79 C5
La Cumbre E 93 B5
Łącznik PL 54 C2
Lad H 74 B2
Ladbergen D 50 A3
Lądek-Zdrój PL 54 C1
Ladelund D 39 E2
Ladendorf A 64 B2
Ladignac-le-Long F 67 C6
Ladíspoli I 102 B5
Ladoeiro P 93 B3
Ladon F 58 C3
La Douze F 77 A3
Ladushkin RUS 47 A6
Ladybank GB 25 B4
Laer D 50 A3
La Espina E 86 A4
La Estrella E 94 C1
La Farga de Moles E 91 A4
La Fatarella E 90 B3
La Felipa E 95 C5
La Fère F 59 A4
La Ferrière
Indre-et-Loire F 58 C1
Vendée F 66 B3
La Ferrière-en-Parthenay
F 67 B4
La-Ferté-Alais F 58 B3
La Ferté-Bernard F 58 B1
La Ferté-Frênel F 58 B1
La Ferté-Gaucher F 59 B4
La Ferté-Imbault F 68 A1
La Ferté-Macé F 57 B5
La Ferté-Milon F 59 A4
La Ferté-sous-Jouarre
F 59 B4
La Ferté-St-Aubin F 58 C2
La Ferté-St-Cyr F 58 C2
La Ferté-Vidame F 58 B1
La Ferté Villeneuil F 58 C2
La Feuillie F 58 A2
Lafkos GR 116 C5
La Flèche F 57 C5
La Flotte F 66 B3
Lafnitz A 73 A6
La Font de la Figuera
E 101 A5
La Fouillade F 77 B5
Lafrançaise F 77 B4
La Fregeneda E 87 D4
La Fresneda E 90 C3
La Fuencubierta E 99 B6
La Fuente de San Esteban
E 87 D4
La Fulioala E 91 B4
La Gacilly F 57 C3
La Galera E 90 C3
Lagan S 40 C3
Laganadi I 109 A4
Lagarde F 77 C4
La Garde-Freinet F 79 C5
Lagares
Coimbra P 92 A3
Porto P 87 C2
La Garnache F 66 B3
Lagaro I 81 B5
La Garriga E 91 B5
La Garrovilla E 93 C4
Lagartera E 93 B5
La Gaubretière F 66 B3
Lågbol S 36 B5
Lage D 51 B4
Lägerdorf D 43 B6
Lagg GB 24 C2
Laggan GB 22 D4
Laggartorp S 35 C6
Łagiewniki PL 54 C1
La Gineta E 95 C4
Láglio I 71 C4
Lagnieu F 69 C5
Lagny-sur-Marne F 58 B3
Lago
Calabria I 106 B3
Veneto I 72 C2
Lagôa P 98 B2
Lagoaça P 87 C4
Lagonegro I 106 A2
Lagos
GR 116 A7
P 98 B2
Lagosanto I 82 B1
Łagów
Lubuskie PL 46 C1
Świętokrzyskie PL 55 C6
La Granadella
Alicante E 96 C3
Lleida E 90 B3
La Grand-Combe F 78 B3
La Grande-Croix F 69 C4
La Grande-Motte F 78 C3
La Granja d'Escarp E 90 B3
La Granjuela E 93 C5
Lagrasse F 77 C5
La Grave F 79 A5
La Gravelle F 57 B4
Laguardia E 89 B4
La Guardia E 95 C3
La Guardia de Jaén
E 100 B2
Laguarres E 90 A3
Laguenne F 68 C1
Laguépie F 77 B4
La Guerche-de-Bretagne
F 57 C4
La Guerche-sur-l'Aubois
F 68 B2
La Guérinière F 66 B2
Laguiole F 78 B1
Laguna de Duera E 88 C2
Laguna del Marquesado
E 95 B5
Laguna de Negrillos
E 88 B1
Lagundo I 71 B6
Lagunilla E 93 A4
La Haba E 93 C5
Laharie F 76 B2
La Haye-du-Puits F 57 A4
La Haye-Pesnel F 57 B4
Lahden D 43 C4
La Herlière F 48 C3
La Hermida E 88 A2
La Herrera E 95 D4
Laheycourt F 59 B6
La Higuera E 101 A4
La Hiniesta E 88 C1
Lahnstein D 50 C3
Laholm S 40 C3
La Horcajada E 93 A5
La Horra E 88 C3
Lahr D 60 B3
Lahti FIN 3 F26
La Hulpe B 49 C5
La Hutte F 57 B6
Laichingen D 61 B5
L'Aigle F 58 B1
La Iglesuela E 94 B2
La Iglesuela del Cid E 90 C2
Laignes F 59 C5
Laiguéglia I 80 C2
L'Aiguillon-sur-Mer F 66 B3
Laimbach am Ostrong
A 63 B6
Laina E 95 A4
Lainio S 113 E11
Lairg GB 23 C4
La Iruela E 100 B3
Laissac F 78 B1
Laisvall S 115 A14
Láives I 71 B6
La Javie F 79 B5
Lajkovac SRB 85 B5
La Jonchère-St Maurice
F 67 B6
La Jonquera E 91 A5
Lajoskomárom H 74 B3
Lajosmizse H 75 A4
Lak H 65 B6
Lakenheath GB 30 B4
Lakitelek H 75 B5
Lakki GR 117 G5
Lakolk DK 39 D1
Łąkorz PL 47 B5
Lakšárska Nová Ves
SK 64 B3
Lakselv N 113 B13
Laksfors N 115 B10
Laktaši BIH 84 B2
La Lantejuela E 99 B5
Lalapaşa TR 118 A1
L'Albagès E 90 B3
Lalbenque F 77 B4
L'Alcudia E 96 B2
L'Aldea E 90 C3
Lalëz AL 105 B5
Lalín E 86 B2
Lalinde F 77 B3
La Línea de la
Concepción E 99 C5
Lalizolle F 68 B3
La Llacuna E 91 B4
Lalley F 79 B4
Lalling D 62 B4
Lalm N 114 F6
La Londe-les-Maures
F 79 C5
La Loupe F 58 B2
La Louvière B 49 C5
L'Alpe-d'Huez F 79 A5
La Luisiana E 99 B5
Laluque F 76 C1
Lam D 62 A4
La Machine F 68 B3
la Maddalena I 110 A2
Lama dei Peligni I 103 A7
Lamadrid E 88 A2
Lamagistére F 77 B3
La Mailleraye-sur-Seine
F 58 A1
La Malène F 78 B2
Lama Mocogno I 81 B4
La Mamola E 100 C2
La Manresana dels Prats
E 91 B4
Lamarche F 60 B1
Lamarche-sur-Saône
F 69 A5
Lamargelle F 69 A4
Lamarosa P 92 B2
Lamarque F 76 A2
Lamas P 92 A2
La Masadera E 90 B2
Lamas de Moaro P 87 B2
Lamastre F 78 B3
La Mata E 94 C2
La Mata de Ledesma
E 94 A1
La Mata de Monteagudo
E 88 B1
Lambach A 63 B4
Lamballe F 56 B3
Lamberhurst GB 31 C4
Lambesc F 79 C4
Lambia GR 117 E3
Lambley GB 25 D5
Lambourn GB 31 C2
Lamego P 87 C3
La Meilleraye-de-Bretagne
F 66 A3
La Ménitré F 67 A4
L'Ametlla de Mar E 90 C3
Lamia GR 116 D4
Lammhult S 40 B4
La Mojonera E 101 C3
La Mole F 79 C5
La Molina E 91 A4
La Monnerie-le-Montel
F 68 C3
La Morera E 93 C4
La Mothe-Achard F 66 B3
Lamothe-Cassel F 77 B4
Lamothe-Montravel F 76 B3
La Mothe-St Héray F 67 B4
Lamotte-Beuvron F 58 C3
La Motte-Chalançon
F 79 B4
La Motte-du-Caire F 79 B5
La Motte-Servolex F 69 C5
Lampertheim D 61 A4
Lampeter GB 28 A3
L'Ampolla E 90 C3
Lamprechtshausen A 62 C3
Lamsfeld D 53 B4
Lamspringe D 51 B6
Lamstedt D 43 B6
La Mudarra E 88 C2
La Muela E 90 B1
La Mure F 79 B4
Lamure-sur-Azergues
F 69 B4
Lana I 71 B6
Lanaja E 90 B2
Lanarce F 78 B2
Lanark GB 25 C4
La Nava E 99 B4
La Nava de Ricomalillo
E 94 C2
La Nava de Santiago
E 93 B4
Lancaster GB 26 A3
Lanchester GB 25 D6
Lanciano I 103 A7
Lancing GB 31 D3
Lançon-Provence F 79 C4
Lancova Vas SLO 73 B5
Landau
Bayern D 62 B3
Rheinland-Pfalz D 61 A4
Landeck A 71 A5
Landen B 49 C6
Landerneau F 56 B1
Landeryd S 40 B3
Landesbergen D 43 C6
Landete E 96 B1
Landévant F 56 C2
Landévennec F 56 B1
Landeyjahöfn IS 111 D5
Landivisiau F 56 B1
Landivy F 57 B4
Landl A 62 C3
Landön S 115 D11
Landos F 78 B2
Landouzy-le-Ville F 59 A5
Landquart CH 71 B4
Landrecies F 49 C4
Landreville F 59 B5
Landriano I 71 C4
Landsberg D 62 B1
Lands-berg D 52 B2
Landsbro S 40 B4
Landscheid D 50 D2
Landshut D 62 B3
Landskrona S 41 D2
Landstuhl D 60 A3
Lanesborough IRL 19 C4
Lanester F 56 C2
Lanestosa E 89 A3
La Neuve-Lyre F 58 B1
La Neuveville CH 70 A2
Langå DK 39 C2
Langada GR 116 D8
Langadas GR 116 B5
Langa de Duero E 89 C3
Langadia GR 117 E4
Langangen N 35 C1
Långared S 40 A2
Långaröd S 41 D3
Långaryd S 40 B3
Långås S 40 C2
Långasjö S 40 C5
Langau A 63 B6
Langeac F 78 A2
Langeais F 67 A5
Langedijk NL 42 C1
Langeln D 51 B6
Langelsheim D 51 B6
Langemark-Poelkapelle
B 48 C3
Langen
Hessen D 51 D4
Niedersachsen D 43 B5
Langenau D 61 B6
Langenberg D 50 B4
Langenbruck CH 70 A2
Langenburg D 61 A5
Längenfeld A 71 A5
Langenfeld D 50 B2
Langenhorn D 43 A5
Langenlois A 63 B6
Langenlonsheim D 60 A3
Langennaudorf D 52 B3
Langenneufnach D 62 B1
Langenthal CH 70 A2
Langenzenn D 62 A1
Langeoog D 43 B4
Langeskov DK 39 D3
Langesund N 35 C1
Langewiesen D 51 C6
Långflon S 34 A4
Langförden D 43 C5
Langhagen D 44 B4
Länghem S 40 B3
Langhirano I 81 B4
Langholm GB 25 C5
Langholt IS 111 D7
Långlöt S 41 C6
Langnau CH 70 B2
Langø DK 39 E4
Langogne F 78 B2
Langon F 76 B2
Langquaid D 62 B3
Långrådna S 37 D3
Langreo E 88 A1
Langres F 59 C6
Långsele S 115 D14
Långserud S 35 C4
Langset N 34 B3
Långshyttan S 36 B3
Langstrand N 113 B12
Långträsk S 115 B17
Langueux F 56 B3
Languidic F 56 C2
Längvik S 37 C5
Langwarden D 43 B5
Langwathby GB 26 A3
Langwedel D 43 C6
Langweid D 62 B1
Langwies CH 71 B4
Lanheses P 87 C2
Lanięta PL 47 C5
Lanildut F 56 B1
Lanjarón E 100 C2
Lanmeur F 56 B2
Lanna
Jönköping S 40 B3
Örebro S 37 C1
Lännaholm S 36 C4
Lannavaara S 113 D10
Lannéanou F 56 B2
Lannemezan F 77 C3
Lanneuville-sur-Meuse
F 59 A6
Lannilis F 56 B1
Lannion F 56 B2
La Nocle-Maulaix F 68 B3
Lanouaille F 67 C6
Lansjärv S 113 F11
Lanškroun CZ 64 A2
Lanslebourg-Mont-Cenis
F 70 C1
Lanta F 77 C4
Lantadilla E 88 B2
Lanton F 76 B1
Lantosque F 79 C6
La Nuez de Arriba E 88 B3
Lanusei I 110 C2
Lanúvio I 102 B5
Lanvollon F 56 B3
Lánycsók H 74 B3
Lanz D 44 B3
Lanza E 86 A2
Lanzada E 86 B2
Lanzahita E 94 B2
Lanžhot CZ 64 B2
Lanzo Torinese I 70 C2
Laole SRB 85 B6
Laon F 59 A4
Laons F 58 B2
La Paca E 101 B4
La Pacaudière F 68 B3
Lapalisse F 68 B3
La Palma d'Ebre E 90 B3
La Palma del Condado
E 99 B4
La Palme F 78 D2
La Palmyre F 66 C3
La Parra E 93 C4
Łapczyna Wola PL 55 C4
La Pedraja de Portillo
E 88 C2
La Peraleja E 95 B4
La Petit-Pierre F 60 B3
Lapeyrade F 76 B2
Lapeyrouse F 68 B2
Lapford GB 28 C4
La Pinilla E 101 B4
Lapithos CY 120 A2
La Plagne F 70 C1
La Plaza E 86 A4
Laplje Selo KOS 85 D6
Laplume F 77 B3
La Pobla de Lillet E 91 A4
La Pobla de Vallbona
E 96 B2
La Pobla Llarga E 96 B2
La Pola de Gordón E 88 B1
la Porta F 102 A2
La Pouëze F 66 A4
Lapoutroie F 60 B3
La Póveda de Soria
E 89 B4
Lapovo SRB 85 B6
Läppe S 37 C2
Lappeenranta FIN 3 F28
Lappoluobbal N 113 C12
La Preste F 91 A5
La Primaube F 77 B5
Lapseki TR 118 B1
Lapua FIN 3 E25
La Puebla de Almoradie
E 95 C3
La Puebla de Cazalla
E 99 B5
La Puebla de los Infantes
E 99 B5
La Puebla del Río E 99 B4
La Puebla de Montalbán
E 94 C2
La Puebla de Roda E 90 A3
La Puebla de Valdavia
E 88 B2
La Puebla de Valverde
E 96 A2
La Pueblanueva E 94 C2
La Puerta de Segura
E 101 A3
La Punt CH 71 B4
L'Áquila I 103 A6
La Quintana E 100 B1
La Quintera E 99 B5
La Rábita
Granada E 100 C2
Jaén E 100 B1
Laracha E 86 A2
Laragh IRL 21 A5
Laragne-Montéglin F 79 B4
La Rambla E 100 B1
l'Arboç E 91 B4
L'Arbresle F 69 C4
Lärbro S 37 E5

Larceveau F 76 C1
Larche
Alpes-de-Haute-Provence F 79 B5
Corrèze F 77 A4
Lårdal N 33 C5
Lærdalsøyri N 32 A4
Lardosa P 92 B3
La Reale I 110 A1
Laredo E 89 A3
La Redondela E 98 B3
La Réole F 76 B2
Largentière F 78 B3
L'Argentière-la-Bessée F 79 B5
Largs GB 24 C3
Lari I 81 C4
La Riera E 86 A4
La Riera de Gaià E 91 B4
La Rinconada E 99 B4
Lariño E 86 B1
Larino I 103 B7
Larisa GR 116 C4
La Rivière-Thibouville F 58 A1
Larkhall GB 25 C4
Larkollen N 35 C2
Larmor-Plage F 56 C2
Larnaca CY 120 B2
Larne GB 19 B6
La Robla E 88 B1
La Roca de la Sierra E 93 B4
La Roche CH 70 B2
La Rochebeaucourtet-Argentine F 67 C5
La Roche-Bernard F 66 A2
La Roche-Canillac F 68 C1
La Roche-Chalais F 67 C5
La Roche Derrien F 56 B2
La Roche-des-Arnauds F 79 B4
La Roche-en-Ardenne B 49 C6
La Roche-en-Brénil F 69 A4
La Rochefoucauld F 67 C5
La Roche-Guyon F 58 A2
La Rochelle F 66 B3
La Roche-Posay F 67 B5
La Roche-sur-Foron F 69 B6
La Roche-sur-Yon F 66 B3
Larochette L 60 A2
La Rochette F 79 B4
La Roda
Albacete E 95 C4
Oviedo E 86 A4
La Roda de Andalucía E 100 B1
Laroquebrou F 77 B5
La Roquebrussanne F 79 C4
Laroque d'Olmes F 77 D4
La Roque-Gageac F 77 B4
La Roque-Ste Marguerite F 78 B2
Laroque-Timbaut F 77 B3
Larouco E 87 B3
Larraga E 89 B5
Larrau F 76 C2
Larrazet F 77 C4
Larsnes N 114 E2
La Rubia E 89 C4
Laruns F 76 C2
Larva E 100 B2
Larvik N 35 C2
La Sagrada E 87 D4
La Salceda E 94 A3
Lasalle F 78 B2
La Salle F 79 B5
la Salute di Livenza I 72 C2
La Salvetat-Peyralés F 77 B5
La Salvetat-sur-Agout F 78 C1
Las Arenas E 88 A2
La Sarraz CH 69 B6
Lasarte E 89 A4
Låsby DK 39 C2
Las Cabezadas E 95 A3
Las Cabezas de San Juan E 99 C5
Las Correderas E 100 A2
Las Cuevas de Cañart E 90 C2
La Seca E 88 C2
La Selva del Camp E 91 B4
La Senia E 90 C3
La Serra E 91 B4
La Seu d'Urgell E 91 A4
La Seyne-sur-Mer F 79 C4
Las Gabias E 100 B2
Las Herencias E 94 C2
Las Herrerias E 98 B3
Łasin PL 47 B5
Lask PL 55 B4
Laska PL 46 B3
Łaskarzow PL 55 B6
Laško SLO 73 B5
Laskowice PL 47 B4
Las Labores E 95 C3
Las Mesas E 95 C4
Las Minas E 101 A4
Las Navas E 100 B1
Las Navas de la Concepción E 99 B5
Las Navas del Marqués E 94 B2
Las Navillas E 94 C2
Las Negras E 101 C4
La Solana E 95 D3
La Souterraine F 67 B6
Las Pajanosas E 99 B4
Laspaules E 90 A3
Las Pedroñas E 95 C4
La Spézia I 81 B3
Las Planes d'Hostoles E 91 A5
Laspuña E 90 A3
Las Rozas
Cantabria E 88 B2
Madrid E 94 B3
Lassan D 45 B5
Lassay-les-Châteaux F 57 B5
Lasseube F 76 C2
Lassigny F 58 A3
La Storta I 102 B5
Lastovo HR 84 D1
Lastras de Cuéllar E 88 C2
Lästringe S 37 D4
Lastrup D 43 C4
Lastva BIH 84 D3
Las Uces E 87 C4
La Suze-sur-Sarthe F 57 C6
Las Veguillas E 94 B1
Las Ventas con Peña Aguilera E 94 C2
Las Ventas de San Julián E 93 A5
Las Villes E 96 A3
Latasa E 76 D1
Látera I 102 A4
Laterza I 104 C2
La Teste F 76 B1
Lathen D 43 C4
Latheron GB 23 C5
La Thuile I 70 C1
Latiano I 105 C3
Latina I 102 B5
Latisana I 72 C3
Látky SK 65 B5
La Toba E 95 B5
La Toledana E 94 C2
La Torre de Cabdella E 90 A3
La Torre de Esteban Hambrán E 94 B2
La Torre del l'Espanyol E 90 B3
La Torresaviñán E 95 B4
La Tour d'Aigues F 79 C4
La Tour de Peilz CH 70 B1
La Tour-du-Pin F 69 C5
Latowicz PL 55 A6
La Tranche-sur-Mer F 66 B3
La Tremblade F 66 C3
La Trimouille F 67 B6
La Trinité F 56 C2
La Trinité-Porhoët F 56 B3
Latrónico I 106 A3
Latronquière F 77 B5
Latterbach CH 70 B2
La Turballe F 66 A2
Laubach D 51 C4
Laubert F 78 B2
Laucha D 52 B1
Lauchhammer D 53 B3
Lauchheim D 61 B6
Lauda-Königshofen D 61 A5
Laudal N 33 D4
Lauder GB 25 C5
Lauenau D 51 A5
Lauenburg D 44 B2
Lauf D 62 A2
Laufach D 51 C5
Laufen
CH 70 A2
D 62 C3
Lauffen D 61 A5
Laugar IS 111 B8
Laugarás IS 111 C5
Laugarbakki IS 111 B5
Laugarvatn IS 111 C5
Laugharne GB 28 B3
Lauingen D 61 B6
Laujar de Andarax E 100 C3
Laukaa FIN 3 E26
Lauker S 115 B16
Laukvik N 112 E3
La Uña E 88 A1
Launceston GB 28 C3
La Unión E 101 B5
Launois-sur-Vence F 59 A5
Laupheim D 61 B5
Lauragh IRL 20 C2
Laureana di Borrello I 106 C3
Laurencekirk GB 25 B5
Laurencetown IRL 20 A3
Laurenzana I 104 C1
Lauria I 106 A2
Laurière F 67 B6
Laurieston GB 24 D3
Laurino I 103 C8
Lausanne CH 69 B6
Laussonne F 78 B3
Lauta D 53 B4
Lautenthal D 51 B6
Lauterach A 71 A4
Lauterbach D 51 C5
Lauterbrunnen CH 70 B2
Lauterecken D 60 A3
Lauterhofen D 62 A2
Lautrec F 77 C5
Lauvsnes N 114 C7
Lauvvik N 33 D3
Lauzerte F 77 B4
Lauzès F 77 B4
Lauzun F 77 B3
Lavagna I 80 B3
Laval F 57 B5
La Vall d'Uixó E 96 B2
Lavamünd A 73 B4
Lavara GR 118 A1
Lavardac F 76 B3
Lavaris P 92 A2
Lavarone I 71 C6
Lavau F 59 C3
Lavaur F 77 C4
La Vecilla de Curueño E 88 B1
La Vega
Asturias E 88 A1
Asturias E 88 A1
Cantabria E 88 A2
Lavelanet F 77 D4
La Velilla E 94 A3
La Velles E 94 A1
Lavello I 104 B1
Lavelsloh D 43 C5
Lavenham GB 30 B4
Laveno I 70 C3
La Ventosa E 95 B4
Lavezzola I 81 B5
Laviano I 103 C8
La Victoria E 100 B1
La Vid E 89 C3
Lavik N 32 A2
La Vilavella E 96 B2
La Vilella Baixa E 90 B3
La Villa de Don Fadrique E 95 C3
Lavilledieu F 78 B3
La Villedieu F 67 B4
La Ville Dieu-du-Temple F 77 B4
Lavinio-Lido di Enea I 102 B5
Lav is I 71 B6
Lavit F 77 C3
Lavoncourt F 60 C1
Lavos P 92 A2
La Voulte-sur-Rhône F 78 B3
Lavoûte-Chilhac F 68 C3
Lavradio P 92 C1
Lavre P 92 C2
Lavrio GR 117 E6
La Wantzenau F 60 B3
Lawers GB 24 B3
Ławy PL 45 C6
Laxå S 37 D1
Laxamýri IS 111 B8
Laxe E 86 A2
Laxey GB 26 A1
Laxford Bridge GB 22 C3
Laxhall S 35 D5
Laxsjö S 115 D11
Laxtjarn S 34 B6
Laxvik S 40 C2
Laxviken S 115 D11
La Yesa E 96 B2
Laza E 87 B3
Lazarevac SRB 85 B5
Lazarev Krst MNE 105 A5
Lazarevo SRB 75 C5
Lazise I 71 C5
Łaziska Grn. PL 54 C3
Lazkao E 89 A4
Lázně Bělohrad CZ 53 C5
Lázně Bohdaneč CZ 53 C5
Lázně Kynžvart CZ 52 C2
Lazonby GB 26 A3
La Zubia E 100 B2
Łazy PL 46 A2
Lazzaro I 109 B4
Lea GB 27 B5
Leadburn GB 25 C4
Leadhills GB 25 C4
Leap IRL 20 C2
Leatherhead GB 31 C3
Łeba PL 46 A3
Lebach D 60 A2
Le Barp F 76 B2
Le Bar-sur-Loup F 79 C5
Le Béage F 78 B3
Le Beausset F 79 C4
Lebedyn UA 7 F13
Lebekke B 49 B5
Lébény H 64 C3
Le Bessat F 69 C4
Le Blanc F 67 B6
Le Bleymard F 78 B2
Łebno PL 47 A4
Leboreiro E 87 B3
Lębork PL 46 A3
Le Boullay-Mivoye F 58 B2
Le Boulou F 91 A5
Le Bourg F 77 B4
Le Bourg-d'Oisans F 79 A5
Le Bourget-du-Lac F 69 C5
Le Bourgneuf-la-Forêt F 57 B5
Le Bousquet d'Orb F 78 C2
Le Brassus CH 69 B6
Le Breuil F 68 B3
Le Breuil-en-Auge F 57 A6
Lebrija E 99 C4
Lebring A 73 B5
Le Brusquet F 79 B5
Le Bry CH 70 B2
Le Bugue F 77 B3
Le Buisson F 77 B3
Lebus D 45 C6
Lebusa D 52 B3
Leca da Palmeira P 87 C2
Le Caloy F 76 C2
Le Cap d'Agde F 78 C2
Le Cateau Cambrésis F 49 C4
Le Caylar F 78 C2
Le Cayrol F 78 B1
Lecce I 105 C4
Lecco I 71 C4
Lécera E 90 B2
Lećevica HR 83 C5
Lech A 71 A5
Le Chambon-Feugerolles F 69 C4
Le Chambon-sur-Lignon F 78 A3
Le Château d'Oléron F 66 C3
Le Châtelard F 69 C6
Le Châtelet F 68 B2
Le Chatelet-en-Brie F 58 B3
Lechbruck D 62 C1
Lechena GR 117 E3
Le Chesne F 59 A5
Le Cheylard F 78 B3
Lechlade GB 29 B6
Lechovice CZ 64 B2
Leciñena E 90 B2
Leck D 39 E1
Le Collet-de-Deze F 78 B2
Le Conquet F 56 B1
Le Creusot F 69 B4
Le Croisic F 66 A2
Le Crotoy F 48 C2
Lectoure F 77 C3
Łęczyca
Łódzkie PL 55 A4
Zachodnio-Pomorskie PL 45 B7
Ledaña E 95 C5
Ledbury GB 29 A5
Lede B 49 C4
Ledečnad Sazavou CZ 63 A6
Ledenice CZ 63 B5
Le Deschaux F 69 B5
Ledesma E 87 C4
Lédignan F 78 C3
Lédigos E 88 B2
Ledmore GB 22 C4
Lednice CZ 64 B2
Lednicke-Rovné SK 64 A4
Le Donjon F 68 B3
Le Dorat F 67 B6
Lędyczek PL 46 B2
Lędziny PL 55 C4
Leeds GB 27 B4
Leek
GB 26 B3
NL 42 B3
Leenaun IRL 18 C2
Leens NL 42 B3
Leer D 43 B4
Leerdam NL 49 B6
Leerhafe D 43 B4
Leese D 43 C6
Leeuwarden NL 42 B2
Leezen D 44 B2
Le Faou F 56 B1
Le Faoüet F 56 B2
Lefka CY 120 A1
Lefkada GR 116 D2
Lefkimis GR 116 C2
Lefkoniko CY 120 A2
Le Folgoet F 56 B1
Le Fossat F 77 C4
Le Fousseret F 77 C4
Le Fugeret F 79 B5
Leganés E 94 B3
Legau D 61 C6
Le Gault-Soigny F 59 B4
Legbąd PL 46 B3
Legé F 66 B3
Lège-Cap-Ferret F 76 B1
Legionowo PL 55 A5
Léglise B 60 A1
Legnago I 71 C6
Legnano I 70 C3
Legnaro I 72 C1
Legnica PL 53 B6
Łęgowo PL 47 A4
Legrad HR 74 B1
Le Grand-Bornand F 69 C6
Le-Grand-Bourg F 67 B6
Le Grand-Lucé F 58 C1
Le Grand-Pressigny F 67 B5
Le Grand-Quevilly F 58 A2
Le Grau-du-Roi F 78 C3
Léguevin F 77 C4
Legutiano E 89 B4
Le Havre F 57 A6
Lehesten D 52 C1
Lehnice SK 64 B3
Lehnin D 52 A2
Le Hohwald F 60 B3
Le Houga F 76 C2
Lehrberg D 61 A6
Lehre D 51 A6
Lehrte D 44 C1
Lehsen D 44 B3
Leibnitz A 73 B5
Leicester GB 30 B2
Leiden NL 49 A5
Leidschendam NL 49 A5
Leigh GB 26 B3
Leighlinbridge IRL 21 B5
Leighton Buzzard GB 31 C3
Leignon B 49 C6
Leikanger N 114 E2
Leimen D 61 A4
Leinefelde D 51 B6
Leinesfjord N 112 E4
Leintwardine GB 29 A5
Leipojärvi S 112 E10
Leipzig D 52 B2
Leira
Nordland N 115 A10
Oppland N 32 B6
Leiråmoen N 112 F3
Leiria P 92 B2
Leirvik
Hordaland N 32 C2
Sogn og Fjordane N 32 A2
Leisach A 72 B2
Leisnig D 52 B2
Leiston GB 30 B5
Leitholm GB 25 C5
Leitrim IRL 18 C3
Leitza E 76 C1
Leitzkau D 52 A1
Lejkowo PL 46 A2
Lekani GR 116 A6
Łękawa PL 55 B4
Łekawica PL 65 A5
Lekbibaj AL 105 A5
Lekeitio E 89 A4
Lekenik HR 73 C6
Lekeryd S 40 B4
Leknes N 112 D2
Łęknica PL 53 B4
Leksand S 36 B1
Leksvik N 114 D7
Lekunberri E 76 C1
Lekvattnet S 34 B4
Le Lardin-St Lazare F 67 C6
Le Lauzet-Ubaye F 79 B5
Le Lavandou F 79 C5
Le Lion-d'Angers F 57 C5
Lelkowo PL 47 A6
Le Locle CH 70 A1
Le Loroux-Bottereau F 66 A3
Le Louroux-Béconnais F 66 A4
Lelów PL 55 C4
Le Luc F 79 C5
Le Lude F 57 C6
Lelystad NL 42 C2
Lem
Ringkøbing DK 39 C1
Viborg Amt. DK 38 C1
Le Malzieu-Ville F 78 B2
Le Mans F 57 B6
Le Mas-d'Azil F 77 C4
Le Massegros F 78 B2
Le Mayet-de-Montagne F 68 B3
Le May-sur-Evre F 66 A4
Lembach F 60 A3
Lemberg F 60 A3
Lembèye F 76 C2
Lemelerveld NL 42 C3
Le Mêle-sur-Sarthe F 58 B1
Le Ménil F 60 B2
Le Merlerault F 57 B6
Le Mesnil-sur-Oger F 59 B5
Lemförde D 43 C5
Lemgo D 51 A4
Le Miroir F 69 B5
Lemland FIN 36 B7
Lemmer NL 42 C2
Le Molay-Littry F 57 A5
Le Monastier-sur-Gazeille F 78 B2
Le Monêtier-les-Bains F 79 B5
Le Mont-Dore F 68 C2
Le Montet F 68 B3
Le Mont-St Michel F 57 B4
Lempdes F 68 C3
Le Muret F 76 B2
Le Muy F 79 C5
Lemvig DK 38 C1
Lemwerder D 43 B5
Lena N 34 B2
Lenart SLO 73 B5
Lenartovce SK 65 B6
Lenauheim RO 75 C5
Lencloître F 67 B5
Lend A 72 A3
Lendalfoot GB 24 C3
Lendava SLO 73 B6
Lendery RUS 3 E29
Lendinara I 81 A5
Lendorf A 72 B3
Lendum DK 38 B3
Le Neubourg F 58 A1
Lengefeld D 52 C3
Lengerich
Niedersachsen D 43 C4
Nordrhein-Westfalen D 50 A3
Lenggries D 62 C2
Lengyeltóti H 74 B2
Lenhovda S 40 C5
Lenk CH 70 B2
Lennartsfors S 35 C3
Lennestadt D 50 B4
Lennoxtown GB 24 C3
Leno I 71 C5
Lénola I 103 B6
Le Nouvion-en-Thiérache F 49 C4
Lens
B 49 C4
F 48 C3
Lensahn D 44 A2
Lens Lestang F 69 C5
Lensvik N 114 D6
Lentellais E 87 B3
Lentföhrden D 44 B1
Lenti H 74 B1
Lentini I 109 B3
Lenungshammar S 35 C4
Lenzburg CH 70 A3
Lenzen D 44 B3
Lenzerheide CH 71 B4
Leoben A 73 A5
Leogang A 72 A2
Leominster GB 29 A5
León E 88 B1
Léon F 76 C1
Leonberg D 61 B5
Léoncel F 79 B4
Leonding A 63 B5
Leonessa I 102 A5
Leonforte I 109 B3
Leonidio GR 117 E4
Leopoldsburg B 49 B6
Leopoldsdorf im Marchfeld A 64 B2
Leopoldshagen D 45 B5
Leova MD 11 C10
Le Palais F 66 A1
Le Parcq F 48 C3
Lepe E 98 B3
Le Péage-de-Roussillon F 69 C4
Le Pellerin F 66 A3
Lepenac
MNE 85 D4
SRB 85 C6
Lepenou GR 116 D3
Le Perthus F 91 A5
Le Pertuis F 78 A3
Le Petit-Bornand F 69 C6
Lephin GB 22 D2
L'Épine F 79 B4
Le Poët F 79 B4
Lepoglava HR 73 B6
Le Poirè-sur-Vie F 66 B3
Le Pont CH 69 B6
Le Pont-de-Montvert F 78 B2
Le Porge F 76 B1
Le Porge-Océan F 76 B1
Le Portel F 48 C2
Le Pouldu F 56 C2
Le Pouliguen F 66 A2
Leppäjärvi FIN 113 D12
Leppävirta FIN 3 E27
Leppin D 44 C3
le Prese I 71 B5
Lepsény H 74 B3
Le Puy-en-Velay F 78 A2
Le Puy-Ste Réparade F 79 C4
Le Quesnoy F 49 C4
Léquile I 105 C4
Le Rayol F 79 C5
Lercara Friddi I 108 B2
Lerdal S 35 D3
Leré F 68 A2
Lérici I 81 B3
Lerin E 89 B5
Lerma E 88 B3
Lerm-et-Musset F 76 B2
Lermoos A 71 A5
Le Roeulx B 49 C5
Le Rouget F 77 B5
Lérouville F 60 B1
Le Rozier F 78 B2
Lerum S 40 B2
Le Russey F 70 A1
Lervik N 35 C2
Lerwick GB 22 A7
Lés E 77 D3
Les Abrets F 69 C5
Les Aix-d'Angillon F 68 A2
Lešak KOS 85 C5
Lesaka E 76 C1
Les Ancizes-Comps F 68 C2
Les Andelys F 58 A2
Les Arcs
Savoie F 70 C1
Les Arcs continued
Var F 79 C5
Les-Aubiers F 67 B4
Les Baux-de-Provence F 78 C3
Les Bézards F 58 C3
Les Bois CH 70 A1
Les Bordes F 58 C3
Les Borges Blanques E 90 B3
Les Borges del Camp E 91 B4
Les Brunettes F 68 B3
Lesbury GB 25 C6
Les Cabannes F 77 D4
L'Escala E 91 A6
Lescar F 76 C2
L'Escarène F 80 C1
Lesce SLO 73 B4
Lescheraines F 69 C6
Lesconil F 56 C1
Les Contamines-Montjoie F 70 C1
les Coves de Vinroma E 90 C3
Les Déserts F 69 C5
Les Deux-Alpes F 79 B5
Les Diablerets CH 70 B2
Lesdins F 59 A4
Les Echelles F 69 C5
Le Sel-de-Bretagne F 57 C4
Le Sentier CH 69 B6
Les Escaldes AND 91 A4
Les Essarts F 66 B3
Les Estables F 78 B3
Les Eyzies-de-Tayac F 77 B4
Les Gets F 70 B1
Les Grandes-Ventes F 58 A2
Les Haudères CH 70 B2
Les Herbiers F 66 B3
Les Hôpitaux-Neufs F 69 B6
Lesično SLO 73 B5
Lésina I 103 B8
Lesjaskog N 114 E5
Lesjöfors S 34 C6
Leskovac SRB 10 E6
Leskova Dolina SLO 73 C4
Leskovec
CZ 64 A3
SLO 73 C5
Leskovice CZ 63 A6
Leskovik AL 116 B2
Leslie GB 25 B4
Les Lucs-sur-Boulogne F 66 B3
Les Mages F 78 B3
Lesmahagow GB 25 C4
Les Mazures F 59 A5
Les Mées F 79 B4
Lesmont F 59 B5
Les Mureaux F 58 B2
Leśna PL 53 B5
Lesneven F 56 B1
Leśnica PL 54 C3
Lešnica SRB 85 B4
Leśniów Wielkoplski PL 53 B5
Lesnoye RUS 7 B13
Les Omergues F 79 B4
Les Ormes-sur-Voulzie F 59 B4
Les Orres F 79 B5
Le Souquet F 76 C1
Lesparre-Médoc F 66 C4
l'Espérance F 59 A4
l'Esperou F 78 B2
Les Pieux F 57 A4
Lesponne F 76 C3
Les Ponts-de-Cé F 67 A4
Les Ponts-de-Martel CH 70 B1
Les Praz F 70 C1
L'Espunyola E 91 A4
Les Riceys F 59 C5
Les Roches F 69 C4
Les Rosaires F 56 B3
Les Rosiers F 67 A4
Les Rousses F 69 B6
Les Sables-d'Olonne F 66 B3
Lessach A 72 A3
Lessay F 57 A4
Lessebo S 40 C5
Les Settons F 68 A4
Lessines B 49 C4
L'Estany E 91 B5
Les Ternes F 78 A1
Lesterps F 67 B5
Les Thilliers en-Vexin F 58 A2
Les Touches F 66 A3
Les Trois Moûtiers F 67 A5
Les Vans F 78 B3
Les Verrières CH 69 B6
Les Vignes F 78 B2
Leswalt GB 24 D2
Leszno
Mazowieckie PL 55 A5
Wielkopolskie PL 54 B1
Leszno Górne PL 53 B5
Letchworth GB 31 C3
Le Teil F 78 B3
Le Teilleul F 57 B5
Le Temple-de-Bretagne F 66 A3
Letenye H 74 B1
Le Theil F 58 B1
Le Thillot F 60 C2
Letino I 103 B7
Letohrad CZ 54 C1
Le Touquet-Paris-Plage F 48 C2
Le Touvet F 69 C5
Letovice CZ 64 A2
Le Translay F 48 D2
Le Tréport F 48 C2
Letschin D 45 C6
Letterfrack IRL 18 C2
Letterkenny IRL 19 B4
Lettermacaward IRL 18 B3
Lettoch GB 23 D5
Letur E 101 A3
Letux E 90 B2
Letzlingen D 44 C3
Leucate F 78 D2
Leuchars GB 25 B5
Leuglay F 59 C5
Leuk CH 70 B2
Leukerbad CH 70 B2
Leumrabhagh GB 22 C2
Leuna D 52 B2
Leusden NL 49 A6
Leutenberg D 52 C1
Leuterschach D 61 C6
Leutershausen D 61 A6
Leutkirch D 61 C6
Leuven B 49 C5
Leuze-en-Hainaut B 49 C4
Le Val F 79 C5
Le Val-André F 56 B3
Le Val-d'Ajol F 60 C2
Levan AL 105 C5
Levanger N 114 D8
Levanjska Varoš HR 74 C3
Lévanto I 80 B3
Levaré F 57 B5
Levata I 71 C5
Leveld N 32 B5
Leven
East Yorkshire GB 27 B5
Fife GB 25 B5
Leverano I 105 C3
Le Verdon-sur-Mer F 66 C3
Leverkusen D 50 B2
Levern D 43 C5
Le Vernet F 79 B5
Levet F 68 B2
Levice SK 65 B4
Lévico Terme I 71 B6
Levie F 102 B2
Levier F 69 B6
Le Vigan F 78 C2
Lévignen F 59 A3
le Ville I 82 C1
Levinovac HR 74 C2
Le Vivier-sur-Mer F 57 B4
Levoča SK 65 A6
Levroux F 67 B6
Lewes GB 31 D4
Lewin Brzeski PL 54 C2
Lewisham GB 31 C3
Leyburn GB 27 A4
Leyland GB 26 B3
Leysdown-on-Sea GB 31 C4
Leysin CH 70 B2
Lezajsk PL 11 A7
Lézardrieux F 56 B2
Lézat-sur-Léze F 77 C4
Lezay F 67 B4
Lezhë AL 105 B5
Lézignan-Corbières F 78 C1
Lezignan-la-Cèbe F 78 C2
Ležimir SRB 75 C4
Lézinnes F 59 C5
Lezoux F 68 C3
Lezuza E 95 D4
Lgov RUS 7 F13
Lhenice CZ 63 B5
Lherm F 77 C4
Lhommaizé F 67 B5
L'Hospitalet F 91 A4
L'Hospitalet de l'Infant E 90 C3
L'Hospitalet de Llobregat E 91 B5
L'Hospitalet-du-Larzac F 78 C2
Lhuître F 59 B5
Liancourt F 58 A3
Liart F 59 A5
Liatorp S 40 C4
Liatrie GB 22 D4
Libáň CZ 53 C5
Libceves CZ 53 C3
Liběchov CZ 53 C4
Liber E 86 B3
Liberec CZ 53 C5
Libiąż PL 55 C4
Libina CZ 64 A3
Libochovice CZ 53 C4
Libofshë AL 105 C5
Libohovë AL 116 B2
Libourne F 76 B2
Libramont B 59 A6
Librazhd AL 116 A2
Librilla E 101 B4
Libros E 96 A1
Licata I 108 B2
Licciana Nardi I 81 B4
Licenza I 102 A5
Liceros E 89 C3
Lich D 51 C4
Lichères-près-Aigremont F 59 C4
Lichfield GB 27 C4
Lichtenau
A 63 B6
D 51 B4
Lichtenberg D 52 C1
Lichtenfels D 52 C1
Lichtensteig CH 71 A4
Lichtenstein D 52 C2
Lichtenvoorde NL 50 B2
Lichtervelde B 49 B4
Lička Jesenica HR 83 A4
Lickershamn S 37 E5
Lički Osik HR 83 B4
Ličko Lešce HR 83 B4
Licodía Eubéa I 109 B3
Licques F 48 C2
Lida BY 7 E8
Lidar N 32 A6
Lidečko CZ 64 A4
Liden S 115 E13
Lidhult S 40 C3
Lidköping S 35 D5
Lido I 72 C2
Lido Azzurro I 104 C3
Lido degli Estensi I 82 B1
Lido degli Scacchi I 82 B1
Lido della Nazioni I 82 B1
Lido di Camaiore I 81 C4
Lido di Casalbordino I 103 A7
Lido di Castél Fusano I 102 B5
Lido di Cincinnato I 102 B5
Lido di Classe I 82 B1
Lido di Fermo I 82 C2
Lido di Fondi I 103 B6
Lido di Jésolo I 72 C2
Lido di Lícola I 103 C7
Lido di Metaponto I 104 C2
Lido di Óstia I 102 B5
Lido di Policoro I 106 A3
Lido di Pomposa I 82 B1
Lido di Savio I 82 B1
Lido di Scanzano I 104 C2
Lido di Siponto I 104 B1
Lido di Squillace I 106 C3
Lido di Volano I 82 B1
Lido Riccio I 103 A7
Lidoriki GR 116 D4
Lido Silvana I 104 C3
Lidsjöberg S 115 C12
Lidzbark PL 47 B5
Lidzbark Warmiński PL 47 A6
Liebenau
A 63 B5
D 43 C6
Liebenwalde D 45 C5
Lieberose D 53 B4
Liebling RO 75 C6
Lieboch A 73 B5
Liège B 49 C6
Lieksa FIN 3 E29
Lienen D 50 A3
Lienz A 72 B2
Liepāja LV 6 C6
Lier B 49 B5
Lierbyen N 34 C2
Liernais F 69 A4
Liesing A 72 B2
Liestal CH 70 A2
Liétor E 101 A4
Lieurac F 77 D4
Lieurey F 58 A1
Liévin F 48 C3
Liezen A 73 A4
Liffol-le-Grand F 60 B1
Lifford IRL 19 B4
Liffré F 57 B4
Ligardes F 77 B3
Lignano Sabbiadoro I 72 C3
Ligne F 66 A3
Lignières F 68 B2
Ligny-en-Barrois F 59 B6
Ligny-le-Châtel F 59 C4
Ligoła Polska PL 54 B2
Ligourio GR 117 E5
Ligowo PL 47 C5
Ligueil F 67 A5
Lijeva Rijeka MNE 85 D4
Likavka SK 65 A5
Likenäs S 34 B5
Likhoslavl RUS 7 C13
Lild Strand DK 38 B1
L'Île-Bouchard F 67 A5
l'Île-Rousse F 102 A1
Lilienfeld A 63 B6
Lilienthal D 43 B5
Lilla Edet S 35 D4
Lilla Tjärby S 40 C3
Lille
B 49 B5
F 49 C4
Lillebonne F 58 A1
Lillehammer N 34 A2
Lillerød DK 41 D2
Lillers F 48 C3
Lillesand N 33 D5
Lillestrøm N 34 C3
Lillhärdal S 115 F11
Lillkyrka S 37 C4
Lillo E 95 C3
Lillögda S 115 C14
Lima S 34 B5
Limanowa PL 65 A6
Limassol CY 120 B2
Limavady GB 19 A5
Limbach-Oberfrohna D 52 C2
Limbaži LV 6 C8
Limbourg B 50 C1
Limburg D 50 C4
Lime DK 39 C3
Limedsforsen S 34 B5
Limenaria GR 116 B6
Limenas Chersonisou GR 117 G7
Limerick IRL 20 B3
Limes I 71 C5
Limésy F 58 A1
Limmared S 40 B3
Limni GR 116 D5
Limoges F 67 C6
Limogne-en-Quercy F 77 B4
Limoise F 68 B3
Limone Piemonte I 80 B1
Limone sul Garda I 71 C5
Limons F 68 C3
Limours F 58 B3
Limoux F 77 C5
Linares E 100 A2
Linares de Mora E 90 C2
Linares de Riofrio E 93 A5
Linaria GR 116 D6
Linas de Broto E 90 A2
Lincoln GB 27 B5
Lind DK 39 C1
Lindås N 32 B2
Lindau D 71 A4
Lindberget N 34 A3
Lindelse DK 39 E3
Lindenberg D 53 A4
Lindenberg im Allgäu D 61 C5
Lindern D 43 C4
Linderöd S 41 D3
Lindesberg S 37 C2
Lindesnäs S 36 B1
Lindesnes N 33 E4
Lindholmen S 37 C5
Lindknud DK 39 D2
Lindlar D 50 B3
Lindö S 37 D3
Lindome S 38 B5
Lindos GR 119 F3
Lindoso P 87 C2
Lindow D 45 C4
Lindsdal S 40 C6
Lindshammar S 40 B5
Lindstedt D 44 C3
Lindved DK 39 D2
Líně CZ 63 A4
Lingbo S 36 A3
Lingen D 43 C4
Linghed S 36 B2
Linghem S 37 D2
Linguaglossa I 109 B4
Linia PL 46 A3
Linie PL 45 B6
Liniewo PL 47 A4
Linkenheim D 61 A4
Linköping S 37 D2
Linksness GB 23 C5
Linlithgow GB 25 C4
Linneryd S 40 C5
Linnes Hammarby S 36 C4
Linnich D 50 C2
Linsell S 115 E10
Linslade GB 31 C3
Linthal CH 70 B4
Linyola E 90 B3
Linz
A 63 B5
D 50 C3
Liomseter N 32 A6
Lionárisso CY 120 A3
Lioni I 103 C8
Lion-sur-Mer F 57 A5
Lipany SK 65 A6
Lipar SRB 75 C4
Lípari I 106 C1
Lipcani MD 11 B9
Liperi FIN 3 E28
Liphook GB 31 C3
Lipiany PL 45 B6
Lipik HR 74 C2
Lipka PL 46 B3
Lipki Wielkie PL 46 C1
Lipnica PL 46 B3
Lipnica Murowana PL 65 A6
Lipnik PL 55 C6
Lipník nad Bečvou CZ 64 A3
Lipno
Kujawsko-Pomorskie PL 47 C5
Łódzkie PL 54 B3
Liposthey F 76 B2
Lipovac HR 84 A4
Lipovec CZ 64 A2
Lipovets UA 11 B10
Lipovljani HR 74 C1
Lipowina PL 47 A5
Lippborg D 50 B4
Lippó H 74 C3
Lippoldsberg D 51 B5
Lippstadt D 51 B4
Lipsko PL 55 B6
Liptál CZ 64 A3
Liptovská-Lúžna SK 65 B5
Liptovská Osada SK 65 B5
Liptovská-Teplička SK 65 B6
Liptovský Hrádok SK 65 A5
Liptovský Milkuláš SK 65 A5
Lipusz PL 46 A3
Lipůvka CZ 64 A2
Liré F 66 A3
Lis AL 105 B6
Lisa SRB 85 C5
Lisac BIH 84 B2
Lisbellaw GB 19 B4
Lisboa = Lisbon P 92 C1
Lisbon = Lisboa P 92 C1
Lisburn GB 19 B5
Liscannor IRL 20 B2
Lisdoonvarna IRL 20 A2
Lisewo PL 47 B4
Lisia Góra PL 55 C6
Lisięcice PL 54 C2
Lisieux F 57 A6
Lisjö S 37 C3
Liskeard GB 28 C3
L'Isle CH 69 B6
L'Isle-Adam F 58 A3
L'Isle-de-Noé F 77 C3
L'Isle-en-Dodon F 77 C3
L'Isle-Jourdain
Gers F 77 C4
Vienne F 67 B5
L'Isle-sur-la-Sorgue F 79 C4
L'Isle-sur-le Doubs F 69 A6
L'Isle-sur-Serein F 59 C5
Lisle-sur-Tarn F 77 C4
Lismore IRL 21 B4
Lisnaskea GB 19 B4
Lišov CZ 63 A5
Lisów
Lubuskie PL 45 C6
Śląskie PL 54 C3
Lisse NL 49 A5
Lissycasey IRL 20 B2
List D 39 D1
Listerby S 41 C5
Listowel IRL 20 B2
Listrac-Médoc F 76 A2
Liszki PL 55 C4
Liszkowo PL 46 B3
Lit S 115 D11
Litava SK 65 B5
Litcham GB 30 B4
Lit-et-Mixe F 76 B1
Litija SLO 73 B4
Litke H 65 B5
Litlabø N 32 C2
Litochoro GR 116 B4
Litoměřice CZ 53 C4
Litomyšl CZ 64 A2
Litovel CZ 64 A3
Litschau A 63 B6
Littlehampton GB 31 D3
Littleport GB 30 B4
Littleton IRL 21 B4
Little Walsingham GB 30 B4
Litvinov CZ 52 C3
Livadero GR 116 B3
Livadhia CY 120 B2
Livadi GR 116 B4
Livadia GR 116 D4
Livarot F 57 B6
Liveras CY 120 A1
Livernon F 77 B4
Liverovici MNE 85 D4
Liverpool GB 26 B3
Livigno I 71 B5
Livingston GB 25 C4
Livno BIH 84 C1
Livold SLO 73 C4
Livorno I 81 C4
Livorno Ferraris I 70 C3
Livron-sur-Drôme F 78 B3
Livry-Louvercy F 59 A5
Lixheim F 60 B3
Lixouri GR 117 D2
Lizard GB 28 D2
Lizy-sur-Ourcq F 59 A4
Lizzano I 104 C3
Lizzano in Belvedere I 81 B4
Lješane KOS 85 D5
Ljig SRB 85 B5
Ljørdalen N 34 A4
Ljosland N 33 D4
Ljubija BIH 83 B5
Ljubinje BIH 84 D3
Ljubljana SLO 73 B4
Ljubno ob Savinji SLO 73 B4
Ljubovija SRB 85 B4
Ljubuški BIH 84 C2
Ljugarn S 37 E5
Ljung S 40 B3
Ljunga S 37 D3
Ljungaverk S 115 E13
Ljungby S 40 C3
Ljungbyhed S 41 C3
Ljungbyholm S 40 C6
Ljungdalen S 115 E9
Ljungsarp S 40 B3
Ljungsbro S 37 D2
Ljungskile S 35 D3
Ljusdal S 115 F13
Ljusfallshammar S 37 D2
Ljusne S 36 A4
Ljusterö S 37 C5
Ljutomer SLO 73 B6
Lladurs E 91 A4
Llafranc E 91 B6
Llagostera E 91 B5
Llanaelhaiarn GB 26 C1
Llanarth GB 28 A3
Llanbedr GB 26 C1
Llanbedrog GB 26 C1
Llanberis GB 26 B1
Llanbister GB 29 A4
Llanbrynmair GB 26 C2
Llançà E 91 A6
Llandeilo GB 28 B4
Llandissilio GB 28 B3
Llandovery GB 28 B4
Llandrillo GB 26 C2
Llandrindod Wells GB 29 A4
Llandudec F 56 B1
Llandudno GB 26 B2
Llandysul GB 28 A3
Llanelli GB 28 B3
Llanerchymedd GB 26 B1
Llanes E 88 A2
Llanfair Caereinion GB 26 C2
Llanfairfechan GB 26 B2
Llanfyllin GB 26 C2
Llangadog GB 28 B4
Llangefni GB 26 B1
Llangollen GB 26 C2
Llangrannog GB 28 A3
Llangurig GB 26 C2
Llanidloes GB 26 C2
Llanilar GB 28 A3
Llanrhystud GB 28 A3
Llanrwst GB 26 B2
Llansannan GB 26 B2
Llansawel GB 28 A3
Llanstephan GB 28 B3
Llanteno E 89 A3
Llanthony GB 29 B4
Llantrisant GB 29 B4
Llantwit-Major GB 29 B4
Llanuwchllyn GB 26 C2
Llanwddyn GB 26 C2
Llanwrda GB 28 B4
Llanwrtyd Wells GB 29 A4
Llanybydder GB 28 A3
Llanymynech GB 26 C2
Llavorsi E 91 A4
Lleida E 90 B3
Llera E 93 C4
Llerena E 99 A4
Lles E 91 A4
Llessui E 91 A4
Llinars E 91 A4
Lliria E 96 B2
Llivia E 91 A4
Llodio E 89 A4
Lloret de Mar E 91 B5
Llosa de Ranes E 96 B2
Lloseta E 97 B2
Llucena del Cid E 96 A2
Llucmajor E 97 B2
Llutxent E 96 C2
Llwyngwril GB 26 C1
Llyswen GB 29 A4
Lnáře CZ 63 A4
Lniano PL 47 B4
Loanhead GB 25 C4
Loano I 80 B2
Loarre E 90 A2
Löbau D 53 B4
Löbejün D 52 B1
Löberöd S 41 D3
Łobez PL 46 B1
Löbnitz D 45 A4
Lobón E 93 C4
Loburg D 52 A2
Łobżenica PL 46 B3
Locana I 70 C2
Locarno CH 70 B3
Loccum D 43 C6
Loče SLO 73 B5
Lochailort GB 24 B2
Lochaline GB 24 B2
Lochans GB 24 D2
Locharbriggs GB 25 C4
Lochau A 71 A4
Loch Baghasdail GB 22 D1
Lochcarron GB 22 D3
Lochearnhead GB 24 B3
Lochem NL 50 A2
Loches F 67 A5
Lochgelly GB 25 B4
Lochgilphead GB 24 B2
Lochgoilhead GB 24 B3
Lochinver GB 22 C3
Loch nam Madadh GB 22 D1
Lochranza GB 24 C2
Ločika SRB 85 C6
Lockenhaus A 73 A6

Lockerbie GB 25 C4
Löcknitz D 45 B6
Locmaria F 66 A1
Locmariaquer F 56 C3
Locminé F 56 C3
Locorotondo I 104 C3
Locquirec F 56 B2
Locri I 106 C3
Locronan F 56 B1
Loctudy F 56 C1
Lodares de Osma E 89 C4
Lodé I 110 B2
Lodeinoye Pole RUS 7 A12
Lodève F 78 C2
Lodi I 71 C4
Løding N 112 E3
Lødingen N 112 D4
Lodosa E 89 B4
Lödöse S 38 A5
Łódź PL 55 B4
Loeches E 95 B3
Løfallstrand N 32 B3
Lofer A 62 C3
Lofsdalen S 115 E10
Loftahammar S 40 B6
Lofthus N 32 B3
Loftus GB 27 A5
Loga N 33 D3
Logatec SLO 73 C4
Lögdeå S 115 D16
Lograto I 71 C5
Logroño E 89 B4
Logrosán E 93 B5
Løgstør DK 38 C2
Løgumgårde DK 39 D1
Løgumkloster DK 39 D1
Lohals DK 39 D3
Lohiniva FIN 113 E14
Lohja FIN 6 A8
Löhlbach D 51 B4
Lohmen
Mecklenburg-Vorpommern D 44 B4
Sachsen D 53 C4
Löhnberg D 50 C4
Lohne D 43 C5
Löhne D 51 A4
Lohr D 51 D5
Lohra D 51 C4
Lohsa D 53 B4
Loiano I 81 B5
Loimaa FIN 3 F25
Lóiri I 110 B2
Loitz D 45 B5
Loivos P 87 C3
Loivos do Monte P 87 C3
Loja E 100 B1
Lojanice SRB 85 B4
Lojsta S 37 E5
Løjt Kirkeby DK 39 D2
Lok SK 65 B4
Lokca SK 65 A5
Løken N 34 C3
Lokeren B 49 B4
Loket CZ 52 C2
Lokhvitsa UA 11 A12
Lokka FIN 113 E16
Løkken
DK 38 B2
N 114 D6
Loknya RUS 7 C11
Lökosháza H 75 B6
Lokot RUS 7 E13
Lokve SRB 75 C6
Lollar D 51 C4
L'Olleria E 96 C2
Lölling-Graben A 73 B4
Lom
BG 11 E7
N 114 F5
SK 65 B5
Lombez F 77 C3
Lomello I 80 A2
Łomianki PL 55 A5
Lomma S 41 D3
Lommaryd S 40 B4
Lommatzsch D 52 B3
Lommel B 49 B6
Lommersum D 50 C2
Lomnice CZ 64 A2
Lomnice nad Lužnici CZ 63 A5
Lomnice-nad Popelkou CZ 53 C5
Lompolo FIN 113 D13
Łomza PL 6 E7
Lönashult S 40 C4
Lønborg DK 39 D1
Londerzeel B 49 B5
Londinières F 58 A2
London GB 31 C3
Lonevåg N 32 B2
Longa GR 117 F3
Longare I 72 C1
Longares E 90 B1
Longarone I 72 B2
Longastrino I 81 B6
Long Bennington GB 27 C5
Longbenton GB 25 C6
Longchamp-sur-Aujon F 59 B5
Longchaumois F 69 B5
Long Eaton GB 27 C4
Longeau F 59 C6
Longecourt-en-Plaine F 69 A5
Longeville-les-St Avold F 60 A2
Longeville-sur-Mer F 66 B3
Longford IRL 19 C4
Longframlington GB 25 C6
Longhope GB 23 C5
Longhorsley GB 25 C6
Longhoughton GB 25 C6
Longi I 109 A3
Long Melford GB 30 B4
Longny-au-Perche F 58 B1
Longobucco I 106 B3
Long Preston GB 26 A3
Longré F 67 B4
Longridge GB 26 B3
Longroiva P 87 D3
Long Sutton GB 30 B4
Longtown
Cumbria GB 25 C5
Herefordshire GB 29 B5
Longueau F 58 A3
Longué-Jumelles F 67 A4
Longuyon F 60 A1
Longvic F 69 A5
Longvilly B 50 C1
Longwy F 60 A1
Lonigo I 71 C6
Löningen D 43 C4
Lonja HR 74 C1
Lönneberga S 40 B5
Lönsboda S 41 C4
Lønset N 114 E6
Lons-le-Saunier F 69 B5
Lønstrup DK 38 B2
Looe GB 28 C3
Loone-Plage F 48 B3
Loon op Zand NL 49 B6
Loosdorf A 63 B6
Lo Pagán E 101 B5
Lopar HR 83 B3
Lopare BIH 84 B3
Lopera E 100 B1
Lopigna F 102 A1
Loppersum NL 42 B3
Łopuszna PL 65 A6
Łopuszno PL 55 C5
Lor F 59 A5
Lora N 114 E5
Lora de Estepa E 100 B1
Lora del Río E 99 B5
Loranca del Campo E 95 B4
Lörby S 41 C4
Lorca E 101 B4
Lorch D 50 C3
Lørenfallet N 34 B3
Lørenskog N 34 C2
Loreo I 82 A1
Loreto I 82 C2
Lorgues F 79 C5
Lorica I 106 B3
Lorient F 56 C2
Lorignac F 67 C4
Lörinci H 65 C5
Loriol-sur-Drôme F 78 B3
Lormes F 68 A3
Loro Ciuffenna I 81 C5
Lorqui E 101 A4
Lörrach D 60 C3
Lorrez-le-Bocage F 59 B3
Lorris F 58 C3
Lorup D 43 C4
Łoś PL 55 B5
Los S 115 F12
Losacino E 87 C4
Los Alcázares E 101 B5
Los Arcos E 89 B4
Losar de la Vera E 93 A5
Los Barios de Luna E 88 B1
Los Barrios E 99 C5
Los Caños de Meca E 99 C4
Los Cerricos E 101 B3
Los Corrales E 100 B1
Los Corrales de Buelna E 88 A2
Los Dolores E 101 B4
Losenstein A 63 C5
Los Gallardos E 101 B4
Losheim
Nordrhein-Westfalen D 50 C2
Saarland D 60 A2
Los Hinojosos E 95 C4
Los Isidros E 96 B1
Los Molinos E 94 B2
Los Morales E 99 B5
Los Navalmorales E 94 C2
Los Navalucillos E 94 C2
Losne F 69 A5
Los Nietos E 101 B5
Løsning DK 39 D2
Los Palacios y Villafranca E 99 B5
Los Pozuelos de Calatrava E 100 A1
Los Rábanos E 89 C4
Los Santos E 93 A5
Los Santos de la Humosa E 95 B3
Los Santos de Maimona E 93 C4
Lossburg D 61 B4
Losse F 76 B2
Losser NL 50 A3
Lossiemouth GB 23 D5
Lössnitz D 52 C2
Loštice CZ 64 A2
Los Tijos E 88 A2
Lostwithiel GB 28 C3
Los Villares E 100 B2
Los Yébenes E 94 C3
Løten N 34 B3
Lotorp S 37 D2
Lottefors S 36 A3
Löttorp S 41 B7
Lotyń PL 46 B2
Lotzorai I 110 C2
Louargat F 56 B2
Loudéac F 56 B3
Loudun F 67 A5
Loué F 57 C5
Loughborough GB 27 C4
Loughbrickland GB 19 B5
Loughrea IRL 20 A3
Louhans F 69 B5
Louisburgh IRL 18 C2
Loukhi RUS 3 C30
Loulay F 67 B4
Loulé P 98 B2
Louny CZ 53 C3
Lourdes F 76 C2
Lourenzá E 86 A3
Loures P 92 C1
Loures-Barousse F 77 C3
Louriçal P 92 A2
Lourinhã P 92 B1
Lourmarin F 79 C4
Loury F 58 C3
Lousa
Bragança P 87 C3
Castelo Branco P 92 B3
Lousã P 92 A2
Lousa P 92 C1
Lousada
E 86 B3
P 87 C2
Louth GB 27 B5
Loutra Edipsou GR 116 D5
Loutraki GR 117 E4
Loutropoli Thermis GR 118 C1
Louverné F 57 B5
Louvie-Juzon F 76 C2
Louviers F 58 A2
Louvigné-du-Désert F 57 B4
Louvois F 59 A5
Lova I 72 C2
Lovasberény H 74 A3
Lövåsen S 34 C5
Lovászpatona H 74 A2
Lövberga S 115 D12
Lovech BG 11 E8
Lövenich D 50 B2
Lóvere I 71 C5
Lövestad S 41 D3
Loviisa FIN 7 A9
Lovikka S 113 E11
Lovinobaňa SK 65 B5
Loviste HR 84 C2
Lovke HR 73 C4
Lovnäs S 34 A5
Lövö H 74 A1
Lovosice CZ 53 C4
Lovozero RUS 3 C31
Lovran HR 73 C4
Lovreć HR 84 C1
Lovrenc na Pohorju SLO 73 B5
Lovrin RO 75 C5
Lövstabruk S 36 B4
Löwenberg D 45 C5
Löwenstein D 61 A5
Lowestoft GB 30 B5
Lowick GB 25 C6
Łowicz PL 55 A4
Loxstedt D 43 B5
Loyew BY 7 F11
Lož SLO 73 C4
Loza CZ 63 A4
Łozina PL 54 B2
Loznica SRB 85 B4
Lozničko Polje SRB 85 B4
Lozorno SK 64 B3
Lozovik SRB 85 B6
Lozoya E 94 B3
Lozoyuela E 94 B3
Lozzo di Cadore I 72 B2
Luanco E 88 A1
Luarca E 86 A4
Lubaczów PL 11 A7
Lubań PL 53 B5
Lubanie PL 47 C4
Lubanów PL 55 B4
Lubars D 52 A2
Lubasz PL 46 C2
Lubawa PL 47 B5
Lubawka PL 53 C6
Lübbecke D 51 A4
Lübben D 53 B3
Lübbenau D 53 B3
Lubczyna PL 45 B6
Lübeck D 44 B2
Lubenec CZ 52 C3
Lubersac F 67 C6
Lübesse D 44 B3
Lubia E 89 C4
Lubian E 87 B4
Lubiatowo PL 45 B7
Lubichowo PL 47 B4
Lubicz Dolny PL 47 B4
Lubień PL 65 A5
Lubienia PL 55 B6
Lubień Kujawski PL 47 C5
Lubieszewo PL 46 B1
Lubin
Dolnośląskie PL 53 B6
Zachodnio-Pomorskie PL 45 B6
Lublin PL 11 A7
Lubliniec PL 54 C3
Lubmin D 45 A5
Lubniewice PL 45 C7
Lubny UA 11 A12
Lubochnia PL 55 B5
Lubomierz
Dolnośląskie PL 53 B5
Małopolskie PL 65 A6
Lubomino PL 47 A6
Luboń PL 54 A1
L'ubotín SK 65 A6
Lubowidz PL 47 B5
Łubowo
Wielkopolskie PL 46 C3
Zachodnio-Pomorskie PL 46 B2
Lubraniec PL 47 C4
Lubrin E 101 B3
Lubrza PL 54 C2
Lubsko PL 53 B4
Lübtheen D 44 B3
Lubuczewo PL 46 A3
Luby CZ 52 C2
Lübz D 44 B4
Luc F 78 B2
Lucainena de las Torres E 101 B3
Lucan IRL 21 A5
Lučani SRB 85 C5
Lúcar E 101 B3
Luçay-le-Mâle F 67 A6
Lucca I 81 C4
Lucciana F 102 A2
Lucé F 58 B2
Luče SLO 73 B4
Lucena
Córdoba E 100 B1
Huelva E 99 B4
Lucenay-les-Aix F 68 B3
Lucenay-l'Evéque F 69 A4
Luc-en-Diois F 79 B4
Lučenec SK 65 B5
Luceni E 90 B1
Lucens CH 70 B1
Lucera I 103 B8
Luceram F 80 C1
Lüchow D 44 C3
Luciana E 94 D2
Lucignano I 81 C5
Lucija SLO 72 C3
Lucka D 52 B2
Luckau D 53 B3
Luckenwalde D 52 A3
Lückstedt D 44 C3
Luco dei Marsi I 103 B6
Luçon F 66 B3
Luc-sur-Mer F 57 A5
Ludanice SK 64 B4
Ludbreg HR 74 B1
Lüdenscheid D 50 B3
Lüderitz D 44 C3
Lüdersdorf D 44 B2
Ludgershall GB 31 C2
Ludgo S 37 D4
Lüdinghausen D 50 B3
Ludlow GB 29 A5
Ludomy PL 46 C2
Ludvika S 36 B2
Ludweiler Warndt D 60 A2
Ludwigsburg D 61 B5
Ludwigsfelde D 52 A3
Ludwigshafen D 61 A4
Ludwigslust D 44 B3
Ludwigsstadt D 52 C1
Ludza LV 7 C9
Luesia E 90 A1
Luftkurort Arendsee D 44 C3
Lug
BIH 84 D3
HR 74 C3
Luga RUS 7 B10
Lugagnano Val d'Arda I 81 B3
Lugano CH 70 B3
Lugau D 52 C2
Lugnas S 35 D5
Lúgnola I 102 A5
Lugny F 69 B4
Lugo
E 86 A3
I 81 B5
Lugoj RO 10 D6
Lugones E 88 A1
Lugros E 100 B2
Luhačovice CZ 64 A3
Luhe D 62 A3
Luino I 70 C3
Luintra E 87 B3
Lújar E 100 C2
Luka nad Jihlavou CZ 63 A6
Lukavac BIH 84 B3
Lukavika BIH 84 B3
Lukovë AL 116 C1
Lukovica SLO 73 B4
Lukovit BG 11 E8
Lukovo
HR 83 B3
SRB 85 C6
Lukovo Šugorje HR 83 B4
Łuków PL 6 F7
Łukowice Brzeskie PL 54 C2
Luksefjell N 33 C6
Łukta PL 47 B6
Lula I 110 B2
Luleå S 3 D25
Lüleburgaz TR 118 A2
Lumbarda HR 84 D2
Lumbier E 90 A1
Lumbrales E 87 D4
Lumbreras E 89 B4
Lumbres F 48 C3
Lummelunda S 37 E5
Lummen B 49 C6
Lumparland FIN 36 B7
Lumpiaque E 90 B1
Lumsås DK 39 D4
Lumsden GB 23 D6
Lumsheden S 36 B3
Lun HR 83 B3
Luna E 90 A2
Lunamatrona I 110 C1
Lunano I 82 C1
Lunas F 78 C2
Lund
N 114 C8
Skåne S 41 D3
Västra Götaland S 35 C4
Lundamo N 114 D7
Lunde
DK 39 D1
Sogn og Fjordane N 32 A3
Sogn og Fjordane N 32 A3
Telemark N 33 C6
S 115 E14
Lundebyvollen N 34 B4
Lunden D 43 A6
Lunderseter N 34 B4
Lunderskov DK 39 D2
Lundsberg S 35 C6
Lüneburg D 44 B2
Lunel F 78 C3
Lünen D 50 B3
Lunéville F 60 B2
Lungern CH 70 B3
Lungro I 106 B3
Luninyets BY 7 E9
Lünne D 43 C4
Lunner N 34 B2
Lunteren NL 49 A6
Lunz am See A 63 C6
Luogosanto I 110 A2
Łupawa PL 46 A3
Lupión E 100 A2
Lupoglav HR 73 C4
Luppa D 52 B2
Luque E 100 B1
Lurago d'Erba I 71 C4
Lúras I 110 B2
Lurcy-Lévis F 68 B2
Lure F 60 C2
Lurgan GB 19 B5
Luri F 102 A2
Lury-sur-Arnon F 68 A2
Lušci Palanka BIH 83 B5
Lusévera I 72 B3
Lushnjë AL 105 C5
Lusignan F 67 B5
Lusigny-sur-Barse F 59 B5
Lusnić BIH 84 C1
Luso P 92 A2
Lusówko PL 46 C2
Luspebryggan S 112 E8
Luss GB 24 B3
Lussac F 76 B2
Lussac-les-Châteaux F 67 B5
Lussac-les-Eglises F 67 B6
Lussan F 78 B3
Lüssow D 44 B4
Lustenau A 71 A4
Luštěnice CZ 53 C4
Luster N 32 A4
Lutago I 72 B1
Lutherstadt Wittenberg D 52 B2
Lütjenburg D 44 A2
Lutnes N 34 A4
Lutocin PL 47 C5
Lutomiersk PL 55 B4
Luton GB 31 C3
Lutry
CH 70 B1
PL 47 A6
Lutsk UA 11 A8
Lutter am Barenberge D 51 B6
Lutterworth GB 30 B2
Lututów PL 54 B3
Lützen D 52 B2
Lutzow D 44 B3
Luusua FIN 113 F16
Luvos S 112 F7
Luxembourg L 60 A2
Luxeuil-les-Bains F 60 C2
Luxey F 76 B2
Luz
Évora P 92 C3
Faro P 98 B2
Faro P 98 B3
Luzarches F 58 A3
Luže CZ 64 A2
Luzech F 77 B4
Luzern CH 70 A3
Luzino PL 47 A4
Luz-St Sauveur F 76 D2
Luzy F 68 B3
Luzzi I 106 B3
L'viv UA 11 B8
Lwówek PL 46 C2
Lwówek Śląski PL 53 B5
Lyakhavichy BY 7 E9
Lybster GB 23 C5
Lychen D 45 B5
Lychkova RUS 7 C12
Lyckeby S 41 C5
Lycksele S 115 C15
Lydd GB 31 D4
Lydford GB 28 C3
Lydney GB 29 B5
Lyepyel BY 7 D10
Lygna N 34 B2
Lykkja N 32 B5
Lykling N 33 C2
Lyme Regis GB 29 C5
Lymington GB 31 D2
Lympne GB 31 C5
Lyndhurst GB 31 D2
Lyneham GB 29 B6
Lyness GB 23 C5
Lyngdal
Buskerud N 32 C6
Vest-Agder N 33 D4
Lyngør N 33 D6
Lyngsa DK 38 B3
Lyngseidet N 112 C9
Lyngsnes N 114 C8
Lynmouth GB 28 B4
Lynton GB 28 B4
Lyntupy BY 7 D9
Lyon F 69 C4
Lyons-la-Forêt F 58 A2
Lyozna BY 7 D11
Lyrestad S 35 D6
Lysánad Labem CZ 53 C4
Lysápod Makytou SK 64 A4
Lysebotn N 33 C3
Lysekil S 35 D3
Lysice CZ 64 A2
Lysomice PL 47 B4
Lysøysund N 114 D6
Lyss CH 70 A2
Lystrup DK 39 C3
Lysvik S 34 B5
Łyszkowice PL 55 B4
Lytham St Anne's GB 26 B2
Lyuban RUS 7 B11
Lyubertsy RUS 7 D14
Lyuboml' UA 11 A8
Lyubytino RUS 7 B12
Lyudinovo RUS 7 E13

M

Maaninkavaara FIN 113 F17
Maarheeze NL 49 B6
Maaseik B 50 B1
Maastricht NL 50 C1
Mablethorpe GB 27 B6
Mably F 68 B4
Macael E 101 B3
Maçanet de Cabrenys E 91 A5
Mação P 92 B2
Macau F 76 A2
Maccagno-Agra I 70 B3
Maccarese I 102 B5
Macchiagódena I 103 B7
Macclesfield GB 26 B3
Macduff GB 23 D6
Maceda E 87 B3
Macedo de Cavaleiros P 87 C4
Maceira
Guarda P 92 A3
Leiria P 92 B2
Macelj HR 73 B5
Macerata I 82 C2
Macerata Féltria I 82 C1
Machault F 59 A5
Machecoul F 66 B3
Mchowo PL 47 B6
Machrihanish GB 24 C2
Machynlleth GB 26 C2
Macieira P 87 C2
Maciejowice PL 55 B6
Macinaggio F 102 A2
Mackenrode D 51 B6
Mačkovci SLO 73 B6
Macomer I 110 B1
Macon B 49 C5
Mâcon F 69 B4
Macotera E 94 B1
Macroom IRL 20 C3
Macugnaga I 70 C2
Madan BG 116 A6
Madängsholm S 35 D5
Madaras H 75 B4
Maddaloni I 103 B7
Made NL 49 B5
Madeley GB 26 C3
Maderuelo E 89 C3
Madetkoski FIN 113 E15
Madley GB 29 A5
Madocsa H 75 B3
Madona LV 7 C9
Madonna di Campíglio I 71 B5
Madrid E 94 B3
Madridejos E 95 C3
Madrigal de las Altas Torres E 94 A1
Madrigal de la Vera E 93 A5
Madrigalejo E 93 B5
Madrigalejo de Monte E 88 B3
Madriguera E 89 C3
Madrigueras E 95 C5
Madroñera E 93 B5
Maël-Carhaix F 56 B2
Maella E 90 B3
Maello E 94 B2
Maesteg GB 29 B4
Mafra P 92 C1
Magacela E 93 C5
Magallon E 89 C5
Magaluf E 97 B2
Magán E 94 C3
Magaña E 89 C4
Magasa I 71 C5
Magaz E 88 C2
Magdeburg D 52 A1
Magenta I 70 C3
Magescq F 76 C1
Maghera GB 19 B5
Magherafelt GB 19 B5
Maghull GB 26 B3
Magilligan GB 19 A5
Magione I 82 C1
Magioto P 92 C1
Maglaj BIH 84 B3
Maglehem S 41 D4
Magliano de'Marsi I 103 A6
Magliano in Toscana I 102 A4
Magliano Sabina I 102 A5
Maglić SRB 75 C4
Máglie I 107 A5
Maglód H 75 A4
Magnac-Bourg F 67 C6
Magnac-Laval F 67 B6
Magnieres F 60 B2
Magnor N 34 C4
Magnuszew PL 55 B6
Magny-Cours F 68 B3
Magny-en-Vexin F 58 A2
Mágocs H 74 B3
Maguilla E 93 C5
Maguiresbridge GB 19 B4
Magyarbóly H 74 C3
Magyarkeszi H 74 B3
Magyarszék H 74 B3
Mahala MNE 105 A5
Mahide E 87 C4
Mahilyow BY 7 E11
Mahmudiye TR 118 C5
Mahora E 95 C5
Mahovo HR 73 C6
Mähring D 62 A3
Maia
E 76 C1
P 87 C2
Maiaelrayo E 95 A3
Maials E 90 B3
Maîche F 70 A1
Máida I 106 C3
Maiden Bradley GB 29 B5
Maidenhead GB 31 C3
Maiden Newton GB 29 C5
Maidstone GB 31 C4
Maienfeld CH 71 A4
Maignelay Montigny F 58 A3
Maijanen FIN 113 E14
Maillezais F 66 B4
Mailly-le-Camp F 59 B5
Mailly-le-Château F 59 C4
Mainar E 89 C5
Mainbernheim D 61 A6
Mainburg D 62 B2
Mainhardt D 61 A5
Maintal D 51 C4
Maintenon F 58 B2
Mainvilliers F 58 B2
Mainz D 50 C4
Maiorca P 92 A2
Mairena de Aljarafe E 99 B4
Mairena del Alcor E 99 B5
Maisach D 62 B2
Maishofen A 72 A2
Maison-Rouge F 59 B4
Maissau A 64 B1
Maisse F 58 B3
Maizières-lès-Vic F 60 B2
Maja HR 73 C6
Majadahonda E 94 B3
Majadas E 93 B5
Majavatn N 115 B10
Majs H 74 C3
Majšperk SLO 73 B5
Makarska HR 84 C2
Makkum NL 42 B2
Maklár H 65 C6
Makó H 75 B5
Makoszyce PL 54 C2
Makov SK 65 A4
Makovac KOS 85 D6
Mąkowarsko PL 46 B3
Maków Podhalański PL 65 A5
Makrakomi GR 116 D4
Malå S 115 B15
Mala Bosna SRB 75 B4
Malacky SK 64 B3
Maladzyechna BY 7 D9
Málaga E 100 C1
Malagón E 94 C3
Malaguilla E 95 B3
Malahide IRL 21 A5
Mala Kladuša BIH 73 C5
Mala Krsna SRB 85 B6
Malalbergo I 81 B5
Malá Lehota SK 65 B4
Malanów PL 54 B3
Mala Pijace SRB 75 B4
Mala Plana SRB 85 C6
Mala Subotica HR 74 B1
Malaucène F 79 B4
Malaunay F 58 A2
Mala Vyska UA 11 B11
Malaya Vishera RUS 7 B12
Malborghetto I 72 B3
Malbork PL 47 A5
Malborn D 60 A2
Malbuisson F 69 B6
Malcésine I 71 C5
Malchin D 45 B4
Malching D 63 B4
Malchow D 44 B4
Malcocinado E 99 A5
Malczyce PL 54 B1
Maldegem B 49 B4
Maldon GB 31 C4
Małdyty PL 47 B5
Malè I 71 B5
Malemort F 67 C6
Malente D 44 A2
Målerås S 40 C5
Males GR 117 G7
Malesherbes F 58 B3
Malesina GR 116 D5
Malestroit F 56 C3
Maletto I 109 B3
Malexander S 40 A5
Malfa I 106 C1
Malgrat de Mar E 91 B5
Malhadas P 87 C4
Malia
CY 120 B1
GR 117 G7
Malicorne-sur-Sarthe F 57 C5
Malijai F 79 B5
Malildjoš SRB 75 C4
Målilla S 40 B5
Mali Lošinj HR 83 B3
Malin IRL 19 A4
Málinec SK 65 B5
Malingsbo S 36 C2
Maliniec PL 54 A3
Malinska HR 83 A3
Maliq AL 116 B2
Maljevac HR 73 C5
Malkara TR 118 B1
Małki PL 47 B5
Malko Tŭrnovo BG 11 E9
Mallaig GB 22 D3
Mallaranny IRL 18 C2
Mallemort F 79 C4
Mallén E 89 C5
Malléon F 77 C4
Mallersdorf-Pfaffenberg D 62 B3
Málles Venosta I 71 B5
Malling DK 39 C3
Mallnitz A 72 B3
Mallow IRL 20 B3
Mallwyd GB 26 C2
Malm N 114 C8
Malmbäck S 40 B4
Malmberget S 112 E9
Malmby S 37 C4
Malmédy B 50 C2
Malmesbury GB 29 B5
Malmköping S 37 C3
Malmö S 41 D3
Malmon S 35 D3
Malmslätt S 37 D2
Malnate I 70 C3
Malo I 71 C6
Maloarkhangelsk RUS 7 E14
Małogoszcz PL 55 C5
Maloja CH 71 B4
Małomice PL 53 B5
Måløy N 114 F2
Maloyaroslovets RUS 7 D14
Malpartida E 93 B4
Malpartida de la Serena E 93 C5
Malpartida de Plasencia E 93 B4
Malpas
E 90 A3
GB 26 B3
Malpica P 92 B3
Malpica de Bergantiños E 86 A2
Malpica de Tajo E 94 C2
Malsch D 61 B4
Malšice CZ 63 A5
Malta A 72 B3
Maltat F 68 B3
Maltby GB 27 B4
Malung S 34 B5
Malungsfors S 34 B5
Maluszów PL 45 C7
Maluszyn PL 55 C4
Malva E 88 C1
Malvaglia CH 70 B3
Malveira P 92 C1
Malvik N 114 D7
Malyn UA 11 A10
Mamarrosa P 92 A2
Mamer L 60 A2
Mamers F 58 B1
Mamirolle F 69 A6
Mammendorf D 62 B2
Mámmola I 106 C3
Mamoiada I 110 B2
Mamonovo RUS 47 A5
Mamuras AL 105 B5
Maňa SK 64 B4
Manacor E 97 B3
Manavgat TR 119 F6
Mancera de Abajo E 94 B1
Mancha Real E 100 B2
Manchester GB 26 B3
Manching D 62 B2
Manchita E 93 C4
Manciano I 102 A4
Manciet F 76 C3
Mandal N 33 D4
Mandanici I 109 A4
Mándas I 110 C2
Mandatoríccio I 107 B3
Mandayona E 95 B4
Mandelieu-la-Napoule F 79 C5
Mandello del Lário I 71 C4
Mandelsloh D 43 C6
Manderfeld B 50 C2
Manderscheid D 50 C2
Mandino Selo BIH 84 C2
Mandoudi GR 116 D5
Mandra GR 117 D5
Mandraki GR 119 F2
Mandúria I 104 C3
Mane
Alpes-de-Haute-Provence F 79 C4
Haute-Garonne F 77 C3
Manérbio I 71 C5
Mañeru E 89 B5
Manetin CZ 52 D3
Manfredónia I 104 B1
Mangalia RO 11 E10
Manganeses de la Lampreana E 88 C1
Manganeses de la Polvorosa E 88 B1
Mangen N 34 C3
Manger N 32 B2
Mangiennes F 60 A1
Mangotsfield GB 29 B5
Mångsbodarna S 34 A5
Mangualde P 92 A3
Maniago I 72 B2
Manilva E 99 C5
Manisa TR 118 D2
Manises E 96 B2
Mank A 63 B6
Månkarbo S 36 B4
Manlleu E 91 B5
Manna DK 38 B2
Männedorf CH 70 A3
Mannersdorf am Leithagebirge A 64 C2
Mannheim D 61 A4
Manningtree GB 31 C5
Manoppello I 103 A7
Manorbier GB 28 B3
Manorhamilton IRL 18 B3
Manosque F 79 C4
Manowo PL 46 A2
Manresa E 91 B4
Månsarp S 40 B4
Månsåsen S 115 D11
Manschnow D 45 C6
Mansfeld D 52 B1
Mansfield GB 27 B4
Mansilla de Burgos E 88 B3
Mansilla de las Mulas E 88 B1
Manskog S 35 C4
Mansle F 67 C5
Manso F 102 A1
Manteigas P 92 A3
Mantel D 62 A3
Mantes-la-Jolie F 58 B2
Mantes-la-Ville F 58 B2
Manthelan F 67 A5
Mantorp S 37 D2
Mántova I 71 C5
Mänttä FIN 3 E26
Manuel E 96 B2
Manyas TR 118 B2
Manzanal de Arriba E 87 B4
Manzanares E 95 C3
Manzanares el Real E 94 B3
Manzaneda
León E 87 B4
Orense E 87 B3
Manzanedo E 88 B3
Manzaneque E 94 C3
Manzanera E 96 A2
Manzanilla E 99 B4
Manzat F 68 C2
Manziana I 102 A5
Manziat F 69 B4
Maó E 97 B4
Maoča BIH 84 B3
Maqueda E 94 B2
Mara E 89 C5
Maramaraereğlisi TR 118 B2
Maraña E 88 A1
Maranchón E 95 A4
Maranello I 81 B4
Marano I 103 C7
Marano Lagunare I 72 C3
Marans F 66 B3
Maratea I 106 B2
Marateca P 92 C2
Marathokambos GR 119 E1
Marathonas GR 117 D5
Marathóvouno CY 120 A2
Marazion GB 28 C2
Marbach
Baden-Württemberg D 61 B5
Hessen D 51 C5
F 60 B2
Marbäck S 40 B3
Mårbacka S 34 C5
Marbella E 100 C1
Marboz F 69 B5
Marburg D 51 C4
Marcali H 74 B2
Marčana HR 82 B2
Marcaria I 81 A4
Marcelová SK 64 C4
Marcenat F 68 C2
March GB 30 B4
Marchamalo E 95 B3
Marchaux F 69 A6
Marche-en-Famenne B 49 C6
Marchegg A 64 B2
Marchena E 99 B5
Marchenoir F 58 C2
Marcheprime F 76 B2
Marciac F 76 C3
Marciana Marina I 81 D4
Marcianise I 103 B7
Marcigny F 68 B4
Marcilla E 89 B5
Marcillac-la-Croisille F 68 C2
Marcillac-Vallon F 77 B5
Marcillat-en-Combraille F 68 B2
Marcille-sur-Seine F 59 B4
Marcilloles F 69 C5
Marcilly-le-Hayer F 59 B4
Marcinkowice PL 46 B2
Marciszów PL 53 C6
Marck F 48 C2
Marckolsheim F 60 B3
Marco de Canevezes P 87 C2
Mårdsele S 115 C16
Mårdsjö S 115 D12
Mareham le Fen GB 27 B5
Marek S 40 B5
Marennes F 66 C3
Maresquel F 48 C2
Mareuil F 67 C5
Mareuil-en-Brie F 59 B4
Mareuil-sur-Arnon F 68 B2
Mareuil-sur-Lay F 66 B3
Mareuil-sur-Ourcq F 59 A4
Margam GB 28 B4
Margariti GR 116 C2
Margate GB 31 C5
Margaux F 76 A2
Margerie-Hancourt F 59 B5
Margès F 69 C5
Margherita di Savóia I 104 B2
Margita SRB 75 C6
Margone I 70 C2
Margonin PL 46 C3
Marguerittes F 78 C3
Margut F 59 A6
Maria E 101 B3
Mariager DK 38 C2
Mariana E 95 B4
Maria Neustift A 63 C5
Mariannelund S 40 B5
Marianópoli I 108 B2
Mariánské Lázně CZ 52 D2
Mariapfarr A 72 A3
Maria Saal A 73 B4
Mariazell A 63 C6
Maribo DK 39 E4
Maribor SLO 73 B5
Marieberg S 37 C2
Mariefred S 37 C4
Mariehamn FIN 36 B6
Marieholm S 41 D3
Mariembourg B 49 C5
Marienbaum D 50 B2
Marienberg D 52 C3
Marienheide D 50 B3
Mariental D 51 A6
Mariestad S 35 D5
Marieux F 48 C3
Marigliano I 103 C7
Marignane F 79 C4
Marigny
Jura F 69 B5
Manche F 57 A4
Marigny-le-Châtel F 59 B4
Marija Bistrica HR 73 B6
Marijampolė LT 6 D7
Marín E 87 B2
Marina HR 83 C5
Marina del Cantone I 103 C7
Marina di Acquappesa I 106 B2
Marina di Alberese I 81 D5
Marina di Amendolara I 106 B3
Marina di Árbus I 110 C1
Marina di Campo I 81 D4
Marina di Carrara I 81 B4
Marina di Castagneto-Donorático I 81 C4
Marina di Cécina I 81 C4
Marina di Gáiro I 110 C2
Marina di Ginosa I 104 C2
Marina di Gioiosa Iónica I 106 C3
Marina di Grosseto I 81 D4
Marina di Léuca I 107 B5
Marina di Massa I 81 B4
Marina di Nováglie I 107 B5
Marina di Pisa I 81 C4
Marina di Ragusa I 109 C3
Marina di Ravenna I 82 B1
Marina di Torre Grande I 110 C1
Marinaleda E 100 B1
Marina Romea I 82 B1
Marine de Sisco F 102 A2
Marinella I 108 B1
Marinella di Sarzana I 81 B4
Marineo I 108 B2
Marines F 58 A2
Maringues F 68 C3
Marinha das Ondas P 92 A2
Marinha Grande P 92 B2
Marinhas P 87 C2
Marino I 102 B5
Marjaliza E 94 C3
Markabygd N 114 D8
Markaryd S 40 C3
Markdorf D 61 C5
Markelo NL 50 A2
Market Deeping GB 30 B3
Market Drayton GB 26 C3
Market Harborough GB 30 B3
Markethill GB 19 B5
Market Rasen GB 27 B5
Market Warsop GB 27 B4
Market Weighton GB 27 B5
Markgröningen D 61 B5
Markhausen D 43 C4
Marki PL 55 A6
Markina-Xemein E 89 A4
Markinch GB 25 B4
Märkische Buchholz D 53 A3
Markitta S 113 E10
Markkleeberg D 52 B2
Marklohe D 43 C6
Marknesse NL 42 C2
Markneukirchen D 52 C2
Markopoulo GR 117 E5
Markovac SRB 85 B6
Markowice PL 54 C3
Markranstädt D 52 B2
Marksuhl D 51 C6
Markt Allhau A 73 A6
Markt Bibart D 61 A6
Marktbreit D 61 A6
Markt Erlbach D 62 A1
Markt-heidenfeld D 61 A5
Markt Indersdorf D 62 B2
Marktl D 62 B3
Marktleuthen D 52 C1
Marktoberdorf D 62 C1
Marktredwitz D 52 C2
Markt Rettenbach D 61 C6
Markt Schwaben D 62 B2
Markt-Übelbach A 73 A5
Markusica HR 74 C3
Markušovce SK 65 B6
Marl D 50 B3
Marlborough
Devon GB 28 C4
Wiltshire GB 29 B6
Marle F 59 A4
Marlieux F 69 B5
Marlow
D 45 A4
GB 31 C3
Marma S 36 B4
Marmagne F 69 B4
Marmande F 76 B3
Marmara TR 118 B2
Marmaris TR 119 F3
Marmelete P 98 B2
Marmolejo E 100 A1
Marmoutier F 60 B3
Marnay F 69 A5
Marne D 43 B6
Marnheim D 61 A4
Marnitz D 44 B3
Maroldsweisach D 51 C6
Marolles-les-Braults F 58 B1
Maromme F 58 A2
Marone I 71 C5
Maronia GR 116 B7
Maroslele H 75 B5
Maróstica I 72 C1
Marotta I 82 C2
Marpisa GR 117 E7
Marquion F 49 C4
Marquise F 48 C2
Marradi I 81 B5
Marrasjärvi FIN 113 F14
Marraskoski FIN 113 F14
Marratxi E 97 B2
Marrúbiu I 110 C1
Marrum NL 42 B2
Marrupe E 94 B2
Marsac F 77 C5
Marsac-en-Livradois F 68 C3
Marságlia I 80 B3
Marsala I 108 B1
Marsberg D 51 B4
Marsciano I 82 D1
Marseillan F 78 C2
Marseille = Marseilles F 79 C4
Marseille en Beauvaisis F 58 A2
Marseilles = Marseille F 79 C4
Mársico Nuovo I 104 C1
Marske-by-the-Sea GB 27 A4
Mars-la-Tours F 60 A1
Marsliden S 115 B12
Marson F 59 B5
Märsta S 37 C4
Marstal DK 39 E3
Marstrand S 38 B4
Marta I 102 A4
Martano I 107 A5
Martel F 77 B4
Martelange B 60 A1
Martfeld D 43 C6
Martfű H 75 A5
Martham GB 30 B5
Marthon F 67 C5
Martiago E 93 A4
Martigné-Briand F 67 A4
Martigné-Ferchaud F 57 C4
Martigne-sur-Mayenne F 57 B5
Martigny CH 70 B2
Martigny-les-Bains F 60 B1
Martigues F 79 C4
Martim-Longo P 98 B3
Martin SK 65 A4
Martina CH 71 B5
Martina Franca I 104 C3
Martinamor E 94 B1
Martin de la Jara E 100 B1
Martinengo I 71 C4
Martin Muñoz de las Posadas E 94 A2
Martinsberg A 63 B6
Martinšćica HR 82 B3
Martinshöhe D 60 A3
Martinsicuro I 82 D2
Martinszell D 61 C6
Mártis I 110 B1
Martofte DK 39 D3
Martonvásár H 74 A3
Martorell E 91 B4
Martos E 100 B2
Martres Tolosane F 77 C3
Martti FIN 113 E17
Marugán E 94 B2
Marúggio I 104 C3
Marvão P 92 B3
Marvejols F 78 B2
Marville F 60 A1
Marwałd PL 47 B5
Marykirk GB 25 B5
Marypark GB 23 D5
Maryport GB 26 A2
Marytavy GB 28 C3
Marzabotto I 81 B5
Marzahna D 52 B2
Marzahne D 45 C4
Marzamemi I 109 C4
Marzocca I 82 C2
Masa E 88 B3
Mas-Cabardès F 77 C5
Máscali I 109 B4
Mascaraque E 94 C3
Mascarenhas P 87 C3
Mascioni I 103 A6
Mas de Barberáns E 90 C3
Mas de las Matas E 90 C2
Masegoso E 101 A3
Masegoso de Tajuña E 95 B4
Masera I 70 B3
Masevaux F 60 C2
Masfjorden N 32 B2
Masham GB 27 A4
Masi N 113 C12
Maside E 87 B2
Maslacq F 76 C2
Maslinica HR 83 C5

Maslovare BIH 84 B2
Masone I 80 B2
Massa I 81 B4
Massa Fiscáglia I 81 B6
Massafra I 104 C3
Massa Lombarda I 81 B5
Massa Lubrense I 103 C7
Massamagrell E 96 B2
Massa Maríttima I 81 C4
Massa Martana I 82 D1
Massanassa E 96 B2
Massarosa I 81 C4
Massat F 77 D4
Massay F 68 A1
Massbach D 51 C6
Masseret F 67 C6
Masseube F 77 C3
Massiac F 68 C3
Massignac F 67 C5
Massing D 62 B3
Massmechelen B 50 C1
Masterud N 34 B4
Mästocka S 40 C3
Masty BY 6 E8
Masúa I 110 C1
Masueco E 87 C4
Masugnsbyn S 113 E11
Mašun SLO 73 C4
Maszewo
Lubuskie PL 53 A4
Zachodnio-Pomorskie PL 45 B7
Mata de Alcântara E 93 B4
Matala GR 117 H6
Matalebreras E 89 C4
Matallana de Torío E 88 B1
Matamala E 89 C4
Mataporquera E 88 B2
Matapozuelos E 88 C2
Mataró E 91 B5
Matarocco I 108 B1
Mataruge MNE 85 C4
Mataruška Banja SRB 85 C5
Matélica I 82 C2
Matera I 104 C2
Mateševo MNE 85 D4
Mátészalka H 11 C7
Matet E 96 B2
Matfors S 115 E14
Matha F 67 C4
Mathay F 70 A1
Matignon F 57 B3
Matilla de los Caños del Río E 94 B1
Matlock GB 27 B4
Matosinhos P 87 C2
Matour F 69 B4
Mátrafüred H 65 C5
Mátraterenye H 65 B5
Matre
Hordaland N 32 B2
Hordaland N 32 C2
Matrei am Brenner A 71 A6
Matrei in Osttirol A 72 A2
Matrice I 103 B7
Matsdal S 115 B12
Mattarello I 71 B6
Mattersburg A 64 C2
Mattighofen A 62 B4
Mattinata I 104 B2
Mattos P 92 B2
Mattsee A 62 C4
Mattsmyra S 36 A2
Matulji HR 73 C4
Maubert-Fontaine F 59 A5
Maubeuge F 49 C4
Mauborguet F 76 C3
Mauchline GB 24 C3
Maud GB 23 D6
Mauer-kirchen A 62 B4
Mauern D 62 B2
Mauguio F 78 C3
Maulbronn D 61 B4
Maule F 58 B2
Mauléon F 67 B4
Mauléon-Barousse F 77 D3
Mauléon-Licharre F 76 C2
Maulévrier F 67 A4
Maum IRL 18 C2
Maurach A 72 A1
Maure-de-Bretagne F 57 C4
Maureilhan F 78 C2
Mauriac F 68 C2
Mauron F 57 B3
Maurs F 77 B5
Maury F 77 D5
Maussane-les-Alpilles F 78 C3
Mautern A 63 B6
Mauterndorf A 72 A3
Mautern im Steiermark A 73 A4
Mauthausen A 63 B5
Mauthen A 72 B2
Mauvezin F 77 C3
Mauzé-sur-le-Mignon F 67 B4
Maxent F 57 C3
Maxey-sur-Vaise F 60 B1
Maxial P 92 B1
Maxieira P 92 B2
Maxwellheugh GB 25 C5
Mayalde E 88 C1
Maybole GB 24 C3
Mayen D 50 C3
Mayenne F 57 B5
Mayet F 58 C1
Mayorga E 88 B1
Mayres F 78 B3
Mayrhofen A 72 A1
Mazagón E 99 B4
Mazaleón E 90 B3
Mazamet F 77 C5
Mazan F 79 B4
Mazara del Vallo I 108 B1
Mazarambroz E 94 C2
Mazarete E 95 B4
Mazaricos E 86 B2
Mazarrón E 101 B4
Mažeikiai LT 6 C7
Mazères F 77 C4
Mazères-sur-Salat F 77 C3
Mazières-en-Gâtine F 67 B4
Mazin HR 83 B4
Mazuelo E 88 B3
Mazyr BY 7 E10
Mazzarino I 109 B3
Mazzarrà Sant'Andrea I 109 A4
Mazzo di Valtellina I 71 B5
Mdzewo PL 47 C6
Mealabost GB 22 C2
Mealhada P 92 A2
Méan B 49 C6
Meana Sardo I 110 C2
Meaulne F 68 B2
Meaux F 59 B3
Mebonden N 114 D8
Mecerreyes E 89 B3
Mechelen B 49 B5
Mechernich D 50 C2
Mechnica PL 54 C3
Mechowo PL 45 B7
Mechterstädt D 51 C6
Mecidiye TR 118 B1
Mecikal PL 46 B3
Mecina-Bombarón E 100 C2
Mecitözü TR 16 A7
Meckenbeuren D 61 C5
Meckenheim
Rheinland-Pfalz D 50 C3
Rheinland-Pfalz D 61 A4
Meckesheim D 61 A4
Mecseknádasd H 74 B3
Meda
I 71 C4
P 87 D3
Medak HR 83 B4
Mede I 80 A2
Medebach D 51 B4
Medelim P 93 A3
Medemblik NL 42 C2
Medena Selista BIH 84 B1
Medesano I 81 B4
Medevi S 37 D1
Medgidia RO 11 D10
Medgyesháza H 75 B6
Medhamn S 35 C5
Mediaș RO 11 C8
Medicina I 81 B5
Medinaceli E 95 A4
Medina de las Torres E 93 C4
Medina del Campo E 88 C2
Medina de Pomar E 89 B3
Medina de Ríoseco E 88 C1
Medina Sidonia E 99 C5
Medinilla E 93 A5
Medja SRB 75 C5
Medjedja BIH 85 C4
Medulin HR 82 B2
Meduno I 72 B2
Medveđa SRB 85 D6
Medvedja SRB 85 C6
Medvedov SK 64 C3
Medvide HR 83 B4
Medvode SLO 73 B4
Medzev SK 65 B6
Medžitlija MK 116 B3
Meerane D 52 C2
Meerle B 49 B5
Meersburg D 61 C5
Meeuwen B 49 B6
Megalo Horio GR 119 F2
Megalopoli GR 117 E4
Megara GR 117 D5
Megève F 69 C6
Meggenhofen A 63 B4
Megra RUS 7 A14
Mehamn N 113 A16
Mehedeby S 36 B4
Méhkerék H 75 B6
Mehun-sur-Yèvre F 68 A2
Meigle GB 25 B4
Meijel NL 50 B1
Meilen CH 70 A3
Meilhan F 76 C2
Meimôa P 93 A3
Meina I 70 C3
Meine D 44 C2
Meinersen D 44 C2
Meinerzhagen D 50 B3
Meiningen D 51 C6
Meira E 86 A3
Meiringen CH 70 B3
Meisenheim D 60 A3
Meissen D 52 B3
Meitingen D 62 B1
Meix-devant-Virton B 60 A1
Meka PL 54 B3
Meka Gruda BIH 84 C3
Mel I 72 B2
Melbu N 112 D3
Melč CZ 64 A3
Meldal N 114 D6
Méldola I 82 B1
Meldorf D 43 A6
Melegnano I 71 C4
Melenci SRB 75 C5
Melendugno I 105 C4
Melfi I 104 C1
Melfjordbotn N 112 F2
Melgaço P 87 B2
Melgar de Arriba E 88 B1
Melgar de Fernamental E 88 B2
Melgar de Yuso E 88 B2
Melhus N 114 D7
Meliana E 96 B2
Melide
CH 70 C3
E 86 B2
Melides P 98 A2
Meligales GR 117 E3
Melilli I 109 B4
Melinovac HR 83 B4
Melisenda I 110 C2
Melisey F 60 C2
Mélito di Porto Salvo I 109 B4
Melk A 63 B6
Melksham GB 29 B5
Mellanström S 115 B15
Mellbystrand S 40 C2
Melle
B 49 B4
D 50 A4
F 67 B4
Mellendorf D 43 C6
Mellerud S 35 D4
Mellieha M 107 C5
Mellösa S 37 C3
Mellrichstadt D 51 C6
Mělnické Vtelno CZ 53 C4
Mělník CZ 53 C4
Melón E 87 B2
Melrose GB 25 C5
Mels CH 71 A4
Melsungen D 51 B5
Meltaus FIN 113 F14
Meltham GB 27 B4
Melton Mowbray GB 30 B3
Meltosjärvi FIN 113 F13
Melun F 58 B3
Melvaig GB 22 D3
Melvich GB 23 C5
Mélykút H 75 B4
Melzo I 71 C4
Memaliaj AL 116 B1
Membrilla E 95 D3
Membrio E 93 B3
Memer F 77 B4
Memmelsdorf D 51 D6
Memmingen D 61 C6
Memoria P 92 B2
Mena UA 7 F12
Menággio I 71 B4
Menai Bridge GB 26 B1
Menasalbas E 94 C2
Menat F 68 B2
Mendavia E 89 B4
Mendaza E 89 B4
Mende F 78 B2
Menden D 50 B3
Menderes TR 119 D2
Mendig D 50 C3
Mendiga P 92 B2
Mendrisio CH 70 C3
Ménéac F 56 B3
Menemen TR 118 D2
Menen B 49 C4
Menesjärvi FIN 113 D15
Menetou-Salon F 68 A2
Menfi I 108 B1
Ménfőcsanak H 64 C3
Mengamuñoz E 94 B2
Mengen
D 61 B5
TR 118 B7
Mengeš SLO 73 B4
Mengibar E 100 B2
Mengkofen D 62 B3
Menou F 68 A3
Mens F 79 B4
Menslage D 43 C4
Mensträsk S 115 B16
Mentana I 102 A5
Menton F 80 C1
Méntrida E 94 B2
Méobecq F 67 B6
Méounes-les-Montrieux F 79 C4
Meppel NL 42 C3
Meppen D 43 C4
Mequinenza E 90 B3
Mer F 58 C2
Mera
Coruña E 86 A2
Coruña E 86 A3
Meråker N 114 D8
Merano I 71 B6
Merate I 71 C4
Mercadillo E 89 A3
Mercatale I 82 C1
Mercatino Conca I 82 C1
Mercato San Severino I 103 C7
Mercato Saraceno I 82 C1
Merching D 62 B1
Merchtem B 49 C5
Merdrignac F 56 B3
Merdžanići BIH 84 C2
Meré E 88 A2
Mere GB 29 B5
Meréville F 58 B3
Merfeld D 50 B3
Méribel F 69 C6
Méribel Motraret F 69 C6
Meriç TR 118 A1
Mérida E 93 C4
Mérignac F 76 B2
Měřín CZ 64 A1
Mering D 62 B1
Merkendorf D 62 A1
Merklin CZ 63 A4
Merksplas B 49 B5
Merlånna S 37 C3
Merlimont Plage F 48 C2
Mern DK 39 D5
Mernye H 74 B2
Mersch L 60 A2
Merseburg D 52 B1
Mers-les-Bains F 48 C2
Merthyr Tydfil GB 29 B4
Mertingen D 62 B1
Mértola P 98 B3
Méru F 58 A3
Merufe P 87 B2
Mervans F 69 B5
Merville F 48 C3
Méry-sur-Seine F 59 B4
Merzen D 43 C4
Merzifon TR 16 A7
Merzig D 60 A2
Mesagne I 105 C3
Mesão Frio P 87 C3
Mesas de Ibor E 93 B5
Meschede D 50 B4
Meschers-sur-Gironde F 66 C4
Meshchovsk RUS 7 D13
Meslay-du-Maine F 57 C5
Mesna N 34 A2
Mesnalien N 34 A2
Mesocco CH 71 B4
Mésola I 82 B1
Mesologi GR 116 D3
Mesopotamo GR 116 C2
Mesoraca I 107 B3
Messac F 57 C4
Messancy B 60 A1
Messdorf D 44 C3
Messei F 57 B5
Messejana P 98 B2
Messelt N 34 A3
Messina I 109 A4
Messingen D 43 C4
Messini GR 117 E4
Messkirch D 61 C5
Messlingen S 115 E9
Messtetten D 61 B4
Mesta GR 117 D7
Mestanza E 100 A1
Městec Králové CZ 53 C5
Mestlin D 44 B3
Město Albrechtice CZ 54 C2
Město Libavá CZ 64 A3
Město Touškov CZ 63 A4
Mestre I 72 C2
Mesvres F 69 B4
Mesztegnyő H 74 B2
Meta I 103 C7
Metajna HR 83 B4
Metelen D 50 A3
Methana GR 117 E5
Methlick GB 23 D6
Methven GB 25 B4
Methwold GB 30 B4
Metković HR 84 C2
Metlika SLO 73 C5
Metnitz A 73 B4
Metslawier NL 42 B3
Metsovo GR 116 C3
Metten D 62 B3
Mettendorf D 50 D2
Mettet B 49 C5
Mettingen D 50 A3
Mettlach D 60 A2
Mettlen CH 70 B2
Mettmann D 50 B2
Metz F 60 A2
Metzervisse F 60 A2
Metzingen D 61 B5
Meulan F 58 A2
Meung-sur-Loire F 58 C2
Meuselwitz D 52 B2
Meuzac F 67 C6
Mevagissey GB 28 C3
Mexborough GB 27 B4
Meximieux F 69 C5
Mey GB 23 C5
Meyenburg D 44 B4
Meyerhöfen D 43 C5
Meylan F 69 C5
Meymac F 68 C2
Meyrargues F 79 C4
Meyrueis F 78 B2
Meyssac F 77 A4
Meysse F 78 B3
Meyzieu F 69 C4
Mèze F 78 C2
Mézériat F 69 B5
Mežica SLO 73 B4
Mézidon-Canon F 57 A5
Mézières-en-Brenne F 67 B6
Mézières-sur-Issoire F 67 B5
Mézilhac F 78 B3
Mézilles F 59 C4
Mézin F 76 B3
Mezőberény H 75 B6
Mezőcsát H 65 C6
Mezőfalva H 74 B3
Mezőhegyes H 75 B5
Mezőkeresztes H 65 C6
Mezőkomárom H 74 B3
Mezőkövácsháza H 75 B5
Mezőkövesd H 65 C6
Mezőörs H 74 A2
Mézos F 76 B1
Mezőszilas H 74 B3
Mezőtúr H 75 A5
Mezquita de Jarque E 90 C2
Mezzano
Emilia Romagna I 81 B6
Trentino Alto Adige I 72 B1
Mezzojuso I 108 B2
Mezzoldo I 71 B4
Mezzolombardo I 71 B6
Mgarr M 107 C5
Mglin RUS 7 E12
Miajadas E 93 B5
Miały PL 46 C2
Mianowice PL 46 A3
Miasteczko Krajeńskie PL 46 B3
Miasteczko Sł. PL 54 C3
Miastko PL 46 A2
Michalovce SK 10 B6
Michałowice PL 55 C4
Michelau D 61 A6
Michelbach D 61 A6
Micheldorf A 63 C5
Michelhausen A 64 B1
Michelsneukirchen D 62 A3
Michelstadt D 61 A5
Michendorf D 52 A3
Mickleover GB 27 C4
Midbea GB 23 B6
Middelburg NL 49 B4
Middelfart DK 39 D2
Middelharnis NL 49 B5
Middelkerke B 48 B3
Middelstum NL 42 B3
Middlesbrough GB 27 A4
Middleton Cheney GB 30 B2
Middleton-in-Teesdale GB 26 A3
Middletown GB 19 B5
Middlewich GB 26 B3
Middlezoy GB 29 B5
Midhurst GB 31 D3
Midleton IRL 20 C3
Midlum D 43 B5
Midsomer Norton GB 29 B5
Midtgulen N 114 F2
Midtskogberget N 34 A4
Midwolda NL 43 B4
Mid Yell GB 22 A7
Miechów PL 55 C5
Miedes de Aragón E 89 C5
Miedes de Atienza E 95 A3
Międzybodzie Bielskie PL 65 A5
Międzybórz PL 54 B2
Międzychód PL 46 C1
Międzylesie PL 54 C1
Międzyrzec Podlaski PL 6 F7
Międzyrzecz PL 46 C1
Międzywodzie PL 45 A6
Międzyzdroje PL 45 B6
Miejska Górka PL 54 B1
Miélan F 76 C3
Mielec PL 55 C6
Mielęcin PL 45 B6
Mielno
Warmińsko-Mazurskie PL 47 B6
Zachodnio-Pomorskie PL 46 A2
Miengo E 88 A3
Mieraslompolo FIN 113 C16
Miercurea Ciuc RO 11 C8
Mieres
Asturias E 88 A1
Girona E 91 A5
Mieroszów PL 53 C6
Mierzyn PL 55 B4
Miesau D 60 A3
Miesbach D 62 C2
Mieścisko PL 46 C3
Mieste D 44 C3
Miesterhorst D 44 C3
Mieszków PL 54 A2
Mieszkowice PL 45 C6
Mietków PL 54 C1
Migennes F 59 C4
Miggiano I 107 B5
Migliánico I 103 A7
Migliarino I 81 B5
Migliónico I 104 C2
Mignano Monte Lungo I 103 B6
Migné F 67 B6
Miguel Esteban E 95 C3
Miguelturra E 94 D3
Mihajlovac SRB 85 B5
Miháld H 74 B2
Mihalgazi TR 118 B5
Mihaliççık TR 118 C6
Mihályi H 74 A2
Mihla D 51 B6
Mihohnić HR 83 A3
Miholjsko HR 73 C5
Mihovljan HR 73 B5
Mijares E 94 B2
Mijas E 100 C1
Mijoska MNE 85 D4
Mike H 74 B2
Mikhnevo RUS 7 D14
Mikines GR 117 E4
Mikkeli FIN 3 F27
Mikkelvik N 112 B8
Mikleuš HR 74 C2
Mikołajki Pomorskie PL 47 B5
Mikolów PL 54 C3
Mikonos GR 117 E7
Mikorzyn PL 54 B3
Mikro Derio GR 116 A8
Mikstat PL 54 B2
Mikulášovice CZ 53 C4
Mikulov CZ 64 B2
Mikulovice CZ 54 C2
Milagro E 89 B5
Miłakowo PL 47 A6
Milan = Milano I 71 C4
Miland N 32 C5
Milano = Milan I 71 C4
Milano Marittima I 82 B1
Milas TR 119 E2
Milazzo I 109 A4
Mildenhall GB 30 B4
Milejewo PL 47 A5
Milelín CZ 53 C5
Miletić SRB 75 C4
Miletićevo SRB 75 C6
Mileto I 106 C3
Milevsko CZ 63 A5
Milford IRL 19 A4
Milford Haven GB 28 B2
Milford on Sea GB 31 D2
Milhão P 87 C4
Milići BIH 85 B4
Miličín CZ 63 A5
Milicz PL 54 B2
Milín CZ 63 A5
Militello in Val di Catánia I 109 B3
Miljevina BIH 84 C3
Milkowice PL 53 B6
Millançay F 68 A1
Millares E 96 B2
Millas F 91 A5
Millau F 78 B2
Millesimo I 80 B2
Millevaches F 68 C2
Millom GB 26 A2
Millport GB 24 C3
Millstatt A 72 B3
Millstreet
Cork IRL 20 B2
Waterford IRL 21 B4
Milltown
Galway IRL 18 C3
Kerry IRL 20 B1
Milltown Malbay IRL 20 B2
Milly-la-Forêt F 58 B3
Milmarcos E 95 A5
Milmersdorf D 45 B5
Milna HR 83 C5
Milnthorpe GB 26 A3
Miločaj SRB 85 C5
Milogórze PL 47 A6
Miłomłyn PL 47 B5
Milos GR 117 F6
Miloševo SRB 85 B6
Miłosław PL 54 A2
Milot AL 105 B5
Milówka PL 65 A5
Miltach D 62 A3
Miltenberg D 61 A5
Milton Keynes GB 31 B3
Miltzow D 45 A5
Milutovac SRB 85 C6
Milverton GB 29 B4
Milzyn PL 47 C4
Mimice HR 84 C1
Mimizan F 76 B1
Mimizan-Plage F 76 B1
Mimoň CZ 53 C4
Mina de Juliana P 98 B2
Mina de São Domingos P 98 B3
Minas de Riotinto E 99 B4
Minateda E 101 A4
Minaya E 95 C4
Minde P 92 B2
Mindelheim D 61 B6
Mindelstetten D 62 B2
Minden D 51 A4
Mindszent H 75 B5
Minehead GB 29 B4
Mineo I 109 B3
Minerbe I 71 C6
Minérbio I 81 B5
Minervino Murge I 104 B2
Minglanilla E 95 C5
Mingorría E 94 B2
Minnesund N 34 B3
Miño E 86 A2
Miño de San Esteban E 89 C3
Minsen D 43 B4
Minsk BY 7 E9
Mińsk Mazowiecki PL 55 A6
Minsterley GB 26 C3
Mintlaw GB 23 D6
Minturno I 103 B6
Mionica
BIH 84 B3
SRB 85 B5
Mios F 76 B2
Mira
E 96 B1
I 72 C2
P 92 A2
Mirabel E 93 B4
Mirabel-aux-Baronnies F 79 B4
Mirabella Eclano I 103 B8
Mirabella Imbáccari I 109 B3
Mirabello I 81 B5
Miradoux F 77 B3
Miraflores de la Sierra E 94 B3
Miralrio E 95 B4
Miramar P 87 C2
Miramare I 82 B1
Miramas F 78 C3
Mirambeau F 67 C4
Miramont-de-Guyenne F 77 B3
Miranda de Arga E 89 B5
Miranda de Ebro E 89 B4
Miranda do Corvo P 92 A2
Miranda do Douro P 87 C4
Mirande F 77 C3
Mirandela P 87 C3
Mirandilla E 93 C4
Mirándola I 81 B5
Miranje HR 83 B4
Mirano I 72 C2
Miras AL 116 B2
Miravet E 90 B3
Miré F 57 C5
Mirebeau F 67 B5
Mirebeau-sur-Bèze F 69 A5
Mirecourt F 60 B2
Mirepoix F 77 C4
Mires GR 117 G6
Miribel F 69 C4
Miričina BIH 84 B3
Mirina GR 116 C7
Mirna SLO 73 C5
Miroslav CZ 64 B2
Mirosławice PL 54 C1
Mirosławiec PL 46 B2
Mirošov CZ 63 A4
Mirotice CZ 63 A5
Mirovice CZ 63 A5
Mirow D 45 B4
Mirsk PL 53 C5
Mirzec PL 55 B6
Misi FIN 113 F15
Misilmeri I 108 A2
Miske H 75 B4
Miskolc H 65 B6
Mislinja SLO 73 B5
Missanello I 104 C2
Missillac F 66 A2
Mistelbach
A 64 B2
D 62 A2
Misten N 112 E3
Misterbianco I 109 B4
Misterhult S 40 B6
Mistretta I 109 B3
Misurina I 72 B2
Mitchelstown IRL 20 B3
Mithimna GR 116 C8
Mithoni GR 117 F3
Mitilini GR 118 C1
Mitilinii GR 119 E1
Mittelberg
Tirol A 71 B5
Vorarlberg A 71 A5
Mittenwald D 71 A6
Mittenwalde D 52 A3
Mitterback A 63 C6
Mitterdorf im Mürztal A 73 A5
Mitter-Kleinarl A 72 A3
Mittersheim F 60 B2
Mittersill A 72 A2
Mitterskirchen D 62 B3
Mitterteich D 62 A3
Mitton F 76 B2
Mittweida D 52 C2
Mitwitz D 52 C1
Mizhhir'ya UA 11 B7
Mjällby S 41 C4
Mjåvatn N 33 D5
Mjöbäck S 40 B2
Mjölby S 37 D2
Mjølfjell N 32 B3
Mjøndalen N 35 C2
Mjørlund N 34 B2
Mladá Boleslav CZ 53 C4
Mladá Vožice CZ 63 A5
Mladé Buky CZ 53 C5
Mladenovac SRB 85 B5
Mladenovo SRB 75 C4
Mladikovine BIH 84 B2
Mława PL 47 B6
Mlinište BIH 84 B1
Młodzieszyn PL 55 A5
Mlogoszyn PL 55 A4
Młynary PL 47 A5
Mnichóvice CZ 63 A5
Mnichovo Hradiště CZ 53 C4
Mniów PL 55 B5
Mnisek nad Hnilcom SK 65 B6
Mnišek pod Brdy CZ 63 A5
Mniszek PL 55 B5
Mniszków PL 55 B5
Mo
Hedmark N 34 B3
Hordaland N 32 B2
Møre og Romsdal N 114 E5
Telemark N 33 C4
Gävleborg S 36 A3
Västra Götaland S 35 D3
Moaña E 87 B2
Moate IRL 21 A4
Mocejón E 94 C3
Močenok SK 64 B3
Mochales E 95 A4
Mochowo PL 47 C5
Mochy PL 53 A6
Mockern D 52 A1
Mockfjärd S 36 B1
Möckmühl D 61 A5
Mockrehna D 52 B2
Moclin E 100 B2
Mocsa H 64 C4
Mőcsény H 74 B3
Modane F 70 C1
Modbury GB 28 C4
Módena I 81 B4
Módica I 109 C3
Modigliana I 81 B5
Modlin PL 47 C6
Mödling A 64 B2
Modliszewice PL 55 B5
Modliszewko PL 46 C3
Modogno I 104 B2
Modra SK 64 B3
Modran BIH 84 B2
Modriča BIH 84 B3
Möðrudalur IS 111 B10
Modrý Kamen SK 65 B5
Moëlan-sur-Mer F 56 C2
Moelfre GB 26 B1
Moelv N 34 B2
Moen N 112 C7
Moena I 72 B1
Moerbeke B 49 B4
Moers D 50 B2
Móes P 87 D3
Moffat GB 25 C4
Mogadouro P 87 C4
Mogata S 37 D3
Móggio Udinese I 72 B3
Mogielnica PL 55 B5
Mogilany PL 65 A5
Mogilno PL 46 C3
Mogliano I 82 C2
Mogliano Véneto I 72 C2
Mogor E 87 B2
Mógoro I 110 C1
Moguer E 99 B4
Mohács H 74 C3
Moheda S 40 B4
Mohedas E 93 A4
Mohedas de la Jara E 93 B5
Mohelnice CZ 64 A2
Mohill IRL 19 C4
Möhlin CH 70 A2
Moholm S 35 D6
Mohorn D 52 B3
Mohyliv-Podil's'kyy UA 11 B9
Moi N 33 D3
Moià E 91 B5
Móie I 82 C2
Moimenta da Beira P 87 D3
Mo i Rana N 115 A11
Moirans F 69 C5
Moirans-en-Montagne F 69 B5
Moisaküla EST 7 B8
Moisdon-la-Rivière F 57 C4
Moissac F 77 B4
Moita
Coimbra P 92 A2
Guarda P 93 A3
Santarém P 92 B2
Setúbal P 92 C1
Moita dos Ferreiros P 92 B1
Moixent E 101 A5
Mojacar E 101 B4
Mojados E 88 C2
Mojkovac MNE 85 D4
Mojmírovce SK 64 B4
Mojtin SK 65 B4
Möklinta S 36 B3
Mokošica HR 84 D3
Mokra Gora SRB 85 C4
Mokronog SLO 73 C5
Mokro Polje HR 83 B5
Mokrzyska PL 55 C5
Møkster N 32 B2
Mol
B 49 B6
SRB 75 C5
Mola di Bari I 104 B3
Molai GR 117 F4
Molare I 80 B2
Molaretto I 70 C2
Molas F 77 C3
Molassano I 80 B2
Molbergen D 43 C4
Mold GB 26 B2
Molde N 114 E4
Møldrup DK 38 C2
Moledo do Minho P 87 C2
Molfetta I 104 B2
Molfsee D 44 A2
Moliden S 115 D15
Molières F 77 B4
Molina de Aragón E 95 B5
Molina de Segura E 101 A4
Molinar E 89 A3
Molinaseca E 86 B4
Molinella I 81 B5
Molinet F 68 B3
Molinicos E 101 A3
Molini di Tures I 72 B1
Molinos de Duero E 89 C4
Molins de Rei E 91 B5
Moliterno I 104 C1
Molkom S 35 C5
Möllbrücke A 72 B3
Mölle S 41 C2
Molledo E 88 A2
Möllenbeck D 45 B5
Mollerussa E 90 B3
Mollet de Perelada E 91 A5
Mollina E 100 B1
Mölln D 44 B2
Molló E 91 A5
Mölnlösund S 35 D3
Mölltorp S 37 D1
Mölnbo S 37 C4
Mölndal S 38 B5
Mölnlycke S 38 B5
Molompize F 68 C3
Moloy F 69 A4
Molsheim F 60 B3
Moltzow D 45 B4
Molve HR 74 B2
Molveno I 71 B5
Molvizar E 100 C2
Molzbichl A 72 B3
Mombaróccio I 82 C1
Mombeltrán E 94 B1
Mombris D 51 C5
Mombuey E 87 B4
Momchilgrad BG 116 A7
Mommark DK 39 E3
Momo I 70 C3
Monaghan IRL 19 B5
Monar Lodge GB 22 D4
Monasterace Marina I 106 C3
Monasterevin IRL 21 A4
Monasterio de Rodilla E 89 B3
Monastir I 110 C2
Monbahus F 77 B3
Monbazillac F 77 B3
Moncada E 96 B2
Moncalieri I 80 A1
Moncalvo I 80 A2
Monção P 87 B2
Moncarapacho P 98 B3
Moncel-sur-Seille F 60 B2
Monchegorsk RUS 3 C30
Mönchengladbach = Munchen-Gladbach D 50 B2
Mónchio della Corti I 81 B4
Monchique P 98 B2
Monclar-de-Quercy F 77 C4
Moncofa E 96 B2
Moncontour F 56 B3
Moncoutant F 67 B4
Monda E 100 C1
Mondariz E 87 B2
Mondavio I 82 C1
Mondéjar E 95 B3
Mondello I 108 A2
Mondim de Basto P 87 C3
Mondolfo I 82 C2
Mondoñedo E 86 A3
Mondorf-les-Bains L 60 A2
Mondoubleau F 58 C1
Mondovì I 80 B1
Mondragon F 78 B3
Mondragone I 103 B6
Mondsee A 63 C4
Monéglia I 80 B3
Monegrillo E 90 B2
Monein F 76 C2
Monemvasia GR 117 F5
Mónesi I 80 B1
Monesíglio I 80 B2
Monesterio E 99 A4
Monestier-de-Clermont F 79 B4
Monestiés F 77 B5
Monéteau F 59 C4
Moneygall IRL 21 B4
Moneymore GB 19 B5
Monfalcone I 72 C3
Monfero E 86 A2
Monflanquin F 77 B3
Monflorite E 90 A2
Monforte P 92 B3
Monforte da Beira
E 92 B3
P 92 B3
Monforte d'Alba I 80 B1
Monforte del Cid E 96 C2
Monforte de Lemos E 86 B3
Monforte de Moyuela E 90 B1
Monghidoro I 81 B5
Mongiana I 106 C3
Monguelfo I 72 B2
Monheim D 62 B1
Moniaive GB 25 C4
Monifieth GB 25 B5
Monikie GB 25 B5
Monistrol-d'Allier F 78 B2
Monistrol de Montserrat E 91 B4
Monistrol-sur-Loire F 68 C4
Mönkebude D 45 B5
Monkton GB 24 C3
Monmouth GB 29 B5
Monnaie F 67 A5
Monnerville F 58 B3
Monnickendam NL 42 C2
Monolithos GR 119 F2
Monópoli I 104 C3
Monor H 75 A4
Monóvar E 101 A5
Monpazier F 77 B3
Monreal
D 50 C3
E 76 D1
Monreal del Campo E 95 B5
Monreale I 108 A2
Monroy E 93 B4
Monroyo E 90 C2
Mons B 49 C4
Monsaraz P 92 C3
Monschau D 50 C2
Monségur F 76 B3
Monsélice I 72 C1
Mønshaug N 32 B3
Monster NL 49 A5
Mönsterås S 40 B6
Monsummano Terme I 81 C4
Montabaur D 50 C3
Montafia I 80 B2
Montagnac F 78 C2
Montagnana I 71 C6
Montaigu F 66 B3
Montaigu-de-Quercy F 77 B4
Montaiguët-en-Forez F 68 B3
Montaigut F 68 B2
Montaigut-sur-Save F 77 C4
Montainville F 58 B2
Montalbán E 90 C2
Montalbán de Córdoba E 100 B1
Montalbano Elicona I 109 A4
Montalbano Iónico I 104 C2
Montalbo E 95 C4
Montalcino I 81 C5
Montaldo di Cósola I 80 B3
Montalegre P 87 C3
Montalieu-Vercieu F 69 C5
Montalivet-les-Bains F 66 C3
Montallegro I 108 B2
Montalto delle Marche I 82 D2
Montalto di Castro I 102 A4
Montalto Pavese I 80 B3
Montalto Uffugo I 106 B3
Montalvão P 92 B3
Montamarta E 88 C1
Montana BG 11 E7
Montana-Vermala CH 70 B2
Montánchez E 93 B4
Montanejos E 96 A2
Montano Antilia I 106 A2
Montans F 77 C4
Montargil P 92 B2
Montargis F 58 C3
Montastruc-la-Conseillère F 77 C4
Montauban F 77 B4
Montauban-de-Bretagne F 57 B3
Montbard F 59 C5
Montbarrey F 69 A5
Montbazens F 77 B5
Montbazon F 67 A5
Montbéliard F 70 A1
Montbenoit F 69 B6
Montbeugny F 68 B3
Montblanc E 91 B4
Montbozon F 69 A6
Montbrison F 68 C4
Montbron F 67 C5
Montbrun-les-Bains F 79 B4
Montceau-les-Mines F 69 B4
Montcenis F 69 B4
Montchanin F 69 B4
Montcornet F 59 A5
Montcuq F 77 B4
Montdardier F 78 C2
Mont-de-Marsan F 76 C2
Montdidier F 58 A3
Monteagudo E 101 A4
Monteagudo de las Vicarías E 89 C4
Montealegre E 88 C2
Montealegre del Castillo E 101 A4
Montebello Iónico I 109 B4
Montebello Vicentino I 71 C6
Montebelluna I 72 C2
Montebourg F 57 A4
Montebruno I 80 B3
Monte-Carlo MC 80 C1
Montecarotto I 82 C2
Montecassiano I 82 C2
Montecastrilli I 102 A5
Montecatini Terme I 81 C4
Montécchio I 82 C1
Montécchio Emilia I 81 B4
Montécchio Maggiore I 71 C6
Montech F 77 C4
Montechiaro d'Asti I 80 A2
Monte Clara P 92 B3
Monte Clérigo P 98 B2
Montecórice I 103 C7
Montecorvino Rovella I 103 C7
Monte da Pedra P 92 B3
Monte de Goula P 92 B3
Montederramo E 87 B3
Montedoro I 108 B2
Monte do Trigo P 92 C3
Montefalco I 82 D1
Montefalcone di Val Fortore I 103 B8
Montefalcone nel Sánnio I 103 B7
Montefano I 82 C2
Montefiascone I 102 A5
Montefiorino I 81 B4
Montefortino I 82 D2
Montefranco I 102 A5
Montefrío E 100 B2
Montegiordano Marina I 106 A3
Montegiórgio I 82 C2
Monte Gordo P 98 B3
Montegranaro I 82 C2
Montehermoso E 93 A4
Montejicar E 100 B2
Montejo de la Sierra E 95 A3
Montejo de Tiermes E 89 C3
Monte Juntos P 92 C3
Montel-de-Gelat F 68 C2
Monteleone di Púglia I 103 B8
Monteleone di Spoleto I 102 A5
Monteleone d'Orvieto I 81 D6
Montelepre I 108 A2
Montelibretti I 102 A5
Montelier F 79 B4
Montélimar F 78 B3
Montella
E 91 A4
I 103 C8
Montellano E 99 B5
Montelupo Fiorentino I 81 C5
Montemaggiore Belsito I 108 B2
Montemagno I 80 B2
Montemayor E 100 B1
Montemayor de Pinilla E 88 C2
Montemésola I 104 C3
Montemilleto I 103 B7
Montemilone I 104 B1
Montemolín E 99 A4
Montemónaco I 82 D2
Montemor-o-Novo P 92 C2
Montemor-o-Velho P 92 A2
Montemurro I 104 C1
Montendre F 67 C4
Montenegro de Cameros E 89 B4
Montenero di Bisáccia I 103 B7
Monteneuf F 57 C3
Monteparano I 104 C3
Montepescali I 81 D5
Montepiano I 81 B5
Monte Porzio I 82 C1
Montepulciano I 81 C5
Monte Real P 92 B2
Montereale I 103 A6
Montereale Valcellina I 72 B2
Montereau-Faut-Yonne F 59 B3
Monte Redondo P 92 B2
Monterénzio I 81 B5
Monte Romano I 102 A4
Monteroni d'Arbia I 81 C5
Monteroni di Lecce I 105 C4
Monterosso al Mare I 80 B3
Monterosso Almo I 109 B3
Monterosso Grana I 79 B6
Monterotondo I 102 A5
Monterotondo Marittimo I 81 C4
Monterrey E 87 C3
Monterroso E 86 B3
Monterrubio de la Serena E 93 C5
Monterubbiano I 82 C2
Montesa E 96 C2
Montesalgueiro E 86 A2
Monte San Giovanni Campano I 103 B6
Montesano sulla Marcellana I 104 C1
Monte San Savino I 81 C5
Monte Sant'Ángelo I 104 B1
Montesárchio I 103 B7
Montescaglioso I 104 C2
Montesclaros E 94 B2
Montesilvano I 103 A7
Montespértoli I 81 C5
Montesquieu-Volvestre F 77 C4
Montesquiou F 77 C3
Montestruc-sur-Gers F 77 C3
Montes Velhos P 98 B2
Montevarchi I 81 C5
Montéveglio I 81 B5
Monte Vilar P 92 B1
Montfaucon F 66 A3
Montfaucon-d'Argonne F 59 A6
Montfaucon-en-Velay F 69 C4
Montferrat
Isère F 69 C5
Var F 79 C5
Montfort-en-Chalosse F 76 C2
Montfort-l'Amaury F 58 B2
Montfort-le-Gesnois F 58 B1
Montfort-sur-Meu F 57 B4
Montfort-sur-Risle F 58 A1
Montgai E 90 B3
Montgaillard F 77 C3
Montgenèvre F 79 B5
Montgiscard F 77 C4
Montgomery GB 26 C2
Montguyon F 67 C4
Monthermé F 59 A5
Monthey CH 70 B1
Monthois F 59 A5
Monthureux-sur-Saône F 60 B1
Monti I 110 B2
Monticelli d'Ongina I 81 A3
Montichiari I 71 C5
Monticiano I 81 C5
Montiel E 100 A3
Montier-en-Der F 59 B5
Montieri I 81 C5
Montiglio I 80 A2
Montignac F 77 A4
Montigny-le-Roi F 60 C1
Montigny-lès-Metz F 60 A2
Montigny-sur-Aube F 59 C5
Montijo
E 93 C4
P 92 C2
Montilla E 100 B1
Montillana E 100 B2
Montilly F 68 B3
Montivilliers F 57 A6
Montjaux F 78 B1
Montjean-sur-Loire F 66 A4
Montlhéry F 58 B3
Montlieu-la-Garde F 67 C4
Mont-Louis F 91 A5
Montlouis-sur-Loire F 67 A5
Montluçon F 68 B2
Montluel F 69 C5
Montmarault F 68 B2
Montmartin-sur-Mer F 57 B4
Montmédy F 59 A6
Montmélian F 69 C6
Montmeyan F 79 C5
Montmeyran F 78 B3
Montmirail
Marne F 59 B4
Sarthe F 58 B1
Montmiral F 69 C5
Montmirat F 78 C3
Montmirey-le-Château F 69 A5
Montmoreau-St Cybard F 67 C5
Montmorency F 58 B3
Montmorillon F 67 B5
Montmort-Lucy F 59 B4
Montoir-de-Bretagne F 66 A2
Montoire-sur-le-Loir F 58 C1
Montoito P 92 C3

Montolieu F 77 C5
Montório al Vomano I 103 A6
Montoro E 100 A1
Montpellier F 78 C2
Montpezat-de-Quercy F 77 B4
Montpezat-sous-Bouzon F 78 B3
Montpon-Ménestérol F 76 A3
Montpont-en-Bresse F 69 B5
Montréal
Aude F 77 C5
Gers F 76 C3
Montredon-Labessonnié F 77 C5
Montréjeau F 77 C3
Montrésor F 67 A6
Montresta I 110 B1
Montret F 69 B5
Montreuil
Pas de Calais F 48 C2
Seine St Denis F 58 B3
Montreuil-aux-Lions F 59 A4
Montreuil-Bellay F 67 A4
Montreux CH 70 B1
Montrevault F 66 A3
Montrevel-en-Bresse F 69 B5
Montrichard F 67 A6
Montricoux F 77 B4
Mont-roig del Camp E 90 B3
Montrond-les-Bains F 69 C4
Montrose GB 25 B5
Montroy E 96 B2
Montsalvy F 77 B5
Montsauche-les-Settons F 68 A4
Montseny E 91 B5
Montsoreau F 67 A5
Mont-sous-Vaudrey F 69 B5
Monts-sur-Guesnes F 67 B5
Mont-St Aignan F 58 A2
Mont-St Vincent F 69 B4
Montsûrs F 57 B5
Montuenga E 94 A2
Montuïri E 97 B3
Monturque E 100 B1
Monza I 71 C4
Monzón E 90 B3
Monzón de Campos E 88 B2
Moorbad Lobenstein D 52 C1
Moordorf D 43 B4
Moorslede B 49 C4
Moos D 61 C4
Moosburg D 62 B2
Moosburg im Kärnten A 73 B4
Mór H 74 A3
Mora E 94 C3
Móra P 92 C2
Mora S 36 A1
Moraby S 36 B2
Mòra d'Ebre E 90 B3
Mora de Rubielos E 96 A2
Moradillo de Roa E 88 C3
Morąg PL 47 B5
Mórahalom H 75 B4
Moraime E 86 A1
Morais P 87 C4
Mòra la Nova E 90 B3
Moral de Calatrava E 100 A2
Moraleda de Zafayona E 100 B2
Moraleja E 93 A4
Moraleja del Vino E 88 C1
Morales del Vino E 88 C1
Morales de Toro E 88 C1
Morales de Valverde E 88 C1
Moralina E 87 C4
Morano Cálabro I 106 B3
Mörarp S 41 C2
Morasverdes E 93 A4
Morata de Jalón E 89 C5
Morata de Jiloca E 89 C5
Morata de Tajuña E 95 B3
Moratalla E 101 A4
Moravče SLO 73 B4
Moravec CZ 64 A2
Moraviţa RO 75 C6
Morávka CZ 65 A4
Moravská Třebová CZ 64 A2
Moravské Budějovice CZ 64 A1
Moravské Lieskové SK 64 B3
Moravske Toplice SLO 73 B6
Moravský-Beroun CZ 64 A3
Moravský Krumlov CZ 64 A2
Moravský Svätý Ján SK 64 B3
Morawica PL 55 C5
Morawin PL 54 B3
Morbach D 60 A3
Morbegno I 71 B4
Morbier F 69 B6
Mörbisch am See A 64 C2
Mörbylånga S 41 C6
Morcenx F 76 B2
Morciano di Romagna I 82 C1
Morcone I 103 B7
Morcuera E 89 C3
Mordelles F 57 B4
Mordoğan TR 119 D1
Moréac F 56 C3
Morebattle GB 25 C5
Morecambe GB 26 A3
Moreda
Granada E 100 B2
Oviedo E 88 A1
Morée F 58 C2
Moreles de Rey E 88 B1
Morella E 90 C2
Moreruela de los Infanzones E 88 C1
Morés E 89 C5
Móres I 110 B1
Morestel F 69 C5
Moretonhampstead GB 28 C4
Moreton-in-Marsh GB 29 B6
Moret-sur-Loing F 58 B3
Moretta I 80 B1
Moreuil F 58 A3
Morez F 69 B6
Mörfelden D 51 D4
Morgat F 56 B1
Morges CH 69 B6
Morgex I 70 C2
Morgongåva S 36 C3
Morhange F 60 B2
Morhet B 49 D6
Mori I 71 C5
Morialmé B 49 C5
Morianes P 98 B3
Moriani Plage F 102 A2
Mórichida H 74 A2
Moriles E 100 B1
Morille E 94 B1
Moringen D 51 B5
Morjärv S 3 C25
Morkarla S 36 B4
Mørke DK 39 C3
Mørkøv DK 39 D4
Morkovice-Slížany CZ 64 A3
Morlaàs F 76 C2
Morlaix F 56 B2
Morley F 59 B6
Mörlunda S 40 B5
Mormanno I 106 B2
Mormant F 59 B3
Mornant F 69 C4
Mornay-Berry F 68 A2
Morokovo MNE 85 D4
Morón de Almazán E 89 C4
Morón de la Frontera E 99 B5
Morović SRB 85 A4
Morozzo I 80 B1
Morpeth GB 25 C6
Morphou CY 120 A1
Mörrum S 41 C4
Morsbach D 50 C3
Mörsch D 61 B4
Mörsil S 115 D10
Morsum D 39 E1
Mørsvikbotn N 112 E4
Mortagne-au-Perche F 58 B1
Mortagne-sur-Gironde F 66 C4
Mortagne-sur-Sèvre F 66 B4
Mortágua P 92 A2
Mortain F 57 B5
Mortara I 70 C3
Morteau F 69 A6
Mortegliano I 72 C3
Mortelle I 109 A4
Mortemart F 67 B5
Mortimer's Cross GB 29 A5
Mortrée F 57 B6
Mörtschach A 72 B2
Mortsel B 49 B5
Morud DK 39 D3
Morwenstow GB 28 C3
Moryń PL 45 C6
Morzeszczyn PL 47 B4
Morzewo PL 47 B5
Morzine F 70 B1
Mosalsk RUS 7 D13
Mosbach D 61 A5
Mosbjerg DK 38 B3
Mosby N 33 D4
Mosca P 87 C4
Moscavide P 92 C1
Moščenica HR 73 C6
Mošćenice HR 73 C4
Moščenicka Draga HR 73 C4
Mosciano Sant'Ángelo I 82 D2
Mościsko PL 54 C1
Moscow = Moskva RUS 7 D14
Mosina PL 54 A1
Mosjøen N 115 B10
Moskog N 32 A3
Moskorzew PL 55 C4
Moskosel S 115 B16
Moskuvarra FIN 113 E15
Moskva = Moscow RUS 7 D14
Moslavina Podravska HR 74 C2
Moşniţa Nouă RO 75 C6
Moso in Passíria I 71 B6
Mosonmagyaróvár H 64 C3
Mošorin SRB 75 C5
Mošovce SK 65 B4
Mosqueruela E 90 C2
Moss N 35 C2
Mossfellsbær IS 111 C4
Mössingen D 61 B5
Møsstrand N 32 C5
Most CZ 52 C3
Mosta M 107 C5
Mostar BIH 84 C2
Mosterhamn N 33 C2
Mostki PL 53 A5
Most na Soči SLO 72 B3
Móstoles E 94 B3
Mostová SK 64 B3
Mostowo PL 46 A2
Mostuéjouls F 78 B2
Mosty PL 45 B6
Mostys'ka UA 11 B7
Mosvik N 114 D7
Mota del Cuervo E 95 C4
Mota del Marqués E 88 C1
Motala S 37 D2
Motherwell GB 25 C4
Möthlow D 45 C4
Motilla del Palancar E 95 C5
Motnik SLO 73 B4
Motovun HR 72 C3
Motril E 100 C2
Motta I 71 C6
Motta di Livenza I 72 C2
Motta Montecorvino I 103 B8
Motta Visconti I 70 C3
Mottisfont GB 31 C2
Móttola I 104 C3
Mou DK 38 C3
Mouchard F 69 B5
Moudon CH 70 B1
Moudros GR 116 C7
Mougins F 79 C5
Mouilleron en-Pareds F 66 B4
Mouliherne F 67 A5
Moulinet F 80 C1
Moulins F 68 B3
Moulins-Engilbert F 68 B3
Moulins-la-Marche F 58 B1
Moulismes F 67 B5
Moult F 57 A5
Mountain Ash GB 29 B4
Mountbellew IRL 20 A3
Mountfield GB 19 B4
Mountmellick IRL 21 A4
Mountrath IRL 21 A4
Mountsorrel GB 30 B2
Moura P 98 A3
Mourão P 92 C3
Mourenx F 76 C2
Mouriés F 78 C3
Mourmelon-le-Grand F 59 A5
Mouronho P 92 A2
Mouscron B 49 C4
Mousehole GB 28 C2
Moussac F 78 C3
Moussey F 60 B2
Mousteru F 56 B2
Moustey F 76 B2
Moustiers-Ste Marie F 79 C5
Mouthe F 69 B6
Mouthier-Haute-Pierre F 69 A6
Mouthoumet F 77 D5
Moutier CH 70 A2
Moûtiers F 69 C6
Moutiers-les-Mauxfaits F 66 B3
Mouy F 58 A3
Mouzaki GR 116 C3
Mouzon F 59 A6
Møvik N 32 B2
Moville IRL 19 A4
Moy
Highland GB 23 D4
Tyrone GB 19 B5
Moycullen IRL 20 A2
Moyenmoutier F 60 B2
Moyenvic F 60 B2
Moylough IRL 18 C3
Mózar E 88 C1
Mozhaysk RUS 7 D14
Mozirje SLO 73 B4
Mözs H 74 B3
Mozzanica I 71 C4
Mramorak SRB 85 B5
Mrčajevci SRB 85 C5
Mrkonjić Grad BIH 84 B2
Mrkopalj HR 73 C4
Mrmoš SRB 85 C6
Mrocza PL 46 B3
Mroczeń PL 54 B2
Mroczno PL 47 B5
Mrozy PL 55 A6
Mrzezyno PL 45 A7
Mšec CZ 53 C3
Mšeno CZ 53 C4
Mstów PL 55 C4
Mstsislaw BY 7 D11
Mszana Dolna PL 65 A6
Mszczonów PL 55 B5
Mtsensk RUS 7 E14
Muć HR 83 C5
Múccia I 82 C2
Much D 50 C3
Mücheln D 52 B1
Much Marcle GB 29 B5
Muchów PL 53 B6
Much Wenlock GB 26 C3
Mucientes E 88 C2
Muckross IRL 20 B2
Mucur TR 16 B7
Muda P 98 B2
Mudanya TR 118 B3
Mudau D 61 A5
Müden D 44 C2
Mudersbach D 50 C3
Mudurnu TR 118 B6
Muel E 90 B1
Muelas del Pan E 88 C1
Muess D 44 B3
Muff IRL 19 A4
Mugardos E 86 A2
Muge P 92 B2
Mügeln
Sachsen D 52 B3
Sachsen-Anhalt D 52 B3
Múggia I 72 C3
Mugnano I 82 C1
Mugron F 76 C2
Mugueimes E 87 C3
Muhi H 65 C6
Mühlacker D 61 B4
Mühlbach am Hochkönig A 72 A3
Mühlberg
Brandenburg D 52 B3
Thüringen D 51 C6
Mühldorf
A 72 B3
D 62 B3
Muhleberg CH 70 B2
Mühleim D 61 B4
Muhlen-Eichsen D 44 B3
Mühlhausen
Bayern D 62 A1
Thüringen D 51 B6
Mühltroff D 52 C1
Muhos FIN 3 D27
Muhr A 72 A3
Muine Bheag IRL 21 B5
Muirkirk GB 24 C3
Muir of Ord GB 23 D4
Muirteira P 92 B1
Mukacheve UA 11 B7
Muker GB 26 A3
Mula E 101 A4
Muğla TR 119 E3
Mulben GB 23 D5
Mulegns CH 71 B4
Mules I 71 B6
Mülheim D 50 B2
Mulhouse F 60 C3
Muljava SLO 73 C4
Mullanys Cross IRL 18 B3
Müllheim D 60 C3
Mullhyttan S 37 C1
Mullinavat IRL 21 B4
Mullingar IRL 21 A4
Mullion GB 28 C2
Müllrose D 53 A4
Mullsjö S 40 B3
Mulseryd S 40 B3
Munaðarnes IS 111 A4
Munana E 94 B1
Muñás E 86 A4
Münchberg D 52 C1
Müncheberg D 45 C6
München = Munich D 62 B2
Munchen-Gladbach = Mönchengladbach D 50 B2
Münchhausen D 51 C4
Mundaka E 89 A4
Münden D 51 B5
Munderfing A 63 B4
Munderkingen D 61 B5
Mundesley GB 30 B5
Munera E 95 C4
Mungia E 89 A4
Munich = München D 62 B2
Muñico E 94 B1
Muniesa E 90 B2
Munka-Ljungby S 41 C2
Munkebo DK 39 D3
Munkedal S 35 D3
Munkflohögen S 115 D11
Munkfors S 34 C5
Munktorp S 37 C3
Münnerstadt D 51 C6
Muñopepe E 94 B2
Muñotello E 94 B1
Münsingen
CH 70 B2
D 61 B5
Munsö S 37 C4
Münster
CH 70 B3
Hessen D 61 A4
Munster D 44 C2
Münster D 50 B3
Munster F 60 B3
Muntibar E 89 A4
Münzkirchen A 63 B4
Muodoslompolo S 113 E12
Muonio FIN 113 E12
Muotathal CH 70 B3
Muradiye TR 118 D2
Murakeresztúr H 74 B1
Murán SK 65 B6
Murano I 72 C2
Muras E 86 A3
Murat F 78 A1
Muratlı TR 118 A2
Murato F 102 A2
Murat-sur-Vèbre F 78 C1
Murau A 73 A4
Muravera I 110 C2
Murazzano I 80 B2
Murça P 87 C3
Murchante E 89 B5
Murchin D 45 B5
Murcia E 101 B4
Murczyn PL 46 C3
Mur-de-Barrez F 77 B5
Mûr-de-Bretagne F 56 B2
Mur-de-Sologne F 67 A6
Mureck A 73 B5
Mürefte TR 118 B2
Muret F 77 C4
Murg CH 71 A4
Murguia E 89 B4
Muri CH 70 A3
Murias de Paredes E 86 B4
Muriedas E 88 A3
Muriel Viejo E 89 C4
Murillo de Rio Leza E 89 B4
Murillo el Fruto E 89 B5
Murino MNE 85 D4
Muriqan AL 105 A5
Murlaggan GB 22 E3
Murmansk RUS 3 B30
Murmashi RUS 3 B30
Murnau D 62 C2
Muro
E 97 B3
F 102 A1
Muro de Alcoy E 96 C2
Murol F 68 C2
Muro Lucano I 103 C8
Muron F 66 B4
Muros E 86 B1
Muros de Nalón E 86 A4
Murowana Goślina PL 46 C3
Mürren CH 70 B2
Murrhardt D 61 B5
Murska Sobota SLO 73 B6
Mursko Središce HR 73 B6
Murtas E 100 C2
Murten CH 70 B2
Murter HR 83 C4
Murtiçi TR 119 F6
Murtosa P 87 D2
Murvica HR 83 B4
Murviel-lès-Béziers F 78 C2
Mürzsteg A 63 C6
Murzynowo PL 46 C1
Mürzzuschlag A 63 C6
Musculdy F 76 C2
Mushqeta AL 105 B5
Muskö S 37 C5
Mušov CZ 64 B2
Musselburgh GB 25 C4
Musselkanaal NL 43 C4
Mussidan F 77 A3
Mussomeli I 108 B2
Musson B 60 A1
Mussy-sur-Seine F 59 C5
Mustafakemalpaşa TR 118 B3
Muszaki PL 47 B6
Muszyna PL 65 A6
Mut TR 16 C6
Muta SLO 73 B5
Muthill GB 25 B4
Mutné SK 65 A5
Mutriku E 89 A4
Muttalip TR 118 C5
Mutterbergalm A 71 A6
Muxia E 86 A1
Muxilka-Ugarte E 89 A4
Muzillac F 66 A2
Mužla SK 65 C4
Muzzano del Turgnano I 72 C3
Mybster GB 23 C5
Myckelgensjö S 115 D14
Myennes F 68 A2
Myjava SK 64 B3
Myking N 32 B2
Mykland N 33 D5
Mykolayiv = Nikolayev UA 11 C12
Myra N 33 D6
Myrdal N 32 B4
Myre
Nordland N 112 C4
Nordland N 112 D4
Myresjö S 40 B4
Myrhorod UA 11 B12
Mýri IS 111 B8
Myrtou CY 120 A2
Mysen N 35 C3
Mysłakowice PL 53 C5
Myślenice PL 65 A5
Myślibórz PL 45 C6
Mysłowice PL 55 C4
Myszków PL 55 C4
Mytishchi RUS 7 D14
Mýtna SK 65 B5
Mýtne Ludany SK 65 B4
Mýto CZ 63 A4

N

Nå N 32 B3
Naaldwijk NL 49 B5
Naantali FIN 6 A6
Naas IRL 21 A5
Nabais P 92 A3
Nabbelund S 41 B7
Nabburg D 62 A3
Načeradec CZ 63 A5
Náchod CZ 53 C6
Nacław PL 46 A2
Nadarzyce PL 46 B2
Nadarzyn PL 55 A5
Nádasd H 74 B1
Nădlac RO 75 B5
Nádudvar H 75 A6
Nadvirna UA 11 B8
Näfels CH 70 A4
Nafpaktos GR 116 D3
Nafplio GR 117 E4
Nagel D 52 D1
Nagele NL 42 C2
Naggen S 115 E13
Nagłowice PL 55 C5
Nagold D 61 B4
Nagore E 76 D1
Nagyatád H 74 B2
Nagybajom H 74 B2
Nagybaracska H 74 B3
Nagybátony H 65 C5
Nagyberény H 74 B3
Nagybörzsöny H 65 C4
Nagycenk H 64 C2
Nagydorog H 74 B3
Nagyfüged H 65 C6
Nagyhersány H 74 C3
Nagyigmánd H 64 C4
Nagyiván H 75 A5
Nagykanizsa H 74 B1
Nagykáta H 75 A4
Nagykonyi H 74 B3
Nagykőrös H 75 A4
Nagykörü H 75 A5
Nagylóc H 65 B5
Nagymágocs H 75 B5
Nagymányok H 74 B3
Nagymaros H 65 C4
Nagyoroszi H 65 B5
Nagyrábé H 75 A6
Nagyréde H 65 C5
Nagyszékely H 74 B3
Nagyszénás H 75 B5
Nagyszokoly H 74 B3
Nagytöke H 75 B5
Nagyvázsony H 74 B2
Nagyvenyim H 74 B3
Naharros E 95 B4
Nahe D 44 B2
Naidăş RO 85 B6
Naila D 52 C1
Nailloux F 77 C4
Nailsworth GB 29 B5
Naintré F 67 B5
Nairn GB 23 D5
Najac F 77 B4
Nájera E 89 B4
Nak H 74 B3
Nakksjø N 33 C6
Nakło nad Notecią PL 46 B3
Nakskov DK 39 E4
Nalda E 89 B4
Nälden S 115 D11
Nálepkovo SK 65 B6
Nalliers F 66 B3
Nallıhan TR 118 B6
Nalzen F 77 D4
Nalžouské Hory CZ 63 A4
Namdalseid N 114 C8
Náměšť nad Oslavou CZ 64 A2
Námestovo SK 65 A5
Namná N 34 B4
Namsos N 114 C8
Namsskogan N 115 C10
Namur B 49 C5
Namysłów PL 54 B2
Nançay F 68 A2
Nanclares de la Oca E 89 B4
Nancy F 60 B2
Nangis F 59 B4
Nannestad N 34 B3
Nant F 78 B2
Nanterre F 58 B3
Nantes F 66 A3
Nanteuil-le-Haudouin F 58 A3
Nantiat F 67 B6
Nantua F 69 B5
Nantwich GB 26 B3
Naoussa
Cyclades GR 117 E7
Imathia GR 116 B4
Napajedla CZ 64 A3
Napiwoda PL 47 B6
Naples = Nápoli I 103 C7
Nápoli = Naples I 103 C7
Nar S 37 E5
Nara N 32 A1
Naraval E 86 A4
Narberth GB 28 B3
Nærbø N 33 D2
Narbonne F 78 C1
Narbonne-Plage F 78 C2
Narbuvollen N 114 E8
Narcao I 110 C1
Nardò I 107 A5
Narken S 113 F11
Narmo N 34 B3
Narni I 102 A5
Naro I 108 B2
Naro Fominsk RUS 7 D14
Narón E 86 A2
Narros del Castillo E 94 B1
Narta HR 74 C1
Naruszewo PL 47 C6
Narva EST 7 B10
Narvik N 112 D6
Narzole I 80 B1
Näs FIN 36 B7
Nås S 36 B1
Näs S 37 E5
Näsåker S 115 D13
Năsăud RO 11 C8
Nasavrky CZ 64 A1
Nasbinals F 78 B2
Næsbjerg DK 39 D1
Näshull S 40 B5
Našice HR 74 C3
Nasielsk PL 47 C6
Naso I 109 A3
Nassau D 50 C3
Nassenfels D 62 B2
Nassenheide D 45 C5
Nassereith A 71 A5
Nässjö S 40 B4
Nastätten D 50 C3
Næstved DK 39 D4
Näsum S 41 C4
Näsviken S 115 D12
Natalinci SRB 85 B5
Naters CH 70 B3
Nater-Stetten D 62 B2
Nattavaara S 112 F9
Natters A 71 A6
Nattheim D 61 B6
Nättraby S 41 C5
Naturno I 71 B5
Naucelle F 77 B5
Nauders A 71 B5
Nauen D 45 C4
Naul IRL 19 C5
Naumburg D 52 B1
Naundorf D 52 C3
Naunhof D 52 B2
Naustdal N 32 A2
Nautijaur S 112 F8
Nautsi RUS 113 D18
Nava E 88 A1
Navacerrada E 94 B2
Navaconcejo E 93 A5
Nava de Arévalo E 94 B2
Nava de la Asunción E 94 A2
Nava del Rey E 88 C1
Navafriá E 94 A3
Navahermosa E 94 C2
Navahrudak BY 7 E8
Naval E 90 A3
Navalacruz E 94 B2
Navalcán E 94 B1
Navalcarnero E 94 B2
Navaleno E 89 C3
Navalmanzano E 94 A2
Navalmoral E 94 B2
Navalmoral de la Mata E 93 B5
Naválón E 96 C2
Navalonguilla E 93 A5
Navalperal de Pinares E 94 B2
Navalpino E 94 C2
Navaltalgordo E 94 B2
Navaltoril E 94 C2
Navaluenga E 94 B2
Navalvillar de Pela E 93 B5
Navan IRL 19 C5
Navaperal de Tormes E 93 A5
Navapolatsk BY 7 D10
Navarclés E 91 B4
Navarredonda de Gredos E 93 A5
Navarrenx F 76 C2
Navarrés E 96 B2
Navarrete E 89 B4
Navarrevisca E 94 B2
Navás E 91 B4
Navascués E 76 D1
Navas del Madroño E 93 B4
Navas del Rey E 94 B2
Navas del Sepillar E 100 B1
Navas de Oro E 94 A2
Navas de San Juan E 100 A2
Navasfrias E 93 A4
Nave I 71 C5
Nave de Haver P 93 A4
Nävekvarn S 37 D3
Navelli I 103 A6
Navenby GB 27 B5
Näverkärret S 37 C2
Naverstad S 35 D3
Navés E 91 B4
Navezuelas E 93 B5
Navia E 86 A4
Navia de Suarna E 86 B4
Navilly F 69 B5
Navlya RUS 7 E13
Năvodari RO 11 D10
Naxos GR 117 E7
Nay F 76 C2
Nazaré P 92 B1
Nazarje SLO 73 B4
Nazilli TR 119 E3
Nazza D 51 B6
Ndroq AL 105 B5
Nea Anchialos GR 116 C4
Nea Epidavros GR 117 E5
Nea Flippias GR 116 C2
Nea Kalikratia GR 116 B5
Nea Makri GR 117 D5
Nea Moudania GR 116 B5
Neap GB 22 A7
Nea Peramos GR 116 B6
Neapoli
Kozani GR 116 B3
Kriti GR 117 G7
Lakonia GR 117 F5
Nea Stira GR 117 D6
Neath GB 28 B4
Nea Visa GR 118 A1
Nea Zichni GR 116 A5
Nebljusi HR 83 B4
Neblo SLO 72 B3
Nebolchy RUS 7 B12
Nebra D 52 B1
Nebreda E 88 C3
Nechanice CZ 53 C5
Neckargemünd D 61 A4
Neckarsulm D 61 A5
Neda E 86 A2
Neded SK 64 B3
Nedelišće HR 73 B6
Nederweert NL 50 B1
Nedreberg N 34 B3
Nedre Gärdsjö S 36 B2
Nedre Soppero S 113 D10
Nedstrand N 33 C2
Nedvědice CZ 64 A2
Nędza PL 54 C3
Neede NL 50 A2
Needham Market GB 30 B5
Needingworth GB 30 B3
Neermoor D 43 B4
Neeroeteren B 50 B1
Neerpelt B 49 B6
Neesen D 51 A4
Neetze D 44 B2
Nefyn GB 26 C1
Negbina SRB 85 C4
Negotin SRB 11 D7
Negotino MK 116 A4
Negrar I 71 C5
Negredo E 95 A4
Negreira E 86 B2
Nègrepelisse F 77 B4
Negru Vodă RO 11 E10
Negueira de Muñiz E 86 A4
Neheim D 50 B3
Neila E 89 B4
Néive I 80 B2
Nejdek CZ 52 C2
Nekla PL 46 C3
Neksø DK 41 D5
Nelas P 92 A3
Nelaug N 33 D5
Nelidovo RUS 7 C12
Nelim FIN 113 D17
Nellingen D 61 B5
Nelson GB 26 B3
Neman RUS 6 D7
Nemea GR 117 E4
Nemesgörzsöny H 74 A2
Nemeskér H 74 A1
Nemesnádudvar H 75 B4
Nemesszalók H 74 A2
Németkér H 74 B3
Nemours F 58 B3
Nemška Loka SLO 73 C5
Nemšová SK 64 B4
Nenagh IRL 20 B3
Nenince SK 65 B5
Nenita GR 117 D8
Nenzing A 71 A4
Neochori GR 116 C3
Neo Chori GR 116 D3
Neon Petritsi GR 116 A5
Nepi I 102 A5
Nepomuk CZ 63 A4
Nérac F 77 B3
Neratovice CZ 53 C4
Nerchau D 52 B2
Néré F 67 C4
Neresheim D 61 B6
Nereto I 82 D2
Nerezine HR 82 B3
Nerežišća HR 83 C5
Neringa LT 6 D6
Néris-les Bains F 68 B2
Nerito I 103 A6
Nerja E 100 C2
Néronde F 69 C4
Nérondes F 68 B2
Nerpio E 101 A3
Nersingen D 61 B6
Nerva E 99 B4
Nervesa della Battáglia I 72 C2
Nervi I 80 B3
Nes
N 114 D6
Buskerud N 34 B1
Hedmark N 34 B2
NL 42 B2
Nesbyen N 32 B6
Neset N 114 F7
Nesflaten N 33 C3
Nesjahverfi IS 111 C10
Neskaupstaður IS 111 B12
Nesland N 33 C4
Neslandsvatn N 33 D6
Nesle F 59 A3
Nesna N 115 A10
Nesoddtangen N 34 C2
Nesovice CZ 64 A3
Nesselwang D 61 C6
Nesslau CH 71 A4
Nessmersiel D 43 B4
Nesso I 71 C4
Nesterov UA 11 A7
Nestorio GR 116 B3
Nesttun N 32 B2
Nesvady SK 64 C4
Nesvatnstemmen N 33 D5
Nether Stowey GB 29 B4
Netland N 33 D3
Netolice CZ 63 A5
Netphen D 50 C4
Netstal CH 70 A4
Nettancourt F 59 B5
Nettetal D 50 B2
Nettlingen D 51 A6
Nettuno I 102 B5
Neualbenreuth D 52 D2
Neubeckum D 50 B4
Neubrandenburg D 45 B5
Neubruchhausen D 43 C5
Neubukow D 44 A3
Neuburg D 62 B2
Neuchâtel CH 70 B1
Neu Darchau D 44 B2
Neudau A 73 A6
Neudietendorf D 51 C6
Neudorf D 61 A4
Neuenbürg D 61 B4
Neuenburg D 43 B4
Neuendorf D 45 A5
Neuenhagen D 45 C5
Neuenhaus D 42 C3
Neuenkirchen
Niedersachsen D 43 B6
Niedersachsen D 43 C5
Nordrhein-Westfalen D 50 A3
Nordrhein-Westfalen D 50 C3
Neuenrade D 50 B3
Neuenwalde D 43 B5
Neuerburg D 50 C2
Neufahrn
Bayern D 62 B2
Bayern D 62 B3
Neuf-Brisach F 60 B3
Neufchâteau
B 60 A1
F 60 B1
Neufchâtel-en-Bray F 58 A2
Neufchâtel-sur-Aisne F 59 A5
Neuflize F 59 A5
Neugersdorf D 53 C4
Neuhardenberg D 45 C6
Neuharlingersiel D 43 B4
Neuhaus
Bayern D 62 A2
Bayern D 63 B4
Niedersachsen D 43 B6
Niedersachsen D 44 B2
Niedersachsen D 51 B5
Neuhaus a Rennweg D 52 C1
Neuhausen
CH 61 C4
D 52 C3
Neuhausen ob Eck D 61 C4
Neuhof
Bayern D 62 A1
Hessen D 51 C5
Neuhofen an der Krems A 63 B5
Neuillé-Pont-Pierre F 67 A5
Neuilly-en-Thelle F 58 A3
Neuilly-le-Réal F 68 B3
Neuilly-l'Évêque F 60 C1
Neuilly-St Front F 59 A4
Neu-Isenburg D 51 C4
Neukalen D 45 B4
Neu Kaliss D 44 B3
Neukirch D 53 B4
Neukirchen
A 62 B4
Neukirchen *continued*
Hessen D 51 C5
Schleswig-Holstein D 39 E1
Neukirchen am Grossvenediger A 72 A2
Neukirchen bei Heiligen Blut D 62 A3
Neukloster D 44 B3
Neulengbach A 64 B1
Neulise F 68 C4
Neu Lübbenau D 53 A3
Neum BIH 84 D2
Neumagen D 60 A2
Neumarkt D 62 A2
Neumarkt am Wallersee A 63 C4
Neumarkt im Hausruckkreis A 63 B4
Neumarkt im Mühlkreis A 63 B5
Neumarkt im Steiermark A 73 A4
Neumarkt Sankt Veit D 62 B3
Neumünster D 44 A1
Neunburg vorm Wald D 62 A3
Neung-sur-Beuvron F 68 A1
Neunkirch
Luzern CH 70 A3
Schaffhausen CH 61 C4
Neunkirchen
A 64 C2
Nordrhein-Westfalen D 50 C3
Saarland D 60 A3
Neunkirchen am Brand D 62 A2
Neuötting D 62 B3
Neupetershain D 53 B4
Neuravensburg D 61 C5
Neureut D 61 A4
Neuruppin D 45 C4
Neusäss D 62 B1
Neusiedl A 64 C2
Neuss D 50 B2
Neussargues-Moissac F 68 C2
Neustadt
Bayern D 62 A1
Bayern D 62 A3
Bayern D 62 B2
Brandenburg D 44 C4
Hessen D 51 C5
Niedersachsen D 43 C6
Rheinland-Pfalz D 61 A4
Sachsen D 53 B4
Schleswig-Holstein D 44 A2
Thüringen D 52 C1
Thüringen D 52 C1
Neustadt-Glewe D 44 B3
Neustift im Stubaital A 71 A6
Neustrelitz D 45 B5
Neutal A 73 A6
Neutrebbin D 45 C6
Neu-Ulm D 61 B6
Neuves-Maisons F 60 B2
Neuvic
Corrèze F 68 C2
Dordogne F 77 A3
Neuville-aux-Bois F 58 B3
Neuville-de-Poitou F 67 B5
Neuville-les-Dames F 69 B5
Neuville-sur-Saône F 69 C4
Neuvy-le-Roi F 58 C1
Neuvy-Santour F 59 B4
Neuvy-St Sépulchre F 68 B1
Neuvy-sur-Barangeon F 68 A2
Neuwied D 50 C3
Neuzelle D 53 A4
Névache F 79 A5
Neveklov CZ 63 A5
Nevel RUS 7 D10
Neverfjord N 113 B12
Nevers F 68 B3
Nevesinje BIH 84 C3
Névez F 56 C2
Nevlunghavn N 35 D1
Nevşehir TR 16 B7
New Abbey GB 25 D4
New Aberdour GB 23 D6
New Alresford GB 31 C2
Newark-on-Trent GB 27 B5
Newbiggin-by-the-Sea GB 25 C6
Newbliss IRL 19 B4
Newborough GB 26 B1
Newbridge IRL 21 A5
Newbridge on Wye GB 29 A4
Newburgh
Aberdeenshire GB 23 D6
Fife GB 25 B4
Newbury GB 31 C2
Newby Bridge GB 26 A3
Newcastle GB 19 B6
Newcastle Emlyn GB 28 A3
Newcastleton GB 25 C5
Newcastle-under-Lyme GB 26 B3
Newcastle upon Tyne GB 25 D6
Newcastle West IRL 20 B2
Newchurch GB 29 A4
New Costessey GB 30 B5
New Cumnock GB 24 C3
Newent GB 29 B5
New Galloway GB 24 C3
Newham GB 31 C4
Newhaven GB 31 D4
Newington GB 31 C5
Newinn IRL 21 B4
Newlyn GB 28 C2
Newmachar GB 23 D6
Newmarket
Suffolk GB 30 B4
Western Isles GB 22 C2
IRL 20 B3
Newmarket-on-Fergus IRL 20 B3
New Mills GB 27 B4
New Milton GB 31 D2
New Pitsligo GB 23 D6
Newport
Isle of Wight GB 31 D2
Newport GB 29 B5
Pembrokeshire GB 28 A3
Telford & Wrekin GB 26 C3
Mayo IRL 18 C2
Tipperary IRL 20 B3
Newport-on-Tay GB 25 B5
Newport Pagnell GB 30 B3
Newquay GB 28 C2
New Quay GB 28 A3
New Radnor GB 29 A4
New Romney GB 31 D4
New Ross IRL 21 B5
Newry GB 19 B5
New Scone GB 25 B4
Newton Abbot GB 29 C4
Newton Arlosh GB 25 D4
Newton Aycliffe GB 27 A4
Newton Ferrers GB 28 C3
Newtonhill GB 23 D6
Newtonmore GB 23 D4
Newton Stewart GB 24 D3
Newtown
Herefordshire GB 29 A5
Powys GB 26 C2
Newtownabbey GB 19 B6
Newtownards GB 19 B6
Newtownbutler GB 19 B4
Newtown Cunningham IRL 19 B4
Newtownhamilton GB 19 B5
Newtownmountkennedy IRL 21 A5
Newtown St Boswells GB 25 C5
Newtown Sands IRL 20 B2
Newtownshandrum IRL 20 B3
Newtownstewart GB 19 B4
Nexon F 67 C6
Neyland GB 28 B3
Nibbiano I 80 B3
Nibe DK 38 C2
Nicaj-Shalë AL 105 A5
Nicastro I 106 C3
Niccone I 82 C1
Nice F 80 C1
Nickelsdorf A 64 C3
Nicolosi I 109 B4
Nicosia
CY 120 A2
I 109 B3
Nicótera I 106 C2
Nidda D 51 C5
Niğde TR 16 C7
Nidzica PL 47 B6
Niebla E 99 B4
Nieborów PL 55 A5
Niebüll D 39 E1
Niechanowo PL 46 C3
Niechorze PL 45 A7
Niedalino PL 46 A2
Niederaula D 51 C5
Niederbipp CH 70 A2
Niederbronn-les-Bains F 60 B3
Niederfischbach D 50 C3
Niedergörsdorf D 52 B2
Niederkrüchten D 50 B2
Niederndorf A 62 C3
Nieder-Olm D 61 A4
Niedersachswerfen D 51 B6
Niederstetten D 61 A5
Niederurnen CH 70 A4
Niederwölz A 73 A4
Niedoradz PL 53 B5
Niedzica PL 65 A6
Niegosławice PL 53 B5
Nieheim D 51 B5
Niemcza PL 54 C1
Niemegk D 52 A2
Niemodlin PL 54 C2
Nienburg
Niedersachsen D 43 C6
Sachsen-Anhalt D 52 B1
Niepołomice PL 55 C5
Nierstein D 61 A4
Niesky D 53 B4
Niestronno PL 46 C3
Nieświń PL 55 B5
Nieszawa PL 47 C4
Nieul-le-Dolent F 66 B3
Nieul-sur-Mer F 66 B3
Nieuw-Amsterdam NL 42 C3
Nieuw-Buinen NL 42 C3
Nieuwegein NL 49 A6
Nieuwe Niedorp NL 42 C1
Nieuwe-Pekela NL 42 B3
Nieuwerkerken B 49 C6
Nieuwe-schans NL 43 B4
Nieuwolda NL 42 B3
Nieuwpoort B 48 B3
Nieuw-Weerdinge NL 42 C3
Nigrita GR 116 B5
Nigüelas E 100 C2
Níjar E 101 C3
Nijemci HR 75 C4
Nijkerk NL 49 A6
Nijlen B 49 B5
Nijmegen NL 50 B1
Nijverdal NL 42 C3
Nikel RUS 113 C19
Nikinci SRB 85 B4
Nikiti GR 116 B5
Nikitsch A 74 A1
Nikkaluokta S 112 E8
Nikla H 74 B2
Niklasdorf A 73 A5
Nikolayev = Mykolayiv UA 11 C12
Nikšić MNE 84 D3
Nilivaara S 113 E10
Nîmes F 78 C3
Nimis I 72 B3
Nimtofte DK 39 C3
Nin HR 83 B4
Nindorf D 43 A6
Ninemilehouse IRL 21 B4
Ninove B 49 C5
Niort F 67 B4
Niš SRB 10 E6
Nisa P 92 B3
Niscemi I 109 B3
Nissafors S 40 B3
Nissan-lez-Ensérune F 78 C2
Nissedal N 33 C5
Nissumby DK 38 C1
Nisterud N 33 C6
Niton GB 31 D2
Nitra SK 64 B4
Nitrianske-Pravno SK 65 B4
Nitrianske Rudno SK 65 B4
Nitry F 59 C4
Nittedal N 34 B2
Nittenau D 62 A3
Nittendorf D 62 A2
Nivala FIN 3 E26
Nivelles B 49 C5
Nivenskoye RUS 47 A6
Nivnice CZ 64 B3
Nizhyn UA 11 A11
Nižná SK 65 A5
Nižná Boca SK 65 B5
Nižne Repaše SK 65 A6
Nizza Monferrato I 80 B2
Njarðvík IS 111 D3
Njegůsevo SRB 75 C4
Njivice HR 73 C4
Njurundabommen S 115 E14
Njutånger S 115 F14
Noailles F 58 A3
Noain E 76 D1
Noale I 72 C2
Noalejo E 100 B2
Noblejas E 95 C3
Noceda E 86 B4
Nocera Inferiore I 103 C7
Nocera Terinese I 106 B3
Nocera Umbra I 82 C1
Noceto I 81 B4
Noci I 104 C3
Nociglia I 107 A5
Nodeland N 33 D4
Nödinge S 38 B5
Nods F 69 A6
Noé F 77 C4
Noépoli I 106 A3
Noeux-les-Mines F 48 C3
Noez E 94 C2
Nogales E 93 C4
Nogara I 71 C6
Nogarejas E 87 B4
Nogaro F 76 C2
Nogent F 59 B6
Nogent l'Artaud F 59 B4
Nogent-le-Roi F 58 B2
Nogent-le-Rotrou F 58 B1
Nogent-sur-Seine F 59 B4
Nogent-sur-Vernisson F 58 C3
Nogersund S 41 C4
Noguera E 95 B5
Noguerones E 100 B1
Nohfelden D 60 A3
Nohn D 50 C2
Noia E 86 B2
Noicáttaro I 104 B2
Noirétable F 68 C3
Noirmoutier-en-l'Île F 66 A2
Noja E 89 A3
Nojewo PL 46 C2

Nokia FIN 3 F25
Nol S 38 B5
Nola I 103 C7
Nolay F 69 B4
Noli I 80 B2
Nolnyra S 36 B4
Nombela E 94 B2
Nomeny F 60 B2
Nomexy F 60 B2
Nonancourt F 58 B2
Nonant-le-Pin F 57 B6
Nonántola I 81 B5
Nonaspe E 90 B3
None I 80 B1
Nontron F 67 C5
Nonza F 102 A2
Noordhorn NL 42 B3
Noordwijk NL 49 A5
Noordwijkerhout NL 49 A5
Noordwolde NL 42 C3
Noppikoski S 36 A1
Nora S 37 C2
Nørager DK 38 C2
Norberg S 36 B2
Norboda S 36 B5
Nórcia I 82 D2
Nordagutu N 33 C6
Nordanås S 115 C15
Nordausques F 48 C3
Nordborg DK 39 D2
Nordby
Aarhus Amt. DK 39 D3
Ribe Amt. DK 39 D1
Norddeich D 43 B4
Norddorf D 43 A5
Norden D 43 B4
Nordenham D 43 B5
Norderhov N 34 B2
Norderney D 43 B4
Norderstapel D 43 A6
Norderstedt D 44 B2
Nordfjord N 113 B19
Nordfjordeid N 114 F3
Nordfold N 112 E4
Nordhalben D 52 C1
Nordhausen D 51 B6
Nordheim vor der Rhön D 51 C6
Nordholz D 43 B5
Nordhorn D 43 C4
Nordingrå S 115 E15
Nordkjosbotn N 112 C8
Nordli N 115 C10
Nördlingen D 61 B6
Nordmaling S 115 D16
Nordmark S 34 C6
Nordmela N 112 C4
Nord-Odal N 34 B3
Nordre Osen N 34 A3
Nordsinni N 34 B1
Nørdstedalsseter N 114 F4
Nordstemmen D 51 A5
Nordvågen N 113 B15
Nordwalde D 50 A3
Noreña E 88 A1
Noresund N 34 B1
Norg NL 42 B3
Norheimsund N 32 B3
Norie S 41 C4
Norma I 102 B5
Nornäs S 34 A5
Norrahammar S 40 B4
Norråker S 115 C12
Norrala S 36 A3
Norra Vi S 40 B5
Nørre Aaby DK 39 D2
Nørre Alslev DK 39 E4
Nørre Lyndelse DK 39 D3
Nørre Nebel DK 39 D1
Norrent-Fontes F 48 C3
Nørre Snede DK 39 D2
Nørresundby DK 38 B2
Nørre Vorupør DK 38 C1
Norrhult Klavreström S 40 B5
Norrköping S 37 D3
Norrskedika S 36 B5
Norrsundet S 36 B4
Norrtälje S 36 C5
Nors DK 38 B1
Norsbron S 35 C5
Norsholm S 37 D2
Norsjö S 115 C16
Nörten-Hardenberg D 51 B5
Northallerton GB 27 A4
Northampton GB 30 B3
North Berwick GB 25 B5
North Charlton GB 25 C6
Northeim D 51 B6
Northfleet GB 31 C4
North Frodingham GB 27 B5
North Kessock GB 23 D4
Northleach GB 29 B6
North Molton GB 28 B4
North Petherton GB 29 B4
Northpunds GB 22 B7
North Somercotes GB 27 B6
North Tawton GB 28 C4
North Thoresby GB 27 B5
North Walsham GB 30 B5
Northwich GB 26 B3
Norton GB 27 A5
Nortorf D 44 A1
Nort-sur-Erdre F 66 A3
Nörvenich D 50 C2
Norwich GB 30 B5
Norwick GB 22 A8
Nøsen N 32 B5
Nosivka UA 11 A11
Nossa Senhora do Cabo P 92 C1
Nossebro S 35 D4
Nössemark S 35 C3
Nossen D 52 B3
Notaresco I 103 A6
Noto I 109 C4
Notodden N 33 C6
Nottingham GB 27 C4
Nottuln D 50 B3
Nouan-le-Fuzelier F 68 A2
Nouans-les-Fontaines F 67 A6
Nougaroulet F 77 C3
Nouvion F 48 C2
Nouzonville F 59 A5
Nova H 74 B1
Nová Baňa SK 65 B4
Nová Bystrica SK 65 A5
Nová Bystřice CZ 63 A6
Nova Crnja SRB 75 C5
Novaféltria I 82 C1
Nova Gorica SLO 72 C3
Nova Gradiška HR 74 C2
Nováky SK 65 B4
Novalaise F 69 C5
Novales E 90 A2
Nova Levante I 71 B6
Novalja HR 83 B3
Nova Odesa UA 11 C11
Nová Paka CZ 53 C5
Nova Pazova SRB 85 B5
Nová Pec CZ 63 B4
Novara I 70 C3
Novara di Sicília I 109 A4
Nova Siri I 106 A3
Novate Mezzola I 71 B4
Nova Topola BIH 84 A2
Nova Varoš SRB 85 C4
Novaya Ladoga RUS 7 A12
Nova Zagora BG 11 E8
Nové Hrady CZ 63 B5
Novelda E 101 A5
Novellara I 81 B4
Nové Město SK 64 B3
Nové Město nad Metují CZ 53 C6
Nové Město na Moravě CZ 64 A2
Nové Město pod Smrkem CZ 53 C5
Nové Mitrovice CZ 63 A4
Noventa di Piave I 72 C2
Noventa Vicentina I 71 C6
Novés E 94 B2
Noves F 78 C3
Nové Sady SK 64 B3
Novés de Segre E 91 A4
Nové Strašeci CZ 53 C3
Nové Zámky SK 64 C4
Novgorod RUS 7 B11
Novhorod-Siverskyy UA 7 F12
Novi Bečej SRB 75 C5
Novi di Módena I 81 B4
Novigrad
Istarska HR 72 C3
Zadarsko-Kninska HR 83 B4
Novigrad Podravski HR 74 B1
Novi Kneževac SRB 75 B5
Novi Lígure I 80 B2
Noville B 50 C1
Novi Marof HR 73 B6
Novion-Porcien F 59 A5
Novi Pazar
BG 11 E9
SRB 85 C5
Novi Sad SRB 75 C4
Novi Slankamen SRB 75 C5
Novi Travnik BIH 84 B2
Novi Vinodolski HR 83 A3
Novo Brdo KOS 85 D6
Novohrad-Volynskyy UA 11 A9
Novo Mesto SLO 73 C5
Novo Miloševo SRB 75 C5
Novomirgorod UA 11 B11
Novorzhev RUS 7 C10
Novoselë AL 105 C5
Novo Selo
BIH 84 A2
KOS 85 D5
SRB 85 C5
Novoselytsya UA 11 B9
Novosil RUS 7 E14
Novosokolniki RUS 7 C10
Novoukrayinka UA 11 B11
Novoveská Huta SK 65 B6
Novovolynsk UA 11 A8
Novozybkov RUS 7 E11
Novska HR 74 C1
Nový Bor CZ 53 C4
Nový Bydžov CZ 53 C5
Novy-Chevrières F 59 A5
Novy Dwór Mazowiecki PL 47 C6
Nový-Hrozenkov CZ 64 A4
Nový Jičín CZ 64 A4
Novy Knin CZ 63 A5
Novyy Buh UA 11 C12
Nowa Cerekwia PL 54 C2
Nowa Karczma PL 47 A4
Nowa Kościoł PL 53 B5
Nowa Ruda PL 54 C1
Nowa Słupia PL 55 C6
Nowa Sól PL 53 B5
Nowa Wieś PL 47 B5
Nowa-Wieś Wielka PL 47 C4
Nowe PL 47 B4
Nowe Brzesko PL 55 C5
Nowe Grudze PL 55 A4
Nowe Miasteczko PL 53 B5
Nowe Miasto
Mazowieckie PL 47 C6
Mazowieckie PL 55 B5
Nowe Miasto Lubawskie PL 47 B5
Nowe Miasto nad Wartą PL 54 A2
Nowe Skalmierzyce PL 54 B3
Nowe Warpno PL 45 B6
Nowica PL 47 A5
Nowogard PL 45 B7
Nowogród Bobrzanski PL 53 B5
Nowogrodziec PL 53 B5
Nowosolna PL 55 B4
Nowy Dwór Gdański PL 47 A5
Nowy Korczyn PL 55 C5
Nowy Sącz PL 65 A6
Nowy Staw PL 47 A5
Nowy Targ PL 65 A6
Nowy Tomyśl PL 46 C2
Nowy Wiśnicz PL 65 A6
Noyalo F 56 C3
Noyal-Pontivy F 56 B3
Noyant F 67 A5
Noyelles-sur-Mer F 48 C2
Noyen-sur-Sarthe F 57 C5
Noyers F 59 C4
Noyers-sur-Cher F 67 A6
Noyers-sur-Jabron F 79 B4
Noyon F 59 A3
Nozay F 66 A3
Nuaillé F 66 A4
Nuaillé-d'Aunis F 66 B4
Nuars F 68 A3
Nubledo E 88 A1
Nuéno E 90 A2
Nuestra Señora Sa Verge des Pilar E 97 C1
Nueva E 88 A2
Nueva Carteya E 100 B1
Nuevalos E 95 A5
Nuits F 59 C5
Nuits-St Georges F 69 A4
Nule I 110 B2
Nules E 96 B2
Nulvi I 110 B1
Numana I 82 C2
Numansdorp NL 49 B5
Nümbrecht D 50 C3
Nunchritz D 52 B3
Nuneaton GB 30 B2
Nunnanen FIN 113 D13
N Unnaryd S 40 B3
Nuñomoral E 93 A4
Nunspeet NL 42 C2
Nuorgam FIN 113 B16
Núoro I 110 B2
Nurallao I 110 C2
Nuremberg = Nürnberg D 62 A2
Nurmes FIN 3 E28
Nürnberg = Nuremberg D 62 A2
Nurri I 110 C2
Nürtingen D 61 B5
Nus I 70 C2
Nusnäs S 36 B1
Nusplingen D 61 B4
Nuštar HR 74 C3
Nyåker S 115 D16
Nyáregyháza H 75 A4
Nyarlörinc H 75 B4
Nyasvizh BY 7 E9
Nybble S 35 C6
Nybergsund N 34 A4
Nybøl DK 39 E2
Nyborg DK 39 D3
Nybro S 40 C5
Nybster GB 23 C5
Nyby DK 39 E5
Nye S 40 B5
Nyékládháza H 65 C6
Nyergesujfalu H 65 C4
Nyhammar S 36 B1
Nyhyttan S 37 C1
Nyirád H 74 A2
Nyirbátor H 11 C7
Nyíregyháza H 10 C6
Nyker DK 41 D4
Nykil S 37 D2
Nykirke N 34 B2
Nykøbing
Falster DK 39 E4
Vestsjællands Amt. DK 39 D4
Nykøbing Mors DK 38 C1
Nyköping S 37 D4
Nykroppa S 35 C6
Nykvarn S 37 C4
Nykyrke S 37 D1
Nyland S 115 D14
Nylars DK 41 D4
Nymburk CZ 53 C5
Nynäshamn S 37 D4
Nyon CH 69 B6
Nyons F 79 B4
Nýřany CZ 63 A4
Nýrsko CZ 62 A4
Nyrud N 113 C18
Nysa PL 54 C2
Nysäter S 35 C4
Nyseter N 114 E5
Nyskoga S 34 B4
Nysted DK 44 A3
Nystrand N 35 C1
Nyúl H 64 C3
Nyvoll N 113 B12

O

Oadby GB 30 B2
Oakengates GB 26 C3
Oakham GB 30 B3
Oanes N 33 D3
Obalj BIH 84 C3
Oban GB 24 B2
O Barco E 86 B4
Obdach A 73 A4
Obejo E 100 A1
Oberammergau D 62 C2
Oberasbach D 62 A1
Oberau D 62 C2
Oberaudorf D 62 C3
Oberbruck F 60 C2
Oberdiessbach CH 70 B2
Oberdorf CH 70 A2
Oberdrauburg A 72 B2
Oberelsbach D 51 C6
Obere Stanz A 73 A5
Ober Grafendorf A 63 B6
Obergünzburg D 61 C6
Obergurgl A 71 B6
Oberhausen D 50 B2
Oberhof D 51 C6
Oberkirch D 61 B4
Oberkirchen D 51 B4
Oberkochen D 61 B6
Obermassfeld-Grimmenthal D 51 C6
Ober-Morlen D 51 C4
Obermünchen D 62 B2
Obernai F 60 B3
Obernberg A 63 B4
Obernburg D 61 A5
Oberndorf D 61 B4
Oberndorf bei Salzburg A 62 C3
Obernkirchen D 51 A5
Oberort A 73 A5
Oberpullendorf A 74 A1
Oberriet CH 71 A4
Oberröblingen D 52 B1
Oberrot D 61 A5
Oberstaufen D 61 C6
Oberstdorf D 71 A5
Obertauern A 72 A3
Obertilliach A 72 B2
Obertraubling D 62 B3
Obertraun A 72 A3
Obertrubach D 62 A2
Obertrum A 62 C4
Oberursel D 51 C4
Obervellach A 72 B3
Oberviechtach D 62 A3
Oberwart A 73 A6
Oberwesel D 50 C3
Oberwinter D 50 C3
Oberwölzstadt A 73 A4
Oberzell D 63 B4
Obice PL 55 C5
Óbidos P 92 B1
Obilić KOS 85 D6
Obing D 62 C3
Objat F 67 C6
Objazda PL 46 A3
Öblarn A 73 A4
Obninsk RUS 7 D14
O Bolo E 87 B3
Oborniki PL 46 C2
Oborniki Śląskie PL 54 B1
Obornjača SRB 75 C4
Oboyan RUS 7 F14
Obrenovac SRB 85 B5
Obrež
Srbija SRB 85 C6
Vojvodina SRB 85 B4
Obrigheim D 61 A5
Obrov SLO 73 C4
Obrovac
HR 83 B4
SRB 75 C4
Obrovac Sinjski HR 83 C5
Obruk TR 16 B6
Obrzycko PL 46 C2
Obudovac BIH 84 B3
Ocaña E 95 C3
O Carballiño E 86 B2
Occhiobello I 81 B5
Occimiano I 80 A2
Očevlja BIH 84 B3
Ochagavía E 76 D1
Ochakiv UA 11 C11
Ochiltree GB 24 C3
Ochla PL 53 B5
Ochotnica-Dolna PL 65 A6
Ochotnica-Górna PL 65 A6
Ochsenfurt D 61 A6
Ochsenhausen D 61 B5
Ochtendung D 50 C3
Ochtrup D 50 A3
Ocieka PL 55 C6
Ockelbo S 36 B3
Öckerö S 38 B4
Ocniţa MD 11 B9
O Corgo E 86 B3
Očová SK 65 B5
Ócsa H 75 A4
Öcseny H 74 B3
Öcsöd H 75 B5
Octeville F 57 A4
Ocypel PL 47 B4
Ödåkra S 41 C2
Odby DK 38 C1
Odda N 32 B3
Odder DK 39 D3
Ödeborg S 35 D3
Odeceixe P 98 B2
Odechów PL 55 B6
Odeleite P 98 B3
Odemira P 98 B2
Ödemiş TR 119 D2
Odensbacken S 37 C2
Odense DK 39 D3
Odensjö
Jönköping S 40 B4
Kronoberg S 40 C3
Oderberg D 45 C6
Oderzo I 72 C2
Odesa = Odessa UA 11 C11
Ödeshög S 37 D1
Odessa = Odesa UA 11 C11
Odiáxere P 98 B2
Odie GB 23 B6
Odiham GB 31 C3
Odintsovo RUS 7 D14
Odivelas P 98 A2
Odolanów PL 54 B2
Odón E 95 B5
Odorheiu Secuiesc RO 11 C8
Odoyevo RUS 7 E14
Odrowaz PL 55 B5
Odry CZ 64 A3
Odrzywół PL 55 B5
Ødsted DK 39 D2
Odžaci SRB 75 C4
Odžak BIH 84 A3
Oebisfelde D 44 C2
Oederan D 52 C3
Oeding D 50 B2
Oegstgeest NL 49 A5
Oelde D 50 B4
Oelsnitz D 52 C2
Oer-Erkenschwick D 50 B3
Oerlinghausen D 51 B4
Oettingen D 62 B1
Oetz A 71 A5
Oeventrop D 50 B4
Offanengo I 71 C4
Offenbach D 51 C4
Offenburg D 60 B3
Offida I 82 D2
Offingen D 61 B6
Offranville F 58 A2
Ofir P 87 C2
Ofte N 33 C5
Ofterschwang D 71 A5
Oggiono I 71 C4
Ogihares E 100 B2
Ogliastro Cilento I 103 C8
Ogliastro Marina I 103 C7
Ogmore-by-Sea GB 29 B4
Ogna N 33 D2
Ogre LV 6 C8
Ogrodzieniec PL 55 C4
Ogulin HR 73 C5
Ögur IS 111 A3
Ohanes E 101 B3
Ohey B 49 C6
Ohlstadt D 62 C2
Ohrdorf D 44 C2
Ohrdruf D 51 C6
Ohrid MK 116 A2
Öhringen D 61 A5
Oia E 87 B2
Oiã P 92 A2
Oiartzun E 76 C1
Oilgate IRL 21 B5
Oimbra E 87 C3
Oiselay-et-Grachoux F 69 A5
Oisemont F 48 D2
Oisterwijk NL 49 B6
Öja S 37 E5
Öje S 34 B5
Ojén E 100 C1
Ojrzeń PL 47 C6
Ojuelos Altos E 99 A5
Okalewo PL 47 B5
Okány H 75 B6
Okehampton GB 28 C3
Okhtyrka UA 7 F13
Oklaj HR 83 C5
Økneshamn N 112 D4
Okoč SK 64 C3
Okoličné SK 65 A5
Okonek PL 46 B2
Okonin PL 47 B4
Okřisky CZ 64 A1
Oksa PL 55 C5
Oksbøl DK 39 D1
Oksby DK 39 D1
Øksfjord N 113 B11
Øksna N 34 B3
Okučani HR 74 C2
Okulovka RUS 7 B12
Ólafsfjörður IS 111 A7
Ólafsvík IS 111 C2
ÖLagnö S 37 C5
Olagüe E 76 D1
Oland N 33 D5
Olargues F 78 C1
Oława PL 54 C2
Olazagutia E 89 B4
Olbernhau D 52 C3
Ólbia I 110 B2
Olching D 62 B2
Oldbury GB 29 B5
Oldcastle IRL 19 C4
Old Deer GB 23 D6
Oldeberkoop NL 42 C3
Oldeboorn NL 42 B2
Olden N 114 F3
Oldenbrok D 43 B5
Oldenburg
Niedersachsen D 43 B5
Schleswig-Holstein D 44 A2
Oldenzaal NL 50 A2
Olderdalen N 112 C9
Olderfjord N 113 B14
Oldersum D 43 B4
Oldervik N 112 C7
Oldham GB 26 B3
Oldisleben D 52 B1
Oldmeldrum GB 23 D6
Olea E 88 B2
Oleby S 34 B5
Olechów PL 55 B6
Oledo P 92 B3
Oléggio I 70 C3
Oleiros
Coruña E 86 A2
Coruña E 86 B1
P 92 B3
Oleksandriya
Kirovohrad UA 11 B12
Rivne UA 11 A9
Oleksandrovka UA 11 B12
Olen B 49 B5
Ølen N 33 C2
Olenegorsk RUS 3 B30
Olenino RUS 7 C12
Olesa de Montserrat E 91 B4
Oleśnica PL 54 B2
Olešnice CZ 64 A2
Olesno PL 54 C3
Oletta F 102 A2
Olette F 91 A5
Olevsk UA 11 A9
Olfen D 50 B3
Olgiate Comasco I 70 C3
Olginate I 71 C4
Ølgod DK 39 D1
Olgrinmore GB 23 C5
Olhão P 98 B3
Olhavo P 92 B1
Oliana E 91 A4
Olias del Rey E 94 C3
Oliena I 110 B2
Oliete E 90 C2
Olimbos GR 119 G2
Olite E 89 B5
Oliva E 96 C2
Oliva de la Frontera E 99 A4
Oliva de Mérida E 93 C4
Oliva de Plasencia E 93 A4
Olivadi I 106 C3
Olival P 92 B2
Olivar E 100 C2
Olivares E 99 B4
Olivares de Duero E 88 C2
Olivares de Júcar E 95 C4
Oliveira de Azeméis P 87 D2
Oliveira de Frades P 87 D2
Oliveira do Conde P 92 A3
Oliveira do Douro P 87 C2
Oliveira do Hospital P 92 A3
Olivenza E 93 C3
Olivet F 58 C2
Olivone CH 70 B3
Öljehult S 41 C5
Olkusz PL 55 C4
Ollerton GB 27 B4
Ollerup DK 39 D3
Olliergues F 68 C3
Ölmbrotorp S 37 C2
Ölme S 35 C5
Olmedilla de Alarcón E 95 C4
Olmedillo de Roa E 88 C3
Olmedo
E 88 C2
Olmedo continued
I 110 B1
Olmeto F 102 B1
Olmillos de Castro E 87 C4
Olmos de Ojeda E 88 B2
Olney GB 30 B3
Ołobok PL 54 B3
Olocau del Rey E 90 C2
Olofström S 41 C4
Olomouc CZ 64 A3
Olonets RUS 3 F30
Olonne-sur-Mer F 66 B3
Olonzac F 78 C1
Oloron-Ste Marie F 76 C2
Olost E 91 B5
Olot E 91 A5
Olovo BIH 84 B3
Olpe D 50 B3
Olsberg D 51 B4
Olsene B 49 C4
Olserud S 35 C5
Olshammar S 37 D1
Olshanka UA 11 B11
Olszanica PL 53 B5
Olsztyn
Śląskie PL 55 C4
Warmińsko-Mazurskie PL 47 B6
Olsztynek PL 47 B6
Olszyna PL 53 B5
Oltedal N 33 D3
Olten CH 70 A2
Olteniţa RO 11 D9
Olula del Rio E 101 B3
Ølve N 32 B2
Olvega E 89 C5
Olvera E 99 C5
Olympia GR 117 E3
Olzai I 110 B2
Omagh GB 19 B4
Omalos GR 117 G5
Omegna I 70 C3
Omiš HR 83 C5
Omišalj HR 73 C4
Ommen NL 42 C3
Omodhos CY 120 B1
Omoljica SRB 85 B5
On B 49 C6
Oña E 89 B3
Onano I 81 D5
O Näsberg S 34 B5
Oñati E 89 A4
Onda E 96 B2
Ondara E 96 C3
Ondarroa E 89 A4
Onesse-et-Laharie F 76 B1
Oneşti RO 11 C9
Onhaye B 49 C5
Onich GB 24 B2
Onil E 96 C2
Onis E 88 A2
Önnestad S 41 C4
Onsala S 38 B5
Ontinyent E 96 C2
Ontur E 101 A4
Onzain F 67 A6
Onzonilla E 88 B1
Oostburg NL 49 B4
Oostende B 48 B3
Oosterend NL 42 B2
Oosterhout NL 49 B5
Oosterwolde NL 42 C3
Oosterzele B 49 C4
Oosthuizen NL 42 C2
Oostkamp B 49 B4
Oostmalle B 49 B5
Oost-Vlieland NL 42 B2
Oostvoorne NL 49 B5
Ootmarsum NL 42 C3
Opalenica PL 54 A1
O Páramo E 86 B3
Opařany CZ 63 A5
Oparić SRB 85 C6
Opatija HR 73 C4
Opatów
Śląskie PL 54 C3
Świętokrzyskie PL 55 C6
Wielkopolskie PL 54 B3
Opatówek PL 54 B3
Opatowiec PL 55 C5
Opava CZ 64 A3
O Pedrouzo E 86 B2
Opeinde NL 42 B3
Oper Thalkirchdorf D 61 C6
Opglabbeerk B 49 B6
Opicina I 72 C3
O Pino E 86 B2
Oplotnica SLO 73 B5
Opmeer NL 42 C1
Opochka RUS 7 C10
Opočno CZ 53 C6
Opoczno PL 55 B5
Opole PL 54 C2
Oporów PL 55 A4
O Porriño E 87 B2
Opovo SRB 85 A5
Oppach D 53 B4
Oppdal N 114 E6
Oppeby
Östergötland S 40 A5
Södermanland S 37 D3
Oppedal N 32 A2
Oppegård N 34 C2
Oppenau D 61 B4
Oppenberg A 73 A4
Oppenheim D 61 A4
Óppido Lucano I 104 C1
Óppido Mamertina I 106 C2
Opponitz A 63 C5
Oppstad N 34 B3
Oprtalj HR 72 C3
Opsaheden S 34 B5
Ópusztaszer H 75 B5
Opuzen HR 84 C2
Ora
CY 120 B2
I 71 B6
Orada P 92 C3
Oradea RO 10 C6
Oradour-sur-Glane F 67 C6
Oradour-sur-Vayres F 67 C5
Oragonja SLO 72 C3
Orah BIH 84 D3
Orahova BIH 84 B2
Orahovica HR 74 C2
Orahovo BIH 74 C2
Oraison F 79 C4
Orajärvi FIN 113 F13
Orange F 78 B3
Orani I 110 B2
Oranienbaum D 52 B2
Oranienburg D 45 C5
Oranmore IRL 20 A3
Orašac SRB 85 B5
Orašje BIH 84 A3
Oravská Lesná SK 65 A5
Oravská Polhora SK 65 A5
Oravské Veselé SK 65 A5
Oravsky-Podzámok SK 65 A5
Orba E 96 C2
Orbacém P 87 C2
Orbais F 59 B4
Ørbæk DK 39 D3
Orbassano I 80 A1
Orbe CH 69 B6
Orbec F 58 A1
Orbetello I 102 A4
Orbetello Scalo I 102 A4
Orbigny F 67 A6
Ørby DK 39 C3
Örbyhus S 36 B4
Orce E 101 B3
Orcera E 101 A3
Orchamps-Vennes F 69 A6
Orches F 67 B5
Orchete E 96 C2
Orchies F 49 C4
Orchowo PL 47 C4
Orcières F 79 B5
Ordes E 86 A2
Ordhead GB 23 D6
Ordino AND 91 A4
Ordizia E 89 A4
Orduña E 89 B4
Ore S 36 A2
Orea E 95 B5
Orebić HR 84 D2
Örebro S 37 C2
Öregcsertö H 75 B4
Öregrund S 36 B5
Orehoved DK 39 E4
Orel RUS 7 E14
Orellana E 93 B5
Orellana de la Sierra E 93 B5
Ören TR 119 E2
Örencik TR 118 C4
Orestiada GR 118 A1
Organyà E 91 A4
Orgaz E 94 C3
Orgelet F 69 B5
Ørgenvika N 34 B1
Orgères-en-Beauce F 58 B2
Orgibet F 77 D3
Orgnac-l'Aven F 78 B3
Orgon F 79 C4
Orgósolo I 110 B2
Orhaneli TR 118 C3
Orhangazi TR 118 B4
Orhei MD 11 C10
Orhomenos GR 116 D4
Oria E 101 B3
Ória I 104 C3
Origny-Ste Benoite F 59 A4
Orihuela E 101 A5
Orihuela del Tremedal E 95 B5
Orikum AL 105 C5
Oriola P 92 C3
Oriolo I 106 A3
Oriovac HR 74 C2
Orissaare EST 6 B7
Oristano I 110 C1
Öriszentpéter H 73 B6
Ørje N 35 C3
Orjiva E 100 C2
Orkanger N 114 D6
Örkelljunga S 41 C3
Örkény H 75 A4
Orlamünde D 52 C1
Orlane KOS 85 D6
Orléans F 58 C2
Orlová CZ 65 A4
Orlovat SRB 75 C5
Ormea I 80 B1
Ormelet N 35 C2
Ormemyr N 33 C6
Ormilia GR 116 B5
Ormos GR 117 E6
Ormož SLO 73 B6
Ormskirk GB 26 B3
Ornans F 69 A6
Ornäs S 36 B2
Ørnes N 112 F2
Orneta PL 47 A6
Ørnhøj DK 39 C1
Ornö S 37 C5
Örnsköldsvik S 115 D15
Orolik HR 75 C3
Orom SRB 75 C4
Oron-la-Ville CH 70 B1
Oronsko PL 55 B5
Oropa I 70 C2
Oropesa
Castellón de la Plana E 96 A3
Toledo E 93 B5
O Rosal E 87 C2
Orosei I 110 B2
Orosháza H 75 B5
Oroslavje HR 73 C5
Oroszlány H 74 A3
Oroszlo H 74 B3
Orotelli I 110 B2
Orozko E 89 A4
Orphir GB 23 C5
Orpington GB 31 C4
Orreaga-Roncesvalles E 76 C1
Orrefors S 40 C5
Orrviken S 115 D11
Orsa S 36 A1
Orsara di Púglia I 103 B8
Orsay F 58 B3
Orscholz D 60 A2
Orsennes F 67 B6
Orserum S 40 A4
Orsha BY 7 D11
Orsières CH 70 B2
Örsjö S 40 C5
Ørslev DK 39 D4
Örslösa S 35 D4
Orsogna I 103 A7
Orsomarso I 106 B2
Orşova RO 11 D7
Ørsta N 114 E3
Ørsted DK 38 C3
Örsundsbro S 37 C4
Ortaca TR 119 F3
Ortakent TR 119 E2
Ortaklar TR 119 E2
Ortaköy TR 16 B7
Orta Nova I 104 B1
Orte I 102 A5
Ortenburg D 63 B4
Orth A 64 B2
Orthez F 76 C2
Ortigueira E 86 A3
Ortilla E 90 A2
Ortisei I 72 B1
Orţişoara RO 75 C6
Ortnevik N 32 A3
Orton GB 26 A3
Ortona I 103 A7
Ortrand D 53 B3
Orubica HR 74 C2
Ørum DK 38 C2
Orune I 110 B2
Orusco E 95 B3
Orvalho P 92 A3
Orvault F 66 A3
Ørvella N 33 C6
Orvieto I 82 D1
Orvínio I 102 A5
Oryakhovo BG 11 E7
Orzesze PL 54 C3
Orzinuovi I 71 C4
Orzivécchi I 71 C4
Os
Hedmark N 34 B3
Hedmark N 114 E8
Osann-Monzel D 60 A2
Osaonica SRB 85 C5
Osbruk S 40 B4
Øsby DK 39 D2
Osby S 41 C3
Oščadnica SK 65 A4
Oschatz D 52 B3
Oschersleben D 52 A1
Óschiri I 110 B2
Osciłowo PL 47 C6
Osdorf D 44 A2
Osečina SRB 85 B4
Osečná CZ 53 C4
Oseja de Sajambre E 88 A1
Osek CZ 53 C3
Osen N 114 C7
Osera de Ebro E 90 B2
Osidda I 110 B2
Osie PL 47 B4
Osieck PL 55 B6
Osieczna
Pomorskie PL 47 B4
Wielkopolskie PL 54 B1
Osieczno PL 46 B1
Osiek
Kujawsko-Pomorskie PL 47 B5
Kujawsko-Pomorskie PL 47 C4
Pomorskie PL 47 B4
Świętokrzyskie PL 55 C6
Osiek nad Notecią PL 46 B3
Osielsko PL 47 B4
Osijek HR 74 C3
Osilnica SLO 73 C4
Ósilo I 110 B1
Ósimo I 82 C2
Osinja BIH 84 B2
Osintorf BY 7 D11
Osipaonica SRB 85 B6
Osjaków PL 54 B3
Oskamull GB 24 B1
Oskarshamn S 40 B6
Oskarström S 40 C2
Oslany SK 65 B4
Oslavany CZ 64 A2
Ošlje HR 84 D2
Oslo N 34 C2
Øsløs DK 38 B1
Osmancık TR 16 A7
Osmaneli TR 118 B4
Ösmo S 37 D4
Osmolin PL 55 A4
Osnabrück D 50 A4
Ośno Lubuskie PL 45 C6
Osoblaha CZ 54 C2
Osor HR 83 B3
Osorno E 88 B2
Øsoyra N 32 A2
Osøyro N 32 B2
Ospakseyri IS 111 B4
Os Peares E 86 B3
Ospedaletti I 80 C1
Ospitaletto I 71 C5
Oss NL 49 B6
Ossa de Montiel E 95 D4
Ossi I 110 B1
Ossjøen N 32 B5
Ossun F 76 C2
Ostanå S 41 C4
Ostanvik S 36 A2
Ostashkov RUS 7 C12
Östavall S 115 E12
Ostbevern D 50 A3
Østborg N 115 C10
Østby N 34 A4
Osted DK 39 D4
Ostenfeld D 43 A6
Oster UA 11 A11
Øster Assels DK 38 C1
Osterburg D 44 C3
Osterburken D 61 A5
Österbybruk S 36 B4
Østerbyhavn DK 38 B4
Österbymo S 40 B5
Ostercappeln D 43 C5
Österfärnebo S 36 B3
Osterfeld D 52 B1
Österforse S 115 D14
Osterhever D 43 A5
Osterhofen D 62 B4
Osterholz-Scharmbeck D 43 B5
Øster Hornum DK 38 C2
Øster Hurup DK 38 C3
Østerild DK 38 B1
Øster Jølby DK 38 C1
Österlövsta S 36 B4
Øster-marie DK 41 D5
Ostermiething A 62 B3
Osterode am Harz D 51 B6
Ostersiel D 43 A5
Östersund S 115 D11
Øster Tørslev DK 38 C3
Östervåla S 36 B4
Östervallskog S 35 C3
Østervrå DK 38 B3
Osterwieck D 51 B6
Osterzell D 62 C1
Ostffyasszonyfa H 74 A2
Östfora S 36 C4
Östhammar S 36 B5
Ostheim F 60 B3
Ostheim vor der Rhön D 51 C6
Osthofen D 61 A4
Ostiano I 71 C5
Ostíglia I 81 A5
Ostiz E 76 D1
Östmark S 34 B4
Östnor S 36 A1
Ostojićevo SRB 75 C5
Ostra I 82 C2
Östra Amtervik S 35 C5
Östraby S 41 D3
Ostrach D 61 C5
Östra Husby S 37 D3
Östra Ljungby S 41 C3
Östra Ryd S 37 D3
Ostrau D 52 B3
Ostrava CZ 64 A4
Østre Halsen N 35 C2
Ostrhauderfehn D 43 B4
Ostritz D 53 B4
Ostróda PL 47 B5
Ostroh UA 11 A9
Ostrołęka PL 6 E6
Ostropole PL 46 B2
Ostroróg PL 46 C2
Ostros MNE 105 A5
Ostrošovac BIH 83 B4
Ostrov
CZ 52 C2
RUS 7 C10
Ostrov nad Oslavou CZ 64 A1
Ostrówek PL 54 B3
Ostrowiec PL 46 A2
Ostrowiec-Świętokrzyski PL 55 C6
Ostrowite PL 47 B5
Ostrów Mazowiecka PL 6 E6
Ostrowo PL 47 C4
Ostrów Wielkopolski PL 54 B2
Ostrožac BIH 84 C2
Ostrzeszów PL 54 B2
Ostseebad Kühlungsborn D 44 A3
Ostuni I 104 C3
Osuna E 99 B5
Osvětimany CZ 64 A3
Oswestry GB 26 C2
Oświęcim PL 55 C4
Osztopán H 74 B2
Oteiza E 89 B5
Otelec RO 75 C5
Oteo E 89 A3
Oterbekk N 35 C2
Otero de Herreros E 94 B2
Otero de O Bodas E 87 C4
Othem S 37 E5
Otley GB 27 B4
Otmuchów PL 54 C2
Otočac HR 83 B4
Otok
Splitsko-Dalmatinska HR 83 C5
Vukovarsko-Srijemska HR 74 C3
Otoka BIH 83 B5
Otranto I 107 A5
Otrić HR 83 B5
Otrícoli I 102 A5
Otrokovice CZ 64 A3
Otta N 114 F6
Ottana I 110 B2
Ottaviano I 103 C7
Ottenby S 41 C6
Ottendorf-Okrilla D 53 B3
Ottenhöfen D 61 B4
Ottenschlag A 63 B6
Ottensheim A 63 B5
Otterbach D 60 A3
Otterbäcken S 35 D6
Otterberg D 60 A3
Otterburn GB 25 C5
Otter Ferry GB 24 B2
Otterndorf D 43 B5
Ottersburg D 43 B6
Ottersweier D 61 B4
Otterup DK 39 D3
Ottery St Mary GB 29 C4
Ottignies B 49 C5
Ottmarsheim F 60 C3
Ottobeuren D 61 C6
Öttömös H 75 B4
Ottone I 80 B3
Ottsjö S 115 D10
Ottweiler D 60 A3
Ötvöskónyi H 74 B2
Otwock PL 55 A6
Ouanne F 59 C4
Ouarville F 58 B2
Oucques F 58 C2
Oud-Beijerland NL 49 B5
Ouddorp NL 49 B4
Oudemirdum NL 42 C2
Oudenaarde B 49 C4
Oudenbosch NL 49 B5
Oudenburg B 48 B3
Oude-Pekela NL 43 B4
Oude-Tonge NL 49 B5
Oudewater NL 49 A5
Oud Gastel NL 49 B5
Oudon F 66 A3
Oue DK 38 C2
Oughterard IRL 20 A2
Ouguela P 93 B3
Ouistreham F 57 A5
Oulainen FIN 3 D26
Oulchy-le-Château F 59 A4
Oullins F 69 C4
Oulmes F 67 B4
Oulton GB 30 B5
Oulton Broad GB 30 B5
Oulu FIN 3 D26
Oulx I 79 A5
Oundle GB 30 B3
Ouranopoli GR 116 B6
Ourém P 92 B2
Ourense E 87 B3
Ourique P 98 B2
Ourol E 86 A3
Ouroux-en-Morvan F 68 A3
Ousdale GB 23 C5
Oust F 77 D4
Outakoski FIN 113 C15
Outeiro P 92 A2
Outeiro de Rei E 86 A3
Outes E 86 B2
Outokumpu FIN 3 E28
Outreau F 48 C2
Outwell GB 30 B4
Ouzouer-le-Marché F 58 C2
Ouzouer-sur-Loire F 58 C3
Ovada I 80 B2
Ovar P 87 D2
Ovelgönne D 43 B5
Overath D 50 C3
Overbister GB 23 B6
Øverbygd N 112 D8
Overdinkel NL 50 A3
Överenhörna S 37 C4
Overhalla N 114 C8
Overijse B 49 C5
Over-jerstal DK 39 D2
Överkalix S 3 C25
Overlade DK 38 C2
Överlida S 40 B2
Överö FIN 36 B7
Overpelt B 49 B6
Overton GB 26 C3
Övertorneå S 3 C25
Överum S 40 B6
Ovidiopol UA 11 C11
Oviedo E 88 A1
Oviglio I 80 B2
Ovíndoli I 103 A6
Ovodda I 110 B2
Øvre Årdal N 32 A4
Øvrebygd N 33 D3
Øvre Rendal N 114 F8
Øvre Sirdal N 33 D3
Övre Soppero S 113 D10
Övre Ullerud S 35 C5
Ovruch UA 7 F10
Ovtrup DK 39 D1
Owińska PL 46 C2
Oxaback S 40 B2
Oxberg S 34 A6
Oxelösund S 37 D4
Oxenholme GB 26 A3
Oxford GB 31 C2
Oxie S 41 D3
Oxilithos GR 116 D6
Oxted GB 31 C4
Oyaca TR 118 C7
Øye N 32 A5
Øyenkilen N 35 C2
Øyer N 34 A2
Øyeren N 34 B4
Oyfiell N 33 C5
Øygärdslia N 33 D5
Oykel Bridge GB 22 D4
Øymark N 35 C3
Oyonnax F 69 B5
Øyslebø N 33 D4
Øystese N 32 B3
Oyten D 43 B6
Øyuvsbu N 33 C4
Ozaeta E 89 B4
Ozalj HR 73 C5
Ożarów PL 55 C6
Ożarów Maz PL 55 A5
Ožbalt SLO 73 B5
Ózd H 65 B6
Ožd'any SK 65 B5
Ozieri I 110 B2
Ozimek PL 54 C3
Ozimica BIH 84 B3
Ozora H 74 B3
Ozorków PL 55 B4
Ozzano Monferrato I 80 A2

P

Paal B 49 B6
Pabianice PL 55 B4
Pacanów PL 55 C6
Paceco I 108 B1
Pachino I 109 C4
Pačir SRB 75 C4
Pack A 73 A5
Paços de Ferreira P 87 C2
Pacov CZ 63 A6
Pacsa H 74 B2
Pacy-sur-Eure F 58 A2
Paczków PL 54 C2
Padany RUS 3 E30
Padborg DK 39 E2
Padej SRB 75 C5
Padene HR 83 B5
Paderborn D 51 B4
Paderne P 98 B2
Padiham GB 26 B3
Padina SRB 75 C5
Padinska Skela SRB 85 B5
Padornelo P 87 C2
Pádova I 72 C1
Padragkút H 74 A2
Padria I 110 B1
Padrón E 86 B2
Padru I 110 B2
Padstow GB 28 C3
Padul E 100 B2
Padula I 104 C1
Paduli I 103 B7
Paesana I 79 B6
Paese I 72 C2
Pag HR 83 B4
Pagani I 103 C7
Pagánica I 103 A6
Pagánico I 81 D5
Pagl ieta I 103 A7
Pagny-sur-Moselle F 60 B2
Páhi H 75 B4
Pahkakumpu FIN 113 F17
Pahl D 62 C2
Paide EST 7 B8
Paignton GB 29 C4
Pailhès F 77 C4
Paimboeuf F 66 A2

Paimpol F 56 B2
Paimpont F 57 B3
Painswick GB 29 B5
Painten D 62 B2
Paisley GB 24 C3
Pajala S 113 E12
Pajares E 88 A1
Pajares de los Oteros E 88 B1
Pajęczno PL 54 B3
Páka H 74 B1
Pakość PL 47 C4
Pakosławice PL 54 C2
Pakoštane HR 83 C4
Pakrac HR 74 C2
Paks H 74 B3
Palacios de la Sierra E 89 C3
Palaciòs de la Valduerna E 88 B1
Palacios del Sil E 86 B4
Palacios de Sanabria E 87 B4
Palaciosrubios E 94 A1
Palafrugell E 91 B6
Palagiano I 104 C3
Palagonía I 109 B3
Paláia I 81 C4
Palaiseau F 58 B3
Palaj AL 105 A5
Palamas GR 116 C4
Palamòs E 91 B6
Palanga LT 6 D6
Palanzano I 81 B4
Palárikovo SK 64 B4
Palas de Rei E 86 B3
Palata I 103 B7
Palatna KOS 85 C6
Palau I 110 A2
Palavas-les-Flots F 78 C2
Palazuelos de la Sierra E 89 B3
Palazzo Adriano I 108 B2
Palazzo del Pero I 81 C5
Palazzolo Acréide I 109 B3
Palazzolo sull Oglio I 71 C4
Palazzo San Gervásio I 104 C1
Palazzuolo sul Senio I 81 B5
Paldiski EST 6 B8
Pale BIH 84 C3
Palekastro GR 117 G8
Palena I 103 B7
Palencia E 88 B2
Palenciana E 100 B1
Paleochora GR 117 G5
Paleometokho CY 120 A2
Palermo I 108 A2
Paleros GR 116 D2
Palestrina I 102 B5
Pálfa H 74 B3
Palfau A 63 C5
Palhaça P 92 A2
Palheiros da Tocha P 92 A2
Palheiros de Quiaios P 92 A2
Paliaopoli GR 117 E6
Palić SRB 75 B4
Palidoro I 102 B5
Palinuro I 106 A2
Paliouri GR 116 C5
Paliseul B 59 A6
Pallanza I 70 C3
Pallares E 99 A4
Pallaruelo de Monegros E 90 B2
Pallas Green IRL 20 B3
Pallerols E 91 A4
Palling D 62 B3
Palluau F 66 B3
Palma P 92 C2
Palma Campánia I 103 C7
Palma del Río E 99 B5
Palma de Mallorca E 97 B2
Palma di Montechiaro I 108 B2
Palmádula I 110 B1
Palmanova I 72 C3
Palma Nova E 97 B2
Palmela P 92 C2
Palmerola E 91 A5
Palmi I 106 C2
Pälmonostora H 75 B4
Palo del Colle I 104 B2
Palojärvi FIN 113 D12
Palojoensuu FIN 113 D12
Palomares E 101 B4
Palomares del Campo E 95 C4
Palomas E 93 C4
Palombara Sabina I 102 A5
Palos de la Frontera E 99 B4
Palotaboszok H 74 B3
Palotás H 65 C5
Pals E 91 B6
Pålsboda S 37 C2
Paluzza I 72 B3
Pamhagen A 64 C2
Pamiers F 77 C4
Pamiętowo PL 46 B3
Pampaneira E 100 C2
Pamparato I 80 B1
Pampilhosa
Aveiro P 92 A2
Coimbra P 92 A3
Pampliega E 88 B3
Pamplona E 76 D1
Pampow D 44 B3
Pamukçu TR 118 C2
Pamukkale TR 119 E4
Pamukova TR 118 B5
Panagyurishte BG 11 E8
Pancalieri I 80 B1
Pančevo SRB 85 B5
Pancey F 59 B6
Pancorvo E 89 B3
Pancrudo E 90 C1
Pandino I 71 C4
Pandrup DK 38 B2
Panenský-Týnec CZ 53 C3
Panes E 88 A2
Panevėžys LT 6 D8
Pangbourne GB 31 C2
Panissières F 69 C4
Panki PL 54 C3
Pannes F 58 B3
Panningen NL 50 B1
Pannonhalma H 74 A2
Pano Lefkara CY 120 B2
Pano Panayia CY 120 B1
Panormos GR 117 E7
Panschwitz-Kuckau D 53 B4
Pansdorf D 44 B2
Pantano de Cíjara E 94 C2
Pantelleria I 108 C1
Panticosa E 76 D2
Pantín E 86 A2
Pantoja E 94 B3
Pantón E 86 B3
Panxon E 87 B2
Páola I 106 B3
Paola M 107 C5
Pápa H 74 A2
Papasídero I 106 B2
Pápateszér H 74 A2
Papenburg D 43 B4
Paphos CY 120 B1
Pappenheim D 62 B1
Paprotnia PL 55 A5
Parábita I 107 A5
Paraćin SRB 85 C6
Parád H 65 C6
Parada
Bragança P 87 C4
Viseu P 92 A2
Paradas E 99 B5
Paradela E 86 B3
Parades de Rubiales E 94 A1
Paradinas de San Juan E 94 B1
Paradiso di Cevadale I 71 B5
Paradyź PL 55 B5
Parainen FIN 6 A7
Parakhino Paddubye RUS 7 B12
Parakka S 113 E10
Paralimni CY 120 A2
Parallo Astros GR 117 E4
Paramé F 57 B4
Paramithia GR 116 C2
Páramo E 86 A4
Páramo del Sil E 86 B4
Parandaça P 87 C3
Paravadella E 86 A3
Paray-le-Monial F 68 B4
Parceiros P 92 B2
Parcey F 69 A5
Parchim D 44 B3
Parcice PL 54 B3
Pardilla E 88 C3
Pardubice CZ 53 C5
Paredes
E 95 B4
P 87 C2
Paredes de Coura P 87 C2
Paredes de Nava E 88 B2
Paredes de Siguenza E 95 A4
Pareja E 95 B4
Parennes F 57 B5
Parenti I 106 B3
Parentis-en-Born F 76 B1
Parey D 44 C3
Parfino RUS 7 C11
Parga GR 116 C2
Pargny-sur-Saulx F 59 B5
Pari-Gagné F 69 B4
Parigné-l'Évêque F 58 C1
Parikkala FIN 3 F28
Paris F 58 B3
Parisot F 77 B4
Parkalompolo S 113 E11
Parkano FIN 3 E25
Parknasilla IRL 20 C2
Parla E 94 B3
Parlavá E 91 A6
Parma I 81 B4
Parndorf A 64 C2
Párnica SK 65 A5
Parnu EST 6 B8
Parolis E 101 A3
Paros GR 117 E7
Parrillas E 94 B1
Parsberg D 62 A2
Parstein D 45 C6
Partakko FIN 113 C16
Partanna I 108 B1
Parthenay F 67 B4
Partinico I 108 A2
Partizani SRB 85 B5
Partizánske SK 65 B4
Partney GB 27 B6
Påryd S 40 C5
Parysów PL 55 B6
Parzymiechy PL 54 B3
Paşcani RO 11 C9
Pasewalk D 45 B5
Pašina Voda MNE 85 C4
Påskallavik S 40 B6
Pasłęk PL 47 A5
Pašman HR 83 C4
Passage East IRL 21 B5
Passage West IRL 20 C3
Passail A 73 A5
Passais F 57 B5
Passau D 63 B4
Passegueiro P 92 A2
Passignano sul Trasimeno I 82 C1
Passo di Tréia I 82 C2
Passopisciaro I 109 B4
Passow D 45 B6
Passy F 70 C1
Pastavy BY 7 D9
Pástena I 103 B7
Pastrana E 95 B4
Pastrengo I 71 C5
Pasym PL 47 B6
Pásztó H 65 C5
Pata SK 64 B3
Patay F 58 B2
Pateley Bridge GB 27 A4
Paterek PL 46 B3
Paterna E 96 B2
Paterna del Campo E 99 B4
Paterna del Madera E 101 A3
Paterna de Rivera E 99 C5
Paternion A 72 B3
Paternò I 109 B3
Paternópoli I 103 C8
Patersdorf D 62 A3
Paterswolde NL 42 B3
Patitiri GR 116 C5
Patmos GR 119 E1
Patna GB 24 C3
Pątnow PL 54 A3
Patoniva FIN 113 C16
Patoprtti FIN 113 E18
Patos AL 105 C5
Patra = Patras GR 117 D3
Patras = Patra GR 117 D3
Patreksfjörður IS 111 B2
Patrickswell IRL 20 B3
Patrimonio F 102 A2
Patrington GB 27 B5
Pattada I 110 B2
Pattensen
Niedersachsen D 44 B2
Niedersachsen D 51 A5
Patterdale GB 26 A3
Patti I 109 A3
Páty H 74 A3
Pau F 76 C2
Pauillac F 66 C4
Paularo I 72 B3
Paulhaguet F 68 C3
Paulhan F 78 C2
Paulilátino I 110 B1
Pauliström S 40 B5
Paullo I 71 C4
Paulstown IRL 21 B4
Pausa D 52 C1
Pauträsk S 115 C14
Pavia
I 71 C4
P 92 C2
Pavias E 96 B2
Pavilly F 58 A1
Pāvilosta LV 6 C6
Pavino Polje MNE 85 C4
Pavullo nel Frignano I 81 B4
Pawłowice PL 54 B2
Pawlowice PL 54 D3
Paxi GR 116 C2
Payallar TR 119 F6
Payerne CH 70 B1
Paymogo E 98 B3
Payrac F 77 B4
Pazardzhik BG 11 E8
Pazaryeri TR 118 B4
Pazin HR 72 C3
Paziols F 78 D1
Pčelić HR 74 C2
Peal de Becerro E 100 B2
Peasmarsh GB 31 D4
Peć KOS 85 D5
Péccioli I 81 C4
Pécel H 75 A4
Pechao P 98 B3
Pechenga RUS 3 B29
Pechenizhyn UA 11 B8
Pecica RO 75 B6
Pećinci SRB 85 B4
Pecka SRB 85 B4
Peckelsheim D 51 B5
Pečory RUS 7 C9
Pécs H 74 B3
Pécsvárad H 74 B3
Pečurice MNE 105 A5
Peczniew PL 54 B3
Pedaso I 82 C2
Pedavena I 72 B1
Pedérobba I 72 C1
Pedersker DK 41 D4
Pedescala I 71 C6
Pedrafita E 86 B3
Pedrajas de San Esteban E 88 C2
Pedralba E 96 B2
Pedralba de la Praderia E 87 B4
Pedraza E 94 A3
Pedreguer E 96 C3
Pedrera E 100 B1
Pedro Abad E 100 B1
Pedro Bernardo E 94 B2
Pedroche E 100 A1
Pedrógão P 98 A3
Pedrogao P 92 A3
Pedrógão P 92 B2
Pedrógão Grande P 92 B2
Pedrola E 90 B1
Pedro-Martinez E 100 B2
Pedro Muñoz E 95 C4
Pedrosa del Rey E 88 C1
Pedrosa del Rio Urbel E 88 B3
Pedrosa de Tobalina E 89 B3
Pedrosillo de los Aires E 94 B1
Pedrosillo el Ralo E 94 A1
Pędzewo PL 47 B4
Peebles GB 25 C4
Peel GB 26 A1
Peenemünde D 45 A5
Peer B 49 B6
Pega P 93 A3
Pegalajar E 100 B2
Pegau D 52 B2
Peggau A 73 A5
Pegli I 80 B2
Pegnitz D 62 A2
Pego E 96 C2
Pegões-Estação P 92 C2
Pegões Velhos P 92 C2
Pęgów PL 54 B1
Pegswood GB 25 C6
Peguera E 97 B2
Pehlivanköy TR 118 A1
Peine D 51 A6
Peisey-Nancroix F 70 C1
Peissenberg D 62 C2
Peiting D 62 C1
Peitz D 53 B4
Péjo I 71 B5
Pelagićevo BIH 84 B3
Pelahustán E 94 B2
Pełczyce PL 46 B1
Pelhřimov CZ 63 A6
Pélissanne F 79 C4
Pelkosenniemi FIN 113 E16
Pellegrino Parmense I 81 B3
Pellegrue F 76 B3
Pellérd H 74 B3
Pellestrina I 72 C2
Pellevoisin F 67 B6
Pellizzano I 71 B5
Pello
FIN 113 F13
S 113 F12
Peloche E 93 B5
Pelplin PL 47 B4
Pelussin F 69 C4
Pély H 75 A5
Pembroke GB 28 B3
Pembroke Dock GB 28 B3
Peñacerrada E 89 B4
Penacova P 92 A2
Peña de Cabra E 94 B1
Peñafiel E 88 C2
Penafiel P 87 C2
Peñaflor E 99 B5
Peñalba de Santiago E 86 B4
Peñalsordo E 93 C5
Penalva do Castelo P 92 A3
Penamacôr P 93 A3
Peñaparda E 93 A4
Peñaranda de Bracamonte E 94 B1
Peñaranda de Duero E 89 C3
Peñarroya de Tastavins E 90 C3
Peñarroya-Pueblonuevo E 93 C5
Peñarrubla E 86 B3
Penarth GB 29 B4
Peñascosa E 101 A3
Peñas de San Pedro E 101 A4
Peñausende E 88 C1
Penc H 65 C5
Pencoed GB 29 B4
Pendalofos GR 116 B3
Pendeen GB 28 C2
Pendine GB 28 B3
Pendueles E 88 A2
Penedono P 87 D3
Penela P 92 A2
Pénestin F 56 C3
Penhas Juntas P 87 C3
Peniche P 92 B1
Penicuik GB 25 C4
Penig D 52 C2
Penilhos P 98 B3
Peñíscola E 90 C3
Penistone GB 27 B4
Penkridge GB 26 C3
Penkun D 45 B6
Penmarch F 56 C1
Pennabilli I 82 C1
Penne I 103 A6
Penne-d'Agenais F 77 B3
Pennes I 71 B6
Pennyghael GB 24 B1
Peno RUS 7 C12
Penpont GB 25 C4
Penrhyndeudraeth GB 26 C1
Penrith GB 26 A3
Penryn GB 28 C2
Pentraeth GB 26 B1
Penybontfawr GB 26 C2
Penygroes
Carmarthenshire GB 28 B3
Gwynedd GB 26 B1
Penzance GB 28 C2
Penzberg D 62 C2
Penzlin D 45 B5
Pepeljevac SRB 85 C6
Pepinster B 50 C1
Peqin AL 105 B5
Pér H 64 C3
Pera Boa P 92 A3
Perachora GR 117 D4
Perafita P 87 C2
Peraleda de la Mata E 93 B5
Peraleda del Zaucejo E 93 C5
Peraleda de San Román E 93 B5
Perales de Alfambra E 90 C1
Perales del Puerto E 93 A4
Perales de Tajuña E 95 B3
Peralta E 89 B5
Peralta de la Sal E 90 B3
Peralva P 98 B3
Peralveche E 95 B4
Perama GR 117 G6
Perast MNE 105 A4
Perbál H 65 C4
Perchtoldsdorf A 64 B2
Percy F 57 B4
Perdasdefogu I 110 C2
Perdiguera E 90 B2
Peredo P 87 C4
Peregu Mare RO 75 B5
Pereiro
Faro P 98 B3
Guarda P 87 D3
Santarém P 92 B2
Pereiro de Aguiar E 87 B3
Perelada E 91 A6
Perelejos de las Truchas E 95 B5
Pereña E 87 C4
Pereruela E 88 C1
Pereyaslav-Khmelnytskyy UA 11 A11
Pérfugas I 110 B1
Perg A 63 B5
Pérgine Valsugana I 71 B6
Pérgola I 82 C1
Pergusa I 109 B3
Periam RO 75 B5
Periana E 100 C1
Périers F 57 A4
Périgueux F 67 C5
Perino I 80 B3
Perjasica HR 73 C5
Perkáta H 74 A3
Perković HR 83 C5
Perleberg D 44 B3
Perlez SRB 75 C5
Përmet AL 116 B2
Pernarec CZ 62 A4
Pernek SK 64 B3
Pernes P 92 B2
Pernes-les-Fontaines F 79 B4
Pernik BG 11 E7
Pernink CZ 52 C2
Pernitz A 64 C1
Peroguarda P 98 A2
Pérols F 78 C2
Péronne F 59 A3
Péronnes B 49 C5
Pero Pinheiro P 92 C1
Perorrubio E 94 A3
Perosa Argentina I 79 B6
Perozinho P 87 C2
Perpignan F 91 A5
Perranporth GB 28 C2
Perranzabuloe GB 28 C2
Perrecy-les-Forges F 69 B4
Perrero I 79 B6
Perrignier F 69 B6
Perros-Guirec F 56 B2
Persan F 58 A3
Persberg S 34 C6
Persenbeug A 63 B6
Pershore GB 29 A5
Perstorp S 41 C3
Perth GB 25 B4
Pertisau A 72 A1
Pertoča SLO 73 B6
Pertuis F 79 C4
Perućac SRB 85 C4
Perúgia I 82 C1
Perušić HR 83 B4
Péruwelz B 49 C4
Pervomaysk UA 11 B11
Perwez B 49 C5
Pesadas de Burgos E 89 B3
Pesaguero E 88 A2
Pésaro I 82 C1
Pescantina I 71 C5
Pescara I 103 A7
Pescasséroli I 103 B6
Peschici I 104 B2
Peschiera del Garda I 71 C5
Péscia I 81 C4
Pescina I 103 A6
Pescocostanzo I 103 B7
Pescopagano I 103 C8
Pesco Sannita I 103 B7
Peshkopi AL 116 A2
Pesmes F 69 A5
Pesnica SLO 73 B5
Peso da Régua P 87 C3
Pesquera de Duero E 88 C2
Pessac F 76 B2
Pestovo RUS 7 B13
Petalidi GR 117 F3
Pétange L 60 A1
Petas GR 116 C3
Peteranec HR 74 B1
Peterborough GB 30 B3
Peterculter GB 23 D6
Peterhead GB 23 D7
Peterlee GB 25 D6
Petersfield GB 31 C3
Petershagen
Brandenburg D 45 C5
Brandenburg D 45 C6
Nordrhein-Westfalen D 43 C5
Petershausen D 62 B2
Peterswell IRL 20 A3
Pétervására H 65 B6
Petilia Policastro I 107 B3
Petin E 87 B3
Pětipsy CZ 52 C3
Petkus D 52 B3
Petlovac HR 74 C3
Petlovača SRB 85 B4
Petőfiszallás H 75 B4
Petra E 97 B3
Petralia Sottana I 109 B3
Petrčane HR 83 B4
Petrelë AL 105 B5
Petrella Tifernina I 103 B7
Petrer E 101 A5
Petreto-Bicchisano F 102 B1
Petrich BG 116 A5
Petrijevci HR 74 C3
Petrinja HR 73 C6
Petrodvorets RUS 7 B10
Pétrola E 101 A4
Petronà I 107 B3
Petronell A 64 B2
Petroşani RO 11 D7
Petrovac
MNE 105 A4
SRB 85 B6
Petrovaradin SRB 75 C4
Petrovice
BIH 84 B3
CZ 53 C3
Pettenbach A 63 C5
Pettigo IRL 19 B4
Petworth GB 31 D3
Peuerbach A 63 B4
Peuntenansa E 88 A2
Peurasuvanto FIN 113 E15
Pevensey Bay GB 31 D4
Peveragno I 80 B1
Pewsey GB 29 B6
Pewsum D 43 B4
Peyrat-le-Château F 68 C1
Peyrehorade F 76 C1
Peyriac-Minervois F 77 C5
Peyrins F 79 A4
Peyrissac F 67 C6
Peyrolles-en-Provence F 79 C4
Peyruis F 79 B4
Pézarches F 59 B3
Pézenas F 78 C2
Pezinok SK 64 B3
Pezuls F 77 B3
Pfaffenhausen D 61 B6
Pfaffenhofen
Bayern D 61 B6
Bayern D 62 B2
Pfaffenhoffen F 60 B3
Pfäffikon CH 70 A3
Pfarrkirchen D 62 B3
Pfeffenhausen D 62 B2
Pfetterhouse F 70 A2
Pforzheim D 61 B4
Pfreimd D 62 A3
Pfronten D 61 C6
Pfullendorf D 61 C5
Pfullingen D 61 B5
Pfunds A 71 B5
Pfungstadt D 61 A4
Pfyn CH 61 C4
Phalsbourg F 60 B3
Philippeville B 49 C5
Philippsreut D 63 B4
Philippsthal D 51 C5
Piacenza I 81 A3
Piacenza d'Adige I 72 C1
Piádena I 71 C5
Piana F 102 A1
Piana Crixia I 80 B2
Piana degli Albanesi I 108 B2
Piana di Monte Verna I 103 B7
Piancastagnáio I 81 D5
Piandelagotti I 81 B4
Pianella
Abruzzi I 103 A7
Toscana I 81 C5
Pianello Val Tidone I 80 B3
Pianoro I 81 B5
Pians A 71 A5
Pías E 87 B4
Pias P 98 A3
Piaseczno PL 55 A6
Piasek PL 45 C6
Piaski PL 47 A5
Piastów PL 55 A5
Piaszcyna PL 46 A3
Piątek PL 55 A4
Piatra Neamţ RO 11 C9
Piazza al Sérchio I 81 B4
Piazza Armerina I 109 B3
Piazza Brembana I 71 C4
Piazze I 81 D5
Piazzola sul Brenta I 72 C1
Picassent E 96 B2
Piccione I 82 C1
Picerno I 104 C1
Picher D 44 B3
Pickering GB 27 A5
Pico I 103 B6
Picón E 94 C2
Picquigny F 58 A3
Piechowice PL 53 C5
Piecnik PL 46 B2
Piedicavallo I 70 C2
Piedicroce F 102 A2
Piedimonte Etneo I 109 B4
Piedimonte Matese I 103 B7
Piedimulera I 70 B3
Piedipaterno I 82 D1
Piedrabuena E 94 C2
Piedraescrita E 94 C2
Piedrafita E 88 A1
Piedrahita E 93 A5
Piedralaves E 94 B2
Piedras Albas E 93 B4
Piedras Blancas E 88 A1
Piegaro I 82 D1
Piekary Śl. PL 54 C3
Piekoszów PL 55 C5
Pieksämäki FIN 3 E27
Pielenhofen D 62 A2
Pielgrzymka PL 53 B5
Pieniężno PL 47 A6
Pieńsk PL 53 B5
Pienza I 81 C5
Piera E 91 B4
Pieranie PL 47 C4
Pierowall GB 23 B6
Pierre-Buffière F 67 C6
Pierrecourt F 60 C1
Pierre-de-Bresse F 69 B5
Pierrefeu-du-Var F 79 C5
Pierrefitte-Nestalas F 76 D2
Pierrefitte-sur-Aire F 59 B6
Pierrefonds F 59 A3
Pierrefontaine-les-Varans F 69 A6
Pierrefort F 78 B1
Pierrelatte F 78 B3
Pierrepont
Aisne F 59 A4
Meurthe-et-Moselle F 60 A1
Piesendorf A 72 A2
Pieštany SK 64 B3
Pieszkowo PL 47 A6
Pieszyce PL 54 C1
Pietarsaari FIN 3 E25
Pietragalla I 104 C1
Pietra Ligure I 80 B2
Pietralunga I 82 C1
Pietramelara I 103 B7
Pietraperzía I 109 B3
Pietrasanta I 81 C4
Pietravairano I 103 B7
Pieve del Cáiro I 80 A2
Pieve di Bono I 71 C5
Pieve di Cadore I 72 B2
Pieve di Cento I 81 B5
Pieve di Soligo I 72 C2
Pieve di Teco I 80 B1
Pievepélago I 81 B4
Pieve Santo Stefano I 82 C1
Pieve Torina I 82 C2
Piges GR 116 C3
Píglio I 102 B6
Pigna I 80 C1
Pignan F 78 C2
Pignataro Maggiore I 103 B7
Pijnacker NL 49 A5
Pikalevo RUS 7 B13
Piła PL 46 B2
Pilar de la Horadada E 101 B5
Pilas E 99 B4
Pilastri I 81 B5
Piława PL 55 B6
Piława Górna PL 54 C1
Piławki PL 47 B5
Pilchowice PL 54 C3
Pilea GR 116 B5
Pilgrimstad S 115 E12
Pili
Dodekanisa GR 119 F2
Trikala GR 116 C3
Pilica PL 55 C4
Pilis H 75 A4
Piliscaba H 65 C4
Pilisszántó H 65 C4
Pilisvörösvár H 65 C4
Pilos GR 117 F3
Pilsting D 62 B3
Pilszcz PL 54 C2
Pilterud N 34 C2
Pilu RO 75 B6
Pilzno PL 55 D6
Pina de Ebro E 90 B2
Piñar E 100 B2
Pınarbaşı TR 118 C1
Pınarhisar TR 118 A2
Pinas F 77 C3
Pincehely H 74 B3
Pinchbeck GB 30 B3
Pińczów PL 55 C5
Pineda de la Sierra E 89 B3
Pineda de Mar E 91 B5
Pinerella I 82 B1
Pinerolo I 79 B6
Pineta Grande I 103 C6
Pineto I 103 A7
Piney F 59 B5
Pinggau A 73 A6
Pinhal Novo P 92 C2
Pinhão P 87 C3
Pinheiro
Aveiro P 87 C2
Aveiro P 87 D2
Pinheiro Grande P 92 B2
Pinhel P 87 D3
Pinhoe GB 29 C4
Pinilla E 101 A4
Pinilla de Toro E 88 C1
Pinkafeld A 73 A6
Pinneberg D 43 B6
Pinnow D 53 B4
Pino F 102 A2
Pino del Rio E 88 B2
Pino de Val E 86 B2
Pinofranqueado E 93 A4
Pinols F 78 A2
Piñor E 86 B2
Pinos del Valle E 100 C2
Pinoso E 101 A4
Pinos Puente E 100 B2
Pinsk BY 7 E9
Pinto E 94 B3
Pinzano al Tagliamento I 72 B2
Pinzio P 93 A3
Pinzolo I 71 B5
Pióbbico I 82 C1
Piombino I 81 D4
Pionki PL 55 B6
Pionsat F 68 B2
Pióraco I 82 C1
Piornal E 93 A5
Piotrkowice PL 55 C5
Piotrków-Kujawski PL 47 C4
Piotrków Trybunalski PL 55 B4
Piotrowice PL 55 A6
Piotrowo PL 46 C2
Piove di Sacco I 72 C2
Piovene I 71 C6
Piperskärr S 40 B6
Pipriac F 57 C4
Piraeus = Pireas GR 117 E5
Piran SLO 72 C3
Pireas = Piraeus GR 117 E5
Piré-sur-Seiche F 57 B4
Pirgi GR 117 D7
Pirgos
Ilia GR 117 E3
Kriti GR 117 G7
Piriac-sur-Mer F 66 A2
Piringsdorf A 73 A6
Pirmasens D 60 A3
Pirna D 53 C3
Pirnmill GB 24 C2
Pirot SRB 11 E7
Pirovac HR 83 C4
Pirttivuopio S 112 E8
Pisa I 81 C4
Pisany F 66 C4
Pisarovina HR 73 C5
Pischelsdorf in der Steiermark A 73 A5
Pişchia RO 75 C6
Pisciotta I 106 A2
Písek CZ 63 A5
Pisogne I 71 C5
Pissos F 76 B2
Pissouri CY 120 B1
Pisticci I 104 C2
Pistóia I 81 C4
Piteå S 3 D24
Piteşti RO 11 D8
Pithiviers F 58 B3
Pitigliano I 102 A4
Pitkyaranta RUS 3 F29
Pitlochry GB 25 B4
Pitomača HR 74 C2
Pitres E 100 C2
Pittentrail GB 23 D4
Pitvaros H 75 B5
Pivka SLO 73 C4
Pivnice SRB 75 C4
Piwniczna PL 65 A6
Pizarra E 100 C1
Pizzano I 71 B5
Pizzighettone I 71 C4
Pizzo I 106 C3
Pízzoli I 103 A6
Pizzolungo I 108 A1
Pjätteryd S 40 C4
Plabennec F 56 B1
Placencia E 89 A4
Plaffeien CH 70 B2
Plaisance
Gers F 76 C3
Haute-Garonne F 77 C4
Tarn F 77 C5
Plaka GR 116 C7
Plan E 90 A3
Planá CZ 62 A3
Planánad Lužnici CZ 63 A5
Plaňany CZ 53 C5
Planchez F 68 A4
Plancoët F 57 B3
Plancy-l'Abbaye F 59 B4
Plan-de-Baix F 79 B4
Plandište SRB 75 C6
Plan-d'Orgon F 78 C3
Plánice CZ 63 A4
Planina
SLO 73 B5
SLO 73 C4
Plankenfels D 62 A2
Plasencia E 93 A4
Plasenzuela E 93 B4
Plaški HR 83 A4
Plassen
Buskerud N 32 B4
Hedmark N 34 A4
Plášťovce SK 65 B5
Plasy CZ 63 A4
Plat HR 84 D3
Platamona Lido I 110 B1
Platania I 106 B3
Platanos GR 117 G5
Platí I 106 C3
Platičevo SRB 85 B4
Platja d'Aro E 91 B6
Plattling D 62 B3
Plau D 44 B4
Plaue
Brandenburg D 44 C4
Thüringen D 51 C6
Plauen D 52 C2
Plav MNE 85 D4
Plavecký Mikuláš SK 64 B3
Plavinas LV 7 C8
Plavna SRB 75 C4
Plavnica SK 65 A6
Plavno HR 83 B5
Plavsk RUS 7 E14
Playben F 56 B2
Pléaux F 68 C2
Pleine-Fourgères F 57 B4
Pleinfeld D 62 A1
Pleinting D 62 B4
Plélan-le-Grand F 57 C3
Plémet F 56 B3
Pléneuf-Val-André F 56 B3
Plentzia E 89 A4
Plérin F 56 B3
Plešivec SK 65 B6
Plessa D 52 B3
Plessé F 66 A3
Plestin-les-Grèves F 56 B2
Pleszew PL 54 B2
Pleternica HR 74 C2
Plettenberg D 50 B3
Pleubian F 56 B2
Pleumartin F 67 B5
Pleumeur-Bodou F 56 B2
Pleurs F 59 B4
Pleven BG 11 E8
Plevlja MNE 85 C4
Plevnik-Drienové SK 65 A4
Pleyber-Christ F 56 B2
Pliego E 101 B4
Pliešovce SK 65 B5
Plitvička Jezera HR 83 B4
Plitvički Ljeskovac HR 83 B4
Ploaghe I 110 B1
Ploče HR 84 C2
Plochingen D 61 B5
Płock PL 47 C5
Ploemeur F 56 C2
Ploërmel F 56 C3
Ploeuc-sur-Lie F 56 B3
Plogastel St Germain F 56 C1
Plogoff F 56 B1
Ploieşti RO 11 D9
Plomari GR 118 D1
Plombières-les-Bains F 60 C2
Plomin HR 82 A3
Plön D 44 A2
Plonéour-Lanvern F 56 C1
Płonia PL 45 B6
Płońsk PL 47 C6
Płoskinia PL 47 A5
Plössberg D 62 A3
Płoty PL 45 B7
Plouagat F 56 B2
Plouaret F 56 B2
Plouarzel F 56 B1
Plouay F 56 C2
Ploubalay F 57 B3
Ploubazlanec F 56 B2
Ploudalmézeau F 56 B1
Ploudiry F 56 B1
Plouescat F 56 B1
Plouézec F 56 B3
Plougasnou F 56 B2
Plougastel-Daoulas F 56 B1
Plougonven F 56 B2
Plougonver F 56 B2
Plougrescant F 56 B2
Plouguenast F 56 B3
Plouguerneau F 56 B1
Plouha F 56 B3
Plouhinec F 56 B1
Plouigneau F 56 B2
Ploumanach F 56 B2
Plounévez-Quintin F 56 B2
Plouray F 56 B2
Plouzévédé F 56 B1
Plovdiv BG 11 E8
Plozévet F 56 C1
Plumbridge GB 19 B4
Pluméliau F 56 C3
Plumlov CZ 64 A3
Plungė LT 6 D6
Pluty PL 47 A6
Pluvigner F 56 C3
Plužine
BIH 84 C3
MNE 84 C3
Płużnica PL 47 B4
Plymouth GB 28 C3
Plymstock GB 28 C3
Płytnica PL 46 B2
Plyusa RUS 7 B10
Plzeň CZ 63 A4
Pniewy PL 46 C2
Pobes E 89 B4
Poběžovice CZ 62 A3
Pobiedziska PL 46 C3
Pobierowo PL 45 A6
Pobla de Segur E 90 A3
Pobladura del Valle E 88 B1
Pobla-Tornesa E 96 A3
Pobra de Trives E 87 B3
Pobra do Brollón E 86 B3
Pobra do Caramiñal E 86 B2
Pobudje BIH 85 B4
Počátky CZ 63 A6
Poceirão P 92 C2
Pochep RUS 7 E12
Pochinok RUS 7 D12
Pöchlarn A 63 B6
Pociecha PL 55 B5
Pockau D 52 C3
Pocking D 63 B4
Pocklington GB 27 B5
Poda MNE 85 D4
Podbořany CZ 52 C3
Podbrdo SLO 72 B3
Podbrezová SK 65 B5
Podčetrtek SLO 73 B5
Poddębice PL 54 B3
Poděbrady CZ 53 C5
Podence P 87 C4
Podensac F 76 B2
Podenzano I 80 B3
Podersdorf am See A 64 C2
Podgaje PL 46 B2
Podgora HR 84 C2
Podgóra PL 55 B6
Podgorač HR 74 C3
Podgorica MNE 105 A5
Podgorie AL 116 B2
Podgrad SLO 73 C4
Podhájska SK 65 B4
Podkova BG 116 A7
Podlapača HR 83 B4
Podlejki PL 47 B6
Podlužany SK 65 B4
Podnovlje BIH 84 B3
Podolie SK 64 B3
Podolínec SK 65 A6
Podolsk RUS 7 D14
Podporozhy RUS 7 A13
Podromanija BIH 84 C3
Podturen HR 74 B1
Podujevo KOS 85 D6
Podvín CZ 64 B2
Podwilk PL 65 A5
Poetto I 110 C2
Poggendorf D 45 A5
Poggiardo I 107 A5
Poggibonsi I 81 C5
Pòggio a Caiano I 81 C5
Poggio Imperiale I 103 B8
Pòggio Mirteto I 102 A5
Pòggio Moiano I 102 A5
Pòggio Renatico I 81 B5
Pòggio Rusco I 81 B5
Pöggstall A 63 B6
Pogny F 59 B5
Pogorzela PL 54 B2
Pogorzelice PL 46 A3
Pogradec AL 116 B2
Pogrodzie PL 47 A5
Pohorelá SK 65 B6
Pohořelice CZ 64 B2
Pohronská Polhora SK 65 B5
Poiares P 92 A2
Poio E 86 B2
Poirino I 80 B1
Poisson F 68 B4
Poissons F 59 B6
Poissy F 58 B3
Poitiers F 67 B5
Poix-de-Picardie F 58 A2
Poix-Terron F 59 A5
Pokka FIN 113 D14
Pokój PL 54 C2
Pokupsko HR 73 C5
Pol E 86 A3
Pola RUS 7 C11
Pol a Charra GB 22 D1
Pola de Allande E 86 A4
Pola de Laviana E 88 A1
Pola de Lena E 88 A1
Pola de Siero E 88 A1
Pola de Somiedo E 86 A4
Polaincourt-et-Clairefontaine F 60 C2
Połajewo PL 46 C2
Polán E 94 C2
Polanica-Zdrój PL 54 C1
Połaniec PL 55 C6
Polanów PL 46 A2
Polatlı TR 118 C7
Polatsk BY 7 D10
Polch D 50 C3
Pólczno PL 46 A3
Połczyn-Zdrój PL 46 B2
Polegate GB 31 D4
Poleñino E 90 B2
Polesella I 81 B5
Polessk RUS 6 D6
Polgárdi H 74 A3
Polhov Gradec SLO 73 B4
Police PL 45 B6
Police nad Metují CZ 53 C6
Polichnitos GR 116 C8
Polička CZ 64 A2
Poličnik HR 83 B4
Policoro I 106 A3
Policzna PL 55 B6
Poligiros GR 116 B5
Polignano a Mare I 104 C3
Poligny F 69 B5
Polis CY 120 A1
Polístena I 106 C3
Polizzi Generosa I 109 B3
Poljana SRB 85 B6
Poljanák HR 83 B4
Poljčane SLO 73 B5
Polje BIH 84 B2
Poljice
BIH 83 B5
BIH 84 B3
Poljna SRB 85 C6
Polkowice PL 53 B6
Polla I 104 C1
Pollas E 88 C1
Pöllau A 73 A5
Polleben D 52 B1
Pollença E 97 B3
Pollenfeld D 62 B2
Pollfoss N 114 F4
Póllica I 106 A2
Polminhac F 77 B5
Polná CZ 63 A6
Polna RUS 7 B10
Polne PL 46 B2
Polomka SK 65 B5
Polonne UA 11 A9
Polperro GB 28 C3
Polruan GB 28 C3
Pöls A 73 A4
Polska Cerekiew PL 54 C3
Poltár SK 65 B5
Põltsamaa EST 7 B8
Polyarny RUS 3 B30
Polyarnyye Zori RUS 3 C30
Polzela SLO 73 B5
Pomarance I 81 C4
Pomarez F 76 C2
Pomárico I 104 C2
Pomáz H 65 C5
Pombal P 92 B2
Pomeroy GB 19 B5
Pomézia I 102 B5
Pomichna UA 11 B11
Pommard F 69 A4
Pommelsbrunn D 62 A2
Pomonte I 81 D4
Pomorie BG 11 E9
Pomos CY 120 A1
Pompei I 103 C7
Pompey F 60 B2
Pomposa I 82 B1
Poncin F 69 B5
Pondorf D 62 B2
Ponferrada E 86 B4
Pongoma RUS 3 D31
Poniec PL 54 B1
Ponikva SLO 73 B5
Poniky SK 65 B5
Pons F 67 C4
Ponsacco I 81 C4
Pont I 70 C2
Pont-a-Celles B 49 C5
Pontacq F 76 C2
Pontailler-sur-Saône F 69 A5
Pont-a-Marcq F 49 C4
Pont-à-Mousson F 60 B2
Pontão P 92 B2
Pontardawe GB 28 B4
Pontarddulais GB 28 B3
Pontarion F 68 C1
Pontarlier F 69 B6
Pontassieve I 81 C5
Pontaubault F 57 B4
Pont-Audemer F 58 A1
Pontaumur F 68 C2
Pont-Aven F 56 C2
Pont Canavese I 70 C2
Pontcharra F 69 C6
Pontcharra-sur-Turdine F 69 C4
Pontchâteau F 66 A2
Pont-Croix F 56 B1
Pont-d'Ain F 69 B5
Pont de-Beauvoisin F 69 C5
Pont-de-Buis-lès-Quimerch F 56 B1
Pont-de-Chéruy F 69 C5
Pont de Dore F 68 C3
Pont-de-Labeaume F 78 B3
Pont-de-l'Arche F 58 A2
Pont de Molins E 91 A5
Pont-de-Roide F 70 A1
Pont-de-Salars F 78 B1
Pont-d'Espagne F 76 D2
Pont de Suert E 90 A3
Pont-de-Vaux F 69 B4
Pont-de-Veyle F 69 B4
Pont d'Ouilly F 57 B5
Pont-du-Château F 68 C3
Pont-du-Navoy F 69 B5
Ponte a Moriano I 81 C4
Ponte Arche I 71 B5
Ponteareas E 87 B2
Pontebba I 72 B3
Ponte Cáffaro I 71 C5
Pontecagnano I 103 C7
Ponte-Caldelas E 87 B2
Ponteceso E 86 A2
Pontecesures E 86 B2
Pontecorvo I 103 B6
Ponte da Barca P 87 C2
Pontedássio I 80 C2
Pontedécimo I 80 B2
Ponte de Lima P 87 C2
Ponte dell'Ólio I 80 B3
Pontedera I 81 C4
Ponte de Sor P 92 B2
Pontedeume E 86 A2
Ponte di Barbarano I 72 C1
Ponte di Legno I 71 B5
Ponte di Nava I 80 B1
Ponte di Piave I 72 C2
Ponte Felcino I 82 C1
Pontefract GB 27 B4
Ponte Gardena I 71 B6
Ponteginori I 81 C4
Pontelagoscuro I 81 B5
Ponteland GB 25 C6
Pontelandolfo I 103 B7
Ponte-Leccia F 102 A2
Pontelongo I 72 C2
Ponte nelle Alpi I 72 B2
Pont-en-Royans F 79 A4
Pontenure I 81 B3
Pontenx-les-Forges F 76 B1
Ponterwyd GB 26 C2
Ponte San Giovanni I 82 C1
Ponte San Pietro I 71 C4
Pontevedra E 86 B2
Pontevico I 71 C5
Pont Farcy F 57 B4
Pontfaverger-Moronvillers F 59 A5
Pontgibaud F 68 C2
Ponticino I 81 C5
Pontigny F 59 C4
Pontijou F 58 C2
Pontínia I 102 B6
Pontinvrea I 80 B2
Pontivy F 56 B3
Pont-l'Abbé F 56 C1
Pont-l'Évêque F 57 A6
Pontlevoy F 67 A6
Pontoise F 58 A3
Pontones E 101 A3
Pontonx-sur-l'Abour F 76 C2
Pontoon IRL 18 C2
Pontorson F 57 B4
Pontrémoli I 81 B3
Pont-Remy F 48 C2
Pontresina CH 71 B4
Pontrhydfendigaid GB 28 A4
Pontrieux F 56 B2
Ponts E 91 B4

Ponts-aux-Dames F 59 B3
Pont Scorff F 56 C2
Pöntsö FIN 113 E13
Pont-Ste Maxence F 58 A3
Pont-St Esprit F 78 B3
Pont-St Mamet F 77 B3
Pont-St Martin
F 66 A3
I 70 C2
Pont-St Vincent F 60 B2
Pont-sur-Yonne F 59 B4
Pontvallain F 57 C6
Pontypool GB 29 B4
Pontypridd GB 29 B4
Ponza I 102 C5
Poo E 88 A2
Poole GB 29 C6
Poolewe GB 22 D3
Poperinge B 48 C3
Pópoli I 103 A6
Popovac SRB 85 C6
Popovača HR 74 C1
Popow PL 55 A4
Poppel B 49 B6
Poppenhausen
Bayern D 51 C6
Hessen D 51 C5
Poppi I 81 C5
Poprad SK 65 A6
Popučke SRB 85 B4
Pópulo P 87 C3
Populónia I 81 D4
Pörböly H 74 B3
Porcuna E 100 B1
Pordenone I 72 C2
Pordic F 56 B3
Poręba PL 55 C4
Poreč HR 72 C3
Pori FIN 3 F24
Porjus S 112 F8
Porkhov RUS 7 C10
Porlezza I 71 B4
Porlock GB 29 B4
Pörnbach D 62 B2
Pornic F 66 A2
Pornichet F 66 A2
Porodin SRB 85 B6
Poronin PL 65 A5
Poros
Attiki GR 117 E5
Kefalonia GR 117 D2
Poroszló H 65 C6
Porozina HR 82 A3
Porquerolles F 79 D5
Porrentruy CH 70 A2
Porreres E 97 B3
Porretta Terme I 81 B4
Porsgrunn N 35 C1
Porspoder F 56 B1
Port-a-Binson F 59 A4
Portacloy IRL 18 B2
Portadown GB 19 B5
Portaferry GB 19 B6
Portaje E 93 B4
Portalegre P 92 B3
Portarlington IRL 21 A4
Port Askaig GB 24 C1
Portavadie GB 24 C2
Portavogie GB 19 B6
Portbail F 57 A4
Port Bannatyne GB 24 C2
Port-Barcarès F 78 D2
Portbou E 91 A6
Port-Camargue F 78 C3
Port Charlotte GB 24 C1
Port d'Andratx E 97 B2
Port-de-Bouc F 78 C3
Port-de-Lanne F 76 C1
Port de Pollença E 97 B3
Port-des-Barques F 66 C3
Port de Sóller E 97 B2
Portegrandi I 72 C2
Portel P 92 C3
Portela P 92 A2
Port Ellen GB 24 C1
Portelo P 87 C4
Portemouro E 86 B2
Port-en-Bessin F 57 A5
Port'Ercole I 102 A4
Port Erin GB 26 A1
Portes-lès-Valence F 78 B3
Portets F 76 B2
Port Eynon GB 28 B3
Portezuelo E 93 B4
Port Glasgow GB 24 C3
Portglenone GB 19 B5
Porthcawl GB 28 B4
Port Henderson GB 22 D3
Porthleven GB 28 C2
Porthmadog GB 26 C1
Porticcio F 102 B1
Portici I 103 C7
Portico di Romagna I 81 B5
Portilla de la Reina E 88 A2
Portillo E 88 C2
Portimao P 98 B2
Portinatx E 97 B1
Portinho da Arrabida
P 92 C1
Port Isaac GB 28 C3
Portishead GB 29 B5
Port-Joinville F 66 B2
Portknockie GB 23 D6
Port-la-Nouvelle F 78 C2
Portlaoise IRL 21 A4
Portlethen GB 23 D6
Port Logan GB 24 D3
Port Louis F 56 C2
Portmagne IRL 20 C1
Portmahomack GB 23 D5
Portman E 101 B5
Port Manech F 56 C2
Portnacroish GB 24 B2
Portnahaven GB 24 C1
Port Nan Giuran GB 22 C2
Port-Navalo F 66 A2
Port Nis GB 22 C2
Porto
F 102 A1
P 87 C2
Porto-Alto P 92 C2
Porto Azzurro I 81 D4
Portocannone I 103 B8
Porto Cerésio I 70 C3
Porto Cervo I 110 A2
Porto Cesáreo I 107 A4
Porto Colom E 97 B3
Porto Covo P 98 B2
Porto Cristo E 97 B3
Porto d'Áscoli I 82 D2
Porto de Lagos P 98 B2
Porto de Mos P 92 B2
Porto de Rei P 98 A2
Porto do Son E 86 B2
Porto Empédocle I 108 B2
Portoferráio I 81 D4
Portofino I 80 B3
Porto Garibaldi I 82 B1
Portogruaro I 72 C2
Portokhelion GR 117 E5
Portomaggiore I 81 B5
Portomarin E 86 B3
Porton GB 29 B6
Portonovo E 87 B2
Portopalo di Capo
Passero I 109 C4
Porto Petro E 97 B3
Porto Pino I 110 D1
Porto Potenza Picena
I 82 C2
Portør N 33 D6
Porto Recanati I 82 C2
Porto San Giórgio I 82 C2
Porto Sant'Elpídio I 82 C2
Porto Santo Stéfano
I 102 A4
Portoscuso I 110 C1
Porto Tolle I 82 B1
Porto Tórres I 110 B1
Porto-Vecchio F 102 B2
Portovénere I 81 B3
Portpatrick GB 24 D2
Portreath GB 28 C2
Portree GB 22 D2
Portroe IRL 20 B3
Portrush GB 19 A5
Port St Mary GB 26 A1
Portsall F 56 B1
Portsmouth GB 31 D2
Portsoy GB 23 D6
Port-Ste Marie F 77 B3
Portstewart GB 19 A5
Port-St-Louis-du-Rhône
F 78 C3
Port-sur-Saône F 60 C2
Port Talbot GB 28 B4
Portugalete E 89 A4
Portumna IRL 20 A3
Port-Vendres F 91 A6
Port William GB 24 D3
Porvoo FIN 7 A8
Porzuna E 94 C2
Posada
Oviedo E 88 A1
Oviedo E 88 A2
I 110 B2
Posada de Valdeón E 88 A2
Posadas E 99 B5
Poschiavo CH 71 B5
Posedarje HR 83 B4
Positano I 103 C7
Possagno I 72 C1
Posseck D 52 C2
Possesse F 59 B5
Pössneck D 52 C1
Posta I 102 A6
Postal I 71 B6
Posta Piana I 104 B1
Postbauer-Heng D 62 A2
Posterholt NL 50 B2
Postioma I 72 C2
Postira HR 83 C5
Postojna SLO 73 C4
Postoloprty CZ 53 C3
Postomino PL 46 A2
Posušje BIH 84 C2
Potamos
Attiki GR 117 F4
Attiki GR 117 G5
Potegowo PL 46 A3
Potenza I 104 C1
Potenza Picena I 82 C2
Potes E 88 A2
Potigny F 57 B5
Potkrajci MNE 85 C4
Potočari BIH 85 B4
Potoci
BIH 83 B5
BIH 84 C2
Potony H 74 C2
Potries E 96 C2
Potsdam D 45 C5
Potštát CZ 64 A3
Pottenbrunn A 63 B6
Pottendorf A 64 C2
Pottenstein
A 64 C2
D 62 A2
Potters Bar GB 31 C3
Pöttmes D 62 B2
Pöttsching A 64 C2
Potworów PL 55 B5
Pouancé F 57 C4
Pougues-les-Eaux F 68 A3
Pouilly-en-Auxois F 69 A4
Pouilly-sous Charlieu
F 68 B4
Pouilly-sur-Loire F 68 A2
Poujol-sur-Orb F 78 C2
Poullaouen F 56 B2
Poulton-le-Fylde GB 26 B3
Poundstock GB 28 C3
Pourcy F 59 A4
Pourrain F 59 C4
Pouyastruc F 76 C3
Pouy-de-Touges F 77 C4
Pouzauges F 66 B4
Pova de Santa Iria P 92 C1
Považská Bystrica
SK 65 A4
Povedilla E 101 A3
Povlja HR 84 C1
Povljana HR 83 B4
Póvoa
Beja P 98 A3
Santarém P 92 B2
Póvoa de Lanhoso P 87 C2
Póvoa de Varzim P 87 C2
Póvoa e Meadas P 92 B3
Powidz PL 46 C3
Poyales del Hoyo E 93 A5
Poynton GB 26 B3
Poyntz Pass GB 19 B5
Poysdorf A 64 B2
Poza de la Sal E 89 B3
Pozaldez E 88 C2
Pozán de Vero E 90 A3
Pozanti TR 16 C7
Požarevac SRB 85 B6
Požega
HR 74 C2
SRB 85 C5
Poznań PL 46 C2
Pozo Alcón E 100 B3
Pozoantiguo E 88 C1
Pozoblanco E 100 A1
Pozo Cañada E 101 A4
Pozo de Guadalajara
E 95 B3
Pozo de la Serna E 100 A2
Pozohondo E 101 A4
Pozondón E 95 B5
Poźrzadło Wielkie
PL 46 B1
Pozuel del Campo E 95 B5
Pozuelo de Alarcón
E 94 B3
Pozuelo de Calatrava
E 100 A2
Pozuelo del Páramo
E 88 B1
Pozuelo de Zarzón E 93 A4
Pozzallo I 109 C3
Pozzomaggiore I 110 B1
Pozzo San Nicola I 110 B1
Pozzuoli I 103 C7
Pozzuolo I 81 C5
Prabuty PL 47 B5
Prača BIH 84 C3
Prachatice CZ 63 A4
Prada E 87 B3
Pradelle F 79 B4
Pradelles F 78 B2
Prades
E 90 B3
F 91 A5
Pradła PL 55 C4
Prado
E 88 A1
P 87 C2
Prado del Rey E 99 C5
Pradoluengo E 89 B3
Pragelato I 79 A5
Pragersko SLO 73 B5
Prägraten A 72 A2
Prague = Praha CZ 53 C4
Praha = Prague CZ 53 C4
Prahecq F 67 B4
Praia P 92 B1
Práia a Mare I 106 B2
Praia da Rocha P 98 B2
Praia da Viera P 92 B2
Praia de Mira P 92 A2
Praiano I 103 C7
Pralboino I 71 C5
Pralognan-la-Vanoise
F 70 C1
Pramanda GR 116 C3
Pranjani SRB 85 B5
Prapatnica HR 83 C5
Præstø DK 39 D5
Praszka PL 54 B3
Prat F 77 C3
Prata I 81 C4
Prata di Pordenone I 72 C2
Pratau D 52 B2
Prat de Compte E 90 C3
Pratdip E 90 B3
Pratella I 103 B7
Prato I 81 C5
Prátola Peligna I 103 A6
Pratola Serra I 103 C7
Prats-de-Mollo-la-Preste
F 91 A5
Prauthoy F 59 C6
Pravia E 86 A4
Praxmar A 71 A6
Prayssac F 77 B4
Prazzo I 79 B6
Prebold SLO 73 B5
Préchac F 76 B2
Précy-sur-Thil F 69 A4
Predáppio I 81 B5
Predazzo I 72 B1
Předin CZ 63 A6
Preding A 73 B5
Predjame SLO 73 C4
Predlitz A 72 A3
Predmeja SLO 72 C3
Predoi I 72 A2
Pré-en-Pail F 57 B5
Prees GB 26 C3
Preetz D 44 A2
Préfailles F 66 A2
Pregarten A 63 B5
Pregrada HR 73 B5
Preignan F 77 C3
Preiļi LV 7 C9
Preitenegg A 73 B4
Prekaja BIH 83 B5
Preko HR 83 B4
Preljina SRB 85 C5
Prelog HR 74 B1
Prelošćica HR 74 C1
Přelouč CZ 53 C5
Prem SLO 73 C4
Premantura HR 82 B2
Prémery F 68 A3
Prémia I 70 B3
Premiàde Mar E 91 B5
Premnitz D 44 C4
Prémont F 49 C4
Prenzlau D 45 B5
Preodac BIH 83 B5
Přerov CZ 64 A3
Prerow D 45 A4
Presencio E 88 B3
Presicce I 107 B5
Presly F 68 A2
Prešov SK 10 B6
Pressac F 67 B5
Pressath D 62 A2
Pressbaum A 64 B2
Prestatyn GB 26 B2
Prestebakke N 35 D3
Presteigne GB 29 A4
Přeštice CZ 63 A4
Preston
Lancashire GB 26 B3
Scottish Borders GB 25 C5
Prestonpans GB 25 C5
Prestwick GB 24 C3
Prettin D 52 B2
Preturo I 103 A6
Pretzchendorf D 52 C3
Pretzier D 44 C3
Pretzsch D 52 B2
Preuilly-sur-Claise F 67 B5
Prevalje SLO 73 B4
Prevenchères F 78 B2
Préveranges F 68 B2
Preveza GR 116 D2
Prevršac HR 73 C6
Prezid HR 73 C4
Priaranza del Bierzo
E 86 B4
Priay F 69 B5
Pribeta SK 64 C4
Priboj
BIH 84 B3
SRB 85 C4
Přibor CZ 64 A4
Příbram CZ 63 A5
Pribylina SK 65 A5
Přibyslav CZ 63 A6
Pričević SRB 85 B4
Pridjel BIH 84 B3
Priego E 95 B4
Priego de Córdoba
E 100 B1
Priekule LV 6 C6
Prien D 62 C3
Prienai LT 6 D7
Prievidza SK 65 B4
Prigradica HR 84 D1
Prigrevica SRB 75 C4
Prijeboj HR 83 B4
Prijedor BIH 83 B5
Prijepolje SRB 85 C4
Prilep MK 116 A3
Priluka BIH 84 C1
Primda CZ 62 A3
Primel-Trégastel F 56 B2
Primišje HR 73 C5
Primorsk
Kaliningrad RUS 47 A6
Severo-Zapadnyy
RUS 7 A10
Primošten HR 83 C4
Primstal D 60 A2
Princes Risborough
GB 31 C3
Princetown GB 28 C3
Principina a Mare I 81 D5
Priolo Gargallo I 109 B4
Prioro E 88 B2
Priozersk RUS 3 F29
Prirechnyy RUS 113 C19
Prisoje BIH 84 C2
Pristen RUS 7 F14
Priština KOS 85 D6
Pritzerbe D 44 C4
Pritzier D 44 B3
Pritzwalk D 44 B4
Privas F 78 B3
Priverno I 102 B6
Privlaka
Vukovarsko-Srijemska
HR 74 C3
Zadarska HR 83 B4
Prizna HR 83 B3
Prizren KOS 10 E6
Prizzi I 108 B2
Prnjavor
BIH 84 B2
HR 73 C5
SRB 85 B4
Proaza E 86 A4
Probstzella D 52 C1
Probus GB 28 C3
Prócchio I 81 D4
Prochowice PL 54 B1
Prócida I 103 C7
Prodhromos CY 120 B1
Prodo I 82 D1
Proença-a-Nova P 92 B3
Proença-a-Velha P 92 A3
Profondeville B 49 C5
Prokuplje SRB 10 E6
Propriano F 102 B1
Prosec CZ 64 A2
Prösen D 52 B3
Prosenjakovci SLO 73 B6
Prosotsani GR 116 A5
Prostějov CZ 64 A3
Prószków PL 54 C2
Proszowice PL 55 C5
Protić BIH 84 B1
Protivanov CZ 64 A2
Protivín CZ 63 A5
Prötzel D 45 C5
Provins F 59 B4
Prozor BIH 84 C2
Prrenjas AL 116 A2
Prudhoe GB 25 D6
Prudnik PL 54 C2
Pruggern A 72 A3
Prüm D 50 C2
Pruna E 99 C5
Prunelli-di-Fiumorbo
F 102 A2
Prunetta I 81 B4
Pruniers F 68 B2
Prusice PL 54 B1
Pruské SK 64 A4
Pruszce PL 47 B4
Pruszcz Gdański PL 47 A4
Pruszków PL 55 A5
Prutz A 71 A5
Prüzen D 44 B4
Pruzhany BY 6 E8
Pružina SK 65 A4
Pryluky UA 11 A12
Pryzlęg PL 46 C1
Przechlewo PL 46 B3
Przecław PL 55 C6
Przedbórz PL 55 B4
Przedecz PL 54 A3
Przejęslav PL 53 B5
Przemków PL 53 B5
Przemocze PL 45 B6
Przemyśl PL 11 B7
Przerąb PL 55 B4
Przewodnik PL 47 B4
Przewóz PL 53 B4
Przezmark PL 47 B5
Przodkowo PL 47 A4
Przybiernów PL 45 B6
Przyborowice PL 47 C6
Przybyszew PL 55 B5
Przybyszów PL 55 B4
Przylęg PL 46 C1
Przysucha PL 55 B5
Przytóczna PL 46 C1
Przytyk PL 55 B5
Przywidz PL 47 A4
Psachna GR 116 D5
Psara GR 116 D7
Psary PL 54 B3
Pskov RUS 7 C10
Pszczew PL 46 C1
Pszczółki PL 47 A4
Pszczyna PL 54 D3
Pszów PL 54 C3
Pteleos GR 116 C4
Ptolemaida GR 116 B3
Ptuj SLO 73 B5
Ptusza PL 46 B2
Puch A 62 C4
Puchberg am Schneeberg
A 64 C1
Puchevillers F 48 C3
Puchheim D 62 B2
Púchov SK 64 A4
Pučišća HR 83 C5
Puck PL 47 A4
Puçol E 96 B2
Puconci SLO 73 B6
Pudasjärvi FIN 3 D27
Puderbach D 50 C3
Puebla de Albortón E 90 B2
Puebla de Alcocer E 93 C5
Puebla de Beleña E 95 B3
Puebla de Don Fadrique
E 101 B3
Puebla de Don Rodrigo
E 94 C2
Puebla de Guzmán E 98 B3
Puebla de la Calzada
E 93 C4
Puebla de la Reina E 93 C4
Puebla de Lillo E 88 A1
Puebla del Maestre E 99 A4
Puebla del Principe
E 100 A3
Puebla de Obando E 93 B4
Puebla de Sanabria E 87 B4
Puebla de Sancho Pérez
E 93 C4
Puente Almuhey E 88 B2
Puente de Domingo
Flórez E 86 B4
Puente de Génave E 101 A3
Puente del Congosto
E 93 A5
Puente de Montañana
E 90 A3
Puente Duero E 88 C2
Puente-Genil E 100 B1
Puente la Reina E 89 B5
Puente la Reina de Jaca
E 90 A2
Puentelarra E 89 B3
Puente Mayorga E 99 C5
Puente Viesgo E 88 A3
Puertas
Asturias E 88 A2
Salamanca E 87 C4
Puerto de Mazarrón
E 101 B4
Puerto de Santa Cruz
E 93 B5
Puerto de San Vicente
E 94 C1
Puerto-Lápice E 95 C3
Puertollano E 100 A1
Puerto Lumbreras E 101 B4
Puerto Moral E 99 B4
Puerto Real E 99 C4
Puerto Rey E 94 C1
Puerto Seguro E 87 D4
Puerto Serrano E 99 C5
Puget-Sur-Argens F 79 C5
Puget-Théniers F 79 C5
Puget-ville F 79 C5
Pugnochiuso I 104 B2
Puigcerdà E 91 A4
Puigpunyent E 97 B2
Puig Reig E 91 B4
Puillon F 76 C2
Puimichel F 79 C5
Puimoisson F 79 C5
Puiseaux F 58 B3
Puisieux F 48 C3
Puisserguier F 78 C2
Puivert F 77 D5
Pujols F 76 B2
Pukanec SK 65 B4
Pukavik S 41 C4
Pukë AL 105 A5
Pula
HR 82 B2
I 110 C1
Puławy PL 10 A6
Pulborough GB 31 D3
Pulfero I 72 B3
Pulgar E 94 C2
Pulheim D 50 B2
Pulkau A 64 B1
Pulpi E 101 B4
Pulsano I 104 C3
Pulsnitz D 53 B4
Pułtusk PL 6 E6
Pumpsaint GB 28 A4
Punat HR 83 A3
Punta Marina I 82 B1
Punta Prima E 97 B4
Punta Sabbioni I 72 C2
Puntas de Calnegre
E 101 B4
Punta Umbria E 99 B4
Puolanka FIN 3 D27
Puoltikasvaara S 112 E10
Puoltsa S 112 E8
Puračić BIH 84 B3
Purbach am Neusiedler
See A 64 C2
Purchena E 101 B3
Purfleet GB 31 C4
Purgstall A 63 B6
Purkersdorf A 64 B2
Purmerend NL 42 C1
Purullena E 100 B2
Pushkin RUS 7 B11
Pushkino RUS 7 C14
Püspökladány H 75 A6
Pustelnik PL 55 A6
Pusté Ulany SK 64 B3
Pustoshka RUS 7 C10
Puszcza Mariańska
PL 55 B5
Puszczykowo PL 54 A1
Pusztamagyaród H 74 B1
Pusztamonostor H 75 A4
Pusztaszabolcs H 74 A3
Pusztavám H 74 A3
Putanges-Pont-Ecrepin
F 57 B5
Putbus D 45 A5
Putignano I 104 C3
Putlitz D 44 B4
Putnok H 65 B6
Putte B 49 B5
Puttelange-aux-Lacs
F 60 A2
Putten NL 49 A6
Puttgarden D 44 A3
Püttlingen D 60 A2
Putzu Idu I 110 B1
Puy-Guillaume F 68 C3
Puylaroque F 77 B4
Puylaurens F 77 C5
Puy-l'Évêque F 77 B4
Puymirol F 77 B3
Puyôo F 76 C2
Puyrolland F 67 B4
Pwllheli GB 26 C1
Pyatykhatky UA 11 B12
Pyetrikaw BY 7 E10
Pyhäjärvi FIN 3 E26
Pyla CY 120 A2
Pyla-sur-Mer F 76 B1
Pyryatyn UA 11 A12
Pyrzyce PL 45 B6
Pysely CZ 63 A5
Pyskowice PL 54 C3
Pytalovo RUS 7 C9
Pyzdry PL 54 A2

Q

Quakenbrück D 43 C4
Quargnento I 80 B2
Quarré-les-Tombes F 68 A3
Quarteira P 98 B2
Quartu Sant'Élena I 110 C2
Quatre-Champs F 59 A5
Quedlinburg D 52 B1
Queensferry
Edinburgh GB 25 C4
Flintshire GB 26 B2
Queige F 69 C6
Queipo E 99 B4
Queixans E 91 A4
Quel E 89 B4
Quelaines-St-Gault F 57 C5
Queljada P 87 C2
Quemada E 89 C3
Queralbs E 91 A5
Quercianella I 81 C4
Querfurt D 52 B1
Quérigut F 77 D5
Quero
E 95 C3
I 72 C1
Querqueville F 57 A4
Quesada E 100 B2
Questembert F 56 C3
Quettehou F 57 A4
Quevauvillers F 58 A3
Quevy B 49 C5
Quiaois P 92 A2
Quiberon F 66 A1
Quiberville F 58 A1
Quickborn D 44 B1
Quiévrain B 49 C4
Quillan F 77 D5
Quillebeuf F 58 A1
Quimper F 56 B1
Quimperlé F 56 C2
Quincampoix F 58 A2
Quincoces de Yuso E 89 B3
Quincy F 68 A2
Quinéville F 57 A4
Quingey F 69 A5
Quinson F 79 C5
Quinssaines F 68 B2
Quinta-Grande P 92 C2
Quintana de la Serena
E 93 C5
Quintana del Castillo
E 86 B4
Quintana del Marco E 88 B1
Quintana del Puenta
E 88 B2
Quintana-Martin Galindez
E 89 B3
Quintanaortuño E 88 B3
Quintanapalla E 89 B3
Quintanar de la Orden
E 95 C3
Quintanar de la Sierra
E 89 C3
Quintanar del Rey E 95 C5
Quintanilla de la Mata
E 88 C3
Quintanilla del Coco
E 89 C3
Quintanilla de Onésimo
E 88 C2
Quintanilla de Somoza
E 87 B4
Quintas de Valdelucio
E 88 B2
Quintela P 87 D3
Quintin F 56 B3
Quinto E 90 B2
Quinzano d'Oglio I 71 C5
Quiroga E 86 B3
Quismondo E 94 B2
Quissac F 78 C2
Quistello I 81 A4

R

Raab A 63 B4
Raabs an der Thaya
A 63 B6
Raahe FIN 3 D26
Raajärvi FIN 113 F15
Raalte NL 42 C3
Raamsdonksveer NL 49 B5
Raanujarvi FIN 113 F13
Raattama FIN 113 D13
Rab HR 83 B3
Rabac HR 82 A3
Rábade E 86 A3
Rábafüzes H 73 B6
Rábahidvég H 74 A1
Rabanales E 87 C4
Rábapatona H 64 C3
Rabapordány H 74 A2
Rabastens F 77 C4
Rabastens-de-Bigorre
F 76 C3
Rabat = Victoria M 107 C5
Rabat M 107 C5
Rabča SK 65 A5
Rabe SRB 75 B5
Rabi CZ 63 A4
Rabino PL 46 B1
Rabka PL 65 A5
Rabrovo SRB 85 B6
Rača
Srbija SRB 85 B6
Srbija SRB 85 C6
Rácale I 107 B5
Rácalmás H 75 A3
Racalmuto I 108 B2
Racconigi I 80 B1
Rače SLO 73 B5
Rachecourt-sur-Marne
F 59 B6
Raciąż PL 47 C6
Racibórz PL 54 C3
Račinovci HR 84 B3
Ráckeve H 75 A3
Racławice PL 55 C5
Racławice Sląskie
PL 54 C2
Racot PL 54 A1
Råda
Skaraborg S 35 D5
Värmland S 34 B5
Radalj SRB 85 B4
Rădăuţi RO 11 C8
Radda in Chianti I 81 C5
Raddusa I 109 B3
Radeberg D 53 B3
Radebeul D 52 B3
Radeburg D 53 B3
Radeče SLO 73 B5
Radekhiv UA 11 A8
Radenci SLO 73 B6
Radenthein A 72 B3
Radevormwald D 50 B3
Radicófani I 81 D5
Radicóndoli I 81 C5
Radišići BIH 84 C2
Radizel SLO 73 B5
Radków PL 54 C1
Radlje ob Dravi SLO 73 B5
Radlów PL 55 C5
Radmer an der Stube
A 73 A4
Radnejaur S 115 B15
Radnice CZ 63 A4
Radohova BIH 84 B2
Radojevo SRB 75 C5
Radolfzell D 61 C4
Radom PL 55 B6
Radomice PL 47 C5
Radomin PL 47 B5
Radomsko PL 55 B4
Radomyshl UA 11 A10
Radomyśl Wielki PL 55 C6
Radošina SK 64 B3
Radošovce SK 64 B3
Radostowo PL 47 B6
Radoszewice PL 54 B3
Radoszyce PL 55 B5
Radotín CZ 53 D4
Radoviš MK 116 A4
Radovljica SLO 73 B4
Radowo Wielkie PL 46 B1
Radstadt A 72 A3
Radstock GB 29 B5
Raduc HR 83 B4
Radviliškis LT 6 D7
Radzanów
Mazowieckie PL 47 C6
Mazowieckie PL 55 B5
Radziejów PL 47 C4
Radziejowice PL 55 A5
Radzovce SK 65 B5
Radzymin PL 55 A6
Radzyń Chełmiński
PL 47 B4
Raeren B 50 C2
Raesfeld D 50 B2
Raffadali I 108 B2
Rafina GR 117 D5
Rafsbotn N 113 B12
Ragachow BY 7 E11
Ragály H 65 B6
Rågeleje DK 41 C2
Raglan GB 29 B5
Ragnitz A 73 B5
Ragusa I 109 C3
Rahden D 43 C5
Råholt N 34 B3
Raiano I 103 A6
Raigada E 87 B3
Rain D 62 B1
Rainbach im Mühlkreis
A 63 B5
Rainham GB 31 C4
Rairiz de Veiga E 87 B3
Raisdorf D 44 A2
Raisio FIN 6 A7
Raiva
Aveiro P 87 C2
Coimbra P 92 A2
Raja-Jooseppi FIN 113 D17
Rajala FIN 113 E15
Rajcza PL 65 A5
Rajec SK 65 A4
Rájec-Jestřebi CZ 64 A2
Rajecké Teplice SK 65 A4
Rajevo Selo HR 84 B3
Rajhrad CZ 64 A2
Rajić HR 74 C2
Rajka H 64 C3
Rakaca H 65 B6
Rakek SLO 73 C4
Rakhiv UA 11 B8
Rakitna SLO 73 C4
Rakkestad N 35 C3
Rákóczifalva H 75 A5
Rakoniewice PL 53 A6
Rakoszyce PL 54 B1
Raková SK 65 A4
Rakovac BIH 84 A2
Rakovica HR 83 B4
Rakovník CZ 53 C3
Rakow D 45 A5
Raków PL 55 C6
Rakvere EST 7 B9
Ralja SRB 85 B5
Rälla S 41 C6
Ramacastañas E 94 B1
Ramacca I 109 B3
Ramales de la Victoria
E 89 A3
Ramberg N 112 D2
Rambervillers F 60 B2
Rambouillet F 58 B2
Rambucourt F 60 B1
Ramdala S 41 C5
Ramerupt F 59 B5
Ramingstein A 72 A3
Ramirás E 87 B2
Ramiswil CH 70 A2
Ramkvilla S 40 B4
Ramme DK 38 C1
Rämmen S 34 B6
Ramnäs S 36 C3
Ramnes N 35 C2
Râmnicu Vâlcea RO 11 D8
Ramonville-St Agne
F 77 C4
Rampside GB 26 A2
Ramsau D 62 C3
Ramsbeck D 51 B4
Ramsberg S 36 C2
Ramsele S 115 D13
Ramsey
Cambridgeshire GB 30 B3
Isle of Man GB 26 A1
Ramseycleuch GB 25 C4
Ramsgate GB 31 C5
Ramsjö S 115 E12
Ramstein-Meisenbach
D 60 A3
Ramsund N 112 D5
Ramundberget S 114 E9
Ramvik S 115 E14
Ranalt A 71 A6
Rånäs S 36 C5
Rånåsfoss N 34 B3
Rance B 49 C5
Ránchio I 82 C1
Randaberg N 33 D2
Randalstown GB 19 B5
Randan F 68 B3
Randazzo I 109 B3
Rånddalen S 115 E10
Randegg A 63 B5
Randers DK 38 C3
Randijaur S 112 F8
Randin E 87 C3
Randsverk N 114 F6
Rânes F 57 B5
Rångedala S 40 B3
Ranis D 52 C1
Rankweil A 71 A4
Rånnaväg S 40 B3
Ränneslöv S 40 C3
Rannoch Station GB 24 B3
Ranovac SRB 85 B6
Ransäter S 34 C5
Ransbach-Baumbach
D 50 C3
Ransta S 36 C3
Ranttila FIN 113 C14
Ranua FIN 3 D27
Ranum DK 38 C2
Ranvalhal P 92 B1
Raon-l'Étape F 60 B2
Ráossi I 71 C6
Rapallo I 80 B3
Rapla EST 6 B8
Rapness GB 23 B6
Rapolano Terme I 81 C5
Rapolla I 104 C1
Raposa P 92 B2
Rapperswil CH 70 A3
Raša HR 82 A3
Rasal E 90 A2
Rascafria E 94 B3
Rasdorf D 51 C5
Raseiniai LT 6 D7
Rašica SLO 73 C4
Rasines E 89 A3
Raška SRB 85 C5
Rasquera E 90 B3
Rássina I 81 C5
Rastatt D 61 B4
Rastede D 43 B5
Rastenberg D 52 B1
Rastošnica BIH 84 B3
Rastovac MNE 84 D3
Rasueros E 94 A1
Rasy PL 55 B4
Raszków PL 54 B2
Rataje SRB 85 C6
Rätan S 115 E11
Rateče SLO 72 B3
Ratekau D 44 B2
Ratež SLO 73 C5
Rathangan IRL 21 A5
Rathcoole IRL 21 A5
Rathcormack IRL 20 B3
Rathdrum IRL 21 B5
Rathebur D 45 B5
Rathenow D 44 C4
Rathfriland GB 19 B5
Rathkeale IRL 20 B3
Rathmelton IRL 19 A4
Rathmolyon IRL 21 A5
Rathmore IRL 20 B2
Rathmullan IRL 19 A4
Rathnew IRL 21 B5
Rathvilly IRL 21 B5
Ratibořské Hory CZ 63 A5
Ratingen D 50 B2
Ratková SK 65 B6
Ratkovo SRB 75 C4
Ratne UA 6 F8
Ratoath IRL 21 A5
Rattelsdorf D 51 C6
Ratten A 73 A5
Rattosjärvi FIN 113 F13
Rattray GB 25 B4
Rättvik S 36 B2
Ratvika N 114 D7
Ratzeburg D 44 B2
Rätzlingen D 44 C3
Raucourt-et-Flaba F 59 A5
Raudeberg N 114 F2
Raufarhöfn IS 111 A10
Raufoss N 34 B2
Rauhala FIN 113 E13
Rauland N 33 C5
Raulhac F 77 B5
Raulia N 115 B11
Rauma FIN 3 F24
Raundal N 32 B3
Raunds GB 30 B3
Rauris A 72 A3
Rautas S 112 E8
Rautavaara FIN 3 E28
Rauville-la-Bigot F 57 A4
Rauzan F 76 B2
Ravanusa I 108 B2
Rava-Rus'ka UA 11 A7
Ravča HR 84 C2
Ravels B 49 B5
Rävemåla S 40 C5
Ravenglass GB 26 A2
Ravenna I 82 B1
Ravensburg D 61 C5
Rävlanda S 40 B2
Ravna Gora HR 73 C4
Ravne na Koroškem
SLO 73 B4
Ravnište SRB 85 C6
Ravnje SRB 85 B4
Ravno BIH 84 D2
Ravno Selo SRB 75 C4
Rawa Mazowiecka PL 55 B5
Rawicz PL 54 B1
Rawtenstall GB 26 B3
Rayleigh GB 31 C4
Ražana SRB 85 B4
Ražanac HR 83 B4
Razboj BIH 84 A2
Razbojna SRB 85 C6
Razes F 67 B6
Razgrad BG 11 E9
Razkrižie SLO 73 B6
Razo E 86 A2
Reading GB 31 C3
Réalmont F 77 C5
Rebais F 59 B4
Reboly RUS 3 E29
Rebordelo P 87 C3
Recanati I 82 C2
Recas
E 94 B3
RO 10 D6
Recco I 80 B3
Recess IRL 18 C2
Recey-sur-Ource F 59 C5
Recezinhos P 87 C2
Rechnitz A 73 A6
Rechytsa BY 7 E11
Recke D 43 C4
Recklinghausen D 50 B3
Recoaro Terme I 71 C6
Recogne B 59 A6
Recoules-Prévinquières
F 78 B1
Recsk H 65 C6
Recz PL 46 B1
Reda PL 47 A4
Redalen N 34 B2
Redange L 60 A1
Redcar GB 27 A4
Redditch GB 29 A6
Redefin D 44 B3
Redhill GB 31 C3
Redics H 74 B1
Redkino RUS 7 C14
Redland GB 23 B5
Redlin D 44 B4
Redon F 57 C3
Redondela E 87 B2
Redondo P 92 C3
Red Point GB 22 D3
Redruth GB 28 C2
Redzikowo PL 46 A3
Reepham GB 30 B5
Rees D 50 B2
Reeth GB 27 A4
Reetz D 44 B3
Reftele S 40 B3
Regalbuto I 109 B3
Regen D 62 B4
Regensburg D 62 A3
Regenstauf D 62 A3
Reggello I 81 C5
Réggio di Calábria I 109 A4
Reggiolo I 81 B4
Réggio nell'Emília I 81 B4
Reghin RO 11 C8
Régil E 89 A4
Regna S 37 D2
Regniéville F 60 B1
Regny F 69 C4
Rego da Leirosa P 92 A2
Regöly H 74 B3
Regueiro E 86 B2
Reguengo
Portalegre P 92 B3
Santarém P 92 B2
Reguengos de Monsaraz
P 92 C3
Rehau D 52 C2
Rehburg D 43 C6
Rehden D 43 C5
Rehna D 44 B3
Reichelsheim D 61 A4
Reichelshofen D 61 A6
Reichenau A 64 C1
Reichenbach
Sachsen D 52 C2
Sachsen D 53 B4
Reichenfels A 73 A4
Reichensachsen D 51 B6
Reichertshofen D 62 B2
Reichshoffen F 60 B3
Reiden CH 70 A2
Reigada
E 86 A4
P 87 D4
Reigate GB 31 C3
Reillanne F 79 C4
Reillo E 95 C5
Reims F 59 A5
Reinach CH 70 A3
Reinbek D 44 B2
Reinberg D 45 A5
Reine N 112 E2
Reinfeld D 44 B2
Reinheim D 61 A4
Reinli N 32 B6
Reinosa E 88 A2
Reinstorf D 44 B3
Reinsvoll N 34 B2
Reisach A 72 B3
Reiss GB 23 C5
Reitan N 114 E8
Reit im Winkl D 62 C3
Rejmyre S 37 D2
Rekavice BIH 84 B2
Rekovac SRB 85 C6
Relleu E 96 C2
Rém H 75 B4
Remagen D 50 C3
Rémalard F 58 B1
Rembercourt-aux-Pots
F 59 B6
Remedios P 92 B1
Remels D 43 B4
Remetea Mare RO 75 C6
Remich L 60 A2
Rémilly F 60 A2
Remiremont F 60 C2
Remolinos E 90 B1
Remoulins F 78 C3
Remscheid D 50 B3
Rémuzat F 79 B4
Rena N 34 A3
Renaison F 68 B3
Renazé F 57 C4
Renchen D 61 B4
Rencurel F 79 A4
Rende I 106 B3
Rendina GR 116 C3
Rendsburg D 43 A6
Renedo E 88 C2
Renens CH 69 B6
Renfrew GB 24 C3
Rengsjö S 36 A3
Reni UA 11 D10
Rennebu N 114 E6
Rennerod D 50 C4
Rennertshofen D 62 B2
Rennes F 57 B4
Rennes-les-Bains F 77 D5
Rennweg A 72 A3
Rens DK 39 E2
Rensjön S 112 D8
Rentería E 76 C1
Rentjärn S 115 B15
Répcelak H 74 A2
Repojoki FIN 113 D14
Repvåg N 113 B14
Requena E 96 B1
Réquista F 77 B5
Rerik D 44 A3
Resana I 72 C1
Resarö S 37 C5
Reschen = Résia I 71 B5
Resen MK 116 A3
Resende P 87 C3
Résia = Reschen I 71 B5
Reşiţa RO 10 D6
Resko PL 46 B1
Resnik SRB 85 B5
Ressons-sur-Matz F 58 A3
Restábal E 100 C2
Resuttano I 109 B3
Retamal E 93 C4
Retford GB 27 B5
Rethel F 59 A5
Rethem D 43 C6
Rethimno GR 117 G6
Retie B 49 B6
Retiers F 57 C4
Retortillo E 87 D4
Retortillo de Soria E 89 C3
Retournac F 68 C4
Rétság H 65 C5
Rettenegg A 73 A5
Retuerta del Bullaque
E 94 C2
Retz A 64 B1
Retzbach D 61 A5
Reuden D 52 A2
Reuilly F 68 A2
Reus E 91 B4
Reusel NL 49 B6
Reuterstadt Stavenhagen
D 45 B4
Reuth D 62 A3
Reutlingen D 61 B5
Reutte A 71 A5
Reuver NL 50 B2
Revel F 77 C4
Revello I 80 B1
Revenga E 94 B2
Revest-du-Bion F 79 B4
Révfülöp H 74 B2
Revigny-sur-Ornain F 59 B5
Revin F 59 A5
Řevnice CZ 63 A5
Řevničov CZ 53 C3
Revo I 71 B6
Revsnes N 32 A4
Revúca SK 65 B6
Rewa PL 47 A4
Rewal PL 45 A7
Rexbo S 36 B2
Reyðarfjörður IS 111 B11
Reyero E 88 B1
Reykhólar IS 111 B3
Reykholt
Árnessýsla IS 111 C5
Borgarfjarðarsýsla
IS 111 C4
Reykjahlið IS 111 B9
Reykjavík IS 111 C4
Rezé F 66 A3
Rēzekne LV 7 C9
Rezovo BG 11 F10
Rezzato I 71 C5
Rezzoáglio I 80 B3
Rhade D 43 B6
Rhaunen D 60 A3
Rhayader GB 29 A4
Rheda-Wiedenbrück
D 50 B4
Rhede
Niedersachsen D 43 B4
Nordrhein-Westfalen
D 50 B2
Rheinau D 60 B3
Rheinbach D 50 C2
Rheinberg D 50 B2

Rheine D 50 A3
Rheinfelden D 70 A2
Rheinsberg D 45 B4
Rhêmes-Notre-Dame
I 70 C2
Rhenen NL 49 B6
Rhens D 50 C3
Rheydt D 50 B2
Rhiconich GB 22 C4
Rhinow D 44 C4
Rhiw GB 26 C1
Rho I 70 C4
Rhoden D 51 B5
Rhodes GR 119 F3
Rhondda GB 29 B4
Rhosllanerchrugog
GB 26 B2
Rhosneigr GB 26 B1
Rhossili GB 28 B3
Rhubodach GB 24 C2
Rhuddlan GB 26 B2
Rhyl GB 26 B2
Rhynie GB 23 D6
Riala S 37 C5
Riallé F 66 A3
Riaño E 88 B1
Riano I 102 A5
Rians F 79 C4
Rianxo E 86 B2
Riaza E 89 C3
Riba E 89 A3
Ribadavia E 87 B2
Ribadeo E 86 A3
Riba de Saelices E 95 B4
Ribadesella E 88 A1
Ribaflecha E 89 B4
Ribaforada E 89 C5
Ribare SRB 85 B6
Ribariće SRB 85 D5
Riba-roja d'Ebre E 90 B3
Riba-Roja de Turia E 96 B2
Ribe DK 39 D1
Ribeauvillé F 60 B3
Ribécourt-Dreslincourt
F 59 A3
Ribeira da Pena P 87 C3
Ribeira de Piquín E 86 A3
Ribemont F 59 A4
Ribera I 108 B2
Ribérac F 67 C5
Ribera de Cardós E 91 A4
Ribera del Fresno E 93 C4
Ribesalbes E 96 A2
Ribes de Freser E 91 A5
Ribiers F 79 B4
Ribnica
BIH 84 B3
SLO 73 C4
SRB 85 C5
Ribnica na Potorju
SLO 73 B5
Ribnik HR 73 C5
Rîbniţa MD 11 C10
Ribnitz-Damgarten D 44 A4
Ribolla I 81 D5
Řicany CZ 64 A2
Ričany CZ 53 D4
Ríccia I 103 B7
Riccione I 82 B1
Ricco Del Golfo I 81 B3
Richebourg F 59 B6
Richelieu F 67 A5
Richisau CH 70 A3
Richmond
Greater London GB 31 C3
North Yorkshire GB 27 A4
Richtenberg D 45 A4
Richterswil CH 70 A3
Rickling D 44 A2
Rickmansworth GB 31 C3
Ricla E 89 C5
Riddarhyttan S 36 C2
Ridderkerk NL 49 B5
Riddes CH 70 B2
Ridjica SRB 75 C4
Riec-sur-Bélon F 56 C2
Ried A 63 B4
Riedenburg D 62 B2
Ried im Oberinntal A 71 A5
Riedlingen D 61 B5
Riedstadt D 61 A4
Riegersburg A 73 B5
Riego de la Vega E 88 B1
Riego del Camino E 88 C1
Riello E 88 B1
Riemst B 49 C6
Rienne B 49 D5
Riénsena E 88 A2
Riesa D 52 B3
Riese Pio X I 72 C1
Riesi I 109 B3
Riestedt D 52 B1
Rietberg D 51 B4
Rieti I 102 A5
Rietschen D 53 B4
Rieumes F 77 C4
Rieupeyroux F 77 B5
Rieux-Volvestre F 77 C4
Riez F 79 C5
Rīga LV 6 C8
Riggisberg CH 70 B2
Rignac F 77 B5
Rignano Gargánico
I 104 B1
Rigolato I 72 B2
Rigside GB 25 C4
Rigutino I 81 C5
Riihimäki FIN 3 F26
Rijeka HR 73 C4
Rijeka Crnojeviča
MNE 105 A5
Rijen NL 49 B5
Rijkevorsel B 49 B5
Rijssen NL 50 A2
Rilić BIH 84 C2
Rilievo I 108 B1
Rillé F 67 A5
Rillo de Gallo E 95 B5
Rimavská Baňa SK 65 B5
Rimavská Seč SK 65 B6
Rimavská Sobota SK 65 B6
Rimbo S 36 C5
Rimforsa S 37 D2
Rímini I 82 B1
Rîmnicu Sărat RO 11 D9
Rimogne F 59 A5
Rimpar D 61 A5
Rimske Toplice SLO 73 B5
Rincón de la Victoria
E 100 C1
Rincón de Soto E 89 B5
Rindal N 114 D6
Rinde N 32 A3
Ringarum S 37 D3
Ringaskiddy IRL 20 C3
Ringe DK 39 D3
Ringebu N 34 A2
Ringkøbing DK 39 C1
Ringsaker N 34 B2
Ringsted DK 39 D4
Ringwood GB 29 C6
Rinkaby S 41 D4
Rinkabyholm S 40 C6
Rinlo E 86 A3
Rinn A 71 A6
Rinteln D 51 A5
Rio E 86 B3
Riobo E 86 B2
Riodeva E 96 A1
Rio do Coures P 92 B2
Rio Douro P 87 C3
Riofrio E 94 B2
Rio Frio P 92 C2
Riofrio de Aliste E 87 C4
Rio frio de Riaza E 95 A3
Riogordo E 100 C1
Rioja E 101 C3
Riola I 81 B5
Riola Sardo I 110 C1
Riolobos E 93 B4
Riom F 68 C3
Riomaggiore I 81 B3
Rio Maior P 92 B2
Rio Marina I 81 D4
Riom-ès-Montagnes
F 68 C2
Rion-des-Landes F 76 C2
Rionegro del Puente
E 87 B4
Rionero in Vúlture I 104 C1
Riopar E 101 A3
Riós E 87 C3
Rioseco E 88 A1
Rioseco de Tapia E 88 B1
Rio Tinto P 87 C2
Riotord F 69 C4
Riotorto E 86 A3
Rioz F 69 A6
Ripač BIH 83 B4
Ripacándida I 104 C1
Ripanj SRB 85 B5
Ripatransone I 82 D2
Ripley GB 27 B4
Ripoll E 91 A5
Ripon GB 27 A4
Riposto I 109 B4
Ripsa S 37 D3
Risan MNE 105 A4
Risbäck S 115 C12
Risca GB 29 B4
Rischenau D 51 B5
Riscle F 76 C2
Risebo S 40 A6
Risnes N 32 A2
Rišňovce SK 64 B3
Risør N 33 D6
Risøyhamn N 112 D4
Rissna S 115 D12
Ritsem S 112 E6
Ritterhude D 43 B5
Riutula FIN 113 D15
Riva del Garda I 71 C5
Riva Lígure I 80 C1
Rivanazzano I 80 B3
Rivarolo Canavese I 70 C2
Rivarolo Mantovano I 81 A4
Rive-de-Gier F 69 C4
Rivedoux-Plage F 66 B3
Rivello I 106 A2
Rivergaro I 80 B3
Rives F 69 C5
Rivesaltes F 78 D1
Rivignano I 72 C3
Rivne UA 11 A9
Rívoli I 80 A1
Rivolta d'Adda I 71 C4
Rixheim F 60 C3
Rixo S 35 D3
Riza GR 116 B5
Rizokarpaso CY 120 A3
Rjukan N 32 C5
Rø DK 41 D4
Rö S 37 C5
Roa
E 88 C3
N 34 B2
Roade GB 30 B3
Roager DK 39 D1
Roaldkvam N 33 C3
Roanne F 68 B4
Robakowo PL 47 B4
Róbbio I 70 C3
Röbel D 45 B4
Roberton GB 25 C5
Robertville B 50 C2
Robin Hood's Bay GB 27 A5
Robleda E 93 A4
Robledillo de Trujillo
E 93 B5
Robledo
Albacete E 101 A3
Orense E 86 B4
Robledo de Chavela
E 94 B2
Robledo del Buey E 94 C2
Robledo del Mazo E 94 C2
Robledollano E 93 B5
Robles de la Valcueva
E 88 B1
Robliza de Cojos E 87 D5
Robres E 90 B2
Robres del Castillo E 89 B4
Rocafort de Queralt E 91 B4
Rocamadour F 77 B4
Roccabernarda I 107 B3
Roccabianca I 81 A4
Roccadáspide I 103 C8
Rocca di Mezzo I 103 A6
Rocca di Papa I 102 B5
Roccagorga I 102 B6
Rocca Imperiale I 106 A3
Roccalbegna I 81 D5
Roccalumera I 109 B4
Roccamena I 108 B2
Roccamonfina I 103 B6
Roccanova I 106 A3
Roccapalumba I 108 B2
Roccapassa I 103 A6
Rocca Priora I 82 C2
Roccaraso I 103 B7
Rocca San Casciano
I 81 B5
Roccasecca I 103 B6
Rocca Sinibalda I 102 A5
Roccastrada I 81 C5
Roccatederighi I 81 C5
Roccella Iónica I 106 C3
Rocchetta Sant'António
I 103 B8
Rocester GB 27 C4
Rochdale GB 26 B3
Rochechouart F 67 C5
Rochefort
B 49 C6
F 66 C4
Rochefort-en-Terre F 56 C3
Rochefort-Montagne
F 68 C2
Rochefort-sur-Nenon
F 69 A5
Roche-lez-Beaupré F 69 A6
Rochemaure F 78 B3
Rocheservière F 66 B3
Rochester
Medway GB 31 C4
Northumberland GB 25 C5
Rochlitz D 52 B2
Rociana del Condado
E 99 B4
Rockenhausen D 60 A3
Rockhammar S 37 C2
Rockneby S 40 C6
Ročko Polje HR 73 C4
Ročov CZ 53 C3
Rocroi F 59 A5
Rodach D 51 C6
Roda de Bara E 91 B4
Roda de Ter E 91 B5
Rodalben D 60 A3
Rødberg N 32 B5
Rødby DK 44 A3
Rødbyhavn DK 44 A3
Rødding
Sonderjyllands Amt.
DK 39 D2
Viborg Amt. DK 38 C1
Rödeby S 41 C5
Rodeiro E 86 B3
Rødekro DK 39 D2
Roden NL 42 B3
Ródenas E 95 B5
Rodenkirchen D 43 B5
Rödental D 52 C1
Rödermark D 51 D4
Rodewisch D 52 C2
Rodez F 77 B5
Rodi Gargánico I 104 B1
Roding D 62 A3
Rödjebro S 36 B4
Rødkærsbro DK 39 C2
Rodolivas GR 116 B5
Rodoñá E 91 B4
Rødvig DK 41 D2
Roermond NL 50 B1
Roesbrugge B 48 C3
Roeschwoog F 61 B4
Roeselare B 49 C4
Roetgen D 50 C2
Roffiac F 78 A2
Röfors S 37 D1
Rofrano I 106 A2
Rogač HR 83 C5
Rogačica SRB 85 B4
Rogalinek PL 54 A1
Rogaška Slatina SLO 73 B5
Rogatec SLO 73 B5
Rogatica BIH 84 C4
Rogatyn UA 11 B8
Rogätz D 52 A1
Roggendorf D 44 B3
Roggiano Gravina I 106 B3
Roghadal GB 22 D2
Rogliano
F 102 A2
I 106 B3
Rognan N 112 E4
Rogne N 32 A6
Rognes F 79 C4
Rogny-les-7-Ecluses
F 59 C3
Rogowo PL 46 C3
Rogóz PL 47 A6
Rogoznica HR 83 C4
Rogoźnica PL 53 B6
Rogoźno PL 46 C2
Rohan F 56 B3
Röhlingen D 61 B6
Rohožnik SK 64 B3
Rohr D 51 C6
Rohrbach A 63 B4
Rohrbach-lès-Bitche
F 60 A3
Rohrberg D 44 C3
Rohr im Gebirge A 63 C6
Röhrnbach D 63 B4
Roisel F 59 A4
Roja LV 6 C7
Rojales E 96 C2
Röjeråsen S 36 B1
Rojewo PL 47 C4
Rokiciny PL 55 B4
Rokietnica PL 46 C2
Rokiškis LT 7 D8
Rokitki PL 53 B5
Rokitno RUS 7 F13
Rokycany CZ 63 A4
Rolampont F 59 C6
Rold DK 38 C2
Røldal N 32 C3
Rolde NL 42 C3
Rollag N 32 B6
Rollán E 94 B1
Rolle CH 69 B6
Roma = Rome I 102 B5
Roma S 37 E5
Romagnano Sésia I 70 C3
Romagné F 57 B4
Romakloster S 37 E5
Roman RO 11 C9
Romana I 110 B1
Romanèche-Thorins
F 69 B4
Romano di Lombardia
I 71 C4
Romanshorn CH 71 A4
Romans-sur-Isère F 79 A4
Rombas F 60 A2
Rome = Roma I 102 B5
Romeán E 86 B3
Romenay F 69 B5
Romeral E 95 C3
Römerstein D 61 B5
Rometta I 109 A4
Romford GB 31 C4
Romhány H 65 C5
Römhild D 51 C6
Romilly-sur-Seine F 59 B4
Romny UA 11 A12
Romodan UA 11 B12
Romont CH 70 B1
Romorantin-Lanthenay
F 68 A1
Romrod D 51 C5
Romsey GB 31 D2
Rømskog N 35 C3
Rønbjerg DK 38 C1
Roncal E 76 D2
Ronce-les-Bains F 66 C3
Ronchamp F 60 C2
Ronchi dei Legionari
I 72 C3
Ronciglione I 102 A5
Ronco Canavese I 70 C2
Ronco Scrivia I 80 B2
Ronda E 99 C5
Rønde DK 39 C3
Rone S 37 E5
Ronehamn S 37 E5
Rong N 32 B1
Rönnäng S 38 B4
Rønne DK 41 D4
Ronneburg D 52 C2
Ronneby S 41 C5
Rönneshytta S 37 D2
Rönninge S 37 C4
Rönnöfors S 115 D10
Rönö S 37 D3
Ronov nad Doubravou
CZ 63 A6
Ronse B 49 C4
Roosendaal NL 49 B5
Roosky IRL 19 C4
Ropczyce PL 55 C6
Ropeid N 33 C3
Ropinsalmi FIN 113 D10
Ropuerelos del Páramo
E 88 B1
Roquebilière F 79 B6
Roquebrun F 78 C2
Roquecourbe F 77 C5
Roquefort F 76 B2
Roquemaure F 78 B3
Roquesteron F 79 C6
Roquetas de Mar E 101 C3
Roquetes E 90 C3
Roquevaire F 79 C4
Røra N 114 D8
Rörbäcksnäs S 34 A4
Rørbæk DK 38 C2
Rore BIH 83 B5
Röro S 38 B4
Røros N 114 E8
Rorschach CH 71 A4
Rørvig DK 39 D4
Rørvik N 114 C8
Rörvik S 40 B4
Rosà I 72 C1
Rosal de la Frontera
E 98 B3
Rosalina Mare I 72 C2
Rosa Marina I 104 C3
Rosans F 79 B4
Rosário P 98 B2
Rosarno I 106 C2
Rosbach D 50 C3
Rosche D 44 C2
Rościszewo PL 47 C5
Roscoff F 56 B2
Roscommon IRL 18 C3
Roscrea IRL 21 B4
Rosdorf D 51 B5
Rose I 106 B3
Rosegg A 73 B4
Rosehall GB 22 D4
Rosehearty GB 23 D6
Rosel GB 57 A3
Rosell E 90 C3
Roselló E 90 B3
Rosendal N 32 C3
Rosenfeld D 61 B4
Rosenfors S 40 B5
Rosenheim D 62 C3
Rosenow D 45 B5
Rosenthal D 51 B4
Rosersberg S 37 C4
Roses E 91 A6
Roseto degli Abruzzi
I 103 A7
Roseto Valfortore I 103 B8
Rosheim F 60 B3
Rosia I 81 C5
Rosice CZ 64 A2
Rosières-en-Santerre
F 58 A3
Rosignano Maríttimo
I 81 C4
Rosignano Solvay I 81 C4
Roşiori-de-Vede RO 11 D8
Roskhill GB 22 D2
Roskilde DK 39 D5
Roskovec AL 105 C5
Röslau D 52 C1
Roslavl RUS 7 E12
Roslev DK 38 C1
Rosmaninhal P 93 B3
Rosmult IRL 21 B4
Rosnowo PL 46 A2
Rosolini I 109 C3
Rosova MNE 85 C4
Rosoy F 59 B4
Rosporden F 56 C2
Rosquete P 92 B2
Rosrath D 50 C3
Rossa CH 71 B4
Rossano I 106 B3
Rossas
Aveiro P 87 D2
Braga P 87 C2
Rossdorf D 51 C6
Rossett GB 26 B3
Rosshaupten D 62 C1
Rossiglione I 80 B2
Rossignol B 60 A1
Rossla D 52 B1
Rosslare IRL 21 B5
Rosslare Harbour IRL 21 B5
Rosslau D 52 B2
Rosslea GB 19 B4
Rossleben D 52 B1
Rossön S 115 D13
Ross-on-Wye GB 29 B5
Rossoszyca PL 54 B3
Rosswein D 52 B3
Röstånga S 41 C3
Roštár SK 65 B6
Rostock D 44 A4
Rostrenen F 56 B2
Røsvik N 112 E4
Rosyth GB 25 B4
Röszke H 75 B5
Rot S 34 A6
Rota E 99 C4
Rota Greca I 106 B3
Rot am See D 61 A6
Rotberget N 34 B4
Rotella I 82 D2
Rotenburg
Hessen D 51 C5
Niedersachsen D 43 B6
Roth
Bayern D 62 A2
Rheinland-Pfalz D 50 C3
Rothbury GB 25 C6
Rothemühl D 45 B5
Röthenbach D 62 A2
Rothenburg D 53 B4
Rothenburg ob der
Tauber D 61 A6
Rothéneuf F 57 B4
Rothenklempenow D 45 B6
Rothenstein D 62 B2
Rotherham GB 27 B4
Rothes GB 23 D5
Rothesay GB 24 C2
Rothwell GB 30 B3
Rotnes N 34 B2
Rotonda I 106 B3
Rotondella I 106 A3
Rotova E 96 C2
Rott
Bayern D 62 C1
Bayern D 62 C3
Rottach-Egern D 62 C2
Röttenbach D 62 A2
Rottenbuch D 62 C1
Rottenburg
Baden-Württemberg
D 61 B4
Bayern D 62 B3
Rottenmann A 73 A4
Rotterdam NL 49 B5
Rotthalmünster D 63 B4
Rottingdean GB 31 D3
Röttingen D 61 A5
Rottleberode D 51 B6
Rottne S 40 B4
Rottneros S 34 C5
Rottofreno I 80 A3
Rottweil D 61 B4
Rötz D 62 A3
Roubaix F 49 C4
Roudnice nad Labem
CZ 53 C4
Roudouallec F 56 B2
Rouen F 58 A2
Rouffach F 60 C3
Rougé F 57 C4
Rougemont F 69 A6
Rougemont le-Château
F 60 C2
Rouillac F 67 C4
Rouillé F 67 B5
Roujan F 78 C2
Roulans F 69 A6
Roundwood IRL 21 A5
Rousínov CZ 64 A2
Roussac F 67 B6
Roussennac F 77 B5
Rousses F 78 B2
Roussillon F 69 C4
Rouvroy-sur-Audry F 59 A5
Rouy F 68 A3
Rovanieman
maalaiskunta FIN 113 F14
Rovaniemi FIN 113 F14
Rovato I 71 C4
Rovensko pod Troskami
CZ 53 C5
Roverbella I 71 C5
Rovereto I 71 C6
Rövershagen D 44 A4
Roverud N 34 B4
Rovigo I 81 A5
Rovinj HR 82 A2
Rovišce HR 74 C1
Rów PL 45 C6
Rowy PL 46 A3
Royal Leamington Spa
GB 30 B2
Royal Tunbridge Wells
GB 31 C4
Royan F 66 C3
Royat F 68 C3
Roybon F 69 C5
Roybridge GB 24 B3
Roye F 58 A3
Royère-de-Vassivière
F 68 C1
Røykenvik N 34 B2
Royos E 101 B3
Røyrvik N 115 C10
Royston GB 30 B3
Rozadas E 86 A4
Rožaj MNE 85 D5
Rozalén del Monte E 95 C4
Rózańsko PL 45 C6
Rožanstvo SRB 85 C4
Rozay-en-Brie F 59 B3
Roždalovice CZ 53 C5
Rozdilna UA 11 C11
Rozental PL 47 B5
Rozhyshche UA 11 A8
Rožmitál pod Třemšínem
CZ 63 A4
Rožňava SK 65 B6
Rožnov pod Radhoštěm
CZ 64 A4
Rozoy-sur-Serre F 59 A5
Rozprza PL 55 B4
Roztoky CZ 53 C4
Rozvadov CZ 62 A3
Rozzano I 71 C4
Rranxë AL 105 B5
Rrëshen AL 105 B5
Rrogozhine AL 105 B5
Ruanes E 93 B5
Rubbestadnesset N 32 C2
Rubi E 91 B5
Rubiá E 86 B4
Rubiacedo de Abajo
E 89 B3
Rubielos Bajos E 95 C4
Rubielos de Mora E 96 A2
Rubiera I 81 B4
Rubik AL 105 B5
Rucandio E 89 B3
Rud
Akershus N 34 B3
Buskerud N 34 B2
Ruda
PL 54 B3
S 40 B6
Rudabánya H 65 B6
Ruda Maleniecka PL 55 B5
Ruda Pilczycka PL 55 B5
Ruda Śl. PL 54 C3
Ruddervorde B 49 B4
Ruden A 73 B4
Rudersberg D 61 B5
Rudersdorf A 73 A6
Rüdersdorf D 45 C5
Ruderting D 63 B4
Rüdesheim D 50 D3
Rudkøbing DK 39 E3
Rudmanns A 63 B6
Rudna
CZ 53 C4
PL 53 B6
Rudnik
KOS 85 D5
SRB 85 B5
Rudniki
Opolskie PL 54 B3
Śląskie PL 55 C4
Rudno
Dolnośląskie PL 54 B1
Pomorskie PL 47 B4
Rudnya RUS 7 D11
Rudo BIH 85 C4
Rudolstadt D 52 C1
Rudowica PL 53 B5
Rudozem BG 116 A6
Rudskoga S 35 C6
Rudston GB 27 A5
Ruds Vedby DK 39 D4
Rudy PL 54 C3
Rue F 48 C2
Rueda E 88 C2
Rueda de Jalón E 90 B1
Ruelle-sur-Touvre F 67 C5
Ruerrero E 88 B3
Ruffano I 107 B5
Ruffec F 67 B5
Rufina I 81 C5
Rugby GB 30 B2
Rugeley GB 27 C4
Ruggstrop S 40 C6
Rugles F 58 B1
Rugozero RUS 3 D30
Rühen D 44 C2
Ruhla D 51 C6
Ruhland D 53 B3
Ruhle D 43 C4
Ruhpolding D 62 C3
Ruhstorf D 63 B4
Ruidera E 95 D4
Ruillé-sur-le-Loir F 58 C1
Ruinen NL 42 C3
Ruiselede B 49 B4
Rulles B 60 A1
Rülzheim D 61 A4
Rum H 74 A1
Ruma SRB 85 A4
Rumboci BIH 84 C2
Rumburk CZ 53 C4
Rumenka SRB 75 C4
Rumia PL 47 A4
Rumigny F 59 A5
Rumilly F 69 C5
Rumma S 37 D3
Rumney GB 29 B4
Rumont F 59 B6
Rumy PL 47 B6
Runa P 92 B1
Runcorn GB 26 B3
Rundmoen N 115 A11
Rungsted DK 41 D2
Runhällen S 36 B3
Runowo PL 47 A6
Runtuna S 37 D4
Ruokojärvi FIN 113 E13
Ruokolahti FIN 3 F28
Ruokto S 112 E8
Ruoms F 78 B3
Ruoti I 104 C1
Rupa HR 73 C4
Ruppichteroth D 50 C3
Rupt-sur-Moselle F 60 C2
Rus E 100 A2
Ruse BG 11 E9
Ruše SLO 73 B5
Rusele S 115 C15
Ruševo HR 74 C3
Rush IRL 21 A5
Rushden GB 30 B3
Rusiec PL 54 B3
Rusinowo
Zachodnio-Pomorskie
PL 46 B1
Zachodnio-Pomorskie
PL 46 B2
Ruskele S 115 C15
Ruski Krstur SRB 75 C4
Ruskington GB 27 B5
Rusovce SK 64 B3
Rüsselsheim D 51 D4
Russelv N 112 C9
Russi I 81 B6
Rust A 64 C2
Rustefjelbma N 113 B17
Rustrel F 79 C4
Ruszki PL 55 A5
Ruszów PL 53 B5
Rute E 100 B1
Rüthen D 51 B4
Rutherglen GB 24 C3
Ruthin GB 26 B2
Ruthven GB 23 D4
Ruthwell GB 25 D4
Rüti CH 70 A3
Rutigliano I 104 B3
Rutledal N 32 A2
Rutoši SRB 85 C4
Ruurlo NL 50 A2
Ruuvaoja FIN 113 E17
Ruvo del Monte I 104 C1
Ruvo di Púglia I 104 B2
Ruynes-en-Margeride
F 78 B2
Ružic HR 83 C5
Ružomberok SK 65 A5
Ruzsa H 75 B4
Ry DK 39 C2
Rybany SK 64 B4
Rybina PL 47 A5
Rybinsk RUS 7 B15
Rybnik PL 54 C3
Rychliki PL 47 B5
Rychlocice PL 54 B3
Rychnov nad Kněžnou
CZ 53 C6
Rychnowo PL 47 B6
Rychtal PL 54 B2
Rychwał PL 54 A3
Ryczywół PL 55 B6
Ryczywół PL 46 C2
Ryd S 40 C4
Rydaholm S 40 C4
Rydal S 40 B2
Rydbo S 37 C5
Rydboholm S 40 B2
Ryde GB 31 D2
Rydöbruk S 40 C3
Rydsgård S 41 D3
Rydsnäs S 40 B5
Rydultowy PL 54 C3
Rydzyna PL 54 B1
Rye GB 31 D4
Rygge N 35 C2
Ryjewo PL 47 B4
Rykene N 33 D5
Rylsk RUS 7 F13
Rymań PL 46 B1
Rýmařov CZ 64 A3
Rynarzewo PL 46 B3
Ryomgård DK 39 C3
Rypefjord N 113 B12
Rypin PL 47 B5
Rysjedalsvika N 32 A2
Ryssby S 40 C4
Rytel PL 46 B3
Rytro PL 65 A6
Rywociny PL 47 B6
Rzeczenica PL 46 B3
Rzeczniów PL 55 B6
Rzeczyca PL 55 B5
Rzęgnowo PL 47 B6
Rzejowice PL 55 B4
Rzemień PL 55 C6
Rzepin PL 45 C6
Rzesznikowo PL 46 B1
Rzeszów PL 10 A6
Rzgów PL 55 B4
Rzhev RUS 7 C13

S

Saal
Bayern D 51 C6
Bayern D 62 B2
Saalbach A 72 A2
Saalburg D 52 C1
Saales F 60 B3
Saalfeld D 52 C1
Saalfelden am Steinernen
Meer A 72 A2
Saanen CH 70 B2
Saarbrücken D 60 A2
Saarburg D 60 A2
Saarijärvi FIN 3 E26
Saarlouis D 60 A2
Saas-Fee CH 70 B2
Šabac SRB 85 B4
Sabadell E 91 B5
Sabáudia I 102 B6
Sabbioneta I 81 B4
Sabero E 88 B1
Sabiñánigo E 90 A2
Sabiote E 100 A2
Sables-d'Or-les-Pins
F 56 B3
Sablé-sur-Sarthe F 57 C5
Sabóia P 98 B2
Saborsko HR 83 A4
Sæbøvik N 32 C2
Sabres F 76 B2
Sabrosa P 87 C3
Sabugal P 93 A3
Sabuncu TR 118 C5
Sæby DK 38 B3
Săcălaz RO 75 C6
Sacecorbo E 95 B4
Saceda del Rio E 95 B4
Sacedón E 95 B4
Săcele RO 11 D8
Saceruela E 94 D2
Sachsenburg A 72 B3
Sachsenhagen D 43 C6
Sacile I 72 C2
Sacramenia E 88 C3
Sada E 86 A2
Sádaba E 90 A1
Saddell GB 24 C2
Sadernes E 91 A5
Sadki PL 46 B3
Sadkowice PL 55 B5
Sadlinki PL 47 B4
Sadów PL 53 A4
Sadská CZ 53 C4
Saelices E 95 C4
Saelices de Mayorga
E 88 B1
Saerbeck D 50 A3
Saeul L 60 A1
Safaalan TR 118 A3
Safara P 98 A3
Säffle S 35 C4
Saffron Walden GB 31 B4
Safonovo RUS 7 D12
Safranbolu TR 16 A6
Säfsnäs S 36 B1
Şag RO 75 C6
Sagard D 45 A5
S'Agaro E 91 B6
Sågmyra S 36 B2
Sagone F 102 A1
Sagres P 98 C2
Ságújfalu H 65 B5
Sagunt E 96 B2
Sagvåg N 32 C2
Ságvár H 74 B3
Sagy F 69 B5
Sahagún E 88 B1
Šahy SK 65 B4
Saignelégier CH 70 A1
Saignes F 68 C2
Saija FIN 113 E17
Saillagouse F 91 A5
Saillans F 79 B4
Sains Richaumont F 59 A4
St Abb's GB 25 C5
St Affrique F 78 C1
St Agnan F 68 B3
St Agnant F 66 C4
St Agnes GB 28 C2
St Agrève F 78 A3
St Aignan F 67 A6
St Aignan-sur-Roë F 57 C4
St Albans GB 31 C3
St Alban-sur-Limagnole
F 78 B2
St Amand-en-Puisaye
F 68 A3
St Amand-les-Eaux F 49 C4
St Amand-Longpré F 58 C2
St Amand-Montrond
F 68 B2
St Amans F 78 B2
St Amans-Soult F 77 C5
St Amant-Roche-Savine
F 68 C3
St Amarin F 60 C2
St Ambroix F 78 B3
St Amé F 60 B2
St Amour F 69 B5
St André-de-Corcy F 69 C4
St André-de-Cubzac
F 76 B2
St André-de-l'Eure F 58 B2
St André-de-
Roquepertuis F 78 B3
St André-de-Sangonis
F 78 C2
St Andre-de-Valborgne
F 78 B2
St André-les-Alpes F 79 C5
St Andrews GB 25 B5
St Angel F 68 C2
St Anthème F 68 C3
St Antoine F 102 A2
St Antoine-de-Ficalba
F 77 B3
St Antönien CH 71 B4
St Antonin-Noble-Val
F 77 B4
St Août F 68 B1
St Armant-Tallende F 68 C3
St Arnoult F 58 B2
St Asaph GB 26 B2
St Astier F 67 C5
St Athan GB 29 B4
St Auban F 79 C5
St Aubin
CH 70 B1
F 69 A5
GB 57 A3
St Aubin-d'Aubigné F 57 B4
St Aubin-du-Cormier
F 57 B4
St Aubin-sur-Aire F 60 B1
St Aubin-sur-Mer F 57 A5
St Aulaye F 67 C5
St Austell GB 28 C3
St Avit F 68 C2
St Avold F 60 A2
St Aygulf F 79 C5
St Bauzille-de-Putois
F 78 C2
St Béat F 77 D3
St Beauzély F 78 B1
St Bees GB 26 A2
St Benim-d'Azy F 68 B3
St Benoît-du-Sault F 67 B6
St Benoit-en-Woëvre
F 60 B1
St Berthevin F 57 B5
St Blaise-la-Roche F 60 B3
St Blazey GB 28 C3
St Blin F 59 B6
St Bonnet F 79 B5
St Bonnet Briance F 67 C6
St Bonnet-de-Joux F 69 B4
St Bonnet-le-Château
F 68 C4
St Bonnet-le-Froid F 69 C4
St Brévin-les-Pins F 66 A2
St Briac-sur-Mer F 57 B3
St Brice-en-Coglès F 57 B4
St Brieuc F 56 B3
St Bris-le-Vineux F 59 C4
St Broladre F 57 B4
St Calais F 58 C1
St Cannat F 79 C4
St Cast-le-Guildo F 57 B3
St Céré F 77 B4
St Cergue CH 69 B6
St Cergues F 69 B6
St Cernin F 77 A5
St Chamant F 68 C1
St Chamas F 79 C4
St Chamond F 69 C4
St Chély-d'Apcher F 78 B2
St Chély-d'Aubrac F 78 B1
St Chinian F 78 C1
St Christol F 79 B4
St Christol-lès-Alès F 78 B3
St Christoly-Médoc F 66 C4
St Christophe-du-
Ligneron F 66 B3
St Christophe-en-
Brionnais F 69 B4
St Ciers-sur-Gironde
F 67 C4
St Clair-sur-Epte F 58 A2
St Clar F 77 C3
St Claud F 67 C5
St Claude F 69 B5
St Clears GB 28 B3
St Columb Major GB 28 C3
St Come-d'Olt F 78 B1
St Cosme-en-Vairais
F 58 B1
St Cyprien
Dordogne F 77 B4
Pyrenées-Orientales
F 91 A6
St Cyr-sur-Loire F 67 A5
St Cyr-sur-Mer F 79 C4
St Cyr-sur-Methon F 69 B4
St David's GB 28 B2
St Denis F 58 B3
St Denis-d'Oléron F 66 B3
St Denis d'Orques F 57 B5
St Didier F 69 B4
St Didier-en-Velay F 69 C4
St Dié F 60 B2
St Dier-d'Auvergne F 68 C3
St Dizier F 59 B5
St Dizier-Leyrenne F 68 B1
St Dogmaels GB 28 A3
Ste Adresse F 57 A6
Ste Anne F 58 B1
Ste Anne-d'Auray F 56 C3
Ste Croix CH 69 B6
Ste Croix-Volvestre F 77 C4
Ste Engrâce F 76 C2
Ste Enimie F 78 B2
St Efflam F 56 B2
Ste Foy-de-Peyrolières
F 77 C4
Ste Foy-la-Grande F 76 B3
Ste Foy l'Argentiere
F 69 C4
Ste Gauburge-Ste
Colombe F 58 B1
Ste Gemme la Plaine
F 66 B3
Ste Geneviève F 58 A3
St Égrève F 69 C5
Ste Hélène F 76 B2
Ste Hélène-sur-Isère
F 69 C6
Ste Hermine F 66 B3
Ste Jalle F 79 B4
Ste Livrade-sur-Lot F 77 B3
St Eloy-les-Mines F 68 B2
Ste Marie-aux-Mines
F 60 B3
Ste Marie-du-Mont F 57 A4
Ste Maure-de-Touraine
F 67 A5
Ste Maxime F 79 C5
Ste Menehould F 59 A5
Ste Mère-Église F 57 A4
St Emiland F 69 B4
St Émilion F 76 B2
St Enoder GB 28 C3
Sainteny F 57 A4
Ste Ode B 49 C6
Saintes F 67 C4
Ste Savine F 59 B5
Ste Sévère-sur-Indre
F 68 B2
Ste Sigolène F 69 C4
St Esteben F 76 C1
St Estèphe F 66 C4
Ste Suzanne F 57 B5
St Étienne F 69 C4
St Etienne-de-Baigorry
F 76 C1
St Étienne-de-Cuines
F 69 C6
St Etienne-de-Fursac
F 67 B6
St Etienne-de-Montluc
F 66 A3
St Etienne-de-St Geoirs
F 69 C5
St Étienne-de-Tinée F 79 B5
St Étienne-du-Bois F 69 B5
St Étienne-du-Rouvray
F 58 A2
St Etienne-les-Orgues
F 79 B4
Ste Tulle F 79 C4
St Fargeau F 59 C4
St Félicien F 78 A3
St Felix-de-Sorgues F 78 C1
St Félix-Lauragais F 77 C4
Saintfield GB 19 B6
St Fillans GB 24 B3
St Firmin F 79 B5
St Florent F 102 A2
St Florentin F 59 C4
St Florent-le-Vieil F 66 A3
St Florent-sur-Cher F 68 B2
St Flour F 78 A2
St Flovier F 67 B6
St Fort-sur-le-Né F 67 C4
St Fulgent F 66 B3
St Galmier F 69 C4
St Gaudens F 77 C3
St Gaultier F 67 B6
St Gély-du-Fesc F 78 C2
St Genest-Malifaux F 69 C4
St Gengoux-le-National
F 69 B4
St Geniez F 79 B5
St Geniez-d'Olt F 78 B1
St Genis-de-Saintonge
F 67 C4
St Genis-Pouilly F 69 B6
St Genix-sur-Guiers
F 69 C5
St Georges Buttavent
F 57 B5
St Georges-d'Aurac F 68 C3
St Georges-de-Commiers
F 79 A4
St Georges-de-Didonne
F 66 C4
St Georges-de-Luzençon
F 78 B1
St Georges-de Mons
F 68 C2
St Georges-de-Reneins
F 69 B4
St Georges d'Oléron
F 66 C3
St Georges-en-Couzan
F 68 C3
St Georges-lès-
Baillargeaux F 67 B5
St Georges-sur-Loire
F 66 A4
St Georges-sur-Meuse
B 49 C6
St Geours-de-Maremne
F 76 C1
St Gérand-de-Vaux F 68 B3
St Gérand-le-Puy F 68 B3
St Germain F 60 C2
St Germain-Chassenay
F 68 B3
St Germain-de-Calberte
F 78 B2
St Germain-de-Confolens
F 67 B5
St Germain-de-Joux
F 69 B5
St Germain-des-Fossés
F 68 B3
St Germain-du-Bois F 69 B5
St Germain-du-Plain
F 69 B4
St Germain-du Puy F 68 A2
St Germain-en-Laye F 58 B3
St Germain-Laval F 68 C4
St Germain-Lembron
F 68 C3
St Germain-les-Belles
F 67 C6
St Germain-Lespinasse
F 68 B3
St Germain-l'Herm F 68 C3
St Gervais-d'Auvergne
F 68 B2
St Gervais-les-Bains
F 70 C1
St Gervais-sur-Mare
F 78 C2
St Gildas-de-Rhuys F 66 A2
St Gildas-des-Bois F 66 A2
St Gilles
Gard F 78 C3
Ille-et-Vilaine F 57 B4
St Gilles-Croix-de-Vie
F 66 B3
St Gingolph F 70 B1
St Girons
Ariège F 77 D4
Landes F 76 C1
St Girons-Plage F 76 C1
St Gobain F 59 A4
St Gorgon-Main F 69 A6
St Guénolé F 56 C1
St Harmon GB 29 A4
St Helens GB 26 B3
St Helier GB 57 A3
St Herblain F 66 A3
St Hilaire
Allier F 68 B3
Aude F 77 C5
St Hilaire-de-Riez F 66 B3
St Hilaire-des-Loges
F 67 B4
St Hilaire-de-Villefranche
F 67 C4
St Hilaire-du-Harcouët
F 57 B4
St Hilaire-du-Rosier F 79 A4
St Hippolyte
Aveyron F 77 B5
Doubs F 70 A1
St Hippolyte-du-Fort
F 78 C2
St Honoré-les-Bains
F 68 B3
St Hubert B 49 C6
St Imier CH 70 A2
St Issey GB 28 C3
St Ives
Cambridgeshire GB 30 B3
Cornwall GB 28 C2
St Izaire F 78 C1
St Jacques-de-la-Lande
F 57 B4
St Jacut-de-la-Mer F 57 B3
St James F 57 B4
St Jaume d'Enveja E 90 C3
St Jean-Brévelay F 56 C3
St Jean-d'Angély F 67 C4
St Jean-de-Belleville
F 69 C6
St Jean-de-Bournay
F 69 C5
St Jean-de-Braye F 58 C2
St Jean-de-Côle F 67 C5
St Jean-de-Daye F 57 A4
St Jean de Losne F 69 A5
St Jean-de-Luz F 76 C1
St Jean-de-Maurienne
F 69 C6
St Jean-de-Monts F 66 B2
St Jean-d'Illac F 76 B2
St Jean-du-Bruel F 78 B2
St Jean-du-Gard F 78 B2
St Jean-en-Royans F 79 A4
St Jean-la-Riviere F 79 C6
St Jean-Pied-de-Port
F 76 C1
St Jean-Poutge F 77 C3
St Jeoire F 69 B6
St Joachim F 66 A2
St Johnstown IRL 19 B4
St Jorioz F 69 C6
St Joris Winge B 49 C5
St Jouin-de-Marnes F 67 B4
St Juéry F 77 C5
St Julien F 69 B5
St Julien-Chapteuil F 78 A3
St Julien-de-Vouvantes
F 57 C4
St Julien-du-Sault F 59 B4
St Julien-du-Verdon
F 79 C5
St Julien-en-Born F 76 B1
St Julien-en-Genevois
F 69 B6
St Julien-l'Ars F 67 B5
St Julien la-Vêtre F 68 C3
St Julien-Mont-Denis
F 69 C6
St Julien-sur-Reyssouze
F 69 B5
St Junien F 67 C5
St Just
F 78 B3
GB 28 C2
St Just-en-Chaussée
F 58 A3
St Just-en-Chevalet F 68 C3

St Justin F 76 C2
St Just-St Rambert F 69 C4
St Keverne GB 28 C2
St Lary-Soulan F 77 D3
St Laurent-d'Aigouze F 78 C3
St Laurent-de-Chamousset F 69 C4
St Laurent-de-Condel F 57 A5
St Laurent-de-la-Cabrerisse F 78 C1
St Laurent-de-la-Salanque F 78 D1
St Laurent-des-Autels F 66 A3
St Laurent-du-Pont F 69 C5
St Laurent-en-Caux F 58 A1
St Laurent-en-Grandvaux F 69 B5
St Laurent-Médoc F 76 A2
St Laurent-sur-Gorre F 67 C5
St Laurent-sur-Mer F 57 A5
St Laurent-sur-Sèvre F 66 B4
St Leger B 60 A1
St Léger-de-Vignes F 68 B3
St Léger-sous-Beuvray F 68 B4
St Léger-sur-Dheune F 69 B4
St Léonard-de-Noblat F 67 C6
St Leonards GB 31 D4
St Lô F 57 A4
St Lon-les-Mines F 76 C1
St Louis F 60 C3
St Loup F 68 B3
St Loup-de-la-Salle F 69 B4
St Loup-sur-Semouse F 60 C2
St Lunaire F 57 B3
St Lupicin F 69 B5
St Lyphard F 66 A2
St Lys F 77 C4
St Macaire F 76 B2
St Maclou F 58 A1
St Maixent-l'École F 67 B4
St Malo F 57 B3
St Mamet-la-Salvetat F 77 B5
St Mandrier-sur-Mer F 79 C4
St Marcel
Drôme F 78 B3
Saône-et-Loire F 69 B4
St Marcellin F 69 C5
St Marcellin sur Loire F 68 C4
St Marcet F 77 C3
St Mards-en-Othe F 59 B4
St Margaret's-at-Cliffe GB 31 C5
St Margaret's Hope GB 23 C6
St Mars-la-Jaille F 66 A3
St Martin-d'Ablois F 59 B4
St Martin-d'Auxigny F 68 A2
St Martin-de-Belleville F 69 C6
St Martin-de-Bossenay F 59 B4
St Martin-de-Crau F 78 C3
St Martin-de-Londres F 78 C2
St Martin-d'Entraunes F 79 B5
St Martin-de-Queyrières F 79 B5
St Martin-de-Ré F 66 B3
St Martin des Besaces F 57 A5
St Martin-d'Estreaux F 68 B3
St Martin-de-Valamas F 78 B3
St Martin-d'Hères F 69 C5
St Martin-du-Frêne F 69 B5
St Martin-en-Bresse F 69 B5
St Martin-en-Haut F 69 C4
St Martin-la-Méanne F 68 C1
St Martin-sur-Ouanne F 59 C4
St Martin-Valmeroux F 77 A5
St Martin-Vésubie F 79 B6
St Martory F 77 C3
St Mary's GB 23 C6
St Mathieu F 67 C5
St Mathieu-de-Tréviers F 78 C2
St Maurice CH 70 B1
St Maurice-Navacelles F 78 C2
St Maurice-sur-Moselle F 60 C2
St Mawes GB 28 C2
St Maximin-la-Ste Baume F 79 C4
St Méard-de-Gurçon F 76 B3
St Médard-de-Guizières F 76 A2
St Médard-en-Jalles F 76 B2
St Méen-le-Grand F 57 B3
St Menges F 59 A5
St Merløse DK 39 D4
St Město CZ 54 C1
St M'Hervé F 57 B4
St Michel
Aisne F 59 A5
Gers F 77 C3
St Michel-Chef-Chef F 66 A2
St Michel-de-Castelnau F 76 B2
St Michel-de-Maurienne F 69 C6
St Michel-en-Grève F 56 B2
St Michel-enl'Herm F 66 B3
St Michel-Mont-Mercure F 66 B4
St Mihiel F 60 B1
St Monance GB 25 B5
St Montant F 78 B3
St Moritz CH 71 B4
St Nazaire F 66 A2
St Nazaire-en-Royans F 79 A4
St Nazaire-le-Désert F 79 B4
St Nectaire F 68 C2
St Neots GB 30 B3
St Nicolas-de-Port F 60 B2
St Nicolas-de-Redon F 57 C3
St Nicolas-du-Pélem F 56 B2
St Niklaas B 49 B5
St Omer F 48 C3
St Pair-sur-Mer F 57 B4
St Palais F 76 C1
St Palais-sur-Mer F 66 C3
St Pardoux-la-Rivière F 67 C5
St Paul-Cap-de-Joux F 77 C4
St Paul-de-Fenouillet F 77 D5
St Paul-de-Varax F 69 B5
St Paulien F 68 C3
St Paul-le-Jeune F 78 B3
St Paul-lès-Dax F 76 C1
St Paul-Trois-Châteaux F 78 B3
St Pé-de-Bigorre F 76 C2
St Pée-sur-Nivelle F 76 C1
St Péravy-la-Colombe F 58 C2
St Péray F 78 B3
St Père-en-Retz F 66 A2
St Peter Port GB 56 A3
St Petersburg = Sankt-Peterburg RUS 7 B11
St Philbert-de-Grand-Lieu F 66 A3
St Pierre F 78 C1
St Pierre-d'Albigny F 69 C6
St Pierre-d'Allevard F 69 C6
St Pierre-de-Chartreuse F 69 C5
St Pierre-de-Chignac F 77 A3
St Pierre-de-la-Fage F 78 C2
St Pierre-d'Entremont F 69 C5
St Pierre-d'Oléron F 66 C3
St Pierre-Eglise F 57 A4
St Pierre-en-Port F 58 A1
St Pierre-le-Moûtier F 68 B3
St Pierre Montlimart F 66 A3
St Pierre-Quiberon F 66 A1
St Pierre-sur-Dives F 57 A5
St Pierreville F 78 B3
St Pieters-Leeuw B 49 C5
St Plancard F 77 C3
St Poix F 57 C4
St Pol-de-Léon F 56 B2
St Polgues F 68 C3
St Pol-sur-Ternoise F 48 C3
St Pons-de-Thomières F 78 C1
St Porchaire F 66 C4
St Pourçain-sur-Sioule F 68 B3
St Priest F 69 C4
St Privat F 68 C2
St Quay-Portrieux F 56 B3
St Quentin F 59 A4
St Quentin-la-Poterie F 78 B3
St Quentin-les-Anges F 57 C5
St Rambert d'Albon F 69 C4
St Rambert-en-Bugey F 69 C5
St Raphaël F 79 C5
St Rémy-de-Provence F 78 C3
St Rémy-du-Val F 57 B6
St Remy-en-Bouzemont F 59 B5
St Renan F 56 B1
St Révérien F 68 A3
St Riquier F 48 C2
St Romain-de-Colbosc F 58 A1
St Rome-de-Cernon F 78 B1
St Rome-de-Tarn F 78 B1
St Sadurní-d'Anoia E 91 B4
St Saëns F 58 A2
St Sampson GB 56 A3
St Samson-la-Poterie F 58 A2
St Saturnin-de-Lenne F 78 B2
St Saturnin-lès-Apt F 79 C4
St Sauflieu F 58 A3
St Saulge F 68 A3
St Sauveur
Finistère F 56 B2
Haute-Saône F 60 C2
St Sauveur-de-Montagut F 78 B3
St Sauveur-en-Puisaye F 59 C4
St Sauveur-en-Rue F 69 C4
St Sauveur-Lendelin F 57 A4
St Sauveur-le-Vicomte F 57 A4
St Sauveur-sur-Tinée F 79 B6
St Savin
Gironde F 76 A2
Vienne F 67 B5
St Savinien F 67 C4
St Savournin F 79 C4
St Seine-l'Abbaye F 69 A4
St Sernin-sur-Rance F 77 C5
St Sevan-sur-Mer F 57 B3
St Sever F 76 C2
St Sever-Calvados F 57 B4
St Sorlin-d'Arves F 69 C6
St Soupplets F 58 A3
St Sulpice F 77 C4
St Sulpice-Laurière F 67 B6
St Sulpice-les-Feuilles F 67 B6
St Symphorien F 76 B2
St Symphorien-de-Lay F 69 C4
St Symphorien d'Ozon F 69 C4
St Symphoriensur-Coise F 69 C4
St Teath GB 28 C3
St Thégonnec F 56 B2
St Thiébault F 60 B1
St Trivier-de-Courtes F 69 B5
St Trivier sur-Moignans F 69 B4
St Trojan-les-Bains F 66 C3
St Tropez F 79 C5
St Truiden B 49 C6
St Vaast-la-Hougue F 57 A4
St Valérien F 59 B4
St Valery-en-Caux F 58 A1
St Valéry-sur-Somme F 48 C2
St Vallier
Drôme F 69 C4
Saône-et-Loire F 69 B4
St Vallier-de-Thiey F 79 C5
St Varent F 67 B4
St Vaury F 68 B1
St Venant F 48 C3
St Véran F 79 B5
St Vincent I 70 C2
St Vincent-de-Tyrosse F 76 C1
St Vit F 69 A5
St Vith B 50 C2
St Vivien-de-Médoc F 66 C3
St Yan F 68 B4
St Ybars F 77 C4
St Yorre F 68 B3
St Yrieix-la-Perche F 67 C6
Saissac F 77 C5
Saja E 88 A2
Šajan SRB 75 C5
Šajkaš SRB 75 C5
Sajókaza H 65 B6
Sajószentpéter H 65 B6
Sajóvámos H 65 B6
Şakarya TR 118 B5
Šakiai LT 6 D7
Sakskøbing DK 39 E4
Sakule SRB 75 C5
Sala S 36 C3
Šal'a SK 64 B3
Sala Baganza I 81 B4
Sala Consilina I 104 C1
Salakovac SRB 85 B6
Salamanca E 94 B1
Salamina GR 117 E5
Salandra I 104 C2
Salaparuta I 108 B1
Salar E 100 B1
Salardú E 90 A3
Salas E 86 A4
Salas de los Infantes E 89 B3
Salau F 77 D4
Salavaux CH 70 B2
Salbertrand I 79 A5
Salbohed S 36 C3
Salbris F 68 A2
Salbu N 32 A2
Salce E 86 B4
Salching D 62 B3
Salcombe GB 28 C4
Saldaña E 88 B2
Saldus LV 6 C7
Sale I 80 B2
Saleby S 35 D5
Salem D 61 C5
Salemi I 108 B1
Salen
Argyll & Bute GB 24 B2
Highland GB 24 B2
N 114 C8
Sälen S 34 A5
Salernes F 79 C5
Salerno I 103 C7
Salers F 68 C2
Salford GB 26 B3
Salgótarján H 65 B5
Salgueiro P 92 B3
Salhus N 32 B2
Sali HR 83 C4
Sálice Salentino I 105 C3
Salientes E 86 B4
Salies-de-Béarn F 76 C2
Salies-du-Salat F 77 C3
Salignac-Eyvigues F 77 B4
Saligney-sur-Roudon F 68 B3
Salihli TR 119 D3
Salihorsk BY 7 E9
Salinas
Alicante E 101 A5
Huesca E 90 A3
Salinas de Medinaceli E 95 A4
Salinas de Pisuerga E 88 B2
Salindres F 78 B3
Saline di Volterra I 81 C4
Salins-les-Bains F 69 B5
Salir P 98 B2
Salisbury GB 29 B6
Salla
A 73 A4
FIN 113 F17
Sallachy GB 23 C4
Sallanches F 70 C1
Sallent E 91 B4
Sallent de Gállego E 76 D2
Salles F 76 B2
Salles-Curan F 78 B1
Salles-sur-l'Hers F 77 C4
Sallins IRL 21 A5
Sällsjö S 115 D10
Salmerón E 95 B4
Salmiech F 77 B5
Salmivaara FIN 113 F17
Salmoral E 94 B1
Salo FIN 6 A7
Salò I 71 C5
Salobreña E 100 C2
Salon-de-Provence F 79 C4
Salonica = Thessaloniki GR 116 B4
Salonta RO 10 C6
Salorino E 93 B3
Salornay-sur-Guye F 69 B4
Salorno I 71 B6
Salou E 91 B4
Šalovci SLO 73 B6
Salsbruket N 114 C8
Salses-le-Château F 78 D1
Salsomaggiore Terme I 81 B3
Salt E 91 B5
Saltaire GB 27 B4
Saltara I 82 C1
Saltash GB 28 C3
Saltburn-by-the-Sea GB 27 A5
Saltcoats GB 24 C3
Saltfleet GB 27 B6
Salto P 87 C3
Saltrød N 33 D5
Saltsjöbaden S 37 C5
Saltvik
FIN 36 B7
S 40 B6
Saludécio I 82 C1
Salussola I 70 C3
Saluzzo I 80 B1
Salvacañete E 95 B5
Salvada P 98 B3
Salvagnac F 77 C4
Salvaleon E 93 C4
Salvaterra de Magos P 92 B2
Salvaterra do Extremo P 93 B4
Salvatierra
Avila E 89 B4
Badajoz E 93 C4
Salvatierra de Santiago E 93 B4
Salviac F 77 B4
Salzburg A 62 C4
Salzgitter D 51 A6
Salzgitter Bad D 51 A6
Salzhausen D 44 B2
Salzhemmendorf D 51 A5
Salzkotten D 51 B4
Salzmünde D 52 B1
Salzwedel D 44 C3
Samadet F 76 C2
Samandıra TR 118 B4
Samassi I 110 C1
Samatan F 77 C3
Sambiase I 106 C3
Sambir UA 11 B7
Samborowo PL 47 B5
Sambuca di Sicília I 108 B2
Samedan CH 71 B4
Samer F 48 C2
Sami GR 117 D2
Şamlı TR 118 C2
Sammichele di Bari I 104 C2
Samnaun CH 71 B5
Samobor HR 73 C5
Samoëns F 70 B1
Samogneux F 59 A6
Samokov BG 11 E7
Samora Correia P 92 C2
Šamorín SK 64 B3
Samos
E 86 B3
GR 119 E1
Samoš SRB 75 C5
Samothraki GR 116 B7
Samper de Calanda E 90 B2
Sampéyre I 79 B6
Sampieri I 109 C3
Sampigny F 60 B1
Samplawa PL 47 B5
Samproniano I 81 D5
Samtens D 45 A5
Samugheo I 110 C1
San Adrián E 89 B5
San Agustín E 101 C3
San Agustin de Guadalix E 94 B3
Sanaigmore GB 24 C1
San Alberto I 82 B1
San Amaro E 87 B2
Sânandrei RO 75 C6
San Andrês del Rabanedo E 88 B1
San Antanio di Santadi I 110 C1
San Antolín de Ibias E 86 A4
San Arcángelo I 104 C2
Sanary-sur-Mer F 79 C4
San Asensio E 89 B4
San Bartoloméde las Abiertas E 94 C2
San Bartoloméde la Torre E 99 B3
San Bartoloméde Pinares E 94 B2
San Bartolomeo in Galdo I 103 B8
San Benedetto del Tronto I 82 D2
San Benedetto in Alpe I 81 C5
San Benedetto Po I 81 A4
San Benito E 100 A1
San Benito de la Contienda E 93 C3
San Biágio Plátani I 108 B2
San Biágio Saracinisco I 103 B6
San Bonifacio I 71 C6
San Calixto E 99 B5
San Cándido I 72 B2
San Carlo
CH 70 B3
I 108 B2
San Carlos del Valle E 100 A2
San Casciano dei Bagni I 81 D5
San Casciano in Val di Pesa I 81 C5
San Cataldo
Puglia I 105 C4
Sicilia I 108 B2
San Cebrián de Castro E 88 C1
Sancergues F 68 A2
Sancerre F 68 A2
San Cesário di Lecce I 105 C4
Sancey-le-Long F 69 A6
Sanchiorian E 94 B2
San Chírico Raparo I 106 A3
Sanchonuño E 88 C2
San Cibrao das Viñas E 87 B3
San Cipirello I 108 B2
San Ciprián E 86 A3
San Clemente E 95 C4
San Clodio E 86 B3
Sancoins F 68 B2
San Colombano al Lambro I 71 C4
San Costanzo I 82 C2
San Crisóbal de Entreviñas E 88 B1
San Cristóbal de la Polantera E 88 B1
San Cristóbal de la Vega E 94 A2
San Cristovo E 87 C3
Sancti-Petri E 99 C4
Sancti-Spiritus E 87 D4
Sand
Hedmark N 34 B3
Rogaland N 33 C3
Sanda S 37 E5
San Damiano d'Asti I 80 B2
San Damiano Macra I 79 B6
Sandane N 114 F3
San Daniele del Friuli I 72 B3
Sandanski BG 116 A5
Sandared S 40 B2
Sandarne S 36 A4
Sandau D 44 C4
Sandbach
D 63 B4
GB 26 B3
Sandbank GB 24 C3
Sandbanks GB 29 C6
Sandbukt N 112 C10
Sandby DK 39 E4
Sande
D 43 B5
Sogn og Fjordane N 32 A2
Vestfold N 35 C2
Sandefjord N 35 C2
Sandeid N 33 C2
San Demétrio Corone I 106 B3
San Demétrio né Vestini I 103 A6
Sandersleben D 52 B1
Sanderstølen N 32 B6
Sandes N 33 D4
Sandesneben D 44 B2
Sandhead GB 24 D3
Sandhem S 40 B3
Sandhorst D 43 B4
Sandhurst GB 31 C3
Sandıklı TR 119 D5
Sandillon F 58 C3
Sandl A 63 B5
Sandnes N 33 D2
Sandness GB 22 A7
Sandnessjøen N 115 A9
Sando E 87 D4
Sandomierz PL 55 C6
San Dónaci I 105 C3
San Donàdi Piave I 72 C2
San Donato Val di Comino I 103 B6
Sándorfalva H 75 B5
Sandown GB 31 D2
Sandøysund N 35 C2
Sandrigo I 72 C1
Sandsele S 115 B14
Sandset N 112 D3
Sandsjöfors S 40 B4
Sandstad N 114 D6
Sandvatn N 33 D3
Sandvig-Allinge DK 41 D4
Sandvika
Akershus N 34 C2
Hedmark N 34 B3
Nord-Trøndelag N 114 D9
Sandviken S 36 B3
Sandvikvåy N 32 C2
Sandwich GB 31 C5
Sandy GB 30 B3
San Emiliano E 86 B5
San Enrique E 99 C5
San Esteban E 86 A4
San Esteban de Gormaz E 89 C3
San Esteban de la Sierra E 93 A5
San Esteban de Litera E 90 B3
San Esteban del Molar E 88 C1
San Esteban del Valle E 94 B2
San Esteban de Valdueza E 86 B4
San Fele I 104 C1
San Felice Circeo I 102 B6
San Felices E 88 B3
San Felices de los Gallégos E 87 D4
San Felice sul Panaro I 81 B5
San Ferdinando di Púglia I 104 B2
San Fernando E 99 C4
San Fernando de Henares E 95 B3
San Fili I 106 B3
San Foca I 105 C4
San Fratello I 109 B3
Sangatte F 48 C2
San Gavino Monreale I 110 C1
San Gémini Fonte I 102 A5
Sangerhausen D 52 B1
San Germano Vercellese I 70 C3
San Giácomo
Trentino Alto Adige I 72 B1
Umbria I 82 D1
San Gimignano I 81 C5
San Ginésio I 82 C2
Sangineto Lido I 106 B2
San Giórgio a Liri I 103 B6
San Giorgio della Richinvelda I 72 B2
San Giórgio del Sánnio I 103 B7
San Giórgio di Lomellina I 70 C3
San Giórgio di Nogaro I 72 C3
San Giorgio di Piano I 81 B5
San Giórgio Iónico I 104 C3
San Giovanni a Piro I 106 A2
San Giovanni Bianco I 71 C4
San Giovanni di Sinis I 110 C1
San Giovanni in Croce I 81 A4
San Giovanni in Fiore I 106 B3
San Giovanni in Persiceto I 81 B5
San Giovanni Reatino I 102 A5
San Giovanni Rotondo I 104 B1
San Giovanni Suérgiu I 110 C1
San Giovanni Valdarno I 81 C5
San Giuliano Terme I 81 C4
San Giustino I 82 C1
San Godenzo I 81 C5
Sangonera la Verde E 101 B4
San Gregorio Magno I 103 C8
Sangüesa E 90 A1
Sanguinet F 76 B1
San Guiseppe Jato I 108 B2
Sanica BIH 83 B5
Sanitz D 44 A4
San Javier E 101 B5
San Jorge P 92 B2
San José E 101 C3
San Juan E 89 B3
San Juan de Alicante E 96 C2
San Juan de la Nava E 94 B2
San Justo de la Vega E 86 B4
Sankt Aegyd am Neuwalde A 63 C6
Sankt Andrä A 73 B4
Sankt Andreasberg D 51 B6
Sankt Anna S 37 D3
Sankt Anna am Aigen A 73 B5
Sankt Anton am Arlberg A 71 A5
Sankt Anton an der Jessnitz A 63 C6
Sankt Augustin D 50 C3
Sankt Blasien D 61 C4
Sankt Englmar D 62 A3
Sankt Gallen
A 63 C5
CH 71 A4
Sankt Gallenkirch A 71 A4
Sankt Georgen
A 63 B5
D 61 B4
Sankt Georgen am Reith A 63 C5
Sankt Georgen ob Judenburg A 73 A4
Sankt Georgen ob Murau A 73 A4
Sankt Gilgen A 63 C4
Sankt Goar D 50 C3
Sankt Goarshausen D 50 C3
Sankt Ingbert D 60 A3
Sankt Jacob A 73 B4
Sankt Jakob in Defereggen A 72 B2
Sankt Johann am Tauern A 73 A4
Sankt Johann am Wesen A 63 B4
Sankt Johann im Pongau A 72 A3
Sankt Johann in Tirol A 72 A2
Sankt Katharein an der Laming A 73 A5
Sankt Kathrein am Hauenstein A 73 A5
Sankt Lambrecht A 73 A4
Sankt Leonhard am Forst A 63 B6
Sankt Leonhard im Pitztal A 71 A5
Sankt Lorenzen A 72 B2
Sankt Marein
Steiermark A 73 A5
Steiermark A 73 A5
Sankt Margarethen im Lavanttal A 73 B4
Sankt Margrethen CH 71 A4
Sankt Michael A 73 A5
Sankt Michael im Burgenland A 73 A6
Sankt Michael im Lungau A 72 A3
Sankt Michaelisdonn D 43 B6
Sankt Niklaus CH 70 B2
Sankt Nikolai im Sölktal A 73 A4
Sankt Olof S 41 D4
Sankt Oswald D 63 B4
Sankt Paul
A 73 B4
F 79 B5
Sankt Peter D 61 B4
Sankt Peter am Kammersberg A 73 A4
Sankt-Peterburg = St Petersburg RUS 7 B11
Sankt Peter-Ording D 43 A5
Sankt Pölten A 63 B6
Sankt Radegund A 73 A5
Sankt Ruprecht an der Raab A 73 A5
Sankt Salvator A 73 B4
Sankt Stefan A 73 B4
Sankt Stefan an der Gail A 72 B3
Sankt Stefan im Rosental A 73 B5
Sankt Valentin A 63 B5
Sankt Veit an der Glan A 73 B4
Sankt Veit an der Gölsen A 63 B6
Sankt Veit in Defereggen A 72 B2
Sankt Wendel D 60 A3
Sankt Wolfgang
A 63 C4
D 62 B3
San Lazzaro di Sávena I 81 B5
San Leo I 82 C1
San Leonardo de Yagüe E 89 C3
San Leonardo in Passiria I 71 B6
San Lorenzo al Mare I 80 C1
San Lorenzo a Merse I 81 C5
San Lorenzo Bellizzi I 106 B3
San Lorenzo de Calatrava E 100 A2
San Lorenzo de El Escorial E 94 B2
San Lorenzo de la Parrilla E 95 C4
San Lorenzo di Sebato I 72 B1
San Lorenzo in Campo I 82 C1
San Lorenzo Nuovo I 81 D5
San Lourenco P 98 A2
San Luca I 106 C3
Sanlúcar de Barrameda E 99 C4
Sanlúcar de Guadiana E 98 B3
Sanlúcar la Mayor E 99 B4
San Lúcido I 106 B3
Sanluri I 110 C1
San Marcello I 82 C2
San Marcello Pistoiese I 81 B4
San Marcial E 88 C1
San Marco I 103 C7
San Marco Argentano I 106 B3
San Marco dei Cavoti I 103 B7
San Marco in Lámis I 104 B1
San Marino RSM 82 C1
San Martin de Castañeda E 87 B4
San Martín de la Vega E 95 B3
San Martin de la Vega del Alberche E 93 A5
San Martín del Tesorillo E 99 C5
San Martin de Luiña E 86 A4
San Martin de Montalbán E 94 C2
San Martin de Oscos E 86 A4
San Martin de Pusa E 94 C2
San Martin de Unx E 89 B5
San Martín de Valdeiglesias E 94 B2
San Martino di Campagna I 72 B2
San Martino di Castrozza I 72 B1
San-Martino-di-Lota F 102 A2
San Martino in Pénsilis I 103 B8
San Mateo de Gallego E 90 B2
San Máuro Forte I 104 C2
San Michele all'Adige I 71 B6
San Michele di Ganzaria I 109 B3
San Michele Mondov ì I 80 B1
San Miguel de Aguayo E 88 A2
San Miguel de Bernuy E 88 C3
San Miguel del Arroyo E 88 C2
San Miguel de Salinas E 101 B5
Sânmihaiu Roman RO 75 C6
San Millán de la Cogolla E 89 B4
San Miniato I 81 C4
San Muñoz E 87 D4
Sänna S 37 D1
Sannazzaro de'Burgondi I 80 A2
Sanne D 44 C3
Sannicandro di Bari I 104 B2
Sannicandro Gargánico I 104 B1
San Nicola del'Alto I 107 B3
San Nicolás del Puerto E 99 B5
Sânnicolau Mare RO 75 B5
San Nicolò I 81 B5
San Nicolò Gerrei I 110 C2
Sannidal N 33 D6
Sanniki PL 47 C5
Sanok PL 11 B7
San Pablo de los Montes E 94 C2
San Pancrázio Salentino I 105 C3
San Pantaleo I 110 A2
San Páolo di Civitate I 103 B8
San Pawl il-Bahar M 107 C5
San Pedro
Albacete E 101 A3
Oviedo E 86 A4
San Pedro de Alcántara E 100 C1
San Pedro de Ceque E 87 B4
San Pedro del Arroyo E 94 B2
San Pedro de Latarce E 88 C1
San Pedro del Pinatar E 101 B5
San Pedro del Romeral E 88 A3
San Pedro de Merida E 93 C4
San Pedro de Valderaduey E 88 B2
San Pedro Manrique E 89 B4
San Pellegrino Terme I 71 C4
San Piero a Sieve I 81 C5
San Piero in Bagno I 81 C5
San Piero Patti I 109 A3
San Pietro I 109 B3
San Pietro in Casale I 81 B5
San Pietro in Gu I 72 C1
San Pietro in Palazzi I 81 C4
San Pietro in Volta I 72 C2
San Pietro Vara I 80 B3
San Pietro Vernótico I 105 C3
San Polo d'Enza I 81 B4
Sanquhar GB 25 C4
San Quírico d'Órcia I 81 C5
San Rafael del Rio E 90 C3
San Remo I 80 C1
San Román de Cameros E 89 B4
San Roman de Hernija E 88 C1
San Román de la Cuba E 88 B2
San Roman de los Montes E 94 B2
San Romao P 92 C3
San Roque E 99 C5
San Roque de Riomera E 88 A3
San Rufo I 104 C1
San Sabastián de los Ballesteros E 100 B1
San Salvador de Cantamuda E 88 B2
San Salvo I 103 A7
San Salvo Marina I 103 A7
San Sebastián de los Reyes E 94 B3
San Sebastiano Curone I 80 B3
San Secondo Parmense I 81 B4
Sansepolcro I 82 C1
San Serverino Marche I 82 C2
San Severino Lucano I 106 A3
San Severo I 103 B8
San Silvestre de Guzmán E 98 B3
Sanski Most BIH 83 B5
San Sosti I 106 B3
San Stéfano di Cadore I 72 B2
San Stino di Livenza I 72 C2
Santa Agnès E 97 B1
Santa Amalia E 93 B4
Santa Ana
Cáceres E 93 B5
Jaén E 100 B2
Santa Ana de Pusa E 94 C2
Santa Barbara E 90 C3
Santa Bárbara P 98 B2
Santa Barbara de Casa E 98 B3
Santa Bárbara de Padrões P 98 B3
Santacara E 89 B5
Santa Catarina P 98 B3
Santa Caterina di Pittinuri I 110 B1
Santa Caterina Villarmosa I 109 B3
Santa Cesárea Terme I 107 A5
Santa Clara-a-Nova P 98 B2
Santa Clara-a-Velha P 98 B2
Santa Clara de Louredo P 98 B3
Santa Coloma de Farners E 91 B5
Santa Coloma de Gramenet E 91 B5
Santa Coloma de Queralt E 91 B4
Santa Colomba de Curueño E 88 B1
Santa Colomba de Somoza E 86 B4
Santa Comba E 86 A2
Santa Comba Dáo P 92 A2
Santa Comba de Rossas P 87 C4
Santa Cristina I 71 C4
Santa Cristina de la Polvorosa E 88 B1
Santa Croce Camerina I 109 C3
Santa Croce di Magliano I 103 B7
Santa Cruz
E 86 A2
P 92 B1
Santa Cruz de Alhama E 100 B2
Santa Cruz de Campezo E 89 B4
Santa Cruz de Grio E 89 C5
Santa Cruz de la Salceda E 89 C3
Santa Cruz de la Sierra E 93 B5
Santa Cruz de la Zarza E 95 C3
Santa Cruz del Retamar E 94 B2
Santa Cruz del Valle E 94 B1
Santa Cruz de Moya E 96 B1
Santa Cruz de Mudela E 100 A2
Santa Cruz de Paniagua E 93 A4
Santadi I 110 C1
Santa Doménica Talao I 106 B2
Santa Doménica Vittória I 109 B3
Santa Elena E 100 A2
Santa Elena de Jamuz E 88 B1
Santaella E 100 B1
Santa Eufemia E 100 A1
Santa Eufémia d'Aspromonte I 106 C2
Santa Eulalia E 95 B5
Santa Eulália P 92 C3
Santa Eulalia de Oscos E 86 A3
Santa Eulàlia des Riu E 97 C1
Santa Fe E 100 B2
Santa Fiora I 81 D5
Sant'Ágata dei Goti I 103 B7
Sant'Ágata di Ésaro I 106 B2
Sant'Ágata di Puglia I 103 B8
Sant'Ágata Feltria I 82 C1
Sant'Ágata Militello I 109 A3
Santa Gertrude I 71 B5
Santa Giustina I 72 B2
Sant Agust ìde Lluçanès E 91 A5
Santa Iria P 98 B3
Santa Leocadia P 87 C2
Santa Lucia del Mela I 109 A4
Santa Lucia-de-Porto-Vecchio F 102 B2
Santa Luzia P 98 B2
Santa Maddalena Vallalta I 72 B2
Santa Magdalena de Polpis E 90 C3
Santa Margalida E 97 B3
Santa Margarida P 92 B2
Santa Margarida do Sado P 98 A2
Santa Margaridao de Montbui E 91 B4
Santa Margherita I 110 D1
Santa Margherita di Belice I 108 B2
Santa Margherita Ligure I 80 B3
Santa Maria
CH 71 B5
E 90 A2
Santa Maria al Bagno I 107 A4
Santa Maria Cápua Vétere I 103 B7
Santa Maria da Feira P 87 D2
Santa Maria de Cayón E 88 A3
Santa Maria de Corco E 91 A5
Santa Maria de Huerta E 95 A4
Santa Maria de la Alameda E 94 B2
Santa Maria de las Hoyas E 89 C3
Santa Maria del Camí E 97 B2
Santa Maria del Campo E 88 B3
Santa Maria del Campo Rus E 95 C4
Santa Maria della Versa I 80 B3
Santa Maria del Páramo E 88 B1
Santa Maria del Taro I 80 B3
Santa Maria de Mercadillo E 89 C3
Santa Maria de Nieva E 101 B4
Santa Maria de Trassierra E 100 B1
Santa Maria di Licodia I 109 B3
Santa Maria-di-Rispéscia I 81 D5
Santa Maria la Palma I 110 B1
Santa María la Real de Nieva E 94 A2
Santa Maria Maggiore I 70 B3
Santa Maria Ribarredonda E 89 B3
Santa Marina del Rey E 88 B1
Santa Marinella I 102 A4
Santa Marta
Albacete E 95 C4
Badajoz E 93 C4
Santa Marta de Magasca E 93 B4
Santa Marta de Penaguião P 87 C3
Santa Marta de Tormes E 94 B1
Santana
Évora P 92 C2
Setúbal P 92 C1
Santana da Serra P 98 B2
Sant'Ana de Cambas P 98 B3
Santana do Mato P 92 C2
Sant'Anastasia I 103 C7
Santander E 88 A3
Sant'Andrea Frius I 110 C2
Sant'Ángelo dei Lombardi I 103 C8
Sant'Angelo in Vado I 82 C1
Sant'Angelo Lodigiano I 71 C4
Santa Ninfa I 108 B1
Sant'Antíoco I 110 C1
Sant Antoni de Calonge E 91 B6
Sant Antoni de Portmany E 97 C1
Sant'Antonio-di-Gallura I 110 B2
Santanyí E 97 B3
Santa Olalla
Huelva E 99 B4
Toledo E 94 B2
Santa Pau E 91 A5
Santa Pola E 96 C2
Santa Ponça E 97 B2
Santarcángelo di Romagna I 82 B1
Santarém P 92 B2
Santa Severa
F 102 A2
I 102 A4
Santa Severina I 107 B3
Santas Martas E 88 B1
Santa Sofia I 81 C5
Santa Susana P 92 C2
Santa Suzana P 92 C3
Santa Teresa di Riva I 109 B4
Santa Teresa Gallura I 110 A2
Santa Uxía E 86 B2
Santa Valburga I 71 B5
Santa Vittória in Matenano I 82 C2
Sant Boi de Llobregat E 91 B5
Sant Carles de la Ràpita E 90 C3
Sant Carlos E 97 B1
Sant'Caterina I 81 D5
Sant Celoni E 91 B5
Sant Climent E 97 B4
Santed E 95 A5
Sant'Egídio alla Vibrata I 82 D2
Sant'Elia a Pianisi I 103 B7
Sant'Elia Fiumerapido I 103 B6
Santelices E 88 A3
San Telmo E 99 B4
Sant'Elpídio a Mare I 82 C2
Santéramo in Colle I 104 C2
Santervas de la Vega E 88 B2
Sant' Eufemia Lamezia I 106 C3
Sant Felíu E 91 B5
Sant Feliu de Codines E 91 B5
Sant Feliu de Guíxols E 91 B6
Sant Feliu Sasserra E 91 B5
Sant Ferran E 97 C1
Sant Francesc de Formentera E 97 C1
Sant Francesc de ses Salines E 97 C1
Santhià I 70 C3
Sant Hilari Sacalm E 91 B5
Sant Hipòlit de Voltregà E 91 A5
Santiago de Alcántara E 92 B3
Santiago de Calatrava E 100 B1
Santiago de Compostela E 86 B2
Santiago de la Espade E 101 A3
Santiago de la Puebla E 94 B1
Santiago de la Ribera E 101 B5
Santiago del Campo E 93 B4
Santiago de Litem P 92 B2
Santiago do Cacém P 98 B2
Santiago do Escoural P 92 C2
Santiago Maior P 92 C3
Santibáñez de Béjar E 93 A5
Santibáñez de la Peña E 88 B2
Santibáñez de Murias E 88 A1
Santibáñez de Vidriales E 87 B4
Santibáñez el Alto E 93 A4
Santibáñez el Bajo E 93 A4
Santillana E 88 A2
Santiponce E 99 B4
San Tirso de Abres E 86 A3
Santisteban del Puerto E 100 A2
Santiuste de San Juan Bautiste E 94 A2
Santiz E 94 A1
Sant Jaume dels Domenys E 91 B4
Sant Joan Baptista E 97 B1
Sant Joan de les Abadesses E 91 A5
Sant Jordi E 90 C3
Sant Josep de sa Talaia E 97 C1
Sant Juliàde Loria AND 91 A4
Sant'Ilario d'Enza I 81 B4
Sant Llorençde Morunys E 91 A4
Sant Llorençdes Carctassar E 97 B3
Sant Llorenç Savall E 91 B5
Sant Luis E 97 B4
Sant Mart ìde Llemaná E 91 A5
Sant Marti de Maldá E 91 B4
Sant Marti Sarroca E 91 B4
Sant Mateu E 90 C3
Sant Miquel E 97 B1
Santo Aleixo P 98 A3
Santo Amado P 98 A3
Santo Amaro P 92 C3
Santo André P 98 A2
Santo Domingo E 93 C3

Santo Domingo de la Calzada E 89 B4
Santo Domingo de Silos E 89 C3
Santo Estêvão
Faro P 98 B3
Santarém P 92 C2
Santok PL 46 C1
Santomera E 101 A4
Santoña E 89 A3
Santo-Pietro-di Tenda F 102 A2
Sant'Oreste I 102 A5
Santo Spirito I 104 B2
Santo Stefano d'Aveto I 80 B3
Santo Stéfano di Camastra I 109 B3
Santo Stefano di Magra I 81 B3
Santo Stéfano Quisquina I 108 B2
Santo Tirso P 87 C2
Santotis E 88 A2
Santo Tomé E 100 A2
Santovenia
Burgos E 89 B3
Zamora E 88 C1
Sant Pau de Seguries E 91 A5
Santpedor E 91 B4
Sant Pere de Riudebitles E 91 B4
Sant Pere Pescador E 91 A6
Sant Pere Sallavinera E 91 B4
Sant Quirze de Besora E 91 A5
Sant Rafel E 97 C1
Sant Ramon E 91 B4
Santu Lussurgiu I 110 B1
Santutzi E 89 A3
Sant Vincençde Castellet E 91 B4
San Valentino alla Muta I 71 B5
San Venanzo I 82 D1
San Vicente de Alcántara E 93 B3
San Vicente de Arana E 89 B4
San Vicente de la Barquera E 88 A2
San Vicente de la Sonsierra E 89 B4
San Vicente de Toranzo E 88 A3
San Vietro E 87 C4
San Vigilio I 72 B1
San Vincente del Raspeig E 96 C2
San Vincenzo I 81 C4
San Vito I 110 C2
San Vito al Tagliamento I 72 C2
San Vito Chietino I 103 A7
San Vito dei Normanni I 104 C3
San Vito di Cadore I 72 B2
San Vito lo Capo I 108 A1
San Vito Romano I 102 B5
Sanxenxo E 86 B2
Sanza I 104 C1
São Aleixo P 92 C3
São Barnabé P 98 B2
São Bartoloméda Serra P 98 A2
São Bartolomeu de Messines P 98 B2
São Bento P 87 C2
São Brás P 98 B3
São Brás de Alportel P 98 B3
São Braz do Reguedoura P 92 C2
São Cristóvão P 92 C2
São Domingos P 98 B2
São Geraldo P 92 C2
São Jacinto P 92 A2
São João da Madeira P 87 D2
São João da Pesqueira P 87 C3
São João da Ribeira P 92 B2
São João da Serra P 87 D2
São João da Venda P 98 B3
São João dos Caldeireiros P 98 B3
São Julião P 92 B3
São Leonardo P 92 C3
São Luis P 98 B2
São Manços P 92 C3
São Marcos da Ataboeira P 98 B3
Saõ Marcos da Serra P 98 B2
São Marcos de Campo P 92 C3
São Martinho da Cortiça P 92 A2
São Martinho das Amoreiras P 98 B2
São Martinho do Porto P 92 B1
São Matias
Beja P 98 A3
Évora P 92 C2
São Miguel d'Acha P 92 A3
São Miguel de Machede P 92 C3
São Pedro da Torre P 87 C2
São Pedro de Cadeira P 92 B1
São Pedro de Muel P 92 B1
São Pedro de Solis P 98 B3
São Pedro do Sul P 87 D2
Saorge F 80 C1
São Romão P 92 C2
São Sebastião dos Carros P 98 B3
São Teotónio P 98 B2
São Torcato P 87 C2
Sapataria P 92 C1
Sapes GR 116 A7
Sapiãos P 87 C3
Sa Pobla E 97 B3
Sappada I 72 B2
Sappen N 112 C10
Sapri I 106 A2
Sarajevo BIH 84 C3
Saramon F 77 C3
Sarandë AL 116 C2
Saranovo SRB 85 B5
Saraorci SRB 85 B6
Sa Rapita E 97 B3
Saray TR 118 A2
Saraycık TR 118 C4
Sarayköy TR 119 E3
Saraylar TR 118 B2
Sarayönü TR 119 D7
Sarbia PL 46 C2
Sarbinowo
Zachodnio-Pomorskie PL 45 C6
Zachodnio-Pomorskie PL 46 A1
Sárbogárd H 74 B3
Sarcelles F 58 A3
Sarche I 71 B5
Sardara I 110 C1
Sardoal P 92 B2
Sardón de Duero E 88 C2
Sare F 76 C1
S'Arenal E 97 B2
Šarengrad HR 75 C4
Sarentino I 71 B6
Sarezzo I 71 C5
Sargans CH 71 A4
Sári H 75 A4
Sarıbeyler TR 118 C2
Sarıcakaya TR 118 B5
Sari-d'Orcino F 102 A1
Sarıgöl TR 119 D3
Sarıkaya TR 16 B7
Sarıköy TR 118 B2
Sarilhos Grandes P 92 C2
Sariñena E 90 B2
Sarıoba TR 118 C7
Sárisáp H 65 C4
Sariyer TR 118 A4
Sarkad H 75 B6
Sárkeresztes H 74 A3
Sárkeresztúr H 74 A3
Särkijärvi FIN 113 E12
Şarkikaraağaç TR 119 D6
Şarköy TR 118 B2
Sarlat-la-Canéda F 77 B4
Sarliac-sur-l'Isle F 67 C5
Sármellék H 74 B2
Särna S 115 F10
Sarnadas P 92 B3
Sarnano I 82 C2
Sarnen CH 70 B3
Sarnesfield GB 29 A5
Sárnico I 71 C4
Sarno I 103 C7
Sarnonico I 71 B6
Sarnow D 45 B5
Sarny UA 11 A9
Särö S 38 B4
Saronno I 70 C4
Sárosd H 74 A3
Šarovce SK 65 B4
Sarpoil F 68 C3
Sarpsborg N 35 C3
Sarracín E 88 B3
Sarral E 91 B4
Sarralbe F 60 A3
Sarrancolin F 77 D3
Sarras F 69 C4
Sarre I 70 C2
Sarreaus E 87 B3
Sarrebourg F 60 B3
Sarreguemines F 60 A3
Sárrétudvari H 75 A6
Sarre-Union F 60 B3
Sarria E 86 B3
Sarriàde Ter E 91 A5
Sarrión E 96 A2
Sarroca de Lleida E 90 B3
Sarroch I 110 C2
Sarron F 76 C2
Sársina I 82 C1
Særslev DK 39 D3
Sarstedt D 51 A5
Sárszentlörinc H 74 B3
Sárszentmihaly H 74 A3
Sárszentmiklós H 74 B3
Sarteano I 81 D5
Sartène F 102 B1
Sartilly F 57 B4
Sartirana Lomellina I 80 A2
Saruhanlı TR 118 D2
Sárvár H 74 A1
Sarvisvaara S 113 F10
Sarzana I 81 B3
Sarzeau F 66 A2
Sarzedas P 92 B3
Sasalli TR 119 D1
Sasamón E 88 B2
Sa Savina E 97 C1
Sásd H 74 B3
Sasino PL 46 A3
Sássari I 110 B1
Sassello I 80 B2
Sassenberg D 50 B4
Sassetta I 81 C4
Sassnitz D 45 A5
Sassocorvaro I 82 C1
Sasso d'Ombrone I 81 D5
Sassoferrato I 82 C1
Sassoleone I 81 B5
Sasso Marconi I 81 B5
Sassuolo I 81 B4
Sástago E 90 B2
Šaštinske Stráže SK 64 B3
Sas van Gent NL 49 B4
Såtåhaugen N 114 E7
Satão P 87 D3
Såtenäs S 35 D4
Säter S 36 B2
Sätila S 40 B2
Satillieu F 69 C4
Satnica Đakovačka HR 74 C3
Sátoraljaújhely H 10 B6
Satow D 44 B3
Sätra-brunn S 36 C3
Sætre N 35 C2
Satrup D 43 A6
Satteins A 71 A4
Satu Mare RO 11 C7
Saturnia I 102 A4
Saucats F 76 B2
Saucelle E 87 C4
Sauda N 33 C3
Sauðarkrókur IS 111 B6
Saudasjøen N 33 C3
Sauerlach D 62 C2
Saugues F 78 B2
Sauherad N 33 C6
Saujon F 66 C4
Sauland N 33 C5
Saulces Monclin F 59 A5
Saulgau D 61 B5
Saulgrub D 62 C2
Saulieu F 69 A4
Saulnot F 60 C2
Sault F 79 B4
Sault-Brénaz F 69 C5
Sault-de-Navailles F 76 C2
Saulx F 60 C2
Saulxures-sur-Moselotte F 60 C2
Saulzais-le-Potier F 68 B2
Saumos F 76 B1
Saumur F 67 A4
Saunavaara FIN 113 E16
Saundersfoot GB 28 B3
Saurat F 77 D4
Saurbær
Borgarfjarðarsýsla IS 111 C4
Dalasýsla IS 111 B4
Eyjafjarðarsýsla IS 111 B7
Sáuris I 72 B2
Sausset-les-Pins F 79 C4
Sauteyrargues F 78 C2
Sauvagnat F 68 C2
Sauve F 78 C2
Sauveterre-de-Béarn F 76 C2
Sauveterre-de-Guyenne F 76 B2
Sauviat-sur-Vige F 67 C6
Sauxillanges F 68 C3
Sauzet
Drôme F 78 B3
Lot F 77 B4
Sauzé-Vaussais F 67 B5
Sauzon F 66 A1
Sava I 104 C3
Sævareid N 32 B2
Savarsin RO 11 C7
Savaştepe TR 118 C2
Savci SLO 73 B6
Säve S 38 B4
Savelletri I 104 C3
Savelli I 107 B3
Savenay F 66 A3
Saverdun F 77 C4
Saverne F 60 B3
Savières F 59 B4
Savigliano I 80 B1
Savignac-les-Eglises F 67 C5
Savignano Irpino I 103 B8
Savignano sul Rubicone I 82 B1
Savigny-sur-Braye F 58 C1
Saviñán E 89 C5
Savines-le-lac F 79 B5
Savino Selo SRB 75 C4
Savio I 82 B1
Sävja S 36 C4
Šavnik MNE 85 D4
Savognin CH 71 B4
Savona I 80 B2
Savonlinna FIN 3 F28
Savournon F 79 B4
Sævråsvåg N 32 B2
Sävsjö S 40 B4
Savsjön S 36 C1
Sävsjöström S 40 B5
Savudrija HR 72 C3
Savukoski FIN 113 E17
Sawbridgeworth GB 31 C4
Sawtry GB 30 B3
Sax E 101 A5
Saxdalen S 36 B1
Saxilby GB 27 B5
Saxmundham GB 30 B5
Saxnäs S 115 C12
Saxthorpe GB 30 B5
Sayalonga E 100 C1
Sayatón E 95 B4
Sayda D 52 C3
Säytsjärvi FIN 113 C16
Śazava CZ 64 A1
Sázava CZ 63 A5
Scaër F 56 B2
Scafa I 103 A7
Scalasaig GB 24 B1
Scalby GB 27 A5
Scalea I 106 B2
Scaletta Zanclea I 109 A4
Scalloway GB 22 A7
Scamblesby GB 27 B5
Scandale I 107 B3
Scandiano I 81 B4
Scandicci I 81 C5
Scandolara Ravara I 81 A4
Scanno I 103 B6
Scansano I 81 D5
Scanzano Jónico I 104 C2
Scarborough GB 27 A5
Scardovari I 82 B1
Scardoy GB 22 D4
Scarinish GB 24 B1
Scarperia I 81 C5
Scarriff IRL 20 B3
Scey-sur-Saône et St Albin F 60 C1
Schachendorf A 73 A6
Schaffhausen CH 61 C4
Schafstädt D 52 B1
Schafstedt D 43 A6
Schäftlarn D 62 C2
Schagen NL 42 C1
Schalkau D 51 C7
Schangnau CH 70 B2
Schapbach D 61 B4
Scharbeutz D 44 A2
Schärding A 63 B4
Scharnitz A 71 A6
Scharrel D 43 B4
Schattendorf A 64 C2
Scheemda NL 42 B3
Scheessel D 43 B6
Schéggia I 82 C1
Scheibbs A 63 B6
Scheibenberg D 52 C2
Scheidegg D 61 C5
Scheifling A 73 A4
Scheinfeld D 61 A6
Schelklingen D 61 B5
Schenefeld
Schleswig-Holstein D 43 A6
Schleswig-Holstein D 44 B1
Schenklengsfeld D 51 C5
Scherfede D 51 B5
Schermbeck D 50 B2
Scherpenzeel NL 49 A6
Schesslitz D 52 D1
Scheveningen NL 49 A5
Schiedam NL 49 B5
Schieder-Schwalenberg D 51 B5
Schierling D 62 B3
Schiers CH 71 B4
Schildau D 52 B2
Schillingen D 60 A2
Schillingsfürst D 61 A6
Schilpário I 71 B5
Schiltach D 61 B4
Schiltigheim F 60 B3
Schio I 71 C6
Schirmeck F 60 B3
Schirnding D 52 C2
Schkeuditz D 52 B2
Schkölen D 52 B1
Schlabendorf D 53 B3
Schladen D 51 A6
Schladming A 72 A3
Schlangen D 51 B4
Schleiden D 50 C2
Schleiz D 52 C1
Schleswig D 43 A6
Schleusingen D 51 C6
Schlieben D 52 B3
Schliengen D 60 C3
Schliersee D 62 C2
Schlitz D 51 C5
Schloss Neuhans D 51 B4
Schlossvippach D 52 B1
Schlotheim D 51 B6
Schluchsee D 61 C4
Schlüchtern D 51 C5
Schmallenberg D 50 B4
Schmelz D 60 A2
Schmidmühlen D 62 A2
Schmiedeberg D 53 C3
Schmiedefeld D 51 C6
Schmirn A 72 A1
Schmölln
Brandenburg D 45 B6
Sachsen D 52 C2
Schnaittach D 62 A2
Schneeberg D 52 C2
Schneizlreuth D 62 C3
Schneverdingen D 44 B1
Schöder A 73 A4
Schoenburg B 50 C2
Schollene D 44 C4
Schöllkrippen D 51 C5
Schomberg D 61 B4
Schönach D 62 B3
Schönau
Baden-Württemberg D 60 C3
Bayern D 62 B3
Schönbeck D 45 B5
Schönberg
Bayern D 63 B4
Mecklenburg-Vorpommern D 44 B2
Schleswig-Holstein D 44 A2
Schönebeck D 52 A1
Schöneck D 52 C2
Schönecken- D 50 C2
Schönermark D 45 B5
Schönewalde D 52 B3
Schongau D 62 C1
Schöngrabern A 64 B2
Schönhagen D 51 B5
Schönhausen D 44 C4
Schöningen D 51 A6
Schönkirchen D 44 A2
Schönsee D 62 A3
Schöntal D 61 A5
Schönthal D 62 A3
Schonungen D 51 C6
Schönwalde D 44 A2
Schoondijke NL 49 B4
Schoonebeek NL 42 C3
Schoonhoven NL 49 B5
Schopfheim D 60 C3
Schöppenstedt D 51 A6
Schörfling A 63 C4
Schorndorf D 61 B5
Schortens D 43 B4
Schotten D 51 C5
Schramberg D 61 B4
Schraplau D 52 B1
Schrattenberg A 64 B2
Schrecksbach D 51 C5
Schrems A 63 B6
Schrobenhausen D 62 B2
Schröcken A 71 A5
Schrozberg D 61 A5
Schruns A 71 A4
Schüpfheim CH 70 B3
Schüttorf D 50 A3
Schwaan D 44 B4
Schwabach D 62 A2
Schwäbisch Gmünd D 61 B5
Schwäbisch Hall D 61 A5
Schwabmünchen D 62 B1
Schwadorf A 64 B2
Schwagstorf D 43 C4
Schwaigern D 61 A5
Schwalmstadt D 51 C5
Schwanberg A 73 B5
Schwanden CH 70 B4
Schwandorf D 62 A3
Schwanebeck D 52 B1
Schwanenstadt A 63 B4
Schwanewede D 43 B5
Schwanfeld D 61 A6
Schwangau D 62 C1
Schwarmstedt D 43 C6
Schwarza D 51 C6
Schwarzach im Pongau A 72 A3
Schwarzau im Gebirge A 63 C6
Schwarzenau A 63 B6
Schwarzenbach D 52 C1
Schwarzenbach am Wald D 52 C1
Schwarzenbek D 44 B2
Schwarzenberg D 52 C2
Schwarzenburg CH 70 B2
Schwarzenfeld D 62 A3
Schwarz-heide D 53 B3
Schwaz A 72 A1
Schwechat A 64 B2
Schwedt D 45 B6
Schwei D 43 B5
Schweich D 60 A2
Schweighausen D 60 B3
Schweinfurt D 51 C6
Schweinitz D 52 B3
Schweinrich D 45 B4
Schwelm D 50 B3
Schwemsal D 52 B2
Schwendt A 62 C3
Schwenningen D 61 B4
Schwepnitz D 53 B3
Schwerin D 44 B3
Schwerte D 50 B3
Schweskau D 44 C3
Schwetzingen D 61 A4
Schwyz CH 70 A3
Sciacca I 108 B2
Scicli I 109 C3
Ściechów PL 45 C6
Scigliano I 106 B3
Scilla I 109 A4
Ścinawa PL 54 B1
Scionzier F 69 B6
Scoglitti I 109 C3
Scole GB 30 B5
Sconser GB 22 D2
Scopello
Piemonte I 70 C3
Sicilia I 108 A1
Scordia I 109 B3
Scorzè I 72 C2
Scotch Corner GB 27 A4
Scotter GB 27 B5
Scourie GB 22 C3
Scousburgh GB 22 B7
Scrabster GB 23 C5
Screeb IRL 20 A2
Scremerston GB 25 C6
Scritto I 82 C1
Scunthorpe GB 27 B5
Scuol CH 71 B5
Scúrcola Marsicana I 103 A6
Seaford GB 31 D4
Seaham GB 25 D6
Seahouses GB 25 C6
Seascale GB 26 A2
Seaton GB 29 C4
Sebazac-Concourès F 77 B5
Sebečevo SRB 85 C5
Seben TR 118 B6
Sebersdorf A 73 A5
Sebezh RUS 7 C10
Sebnitz D 53 C4
Seborga I 80 C1
Seby S 41 C6
Seč
Vychodočeský CZ 63 A6
Západočeský CZ 63 A4
Sečanj SRB 75 C5
Secemin PL 55 C4
Séchault F 59 A5
Seckau A 73 A4
Seclin F 49 C4
Secondigny F 67 B4
Seda P 92 B3
Sedan F 59 A5
Sedano E 88 B3
Sedbergh GB 26 A3
Sedella E 100 C1
Séderon F 79 B4
Sedgefield GB 27 A4
Sedico I 72 B2
Sédilo I 110 B1
Sédini I 110 B1
Sedlarica HR 74 C2
Sedlčany CZ 63 A5
Sedlec-Prčice CZ 63 A5
Sedlice CZ 63 A4
Sędziejowice PL 55 B4
Sędziszów PL 55 C5
Sędziszów Małapolski PL 55 C6
Seebach F 60 B3
Seeboden A 72 B3
Seefeld
Brandenburg D 45 C5
Niedersachsen D 43 B5
Seefeld in Tirol A 71 A6
Seeg D 62 C1
Seehausen
Sachsen-Anhalt D 44 C3
Sachsen-Anhalt D 52 A1
Seeheim-Jugenheim D 61 A4
Seelbach D 60 B3
Seelow D 45 C6
Seelze D 43 C6
Seerhausen D 52 B3
Sées F 57 B6
Seesen D 51 B6
Seeshaupt D 62 C2
Seewalchen A 63 C4
Seferihisar TR 119 D1
Sefkerin SRB 85 A5
Segård N 34 B2
Segerstad S 35 C5
Segesd H 74 B2
Seglinge FIN 36 B7
Segmon S 35 C5
Segonzac F 67 C4
Segorbe E 96 B2
Segovia E 94 B2
Segré F 57 C5
Segura
E 89 B4
P 93 B3
Segura de León E 99 A4
Segura de los Baños E 90 C2
Ségur-les-Villas F 68 C2
Segurrilla E 94 B2
Sehnde D 51 A5
Seia P 92 A3
Seiches-sur-le-Loir F 67 A4
Seifhennersdorf D 53 C4
Seignelay F 59 C4
Seijo E 87 C2
Seilhac F 68 C1
Seilles B 49 C6
Seim N 32 B2
Seinäjoki FIN 3 E25
Seissan F 77 C3
Seitenstetten Markt A 63 B5
Seixal P 92 C1
Seiz A 73 A4
Seizthal A 73 A4
Sejerslev DK 38 C1
Seksna RUS 7 B15
Selárdalur IS 111 B1
Selárgius I 110 C2
Selb D 52 C2
Selby GB 27 B4
Selca HR 84 C1
Selcë AL 105 A5
Selce HR 73 C4
Selçuk TR 119 E2
Selde DK 38 C2
Selenča SRB 75 C4
Selendi
Manisa TR 118 D2
Manisa TR 118 D3
Selenicë AL 105 C5
Sélestat F 60 B3
Seleuš SRB 75 C5
Selevac SRB 85 B5
Selfoss IS 111 D5
Selgua E 90 B3
Selice SK 64 B3
Seligenstadt D 51 C4
Seligenthal D 51 C6
Selimiye TR 119 E2
Selizharovo RUS 7 C12
Selja S 36 A1
Selje N 114 E2
Seljelvnes N 112 C8
Seljord N 33 C5
Selkirk GB 25 C5
Sellano I 82 D1
Selles-St Denis F 68 A1
Selles-sur-Cher F 67 A6
Sellières F 69 B5
Sellin D 45 A5
Sellye H 74 C2
Selm D 50 B3
Selnica ob Dravi SLO 73 B5
Selongey F 59 C6
Selonnet F 79 B5
Selow D 44 B3
Selsey GB 31 D3
Selsingen D 43 B6
Selters D 50 C3
Seltso RUS 7 E13
Seltz F 61 B4
Selva E 97 B2
Selva di Cadore I 72 B2
Selva di Val Gardena I 72 B1
Selvik
Sogn og Fjordane N 32 A2
Vestfold N 35 C2
Selvino I 71 C4
Selyatyn UA 11 C8
Sem N 35 C2
Semeljci HR 74 C3
Semenovka
Chernihiv UA 7 E12
Kremenchuk UA 11 B12
Semič SLO 73 C5
Semide
F 59 A5
P 92 A2
Semily CZ 53 C5
Seminara I 106 C2
Semlac RO 75 B5
Şemmen-stedt D 51 A6
Šempeter SLO 73 B5
Semriach A 73 A5
Semur-en-Auxois F 69 A4
Sena E 90 B2
Sena de Luna E 88 B1
Senarpont F 58 A2
Sénas F 79 C4
Senćanski Trešnjevac SRB 75 C4
Sencelles E 97 B2
Senčur SLO 73 B4
Senden
Bayern D 61 B6
Nordrhein-Westfalen D 50 B3
Sendenhorst D 50 B3
Sendim P 87 C4
Senec SK 64 B3
Seneffe B 49 C5
Séneghe I 110 B1
Senés E 101 B3
Senez F 79 C5
Senftenberg D 53 B3
Sengouagnet F 77 D3
Sengwarden D 43 B5
Senica SK 64 B3
Senice na Hané CZ 64 A3
Senigállia I 82 C2
Senirkent TR 119 D5
Sénis I 110 C1
Senise I 106 A3
Senj HR 83 B3
Senje SRB 85 C6
Senjehopen N 112 C6
Senjski Rudnik SRB 85 C6
Senlis F 58 A3
Sennan S 40 C2
Sennecey-le-Grand F 69 B4
Sennen GB 28 C2
Senno BY 7 D10
Sénnori I 110 B1
Sennwald CH 71 A4
Sennybridge GB 29 B4
Senohrad SK 65 B5
Senonches F 58 B2
Senones F 60 B2
Senorb ì I 110 C2
Senovo SLO 73 B5
Senožeče SLO 73 C4
Senožeti SLO 73 B4
Sens F 59 B4
Sens-de-Bretagne F 57 B4
Senta SRB 75 C5
Senterada E 90 A3
Şentilj SLO 73 B5
Šentjernej SLO 73 C5
Šentjur SLO 73 B5
Senumstad N 33 D5
Seoane E 86 B3
Seon CH 70 A3
Sépeaux F 59 C4
Sépey CH 70 B2
Sepino I 103 B7
Sępólno Krajeńskie PL 46 B3
Seppenrade D 50 B3
Seppois F 70 A2
Septeuil F 58 B2
Sepúlveda E 88 C3
Sequals I 72 B2
Sequeros E 93 A4
Seraincourt F 59 A5
Seraing B 49 C6
Seravezza I 81 C4
Sered' SK 64 B3
Seredka RUS 7 B10
Şereflikoçhisar TR 16 B6
Seregélyes H 74 A3
Seregno I 71 C4
Sérent F 56 C3
Serfaus A 71 A5
Sergiyev Posad RUS 7 C15
Seriate I 71 C4
Sérifontaine F 58 A2
Serifos GR 117 E6
Sérignan F 78 C2
Serik TR 119 F6
Serina I 71 C4
Serinhisar TR 119 E4
Sermaises F 58 B3
Sermaize-les-Bains F 59 B5
Sérmide I 81 B5
Sermoneta I 102 B5
Sernache de Bonjardim P 92 B2
Sernancelhe P 87 D3
Serón E 101 B3
Serón de Najima E 89 C4
Serooskerke NL 49 B4
Seròs E 90 B3
Serpa P 98 B3
Serpukhov RUS 7 D14
Serracapriola I 103 B8
Serrada E 88 C2
Serra de Outes E 86 B2
Serradifalco I 108 B2
Serradilla E 93 B4
Serradilla del Arroyo E 93 A4
Serradilla del Llano E 93 A4
Serramanna I 110 C1
Serramazzoni I 81 B4
Serranillos E 94 B2
Serrapetrona I 82 C2
Serra San Bruno I 106 C3
Serra San Quírico I 82 C2
Serrastretta I 106 B3
Serravalle
Piemonte I 70 C3
Umbria I 82 D2
Serravalle di Chienti I 82 C1
Serravalle Scrívia I 80 B2
Serre I 103 C8
Serrejón E 93 B5
Serres
F 79 B4
GR 116 A5
Serrières F 69 C4
Serrières-de-Briord F 69 C5
Sersale I 106 B3
Sertã P 92 B2
Sertig Dörfli CH 71 B4
Servance F 60 C2
Serverette F 78 B2
Servia GR 116 B4
Servian F 78 C2
Serviers F 78 B3
Servigliano I 82 C2
Serzedelo P 87 C2
Seseña Nuevo E 95 B3
Sesimbra P 92 C1
Seskinore GB 19 B4
Sesma E 89 B4
Sessa Aurunca I 103 B6
Ses Salines E 97 B3
Şesta Godano I 80 B3
Šestanovac HR 84 C1
Sestao E 89 A4
Sestino I 82 C1
Sesto I 72 B2
Sesto Calende I 70 C3
Sesto Fiorentino I 81 C5
Séstola I 81 B4
Sesto San Giovanni I 71 C4
Sestriere I 79 B5
Sestri Levante I 80 B3
Sestroretsk RUS 7 A11
Sestu I 110 C2
Sesvete HR 73 C6
Setcases E 91 A5
Sète F 78 C2
Setenil E 99 C5
Şetermoen N 112 D7
Šetonje SRB 85 B6
Setskog N 34 C3
Settalsjølia N 114 E7
Séttimo Torinese I 70 C2
Settimo Vittone I 70 C2
Settle GB 26 A3
Setúbal P 92 C2
Seubersdort D 62 A2
Seúi I 110 C2
Seúlo I 110 C2
Seurre F 69 B5
Sevaster AL 105 C5
Sevel DK 38 C1
Sevenoaks GB 31 C4
Sévérac-le-Château F 78 B2
Sever do Vouga P 87 D2
Severin HR 73 C5
Severomorsk RUS 3 B30
Şéveso I 71 C4
Ševětin CZ 63 A5
Sevettijärvi FIN 113 C17
Sévigny F 59 A5
Sevilla = Seville E 99 B5
Sevilla la Nueva E 94 B2
Seville = Sevilla E 99 B5
Sevilleja de la Jara E 94 C2
Sevlievo BG 11 E8
Sevnica SLO 73 B5
Sevojno SRB 85 C4
Sevrier F 69 C6
Sevsk RUS 7 E13
Sexdrega S 40 B3
Seyches F 76 B3
Seyda D 52 B2
Seydişehir TR 119 E6
Seyðisfjörður IS 111 B12
Seyitgazi TR 118 C5
Seyitömer TR 118 C4
Seymen TR 118 A2
Seyne F 79 B5
Seynes F 78 B3
Seyssel F 69 C5
Sežana SLO 72 C3
Sézanne F 59 B4
Sezulfe P 87 C3
Sezze I 102 B6
Sfântu Gheorghe RO 11 D8
Sforzacosta I 82 C2
Sgarasta Mhor GB 22 D1
's-Gravendeel NL 49 B5
's-Gravenhage = The Hague NL 49 A5
's-Gravenzande NL 49 B5
Shaftesbury GB 29 B5
Shaldon GB 29 C4
Shanagolden IRL 20 B2
Shanklin GB 31 D2
Shannon IRL 20 B3
Shap GB 26 A3
Sharpness GB 29 B5
Shawbury GB 26 C3
Shchekino RUS 7 D14
Shchigry RUS 7 F14
Shchors UA 7 F11
's-Heerenberg NL 50 B2
Sheerness GB 31 C4
Sheffield GB 27 B4
Shefford GB 31 B3
Shenfield GB 31 C4
Shëngjergj AL 116 A2
Shëngjin AL 105 B5
Shepetivka UA 11 A9
Shepshed GB 27 C4
Shepton Mallet GB 29 B5
Sherborne GB 29 C5
Shercock IRL 19 C5
Sheringham GB 30 B5
's-Hertogenbosch NL 49 B6
Shiel Bridge GB 22 D3
Shieldaig GB 22 D3
Shijak AL 105 B5
Shillelagh IRL 21 B5
Shimsk RUS 7 B11
Shipston-on-Stour GB 29 A6
Shirgjan AL 105 B6
Shklow BY 7 D11
Shkodër AL 105 A5
Shoeburyness GB 31 C4
Shoreham-by-Sea GB 31 D3
Shostka UA 7 F12
Shotley Gate GB 31 C5
Shpola UA 11 B11
Shrewsbury GB 26 C3
Shugozero RUS 7 B13
Shumen BG 11 E9
Siabost GB 22 C2
Siamanna I 110 C1
Sianów PL 46 A2
Siatista GR 116 B3
Şiauges-St Romain F 78 A2
Šiauliai LT 6 D7
Sibari I 106 B3
Şibbhult S 41 C4
Šibenik HR 83 C4
Sibinj HR 74 C2
Sibiu RO 11 D8
Sibnica SRB 85 B5
Sibsey GB 27 B6
Şiculiana I 108 B2
Šid SRB 85 A4
Sidari GR 116 C1
Siddeburen NL 42 B3
Sidensjö S 115 D15
Siderno I 106 C3
Sidirokastro GR 116 A5
Sidmouth GB 29 C4
Sidzina PL 65 A5
Siebe N 113 D12
Siebenlehn D 52 B3
Siedlce PL 6 E7
Siedlice PL 46 B1
Siedlinghausen D 51 B4
Siedlisko PL 46 C2
Siegburg D 50 C3
Siegen D 50 C4
Siegenburg D 62 B2
Sieghartskirchen A 64 B2
Siegsdorf D 62 C3
Siekierki PL 45 C6
Sielpia PL 55 B5
Siemiany PL 47 B5
Siena I 81 C5
Sieniawka PL 53 C4
Siennica PL 55 A6
Sienno PL 55 B6
Sieppijärvi FIN 113 E13
Sieradz PL 54 B3
Sieraków
Śląskie PL 54 C3
Wielkopolskie PL 46 C2
Sierakowice PL 46 A3
Sierck-les-Bains F 60 A2
Sierentz F 60 C3
Sierning A 63 B5
Sierpc PL 47 C5
Sierra de Fuentes E 93 B4
Sierra de Luna E 90 A2
Sierra de Yeguas E 100 B1
Sierre CH 70 B2
Siestrzeń PL 55 A5
Sietamo E 90 A2
Siewierz PL 55 C4
Sigdal N 34 B1
Sigean F 78 C1
Sigerfjord N 112 D4
Sighetu-Marmatiei RO 11 C7
Sighişoara RO 11 C8
Sigillo I 82 C1
Siglufjörður IS 111 A7
Sigmaringen D 61 B5
Signa I 81 C5
Signes F 79 C4
Signy-l'Abbaye F 59 A5
Signy-le-Petit F 59 A5
Sigogne F 67 C4
Sigri GR 116 C7
Sigtuna S 37 C4
Sigueiro E 86 B2
Sigüenza E 95 A4
Sigües E 90 A1
Sigulda LV 6 C8
Siilinjärvi FIN 3 E27
Sikenica SK 65 B4
Sikia GR 116 B5
Sikinos GR 117 F7
Sikkilsdalseter N 32 A6
Siklós H 74 C3
Sikórz PL 47 C5
Sikselet S 115 A14
Silandro I 71 B5
Silánus I 110 B1
Silbaš SRB 75 C4
Silbersted D 43 A6
Şile TR 118 A4
Siles E 101 A3
Silgueiros P 92 A3
Silifke TR 16 C6
Silíqua I 110 C1
Silistra BG 11 D9
Silivri TR 118 A3
Siljan N 35 C1
Siljansnäs S 36 B1
Silkeborg DK 39 C2
Silla E 96 B2
Sillamäe EST 7 B9
Silleda E 86 B2
Sillé-le-Guillaume F 57 B5
Sillenstede D 43 B4
Sillerud S 35 C4
Sillian A 72 B2
Silloth GB 25 D4
Silno PL 46 B3
Silnowo PL 46 B2
Silo HR 73 C4
Sils E 91 B5
Silsand N 112 C6
Şilte S 37 E5
Šilute LT 6 D6
Silvalen N 114 B9
Silvaplana CH 71 B4
Silvares P 92 A3
Silvberg S 36 B2
Silverdalen S 40 B5
Silvermines IRL 20 B3
Silverstone GB 30 B2
Silverton GB 29 C4
Silves P 98 B2
Silvi Marina I 103 A7
Şimandre F 69 B4
Šimanovci SRB 85 B5
Simard F 69 B5
Simat de Valldigna E 96 B2
Simav TR 118 C3
Simbach
Bayern D 62 B3
Bayern D 62 B4
Simbário I 106 C3
Simeria RO 11 D7
Simi GR 119 F2
Simićevo SRB 85 B6
Simlångsdalen S 40 C3
Simmerath D 50 C2
Simmerberg D 61 C5
Simmern D 50 D3
Şimo FIN 3 D26
Šimonovce SK 65 B6
Simonsbath GB 28 B4
Simonstorp S 37 D3
Simontornya H 74 B3
Simplon CH 70 B3
Simrishamn S 41 D4
Sinaia RO 11 D8
Sinalunga I 81 C5
Sinanaj AL 105 C5
Sinarcas E 96 B1
Sincan TR 118 C7
Sincanlı TR 118 D5
Sindal DK 38 B3
Sindelfingen D 61 B5
Sindia I 110 B1
Sındırgı TR 118 C3
Sinekli TR 118 A3
Sines P 98 B2
Sinetta FIN 113 F14
Sineu E 97 B3
Singen D 61 C4
Singleton GB 31 D3
Singsås N 114 E7
Siniscóla I 110 B2
Sinj HR 83 C5
Sinlabajos E 94 A2
Sinn D 50 C4
Sínnai I 110 C2
Sinnes N 33 D3
Sinop TR 16 A7
Sins CH 70 A3
Sinsheim D 61 A4
Sint Annaland NL 49 B5
Sint Annaparochie NL 42 B2
Sint Athonis NL 50 B1
Sint Nicolaasga NL 42 C2
Sint Oedenrode NL 49 B6
Sintra P 92 C1
Sinzheim D 61 B4
Sinzig D 50 C3
Siófok H 74 B3
Sion CH 70 B2
Sion Mills GB 19 B4
Şiorac-en-Périgord F 77 B3
Šipanska Luka HR 84 D2
Šipovo BIH 84 B2
Sira N 33 D3
Siracusa I 109 B4
Siret RO 11 C9
Sirevåg N 33 D2
Sirig SRB 75 C4
Sirkka FIN 113 E13
Sirmione I 71 C5
Şirok H 65 C6
Široké SK 65 B6
Široki Brijeg BIH 84 C2
Sirolo I 82 C2
Siruela E 94 D1
Sisak HR 73 C6
Şisante E 95 C4
Šišljavić HR 73 C5
Sissach CH 70 A2
Sissonne F 59 A4
Sistelo P 87 C2
Sisteron F 79 B4
Sistiana I 72 C3
Sistranda N 114 D5
Sitasjaurestugorna S 112 E6
Sitges E 91 B4
Sitia GR 117 G8
Sittard NL 50 B1
Sittensen D 43 B6
Sittingbourne GB 31 C4
Sitzenroda D 52 B2
Sivac SRB 75 C4
Sivaslı TR 119 D4
Siverić HR 83 C5
Sivrihisar TR 118 C6
Sixt-Fer-á-Cheval F 70 B1
Siziano I 71 C4
Sizun F 56 B1
Sjenica SRB 85 C5
Sjoa N 114 F6
Sjøåsen N 114 C8
Sjöbo S 41 D3
Sjøenden
Hedmark N 34 A3
Hedmark N 34 B3
Sjøholt N 114 E3
Sjøli N 34 A3
Sjølstad N 114 C9
Sjölunda S 37 C2
Sjømarken S 40 B2
Sjørring DK 38 C1
Sjötofta S 40 B3
Sjötorp S 35 D5
Sjoutnäset S 115 C11
Sjøvegan N 112 D6
Sjuntorp S 35 D4
Skåbu N 32 A6
Skadovsk UA 11 C12
Skafså N 33 C5
Skaftafell IS 111 D9
Skagaströnd IS 111 B5
Skagen DK 38 B3
Skagersvik S 35 D6
Skaiå N 33 D4
Skaidi N 113 B13
Skala GR 117 D2
Skała PL 55 C4
Skaland N 112 C6
Skala Oropou GR 117 D5
Skala-Podilska UA 11 B9
Skalat UA 11 B8
Skalbmierz PL 55 C5
Skålevik N 33 D5
Skalica SK 64 B3
Skalité SK 65 A4
Skällinge S 40 B2
Skalná CZ 52 C2
Skals DK 38 C2
Skælskør DK 39 D4
Skalstugan S 114 D9
Skanderborg DK 39 C2
Skånes-Fagerhult S 41 C3
Skåne-Tranås S 41 D3
Skånevik N 33 C2
Skänninge S 37 D2
Skanör med Falsterbo S 41 D2
Skåpafors S 35 C4
Skąpe PL 53 A5
Skara S 35 D5
Skærbæk DK 39 D1
Skarberget N 112 D5
Skärblacka S 37 D2
Skarð IS 111 B3
Skarda S 115 C15
Skare N 32 C3
Skåre S 35 C5
Skärhamn S 38 B4
Skarnes N 34 B3
Skärplinge S 36 B4
Skarpnatö FIN 36 B6
Skarp Salling DK 38 C2
Skarrild DK 39 D1
Skarstad N 112 D5
Skärstad S 40 B4
Skarsvåg N 113 A14
Skarszewy PL 47 A4
Skårup DK 39 D3
Skärvången S 115 D11
Skarvsjöby S 115 C14
Skaryszew PL 55 B6
Skarżysko-Kamienna PL 55 B5
Skarzysko Ksiazece PL 55 B5
Skatøy N 33 D6
Skattkärr S 35 C5
Skattungbyn S 36 A1
Skatval N 114 D7
Skaulo S 112 E10
Skave DK 39 C1
Skawina PL 55 D4
Skebobruk S 36 C5
Skebokvarn S 37 C3
Skedala S 40 C2
Skedevi S 37 D2
Skedsmokorset N 34 B3
Skee S 35 D3
Skegness GB 27 B6
Skela SRB 85 B5
Skelani BIH 85 C4
Skellefteå S 3 D24
Skelleftehamn S 3 D24
Skelmersdale GB 26 B3
Skelmorlie GB 24 C3
Skelund DK 38 C3
Skender Vakuf BIH 84 B2
Skene S 40 B2
Skępe PL 47 C5
Skepplanda S 40 B2
Skeppshult S 40 B3
Skerries IRL 19 C5
Ski N 35 C2
Skiathos GR 116 C5
Skibbereen IRL 20 C2
Skibotn N 112 C9
Skidra GR 116 B4
Skien N 35 C1
Skierniewice PL 55 B5
Skillingaryd S 40 B4
Skillinge S 41 D4
Skillingmark S 34 C4
Skilloura CY 120 A2
Skinnardai S 37 C5
Skinnskatteberg S 36 C2

Sulzbach
Baden-Württemberg D 61 A5
Baden-Württemberg D 61 B5
Bayern D 61 A5
Saarland D 60 A3
Sulzbach-Rosenberg D 62 A2
Sülze D 44 C2
Sulzfeld D 51 C6
Sumartin HR 84 C1
Sumburgh GB 22 B7
Sümeg H 74 B2
Sumiswald CH 70 A2
Šumná CZ 64 B1
Šumperk CZ 54 D1
Šumvald CZ 64 A3
Sumy UA 7 F13
Sunbilla E 76 C1
Sünching D 62 B3
Sund
FIN 36 B7
S 35 C3
Sundborn S 36 B2
Sundby DK 38 C1
Sunde N 32 C2
Sunde bru N 33 D6
Sunderland GB 25 D6
Sundern D 50 B4
Sundhultsbrunn S 40 B4
Sundnäs S 115 A14
Sunds DK 39 C2
Sundsfjord N 112 F3
Sundsvall S 115 E14
Sungurlu TR 16 A7
Suni I 110 B1
Sunja HR 74 C1
Sunnansjö S 36 B1
Sunnaryd S 40 B3
Sunndalsøra N 114 E5
Sunne S 34 C5
Sunnemo S 34 C5
Sunnersberg S 35 D5
Suolovuopmio N 113 C12
Suomussalmi FIN 3 D28
Suoyarvi RUS 3 E30
Super Sauze F 79 B5
Supetar HR 83 C5
Supetarska Draga HR 83 B3
Supino I 102 B6
Šuplja Stijena MNE 84 C4
Surahammar S 37 C3
Šurany SK 64 B4
Surazh
BY 7 D11
RUS 7 E12
Surbo I 105 C4
Surčin SRB 85 B5
Surgères F 66 B4
Surhuisterveen NL 42 B3
Súria E 91 B4
Surin F 67 B5
Surka N 34 B2
Surnadalsøra N 114 E5
Sursee CH 70 A3
Surte S 38 B5
Surwold D 43 C4
Sury-le-Comtal F 69 C4
Susa I 70 C2
Šušara SRB 85 B6
Susch CH 71 B5
Susegana I 72 C2
Süsel D 44 A2
Sušice CZ 63 A4
Šušnjevica HR 73 C4
Sussen D 61 B5
Susurluk TR 118 C3
Susz PL 47 B5
Sütçüler TR 119 E5
Sutivan HR 83 C5
Sutjeska SRB 75 C5
Sutomore MNE 105 A5
Sutri I 102 A5
Sutton GB 31 C3
Sutton Coldfield GB 27 C4
Sutton-in-Ashfield GB 27 B4
Sutton-on-Sea GB 27 B6
Sutton-on-Trent GB 27 B5
Sutton Scotney GB 31 C2
Sutton Valence GB 31 C4
Suvaja BIH 83 B5
Suvereto I 81 C4
Suvorov RUS 7 D14
Suwałki PL 6 D7
Suze-la-Rousse F 78 B3
Suzzara I 81 B4
Svabensverk S 36 A2
Svalbarð IS 111 A10
Svalöv S 41 D3
Svanabyn S 115 C13
Svanberga S 36 C5
Svaneke DK 41 D5
Svanesund S 35 D3
Svängsta S 41 C4
Svannäs S 115 A15
Svanskog S 35 C4
Svanstein S 113 F12
Svappavaara S 112 E10
Svärdsjö S 36 B2
Svarstad N 35 C1
Svartå S 37 C1
Svärta S 37 D4
Svartå S 34 C5
Svärtinge S 37 D3
Svartnäs S 36 B3
Svartnes N 112 E3
Svarttjärn S 115 B13
Svatsum N 34 A1
Svätý Jur SK 64 B3
Svätý Peter SK 64 C4
Svedala S 41 D3
Sveg S 115 E11
Sveindal N 33 D4
Sveio N 33 C2
Svejbæk DK 39 C2
Svelgen N 114 F2
Svelvik N 35 C2
Svendborg DK 39 D3
Svene N 32 C6
Svenljunga S 40 B3
Svennevad S 37 C2
Svenstavik S 115 E11
Svenstrup DK 38 C2
Švermov CZ 53 C4
Sveti Ivan Zabno HR 74 C1
Sveti Ivan Zelina HR 73 C6
Sveti Nikola MNE 105 B5
Sveti Rok HR 83 B4
Sveti Stefan MNE 105 A4
Světlá nad Sázavou CZ 63 A6
Svetlyy RUS 47 A6
Svetvinčenat HR 82 A2
Švica HR 83 B4
Svidník SK 10 B6
Švihov CZ 63 A4
Svilajnac SRB 85 B6
Svilengrad BG 11 F9
Svindal N 35 C3
Svinhult S 40 B5
Svinna SK 64 B4
Svinninge
DK 39 D4
S 37 C5
Sviritsa RUS 7 A12
Svishtov BG 11 E8
Svislach BY 6 E8
Svit SK 65 A6
Svitavy CZ 64 A2
Svitlovodsk UA 11 B12
Svodin SK 65 C4
Svolvær N 112 D3
Svortemyr N 32 A2
Svortland N 32 C2
Svratka CZ 64 A2
Svrčinovec SK 65 A4
Svullrya N 34 B4
Svyetlahorsk BY 7 E10
Swadlincote GB 27 C4
Swaffham GB 30 B4
Swanage GB 29 C6
Swanley GB 31 C4
Swanlinbar IRL 19 B4
Swansea GB 28 B4
Swarzędz PL 46 C3
Swatragh GB 19 B5
Świątki PL 47 B6
Świdnica
Dolnośląskie PL 54 C1
Lubuskie PL 53 B5
Świdnik PL 11 A7
Świdwin PL 46 B1
Świebodzice PL 53 C6
Świebodzin PL 53 A5
Świecie PL 47 B4
Świedziebnia PL 47 B5
Świeradów Zdrój PL 53 C5
Świerki PL 54 C1
Swierzawa PL 53 B5
Swierzno PL 45 B6
Swięta PL 45 B6
Swieta Anna PL 55 C4
Świętno PL 53 A6
Swifterbant NL 42 C2
Swindon GB 29 B6
Swineshead GB 30 B3
Swinford IRL 18 C3
Świnoujście PL 45 B6
Swinton GB 25 C5
Swobnica PL 45 B6
Swords IRL 21 A5
Swornegacie PL 46 B3
Sya S 37 D2
Syasstroy RUS 7 A12
Sycewice PL 46 A2
Sychevka RUS 7 D13
Syców PL 54 B2
Sycowice PL 53 A5
Sydnes N 33 C2
Syfteland N 32 B2
Syke D 43 C5
Sykkylven N 114 E3
Sylling N 34 C2
Sylte N 114 E4
Symbister GB 22 A7
Symington GB 25 C4
Symonds Yat GB 29 B5
Sypniewo
Kujawsko-Pomorskie PL 46 B3
Wielkopolskie PL 46 B2
Syserum S 40 B6
Sysslebäck S 34 B4
Syväjärvi FIN 113 E14
Szabadbattyán H 74 A3
Szabadegyháza H 74 A3
Szabadszállás H 75 B4
Szadek PL 54 B3
Szajol H 75 A5
Szakály H 74 B3
Szakcs H 74 B3
Szakmár H 75 B4
Szalánta H 74 C3
Szałas PL 55 B5
Szalkszentmárton H 75 B4
Szalonna H 65 B6
Szamocin PL 46 B3
Szamotuły PL 46 C2
Szany H 74 A2
Szarvas H 75 B5
Szarvaskő H 65 C6
Szászvár H 74 B3
Százhalombatta H 74 A3
Szczawa PL 65 A6
Szczawnica PL 65 A6
Szczecin PL 45 B6
Szczecinek PL 46 B2
Szczekociny PL 55 C4
Szczerców PL 55 B4
Szczucin PL 55 C6
Szczuczarz PL 46 B2
Szczurkowo PL 47 A6
Szczurowa PL 55 C5
Szczyrk PL 65 A5
Szczytna PL 54 C1
Szczytno PL 6 E6
Szczyty PL 54 B3
Szécsény H 65 B5
Szederkény H 74 C3
Szedres H 74 B3
Szeged H 75 B5
Szeghalom H 75 A6
Szegvár H 75 B5
Székesfehérvár H 74 A3
Székkutas H 75 B5
Szekszárd H 74 B3
Szemplino Czarne PL 47 B6
Szemud PL 47 A4
Szendehely H 65 C5
Szendrő H 65 B6
Szentendre H 65 C5
Szentes H 75 B5
Szentgotthárd H 73 B6
Szentlászló H 74 B2
Szentlőrinc H 74 B3
Szentmártonkáta H 75 A4
Szenyér H 74 B2
Szeremle H 74 B3
Szerep H 75 A6
Szigetszentmiklós H 75 A4
Szigetvár H 74 B2
Szikáncs H 75 B5
Szikszó H 65 B6
Szil H 74 A2
Szilvásvárad H 65 B6
Szklarska Poreba PL 53 C5
Szlichtyngowa PL 53 B6
Szob H 65 C4
Szolnok H 75 A5
Szombathely H 74 A1
Szorosad H 74 B3
Szpetal Graniczny PL 47 C5
Szprotawa PL 53 B5
Szreńsk PL 47 B6
Sztum PL 47 B5
Sztutowo PL 47 A5
Szubin PL 46 B3
Szücsi H 65 C5
Szulmierz PL 47 C6
Szulok H 74 B2
Szumanie PL 47 C5
Szwecja PL 46 B2
Szydłów
Łódzkie PL 55 B4
Świętokrzyskie PL 55 C6
Szydłowiec PL 55 B5
Szydlowo PL 47 B6
Szydłowo PL 46 B2
Szymanów PL 55 A5
Szynkielów PL 54 B3
Szynwald PL 55 D6

T

Taastrup DK 41 D2
Tab H 74 B3
Tabanera la Luenga E 94 A2
Tabaqueros E 96 B1
Tábara E 88 C1
Tabenera de Cerrato E 88 B2
Taberg S 40 B4
Tabernas E 101 B3
Tabiano Bagni I 81 B4
Taboada E 86 B3
Taboadela E 87 B3
Tábor CZ 63 A5
Táborfalva H 75 A4
Taborište HR 73 C6
Tábua P 92 A2
Tabuaco P 87 C3
Tabuenca E 89 C5
Tabuyo del Monte E 87 B4
Täby S 37 C5
Tác H 74 A3
Tachov CZ 62 A3
Tadcaster GB 27 B4
Tadley GB 31 C2
Tafalla E 89 B5
Tafjord N 114 E4
Taganheira P 98 B2
Tågarp S 41 D2
Tággia I 80 C1
Tagliacozzo I 102 A6
Táglio di Po I 82 A1
Tagnon F 59 A5
Tahal E 101 B3
Tahitótfalu H 65 C5
Tahtaköprü TR 118 C4
Tailfingen D 61 B5
Taillis F 57 B4
Tain GB 23 D4
Tain-l'Hermitage F 78 A3
Taipadas P 92 C2
Taivalkoski FIN 3 D28
Takene S 35 C5
Takovo SRB 85 B5
Taksony H 75 A4
Tal E 86 B2
Talachyn BY 7 D10
Talamello I 82 C1
Talamone I 102 A4
Talant F 69 A4
Talarrubias E 93 B5
Talas TR 16 B7
Talaván E 93 B4
Talavera de la Reina E 94 C2
Talavera la Real E 93 C4
Talayuela E 93 B5
Talayuelas E 96 B1
Talgarth GB 29 B4
Talgje N 33 C2
Talhadas P 92 A2
Táliga E 93 C3
Talizat F 78 A2
Tálknafjörður IS 111 B2
Talla I 81 C5
Talladale GB 22 D3
Tallaght IRL 21 A5
Tallard F 79 B5
Tällberg S 36 B1
Tallinn EST 6 B8
Talloires F 69 C6
Tallow IRL 21 B4
Tallsjö S 115 C15
Talmay F 69 A5
Talmont-St Hilaire F 66 B3
Talmont-sur-Gironde F 66 C4
Talne UA 11 B11
Talsano I 104 C3
Talsi LV 6 C7
Talvik N 113 B11
Talybont GB 26 C2
Tal-Y-Llyn GB 26 C2
Tamajón E 95 B3
Tamame E 88 C1
Tamames E 93 A4
Tamarit de Mar E 91 B4
Tamarite de Litera E 90 B3
Tamariu E 91 B6
Tamási H 74 B3
Tambach-Dietharz D 51 C6
Tameza E 86 A4
Tammisaari FIN 6 A7
Tampere FIN 3 F25
Tamsweg A 72 A3
Tamurejo E 94 D2
Tamworth GB 27 C4
Tana bru N 113 B17
Tañabueyes E 89 B3
Tanakajd H 74 A1
Tananger N 33 D2
Tanaunella I 110 B2
Tancarville F 58 A1
Tandsjöborg S 115 F11
Tånga S 41 C2
Tangelic H 74 B3
Tangen N 34 B3
Tangerhütte D 44 C3
Tangermünde D 44 C3
Tanhua FIN 113 E16
Taninges F 69 B6
Tankavaara FIN 113 D16
Tann D 51 C6
Tanna D 52 C1
Tannadice GB 25 B5
Tannåker S 40 C3
Tännäs S 115 E9
Tannay
Ardennes F 59 A5
Nièvre F 68 A3
Tannenbergsthal D 52 C2
Tännesberg D 62 A3
Tannheim A 71 A5
Tanowo PL 45 B6
Tanum S 35 D3
Tanumshede S 35 D3
Tanus F 77 B5
Tanvald CZ 53 C5
Taormina I 109 B4
Tapa EST 7 B8
Tapfheim D 62 B1
Tapia de Casariego E 86 A4
Tapio F 77 C4
Tápióbicske H 75 A4
Tápiógyörgye H 75 A4
Tápióság H 75 A4
Tápiószecső H 75 A4
Tápiószele H 75 A4
Tápiószentmárton H 75 A4
Tapolca H 74 B2
Tapolcafő H 74 A2
Tar HR 72 C3
Tarabo S 38 B5
Taradell E 91 B5
Taraklı TR 118 B5
Taramundi E 86 A3
Tarancón E 95 B3
Táranto I 104 C3
Tarare F 69 C4
Tarascon F 78 C3
Tarascon-sur-Ariège F 77 D4
Tarashcha UA 11 B11
Tarazona E 89 C5
Tarazona de la Mancha E 95 C5
Tarbena E 96 C2
Tarbert
GB 24 C2
IRL 20 B2
Tarbes F 76 C3
Tarbet GB 24 B3
Tarbolton GB 24 C3
Tarcento I 72 B3
Tarčin BIH 84 C3
Tarczyn PL 55 B5
Tardajos E 88 B3
Tardelcuende E 89 C4
Tardets-Sorholus F 76 C2
Tardienta E 90 B2
Tärendö S 113 E11
Targon F 76 B2
Târgoviște RO 11 D8
Târgu-Jiu RO 11 D7
Târgu Mureș RO 11 C8
Târgu Ocna RO 11 C9
Târgu Secuiesc RO 11 D9
Tarifa E 99 C5
Tariquejas E 98 B3
Tarján H 65 C4
Tárkány H 64 C4
Tarland GB 23 D6
Tarłów PL 55 B6
Tarm DK 39 D1
Tarmstedt D 43 B6
Tärnaby S 115 B12
Tarnalelesz H 65 B6
Tarnaörs H 65 C6
Târnăveni RO 11 C8
Tärnet N 113 C19
Tarnobrzeg PL 55 C6
Tarnos F 76 C1
Tarnów
Lubuskie PL 45 C6
Małopolskie PL 55 C5
Tarnowo Podgórne PL 46 C2
Tarnowskie Góry PL 54 C3
Tärnsjö S 36 B3
Tärnvik N 112 E4
Tarouca P 87 C3
Tarp D 43 A6
Tarquínia I 102 A4
Tarquínia Lido I 102 A4
Tarragona E 91 B4
Tàrrega E 91 B4
Tarrenz A 71 A5
Tårs
Nordjyllands DK 38 B3
Storstrøms DK 39 E4
Tarsia I 106 B3
Tarsus TR 16 C7
Tartas F 76 C2
Tartu EST 7 B9
Tarussa RUS 7 D14
Tarves GB 23 D6
Tarvísio I 72 B3
Taşağıl TR 119 F6
Täsch CH 70 B2
Taşköprü TR 16 A7
Tasov CZ 64 A2
Tasovčići BIH 84 C2
Taşucu TR 16 C6
Tát H 65 C4
Tata H 65 C4
Tatabánya H 74 A3
Tataháza H 75 B4
Tatarbunary UA 11 D10
Tatárszentgyörgy H 75 A4
Tatranská-Lomnica SK 65 A6
Tau N 33 C2
Tauberbischofsheim D 61 A5
Taucha D 52 B2
Taufkirchen D 62 B3
Taufkirchen an der Pram A 63 B4
Taulé F 56 B2
Taulignan F 78 B3
Taulov DK 39 D2
Taunton GB 29 B4
Taunusstein D 50 C4
Tauragė LT 6 D7
Taurianova I 106 C3
Taurisano I 107 B5
Tauste E 90 B1
Tauves F 68 C2
Tavankut SRB 75 B4
Tavannes CH 70 A2
Tavarnelle val di Pesa I 81 C5
Tavas TR 119 E4
Tavaux F 69 A5
Tävelsås S 40 C4
Taverna I 106 B3
Taverne CH 70 B3
Tavernelle I 82 C1
Tavernes de la Valldigna E 96 B2
Tavérnola Bergamasca I 71 C5
Taverny F 58 A3
Tavescan E 91 A4
Taviano I 107 B5
Tavira P 98 B3
Tavistock GB 28 C3
Tavnik SRB 85 C5
Tavşanlı TR 118 C4
Tayinloan GB 24 C2
Taynuilt GB 24 B2
Tayport GB 25 B5
Tázlár H 75 B4
Tazones E 88 A1
Tczew PL 47 A4
Tczów PL 55 B6
Teangue GB 22 D3
Teano I 103 B7
Teba E 100 C1
Tebay GB 26 A3
Techendorf A 72 B3
Tecklenburg D 50 A3
Tecko-matorp S 41 D3
Tecuci RO 11 D9
Tefenni TR 119 E4
Tegelsmora S 36 B4
Tegernsee D 62 C2
Teggiano I 104 C1
Tegoleto I 81 C5
Teichel D 52 C1
Teignmouth GB 29 C4
Teillay F 57 C4
Teillet F 77 C5
Teisendorf D 62 C3
Teistungen D 51 B6
Teixeiro E 86 A2
Tejada de Tiétar E 93 A5
Tejado E 89 C4
Tejares E 94 B1
Tejn DK 41 D4
Teke TR 118 A4
Tekirdağ TR 118 B2
Tekovské-Lužany SK 65 B4
Telavåg N 32 B1
Telč CZ 63 A6
Telese Terme I 103 B7
Telford GB 26 C3
Telfs A 71 A6
Telgárt SK 65 B6
Telgte D 50 B3
Tellingstedt D 43 A6
Telšiai LT 6 D7
Telti I 110 B2
Teltow D 45 C5
Tembleque E 95 C3
Temelín CZ 63 A5
Temerin SRB 75 C4
Temiño E 89 B3
Témpio Pausánia I 110 B2
Templederry IRL 20 B3
Templemore IRL 21 B4
Temple Sowerby GB 26 A3
Templin D 45 B5
Temse B 49 B5
Tenay F 69 C5
Ten Boer NL 42 B3
Tenbury Wells GB 29 A5
Tenby GB 28 B3
Tence F 78 A3
Tende F 80 B1
Tenhult S 40 B4
Tenja HR 74 C3
Tenneville B 49 C6
Tennevoll N 112 D6
Tensta S 36 B4
Tenterden GB 31 C4
Teo E 86 B2
Teora I 103 C8
Tepasto FIN 113 E13
Tepelenë AL 116 B2
Teplá CZ 52 D2
Teplice CZ 53 C3
Teplička nad Váhom SK 65 A4
Tepsa FIN 113 E14
Tera E 89 C4
Téramo I 103 A6
Ter Apel NL 43 C4
Terborg NL 50 B2
Terchová SK 65 A5
Terebovlya UA 11 B8
Teremia Mare RO 75 C5
Terena P 92 C3
Teresa de Cofrentes E 96 B1
Terešov CZ 63 A4
Terezín CZ 53 C4
Terezino Polje HR 74 C2
Tergnier F 59 A4
Teriberka RUS 3 B31
Terlizzi I 104 B2
Termas de Monfortinho P 93 A4
Terme di Súio I 103 B6
Terme di Valdieri I 79 B6
Termens E 90 B3
Termes F 78 B2
Términi Imerese I 108 B2
Terminillo I 102 A5
Térmoli I 103 B8
Termonfeckin IRL 19 C5
Ternberg A 63 C5
Terndrup DK 38 C3
Terneuzen NL 49 B4
Terni I 102 A5
Ternitz A 64 C2
Ternopil UA 11 B8
Terpni GR 116 B5
Terracina I 102 B6
Terråk N 115 B9
Terralba I 110 C1
Terranova di Pollino I 106 B3
Terranova di Sibari I 106 B3
Terras do Bouro P 87 C2
Terrasini I 108 A2
Terrassa E 91 B5
Terrasson-la-Villedieu F 77 A4
Terrazos E 89 B3
Terriente E 95 B5
Terrugem P 92 C3
Tertenia I 110 C2
Teruel E 90 C1
Tervola FIN 3 C26
Tervuren B 49 C5
Terzaga E 95 B5
Tešanj BIH 84 B3
Tesáske-Mlyňany SK 65 B4
Teslić BIH 84 B2
Tessin D 44 A4
Tessy-sur-Vire F 57 B4
Tét H 74 A2
Tetbury GB 29 B5
Teterchen F 60 A2
Teterow D 45 B4
Teteven BG 11 E8
Tetiyev UA 11 B10
Tetovo MK 10 E6
Tettau D 52 C1
Tettnang D 61 C5
Teublitz D 62 A3
Teuchern D 52 B2
Teulada
E 96 C3
I 110 D1
Teupitz D 52 A3
Teurajärvi S 113 F11
Teutschenthal D 52 B1
Tevel H 74 B3
Teviothead GB 25 C5
Tewkesbury GB 29 B5
Thale D 52 B1
Thalfang D 60 A2
Thalgau A 63 C4
Thalkirch CH 71 B4
Thalmässing D 62 A2
Thalwil CH 70 A3
Thame GB 31 C3
Thann F 60 C3
Thannhausen D 61 B6
Thaon-les-Vosges F 60 B2
Tharandt D 52 C3
Tharsis E 99 B3
Thasos GR 116 B6
Thatcham GB 31 C2
Thaxted GB 31 C4
Thayngen CH 61 C4
Theale GB 31 C2
The Barony GB 23 B5
Thebes = Thiva GR 117 D5
Theding-hausen D 43 C6
Theessen D 52 A2
The Hague = 's-Gravenhage NL 49 A5
Themar D 51 C6
The Mumbles GB 28 B4
Thénezay F 67 B4
Thenon F 67 C6
Therouanne F 48 C3
Thessaloniki = Salonica GR 116 B4
Thetford GB 30 B4
Theth AL 105 A5
Theux B 50 C1
Thézar-les-Corbières F 78 C1
Thèze F 76 C2
Thiberville F 58 A1
Thibie F 59 B5
Thiéblemont-Farémont F 59 B5
Thiendorf D 53 B3
Thiene I 71 C6
Thierrens CH 70 B1
Thiers F 68 C3
Thiesi I 110 B1
Thiessow D 45 A5
Thiezac F 77 A5
Þingeyri IS 111 B2
Þingvellir IS 111 C4
Thionville F 60 A2
Thira GR 117 F7
Thiron-Gardais F 58 B1
Thirsk GB 27 A4
Thisted DK 38 C1
Thiva = Thebes GR 117 D5
Thivars F 58 B2
Thiviers F 67 C5
Thizy F 69 B4
Tholen NL 49 B5
Tholey D 60 A3
Thomas Street IRL 20 A3
Thomastown IRL 21 B4
Thônes F 69 C6
Thonnance-les-Joinville F 59 B6
Thonon-les-Bains F 69 B6
Thorame-Basse F 79 B5
Thorame-Haute F 79 B5
Thorens-Glières F 69 B6
Thorigny-sur-Oreuse F 59 B4
Thörl A 73 A5
Þorlákshöfn IS 111 D4
Thornaby on Tees GB 27 A4
Thornbury GB 29 B5
Thorne GB 27 B5
Thornhill
Dumfries & Galloway GB 25 C4
Stirling GB 24 B3
Thornthwaite GB 26 A2
Thornton-le-Dale GB 27 A5
Þórshöfn IS 111 A10
Thouarcé F 67 A4
Thouars F 67 B4
Thrapston GB 30 B3
Threlkeld GB 26 A2
Thrumster GB 23 C5
Thueyts F 78 B3
Thuin B 49 C5
Thuir F 91 A5
Thumau D 52 C1
Thun CH 70 B2
Thuret F 68 C3
Thurey F 69 B5
Thüringen A 71 A4
Thurins F 69 C4
Thürkow D 45 B4
Thurles IRL 21 B4
Thurmaston GB 30 B2
Thurø By DK 39 D3
Thursby GB 25 D4
Thurso GB 23 C5
Thury-Harcourt F 57 B5
Thusis CH 71 B4
Thyborøn DK 38 C1
Þykkvibær IS 111 D5
Thyregod DK 39 D2
Tibi E 96 C2
Tibro S 35 D6
Tidaholm S 35 D5
Tidan S 35 D6
Tidersrum S 40 B5
Tiedra E 88 C1
Tiefenbach D 62 A3
Tiefencastel CH 71 B4
Tiefenort D 51 C6
Tiefensee D 45 C5
Tiel NL 49 B6
Tielmes E 95 B3
Tielt B 49 B4
Tienen B 49 C5
Tiengen D 61 C4
Tiercé F 57 C5
Tierga E 89 C5
Tiermas E 90 A1
Tierp S 36 B4
Tierrantona E 90 A3
Tighina MD 11 C10
Tighnabruaich GB 24 C2
Tignes F 70 C1
Tigy F 58 C3
Tihany H 74 B2
Tijnje NL 42 B2
Tijola E 101 B3
Tikhvin RUS 7 B12
Tilburg NL 49 B6
Til Châtel F 69 A5
Tilh F 76 C2
Tillac F 76 C3
Tillberga S 37 C3
Tille F 58 A3
Tillicoultry GB 25 B4
Tilloy Bellay F 59 A5
Tilly F 67 B6
Tilly-sur-Seulles F 57 A5
Tim DK 39 C1
Timau I 72 B3
Timbaki GR 117 G6
Timi CY 120 B1
Timişoara RO 75 C6
Timmele S 40 B3
Timmendorfer Strand D 44 B2
Timmernabben S 40 C6
Timmersdala S 35 D5
Timoleague IRL 20 C3
Timolin IRL 21 B5
Timrå S 115 E14
Timsfors S 40 C3
Timsgearraidh GB 22 C1
Tinajas E 95 B4
Tinalhas P 92 B3
Tinchebray F 57 B5
Tincques F 48 C3
Tineo E 86 A4
Tinglev DK 39 E2
Tingsryd S 40 C5
Tingstäde S 37 E5
Tingvoll N 114 E5
Tinlot B 49 C6
Tinnoset N 33 C6
Tinos GR 117 E7
Tintagel GB 28 C3
Tinténiac F 57 B4
Tintern GB 29 B5
Tintigny B 60 A1
Tione di Trento I 71 B5
Tipperary IRL 20 B3
Tiptree GB 31 C4
Tirana = Tiranë AL 105 B5
Tiranë = Tirana AL 105 B5
Tirano I 71 B5
Tiraspol MD 11 C10
Tire TR 119 D2
Tires I 71 B6
Tiriez E 95 D4
Tirig E 90 C3
Tiriolo I 106 C3
Tirnavos GR 116 C4
Tirrénia I 81 C4
Tirschenreuth D 62 A3
Tirstrup DK 39 C3
Tirteafuera E 100 A1
Tisno HR 83 C4
Tišnov CZ 64 A2
Tisovec SK 65 B5
Tisselskog S 35 D4
Tistedal N 35 C3
Tistrup DK 39 D1
Tisvildeleje DK 39 C5
Tiszaalpár H 75 B4
Tiszabő H 75 A5
Tiszadorogma H 65 C6
Tiszaföldvár H 75 B5
Tiszafüred H 65 C6
Tiszajenő H 75 A5
Tiszakécske H 75 B5
Tiszakürt H 75 B5
Tiszanána H 75 A5
Tiszaörs H 75 A5
Tiszaroff H 75 A5
Tiszasüly H 75 A5
Tiszasziget H 75 B5
Tiszaszőlős H 75 A5
Titaguas E 96 B1
Titel SRB 75 C5
Titisee-Neustadt D 61 C4
Tito I 104 C1
Titova Korenica HR 83 B4
Titran N 114 D5
Tittling D 63 B4
Tittmoning D 62 B3
Titz D 50 B2
Tiurajärvi FIN 113 E13
Tived S 37 D1
Tiverton GB 29 C4
Tivisa E 90 B3
Tívoli I 102 B5
Tjällmo S 37 D2
Tjämotis S 112 F7
Tjæreborg DK 39 D1
Tjautjas S 112 E9
Tjøme N 35 C2
Tjong N 112 F2
Tjonnefoss N 33 D5
Tjörn IS 111 B5
Tjörnarp S 41 D3
Tjøtta N 115 B9
Tkon HR 83 C4
Tleń PL 47 B4
Tlmače SK 65 B4
Tłuchowo PL 47 C5
Tlumačov CZ 64 A3
Tóalmas H 75 A4
Toano I 81 B4
Toba D 51 B6
Tobarra E 101 A4
Tobermore GB 19 B5
Tobermory GB 24 B1
Toberonochy GB 24 B2
Tobha Mor GB 22 D1
Tobo S 36 B4
Tocane-St Apre F 67 C5
Tocha P 92 A2
Tocina E 99 B5
Töcksfors S 35 C3
Tocón E 100 B2
Todal N 114 E5
Todi I 82 D1
Todmorden GB 26 B3
Todorici BIH 84 B2
Todtmoos D 61 C4
Todtnau D 60 C3
Toén E 87 B3
Tofta
Gotland S 37 E5
Skaraborg S 35 D5
Toftbyn S 36 B2
Tofte N 35 C2
Töftedal S 35 D3
Tofterup DK 39 D1
Toftlund DK 39 D2
Tófű H 74 B3
Tohmo FIN 113 F16
Tokarnia PL 55 C5
Tokary PL 54 B3
Tokod H 65 C4
Tököl H 75 A3
Tolastadh bho Thuath GB 22 C2
Toledo E 94 C2
Tolentino I 82 C2
Tolfa I 102 A4
Tolg S 40 B4
Tolga N 114 E8
Tolkmicko PL 47 A5
Tolko PL 47 A6
Tollarp S 41 D3
Tollered S 40 B2
Tølløse DK 39 D4
Tolmachevo RUS 7 B10
Tolmezzo I 72 B3
Tolmin SLO 72 B3
Tolna H 74 B3
Tolnanémedi H 74 B3
Tolob GB 22 B7
Tolosa
E 89 A4
P 92 B3
Tolox E 100 C1
Tolpuddle GB 29 C5
Tolva E 90 A3
Tolve I 104 C2
Tomar P 92 B2
Tomarza TR 16 B7
Tomaševac SRB 75 C5
Tomašica BIH 83 B5
Tomášikovo SK 64 B3
Tomašouka BY 6 F7
Tomašovce SK 65 B5
Tomaszów Mazowiecki PL 55 B5
Tomatin GB 23 D5
Tombeboeuf F 77 B3
Tomdoun GB 22 D3
Tomelilla S 41 D3
Tomellosa E 95 B4
Tomelloso E 95 C3
Tomiño E 87 C2
Tomintoul GB 23 D5
Tomislavgrad BIH 84 C2
Tomisław PL 53 B5
Tomisławice PL 47 C4
Tomnavoulin GB 23 D5
Tompa H 75 B4
Tompaládony H 74 A1
Tomra N 114 E3
Tomter N 35 C2
Tona E 91 B5
Tonara I 110 B2
Tonbridge GB 31 C4
Tondela P 92 A2
Tønder DK 39 E1
Tongeren B 49 C6
Tongue GB 23 C4
Tönisvorst D 50 B2
Tonjum N 32 A4
Tonkopuro FIN 113 F17
Tonnay-Boutonne F 67 C4
Tonnay-Charente F 66 C4
Tonneins F 77 B3
Tonnerre F 59 C4
Tonnes N 115 A10
Tönning D 43 A5
Tonsåsen N 32 B6
Tønsberg N 35 C2
Tonstad N 33 D3
Toomyvara IRL 20 B3
Toormore IRL 20 C2
Topares E 101 B3
Topas E 94 B1
Toplița RO 11 C8
Topola SRB 85 B5
Topolčani MK 116 A3
Topoľčany SK 64 B4
Topoľčianky SK 65 B4
Topolje HR 73 C6
Topólka PL 47 C4
Topoľ'niky SK 64 C3
Toponár H 74 B2
Toporów PL 53 A5
Topsham GB 29 C4
Topusko HR 73 C5
Toques E 86 B3
Torà E 91 B4
Toral de los Guzmanes E 88 B1
Toral de los Vados E 86 B4
Torbalı TR 119 D2
Torbjörntorp S 35 D5
Torbole I 71 C5
Torchiarolo I 105 C4
Torcross GB 29 C4
Torcy-le-Petit F 58 A2
Torda SRB 75 C5
Tørdal N 33 C5
Tordehumos E 88 C1
Tordera E 91 B5
Tordesillas E 88 C1
Tordesilos E 95 B5
Töre S 3 D25
Töreboda S 35 D6
Toreby DK 39 E4
Torekov S 41 C2
Torella dei Lombardi I 103 C8
Torellò E 91 A5
Toreno E 86 B4
Torfou F 66 A3
Torgau D 52 B3
Torgelow D 45 B6
Torgueda P 87 C3
Torhamn S 41 C5
Torhop N 113 B16
Torhout B 49 B4
Torigni-sur-Vire F 57 A5
Torija E 95 B3
Toril E 95 B5
Torino = Turin I 80 A1
Toritto I 104 C2
Torkovichi RUS 7 B11
Torla E 90 A2
Tormänen FIN 113 D16
Tormestorp S 41 C3
Tórmini I 71 C5
Tornada P 92 B1
Tornal'a SK 65 B6
Tornavacas E 93 A5
Tornby DK 38 B2
Tornesch D 43 B6
Torness GB 23 D4
Torniella I 81 C5
Tornimparte I 103 A6
Torning DK 39 C2
Tornio FIN 3 D26
Tornjoš SRB 75 C4
Tornos E 95 B5
Toro E 88 C1
Törökszentmiklós H 75 A5
Toropets RUS 7 C11
Torpa S 40 C3
Torpè I 110 B2
Torphins GB 23 D6
Torpo N 32 B5
Torpoint GB 28 C3
Torpsbruk S 40 B4
Torquay GB 29 C4
Torquemada E 88 B2
Torralba de Burgo E 89 C4
Torralba de Calatrava E 94 C3
Torrão P 98 A2
Torre Annunziata I 103 C7
Torreblacos E 89 C4
Torreblanca E 96 A3
Torreblascopedro E 100 A2
Torrecaballeros E 94 A2
Torrecampo E 100 A1
Torre Canne I 104 C3
Torre Cardela E 100 B2
Torrecilla E 95 B4
Torrecilla de la Jara E 94 C2
Torrecilla de la Orden E 94 A1
Torrecilla del Pinar E 88 C2
Torrecilla en Cameros E 89 B4
Torrecillas de la Tiesa E 93 B5
Torre das Vargens P 92 B3
Torre de Coelheiros P 92 C3
Torre de Dom Chama P 87 C3
Torre de Juan Abad E 100 A2
Torre de la Higuera E 99 B4
Torre del Bierzo E 86 B4
Torre del Burgo E 95 B3
Torre del Campo E 100 B2
Torre del Greco I 103 C7
Torre del Lago Puccini I 81 C4
Torre dell'Orso I 105 C4
Torre del Mar E 100 C1
Torredembarra E 91 B4
Torre de Miguel Sesmero E 93 C4
Torre de Moncorvo P 87 C3
Torre de Santa Maria E 93 B4
Torredonjimeno E 100 B2
Torre do Terranho P 87 D3
Torre Faro I 109 A4
Torregrosa E 90 B3
Torreira P 87 D2
Torrejoncillo E 93 B4
Torrejón de Ardoz E 95 B3
Torrejón de la Calzada E 94 B3
Torrejón del Rey E 95 B3
Torrejon el Rubio E 93 B4
Torrelaguna E 95 B3
Torrelapaja E 89 C5
Torre la Ribera E 90 A3
Torrelavega E 88 A2
Torrelobatón E 88 C1
Torrelodones E 94 B3
Torre los Negros E 90 C1
Torremaggiore I 103 B8
Torremanzanas E 96 C2
Torremayor E 93 C4
Torremezzo di Falconara I 106 B3
Torremocha E 93 B4
Torremolinos E 100 C1
Torrenieri I 81 C5
Torrenostra E 96 A3
Torrenova I 102 B5
Torrent E 96 B2
Torrente de Cinca E 90 B3
Torrenueva
Ciudad Real E 100 A2
Granada E 100 C2
Torreorgaz E 93 B4
Torre Orsáia I 106 A2
Torre-Pacheco E 101 B5
Torre Péllice I 79 B6
Torreperogil E 100 A2
Torres E 100 B2
Torresandino E 88 C3
Torre Santa Susanna I 105 C3
Torres-Cabrera E 100 B1
Torres de la Alameda E 95 B3
Torres Novas P 92 B2
Torres Vedras P 92 B1
Torrevieja E 96 D2
Torricella I 104 C3
Torri del Benaco I 71 C5
Torridon GB 22 D3
Torriglia I 80 B3
Torrijos E 94 C2
Tørring DK 39 D2
Torrita di Siena I 81 C5
Torroal P 92 C2
Torroella de Montgrì E 91 A6
Torrox E 100 C2
Torrskog S 35 C4
Torsåker S 36 B3
Torsang S 36 B2
Torsås S 41 C6
Torsby S 34 B4
Torsetra N 34 B2
Torshälla S 37 C3
Tórshavn FO 2 E10
Torslanda S 38 B4
Torsminde DK 39 C1
Torsnes N 32 B3
Törtel H 75 A4
Tórtoles E 93 A5
Tórtoles de Esgueva E 88 C2
Tortol ì I 110 C2
Tortona I 80 B2
Tórtora I 106 B2
Tortoreto Lido I 82 D2
Tortorici I 109 A3
Tortosa E 90 C3
Tortosendo P 92 A3
Tortuera E 95 B5
Tortuero E 95 B3
Toruń PL 47 B4
Torup S 40 C3
Tor Vaiánica I 102 B5
Torver GB 26 A2
Tørvikbygde N 32 B3
Torviscón E 100 C2
Torzhok RUS 7 C13
Torzym PL 53 A5
Tosbotn N 115 B9
Toscelanor-Maderno I 71 C5
Tosno RUS 7 B11
Tossa de Mar E 91 B5
Tossåsen S 115 E10
Tosse F 76 C1
Tösse S 35 D4
Tossicia I 103 A6
Tostedt D 43 B6
Tosya TR 16 A7
Tószeg H 75 A5
Toszek PL 54 C3
Totana E 101 B4
Totebo S 40 B6
Tôtes F 58 A2
Tótkomlós H 75 B5
Totland N 114 F2
Tøtlandsvik N 33 C3
Totnes GB 28 C4
Tótszerdahely H 74 B1
Tøttdal N 114 C8
Totton GB 31 D2
Touça P 87 C3
Toucy F 59 C4
Toul F 60 B1
Toulon F 79 C4
Toulon-sur-Allier F 68 B3
Toulon-sur-Arroux F 68 B4
Toulouse F 77 C4
Tourcoing F 49 C4
Tour de la Parata F 102 B1
Tourlaville F 57 A4
Tournai B 49 C4
Tournan-en-Brie F 58 B3
Tournay F 76 C3
Tournon-d'Agenais F 77 B3
Tournon-St Martin F 67 B5
Tournon-sur-Rhône F 78 A3
Tournus F 69 B4
Touro
E 86 B2
P 87 D3
Tourouvre F 58 B1
Tourriers F 67 C5
Tours F 67 A5
Tourteron F 59 A5
Tourves F 79 C4
Toury F 58 B2
Touvedo P 87 C2
Touvois F 66 B3
Toužim CZ 52 C2
Tovačov CZ 64 A3
Tovariševo SRB 75 C4
Tovarnik HR 75 C4
Tovdal N 33 D5
Tovrljane SRB 85 C6
Towcester GB 30 B3
Town Yetholm GB 25 C5
Tråastølen N 32 B4
Trabada E 86 A3
Trabadelo E 86 B4
Trabanca E 87 C4
Trabazos E 87 C4
Traben-Trarbach D 50 D3
Trabia I 108 B2
Tradate I 70 C3

Trädet S 40 B3
Trafaria P 92 C1
Tragacete E 95 B5
Tragwein A 63 B5
Traiguera E 90 C3
Trainel F 59 B4
Traisen A 63 B6
Traismauer A 64 B1
Traitsching D 62 A3
Trákhonas CY 120 A2
Tralee IRL 20 B2
Tramacastilla de Tena E 76 D2
Tramagal P 92 B2
Tramariglio I 110 B1
Tramatza I 110 B1
Tramelan CH 70 A2
Tramonti di Sopra I 72 B2
Tramore IRL 21 B4
Trampot F 60 B1
Trana I 80 A1
Tranås S 40 A4
Tranbjerg DK 39 C3
Tranby N 34 C2
Trancoso P 87 D3
Tranebjerg DK 39 D3
Tranekær DK 39 E3
Tranemo S 40 B3
Tranent GB 25 C5
Tranevåg N 33 D3
Trängslet S 34 A5
Tranhult S 40 B3
Trani I 104 B2
Trans-en-Provence F 79 C5
Transtrand S 34 A5
Tranum DK 38 B2
Tranvik S 37 C5
Trápani I 108 A1
Trappes F 58 B3
Traryd S 40 C3
Trasacco I 103 B6
Trasierra E 99 A4
Träslövsläge S 40 B2
Trasmiras E 87 B3
Traspinedo E 88 C2
Trate SLO 73 B5
Trauchgau D 62 C1
Traun A 63 B5
Traunreut D 62 C3
Traunstein D 62 C3
Traunwalchen D 62 C3
Tråvad S 35 D5
Travemünde D 44 B2
Traversétolo I 81 B4
Travnik
BIH 84 B2
SLO 73 C4
Travo
F 102 B2
I 80 B3
Trawsfynydd GB 26 C2
Trbovlje SLO 73 B5
Trbušani SRB 85 C5
Treban F 68 B3
Třebařov CZ 64 A2
Trebatsch D 53 A4
Trebbin D 52 A3
Třebechovice pod Orebem CZ 53 C5
Trebel D 44 C3
Třebenice CZ 53 C3
Trébeurden F 56 B2
Třebíč CZ 64 A1
Trebinje BIH 84 D3
Trebisacce I 106 B3
Trebitz D 52 B2
Trebnje SLO 73 C5
Třeboň CZ 63 A5
Třebovice CZ 64 A2
Trebsen D 52 B2
Trebujena E 99 C4
Trecastagni I 109 B4
Trecate I 70 C3
Trecenta I 81 A5
Tredegar GB 29 B4
Tredózio I 81 B5
Treffen A 72 B3
Treffort F 69 B5
Treffurt D 51 B6
Trefnant GB 26 B2
Tregaron GB 28 A4
Trégastel-Plage F 56 B2
Tregnago I 71 C6
Tregony GB 28 C3
Tréguier F 56 B2
Trégunc F 56 C2
Treharris GB 29 B4
Trehörningsjö S 115 D15
Tréia I 82 C2
Treignac F 68 C1
Treignat F 68 B2
Treignes B 49 C5
Treis-Karden D 50 C3
Trekanten S 40 C6
Trélazé F 67 A4
Trelech GB 28 B3
Trélissac F 67 C5
Trelleborg S 41 D3
Trélon F 49 C5
Trélou-sur-Marne F 59 A4
Tremblay-le-Vicomte F 58 B2
Tremés P 92 B2
Tremezzo I 71 C4
Třemošná CZ 63 A4
Tremp E 90 A3
Trenčianska Stankovce SK 64 B3
Trenčianska Turná SK 64 B4
Trenčianske Teplá SK 64 B4
Trenčianske Teplice SK 64 B4
Trenčín SK 64 B4
Trendelburg D 51 B5
Trengereid N 32 B2
Trensacq F 76 B2
Trent D 45 A5
Trento I 71 B6
Treorchy GB 29 B4
Trepča KOS 85 D5
Trept F 69 C5
Trepuzzi I 105 C4
Trescore Balneário I 71 C4
Tresenda I 71 B5
Tresfjord N 114 E4
Tresigallo I 81 B5
Trešnjevica SRB 85 C6
Tresnurághes I 110 B1
Trespaderne E 89 B3
Třešt CZ 63 A6
Trestina I 82 C1
Tretower GB 29 B4
Trets F 79 C4
Tretten N 34 A2
Treuchtlingen D 62 B1
Treuen D 52 C2
Treuenbrietzen D 52 A2
Treungen N 33 C5
Trevelez E 100 C2
Trevi I 82 D1
Treviana E 89 B3
Trevíglio I 71 C4
Trevignano Romano I 102 A5
Trevi nel Lázio I 102 B6
Treviso I 72 C2
Trévoux F 69 C4
Treysa D 51 C5
Trézelles F 68 B3
Trezzo sull'Adda I 71 C4
Trhová Kamenice CZ 64 A1
Trhové Sviny CZ 63 B5
Triacastela E 86 B3
Triaize F 66 B3
Trianda GR 119 F3
Triaucourt-en-Argonne F 59 B6
Tribanj Kruščica HR 83 B4
Triberg D 61 B4
Tribsees D 45 A4
Tribuče SLO 73 C5
Tricárico I 104 C2
Tricase I 107 B5
Tricésimo I 72 B3
Trieben A 73 A4
Triebes D 52 C2
Triepkendorf D 45 B5
Trier D 60 A2
Trieste I 72 C3
Trie-sur-Baïse F 77 C3
Triggiano I 104 B2
Triglitz D 44 B4
Trignac F 66 A2
Trigueros E 99 B4
Trigueros del Valle E 88 C2
Trijebine SRB 85 C4
Trikala GR 116 C3
Trikeri GR 116 C5
Trikomo CY 120 A2
Trilj HR 83 C5
Trillo E 95 B4
Trilport F 59 B3
Trim IRL 21 A5
Trimdon GB 25 D6
Trindade
Beja P 98 B3
Bragança P 87 C3
Třinec CZ 65 A4
Tring GB 31 C3
Trinità d'Agultu I 110 B1
Trinitápoli I 104 B2
Trino I 70 C3
Trinta P 92 A3
Triora I 80 C1
Tripoli GR 117 E4
Triponzo I 82 D1
Triptis D 52 C1
Triste E 90 A2
Trittau D 44 B2
Trivento I 103 B7
Trivero I 70 C3
Trivigno I 104 C1
Trn BIH 84 B2
Trnava
HR 74 C3
SK 64 B3
Trnovec SK 64 B3
Trnovo BIH 84 C3
Trnovska vas SLO 73 B5
Troarn F 57 A5
Trochtelfingen D 61 B5
Trödje S 36 B4
Troense DK 39 D3
Trofa P 87 C2
Trofaiach A 73 A5
Trofors N 115 B10
Trogir HR 83 C5
Trøgstad N 35 C3
Tróia I 103 B8
Troia P 92 C2
Troina I 109 B3
Troisdorf D 50 C3
Trois-Ponts B 50 C1
Troisvierges L 50 C2
Trojane SLO 73 B4
Trojanów PL 55 B6
Troldhede DK 39 D1
Trollhättan S 35 D4
Trolog BIH 84 C1
Tromello I 70 C3
Tromøy N 33 D5
Tromsø N 112 C8
Trondheim N 114 D7
Tronget F 68 B3
Trönninge S 40 C2
Trönningeby S 40 B2
Trönö S 36 A3
Tronzano-Vercellese I 70 C3
Trôo F 58 C1
Troon GB 24 C3
Tropea I 106 C2
Tropojë AL 105 A6
Tropy Sztumskie PL 47 B5
Trosa S 37 D4
Trösken S 36 B3
Trosly-Breuil F 59 A4
Trossingen D 61 B4
Trostberg D 62 B3
Trostyanets UA 7 F13
Trouville-sur-Mer F 57 A6
Trowbridge GB 29 B5
Troyes F 59 B5
Trpanj HR 84 C2
Trpezi MNE 85 D5
Trpinja HR 74 C3
Tršće HR 73 C4
Tršice CZ 64 A3
Trstená SK 65 A5
Trstenci BIH 84 A2
Trstenik
KOS 85 D5
SRB 85 C6
Trsteno HR 84 D2
Trstice SK 64 B3
Trstin SK 64 B3
Trubchevsk RUS 7 E12
Trubia E 88 A1
Trubjela MNE 84 D3
Truchas E 87 B4
Trujillanos E 93 C4
Trujillo E 93 B5
Trumieje PL 47 B5
Trun
CH 70 B3
F 57 B6
Truro GB 28 C2
Trusetal D 51 C6
Truskavets' UA 11 B7
Trustrup DK 39 C3
Trutnov CZ 53 C5
Tryserum S 37 D3
Trysil N 34 A4
Tryszczyn PL 46 B3
Trzcianka PL 46 B2
Trzciel PL 46 C1
Trzcińsko Zdrój PL 45 C6
Trzebiatów PL 45 A7
Trzebiel PL 53 B4
Trzebielino PL 46 A3
Trzebień PL 53 B5
Trzebiez PL 45 B6
Trzebinia PL 55 C4
Trzebnica PL 54 B2
Trzebnice PL 53 B6
Trzeciewiec PL 47 B4
Trzemeszno PL 46 C3
Trzemeszno-Lubuskie PL 46 C1
Trzetrzewina PL 65 A6
Tržič SLO 73 B4
Tsamandas GR 116 C2
Tschagguns A 71 A4
Tschernitz D 53 B4
Tsebrykove UA 11 C11
Tsvetkovo UA 11 B11
Tsyelyakhany BY 7 E8
Tua P 87 C3
Tuam IRL 20 A3
Tubbercurry IRL 18 B3
Tubbergen NL 42 C3
Tubilla del Lago E 89 C3
Tübingen D 61 B5
Tubize B 49 C5
Tučapy CZ 63 A5
Tučepi HR 84 C2
Tuchan F 78 D1
Tüchen D 44 B4
Tuchola PL 46 B3
Tuchomie PL 46 A3
Tuchów PL 65 A7
Tuczno PL 46 B2
Tuddal N 32 C5
Tudela E 89 B5
Tudela de Duero E 88 C2
Tudweiliog GB 26 C1
Tuejar E 96 B1
Tuffé F 58 B1
Tufsingdalen N 114 E8
Tuhaň CZ 53 C4
Tui E 87 B2
Tukums LV 6 C7
Tula
I 110 B1
RUS 7 D14
Tulcea RO 11 D10
Tul'chyn UA 11 B10
Tulette F 78 B3
Tuliszków PL 54 A3
Tulla IRL 20 B3
Tullamore IRL 21 A4
Tulle F 68 C1
Tullins F 69 C5
Tulln A 64 B2
Tullow IRL 21 B5
Tułowice PL 54 C2
Tulppio FIN 113 E18
Tulsk IRL 18 C3
Tumba S 37 C4
Tummel Bridge GB 24 B3
Tun S 35 D4
Tuna
Kalmar S 40 B6
Uppsala S 36 B5
Tuna Hästberg S 36 B2
Tunçbilek TR 118 C4
Tunes P 98 B2
Tungelsta S 37 C5
Tunje AL 105 C6
Tunnerstad S 40 A4
Tunnhovd N 32 B5
Tunstall GB 30 B5
Tuohikotti FIN 3 F27
Tuoro sul Trasimeno I 82 C1
Tupadły PL 47 C4
Tupanari BIH 84 B3
Tupik RUS 7 D12
Tuplice PL 53 B4
Tura H 65 C5
Turanj HR 83 C4
Turany SK 65 A5
Turbe BIH 84 B2
Turbenthal CH 70 A3
Turcia E 88 B1
Turčianske Teplice SK 65 B4
Turcifal P 92 B1
Turckheim F 60 B3
Turda RO 11 C7
Turégano E 94 A3
Turek PL 54 A3
Tŭrgovishte BG 11 E9
Turgutlu TR 119 D2
Turi I 104 C3
Turin = Torino I 80 A1
Turis E 96 B2
Türje H 74 B2
Turka UA 11 B7
Túrkeve H 75 A5
Türkheim D 62 B1
Türkmenli TR 118 C1
Turku FIN 6 A7
Turleque E 94 C3
Turňa nad Bodvou SK 65 B6
Turnberry GB 24 C3
Turnhout B 49 B5
Türnitz A 63 C6
Turnov CZ 53 C5
Turnu RO 75 B6
Turnu Măgurele RO 11 E8
Turón E 100 C2
Turoszów PL 53 C4
Turowo PL 47 B6
Turquel P 92 B1
Turri I 110 C1
Turries F 79 B5
Turriff GB 23 D6
Tursi I 104 C2
Turtmann CH 70 B2
Turtola FIN 113 F12
Turze PL 54 B2
Turzovka SK 65 A4
Tusa I 109 B3
Tuscánia I 102 A4
Tuse DK 39 D4
Tušilovic HR 73 C5
Tuszyn PL 55 B4
Tutin SRB 85 D5
Tutow D 45 B5
Tutrakan BG 11 D9
Tuttlingen D 61 C4
Tutzing D 62 C2
Tuzi MNE 105 A5
Tuzla
BIH 84 B3
TR 16 C7
Tuzlukçu TR 119 D6
Tvååker S 40 B2
Tväråkund S 115 C16
Tvärskog S 40 C6
Tvedestrand N 33 D5
Tveit
Hordaland N 32 B4
Rogaland N 33 C3
Tver RUS 7 C13
Tverrelvmo N 112 D8
Tversted DK 38 B3
Tving S 41 C5
Tvrdošin SK 65 A5
Tvrdošovce SK 64 B4
Twardogóra PL 54 B2
Twatt GB 23 B5
Twello NL 50 A2
Twimberg A 73 B4
Twist D 43 C4
Twistringen D 43 C5
Tworóg PL 54 C3
Twyford
Hampshire GB 31 C2
Wokingham GB 31 C3
Tyachiv UA 11 B7
Tychówka PL 46 B2
Tychowo PL 46 B2
Tychy PL 54 C3
Tydal N 114 D8
Týec nad Labem CZ 53 C5
Tyfors S 34 B6
Tygelsjö S 41 D2
Tylldal N 114 E7
Tylstrup DK 38 B2
Tymbark PL 65 A6
Tymowa PL 65 A6
Tyndrum GB 24 B3
Týnec nad Sázavou CZ 63 A5
Tynemouth GB 25 C6
Tyngsjö S 34 B5
Týništěnad Orlicí CZ 53 C6
Týn nad Vltavou CZ 63 A5
Tynset N 114 E7
Tyresö S 37 C5
Tyringe S 41 C3
Tyrislöt S 37 D3
Tyristrand N 34 B2
Tyrrellspass IRL 21 A4
Tysnes N 32 B2
Tysse N 32 B2
Tyssebotn N 32 B2
Tyssedal N 32 B3
Tystberga S 37 D4
Tysvær N 33 C2
Tywyn GB 26 C1
Tzermiado GR 117 G7
Tzummarum NL 42 B2

U

Ub SRB 85 B5
Ubby DK 39 D4
Úbeda E 100 A2
Überlingen D 61 C5
Ubidea E 89 A4
Ubli
HR 84 D1
MNE 105 A5
Ubrique E 99 C5
Ucero E 89 C3
Uchaud F 78 C3
Uchte D 43 C5
Uckerath D 50 C3
Uckfield GB 31 D4
Ucklum S 38 A4
Uclés E 95 C4
Ucria I 109 A3
Udbina HR 83 B4
Uddebo S 40 B3
Uddeholm S 34 B5
Uddevalla S 35 D3
Uddheden S 34 C4
Uden NL 49 B6
Uder D 51 B6
Udiča SK 65 A4
Údine I 72 B3
Udvar H 74 C3
Ueckermünde D 45 B6
Uelsen D 42 C3
Uelzen D 44 C2
Uetendorf CH 70 B2
Uetersen D 43 B6
Uetze D 44 C2
Uffculme GB 29 C4
Uffenheim D 61 A6
Ugarana E 89 A4
Ugento I 107 B5
Ugerldse DK 39 D4
Uggerby DK 38 B3
Uggerslev DK 39 D3
Uggiano la Chiesa I 107 A5
Ugíjar E 100 C2
Ugine F 69 C6
Uglejevik BIH 84 B4
Uglenes N 32 B2
Uglich RUS 7 C15
Ugljane HR 84 C1
Ugod H 74 A2
Uherské Hradiště CZ 64 A3
Uherský Brod CZ 64 A3
Uherský Ostroh CZ 64 B3
Uhingen D 61 B5
Uhlířské-Janovice CZ 63 A6
Uhříněves CZ 53 C4
Uhyst D 53 B4
Uig GB 22 D2
Uitgeest NL 42 C1
Uithoorn NL 49 A5
Uithuizen NL 42 B3
Uithuizermeeden NL 42 B3
Uivar RO 75 C5
Ujazd
Łódzkie PL 55 B4
Opolskie PL 54 C3
Ujezd u Brna CZ 64 A2
Ujhartyán H 75 A4
Újkigyós H 75 B6
Ujpetre H 74 C3
Ujście PL 46 B2
Ujsolt H 75 B4
Újszász H 75 A5
Ujué E 89 B5
Ukanc SLO 72 B3
Ukmergė LT 6 D8
Ukna S 40 A6
Ula TR 119 E3
Ul'anka SK 65 B5
Ulaş TR 118 A2
Ulássai I 110 C2
Ulbjerg DK 38 C2
Ulbster GB 23 C5
Ulceby GB 27 B5
Ulcinj MNE 105 B5
Uldum DK 39 D2
Ulefoss N 33 C6
Uleila del Campo E 101 B3
Ulëz AL 105 B5
Ulfborg DK 39 C1
Uljma SRB 85 A6
Ullånger S 115 D15
Ullapool GB 22 D3
Ullared S 40 B2
Ullatti S 113 E10
Ullatun N 33 C3
Ulldecona E 90 C3
Ulldemolins E 90 B3
Ullerslev DK 39 D3
Ullervad S 35 D5
Üllés H 75 B4
Üllö H 75 A4
Ulm D 61 B5
Ulme P 92 B2
Ulmen D 50 C2
Ulnes N 32 B6
Ulog BIH 84 C3
Ulricehamn S 40 B3
Ulrichstein D 51 C5
Ulrika S 37 D2
Ulriksfors S 115 D12
Ulrum NL 42 B3
Ulsberg N 114 E6
Ulsta GB 22 A7
Ulsted DK 38 B3
Ulsteinvik N 114 E2
Ulstrup
Vestsjællands Amt. DK 39 D3
Viborg Amt. DK 39 C2
Ulsvåg N 112 D4
Ulubey TR 119 D4
Uluborlu TR 119 D5
Ulukışla TR 16 C7
Ulverston GB 26 A2
Ulvik N 32 B3
Umag HR 72 C3
Uman UA 11 B11
Umba RUS 3 C31
Umbértide I 82 C1
Umbriático I 107 B3
Umčari SRB 85 B5
Umeå S 3 E24
Umgransele S 115 C15
Umhausen A 71 A5
Umka SRB 85 B5
Umljanovic HR 83 C5
Umnäs S 115 B13
Umurbey TR 118 B1
Unaðsdalur IS 111 A3
Unapool GB 22 C3
Unari FIN 113 E14
Uncastillo E 90 A1
Undenäs S 37 D1
Undersaker S 115 D10
Undredal N 32 B4
Unecha RUS 7 E12
Unešić HR 83 C5
Úněšov CZ 62 A4
Ungheni MD 11 C9
Unhais da Serra P 92 A3
Unhošt CZ 53 C4
Unichowo PL 46 A3
Uničov CZ 64 A3
Uniejów PL 54 B3
Unisław PL 47 B4
Unkel D 50 C3
Unken A 62 C3
Unna D 50 B3
Unnaryd S 40 C3
Unquera E 88 A2
Unterach A 63 C4
Unterägeri CH 70 A3
Unterammergau D 62 C2
Unterhaching D 62 B2
Unteriberg CH 70 A3
Unterkochen D 61 B6
Unter Langkampfen A 72 A2
Unterlaussa A 63 C5
Unterlüss D 44 C2
Untermünkheim D 61 A5
Unterschächen CH 70 B3
Unterschleissheim D 62 B2
Unterschwaningen D 62 A1
Untersiemau D 51 C6
Unter-steinbach D 61 A6
Unterweissenbach A 63 B5
Unterzell D 62 A3
Upavon GB 29 B6
Úpice CZ 53 C6
Upiłka PL 46 B3
Upphärad S 35 D4
Uppingham GB 30 B3
Upplands-Väsby S 37 C4
Uppsala S 36 C4
Uppsjøhytta N 34 A1
Upton-upon-Severn GB 29 A5
Ur F 91 A4
Ura e Shtrenjte AL 105 A5
Uras I 110 C1
Ura-Vajgurorë AL 105 C5
Uraz PL 54 B1
Urbánia I 82 C1
Urbino I 82 C1
Urçay F 68 B2
Urda E 94 C3
Urdax E 76 C1
Urdilde E 86 B2
Urdos F 76 D2
Urk NL 42 C2
Úrkút H 74 A2
Urla TR 119 D1
Urlingford IRL 21 B4
Urnäsch CH 71 A4
Urnes N 32 A4
Uroševac KOS 10 E6
Urracal E 101 B3
Urries E 90 A1
Urroz E 76 D1
Ursensollen D 62 A2
Urshult S 40 C4
Uršna Sela SLO 73 C5
Urszulewo PL 47 C5
Ury F 58 B3
Urziceni RO 11 D9
Urzulei I 110 B2
Usagre E 93 C4
Uşak TR 118 D4
Ušće SRB 85 C5
Usedom D 45 B5
Useldange L 60 A1
Uséllus I 110 C1
Ushakovo RUS 47 A6
Usingen D 51 C4
Usini I 110 B1
Usk GB 29 B5
Uskedal N 32 C2
Üsküdar TR 118 A4
Uslar D 51 B5
Úsov CZ 64 A3
Usquert NL 42 B3
Ussássai I 110 C2
Ussé F 67 A5
Usséglio I 70 C2
Ussel
Cantal F 78 A1
Corrèze F 68 C2
Usson-du-Poitou F 67 B5
Usson-en-Forez F 68 C3
Usson-les-Bains F 77 D5
Ustaoset N 32 B5
Ustaritz F 76 C1
Úštěk CZ 53 C4
Uster CH 70 A3
Ústi CZ 64 A3
Ustibar BIH 85 C4
Ustikolina BIH 84 C3
Ústínad Labem CZ 53 C4
Ústínad Orlicí CZ 54 D1
Ustipračà BIH 84 C4
Ustka PL 46 A2
Ust Luga RUS 7 B10
Ustroń PL 65 A4
Ustronie Morskie PL 46 A1
Ustyuzhna RUS 7 B14
Uszód H 74 B3
Utåker N 32 C2
Utansjö S 115 E14
Utebo E 90 B2
Utena LT 7 D8
Utery CZ 62 A4
Uthaug N 114 D6
Utiel E 96 B1
Utne N 32 B3
Utö S 37 D5
Utrecht NL 49 A6
Utrera E 99 B5
Utrillas E 90 C2
Utsjoki FIN 113 C16
Utstein kloster N 33 C2
Uttendorf A 72 A2
Uttenweiler D 61 B5
Utterslev DK 39 E4
Uttoxeter GB 27 C4
Utvälinge S 41 C2
Utvorda N 114 C7
Uusikaarlepyy FIN 3 E25
Uusikaupunki FIN 3 F24
Uvac BIH 85 C4
Uvaly CZ 53 C4
Uvdal N 32 B5
Uza F 76 B1
Uzdin SRB 75 C5
Uzdowo PL 47 B6
Uzein F 76 C2
Uzel F 56 B3
Uzerche F 67 C6
Uzès F 78 B3
Uzhhorod UA 11 B7
Uzhok UA 11 B7
Užice SRB 85 C4
Uznach CH 70 A3
Uznovë AL 105 C6
Üzümlü
Konya TR 119 E6
Muğla TR 119 F4
Uzunköprü TR 118 A1

V

Vaalajärvi FIN 113 E15
Vaas F 58 C1
Vaasa FIN 3 E24
Vaasen NL 50 A1
Vabre F 77 C5
Vác H 65 C5
Vacha D 51 C6
Váchartyán H 65 C5
Väckelsång S 40 C4
Vacqueyras F 78 B3
Vad S 36 B2
Vada I 81 C4
Väddö S 36 C5
Väderstad S 37 D1
Vadheim N 32 A2
Vadillo de la Sierra E 93 A5
Vadillos E 95 B4
Vadla N 33 C3
Vado I 81 B5
Vado Lígure I 80 B2
Vadsø N 113 B18
Vadstena S 37 D1
Vadum DK 38 B2
Vaduz FL 71 A4
Vafos N 33 D6
Vág H 74 A2
Vågåmo N 114 F6
Væggerløse DK 44 A3
Vaggeryd S 40 B4
Vaghia GR 117 D5
Vaglia I 81 C5
Váglio Basilicata I 104 C1
Vagney F 60 B2
Vagnhärad S 37 D4
Vagnsunda S 37 C5
Vagos P 92 A2
Vai GR 117 G8
Vaiano I 81 C5
Vaiges F 57 B5
Vaihingen D 61 B4
Vaillant F 59 C6
Vailly-sur-Aisne F 59 A4
Vailly-sur Sauldre F 68 A2
Vairano Scalo I 103 B7
Vaison-la-Romaine F 79 B4
Vaite F 60 C1
Väjern S 35 D3
Vajszló H 74 C2
Vaksdal N 32 B2
Vál H 74 A3
Valaam RUS 3 F29
Valada P 92 B2
Vålådalen S 115 D10
Valadares P 87 C2
Valado P 92 B1
Valandovo MK 116 A4
Valaská SK 65 B5
Valaská Belá SK 65 B4
Valaská Dubová SK 65 A5
Valašská Polanka CZ 64 A3
Valašské Klobouky CZ 64 A4
Valašské Meziříčí CZ 64 A3
Valberg F 79 B5
Vålberg S 35 C5
Valbo S 36 B4
Valbom P 87 C2
Valbondione I 71 B5
Valbonë AL 105 A5
Valbonnais F 79 B4
Valbuena de Duero E 88 C2
Vălcani RO 75 C5
Valdagno I 71 C6
Valdahon F 69 A6
Valdaracete E 95 B3
Valday RUS 7 C12
Valdealgorfa E 90 C2
Valdecaballeros E 93 B5
Valdecabras E 95 B4
Valdecarros E 94 B1
Valdeconcha E 95 B4
Valdeflores E 99 B4
Valdefresno E 88 B1
Valdeganga E 95 C5
Valdelacasa E 93 A5
Valdelacasa de Tajo E 93 B5
Valdelarco E 99 B4
Valdelosa E 94 A1
Valdeltormo E 90 C3
Valdelugeros E 88 B1
Valdemanco de Esteras E 94 D2
Valdemarsvik S 37 D3
Valdemorillo E 94 B2
Valdemoro E 94 B3
Valdemoro Sierra E 95 B5
Valdenoceda E 89 B3
Valdeobispo E 93 A4
Valdeolivas E 95 B4
Valdepeñas E 100 A2
Valdepeñas de Jaén E 100 B2
Valdepiélago E 88 B1
Valdepolo E 88 B1
Valderas E 88 B1
Valdérice I 108 A1
Valderrobres E 90 C3
Valderrueda E 88 B2
Val de San Lorenzo E 86 B4
Val de Santo Domingo E 94 B2
Val d'Esquières F 79 C5
Valdestillas E 88 C2
Valdetorres E 93 C4
Valdetorres de Jarama E 95 B3
Valdeverdeja E 93 B5
Valdevimbre E 88 B1
Valdieri I 80 B1
Valdilecha E 95 B3
Val-d'Isère F 70 C1
Valdobbiádene I 72 C1
Valdocondes E 89 C3
Valdoviño E 86 A2
Valea lui Mihai RO 11 C7
Vale de Açor
Beja P 98 B3
Portalegre P 92 B3
Vale de Água P 98 B2
Vale de Cambra P 87 D2
Vale de Lobo P 98 B2
Vale de Prazeres P 92 A3
Vale de Reis P 92 C2
Vale de Rosa P 98 B3
Vale de Santarém P 92 B2
Vale de Vargo P 98 B3
Vale do Peso P 92 B3
Valega P 87 D2
Valéggio sul Mincio I 71 C5
Valeiro P 92 C2
Valença P 87 B2
Valençay F 67 A6
Valence
Charente F 67 C5
Drôme F 78 B3
Valence d'Agen F 77 B3
Valence-d'Albigeois F 77 B5
Valence-sur-Baise F 77 C3
Valencia E 96 B2
Valencia de Alcántara E 93 B3
Valencia de Don Juan E 88 B1
Valencia de las Torres E 93 C4
Valencia del Ventoso E 99 A4
Valencia de Mombuey E 99 A3
Valenciennes F 49 C4
Valensole F 79 C4
Valentano I 102 A4
Valentigney F 70 A1
Valentine F 77 C3
Valenza I 80 A2
Valenzuela E 100 B1
Valenzuela de Calatrava E 100 A2
Våler
Hedmark N 34 B3
Østfold N 35 C2
Valera de Abajo E 95 C4
Valeria E 95 C4
Valestrand N 33 C2
Valestrandsfossen N 32 B2
Valevåg N 33 C2
Valfabbrica I 82 C1
Valflaunes F 78 C2
Valga EST 7 C9
Valgorge F 78 B3
Valgrisenche I 70 C2
Valguarnera Caropepe I 109 B3
Valhelhas P 92 A3
Valjevo SRB 85 B4
Valka LV 7 C8
Valkeakoski FIN 3 F26
Valkenburg NL 50 C1
Valkenswaard NL 49 B6
Valkó H 75 A4
Valla S 37 C3
Vallada E 96 C2
Vallado E 86 A4
Valladolid E 88 C2
Vallåkra S 41 D2
Vallata I 103 B8
Vallberga S 40 C3
Vall d'Alba E 96 A2
Valldemossa E 97 B2
Valle N 33 C4
Valle Castellana I 82 D2
Valle de Abdalajís E 100 C1
Valle de Cabuérniga E 88 A2
Valle de la Serena E 93 C5
Valle de Matamoros E 93 C4
Valle de Santa Ana E 93 C4
Valledolmo I 108 B2
Valledoria I 110 B1
Vallelado E 88 C2
Vallelunga Pratameno I 108 B2
Valle Mosso I 70 C3
Vallendar D 50 C3
Vallentuna S 37 C5
Vallerås S 34 B5
Valleraugue F 78 B2
Vallermosa I 110 C1
Vallet F 66 A3
Valletta M 107 C5
Valley GB 26 B1
Vallfogona de Riucorb E 91 B4
Valli del Pasúbio I 71 C6
Vallo della Lucánia I 103 C8
Valloire F 69 C6
Vallombrosa I 81 C5
Vallon-Pont-d'Arc F 78 B3
Vallorbe CH 69 B6
Vallouise F 79 B5
Valls E 91 B4
Vallset N 34 B3
Vallsta S 36 A3
Vallstena S 37 E5
Valmadrid E 90 B2
Valmiera LV 7 C8
Valmojado E 94 B2
Valmont F 58 A1
Valmontone I 102 B5
Valö S 36 B5
Valognes F 57 A4
Valonga P 92 A2
Valongo P 87 C2
Válor E 100 C2
Valoria la Buena E 88 C2
Valøy N 114 C7
Valozhyn BY 7 D9
Valpaços P 87 C3
Valpelline I 70 C2
Valpiana I 81 C4
Valpovo HR 74 C3
Valras-Plage F 78 C2
Valréas F 78 B3
Vals CH 71 B4
Valsavarenche I 70 C2
Vålse DK 39 E4
Valsequillo E 93 C5
Valsjöbyn S 115 C11
Vals-les-Bains F 78 B3
Valsonne F 69 C4
Valstagna I 72 C1
Val-Suzon F 69 A4
Valtablado del Rio E 95 B4
Valþjofsstaður IS 111 B11
Val Thorens F 69 C6
Valtice CZ 64 B2
Valtiendas E 88 C3
Valtierra E 89 B5
Valtopina I 82 C1
Valtorta I 71 C4
Valtournenche I 70 C2
Valverde E 89 C5
Valverde de Burguillos E 93 C4
Valverde de Júcar E 95 C4
Valverde de la Vera E 93 A5
Valverde de la Virgen E 88 B1
Valverde del Camino E 99 B4
Valverde del Fresno E 93 A4
Valverde de Llerena E 99 A5
Valverde de Mérida E 93 C4
Vamberk CZ 53 C6
Vamdrup DK 39 D2
Våmhus S 34 A6
Vamlingbo S 37 F5
Vammala FIN 3 F25
Vamos GR 117 G6
Vámosmikola H 65 C4
Vámosszabadi H 64 C3
Vanault-les-Dames F 59 B5
Vandel DK 39 D2
Vandenesse F 68 B3
Vandenesse-en-Auxois F 69 A4
Vandóies I 72 B1
Väne-Åsaka S 35 D4
Vänersborg S 35 D4
Vänersnäs S 35 D4
Vang N 32 A5
Vänge S 36 C4
Vangsnes N 32 A3
Vänjaurbäck S 115 C15
Vännacka S 35 C4
Vannareid N 112 B8
Vännäs S 115 D16
Vannes F 56 C3
Vannsätter S 36 A3
Vannvåg N 112 B8
Vansbro S 34 B6
Vanse N 33 D3
Vantaa FIN 6 A8
Vanviken N 114 D7
Vanyarc H 65 C5
Vaour F 77 B4
Vapnyarka UA 11 B10
Vaprio d'Adda I 71 C4
Vaqueiros P 98 B3
Vara S 35 D4
Varacieux F 69 C5
Varades F 66 A3
Varages F 79 C4
Varaldsøy N 32 B2
Varallo I 70 C3
Varangerbotn N 113 B17
Varano de'Melegari I 81 B4
Varaždin HR 73 B6
Varaždinske Toplice HR 73 B6
Varazze I 80 B2
Varberg S 40 B2
Vardal N 34 B2
Varde DK 39 D1
Vårdö FIN 36 B7
Vardø N 113 B20
Vardomb H 74 B3
Varel D 43 B5
Varėna LT 6 D8
Vårenes N 33 C2
Varengeville-sur-Mer F 58 A1
Varenna I 71 B4
Varennes-en-Argonne F 59 A6
Varennes-le-Grand F 69 B4
Varennes-St Sauveur F 69 B5
Varennes-sur-Allier F 68 B3
Varennes-sur-Amance F 60 C1
Vareš BIH 84 B3
Varese I 70 C3
Varese Ligure I 80 B3
Vârfurile RO 11 C7
Vårgårda S 40 A2
Vargas
E 88 A3
P 92 B2
Vargön S 35 D4
Varhaug N 33 D2
Variaş RO 75 B5
Variaşu Mic RO 75 B6
Varilhes F 77 C4
Varin SK 65 A4
Väring S 35 D5
Váriz P 87 C4
Varkaus FIN 3 E27
Varmahlíð IS 111 B6
Varmaland IS 111 C4
Värmlands Bro S 35 C5
Värmskog S 35 C4
Varna
BG 11 E9
SRB 85 B4
Värnamo S 40 B4
Varnhem S 35 D5
Varnsdorf CZ 53 C4
Värö S 40 B2
Varoška Rijeka BIH 83 A5
Városlöd H 74 A2
Várpalota H 74 A3
Varreddes F 59 B3
Vars F 79 B5
Varsi I 81 B3
Varsseveld NL 50 B2
Vårsta S 37 C4
Vartdal N 114 E3
Vartofta S 40 A3
Varvarin SRB 85 C6
Várvik S 35 C4
Várvölgy H 74 B2
Varzi I 80 B3
Varzjelas P 92 A2
Varzo I 70 B3
Varzy F 68 A3
Vasad H 75 A4
Väse S 35 C5
Vašica SRB 85 A4
Vasilevichi BY 7 E10
Väskinde S 37 E5
Vaskút H 75 B3
Vaslui RO 11 C9
Vassbotn N 33 D5
Vassenden N 32 A6
Vassieux-en-Vercors F 79 B4
Vassmolösa S 40 C6
Vassy F 57 B5
Västansjö S 115 B12
Västanvik S 36 B1
Västerås S 37 C3
Västerby S 36 B2
Västerfärnebo S 36 C3
Västergarn S 37 E5
Västerhaninge S 37 C5
Västervik S 40 B6
Vasto I 103 A7
Västra Ämtervik S 35 C5
Västra-Bodarne S 40 B2
Västra Karup S 41 C2
Vasvár H 74 A1
Vasylkiv UA 11 A11
Vát H 74 A1
Vatan F 68 A1
Väte S 37 E5
Vathia GR 117 F4
Vatican City = Cittádel Vaticano I 102 B5
Vatili CY 120 A2
Vatin SRB 75 C6
Vatland N 33 D4
Vatnar N 33 C6
Vatnås N 32 C6
Vatne N 33 D4
Vatnestrøm N 33 D5
Vätö S 36 C5
Vatra-Dornei RO 11 C8
Vatry F 59 B5
Vattholma S 36 B4
Vättis CH 71 B4
Vauchamps F 59 B4
Vauchassis F 59 B4
Vaucouleurs F 60 B1
Vaudoy-en-Brie F 59 B4
Vaulen N 33 D2
Vaulruz CH 70 B1
Vaulx Vraucourt F 48 C3
Vaumas F 68 B3
Vausseroux F 67 B4
Vauvenargues F 79 C4
Vauvert F 78 C3
Vauvillers F 60 C2
Vaux-sur-Sure B 60 A1
Vawkavysk BY 6 E8
Vaxholm S 37 C5
Växjö S 40 C4
Våxtorp S 41 C3
Vayrac F 77 B4
Važec SK 65 A5
Veberöd S 41 D3
Vechelde D 51 A6
Vechta D 43 C5
Vecinos E 94 B1
Vecsés H 75 A4
Vedavågen N 33 C2
Veddige S 40 B2
Vedersø DK 39 C1
Vedeseta I 71 C4
Vedevåg S 37 C2
Vedra E 86 B2
Vedum S 35 D4
Veendam NL 42 B3
Veenendaal NL 49 A6
Vega
Asturias E 88 A1
Asturias E 88 A1
Vega de Espinareda E 86 B4
Vega de Infanzones E 88 B1
Vegadeo E 86 A3
Vega de Pas E 88 A3
Vega de Valcarce E 86 B4
Vega de Valdetronco E 88 C1
Vegårshei N 33 D5
Vegas de Coria E 93 A4
Vegas del Condado E 88 B1
Vegby S 40 B3
Vegger DK 38 C2
Veggli N 32 B6
Veghel NL 49 B6
Veglast D 45 A4
Véglie I 105 C3
Veguillas E 95 B3
Vegusdal N 33 D5
Veidholmen N 114 D4
Veidnes N 113 B15
Veikåker N 34 B1
Veinge S 40 C3
Vejbystrand S 41 C2
Vejen DK 39 D2
Vejer de la Frontera E 99 C5
Vejle DK 39 D2
Vejprty CZ 52 C3
Velada E 94 B2
Vela Luka HR 83 D5
Velayos E 94 B2
Velbert D 50 B3
Velburg D 62 A2
Velde N 114 C8
Velden
Bayern D 62 A2
Bayern D 62 B3
Velden am Worther See A 73 B4
Velefique E 101 B3
Velen D 50 B2
Velenje SLO 73 B5
Veles MK 116 A3
Velesevec HR 73 C6
Velešin CZ 63 B5
Velestino GR 116 C4
Velez Blanco E 101 B3
Vélez de Benaudalla E 100 C2
Vélez-Málaga E 100 C1
Vélez Rubio E 101 B3
Veliiki Radinci SRB 85 A4
Velika
HR 74 C2
MNE 85 D4
Velika Drenova SRB 85 C6
Velika Gorica HR 73 C6
Velika Grdevac HR 74 C2
Velika Greda SRB 75 C6
Velika Ilova BIH 84 B2
Velika Kladuša BIH 73 C5
Velika Kopanica HR 74 C3
Velika Krsna SRB 85 B5
Velika Obarska BIH 85 B4
Velika Pisanica HR 74 C2
Velika Plana
Srbija SRB 85 B6
Srbija SRB 85 C6
Velika Zdenci HR 74 C2
Velike Lašče SLO 73 C4
Veliki Gaj SRB 75 C6
Veliki Popović SRB 85 B6
Veliki Šiljegovac SRB 85 C6
Velikiye Luki RUS 7 C11
Veliko Gradište SRB 85 B6
Veliko Orašje SRB 85 B6
Veliko Selo SRB 85 B6
Veliko Tŭrnovo BG 11 E8
Velilla del Río Carrió E 88 B2
Velilla de San Antonio E 95 B3
Veli Lošinj HR 83 B3
Velipojë AL 105 B5
Velizh RUS 7 D11
Veljun HR 73 C5
Velká Bíteš CZ 64 A2
Velka Hled'scbe CZ 52 D2

Velká Lomnica SK 65 A6
Velkánad Veličkou CZ 64 B3
Velké Bystřice CZ 64 A3
Velké Heraltice CZ 54 D2
Velké Karlovice CZ 64 A4
Vel'ke'Kostol'any SK 64 B3
Vel'ké Leváre SK 64 B3
Velké Losiny CZ 54 C2
Velké Meziříčí CZ 64 A2
Velké Pavlovice CZ 64 B2
Vel'ké Rovné SK 65 A4
Vel'ké Uherce SK 65 B4
Vel'ké Zálužie SK 64 B3
Vel'ký Blahovo SK 65 B6
Velky Bor CZ 63 A4
Vel'ký Cetin SK 64 B4
Vel'ký Krtíš SK 65 B5
Vel'ký Meder SK 64 C3
Velky Ujezd CZ 64 A3
Vellahn D 44 B2
Vellberg D 61 A5
Velles F 67 B6
Velletri I 102 B5
Vellinge S 41 D3
Vellisca E 95 B4
Velliza E 88 C2
Vellmar D 51 B5
Velp NL 50 A1
Velten D 45 C5
Velvary CZ 53 C4
Velvendos GR 116 B4
Vemb DK 39 C1
Vemdalen S 115 E10
Veme N 34 B2
Véménd H 74 B3
Vemmedrup DK 39 D5
Vena S 40 B5
Venaco F 102 A2
Venafro I 103 B7
Venarey-les-Laumes F 69 A4
Venaría I 70 C2
Venasca I 80 B1
Venčane SRB 85 B5
Vence F 79 C6
Venda Nova
Coimbra P 92 A2
Leiria P 92 B2
Vendas Novas P 92 C2
Vendays-Montalivet F 66 C3
Vendel S 36 B4
Vendelso S 37 C5
Vendeuil F 59 A4
Vendeuvre-sur-Barse F 59 B5
Vendoeuvres F 67 B6
Vendôme F 58 C2
Venelles F 79 C4
Veness GB 23 B6
Venézia = Venice I 72 C2
Venialbo E 88 C1
Venice = Venézia I 72 C2
Vénissieux F 69 C4
Venjan S 34 B5
Venlo NL 50 B2
Vennesla N 33 D4
Vennesund N 114 B9
Vennezey F 60 B2
Venn Green GB 28 C3
Venosa I 104 C1
Venray NL 50 B1
Vent A 71 B5
Venta de Baños E 88 C2
Venta del Moro E 96 B1
Venta de los Santos E 100 A2
Venta las Ranas E 88 A1
Ventanueva E 86 A4
Ventas de Huelma E 100 B2
Ventas de Zafarraya E 100 C1
Ventavon F 79 B4
Ventimíglia I 80 C1
Ventnor GB 31 D2
Ventosa de la Sierra E 89 C4
Ventosilla E 89 C4
Ventspils LV 6 C6
Venturina I 81 C4
Venzolasca F 102 A2
Venzone I 72 B3
Vép H 74 A1
Vera
E 101 B4
N 115 D9
Vera Cruz P 98 A3
Vera de Bidasoa E 76 C1
Vera de Moncayo E 89 C5
Verbánia I 70 C3
Verberie F 58 A3
Verbicaro I 106 B2
Verbier CH 70 B2
Vercelli I 70 C3
Vercel-Villedieu-le-Camp F 69 A6
Verchen D 45 B4
Vercheny F 79 B4
Verclause F 79 B4
Verdalsøra N 114 D8
Verden D 43 C6
Verdens Ende N 35 C2
Verdikoussa GR 116 C3
Verdille F 67 C4
Verdú E 91 B4
Verdun F 59 A6
Verdun-sur-Garonne F 77 C4
Verdun-sur-le-Doubs F 69 B5
Veresegyház H 65 C5
Verfeil F 77 C4
Vergato I 81 B5
Vergel E 96 C3
Vergeletto CH 70 B3
Verges E 91 A6
Vergiate I 70 C3
Vergt F 77 A3
Veria GR 116 B4
Verín E 87 C3
Veringenstadt D 61 B5
Verkhovye RUS 7 E14
Verl D 51 B4
Verma N 114 E5
Vermand F 59 A4
Vermelha P 92 B1
Vermenton F 59 C4
Vermosh AL 85 D4
Vernago I 71 B5
Vernante I 80 B1
Vernantes F 67 A5
Vernár SK 65 B6
Vernasca I 81 B3
Vernayaz CH 70 B2
Vernazza I 81 B3
Vern-d'Anjou F 57 C5
Verneřice CZ 53 C4
Vernet F 77 C4
Vernet-les-Bains F 91 A5
Verneuil F 59 A4
Verneuil-sur-Avre F 58 B1
Vernier CH 69 B6
Vérnio I 81 B5
Vérnole I 105 C4
Vernon F 58 A2
Vernoux-en-Vivarais F 78 B3
Veróce H 65 C5
Verolanuova I 71 C5
Véroli I 103 B6
Verona I 71 C6
Verpelét H 65 C6
Verrabotn N 114 D7
Verrès I 70 C2
Verrey-sous-Salmaise F 69 A4
Verrières F 67 B5
Versailles F 58 B3
Versam CH 71 B4
Verseg H 65 C5
Versmold D 50 A4
Versoix CH 69 B6
Verteillac F 67 C5
Vértesacsa H 74 A3
Vertou F 66 A3
Vertus F 59 B4
Verviers B 50 C1
Vervins F 59 A4
Verwood GB 29 C6
Veryan GB 28 C3
Veržej SLO 73 B6
Verzuolo I 80 B1
Verzy F 59 A5
Vescovato F 102 A2
Vése H 74 B2
Veselínad Lužnicí CZ 63 A5
Veselínad Moravou CZ 64 B3
Veseliy BG 11 E9
Vésime I 80 B2
Veskoniemi FIN 113 D16
Vesoul F 60 C2
Vespolate I 70 C3
Vessigebro S 40 C2
Vestbygd N 33 D3
Vestenanova I 71 C6
Vester Husby S 37 D3
Vester Nebel DK 39 D2
Vesterøhavn DK 38 B3
Vester Torup DK 38 B2
Vester Vedsted DK 39 D1
Vestervig DK 38 C1
Vestfossen N 35 C1
Vestmannaeyjar IS 111 D5
Vestmarka N 34 C3
Vestnes N 114 E4
Vestone I 71 C5
Vestre Gausdal N 34 A2
Vestre Jakobselv N 113 B18
Vestre Slidre N 32 A5
Vesyegonsk RUS 7 B14
Veszprém H 74 A2
Veszprémvarsány H 74 A2
Vésztö H 75 B6
Vetlanda S 40 B5
Vetovo HR 74 C2
Vetralla I 102 A5
Větrný Jeníkov CZ 63 A6
Vétroz CH 70 B2
Vetschau D 53 B4
Vettasjärvi S 113 E10
Vetto I 81 B4
Vetulónia I 81 D4
Veules-les-Roses F 58 A1
Veulettes-sur-Mer F 58 A1
Veum N 33 C5
Veurne B 48 B3
Veverská Bítýška CZ 64 A2
Vevey CH 70 B1
Vevi GR 116 B3
Vevring N 32 A2
Vex CH 70 B2
Veynes F 79 B4
Veyre-Monton F 68 C3
Veyrier F 69 C6
Vézelay F 68 A3
Vézelise F 60 B2
Vézenobres F 78 B3
Vezins F 67 A4
Vézins-de-Lévézou F 78 B1
Vezirhan TR 118 B5
Vezirköprü TR 16 A7
Vezza di Óglio I 71 B5
Vezzani F 102 A2
Vezzano I 71 B6
Vezzano sul Cróstolo I 81 B4
Vi S 115 E14
Viadana I 81 B4
Via Gloria P 98 B3
Viana E 89 B4
Viana do Alentejo P 92 C2
Viana do Bolo E 87 B3
Viana do Castelo P 87 C2
Vianden L 60 A2
Viannos GR 117 G7
Viaréggio I 81 C4
Viator E 101 C3
Vibble S 37 E5
Viborg DK 38 C2
Vibo Valéntia I 106 C3
Vibraye F 58 B1
Vic E 91 B5
Vícar E 101 C3
Vicarello I 81 C4
Vicari I 108 B2
Vicchio I 81 C5
Vicdesses F 77 D4
Vic-en-Bigorre F 76 C3
Vicenza I 71 C6
Vic-Fézensac F 76 C3
Vichy F 68 B3
Vickan S 38 B5
Vickerstown GB 26 A2
Vic-le-Comte F 68 C3
Vico F 102 A1
Vico del Gargano I 104 B1
Vico Equense I 103 C7
Vicopisano I 81 C4
Vicosoprano CH 71 B4
Vicovaro I 102 A5
Vic-sur-Aisne F 59 A4
Vic-sur-Cère F 77 B5
Victoria = Rabat M 107 C5
Vidago P 87 C3
Vidauban F 79 C5
Vide P 92 A3
Videbæk DK 39 C1
Videm SLO 73 C4
Videseter N 114 F4
Vidigueira P 98 A3
Vidin BG 11 E7
Vidlin GB 22 A7
Vidzy BY 7 D9
Viechtach D 62 A3
Vieille-Brioude F 68 C3
Vieira P 92 B2
Vieira do Minho P 87 C2
Vieiros P 92 C3
Vielha E 90 A3
Vielle-Aure F 77 D3
Viellespesse F 68 C3
Viellevigne F 66 B3
Vielmur-sur-Agout F 77 C5
Vielsalm B 50 C1
Viels Maison F 59 B4
Vienenburg D 51 B6
Vienna = Wien A 64 B2
Vienne F 69 C4
Vieritz D 44 C4
Viernheim D 61 A4
Vierraden D 45 B6
Viersen D 50 B2
Vierville-sur-Mer F 57 A5
Vierzon F 68 A2
Vieselbach D 52 C1
Vieste I 104 B2
Vietas S 112 E7
Vieteren B 48 C3
Vietri di Potenza I 104 C1
Vietri sul Mare I 103 C7
Vieux-Boucau-les-Bains F 76 C1
Vif F 79 A4
Vig DK 39 D4
Vigásio I 71 C5
Vigaun A 63 C4
Vigeland N 33 D4
Vigeois F 67 C6
Vigévano I 70 C3
Viggianello I 106 B3
Viggiano I 104 C1
Vigliano I 102 A6
Vigmostad N 33 D4
Vignale I 80 A2
Vignanello I 102 A5
Vigneulles-lès-Hattonchâtel F 60 B1
Vignevieille F 77 D5
Vignola I 81 B5
Vignory F 59 B6
Vignoux-sur Barangeon F 68 A2
Vigo E 87 B2
Vigo di Fassa I 72 B1
Vigone I 80 B1
Vigrestad N 33 D2
Vihiers F 67 A4
Viitasaari FIN 3 E26
Vík IS 111 D6
Vik
Nordland N 114 B9
Rogaland N 33 D2
Sogn og Fjordane N 32 A3
S 41 D4
Vika S 36 B2
Vikajärvi FIN 113 F15
Vikane N 35 C2
Vikarbyn S 36 B2
Vike N 32 B2
Vikedal N 33 C2
Vikeland N 33 D4
Viken
Jämtland S 115 C10
Skåne S 41 C2
Viker N 34 B2
Vikersund N 34 C1
Vikeså N 33 D3
Vikevåg N 33 C2
Vikingstad S 37 D2
Vikmanshyttan S 36 B2
Vikna N 114 C7
Vikøy N 32 B3
Vikran
Troms N 112 C7
Troms N 112 D5
Viksjö S 115 E14
Viksøyri N 32 A3
Viksta S 36 B4
Vila Boim P 92 C3
Vila Chãde Ourique P 92 B2
Viladamat E 91 A6
Vila de Cruces E 86 B2
Vila de Rei P 92 B2
Vila do Bispo P 98 B2
Vila do Conde P 87 C2
Viladrau E 91 B5
Vila Flor P 87 C3
Vila Franca das Navas P 87 D3
Vilafranca del Maestrat E 90 C2
Vilafranca del Penedès E 91 B4
Vila Franca de Xira P 92 C1
Vila Fresca P 92 C1
Vilagarcía de Arousa E 86 B2
Vilajuiga E 91 A6
Vilamarin E 86 B3
Vilamartín de Valdeorras E 86 B3
Vila Nogueira P 92 C1
Vila Nova da Baronia P 98 A2
Vilanova de Castelló E 96 B2
Vila Nova de Cerveira P 87 C2
Vila Nova de Famalicão P 87 C2
Vila Nova de Foz Côa P 87 C3
Vila Nova de Gaia P 87 C2
Vila Nova de Milfontes P 98 B2
Vila Nova de Paiva P 87 D3
Vila Nova de São Bento P 98 B3
Vilanova de Sau E 91 B5
Vilanova i la Geltrú E 91 B4
Vilapedre E 86 A3
Vila Pouca de Aguiar P 87 C3
Vila Praja de Ancora P 87 C2
Vilarandelo P 87 C3
Vilar de Santos E 87 B3
Vilardevós E 87 C3
Vila Real P 87 C3
Vila-real de los Infantes E 96 B2
Vila Real de Santo António P 98 B3
Vilar Formosa P 93 A4
Vila-Rodona E 91 B4
Vila Ruiva P 98 A3
Vilasantar E 86 A2
Vilaseca E 91 B4
Vila Seca P 92 A2
Vilassar de Mar E 91 B5
Vilasund S 115 A11
Vila Velha de Ródão P 92 B3
Vila Verde
Braga P 87 C2
Lisboa P 92 B1
Vila Verde de Filcalho P 98 B3
Vila Viçosa P 92 C3
Vilches E 100 A2
Vildbjerg DK 39 C1
Vilémov CZ 63 A6
Vileyka BY 7 D9
Vilhelmina S 115 C13
Vilia GR 117 D5
Viljandi EST 7 B8
Villabáñez E 88 C2
Villablanca E 98 B3
Villablino E 86 B4
Villabona E 89 A4
Villabragima E 88 C1
Villabuena del Puente E 88 C1
Villacadima E 95 A3
Villacañas E 95 C3
Villacarriedo E 88 A3
Villacarrillo E 100 A2
Villa Castelli I 104 C3
Villacastín E 94 B2
Villach A 72 B3
Villacidro I 110 C1
Villaconejos E 95 B3
Villaconejos de Trabaque E 95 B4
Villa Cova de Lixa P 87 C2
Villada E 88 B2
Villadangos del Páramo E 88 B1
Villadecanes E 86 B4
Villa del Prado E 94 B2
Villa del Rio E 100 B1
Villadepera E 87 C4
Villa de Peralonso E 87 C4
Villa di Chiavenna I 71 B4
Villadiego E 88 B2
Villadompardo E 100 B1
Villadóssola I 70 B3
Villaeles de Valdavia E 88 B2
Villaescusa de Haro E 95 C4
Villafáfila E 88 C1
Villafeliche E 95 A5
Villaflores E 94 A1
Villafrades de Campos E 88 B2
Villafranca
Avila E 93 A5
Navarra E 89 B5
Villafranca de Córdoba E 100 B1
Villafranca del Bierzo E 86 B4
Villafranca de los Barros E 93 C4
Villafranca de los Caballeros E 95 C3
Villafranca di Verona I 71 C5
Villafranca in Lunigiana I 81 B3
Villafranca-Montes de Oca E 89 B3
Villafranca Tirrena I 109 A4
Villafranco del Campo E 95 B5
Villafranco del Guadalquivir E 99 B4
Villafrati I 108 B2
Villafrechós E 88 C1
Villafruela E 88 C3
Villagarcia de las Torres E 93 C4
Villaggio Mancuso I 106 B3
Villagonzalo E 93 C4
Villagotón E 86 B4
Villagrains F 76 B2
Villaharta E 100 A1
Villahermosa E 100 A3
Villaherreros E 88 B2
Villahoz E 88 B3
Villaines-la-Juhel F 57 B5
Villajoyosa E 96 C2
Villalago I 103 B6
Villalba
E 86 A3
I 108 B2
Villalba de Calatrava E 100 A2
Villalba de Guardo E 88 B2
Villalba del Alcor E 99 B4
Villalba de la Sierra E 95 B4
Villalba de los Alcores E 88 C2
Villalba de los Barros E 93 C4
Villalba del Rey E 95 B4
Villalcampo E 87 C4
Villalcázar de Sirga E 88 B2
Villalengua E 89 C5
Villalgordo del Júcar E 95 C4
Villalgordo del Marquesado E 95 C4
Villalmóndar E 89 B3
Villalón de Campos E 88 B1
Villalonga E 96 C2
Villalonso E 88 C1
Villalpando E 88 C1
Villaluenga E 94 B3
Villalumbroso E 88 B2
Villálvaro E 89 C3
Villamalea E 95 C5
Villamanán E 88 B1
Villamanín E 88 B1
Villamanrique E 100 A3
Villamanrique de la Condesa E 99 B4
Villamanta E 94 B2
Villamantilla E 94 B2
Villamar I 110 C1
Villamartín E 99 C5
Villamartin de Campos E 88 B2
Villamartin de Don Sancho E 88 B1
Villamassárgia I 110 C1
Villamayor E 88 A1
Villamayor de Calatrava E 100 A1
Villamayor de Campos E 88 C1
Villamayor de Santiago E 95 C4
Villamblard F 77 A3
Villamejil E 86 B4
Villamesias E 93 B5
Villaminaya E 94 C3
Villa Minozzo I 81 B4
Villamor de los Escuderos E 88 C1
Villamoronta E 88 B2
Villamuelas E 94 C3
Villamuriel de Cerrato E 88 C2
Villandraut F 76 B2
Villanova I 104 C3
Villanova d'Asti I 80 B1
Villanova del Battista I 103 B8
Villanova Mondov ì I 80 B1
Villanova Monteleone I 110 B1
Villante E 88 B3
Villantério I 71 C4
Villanubla E 88 C2
Villanueva de Alcardete E 95 C3
Villanueva de Alcorón E 95 B4
Villanueva de Algaidas E 100 B1
Villanueva de Argaña E 88 B3
Villanueva de Bogas E 95 C3
Villanueva de Córdoba E 100 A1
Villanueva de Gállego E 90 B2
Villanueva del Aceral E 94 A2
Villanueva de la Concepcion E 100 C1
Villanueva de la Fuente E 101 A3
Villanueva de la Jara E 95 C5
Villanueva de la Reina E 100 A2
Villanueva del Arzobispo E 100 A3
Villanueva de la Serena E 93 C5
Villanueva de la Sierra E 93 A4
Villanueva de las Manzanas E 88 B1
Villanueva de las Peras E 88 C1
Villanueva de las Torres E 100 B2
Villanueva de la Vera E 93 A5
Villanueva del Campo E 88 C1
Villanueva del Duque E 100 A1
Villanueva del Fresno E 93 C3
Villanueva del Huerva E 90 B1
Villanueva de los Castillejos E 98 B3
Villanueva de los Infantes E 100 A3
Villanueva del Rey E 99 A5
Villanueva del Rio E 99 B5
Villanueva del Río y Minas E 99 B5
Villanueva del Rosario E 100 C1
Villanueva del Trabuco E 100 B1
Villanueva de Mesia E 100 B2
Villanueva de Nía E 88 B2
Villanueva de Oscos E 86 A4
Villanueva de San Carlos E 100 A2
Villanueva de San Juan E 99 B5
Villanueva de Tapia E 100 B1
Villanueva de Valdegovia E 89 B3
Villány H 74 C3
Villaputzu I 110 C2
Villaquejida E 88 B1
Villaquilambre E 88 B1
Villaquiran de los Infantes E 88 B2
Villaralto E 100 A1
Villarcayo E 89 B3
Villard-de-Lans F 79 A4
Villar de Barrio E 87 B3
Villar de Cañas E 95 C4
Villar de Chinchilla E 96 C1
Villar de Ciervo E 87 D4
Villardeciervos E 87 C4
Villar de Domingo Garcia E 95 B4
Villardefrades E 88 C1
Villar del Arzobispo E 96 B2
Villar del Buey E 87 C4
Villar del Cobo E 95 B5
Villar del Humo E 95 C5
Villar de los Navarros E 90 B1
Villar del Pedroso E 93 B5
Villar del Rey E 93 B4
Villar del Rio E 89 B4
Villar del Saz de Navalón E 95 B4
Villar de Rena E 93 B5
Villarejo E 95 A3
Villarejo de Fuentes E 95 C4
Villarejo de Orbigo E 88 B1
Villarejo de Salvanes E 95 B3
Villarejo-Periesteban E 95 C4
Villares del Saz E 95 C4
Villaretto I 79 A6
Villargordo del Cabriel E 96 B1
Villarino E 87 C4
Villarino de Conso E 87 B3
Villarluengo E 90 C2
Villarobe E 89 B3
Villarosa I 109 B3
Villar Perosa I 79 B6
Villarramiel E 88 B2
Villarrasa E 99 B4
Villarreal de San Carlos E 93 B4
Villarrin de Campos E 88 C1
Villarrobledo E 95 C4
Villarroya de la Sierra E 89 C5
Villarroya de los Pinares E 90 C2
Villarrubia de los Ojos E 95 C3
Villarrubia de Santiago E 95 C3
Villarrubio E 95 C4
Villars-les-Dombes F 69 B5
Villarta E 95 C5
Villarta de los Montes E 94 C2
Villarta de San Juan E 95 C3
Villasana de Mena E 89 A3
Villasandino E 88 B2
Villa San Giovanni I 109 A4
Villa Santa Maria I 103 B7
Villasante E 89 A3
Villa Santina I 72 B2
Villasarracino E 88 B2
Villasayas E 89 C4
Villasdardo E 87 C4
Villaseca de Henares E 95 B4
Villaseca de Laciana E 86 B4
Villaseca de la Sagra E 94 C3
Villaseco de los Gamitos E 87 C4
Villaseco de los Reyes E 87 C4
Villasequilla de Yepes E 94 C3
Villasimíus I 110 C2
Villasmundo I 109 B4
Villasor I 110 C1
Villastar E 90 C1
Villastellone I 80 B1
Villatobas E 95 C3
Villatorp E 93 A5
Villatoya E 96 B1
Villavaliente E 96 B1
Villavelayo E 89 B4
Villavella E 87 B3
Villaver de de Guadalimar E 101 A3
Villaverde del Rio E 99 B5
Villaviciosa E 88 A1
Villaviciosa de Córdoba E 99 A6
Villaviciosa de Odón E 94 B3
Villavieja de Yeltes E 87 D4
Villayón E 86 A4
Villé F 60 B3
Villebois-Lavalette F 67 C5
Villecerf F 59 B3
Villecomtal F 77 B5
Villedieu-les-Poêles F 57 B4
Villedieu-sur-Indre F 67 B6
Ville-di-Pietrabugno F 102 A2
Villedômain F 67 A6
Villefagnan F 67 B5
Villefontaine F 69 C5
Villefort F 78 B2
Villefranche-d'Albigeois F 77 C5
Villefranche-d'Allier F 68 B2
Villefranche-de-Lauragais F 77 C4
Villefranche-de-Lonchat F 76 B3
Villefranche-de-Panat F 78 B1
Villefranche-de-Rouergue F 77 B5
Villefranche-du-Périgord F 77 B4
Villefranche-sur-Cher F 68 A1
Villefranche-sur-Mer F 80 C1
Villefranche-sur-Saône F 69 B4
Villegenon F 68 A2
Villel E 96 A1
Villemaur-sur-Vanne F 59 B4
Villemontais F 68 C3
Villemur-sur-Tarn F 77 C4
Villena E 101 A5
Villenauxe-la-Grande F 59 B4
Villenave-d'Ornon F 76 B2
Villeneuve
CH 70 B1
F 77 B5
Villeneuve-d'Ascq F 49 C4
Villeneuve-de-Berg F 78 B3
Villeneuve-de-Marsan F 76 C2
Villeneuve-de-Rivière F 77 C3
Villeneuve-la-Guyard F 59 B4
Villeneuve-l'Archevêque F 59 B4
Villeneuve-le-Comte F 58 B3
Villeneuve-lès-Avignon F 78 C3
Villeneuve-les-Corbières F 78 D1
Villeneuve-St Georges F 58 B3
Villeneuve-sur-Allier F 68 B3
Villeneuve-sur-Lot F 77 B3
Villeneuve-sur-Yonne F 59 B4
Villeréal F 77 B3
Villerias E 88 C2
Villeromain F 58 C2
Villers-Bocage
Calvados F 57 A5
Somme F 48 D3
Villers-Bretonneux F 58 A3
Villers-Carbonnel F 59 A3
Villers-Cotterêts F 59 A4
Villersexel F 60 C2
Villers-Farlay F 69 B5
Villers-le-Gambon B 49 C5
Villers-le-Lac F 70 A1
Villers-sur-Mer F 57 A6
Villerupt F 60 A1
Villerville F 57 A6
Villeseneux F 59 B5
Ville-sous-la-Ferté F 59 B5
Ville-sur-Illon F 60 B2
Ville-sur-Tourbe F 59 A5
Villetrun F 58 C2
Villetta Barrea I 103 B6
Villeurbanne F 69 C4
Villeveyrac F 78 C2
Villevocance F 69 C4
Villiers-St Benoit F 59 C4
Villiers-St Georges F 59 B4
Villingen D 61 B4
Villmar D 50 C4
Villoldo E 88 B2
Villon F 59 C5
Villoria E 94 B1
Vilnes N 32 A1
Vilnius LT 7 D8
Vils
A 62 C1
DK 38 C1
Vilsbiburg D 62 B3
Vilseck D 62 A2
Vilshofen D 63 B4
Vilshult S 41 C4
Vilusi MNE 84 D3
Vilvestre E 87 C4
Vilvoorde B 49 C5
Vimeiro P 92 B1
Vimercate I 71 C4
Vimianzo E 86 A1
Vimieiro P 92 C3
Vimioso P 87 C4
Vimmerby S 40 B5
Vimoutiers F 57 B6
Vimperk CZ 63 A4
Vimy F 48 C3
Vinadi CH 71 B5
Vinadio I 79 B6
Vinaixa E 90 B3
Vinarós E 90 C3
Vinäs S 36 B1
Vinay F 69 C5
Vinberg S 40 C2
Vinca F 91 A5
Vinča SRB 85 B5
Vinchiaturo I 103 B7
Vinci I 81 C4
Vindeby DK 39 D3
Vindelgransele S 115 B15
Vindeln S 115 C16
Vinderup DK 38 C1
Vindsvik N 33 C3
Vinets F 59 B5
Vineuil F 58 C2
Vinga RO 75 B6
Vingåker S 37 C2
Vingnes N 34 A2
Vingrau F 78 D1
Vingrom N 34 A2
Vinhais P 87 C4
Vinica
HR 73 B6
SK 65 B5
SLO 73 C5
Vinicka MNE 85 D4
Viniegra de Arriba E 89 B4
Vinje
Hordaland N 32 B3
Sør-Trøndelag N 114 D6
Telemark N 33 C4
Vinkovci HR 74 C3
Vinliden S 115 C14
Vinninga S 35 D5
Vinnytsya UA 11 B10
Vinon F 68 A2
Vinon-sur-Verdon F 79 C4
Vinslöv S 41 C3
Vintjärn S 36 B3
Vintrosa S 37 C1
Viñuela E 100 C1
Viñuela de Sayago E 87 C5
Viñuelas E 95 B3
Vinuesa E 89 C4
Vinzelberg D 44 C3
Viöl D 43 A6
Viola I 80 B1
Violay F 69 C4
Vipava SLO 72 C3
Vipiteno I 71 B6
Vipperow D 45 B4
Vir
BIH 84 C2
HR 83 B4
Vira CH 70 B3
Vire F 57 B5
Vireda S 40 B4
Vireux F 49 C5
Virgen A 72 A2
Virgen de la Cabeza E 100 A1
Virginia IRL 19 C4
Virieu F 69 C5
Virieu-le-Grand F 69 C5
Virje HR 74 B1
Virklund DK 39 C2
Virovitica HR 74 C2
Virpazar MNE 105 A5
Virsbo S 36 C3
Virserum S 40 B5
Virtaniemi FIN 113 D17
Virton B 60 A1
Virtsu EST 6 B7
Viry F 69 B6
Vis HR 83 C5
Visbek D 43 C5
Visby
DK 39 D1
S 37 E5
Visé B 50 C1
Višegrad BIH 85 C4
Viserba I 82 B1
Viseu P 92 A3
Visiedo E 90 C1
Viskafors S 40 B2
Visland N 33 D3
Vislanda S 40 C4
Visnes N 33 C2
Višnja Gora SLO 73 C4
Višnjan HR 72 C3
Višnové CZ 64 B2
Visnums-Kil S 35 C6
Viso del Marqués E 100 A2
Visoko
BIH 84 C3
SLO 73 B4
Visone I 80 B2
Visp CH 70 B2
Vissefjärda S 40 C5
Visselhövede D 43 C6
Vissenbjerg DK 39 D3
Visso I 82 D2
Vistabella del Maestrat E 96 A2
Vita I 108 B1
Vitanje SLO 73 B5
Vitanovac SRB 85 C5
Vitebsk = Vitsyebsk BY 7 D11
Viterbo I 102 A5
Vitez BIH 84 B2
Vithkuq AL 116 B2
Vitigudino E 87 C4
Vitina
BIH 84 C2
GR 117 E4
Vitis A 63 B6
Vítkov CZ 64 A3
Vitkovac SRB 85 C5
Vitomirica KOS 85 D5
Vitoria-Gasteiz E 89 B4
Vitré F 57 B4
Vitrey-sur-Mance F 60 C1
Vitry-en-Artois F 48 C3
Vitry-le-François F 59 B5
Vitry-sur-Seine F 58 B3
Vitsand S 34 B4
Vitsyebsk = Vitebsk BY 7 D11
Vittangi S 113 E10
Vittaryd S 40 C3
Vitteaux F 69 A4
Vittel F 60 B1
Vittinge S 36 C4
Vittória I 109 C3
Vittório Véneto I 72 C2
Vittsjö S 41 C3
Viù I 70 C2
Viul N 34 B2
Vivario F 102 A2
Viveiro E 86 A3
Vivel del Rio Martin E 90 C2
Viver E 96 B2
Viverols F 68 C3
Viveros E 101 A3
Viviers F 78 B3
Vivonne F 67 B5
Vivy F 67 A4
Vize TR 118 A2
Vizille F 79 A4
Viziñada HR 72 C3
Viziru RO 11 D9
Vizovice CZ 64 A3
Vizvár H 74 B2
Vizzavona F 102 A2
Vizzini I 109 B3
Vlachiotis GR 117 F4
Vlachovice CZ 64 A3
Vlachovo SK 65 B6
Váchovo Březi CZ 63 A4
Vladimirci SRB 85 B4
Vladimirovac SRB 85 A5
Vladislav CZ 64 A1
Vlagtwedde NL 43 B4
Vlajkovac SRB 85 A6
Vlasenica BIH 84 B3
Vlašim CZ 63 A5
Vlatkovići BIH 84 B2
Vledder NL 42 C3
Vlissingen NL 49 B4
Vlkolínec SK 65 A5
Vlorë AL 105 C5
Vlotho D 51 A4
Vnanje Gorice SLO 73 C4
Vobarno I 71 C5
Voćin HR 74 C2
Vöcklabruck A 63 B4
Vöcklamarkt A 63 C4
Vodanj SRB 85 B5
Voderady SK 64 B3
Vodice
Istarska HR 73 C4
Šibenska HR 83 C4
SLO 73 B4
Vodňany CZ 63 A5
Vodnjan HR 82 B2
Vodskov DK 38 B3
Voe GB 22 A7
Voerså DK 38 B3
Voghera I 80 B3
Vogogna I 70 B3
Vogošća BIH 84 C3
Vogué F 78 B3
Vohburg D 62 B2
Vohenstrauss D 62 A3
Vöhl D 51 B4
Vöhrenbach D 61 B4
Vöhringen D 61 B6
Void-Vacon F 60 B1
Voiron F 69 C5
Voise F 58 B2
Voisey F 60 C1
Voiteg RO 75 C6
Voiteur F 69 B5
Voitsberg A 73 A5
Vojens DK 39 D2
Vojka SRB 85 B5
Vojlovica SRB 85 B5
Vojnić HR 73 C5
Vojnice SK 65 C4
Vojnik SLO 73 B5
Vojvoda Stepa SRB 75 C5
Volada GR 119 G2
Volargne I 71 C5
Volary CZ 63 B4
Volče SLO 72 B3
Volda N 114 E3
Volendam NL 42 C2
Volga RUS 7 B15
Volimes GR 117 E2
Volissos GR 116 D7
Volkach D 61 A6
Völkermarkt A 73 B4
Volkhov RUS 7 B12
Völklingen D 60 A2
Volkmarsen D 51 B5
Voll N 114 E4
Vollenhove NL 42 C2
Vollore-Montagne F 68 C3
Vollsjö S 41 D3
Volodymyr-Volyns'kyy UA 11 A8
Volokolamsk RUS 7 C13
Volos GR 116 C4
Volosovo RUS 7 B10
Volovets UA 11 B7
Voltággio I 80 B2
Volta Mantovana I 71 C5
Volterra I 81 C4
Voltri I 80 B2
Volturara Áppula I 103 B8
Volturara Irpina I 103 C7
Volvic F 68 C3
Volx F 79 C4
Volyně CZ 63 A4
Vonitsa GR 116 D2
Vönöck H 74 A2
Vonsild DK 39 D2
Voorschoten NL 49 A5
Vopnafjörður IS 111 B11
Vorau A 73 A5
Vorbasse DK 39 D2
Vorchdorf A 63 C4
Vorden
D 43 C5
NL 50 A2
Vordernberg A 73 A4
Vordingborg DK 39 D4
Vorë AL 105 B5
Voreppe F 69 C5
Vorey F 68 C3
Vorgod DK 39 C1
Vormsund N 34 B3
Voronezh UA 7 F12
Vöru EST 7 C9
Voskopojë AL 116 B2
Voss N 32 B3
Votice CZ 63 A5
Voué F 59 B5
Vouillé F 67 B5
Voulx F 59 B3
Voussac F 68 B3
Vouvray F 67 A5
Vouvry CH 70 B1
Vouzela P 87 D2
Vouziers F 59 A5
Voves F 58 B2
Voxna S 36 A2
Voy GB 23 B5
Voynitsa RUS 3 D29
Voznesensk UA 11 C11
Voznesenye RUS 7 A13
Vrå
DK 38 B2
S 40 C3
Vráble SK 64 B4
Vračenovići MNE 84 D3
Vračev Gaj SRB 85 B6
Vraćevsnica SRB 85 B5
Vrådal N 33 C5
Vrakneika GR 117 D3
Vrana HR 83 B3
Vranduk BIH 84 B2
Vrångö S 38 B4
Vrani RO 85 A6
Vranić SRB 85 B5
Vraniči BIH 84 C3
Vranja HR 73 C4
Vranjak BIH 84 B3
Vranje SRB 10 E6
Vranovice CZ 64 B2
Vranov nad Dyje CZ 64 B1
Vransko SLO 73 B4
Vrapčići BIH 84 C2
Vratimov CZ 64 A4
Vratsa BG 11 E7
Vrbanja HR 84 B3
Vrbanjci BIH 84 B2
Vrbas SRB 75 C4
Vrbaška BIH 84 A2
Vrbnik
Primorsko-Goranska HR 83 A3
Zadarsko-Kninska HR 83 B5
Vrbno pod Pradědem CZ 54 C2
Vrboska HR 83 C5
Vrbov SK 65 A6
Vrbovce SK 64 B3
Vrbové SK 64 B3
Vrbovec HR 73 C6
Vrbovski SRB 85 B5
Vrbovsko HR 73 C5
Vrchlabí CZ 53 C5
Vrčin SRB 85 B5
Vrdy CZ 63 A6
Vrebac HR 83 B4
Vreden D 50 A2
Vrela KOS 85 D5
Vreoci SRB 85 B5
Vretstorp S 37 C1
Vrginmost HR 73 C5
Vrgorac HR 84 C2
Vrhnika SLO 73 C4
Vrhovine HR 83 B4
Vrhpolie SRB 85 B4
Vriezenveen NL 42 C3
Vrigne-aux-Bois F 59 A5
Vrigstad S 40 B4
Vrlika HR 83 C5
Vrmbaje SRB 85 C5
Vrnjačka Banja SRB 85 C5
Vrnograč BIH 73 C5
Vron F 48 C2
Vroomshoop NL 42 C3
Vroutek CZ 52 C3
Vrpolje HR 74 C3
Vršac SRB 85 A6
Vrsar HR 82 A2
Vrsi HR 83 B4
Vrtoče BIH 83 B5
Vrútky SK 65 A4
Všeruby CZ 62 A3
Všestary CZ 53 C5
Vsetín CZ 64 A3
Vuča MNE 85 D5
Vučitrn KOS 85 D5
Vučkovica SRB 85 C5
Vught NL 49 B6
Vuillafans F 69 A6
Vukovar HR 75 C4
Vuku N 114 D8
Vulcan RO 11 D7
Vulcăneşti MD 11 D10
Vuoggatjålme S 112 F5
Vuojärvi FIN 113 E15
Vuolijoki FIN 3 D27
Vuotso FIN 113 D16
Vuzenica SLO 73 B5
Vyartsilya RUS 3 E29
Vyazma RUS 7 D13
Vyborg RUS 3 F28
Výčapy CZ 64 A1
Výčapy-Opatovce SK 64 B4
Východna SK 65 A5
Vydrany SK 64 B3
Vyerkhnyadzvinsk BY 7 D9
Vyhne SK 65 B4
Vy-lès Lure F 60 C2
Vylkove UA 11 D10
Vynohradiv UA 11 B7
Vyshniy Volochek RUS 7 C13
Vyškov CZ 64 A3
Vysokánad Kysucou SK 65 A4
Vysoké Mýto CZ 53 D6
Vysokovsk RUS 7 C14
Vyšší Brod CZ 63 B5
Vytegra RUS 7 A14

W

Waabs D 44 A1
Waalwijk NL 49 B6
Waarschoot B 49 B4
Wabern D 51 B5
Wąbrzeźno PL 47 B4
Wąchock PL 55 B6
Wachow D 45 C4
Wachów PL 54 C3
Wächtersbach D 51 C5
Wackersdorf D 62 A3
Waddington GB 27 B5
Wadebridge GB 28 C3
Wadelsdorf D 53 B4
Wädenswil CH 70 A3
Wadern D 60 A2
Wadersloh D 50 B4
Wadlew PL 55 B4
Wadowice PL 65 A5
Wagenfeld D 43 C5
Wageningen NL 49 B6
Waghäusel D 61 A4
Waging D 62 C3
Wagrain A 72 A3
Wagrowiec PL 46 C3
Wahlsdorf D 52 B3
Wahlstedt D 44 B2
Wahrenholz D 44 C2
Waiblingen D 61 B5
Waidhaus D 62 A3
Waidhofen an der Thaya A 63 B6
Waidhofen an der Ybbs A 63 C5
Waimes B 50 C2
Wainfleet All Saints GB 27 B6
Waizenkirchen A 63 B4
Wakefield GB 27 B4
Wałbrzych PL 53 C6
Walchensee D 62 C2
Walchsee A 62 C3
Wałcz PL 46 B2
Wald CH 70 A3
Waldaschaff D 51 D5
Waldbach A 73 A5
Waldböckelheim D 60 A3
Waldbröl D 50 C3
Waldeck D 51 B5
Waldenburg D 52 C2
Waldfischbach-Burgalben D 60 A3
Waldheim D 52 B3
Waldkappel D 51 B5
Waldkirch D 60 B3
Waldkirchen D 63 B4
Waldkirchen am Wesen A 63 B4
Waldkraiburg D 62 B3
Wald-Michelbach D 61 A4
Waldmohr D 60 A3
Waldmünchen D 62 A3
Waldring A 62 C3
Waldsassen D 52 C2
Waldshut D 61 C4

X

Y

Z